COAT OF ARMS OF ANCIENT HERR FAMILY.

See description on opposite page.

The following translation from the German is of much
interest :

"The race of Herr descended from a very ancient family ; is free—that is to say, of noble origin. . . . Like-
wise from time immemorial, its knights were brave and
worthy. .   . Possessing in Schwaben vast and rich
estates, the name of which was called and written Hern von
Bilried.   . . The father of this race was called the
Schwabish Knight Hugo, the Herr or Lord of Bilried. . .
. In the year 1009 flourished and was known to all, the
family from whom that of Herr is descended. . . . But
in the fifteenth century several of the race resigned their
nobility and settled as citizens   . . They, however, re-
tained their noble name and their Coat of Arms, and in the
year 1593 John Herr, or Lord of Bilried, obtained from the
Emperor Ferdinand, in *Schwabish Hall*, a written testimo-
nial, proving for his flourishing family their Coat of Arms,
their free and noble descent and the possession of their race
to the latest generation."

"And this *Coat of Arms* yet rightly belongs to the
present living family of Herr."

E. B. VIEN.

Recorded in the Register of noble families, with their Coat of
Arms. *Book 5, page 258.*

GENEALOGICAL RECORD

OF

REVEREND HANS HERR

AND HIS

DIRECT LINEAL DESCENDANTS

FROM HIS BIRTH A. D. 1639 TO THE PRESENT TIME
CONTAINING THE NAMES, ETC.,
OF 13223 PERSONS

———

COMPILED, ARRANGED, INDEXED IN
ALPHABETICAL ORDER, AND
PUBLISHED BY

THEODORE W. HERR, GENEALOGIST

———

LANCASTER, PA.

1908

THE EXAMINER PRINTING HOUSE
LANCASTER, PA.

PORTRAIT OF REV. HANS HERR

From a painting by John Funk.

PREFACE.

Obtaining the data and information required to enable the undersigned compiler to have the genealogical record of Rev. Hans Herr and his descendants published, was commenced in 1850, with the assistance of Milton B. Eshleman, an honored cousin, long since deceased. Both spent several years very industriously in visiting the oldest residents of Lancaster, Dauphin and Cumberland counties in Pennsylvania, where most of the descendants then lived. Information was obtained from them, their relatives, and neighbors, of all they could furnish or remember, relating to residences, births, marriages and deaths of Rev. Hans Herr and his descendants, and of all the persons any of them married, and the names of the parents of the latter.

All old papers, Bible records, deeds, mortgages, wills, and much memoranda were carefully examined, as well as tombstones in many of the old burying grounds. All was verified by family records, traditions, memories, etc., as fully as possible. Many old records in Philadelphia, Harrisburg, Lancaster, and West Chester, were investigated to ascertain what lands they owned and last places of residences. Much time was occupied and expense incurred in persistent efforts to obtain the fullest reliable data of these early settlers, as they and their companions were the first white settlers in what is now Lancaster county, Penna. Great care was taken to insure absolutely correct information as complete as possible of these early pioneers, but it has been impossible to obtain much desirable matter. It is to be hoped this publication will be the means of calling out much that is now wanting of names, dates and addresses.

It should be understood that this Record is not a history, but a genealogical record of names, last residences, dates of births, marriages and deaths and names of parents of the consorts.

This record contains all the data obtained at this office up to the time of going to press. The records of many families are complete, but many failed to report changes of address, births, marriages and deaths occurring since former entries were made, even when frequently requested to do so. No question has or will be asked unless the record shows the information asked for is wanting, or to verify the record. This data is important, or may be sometime, to every person in the record. In some cases, the information has been asked from several persons simultaneously, or at various times, so as to be more likely to receive the correct data, as so many fail to answer promptly, even when it would require but little time or trouble.

Much time in thought, research and investigation, with numerous clerks and assistants from time to time, was required. Many thanks are due to those who have gone to the trouble to obtain and furnish facts for this work without recompense, *except* in the knowledge that they were aiding a worthy enterprise, in which all in the record, now living, and their descendants are or may hereafter be much interested.

The publication shows all the information obtained in each case. Wherever the last place of residence, births, marriages, deaths and names do not correctly appear, or spelling of names, etc., is wrong, any one who will notice it and send or bring correct data to the The Geneaogical Bureau, will confer a great favor. All may realize it will be of much benefit to the many interested. Strenuous effort has been made to have all as complete as possible; but, mistakes will occur. Many in writing are not always particular in dotting an "i" or crossing a "t," etc., and they may be taken for "c," "e," "b," "l," "w" for "u" and so on. Errors often occur in entering data from such causes. The Genealogical Bureau is established at Lancaster, Pa., to perfect these Records, and any others of like character that may hereafter be compiled. All persons are earnestly requested to notify The Bureau of any errors or omissions that may be found, and to answer all inquiries promptly.

In some cases the names of the members of the same family have lower or higher numbers than others. This occurs because the irregularly numbered ones were not reported to this office until the numbers were assigned, and then unassigned numbers were given them, as occasion seemed to require. While it may seem strange that such differences appear, it is really immaterial, as the references always show to what family each belongs.

It has recently been decided to add an index to the Record, to show the number and name of each descendant in alphabetical order so that the record of each may be readily found; by referring to any person's number, the name and number of one or both parents will be seen from which can readily be traced any connections, either in the ascending or descending line by references from one family to another. This index is a valuable and important addition, and will appear at the end of the Record in each volume. It required much time and labor to accurately complete it, but it is a very desirable feature, and adds much to the value of the Record.

At the end of the Hans Herr record appears the name and what facts are known of the father of Rev. Hans Herr and of four of his brothers. The numbers relating to them and their respective descendants are indicated by prefixing the initial letter of the name of these brothers to their own numbers and to those of their respective descendants. Little is known of them except of descendants of Christian Herr, some of whom emigrated to the United States.

LOCATION OF FIRST RESIDENCE OF REV. HANS HERR, (A. D. 1709)

ONE MILE EAST OF WILLOW STREET, IN LANCASTER COUNTY, PENNA.

HISTORICAL INTRODUCTION.

Prior to the year 1492, when America was discovered by Christopher Columbus, up to the year 1681, when Charles II., King of England, Scotland and Ireland, granted a charter to William Penn, Esquire, conveying to him that portion of North America now called Pennsylvania, and until the year 1709, no settlement of any white people had been made in any part of what is now known as Lancaster county, Pennsylvania.

In 1681 Penn published the fact of the grant having been made to him, especially by distributing printed circulars and by lectures in Switzerland and Germany, describing the fertility of the soil, wrote kind and conciliatory letters to different Indian tribes, visited many of them later and by presents, and payments to them for their claims to the land, succeeded in making them his confidential and permanent friends, which friendship continued until the date of his death in 1718.

In 1682 the Duke of York, who then owned large tracts of land at the mouth of, and along the Delaware river, and, what is now New Jersey, after much hesitancy, and at the earnest solicitation of Penn, conveyed to the latter for satisfactory considerations, all his rights to such lands. This gave to Penn full and unobstructed access to his Pennsylvania acquisitions up the Delaware river from its mouth by ships from the old countries. During the same year he made a voyage from England to America and took full possession of his property, being received by great demonstrations of joy and good will by the people then living there.

The lower, or southeastern, part of Pennsylvania was divided into three counties—Philadelphia, Bucks and Chester. The latter included what is now Lancaster county, which was not organized into a separate county until 1729.

In 1684 Penn went to Europe and returned in 1699 with his wife and children. During his absence many emigrants from Europe had arrived and settled on the eastern portions of his lands. He had been to Switzerland and Germany several times, distributing many circulars and pamphlets in different languages, and in conversations and lectures, described his lands, the fruitfulness, salubrity of climate and many other advantages of the country, and especially the freedom from religious persecution, which settlers would enjoy. Thus he laid the foundation for the large colonies that were later to settle on his large landed estate in Pennsylvania.

In 1701 Penn again returned to England. Many Swiss, Germans and others were being relentlessly persecuted for religious beliefs, about the close of the seventeenth century. Rulers were being changed frequently, and the dominant religion one year often became changed the next, as one set of rulers was deposed and another substituted. Many of the people were of deep religious feelings and not disposed to change their opinions either by force or other considerations, and so be subject to the whim or caprice of those temporarily in power. The Swiss and German Mennonites, and others, being non-resistants, and opposed to bearing arms, or going to wars, unable to agree with many of the tenets of those who happened to be in power, were especially subject to persecution, which they suffered to an exceedingly sorrowful and painful degree. For a more complete history of the Mennonites, the causes which led to their origin, and the persecutions and sufferings they endured, the reader is referred to the writings of Menno Simon about the middle of the sixteenth century, and to other histories since A. D. 1531, and for especial information about the Pioneer Settlers of Lancaster County, Pa., to the writings of I. D. Rupp and other historians of the county, many of whom have graphically and interestingly described events, localities and persons in books which can readily be obtained.

The edict of Nantes issued in 1598 in favor of the Huguenots was revoked in 1685 by Louis XIV. One of the most cruel and terrible persecutions ever known occurred in France, Switzerland and Germany, especially in the Palatinate, from that and other causes. It is estimated that over 500,000 Huguenots (confederated protestants) escaped from France alone from 1685 to 1720. Many also from Zurich, Berne, etc., in Switzerland, suffered severely from religious persecution about this time. Some of the persecuted Swiss and German Mennonites, by the invitation and encouragement of William Penn, settled, as early as 1683, at what is now Germantown, Pa.

Hans Herr was born in 1639, in Switzerland, at, or near Zurich, Canton of Zurich, became a member of the Mennonite religious society and a prominent minister of that denomination.

When religious persecution became unendurable, many of his congregation emigrated with him to the Palatinate in Germany, which was then governed by a ruler who promised them protection and religious freedom. This was satisfactory until the Palatinate fell into the hands of other rulers, when the Mennonites were again subject to severe religious persecution.

When this occurred, a number of them visited Penn in London, in 1707, and arranged terms with him to colonize a portion of what is now Lancaster county, and in 1709 Hans Herr, John R. Bundely, Hans Mylin, Martin Kendig, Jacob Miller, Hans Funk, Martin Oberholtzer, Wendel Bowman and others bought 10,000 acres of land on the south side of Pequea creek. A warrant was issued for the land October 10, 1710, and it was surveyed Oct. 23, 1710. The tradition, which is no doubt true, is, that these people held a conference as to what steps should be taken to inform their relatives and friends left behind in Europe of their opinions and expectations, and it was determined by lot that Hans Herr, their revered minister, should return, explain the situation and the great advantages of emigration, and bring with him those he could induce to come. There is a tradition that the "lot" fell upon Christian Herr, son of Hans Herr, instead of on his father, but it does not seem to be supported by historical evidence. Hans consented to go, but many argued that their beloved pastor, head and leader, then over seventy years of age, should not leave them at this juncture, and at last it was agreed that his brother-in-law, Martin Kendig, should go. Accordingly, without delay, he embarked for Europe and returned in 1710 with six sons and one daughter of the venerable Hans Herr, and members of the families of those who had come over in 1709. John Houser, John Bachman, Hans Tshantz Jacob Weaver, Henry Funk and others, also came with them. The six sons of Hans Herr, John, Emanuel, Abraham, Christian, Henry and Samuel, and the daughter, Maria, were married and had families. Tradition asserts that several of his sons and daughters remained in Europe. One son, at least, went with a colony to London, England, in 1709, or about that date, and shortly after settled in Ireland. Some of his descendants came to the United States about fifty years ago.

The peope who came to what is now Lancaster county, Pa., in 1709, settled in Lampeter, Manor, Pequea and Strasburg townships. From this beginning of the The Pioneer Settlers, they and their descendants now number many thousands of the best native population of this county and other sections of the United States, also many in other countries. They comprise the families of Allen, Bare, Baer, Bair, Bear, Bachman, Baldwin, Barr, Bauman, Bomgardner, Bowman, Brackbill, Breneman, Brown, Brinton, Brubaker, Bryan, Buckwalter, Burkholder, Carpenter, Charles, Clark, Davis, DuBois, Eaby, Edwards, Ellis, Erisman, Eshleman, Evans, Ferree, Forrer, Foulk, Frick, Fry, Fulton, Funk, Galbraith, Galt, Gardner, Good, Graeff, Grant, Gray, Graybill, Greider, Groff, Grove, Haines, Harnish, Harris, Hartman, Hay, Hendrickson, Herr, Hershey, Hess, Hoover, Hostetter, Houser, Howard, Howell, Huber, Immel, Johns, Jones, Kauffman, Keagy, Kendig, Kendrick, King, Kreider, Landis, Leaman, Lefever, Lemon, Levis, Lewis, Lightner, Lines. Linville, Lloyd, Long, Martin, Mason, McClure, Middleton, Miller, Moore, Moser, Moyer, Musselman, Musser, Myers, Mylin, Neff, Newcomer, Nissley, Patterson, Pickel, Price, Rife, Robinson, Rowe, Rutter, Sample, Seldomridge, Shank, Shenk, Smith, Snavely, Stehman, Steinman, Stewart, Stoneman, Swarr, Swope, Taylor, Thompson, Walker, Weaver, White, Whiteside, Wilkins, Williams, Witmer, Zorty, and many others, and are scattered all over the United States and elsewhere.

The illustrations of the Portrait and Coat of Arms used in this Record were made originally for the Hans Herr Memorial Association in 1895.

Hans Herr settled near Lampeter, and later lived with his son, Rev. Christian Herr, near Willow Street, where the latter built a large stone dwelling in 1719, which is still standing. This house is a most interesting specimen of architecture, when it is remembered that it was erected in a location that only a few years before was in the midst of a vast forest, far from sawmills or other facilities for obtaining materials. Here the venerable Hans Herr died in 1725. His children settled in Strasburg, Lampeter, Lancaster and Manor townships, in Lancaster county, Pa. Their descendants are now scattered in all parts of the United States and in other countries. Many became prominent as ministers, physicians, lawyers, statesmen, civil and mechanical engineers and other professions. A number settled early in Virginia. John Herr (897) went to York county, Pa., and afterwards, about 1830, settled in Kentucky. His descendants, who are numerous, became famous for their fine horses.

Benjamin Herr (80), in 1798, went to Pittsburg, Pa., became the owner of Herr's Island, in the Allegheny river. The descendants are numerous; many settled in Kansas and other western States.

Rev. John Herr (494) became bishop of the Reformed Mennonite denomination, which he, with others, organized. It is now composed of many members.

John Herr (160) went to Red Haw, O., where he and his wife were both killed by a tree blown down in a storm, falling on their carriage. Their descendants settled in Indiana, Kansas, Missouri, and Wyoming.

John Strohm (523), and A. Herr Smith (1005), were members of Congress, U. S. Dr. John H. Musser (4899), of Philadelphia, was lately president of the American Medical Association of U. S. John Neff (431) became a prominent Mormon, his numerous descendants are mostly in Utah. Descendants of Henry Forrer (1317) settled mostly in Ohio and Nebraska. John W. Forney (2164), of Philadelphia, Pa., was a celebrated journalist; the descendants of his father, Peter Forney (649), are mostly in Washington, D. C., and in Philadelphia, Harrisburg and Lebanon, Pa. The descendants of Abraham Frantz (2433) are scattered in Pennsylvania, Maryland and elsewhere. Abraham Groff (665) has many descendants in Pennsylvania, Maryland, Washington and in Washington, D. C. John Eshleman (667) has descendants in Pennsylvania and Iowa.

This list might be continued indefinitely, suffice it to say, many have acquired eminence in all parts of the world as judges, legislators, railroaders, inventors, college presidents, instructors, missionaries, etc., in this country, in Australia, Mexico, South America, the Philippines, Egypt, Siberia, and in other places. By reference to the Genealogical Record, the last known residence or address of each person can easily be found.

CONTENTS

ILLUSTRATIONS

Last Residence of Rev. Hans Herr, One-Half Mile East of Willow Street, in Lancaster County, Penna., Built of Sandstone, A. D. 1719, and Still Standing.

GENEALOGICAL RECORD

OF

REV. HANS HERR AND HIS DIRECT LINEAL DESCENDANTS.

ABBREVIATIONS.—b. = born; d. = died; m. = married; dau. = daughter; wid. = widow or widower.

1. **REV. HANS HERR,** Lampeter, Pa., b. Sept. 17, 1639; d. 1725; m. 1660, Elizabeth Kendig, b. 1644; d. 1730; dau. John Kendig and Jane Mylin.

   Family of REV. HANS HERR (1) and ELIZABETH KENDIG.

2. Abraham, Manor, Pa., b. 1660; m. Anna ———.
3. Rev. Christian, Willow Street, Pa., m. Anna ———.
4. John, Lampeter, Pa., b. 1685; d. 1765; m. Frances ———.
5. Samuel, Letort, Pa., b. 1686.
6. Emanuel, Wheatland Mills, Pa., b. 1689; d. 1740; m. 1720, Maudlin Brackbill (40).
7. Henry, New Providence, Pa., d. 1785.
8. Maria, Strasburg, Pa., d. Dec. 1, 1725; m. 1701, Rev. Benedict Brackbill, d. Apr. 27, 1720.

   Family of ABRAHAM HERR (2) and ANNA ———.

9. Abraham, Manor, Pa., b. June 25, 1700; d. Sept. 5, 1785; m. Anna Miller; m. Fanny Martin, d. July 5, 1803.
10. Rudolph, Manor, Pa., b. 1701; d. 1775; m. Barbara Brubaker; m. Ann ———.
11. Christian, Lancaster, Pa., b. 1720; d. 1822; m. Barbara ———.
12. John, Manor, Pa., d. 1796.

13. Barbara, Manor, Pa., m. David Martin.
14. Elizabeth, Manor, Pa., d. 1735; m. Jacob Bartzell.

Family of REV. CHRISTIAN HERR (3) and ANNA ———.

16. John, Willow Street, Pa., d. 1773; m. Annie ———.
17. Christian, Willow Street, Pa., d. 1763; m. Barbara ———.
18. Abraham, Lampeter, Pa., d. 1756; m. Fronica ———.
19. Elizabeth, Lampeter, Pa., m. 1740, Michael Groff.
20. Anna, Strasburg, Pa., m. Martin Mylin.
21. Maria, Quarryville, Pa., m. Martin Barr, son Rev. John Barr.
22. Susanna, Quarryville, Pa., m. George Graff.
23. Barbara, Lampeter, Pa., b. Dec. 15, 1769; d. May 22, 1854; m. John Jacob Miller, b. Nov. 24, 1750; d. Aug. 18, 1828; m. Henry Shaub.

Family of JOHN HERR (4) and FRANCES ———.

24. Rev. John, Lime Valley, Pa., d. 1783.
25. Fanny, Strasburg, Pa., b. June 8, 1709; d. May 20, 1780; m. Oct. 21, 1722, Rev. Uhlrich Brackbill (41).
26. Anna, Strasburg, Pa., m. John Burkholder.
27. Christian, Willow Street, Pa., d. May 18, 1772; m. 1751, Mary Kendig, dau. Jacob Kendig and Alice Wade, m. 1762, Fanny Groff (180).
28. Mary, New Danville, Pa., m. Christian Forrer.
29. Elizabeth, Strasburg, Pa., m. Martin Barr, son Rev. John Barr.

Family of SAMUEL HERR (5) and ——— ———.

30. Samuel, Millersville, Pa., b. 1722; d. May 30, 1787; m. Anna E. ———.
31. Christian, Millersville, Pa., b. 1726; d. 1796.
32. Anna, Millersville, Pa., m. Christian Bachman.

Family of EMANUEL HERR (6) and MAUDLIN BRACKBILL (40).

33. Rev. John, Lampeter, Pa., b. 1720; d. Aug., 1797; m. 1744, Esther Neff, dau. Dr. John Henry Neff and Frances ———; m. Esther Shenk, dau. Henry Shenk and Margaret ———.

34. Emanuel, Wheatland Mills, Pa., b. 1722; m. Nov. 16, 1747, Mary Smith.
35. Martin, Strasburg, Pa., d. Oct., 1805; m. Elizabeth Bowman.
36. Susanna, Enterprise, Pa., m. Christian Carpenter, son Gabriel Carpenter and Apalonia Herman.
37. Elizabeth, Wheatland Mills, Pa., d. Mar. 26, 1760; m. May 12, 1746, Jacob Carpenter, b. Apr. 3, 1726; d. Dec. 3, 1772; son Henry Carpenter and Salome Ruffner.
38. Mary, Wheatland Mills, Pa., m. Dariel Carpenter, son Gabriel Carpenter and Apalonia Herman; m. 1765, Peter Good.

Family of HENRY HERR (7) and ——.
39. Isaac, New Providence, Pa., m. 1785.

Family of MARIA HERR (8) and Rev. BENEDICT BRACKBILL.
40. Maudlin, Strasburg, Pa., b. 1702; m. 1720, Emanuel Herr (6).
41. Uhlrich, Strasburg, Pa., b. July 4, 1703; d. Nov. 17, 1739; m. Oct. 1722, Fanny Herr (25).
42. Barbara, Strasburg, Pa., b. May 10, 1714; m. Jacob Groff: b. Apr. 2, 1699; d. 1766.

Family of ABRAHAM HERR (9) and ANNA MILLER.
43. Abraham, Manor, Pa., m. —— Witmer.
44. John, Manor, Pa., d. May 2, 1792; m. Mary Myers; d. May 5, 1805.
45. Magdalena, Neffsville, Pa., b. June 11, 1739; d. Oct. 17, 1793; m. Jacob Frick; b. Sept. 4, 1728; d. Oct. 26, 1781; son Jacob Frick and Mary Stroheim.
46. Frances, Strasburg, Pa., b. 1740; d. 1775; m. Uhlrich Eshleman; b. 1738; d. May 1, 1802.
47. Christian, Manor, Pa., b. Dec. 30, 1746; d. 1822; m. Jan. 13, 1767, Frances Martin; b. Nov. 18, 1747; dau. Jacob Martin and ——; m. Wid. Barbara Dombach Funk, dau. —— Dombach and ——.
48. Mary, Manor, Pa., m. —— Long.
49. Barbara, Manor, Pa., m. —— Myers.
50. Elizabeth, Manor, Pa., m. Jacob Stoner.
51. Christiana, Strasburg, Pa., m. —— Hoffman.
15. David, Manor, Pa., b. 1722; d. 1771; m. Barbara Hershey.

Family of Wid. ABRAHAM HERR (9) and FANNY MARTIN.

52. Christian, Millersville, Pa., m. Anna Hostetter.
53. Anna, Millersville, Pa., m. Jacob Groff.
54. Magdalene, Millersville, Pa., m. Jacob Smth.
55. Fanny, Millersville, Pa., m. Henry Kauffman.

Family of RUDOLPH HERR (10) and BARBARA BRUBAKER.

56. Abraham, Manor, Pa.
57. Daughter, m. Christian Breneman.
58. Henry, Manor, Pa., d. July 26, 1780; m. Esther Hershey.
59. John, Cocalico, Pa., b. 1727; d. 1775; m. Barbara Groff (97).
60. David, Manor, Pa., d. 1789.
61. Rudolph, Manor, Pa., d. Dec. 17, 1796; m. Frances ———.
62. Barbara, Manor, Pa., m. Jacob Erisman.
63. Magdalene, Manor, Pa.
64. Anna, Manor, Pa., m. Isaac Breneman.

Family of CHRISTIAN HERR (11) and BARBARA ———.

65. Christian, Manor, Pa., d. 1811; m. Frances ———; m. Christiana
    Eyerman.
66. Abraham, Donegal, Pa., d. July 13, 1807.
67. David, Hawksville, Pa., b. 1740; d. 1834; m. Christiana Martin;
    b. June 15, 1744; d. 1825.
68. Daniel, Lancaster, Pa.
69. Emanuel, Lancaster, Pa., b. 1745; m. three times.
70. Barbara, Bart, Pa., m. Abraham Beam.
71. Maria, Lebanon, Pa., m. John Baughman.

Family of DAVID HERR (15) and BARBARA HERSHEY.

72. Fanny, Millersville, Pa., b. Jan. 19, 1747; m. Henry Binkley, son
    Christian Binkley, and ———; m. Baltzer Shertzler.
73. Christian, Millersville, Pa., b. June 7, 1748; d. 1817; m. Mary
    Hershey, dau. Christian Hershey and ———.
74. Esther, Millersville,, Pa., b. July 30, 1750; d. 1750.
75. Abraham, Millersville, Pa., b. Oct. 7, 1751; d. Nov. 26, 1823; m.
    Barbara Eshleman, b. May 22, 1757; d. Sept. 16, 1839; dau.
    Benedict Eshleman and ———.

76. John, Millersville, Pa., b. Dec. 30, 1753; m. Anna Hershey, dau. Christian Hershey, and ———.
77. Esther, Millersville, Pa., b. July 18, 1755; m. Christian Habecker, d. 1822, son Christian Habecker and ———.
78. David, Creswell, Pa., b. Aug. 25, 1758; d. 1846; m. ——— Jumper; m. Susan Yertz, dau. Peter Yertz, and ———; m. Wid. Anna Whitestick, dau. Michael Shenk and ———.
79. Son ———, Millersville, Pa., b. 1760; d. 1760.
80. Benjamin, Troy Hill, Pa., b. Dec. 7, 1760; d. May 9, 1846; m. Apr. 29, 1794, Magdalena Lichte; b. 1769; d. Oct. 13, 1842.

Family of JOHN HERR (16) and ANNA ———.

81. Abraham, Strasburg, Pa., m. Ann Miller; d. 1815; dau. ——— Miller and ——— Souders.
82. John, Soudersburg, Pa., b. Mar. 10, 1740; m. Dec. 21, 1770, Mary Groff, (181); m. Wid. Maria Strohm.
83. Benjamin, Strasburg, Pa., d. 1772; m. Ann Herr (114).
84. Christian, Willow Street, Pa., m. Ann Barr (124).
85. David, Willow Street, Pa., m. Eve Barr; m. Betsey Kendig, b. Aug. 22, 1768; dau. Martin Kendig and Betsey Neff.
86. Christiana, Wheatland Mills, Pa., b. Mar. 15, 1749; d. June 4, 1818; m. John Herr (139).

Family of CHRISTIAN HERR (17) and BARBARA ———.

87. Barbara, Willow Street, Pa., m. Henry Kendig, son Jacob Kendig and Alice Wade.
88. Ann, Willow Street, Pa., m. John Kendig, son Jacob Kendig and Alice Wade; m. Michael Withers.

Family of ABRAHAM HERR (18) and FRONICA ———.

89. Maria, Quarryville, Pa., m. Martin Barr, son Jacob Barr and Anna Groff.
90. Fannie, Willow Street, Pa., m. John Barr, son Jacob Barr and Anna Groff; m. James Keech.
91. Barbara, Willow Street, Pa., m. Henry Shaub.
92. Anna, Willow Street, Pa., m. Christian Hoover.

Family of ELIZABETH HERR (19) and MICHAEL GROFF.

93. Anna, Willow Street, Pa., m. Henry Kendig; m. Wid. Jacob Barr, b. Jan. 8, 1723, son Rev. John Barr and ———.
94. Susanna, New Providence, Pa., b. Dec. 10, 1746; d. 1830; m. May 16, 1769, Isaac Herr (658).
95. Fanny, Willow Street, Pa., m. John Miller.
96. Elizabeth, Willow Street, Pa., m. John Lyons.
97. Barbara, Willow Street, Pa., m. John Herr (59).
98. Mary, Willow Street, Pa., m. Christian Shultz.
99. John, Willow Street, Pa.
100. Jacob, Strasburg, Pa.
101. Christian, Willow Street, Pa.

Family of Rev. JOHN HERR (24) and ——— ———.

102. Christian, Lime Valley, Pa., b. Sept. 19, 1732; d. Nov. 26, 1815; m. Maria Bowman, b. Oct. 24, 1738; d. Mar. 20, 1815.
103. Abraham, Refton, Pa., b. Jan. 16, 1743; m. 1764, Barbara Weaver, dau. Jacob Weaver and Magdalene Barr.
104. Fannie, Strasburg, Pa., m. John Buskaston.
105 Ann, Lampeter, Pa., b. 1751; d. 1843.

Family of FANNY HERR (25) and Rev. UHLRICH BRACKBILL (41).

106. Son, Strasburg, Pa., b. Mar. 29, 1724; d. Mar. 29, 1724.
107. Fanny, Strasburg, Pa., b. Oct. 14, 1725; d. Nov. 30, 1735.
108. John, Strasburg, Pa., b. Jan. 6, 1728; d. Aug. 20, 1813; m. Dec. 25, 1754, Anna Landis, b. Jan. 8, 1730; d. May 30, 1760; dau. Benjamin Landis and ———.
109. Benedict, Strasburg, Pa., b. Oct. 24, 1730; d. June 4, 1823; m. Apr. 13, 1762, Mary Kendig, b. Apr. 13, 1741; d. Apr. 4, 1817; dau. Henry Kendig and Maria Wolfe.
110. Anna, Strasburg, Pa., b. Jan. 8, 1733; d. Nov. 18, 1825; m. Aug. 20, 1755, Rev. Jacob Neff; b. Feb. 16, 1724; d. Feb. 16, 1814; son Dr. John H. Neff and ———.
111. Fanny, Strasburg, Pa., b. Feb. 15, 1736; d. Aug. 23, 1793; m. Nov. 30, 1758, George Weaver, b. 1733; d. Sept. 17, 1781; son Jacob Weaver and Anna ———.
112. Henry, Strasburg, Pa., b. Dec. 10, 1738; d. Oct. 18, 1743.

Family of CHRISTIAN HERR (27) and MARY KENDIG.

113. Mary, Lancaster, Pa., b. 1752; d. Oct. 8, 1848; m. Abraham Witmer, b. 1748; d. July 10, 1818; son John Witmer and Frances Roland.
114. Ann, Strasburg, Pa., m. Benjamin Herr (83).
115. Fannie, Strasburg, Pa., b. Oct. 24, 1749; d. Oct. 22, 1836; m. George Bressler, b. Oct. 10, 1738; d. Aug. 16, 1806; son John Bressler and Eve Kendig.

Family of Wid. CHRISTIAN HERR (27) and FANNIE GROFF (180).

116. Barbara, Strasburg, Pa., b. July 28, 1762; d. Oct. 12, 1821; m. John Neff (411).
117. Elizabeth, Strasburg, Pa., b. Aug. 29, 1765; d. June 23, 1848; m. May 10, 1787, Rev. Jacob Neff (409).
118. Christian, Lampeter, Pa., b. Mar. 29, 1772; d. May 13, 1846; m. 1796, Elizabeth Withers, b. Nov. 5, 1774; d. Mar. 24, 1801; dau. John Withers and ———; m. 1802, Mary Rohrer, b. Nov. 18, 1780; d. Feb. 26, 1827; dau. John Rohrer and Mary Neff.

Family of MARY HERR (28) and CHRISTIAN FORRER.

119. John, Lampeter, Pa., m. Elizabeth Mylin.
120. Christian, Willow Street, Pa., m. Barbara Barr, dau. Jacob Barr and Ann Groff.
121. Fannie, New Danville, Pa., m. Isaac Breneman.
122. Anna, Strasburg, Pa., m, John Groff, son Jacob Groff and Alice Kendig.

Family of ELIZABETH HERR (29) and MARTIN BARR.

123. Mary, Martinsville, Pa., d. May 24, 1828; m. Christian Martin.
124. Annie, Willow Street, Pa., m. Christian Herr (84).
125. Fannie, Wheatland Mills, Pa., d. 1815; m. Francis Herr (140).
126. John, Strasburg, Pa., m. Elizabeth Robinson.
127. Lizzie, Strasburg, Pa., m. Wid. James Barr, son John Barr and Elizabeth Stehman.
128. Martin, Strasburg, Pa., b. Aug. 20, 1756; d. June 20, 1844; m. June 10, 1788, Fannie Neff (410).
129. Martha, Strasburg, Pa.; m. Martin Miller, son Samuel Miller and Rachael Haines.

Family of **SAMUEL HERR** (30) and **ANNA ELIZABETH** ———.

130. Daughter, Millersville, Pa., m. Jacob Kauffman.
131. Ann, Millersville, Pa., b. 1751; d. 1843; m. Henry Hartman, b. 1735; d. 1830; son Rev. John J. Hartman and ———.
132. Son, Millersville, Pa.

Family of **CHRISTIAN HERR** (31) and ——— ———.

133. Abraham, Millersville, Pa., b. 1771.
134. Christian, Millersville, Pa., b. 1777.
135. Veronica, Millersville, Pa., b. 1779.
136. Catherine, Millersville, Pa., b. 1781; m. ——— Sternaman.
137. ———.
138. ———.

Family of Rev. **JOHN HERR** (33) and **ESTHER NEFF**.

139. John, Wheatland Mills, Pa., b. Aug. 30, 1745; d. Jan. 30, 1827; m. Christiana Herr (86).
140. Francis, Wheatland Mills, Pa., b. Aug. 6, 1748; d. Jan. 2, 1810; m. Fanny Barr (125).

Family of Wid. Rev. **JOHN HERR** (33) and **ESTHER SHENK**.

141. Esther, Strasburg, Pa., m. Peter Witmer.
142. Henry, Strasburg, Pa., b. Mar. 17, 1755; d. Nov. 17, 1810; m. Magdalena Herr (150).
143. Martin, Strasburg, Pa., b. Aug. 11, 1763; d. Jan. 18, 1821; m. Christiana Strohm, b. May 8, 1767; dau. John Strohm and Maria Huetwohl; m. Christiana Herr (317); m. Susan Buckwalter, dau. Abraham Buckwalter and Maria Landis.
144. Ann, Strasburg, Pa., b. June 27, 1776; d. May 16, 1838; m. Nov. 6, 1791, David Strohm, b. Apr. 25, 1761; d. 1846; son John Strohm and Maria Huetwohl.
145. Adam, Strasburg, Pa., b. Sept. 16, 1768; d. Sept. 27, 1847; m. Mar. 15, 1800, Betsey Herr (324).
146. Eve, Strasburg, Pa., b. Apr. 30, 1771; d. June 1, 1844; m. Tobias Herr (310).
147. Susan, Strasburg, Pa., m. Jacob Witmer.
148. David, Strasburg, Pa., b. Dec. 21, 1773; d. May 6, 1825; m. Esther Witmer; m. Mary Herr (559).

Family of EMANUEL HERR (34) and MARY SMITH.

149. John, Strasburg, Pa., b. June 30, 1748; m. Sarah Randall.
150. Magdalena, Williamsville, N. Y., b. June 13, 1753; d. Jan. 13, 1832; m. Henry Herr (142).
151. Susan, Strasburg, Pa., b. Jan. 2, 1760; d. Dec. 23, 1827; m. Jacob Kendig, son Abraham Kendig and Martha Martin.
152. Esther, Strasburg, Pa., b. Nov. 16, 1764; d. Apr. 1807; m. Abraham Kendig, son Abraham Kendig and Martha Martin; m. John Hagy, son Noah Hagy and Hannah ———; m. John Brua, son John Brua and ———; m. Jacob Froelich; d. 1825.
153. Samuel, Strasburg, Pa., b. Sept. 9, 1767; m. Mar. 1, 1791, Ann Herr (315).
154. Sarah, Strasburg, Pa., b. June 4, 1771; d. Mar. 5, 1858; m. Dec. 14, 1790, Henry Miller, b. Mar. 28, 1765; d. Aug. 18, 1847; son Samuel Miller and Rachel Haines.

Family of MARTIN HERR (35) and ELIZABETH BOWMAN.

155. Joel, Salona, Pa., b. Oct. 27, 1774; d. Feb. 3, 1852; m. 1800, Fanny Bressler (427).
156. Daniel, Columbia, Pa., b. Aug. 10, 1777; d. 1815; m. Rebecca Bressler (426).
157. Martha, Strasburg, Pa., m. Martin Pfoutz.
158. Ann, Strasburg, Pa., m. David Longenecker.
159. Samuel, Salona, Pa., b. Sept. 2, 1784; d. July 30, 1859; m. Isabella Miller, b. 1784; d. Apr. 14, 1846.
160. John, Red Haw, O., d. Sept. 29, 1829; m. Elizabeth Contner, d. Sept. 29, 1829.

Family of SUSANNA HERR (36) and CHRISTIAN CARPENTER.

161. Joel, Reamstown, Pa., b. 1754; d. 1834; m. Margaret Diffenderfer, dau. John Diffenderfer and ———.
162. Daniel, Reamstown, Pa.
163. Mary, Reamstown, Pa., m. Michael Cover.
164. Catherine, Earlville, Pa., m. Henry Carpenter, son Henry Carpenter and Susan Forney.
165. Jacob, Earlville, Pa.,

166. Salome, Earlville, Pa.
167. John, Earlville, Pa.
168. Christion, Earlville, Pa., b. 1768; m. Mary Carpenter, dau. Emanuel Carpenter and Maria Smith.
169. Susan, Lititz, Pa., b. Oct. 24, 1766; d. Nov. 9, 1828; m. 1787, Jacob Forney, b. 1721; d. 1806; son Peter Forney and ——— Smith.

Family of ELIZABETH HERR (37) and JACOB CARPENTER.

170. Salome, Wheatland Mills, Pa., b. Mar. 15, 1747; m. ——— Herr; m. John Miller.
171. Elizabeth, Wheatland Mils, Pa., b. Nov. 7, 1749; m. John Ferree.
172. Susanna, Wheatland Mills, Pa., b. Dec. 1753; m. Abraham Haines.
173. Mary, Wheatland Mills, Pa., b. Nov. 16, 1755; m. Benjamin Elliott.
174. Martha, Wheatland Mills, Pa., b. Jan. 25, 1758.

Family of MARY HERR (38) and DANIEL CARPENTER.

175. Gabriel, Leacock, Pa.

Family of ISAAC HERR (39) and ——— ———.

176. Henry, New Providence, Pa.
177. Catherine, New Providence, Pa., b. Nov. 19, 1727; d. May 9, 1781; m. Jan. 15, 1745, Wid. Jacob Eshleman, b. Dec. 9, 1707; d. Dec. 16, 1758; son John J. Eshleman and ———; m. 1761, Wid. John Groff; m. Mar. 23, 1774, Wid. Benjamin Groff (178).

Family of BARBARA BRACKBILL (42) and JACOB GROFF.

178. Benjamin, Strasburg, Pa., b. Jan. 18, 1727; d. July 10, 1803; m. Dec. 14, 1748, Elizabeth Barr, b. May 10, 1725; d. Dec. 24, 1780; dau. Rev. John Barr and ———; m. Mar. 23, 1774, Wid. Catherine Herr Groff (177).
179. Jacob, Strasburg, Pa., b. July 4, 1730; m. May 21, ———, Alice Kendig, b. June 1, 1734; d. Sept. 3, 1823; dau. Jacob Kendig and Alice Wade.
180. Frances, Willow Street, Pa., b. Mar. 20, 1732; d. Feb. 5, 1826; m. Wid. Christian Herr (27).

181. Mary, Strasburg, Pa., b. Aug. 5, 1735; d. July 10, 1801; m. Dec. 21, 1770, John Herr (82).
182. Ann, Camargo, Pa., b. July 20, 1740; d. Aug. 30, 1777; m. Nov. 18, 1761, Jacob Barr, b. Jan. 8, 1723; son Rev. John Barr and ———.
183. Barbara, Strasburg, Pa., b. Mar. 5, 1747; d. May 22, 1811; m. Jan. 15, 1767, Jacob Eshleman, b. Nov. 17, 1742; d. June 13, 1813; son Jacob Eshleman and Barbara Barr.

Family of JOHN HERR (44) and MARY MYERS.

184. Abraham, Lancaster, Pa., b. Jan. 16, 1762; d. 1855; m. Anna Witmer, dau. John Witmer; m. Wid. Magdalene Brandt, dau. John Getz and ———.
185. Elizabeth, Millersville, Pa., b. May 4, 1765; d. Nov. 7, 1801; m. Apr. 19, 1788, George Hyde, b. 1756; d. 1810; son George Hyde and ———.
186. Fanny, Millersville, Pa., b. May 4, 1765; m. John Sechrist.
187. John, Millersville, Pa., m. Wid. ——— Zimmerman, dau. ——— Sharer and ———; m. Barbara Good; m. Wid. Elizabeth Fehl, dau. John Kline and ———.
188. Mary, Millersville, Pa., m. Andrew Kauffman.
189. Barbara, Millersville, Pa., m. Jacob Bixler.
190. Anna, Millersville, Pa., m. Jacob Kendig.

Family of MAGDALENE HERR (45) and JACOB FRICK.

191. Christian H., Williamsville, N. Y., b. Sept. 2, 1754; m. Nov. 19, 1780, Anna Witmer, b. Feb. 17, 1759; d. July 23, 1790; m. Jan. 25, 1791, Elizabeth Herr (210).
192. Maria, Williamsville, N. Y., b. Mar. 9, 1758; d. May 30, 1758.
193. Abraham Herr, Neffsville, Pa., b. June 20, 1759; d. Feb. 5, 1842; m. Wid. Christiana Long Zug, b. June 2, 1764; d. Dec. 15, 1851; dau. Christopher Royer and Anna Landis; m. ———.
194. John, Williamsville, N. Y., b. July 12, 1761; m. Anna Hershey.
195. Anna, Neffsville, Pa., b. Feb. 29, 1764; m. Jonathan Royer, son Philip Royer and ———.
196. Jacob, Williamsville, N. Y., b. Mar. 13, 1766; d. Mar. 4, 1832; m. Esther Longenecker, b. May 5, 1773; d. June 7, 1854.

197. Martin, Sporting Hill, Pa., b. June 10, 1768; d. May 2, 1830; m. Wid. Maria Erisman, b. Dec. 1, 1763; d. Dec. 1, 1828; dau. ———— Strickler and ————.

198. David Herr, Lancaster, Pa., b. Mar. 24, 1774; m. Anna Landis, dau. Henry Landis and Anna Landis.

199. Magdalena, Williamsville, N. Y., b. Jan. 13, 1776; m. John Blocher.

200. Daniel, Neffsville, Pa., b. Jan. 27, 1778.

201. Maria, Lancaster, Pa., b. June 14, 1781; m. John Brown.

Family of FRANCES HERR (46) and UHLRICH ESHLEMAN.

202. Anna, Strasburg, Pa., b. Mar. 18, 1761; m. ———— Gingrich.

203. John, Strasburg, Pa., b. July 6, 1762; d. infant.

204. Barbara, Strasburg, Pa., b. Nov. 28, 1764; m. ———— Hoover.

205. Abraham, Warwick, Twp., Lanc. Co., Pa., b. June 19, 1765; d. Apr. 7, 1838; m. Susanna Graybill, b. May 5, 1773; d. Apr. 5, 1814.

206. Elizabeth, Strasburg, Pa., b. Feb. 3, 1767; d. May 4, 1844; m. John Strite, b. Mar. 28, 1775; d. Nov. 21, 1840; son Christian Strite and ———— Myers.

207. John, Warwick Twp., Lanc. Co., Pa., b. Sept. 8, 1768; d. 1830.

Family of CHRISTIAN HERR (47) and FRANCES MARTIN.

208. Anna, Conestoga, Pa., b. Oct. 21, 1767; d. May 6, 1854; m. Daniel Steinman, b. Nov. 4, 1767; d. Jan 1, 1851; son Peter Steinman and ————.

209. Frances, Buffalo, N. Y., b. Nov. 26, 1768.

210. Elizabeth, Buffalo, N. Y., b. Jan. 14, 1770; m. Jan. 25, 1791, Wid. Christian H. Frick (191).

211. Abraham, Millersville, Pa., b. Oct. 18, 1771; m. Maria Funk, dau. Rudolph Funk and Catherine Krebell; m. Susan Hostetter, dau. John Hostetter and ————.

212. Fanny, Manor, Pa., b. Jan. 1, 1774; m. Christian Horst.

213. Christian, Millersville, Pa., b. Feb. 22, 1775; d. Aug. 5, 1804; m. Mary Neff, dau. Henry Neff and Elizabeth Brubaker.

214. Mary, Manor, Pa., b. Aug. 14, 1776; m. Henry Schock, son Jacob Schock and Esther Bauman.

215. Magdalena, Carlisle, Pa., b. Nov. 13, 1777.
216. Maria, Millersville, Pa., b. Dec. 6, 1779.
217. Barbara, Millersville, Pa., b. Apr. 11, 1781.
218. Barbara, Millersville, Pa., b. Oct. 19, 1783; d. 1857; m. 1802, Henry Funk, b. Sept. 7, 1781; d. 1819; son Rudolph Funk and Catherine Krebell; m. ———— Hertzler.
219. Frederick, Gettysburg, Pa., b. Feb. 27, 1787; d. Apr. 20, 1870; m. Catherine Pfifer; d. 1822; dau. John Pfifer and Mary ————; m. Susan Lind, b. Mar. 24, 1797; d. Jan. 10, 1869.
220. Magdalene, Carlisle, Pa., b. Aug. 15, 1788; m. John Bowman, son Emanuel Bowman and ————.
221. John, Manor, Pa., b. Apr. 2, 1790; d. Oct. 19, 1794.

Family of CHRISTIAN HERR (52) and ANNA HOSTETTER.

222. Abraham, Millersville, Pa., d. Apr. 18, 1864; m. Barbara Breneman.
223. Christian, Millersville, Pa., m. Nancy Brubaker, dau. David Brubaker and ————; m. Esther Eaby.
224. Anna, Millersville, Pa., m. Rev. Jacob Brubaker.
225. David, Millersville, Pa., b. Feb. 9, 1789; m. Susan Shenk, b. Jan. 21, 1792.
226. Catherine, Millersville, Pa., b. Nov. 7, 1792; m. Christian Kilheffer, b. Nov. 30, 1789; d. Dec. 25, 1846.

Family of FANNY HERR (55) and HENRY KAUFFMAN.

227. Andrew, Millersville, Pa., m. Anna Kreider.
228. Henry, Millersville, Pa., m. Catherine Kreider.
229. John, Millersville, Pa., m. Anna Brubaker, dau. Rev. Jacob Brubaker, and ————.

Family of ABRAHAM HERR (56) and ———— ————.

230. Anna, Millersville, Pa.

Family of HENRY HERR (58) and ESTHER HERSHEY.

231. Rudolph, Manor, Pa., b. Aug. 30, 1752; m. Anna Charles, dau. Joseph Charles and Elizabeth Bachman.

232. Anna, Manor, Pa., b. Oct. 12, 1753; m. Christian Kauffman.
233. Christian, Manor, Pa., b. May 27, 1756; d. 1758.
234. Christian, Manor, Pa., b. Nov. 26, 1759; d. Mar. 27, 1842; m.
     Magdalene Charles, b. Aug. 5, 1759; d. Aug. 26, 1829; dau.
     Joseph Charles and Elizabeth Bachman.
235. Abraham, Annville, Pa., b. Feb. 10, 1762; m. ——— Reist.
236. Henry, Manor, Pa., b. Feb. 16, 1764; m. Elizabeth Kilheffer.
237. Samuel, Manheim, Pa., b. Nov. 22, 1766; m. Wid. Barbara Kil-
     heffer Gochenour, b. Nov. 2, 1772; d. Feb. 13, 1846.

Family of JOHN HERR (59) and BARBARA GROFF (97).

238. John, Cocalico, Pa.
239. Abraham, Cocalico, Pa.
240. Christian, Cocalico, Pa., b. 1744; d. 1819.
241. Michael, Cocalico, Pa., b. 1748; d. Sept. 30, 1778; m. Elizabeth
     ———.
242. Barbara, Cocalico, Pa.
243. Elizabeth, Cocalico, Pa.
244. Fanny, Cocalico, Pa., m. John Witmer.
245. Anna, Cocalico, Pa., m. ——— Hamerker.
246. Maria, Cocalico, Pa.

Family of RUDOLPH HERR (61) and FRANCES ———.

247. Christian, Manor, Pa., m. ——— Brubaker.
248. Rudolph, Manor, Pa., m. ——— Hayes.
249. Susan, Lampeter, Pa., m. John Binkley.
250. Anna, Levan's Mill, Pa., m. Benjamin Kauffman.
251. Elizabeth, Bausman, Pa., m. Christian Stehman.

Family of BARBARA HERR (62) and JACOB ERISMAN.

252. Esther, Manor, Pa.
253. Barbara, Manor, Pa.
254. Ann, Manor, Pa., m. ——— Kauffman.

Family of ABRAHAM HERR (66) and ——— ———.

255. Christian, Millersville, Pa., m. Ann Breneman.
256. Elizabeth, Rohrerstown, Pa., m. Christian Barr.

257. Mary, Manor, Pa., m. Andrew Hershey.
258. Ann, Manor, Pa., m. John Hershey.
259. Esther, Lampeter, Pa., m. Christian Rohrer.

Family of DAVID HERR (67) and CHRISTIANA MARTIN.

260. Christian, Hawksville, Pa., b. June 30, 1765.
261. Barbara, Hawksville, Pa., b. June 14, 1767.
262. Mary, Belmont Co., O., b. Oct. 25, 1769; d. Feb. 2, 1848; m. David Newswenger, son David Newswenger and ———.
263. John, Stumptown, Pa., b. Dec. 15, 1771; m. Magdalene Sides; m. Susan Breneman.
264. David, Camargo, Pa., b. June 15, 1774; d. Mar, 13, 1859; m. June 12, 1808, Catherine Bumbarger, b. Nov. 1, 1791; d. April 26, 1880; dau. Michael Bumbarger and Elizabeth Hawk.
265. Abraham, Hawksville, Pa., b. Dec. 3, 1778; d. Apr. 20, 1851; m. Margaret Mowry, b. June 12, 1767; d. Mar. 30, 1854; dau. Baltzer Mowry and ———.
266. Henry, Hawksville, Pa., b. July 19, 1781; d. Dec. 5, 1848.
267. Susanna, Hawksville, Pa., b. Dec. 9, 1784; d. Sept. 19, 1826; m. Jan. 4, 1803, Abraham Barr (338).
268. Elizabeth, Hawksville, Pa., b. Apr. 10, 1788.

Family of EMANUEL HERR (69) and ——— ———.

269. Emanuel, Millersville, Pa., b. July 13, 1774; d. Sept. 15, 1840; m. Mary Rohrer, b. July 8, 1786; d. Jan. 21, 1842; dau. Henry Rohrer and Mary Musselman.
270. Christian, Lancaster, Pa., b. Feb. 2, 1779; d. June 6, 1824; m. Jan. 28, 1801, Catherine Kauffman, b. June 29, 1782; d. Nov. 6, 1845; dau. John Kauffman and Catherine Witmer.

Family of FANNY HERR (72) and HENRY BINKLEY.

271. David, Millersville, Pa., m. -——— Yertz, dau. Peter Yertz and ———.

Family of Wid. FANNY HERR BINKLEY (72) and BALTZER SHERTZLER.

272. Elizabeth, Millersville, Pa., m. John Doner.
273. Barbara, Millersville, Pa.

Family of CHRISTIAN HERR (73) and MARY HERSHEY.

274. Barbara C., Mountville, Pa., m. Jacob Charles, son Jacob Charles and ———.

275. Christian, Washington, Pa., b. Nov. 16, 1777; d. Mar. 1, 1850; m. Elizabeth Hart, dau. John Hart and ———; m. Susan Stehman, b. June 18, 1790, dau. Abraham Stehman and Elizabeth Bucher.

276. Anna, Lancaster, Pa., m. John Beam, son Jacob Beam, and ———.

277. Mary, Creswell, Pa., m. Rev. Abraham Hershey, son Andrew Hershey and ———.

278. David Creswell, Pa., b. Aug. 1, 1793; d. Apr. 11, 1881; m. 1818, Barbara Ohlwiler, b. June 30, 1780; d. July 28, 1869; dau. Frederick Ohlwiler and Barbara Rider.

Family of ABRAHAM HERR (75) and BARBARA ESHLEMAN.

279. Benjamin, Millersville, Pa., b. Nov. 20, 1776; d. Mar., 1849; m. May 7, 1800, Mary Bachman, dau. Michael Bachman and Elizabeth Swarr.

280. Barbara, Millersville, Pa., m. John Shenk.

281. Abraham, Canton, Ill., m. Fanny Donor, b. 1805; d. Aug. 14, 1837; m. ——— Shaef.

282. Elizabeth, Willow Street, Pa., b. Jan. 18, 1783; d. June 28, 1827; m. Jacob Smith, b. July 7, 1774; d. Feb. 23, 1818; son Jacob Smith and ——— Good.

283. Fanny, Willow Street, Pa., b. Apr. 13, 1790; d. Dec. 5, 1849; m. John Kendig, b. July 28, 1774; d. Oct. 31, 1822.

284. Hettie, Willow Street, Pa.

285. John, Willow Street, Pa.

286. Nancy, Willow Street, Pa.

287. Mary, Willow Street, Pa.

Family of ESTHER HERR (77) and CHRISTIAN HABECKER.

288. Joseph, Suspension Bridge, N. Y.

289. Barbara, Suspension Bridge, N. Y., b. Oct. 23, 1782; d. July 4, 1859; m. Oct. 8, 1804, Abraham Witmer, b. Sept., 1771; d. Aug. 4, 1851; son Christian Witmer and Maria Schallenberger.

290. Esther, Suspension Bridge, N. Y., d. 1816; m. John Charles, son Jacob Charles and ———.
291. Christian, Rohrerstown, Pa., m. Elizabeth Kauffman, dau. Isaac Kauffman and ———.
292. Frances, Rohrerstown, Pa., m. John Shoff.
293. David, Rohrerstown, Pa., m. Barbara Newcomer.

Family of Wid. DAVID HERR (78) and SUSAN YERTZ.

294. Christian, Creswell, Pa., m. Esther Whitestick.
295. Barbara, Washington, Pa., d. 1852; m. Jacob Stoner.
296. Abraham, Creswell, Pa.

Family of BENJAMIN HERR (80) and MAGDALENA LICHTE.

297. Infant, Pittsburg, Pa., b. Jan. 26, 1795; d. Feb. 2, 1795.
298. Jacob, Pittsburg, Pa., b. Feb. 14, 1796; d. Mar. 24, 1796.
299. David, Pittsburg, Pa., b. Feb. 14, 1796; d. May 31, 1797.
300. Barbara, Allegheny City, Pa., b. Sept. 6, 1797; d. Mar. 30, 1874; m. June, 1820, John Croft, b. 1794; d. Aug. 22, 1868.
301. Christiana, Pittsburg, Pa., b. Nov. 26, 1799; d. Nov. 5, 1801.
302. Benjamin, Dehaven, Pa., b. Aug. 16, 1802; d. July, 1867; m. 1847, Wid. Elizabeth Smith Sener, d. Nov., 1889; dau. ——— Smith and ———.
303. Henry, Bennett, Pa., b. June 4, 1805; d. Oct. 3, 1893; m. June 15, 1834, Mary P. Matthias, b. Mar. 30, 1803; d. Mar. 30, 1884; dau. Daniel Matthias and Charlotte Lease.
304. Daniel, Sharpsburg, Pa., b. June 7, 1808; d. June 4, 1838; m. Nov. 28, 1829, Ann Snively, b. Feb. 9, 1809; d. Oct. 22, 1899; dau. Henry Snively and Mary M. Whitmore.
305. John, Cleveland, O., b. Dec. 21, 1810; d. June 20, 1900; m. June 16, 1834, Barbara Ziegler, b. Dec. 31, 1813; d. Jan. 14, 1892; dau. Abraham Ziegler and ———.
306. Elizabeth, Bennett, Pa., b. Oct. 12, 1815; d. Apr. 11, 1900; m. Apr. 2, 1835, Louis Feilbach, b. Jan. 3, 1811; d. Apr. 11, 1886; son Christian Feilbach and Katherine Schraeder.
307. Magdalena, Erie, Pa., b. June 10, 1818; d. 1862; m. Samuel Hershey.

2

Family of ABRAHAM HERR (81) and ANNA MILLER.

308. John, Strasburg, Pa., m. Ann Howry.
309. Abraham, Strasburg, Pa., d. July, 1805; m. Ann Hoover (360).
310. Tobias, Strasburg, Pa., b. Oct. 24, 1775; d. Sept, 28, 1833; m. Eve Herr (146).
311. David, Strasburg, Pa., m. Mary Wiker.
312. Mary, Lime Valley, Pa., m. John Hoover (364).
313. Emanuel, Marticville, Pa., m. Mary Good, dau. John Good and Prudence Kendig.

Family of JOHN HERR (82) and MARY GROFF (181).

314. John, Strasburg, Pa., b. Oct. 8, 1773; d. Feb. 3, 1823; m. Feb. 25, 1800, Susanna Brackbill (404).
315. Ann, Strasburg, Pa., d. Oct. 4, 1823; m. Samuel Herr (153).
316. Barbara, Strasburg, Pa., m. Abraham Groff, son Jacob Groff and Alice Kendig.

Family of CHRISTIAN HERR (84) and ANNA BARR (124).

317. Christiana, Willow Street, Pa., m. Wid. Martin Herr (143).
318. Elizabeth, Willow Street, Pa., m. Martin Mylin.
319. Anna, Willow Street, Pa., m. Martin Light.
320. Benjamin, Johnsville, O., b. Sept. 9, 1775; d. Sept. 23, 1840; m. Apr. 22, 1799, Hannah Withers, b, Mar. 29, 1780; d. July 5, 1831; dau. John Withers and ————.
321. Fanny, Willow Street, Pa., m. Christian Snavely, son John Snavely and Elizabeth Barr.
322. Christian, Willow Street, Pa., m. Lizzie Haverstick.
323. Maria, Willow Street, Pa., m. Jacob Breneman, b. 1775.

Family of DAVID HERR (85) and EVE BARR.

324. Betsey, Willow Street, Pa., b. Sept. 12, 1780; d. Feb. 13, 1845; m. Adam Herr (145).

Family of Wid. DAVID HERR (85) and BETSEY KENDIG.

325. Magdalene, Willow Street, Pa., b. Jan. 9, 1789; d. Mar. 18, 1863; m. Sept. 17, 1807, Christian Brackbill (406).

Family of CHRISTIANA HERR (86) and JOHN HERR (139).

326. Francis, Wheatland Mills, Pa., b. Nov. 19, 1772; d. July 1, 1804.
327. John, Wheatland Mills, Pa., b. Dec. 11, 1774; d. Mar. 8, 1828; m. Apr. 30, 1800, Christiana Mylin, b. Mar. 10, 1778; d. Mar. 21, 1854; dau. Martin Mylin and ———.

Family of BARBARA HERR (87) and HENRY KENDIG.

328. Barbara, Lampeter, Pa.
329. John, ———, Md.
330. Elizabeth, Lampeter, Pa., m. Hieronimus Eckman; m. Henry Kendig, son Isaac Kendig and Rebecca Carpman.
331. Alice, Lampeter, Pa., m. John Martin (467).
332. Henry, New Providence, Pa., b. 1777; d. Sept. 26, 1849; m. 1806, Salome Smith, b. Nov. 24, 1785; d. Jan. 10, 1863.
333. Michael, Sporting Hill, Pa., b. May 24, 1785; d. Apr. 26, 1843; m. Elizabeth Rohr, b. Aug. 17, 1788; d. Nov. 24, 1878.
334. Mary, Martic, Pa., m. Richard Johnson; m. Solomon Cramer.

Family of ANN HERR (88) and JOHN KENDIG.

335. Christian, Strasburg, Pa., b. Dec. 3, 1761; d. Jan 27, 1781.
336. Martin, Strasburg, Pa., b. Oct. 23, 1764; d. 1765.
337. Nancy, Strasburg, Pa., b. Mar. 14, 1769; d. June 30, 1861; m. George Withers, b. 1747; d. 1811.

Family of MARIA HERR (89) and MARTIN BARR.

338. Abraham, Quarryville, Pa., b. Dec. 10, 1770; d. July 23, 1836; m. Jan. 4, 1803, Susanna Herr (267).
339. Jacob, Quarryville, Pa., b. Oct. 10, 1772; d. Dec. 15, 1826; m. Elizabeth Getz, b. July 8, 1770; d. Oct. 20, 1852.
340. Martin, Quarryville, Pa., b. Dec. 2, 1774; d. Dec. 11, 1826; m. Nancy Herr (377).
341. John, Quarryville, Pa.
342. Ann, New Providence, Pa.
343. Fanny, New Providence, Pa.
344. Susan, New Providence, Pa., m. John Longenecker, d. Mar. 27, 1849; son Daniel Longenecker and ———.
345. Mary, Lampeter, Pa., m. Wid. Frederick Myers.

Family of FANNY HERR (90) and JOHN BARR.

346. Jacob, Quarryville, Pa., m. Nancy Bowman; m. Wid. Theodocia Steel.
347. Mary, Quarryville, Pa.

Family of Wid. FANNY HERR BARR (90) and JAMES KEECH.

348. Fanny, Quarryville, Pa., m. Henry Bird.
349. Ann, Quarryville, Pa., m. Samuel Keech.
350. Barbara, Quarryville, Pa.

Family of BARBARA HERR (91) and HENRY SHAUB.

351. Henry, New Providence, Pa., m. Elizabeth Denlinger; m. Mary Eckman.
352. John, Lampeter, Pa., m. Esther Denlinger.
353. Abraham, Lampeter, Pa., d. Sept., 1822; m. Christiana Herr (382).
354. Christian, Lampeter, Pa., m. Nancy Witmer, dau. John Witmer and Fanny Herr (244).
355. Martin, New Providence, Pa., m. Catharine Book.
356. Fanny, Lampeter, Pa., m. Jacob Denlinger.
357. Barbara, New Providence, Pa., m. Abraham Herr (395).
358. Annie, Strasburg, Pa., m. Christian Hoover (365).

Family of ANNA HERR (92) and CHRISTIAN HOOVER.

359. Fanny, Strasburg, Pa., m. Henry Rush.
360. Anna, Strasburg, Pa., d. Mar. 28, 1851; m. Abraham Herr (309).
361. Maria, Strasburg, Pa.
362. Henry, Willow Street, Pa., m. Fanny Buckwalter.
363. Abraham, Strasburg, Pa., m. Esther Brubaker.
364. John, Strasburg, Pa., d. 1856; m. Mary Herr (312).
365. Christian, Strasburg, Pa., m. Anna Shaub (358).
366. David, Strasburg, Pa., m. Susan Eaby.
367. Jacob, Willow Street, Pa., b. Nov. 16, 1792; d. May 29, 1834; m. Mary Herr (513).

Family of ANNA GROFF (93) and HENRY KENDIG.

368. Susan, New Providence, Pa.. m. John Groff, son John Groff and Ann Groff.

369. Daniel, Orrville, O., m. Ann Forrer (448).
370. Elizabeth, Strasburg, Pa., m. Martin Eshleman, son Martin Eshleman and Lizzie Groff.
371. Nancy ———, Md. m. John Forrer (445); m. Wid. Abraham Groff, son Jacob Groffff and Alice Kendig.
372. Barbara, Strasburg, Pa., m. Benjamin Groff (660).
373. Kittie, Willow Street, Pa., m. Martin Forrer (446).

Family of SUSANNA GROFF (94) and ISAAC HERR (658).

374. Henry, Buck, Pa., b. Mar. 19, 1770; m. Elizabeth Harnish, dau. John Harnish and ———.
375. Elizabeth, New Providence, Pa., b. July 3, 1772; m. Frederick Krug.
376. Daniel, Smithville, Pa., b. Feb. 4, 1775; d. Oct. 15, 1828; m. Dec. 1803, Betsey Miller, b. Nov. 1, 1783; d. July 13, 1866; dau. Joseph Miller and Mary ———.
377. Nancy, Quarryville, Pa., b. Jan. 3, 1777; m. Martin Barr (340).
378. Susan, Quarryville, Pa., b. Mar. 19, 1779; d. Mar. 28, 1842; m. Martin Herr (396).
379. Barbara, New Providence, Pa., b. Mar. 13, 1781; m. Peter Lines, son Christian Lines and ———.
380. John, New Providence, Pa., b. June 11, 1784: d. July 16, 1789.
381. Isaac, Smithville, Pa., b. Oct. 12, 1786; d. Jan. 11, 1864; m. 1811, Catherine Miller, b. Jan. 18, 1785; dau. Peter Miller and Susan Rohrer.
382. Christiana, Lampeter, Pa., b. Dec. 12, 1788; d. Oct. 19, 1858; m. Abraham Shaub (353).

Family of CHRISTIAN HERR (102) and MARIA BOWMAN.

383. Ann, Strasburg, Pa., b. May 20, 1756; d. Aug. 13, 1837; m. Apr. 3, 1775, John Funk, b. Mar. 5, 1755; d. May 31, 1831.
384. Elizabeth, Strasburg, Pa., b. May 27, 1759; m. Daniel Miller, b. 1760.
385. Maria, Strasburg, Pa., b. Aug. 13, 1761; d. June 16, 1843; m. May, 1779, George Diffenbaugh, b. Nov. 9, 1754; d. Mar. 16, 1837.

386. Susan, Strasburg, Pa., b. Feb. 13, 1764; d. Sept. 16, 1825.
387. Esther, Refton, Pa., b. May 21, 1766; d. Dec. 16, 1846; m. Henry
    Bowman, b. Feb. 8, 1763; d. Sept. 21, 1841.
388. Catherine, Strasburg, Pa., b. Aug. 26, 1768.
389. Barbara, Strasburg, Pa., b. Jan. 9, 1771.
390. Magdalene, Refton, Pa., b. Aug. 12, 1775; m. Christian Rohrer,
    b. Jan. 3, 1772; d. 1825; son Jacob Rohrer and Magdalene
    Weaver.
391. Rev. Christian, Lime Valley, Pa., b. Oct. 31, 1780; d. June 23,
    1853; m. Apr. 8, 1800, Anna Forrer (453).

Family of ABRAHAM HERR (103) and BARBARA WEAVER.

392. Jacob, Willow Street, Pa., b. Nov. 16, 1765; d. 1801; m, Mary
    Carpman, d. 1801.
393. John L., Willow Street, Pa., b. Dec. 19, 1767; d. July 7, 1831; m.
    1791, Fanny Shultz, dau. Christian Shultz and ———; m. Mar.
    20, 1809. Wid. Ann B. Stauffer (403).
394. Daniel, Willow Street, Pa., b. Feb. 1, 1771.
395. Abraham, Quarryville, Pa., b. Oct. 24, 1774; d. Feb. 4, 1860; m.
    Feb. 19, 1798, Barbara Shaub (357).
396. Martin, Quarryville, Pa., b. July 17, 1777; d. Mar. 22, 1867; m.
    Susan Herr (378).
397. Joseph, Lampeter, Pa., b. Aug. 15, 1780; d. Oct. 12, 1857; m. Apr.
    6, 1802, Maria Forrer (454).
398. David, Quarryville, Pa., b. Feb. 4, 1783.

Family of BENEDICT BACKBILL (109) and MARY KENDIG.

399. John, Strasburg, Pa., b. Jan. 20, 1763; d. July 19, 1825; m. Jan.
    3, 1793, Elizabeth Landis, b. Dec. 15, 1768; d. Feb. 4, 1857; dau.
    Benjamin Landis and Anna Snavely.
400. Elizabeth, Landis Valley, Pa., b. Dec. 10, 1764; d. May 28, 1789;
    m. Apr. 8, 1783, Benjamin Landis, b. May 20, 1755; d. Mar. 8,
    1811; son Benjamin Landis and Anna Snavely.
401. Mary, Strasburg, Pa., b. Sept. 26, 1769; d. May 2, 1848; m. Mar.
    15, 1791, Jacob Eshleman (666).
402. Henry, Strasburg, Pa., b. Aug. 25, 1771; d. July 6, 1837; m. Mar.
    26, 1798, Susanna Eshleman (668).

403. Anna, Marietta, Pa., b. Dec. 25, 1773; d. Jan. 31, 1828; m. Oct. 30, 1794, John Stauffer, b. May 1, 1770; d. Dec. 4, 1797; son Jacob Stauffer and Fanny Snyder; m. Mar. 20, 1809, Wid. John L. Herr (393).

404. Susanna, Soudersburg, Pa., b. Sept. 10, 1776; d. Dec. 10, 1859; m. Feb. 25, 1800, John Herr (314).

405. Benjamin, Bethania, Pa., b. June 8, 1779; d. May 15, 1827; m. Feb. 12, 1805, Elizabeth Hershey, b. May 27, 1783; dau. Jacob Hershey and Anna Newcomer.

406 Christian, Strasburg, Pa., b. Jan 9, 1781; d. July 20, 1857; m. Sept. 17, 1807, Magdalene Herr (325).

Family of ANNA BRACKBILL (110) and Rev. JACOB NEFF.

407. Esther, Strasburg, Pa., b. Sept. 27, 1756; d. Feb. 2, 1817; m. Nov. 8, 1779, Jacob Weaver, b. July 4, 1750; son Jacob Weaver and Magdalene Barr.

408. Anna, Lampeter, Pa., b. Oct. 21, 1757; d. Apr. 16, 1844; m. Oct. 15, 1787, Francis Kendig, b. Apr. 23, 1766; d. Nov. 25, 1840; son Jacob Kendig and Catherine Neff.

409. Rev. Jacob, Strasburg, Pa., b. Sept. 25, 1760; d. June 17, 1849; m. May 12, 1787, Elizabeth Herr (117).

410. Fanny, Strasburg, Pa., b. Oct. 3, 1763; d. July 3, 1840; m. June 10, 1788, Martin Barr (128).

411. John, Strasburg, Pa., b. Jan. 1, 1769; d. July 12, 1837; m. Barbara Herr (116).

Family of FANNY BRACKBILL (111) and GEORGE WEAVER.

412. Henry, Winchester, Pa., b. Oct. 10, 1763; d. July 25, 1798; m. 1788, Mary Good, b. 1766; d. June, 1814; dau. Robert Good and Jane Davis.

413. Anna, Uniontown, O., b. Dec. 25, 1765; d. Mar. 25, 1855; m. Oct. 21, 1784, Matthias Shirk, b. Aug. 20, 1761; d. Oct. 21, 1828; son David Shirk and Frances Brackbill.

414. Frances, Lawrenceburg, Ind., b. May 10, 1768; d. Apr. 25, 1796; m. ———— Perry.

415. George, Lawrenceburg, Ind., b. Dec. 20, 1770; d. Jan. 29, 1853.

416. Elizabeth, Lawrenceburg, Ind., b. Dec. 1, 1772; d. Mar. 14, 1864; m. Elijah Sparks; d. May 1, 1815.

417. Samuel, Natches, Miss., b. Oct. 15, 1775; d. Oct. 4, 1808.

418. John, Lawrenceburg, Ind., b. May 21, 1777; d. Oct. 1, 1841.

Family of MARY HERR (113) and ABRAHAM WITMER.

419. John, Mechanicsburg, Pa., b. Mar. 1, 1770; d. May 22, 1857.

420. Abraham, Lancaster, Pa., b. Feb. 24, 1773; d. Jan. 13, 1819; m. May 19, 1804, Anna C. Burg, b. Oct. 13, 1784; d. Mar. 9, 1869; dau. John Burg and Barbara Eberly.

421. Elizabeth, Lancaster, Pa., b. Dec. 23, 1774; d. 1828; m. June 15, 1805, Patten Ross, b. Mar. 13, 1778; son George Ross and ———.

422. Mary, Mechanicsburg, Pa., b. Sept. 9, 1776; d. June 6, 1862; m. Mar. 4, 1812, John Groff, b. Oct. 31, 1769; d. Feb. 10, 1850; son Andrew Groff and Catherine Groford.

Family of FANNIE HERR (115) and GEORGE BRESSLER.

423. Mary, Canton, O., b. Sept. 14, 1768; d. 1830; m. Joel Ferree, b. 1760.

424. Catherine, Salona, Pa., b. Nov. 11, 1770; d. June 1, 1853; m. Samuel Wilson, b. Nov. 1, 1759.

425. Elizabeth, Salona, Pa., b. Aug. 12, 1775; d. Aug. 15, 1829; m. 1796, Jacob Hartman (488).

426. Rebecca, Salona, Pa., b. Feb. 16, 1778; d. Sept. 11, 1873; m. Daniel Herr (156).

427. Fannie, Salona, Pa., b. Sept. 30, 1782; d. Feb. 10, 1866; m. 1800, Joel Herr (155).

428. Charlotte, Lancaster, Pa., b. Apr. 6, 1785; d. Feb. 7, 1877; m. Mar. 12, 1811, Henry Barnet, b. 1782; d. Oct. 21, 1828; son William Barnet and Elizabeth Keeser.

429. George, Mill Hall, Pa., b. Mar. 17, 1788; d. Mar. 14, 1864; m. July 28, 1812, Ann E. Dornic, b. Sept. 15, 1791; d. Jan. 31, 1853; dau. Henry Dornic and Elizabeth Wilson.

430. Harriet, Salona, Pa., b. Oct. 10, 1791; d. June 13, 1869; m, Jan. 15, 1811, Samuel Miller, b. Feb. 13, 1785; d. Sept. 29, 1828; son Matthias Miller and Anna Baer.

Family of BARBARA HERR (116) and JOHN NEFF (411).

431. John, East Mill Creek, Utah, b. Sept. 19, 1794; d. May 9, 1869; m. Jan. 12, 1822, Mary Barr, b. Dec. 1, 1801; d. Dec. 1, 1875; dau. Christian Barr and Susan Breneman.
432. Benjamin, Paris, Ohio, b. Oct. 27, 1805; d. July 19, 1828.
433. Elizabeth, Strasburg, Pa., b. 1806; d. 1810.

Family of ELIZABETH HERR (117) and Rev. JACOB NEFF (409).

434. Fannie, Wheatland Mills, Pa., b. Oct. 26, 1791; d. July 10, 1871; m, May 25, 1813, Francis Herr (405).
435. Jacob, Strasburg, Pa., b. Dec. 5, 1793; d. Feb. 8, 1859; m, Apr. 29, 1822, Fannie Barr (486); m. May 15, 1828, Anna Barr (487).
436. Elizabeth, Strasburg, Pa., b. July 8, 1796; d. Nov. 8, 1870; m. June 1, 1819; Henry Breneman, b. Jan. 25, 1795; d. May 10, 1859; son Rev. Henry Breneman and Anna Musser.

Family of CHRISTIAN HERR (118) and ELIZABETH WITHERS.

437. Fanny, Lampeter, Pa., b. Nov. 11, 1797; d. Dec. 28, 1857; m. 1820, Samuel Herr (1095); m. Oct. 24, 1839, Wid. Henry Herr (521).
438. Susan, Strasburg, Pa., b. Aug. 8, 1800; d. Dec. 12, 1864; m. May 6, 1823, Benjamin Breneman, b. Nov. 15, 1797; d. Mar. 13, 1877; son Rev. Henry Breneman and Anna Musser.

Family of Wid. CHRISTIAN HERR (118) and MARY ROHRER.

439. Elizabeth, Lampeter, Pa., b. June 22, 1803; d. Dec. 21, 1875.
440. Christian, Willow Street, Pa., b. Mar. 11, 1805; d. Jan. 2, 1875; m. Dec. 23, 1830, Mary Herr (1685).
441. John, Lampeter, Pa., b. Oct. 23, 1807; d. Sept. 17, 1848; m. Feb. 15, 1835, Susan Rohrer, b. Aug. 30, 1809; d. Jan. 29, 1887; dau. Christian Rohrer and Wid. Susan Hoover.
442. Benjamin, Lampeter, Pa., b. Oct. 21, 1811; d. Apr. 2, 1888; m. Dec. 22, 1836, Catherine Barr (4272); m. Mar. 25, 1845, Ann E. Sener, b. Mar. 13, 1817; d. May 25, 1904; dau. Gottlieb Sener and Eve Eberly.

443. Jacob, Lampeter, Pa., b. Apr. 27, 1815; d. May 18, 1878; m. Nov. 17, 1846, Anna Musser, b. Apr. 12, 1821; d. Jan. 18, 1887; dau. Benjamin Musser and Barbara Miller.

444. Samuel, Lampeter, Pa., b. Jan. 29, 1819; d. Apr. 2, 1821.

Family of JOHN FORRER (119) and ELIZABETH MYLIN.

445. John, Lampeter, Pa., d. 1799; m. Nancy Kendig (371).

446. Martin, Lampeter, Pa., m. Kittie Kendig (373).

447. Christian, Orrville, O., m. ——— Yertz; m. Susan Boham, dau. John Boham and ———.

448. Ann, Orrville, O., m. Daniel Kendig (369); m. Wid. Tobias Kreider.

449. Maria, Lampeter, Pa., b. Dec. 7, 1769; d. Feb. 27, 1853; m. Christian Rohrer, b. Nov. 12, 1768; d. June 16, 1825; son Christian Rohrer and Lizzie Neff.

450. Lizzie, Lampeter, Pa., m. George Knaisley; m. Wid. ——— Shenk.

451. Barbara, Elizabethtown, Pa., b. May 9, 1776; d. Dec. 4, 1864; m. Oct. 30, 1792, Henry Hyers, b. July 3, 1770; d. Jan. 27, 1820; m. Abraham Gish.

452. Christiana, Orrville, O., m. Daniel Knaisley.

Family of CHRISTIAN FORRER (120) and BARBARA BARR.

453. Anna, Refton, Pa., b. Feb. 9, 1783; d. Mar. 12, 1831; m. Apr. 8, 1800, Rev. Christian Herr (391).

454. Maria, Refton, Pa., d. 1852; m. Joseph Herr (397).

455. Magdalene, Strasburg, Pa., m. Jacob Herr (1399).

456. Christian, Cumberland Co., Pa., d. Oct., 1853; m. Elizabeth Light (1126).

457. Barbara, Willow Street, Pa., b. Sept. 3, 1812; d. 1867.

Family of FANNIE FORRER (121) and ISAAC BRENNEMAN.

458. Christian, New Danville, Pa.

459. Martin, New Danville, Pa., m. Fannie Kendig, dau. George Kendig and Elizabeth Eshleman.

460. Fannie, New Danville, Pa., b. July 29, 1769; d. Feb. 29, 1828; m.

Apr. 21, 1789, Isaac Heiney; d. May 3, 1832; son Isaac Heiney and ———.

461. Ann, New Danville, Pa.

162. Maria, New Danville, Pa.

Family of ANNA FORRER (122) and JOHN GROFF.

463. Christian, Strasburg, Pa., b. July 1, 1786; d. July 12, 1852; m. 1815, Hettie Groff; d. 1825; dau. Jacob Groff and Anna Groff; m. 1825, Mary Stofer; d. 1840; dau. Daniel Stofer and ———.

464. Mary, Strasburg, Pa., b. Apr. 10, 1788; d. July 15, 1869; m. Mar. 18, 1806, David Eshleman (671).

465. Betsey, Strasburg, Pa., b. July 13, 1789; d. July 23, 1871; m. Apr. 7, 1807, Rev. John Herr (494).

466. John, Lycoming Co., Pa., b. 1790; m. Sallie Downing.

Family of MARY BARR (123) and CHRISTIAN MARTIN.

467. John, Lampeter, Pa., m. Alice Kendig (331).

468. Elizabeth, Mt. Joy, Pa., m. Daniel Longenecker, son Abraham Longenecker and ———.

469. Christian, Mt. Joy, Pa., b. Sept. 10, 1771; d. Aug. 3, 1841; m. Elizabeth Frank, b. Mar. 27, 1768; d. July 5, 1815; dau. John Frank and ———; m. Mary Robinson, b. Apr. 14, 1771; d. Aug. 3, 1841; dau. John Robinson and Mary ———.

470. Nancy, Strasburg, Pa., b. Apr. 1, 1773; d. June 11, 1855; m. 1805, Samuel Eshleman, b. Oct. 22, 1770; d. July 3, 1843; son Martin Eshleman and Lizzie Groff.

471. Martha, Strasburg, Pa., m. John Shaub, son Martin Shaub and ———.

472. David, Willow Street, Pa., m. Susan Eshleman, dau. Martin Eshleman and Lizzie Groff.

473. Maria, Willow Street, Pa., m. Daniel Musser, son Peter Musser and Elizabeth ———.

474. Samuel, Strasburg, Pa., b. 1781; d. Mar. 18, 1867; m. Hary Dunning, b. 1791; d. June 11, 1867.

475. Jacob, Martinsville, Pa., b. Feb. 3, 1784; d. May 18, 1873; m. Apr. 24, 1817, Esther Kendig, b. Oct. 22, 1786; d. Feb. 19, 1870; dau. Jacob Kendig and Susan Kissel.

476. ———.
477. ———.

Family of JOHN BARR (126) and ELIZABETH ROBINSON.

478. John, Baltimore, Md.
479. Dr. Martin, Baltimore, Md., m. Jane Adams.

Family of MARTIN BARR (128) and FANNIE NEFF (410).

480. John, New Providence, Pa., b. Apr. 11, 1789; d. June 10, 1811; m. Sept. 8, 1810, Susanna Herr (1400).
481. Benjamin, Strasburg, Pa., b. Mar. 3, 1791; d. Jan. 6, 1862; m. Dec. 24, 1816, Catherine Kendig (1474).
482. Magdalene. Strasburg, Pa., b. Mar. 15, 1793; d. Jan. 10, 1798.
483. Martin, Strasburg, Pa., b. June 11, 1795; d. Dec. 20, 1867; m. Jan. 13, 1819, Susan Miller, b. Jan. 1, 1798; d. Mar. 8, 1838; dau. Samuel Miller and Anna Witmer; m. Sept. 20, 1847, Elizabeth Johnson, b. June 10, 1810; d. Mar. 2, 1886; dau. Richard Johnson and Mary Galsbach.
484. Elizabeth, Strasburg, Pa., b. Aug. 26, 1797; d. May 24, 1821; m. Mar. 28, 1820, Francis Kendig (1475).
485. Jacob, Strasburg, Pa., b. Dec. 4, 1800; d. Apr. 8, 1803.
486. Fannie, Strasburg, Pa., b. Nov. 18, 1803; d. Nov. 3, 1826; m. Apr. 28, 1822, Jacob Neff (435).
487. Annie, Strasburg, Pa., b. June 7, 1806; d. Feb. 12, 1874; m. May 15, 1828, Wid. Jacob Neff (435).

Family of ANNA HERR (131) and HENRY HARTMAN.

488. Jacob, Lampeter, Pa., b. Mar. 4, 1772; d. Sept. 19, 1849; m. Elizabeth Bressler (425).
489. Christian, Harrisburg, Pa., d. Sept. 17, 1830; m. Anna Brubaker; d. Apr. 1861.

Family of FRANCIS HERR (140) and FANNY BARR (125).

490. Lizzie, Wheatland Mills, Pa., d. 1813.
491. Esther, Greenland, Pa., b. Jan. 19, 1776; d. Mar. 16, 1870; m. Martin Eshleman, b. May 8, 1775; d. Nov. 3, 1849.

492. Anna, Wheatland Mills, Pa., b. June 10, 1779; d. June 8, 1823; m. Henry Mylin, b. 1776; d. 1806; son Martin Mylin and ——— Baer; m. Dec. 28, 1808, Jacob Weaver (1462).
493. Martha, Strasburg, Pa., m. Abraham Groff (665).
494. Rev. John, Strasburg, Pa., b. Sept. 18, 1781; d. May 3, 1850; m. Apr. 7, 1807, Betsey Groff (465).
495. Francis, Wheatland Mills, Pa., b. Mar. 24, 1783; d. Dec. 10, 1852; m. May 25, 1813, Fanny Neff (434).
496. Fanny, Strasburg, Pa., b. Oct. 11, 1786; d. Oct. 6, 1862; m. Jan. 12, 1807, Benjamin Eshleman (670).
497. Martin, Lancaster, Pa., b. June 12, 1788; d. Mar. 25, 1869; m. Apr. 28, 1817, Mary Herr (1402).

Family of ESTHER HERR (141) and PETER WITMER.

498. Martin, ———. Canada, m. Susan Kendig, b. Dec. 7, 1798; dau. Henry Kendig and Ann Rush.
499. Esther, ——— Va., b. June 3, 1785; d. Oct. 17, 1824; m. Oct. 20, 1807, Benjamin Kendig (2203).
500. Susan, Strasburg, Pa., m. Martin Kendig (2209).
501. John, Willow Street, Pa., b. 1799; d. 1839; m. 1823, Anna Brubaker, b. Feb. 2, 1804; d. May 29, 1883; dau. Martin Brubaker and Maria ———.
502. Nancy, Strasburg, Pa., b. May 27, 1793; d. May 18, 1832; m. Jan. 17, 1815, Michael Martin, b. Oct. 13, 1791; d. Oct. 3, 1823; son David Martin and ——— Groff; m. Mar. 4, 1826, Wid. Jacob Denlinger; d. Apr. 1835; son John Denlinger and ———.
503. Martha, Quarryville, Pa., b. Feb. 25, 1800; m. Jan 1, 1822, Samuel Martin (1725).
504. David, Quarryville, Pa., b. July 16, 1806; d. Mar. 24, 1864; m. Oct. 5, 1828, Elizabeth McComsey, b. Sept. 24, 1809; d. 1890; dau. William McComsey and Mary Eckman.
505. Betsey, Quarryville, Pa., b. Sept. 24, 1809.
506. Catherine, Quarryville, Pa.

Family of HENRY HERR (142) and MAGDALENA HERR (150).

507. Susan, Williamsville, N. Y., b. Oct. 10, 1782; d. June 26, 1865.

508. John, Williamsville, N. Y., b. July 31, 1784; d. Apr. 30, 1869; m. July 10, 1817, Mary Long, b. Dec. 1, 1789; d. Jan. 1, 1871; dau. John Long and Mary Hershey.

509. Mary, Williamsville, N. Y., b. Sept. 24, 1786; d. Apr. 11, 1838; m. Aug. 14, 1817, John Long, b. June 5, 1792; d. Apr. 25, 1849; son John Long and Mary Hershey.

510. Henry, Williamsville, N. Y., b. Aug. 6, 1788; d. Dec. 19, 1862.

511. Esther, Williamsville, N. Y., b. Jan. 28, 1791; d. Nov. 7, 1855.

512. Emanuel, Buffalo, N. Y., b. Dec. 25, 1793; d. July 6, 1877; m. June 11, 1833, Nancy Snearly, b. 1812; d. Feb. 2, 1871; dau. George Snearly and Susan Graybill.

Family of Wid. MARTIN HERR (143) and SUSAN BUCKWALTER.

513. Mary, Lampeter, Pa., b. June 17, 1797; d. May 1, 1858; m. Jacob Hoover (367).

514. Esther, Centreville, Pa., b. Mar. 16, 1799; d. Sept. 25, 1867; m Oct. 27, 1818, John Metzler, b. Jan. 20, 1795; d. June 18. 1865; son Henry Metzler and Mary Landis.

515. Abraham, Lancaster. Pa., b. Nov. 25, 1800; d. Feb. 2, 1881; m. Jan. 27, 1820, Susan Hess, b. Dec. 29, 1795; d. Jan. 1, 1867; dau. Christian Hess and Barbara Metzler.

516. Elizabeth, Lampeter, Pa., b. Dec. 18, 1802; d. May 19, 1877; m. Aug. 6, 1822, Daniel Kreider, b. Apr. 27, 1797; d. Mar. 2, 1869; son Daniel Kreider and Martha Stehman.

517. Susanna, Strasburg, Pa., b. Jan. 18, 1805; d. Oct. 1, 1861; m. 1828, John Kieports, b. Apr. 25, 1800; d. Aug. 29, 1880; son Daniel Kieports and Barbara Shenk.

518. John, Lancaster, Pa., b. Nov. 18, 1807; d. Oct. 11, 1894; m. Dec. 23, 1832, Fannie Kreider, b. July 12, 1810; d. Aug. 26, 1888; dau. Christian Kreider and Anna Harnish.

519. Adam, Strasburg, Pa., b. May 7. 1810; d. Aug. 29, 1831.

520. Annie, Medway, O., b. Nov. 9, 1811; d. Sept. 28, 1831; m. Aug. 3, 1830, Abner Rohrer, b. July 7, 1808; d. Feb. 9, 1885, son Martin Rohrer and Anna Miller.

521. Henry, Lancaster, Pa., b. Jan. 27, 1814; d. Sept. 28, 1895; m. Nov. 16, 1834, Mary Rohrer, b. Dec. 15, 1811; d. Mar. 5, 1838;

dau. Martin Rohrer and Anna Miller; m. Oct. 24, 1839, Wid. Fanny Herr (437); m. Dec. 4, 1859; Charlotte Herr (1556).

522. Martha, Lancaster, Pa., b. Oct. 15, 1817; d. July 6, 1866; m. Dec. 21, 1837, Christian H. Miller (12032).

Family of ANN HERR (144) and DAVID STROHM.

523. Hon. John, Lancaster, Pa., b. Oct. 16, 1793; d. Dec. 14, 1884; m. Dec. 23, 1817, Wid. Susanna Herr Barr (1400); m. 1857, Wid. Ann B. Witmer; d. 1883; dau. Martin Brubaker and ————.

524. Esther, New Providence, Pa., b. Nov. 26, 1795; d. Sept. 20, 1817.

525. Mary, Smithville, Pa., b. June 12, 1798; d. Jan. 12, 1799.

526. Mary, Smithville, Pa., b. Dec. 27, 1799; d. Jan. 30, 1888.

527. David, New Providence, Pa., b. May 28, 1804.

528. Emanuel, St. Louis, Mo., b. June 8, 1807; m. Apr. 4, 1839, Mary J. McGuire, b. Jan. 30, 1817; dau. Thomas McGuire and Mary Knott.

529. Susanna, New Providence, Pa., b. Apr. 4, 1812.

Family of ADAM HERR (145) and BETSEY HERR (324).

530. David, Strasburg, Pa., b. Feb. 15, 1801; d. July 30, 1805.

531. Daniel, Greenland, Pa., b. Aug. 3, 1803; d. Mar. 27, 1873; m. Feb. 23, 1830, Sarah Strohm, b. July 27, 1803; d. Feb. 5, 1887; dau. Henry Strohm and Mary Lefevre.

532. Martha, Lancaster, Pa., b. Dec. 4, 1805; d. Sept. 19, 1873; m. Mar. 1, 1838, David Herr (541).

533. Christian B., Lancaster, Pa., b. May 18, 1808; d. Apr. 25, 1847; m. Nov. 16, 1837, Maria Light (1133).

534. John, Refton, Pa., b. Mar. 10, 1811; d. May 24, 1879; m. Dec. 23, 1845, Ann F. Herr (1398).

535. Adam, Strasburg, Pa., b. Feb. 13, 1814; d. May 4, 1890; m. Dec. 14, 1841, Elizabeth Herr (1552).

536. Elizabeth, Strasburg, Pa., b. July 16, 1816; d. July 23, 1875; m. Apr. 19, 1854, Levi Lefevre, b. Feb. 12, 1804; d. June 25, 1879; son Dr. Peter Lefevre and Mary Lefevre.

537. David H., Orrville, O., b. Mar. 12, 1819; d. Sept. 7, 1864; m. Jan. 1, 1846, Mary A. Landis, b. Oct. 31, 1828; dau. Abraham Landis and Mary Witmer.

538. Eve Ann, Strasburg, Pa., b. Jan. 12, 1822; d. Mar. 30, 1849.

Family of EVE HERR (146) and TOBIAS HERR (310).

539. Benjamin, Dillerville, Pa., b. Mar. 16, 1797; d. Sept. 17, 1866; m. Jan. 31, 1822, Sarah Kendig (573); m. Aug. 18, 1829, Susan Strohm, b. Jan. 17, 1798; d. Apr. 1881; dau. Henry Strohm and Mary Lefevre.

540. John, New Danville, Pa., b. June 8, 1799; d. Dec. 18, 1882; m. Dec. 16, 1830, Eliza Herr (1139); m. Feb. 14, 1841, Maria Herr (1142).

541. David, Lampeter, Pa., b. Oct. 24, 1801; d. Oct. 3, 1877; m. Mar. 1, 1838, Martha Herr (532).

542. Ann, Lampeter, Pa., b. Aug. 23, 1804; d. Jan. 23, 1864; m. John Shenk, b. 1804; d. 1867; son John Shenk and ———.

543. Elizabeth, Lampeter, Pa., b. Oct. 3, 1807; d. June 28, 1845; m. Jan. 31, 1840, John Hoffman, b. Oct. 5, 1808; son Nicholas Hoffman and Elizabeth Miller.

544. Esther, Lampeter, Pa., b. Feb. 6, 1810; d. Oct., 1848; m. Jan. 4, 1848, Wid. John Hoffman, b. Oct. 5. 1808; son Nicholas Hoffman and Elizabeth Miller.

545. Tobias, Strasburg, Pa., b. May 29, 1813; d. June 14, 1865; m. Feb, 15, 1838, Susan Landis, b. Apr. 7, 1814; d. July 1, 1851; dau. John Landis and Eve Groff.

Family of SUSAN HERR (147) and JACOB WITMER.

546. Daniel, Strasburg, Pa., b. 1800.
547. John, Manor, Pa.

Family of DAVID HERR (148) and ESTHER WITMER.

548. John, Millersville, Pa., b. Sept. 12, 1797; d. 1854; m. Mar. 6, 1821, Maria Binkley, b. Dec. 13, 1799; d. Mar. 20, 1890; dau. David Binkley and Maria Yardey.

549. David, Columbia, Pa., b. July 7, 1799; d. July 28, 1851; m. May 15, 1821, Magdalene Clepper, b. Sept. 19, 1801; d. Oct. 29, 1884; dau. Joseph Clepper and Catharine Shuldy.

550. Daniel, Columbia, Pa., b. July 20, 1804; d. Oct. 10, 1865; m. 1827,

Mary M. Kurtz, b. 1807; d. 1830; dau. Christopher Kurtz and
———; m. Sept. 22, 1835, Sarah A. Martin, b. Dec. 17, 1810;
d. Feb. 27, 1894; dau. Henry Martin and Mary E. Trainor.
551. Catharine, Columbia, Pa., m. Christian Shock.
552. Esther, Columbia, Pa., m. ——— Stoner.

Family of Wid. DAVID HERR (148) and MARY HERR (559).

553. Henry, Manor, Pa.
554. Benjamin, Manor, Pa., b. Oct. 10, 1810; d. Nov. 26, 1830.
555. Levi, Manor, Pa.
556. Susan, Manor, Pa., m. Andrew Denison.
557. Sarah, Manor, Pa.
558. Martin, Manor, Pa.

Family of JOHN HERR (149) and SALLIE RANDALL.

559. Mary, Strasburg, Pa., m. Wid. David Herr (148).
560. Susan, Strasburg, Pa.
561. Joseph, Strasburg, Pa., b. 1800; m. Ann Smith.
562. Sallie, Strasburg, Pa.
563. Rachel, Strasburg, Pa.
564. Levi, Jamton, O., m. Oct. 18, 1827, Susanna Herr (1349).

Family of SUSAN HERR (151) and JACOB KENDIG.

565. Abraham, Strasburg, Pa., b. Oct. 20, 1782; d. Apr. 7, 1809.
566. Samuel, Strasburg, Pa., b. Feb. 25, 1784; d. Feb. 3, 1839.
567. John, Strasburg, Pa., b. June 2, 1785; d. Oct. 15, 1865.
568. Henry, Strasburg, Pa., b. Aug. 31, 1787; d. July 1, 1830.
569. Martha, Strasburg, Pa., b. Feb. 3, 1790; m. Christian Miller, b, 1787.
570. Emanuel, Strasburg, Pa., b. Dec. 3, 1792; d. July 12, 1824.
571. Jacob, Strasburg, Pa., b. Apr. 3, 1795; d. Feb. 12, 1828.
572. Susan, Strasburg, Pa., b. May 3, 1799; d. Oct. 10, 1820.
573. Sarah, Strasburg, Pa., b. Nov. 5, 1800; d. Sept. 4, 1827; m. Benj. Herr (539).
574. David, Strasburg, Pa., b. Mar. 10, 1804; d. Jan. 1, 1828; m. Mar. 10, 1823, Ann Egner, b. Apr. 4, 1799; dau. Peter Egner and Susan Wilson.

3

Family of **ESTHER HERR** (152) and **ABRAHAM KENDIG**.

575. Sarah, Strasburg, Pa., b. Mar. 27, 1791; m. Feb. 25, 1823, John Carpenter, b. Dec. 3, 1787; d. May 18, 1848; son Andrew Carpenter and Mary Stoutzenberger.

Family of Wid. **ESTHER HERR KENDIG** (152) and **JOHN HAGY**.

576. Ann, Strasburg, Pa., b. Feb. 27, 1796.

Family of Wid. **ESTHER HERR K. HAGY** (152) and **JOHN BRUA**.

577. Catharine, Williamsville, N. Y., b. July 4, 1803; m. Apr. 13, 1830, Daniel Snearly, b. Mar. 29, 1804; son George Snearly and Susanna Graybill.

Family of **SAMUEL HERR** (153) and **ANN HERR** (315).

578. John S., Strasburg, Pa., b. Nov. 7, 1791; d. 1871; m. Nov. 27, 1838, Mary Conner, b. Oct. 7, 1810; d. Nov. 2, 1892; dau. Thomas Conner and Elizabeth Hubert.
579. Benjamin, Paradise, Pa.
580. Emanuel, Westminster, Md., b. Dec. 1799; d. July 23, 1861; m. Dec. 12, 1838, Ann Espenshade, b. Feb. 7, 1822; d. Nov. 30, 1886; dau. Daniel Espenshade and ———.
581. Sarah, Reisterstown, Md., m. Abraham Keagy, son Rudolph Keagy and Esther Bowman.
582. Ann, Pikesville, Md., b. Aug. 20, 1806; m. June 15, 1824. Wid. Francis Kendig (1475).

Family of **JOEL HERR** (155) and **FANNY BRESSLER** (427).

583. Charlotte Bressler, Hannibal, Mo., b. May 24, 1804; d. Mar. 17, 1890; m. Jan. 24, 1824, George C. Moore, b. July 26, 1802: d. Feb. 3, 1843; son George C. Moore and Janet Boyd.
584. Elizabeth, Salona, Pa., b. Sept. 19, 1806; d. July 25, 1894; m. Apr. 13, 1826, Samuel Wilson (1515).
585. George B., Cedar Springs, Pa., b. Nov. 18, 1808; d. May 28, 1871; m. Apr. 12, 1835, Clarissa Miller (1535); m. Apr. 18, 1861, Wid. Rachel A. Hamilton, d. 1862; dau. ——— Douty and ———; m.

Jan. 26, 1865, Wid. Lucy Fritz, b. July 20, 1819; d. Nov. 15, 1893; dau. —— Hazen and ——.

586. Martin, Salona, Pa., b. Apr. 10, 1811; d. June 22, 1893; m. July 22, 1843, Catharine Hartman (4427).

587. Uriah, Salona, Pa., b. Feb. 8, 1814; d. June 1, 1901; m. Nov. 23, 1854, Ann Hoover, b. Oct. 6, 1814; d. Jan. 18, 1886.

588. Catharine, Salona, Pa., b. Oct. 7, 1816; d. Aug. 21, 1845.

589. Rebecca, Salona, Pa., b. Mar. 14, 1819; m. Nov. 23, 1854, John Miller, b. Sept. 1, 1816; d. Mar. 9, 1890; son Robert Miller and Elizabeth Jackson.

590. Fanny Ann, Williamsport, Pa., b. Oct. 7, 1821; d. Aug. 13, 1855; m. Jan. 5, 1843, Prof. John W. Ferree, b. Feb. 2, 1814; d. May 8, 1896; son George Ferree and Margaret Haslet.

591. Harriet, Salona, Pa., b. Oct. 28, 1825; d. Feb. 8, 1899.

592. Daniel, Salona, Pa., b. Feb. 28, 1828; d. Sept. 24, 1904; m. Sept. 18, 1856, Mary J. Leidigh, b. Oct. 24, 1834; d. Nov. 17, 1904; dau. John Leidigh and Catharine Stover.

Family of DANIEL HERR (156) and REBECCA BRESSLER (426).

593. George, Salona, Pa., b. Feb. 24, 1805; d. Jan. 15, 1884; m. Aug. 3, 1834, Charlotte Miller (1534); m. 1847, Catharine Wilson (1517).

594. Elizabeth, Lancaster, Pa., b. Sept. 6, 1807; d. June 2, 1858; m. 1833, Dr. Ely Parry, b. Oct. 11, 1804; d. Apr. 19, 1874; son David Parry and Elizabeth Eby.

595. Rebecca, Mill Hall, Pa., d. 1827; m. Abraham Shoff, son Abraham Shoff and ——.

Family of MARTHA HERR (157) and MARTIN PFOUTZ.

596. Elizabeth, Strasburg, Pa., m. John Reese, b. 1797.

597. Anna. Strasburg, Pa., m. William Reese.

Family of SAMUEL HERR (159) and ISABELLA MILLER.

598. Rev. Martin, Salona, Pa., b. 1804; d. Nov. 24, 1843; m. 1826, Elizabeth Miller, b. 1805; d. Oct, 8, 1884; dau. John Miller and —— Helman.

599. Sarah, Salona, Pa., b. 1806; m. Jesse Wilson (1516).
600. Joel, Mexico, Pa., b. 1808; d. Sept. 9, 1844; m. Jan., 1835, Jane Irvin, b. Feb. 21, 1811; d. Feb. 19, 1890; dau. William Irvin and Jane Holmes.
601. David, Lock Haven, Pa., b. Feb. 26, 1810; d. Feb. 14, 1872; m. Oct. 3, 1839, Mary A. Rockey, b. July 1, 1818; d. Feb. 26, 1886; dau. William Rockey and Elizabeth Maize.
602. Ann Eliza, Lock Haven, Pa., b. Jan. 22, 1812; m. Aug. 4, 1829, Robert Williamson, b. Apr. 27, 1805, son Col. Moses Williamson and Barbara Walters.
603. Samuel, Mexico, Pa., b. 1814; d. Dec. 23, 1876; m. Wid. Eliza McCurdy; d. Feb. 14, 1843; dau. ——— Stewart and ———; m. 1852, Sarah Davis, b. 1820; d. Sept. 23, 1877; dau. Dr. Elijah Davis and Sarah Percil.
604. Rebecca, Kendallville, Ind., b. 1816; d. Oct, 17, 1869; m. ——— Earle.
605. Louisa, Wooster, O., b. 1818; m. ——— Castor.
606. Jane, Wooster, O., b. 1820; m. Henry E. Miller.
607. Martha, Salona, Pa., b. 1824; d. Nov. 8, 1888; m. John Best, d. Feb. 13, 1881; son Peter Best and Mary ———.
608. George Leidy, Thompsontown, Pa., b. Feb. 23, 1826; d. Oct., 1901; m. Mar., 1860, Emma A. Wolcott, b. 1833; d. Mar. 25, 1869; dau. William Wolcott and ———; m. 1870, Ann Funk, b. Apr. 17, 1833; dau. John Funk and ———.

Family of **JOHN HERR** (160) and **ELIZABETH CONTNER.**

609. John, Jr., West Salem, O., b. Mar. 21, 1807; d. Jan. 27, 1895; m. Mar. 23, 1834, Christiana Shreffler, b. May 3, 1815; d. Nov. 1901.
610. Mary, Joliet, Ill., b. Jan. 25, 1809; d. Nov. 1901; m. Aug. 27, 1832, Samuel Shreffler.
611. Catharine, Pine Bluffs, Wyo., b. July 5, 1810; d. Feb. 25, 1887; m. Nov. 15, 1831, Daniel Adams, b. Oct. 2, 1809; d. Oct. 11, 1901; dau. Elijah Adams and Eve Griffith.
612. Samuel, Red Haw, O., b. Aug. 26, 1812; d. Aug. 25, 1885; m. Margaret Myers.

613. Elizabeth, Red Haw, O., b. Feb. 15, 1815; d. Oct. 18, 1902; m. July 20, 1834, Michael Fuhrman, b. Nov. 15, 1804; d. June 2, 1891.

614. Anna, West Salem, O., b. Apr. 17, 1817; d. Oct. 22, 1898; m. 1836, George Myers, b. Aug. 7, 1814; d. July 16, 1895; son Henry Myers and Barbara Fuhrman.

615. Susan, Bristol, Ind., b. Apr. 7, 1819; d. Oct. 15, 1890; m. Elijah Adams, b. Jan. 13, 1815; d. Aug. 23, 1888; son Elijah Adams and Eve Griffith.

616. David, West Salem, O., b. July 13, 1821; d. Oct. 16, 1876; m. Susanna Myers, b. Mar. 29, 1823; d. May 23, 1900; dau. Henry Myers and Barbara Fuhrman.

617. Henry, Cleveland, O., b. June 20, 1825; d. Dec. 3, 1895; m. Mar., 1850, Sarah E. Elgin, b. Dec., 1831.

618. Dr. Levi S., Evansville, Ind., b. Feb. 3, 1828; d. Apr. 6, 1893; m. 1858, Sophia L. Fetter, b. 1834; dau. Dr. Christian Fetter and Sarah Lobinger.

Family of JOEL CARPENTER and MARGARET DIFFENDERFER.

619. Ephraim, Hahnstown, Pa., m. Julianna Kline, dau. Michael Kline and ———.

620. Catharine, Hahnstown, Pa., m. Christian Knopp, son Christian Knopp and ———.

621. Elizabeth, Reamstown, Pa.

622. Miles, Brunnerville, Pa., b. Sept. 15, 1791; m. Feb. 1, 1818, Mary Habecker, dau. Jacob Habecker and Mary Roth.

623. Susanna, Brunnersville, Pa., m. George Lied, son George Lied and ——— Glaze.

624. Allen, Brunnersville, Pa., m. Susanna Breneisen, dau. Daniel Breneisen and ———; m. Mary Keizer.

625. Hester, Reamstown, Pa.

626. Giles, Brunnersville, Pa., m. Jane McClintock, dau. James McClintock and ———

627. Sophia, Reamstown, Pa.

628. Bryan, Hamilton, Can., m. ———; m. ——— Johnson; m. ———.

629. Charles, Reamstown, Pa., b. Dec. 3, 1803; m. Oct. 28, 1829, Elizabeth Johnson, dau. John Johnson and Catharine Steaffy.

630. Aaron, Reamstown, Pa., m. Rebecca Althouse, dau. John Althouse and Catharine Stehley.

Family of MARY CARPENTER (163) and MICHAEL COVER.

631. Susanna, Ephrata, Pa., m. Abraham Konigmacher.
632. Joel, Ephrata, Pa., m. Elizabeth Kieffer.
633. Isaac, Ephrata, Pa.
634. John, Ephrata, Pa., m. Catharine Steinmetz.
635. Mary, Ephrata, Pa., m. David Bricker.

Family of CHRISTIAN CARPENTER (168) and MARY CARPENTER.

636. Levi, Lancaster, Pa.
637. Lucy, Lancaster, Pa., m. Peter J. Eckert.
638. Charles, Lancaster, Pa.
639. Israel, Lancaster, Pa.
640. Mary, Lancaster, Pa.
641. Elizabeth, Lancaster, Pa., m. John Levering.
642. Charles, Lancaster, Pa.
643. Gabriel, Lancaster, Pa., m. Matilda Connell.
644. Paul, Lancaster, Pa., m. Mary Cannon; m. Mary Fetter.
645. William, Lancaster, Pa., m. Caroline Eichler,
646. Sarah, Lancaster, Pa., m. John K. Reed.
647. Daughter, Lancaster, Pa.
648. Francis, Lancaster, Pa., m. Josephine Waltz.

Family of SUSAN CARPENTER (169) and JACOB FORNEY.

649. Peter, Lancaster, Pa., b. June 7, 1789; d. Sept. 30, 1825; m. Aug. 24, 1813, Margaret Wien, b. Dec. 3, 1792; d. Sept. 14, 1869; dau. John Wien and Eve Brungard.
650. Barbara, Lancaster, Pa., b. Jan. 3, 1791; d. Sept. 11, 1862.
651. Susanna, Lancaster, Pa., b. Nov. 14, 1792; d. Feb. 2, 1793.
652. Jacob, Lancaster, Pa., b. Apr. 9, 1794; d. Jan. 22, 1848; m. 1815, Christiana Wien, b. 1794; d. 1868; dau. John Wien and Eve Brungard.
653. Sarah, Lancaster, Pa., b. Nov. 21, 1796; d. Jan. 31, 1862.
654. Catharine, Lancaster, Pa., b. Mar. 30, 1799; d. Feb. 13, 1800.

655. Isaac, Baltimore, Md., b. Oct. 28, 1802; m. Catharine Smith.
656. Charles C., Baltimore, Md., b. Mar. 25, 1806; d. Sept. 11, 1842.

Family of HENRY HERR (176) and ———— ————.

657. Catharine, New Providence, Pa., m. Joseph Groff (661).
658. Isaac, New Providence, Pa., b. Dec. 10, 1746; d. Aug. 2, 1817; m. May 16, 1769, Susanna Groff (94).
659. Esther, New Providence, Pa., b. Jan. 8, 1763; m. Joseph Gochenour, b. Feb. 3, 1756; d. Dec. 3, 1816; son Joseph Gochenour and ————.

Family of Wid. CATHARINE HERR ESHLEMAN (177) and Wid. JOHN GROFF.

660. Benjamin, Hermitage, Pa., b. June 4, 1762; m. Barbara Kendig (372).
661. Joseph, New Providence, Pa., b. Dec. 16, 1763; m. Catharine Herr (657); m. Barbara Shaub; m. Wid. Maria Stauffer, dau. ———— Whitestick and ————.
662. Maria, Strasburg, Pa., b. Oct. 11, 1767; d. Nov. 21, 1842; m. May 1, 1784, Henry Kendig, b. Dec. 1, 1763; d. Oct. 14, 1825; son Henry Kendig and Anna Miller.
663. Jacob, Hawksville, Pa., b. Sept. 25, 1768; m. Susanna Barr, dau. Wid. Jacob Barr and ———— Brubaker.
664. Martin, Hermitage, Va., b. Aug. 22, 1772; d. Oct. 14, 1855; m. Anna Kendig, b. May 1, 1773; d. Aug. 14, 1850; dau. Henry Kendig and Anna Miller.
665. Abraham, Strasburg, Pa., b. Dec. 13, 1773; d. July 22, 1846; m. Mattie Herr (493); m. Maria Barr, b. Nov. 24, 1791; d. Sept. 23, 1853; dau. Jacob Barr and Anna Kendig.

Family of BARBARA GROFF (183) and JACOB ESHLEMAN.

666. Jacob, Paradise, Pa., b. Feb. 20, 1768; d. June 29, 1851; m. Mar. 15, 1791, Mary Brackbill (401).
667. John, Strasburg, Pa., b. May 17, 1770; d. Jan. 20, 1851; m. Oct. 17, 1798, Mary Weaver, b. May 11, 1774; d. Nov. 8, 1801; dau. John Weaver and Anna Landis; m. Nov. 1, 1802, Alice Groff, b. Aug. 19, 1776; d. July 12, 1842; dau. Jacob Groff and Annie Groff.

668. Susanna, Strasburg, Pa., b. Apr. 11, 1776; d. Nov. 11, 1863; m. Mar. 26, 1798, Henry Brackbill (402).

669. Fanny, Strasburg, Pa., b. June 26, 1778; d. June 14, 1854; m. Jan. 8, 1802, Joseph Potts, b. May 19, 1774; d. Sept. 12, 1826; son John Potts and ———.

670. Benjamin, Strasburg, Pa., b. Oct. 5, 1782; d. Mar. 25, 1809; m. Jan. 12, 1807, Fanny Herr (496).

671. David, Strasburg, Pa., b. Apr. 15, 1784; d. Mar. 25, 1819; m. Mar. 18, 1806, Mary Groff (464).

672. Barbara, Strasburg, Pa., b. Jan. 30, 1789; m. Mar. 31, 1814, Jacob Bachman, b. Apr. 25, 1782; d. May 10, 1849; son John Bachman and Maria Rohrer.

673. Maria, Carlisle, Pa., b. Mar. 15, 1791; m. Apr. 3, 1816, David Miller, b. Dec. 24, 1790; d. Nov. 29, 1863; son David Miller and Mary Souders.

Family of ABRAHAM HERR (184) and ANNA WITMER.

674. Fanny, Manor, Pa., m. Christian Kauffman, son Andrew Kauffman and ———.

675. Annie, Dillsburg, Pa., m. Jacob Getz.

676. Mary, Manor, Pa., m. Henry Kauffman.

677. Elizabeth, Manheim, Pa., m. Christian Kendig, son Christian Kendig and ———.

678. Magdalene, Lititz, Pa., m. John Bender, son John Bender and ———.

679. Abraham, Urbana, O., d. Sept., 1864; m. Barbara Herr (909); m. Fanny Resh, dau. John Resh and ———.

Family of Wid. ABRAHAM HERR (184) and Wid. MAGDALENE BRANDT.

680. Catharine, Millersville, Pa., b. July 10, 1805; d. Feb. 24, 1865; m. Henry Herr (802).

Family of ELIZABETH HERR (185) and GEORGE HYDE.

681. John, Millersville, Pa., b. Jan. 14, 1789.

682. Barbara, Rohrerstown, Pa., b. Mar. 14, 1790; d. 1887; m. Stephen Hornberger, d. 1845; son Stephen Hornberger and Susan Gross.

683. Anna Mary, Millersville, Pa., b. Dec. 22, 1791; m. Jacob Metzger, son Jacob Metzger and Mary Tangert.

684. George, Sheppardstown, Pa., b. Dec. 22, 1794; m. Leah Gross.

Family of FANNY HERR (186) and JOHN SEACHRIST.

685. Christian, Millersville, Pa., m. Fanny Landis, dau. Abraham Landis and —— Breneman.
686. John, Millersville, Pa., m. Anna Kreider, dau. Jacob Kreider and Elizabeth Denlinger.
687. Michael, Millersville, Pa., m. Mary Buckwalter.
688. Maria, Millersville, Pa., m. Abraham Hershey.

Family of Wid. JOHN HERR (187) and BARBARA GOOD.

689. John, York, Pa., m. Fanny Kauffman (876).
690. Henry, Witmer, Pa., b. July 25, 1812; d. June 7, 1868; m. Nov. 17, 1835, Anna Herr (837).
691. Mary, Windom, Pa., m. John Funk, son Henry Funk and ——.
692. Anna, Manor, Pa., m. Benjamin Eshleman.
693. Barbara, Manor, Pa.
694. Elizabeth, Rohrerstown, Pa., b. Mar. 18, 1811; d. Dec. 19, 1891; m. Peter Musser, son Henry Musser and Mary Musselman; m. Daniel Brenner, d. Oct. 4, 1885; son Daniel Brenner and Catherine Ensminger.
695. Catharine, Witmer, Pa., b. Oct. 18, 1815; m. Nov., 1835, Solomon Herr (835).

Family of MARY HERR (188) and ANDREW KAUFFMAN.

696. Anna, Millersville, Pa., m. —— Mellinger.

Family of BARBARA HERR (189) and JACOB BIXLLER.

697. John, Millersville, Pa.

Family of ANNA HERR (190) and JACOB KENDIG.

698. John, Millersville, Pa.
699. Henry, Millersville, Pa.
700. Mary, Millersville, Pa.
701. Jacob, Millersville, Pa.

702. Fanny, Millersville, Pa.
703. Christian, Millersville, Pa.
704. Daniel, Millersville, Pa.
705. Samuel, Millersville, Pa.
706. Martin, Millersville, Pa.

Family of CHRISTIAN H. FRICK (191) and ANNA WITMER.

707. Catharine Witmer, Lititz, Pa,; m. Frederick Sheetz.
708. Jacob W., Manchester, Md., b. Nov. 26, 1782; d. Apr. 12, 1835;
     m. Dec. 3, 1811, Magdalena Peifer, b. Nov. 12, 1793; d. Oct. 8,
     1822; m. Jan. 12, 1825, Elizabeth Arnold, b. Apr. 24, 1796; d.
     Aug. 15, 1882.
709. John, Manchester, Md., b. Sept. 16, 1784; d. May 16, 1788.
710. Anna, Manchester, Md., b. Mar. 18, 1789; d. 1792.

Family of Wid. CHRISTIAN H. FRICK (191) and ELIZABETH HERR (210).

711. Veronica, Amherst, N. Y., b. Oct. 29, 1791; d. Nov. 11, 1881; m.
     David Martin, b. Dec. 15, 1786; d. Jan. 4, 1877; son Christian
     Martin and ———.
712. Magdalene, Lancaster, Pa., b. Jan. 26, 1793; m. Joseph Hershey.
713. Christian, Williamsville, N. Y., b. Apr. 12, 1794; d. Mar. 27, 1885;
     m. 1818, Elizabeth Long, b. Feb. 13, 1797; d. Dec. 22, 1883; dau.
     John Long and Maria Hershey.
714. Elizabeth, Williamsville, N. Y., b. Dec. 26, 1795; m. Jacob Frick
     (732).
715. Maria, Williamsville, N. Y., b. Aug. 20, 1797; d. Jan. 11, 1882;
     m. Henry Rhodes.
716. Anna, Williamsville, N. Y., b. Jan. 1, 1799; d. Jan. 18, 1879; m.
     Rev. John Reist.
717. Barbara, Neffsville, Pa., b. Mar. 28, 1801; d. Nov. 20, 1801.
718. Abraham, Neffsville, Pa., b. Dec. 4, 1802; m. Rachael Stover.
719. John, Eggertsville, N. Y., b. Jan. 6, 1805; m. Susanna Shenk.
720. Barbara, Eggertsville, N. Y., b. Aug. 13, 1806; m. Benjamin Bru-
     baker.
721. Martin, Eggertsville, N. Y., b. Nov. 23, 1808; m. Catharine Miller.
722. Susanna, Washington, D. C., b. Feb. 26, 1812; m. May 21, 1833,

Benjamin Summy, b. Mar. 19, 1811; d. Dec. 24, 1898; son Jacob Summy and Susan Eby.

Family of Wid. ABRAHAM HERR FRICK (193) and CHRISTIANA LONG ZUG.

723. Anna, Waynesboro, Pa., b. Oct. 12, 1787; d. Apr. 8, 1836; m. Nov. 21, 1808, Rev. Christian H. Frantz, b. Dec. 17, 1786; d. Feb. 7, 1862; son John Frantz and Maria Hostetter.

724. Maria, Waynesboro, Pa., b. July 22, 1789; d. Jan. 22, 1792.

725. Magdalena, Medway, O., b. Feb. 19, 1791; d. Sept. 21, 1875; m. Peter Baker, b. Mar. 11, 1789; d. Oct. 20, 1874.

726. Abraham, Waynesboro, Pa., b. May 8, 1793; d. Feb. 4, 1879; m. Catharine Diffenbach (1379).

727. Maria, Ringgold, Md., b. Dec. 18, 1797; d. Mar. 8, 1861.

728. John R., Waynesboro, Pa., b. Apr. 7, 1799; d. Apr. 20, 1878; m. Feb. 10, 1827, Annie Kelso, b. Jan. 1, 1800; d. Jan. 20, 1876.

729. Jacob Royer, Neffsville, Pa., b. Mar. 17, 1801; d. Jan. 31, 1897; m. 1822, Mary H. Pfoutz; b. Jan. 8, 1801; d. Mar. 14, 1869; dau. John M. Pfoutz and Elizabeth E. Heller.

Family of JOHN HERR FRICK (194) and ANNA HERSHEY.

730. Martha, Williamsville, N. Y., m. Samuel Tackles.

731. Barbara, Bowmansville, N. Y., m. Benjamin Bowman.

732. Jacob, Williamsville, N. Y., m. Elizabeth Frick (714).

733. Anna, Williamsville, N. Y., b. July 9, 1792; d. Nov. 11, 1883; m. David Spayth, b. Sept. 2, 1794; d. Feb. 2, 1870.

734. Elizabeth, Williamsville, N. Y., m. Henry Lehn.

735. Abraham, Williamsville, N. Y.

Family of ANNA FRICK (195) and JONATHAN ROYER.

736. Henry, New Holland, Pa., b. Dec. 12, 1786; d. Mar. 28, 1852.

737. John, New Holland, Pa., m. Rebecca Lyons.

738. Anna, New Holland, Pa., b. Nov. 1, 1789; d. Dec. 13, 1875; m. Wid. John Rutter, b. Mar. 15, 1795; d. Oct. 30, 1869.

739. Magdalena, New Holland, Pa., b. Oct. 9, 1792; d. Dec. 23, 1824; m. John Rutter, b. Mar. 15, 1795; d. Oct. 30, 1869.

740. Esther, New Holland, Pa., b. Sept. 5, 1795; d. Feb. 5, 1859; m.

Nov. 21, 1816, Amos Rutter, b. Apr. 5, 1791; d. July 21, 1868; son Joseph Rutter and Margaret Bashore.

741. Elizabeth, New Holland, Pa., b. June 26, 1791; d. Jan. 29, 1839; m. Henry Rutter, b. Dec. 12, 1786; d. Mar. 28, 1852; son Joseph Rutter and Margaret Bashore.

742. Mary, New Holland, Pa., m. Martin Rutter.

Family of JACOB FRICK (196) and ESTHER LONGENECKER.

743. John, Neffsville, Pa.

744. Jacob, Williamsville,, N. Y., b. Dec. 25, 1802; d. Mar. 4, 1871; m. Barbara Longenecker, b. Apr. 15, 1805; d. July 7, 1868.

745. David, Williamsville, N. Y.

746. Saphronia, Williamsville, N. Y.

747. Elizabeth, Williamsville, N. Y.

748. Nancy, Williamsville, N. Y.

749. Martha, Williamsville, N. Y.

750. Esther, Williamsville, N. Y.

751. Susan, Williamsville, N. Y.

752. Mary, Williamsville, N. Y.

Family of MARTIN FRICK (197) and Wid. MARIA ERISMAN.

753. Nancy S., Hummelstown, Pa., b. Aug. 8, 1800; d. Oct. 8, 1853; m. Feb. 19, 1824, Rev. John F. Hershey, b. June 28, 1800; d. May 28, 1851; son Isaac Hershey and Anna Frantz.

754. Mary S., Sporting Hill, Pa., b. Jan. 4, 1802; d. Dec. 25, 1881; m. John Balmer, b. Mar. 18, 1812; d. Oct. 5, 1898; son Martin Balmer and Elizabeth Metz.

755. Christian, Sporting Hill, Pa., b. Dec. 30, 1804; d. Apr. 17, 1859.

Family of DAVID HERR FRICK (198) and ANNA LANDIS.

756. Jacob. Fairfield, O., b. Sept. 2, 1802; d. May 28, 1878; m. Aug. 15, 1825, Margaret Jones, b. Aug. 8, 1801; d. Apr. 30, 1882; dau. William Jones and Margaret ———.

757. Elizabeth, Fairfield, O., m. Jacob Falck.

Family of MAGDALENA FRICK (199) and JOHN BLOCHER.

758. Christian, Buffalo, N. Y., m. Catharine Beam.

759. John, Buffalo, N. Y., m. Catharine Bomberger.
760. Mathias, Buffalo, N. Y., m. Susan Fox; m. Margaret ———.
761. Peter, Buffalo, N. Y., m. Hettie Grove; m. Mary Shissler.
762. David, Buffalo, N. Y.
763. Mary, Buffalo, N. Y.
764. Sophia, Buffalo, N. Y., m. George Urban.
765. Nancy, Buffalo, N. Y., m. John Reigle.
766. Martha, Buffalo, N. Y., m. Christian Overholtzer.
767. Jacob, Buffalo, N. Y., m. Hannah ———.
768. Susan, Buffalo, N. Y., m. ——— Grove.

Family of MARIA FRICK (201) and JOHN BROWN.

769. Jacob, Lancaster, Pa.
770. John F., Lancaster, Pa.
771. Peter, Lancaster, Pa.
772. Maria, Lancaster, Pa., b. Feb. 26, 1820; m. Amos Weidler.

Family of ABRAHAM ESHLEMAN (205) and SUSANNA GRAYBILL.

773. Christian, Cearfoss, Md., b. July 8, 1797; m. Lydia Weber, b. Jan. 16, 1812; d. Aug. 20, 1787.
774. Peter, Reid, Md., b. Nov. 8, 1798; d. May 12, 1876; m. Mary Reiff.
775. Abraham, Stark Co., Md., b. Feb. 6, 1800; d. Aug. 9, 1870; m. 1837, Elizabeth Horst.
776. Elizabeth, Maugansville, Md., b. Sept. 24, 1801; d. Dec. 22, 1865; m. John Horst, b. Dec. 11, 1801; d. Apr. 15, 1875.
777. John, Greencastle, Pa., b. Apr. 4, 1803; d. Oct. 28, 1878; m. Sarah Gibble, b. Apr. 11, 1810; d. Nov. 22, 1891.
778. Susanna, Maugansville, Md., b. Jan. 8, 1805; d. July 9, 1868; m. Samuel Weber, b. Dec. 2, 1806; d. Apr. 26, 1872.
779. Samuel, Lancaster, Pa., b. Dec. 15, 1806; d. Feb. 10, 1847; m. Mary Minnich.
780. Catharine, Landisville, Pa., b. Mar. 8, 1808; m. John Miller.
781. Feronica, Franklin Co., Pa., b. Oct. 22, 1809; d. June 12, 1890; m. ——— Gearhart.
782. Anna, Dauphin Co., Pa., b. Feb. 12, 1811; d. June 16, 1857; m. Emanuel Ziegler.

783. Daniel, Lancaster Co., Pa., b. Oct. 15, 1812; d. Sept. 14, 1884; m. Oct. 15, 1839; m. ——— Netzley, b. Apr. 15, 1819; d. Mar. 29, 1894; dau. Rev. Henry Netzley and Sarah ———.

784. David, Dauphin Co., Pa., b. Apr. 4, 1814; d. Dec. 22, 1891; m. 1837, Christiana Stauffer, b. July 9, 1817; d. Nov. 9, 1903.

Family of ELIZABETH ESHLEMAN (206) and JOHN STRITE.

785. Abraham, Leitersburg, Md., b. Jan. 31, 1795; d. Nov. 14, 1863; m. Elizabeth Mentzer, b. May 3, 1798; d. May 19, 1879; dau. John Mentzer and ———.

786. John, Leitersburg, Md., b. Oct. 25, 1796; d. Feb. 19, 1854; m. Elizabeth Summers, b. Jan. 21, 1799; d. Dec. 19, 1866; dau. Jacob Summers and ———.

787. Christian, Leitersburg, Md., b. Dec. 6, 1798; d. Apr. 15, 1862; m. Catharine Schnebley, b. Aug. 22, 1810; d. Jan. 18, 1862; dau. John Schnebley and Anna Hege.

788. Samuel, Clear Spring, Md., b. Dec. 10, 1800; d. May 1, 1878; m. Martha Schnebley, dau. John Schnebley and Anna Hege.

789. Nancy, Leitersburg, Md., b. June 6, 1803; d. Feb. 19, 1832; m. 1820, Jacob Miller, b. July 17, 1797; d. Sept. 7, 1868; son Jacob Miller and Susan ———.

790. Joseph, Leitersburg, Md., b. Aug. 31, 1805; d. June 8, 1858; m. Elizabeth Strite, b. Feb. 7, 1808; d. Dec. 21, 1894; dau. Christian Strite and Elizabeth Eaby.

Family of ANNA HERR (208) and DANIEL STEINAMAN.

791. Christian, Grand View, Ia., b. June 15, 1791; d. Jan. 27, 1857; m. Jan. 27, 1816, Anna Rohrer, b. Oct. 27, 1798; d. Mar. 21, 1867; dau. David Rohrer and Mary Sheirick.

Family of ABRAHAM HERR (211) and MARIA FUNK.

792. Frances, Manor, Pa., m. Christian Eby.

793. Rudolph, Elizabethtown, Pa., b. May 10, 1801; d. Mar. 23, 1888; m. Anna Hostetter, b. Sept. 26, 1796; d. Sept. 28, 1884.

794. Christian, Hagerstown, Md., m. Mary Shertzer; m. Elizabeth Fisher.

795. Abraham, Landisville, Pa., d. July 17, 1887; m. Mary Kreider; d. Jan. 24, 1887.
796. Mary, Elkhart, Ind., m. Abraham Herr (839).
797. John, Hanover, Pa., b. Sept. 23, 1819; d. Nov. 6, 1896; m. Barbara Lutz, b. July 27, 1820; d. Sept. 29, 1901; dau. John Lutz and Barbara ———.
798. Catharine, Hanover, Pa., m. Jacob Kreider, son John Kreider and ———.
799. Elizabeth, Columbia, Pa., m. Martin Dombach, son Adam Dombach and ———.
800. Henry F., Columbia, Pa., b. Oct. 27, 1822; d. Apr. 1, 1895; m. Jan. 16, 1845, Catherine Binkley, b. Sept. 27, 1826; d. Mar. 3, 1882; dau. Christian Binkley and Eliza Miller.

Family of FANNY HERR (212) and CHRISTIAN HORST.

801. Christian, Millersville, Pa.

Family of CHRISTIAN HERR (213) and MARY NEFF.

802. Henry, Millersville, Pa., b. Nov. 4, 1801; d. Dec. 19, 1884; m. Catherine Herr (680).
803. Fanny, Cambridge, Ind., b. Sept. 2, 1803; d. Oct. 7, 1882; m. Dec. 16, 1823, Rudolph Ellenberger, b. Oct. 27, 1799; d. Feb. 3, 1890, son Uhlrich Ellenberger and Martha Funk.
804. Christian, Cambridge, Ind., d. Mar. 12, 1875; m. Elizabeth Shenck; d. 1877; dau. ——— Shenk and ——— Hubley.

Family of MARY HERR (214) and HENRY SHOCK.

805. Frances, Millersville, Pa., m. Jacob Souder, son John Souder and Susan Funk.
806. Esther, Millersville, Pa., m. John Shertzer.
807. Christian, Millersville, Pa., m. Anna Doestler, dau. Adam Doestler and Anna Miller.
808. Jacob, Millersville, Pa.
809. Emanuel, Millersville, Pa.

Family of BARBARA HERR (218) and HENRY FUNK.

810. Henry H., Millersville, Pa., b. Feb. 2, 1804; d. Dec. 28, 1887; m. Feb. 3, 1831, Catherine H. Kilheffer (865).

811. Christian, Millersville, Pa., m. Fanny Witmer, dau. Jacob Witmer and ———.
812. John, Springfield, O., b. Sept. 12, 1808; d. June 25, 1888; m. Feb. 3, 1831, Martha Kauffman; b. Dec. 1, 1811; d. Mar, 10, 1860; dau. Isaac Kauffman and Catherine Baughman; m. March 31, 1863. Wid. Elizabeth Stoner.
813. Fanny, Strasburg, Pa., b. Nov. 12, 1806; d. Nov. 25, 1882; m. Rev. Jacob Andrews; b. Apr. 26, 1797; d. Dec. 3, 1873.
814. Catherine, Millersville, Pa., m. Henry Shuldy, son William Shuldy and ———.

Family of FREDERICK HERR (219) and CATHERINE PFIFER.

815. Christian, Cumberland, Md., m. Jane Wilson, dau. James Wilson and ———.
816. John, Altoona, Pa., b. Dec. 7, 1810; d. Jan. 6, 1898; m. 1848, Rebecca Otto; b. July 2, 1829; d. Sept. 6, 1893; dau. William Otto and ——— Appleman.
817. Abraham, Mansfield, O., b. June 20, 1815; d. Aug. 24, 1894; m. Feb. 24, 1853, Mary M. Herring; b. July 24, 1833.
818. Benjamin, Gettysburg, Pa., m. Mary Plank.

Family of Wid. FREDERICK HERR (219) and SUSAN LIND.

819. Susan, Gettysburg, Pa., b. Sept. 28, 1823.
820. Frederick, Cashtown, Pa., b. May 25, 1825; m. Hannah Hartzell.
821. Harriet, Aspers, Pa., b. Dec. 23, 1827; m. Sept. 5, 1848, James A. Miller; b. Sept. 3, 1826; d. Dec. 2, 1904; son Abraham Miller and ———.
822. Elizabeth Ann, Gettysburg, Pa., b. Dec. 20, 1829; d. 1904; m. 1852, John F. Slentz; b. Aug. 24, 1822; son John Slentz and Susan Tsopel.
823. Henry, Gettysburg, Pa., b. Mar. 4, 1832; d. Mar. 4, 1862; m. Mar. 18, 1858. Clarissa F. Little; b. Jan. 28, 1832; d. Mar. 5, 1868; dau. Joseph Little and Hannah ———.
824. Catherine, Gettysburg, Pa., b. July 25, 1835; d. Aug. 9, 1862; m. Mar. 30, 1858, Ephraim H. Minnigh.
825. Rebecca, Hagerstown, Md., b. Sept. 25, 1837; m. Aug. 18, 1860, Alexander A. Lechlider; b. May 16, 1835; d. Sept. 16, 1898.

826. Susanna, Hanover, Pa., b. June 26, 1844; d. Nov. 12, 1882; m. Feb. 5, 1865, Jacob Gundrum; b. Dec. 22, 1837; d. Sept. 23, 1904.

Family of MAGDALENE HERR (220) and JOHN BOWMAN.

827. John, Carlisle, Pa.
828. Christian, Carlisle, Pa.
829. Abraham, Carlisle, Pa.
830. Henry, Carlisle, Pa.
831. Mary, Carlisle, Pa.
832. Annie, Carlisle, Pa.
833. Esther, Carlisle, Pa.

Family of ABRAHAM HERR (222) and BARBARA BRENEMAN.

834. Peter, Strasburg, Pa., m. Elizabeth Rush.
835. Solomon, Witmer, Pa., b. Jan. 6, 1806; d. Nov. 29, 1868; m. Nov. 1835, Catherine Herr (695).
836. Abraham, Witmer, Pa., m. Barbara Hostetter.
837. Anna, Mascot, Pa., b. Nov. 22, 1817; d. Dec. 3, 1886; m. Nov. 17, 1835; Henry Herr (690).

Family of CHRISTIAN HERR (223) and NANCY BRUBAKER.

838. Benjamin, Mountville, Pa., m. Martha Newcomer.
839. Abraham, Elkhart, Ind., m. Mary Herr (796).
840. Fanny, Hempfield, Pa., m. John Mumma, son John Mumma and ——— Frantz; m. Jacob Kreider, son John Kreider and Esther Denlinger.

Family of Wid. CHRISTIAN HERR (223) and ESTHER EABY.

841. Christian, Millersville, Pa., m. Mary Hostetter; dau. John Hostetter and Catherine Eby.
842. Anna H., Millersville, Pa., b. Apr. 28, 1818; d. Apr. 28, 1876; m. Aug. 22, 1837, John K. Herr (942); m. June 12, 1856, Isaac Brubaker, son Jacob Brubaker and Maria Eby.
843. John E., Millersville, Pa., b. Sept. 15, 1822; m. Oct. 14, 1847, Mary Snyder; b. May 3, 1819.

4

844. Hettie, Millersville, Pa., m. Daniel Barrier.
845. Betsey, Millersville, Pa., m. John Shirick.
846. Mary, Millersville, Pa., m. Abraham Snyder.
847. Susan, Millersville, Pa., b. Aug. 14, 1829; d. Aug. 8, 1903; m.
    Feb. 8, 1853, Wid. David Shelly; b. Nov. 18, 1813; d. Sept. 13,
    1880; son Abraham Shelly and Elizabeth Brand.
848. Jacob, Maytown, Pa., m. Catharine Lanhart.
849. Catherine, Millersville, Pa., m. Wid. Daniel Barrier.

Family of ANNA HERR (224) and Rev. JACOB BRUBAKER.

850. Nancy, Millersville, Pa., m. Rev. Christian Baker.
851. Christian, Millersville, Pa., b. Dec. 13, 1802; m. May 10, 1825,
    Susanna Brubaker; b. June 14, 1809.
852. Jacob, Millersville, Pa., m. Mary Brubaker; m. ———.

Family of DAVID HERR (225) and SUSAN SHENK.

853. Rev. Christian S., Millersville, Pa., b. May 26, 1812; d. Aug. 26,
    1880; m. Hettie Charles; dau. John Charles and ———; m.
    Anna Hostetter; b. Apr. 17, 1822; d. 1895; dau. Abraham Hos-
    tetter and ———.
854. Susan, Millersville, Pa., b. June 25, 1814; d. 1885; m. John
    Charles (1025).
855. Daniel S., Mountville, Pa., b. June 14, 1816; d. 1840; m. Elizabeth
    Denlinger; b. 1822; d. 1865; dau. John Denlinger and ———.
856. Elizabeth, Mountville, Pa., b. Aug. 27, 1818; d. July 10, 1821.
857. Henry S., Lancaster, Pa., b. June 1, 1821; m. 1845, Mary Esh-
    bach; b. 1833; d. 1899; dau. Christian Eshbach and ———.
858. Jacob, Lancaster, Pa., b. Oct. 12, 1823; d. Feb. 13, 1824.
859. Ann S., Millersville, Pa., b. Jan. 10, 1825; d. Aug. 31, 1896; m.
    Feb. 26, 1852, Jacob H. Landis (4189).
860. Rudolph S., Lancaster, Pa., b. Feb. 17, 1827; m. Nov. 25, 1852,
    Magdalene Landis (4192).
861. Daniel S., East Petersburg, Pa., b. Oct. 17, 1828; m. Feb. 12,
    1856, Catherine Gamber (8502).
862. Fanny, Lancaster, Pa., b. Oct. 20, 1830; d. Oct. 8, 1836.
863. Abraham, Lancaster, Pa., b. Oct. 24, 1832; m. Susan Seitz; b.

Mar. 20, 1848; d. Dec. 29, 1892; dau. John Seitz and Mary Mellinger.

864. Mary, Lancaster, Pa., b. Oct. 7, 1836; m. Mar. 15, 1859, Philip Bausman; b. May 30, 1821; d. Dec. 31, 1896; son John Bausman and Elizabeth Peters.

Family of CATHARINE HERR (226) and CHRISTIAN KILHEFFER.

865. Catharine, Millersville, Pa., b. Mar. 14, 1813; d. Mar. 10, 1894; m. Feb. 3, 1831, Henry H. Funk (810).
866. Elizabeth, Manor, Pa., b. Dec. 23, 1815; m. John Stofer.
867. Mary, Lancaster, Pa., b. Apr. 10, 1818; m. Dec. 11, 1842, John Brenner.
868. David, Manor, Pa., b. Mar. 7, 1820; d. May, 1859; m. Mar. 1841, Nancy Brenner; dau. Jacob Brenner and Susan Eshbach.
869. Christian, Millersville, Pa., b. Apr. 21, 1822; m. Elizabeth Ludwig; dau. John Ludwig and ——— Dellet.
870. Anna, Lancaster, Pa., b. Aug. 18, 1826; m. Feb. 26, 1852, John Eshbach.
871. Daniel, Lancaster, Pa., b. Mar. 18, 1830; m. Apr. 28, 1857, Catharine Doerstler.
872. Jacob H., Lancaster, Pa., b. May 5, 1832; d. Dec. 16, 1897; m. Mar. 3, 1853, Susan Haines; b. Dec. 17, 1829; d. July 14, 1907; dau. Samuel Haines and Catharine Brubaker.
873. John, Lancaster, Pa., b. Feb. 21, 1834; d. 1856; m. Martha Kendig.
874. Henry H., Lancaster, Pa., b. Apr. 5, 1836; d. Feb. 28, 1903; m. Mar. 4, 1862, Lizzie Erisman; b. Mar. 12, 1838; d. Apr. 18, 1902; dau. George Erisman and Mary M. Hoffman.

Family of ANDREW KAUFFMAN (227) and ANNA KREIDER.

875. Mary, Millersville, Pa., m. ——— Stoner.
876. Fanny, Millersville, Pa., m. John Herr (689).
877. Barbara, Millersville, Pa., m. ——— Fisher.

Family of HENRY KAUFFMAN (228) and CATHERINE KREIDER.

878. John, Millersville, Pa., m. Wid. ——— Miller; dau. ——— Landis and ———.

Family of JOHN KAUFFMAN (229) and ANNA KREIDER.

879. Henry, Millersville, Pa.
880. Elizabeth, Millersville, Pa.
881. Jacob, Rohrerstown, Pa., m. ——— Herr.
882. Anna, Millersville, Pa., m. Jacob Brenner; son Jacob Brenner and Susan Shenk.

Family of CHRISTIAN HERR (234) and MAGDALENE CHARLES.

883. Henry, Manor, Pa., b. Aug. 29, 1786.
884. Anna, Manor, Pa., b. Dec. 10, 1787; m. Henry Bear; son Martin Bear and Elizabeth Bear.
885. Elizabeth, Manor, Pa., b. Apr. 1, 1791; m. John Baker; b. Jan. 5, 1785; d. Sept. 3, 1847; son Peter Baker and Barbara Bear.

Family of ABRAHAM HERR (235) and ——— REIST.

886. Henry, Annville, Pa., m. Sarah Forney.
887. Abraham, Annville, Pa., d. Oct. 25, 1857; m. Elizabeth Ensminger; d. Aug. 1, 1877.
888. Samuel, Englewood, O., b. Oct. 26, 1796; m. Frances Long.
889. Christian B., Campbellstown, Pa., m. Elizabeth Shenk; dau. Joseph Shenk and Fanny Ober.
890. Rudolph, Campbellstown, Pa.
891. Anna, Annville, Pa., m. Samuel Shenk, son Joseph Shenk and ———.

Family of HENRY HERR (236) and ELIZABETH KILHEFFER.

892. Henry, Lancaster, Pa.
893. Anna, Lancaster, Pa.

Family of SAMUEL HERR (237) and Wid. BARBARA KILHEFFER GOCHENAUR.

894. Abraham, Manheim, Pa.
895. Henry, Harrisburg, Pa., b. Feb. 7, 1798; d. June 9, 1853; m. Fanny Shopp; b. Feb. 11, 1802; d. Sept. 26, 1882; dau. John Shopp and Anna Hershey.
896. Elizabeth, Harrisburg, Pa.

Family of MICHAEL HERR (241) and ELIZABETH ———.

897. John, Louisville, Ky., b. Apr. 2, 1771; d. Apr. 3, 1852; m. 1795, Elizabeth Rudy; d. July 9, 1814; dau. Jacob Rudy and Catharine ———; m. Mar. 28, 1816, Wid. Elizabeth W. Simcoe.

898. Elizabeth, Taneytown, Md., b. Sept. 26, 1774; d. June 13, 1843; m. 1792, Henry Swope; b. Sept. 26, 1767; d. Feb. 13; 1842; son Conrad Swope and Clara Shriner.

Family of CHRISTIAN HERR (255) and ANN BRENEMAN.

899. Elizabeth, Millersville, Pa.

900. Christian B., Millersville, Pa., b. 1834; d. Apr. 7, 1895; m. Elizabeth Shenk.

Family of ELIZABETH HERR (256) and CHRISTIAN BARR.

901. Martin, Rohrerstown, Pa.

902. John, Rohrerstown, Pa.

Family of ANN HERR (258) and JOHN HERSHEY.

903. Elizabeth, Manor, Pa.

904. Christian, Manor, Pa.

905. Ann, Manor, Pa.

Family of ESTHER HERR (259) and CHRISTIAN ROHRER.

906. Barbara, Lampeter, Pa.

907. Henry, Lampeter, Pa.

Family of JOHN HERR (263) and MAGDALENE SIDES.

908. Christian, Urbana, O.

909. Barbara, Urbana, O., b. Jan. 20, 1802; d. 1825; m. Ahraham Herr (679).

Family of DAVID HERR (264) and CATHERINE BUMBERGER.

910. John, Camargo, Pa., b. Jan. 27, 1809; d. May 27, 1888; m. Jan., 1831, Ann Hess; b. July 7, 1813; d. Nov. 24, 1842; dau. John Hess and Martha Musser; m. Jan. 15, 1852, Margaret A. Ral-

ston; b. Dec. 26, 1824; d. Apr. 7, 1894; dau. William Ralston and Barbara Bucher.

911. Elizabeth, Camargo, Pa., b. Mar. 10, 1810; m. Aug. 24, 1829, Martin Barr (1210); m. Dec. 19, 1839, James Creswell; b. Aug. 30, 1809; d. Oct. 4, 1886; son George Creswell and Sarah Gray.

912. Christiana, Camargo, Pa., b. Jan. 2, 1812; d. Sept. 2, 1813.

913. Julia Ann, Camargo, Pa., b. Aug. 24, 1814; m. Jacob Barr; son Christian Barr and Susan Breneman.

914. Maria, Bartville, Pa., b. Oct. 5, 1817; m. Joseph Smith; d. Nov. 7, 1884; son ———— and Sarah Reach.

915. Samuel B., Bridgeport, Pa., b. Jan. 29, 1822; d. Aug. 25, 1902; m. June 18, 1841, Magdalene Brubaker; b. July 17, 1823; d. Aug. 6, 1901; dau. Martin Brubaker and Susan Goodheart.

916. Catharine, Bridgeport, Pa., b. Aug. 9, 1827; m. John Herr (922).

Family of ABRAHAM HERR (265) and MARGARET MOWRY.

917. Benjamin, Bird-in-Hand, Pa., b. Apr. 27, 1802; d. Feb. 16, 1879; m. Feb. 2, 1826, Mary Ranck, b. Jan. 20, 1802; d. Mar. 13, 1881; dau. Jacob R. Ranck and Anna Steuck.

918. Betsey, Lancaster, Pa., m. Samuel L. Kauffman; son Frederick L. Kauffman and ————.

919. Abraham, May, Pa., b. 1807; d. June 24, 1851; m. Anna Byerly; dau. John Byerly and Frances Erb.

920. Mary, May, Pa., b. 1810; d. Aug. 3, 1852; m. Elisha Hamil.

921. Henry, May, Pa., b. 1813; d. Nov. 13, 1847.

922. John, May, Pa., m. Catharine Herr (916); m. Catharine Templeton, dau. John Templeton and Peggy Maurer.

923. Adam, Masonville, Pa., m. Maria Breneman; dau Henry Breneman and ————; m. Sophia Mann.

Family of SUSANNA HERR (267) and ABRAHAM BARR (338).

924. Mary, Quarryville, Pa., b. Sept. 13, 1803; m. 1835, David Newswenger; son Christian Newswenger and Barbara Martin.

925. Christiana, Camargo, Pa., b. Aug. 7, 1806; d. Aug. 19, 1862; m. 1836, Elijah Eshleman, son Jacob Eshleman and Anna Groff.

926. Betsey, Strasburg, Pa., b. Jan. 6, 1810; m. Jan. 27, 1831, Henry Harsh, son George Harsh and Mary Warfel.

927. Susan, New Providence, Pa., b. Nov. 29, 1813; d. Feb. 23, 1853; m. 1852, Wid. Adam Mowrer, son Adam Mowrer and Elizabeth Hawk.

928. Fanny, New Providence, Pa., b. June 18, 1817; d. Aug. 25, 1857; m. 1838, Henry S. Hoover (1281).

929. Nancy, New Providence, Pa., b. Apr. 28, 1820; m. 1859, Wid. Henry S. Hoover (1281).

930. Catharine, New Providence, Pa., b. Oct. 22, 1822; m. 1845, George Mowrer, son Adam Mowrer and Elizabeth Hawk.

931. Abraham, Quarryville, Pa., b. Sept. 11, 1826; m. 1847, Elizabeth Groff, dau. Abraham Groff and Ann Newswenger.

Family of EMANUEL HERR (269) and MARY ROHRER.

932. Christian R., New Danville, Pa., b. Oct. 21, 1804; d. Sept. 19, 1879; m. Sept. 28, 1828, Eliza Balmer, b. Mar. 4, 1809; d. Apr. 24, 1845; dau Daniel Balmer and Anna Bachman; m. Aug. 20, 1846, Elizabeth Barr, b. Oct. 10, 1825; d. Aug. 13, 1888; dau. Emanuel Barr and Catherine Rohrer.

933. Emanuel, Millersville, Pa., b. Nov. 4, 1806; d. July 5, 1881; m. May, 1839, Mary Musselman, b. Dec. 15, 1819; d. July 3, 1891; dau. John Musselman and ———.

934. Mary, Millersville, Pa., b. Oct. 7, 1812; d. Apr. 8, 1888; m. Jacob K. Shenk, b. Oct., 1803; d. Jan. 3, 1879; son Christian Shenk and Elizabeth Grabill.

935. Henry, Landisville, Pa., b. Sept. 26, 1815; d. Apr. 11, 1863; m. 1844, Elizabeth Breneman, b. Jan. 22, 1822.

Family of CHRISTIAN HERR (270) and CATHARINE KAUFFMAN.

936. Emanuel, Millersville, Pa., b. Feb. 22, 1802; d. 1837.

937. Catharine, Millersville, Pa., b. Aug. 31, 1803; d. 1837; m. Jacob Hertzler, son Christian Hertzler and ——— Brubaker.

938. Christian, Boiling Springs, Pa., b. May 27, 1807; d. Apr. 29, 1865; m. June 16, 1829, Mary Myers, b. Nov. 11, 1812; d. Dec. 27, 1897; dau. Samuel Myers and ——— Harnish.

939. Daniel, Binkley's Bridge, Pa., b. June 6, 1809; d. Sept. 12, 1852; m. Mar. 9, 1830, Susan M. Hornberger, b. July 1, 1812; d.

Sept. 16, 1876; dau. Stephen Hornberger and Elizabeth Gross.
940. Mary, Millersville, Pa., b. July 15, 1811; d. Oct., 1879; m. Daniel
Lintner, son Christian Lintner and ———.
941. Anna, Millersville, Pa., b. Mar. 30, 1813; d. 1815.
942. John K., Lancaster, Pa., b. July 14, 1815; d. Feb. 1, 1847; m.
Aug. 22, 1837, Anna H. Herr (842).
943. Jacob, Lancaster, Pa., b. Nov. 17, 1817; m. Oct. 15, 1846, Mary
Kreider, b. Nov. 4, 1822; dau. George Kreider and Maria Swarr.
944. Elizabeth, New Danville, Pa., b. Apr. 23, 1823; m. George
Kreider.

Family of BARBARA HERR (274) and JACOB CHARLES.

945. Mary, Millersville, Pa., m. ——— Froelich.
946. Betsey, Millersville, Pa., m. John Hertzler.
947. Jacob, Millersville, Pa.
948. Anna, Millersville, Pa., m. Wid. Jacob Sides.
949. Christian, Millersville. Pa., m. Fanny Forrey.
950. Barbara, Millersville, Pa., m. Jacob Sides.
951. Fanny, Millersville, Pa., m. John Newcomer.
952. Catharine, Millersville, Pa.

Family of CHRISTIAN HERR (275) and ELIZABETH HART

953. Anna, Washington, Pa., m. John Sailor.
954. Daughter, Washington, Pa.

Family of Wid. CHRISTIAN HERR (275) and SUSAN STEHMAN.

955. Abraham, Washington, Pa., b. 1807; d. May 27, 1889; m. May,
1833, Anna Haldeman, dau. John Haldeman and Anna Staman.
956. Mary Ann, York, Pa., b. 1809; d. Jan. 1863; m. Abraham Forrey,
son Rudolph Forrey and ———.
957. Susan, Washington, Pa., b. Sept., 1811; d. Jan., 1851; m. Nov.,
1836, Israel Brady, son David Brady and ———.
958. Christian S., Washington, Pa., b. Feb. 14, 1820; d. Dec. 15, 1852;
m. Mar., 1841, Carolina Stoner, b. Nov. 1, 1823; dau. Christian
Stoner and Martha Wertz.

959. David B., Washington, Pa., b. June 8, 1823; m. Dec. 24, 1846, Barbara Groh, b. June 9, 1819; dau, Christian Groh and Frances Coble.

960. Fanny, Camden, O., b. May, 1826; m. 1845, Josiah Clap, son Daniel Clap and Susan Staman; m. John Lehman, son Benjamin Lehman and ———.

Family of ANNA HERR (276) and JOHN BEAM.

961. Mary, Lancaster, Pa., m. Dr. Jacob Hies.

962. Abraham T., Lancaster, Pa.

Family of MARY HERR (277) and Rev. ABRAHAM HERSHEY.

963. Betsey, Creswell, Pa.

964. Barbara, Creswell, Pa., m. Daniel Pifer.

965. Abraham, Creswell, Pa., m. ——— Martin.

966. Christian, Creswell, Pa.

967. Mary, Creswell, Pa., m. John Hertzler.

968. Anne, Mountville, Pa., b. Dec. 31, 1808; d. 1870; m. Feb. 18, 1830, Daniel W. Witmer, b. Oct. 1, 1808; d. Dec. 4, 1846.

969. Catharine, Mountville, Pa., m. ——— Stoner.

970. John, Mountville, Pa., m. Barbara Peters.

971. David, Mountville, Pa., m. ——— Kauffman.

972. Jacob, Mountville, Pa., m. Fanny Kauffman.

Family of DAVID HERR (278) and BARBARA OHLWEILER.

973. Christian O., Creswell, Pa., b. Aug. 13, 1819; d. July 23, 1875; m. June 18, 1843, Amelia Stoner, b. Mar. 15, 1825; dau. Christian Stoner and Martha Wertz.

974. Anna, Creswell, Pa., b. Feb. 8, 1821; d. Aug. 27, 1874.

975. Catharine, Creswell, Pa., b. Oct. 10, 1822; d. Aug. 23, 1893.

976. Son, Creswell, Pa., b. 1824; d. 1824.

977. David O., Creswell, Pa., b. June 30, 1825; d. Aug. 6, 1890; m. Aug. 2, 1850, Mary A. Huber (3188); m. Wid. Elizabeth Frey, dau. Christian Lintner and ——— Sener.

978. Daughter, Creswell, Pa., b. 1828; d. 1828.

979. Susan, Millersville, Pa., b. 1830; m. Jan. 7, 1851, George Kendig (1012).

980. Dr. Elias B., Lancaster, Pa., b. May 1, 1833; d. Apr. 28, 1904; m. Apr. 30, 1855, Lizzie S. Miller, b. Jan. 1, 1833; dau. Christian Miller and Elizabeth Shenk.

981. Barbara, Millersville, Pa., b. Dec. 15, 1834; m. Apr. 17, 1855, Henry H. Stehman (3143).

982. Isaiah, Millersville, Pa., b. Dec. 27, 1836; m. Anna E. Brady, dau. John S. Brady and Elizabeth Welch.

Family of BENJAMIN HERR (279) and MARY BACHMAN.

983. Anna, Millersville, Pa., b. Sept. 5, 1801; d. June 18, 1886; m. John Stehman, b. July 15, 1801; d. June 4, 1887; son John Stehman and Elizabeth Brubaker.

984. Mary, Millersville, Pa., b. Mar. 30, 1804.

985. John, York, Pa., b. Feb. 19, 1806; d. 1876; m. Elizabeth Reinecker, d. Feb., 1896.

986. Benjamin, Maytown, Pa., b. Dec. 2, 1808; m. Elizabeth Stehman.

987. Christian B., Lancaster, Pa., b. Jan. 13, 1810; m. Eliza Haldeman, dau. John Haldeman and Anna Stehman.

988. Elizabeth, Columbia, Pa., b. June 9, 1812; m. Ephraim Hershey.

989. Abraham H., Georgetown, D. C., b. Oct. 22, 1814; d. May 16, 1886; m. Feb. 28, 1850, Narcissa Hoffman, b. Nov. 4, 1829; d. Feb. 20, 1865.

990. Michael, Mt. Joy, Pa., b. Sept. 3, 1815.

991. Henry C., Mt. Joy, Pa., b. Aug. 5, 1818; m. Mary A. Breneman, dau. —— and —— Heilman.

992. Son, Mt. Joy, Pa., b. 1819; d. 1819.

993. Infant, Millersville, Pa., b. May 30, 1820; d. May 30, 1820.

994. Adaline S., Lancaster, Pa., b. May 28, 1822; m. John Johnson, son Samuel Johnson and ——; m. Henry Bechtold, b. Apr. 20, 1820; son Samuel Bechtold and Mary Horstick.

995. Amos, Lancaster, Pa., b. June 3, 1825; d. June 3, 1825.

Family of BARBARA HERR (280) and JOHN SHENK.

996. Abraham, Millersville, Pa.

997. Fanny, Millersville, Pa., m. Joseph Hogentogler.

998. John, Millersville, Pa., m. ——; m. —— Long.

999. Eliza, Millersville, Pa.
1000. Henry, Millersville, Pa., m. ——— Hiestand.

Family of ABRAHAM HERR (281) and FANNY DONER.

1001. Abraham D., Canton, Ill., b. Oct. 8, 1823; d. Oct. 8, 1893; m. Dec. 17, 1844, Mary A. Mulvaney, b. Dec. 24. 1827; d. Apr. 30, 1902; dau. Michael Mulvaney and Margaret Long.
1002. Henry, Riverside, Cal., b. 1825; m. Susan Sheaff.
1003. Elizabeth, Canton, Ill., m. Henry Miflin; m. ——— Narcot.
1004. Joseph, Riverside, Cal.

Family of ELIZABETH HERR (282) and JACOB SMITH.

1005. Abraham Herr, Lancaster, Pa., b. Mar. 7, 1815; d. Feb. 10, 1894.
1006. Eliza E., Lancaster, Pa., b. Sept. 8, 1816; d. Mar. 27, 1904.

Family of FANNY HERR (283) and JOHN KENDIG.

1007. Abraham, Willow Street, Pa., d. infant.
1008. Elizabeth, Willow Street, Pa., m. John Huber.
1009. Fanny, Willow Street, Pa.
1010. Barbara, Lancaster, Pa., b. May 13, 1814; d. May 9, 1904; m. Nov. 17, 1832, Martin Mylin, b. May 16, 1807; d. July 9, 1869; son Martin Mylin and Elizabeth Barr.
1011. John, Willow Street, Pa., m. Sept. 28, 1841, Mary Herr (1784).
1012. George, Millersville, Pa., b. May 17, 1821; d. May 11, 1901; m. Susan Herr (979).
1013. Abraham H., Dayton, O., b. May 15, 1823; m. Maria Rohrer; d. Feb. 27, 1851; dau. Henry Rohrer and ———; m. Feb. 10, 1852, Elizabeth Shepherd, b. May 4, 1828; dau. Henry L. Shepherd and Susan Sener.

Family of BARBARA HABECKER (289) and ABRAHAM WITMER.

1014. Son, Suspension Bridge, N. Y., b. 1805; d. 1805.
1015. Christian H., Suspension Bridge, N. Y., b. Mar. 29, 1806; d. Sept. 17, 1859; m. May 31, 1831, Maria S. Mann, b. Jan. 11, 1808; d. Aug. 30, 1885; dau. John Mann and Elizabeth Snyder.
1016. Son, Suspension Bridge, N. Y., b. Aug. 27, 1807; d. 1807.

1017. Abraham, Lockport, N. Y., b. Dec. 18, 1808; m. Feb. 5, 1835, Catharine Strickler, b. 1815; dau. John Strickler and Magdalena Martin.

1018. David, Niagara Falls, N. Y., b. Dec. 5, 1810; m. Jan. 1, 1839, Fanny Martin (2414).

1019. Joseph, Niagara Falls, N. Y., b. Sept. 21, 1812; d. Oct. 20, 1898; m. Sept. 4, 1846, Catharine Kauffman, b. Aug. 2, 1825; dau. Michael Kauffman and —— Newcomer.

1020. Esther, Suspension Bridge, N. Y., b. May 13, 1814; d. Jan. 16, 1834.

1021. Tobias, Williamsville, N. Y., b. Oct. 8, 1816; d. Aug. 14, 1897; m. Nov. 16, 1837, Anna L. Frick (2421).

1022. Elias, Suspension Bridge, N. Y., b. Oct. 8, 1816.

1023. Francis Maria, Fortuna, Mo., b. Sept. 24, 1824; m. Mar. 13, 1849, Jacob S. Leib, b. May 27, 1824; d. Apr. 30, 1893; son Abraham Leib and Elizabeth Schuh.

Family of ESTHER HABECKER (290) and JOHN CHARLES.

1024. Elizabeth, Suspension Bridge, N. Y., b. Aug. 21, 1807; m. John Stauffer, son Henry Stauffer and —— Newcomer.

1025. John, Suspension Bridge, N. Y., b. Sept. 3, 1809; d. June, 1893; m. Susan Herr (854).

1026. Christian, Suspension Bridge, N. Y., b. June 2, 1812; m. Elizabeth Funk, dau. Martin Funk and ——; m. Elizabeth Witmer, dau. Abraham Witmer and ——.

1027. Esther, Suspension Bridge, N. Y., b. June 10, 1814.

1028. Anna, Suspension Bridge, N. Y., b. Feb. 8, 1822.

1029. Joseph, Suspension Bridge, N. Y., b. Feb. 25, 1825.

Family of CHRISTIAN HABECKER (291) and ELIZABETH KAUFFMAN.

1030. Isaac, Rohrerstown, Pa.

1031. Esther, Rohrerstown, Pa., m. Ephraim Rohrer, son Abraham Rohrer and —— Eaby.

1032. John, Rohrerstown, Pa.

1033. Elizabeth, Rohrerstown, Pa., m. Christian B. Habecker, son Christian Habecker and —— Brubaker.

1034. Joseph, Mountville, Pa., m. Esther Charles (3450).
1035. Maria, Mountville, Pa., b. Apr. 26, 1829; m. Jan. 6, 1856, Dr. Peter W. Hiestand, b. Dec. 15, 1831; son Peter Hiestand and Elizabeth Wissler.

Family of FRANCES HABECKER (292) and JOHN SHOFF.

1036. Esther, Rohrerstown, Pa., b. Sept. 14, 1815; m. Mar. 12, 1835, Benjamin Landis (4183).

Family of DAVID HABECKER (293) and BARBARA NEWCOMER.

1037. Joseph, Sanborn, N. Y., b. Jan. 11, 1817; d. Nov. 26, 1855; m. May 29, 1845, Anna Herr (1835).
1038. Barbara, Sanborn, N. Y., m. Pennel Smeck.

Family of CHRISTIAN HERR (294) and ESTHER WHITESTICK.

1039. John, Washington, Pa., b. 1800; m. Mary Kendrick.
1040. Susan, Washington, Pa., m. John Wimer.
1041. Elizabeth, Washington, Pa., m. Abraham Everly.
1042. Daniel, Washington, Pa., m. Elizabeth Shenk; m. ———.
1043. Benjamin, Washington, Pa., b. Feb. 3, 1833; m. Aug. 13, 1853, Mary A. Herr (3748).
1044. Esther Ann, Washington, Pa., b. Feb. 3, 1833; m. William ———.

Family of BARBARA HERR (295) and JACOB STONER.

1045. Hannah, Washington, Pa.
1046. Anderson, Washington, Pa., m. Maria Shellenberger.
1047. Mary Ann, Washington, Pa., m. John Dobson; m. Isaac Hogentogler.
1048. Elizabeth, Washington, Pa., m. Joseph McClain.
1049. Thomas, Washington, Pa.
1050. Susan Jane, Washington, Pa., m. John Derrick; m. Christian W. Sener.

Family of BARBARA HERR (300) and JOHN CROFT.

1051. Edward, Allegheny City, Pa., b. May 30, 1822; d. Dec. 15, 1824.

1052. David, Allegheny City, Pa., b. Dec. 16, 1824; d. Nov., 1904; m. Mar. 19, 1850, Mary Fleming, b. June 22, 1825; d. Aug. 9, 1858; dau. Andrew Fleming and ―――― Murray; m. Apr. 5, 1860, Sarah Smith, b. Dec. 12, 1822; d. Oct. 16, 1889.

1053. Magdalene, Phillipsburg, Pa., b. Apr. 10, 1827; d. Nov. 27, 1854; m. Mar. 10, 1849, John Bunyan Campbell, b. 1825; d. 1907.

1054. Sarah, Allegheny City, Pa., b. Apr. 14, 1830; m. Jan. 21, 1857, Ephraim McKelvey, b. Apr. 30, 1813; d. Aug. 9, 1865; son James McKelvey and Margaret Wallace.

1055. John, Iola, Kas., b. June 17, 1833; d. Feb. 8, 1886; m. Nov. 12, 1857, Wid. Marietta W. Pierce, b. Mar. 31, 1834; dau. Robert Webb and Sarah A. Brandon.

1056. Benjamin H., Sedalia, Mo., b. Aug. 12, 1836; d. Apr. 2, 1883; m. Elizabeth Causley.

1057. Samuel W., Allegheny City, Pa., b. Aug. 19, 1839; d. July 2, 1863.

Family of BENJAMIN HERR (302) and Wid. ELIZABETH SENER.

1058. Sarah, Allegheny, Pa., b. Feb. 20, 1848; m. Joseph A. Spang; b. Dec. 26, 1847; son Jacob Spang and Hannah Buffington.

1059. Elizabeth, Sharpsburg, Pa., b. Nov. 15, 1849; m. Samuel H. Sutter, b. Mar. 6, 1847; son John Sutter and Ursula Durrein.

1060. Magdalene, DeHaven, Pa., b. Mar. 10, 1852.

1061. John, Bennett, Pa., b. May 14, 1854; m. Nov. 4, 1873, Louisa J. Rice, b. July 1, 1853; dau. Theodore Rice and Hannah A. Armstrong; m. May 2, 1900, Mary A. Greer, b. Oct. 14, 1868; dau. William Greer and Elinor Mann.

1062. Benjamin, Lancaster, Pa., b. Feb. 7, 1857; m. V. Ellen Wright.

1063. Mary, Warren, O., b. Sept. 30, 1859; m. William Stevenson.

1064. Daniel, DeHaven, Pa., b. Oct. 30, 1861.

1065. Samuel, DeHaven, Pa., b. Oct. 9, 1864.

Family of HENRY HERR (303) and MARY P. MATTHIAS.

1066. Samuel F., Millvale, Pa., b. Oct. 7, 1838; d. May 18, 1864.

1067. Hiram, Lancaster, Pa., b. Sept. 5, 1840; m. Sept. 6, 1866, Mary A. Johnston, b. Nov. 19, 1837; d. June 8, 1902; dau. Andrew McF. Johnston and Isabella McBane.

Family of DANIEL HERR (304) and ANN SNIVELY.

1068. Mary Elinor, Moline, Ill., b. Jan. 6, 1832; m. May 16, 1850, Dr.
Jacob Stewart, d. Nov. 17, 1900; son John Stewart and Mary
Covotte.

1069. Magdalena, E. Somerville, Mass., b. June 4, 1833; m. Apr. 16,
1863, Rev. David Williams, b. Feb. 27, 1811; d. Feb. 21, 1888;
son Thomas Williams and Elizabeth Pean.

1070. Sarah A., Adrian, Mich., b. July 13, 1835; m. Feb. 14, 1861,
Rev. David Jones, b. Dec. 1, 1835; son John Jones and Jane
Jones.

1071. Joseph Daniel, Norwich, Conn., b. Feb. 23, 1837; d. Feb. 29,
1904; m. June 20, 1859, Mary E. Wood, b. June 21, 1841; d.
Jan. 20, 1862; dau. Benjamin Wood and Ann Baker; m. Oct.
27, 1863, Anna M. Given, b. Dec. 11, 1842; dau. John M. Given
and Nancy Dean.

Family of JOHN HERR (305) and BARBARA ZEIGLER.

1072. Abraham. Old Harmony, Pa., b. June 11, 1835; d. Nov. 14,
1837.

1073. John, Old Harmony, Pa., b. June 24, 1837; d. Aug. 7, 1839.

1074. Benjamin, Brooklyn, O., b. Feb. 24, 1839; d. Aug. 12, 1864; m.
Apr. 10, 1860, Mary Henritze, b. July 6, 1839; dau. Charles
Henritze and Elizabeth Harz.

1075. Daniel, Monroe, Mich., b. Jan. 15, 1841; m. Mar. 6, 1866, Magdalene Walz.

1076. David Z., Cleveland, O., b. Dec. 27, 1842; m. Dec. 17, 1867,
Hattie A. Schmuck, d. Mar. 30, 1879; dau. Jacob Schmuck and
————; m. June, 1885, Emma L. Gish, b. May 29, 1841; dau.
Abraham Gish and Elizabeth Hummel.

1077. Christiana, Bennington, Mich., b. Dec. 25, 1844; m. Apr. 23,
1867, Gottleib Ruhs.

1078. Henry S., Cleveland, O., b. Dec. 14, 1846; m. Apr. 12, 1870,
Rebecca A. Bash, b. July 1, 1845; dau. Jacob Bash and Mary
McKelvey..

1079. Franklin L., Cleveland, O., b. Jan. 18, 1849; d. Sept. 10, 1865.

1080. Mary, Cleveland, O., b. Jan. 10, 1851; d. Jan. 11, 1851.

1081. Elizabeth C., Cleveland, O., b. Mar. 22, 1852.

1082. Josephine A., Avon Park, Fla., b. Aug. 31, 1854; m. Nov. 4, 1875, Rev. William F. Sanders.

1083. Sarah Z., Lancaster, O., b. Feb. 4, 1856; m. Jan. 27, 1876, Rev. B. F. Schubert.

Family of ELIZABETH HERR (306) and LOUIS FEILBACH.

1084. Esther, Macomb, Ill., b. Mar. 27, 1837; m. Apr. 24, 1862, George C. Gumbart, b. May 14, 1826; son Charles M. Gumbart and Catharine E. Dumont.

1085. Elizabeth, Aspinwall, Pa., b. Mar. 2, 1840; d. Sept. 22, 1902; m. Dec. 24, 1860, Charles A. Burrows, b. Jan. 6, 1838; son George Burrows and Ann Close.

1086. Mary M., Philadelphia, Pa., b. Mar. 24, 1842; m. July 30, 1861, Theodore Lougeay, b. May 8, 1840; son Charles Lougeay and Martha Ramsey.

1087. Henrietta F., Etna, Pa., b. Apr. 18, 1844; m. Apr. 6, 1869, James L. McKee, b. Mar., 1840; son James McKee and Rebecca Paulson.

1088. Benjamin H., Pittsburg, Pa., b. Mar. 21, 1846; d. Aug. 14, 1897; m. Dec. 24, 1865, Mary L. Lantz, b. Nov. 7, 1848; dau. David Lantz and Mary Tesh.

1089. Catharine, Hamilton, Ill., b. July 27, 1853; d. Apr. 12, 1874.

Family of MAGDALENE HERR (307) and SAMUEL HERSHEY.

1090. Mary Elizabeth, Erie, Pa., b. Mar. 21, 1845; m. July 12, 1866, George Lehman.

1091. John R., Erie, Pa., b. Apr. 20, 1847; d. 1863.

1092. Sarah B., Erie, Pa., b. Nov. 19, 1850; d. 1859.

1093. Saloma M., Erie, Pa., b. July 19, 1853; d. 1859.

1094. Samuel, Erie, Pa., b. Oct. 10, 1855; d. 1859.

Family of JOHN HERR (308) and ANN HOWRY.

1095. Samuel, Strasburg, Pa., b. Oct. 10, 1793; d. Dec. 25, 1836; m. 1820, Fanny Herr (437).

Family of **ABRAHAM HERR** (309) and **ANN HOOVER** (360).

1096. Henry, Strasburg, Pa., b. June 29, 1797.
1097. John, Strasburg, Pa., b. Feb. 1, 1800; d. Oct. 6, 1856; m. 1840,
Eliza Morrison, b. June 25, 1820; d. Jan. 23, 1856; dau. Matthew Morrison and Ann Kizer.
1098. Jacob, Lampeter, Pa., b. 1803.
1099. Abraham, Strasburg, Pa., b. May 16, 1805; d. Aug. 23, 1869; m.
Mar. 22, 1831, Leah Mayer, b. July 28, 1809; d. June 24, 1888;
dau. Christian Mayer and Mary Miller.

Family of **DAVID HERR** (311) and **MARY WIKER**.

1100. Susan, Strasburg, Pa., m. Adam Beck.
1101. Benjamin, Strasburg, Pa., d. 1830.
1102. Esther Ann, Lancaster, Pa., m. Matthew Bartholomy, son David
Bartholomy and ———.

Family of **MARY HERR** (312) and **JOHN HOOVER** (364).

1103. John, Sterling, Ill., b. Feb. 2, 1805; d. Feb. 1, 1884; m. Jan. 18,
1833, Martha Kreider, b. Jan. 28, 1813; d. Oct. 20, 1869; dau.
John Kreider and ——— Hostetter.
1104. Jacob, Lampeter, Pa., b. 1807; d. 1872; m. Esther Hoffman,
dau. Nicholas Hoffman and ———.
1105. Fanny, Sterling, Ill., b. Jan. 6, 1810; d. Aug. 11, 1882; m. 1848,
Wid. Rev. John Weaver, b. Oct. 12, 1806; d. Apr. 3, 1887; son
John Weaver and Barbara Landis.
1106. Mary, Enterprise, Pa., b. 1812; d. 1857; m. Benjamin Landis,
son John Landis and ——— Resh.
1107. Anna, Fertility, Pa., b. 1815; m. John Miller, son Emanuel Miller
and ———.
1108. Elizabeth, Lancaster, Pa., b. 1817; m. Benjamin Groff (3802).
1109. Susan, Sterling, Ill., b. June 9, 1820; d. June 8, 1901; m. Feb. 13,
1838, John N. Landis, b. Apr. 29, 1817; d. July 8, 1854; son
Rev. Abraham Landis and Anna Neff; m. Dec. 28, 1867,
Emanuel Landis, b. Dec., 1816; d. Sept. 26, 1896.
1110. Benjamin, Sterling, Ill., b. May 1, 1822.

5

1111. Martha, Fertility, Pa., b. 1825; m. Isaac Weaver, son Daniel Weaver and ——— Houser.
1112. Isaac, Lancaster, Pa., b. Oct. 3, 1827; m. Nov. 7, 1854, Margaret Fry, dau. John Fry and Mary ———; m. Dec. 31, 1874, Martha Rhinehart, b. May 15, 1847.

Family of EMANUEL HERR (313) and MARY GOOD.

1113. John, Marticville, Pa.
1114. Levi, Marticville, Pa., m. Leah Warfel.

Family of JOHN HERR (314) and SUSANNA BRACKBILL (404).

1115. Maria, Soudersburg, Pa., b. Apr. 12, 1801; d. Dec. 24, 1846.
1116. Benjamin B., Soudersburg, Pa., b. Jan. 23, 1803; d. Sept. 2, 1889; m. Dec. 12, 1861, Catharine Draucher, b. Apr. 11, 1822; d. Dec. 28, 1894; dau. Adam Draucher and Catharine Eckman.
1117. John Kendig, Soudersburg, Pa., b. May 25, 1805; d. Oct. 25, 1892.
1118. Henry G., Lancaster, Pa., b. Apr. 16, 1808; d. Dec. 7, 1887; m. Dec. 21, 1843, Naomi A. Diller, b. Sept. 6, 1821; d. Feb. 20, 1895; dau. Adam Diller and Mary Eckert.
1119. Eliza, Lancaster, Pa., b. Aug. 2, 1811; d. Feb. 2, 1836.
1120. Susanna, Paradise, Pa., b. Apr. 2, 1813; d. July 17, 1883; m. Feb. 15, 1842, Wid. Henry Witmer, b. July 18, 1798; d. Apr. 3, 1847; son David Witmer and Esther Kendig.
1121. Ann, Lancaster, Pa., b. Mar. 31, 1815; m. Feb. 14, 1837, George Lefevre, b. Nov. 15, 1810; d. Apr. 22, 1852; son George Lefevre and Susanna Hartman.
1122. Amanda, Paradise, Pa., b. Jan. 27, 1818; d. Jan. 2, 1894; m. Dec. 17, 1839, Amos L. Witmer, b. Sept. 12, 1816; d. Nov. 30, 1883; son David Witmer and Jane Lightner.

Family of BARBARA HERR (316) and ABRAHAM GROFF.

1123. David, Dayton, O., m. Nancy Groff (1322).
1124. Ann, Dayton, O., m. Henry Weaver, son John Weaver and Anna Landis.
1125. Elizabeth, Waynesboro, Pa., b. Mar. 1, 1794; d. Feb. 27, 1879; m. Emanuel Kendig (2206).

Family of ANNA HERR (319) and MARTIN LIGHT.

1126. Lizzie, Cumberland, Pa., b. Nov. 4, 1800; d. 1839; m. Christian Forrer (456).

1127. Christian, Willow Street, Pa., b. Aug. 3, 1802.

1128. Ann, York, Pa., b. Mar. 16, 1804; m. Jacob Tanger.

1129. Hannah, Lancaster, Pa., b. Dec. 16, 1805; m. Samuel Miller.

1130. Fanny, Millersville, Pa., b. May 10, 1808; m. Benjamin Hess.

1131. Martin, St. Louis, Mo., b. Aug. 13, 1810; m. Elizabeth Lawman.

1132. Jacob, Lancaster, Pa., b. Jan. 7, 1813; m. Anna Gall.

1133. Maria, Willow Street, Pa., b. Aug. 9, 1815; d. Apr. 2, 1898; m. Nov. 16, 1837, Christian B. Herr (533).

1134. Samuel, Willow Street, Pa., b. Aug. 31, 1817; m. Mary Lawman.

1135. John, Willow Street, Pa., b. Sept. 28, 1819.

Family of BENJAMIN HERR (320) and HANNAH WITHERS.

1136. Martin, New Danville, Pa., b. July 18, 1800; d. Aug. 22, 1896; m. Feb. 19, 1824, Maria Brubaker, b. July 25, 1806; d. Apr. 22, 1890; dau. Abraham Brubaker and Elizabeth ———.

1137. George L., Wilton Junc., Ia., b. Jan. 23, 1802; m. Mary E. Herr (1153).

1138. Anna, Willow Street, Pa., b. Sept. 10, 1803; d. Dec. 13, 1871; m. Dec. 10, 1822, John Bachman, b. Oct. 5, 1799; d. Sept. 9, 1876; son John Bachman and Esther Kreider.

1139. Eliza, Willow Street, Pa., b. Nov. 22, 1806; d. Dec. 18, 1835; m. Dec. 16, 1830, John Herr (540).

1140. Christian, West Liberty, Ia., b. Oct. 14, 1807; d. Aug. 24, 1890; m. Jan. 14, 1834, Susanna Stiver, b. Sept. 10, 1810; d. July, 1854; dau. John Stiver and Margaret Wolf: m. Mar. 15, 1856, Sarah J. Chadwick, d. Mar., 1876: dau. William Chadwick and Abby Spriger.

1141. Hannah, West Liberty, Ia., b. Sept. 26, 1809.

1142. Maria, Willow Street, Pa., b. Feb. 20, 1811; d. Mar. 18, 1891; m. Feb. 14, 1841, Wid. John Herr (540).

1143. Benjamin, Smithville, Pa., b. Mar. 25, 1812; d. Dec. 28, 1867; m. Dec. 3, 1841, Eliza Herr (1370).

1144. Rudolph, Mountville, Pa., b. Nov. 20, 1814; m. Barbara Breneman.
1145. David, Slackwater, Pa., b. Nov. 28, 1816; d. 1883; m. Mary
Howry, d. 1886.
1146. Hannah, Iowa City, Ia., b. Aug. 10, 1820; m. Jonas Miller.
1147. Frances, Lancaster, Pa., b. Jan. 3, 1823; m. Oct. 20, 1846, Benjamin W. Lantz (4346).

Family of FANNY HERR (321) and CHRISTIAN SNAVELY.

1148. Benjamin, Willow Street, Pa., b. Jan. 13, 1810; m. Feb. 20, 1834,
Frances Herr (1405); m. Wid. Elizabeth Mylin, dau. Christian
Kendig and Barbara Mylin.
1149. Eliza, Wheatland Mills, Pa., b. Feb. 8, 1812; m. Apr. 7, 1842,
Martin Herr (1162).
1150. Fanny S., West Willow, Pa., b. May 22, 1815; d. Aug. 6, 1903;
m. Jan. 25, 1844, Joseph Herr (1414).
1151. Maria, Willow Street, Pa., b. 1818; d. Mar. 4, 1900.
1152. Ann, New Providence, Pa., m. Francis Mylin, son Martin Mylin
and ——— Kendig.

Family of CHRISTIAN HERR (322) and ELIZABETH HAVERSTICK.

1153. Mary Elizabeth, Muscatine, Ia., b. July 2, 1815; m. George L.
Herr (1137).
1154. Elizabeth, Medway, O., m. Abraham Harnish.
1155. Jacob, Medway, O.

Family of MARIA HERR (323) and JACOB BRENEMAN.

1156. Christian, Harrisburg, Pa., m. Anna Kline.
1157. Anna, Harrisburg, Pa., m. ——— Kemrer.
1158. Maria, Harrisburg, Pa.

Family of MAGDALENE HERR (325) and CHRISTIAN BRACKBILL (406).

1159. David H., Strasburg, Pa., b. June 20, 1808; d. June 22, 1872; m.
Jan. 12, 1864, Wid. Martha B. Reiley, b. Jan. 31, 1822; d. Aug.
31, 1890; dau. John Bushman and Susan Higgins.

1160. Eliza A., Lancaster, Pa., b. Oct. 21, 1810; d. Nov. 22, 1888; m. Feb. 13, 1834, John Musselman; b. Nov. 9, 1811; d. June 28, 1903; son Michael Musselman and Barbara Sherer.

Family of JOHN HERR (327) and CHRISTIANA MYLIN.

1161. Francis, Wheatland Mills, Pa., b. May 18, 1802; d. July 22, 1838; m. Mar. 24, 1825, Lydia Barr, b. Mar. 5, 1800; d. Feb. 4, 1848; dau. John Barr and Catharine Bachman.
1162. Martin, Wheatland Mills, Pa., b. Feb. 25, 1805; d. Nov. 4, 1880; m. Apr. 7, 1842, Eliza Snavely (1149).
1163. John, Wheatland Mills, Pa., b. May 9, 1809; d. Nov. 9, 1810.
1164. Betsey, Philadelphia, Pa., b. Feb. 2, 1816; d. June 11, 1887; m. Frederick Zaracher, d. July 27, 1894; son George Zaracher and —— Shoff.

Family of ELIZABETH KENDIG (330) and HIERONIMUS ECKMAN.

1165. Henry, Lampeter, Pa., m. Elizabeth McMullen; m. Mary Silvius.
1166. Hettie, Lampeter, Pa.

Family of ALICE KENDIG (331) and JOHN MARTIN (467).

1167. Ann, Lampeter, Pa., b. July 28, 1795; d. Mar. 1843; m. 1814, Jonathan Bushong, b. Mar. 12, 1796; d. 1832; son Philip Bushong and Margaret Smith.
1168. Mattie, Lampeter, Pa., b. 1797; d. May 11, 1838; m. 1830, Henry Mehaffey, b. Feb. 22, 1804; d. July 2, 1885; son John Mehaffey and —— Mundeback.
1169. John, Conestoga Center, Pa., b. June 28, 1798; m. May 12, 1818, Hannah Fagan, b. Dec. 1, 1798; d. 1885; dau. George Fagan and —— Aument.
1170. George, Lancaster, Pa., b. July 12, 1801; d. June 6, 1869; m. Jan. 1820, Alice A. Shaub (1719); m. Apr., 1833, Wid. Ann Tanger, b. Sept. 11, 1803; d. June 16, 1876; dau. Abraham Gochenour and Susan Huber.
1171. Henry, Lancaster, Pa., b. Feb. 22, 1804; d. July 2, 1885; m. Feb. 25, 1827, Catharine Smith, b. Dec. 20, 1812; d. Jan. 26, 1891; dau. Jacob Smith and Margaret Bushong.

1172. Elizabeth, New Providence, Pa., b. Aug. 2, 1809; d. Feb. 2, 1875; m. John E. Lefevre, b. Sept. 9, 1809; d. Sept. 19, 1887; son Adam Lefevre and Catharine Erb.

1173. Samuel, Smithville, Pa., b. Oct. 20, 1812; d. Feb. 4, 1883; m. Feb., 1833, Maria Marron, b. Sept. 4, 1812; d. Nov. 29, 1891; dau. John Marron and Hannah Gamille.

Family of HENRY KENDIG (332) and SALOME SMITH.

1174. Edward S., Middletown, Pa., b. Apr. 12, 1807; d. 1877; m. Wid. Sarah Kissecker.

1175. Sarah, Middletown, Pa., b. Mar. 17, 1809; d. 1809.

1176. Christian S., Middletown, Pa., b. Dec. 15, 1810; d. Mar. 8, 1859.

1177. Abraham S., Philadelphia, Pa., b. Nov. 29, 1812; d. Dec. 27, 1861; m. Lydia Reese.

1178. John C., New Providence, Pa., b. Feb. 20, 1815; m. Eliza String.

1179. Mary A., Harrisburg, Pa., b. Mar. 4, 1817; d. Apr. 29, 1886; m. Dec. 18, 1849, Hother Hagy, b. Apr. 9, 1800; d. June 27, 1872.

1180. Sarah Ann, Harrisburg, Pa., b. July 10, 1819; d. Jan. 5, 1895; m. Feb. 14, 1851, John Horter Ziegler, b. Oct. 12, 1822; son Jacob Ziegler and Elizabeth Horter.

1181. Barbara Ann, Philadelphia, Pa., b. Feb. 7, 1822; d. Dec. 10, 1895.

1182. Elizabeth, Lancaster, Pa., b. Sept. 1, 1823.

1183. Henry S., Tiffin, O., b. June 20, 1826; d. Oct. 30, 1896; m. May 20, 1856, Lamyra V. Pittenger, b. Nov. 4, 1832; d. Apr. 24, 1903; dau. John Pittenger and Julia Ann Gibson.

1184. Maria Jane, Harrisburg, Pa., b. Feb. 22, 1830; d. 1830.

Family of MICHAEL KENDIG (333) and ELIZABETH ROHR.

1185. Harry, Lancaster, Pa., b. Dec. 3, 1807; m. Mary Hubley.

1186. Margaret, Lancaster, Pa., b. Oct. 2, 1809; d. July 23, 1893; m. David Weaver; m. Oct. 10, 1864, Wid. Elias Herr (1392).

1187. George, Newark, N. J., b. Aug. 22, 1813; m. Elizabeth Eshleman; m. Barbara Shenk.

1188. Samuel, Quarryville, Pa., b. Sept. 25, 1811; m. Catharine Aument.

1189. Michael, Junction, Pa., b. Dec. 4, 1815; d. Nov. 2, 1894; m. Mar. 16, 1843, Catharine Shelley, b. Apr. 27, 1823; d. June 4, 1889.

1190. William, Sporting Hill, Pa., b. Nov. 8, 1818; d. Jan. 6, 1832.

1191. Maria, Willow Street, Pa., b. Oct, 5, 1820; d. Oct. 7, 1907; m. John Hoover, d. Sept. 7, 1889.

1192. Hiram, Lancaster, Pa., b. Aug. 23, 1822; d. Apr. 12, 1871; m. Jan. 28, 1848, Anna E. Fetter, b. July 29, 1825; dau. Jacob George Fetter and Margaret Maria Ernest.

1193. Elizabeth, Strasburg, Pa., b. Sept. 13, 1824; d. Apr. 1, 1903; m. John Pennel, d. Apr. 3, 1853; m. Jacob Hildebrand; d. Apr., 1906.

Family of MARY KENDIG (334) and RICHARD JOHNSON.

1194. John, Marticville, Pa., m. Wid. Elizabeth McCurdle.

Family of Wid. MARY K. JOHNSON (334) and SOLOMON CRAMER.

1195. Matilda, Martic, Pa., m. Henry Goodhart.

1196. Solomon, Martic, Pa.

1197. Harriet, Martic, Pa., m. George Daily; m. ———.

Family of NANCY KENDIG (337) and GEORGE WITHERS.

1198. Catharine, Baltimore, Md., b. 1789; d. 1817; m. John R. Hopkins.

1199. Michael, Lancaster, Pa., b. 1791; d. 1873; m. Anna M. Smith, dau. Chester C. Smith and Anna Hubley.

1200. Ann, Cincinnati, O., b. 1796; d. 1862; m. Dr. Richard T. Houghy.

1201. George, Lancaster, Pa., b. 1798; d. Apr. 17, 1876; m. Elizabeth Metzger, d. Oct. 17, 1891; dau. Jonas Metzger and Mary Fowler.

Family of JACOB BARR (339) and ELIZABETH GETZ.

1202. David, Buck, Pa., b. June 13, 1799; d. Feb. 16, 1835; m. Barbara Rush, b. Aug. 13, 1794; d. Dec. 28, 1843.

1203. Christiana, Quarryville, Pa., m. John Mowry.

1204. Jacob, Quarryville, Pa., m. Susan Barr (1229).

1205. Martin, Quarryville, Pa., m., Esther Bleecher.

Family of NANCY HERR (377) and MARTIN BARR (340).

1206. Isaac, Quarryville, Pa.
1207. Mary, Quarryville, Pa., m. Daniel Bleecher, son Michael Bleecher and Mary Lines
1208. Nancy, Quarryville, Pa., m. William Horner; m. ———.
1209. Fanny, Quarryville, Pa., m. James Horner.
1210. Martin, Quarryville, Pa., b. 1804; d. Aug., 1838; m. Aug. 24, 1829, Elizabeth Herr (911).
1211. John, Quarryville, Pa., b. Dec. 15, 1807; d. Dec. 4, 1845; m. Anna Groff, dau. Henry Groff and Rosanna Myers.
1212. Christian, Buffalo, N. Y.
1213. Simon, Buffalo, N. Y.
1214. Benjamin, Buffalo, N. Y.
1215. Susan, Buffalo, N. Y., b. 1829; d. Mar. 7, 1830; m. 1829, Benjamin Gochenour (2192).

Family of SUSAN BARR (344) and JOHN LONGENECKER.

1216. Martin B., Paradise, Pa., b. Sept. 17, 1820; m. June 1, 1843, Harriet Hawke, b. Aug. 29, 1814; dau. Jacob Hawke and Elizabeth ———.
1217. Mary, Paradise, Pa., m. Jacob Martin, son Samuel Martin and Mary ———.
1218. Eliza, New Providence, Pa., m. John Hickman.
1219. Fanny, New Providence, Pa.
1220. John F., Colerain, Pa., b. Sept. 28, 1836; d. Jan. 26, 1863; m. Mary J. Atchison.

Family of MARY BARR (345) and Wid. FREDERICK MYERS.

1221. Eliza, Strasburg, Pa.

Family of JACOB BARR (346) and NANCY BOWMAN.

1222. Elizabeth, Quarryville, Pa., m. David Tennet.
1223. Fanny, Quarryville, Pa., m. Thomas Lyle.
1224. John, Quarryville, Pa., m. Anna Kauffman.
1225. Benjamin, Quarryville, Pa., m. Martha Barr, dau. Abraham Barr and Wid. ——— Howry.

1226. Mary B., Camargo, Pa., b. July 30, 1803; d. 1882; m. 1819, John Harsh, b. 1792; d. 1823; m. Jan. 16, 1825, Oliver Watson, b. July 30, 1802; d. June 1, 1865; son Gabriel Watson and Margaret Burns.

1227. Jacob, Camargo, Pa., m. Betsey McMichael.

1228. Anna, Colerain, Pa., m. Frederick Stively.

1229. Susan, Quarryville, Pa., m. Jacob Barr (1204).

1230. Martha, Quarryville, Pa., m. Jacob King.

1231. Christian, Quarryville, Pa., m. Mary Miles.

1232. Esther, Quarryville, Pa., m. Jacob Landis.

1233. Augustus, Quarryville, Pa.

1234. Tobias, Quarryville, Pa., m. ———; m. Margaret ———.

Family of Wid. FANNY HERR BARR KEECH(348) and HENRY BIRD.

1235. James, Quarryville, Pa.

Family of Wid. HENRY SHAUB (351) and MARY ECKMAN.

1236. Martha, New Providence, Pa., m. Henry Denlinger.

1237. Barbara, New Providence, Pa.

1238. Elizabeth, Lampeter, Pa., m. Abraham Metz.

1239. Henry, Lampeter, Pa., b. July 31, 1811; d. Oct. 12, 1877; m. Eliza Miller, b. Jan. 31, 1807; d. Oct. 19, 1882; dau. Jacob Miller and Esther Groff.

1240. Martin, New Providence, Pa., m. Ann Gochenour.

1241. Samuel, Strasburg, Pa., m. Mattie Miller.

1242. Susan, Willow Street, Pa., b. Feb. 19, 1819; m. Nov. 20, 1840, John W. Martin (1813).

1243. Abraham, Willow Street, Pa.

1244. Jacob, Strasburg, Pa., m. Elizabeth Eckman.

Family of JOHN SHAUB (352) and ESTHER DENLINGER.

1245. Elizabeth, Lampeter, Pa., m. Abraham Lefevre.

1246. Jacob, St. Louis, Mo.

1247. Barbara, Strasburg, Pa., m. William Given.

1248. John, Lampeter, Pa.

Family of **ABRAHAM SHAUB** (353) and **CHRISTIANA HERR** (382).

1249. Henry, Exeter, Neb., m. Harriet Hoover; m. Rebecca Somerville.

1250. Martin, Exeter, Neb., b. Oct. 12, 1812; d. Dec. 29, 1887; m. Apr. 5, 1838, Esther Strohm (1876).

1251. Jacob, Concord, O., b. Feb. 15, 1815; d. Jan. 19, 1878; m. Oct. 27, 1836, Leah E. Bushong, b. Jan. 11, 1817; d. Nov. 23, 1890; dau. Jonathan Bushong and Ann Martin.

1252. Isaac, Johnson, O., b. Sept. 12, 1818; d. Apr. 25, 1886; m. Nov. 30, 1843, Ann Thorn, b. Jan. 11, 1824; d. June 19, 1863; dau. James Thorn and Elenora Davidson; m. Elizabeth Faultenburg.

1253. Christiana, Johnson, O., b. July 1, 1821; m. June 24, 1841, Lewis Jamison, b. Dec. 25, 1814; d. Dec. 15, 1878; son Alexander Jamison and Mary Jones.

1254. Abraham, Johnson, O.

Family of **CHRISTIAN SHAUB** (354) and **NANCY WITMER**.

1255. John, Willow Street, Pa., m. Barbara Metz; m. Susan Fry.

1256. Anna, Willow Street, Pa., m. Dr. Benjamin Frick.

1257. Christian, Willow Street, Pa., m. Mary Shroder.

Family of **MARTIN SHAUB** (355) and **CATHARINE BOOK**.

1258. Mary, New Providence, Pa., m. Jacob Hoak.

1259. Barbara, New Providence, Pa., m. ———— Leonard; m. ————
Lines.

1260. David, New Providence, Pa.

1261. Catharine, New Providence, Pa., m. Christian Hoover, son Christian Hoover and Annie Shaub.

1262. Elizabeth, New Providence, Pa., m. Amos Sides.

1263. Martha, New Providence, Pa., m. John Rowe.

1264. Henry, New Providence, Pa., m. Emma Baldwin.

1265. Martin, New Porvidence, Pa.

Family of **FANNY SHAUB** (356) and **JACOB DENLINGER**.

1266. Nancy, Strasburg, Pa.

1267. Jacob, Strasburg, Pa.

1268. Henry, Strasburg, Pa., m. ——— Sides; m. ———.
1269. Christian, Strasburg, Pa.
1270. Elizabeth, Strasburg, Pa.
1271. Abraham, Strasburg, Pa.
1272. David, Harrisburg, Pa., m. Mahala ———.

Family of ABRAHAM HERR (395) and BARBARA SHAUB (357).

1273. Mary, Quarryville, Pa., b. Mar. 6, 1799; d. 1879; m. Sept. 13, 1855, Wid. Jacob Groff, b. Oct. 9, 1793; son Joseph Groff and ———.

1274. Henry, Quarryville, Pa., b. June 4, 1800; d. Apr. 27, 1823.

1275. Barbara, Strasburg, Pa., b. May 9, 1802; d. Apr. 4, 1847; m. David Groff, son John Groff and Susan Rife.

1276. Abraham, Mountville, Pa., b. Nov. 23, 1803; d. Jan. 17, 1892; m. Sept., 1823, Hannah White, b. Oct. 11, 1804; d. Apr. 17, 1861; dau. William White and Mary Marks; m. Sept., 1865, Wid. Nancy Long; d. 1882.

1277. John, Strasburg, Pa., b. Aug. 26, 1807; d. Apr. 14, 1880; m. Aug. 20, 1835, Susanna Mowrer, b. May 9, 1809; d. Oct. 8, 1837; dau. George Mowrer and Susan Shaeffer; m. Dec. 9, 1841, Mary Bartholomew, b. Apr. 20, 1815; d. Aug. 6, 1888; dau. Henry Bartholomew and Elizabeth Mowrer.

1278. Nancy, New Provdience, Pa., b. Nov. 8, 1809; d. 1875; m. William Shanes, b. 1810; d. 1866.

1279. Martin, New Providence, Pa., b. Feb. 5, 1812; d. Sept. 29, 1892; m. July 25, 1833, Elizabeth Miller, b. Oct. 7, 1811; d. Sept 27, 1891; dau. Frederick Miller and Sarah Marks.

Family of ANNIE SHAUB (358) and CHRISTIAN HOOVER (365).

1280. Barbara, Strasburg, Pa., m. Martin Groff; m. Samuel Wenger.
1281. Henry S., Strasburg, Pa., m. 1838, Frances Barr (928), m. 1859, Anna Barr (929).
1282. Nancy, Strasburg, Pa., b. 1817; m. Jacob H. Hoover (1288).
1283. Mattie, Strasburg, Pa.
1284. Fanny, Strasburg, Pa.

1285. Maria, Strasburg, Pa., b. Sept. 18, 1825; m. Nov., 1846, Martin Hoover (1289).
1286. Christian, Strasburg, Pa., m. Catharine Shaub, dau. Martin Shaub and Catharine Book.
1287. Christiana, Strasburg, Pa., b. 1828; m. Henry Hoover (1290).

Family of JACOB HOOVER (367) and MARY HERR (513).

1288. Jacob H., White Oak, Pa., b. May 1, 1819; m. Ann Hoover (1282).
1289. Martin, Willow Street, Pa., b. July 23, 1824; m. Nov., 1846, Maria Hoover (1285).
1290. Henry, Willow Street, Pa., b. Nov. 16, 1825; m. Christiana Hoover (1287).
1291. Susanna, Lancaster, Pa., b. Dec. 4, 1831.
1292. Eliza, Lampeter, Pa., b. Feb. 1, 1835; m. Dec. 12, 1855, Cyrus Zittle, b. Dec. 4, 1820; son Daniel Zittle and Esther Erb.
1293. Samuel, Lampeter, Pa.
1294. Elias, Willow Street, Pa.

Family of SUSAN KENDIG (368) and JOHN GROFF.

1295. Henry, New Providence, Pa., m. Rosanna Myers.
1296. Isaac, Quarryville, Pa., m. Betsey Eshleman.
1297. Michael, Bart, Pa., m. Rebecca Carpman; m. Mattie Wade.
1298. John, Paradise, Pa., m. Elizabeth Groff, dau. Jacob Groff and Annie Groff.
1299. Simon, New Providence, Pa., b. Apr. 14, 1788; d. Sept. 16, 1884; m. Susan Gochenour; m. Nov. 17, 1840, Barbara Herr (1359).
1300. Jacob, Linestown, Pa., m. Mary Rush.
1301. Daniel, Linestown, Pa., m. Susan Sides.
1302. Joseph, Nickel Mines, Pa., b. May, 1801; d. Sept., 1874; m. Barbara Sides; m. Elizabeth Rice.
1303. Martin, Nickel Mines, Pa., m. Susan Mooney.
1304. Susan, New Providence, Pa., m. John Eckman.
1305. Elizabeth, Willow Street, Pa., m. John Gochenour; m. Frederick Gull.
1306. Annie, Willow Street, Pa., m. Martin Gull.

Family of DANIEL KENDIG (369) and ANN FORRER (448).

1307. Henry, Orrville, O., m. Leah Keesey.
1308. Daniel, Orrville, O., m. Mary Kreider.
1309. John, Orrville, O., m. Susan Reinhart.

Family of ELIZABETH KENDIG (370) and MARTIN ESHLEMAN.

1310. Henry, Strasburg, Pa., m. ——— Harnish.
1311. Benjamin, Strasburg, Pa., m. Martha Martin.
1312. Jacob, Strasburg, Pa., m. Elizabeth Miller.
1313. David, Strasburg, Pa., m. ——— Harnish.
1314. Martin, Strasburg, Pa., m. ——— Warfel.
1315. Elizabeth, Strasburg, Pa., m. Henry Rush.

Family of NANCY KENDIG (371) and JOHN FORRER (445).

1316. John, Orrville, O., b. Jan. 1, 1787; d. Oct. 3, 1863; m. Elizabeth Kendig, b. 1783; d. Aug. 2, 1865; dau. George Kendig and Elizabeth Eshleman.
1317. Henry, Orrville, O., b. Mar. 15, 1788; d. Mar. 10, 1877; m. Magdalena Eyman, b. Mar, 17, 1802; d. Apr. 26, 1862.
1318. Daniel, Fayette City, Pa., b. 1796; d. 1863; m. ———; m. ———.

Family of BARBARA KENDIG (372) and BENJAMIN GROFF (660.

1319. Simon, Hermitage, Va., m. Betty Reinhart.
1320. Benjamin, Hermitage, Va., m. Susan Browning.
1321. Mary, Hermitage, Va., m. Abraham Reinhart.
1322. Ann, Hermitage, Va., m. David Grofft (1123).
1323. Abraham, Hemitage, Va., m. Sarah Griner.
1324. Elizabeth, Hermitage, Va., b. June 10, 1802; d. Aug. 14, 1859; m. Mar. 9, 1820, John Groff (2223).
1325. Jacob, Waynesboro, Va., m. Peggy Hoover.
1326. Henry, Hermitage, Va., m. Elizabeth Hoover.

Family of KITTIE KENDIG (373) and MARTIN FORRER (466).

1327. Susan, Willow Street, Pa., m. John Meck, son Philip Meck and ———.

1328. Betsey, Willow Street, Pa., m. Christian Mylin, son Martin Mylin and ———— Eshleman.
1329. Mary, Willow Street, Pa., m. Martin Kendig, son George Kendig and Elizabeth Eshleman.
1330. Ann, Orrville, O., m. Jacob Lefevre.
1331. Christiana, Lampeter, Pa., m. George Lefevre.
1332. Henry, Orrville, O., m. Charlotte Kendig, dau. George Kendig and Barbara Shenk.
1333. John, Orrville, O., m. Mary Meck.
1334. Christian, Bloomfield, Pa., m. Caroline Kendig, dau. George Kendig and Barbara Shenk.

Family of HENRY HERR (374) and ELIZABETH HARNISH.

1335. Henry, New Providence, Pa., m. Katie Garber, b. Jan. 31, 1797; d. Feb. 24, 1880; dau. Peter Garber and ———— Hallacher.
1336. Isaac, New Providence, Pa., b. Aug. 29, 1798; d. Aug. 16, 1868; m. 1821, Elizabeth Royer, b. Feb. 22, 1801; d. July 29, 1882; dau. Benjamin Royer and Anna Hallacher.
1337. Fanny, Chester, Pa., m. John Urban.

Family of ELIZABETH HERR (375) and FREDERICK KRUG.

1338. Henry, New Providence, Pa., m. Susan Grimes; m. Elizabeth Hoover.
1339. Susan, New Providence, Pa.
1340. Daniel, Lancaster, Pa., m. Susan Johnson.
1341. Frederick, New Providence, Pa., m. Margaret Grimes.
1342. Betsey, Lancaster, Pa.
1343. Mary, Union, O., m. John Williams.
1344. Christiana, Union, O., m. Samuel Myers.
1345. Samuel, Union, O., m. Dorothy A. Myers.
1346. Barbara, Lycoming, Pa., m. Jonathan Steele.

Family of DANIEL HERR (376) and BETSEY MILLER.

1347. Samuel M., Union, O., b. Jan. 27, 1805; d. Mar. 11, 1875; m. Apr. 23, 1835, Mary Bowman (1386).
1348. Henry, Ithica, O., b. Sept. 8, 1806; d. Oct. 2, 1810.

1349. Susanna, Union, O., b. Nov. 25, 1808; m. Oct. 18, 1827, Levi Herr (564).

1350. Mary, Seven Mile, O., b. Nov. 1, 1810; d. Apr. 20, 1850; m. Apr. 7, 1831, Jesse Brenberger, b. July 9, 1809; d. Nov. 25, 1891; son Frederick Brenberger and Christiana ———.

1351. Elizabeth, Johnsville, O., b. Apr. 21, 1813; d. Feb. 6, 1824.

1352. Joseph, Union, O., b. June 9, 1815; d. Mar. 7, 1879.

1353. Benjamin, Helena, O., b. Aug. 6, 1816; d. Feb. 13, 1873; m. Sept. 6, 1838, Mary Miller, b. Mar. 21, 1815; d. July 6, 1886; dau. George Miller and Christiana Wise.

1354. Martha, Osborn, O., b. Oct. 25, 1819; d. Sept. 19, 1885.

1355. Ann, Enon, O., b. Oct. 9, 1821; d. Sept. 21, 1827.

1356. Christiana, Rohrerstown, Pa., b. July 3, 1824; m. Oct. 2, 1845, Jacob M. Huber, b. Feb. 18, 1822; d. Apr. 20, 1890; son Daniel Huber and Susan Myers.

1357. Rachel, Medway, O., b. Nov. 15, 1826; d. Dec. 18, 1893; m. Dec. 29, 1850, Samuel Kline, b. Sept. 19, 1826; d. May 16, 1904; son, Samuel Kline and Ann Lutz.

Family of SUSAN HERR (378) and MARTIN HERR (396).

1358. Susan, Huber, Pa., b. 1801; m. Benjamin Hoover, son Christian Hoover and Elizabeth Rohrer.

1359. Barbara, New Providence, Pa., b. Oct. 10, 1803; d. May 20, 1871; m. Nov. 17, 1840, Wid. Simon Groff (1299).

1360. Christiana, Dayton, O., m. Rudolph Groff (3799).

1361. Ann, Ashland, O., b. Apr. 27, 1807; m. Oct. 16, 1828, John Groff (3781).

1362. Joseph, Ashland, O., m. Elizabeth Miller, dau. John Miller and Susan Raub.

1363. Elizabeth, Lampeter, Pa., b. Mar. 17, 1812; d. Sept. 26, 1879; m. John C. Baldwin, b. Nov. 1, 1808; d. Oct. 19, 1900; son Anthony Baldwin and Maria Bowman.

1364. Martin, Quarryville, Pa., b. Oct, 23, 1814; d. Sept. 12, 1903; m. Sept. 18, 1838, Maria Martin (1753).

1365. Benjamin, New Providence, Pa., m. Elizabeth Barr.

1366. Fannie, New Providence, Pa., m. Peter Reese, b. 1820; son Peter Reese and ———.

Family of ISAAC HERR (381) and CATHERINE MILLER.

1367. Susan, Buck, Pa., m. George Tshudy.

1368. Peter, Buck, Pa.

1369. Mary, Buck, Pa., m. Benjamin Bleacher, son Michael Bleacher and Mary ———.

1370. Eliza, Smithville, Pa., b. Apr. 26, 1820; d. June 17, 1891; m. Dec. 3, 1841, Benjamin Herr (1143).

1371. Isaac, Herrville, Pa., b. July 14, 1823; d. Feb. 27, 1899; m. 1849, Mary B. Shaub, b. Oct. 1, 1826; d. Jan. 26, 1853; dau. Joseph Shaub and Susan Bleacher; m. Nov. 18, 1855, Frances Breneman, b. Dec. 18, 1832; dau. John Breneman and Rebecca Miller.

1372. Jacob, Lancaster, Pa., m. Eliza Barr, dau. David Barr and Barbara Resh.

Family of MARIA HERR (385) and GEORGE DIFFENBACH.

1373. Susan, Strasburg, Pa., b. Mar. 11, 1780; d. Mar. 15, 1829; m. David Buckwalter.

1374. John, Strasburg, Pa., b. Nov. 24, 1781; d. June 20, 1840.

1375. George, Strasburg, Pa., b. Feb. 27, 1784; d. Nov. 22, 1860; m. Feb. 7, 1805, Barbara Rohrer, b. Mar. 10, 1786; d. Mar. 30, 1869; dau. John Rohrer and Fanny Neff.

1376. Maria, Strasburg, Pa., b. Jan. 6, 1787; d. Jan. 7, 1873.

1377. Betsey, Strasburg, Pa., b. Mar. 19, 1789; d. Feb. 27, 1867.

1378. Daughter, Strasburg, Pa., b. May 9, 1791; d. May 17, 1791.

1379. Catherine, Waynesboro, Pa., b. Jan. 20, 1793; d. Sept. 9, 1872; m. Abraham Frick (726).

1380. Mattie, Strasburg, Pa., b. May 16, 1795; m. John Lantz, b. 1790.

1381. Christian, Strasburg, Pa., b. Oct. 18, 1797; d. Oct., 1873; m. Ann Downer, d. 1883.

1382. Anna, Lancaster, Pa., b. Feb. 10, 1800; d. May 30, 1875; m. July 10, 1831, Dr. James Rodgers, d. Feb. 19, 1867.

1383. Infant, Strasburg, Pa., b. Dec. 28, 1801; d. Dec. 29, 1801.

Family of ESTHER HERR (387) and HENRY BOWMAN.

1384. John, Smithville, Pa., b. May 5, 1791; m. Wid. Elizabeth Winters, d. 1868.

1385. Rev. Henry, Refton, Pa., b. Oct. 6, 1795; d. Aug. 4, 1863; m.
May 18, 1819, Betsey Weaver (1470); m. Nov. 12, 1822, Susan
Weaver, b. Jan. 6, 1797; d. Jan. 13, 1832; dau. John Weaver
and Anna Landis; m. Sept. 21, 1834, Wid. Mary Breneman, b.
1793; d. Apr. 16, 1850; dau. Jacob Barr and Mary Barr.
1386. Mary, Union, O., b. Sept. 14, 1803; d. May 6, 1888; m. Apr. 23,
1835, Samuel M. Herr (1347).
1387. Esther, Medway, O., b. July 24, 1805; m. Dec. 6, 1829, John
Harnish, b. Feb. 13, 1801; d. Aug. 29, 1870; son Jacob Harnish
and Annie Shenk.
1388. Lizzie, Conestoga Center, Pa., b. Nov. 16, 1810; d. Mar. 16,
1849; m. George Rathfon.

Family of MAGDALENE HERR (390) and CHRISTIAN ROHRER.

1389. David, Lampeter, Pa., m. Susan McCallister, dau. Archibald
McAllister and —— Hackman.
1390. Elias, Lancaster, Pa., m. Wid. Henrietta Myers, dau. ——
Eberman and ——.

Family of Rev. CHRISTIAN HERR (391) and ANNA FORRER (453).

1391. Rev. Benjamin, Lime Valley, Pa., b. Oct. 12, 1801; d. Aug. 25,
1888; m. Nov. 21, 1822, Nancy Breneman, b. July 1, 1781; d.
Apr. 28, 1872; dau. Henry Breneman and Anna Musser.
1392. Elias, Lime Valley, Pa., b. May 4, 1804; d. Oct. 11, 1881; m.
Sept. 29, 1835, Betsey Hershey, b. Jan. 20, 1809; d. Feb. 5,
1848; dau. Andrew Hershey and Mary Sechrist; m. Oct. 10,
1849, Catherine Hershey, b. Mar. 20, 1797; d. Mar. 15, 1863;
dau. Andrew Hershey and Mary Sechrist; m. June 27, 1864,
Wid. Margaret K. Weaver (1186).
1393. Maria, Strasburg, Pa., b. Oct. 28, 1806; d. May 7, 1871; m.
Mar. 13, 1827, John Brackbill (1425).
1394. Christian, Lime Valley, Pa., b. Oct. 2, 1808; d. Jan. 14, 1885; m.
Dec. 15, 1831, Susanna Brackbill (1426).
1395. Joseph, Willow Street, Pa., b. Oct. 11, 1812; d. Sept. 27, 1894;
m. Nov., 1852, Esther Stauffer, b. Mar. 28, 1820; d. Nov. 7,
1901; dau. Daniel Stauffer and Mary Rohrer.

6

1396. Rev. Amos, Lime Valley, Pa., b. Feb. 13, 1816; d. June 19, 1897; m. Nov. 17, 1840, Betsey Rohrer, b. June 21, 1820; d. Apr. 21, 1878; dau. Henry Rohrer and Anna Forrer; m. Sept. 22, 1874, Wid. Sarah Groff, b. Dec. 17, 1825; dau. Jacob Witmer and Sarah Lefevre.

1397. Daniel, Refton, Pa., b. Sept. 2, 1818; d. Oct. 18, 1894; m. Nov. 17, 1840, Ann C. Breneman (1570).

1398. Anna F., Lancaster, Pa., b. Dec. 21, 1821; m. Dec. 23, 1845, John Herr (534).

Family of JACOB L. HERR (392) and MARY CARPMAN.

1399. Jacob, Willow Street, Pa., m. Magdalena Forrer (455).

Family of JOHN L. HERR (393) and FANNY SHULTZ.

1400. Susanna, Refton, Pa., b. Sept. 17, 1792; d. July 2, 1832; m. Sept. 8, 1810, John Barr (480); m. Dec. 23, 1817, Hon. John Strohm (523).

1401. John, Columbus, O., b. Jan. 1, 1795; d. 1867; m. Dec. 26, 1815, Anna Stauffer (1449).

1402. Mary, Refton, Pa., b. Nov. 25, 1797; d. Mar. 5, 1823; m. Apr. 28, 1817, Martin Herr (497).

1403. Barbara, Refton, Pa., m. David Strohm, son Henry Strohm and Mary Lefevre.

Family of Wid. JOHN HERR (393) and ANNA B. STAUFFER (403).

1404. Elizabeth, Willow Street, Pa., b. Apr. 16, 1810; m. Apr. 22, 1828, Henry Hess, b. Sept. 23, 1802; son Henry Hess and Fanny Hartman.

1405. Frances, Willow Street ,Pa., b. Mar. 18, 1813; d. May 8, 1859; m. Feb. 20, 1834, Benjamin Snavely (1148).

Family of JOSEPH HERR (397) and MARIA FORRER (454).

1406. Abraham, Millersville, Pa., b. Dec. 19, 1803; d. Feb. 18, 1885; m. Jan. 26, 1832, Ann Stoner, b. Feb. 9, 1806; d. Nov. 30, 1838; dau. Jacob Stoner and ———.

1407. Ann, Petersburg, Pa., b. June 18, 1806; d. Oct. 4, 1857; m. John Stoner, son Jacob Stoner and ———.

1408. Christian, Lancaster, Pa., b. Nov. 25, 1807; d. June 29, 1883; m. Nov. 30, 1839, Susan Hess, b. Apr. 25, 1815; d. Oct. 26, 1900; dau. Jacob Hess and Elizabeth Leichty.

1409. John, Lancaster, Pa., b. Apr. 19, 1810; d. May 24, 1810.

1410. Barbara, Lampeter, Pa., b. June 13, 1811; d. Apr. 3, 1883; m. Isaac Houser, son Christian Houser and Elizabeth Landis.

1411. Joseph, Lampeter, Pa., b. July 12, 1813; d. Sept. 24, 1813.

1412. Magdalena, Lampeter, Pa., b. Oct. 11, 1814; d. Apr. 24, 1817.

1413. Maria, Willow Street, Pa., b. Apr. 25, 1819; d. Dec. 15, 1893; m. Sept. 5, 1839, John Harnish, b. Aug. 23, 1815; d. June 13, 1887; son David Harnish and Elizabeth Snavely.

1414. Joseph, Willow Street, Pa., b. Dec. 23, 1816; d. May 15, 1896; m. Jan. 25, 1844, Fanny Snavely (1150).

1415. Martin, Quarryville, Pa., b. Dec. 31, 1820; d. Aug. 2, 1865; m. Nov. 2, 1848, Catherine E. Miller, dau. Benjamin Miller and ——— Haines.

1416. David, Quarryville, Pa., b. Mar. 20, 1823; d. May 2, 1892; m. Mary Groff, dau. David Groff and ———.

1417. Magdalena, Lampeter, Pa., b. Jan. 11, 1825; d. Aug. 16, 1833.

1418. Jacob, Lampeter, Pa., b. May 14, 1827; d. Sept. 15, 1827.

Family of JOHN BRACKBILL (399) and ELIZABETH LANDIS.

1419. Maria, Strasburg, Pa., b. Mar. 2, 1794; d. July 12, 1813.

1420. Daughter, Strasburg, Pa., b. Oct. 2, 1796; d. Oct. 3, 1796.

1421. Anna, Strasburg, Pa., b. Mar. 30, 1798; d. Mar. 25, 1862.

1422. Benjamin, Soudersburg, Pa., b. Nov. 5, 1800; m. July 26, 1827, Ann E. Bair (2871); m. Dec. 28, 1859, Ann Weaver, b. May 7, 1812; dau. David Weaver and Mary Dieffenbach.

1423. John, Strasburg, Pa., b. Dec. 7, 1802; m. Mar. 13, 1827, Maria Herr (1393).

1424. Elizabeth, Lampeter, Pa., b. July 31, 1805; d. Sept. 19, 1887; m. Nov. 22, 1827, Jacob Houser, b. Oct. 17, 1800; son Christian Houser and Elizabeth Landis.

1425. Christian, Fairview, Pa., b. Nov. 14, 1807; d. July 4, 1841; m. Nov. 22, 1829, Barbara Landis, b. Mar. 14, 1809; dau. Henry Landis and Nancy Long.

1426. Susanna, Lampeter, Pa., b. Oct. 14, 1811; d. Sept. 19, 1887; m. Dec. 15, 1831, Christian Herr (1394).

Family of ELIZABETH BRACKBILL (400) and BENJAMIN LANDIS.

1427. Anna, Landis Valley, Pa., b. Mar. 30, 1784; d. Jan. 11, 1790.
1428. John, Manor, Pa., b. June 9, 1786; m. Nov. 10, 1805, Elizabeth Rudy, b. Aug. 30, 1788; d. Mar. 4, 1816; dau. Daniel Rudy and Barbara Long; m. Mar. 3, 1817, Anna Hoover, b. Apr. 2, 1787; d. May 19, 1857; dau. John Hoover and Susan Hess.
1430. Benjamin, Landis Valley, Pa., b. Mar. 29, 1788; d. Sept. 30, 1824; m. Jan. 29, 1810, Magdalene Brubaker, b. Sept. 20, 1790; d. Oct. 27, 1858; dau. Christian Brubaker and Magdalene Hershey.

Family of MARY BRACKBILL (401) and JACOB ESHLEMAN (666).

1431. Susanna, Strasburg, Pa., b. Dec. 22, 1791; d. Jan. 6, 1864; m. Dec. 23, 1813, Michael B. Barr, b. May 15, 1793; d. Dec. 13, 1860; son Christian Barr and Susan Breneman.
1432. Benjamin B., Camargo, Pa., b. Oct 28, 1793; d. Aug. 1, 1854; m. Mar. 17, 1818, Mary E. Stauffer, b. Aug. 4, 1797; d. Apr. 22, 1875; dau. John Stauffer and Sarah Deshong.
1433. Elizabeth, Camargo, Pa., b. Oct. 28, 1795; d. Feb. 20, 1796.
1434. Maria, Lancaster, Pa., b. Oct. 5, 1797; d. Jan. 1, 1871; m. Apr. 20, 1824, John Warfel, b. Mar. 22, 1798; d. May 25, 1846; son Jacob Warfel and Mary Stoutzenberger.
1435. Barbara, Paradise, Pa., b. Sept. 24, 1799; d. Apr. 9, 1873; m. Feb. 8, 1825, Jacob Frantz, b. Mar. 27, 1800; d. July 17, 1870; son Jacob Frantz and Elizabeth Hershey.
1436. Jacob, Paradise, Pa., b. Mar. 23, 1802; d. July 31, 1877; m. Feb. 22, 1831, Jane J. Witmer, b. Mar. 22, 1810; d. Mar. 29, 1886; dau. David Witmer and Jane Lightner.
1437. Ann, Paradise, Pa., b. Mar. 22, 1804; d. Jan. 31, 1875; m. Mar. 10, 1835, George Groff (3810).
1438. Frances, Strasburg, Pa., b. Oct. 16, 1807; d. Nov. 20, 1891.
1439. Henry, Strasburg, Pa., b. Dec. 16, 1808; d. Mar. 31, 1809.
1440. Dr. John Kendig, Downingtown, Pa., b. Mar. 2, 1810; d. Oct. 6,

1897; m. June 2, 1840, Fanny Edge, b. Oct. 10, 1817; d. Aug. 16, 1901; dau. John Edge and Ruth Wilkinson.

1441. Eliza, Paradise, Pa., b. Feb. 16, 1812; d. Aug. 24, 1896.

1442. Martha, Lancaster, Pa., b. Jan. 8, 1815; d. June 18, 1876; m. Apr. 2, 1840, Christian H. Lefevre, b. Jan. 24, 1813; d. Jan. 26, 1890; son George Lefevre and Susan Hartman.

Family of HENRY BRACKBILL (402) and SUSANNA ESHLEMAN (668).

1443. John, Strasburg, Pa., b. Apr. 19, 1799; d. Sept. 2, 1849; m. Feb. 8, 1825, Ann Groff, b. Nov. 4, 1798; dau. John Groff and Mary Hackman.

1444. Maria, Strasburg, Pa., b. Mar. 19, 1801; d. Apr. 28, 1839.

1445. Benjamin, Harristown, Pa., b. Nov. 10, 1803; d. Sept. 11, 1891; m. Jan. 5, 1837, Susanna Howry, b. Mar. 14, 1813; d. Feb. 16, 1865; dau. John Howry and Elizabeth Funk.

1446. Jacob, Strasburg, Pa., b. Dec. 16, 1806; d. Dec. 20, 1882.

1447. Henry, Strasburg, Pa., b. Jan. 21, 1810; m. Feb. 24, 1847, Maria Eaby, b. Sept. 5, 1819; d. Aug. 28, 1904; dau. Christian Eaby and Rebecca Witmer.

Family of ANNA BRACKBILL (403) and JOHN STAUFFER.

1448. Maria, Willow Street, Pa., b. Aug. 14, 1795; d. Apr. 5, 1854; m. Dec. 26, 1815, Samuel Barr, b. Jan. 17, 1793; d. May 25, 1866; son Benjamin Barr and Catherine Myers.

1449. Anna, Columbus, O., b. Dec. 6, 1796; d. Aug. 3, 1840; m. Dec. 26, 1815, John Herr (1401).

Family of BENJAMIN BRACKBILL (405) and ELIZABETH HERSHEY.

1450. Maria, Strasburg, Pa., b. Nov. 17, 1805.

1451. Annie, Strasburg, Pa., b. Jan. 26, 1807; d. Apr. 2, 1840.

1452. Jacob, Salisburyville, Pa., b. Feb. 18, 1809; m. Nov. 15, 1832, Barbara Greenleaf, b. Apr. 8, 1808; d. Feb. 24, 1846; dau. Jacob Greenleaf and Fanny Bruner.

1453. John, Strasburg, Pa., b. Mar. 25, 1811; d. Apr. 3, 1812.

1454. Elizabeth, Strasburg, Pa., b. Jan. 22, 1813.

1455. Barbara, Strasburg, Pa., b. Nov. 27, 1815; d. Sept. 25, 1892; m.

Nov. 22, 1836, Benj. Hoover, b. Jan. 2, 1809; d. Dec. 6, 1876; son Christian Hoover and Elizabeth Huber.

1456. Benjamin, Kinzer's, Pa., b. May 5, 1818; d. Nov. 19, 1903; m. Nov. 8, 1837, Magdalene Carpenter, b. Feb. 3, 1817; d. Mar. 5, 1904; dau. John Carpenter and Barbara Acker.

1457. Susanna, Strasburg, Pa., b. Aug. 9, 1820; m. Nov. 7, 1850, Levi Hoover, b. Oct. 23, 1823; son Christian Hoover and Elizabeth Huber.

1458. Martha, Strasburg, Pa., b. Sept. 29, 1822; d. Dec. 2, 1863.

1459. Joseph, Kinzer's Pa., b. Jan. 14, 1825; d. Oct. 3, 1866; m. Jan. 4, 1853, Elizabeth Metzler, b. May 19, 1827; dau. Christian Metzler and Annie Warner.

Family of ESTHER NEFF (407) and JACOB WEAVER.

1460. John, Strasburg, Pa., b. Oct. 3, 1777; d. Nov. 10, 1779.

1461. Susanna, Strasburg, Pa., b. Mar. 23, 1779; d. Apr. 30, 1805.

1462. Jacob, Lampeter, Pa., b. Sept. 12, 1780; m. Dec. 28, 1808, Wid. Anna Mylin (492).

1463. Samuel, Lampeter, Pa., b. Mar. 8, 1782; d. Oct. 23, 1840; m. Dec. 18, 1809, Magdalene Rush, b. Sept. 25, 1788; dau. Jacob Rush and Martha Kendig.

1464. Anna, Lampeter, Pa., b. Mar. 24, 1784; d. 1865.

1465. David, Strasburg, Pa., b. Nov. 25, 1785; d. Oct. 2, 1817.

1466. Mattie, Conestoga Center, Pa., b. May 16, 1787; d. Dec. 10, 1864; m. Jan. 10, 1822, Martin Harnish, b. Sept. 20, 1792; son David Harnish and Elizabeth Groff.

1467. John. Lampeter, Pa., b. June 12, 1789; d. Aug. 24, 1869; m. June 2, 1818, Betsey Kreider, b. Jan. 23, 1797; d. May 26, 1886; dau. Christian Kreider and Ann Harnish.

1468. Rev. Joseph, Wheatland Mills, Pa., b. Apr. 5, 1792; d. Apr. 5, 1872; m. Nov. 8, 1818, Barbara Barr, b. Mar. 2, 1794; d. Mar. 4, 1840; dau. Jacob Barr and Anna Kendig; m. Mar. 5, 1843, Wid. Esther Brubaker, b. May 12, 1807; d. May 11, 1890; dau. John Stehman and Elizabeth Bowman.

1470. Elizabeth, Refton, Pa., b. Mar. 10, 1794; d. Sept. 9, 1820; m. May 18, 1819, Rev. Henry Bowman (1385.)

1471. Hettie, Lampeter, Pa., b. Apr. 5, 1798; m. May 28, 1819, Jacob Lantz, b. Aug. 17, 1798; d. Nov. 6, 1881; son Jacob Lantz and Elizabeth Rodecker.

Family of ANNA NEFF (408) and FRANCIS KENDIG.

1472. Jacob, Lampeter, Pa., b. Jan. 20, 1789; d. Oct. 6, 1811.
1473. Son, Lampeter, Pa., b. Dec. 22, 1790; d. Jan. 1, 1791.
1474. Catherine, Lampeter, Pa., b. Feb. 18, 1793; m. Dec. 24, 1816, Benjamin Barr (481).
1475. Francis, Reisterstown, Md., b. Mar. 18, 1796; m. Mar. 28, 1820, Elizabeth Barr (484); m. June 15, 1824, Anna Herr (582).
1476. Samuel, Lampeter, Pa., b. Mar. 3, 1799; d. Oct. 3, 1835; m. Mar. 26, 1822, Susan Barr, b. Jan. 9, 1800; d. Jan. 16, 1832; dau. Christian Barr and Susan Breneman; m. Sept. 15, 1835, Fanny Hiestand, dau. Peter Hiestand and ———.

Family of HENRY WEAVER (412) and MARY GOOD.

1477. Mary, Boston, Ky., b. 1789; d. Oct. 30, 1830; m. 1809, James Scott, d. Sept. 7, 1824.
1478. Henry Good, Cleveland, O., b. Nov. 25, 1791; d. Aug. 3, 1852; m. Sept. 25, 1815, Anna M. Shirk (1485).
1479. Davies, Lawrenceburg, Ind., b. 1793; d. Oct. 24, 1837; m. Frances Perry, dau. ——— and Frances Weaver.
1480. Elizabeth, Lawrenceburg, Ind., m. Christopher Bieler, b. 1807; d. 1892.
1481. Harriet, Lawrenceburg, Ind., m. Samuel Hancock.

Family of ANNA WEAVER (413) and MATTHIAS SHIRK.

1482. Elizabeth, Lake, O., b. 1785; d. Dec. 31, 1865; m. Mar. 29, 1807, David Diffenderfer, b. Oct. 12, 1781; d. Mar. 13, 1863; son David Diffenderfer and ———.
1483. George, Lake, O., b. Oct. 1, 1787; d. Oct. 12, 1787.
1484. David, Lake, O., b. Jan. 20, 1789; d. Aug. 25, 1805.
1485. Anna Maria, Lake, O., b. Aug. 4, 1791; d. Nov. 23, 1876; m. Sept. 25, 1815, Henry G. Weaver (1478).
1486. Ann, Lake, O., b. 1794; d. July 12, 1868; m. Sept. 23, 1849, Henry Grim.

1487. Frances, Varich, N. Y., b. Nov. 28, 1797; d. Nov. 24, 1879; m. June 24, 1823, Rev. Diedrich Willers, b. Feb. 6, 1798; d. May 13, 1883.

1488. Margaret, Lake, O., b. Aug. 6, 1799; d. Jan. 12, 1836; m. Apr. 2, 1835, William Lemmon.

1489. Catherine, Lake, O., b. Feb. 22, 1801; d. Oct. 10, 1803.

1490. Lydia, Lake, O., b. June 21, 1803; d. Mar. 1, 1886; m. June 12, 1839, Daniel Gambee, b. June 21, 1792.

1491. Caroline Ann, Canton, O., b. Nov. 21, 1806; d. Sept. 22, 1900; m. Mar. 25, 1833, Thomas Cunningham.

1492. Matthias W., Wooster, O., b. 1809; d. Feb. 9, 1869; m. Oct. 30, 1837, Margaret Schultz, b. 1820; d. Nov., 1885.

Family of ABRAHAM WITMER (420) and ANNA CATHERINE BURG.

1493. Ann Catherine, Greenfield, Mass., b. Mar. 16, 1807; d. Nov. 15, 1853; m. Alston Boyd.

1494. Mary, Greenfield, Mass., b. Aug. 16, 1809; d. Dec. 21, 1818.

1495. Juliana, Greenfield, Mass., b. May 11, 1813; d. Nov. 1, 1885; m. Feb. 15, 1830, John Russel, b. Mar. 30, 1797; d. Dec. 27, 1874; son John Russel and Electa Edwards.

1496. Theodore Burg, Greenfield, Mass., b. Apr. 25, 1817; d. Mar. 29, 1856.

Family of MARY WITMER (422) and JOHN GROFF.

1497. Mary C., Mechanicsburg, Pa., b. Dec. 15, 1813; m. Jan. 28, 1834, Abraham T. Hamilton, b. Nov. 16, 1809; d. Sept. 2, 1849; son Hugh Hamilton and Elizabeth Thauley; m. Jan 23, 1855, Jacob G. Kister, b. Nov. 15, 1800; d. Aug. 15, 1875; son George Kister and Annie Shank.

1498. Abraham Witmer, Milroy, Pa., b. Jan. 14, 1816; d. Apr. 5, 1892; m. July 25, 1848, Wid. Caroline McMurtrie, b. Feb. 3, 1823; d. July 22, 1872; dau. ——— Flick and ———.

Family of MARY BRESSLER (423) and JOEL FERREE.

1499. George, Mill Hall, Pa., b. 1787; d. Sept. 9, 1866; m. Margaret Hazlet, b. Apr. 10, 1787; d. Aug. 27, 1854.

1500. Charlotta, Mill Hall, Pa., b. June 4, 1788; m. Dec. 27, 1808, David Logan.

1501. Mary, Salona, Pa., m. ——— Donahay; m. George Whitemier.

1502. Eliza, Mill Hall, Pa., m. Peter Robinson; m. Isaac Ditsworth.

1504. Fannie, Mill Hall, Pa.

1505. Joel, Canton, O., m. Jane Furgus.

1506. Rebecca, Canton, O., m. Jacob Kauffman, son Solomon Kauffman and ———.

1507. Harriet, Mill Hall, Pa.

Family of CATHERINE BRESSLER (424) and SAMUEL WILSON.

1508. Fannie, Salona, Pa., b. Dec. 24, 1787; d. Dec., 1787.

1509. Mary, Salona, Pa., b. July 3, 1789; d. 1789.

1510. Elizabeth, Salona, Pa., b. Feb. 24, 1792; d. 1872.

1511. George, Salona, Pa., b. May 19, 1795.

1512. Mark, Wooster, O., b. Aug. 27, 1797; d. May 17, 1875; m. Dec. 11, 1817, Harriet Hartman (1519).

1513. John, Salona, Pa., b. Feb. 3, 1800; d. Feb. 4, 1877; m. Mary Elder, b. Jan. 14, 1805; d. Oct. 24, 1875.

1514. Sarah, Salona, Pa., b. May 9, 1802; d. Dec. 2, 1877; m. Mar. 16, 1820, George Hartman (1518).

1515. Samuel, Salona, Pa., b. July 10, 1804; d. June 11, 1885; m. Apr. 13, 1826, Elizabeth Herr (584).

1516. Jesse, Salona, Pa., b. Mar. 16, 1807; m. Sarah Herr (599).

1517. Catharine, Salona, Pa., b. Sept. 28, 1809; d. Jan. 13, 1897; m. 1847, Wid. George Herr (593).

Family of ELIZABETH BRESSLER (425) and JACOB HARTMAN (661).

1518. George, Salona, Pa., b. Mar. 20, 1797; d. Sept. 30, 1868; m. Mar. 16, 1820, Sarah Wilson (1514).

1519. Harriet, Wooster, O., b. Feb. 22, 1802; d. Apr. 10, 1873; m. Dec. 17, 1817, Mark Wilson (1512).

1520. David, Lancaster, Pa., b. Dec. 13, 1802; d. Oct. 10, 1881; m. Sept. 23, 1829, Mary Miller, b. Feb. 4, 1809; d. Jan. 6, 1893; dau. Tobias Miller and Anna Huber.

1521. Christian, Carthage, Mo., b. Sept. 2, 1804; d. Feb. 4, 1882; m.

Feb. 23, 1837, Caroline V. Boyd, b. Aug. 15, 1812; d. May 9, 1889; dau. Col. John Boyd and Frances Woodward.

1522. Samuel, Salona, Pa., b. Dec. 3, 1807; d. Aug. 27, 1900; m. 1832, Lucy Holcomb, b. Sept. 15, 1810; d. Sept. 4, 1880; m. Nov. 2, 1881, Henrietta F. Miller (1540).

1523. Rev. Daniel, West Chester, Pa., b. July 8, 1810; d. Mar. 14, 1891; m. Feb. 14, 1839, Mary E. Davis, b. Nov. 15, 1819; d. June 12, 1874; dau. John F. Davis and Elizabeth Bowles.

1524. Elizabeth, Salona, Pa.

1525. Fannie Ann, Island, Pa., b. Mar. 10, 1817; d. Oct. 4, 1902; m. Apr. 11, 1844, Benjamin H. Baird, b. Oct. 15, 1808; d. May 6, 1888, son Benjamin Baird and Frances Siggins.

Family of GEORGE BRESSLER (429) and ANN ELIZA DORNIC.

1526. Sarah Ann, Mill Hall, Pa., b. Feb. 9, 1816; d. July 8, 1879; m. Sept. 15, 1840, John D. McCormick, b. Aug. 14, 1814; d. Feb. 27, 1848; son Alexander McCormick and Eleanor Montgomery.

1527. George, Mill Hall, Pa., b. June 8, 1818; d. Jan. 28, 1901; m. 1842, Phœbe A. Badger, b. 1823; d. 1850; dau. John Badger and Elizabeth Darrah; m. 1852, Eliza Hindershott, d. 1852; m. 1862, Josephine Vanatta, b. 1843; d. 1875; dau. Peter Vanatta and Elizabeth Holland.

1528. Dr. Charles, York ,Pa., b. Feb. 4, 1821; d. Feb. 22, 1894; m. 1849, Sarah Towner, b. Aug. 3, 1829; d. Aug. 6, 1868; dau. Rev. John Towner and ———.

1529. Henry, Lock Haven, Pa., b. Apr. 4, 1824; d. Apr. 15, 1873; m. Sept. 9, 1845, Isabella Henderson, b. July 22, 1826; d. Aug. 8, 1896; dau. John Henderson and ———.

1530. John J., Flemington, Pa., b. Nov. 18, 1826; d. July 18, 1879; m. July 18, 1847, Rebecca Slenker, b. Jan. 1, 1828; dau, Abraham Slenker and Catherine Lantzer.

1531. Daniel W., Chattanooga, Tenn., b. Jan. 19, 1832; m. Dec. 19, 1860, Harriet F. Hartman (4431); m. ———.

1532. Houston, Mill Hall, Pa., b. Jan. 18, 1836.

1533. Charlotte, Mill Hall, Pa., b. Feb. 7, 1839.

. Family of **HARRIET BRESSLER** (430) and **SAMUEL MILLER.**

1534. Charlotte, Salona, Pa., b. Jan. 6, 1812; d. May 9, 1845; m. Aug. 3, 1834, George Herr (593).

1535. Clarissa, Cedar Springs, Pa., b. July 14, 1813; d. Sept. 29, 1859; m. Apr. 12, 1835, George B. Herr (585).

1536. Ann Eliza, Lock Haven, Pa., b. Nov. 27, 1815; m. William Mc-Cormick, son Alexander McCormick and Eleanor Montgomery.

1537. Josiah, Strasburg, Pa., b. Mar. 29, 1818; d. Sept. 21, 1823.

1538. Samuel, Lancaster, Pa., b. Sept. 20, 1820; d. June 9, 1853.

1539. Cyrus, Lancaster, Pa., b. Dec. 7, 1822; d. Mar. 11, 1824.

1540. Henrietta Frances, Salona, Pa., b. July 8, 1825; m. Nov. 2, 1881, Wid. Samuel Hartman (1522).

1541. Albert Barnet, Salona, Pa., b. Oct. 22, 1827; d. Sept. 22, 1853.

Family of **JOHN NEFF** (431) and **MARY BARR.**

1542. Barbara Matilda, East Mill Creek, U., b. Oct. 28, 1822; d. May 29, 1890; m. Mar. 25, 1845, Julian Moses, b. Apr. 11, 1810; son Jesse Moses and Esther Brown.

1543. Franklin, East Mill Creek, U., b. Feb. 18, 1824; d. Nov. 17, 1882; m. Mar. 5, 1846, Elizabeth Musser, b. Dec. 7, 1825; d. Feb. 24, 1853; dau. Samuel Musser and Ann Barr; m. Jan. 1, 1855, Frances M. Stillman, b. May 29, 1830; dau. Jason Stillman and Harriet Seymour.

1544. Amos Herr, East Mill Creek, U., b. May 20, 1825; m. Apr. 15, 1848, Martha A. Dilworth, b. Jan. 29, 1827; d. May, 1862; dau. Caleb Dilworth and Eliza Walerton; m. Dec. 14, 1864, Catherine E. Thomas, b. Apr. 18, 1844; dau. David Thomas and Mary Davis; m. Dec. 6, 1875, Eliza A. Hughes, b. Nov. 5, 1854; dau. William Hughes and Hannah Crook.

1545. Cyrus N., Florence, Neb., b. Jan. 16, 1827; d. Mar. 4, 1847.

1546. Mary Ann, Salt Lake, U., b. Aug. 5, 1829; d. Sept. 28, 1866; m. Oren P. Rockwell, b. June 15, 1813; d. June 9, 1878; son Oren Rockwell and Sarah Witt.

1547. Susanna, Brigham, U., b. Mar. 26, 1831; d. July 8, 1894; m. Nov. 21, 1850, Eli H. Pierce, b. July 29, 1827; d. Aug. 12, 1858;

son Robert Pierce and Hannah Harvey; m. Mar. 8, 1869, Willis H. Boothe, b. Feb. 3, 1835; d. Feb. 8, 1897; son Henry Boothe and Susanna Henley.

1548. Benjamin Barr, Draper, U., b. May 6, 1834; d. Feb. 18, 1883; m. Martha A. Bitner, b. Nov. 13, 1840; d. July 24, 1868; dau. Samuel Bitner and Ann Barr; m. Oct. 10, 1870, Mary E. Love, b. Apr. 18, 1850; dau. Andrew Love and Nancy M. Bigelow; m. Oct. 10, 1870, Maria A. Bowthorpe, b. May 6, 1843; dau. William Bowthorpe and Mary A. Tuttle.

1549. Amanda, Strasburg, Pa., b. June 7, 1836; d. May 26, 1840.

1550. John, East Mill Creek, U., b. Dec. 28, 1837; m. Jan. 31, 1863, Ann E. Benedict, b. Feb. 8, 1845; dau. Joshua Benedict and Fidelia Moses.

1551. Elizabeth, East Mill Creek, U., b. Nov. 15, 1840; m. Jan. 12, 1858, Charles Stillman, b. June 1, 1834; son Jason Stillman and Harriet Seymour.

Family of FRANCIS HERR (495) and FANNY NEFF (434).

1552. Elizabeth, Strasburg, Pa., b. Mar. 16, 1814; m. Dec. 14, 1841, Adam Herr (535).

1553. Anna Catherine, Enterprise, Pa., b. Jan. 26, 1816; d. Sept. 7, 1882; m. Nov. 28, 1843, Martin Weaver (4327).

1554. Amos F., Wheatland Mills, Pa., b. May 8, 1818; m. Oct. 19, 1849, Ann M. Frantz, b. Dec. 4, 1829; dau. Christian N. Frantz and Elizabeth Miller.

1555. Fanny, Lancaster, Pa., b. Mar. 25, 1820.

1556. Charlotte, Lancaster, Pa., b. Oct. 28, 1822; m. Dec. 4, 1859, Wid. Henry Herr (521).

1557. Cyrus N., Lancaster, Pa., b. Mar. 19, 1825; m. May 15, 1855, Mary A. Brackbill (4255).

1558. Amanda, Lancaster, Pa., b. Nov. 20, 1827.

1559. Mary Ann, Wheatland Mills, Pa., b. Aug. 16, 1830; d. Aug. 1, 1832.

1560. Franklin J., Lancaster, Pa., b. Feb. 7, 1834; d. Jan. 24, 1891; m. May 24, 1858, Sallie M. Frantz, b. June 19, 1833; dau. Christian N. Frantz and Elizabeth Miller.

Family of JACOB NEFF (435) and FANNIE BARR (486).

1561. Letitia, Strasburg, Pa., b. Dec. 25, 1824; d. Oct. 15, 1848; m. May 5, 1846, Dr. Benjamin Musser, b. Sept. 1, 1820; d. July 14, 1883, son Dr. Martin Musser and Anna Hostetter.
1562. Son, Strasburg, Pa., b. Oct. 23, 1826: d. Nov. 4, 1826.

Family of Wid. JACOB NEFF (435) and ANNA BARR (487).

1563. Aldus Jacob, Strasburg, Pa., b. Sept. 2, 1830; d. Aug. 6, 1862.
1564. Jefferson N., Strasburg, Pa., b. July 10, 1834; d. Apr. 21, 1863; m. May 9, 1860, Emma Musser, b. Nov. 25, 1838; d. Dec. 25, 1904; dau. Dr. Martin Musser and Anna Hostetter.
1565. Fannie Elizabeth, Strasburg, Pa., b. Nov. 18, 1836; d. Apr. 13, 1837.
1566. Livingston M., Strasburg, Pa., b. Aug. 26, 1838; d. Jan. 24, 1839.
1567. Ella Ann, Strasburg, Pa., b. Dec. 8, 1842; d. May 13, 1843.
1568. Emily, Strasburg, Pa., b. Aug. 1, 1844; d. Oct. 19, 1844.
1569. Mary Virginia, Strasburg, Pa, b. May 18, 1847; d. Nov. 6, 1872: m. Oct. 11, 1868, John E. Hershey (5644).

Family of ELIZABETH NEFF (436) and HENRY BRENEMAN.

1570. Ann Catherine, Refton, Pa., b. May 25, 1820; d. Mar. 31, 1884; m. Nov. 17, 1840, Daniel Herr (1397).
1571. Jacob N., Strasburg, Pa., b. Oct. 19, 1822; d. Feb. 29, 1824.
1572. Elizabeth, Strasburg, Pa., b. Jan. 18, 1825; d. Feb., 1879; m. Sept. 2, 1845, Henry Musser, b. Oct. 5, 1822; d. Oct. 27, 1889; son Dr. Martin Musser and Anna Hostetter.
1573. Fannie, Strasburg, Pa., b. Dec. 10, 1826; d. Feb. 21, 1828.
1574. Henry N., Lanacster, Pa., b. Jan. 13, 1830; d. Oct. 10, 1901; m. Mar. 17, 1858, Ann M. Potts (5975).
1575. Enos, Strasburg, Pa., b. Mar. 10, 1834; d. Aug. 12, 1836.
1576. Emma, Strasburg, Pa., b. Aug. 26, 1837; d. Apr. 16, 1838.
1577. Susan, Strasburg, Pa., b. Jan. 4, 1839; d. Mar. 27, 1875; m. May 3, 1860, Amaziah M. Herr (1582).

Family of SUSAN HERR (438) and BENJAMIN BRENEMAN.

1578. Christian H., Lancaster, Pa., b. May 20, 1824; d. Oct. 5, 1866;

m. Nov. 2, 1853, Louisa A. Brenner, b. Aug. 28, 1827; dau. Henry Brenner and Eliza Fordney.

1579. Henry H., Denver, Col., b. Sept. 5, 1826; d. Mar. 29, 1885; m. Sept. 29, 1846, Susan Kendig (4360) ; m. Dec. 22, 1864, Emma B. Shenk (9728).

1580. B. Frank, Lancaster, Pa., b. Nov. 21, 1836; d. Dec. 31, 1905.

Family of CHRISTIAN HERR (440) and MARY HERR (1685).

1581. Aldus B. Willow Street, Pa., b. Mar. 14, 1834; d. July 15, 1834.

1582. Amaziah Musser, Strasburg, Pa., b. Dec. 6, 1835; m. May 30, 1860, Susan Breneman (1577) ; m. Oct. 17, 1878, Frances E. Herr (1905).

1583. Francis Henry, Willow Street, Pa., b. Nov. 20, 1837; d. Aug. 8, 1839.

1584. Emma Elizabeth, Willow Street, Pa., b. Sept. 4, 1839; d. Sept. 20, 1867.

1585. Benjamin Ezra, Willow Street, Pa., b. Jan. 22, 1842; m. Jan. 25, 1876, Esther Pfoutz, b. Dec. 21, 1844; d. Feb. 15, 1906; dau. Martin Pfoutz and Esther Miller.

1586. Daughter, Willow Street, Pa., b. Apr. 12, 1845; d. July 20, 1845.

1587. Mary Louise, Landisburg, Pa., b. Sept. 20, 1847; m. Nov. 21, 1876, Wesley W. Nissley, b. July 7, 1840; d. Dec. 21, 1898; son Samuel Nissley and Catharine Norton.

1588. Ada Naomi, Lancaster, Pa., b. Oct. 20, 1850; m. Nov. 21, 1876, Dr. Samuel B. Foreman, b. Oct. 27, 1849; d. Feb. 23, 1888; son Frederick Foreman and Elizabeth Byers.

Family of JOHN HERR (441) and SUSAN ROHRER.

1589. Sarah Ann, Lampeter, Pa., b. Feb. 1, 1836.

1590. Fanny, Strasburg, Pa., b. May 26, 1839; m. Feb. 15, 1860, John H. Brackbill (4088).

1591. Aldus C., Lancaster, Pa., b. Nov. 23, 1841.

1592. Elizabeth M., Lampeter, Pa., b. Sept. 15, 1843.

1593. Henry M., Pottsville, Pa., b. Oct. 11, 1846.

1594. Daughter, Lampeter, Pa.

Family of BENJAMIN HERR (442) and CATHARINE BARR (4272).

1595. Mary Ann, Soudersburg Pa., b. June 11, 1837; d. Dec. 19, 1874; m. Nov. 8, 1868, Wid. Rev. Christian N. Witmer, b. Apr. 16, 1831; d. Sept. 2, 1879; son Abraham Witmer and Susan Newcomer.

1596. Christian B., Lancaster, Pa., b. Sept. 11, 1838; d. Feb. 21, 1884; m. Sept. 29, 1868, Elizabeth A. Herr (4111).

Family of Wid. BENJAMIN HERR (442) and ANN SENER.

1503. Rohrer Eberle Sener, Lampeter, Pa., b. Feb. 3, 1846; d. Nov. 22, 1874.

1597. Sener Millo, Lampeter, Pa., b. Dec. 26, 1847; m. Oct. 12, 1876, Mary Maud Herr (4895).

1598. Jefferson M., Lampeter, Pa., b. Aug. 17, 1849; d. Feb. 7, 1854.

1599. Elizabeth L., Lampeter, Pa., b. Mar. 18, 1851; d. Feb. 18, 1854.

1600. Jefferson, Lampeter, Pa., b. July 3, 1855; d. May 14, 1861.

1601. Alma Frances, Lampeter, Pa., b. July 7, 1856; d. July 10, 1867.

1602. Henry, Lampeter, Pa., b. July 3, 1857; d. June 24, 1863.

1603. Benjamin F., Lampeter, Pa., b. Nov. 22, 1859; d. June 30, 1864.

1604. John Aldus, Willow Street, Pa., b. Nov. 22, 1859; m. Jan. 27, 1897, Mary Bowman (8240).

Family of JACOB HERR (443) and ANNA MUSSER.

1605. Amanda, Lampeter, Pa., b. Feb. 17, 1848; d. June 19, 1871; m. Sept. 4, 1867, David Hess, b. Dec. 12, 1845; son John Hess and Elizabeth Landis.

1606. Benjamin M., Willow Street, Pa., b. July 24, 1849; d. Jan. 11, 1883; m. Oct. 23, 1877, Alice W. Moyer, b. Aug. 29, 1856; dau. Benjamin D. Moyer and Elizabeth Wenger.

1607. Hebron M., Lancaster, Pa., b. Oct. 14, 1851; m. Sept. 16, 1874, Rebecca A. Hershey, b. Dec. 18, 1851; dau. J. H. Hershey and Barbara Breneman.

1608. Jacob R., Strasburg, Pa., b. Mar. 7, 1852; m. Nov. 18, 1878, Susan Breneman, b. July 8, 1857; dau. John Breneman and Maria Hess.

1609. Barbara Ann, Lampeter, Pa., b. Jan. 15, 1854; d. Oct. 30, 1861.
1610. Rev. Frank M., Lancaster, Pa., b. Oct. 3, 1855; m. Oct. 28, 1879, Mary E. Hershey, b. July 3, 1857; dau. J. H. Hershey and Barbara Breneman.
1611. Amos C., Strasburg, Pa., b. Oct. 17, 1857; m. Feb. 28, 1882, Mary Shenk (7433).
1612. Elizabeth, Lampeter, Pa., b. Sept. 4, 1859; d. Oct. 2, 1863.
1613. Mary Ann, Conestoga Centre, Pa., b. Apr. 16, 1862; m. Oct. 11, 1883, Amos H. McAllister, b. Mar. 17, 1858; son Amos McAllister and Fanny L. Hess.

Family of CHRISTIAN FORRER (447) and ——— YERTZ.

1614. Lizzie, Orrville, O., m. Jacob Brubaker.
1615. Catharine, Orrville, O., m. Daniel Andrews.

Family of Wid. CHRISTIAN FORRER (447) and SUSAN BOHAM.

1616. Rudolph, Orrville, O.
1617. John, Orrville, O.
1618. Daniel, Orrville, O.
1619. Benjamin, Orrville, O.
1620. Christian, Orrville, O.
1621. Maria, Orrville, O.
1622. Fanny, Orrville, O.

Family of MARIA FORRER (449) and CHRISTIAN ROHRER.

1623. Henry, Strasburg, Pa., b. Feb. 20, 1790; d. Mar. 4, 1852; m. Mar. 4, 1816, Elizabeth Stoner, b. July 29, 1795; d. June 17, 1874; dau. Jacob Stoner and ———.
1624. John, Lampeter, Pa., b. Aug. 8, 1793; d. Nov. 27, 1878.
1625. Martin, Dayton, O., b. Nov. 3, 1795; d. Dec. 5, 1843; m. Elizabeth Kreider, dau. Tobias Kreider and ——— Diffenbach.
1626. Elizabeth, Lancaster, Pa., b. Apr. 21, 1799; d. Nov. 15, 1885; m. Martin Kreider, son Tobias Kreider and ———.
1627. Catharine, New Danville, Pa., b. Apr. 15, 1802; d. Oct. 4, 1884; m. May 27, 1823, Emanuel Barr, b. May 17, 1791; d. Apr. 8, 1870; son John Barr and Catharine Bachman.

1628. Christian, Germantown, O., b. Dec. 2, 1804; d. July 30, 1883; m. Nov. 29, 1832, Margaret Emerich, dau. Christopher Emerich and ———.

1629. Samuel, Dayton, O., b. Aug. 27, 1807; d. May 19, 1892; m. Rebecca Wise.

1630. Daniel, Urbana, O., b. June 15, 1810; d. Sept. 4, 1847; m. Sarah Lauderbach.

1631. Jacob, Tippecanoe City, O., b. Oct. 15, 1815; m. Dec. 25, 1838, Elizabeth Kendig, b. Sept. 16, 1821; d. Feb. 20, 1894; dau. John Kendig and Susan Reinheart.

Family of BARBARA FORRER (451) and HENRY MYERS.

1632. Henry, Elizabethtown, Pa., b. Oct. 3, 1803; d. Sept. 2, 1890; m. Sarah Ober, b. Feb. 28, 1802; d. Oct. 24, 1837; m. Sarah Coble, b. Nov. 21, 1816; d. Mar. 27, 1852; m. Maria Zimmerman, b. Jan. 19, 1832; d. Sept. 9, 1902.

1633. Catharine, Elizabethtown, Pa., b. Sept. 4, 1795; m. Isaac Over.

1634. Samuel, Elizabethtown, Pa., b. Nov. 10, 1797.

12194. Elias, Elizabethtown, Pa., b. Jan. 3, 1794.

12195. Joanna, Elizabethtown, Pa., b. Dec. 31, 1800.

12196. Daniel, Elizabethtown, Pa., b. Sept. 11, 1806.

12197. Benjamin, Elizabethtown, Pa., b. May 11, 1809.

12198. Annie, Elizabethtown, Pa., b. Jan. 28, 1812.

12199. Elizabeth, Elizabethtown, Pa., b. Sept. 20, 1814.

Family of CHRISTIANA FORRER (452) and DANIEL KNAISLEY.

1635. Eliza, Orrville, O., m. William Keplinger.

1636. Barbara, Orrville, O., m. ——— Houser.

1637. Mary, Orrville, O., m. Benjamin Knaisley.

1638. John, Orrville, O.

1639. Daniel, Orrville, O.

1640. George, Orrville, O.

1641. Samuel, Orrville, O.

1642. Christian, Orrville, O., m. Mary Eby.

7

Family of MAGDALENE FORRER (455) and JACOB HERR (1399).

1643. Mary, Willow Street, Pa., b. Nov., 1810; d. Aug., 1837.

1644. Barbara, Bird-in-Hand, Pa., b. Sept. 3, 1812; m. Aug., 1852, Rev.
Tobias Kreider, b. Sept. 10, 1811; d. Oct., 1864; son Rev. John
Kreider and Esther Denlinger.

1645. Ann, Willow Street, Pa., b. Feb., 1814; d. Nov., 1840.

1646. Jacob F., Strasburg, Pa., b. July 11, 1817; d. Jan. 25, 1899; m.
Jan. 13, 1846, Susan Witmer, b. Dec. 4, 1823; d. Feb. 21, 1874;
dau. Jacob Witmer and Sarah Lefever.

Family of CHRISTIAN FORRER (456) and ELIZABETH LIGHT (1126.

1647. Elizabeth, Carlisle, Pa., m. John Vineland.

1648. Barbara, Carlisle, Pa., m. ———— Zook.

1649. Magdalene, Carlisle, Pa., m. George Langstow.

1650. Mary, Carlisle, Pa., m. Henry Stauffer.

1651. Fanny, Carlisle, Pa.

1652. John, Carlisle, Pa.

1653. Lydia, Carlisle, Pa.

1654. Amanda, Carlisle, Pa., m. John Koons.

Family of FRANCES BRENEMAN (460) and ISAAC HEINEY.

1655. Martha, New Danville, Pa., b. Feb. 15, 1790; d. Feb. 24, 1836;
m. Michael Haverstick, b. Jan. 20, 1789; d. June 29, 1828.

1656. Elizabeth, New Danville, Pa., b. Aug. 20, 1791; m. William
Ream.

1657. Jacob, New Danville, Pa., b. Dec. 1, 1792.

1658. Mary, New Danville, Pa., b. Jan. 9, 1794.

1659. George, New Danville, Pa., b. May 2, 1796.

1660. Frances, Marticville, Pa., b. Feb. 11, 1798; m. David S. Heiney,
b. May 5, 1803; son ———— and Fanny Stone.

1661. Isaac, Marticville, Pa., b. May 3, 1800.

1662. Polly, Marticville, Pa., b. Sept. 10, 1804.

1663. Nancy, Marticville, Pa., b. Jan. 20, 1806.

1664. George, Marticville, Pa., b. Apr. 1, 1808.

1665. Isaac, Lancaster, Pa., b. May 26, 1810; d. Nov. 17, 1883; m. Oct.

14, 1839, Wid. Elizabeth Zercher, b. Dec. 22, 1800; d. May 11, 1868; dau. George Debudd and ———.

1666. Infant, Lancaster, Pa., b. Apr. 26, 1812; d. 1812.

1667. Susan, Millersville, Pa., b. Sept. 8, 1813; d. Jan. 20, 1836; m. Mar. 28, 1834, Jacob Kauffman, b. Mar. 28, 1817; son Jacob Kauffman and Sarah Groff.

1668. George, Millersville, Pa., b. May 20, 1822.

Family of CHRISTIAN GROFF (463) and HETTIE GROFF.

1669. Jacob, Paradise, Pa., Jan. 12, 1816; d. Sept. 4, 1874; m. Dec. 19, 1841, Mary Howry, b. July 8, 1815; d. Aug. 31, 1870; dau. John Howry and ——— Doner.

1670. Richard B., Marengo, Ia., b. Nov. 12, 1817; d. Aug. 24, 1896; m. Oct. 27, 1842, Wid. Judith Eshleman, b. Sept. 29, 1815; dau. Christian Barr and Susan Breneman.

1671. Benjamin, Pope Creek, Ill., d. Mar., 1845; m. Eveline Decker, b. 1819; d. Dec., 1859; dau. Moses Decker and Elizabeth ———.

1672. John E., Strasburg, Pa.

Family of Wid. CHRISTIAN GROFF (463) and MARY STOFER.

1673. Susan, Miamiville, O., b. July 11, 1826; m. Jan. 6, 1853, Thomas Wiggins, b. Aug. 10, 1822; d. Mar. 9, 1878; son Thomas Wiggins and Sarah Varner.

1674. David, Lawrenceville, Ill., b. Mar. 3, 1829; d. Dec. 9, 1900; m. Jan. 1, 1856, Sara Major, b. Feb. 24, 1838; dau. Peter Major and Mary Colgan.

1675. Martin Luther, Weston, O., b. Feb. 22, 1831; m. Dec. 8, 1861, Elizabeth Campbell, b. Nov. 25, 1825; dau. Edward Campbell and Hannah Jones.

1676. Catharine, Shell Rock, Ia., b. Nov. 16, 1833; d. Oct. 5, 1888; m. Mar. 24, 1853, Hiram Hall, b. Oct. 24, 1829.

1677. Lizzie S., Soudersburg, Pa., b. July 18, 1837; m. Feb. 15, 1859, Jacob Baker, b. Feb. 11, 1833; son Peter Baker and Rebecca Caskey.

1678. Mary, Weston, O., b. June 22, 1839; m. Nov. 19, 1857, Eli Capella, b. Apr. 20, 1828; son John Capella and Mary Bolim.

Family of MARY GROFF (464) and DAVID ESHLEMAN (671).

1679. Annie, Strasburg, Pa., b. Apr. 12, 1807; d. May 4, 1884; m. Jan. 3, 1828, Henry Musselman, b. June 14, 1802; d. Nov. 26, 1870; son Christian Musselman and Susanna Forrer.

1680. Samuel, Strasburg, Pa., b. May 31, 1809; d. Sept. 15, 1821.

1681. Son, Strasburg, Pa., b. Aug. 30, 1811; d. Sept. 1, 1811.

1682. David G., Lancaster, Pa., b. July 3, 1816; d. Apr. 30, 1895; m. Nov. 14, 1848, Caroline O. Carpenter, b. Nov. 14, 1828; d. Apr. 11, 1900; dau. Abraham Carpenter and Julia E. Ross.

Family of Rev. JOHN HERR (494) and BETSEY GROFF (465).

1683. Benjamin Groff, Strasburg, Pa., b. Mar. 6, 1808; d. Nov. 4, 1878; m. Jan. 15, 1833, Mary Emma Witmer, b. Oct. 4, 1814; d. Sept. 8, 1886; dau. David Witmer and Jane Lightner.

1684. Veronica, Strasburg, Pa., b. July 9, 1810; d. June 9, 1850.

1685. Mary, Willow Street, Pa., b. Mar. 13, 1812; d. Nov. 12, 1890; m. Dec. 23, 1830, Christian Herr (440).

1686. Betsey, Lampeter, Pa., b. Jan. 15, 1814; d. Nov. 3, 1870; m. Nov. 27, 1832, Rev. Dr. Daniel Musser, b. Nov. 2, 1809; d. May 20, 1877; son Rev. Henry Musser and Susan Neff.

1687. Anna, Rock Island, Ill., b. Jan. 21, 1817; d. Aug. 23, 1884; m. Dec. 20, 1836, Henry Frantz, b. June 11, 1814; d. Oct. 29, 1874; son Jacob Frantz and Elizabeth Hershey.

1688. Martha Magdalena, Witmer, Pa., b. Oct. 12, 1820; d. May 6, 1898; m. Oct. 20, 1840, Dr. Jacob H. Musser, b. Jan. 24, 1819; d. Mar. 4, 1890; son Dr. Martin Musser and Anna Hostetter.

1689. John Forrer, Strasburg, Pa., b. Nov. 14, 1823; d. Feb. 16, 1893; m. Sept. 8, 1846, Martha Musser, b. June 12, 1825; d. Jan. 26, 1892; dau. Dr. Martin Musser and Anna Hostetter.

1690. Esther, Strasburg, Pa., b. Jan. 15, 1827; d. Jan. 15, 1827.

1691. Naomi, Strasburg, Pa., b. Feb. 4, 1831; d. Mar. 7, 1859; m. May 16, 1854, Wid. Dr. Benjamin Musser, b. Sept. 1, 1820; d. July 14, 1883; son Dr. Martin Musser and Anna Hostetter.

1692. Frances, Strasburg, Pa., b. Aug. 9, 1832; d. Nov. 12, 1835.

Family of JOHN GROFF (466) and SALLIE DOWNING.

1693. Samuel, Strasburg, Pa.
1694. Mary, Strasburg, Pa.
1695. John, Strasburg, Pa.
1696. Anna, Strasburg, Pa.
1697. Benjamin, Strasburg, Pa.
1698. Eliza, Strasburg, Pa.

Family of ELIZABETH MARTIN (468) and DANIEL LONGENECKER.

1699. Susan, Strasburg, Pa., m. Henry Eckman.
1700. Benjamin, Camargo, Pa.
1701. John, Strasburg, Pa., m. Susan Barr, dau. Abraham Barr and ———.
1702. Polly, Strasburg, Pa., m. John Aston, son John Aston and ———.
1703. Lizzie, Strasburg, Pa., m. Daniel Eckman.
1704. Nancy, Strasburg, Pa., m. David Groff, son Jacob Groff and ———.
1705. Daniel, Lampeter, Pa., b. 1800; m. Mary Holsehouse, dau. Peter Holsehouse and ———.
1706. Mattie, Lampeter, Pa., m. Michael Kiester.
1707. Fanny, Lampeter, Pa., m. John Groff, son Michael Groff and ——— Carpman.
1708. Abraham, Harrisburg, Pa.

Family of CHRISTIAN MARTIN (469) and ELIZABETH FRANK.

1709. John, Mt. Joy, Pa., m. Catharine Wall.
1710. Martha, Mt. Joy, Pa., m. Benjamin Eshleman, son Martin Eshleman and Betsey Kendig.
1711. Daniel, Mt. Joy, Pa.
1712. Christian, Mt. Joy, Pa., m. ——— Kendig, dau. George Kendig and ———.
1713. Charlotte, Mt. Joy, Pa.
1714. Annie, Mt. Joy, Pa., b. Dec. 21, 1806; d. Feb. 3, 1888; m. John Swisher; m. Wid. Jacob Redsecker, b. June 16, 1800; d. Oct. 14, 1868; son George Redsecker and Susan Ream.

1715. Harriet, Mt. Joy, Pa., b. Dec. 21, 1808; d. June 20, 1847; m. Jacob Redsecker, b. June 16, 1800; d. Oct. 14, 1868; son George Redsecker and Susan Ream.

Family of NANCY MARTIN (470) and SAMUEL ESHLEMAN.

1716. Jacob, Strasburg, Pa., b. Jan. 7, 1807; d. Nov. 27, 1850; m. 1829, Barbara A. Miller, b. Jan. 7, 1807; d. Jan. 25, 1893; dau. Jacob Miller and Barbara Herr.
1717. Ann, Strasburg, Pa., b. Mar. 6, 1812; d. Mar. 16, 1902.

Family of MARTHA MARTIN (471) and JOHN SHAUB.

1718. Elizabeth, Mt. Joy, Pa., m. Benjamin Shaub, son Martin Shaub and Lizzie Myers.
1719. Alice A., Lancaster, Pa., d. 1828; m. Jan., 1820, George Martin (1170).
1720. Christian, Lancaster, Pa., m. Clarissa Griffith.
1721. Mary, Lancaster, Pa., m. Jacob Gorman.
1722. Barbara, Lancaster, Pa., m. George Gorman.
1723. John, Lancaster, Pa., m. Fanny Shaub, dau. Martin Shaub and Lizzie Myers.
1724. Martha, Lancaster, Pa., m. John Binly.

Family of DAVID MARTIN (472) and SUSAN ESHLEMAN.

1725. Samuel, Safe Harbor, Pa., b. Nov. 10, 1799; m. Jan. 1, 1822, Mattie Witmer (503).
1726. Betsey, Willow Street, Pa., m. John Kreider.
1727. David, Willow Street, Pa.
1728. Benjamin, Willow Street, Pa., m. Barbara Good.
1729. Ann, Willow Street, Pa.
1730. Susan, Willow Street, Pa., m. ——— Spear.
1731. Mary, Willow Street, Pa., m. Christian Oyman.

Family of MARIA MARTIN (473) and DANIEL MUSSER.

1732. Elizabeth, Willow Street, Pa., m. John Baker.
1733. Christian, Willow Street, Pa.
1734. Dr. John, Willow Street, Pa.
1735. Nancy, Willow Street, Pa.

1736. Martha, Willow Street, Pa.
1737. Daniel, Willow Street, Pa.
1738. Mary, Willow Street, Pa.
1739. Benjamin, Willow Street, Pa.
1740. Martin, Willow Street, Pa.
1741. Fanny, Willow Street, Pa.
1742. Hettie, Willow Street, Pa.
1743. Samuel, Willow Street, Pa.

Family of SAMUEL MARTIN (474) and MARY DUNNING.

1744. Christian, Washington, Pa., m. Mary Kemmory.
1745. Martha, Lancaster, Pa., m. Daniel Stauffer.
1746. Mary, Iola, Kans., m. Adam Hoke.
1747. Eliza, Lancaster, Pa., b. Dec. 30, 1821; m. Frank Skeen.
1748. Susan, Strasburg, Pa., b. Dec. 30, 1821; m. Oct. 19, 1843, Christian W. Binkley, b. Oct. 14, 1819; d. Sep. 6, 1892.
1749. Samuel, Lancaster, Pa., m. Martha Styer.
1750. Ann, Lancaster, Pa., m. George M. Leary.
1751. Jacob, Strasburg, Pa., b. Apr. 27, 1808; m. Mary Longenecker, dau. Daniel Longenecker and Elizabeth Martin.
1752. Fanny, Lancaster, Pa., b. Apr. 27, 1808.

Family of JACOB MARTIN (475) and ESTHER KENDIG.

1753. Maria, Quarryville, Pa., m. May 27, 1818; m. Sept. 18, 1838, Martin Herr (1364).
1754. Hettie Ann, Lancaster, Pa., b. Sept. 27, 1825; m, Jan. 23, 1845, George H. Miller, b. Aug. 7, 1820; d. Jan. 3, 1894; son Benjamin Miller and Catharine Haines.

Family of JOHN BARR (480) and SUSANNA HERR (1400).

1755. Fanny, New Providence, Pa., b. Aug. 17, 1811; d. Feb. 18, 1844; m. Feb. 3, 1835, Jacob M. Mayer, b. Mar. 21, 1813; d. Nov. 22, 1872; son Christian Mayer and Mary Miller.

Family of BENJAMIN BARR (481) and CATHARINE KENDIG (1474).

1756. Anna, Towson, Md., b. Feb. 13, 1818; m. Aug. 31, 1841, John H. Longenecker, b. Mar. 3, 1818: son David Longenecker and Catharine Stoner.

1757. Martin, Glyndon, Md., b. Apr. 8, 1819; m. Feb. 6, 1855, Margaret Gore, b. Dec. 21, 1825; dau. George Gore and Catharine Wilderson.

1758. Elizabeth, Towson, Md., b. May 17, 1822; m. Feb. 27, 1847, John Groff (3814).

1759. Jacob, Towson, Md., b. May 14, 1824; d. Apr. 10, 1842.

1760. John, Towson, Md., b. Apr. 17, 1828; d. Aug. 27, 1846.

1761. Catharine, Towson, Md., b. July 14, 1836; m. Sept. 11, 1855, John B. Keagy (1989).

Family of MARTIN BARR (483) and SUSAN MILLER.

1762. Eliza Ann, Strasburg, Pa., b. Oct. 4, 1819; d. Sept. 25, 1820.

1763. Fanny B., Owings Mills, Pa., b. Apr. 3, 1821; m. Oct. 23, 1844. John H. Harman, b. Nov. 25, 1819; son Daniel Harman and Susanna Hurbst.

1764. Hettie Ann, Philadelphia, Pa., b. Mar. 10, 1823; d. Aug. 24, 1899; m. Sept. 4, 1848, Francis B. Groff (2235).

1765. John N., Brunswick, Mo., b. May 4, 1825; d. Mar. 21, 1867 · m. Sept. 12, 1854, Sallie M. Darr, b. Apr. 2, 1835; dau. Bushrod Darr and Elily S. Darr.

1766. Martin W., Washington, D. C., b. Oct. 31, 1827; m. Mar. 1, 1855, Harriet Cornelius, b. Jan. 21, 1834; dau. Benjamin Cornelius and Ellen Burd.

1767. Ann Catharine, Sterling, Ill., b. May 7, 1830; m. Sept. 10, 1850, Martin H. Krieder (1860).

1768. Samuel, Strasburg, Pa., b. Oct. 12, 1833.

1769. Dr. David Miller, Long Branch, N. J., b. Nov. 12, 1836; m. July 28, 1864, Susan L. Dickson, b. May 31, 1842; d. Aug., 1891; dau. Isaac Dickson and Mary J. Sears; m. Jan. 22, 1892, Wid. Emma B. Breneman (9728).

Family of Wid. MARTIN BARR (483) and ELIZABETH JOHNSON.

1770. Jacob Neff, Chicago, Ill., b. July 9, 1848; d. May 16, 1904; m. ——— Brooks.

1771. Mary Galebaugh, Strasburg, Pa., b. Dec. 25, 1849.

1772. Letitia Musser, Strasburg, Pa., b. Feb. 2, 1854; d. Nov. 1, 1860.

Family of ELIZABETH BARR (484) and FRANCIS KENDIG (1475).

1773. Jacob, Lampeter, Pa., b. Oct. 14, 1821; d. Aug. 8, 1827.

Family of CHRISTIAN HARTMAN (489) and ANNA BRUBAKER.

1774. Anna, Millersville, Pa., b. July 11, 1814; d. Aug. 24, 1897; m.
Sept. 8, 1836, John Stauffer, b. Jan. 5, 1816; d. June, 1881; son
Daniel Stauffer and ——— Thomas.
1775. Henry, Millersville, Pa., b. Sept. 8, 1816; m. Frances Dellett.
1776. Dr. Abraham, Millersville, Pa., b. 1818; m. ———; m. ———.
1777. Christian B., Hill Grove, O., b. Mar. 7, 1820; d. Sept. 16, 1900;
m. Dec., 1844, Catharine Immel, b. June 22, 1828; d. Sept. 3,
1849; m. Catharine Brooks; m. Catharine O'Donnell.
1778. John B., Hill Grove, O., d. June 15, 1902; m. Nancy Neff.
1779. Elizabeth, Hill Grove, O., m. Henry Kauffman.
1780. Henrietta, New Holland, Pa., b. Sept. 19, 1827; m. Dec. 26, 1847,
Joseph Rutter (2479).
1781. Dr. Samuel B., Columbus, O., b. Apr. 1, 1830; m. 1859, Sarah
A. Martzell, dau. Wendell Martzell and Catharine Ackerman.

Family of FANNY HERR (496) and BENJAMIN ESHLEMAN (670).

1782. Benjamin, Lancaster, Pa., b. Feb. 18, 1809; d. Dec. 2, 1876; m.
Mar. 15, 1832, Elizabeth Gyger, b. May 27, 1814; d. Nov. 24,
1904; dau. John Gyger and Mary Bowman.

Family of MARTIN HERR (497) and MARY HERR (1402).

1783. Frances, Lampeter, Pa., b. Mar. 28, 1818; d. Oct. 26, 1822.
1784. Mary, Lancaster, Pa., b. May 31, 1820; d. Mar. 1, 1905; m. Sept.
28, 1841, John Kendig (1011).
1785. Martha, Lampeter, Pa., b. Aug. 23, 1822; m. Gabriel Wenger,
b. Oct. 28, 1819; d. Apr. 2, 1887; son Michael Wenger and Elizabeth Groff.

Family of MARTIN WITMER (498) and SUSAN KENDIG.

1786. Daniel, Strasburg, Pa., b. Dec. 31, 1815; d. 1850.
1787. Esther, Strasburg, Pa., b. Dec. 15, 1816; d. Sept. 14, 1840.

1788. Benjamin, Strasburg, Pa., b. Feb. 5, 1818; d. 1821.

1789. Anna, Strasburg, Pa., b. May 31, 1819.

1790. Elizabeth, Strasburg, Pa., b. July 18, 1820.

1791. John K., Strasburg, Pa., b. Sept. 16, 1821 ; m. Laura Fritter.

1792. Judith W., Strasburg, Pa., b. Oct. 28, 1822; m. June 4, 1850, William Stacy, b. 1807; d. Nov. 6, 1857.

1793. Susanna, Strasburg, Pa., b. Oct. 20, 1823; d. June, 1824.

Family of ESTHER WITMER (499) and BENJAMIN KENDIG (2203).

1794. Benjamin W., Washington, Ill., b. Aug. 29, 1808; d. Jan., 1887; m. Dec. 12, 1833, Eliza Kendig (3432) ; m. Sept. 26, 1844, Elizabeth T. Page, b. Jan. 11, 1812; d. Aug. 15, 1868; m. Oct. 14, 1869, Wid. Elizabeth A. Kendig, b. Sept. 27, 1829; dau. ——— Arnold and ———.

1795. Esther, Washington, Ill., b. Feb. 12, 1810; d. 1843; m. Jeremiah Smith.

1796. Mary, Washington, Ill., b. Sept. 24, 1811 ; m. Andrew Cress.

1797. Magdalena, Washington, Ill., b. Oct. 3, 1813; d. 1883; m. Jacob J. Banta.

1798. David, Washington, Ill., b. Sept. 12, 1816; d. Sept. 23, 1892; m. Jan. 13, 1844, Elizabeth J. McCord, b. Mar. 23, 1821; d. Apr. 9, 1856; dau. William McCord and Jane McMurtrey; m. Feb. 26, 1857, Ellen Conn, b. Aug. 9, 1824; dau. George W. Conn and Keziah Burris.

1799. Henry W., Washington, Ill., b. Aug. 28, 1823; d. Mar. 13, 1864; m. Elizabeth Arnold.

1800. Leah, Washington, Ill., b. Nov. 20, 1820; m. Jacob Grove.

Family of SUSAN WITMER (500) and MARTIN KENDIG (2209).

1801. Hettie, Waynesboro, Va., b. Sept. 18, 1819; m. David Hildebrand, b. July 23, 1813.

1802. Mary, Waynesboro, Va., b. Mar. 3, 1822; m. John Ruebush.

Family of JOHN WITMER (501) and ANNA BRUBAKER.

1803. Maria, Mt. Nebo, Pa., b. Feb. 2, 1824; m. Aug. 13, 1840, John Erb, b. Aug. 25, 1814; d. Dec. 31, 1894; son Joseph Erb and Susan Bowman.

1804. Elias, Strasburg, Pa., b. 1815; m. Susan Markley.

1805. Esther, New Providence, Pa., m. Miller Raub, b. 1810; son John Raub and ———.

1806. Martin B., Lancaster, Pa., m. Barbara Hiller, dau. John Hiller and Anna Rush.

1807. Ann Elizabeth, New Providence, Pa.

1808. Christiana, New Providence, Pa.

1809. John, New Providence, Pa.

1810. Benjamin Henry, New Providence, Pa.

1811. Julia, Baltimore, Md., m. Wid. Miller Raub, b. 1810; son John Raub and ———.

1812. Martha, New Providence, Pa.

Family of NANCY WITMER (502) and MICHAEL MARTIN.

1813. John W., Willow Street, Pa., b. July 17, 1816; m. Nov. 20, 1840, Susan Shaub (1242).

1814. Esther, Intercourse, Pa., b. Oct. 12, 1818; m. Nov. 9, 1852, Jacob S. Hershey, b. Nov. 27, 1812; son Abraham Hershey and Mary Seachrist.

Family of MARTHA WITMER (503) and SAMUEL MARTIN (1725).

1815. Hettie, Willow Street, Pa., b. Oct. 6, 1822; m. June 7, 1855, Benjamin Gochenour, b. Mar. 31, 1823; son Jacob Gochenour and Anna Hess.

1816. Susan, Duncannon, Pa., b. Oct. 9, 1823; d. Feb. 27, 1883; m. Mar. 9, 1843, James Spence, b. Nov. 26, 1820; d. Sept. 11, 1885; son John Spence and Rosanna Snodgrass.

1817. Mary, Duncannon, Pa., b. June 26, 1826; m. Oct. 20, 1847, David Miller, b. Nov. 21, 1817; son John Miller and Elizabeth Cramer.

1818. David, Duncannon, Pa., b. Sept. 15, 1828; m. 1860, Lizzie Ressel, dau. Samuel Ressel and Anna Kline.

1819. Samuel, Duncannon, Pa., b. Dec. 25, 1830.

1820. John, Duncannon, Pa., b. Mar. 10, 1833.

1821. Martha, Duncannon, Pa., b. Mar. 8, 1835.

1822. Simon Peter, Duncannon, Pa., b. Mar. 26, 1837.

1823. Benjamin W., Duncannon, Pa., b. Oct. 4, 1839; m. Nov. 12, 1863, Susan Good, b. July 30, 1841; dau. John Good and Frances Miller.

1824. Elizabeth, Duncannon, Pa., b. Dec. 1, 1842; m. Samuel B. Kendig, son Samuel Kendig and Martha Bossler.

Family of DAVID WITMER (504) and ELIZABETH McCOMSEY.

1825. Esther Ann, Quarryville, Pa., b. Oct. 7, 1830; d. Dec. 8, 1830.

1826. Benjamin, Quarryville, Pa., b. Nov. 27, 1831; m. Aug. 10, 1854, Lydia A. Lefevre, dau. Daniel Lefevre and Elizabeth Lefevre.

1827. Amos, Quarryville, Pa., b. Feb. 18, 1833; d. Aug. 22, 1833.

1828. Franklin, Quarryville, Pa., b. Apr. 11, 1834; m. Dec. 25, 1856, Hettie Lefevre, dau. Daniel Lefevre and Martha Shenk.

1829. Samuel, Quarryville, Pa., b. Apr. 22, 1837; m. July 30, 1861, Maggie Lyle, dau. Thomas Lyle and Fanny Barr.

1830. John, Quarryville, Pa., b. Oct. 31, 1839.

1831. Mary, Quarryville, Pa., b. Feb. 13, 1842; m. July 31, 1862.

1832. Martha Ann, Quarryville, Pa., b. Jan. 26, 1845; d. Dec. 25, 1845.

1833. George, Quarryville, Pa., b. Mar. 17, 1846.

1834. Lavenia, Quarryville, Pa., b. July 26, 1849.

1835. D. Herr, Parkesburg, Pa., b. Aug. 20, 1852.

Family of JOHN HERR (508) and MARY LONG.

1836. Henry, Shawnee, N. Y., b. Sept. 1, 1818; d. July 15, 1859; m. Aug. 16, 1849, Harriet Metz, b. Nov. 22, 1828; d. July 12, 1862; dau. Christian Metz and Barbara Kauffman.

1837. Ann, Sanborn, N. Y., b. July 28, 1820; d. Apr. 3, 1889; m. May 29, 1845, Joseph Habecker (1026).

1838. Rev. Eli, Williamsville, N. Y., b. Nov. 10, 1822; d. Oct. 8, 1900; m. June 2, 1850, Melvina L. Eggert, b. Oct. 24, 1826; d. Nov. 14, 1894; dau. Christian Eggert and Anna Hershey.

1839. Mary, Sanborn, N. Y., b. May 16, 1825; m. May 18, 1848, Henry Treichler, b. Aug. 19, 1819; son Daniel Treichler and Catharine Schaull.

1840. Susan, Sanborn, N. Y., b. July 20, 1827; m. Jan. 1, 1852, Andrew Reigle, b. Sep. 15, 1829; son David Reigle and Catharine Walkemiller.

1841. Betsey, Pekin, N. Y., b. Mar. 2, 1830; m. Jan. 9, 1862, John Schmeck, b. Oct. 27, 1825; d. Mar. 6, 1901; son Valentine Schmeck and Susan Wagner.

1842. Esther, Niagara Falls, N. Y., b. Feb. 21, 1832; d. Feb. 3, 1865; m. May 20, 1852, Abraham B. Gantz, b. Mar. 28, 1829; d. Apr. 11, 1891; son George Gantz and Catharine Bishop.

Family of MARY HERR (509) and JOHN LONG.

1843. David, Williamsville, N. Y., b. Dec. 18, 1818; d. Mar. 31, 1883; m. Feb. 16, 1841, Mary K. Miller, b. Jan. 2, 1819; d. Nov. 20, 1896; dau. Daniel Miller and Elizabeth Kregloh.

1844. Daniel, Williamsville, N. Y., b. Mar. 5, 1821; d. Mar. 23, 1851; m. July 28, 1844, Sarah Miller, b. Aug. 30, 1822; d. Sept. 8, 1901; dau. Daniel Miller and Elizabeth Kregloh.

Family of EMANUEL HERR (512) and NANCY SNEARLY.

1845. Susan, Buffalo, N. Y., b. Apr. 30, 1834; m. Mar. 26, 1853, Elias Fogelsonger, b. July 10, 1832; son John Fogelsonger and Susan Eby.

1846. Emanuel, Bath, N. Y., b. Jan. 18, 1839.

1847. Anna, Williamsville, N. Y., b. Mar. 10, 1841; d. Feb. 11, 1863.

1848. Henry S., Buffalo, N. Y., b. July 21, 1844; m. Feb. 19, 1871, Georgiana Howard, b. Feb. 19, 1849; dau. Asa Howard and Margaret Siver.

1849. Mary Jane, Williamsville, N. Y., b. July 18, 1846; m. Sept. 1886, Philander Fogelsonger, b. Mar. 2, 1844; son George Fogelsonger and Rachel Long.

1850. Lucius P., Buffalo, N. Y., b. Mar. 6, 1848; d. Aug. 2, 1885.

1851. George Washington, Rochester, N. Y., b. Apr. 13, 1852; m. Oct. 5, 1876, Caroline J. Holton, b. July 7, 1856; dau. John B. Holton and Catharine Ainston.

Family of ESTHER HERR (514) and JOHN METZLER.

1852. Henry H., Old Line, Pa., b. Sep. 25, 1820; d. Jan. 4, 1880; m. Dec. 19, 1843, Nancy Hershey, b. Feb. 14, 1824; dau. Jacob Hershey and Catharine Witmer.

1853. Martin, Sporting Hill, Pa., b. Nov. 3, 1823; d. Aug. 29, 1885; m. Dec. 24, 1846, Susan Metzler, b. June 28, 1826; d. Jan. 3, 1898; dau. Abraham Metzler and Elizabeth Shaub.

1854. John H., Mt. Joy, Pa., b. May 24, 1826; d. Dec. 13, 1901; m. Oct. 12, 1852, Esther Shelly, b. Nov. 6, 1827; d. Dec. 26, 1873; dau. Abraham Shelly and Esther Shoemaker; m. Mar. 18, 1875, Mary Bradley, b. Mar. 22, 1843; dau. Henry Bradley and Esther Shelly.

1855. Susan, Mastersonville, Pa., b. Aug. 9, 1828; m. Nov. 15, 1849, Martin Gepher, b. Oct. 29, 1819; d. Nov. 20, 1884; son Henry Gepher and Barbara Greiner.

1856. Benjamin, Centreville, Pa., b. July 16, 1831; m. Oct. 31, 1855, Barbara W. Nissley, b. Aug. 19, 1832; d. Dec. 2, 1887; dau. Jacob Nissley and Barbara Witmer.

1857. Eliza, Mastersonville, Pa., b. Aug. 8, 1833; m. Sep. 23, 1858, Samuel S. Stauffer, b. Mar. 22, 1831; son Henry Stauffer and Catharine Snyder.

1858. Abraham, Sterling, Ill., b. May 22, 1837; d. Oct. 5, 1886; m. Oct. 12, 1875, Levicia A. Alexander, b. Nov. 5, 1848; dau. Clement C. Alexander and Eliza J. Tedford.

1859. Fanny, Manheim, Pa., b. Aug. 1, 1841; m. Apr. 27, 1865, Samuel Barnes, b. Jan. 30, 1838; son David Barnes and Elizabeth Ebersole.

Family of ELIZABETH HERR (516) and DANIEL KREIDER.

1860. Martin H., Sterling, Ill., b. Feb. 4, 1824; d. Aug. 13, 1880; m. Sept. 10, 1850, Ann C. Barr (1767).

1861. Daniel, Lancaster, Pa., b. Mar. 26, 1826; d. 1826.

1862. Ely H., Strasburg, Pa., b. Nov. 22, 1827; d. 1848.

1863. Susan, Waynesville, O., b. Jan. 19, 1831; m. Dec. 1, 1859, Wid. Peter Eberly, b. Apr. 5, 1826; d. Nov. 2, 1891; son David Eberly and Elizabeth Siddenberger.

1864. Isaac, West Philadelphia, Pa., b. Mar. 12, 1835; d. 1886; m. 1863, Maggie O'Donnell, b. Jan. 26, 1837; d. Aug. 22, 1875; dau. James O'Donnell and Mary ———; m. Sallie Billings.

1865. Martha, Lancaster, Pa., b. June 27, 1838; m. Dec. 23, 1863, John S. Smith, b. June 27, 1838; d. Dec. 18, 1892; son Abraham C. Smith and Elizabeth Shultz.

Family of JOHN HERR (518) and FANNY KREIDER.

1866. Christian, Lancaster, Pa., b. Nov. 2, 1833; d. Dec. 6, 1855.

1867. Abraham, Lancaster, Pa., b. Mar. 9, 1835; d. Nov. 7, 1896; m. Serena Diller.

1868. Anna, Lancaster, Pa., b. Aug. 21, 1837; d. Mar. 21, 1886; m. Nov. 7, 1859, Frank Bowman (4065).

1869. Amos K., Lancaster, Pa., b. Nov. 15, 1839; m. Feb. 2, 1879, Elizabeth Kohr, b. Nov. 17, 1839; dau. Rev. John Kohr and Esther Denlinger.

1870. Fannie, Greenland, Pa., b. Mar. 30, 1844; m. Nov. 14, 1883, George L. Buckwalter, son Martin Buckwalter and Anna Lefevre.

1871. Susanna, Millersville, Pa., b. Feb. 5, 1851; m. Dr. Benjamin F. Herr (5135).

Family of HENRY HERR (521) and MARY ROHRER.

1872. Susanna, Lancaster, Pa., b. Mar. 17, 1836; m. Nov. 7, 1858, Daniel Musser, b. June 18, 1829; d. Dec. 11, 1904; son Martin Musser and Anna Hostetter.

1873. Daniel K., Lancaster, Pa., b. Dec. 2, 1837; m. Jan. 16, 1859, Susanna Musser, b. Apr. 27, 1835; d. Mar. 5, 1870; dau. Martin Musser and Anna Hostetter; m. Jan. 28, 1894, Emma Hess, b. Oct. 7, 1847; dau. John Hess and Louisa Hetler.

Family of Wid. HENRY HERR (521) and CHARLOTTE HERR (1556).

1874. Elizabeth Frances, Lancaster, Pa., b. Jan. 24, 1861; d. Feb. 9, 1890.

Family of MARTHA HERR (522) and CHRISTIAN H. MILLER (12032).

1875. Emma S., Lancaster, Pa., b. Dec. 20, 1845; m. Nov. 1, 1864, Christian Herr, Jr. (4099).

Family of Hon. JOHN STROHM (523) and Wid. SUSANNA BARR (1400).

1876. Esther, Exeter, Neb., b. Dec. 1, 1818; d. Dec. 16, 1894; m. Apr. 5, 1838, Martin Shaub (1250).

1877. Henry, Iowa City, Ia., b. Feb. 7, 1821; m. Mary Kauffman, dau. Jacob Kauffman and M. Witmer.

1878. Mary, Lancaster, Pa., b. Jan. 25, 1823.

1879. John, Lancaster, Pa., b. Dec. 14, 1824; m. Nov. 23, 1853, Fanny Mylin, aau. Daniel Mylin and Elizabeth Hess.

1880. Samuel, Wilton Junction, Ia., b. Dec. 29, 1826; m. Susan Tanger, dau. John Tanger and Ann Gochenour.

1881. Anna, Lancaster, Pa., b. Oct. 14, 1829; d. Aug. 17, 1832.

1882. Martin, Lancaster, Pa., b. Mar. 28, 1832; d. Apr. 30, 1837.

Family of EMANUEL STROHM (528) and MARY J. McGUIRE.

1883. John Franklin, St. Louis, Mo., b. Jan. 28, 1840; m. July 18, 1864, Elizabeth J. Lord, dau. Edwin Lord and Harriet ————.

1884. Samuel Hamford, St. Louis, Mo., b. Nov. 6, 1843.

1885. Charles H. Hall, St. Louis, Mo., b. Mar. 22, 1855; d. Sept. 10, 1861.

Family of DANIEL HERR (531) and SARAH STROHM.

1886. Henry, Strasburg, Pa., b. Nov. 30, 1830; d. Dec. 31, 1832.

1887. Eliza Ann, Strasburg, Pa., b. July 17, 1832; d. Dec. 8, 1896; m. Dec. 6, 1855, Daniel Esbenshade, b. Jan. 18, 1827; d. July 19, 1903; son Adam Esbenshade and Mary Kreider.

1888. Elam L., Strasburg, Pa., b. Mar. 14, 1834; m. Nov. 29, 1866, Anna M. Herr (4020).

1889. Mary Emma, Lancaster, Pa., b. Sept. 27, 1835.

1890. Thaddeus S., Strasburg, Pa., b. Apr. 29, 1837; d. Feb. 4, 1862.

1891. Sarah, Strasburg, Pa., b. May 5, 1839; m. Dec. 24, 1883, Samuel Hess, b. 1840; son Moses Hess and Mary Stauffer.

1892. Daniel, Strasburg, Pa., b. July 1, 1841; d. Jan. 30, 1843.

1893. Susanna, Strasburg, Pa., b. June 14, 1844; d. Mar. 17, 1848.

1894. Serenus B., Roanoke, Va., b. May 10, 1848; m. May 14, 1872, Addie Miller, d. Mar. 18, 1877; dau. William Miller and ————.

Family of MARTHA HERR (532) and DAVID HERR (541).

1895. Hanford B., Lancaster, Pa., b. Oct. 27, 1841; d. Sept. 24, 1892; m. Jan. 17, 1867, Hannah G. Stephens, b. Mar. 24, 1838; dau. Nelson Stephens and Nancy Osmond.

1896. Ann Elizabeth, Reading. Pa., b. Aug. 24, 1843; m. July 26, 1866, David A. Stephens, b. Aug. 10, 1844: son William Stephens and Mary A. Steele.

1897. Mary Louisa, Strasburg, Pa., b. Dec. 19, 1845; d. Dec. 17, 1847.

Family of CHRISTIAN B. HERR (533) and MARIA LIGHT (1133).

1898. Dr. Martin Light, Lancaster, Pa., b. Sept. 13, 1838; d. Feb. 8, 1902; m. Sept., 1870, Rosina E. Hubley, d. Apr. 2, 1889; dau. John A. Hubley and Sarah Young; m. Mar. 15, 1894, Elizabeth H. Hager, b. Apr. 13, 1856; dau. John C. Hager and Margaret Henderson.

1900. Adam Franklin, Lancaster, Pa., b. Feb. 5, 1840; d. Sept. 29, 1879; m. Mar. 13, 1873, Maria Benedict, b. Mar. 14, 1842; dau. John L. Benedict and Maria Bundel.

1901. Annie Elizabeth, Lancaster, Pa., b. Aug. 8, 1842; m. June 1, 1871. Joseph W. Yocum, b. June 27, 1843.

1902. Fanny, Lancaster, Pa., b. July 22, 1845; d. June 15, 1901; m. Apr. 5, 1874, Jerome Kieffer; d. 1880.

Family of JOHN HERR (534) and ANNA F. HERR (1398).

1903. Emma Salome, Refton, Pa., b. Oct. 25, 1847: d. Feb. 17, 1854.
1904. Benjamin H., Refton, Pa., b. Nov. 2, 1851; d. Feb. 12, 1875.

Family of ADAM HERR (535) and ELIZABETH HERR (1552).

1905. Frances E., Strasburg. Pa., b. Nov. 15, 1842; d. June 14, 1888; m. Oct. 17, 1878, Wid. Amaziah M. Herr (1582).

1906. Alpheus N., Strasburg, Pa., b. Aug. 8, 1845; d. Dec. 5, 1903; m. Oct. 27, 1868, Esther M. Miller, b. Mar. 27, 1842; d. Oct. 3, 1875: dau. Henry Miller and Frances Reigart.

8

Family of DAVID H. HERR (537) and MARY A. LANDIS.

1907. Francis W., Orrville, O., b. Aug. 11, 1847; m. Oct. 11, 1871, Arvilla J. Sergeant, b. Aug. 22, 1850; dau. Ephraim E. Sergeant and Harriet Freeman.

1908. Lettie Anna, Orrville, O., b. May 22, 1849; d. July 19, 1897; m. July 19, 1870, Samuel T. Gailey, son William M. Gailey and Eliza A. ———.

1909. Lizzie Ann, Orrville, O., b. Mar. 22, 1850; d. Nov. 22, 1864.

1910. Catharine Naomi, Orrville, O., b. Aug. 9, 1853; m. June 26, 1873, Levi Breneman, b. Aug. 21, 1849; son Samuel Breneman and Elizabeth Neiswanger.

1911. Mary Malinda, Mt. Vernon, O., b. Sept. 12, 1855; m. Sept. 12, 1878, Samuel Trout.

1912. Emma Theresa, Gambier, O., b. Jan. 19, 1862; d. June 9, 1902; m. Sept. 10, 1900, Frank T. Moore, b. Feb. 7, 1869; son Daniel T. Moore and Georgiana ———.

1913. David Grant, Orrville, O., b. Mar. 4, 1864; d. Jan. 24, 1903; m. Jan. 15, 1891, Ida M. Kurtz, b. Sept. 10, 1860.

Family of BENJAMIN HERR (539) and SARAH KENDIG (573).

1914. Lavinia, Lampeter, Pa., b. June 30, 1823; d. May 13, 1848.

1915. Elmira, Lampeter, Pa., b. Sept. 4, 1825; d. May 18, 1863.

Family of Wid. BENJAMIN HERR (539) and SUSAN STROHM.

1916. Benjamin Franklin, Livingston, Ala., b. May 16, 1830; d. Nov. 8, 1898; m. Nov. 6, 1856, Mary A. Wilkinson, b. Aug. 13, 1835; dau. Aaron Wilkinson and Annie Ratcliff.

1917. Henry Clay, Moorestown, N. J., b. Sept. 4, 1832; d. Apr. 8, 1899; m. Sept. 29, 1859, Fanny A. Kinsey, b. May 1, 1834; dau. Samuel Kinsey and Rachel Eastburn.

1918. Sarah Ann, Phila., Pa., b. Jan. 9, 1835; m. Oct. 5, 1859, Joseph Cooper, b. Aug. 18, 1835; d. Jan. 19, 1900; son Joseph Cooper and Mary Horning.

1919. Jesse, Strasburg, Pa., b. Jan. 29, 1837; d. Mar. 19, 1837.

Family of JOHN HERR (540) and ELIZA HERR (1139).

1920. Tobias W., Strasburg, Pa., b. Oct. 2, 1831; d. Dec. 9, 1907; m. Nov. 18, 1856, Mary Shaub (3665).

1921. Eve Ann, Willow Street, Pa., b. Jan. 6, 1833; m. Nov. 10, 1856, Christian Breneman, b. Jan. 8, 1818; d. Sept. 28, 1874; son Jacob Breneman and Maria Good; m. Mar. 19, 1878, Abraham R. Burkholder, b. Mar. 15, 1830; son Joseph Burkholder and Elizabeth Kendig.

1922. Benjamin M., Bloomington, Ill., b. Apr. 23, 1835; d. July 7, 1896; m. Feb. 16, 1865, Anna M. Morgan, b. July 20, 1841; dau. William Morgan and Sarah McCall.

Family of Wid. JOHN HERR (540) and MARIA HERR (1142).

1923. Elizabeth, New Danville, Pa., b. Aug. 13, 1850; d. Nov. 18, 1895; m. Benjamin Gochenour.

Family of ELIZABETH HERR (543) and JOHN HOFFMAN.

1924. John, Lampeter, Pa., b. Mar. 3, 1841; d. Feb. 24, 1853.
1925. Tobias, Lampeter, Pa., b. Feb. 5, 1843; d. Aug. 1, 1844.
1926. Benjamin, Lampeter, Pa., b. Feb. 17, 1845; m. Catharine Huber; dau. Levi Huber and ———.

Family of TOBIAS HERR (545) and SUSAN LANDIS.

1927. Salina, Windom, Pa., b. Mar. 12, 1839; m. Jan. 13, 1859, Benjamin L. Gamber (8501).
1928. John L., Lancaster, Pa., b. Aug. 29, 1840; m. Dec. 23, 1863, Fanny L. Brubaker (8537).

Family of JOHN HERR (548) and MARIA BINKLEY.

1929. Barbara, Millersville, Pa., b. Oct. 25, 1821; d. Oct. 26, 1821.
1930. Maria, Millersville, Pa., b. July 27, 1823; d. July 6, 1902.
1931. Elizabeth, Millersville, Pa., b. Mar. 25, 1825; d. Aug. 14, 1827.
1932. Esther, Millersville, Pa., b. Oct. 18, 1828; d. 1883; m. 1845, Martin Henry, b. 1816; d. 1872.

1933. Francis, Millersville, Pa., b. May 20, 1830; d. Oct. 8, 1831.

1934. Ann, Millersville, Pa., b. Mar. 21, 1832; d. 1863; m. Oct. 16, 1855, Solomon Martin, b. May 24, 1836; son Michael Martin and Catharine Horst.

1935. John B., Millersville, Pa., b. Aug. 14, 1835; m. 1858, Susan Eshleman, b. May 1, 1836; d. Feb. 25, 1897; dau. Jacob Eshleman and Susan Eshleman.

1936. Catharine, Maytown, Pa., b. June 7, 1837; m. Feb. 21, 1860, John A. Garber, b. Dec. 1, 1832; son Jacob B. Garber and Susan Stauffer.

1937. David S., Millersville, Pa., b. Dec. 8, 1838; m. Nov. 18, 1866, Elizabeth Neff, b. Oct. 4, 1841; dau. John Neff and Mary Buckwalter.

1938. Susan, Maytown, Pa., b. June 13, 1841; d. Sept. 19, 1847.

Family of DAVID HERR (549) and MAGDALENE CLEPPER.

1939. Daniel, Columbia, Pa., b. Feb. 28, 1822; d. Mar. 28, 1822.

1940. Son, Columbia, Pa., b. July 13, 1823; d. July 13, 1823.

1941. Jacob K., Columbia, Pa., b. Sept. 6, 1824; m. Malila Middow.

1942. Catharine, Columbia, Pa., b. Aug. 27, 1826; d. Jan. 16, 1833.

1943. David, Columbia, Pa., b. Aug. 27, 1828; d. April 16, 1857.

1944. Magdalena, Millersville, Pa., b. Nov. 20, 1830; m. Feb. 14, 1865, Christian E. Hostetter, b. Aug. 16, 1823; d. Feb. 27, 1879; son Uhlrich Hostetter and Maria Erisman.

1945. John C. Millersville, Pa., b. Dec. 11, 1832; d. 1868; m. Mary Kauffman, dau. Isaac Kauffman and Mary Hertzler.

1946. Martin, Columbia, Pa., b. May 16, 1835; d. April 19, 1856.

1947. Joseph C., Columbia Pa., b. Apr. 24, 1837; d. 1877; m. Mar. 24, 1865, Elmira Hickman.

1948. Esther, Columbia, Pa., b. Feb. 28, 1839; d. July, 1886; m. Aug. 1859, Hiram T. Albert.

1949. Elizabeth, Lancaster, Pa., b. Sept. 17, 1841; m. Jan. 22, 1865, Henry N. Snyder, son Henry Snyder and Caroline Neely.

Family of DANIEL HERR (550) and MARY M. KURTZ.

1950. Adeline E., Addison, N. Y., b. Apr. 13, 1828; d. Feb. 27, 1903; m. June 18, 1850, Rulef S. Gile, b. Sept. 26, 1825; d. May 7, 1858; son William Gile and Ann Stevens.

Family of Wid. DANIEL HERR (550) and SARAH A. MARTIN.

1951. Leander Jefferson, Columbia, Pa., b. Apr. 7, 1837; d. Jan. 6, 1839.
1952. Lucretia Irene, Columbia, Pa., b. Nov. 17, 1839; d. June 15, 1841.
1953. Elbridge Gerry, Goshen, Ind., b. Mar. 25, 1842; d. Oct. 27, 1898; m. Sept. 25, 1866, Mary E. Child, b. Sept. 26, 1840; dau. William Child and Susan Kepner.
1954. Olivia Salome, Columbia, Pa., b. Sept. 1, 1844; d. Nov. 4, 1845.
1955. Ada Serastene, Goshen, Ind., b. Sept. 17, 1846.
1956. Eugene Markham, South Bend, Ind., b. Sept. 27, 1848; m. Dec. 15, 1880, Nettie E. Roe, b. Feb. 14, 1856; dau. Jeremiah B. Roe and Maleta A. Caldwell.

Family of SUSAN HERR (556) and ANDREW DENISON.

1957. Joseph, Falmouth, Pa.
1958. Conrad, Falmouth, Pa., d. 1863.
1959. Noah, Falmouth, Pa.

Family of MARTHA KENDIG (569) and CHRISTIAN MILLER.

1960. Abraham, Strasburg, Pa., m. ——— Buckwalter, dau. Jacob Buckwalter and ———.
1961. Christian, Strasburg, Pa., m. Mary Miller.
1962. Susan, Strasburg, Pa., m. John Frantz.
1963. Amos, Strasburg, Pa., m. ———; m. ——— Harnish.
1964. Abner, Strasburg, Pa., m. Lizzie Shenk, dau John Shenk and ———.
1965. Martha, Strasburg, Pa., m. ——— Nestleward.
1966. John, Strasburg, Pa., m. ——— Erb.

Family of DAVID KENDIG (574) and ANN EGNER.

1967. Susan, Millersville, Pa., b. Feb. 7, 1824; m. Sept. 24, 1843, Samuel Fondersmith, b. Oct. 19, 1815; son George Fondersmith and Catharine Shindle.
1968. Martha, Millersville, Pa., b. Sept. 25, 1825; d. June 5, 1865; m. Feb. 17, 1846, Wid. William Frazer, b. June 26, 1814; d. Feb. 16, 1865; son Chas. Frazer and ———.

1969. Emanuel, Millersville, Pa., b. April 4, 1827; d. Jan. 1, 1828.

Family of SARAH KENDIG (575) and JOHN CARPEN TER.

1970. Sarah Ann, Strasburg, Pa., b. May 5, 1827; m. Jan. 5, 1859,
David Hoover, b. April 10, 1825; son David Hoover and Susan
Eby.

1971. Mary, Strasburg, Pa., b. Feb. 15, 1829; m. Jan. 20, 1853, Abraham Hoover, b. Feb. 4, 1827; son David Hoover and Susan Eby.

1972. Susan, Strasburg, Pa., b. Dec. 4, 1831; m. Dec. 25, 1855, B.
Landis Brackbill, b. Dec. 28, 1833; son Jacob Brackbill and
Barbara Greenleaf.

Family of CATHARINE BRUA (577) and DANIEL SNEARLY.

1973. Esther Ann, Williamsville, N. Y., b. May 8, 1831; m. May 8,
1854, Christian C. Metz, b. Dec. 26, 1827; son John Metz and
Elizabeth Martin.

1974. Mary M., Williamsville, N. Y., b. Oct. 16, 1832; d. Feb. 2, 1872;
m. Nov. 17, 1853, Jacob S. Lapp, son Abraham Lapp and Anna
Smith.

1975. Sarah, Williamsville, N. Y., b. June 26, 1836; m. Mar. 4, 1874,
Franklin Metz, b. Mar. 8, 1840; son John Metz and Leah Got-
walt.

1976. Emanuel, Williamsville, N. Y., b. July 8, 1839; d. July 17, 1864.

Family of JOHN S. HERR (578) and MARY CONRAD.

1977. Anna, Lancaster, Pa.

1978. Amanda, Lancaster, Pa., m. Dec. 24, 1874, B. Frank Sides, son
Henry Sides and Elizabeth ———.

1979. Sarah, Lancaster, Pa.

Family of EMANUEL HERR (580) and ANN ESBENSHADE.

1980. Elizabeth Lefever, Westminster, Md., b. Aug. 22, 1841.

1981. Samuel Kendig, Westminster, Md., b. July 7, 1843; m. Wid.
Emily Buchingham, b. Nov. 8, 1845; dau. Nathan Gorsuch and
Emily ———.

1982. Anna Maria, Baltimore, Md., b. Jan. 1, 1845; m. Edward J.
Shaffer, son David Shaffer and Mary ———.

1983. Francis Kendig, Westminster, Md., b. May 22, 1846; m. Nov 12, 1874, Ellen R. Trump, b. Apr. 10, 1846; dau. George Trump and Elizabeth Kraatz.
1984. Hettie Herr, Manchester, Md., b. Feb. 2, 1848; m. Dr. Luther Trump, son George Trump and Elizabeth Kraatz.
1985. Sallie, Westminster, Md., b. Mar. 15, 1851.

Family of SARAH HERR (581) and ABRAHAM KEAGY.

1986. Samuel Westminster, Md.
1987. Ann, Mt. Joy, Pa., m. George Heckroth.
1988. Amanda, Marietta, Pa., m. Martin Hildebrand, b. 1830.
1989. John B., Marietta, Pa., b. Oct. 29, 1832; d. Sept. 14, 1863; m. Sept. 11, 1855, Catharine Barr (1761).
1990. Levi, Marietta, Pa.
1991. Sarah K., Baltimore, Md., m. Edwin Storm, b. Sept. 16, 1833; d. Apr., 1866.
1992. Elizabeth, Washington, Pa., m. ——— Mathiot.

Family of ANN HERR (582) and Wid. FRANK KENDIG (1475).

1993. Amos. Westminster, Md., b. Sept. 30, 1825; d. June 13, 1829.
1994. Samuel Herr, Pikeville, Md., b. Mar. 4, 1828; d. Dec. 18, 1863.
1995. Annie, Mt. Airy, Md., b. May 10, 1833.
1996. Sarah, Mt. Airy, Md., b. Sept. 14, 1838.
1997. Elizabeth, Mt. Airy, Md., b. Oct. 12, 1840.

Family of CHARLOTTE B. HERR (583) and GEORGE C. MOORE.

1998. Elizabeth, Springfield, Ill., b. Sept. 24, 1824; m. July 3, 1842, Joseph Dudding, b. Sept. 24, 1817; d. Jan. 15, 1879; son Joseph Dudding and Charlotte ———.
1999. Frances Herr, Quincy, Ill., b. Aug. 4, 1826; m. April 5, 1854, John P. Cadogan, b. Mar. 10, 1825; d. Mar. 6, 1887; son Wm. P. Cadogan and Christine Lindamyer.
2000. William Henry, Willston, Mo., b. Oct. 27, 1828; d. Mar. 13, 1892; m. Jan 21, 1855, Susan M. Boynton, b. July 16, 1838; dau. Lemuel H. Boynton and Sarah A. Wash.
2001. Sarah Catharine, Quincy, Ill., b. Feb. 27, 1831; d. July 25. 1893;

m. Oct. 6, 1853, George Lewis, b. Jan. 3, 1829; d. April 10, 1863; son John B. Lewis and Charlotte Packer; m. 1865, J. Brooks, d. 1872.

2002. Uriah Brison, Canton, O., b. Dec. 29, 1834; m. Mary Esselbum.

2003. George Crane, Hanibal, Mo., b. May 10, 1836; m. 1864, Mary E. Hatcher, b. 1840; d. Jan. 3, 1886; dau. Solomon J. Hatcher and Mary E. Menert; m. 1888, Julia T. Thorndike, b. Mar. 18, 1847; dau. William H. Thorndike and Eliza Boggs.

2004. John Samerfield, Hanibal, Mo., b. July 23, 1839; d. Aug. 17, 1879; m. July 26, 1865, Ethlinda Rockwood, b. Mar. 20, 1844; dau. Thomas B. Rockwood and Fidelia Deckerson.

Family of ELIZABETH HERR (584) and SAMUEL WILSON (1515).

2005. Edmond Francis, Salona, Pa., b. Apr. 29, 1827; d. June 25, 1847.

2006. Amanda, Salona, Pa., b. July 25, 1829; d. Feb. 22, 1854.

2007. George Leidy, Newberry, Pa., b. Dec. 10, 1831; d. Aug. 7, 1892; m. Jan. 5, 1862, Sallie B. Gray, b. Nov. 14, 1841; dau. Peter B. Gray and Elizabeth Perdue.

2008. Sarah Catharine, Salona, Pa., b. June 11, 1834; d. Dec. 1, 1862; m. Nov. 15, 1857, John E. Wilson, b. Jan. 3, 1833; d. April 18, 1870; son John Wilson and Mary Elder.

2009. Martin Herr, Salona, Pa., b. May 21, 1838; d. July 27, 1849.

2010. Charlotte Elizabeth, Salona, Pa., b. Dec. 7, 1842; m. May 30, 1870, Ira C. Stoner, b. Aug. 30, 1842; son Hines Stoner and Mary Black.

Family of GEORGE B. HERR (585) and CLARISSA MILLER (1535).

2011. Joel Adrian, Cedar Springs, Pa., b. Mar. 1, 1838.

2012. John Carvosso, Cedar Springs, Pa., b. July 19, 1839; d. Feb. 7, 1873.

2013. Albert Miller, Wiliamsport, Pa., b. Nov. 14, 1841; d. Mar. 26, 1845.

2014. Mary Frances, Cedar Springs, Pa., b. July 23, 1845.

2015. Harriet Elizabeth, Cedar Springs, Pa., b. Dec. 19, 1847; d. Oct. 18, 1861.

2016. Edmund Wilson, Cedar Springs, Pa., b. Apr. 22, 1851; d. Mar. 23, 1892.

Family of MARTIN HERR (586) and CATHARINE HARTMAN (4427).

2017. Sarah Frances, Lock Haven, Pa., b. Aug. 24, 1848; m. Dec. 14, 1868, George W. H. Schreffler; b. Aug. 16, 1845; son Henry Schreffler and Sarah Worrick.

2018. Mary Amanda, Phila., Pa., b. Oct. 19, 1851; m. Apr. 16, 1870, J. Reese Crispin, b. Jan. 26, 1845; d. Dec. 22, 1884; son John Crispin and Martha Linn.

2019. Ellen Amelia, Phila., Pa., b. June, 1853.

2020. Lucy Ophelia, Salona, Pa., b. Apr. 4, 1857; d. Nov. 19, 1874.

2021. Anson Martin, Burlington, N. J., b. Oct. 20, 1859; m. Dec. 14, 1898, Alverna M. Keller, d. June 15, 1869; dau. Peter Keller and Lavina Springer.

2022. Charles George, Salona, Pa., b. Oct. 2, 1863; d. Nov. 19, 1865.

Family of URIAH HERR (587) and ANN HOOVER.

2023. Wesley Uriah, Salona, Pa., b. Dec. 29, 1857; m. Sept. 28, 1887, Margaret Walters, b. Nov. 23, 1859; d. May 28, 1895; m. April 11, 1900, Myrtle Bennet, b. Feb. 14, 1879; dau. Dr. Thomas J. Bennet and Susan Hoover.

Family of REBECCA HERR (589) and JOHN MILLER.

2025. Infant, Salona, Pa.

Family of DANIEL HERR (592) and MARY JANE LEIDY.

2026. George Leidy, Mill Hall, Pa., b. July 8, 1857; m. June 26, 1879, Christina R. Myers, b. Dec. 11, 1859; dau. John Myers and Amanda Walker.

2027. John Mayberry, Indianapolis, Ind., b. May 22, 1859; m. Dec. 24, 1885, Rose A. Brumgard, dau. Geo. Brumgard and Elizabeth Wolford.

2028. Emory Else, Scranton, Pa., b. July 12, 1862; m. June 6, 1889, Cora B. Guyer, b. June 23, 1866; d. Mar. 14, 1894; dau. George Guyer and Catharine Hoke; m. Apr. 9, 1901, Mae Cook Myer, b. May 23, 1872; d. May 4, 1902; dau. Arthur Cook and Alice C. ———; m. Aug. 9, 1903, Mary S. Gillies, b. June 30, 1863; dau. William T. Reynolds and Rachel Morris.

2029. Fannie Catharine, Salona, Pa., b. Oct. 12, 1867; d. Feb. 28, 1869.
2030. Harry Hastings, Salona Pa., b. June 19, 1870; d. June 20, 1877.

Family of GEORGE HERR (593) and CHARLOTTE MILLER (1534).

2031. Emma F., Salona, Pa., b. Mar. 15, 1836; m. Nov. 11, 1856, Ely
   E. Hyatt, b. June 12, 1832; d. Apr. 2, 1894; son Thomas Hyatt
   and Sobrina Griffith.
2032. Henry E., Salona, Pa., b. Jan. 29, 1837; d. Apr. 12, 1879.
2033. Daniel Barnet, Salona, Pa., b. Jan. 7, 1840; m. Oct. 31, 1867,
   Gertrude C. Hills, b. Feb. 11, 1851; dau. Gilbert M. Hills and
   Ellen Shaffer.
2034. Samuel M., Salona, Pa., b. Dec. 3, 1841; d. Aug. 11, 1844.
2035. Elizabeth, Salona, Pa., b. Apr. 2, 1844; d. Aug. 25, 1844.

Family of Wid. GEORGE HERR (593) and CATHARINE WILSON (1517).

2036. George W., Salona, Pa., b. July 18, 1848; m. Feb. 2, 1871, Annie
   E. Frederick, b. Jan. 23, 1848; d. Feb. 3, 1902; dau. John Frederick and Rachel Walter.
2037. Rebecca C., Salona, Pa., b. Dec. 1, 1849.
2038. Sarah Jane, Quincy, Ill., b. Mar. 19, 1852; m. Feb. 5, 1879, Wm.
   H. Cadogan (5476).
2039. Charlotte E., Salona, Pa., b. Mar. 19, 1852; d. May 15, 1866.

Family of ELIZABETH HERR (594) and Dr. ELY PARRY.

2040. Dr. Henry B., Lancaster, Pa., b. Oct, 10, 1834; m. Sept. 16, 1858,
   Lizzie Gray, b. Dec. 5, 1835; dau. Justus Gray and Barbara
   Getz.
2041. John E., Lancaster, Pa., b. May 2, 1846; m. Jan. 10, 1867, Annie
   J. Smith, dau Edward K. Smith and Annie Stranger.
2042. Charlotte R., Lancaster, Pa., b. Mar. 18, 1850.
2043. George A., Phila., Pa.

Family of REBECCA HERR (595) and ABRAHAM SHOFF.

2044. Elizabeth, Flemington, Pa., b. 1820; m. William Furst, son
   Thomas Furst and ———.
2045. Abraham, Lock Haven, Pa., b. Dec. 14, 1822; m. 1844, Jane

Simmons, b. Oct. 11, 1823; d. Apr. 26, 1871; dau. John Simmons and Elizabeth Barrell; m. Jan. 12, 1893, Eva Glosser, b. June 18, 1836; dau. Abraham Glosser and Mary Smith.

Family of ELIZABETH PFOUTZ (596) and JOHN REESE.

2046. Joel, Strasburg, Pa.
2047. Samuel, Strasburg, Pa.

Family of Rev. MARTIN HERR (598) and ELIZABETH MILLER.

2048. Isabella, Salona, Pa., b. Nov., 1828; d. 1831.
2049. Sarah Ann, Salona, Pa., b. Oct. 22, 1830.
2050. Cynthia Jane, Ridgeway, Pa., b. Aug. 26, 1832; m. Nov. 30, 1854, Robinson M. Thompson, b. Nov. 7, 1830; d. Apr. 23, 1880; son Moses Thompson and Hannah Betts.
2051. Eliza, Williamsport, Pa., b. Feb. 22, 1835; m. Aug. 5, 1862, Joseph Farley, b. Jan. 28, 1837; son Henry Farley and Catharine Sypher.
2052. John Miller, Beech Creek, Pa., b. May 23, 1837; m. Dec., 1871, Eliza R. Winkbleck, b. Sept. 16, 1850; dau. Adam Winklebleck and Caroline Groinet.
2053. Samuel G., Salona, Pa., b. 1839; d. Nov. 1, 1845.
2054. Daniel H., Salona, Pa., b. Dec. 2, 1841.
2055. Martin Wilson, Salona, Pa., b. Jan. 17, 1844; d. Aug. 21, 1900; m. Mar. 12, 1874, Lydia A. Burrell, d. Oct. 12, 1879; dau. Samuel Burrell and Lydia Ilgen.

Family of SARAH HERR (599) and JESSE WILSON (1516).

2056. Edward, Salona, Pa.
2057. Charles, Salona, Pa.
2058. Ann Eliza, Salona, Pa.
2059. Ira, Salona, Pa.
2060. Rebecca, Salona, Pa.

Family of JOEL HERR (600) and JANE IRVIN.

2061. James Edwin, Bennington, Kans., b. June 22, 1836; m. Oct. 18, 1865, Annetta M. Young, b. Feb. 26, 1845; dau. William Young and Eleanor Snodgrass.

2062. Ida Jane, Mifflinburg, Pa., b. Oct. 9, 1837; d. June 28, 1888.

2063. Elmira Pellman, Mifflinburg, Pa., b. Nov. 2, 1839.

Family of DAVID HERR (601) and MARY ANN ROCKEY.

2064. Katharine Elizabeth, Lock Haven, Pa., b. Dec. 19, 1840.

2065. Ceniah Furman, Mifflinburg, Pa., b. Dec. 18, 1842; d. Dec. 6, 1850.

2066. Isabella Thompson, Mifflinburg, Pa., b. Feb. 1, 1844; d. Apr. 10, 1844.

2067. Emily Shriner, Mifflinburg, Pa., b. Apr. 19, 1845; d. Jan. 14, 1883; m. Joseph Hanna, d. 1876; son Joseph Hanna and Eliza Watson; m. Thomas A. Blackburn, d. Dec. 21, 1886.

2068. Harry Graham, Athens, N. Y., b. June 14, 1847; m. Nov. 22, 1871, Augusta Hotaling, b. Apr. 5, 1848; dau. Richard Hotaling and Helen Miller.

2069. George Edward, Lock Haven, Pa., b. May 1, 1849; m. Jan. 7, 1871, Catharine C. Gritner, b. Nov. 12, 1849; dau. James Gritner and Elizabeth ———.

2070. Mary Louise, Saxton, Pa., b. Aug. 17, 1851; m. Mar. 20, 1877, Algernon S. Fleming, b. Feb. 8, 1852; son Algernon and Julia Karskaddon.

2071. William R., Lock Haven, Pa., b. June 6, 1853; m. Mar. 17, 1884, Ida Shires, b. May 5, 1860; dau. Andrew J. Shires and Sarah Corson.

2072. Laura, Mifflinburg, Pa., b. Dec. 14, 1854; d. June 18, 1855.

2073. Annie M., Lock Haven, Pa., b. Feb. 10, 1856; m. May 10, 1884, Dr. George W. Rae, b. Jan 14, 1854; son George Rae and ——— Wallace.

2074. Charles, Lock Haven, Pa., b. Sept. 16, 1858; d. Dec. 30, 1873.

2075. Walter Diffenbach, Lock Haven, Pa., b. Nov. 1, 1861; m. Nov. 4, 1884, Catharine Hufford, b. Nov. 6, 1861; dau. Barnhart Hufford and Rebecca Smith.

2076. David Longenecker, Lock Haven, Pa., b. Mar. 11, 1864; m. Dec. 8, 1886, Margaret McLaughlin, b. Mar. 16, 1866; dau. John McLaughlin and Bridget Horn.

Family of ANN ELIZA HERR (602) and ROBERT WILLIAMSON.

2077. Samuel, Mifflinburg, Pa.
2078. Harriet, Mifflinburg, Pa.

Family of Wid. SAMUEL HERR (603) and SARAH DAVIS.

2079. Anna Mary, Port Royal, Pa., b. Aug. 6, 1854; m. Dec. 3, 1874, Dr. Amos W. Shelley, b. July 26, 1850; son Rev. Henry Shelley and Catharine Gingrich.

Family of GEORGE LEIDY HERR (608) and EMMA A. WOLCOTT.

2080. Clara Jane, Chicago, Ill., b. Feb. 1, 1861.
2081. Edwin, Polo, Ill., b. Aug. 15, 1864; d. Sept. 12, 1864.

Family of Wid. GEORGE LEIDY HERR (608) and ANN FUNK.

2082. Mary, Thompsontown, Pa., b. Feb. 7, 1872.
2083. J. Wilbert, Thompsontown, Pa., b. Apr. 3, 1876.

Family of CATHERINE HERR (611) and DANIEL ADAMS.

2084. John, Sacramento, Cal., b. Jan. 25, 1833; d. Oct. 31, 1852.
2085. Clara Ann, Bristol, Ind., b. July 20, 1835; m. Aug. 29, 1856, A. Washington McCoy, b. May 28, 1823; son James McCoy and Nancy Southerland.
2086. Elijah, Bellefontaine, O., b. May 11, 1837; d. Feb. 5, 1839.
2087. Elsie C., Garden City, Kans., b. Oct. 9, 1839; m. Apr. 24, 1863, Phoebe J. Spencer, b. Nov. 22, 1842; d. Apr. 7, 1867; dau. Platte R. Spencer and Persis R. Duty; m. Jan. 11, 1868, Carrie E. Stevens, b. Oct. 3, 1843; dau. Thomas R. Stevens and Sarah A. Duty.
2088. Joseph Henry, Middleburg, Ind., b. Mar. 3, 1847; d. Sept. 8, 1848.
2089. Mary Jennie, Pine Bluffs, Wyo., b. Apr. 6, 1845; m. June 24, 1866, James Newell, b. July 21, 1841; son Joseph Newell and Elizabeth Craig.

Family of SAMUEL HERR (612) and MARGARET MYERS.

2090. Lucinda, West Salem, O., m. J. Scheneman.
2091. Henry, Red Haw, O., m. Linda Wikel.

Family of ELIZABETH HERR (613) and MICHAEL FUHRMAN.

2092. Amy, Red Haw, O., b. May 31, 1835; d. Mar. 2, 1842.
2093. Mary L., Polk, O., b. Jan. 24, 1838; m. Feb. 5, 1865, Lewis Himmelright, b. Dec. 30, 1836; son John Himmelright and Catherine Hankey.
2094. Samuel, Red Haw, O., b. May 13, 1841; d. Jan. 16, 1863.
2095. William Henry, Red Haw, O., b. Jan. 17, 1854; d. July 21, 1862.

Family of ANNA HERR (614) and GEORGE MYERS.

2096. Henry, Argyle, Mich., b. Dec. 7, 1844; m. Catharine Breneman.
2097. Sarah, Shablona, Mich., b. Aug. 28, 1851; m. Sept. 7, 1870, Harmon Smith, d. Oct. 29, 1900.
2098. John, West Salem, Ore.
2099. Rebecca, West Salem, Ore.
2100. Mary, West Salem, Ore.

Family of SUSAN HERR (615) and ELIJAH ADAMS.

2101. Eve Rebecca, Bristol, Ind., b. Sept., 1841; d. Sept., 1846.
2102. Daughter, Bristol, Ind., b. Dec. 7, 1842; d. Dec. 7, 1842.
2103. Arthur Alvin, Bristol, Ind., b. Apr. 2, 1844; d. May 21, 1865.
2104. Aaron Elijah, Redford, Mo., b. Feb. 20, 1847; d. Nov. 1, 1901; m. Sept. 23, 1866, Ella J. Paxson, b. Sept. 25, 1847; dau. Eli Paxson and Elizabeth Vesey.
2105. Ambrose Ira, Bristol, Ind., b. Apr. 26, 1849; m. Jan. 6, 1870, Amanda J. White, dau. Thomas White and ――― Wirt.
2106. Martha Ann, Baltimore, Md., b. Dec. 9, 1851; m. Jan. 27, 1873, Henry T. Menges, b. Jan. 3, 1848; d. Nov. 1, 1887; son George Menges and Susan Teats.

Family of DAVID HERR (616) and SUSANNA MYERS.

2107. Lena, Cleveland, O., b. Nov. 18, 1852; m. Nov. 16, 1871, Dr. Charles Kinnaman, b. June 15, 1852.

2108. Harry Leander, Bucyrus, O., b. 1851; d. May 16, 1903; m. Floy Chesney.
2109. ———, Bucyrus, O.
2110. ———, Bucyrus, O.
2111. ———, Bucyrus, O.
2112. ———, Bucyrus, O.
2113. ———, Bucyrus, O.

Family of HENRY HERR (617) and SARAH ELIZABETH ELGIN.

2114. Ophelia A., Richmond, O., b. Jan. 9, 1853; d. July 12, 1895: m. 1871, Porter E. Barnes.
2115. Oscar O., Cleveland, O., b. Dec. 11, 1854; d. Apr. 24, 1864.
2116. Leon Devitt, West Salem, O., b. May 9, 1857; d. Sept. 22, 1895; m. Flora Farris.
2117. Mary Alice, Cleveland, O., b. Jan. 19, 1859; m. Dec. 2, 1878, Tilman S. Balliett.
2118. Clara Jane, Cleveland, O., b. Jan. 3, 1861.
2119. Harriet Christina, Richmond, O., b. Jan. 14, 1863; d. Dec. 2, 1882.

Family of Dr. LEVI S. HERR (618) and SOPHIA LOBINGER FETTER.

2120. Infant, Evansville, Ind., b. 1859; d. 1859.

Family of EPHRAIM CARPENTER (619) and JULIANNA KLINE.

2121. Leah, Hahnstown, Pa., m. Chambers Hahn.
2122. Ephraim, Naperville, Ill., b. Apr. 23, 1813; d. June 20, 1896; m. Aug. 25, 1839, Harriet Rhodes, b. Dec. 18, 1818; d. June 16, 1888; dau. Philip Rhodes and Julianna Horting.
2123. Harriet, Lancaster, Ill., b. Dec. 18, 1818; d. June 16, 1888; m. Abraham Killian, son Abraham Killian and ———.
2124. Michael, Cincinnati, O.

Family of CATHARINE CARPENTER (620) and CHRISTIAN KNAPP.

2125. Isaac, Hahnstown, Pa.
2126. Sophia, Hahnstown, Pa.
2127. Susanna, Hahnstown, Pa.

2128. Mary, Ephrata, Pa.
2129. Rebecca, Ephrata, Pa.

Family of NILES CARPENTER (622) and MARY HABECKER.

2130. Fianna. Brunnersville, Pa., b. Sept. 18, 1819; m. May 16, 1853, Jacob Sheets, son John Sheets and Elizabeth Gingrich.
2131. Uriah, Brunnersville, Pa., b. Apr. 8, 1825; m. Nov. 24, 1853, Harriet Miller, dau. Samuel Miller and Rebecca Wechter.

Family of SUSANNA CARPENTER (623) and GEORGE LIED.

2132. Israel, Brunnersville, Pa., m. ——— Fasnacht.
2133. Allan, Brunnersville, Pa.
2134. Mary, Brunnersville, Pa., m. Samuel Schlabach.
2135. Catharine, Brunnersville, Pa., m. ——— Swartz.
2136. Isaac, Brunnersville, Pa.

Family of GILES CARPENTER (626) and JANE McCLINTOCK.

2137. James. Mechanicsburg, Pa.
2138. Samuel, Mechanicsburg, Pa.

Family of CHARLES CARPENTER (629) and ELIZABETH JOHNSON.

2139. Gabriella, Reamstown, Pa., m. Jacob Mohler, son John Mohler and ———.
2140. Jane Ann, Reamstown, Pa., m. Rudy W. Hahn, son Daniel Hahn and ——— Shirk.
2141. Miranda, Lancaster, Pa., m. Christian Flick.
2142. Bushrod Washington, Lancaster. Pa., m. Elizabeth Frick.
2143. Cordianna, Lancaster, Pa., m. Davison Horting.
2144. Josephine, Reamstown, Pa., m. Israel Dissinger.
2145. Elizabeth, Reamstown, Pa.
2146. Virdilla Catharine, Reamstown, Pa.
2147. Johnson Joel, Reamstown, Pa.
2148. Augustine Almeda, Lancaster, Pa.

Family of AARON CARPENTER (630) and REBECCA ALTHOUSE.

2149. Raphaella, Reamstown, Pa., m. Aug. 16, 1867, Lemon Royer.
2150. Clayton W., Reamstown, Pa.

2151. Lucy, New Berlin, Pa., m. William Weinhold.
2152. Joel, New Berlin, Pa.
2153. Cecelia, New Berlin, Pa.

Family of JOHN COVER (634) and CATHERINE STEINMETZ.

2154. Michael, Ephrata, Pa., m. Ann Mohler.
2155. Charles, Ephrata, Pa.
2156. Mary, Ephrata, Pa., m. David Hauck.
2157. Eliza, Ephrata, Pa.
2158. Sarah, Ephrata, Pa.
2159. Rebecca, Ephrata, Pa.
2160. Charles, Ephrata, Pa.
2161. Isaac, Ephrata, Pa.
2162. John, Ephrata, Pa.

Family of PETER FORNEY (649) and MARGARET WIEN.

2163. Susan Carpenter, Lancaster, Pa., b. Dec. 15, 1815; d. Dec. 10, 1901.
2164. John Wien, Phila., Pa., b. Sept. 30, 1817; d. Dec. 9, 1881; m. Oct. 22, 1839, Matilda Reitzel, b. Sept. 1, 1820; d. Oct. 22, 1898; dau. Philip Reitzel and Maria Shindle.

Family of JACOB FORNEY (652) and CHRISTIANNA WIEN.

2165. George, Lancaster, Pa.
2166. Frederick, Lancaster, Pa.
2167. Charles B., Lebanon, Pa., b. July 18, 1820; m. 1845, Amelia Stehman, d. 1879; dau. John Stehman and Ann Stoner; m. Rachael G. Pierie.
2168. Sarah, Harrisburg, Pa., m. John Lingle.
2169. Wien. Harrisburg, Pa., b. June 30, 1825; d. Jan. 15, 1898; m. 1850, Lydia Gumph, b. May 15, 1824; d. Aug. 29, 1869; dau. Jacob Gumph and Lydia Getz.
2170. Daniel Carpenter, Washington, D. C., b. Dec. 23, 1827; d. 1897; m. 1850, Catharine Rhinehart.
2171. Jacob, Lancaster, Pa., b. 1829; d. 1865; m. Emma Debolt.
2172. George, Phila., Pa., b. 1831; d. 1895; m. Lessie Briggs.

9

Family of ISAAC FORNEY (655) and CATHARINE SMITH.

2173. George, Baltimore, Md.
2174. William, Baltimore, Md.
2175. Isaac, Baltimore, Md.
2176. Amanda, Baltimore, Md., m. ———— Reed.
2177. Sarah, Baltimore, Md., m. ———— Taylor.
2178. Susanna, Baltimore, Md.

Family of CATHARINE HERR (657) and JOSEPH GROFF. (661).

2179. Henry, New Providence, Pa., m. ———— Gochenour.
2180. John, New Providence, Pa., m. Catharine Eshleman, dau. Martin Eshleman and Lizzie Groff; m. Leah Kendig (2210).
2181. Jacob, New Providence, Pa., m. ———— Bleecher; m. Barbara Niles.
2182. Joseph, New Providence, Pa., m. Nancy Smith.
2183. Abraham, Georgetown, Pa., m. Fanny Groff.
2184. Hettie, Georgetown, Pa.
2185. Samuel, New Providence, Pa., m. Barbara Rank.
2186. Anna, New Providence, Pa., m. Jacob Eshleman, son Martin Eshleman and Lizzie Groff.
2187. Betsey, Hawksville, Pa., m. David Newswenger.

Family of ESTHER HERR (659) and JOSEPH GOCHENOUR.

2188. John, New Providence, Pa., b. July 3, 1782; m. Susan Winters, dau. Christopher Winters and ———— Sides.
2189. Henry, New Providence, Pa., b. April 17, 1784; m. Elizabeth Rohrer; m. Elizabeth Reigle.
2190. Elizabeth, New Providence, Pa., b. Jan. 2, 1787; m. John Shaub.
2191. Joseph, New Providence, Pa., b. Mar. 20, 1789; d. Feb. 24, 1823.
2192. Benjamin, New Providence, Pa., b. Jan. 25, 1791; d. Dec. 30, 1851; m. 1829, Susan Barr (1215); m. Dec. 24, 1844, Barbara Newswenger, b. Oct. 3, 1800; dau. Christian Newswenger and Barbara Martin.
2193. Esther, New Providence, Pa., b. Nov. 17, 1792; d. Sept. 23, 1839; m. Christopher Winters, son Christopher Winters and ———— Sides.

2194. Catharine, New Providence, Pa., b. Jan. 18, 1794; d. Apr. 24, 1861; m. May 9, 1809, John Shenk, b. Nov. 10, 1786; d. Mar. 31, 1826; son John Shenk and Martha Stauffer.

2195. Jacob, New Providence, Pa., b. Feb. 3, 1796.

2196. Susanna, New Providence, Pa., b. Apr. 5, 1799; m. Samuel Broom, son William Broom and ———.

2197. Anna, New Providence, Pa.

Family of Wid. JOSEPH GROFF (561) and Wid. MARIA STAUFFER.

2198. Benjamin, New Providence, Pa., m. Lizzie Lefever; m. Ann Shaub.

2199. David, New Providence, Pa., m. Catharine Kendig, dau. Joseph Kendig and Barbara Kreider.

2200. Amos, Lancaster, Pa., m. Susan Harman.

2201. Martha. Martic, Pa., m. John Miller.

2202. Frank, Martic, Pa., m. Abigail J. McCrabb; m. Marie Breckwell.

Family of MARIA GROFF (562) and HENRY KENDIG.

2203. Benjamin, Washington, Ill., b. Mar. 31, 1785; d. Jan. 17, 1856; m. Oct. 20, 1807, Esther Witmer (499); m. 1825, Abigail Patterson, b. 1807; d. July 19, 1835; m. Oct. 20, 1840, Betsey Page, b. Sept. 21, 1796; d. July 5, 1871; dau. John Page and ———.

2204. Simon, Washington, Ill., b. Feb. 23, 1787; d. Mar. 22, 1789.

2205. Isaac, Waynesboro, Va., b. Sept. 22, 1789; d. May, 1825; m. Mary Groff.

2206. Emanuel, Washington, Ill., b. June 17, 1791; d. June 12, 1862; m. Betsey Groff (1125).

2207. Joseph, Washington, Ill., b. June 10, 1793; d. May 19, 1862; m. Barbara Kreider, dau. Tobias Kreider and ———.

2208. Mary, Lampeter, Pa., b. Dec. 6, 1795; d. May 30, 1842; m. Peter Andrews.

2209. Martin, Waynesboro, Va., b. May 7, 1797; d. Feb. 27, 1873; m. Susan Witmer (500); m. Maria Stauffer.

2210. Leah, New Providence, Pa., b. May 7, 1800; d. May 5, 1852; m. Wid. John Groff (2180).

2211. Samuel, Martinsville, Pa., b. Jan. 6, 1803; d. Jan. 9, 1879; m. Martha Bosler, dau. Joseph Bosler and ———.

2212. John G., Strasburg, Pa., b. Sept. 20, 1805; d. July 31, 1876; m. Jan. 8, 1829, Susan Hartman, b. Jan. 12, 1808; d. Aug. 15, 1865; dau. Christian Hartman and Susanna Lefever.

2213. Abraham, Vogansville, Pa., b. Oct. 14, 1808; m. Wid. Catharine Hartman, dau. ——— Rohrer and ———.

2214. Henry, Enterprise, Pa., b. Aug. 28, 1813; d. Sept. 7, 1878; m. Anna Eaby.

Family of JACOB GROFF (663) and SUSANNA BARR.

2215. Catharine, Hawksville, Pa., m. John Welsh.

2216. Elizabeth, Drumore, Pa., m. John Brown.

2217. David, York, Pa., m. Ann Longenecker.

2218. Benjamin, Harrisburg, Pa., m. Maria Balsley.

2219. Martin, Strasburg, Pa., b. Dec. 13, 1803; m. Sept. 20, 1831, Mary Eshleman (2245).

2220. Susan, Strasburg, Pa., m. Christian Lefever.

2221. Jacob, Strasburg, Pa., m. Jane Steele.

Family of MARTIN GROFF (664) and ANNA KENDIG.

2222. Martin, Dayton, O., d. Jan. 19, 1856.

2223. John, Hermitage, Va., b. May 28, 1796; d. June 24, 1865; m. Elizabeth Groff (1324).

2224. Henry, Waynesboro, Va., b. July 8, 1798; m. Jan. 28, 1823, Anna Stover.

2225. Joseph, Hermitage, Va., b. Mar. 13, 1803; m. Nancy Brower, b. Aug. 7, 1812.

2226. Mary, Spring Mill, Va., b. Feb., 1805; m. Joseph Wenger, b. 1800.

2227. Abraham, Waynesboro, Va.

2228. Emanuel, Harrisonburg, Va.

2229. Isaac, Koiner's Store, Va., b. May 16, 1820; d. May 24, 1899; m. Aug. 30, 1838, Catharine Wenger, b. Mar. 20, 1819; d. June 27, 1890; dau. Joseph Wenger and Barbara Berry.

2230. Martha, New Hope, Va., m. ——— Miller.

2231. Nancy, Clyde, O., m. ——— Breneman.

2232. Lydia, Harrisonburg, Va., m. ——— Berry.

2233. Susan, Washington, Ind., m. ——— Hildebrand.

Family of Wid. ABRAHAM GROFF (665) and MARIA BARR.

2234. Martha, Waynesboro, Pa., b. Dec. 25, 1818; d. Mar. 22, 1898; m. Mar. 13, 1838, Abraham Frantz (2433).

2235. Francis B., Philadelphia, Pa., b. Apr. 14, 1820; m. Sept. 4, 1848, Hettie A. Barr (1764).

2236. Betsey, Catonsville, Md., b. June 4, 1822; d. Mar 23, 1886.

2237. Abraham, Catonsville, Md., b. Nov. 15, 1824; d. May 19, 1888; m. Apr. 5, 1857, Susan Hoffman, b. Dec. 6, 1826; d. July 18, 1866; dau. Henry Hoffman and Susan Garver; m. Feb. 19, 1874, Mary Hoffman, b. Oct. 4, 1830; dau. Henry Hoffman and Susan Garver.

2238. Jacob B., Washington, D. C., b. Oct. 25, 1826; m. Mary A. Miller, dau. David Miller and Catharine Carpenter.

2239. Mary, Lampeter, Pa., b. June 12, 1830; d. Jan. 22, 1886; m. May 22, 1849, Martin Pfoutz, b. May 2, 1825; son Martin Pfoutz and Hettie Miller.

2240. Benjamin F., Owings Mill, Md., b. Feb. 13, 1834; d. Oct. 27, 1895; m. Apr. 19, 1870, Elizabeth A. Denmead, b. June 11, 1844; d. Mar. 10, 1907; dau. Wm. Denmead and Rachael Baldwin.

Family of JOHN ESHLEMAN (667) and MARY WEAVER.

2241. Susanna, Strasburg, Pa., b. Aug. 18, 1800; d. Feb. 10, 1858; m. Mar. 6, 1828, Isaac Girvin, b. Sept. 23, 1800; d. Mar. 1, 1862; son Robert Girvin and Mary Smith.

2242. Nancy, Strasburg, Pa., b. Oct. 19, 1801; d. Apr. 4, 1880; m. Sept. 10, 1826, Daniel Potts (2252).

Family of Wid. JOHN ESHLEMAN (667) and ALICE GROFF.

2243. John, Strasburg, Pa., b. Sept. 23, 1803; d. Sept. 29, 1808.

2244. Jacob, Strasburg, Pa., b. Mar. 17, 1805; d. Mar. 23, 1823.

2245. Mary, Strasburg, Pa., b. Apr. 30, 1807; m. Sept. 20, 1831, Martin Groff (2219).

2246. John, Strasburg, Pa., b. Jan. 11, 1809; d. Jan. 15, 1811.

2247. Benjamin, Strasburg, Pa., b. June 14, 1810; d. June 1, 1833; m.

Mar. 19, 1833, Judith Barr, b. Sept. 29, 1815; dau. Christian
Barr and Susanna Breneman.

2248. John, Strasburg, Pa., b. June 23, 1812; d. Feb. 2, 1849.

2249. Alice, Strasburg, Pa., b. Dec. 1, 1815; d. Oct. 5, 1816.

2250. Dr Abraham, Strasburg, Pa., b. Sept. 12, 1818; m. Apr. 14, 1853,
Lizzie Mason, b. Sept. 15, 1830; dau. Samuel P. Mason and
Narcissa Burton.

Family of FANNY ESHLEMAN (669) and JOSEPH POTTS.

2251. Daniel, Fertility, Pa., b. Dec. 10, 1801; d. May 11, 1803.

2252. Daniel, Fertility, Pa., b. Sept. 20, 1803; d. Sept. 30, 1853; m.
Sept. 10, 1826, Nancy Eshleman (2242).

2253. Samuel, Fertility, Pa., b. Apr. 14, 1805; d. Jan. 31, 1829.

2254. Maria, Buck, Pa., b. Jan. 2, 1808; d. Jan. 16, 1865; m. Mar. 20,
1828, Stephen Hastings, b. Nov. 2, 1799; d. Apr. 19, 1832; son
John Hastings and Mary Mackon; m. Mar. 1, 1838, John Echternach, b. Feb. 5, 1805; son Conrad Echternach and Margaret
Wills.

2255. Fanny, Soudersburg, Pa., b. Aug. 11, 1809; m. Feb. 24, 1831,
Matthias Shirk, b. Apr. 3, 1805; son David Shirk and Susanna
Mark.

2256. Jacob E., Strasburg, Pa., b. Dec. 25, 1810; d. Dec. 4, 1856; m.
Mar. 29, 1838, Elizabeth A. Durham, b. Nov. 15, 1821; d. Jan.
18, 1841; dau. Fleming Durham and ———; m. Mar. 18, 1842,
Wid. Catherine McElroy, b. Jan. 10, 1805; dau. John Herr and
Catherine Miller.

2257. John, Strasburg, Pa., b. Feb. 6, 1812; d. Feb. 10, 1812.

2258. Joseph, Fertility, Pa., b. Aug. 10, 1813; d. July 19, 1856; m. Dec.
18, 1834, Eliza Miller, b. Feb. 1, 1813; dau. Samuel Miller and
Nancy Witmer.

2259. Benjamin, Strasburg, Pa., b. May 13, 1815; d. Mar. 14, 1829.

2260. David E., Lancaster, Pa., b. Feb. 21, 1817; m. Dec. 31, 1840,
Catherine Warren, b. Jan. 27, 1821; d. Nov. 7, 1863; dau. James
Warren and Catherine Aument.

2261. Son, Strasburg, Pa.

2262. Son, Strasburg, Pa.

Family of BARBARA ESHLEMAN (672) and JACOB BACHMAN.

2263. Maria, Greencastle, Ill., b. Jan. 4, 1815; d. May 13, 1854; m. Nov. 21, 1844, William P. Parker, b. Mar. 27, 1799; son Rev. Benjamin Parker and Sarah Miller.
2264. Susan, Strasburg, Pa., b. Sept. 9, 1816.
2265. John, Strasburg, Pa., b. Oct. 17, 1818; m. ――――― Rohrer.
2266. Anna, Owings Mills, Md., b. Sept. 12, 1820; m. May 8, 1849, David S. Longenecker, b. Apr. 24, 1821; son David Longenecker and Catherine Stoner.
2267. Jacob, Strasburg, Pa., b. Aug. 17, 1822; d. Dec. 18, 1823.
2268. Jacob, Strasburg, Pa., b. Jan. 21, 1825; m. Jan. 26, 1858, Ann E. Eshleman, b. Oct. 30, 1832; dau. Benjamin Eshleman and Mary E. Stauffer.
2269. Fanny, Quincy, Ill., b. May 10, 1827; m. Nov. 13, 1855, John R. Jameson, b. Jan. 22, 1826; d. Nov. 19, 1859; son Samuel Jameson and Nancy Myers.
2270. Benjamin F., San Francisco, Cal., b. Feb. 25, 1829.
2271. Elizabeth, Strasburg, Pa., b. Jan. 18, 1832; d. July 13, 1834.

Family of MARIA ESHLEMAN (673) and DAVID MILLER.

2272. Frances, Colerain, Pa., b. July 28, 1817; d. Dec. 13, 1846; m. Nov. 22, 1836, William Hastings, b. Dec. 4, 1811; d. Jan. 31, 1840; son John Hastings and Mary Mackon.
2273. John, Carlisle, Pa., b. Mar. 15, 1819; m. Jan. 29, 1846, Lucetta M. Culver, b. July 3, 1825; dau. Joseph Culver and Elizabeth Cary.
2274. Samuel, Lebanon, Pa., b. Oct. 4, 1820; m. Jan. 21, 1847, Martha I. Evans, b. Aug. 15, 1826; dau. Robert Evans and Sarah Carpenter.
2275. David, Middlesex, Pa., b. Sept. 18, 1825; m. Jan. 18, 1855, Elizabeth Stauffer, b. Jan. 18, 1834; dau. Jacob Stauffer and Elizabeth Rider.
2276. Elizabeth, Carlisle, Pa., b. Aug. 27, 1827; d. Nov. 10, 1835.
2277. Jacob, Carlisle, Pa., b. Feb. 1, 1831; d. Feb. 8, 1831.
2278. Abner, Boiling Springs, Pa., b. Jan. 10, 1832; m. Feb. 10, 1861,

Elizabeth Stoner, b. Apr. 4, 1840; dau.   Samuel Stoner and Martha Stauffer.

2279. Amos, Chambersburg, Pa., b. Mar. 26, 1834; m. Feb. 12, 1860, Catharine Stauffer, b. Mar. 11, 1837; dau. Jacob Stauffer and Elizabeth Rider.

Family of MARY HERR (676) and HENRY KAUFFMAN.

2280. Elizabeth, Washington, Pa., m. Augustus Haines.
2281. Abraham, Washington, Pa.
2282. Catharine, Washington, Pa., m. Jacob Beech.
2283. Henry, Washington, Pa.
2284. Magdalene, Washington, Pa.

Family of MAGDALENE HERR (678) and JOHN BENDER.

2285. Ann, Lititz, Pa.
2286. Ephraim, Lititz, Pa., m. Hannah Netzley.
2287. John, Lititz, Pa., m. Elvina Spickler.
2288. Levi, Lititz, Pa., m. Hanna Cotton.
2289. Jacob, Lititz, Pa.
2290. Joseph, Lititz, Pa., m. Levina Royer.
2291. Martha, Lititz, Pa.
2292. Elizabeth, Lititz, Pa., m. Martin Rudy.
2293. Mary, Lititz, Pa., m. Joseph Eaby.
2294. Michael, Lititz, Pa.
2295. Rebecca, Lititz, Pa.

Family of ABRAHAM HERR (679) and BARBARA HERR (909).

2296. Rudolph, New Danville, Pa., b. Mar. 4, 1820; m. Nov. 4, 1849, Wid. Mary Bender, b. Nov. 1, 1823; dau. John Kendig and Mary Mellinger; m. Dec. 28, 1865, Anna Stoner, b. July 16, 1836; dau. Jacob Stoner and Anna Souder.
2297. Benjamin, New Danville, Pa., b. 1821; d. 1833.
2298. Adam, New Danville, Pa.

Family of Wid. ABRAHAM HERR (679) and FANNY RESH.

2299. Jacob, Urbana, O.
2300. Abraham, Urbana, O.

2301. David, Urbana, O.
2302. Frances, Urbana, O.
2303. Elizabeth, Urbana, O.
2304. Barbara, Urbana. O.
2305. Benjamin, Urbana, O.

Family of CATHARINE HERR (680) and HENRY HERR (802).

2306. Mary, Sterling, Ill., b. July 10, 1825; m. Dec. 17, 1850, Martin Baer, b. Nov. 7, 1824; d. May 3, 1887; son Martin Baer and Elizabeth Harnish.

2307. Tobias H., Millersville, Pa., b. Apr. 30, 1827; d. Jan. 15, 1901; m. Annie H. Mellinger, b. Apr. 5, 1828; dau. Henry Mellinger and Anna Hertzler.

2308. Henry H., Millersville, Pa., b. Oct. 20, 1829; m. Eliza Rutt; dau. David Rutt and Martha Miller.

2309. Martha, Freeport, Ill., b. Sept. 12, 1831; m. Nov. 30, 1858, Nicholas C. Baker, b. Mar. 5, 1821; son Christian Baker and Mary Denlinger.

2310. Amos H., Neffsville, Pa., b. Nov. 28, 1834; m. Aug. 3, 1858, Mary F. Harnish, b. Apr. 12, 1839; dau. David Harnish and Susan Forry.

2311. Frances, Mountville, Pa., b. Sept. 25, 1836; m. Isaac Kauffman, b. Jan. 23, 1834; d. Dec. 27, 1893; son Isaac Kauffman and Annie Hess.

2312. Abraham, E. Petersburg, Pa., b. May 17, 1840; m. Feb. 24, 1863, Martha Shenk, dau. John Shenk and Susanna Rush.

2313. Catharine, Millersville, Pa., b. Apr. 7, 1842; d. Jan. 31, 1845.

2314. Elizabeth, Lancaster, Pa., b. July 25, 1845; m. Jacob Good.

2315. Christian, Lancaster, Pa., b. Dec. 20, 1846; m, Oct. 17, 1869, Mary Funk, dau. Martin Funk and Magdalene Greider.

Family of BARBARA HYDE (682) and STEPHEN HORNBERGER.

2316. Elizabeth, Springfield, O., b. July 31, 1815; d. Nov. 18, 1862; m. Sept. 22, 1836, David Snavely, b. Sept. 9, 1805; d. Apr. 28, 1901; son Jacob Snavely and Fanny Hess.

2317. George, Reading, Pa., m. Fanny Peters, dau. Abraham Peters and Fanny Gamber.

2318 Stephen, Roadhouse, Ill., b. July 15, 1819; m. 1842, Anna Keplinger, d. 1858; dau. Jacob Keplinger and Mary ———.

2319. Susan, Philadelphia, Pa., m. Benjamin H. Kauffman, son John Kauffman and Maria Hershey.

2320. Mary Ann, Philadelphia, Pa., m. Henry R. Minnich, son John Minnich and ———.

2321. Henry, Philadelphia, Pa.

Family of ANNA MARY HYDE (683) and JACOB METZGAR.

2322. George, Millersville, Pa.

2323. Jacob, Millersville, Pa.

2324. John, Millersville, Pa., m. Mary Metzgar, dau. Michael Metzgar and Elizabeth Shindle.

2325. Henry, Millersville, Pa., m. Margaret Dorwart, dau. John Dorwart and Mary Stone.

2326. Emanuel, Millersville, Pa., m. Elizabeth Eshleman, dau. Martin Eshleman and Catharine Dorwart.

2327. Mary, Millersville, Pa., m. Reuben Monderbach, son Martin Monderbach and ———.

2328. Martin, Millersville, Pa., m. Elizabeth Dorwart, dau. John Dorwart and Mary Stone.

2329. William, Millersville, Pa.

2330. Elizabeth, Millersville, Pa.

2331. Barbara, Millersville, Pa.

2332. David, Millersville, Pa.

Family of GEORGE HYDE (684) and LEAH GRASS.

2333. Rebecca, Millersville, Pa.,

2334. Jacob L., Shepherdstown, Pa., m. Anna Coover.

2335. George, Shepherdstown, Pa.

2336. Henry, Shepherdstown, Pa., m. ——— Boyer.

2337. Elizabeth, Shepherdstown, Pa.

2338. Emanuel, Shepherdstown, Pa.

2339. Mary, Mechanicsburg, Pa., m. Jacob Brant.

Family of CHRISTIAN SEACHRIST (685) and FANNY LANDIS.

2340. John, Millersville, Pa.

2341. Abraham, Enterprise, Pa., m. ——— Wenger.

2342. Christian, Millersville, Pa., m. ——— Wenger.
2343. Jacob, Enterprise, Pa.
2344. Fanny, Enterprise, Pa., m. Abraham Denlinger, son John Denlinger and ——— Groff.
2345. Mary, Enterprise, Pa.
2346. Elizabeth, Enterprise, Pa.
2347. Anna, Enterprise, Pa.
2348. Esther, Enterprise, Pa.

Family of JOHN SEACHRIST (686) and ANNA KREIDER.

2349. Tobias, Millersville, Pa., m. ——— Hershey; m. Elizabeth Hershey.

Family of MICHAEL SEACHRIST (687) and MARY BUCKWALTER.

2351. Anna, Millersville, Pa.
2352. Fanny, Osnaburg, O., m. Benjamin Gayman.
2353. Mary, Millersville, Pa., m. Jacob Kreider, son John Kreider and Esther Denlinger.
2354. Elizabeth, Millersville, Pa., m. Randolph Brubaker, son John Brubaker and Barbara Kilheffer
2355. Michael, Millersville, Pa.
2356. Judith, Farmersville, Pa., m. Daniel Myers, son Christian Myers and ———.

Family of MARIA SEACHRIST (688) and ABRAHAM HERSHEY.

2357. Jacob, Millersville, Pa., m. Esther Kreider, dau. John Kreider and Esther Denlinger; m. Esther Martin.

Family of JOHN HERR (689) and FANNY KAUFFMAN (876).

2358. Elizabeth, Windsor, Pa.
2359. Barbara, Windsor, Pa
2360. John, Highville, Pa., m. Annie Frey, dau. George Frey and ———.
2361. Andrew, Windsor, Pa.
2362. Adaline, Windsor, Pa., m. John Peach.
2363. Anna, Windsor, Pa.

2364. Abraham, Windsor, Pa.
2365. Catharine, Windsor, Pa.
2366. Mary, Windsor, Pa.
2367. Fanny, York Co., Pa.

Family of HENRY HERR (690) and ANNA HERR 837).

2368. Barbara, Buyerstown, Pa., b. Oct. 9, 1836; d. Mar. 12, 1870; m. 1859, Henry Eaby, d. 1873; son Henry Eaby and Susan Sensenig.
2369. Elizabeth, New Providence, Pa., b. Feb. 11, 1838; m. Feb. 3, 1863, Simon Resler, son Martin Resler and Martha Andrews.
2370. Mary, Smithville, Pa., b. July 17, 1839; m. Sept. 7, 1862, Charles Foreman, son Philip Foreman and ———.
2371. Anna, Mascot, Pa., b. May 6, 1841.
2372. Susan, Cains, Pa., b. Nov. 9, 1843; m. Dec. 2, 1875, Elias K. Souders, son Henry Souders and ———.
2373. Henry, New Providence, Pa., b. May 28, 1845; d. Dec. 24, 1900; m. Dec. 19, 1865, Magdalene Buckwalter, b. Sept. 20, 1844; dau. John Buckwalter and Fanny Resh.
2374. Hettie, Mascot, Pa., b. Apr. 5, 1848.
2375. Abraham B., Bird-in-Hand, Pa., b. July 10, 1850; m. Sept. 27, 1872, Susanna S. Rohrer, b. June 11, 1851; dau. Jacob Rohrer and Maria Shaeffer.
2376. Lydia, Bareville, Pa., b. Mar. 18, 1852; m. Oct. 13, 1872, Henry Good, son Henry Good and Mary Burkhart.
2377. Amos, Bird-in-Hand, Pa., b. Mar. 30, 1854; d. Nov. 9, 1857.
2378. Ezra G., Chicago, Ill., b. Feb. 15, 1857; m. June 19, 1883, Elizabeth Kreuger, b. May 5, 1865; dau. John H. Kreuger and Laura Nulty.
2379. Mattie, Mascot, Pa., b. Jan. 24, 1859

Family of MARY HERR (691) and JOHN FUNK.

2380. Elizabeth, Turkey Hill, Pa., m. Benjamin Shertzer.
2381. Anna, Bird-in-Hand, Pa., m. Adam Manning.
2382. Fanny, Bird-in-Hand, Pa., m. Rudolph Kauffman.
2383. Lydia, Bird-in-Hand, Pa., m. Jacob Sheck, son Henry Sheck and ———.

2384. Barbara, Bird-in-Hand, Pa., m. Jacob Souders, son Jacob Souders and ———.
2385. Catharine, Bird-in-Hand, Pa., m. David Stauffer.
2386. Magdalene, Bird-in-Hand, Pa., m. Michael Yolk.
2387. John, Bird-in-Hand, Pa., m. Catharine Shertzer, dau. David Shertzer and ——— .

Family of ANNA HERR (692) and BENJAMIN ESHLEMAN.

2388. Benjamin, Manor, Pa., m. ——— Harnish.
2389. John, Manor, Pa.

Family of ELIZABETH HERR (694) and PETER MUSSER.

2390. Mary, Rohrerstown, Pa.
2391. Fanny, Mountville, Pa., m. Abraham Shenk, son Abraham Shenk and Anna Landis.

Family of Wid. ELIZABETH HERR MUSSER (694) and DANIEL BRENNER.

2392. John, Millersville, Pa.
2393. Barbara, Rohrerstown, Pa.
2394. Elizabeth H., Rohrerstown, Pa., b. Mar. 24, 1848; m. Oct. 27, 1872, Samuel D. Shenk, b. Sept. 16, 1848; son Reuben Shenk and Mary Dabler.
2395. Catharine, Rohrerstown, Pa., b. Jan., 1838.

Family of CATHARINE HERR (695) and SOLOMON HERR (835).

2396. Emanuel, Witmer, Pa., b. Aug. 30, 1839; m. Mary Witmer, dau. Rev. David Witmer and ——— Rutt.
2397. Elias, Greenland, Pa., b. Aug. 12, 1842; m. Nov. 5, 1863, Mary L. Rohrer, b. Dec. 6, 1843; dau. John G. Rohrer and Susanna Landis.
2398. Abraham, Greenland, Pa., b. Aug. 12, 1842; m. Jan. 12, 1865. Louisa Landis, b. Aug. 3, 1846; dau. David Landis and Elizabeth Hostetter.
2399. Adam H., Lancaster, Pa., b. Jan. 25, 1854; m. Jan. 25, 1880, Catharine Kilheffer (2862).

Family of CATHARINE WITMER FRICK (707) and FREDERICK SCHEETZ.

2400. Christian, Millersville, Pa., b. 1812; d. 1868; m. Catharine Grabill, b. 1820.

2401. Frederick, Petersburg, Pa., b. Feb. 16, 1815; m. Fannie Rohrer.

2402. Sophia, St. Joseph, Mo., b. Jan. 16, 1816; m. ——— Debbin.

2403. John, New Berlin, O.

2404. Jacob Killinger, Lykens Valley, Pa.

2405. Barbara, Maytown, Pa., m. George Lenhart.

2406. Nancy, Salunga, Pa., m. Michael Minnich.

2407. Catharine, Kissel Hill, Pa., m. Emanuel Grube.

Family of JACOB WITMER FRICK (708) and MAGDALENA PEIFER.

2408. John Peifer, York, Pa., b. Dec. 6, 1812; d. Dec. 7, 1891; m. Nov. 26, 1839, Hannah Hershey; b. Feb. 3, 1815; d. May 23, 1889; dau. John Hershey and Magdalena Roth.

2409. Maria, Manchester, Md., b. Apr. 21, 1815; d. Jan. 26, 1887; m. Aug. 9, 1836, Levi S. Winterode, b. Aug. 17, 1812; d. Jan. 26, 1874; son ——— and Anna Slagle.

2410. Christian, Manchester, Md., b. Dec. 17, 1817; d. Aug. 15, 1863; m. Feb. 2, 1851, Matilda J. Speck, b. Dec. 7, 1821; d. Oct. 17, 1894; dau. Martin Speck and Elizabeth Leighty.

Family of Wid. JACOB WITMER FRICK (708) and ELIZABETH ARNOLD.

2411. Annie E., Baltimore, Md., b. Dec. 13, 1825; d. Feb., 1866; m. Daniel Bond.

2412. Jacob, Manchester, Md., b. Aug. 27, 1827; d. 1857.

2413. Englehart Arnold, Baltimore, Md., b. Jan. 4, 1830; d. Jan. 2, 1885; m. Nov. 24, 1859, Cecelia J. Shower, b. June 6, 1833; dau. George Shower and Rachael Everhart.

Family of FANNY FRICK (711) and DAVID MARTIN.

2414. Fanny, Niagara Falls, N. Y., b. July 9, 1815; m. Jan. 1, 1839, David Witmer (1018).

2415. Elizabeth, Amherst, N. Y., b. Nov. 5, 1816; d. Apr. 4, 1887.

2416. Magdalene, Amherst, N. Y., m. ——— Strickler.

2417. Christian, F., Amherst, N. Y.
2418. David, Amherst, N. Y.
2419. Henry C., Sabetha, Kans.
2420. Anna, Amherst, N. Y., m. ———— Netzley.

Family of CHRISTIAN FRICK (713) and ELIZABETH LONG.

2421. Anna Long, Snyder, N. Y., b. May 18, 1819; m. Nov. 16, 1837, Tobias Witmer (1021).

Family of ABRAHAM FRICK (718) and RACHEL STONER.

2422. Abraham, Neffsville, Pa.
2423. John, Neffsville, Pa.

Family of SUSANNA FRICK (722) and BENJAMIN SUMMY.

2424. Anna Eliza, Washington, D. C., b. Mar. 4, 1834; m. Sept. 22, 1853, Nelson J. Hillman, b. Apr. 12, 1829; son Beriah Hillman and Charlotte Young.
2425. Susan Maria, Lancaster, N. Y., b. Feb. 11, 1836; d. Mar. 10, 1841.
2426. David, Lancaster, N. Y., b. Nov. 25, 1838; d. Mar. 16, 1841.
2427. Orlando David, Washington, D. C., b. Oct. 1, 1841; m. Jan. 3, 1871, Ida M. Irwin, b. May 31, 1847; dau. John W. Irwin and Mary A. McDonnell.
2428. Susan Alvira, Washington, D. C., b. Oct. 14, 1843.
2429. Benjamin West, Vienna, Va., b. June 30, 1847; m. Apr. 29, 1886, Kate Strong, b. Mar. 25, 1859; dau. Col, James W. Strong and Eliza J. Hedenburg.
2430. Frank L., Washington, D. C., b. May 11, 1850; m. Mar. 3, 1880, Isabelle M. Stephenson, b. Jan. 18, 1858; dau. John Stephenson and Mary Gaw.

Family of ANNA FRICK (723) and Rev. CHRISTIAN H. FRANTZ.

2431. Isaac, Waynesboro, Pa., b. Nov. 11, 1809; d. Sept. 18, 1846; m. Mar. 28, 1839, Anna Newcomer, b. Mar. 18, 1814; d. Sept. 18, 1888; dau. Abraham Newcomer and Maria Musselman.

2432. John, Waynesboro, Pa., b. Aug. 10, 1811; d. Mar. 4, 1877; m. Nov. 19, 1844, Anna Weaver, b. July 25, 1825; d. Sept. 11, 1845; dau. Joseph Weaver and ————; m. Dec. 19, 1847, Catharine Ryder, b. May 11, 1814; d. Jan. 28, 1891; dau. Adam Ryder and Elizabeth Longenecker.

2433. Abraham, Waynesboro, Pa., b. Sept. 20, 1813; d. Jan. 31, 1884; m. Mar. 13, 1848, Martha Groff (2234).

2434. Rev. Jacob, Waynesboro, Pa., b. Oct. 13, 1815; d. Feb. 25, 1880; m. Feb. 23, 1837, Frances Hoffman, b. June 1, 1816; d. Aug. 30, 1854; dau. Christian Hoffman and Anna Newcomer; m. Feb. 17, 1867, Anna M. Landis, b. Mar. 2, 1820; d. Oct., 1907; dau. Abraham Landis and Anna Neff.

2435. Christian, Mercersburg, Pa., b. May 4, 1819; d. Mar. 10, 1884; m. Oct. 4, 1842, Leah Stauffer, b. Nov. 7, 1823; d. Oct. 31, 1897; dau. Jacob Stauffer and Elizabeth Oberholser.

2436. Samuel, Waynesboro, Pa., b. Sept. 1, 1821; d. Sept 14, 1901; m. Sept. 22, 1846, Barbara Stauffer, b. Mar. 16, 1822; d. Aug. 13, 1884; dau. Jacob Stauffer and Elizabeth Oberholser.

2437. Dr. Benjamin, Waynesboro, Pa., b. Oct. 17, 1824; d. Feb. 1, 1907; m. Oct. 7, 1849, Mary A. Ryder, b. Apr. 15, 1830; d. Feb. 21, 1898; dau. Michael Ryder and Mary Ryder.

2438. Anna, Waynesboro, Pa., b. Feb. 23, 1828; d. Feb. 7, 1861; m. Dec. 4, 1853, Rev. Martin Hoover, b. Feb. 23, 1822; d. Dec. 26, 1900, son Peter Hoover and Christiana Martin.

Family of ABRAHAM FRICK (726) and CATHARINE DIFFENBACH (1379).

2439. John D., Waynesboro, Pa., b. July 10, 1820; m. Oct. 28, 1849, Louisa Stoner, b. Oct. 5, 1827; dau. Martin Stoner and Anna Bechtel.

2440. Mary, Waynesboro, Pa., b. Sept. 26, 1823; d. May 27, 1848; m. Sept. 1841, Samuel Hirshman, d. 1860; son Jacob Hirshman and Anna Frederick.

2441. Anna, Waynesboro, Pa., b. Jan. 20, 1825; m. Nov. 18, 1841, Jacob Beaver, b. Mar. 19, 1820; son David W. Beaver and Anna Fields.

2442. George, Waynesboro, Pa., b. Nov. 7, 1826; d. Dec. 23, 1892; m.

Dec. 9, 1849, Frederick Oppenlander, b. Aug. 12, 1824; d. Apr. 10, 1901; dau. Frederick Oppenlander and Frederica Miller.

2443. Jacob, Waynesboro, Pa., b. Apr. 27, 1830; m. Sept. 5, 1854, Anna Gantz, b. Dec. 23, 1835; dau. David Gantz and Susan Nicodemus.

2444. Christian, Waynesboro, Pa.

2445. Abraham, Waynesboro, Pa.

Family of JOHN R. FRICK (728) and ANNIE KELSO.

2446. Maria, Waynesboro, Pa., b. Nov. 18, 1828; m. Mar. 19, 1850, Jacob Bonebrake, b. Nov. 28, 1826; son Jacob Bonebrake and Susan Hollinger.

2447. Anna, Chambersburg, Pa., b. Jan. 21, 1830; m. Benjamin Ryder, son Adam Ryder and ———.

2448. Jacob, Waynesboro, Pa., b. Sept. 17, 1832; m, Nov. 16, 1857, Mary A. Funk, b. Sept. 11, 1836; dau. John Funk and Nancy Shenk.

2449. Benjamin, Waynesboro, Pa., b. Dec. 1, 1835; d. Aug. 4, 1876; m. Alice Heitshu, dau. Charles Heitshu and Caroline Ryder.

2450. Elizabeth, Roadside, Pa., b. Feb. 21, 1838; m. Dec. 11, 1856, Aaron Funk, b. Apr. 29, 1835; d. Sept. 4, 1886; son John Funk and Nancy Shenk.

2451. John, Ringgold, Md., b. Mar. 7, 1841; d. Aug. 7, 1873.

2452. Abraham, Ringgold, Md., b. Oct. 17, 1843; m. Nov. 12, 1878, Laura Martin, b. Feb. 21, 1851; dau. Stephen Martin and Anna Funk.

Family of JACOB R. FRICK (729) and MARY HELLER PFOUTZ.

2453. Elizabeth, Lime Valley, Pa., b. July 2, 1823; d. Jan. 7, 1896; m. 1846, Jacob N. Haverstick, b. Jan. 5, 1820; d. Nov. 15, 1887; son John Haverstick and Magdalena Neff.

2454. Lydia P., Waynesboro, Pa., b. Nov. 28, 1824; d. Jan. 14, 1902; m. Oct. 27, 1843, Benjamin N. Landis, b. Nov. 16, 1822; d. Nov. 11, 1855; son Abraham Landis and Anna Neff.

2455. Anna, Lancaster, Pa., b. July 25, 1826; m. Oct. 21, 1845, Jacob M. Frantz, b. Dec. 18, 1823; son Christian N. Frantz and Elizabeth Miller.

10

2456. Maria P., Forgy, O., b. Aug. 8, 1830; m. Nov. 9, 1852, John Bowman (4061).

2457. Dr. Abraham P., Aransas Pass, Tex., b. Aug. 19, 1835; m. Mar. 19, 1861, Mary K. Smith, b. Sept., 1842; dau. Nathan S. Smith and Lavinia S. Tennis.

2458. Salinda, Lancaster, Pa., b. Sept. 5, 1839; m. Dec. 7, 1879, Noah D. Swartley, b. Dec. 12, 1840; son Jacob Swartley and Magdalena Delk.

Family of ANNA FRICK (733) and DAVID SPAYTH.

2459. Elizabeth, Williamsville, N. Y., b. Jan. 16, 1818; d. Sept. 10, 1832.

2460. Mary, Williamsville, N. Y., b. Apr. 3, 1820; d. Oct. 31, 1902.

2461. Daniel, Williamsville, N. Y., b. Mar. 8, 1822; d. Jan. 22, 1892.

2462. Henry, Williamsville, N. Y., b. July 29, 1825.

2463. Martha, Williamsville, N. Y., b. Feb. 1, 1828; d. Feb. 12, 1902.

2464. Abraham, Williamsville, N. Y., b. Sept. 1, 1831; d. Mar. 1, 1874.

2465. John, Williamsville, N. Y., b. Mar. 16, 1834.

Family of JOHN ROYER (737) and REBECCA LYONS.

2466. Anna, Leacock, Pa., b. May 30, 1826; d. Apr. 4, 1898; m. Dec. 22, 1846, Moyer Hoover, b. Apr. 22, 1826; d. Oct. 4, 1898.

2467. Rachael, Vintage, Pa., b. Oct. 31, 1827; m. Feb. 10, 1853, Jacob A. Bair, b. Jan. 30, 1833.

2468. Saloma, Leacock, Pa., b. Apr. 3, 1829; m. Christian Kreider.

2469. Rebecca, Leacock, Pa., b. Feb. 8, 1831.

2470. Mary, Leacock, Pa., m. Martin Severs.

2471. John, Leacock, Pa., m. Ella Bair.

2472. Elizabeth, Leacock, Pa., b. Feb. 16, 1839; m. George W. Laub.

Family of MAGDALENA ROYER (739) and JOHN RUTTER.

2473. Jonathan, Leacock, Pa., b. July 22, 1818; m. Barbara Horst; m. Elizabeth Good.

2474. Anna, Leacock, Pa., b. July 13, 1821; d. July 23, 1882; m. Christian Good.

2475. Martha, Leacock, Pa., b. Dec. 23, 1824; m. Feb. 22, 1844, Andrew Bair, b. Apr. 26, 1853.

Family of ESTHER ROYER (740) and AMOS RUTTER.

2476. John R., New Holland, Pa., b. Aug. 20, 1817; d. Jan. 19, 1889; m. May 12, 1840, Caroline Snader, b. Mar. 20, 1818; d. Sept. 26, 1854; m. Sept. 13, 1855, Anna Freymeyer, b. July 4, 1830.

2477. Anna, New Holland, Pa., b. Apr. 3, 1819; d. Sept. 30, 1896; m. Nov. 9, 1843, Levi Good

2478. Mary, Paradise, Pa., b. Jan. 11, 1821; d. Aug. 3, 1896; m. Sept. 21, 1843, Rudolph Evans, b. May 21, 1821: d. Mar. 11, 1874.

2479. Joseph, New Holland, Pa., b. Sept. 17, 1822; d. Aug. 15, 1900; m. Dec. 26, 1847, Henrietta Hartman (1780).

2480. Catharine, New Holland, Pa., b. Feb. 14, 1826; d. Oct. 24, 1898; m. Oct., 1848, Rolandus Wenger.

2481. Jonathan R., Intercourse, Pa., b. Dec. 28, 1827; m. Sept. 22, 1853. Rachael Hoover, b. Mar. 8, 1829; dau. Benjamin Hoover and Catherine ———.

2482. Amos, New Holland, Pa., b. May 24, 1830; d. Aug. 15, 1902; m. Sept. 2, 1856, Catherine E. Mentzer; b. Aug. 5, 1835; dau. Paul Mentzer and Sarah Kurtz.

2483. Esther, Paradise, Pa., b. Jan. 17, 1833: m. Nov. 15, 1855, Dr. Isaac Miller; d. May, 1898.

2484. Jeremiah H., New Holland, Pa., b. Dec. 2, 1835; d. Oct. 24, 1882: m. Feb. 5, 1861, Christiana Bair.

Family of ELIZABETH ROYER (741) and HENRY RUTTER.

2485. Leah, Bareville, Pa., b. Aug. 25, 1815: m. Mar. 20, 1837, Philip Shaeffer, b. Dec., 1803; d. Apr. 13, 1864.

2486. Rachael, Lancaster, Pa., b. May, 1817; m. William Shaeffer.

2487. Elizabeth, Lancaster, Pa., m. Roland Good.

2488. John, Chester, Pa., b. May 19, 1826; d. July 5, 1876; m. Oct. 12, 1848. Margaret Sweigart, b. May 27, 1824; d. Jan. 11, 1876.

2489. Isaac, Lancaster, Pa., b. Aug. 20, 1831: d. Nov. 30, 1884; m. Oct. 10, 1856, Serena Kulp, b. Dec., 1838; d. Dec. 12, 1898.

2490. Anna, New Holland, Pa., b. Sept. 30, 1832; d. May 23, 1871.

Family of MARY ROYER (742) and MARTIN RUTTER.

2491. Anna, Leacock, Pa., b. May 28, 1830.

2492. Cyrus, New Holland, Pa.

Family of JACOB FRICK (744) and BARBARA LONGENECKER.

2493. Henry, Williamsville, N. Y., b. Jan. 23, 1828; m. May 20, 1852, Maria Metz, b. Feb. 7, 1832; d. Aug. 4, 1879.

2494. Anna, Williamsville, N. Y., b. Apr. 6, 1833.

2495. Elizabeth, Williamsville, N. Y., b. Sept. 19, 1835.

2496. Susan, Williamsville, N. Y., b. Dec. 28, 1841.

Family of NANCY S. FRICK (753) and Rev. JOHN FRANTZ HERSHEY.

2497. Annie, Bachmansville, Pa., b. July 5, 1826; m. Nov. 26, 1852, Isaac Kulp, b. Sept. 17, 1828; d. Nov. 13, 1892.

2498. Martin, Hockersville, Pa., b. Dec. 27, 1829; m. Jan. 25, 1861, Mary A. Shartle, b. Sept. 15, 1830; dau. John Shartle and Anne M. Hoffer.

2499. Elizabeth, Waynesboro, Pa., b. Mar. 21, 1831; d. Dec. 16, 1882; m. Jan. 29, 1866, Wid. Rev. Martin Hoover, b. Feb. 23, 1822; d. Dec. 26, 1901; son Peter Hoover and Christiana Martin.

2500. Fannie, Waynesboro, Pa., b. Aug. 29, 1832; d. Dec. 10, 1900.

2501. Priscilla, Palmyra, Pa., b. Dec. 27, 1834; m. Nov. 11, 1866, Jacob Kulp, b. Nov. 18, 1835; son John Kulp and Mary Moyer.

2502. Lydia, Hockersville, Pa., b. Dec. 4, 1836.

2503. Menno, Campbellstown, Pa., b. Dec. 9, 1838; m. May 12, 1863, Malinda Motter, b. June 4, 1845; dau. Philip Motter and Elizabeth Reed.

2504. Leah, Campbellstown, Pa., b. Sept. 2, 1840; d. Feb. 27, 1886.

2505. Maria, Paradise, Pa., b. Nov. 29, 1842; m. Nov. 1, 1868, Jacob Wenger, b. Apr. 14, 1840; son John B. Wenger and Mary ———.

Family of MARY S. FRICK (754) and JOHN BALMER.

2506. Mary, Sporting Hill, Pa., b. Sept. 27, 1838; d. Aug. 30, 1891; m. Reuben Strickler.

2507. Anna F., Manheim, Pa., b. Jan. 21, 1840; m. Nov. 28, 1865, Henry Beamsderfer, b. Jan. 14, 1840.

2508. Harriet, Sporting Hill, Pa., b. June 4, 1844; d. Sept. 22, 1848.

Family of JACOB FRICK (756) and MARGARET JONES.

2509. Caroline, Coldwater, O., b. Mar. 8, 1826; d. Oct. 3, 1889; m. Joseph Smith.

2510. Margaret Ann, Coldwater, O., b. Oct. 21, 1827; d. Oct. 8, 1894; m. James Rall.

2511. Anna Maria, Coldwater, O., b. Apr. 25, 1829; m. Edward C. Smith, b. Sept. 5, 1821; d. Aug. 14, 1891.

2512. Henry Landis, Coldwater, O., b. Feb. 7, 1831; m. Sarah E. Greiner, d. Apr. 10, 1893.

2513. Louisa, Osborne, O., b. Sept. 10, 1832; d. Feb. 6, 1900.

2514. Leah, Dayton, O., b. Oct. 16, 1833; m. Joseph F. Dunkle.

2515. Angeline, Osborne, O., b. Dec. 8, 1835; m. Jacob Snider, son Daniel Snider and Minerva Richardson.

2516. David Washington, Coldwater, O., b. July 4, 1838; m. Nov. 8, 1866, Margaret A. Snider, b. Aug. 17, 1846; dau. Daniel Snider and Minerva Richardson.

2517. Elizabeth, Zenus, Ind., b. Sept. 8, 1820; d. June 17, 1897; m. Daniel Miller.

2518. Jacob Samuel, Coldwater, O., b. Sept. 23, 1840; d. Mar. 5, 1894.

Family of CHRISTIAN BLOCHER (758) and CATHARINE BEAM.

2519. David, Buffalo, N. Y., m. Catherine Winnower.

2520. Christian, Buffalo, N. Y., m. Susanna Martin.

2521. Peter, Buffalo, N. Y., m. Mary ———.

2522. Betsey, Buffalo, N. Y., m. John Roads.

2523. John, Buffalo, N. Y.

2524. Catharine, Buffalo, N. Y., m. Jacob Bessey.

Family of JOHN BLOCHER (759) and CATHARINE BOMBERGER.

2525. Daniel, Buffalo, N. Y., b. 1812; m. Elizabeth Metz.

2526. Henry, Buffalo, N. Y., m. Catharine Leopard.

2527. John, Buffalo, N. Y., b. July 22, 1825; m. Eliza Neff. b. Feb., 1828.

Family of MARIA BROWN (772) and AMOS WEIDLER.

2528. Emanuel, Lancaster, Pa.

2529. Salinda, Lancaster, Pa., d. Aug. 7, 1842.

2530. Ann Eliza, Lancaser, Pa., d. July 22, 1883.

2531. Benjamin, Lancaster, Pa., d. July 6, 1863

2532. Margaret, Lancaster, Pa., d. July 11, 1853.

2533. Milton, Lancaster, Pa.

2534. Emma, Lancaster, Pa.

2535. Alice, Lancaster, Pa.

2536. John, Lancaster, Pa.

Family of CHRISTIAN ESHLEMAN (773) and LYDIA WEBER.

2537. Benjamin F., Cearfoss, Md., b. Sept. 18, 1835; d. July 28, 1905; m. Fanny Grumbine, b. May 13, 1843; m. Mary Showalter; m. Elizabeth Latshaw.

2538. Samuel, Maugansville, Md., m. ——— Cearfoss.

2539. Christian, Chambersburg, Pa.

Family of PETER ESHLEMAN (774) and MARY REIFF.

2540. Barbara, Reid, Md., b. Aug. 29, 1820; d. Oct. 16, 1858; m. Abraham Horst.

2541. Susanna, Reid, Md., b. Dec. 23, 1821; d. Apr. 4, 1854; m. Frederick Shank.

2542. Abraham, Reid, Md., b. Sept. 9, 1823; d. Mar. 20, 1902; m. Nancy Lesher.

2543. Joseph, Reid, Md., b. Dec. 29, 1825; d. Nov. 11, 1890; m. 1846, Susanna Horst, b. Oct. 16, 1826; d. Aug. 14, 1894; dau. John Horst and Elizabeth Eshleman.

2544. John, Franklin Co., Pa., b. Mar. 12, 1828; d. Jan. 27, 1892; m. Aug. 31, 1848, Elizabeth Strite (2600); m. Sept. 17, 1862, Sarah Jane Spear, b. Nov. 30, 1837; d. Mar. 22, 1863; m. 1886, Fanny Siegrist, b. Jan. 10, 1833; d. July 3, 1885; dau. John Siegrist and Leah Kauffman.

2545. Samuel, Reid, Md., b. Dec. 20, 1829; d. Oct. 6, 1856; m. Susan Lesher.

2546. Jonas, Landisville, Pa., b. Feb. 14, 1831; m. Oct. 18, 1853, Mary Whisler; m. ——— Bally; m. Elizabeth Miller.

2547. Peter, Reid, Md., b. Mar. 2, 1824; m. Martha Hege; m. Elizabeth Martin, dau. Jacob Martin and ——— Hege.

2548. Mary, Greencastle, Pa., b. Oct. 13, 1835; d. 1840.
2549. David, Greencastle, Pa., b. Oct. 8, 1837; m. ———— Ledy.

Family of ABRAHAM ESHLEMAN (775) and ELIZABETH HORST.

2550. Susan, N. Lawrence, O., b. Sept. 17, 1820; d. infant.
2551. Nancy, N. Lawrence, O., b. Sept. 5, 1821; m. Henry Kurtz, d. 1843; m. Samuel Showalter.
2552. Christian, N. Lawrence, O., b. Feb. 17, 1823; m. Mary Gardner.
2553. Elizabeth, Goshen, Ind., b. Sept. 14, 1824; m. Levi Weaver.
2554. Susanna, Goshen, Ind., b. Aug. 22, 1826; m. John A. Hoover.
2555. Abraham, Butler Co., Neb., b. Mar. 1, 1828; m. Mary Horst.
2556. David, Mt. Caln, Texas, b. May 17, 1830; m. Harriet Rowland.
2557. John, N. Lawrence, O., b. Oct. 24, 1831; d. 1834.
2558. Samuel, N. Lawrence, O., b. May 29, 1833; m. Anna Martin.
2559. Jonas, N. Lawrence, O., b. May 2, 1834; m. 1855, Fanny Martin, d. 1861; m. 1863, Martha Martin, d. 1891.

Family of ELIZABETH ESHLEMAN (776) and JOHN HORST.

2560. Christian, Maugansville, Md.
2561. Martin, Maugansville, Md.
2562. John, Maugansville, Md.
2563. David, Maugansville, Md.
2564. Joseph, Maugansville, Md.
2565. David, Jr., Maugansville, Md.
2566. John V., Maugansville, Md.
2567. Daniel, Maugansville, Md.

Family of JOHN ESHLEMAN (777) and SARAH GIBBLE.

2568. Fanny, Franklin Co., Pa., b. Apr. 3, 1826; d. Apr. 14, 1871; m. John E. Stover.
2569. ————, State Line, Pa., m. Samuel Musselman, b. July 26, 1835; d. Apr. 22, 1902.
2570. John S., State Line, Pa., b. Oct. 27, 1842; d. Feb. 27, 1864.
2571. ————.

Family of SUSANNA ESHLEMAN (778) and SAMUEL WEBER.

2572. Samuel, Maugansville, Md.
2573. Abraham, Maugansville, Md.
2574. ————.

Family of SAMUEL ESHLEMAN (779) and MARY MINNICH.

2575. Rev. Daniel M., Rheems', Pa., b. Jan. 18, 1845; m. Mary Shank, dau. Joseph Shank and Magdalena Buckwiler; m. Sarah Eshleman, dau. John Eshleman and Barbara Witmer.

2576. Samuel, Elm, Pa.

2577. Mary, Rapho Twp., Pa., m. Abraham Miller.

Family of CATHERINE ESHLEMAN (780) and JOHN MILLER.

2578. Elizabeth, Landisville, Pa.

2579. John, Landisville, Pa.

2580. ———, Landisville, Pa.

Family of FERONICA ESHLEMAN (781) and JACOB GEARHART.

2581. Jacob, Greencastle, Pa.

2582. ———, Greencastle, Pa.

2583. ———, Greencastle, Pa.

Family of ANNA ESHLEMAN (782) and EMANUEL ZIEGLER.

2584. ———, Dauphin Co., Pa.

2585. ———, Dauphin Co., Pa.

2586. ———, Dauphin Co., Pa.

Family of DANIEL ESHLEMAN (783) and ——— NETZLY.

2587. ———, Manheim, Pa., b. Dec. 5, 1845; m. A. I. K. Mumma; m. Abram H. Siegrist.

2588. ———, Manheim, Pa.

2589. ———, Manheim, Pa.

Family of DAVID ESHLEMAN (784) and CHRISTIANA STAUFFER.

2590. Maria, Bethel, Pa., m. Michael Basehore.

2591. John, Penbrook, Pa., b. Sept. 5, 1841; m. Oct 1, 1863, Ellen Steinbaugh, b. Mar. 29, 1843; d. Nov. 17, 1875; m. June 26, 1877, Mary A. Stoffel, b. Jan. 8, 1858.

2592. Anna, Penbrook, Pa.

2593. Susan, Progress, Pa., m. ——— Smith.

Family of ABRAHAM STRITE (785) and ELIZABETH MENTZER.

2594. ———, Leitersburg, Md.
2595 ———, Leitersburg, Md.
2596. ———, Leitersburg, Md.

Family of JOHN STRITE (786) and ELIZABETH SUMMERS.

2597. David, Leitersburg Md., b. Jan. 6, 1822; d. Feb. 4, 1896; m. 1846, Elizabeth Horst, dau. David Horst and Magdalena Gribell.
2598. Nancy, Leitersburg, Md., d. infant.
2599. John, Leitersburg, Md., b. July 19, 1825; d. Oct. 19, 1870; m. 1850, Catherine Horst, b. Sept. 1, 1830; d. Oct. 7, 1851; dau. John Horst and Elizabeth Eshleman; m. 1853, Eva Shank, b. Oct. 31, 1834; d. Feb. 7, 1861; dau. John Shank and Lydia Myers; m. 1867, Mary Shank, dau. Frederick Shank and Susan Eshleman.
2600. Elizabeth, Leitersburg, Md., b. Sept. 14, 1827; d. Feb. 10, 1862; m. Aug. 31, 1848, John Eshleman (2544).
2601. Jacob, Leitersburg, Md., d. infant.
2602. Martha, Mason and Dixon, Pa., b. Dec. 5, 1834; d. Sept. 30, 1861; m. Jacob Shank.
2603. Catherine, Mason and Dixon, Pa., b. Dec. 5, 1834; d. Sept. 30, 1861; m. Lewis Harbaugh.
2604. Samuel, Leitersburg, Md., b. May 23, 1837; d. July 11, 1907; m. Nov. 25, 1858, Esther Ann H. Shank, dau. Jacob R. Shank and Mary Hoover.
2605. Daniel, Grand Junction, Ia., d. 1871; m. Jennie Virginia Young.
2606. Mary, Waynesboro, Pa., m. 1864, J. Lemuel Gilbert. b. June 12, 1840; d. Feb. 7, 1895; son David Gilbert and Elizabeth Leeron.

Family of CHRISTIAN STRITE (787) and CATHERINE SNIVELY

2607. ———, Leitersburg, Md.
2608. ———, Leitersburg, Md.
2609. ———, Leitersburg, Md.

Family of SAMUEL STRITE (788) and MARTHA SNIVELY.

2610. John, Clear Spring, Md.
2611. Anna, Clear Spring, Md., m. Abraham Ditto.
2612. Henry, Clear Spring, Md.

Family of NANCY STRITE (789) and JACOB MILLER.

2613. ———, Leitersburg, Md.
2614. ———, Leitersburg, Md.
2615. ———, Leitersburg, Md.

Family of JOSEPH STRITE (790) and ELIZABETH STRITE.

2616. Elizabeth, Shady Grove, Pa., b. Nov. 20, 1830; m. Adam Baker.
2617. Abraham, Leitersburg, Md., b. Nov. 7, 1831; d. Dec. 3, 1894; m. Fanny Hoover, dau. John Hoover and ———.
2618. Joseph, Leitersburg, Md., b. Mar. 25, 1833; d. July 4, 1891; m Catherine Lesher, dau. Andrew Lesher and Magdalena Shank.
2619. Catherine, Smithburg, Md., b. Mar. 20, 1836; d. Sept. 3, 1896; m. Tobias Shank, son Henry Shank and Emma Smith.
2620. Martha, Wingerton, Pa., b. Oct. 21, 1847; m. Noah Shank, son Frederick Shank and Susanna Eshleman.
2621. John, Leitersburg, Md., b. Jan. 24, 1846; m. Catherine ———
2622. Mary, Maugansville, Md., b. Sept. 6, 1850; m. Christian Shank, b. Jan. 1, 1848; d. Apr. 5, 1905; son Frederick Shank and Susanna Eshleman.
2623. Christian, Reid, Md., b. May 23, 1844; d. July 6, 1894; m. Mary ———.

Family of CHRISTIAN STEINMAN (791) and ANNA ROHRER.

2624. Daniel, Muscatine, Ia., b. Dec. 15, 1818; m. Wid. Elizabeth Smith.
2625. Christian, Cedar Valley, Ia., b. June 10, 1820; m. Sarah Stamm.
2626. David, Cedar Valley, Pa., b. Dec. 3, 1822; m. Anna Eckman.
2627. Fanny, Grand View, Ia., b. June 2, 1825; d. Feb., 1830.
2628. Maria, Grand View, Pa., b. Jan. 15, 1829; m. Sept. 25, 1855, Henry Daveler, b. July 20, 1830.
2629. Anna, Maytown, Pa., b. June 6, 1832; m. Henry Dougherty.
2630. Elizabeth, Willow Street, Pa., b. June 16, 1837; m. Adam Groff, son Jacob Groff and ——— Resh.
2631. Jonas, Grand View, Ia., b. Oct. 26, 1839.

Family of FRANCES HERR (792) and CHRISTIAN EABY.

2632. Mary, Elizabethtown, Pa.
2633. Abraham, Elizabethtown, Pa.
2634. Frances, Elizabethtown, Pa., m. Joseph Garlack, son John Garlach and ———.
2635. Christian, Elizabethtown, Pa.
2636. Henry, Elizabethtown, Pa.

Family of RUDOLPH HERR (793) and ANNA HOSTETTER.

2637. Abraham, Elizabethtown, Pa., b. Jan. 1, 1824; m. Oct. 26, 1843, Anna Reider, b. May 15, 1822; dau. George Reider and Catherine ———.
2638. Martha, Elizabethtown, Pa.
2639. Mary, York, Pa., b. Apr. 21, 1827; m. Dec. 25, 1856, John Shiffer, b. Nov. 16, 1827; d. Jan. 25, 1901; son Jacob Shiffer and Elizabeth Gepfer.
2640. Rudy H., Elizabethtown, Pa., m. ——— Shearer.
2641. John, Manheim, Pa., b. Jan. 11, 1834; m. Nov. 23, 1856, Barbara Peters, b. Oct. 2, 1838; dau. John Peters and Elizabeth Shank.
2642. Catherine, Mt. Joy, Pa., d. Nov. 11, 1900.
2643. Susan, Columbia, Pa.
2644. Eliza, Maytown, Pa., m. Hiram Beatty.
2645. Annie, Mt. Joy, Pa., b. July 8, 1830; m. Aug. 6, 1861, Samuel Shearer, b. Mar. 7, 1821.

Family of CHRISTIAN HERR (794) and MARY SHERTZER.

2646. John, Hagerstown, Md., m. Frances Miller, dau. John Miller and ———.
2647. Abraham, Hagerstown, Md.
2648. Mary, Hagerstown, Md., m. Abraham Breneman, son Abraham Breneman and ———.
2649. Tobias, Hagerstown, Md., m. Elizabeth Garlack, dau. John Garlack and ———.
2650. Elizabeth, Easton, Pa.

Family of Wid. CHRISTIAN HERR (794) and ELIZABETH FISHER.

2651. Christian F., Rohrersville, Md.

Family of ABRAHAM HERR (795) and MARY KREIDER.

2652. John G., Grand Rapids, Mich., b. Feb. 21, 1832; d. Nov. 29, 1899; m. Sept. 16, 1856, Leah K. Stauffer, b. Nov. 24, 1835; d. Oct. 5, 1899; dau. ———— and Elizabeth Kauffman.
2653. Abraham, Grand Rapids, Mich., m. Elizabeth Balmer.
2654. Martha, Grand Rapids, Mich., m. Henry Wertz, son David Wertz and Mary Walk.
2655. Mary, Grand Rapids, Mich., m. Henry Breneman.
2656. Benjamin, Grand Rapids, Mich., m. Mary Strickler.
2657. Frances, May, Pa., m. Levi Rhoads, son George Rhoads and Elizabeth ————.
2658. Elizabeth, Easton, Pa.

Family of MARY HERR (796) and ABRAHAM HERR (839).

2659. Susan, Elkhart, Ind., m. ———— Hershey.
2660. Jonas, Elkhart, Ind.
2661. Abraham, Goshen, Ind.
2662. Christian, Elkhart, Ind.
2663. Anna, Elkhart, Ind.

Family of JOHN HERR (797) and BARBARA LUTZ.

2664. Abraham, Quarryville, Pa., b. Sept. 29, 1844; m. Lavina Slegel, dau. Simon Slegel and Permelia ————.
2665. Levi, Osborn, O., b. Oct. 26, 1846; m. Mary Deal.
2666. John L., Windom, Pa., b. Apr. 18, 1849; m. Susanna Myers, dau. Rev. Samuel Myers and Magdalene ————.
2667. Henry, Hanover, Pa., b. June 17, 1851.
2668. Maria, Hanover, Pa., b. May 1, 1854; m. Oct. 1878, Ezra E. Myers, b. Dec. 31, 1854; son Samuel B. Myers and ————.
2669. David, Hanover, Pa., b. Feb. 4, 1857; m. Emma Hershey, dau. Samuel Hershey and ————.
2670. Barbara, Hanover, Pa., b. Oct. 22, 1863; m. Harry Shenk.

2671. Emma, Hanover, Pa., b. Dec. 27, 1865; m. John M. Frey, son Jacob Frey and Magdalene ———.

Family of CATHERINE HERR (798) and JACOB KREIDER.

2672. Abraham, Hanover, Pa.
2673. Mary, Hanover, Pa.
2674. John, Hanover, Pa.
2675. Catherine, Hanover, Pa.
2676. Elizabeth, Hanover, Pa.
2677. Frances, Hanover, Pa.
2678. Susan, Hanover, Pa.
2679. Tobias, Hanover, Pa.
2680. Jacob, Hanover, Pa.
2681. Martha, Hanover, Pa.

Family of ELIZABETH HERR (799) and MARTIN DOMBACH.

2682. Mary, Columbia, Pa., m. Jacob ———.
2683. Susan, Columbia, Pa., m. John Heagy.
2684. John, Columbia, Pa.
2685. Martin, Columbia, Pa.
2686. Henry, Columbia, Pa.
2687. Joseph, Columbia, Pa.
2688. Adam, Columbia, Pa.
2689. Amos, Columbia, Pa.
2690. Elizabeth, Columbia, Pa.
2691. Catharine, Columbia, Pa.
2692. David, Columbia, Pa.

Family of HENRY F. HERR (800) and KATHARINE BINKLEY.

2693. Mary, Columbia, Pa., b. July 2, 1847; d. Apr. 26, 1866.
2694. Elizabeth, Columbia, Pa., b. Feb. 4, 1849; d. May 16, 1905; m. Abraham Kauffman, d. Apr. 10, 1873.
2695. Christian B., Millersville, Pa., b. May 8, 1850; m. Oct. 3, 1875, Susan J. Young, b. Jan. 2, 1854; dau. Abraham M. Young and Elizabeth Johnson.
2696. Abraham, Lancaster, Pa., b. Aug. 28, 1851; m. Maggie Myers.

2697. Jacob, Neffsville, Pa., b. Jan. 1, 1853.

2698. Henry, Neffsville, Pa., b. Oct. 28, 1854.

2699. Catharine, Lancaster, Pa., b. May 13, 1856; m. Oct. 23, 1877, Benjamin Eshbach, b. May 27, 1854.

2700. John, Lancaster, Pa., b. Apr. 24, 1858; d. Mar. 31, 1864.

2701. Frances, Lancaster, Pa., b. Oct. 22, 1860; d. Mar. 21, 1864.

2702. Barbara, Lancaster, Pa., b. Mar. 23, 1862.

2350. Anna, Lancaster, Pa., b. Oct. 4, 1868.

Family of FANNY HERR (803) and RUDOLPH ELLENBERGER.

2703. Rudolph, Cambridge, Ind., b. Dec. 18, 1825; d. Apr. 2, 1833.

2704. Fanny, Cambridge, Ind., b. July 11, 1827; m. Sept. 12, 1847, John M. Hoover, b. Mar. 1, 1824; d. Sept. 27, 1867; son John Hoover and Elizabeth Myers.

2705. Mary, Cambridge, Ind., b. Mar. 6, 1829; d. Feb. 27, 1883; m. July 29, 1855, Moses Myers, b. Aug. 9, 1828; son Moses Myers and Barbara Heiney.

2706. Christian, Cambridge, Ind., b. Nov. 1, 1830; d. Feb. 24, 1860; m. Dec. 3, 1857, Catharine Leonard, b. Apr. 6, 1838; dau. George Leonard and Frances Schock.

2707. David, Cambridge, Ind., b. Oct. 20, 1832; d. July 18, 1837.

2708. Magdalena, Millersville, Pa., b. Feb. 15, 1835; d. Aug. 5, 1884.

2709. Neff, Cambridge, Ind., b. Dec. 8, 1841; d. Oct. 28, 1845.

Family of CHRISTIAN HERR (804) and ELIZABETH SHENK.

2710. Elizabeth, New Lisbon, Ind., b. Mar. 24, 1825; m. Nov. 29, 1846, John M. Wissler, b. Mar. 7, 1823; son Peter Wissler and Frances Martin.

2711. Frances, Arcadia, Ind., b. July 5, ——; d. Oct. 17, 1891; m. Henry Good.

2712. Jacob Neff, Cambridge, Ind., b. Dec. 24, 1829; d. Mar. 16, 1854; m. Sept. 19, 1850, Margaret E. Malin, b. Apr. 12, 1832.

2713. Catharine, Notherville, Ind., b. Jan. 16, 1832; d. Jan. 31, 1878; m. Tobias Gascho, son John Gascho and ———.

2714. Mary, Dublin, Ind., b. Apr. 8, 1834; m. Nov. 22, 1855, John W. Elabarger, b. Aug. 10, 1829; son Daniel Elabarger and Catharine Warfel.

2715. Anna, Cambridge, Ind., b. Aug. 25, 1836; m. Jan. 29, 1860, John Graver.
2716. Susan, Dublin, Ind., b. Apr. 7, 1838; d. Feb. 20, 1882; m. Isaiah Elabarger, son Daniel Elabarger and Catharine Warfel.
2717. Christian, N. Hampton, Ind., b. Mar. 28, 1841; m. Mar. 30, 1865, Catharine Byers, b. Mar. 22, 1844; dau. John Byers and Elizabeth Wingart.
2718. Benjamin S., New Lisbon, Ind., b. June 16, 1844; m. Feb. 22, 1869, Elizabeth Elabarger, b. Apr. 22, 1842; d. Aug. 24, 1898; dau. Daniel Elabarger and Catharine Warfel.

Family of JOHN FUNK (812) and MARTHA KAUFFMAN.

2719. Martha A., b. Nov. 27, 1831; d. Aug. 14, 1833.
2720. Barbara Elizabeth, Springfield, O., b. Oct. 22, 1833; m. Mar. 11, 1856, George S. Steinberger, b Aug. 10, 1830; son David Steinberger and Elizabeth Pence.
2721. Henry Jefferson, Springfield, O., b. Nov. 9, 1835; d. 1898; m. Aug. 30, 1859, Courtney Lemon, b. June 27, 1832; d. Aug. 25, 1884; dau. Nathaniel Lemon and Anna ———; m. 1888, Mary E. Baker, b. May 8, 1870; dau. William Baker and Mercinda Sneazley.
2722. Catharine C., Springfield, O., b. Feb. 21, 1838; m. Oct. 16, 1862, George W. Deaver, d. Sept., 1904.
2723. Rev. Isaac K., Brooklyn, N. Y., b. Sept. 10, 1839; m. Oct. 10, 1863, Elizabeth E. Turner, b. Jan. 20, 1840; d. Feb. 29, 1868; dau. James Turner and Jeanette McDonald; m. Mar. 15, 1869, Helen G. Thompson, b. Feb. 19, 1841.
2724. Christian C., Springfield, O., b. Feb. 25, 1842; d. Mar. 24, 1896; m. Nov. 2, 1870, Ida Olive Corbly.
2725. John A., Germantown, Pa., b. July 17, 1844; m. Oct. 12, 1871, Jennie M. Martin.
2726. Anna Martha, Springfield, O., b. July 18, 1849; d. May 25, 1900; m. Aug. 15, 1865, Dr. Brown F. Brownfield, d. Apr. 24, 1878.
2727. Benjamin F., New Brighton, N. Y., b. Jan. 21, 1850; m. Sept. 17, 1872, Cynthia E. Layton, b. Jan. 6, 1853; dau. Arthur Layton and Rhoda Lowman.

Family of JOHN HERR (816) and REBECCA OTTO.

2728. Infant, Altoona, Pa., b. 1848; d. 1848.

2729. John, Cessna, Pa., b. Aug. 2, 1849; d. Dec. 9, 1852.

2730. Henry H., Altoona, Pa., b. Dec. 16, 1850; d. Oct. 4, 1890; m. 1875, Lydia Smyser.

2731. Dr. Franklin Pierce, Ridgley, Md., b. Mar. 15, 1852; m. Dec. 23, 1881, Rachael L. Fries, b. Jan. 8, 1859; dau. Jacob Fries and Eliza Lingenfelter.

2732. William H., Altoona, Pa., b. July 30, 1856; m. Nov. 25, 1879, Clara S. Bobbits, b. Feb. 9, 1860; dau. Samuel K. Bobbits and Elizabeth J. Work.

2733. Mary Bell, Altoona, Pa., b. Sept. 5, 1857; d. Aug. 10, 1877.

2734. Frederick, Altoona, Pa., b. Apr. 18, 1859; m. May 6. 1885, Jennie Donnelly, b. Jan. 29, 1862; dau. William Donnelly and Sarah Gillan.

2735. Sarah Alice, Claysburg, Pa., b. July 9, 1860; d. Feb. 14, 1868.

2736. Hannah Elizabeth, Altoona, Pa., b. Nov. 17, 1861 ; d. Mar. 20, 1884.

2737. Minerva, Altoona, Pa., b. Feb. 14, 1864; m. Nov. 25, 1890, Charles Metzgar, b. Dec. 20, 1853; son David Metzgar and Elizabeth Levan.

2738. Cora, Altoona, Pa., b. July 30, 1866; d. July 14, 1898.

2739. George Elmer, Altoona, Pa., b. July 23, 1867; d. July 30, 1869.

Family of ABRAHAM HERR (817) and MARY MAGDALENA HERRING.

2740. Anna America, Indianapolis, Ind., b. Feb. 7, 1854; m. Dec. 16, 1874, Albert F. Wyon, b. Aug. 18, 1849; son Solomon Wyon and Catharine Ferry.

2741. Charles Edward, Mansfield, O., b. May 29, 1855; m. Jan. 18, 1883, Emma Anderson.

2742. Esther Eugene, Pasadena. Cal., b. Jan. 28, 1857; m. Sept. 6, 1876, J. S. J. Cox.

2743. Mary Catharine, Mansfield, O., b. June 20, 1858; d. July 8, 1858.

2744. Ida Belle, Indianapolis, Ind., b. Mar. 21, 1860.

2745. Mary Emma, Indianapolis, Ind., b. Aug. 31, 1864; m. Nov. 25, 1896, E. J. Willits.

2746. Abraham Seymour, Shelby, O., b. Feb. 28, 1867; m. July 3, 1889, Ella E. Foster, b. May 27, 1870; dau. Amos E. Foster and Sarah ———.

2747. Dr. Milton Frey, Indianapolis, Ind., b. Apr. 4, 1870.

Family of FREDERICK HERR (820) and HANNAH HARTZELL.

2748. Frederica Ann, Cashtown, Pa., m. George Stallsmith.

Family of HARRIET HERR (821) and JAMES A. MILLER.

2749. Susan Rebecca, Aspers, Pa., b. Jan. 15, 1850; d. Jan. 30, 1850.

2750. Clara Louisa, Biglerville, Pa., b. Mar. 12, 1852; m. Jan. 18, 1872, Peter H. Slaybaugh.

2751. Florence V., Biglerville, Pa., b. May 24, 1854; m. Dec. 9, 1875, Daniel S. Bricker.

2752. John Henry, Aspers, Pa., b. Aug. 19, 1855; m. Jan. 15, 1883, Alice Eppleman.

2753. Rosanna Margaret, Gettysburg, Pa., b. Mar. 12, 1859; m. Feb. 8, 1876, Howard Brame.

2754. Elmer Herr, Aspers, Pa., b. Dec. 16, 1861; m. Nov. 5, 1895, Laura Brame.

2755. Annie Jane, York, Pa., b. Aug. 21, 1867; m. Oct. 21, 1890, Jerome R. Emery.

Family of ELIZABETH ANN HERR (822) and JOHN F. SLENTZ.

2756. Mary G., New Chester, Pa., m. Nov., 1879.

2757. Ida B., Fairfield, Pa., m. Nov. 21, 1886.

2758. Julia Katie, Aspers, Pa.

2759. Sarah J., Gettysburg, Pa., b. Apr. 5, 1860.

2760. John Edward, Philadelphia, Pa., m. May 18, 1893.

2761. William H., Quarryville, Pa., m. Feb. 20, 1894.

2762. Eliza Margaret, Wilmington, Del., m. Dec., 1890.

2763. Charles Jacob, Gettysburg, Pa., b. Nov. 14, 1868; m. Nov. 6, 1894.

2764. Luther M., Gettysburg, Pa., b. Oct. 14, 1873.

2765. Franklin C., Philadelphia, Pa.

11

Family of CATHARINE HERR (824) and EPHRAIM H. MINNICH.

2766. Annie K., Gettysburg, Pa., m. George F. Young.
2767. Infant, Gettysburg, Pa.
2768. Infant, Gettysburg, Pa.

Family of REBECCA HERR (825) and ALEXANDER A. LECHLIDER.

2769. William, Hagerstown, Pa., b. May 3, 1862.
2770. Lillie May, Gettysburg, Pa., b. July 2, 1865; m. R. L. Hame.
2771. Francis Alexander, Hagerstown, Pa., b. May 12, 1867.
2772. Martin Luther, Mechanicsburg, Pa., b. Oct. 31, 1869; m. Nov. 8, 1893, Julia R. Houck, b. Jan. 24, 1873; dau. George Houck and E. Frencena Dudnar.
2773. Fannie Boyer, Hagerstown, Md., b. May 7, 1875.
2774. Leonora Grace, Hagerstown, Md., b. Dec. 2, 1879; m. G. A. Mantz.

Family of PETER HERR (834) and ELIZABETH RUSH.

2775. Fanny, Strasburg, Pa., m. John Krantz.
2776. Mattie, Strasburg, Pa., m. Christian Hoover (3762).
2777. Israel, Strasburg, Pa., m. Elizabeth Bleecher.
2778. Peter Witmer, Strasburg, Pa., m. Catharine Harnish.
2779. Anna, Strasburg, Pa., m. Maurice Mylin.

Family of ABRAHAM HERR (836) and BARBARA HOSTETTER.

2780. Mary, Witmer, Pa.

Family of BENJAMIN HERR (838) and MARTHA NEWCOMER.

2781. Barbara, Mountville, Pa.
2782. Elizabeth, Mountville, Pa.
2783. Anna, Mountville, Pa.
2784. Benjamin, Columbia, Pa.
2785. Elias, Columbia, Pa.
2786. Abraham, Columbia, Pa.

Family of FANNY HERR (840) and JOHN MUMMA.

2787. Elizabeth, Hempfield, Pa., m. Samuel Erb, son John Erb and —— Balmer.

2788. Christian, Hempfield, Pa., m. Anna Bowers, dau. Jacob Bowers and ——— Garber; m. Wid. Anna Barr, dau. John Hoffman and ——— Garber.

2789. Jonas, Hempfield, Pa., m. Mary A. Brubaker, dau. Isaac Brubaker and Anna Herr (842).

2790. Fanny, Hempfield, Pa., m. Joseph Hersh, son Henry Hersh and Rebecca Hershey.

Family of ANNA H. HERR (842) and JOHN K. HERR (942).

2791. Reuben H., Mt. Joy, Pa., b. May 14, 1839; m. Mary Reidlinger
2792. ———. Mt. Joy.
2793. Amos H., Creswell, Pa., b. June 30, 1840; d. May 25, 1905; m. May 28, 1861, Mary H. Doerstler, b. June, 1842; d. Dec. 13, 1905; dau. Michael Doerstler and Elizabeth Hertzler.
2794. Tobias H., Neffsville, Pa., b. June 30, 1840; m. Elmira Fry.
2795. Isaac, Maytown, Pa., b. Apr. 3, 1842; d. Feb., 1907; m. Anna Coble.
2796. Christian H., Maytown, Pa., b. Oct. 26, 1845; d. Apr. 28, 1846.
2797. John H., Salunga, Pa., b. Apr. 19, 1844; m. Dec. 5, 1865, Elizabeth Weaver Balmer, dau. Abraham M. Balmer and Elizabeth ———.

Family of JOHN E. HERR (843) and MARY SNYDER.

2798. Son, Millersville, Pa., b. July 4, 1848; d. July 4, 1848.
2799. Susanna, Millersville, Pa., b. Oct. 13, 1849; d. Apr. 15, 1852.
2800. Daughter, Millersville, Pa., b. June 24, 1852; d. June 24, 1852.
2801. Barbara, Milersville, Pa., b. Oct. 10, 1853; d. Nov. 12, 1863.
2802. Mary, Millersville, Pa., b. Nov. 27, 1854; m. John K. Shriner.
2803. Amanda, Millersville, Pa., b. Feb. 27, 1856; d. July 23, 1856.
2804. Fanny, Millersville, Pa., b. Aug. 4, 1857.
2805. Hettie Ann, Millersville, Pa., b. Dec. 5, 1859.

Family of SUSAN HERR (847) and Wid. DAVID SHELLY.

2806. Amos, Mt. Joy, Pa., b. July 30, 1857; m. May 14, 1878, Frances Nissley, b. May 13, 1858; dau. Christian Nissley and Frances Breneman.

2807. Elias, Marietta, Pa., b. Aug. 30, 1865; m. Jan. 8, 1889, Minnie Myers, b. July 26, 1868; dau. Edwin Myers and Elizabeth Hake.
2808. David, Marietta, Pa., b. May 13, 1863; d. Mar. 24, 1864.

Family of NANCY BRUBAKER (850) and Rev. CHRISTIAN BAKER.

2809. Christian, Millersville, Pa., m. Mary Shriner.
2810. Jacob, Millersville, Pa., m. Mattie Stehman.
2811. Henry, Millersville, Pa., m. Barbara Habecker.
2812. Anna, Millersville, Pa., m. John Landis.

Family of CHRISTIAN BRUBAKER (851) and SUSANNA BRUBAKER.

2813. John, Millersville, Pa., b. Mar. 14, 1826; d. Mar. 14, 1826.
2814. David, Millersville, Pa., b. Jan. 16, 1827; d. July 1, 1827.
2815. Jacob B., Millersville, Pa., b. Sept. 27, 1829; m. Maria Erb.
2816. Christian B., Bausman, Pa., b. Jan. 28, 1832; m. Anna S. Herr (2932); m. Mary Hershey.
2817. Mary, Millersville, Pa., b. Nov. 29, 1836; d. Mar. 9, 1837.
2818. Elizabeth, Millersville, Pa., b. Oct. 6, 1851.

Family of JACOB BRUBAKER (852) and MARY BRUBAKER.

2819. Christian, Millersville, Pa.
2820. Anna, Millersville, Pa., m. Emanuel Minic.
2821. Eliza, Millersville, Pa., m. John Myers.
2822. Mary, Millersville, Pa., m. Benjamin Hershey.
2823. Henry, Millersville, Pa., m. Anna Minic.
2824. Susanna, Millersville, Pa., m. ——— Wademan.
2825. Fanny, Millersville, Pa.

Family of Rev. CHRISTIAN HERR (853) and HETTIE CHARLES.

2826. Anna C., Liberty Square, Pa., m. Elias Wisler.
2827. Susan C., Millersville, Pa., m. Amos Shenk.
2828. Fanny C., Rohrerstown, Pa., m. Jacob Brubaker (8539).
2829. John C., Millersville, Pa.

Family of DAVID S. HERR (855) and ELIZABETH DENLINGER.

2830. Frances, Mountville, Pa., b. Dec. 12, 1841; m. Aug. 27, 1861, John L. Gamber (8504).

2831. Daniel D., Mountville, Pa., b. Feb. 28, 1845; m. Nov. 27, 1865, Adaline S. Harnish, dau. Michael Harnish and Anna Shenk.

Family of JACOB H. LANDIS (4189) and ANNA S. HERR (859).

2832. John H., Millersville, Pa., b. Jan. 31, 1853; m. Nov. 6, 1879, Elizabeth A. Thomas, b. Apr. 9, 1852; dau. Henry Thomas and Mary Daniel.

2833. Aaron, Windom, Pa., b. Dec. 25, 1854; d. Feb. 27, 1855.

2834. Mary Ann, W. Earl, Pa., b. Jan. 27, 1856; m. Dec. 5, 1876, Clayton S. Wenger, b. Aug. 14, 1850; son R. Joel G. Wenger and Annie M. Swarr.

2835. Susan, Lancaster, Pa., b. Dec. 2, 1857; m. Oct. 21, 1879, Linnæus R. Riest, b. June 14, 1855; son Simon Riest and Mary Rohrer.

2836. Elizabeth, Rohrerstown, Pa., b. Aug. 7, 1859; m. June 17, 1880, Henry L. Stehman, b. Nov. 2, 1852; son Hon. John M. Stehman and Eliza Landis.

2837. Fanny, Millersville, Pa., b. Sept. 27, 1861; d. July 10, 1890.

2838. David, Windom, Pa., b. Aug. 28, 1864; m. Sept. 6, 1890, Ella H. Shelly, b. July 22, 1866; dau. John Shelly and Mary G. Thomas.

Family of RUDOLPH S. HERR (860) and MAGDALENE LANDIS (4192).

2839. David, Lancaster, Pa., b. Oct. 12, 1853; d. Apr. 16, 1860.

2840. Anna, Lancaster, Pa., b. Dec. 24, 1854; d. Aug. 16, 1855.

2841. Susanna, Lancaster, Pa., b. Feb. 15, 1856; d. Aug. 22, 1856.

2842. Elizabeth, Lancaster, Pa., b. Mar. 14, 1857.

2843. John, Lancaster, Pa., b. Apr. 7, 1858.

2844. Rudolph, Lancaster, Pa., b. Oct. 17, 1859.

2845. Christian, Lancaster, Pa., b. Apr. 4, 1861.

2846. Abraham, Lancaster, Pa., b. Apr. 6, 1862; d. Aug. 7, 1862.

2847. Son, Lancaster, Pa., b. May 12, 1864; d. May 12, 1864.

2848. Son, Lancaster, Pa., b. Dec., 1866.

Family of DANIEL S. HERR (861) and CATHARINE GAMBER (8502).

2849. Susanna, E. Petersburg, Pa., b. Nov. 15, 1856; m. 1877, Jonas B. Nissley, b. Jan. 31, 1850.

2850. Mary, East Petersburg, Pa., b. June 20, 1858.
2851. Anna, East Petersburg, Pa., b. Sept. 15, 1859.
2852. David, Lancaster, Pa., b. July 28, 1861 ; d. Sept. 24, 1861.
2853. Daniel, Lancaster, Pa., b. Sept. 20, 1862.
2854. Rudolph, Lancaster, Pa., b. Aug. 6, 1864.

Family of MARY S. HERR (864) and PHILIP BAUSMAN.

2855. Susanna, Lancaster, Pa., b. Oct. 18, 1859; m. July 26, 1881, Andrew F. Frantz (6239).
2856. John H., Lancaster, Pa., b. Feb. 20, 1861.
2857. David Herr, Bausman, Pa., b. Mar. 6, 1864; m. Mar. 3, 1891, Annie E. Myers.
2858. Daughter, Lancaster, Pa., b. Sept. 20, 1868; d. Sept. 20. 1868.

Family of JACOB H. KILLHEFFER (872) and SUSAN HAINES.

2859. Barbara E., West Toledo, O., b. June 20, 1853 ; m. Aug. 10, 1882, John F. Kohne.
2860. Sarah E., W. Toledo, O., b. Feb. 22, 1855; m. Aug., 1879, M. W. Tshudy; m. Apr. 27, 1899, S. H. Harmon.
2861. Alexander C., Cleveland, Tenn., b. Oct. 3, 1856; m. Feb. 20, 1895, Mary L. Ayres.
2862. Catharine, Lancaster, Pa., b. Sept. 17, 1858; m. Jan. 25, 1880, Adam H. Herr (2399).
2863. Edmund H., Lancaster, Pa., b. July 13, 1860; d. Apr. 2, 1889; m. Feb. 3, 1885, Alice Erisman, dau. Henry Erisman and Mary ———.
2864. Mary H., Shoff, Pa., b. May 16, 1862; m. Nov., 1891, W. F. Wagner.
2865. Annie, Shoff, Pa., b. Jan. 4, 1864; d. Jan. 18. 1907 ; m. Apr. 30, 1885, Harry J. Lind, d. Dec., 1888.
2866. Josie R., Lancaster, Pa., b. Aug. 6, 1865.

Family of JOHN KILLHEFFER (873) and MARTHA KENDIG.

2867. Infant, Lancaster, Pa.
2868. Infant, Lancaster, Pa.

Family of HENRY H. KILLHEFFER (874) and ELIZABETH ERISMAN.

2869. Son, Millersville, Pa., b. Jan. 1, 1866; d. Jan. 1, 1866.
2870. Alice May, Lancaster, Pa., b. Dec. 8, 1871; m. Apr. 12, 1903, Samuel Joseph Brillhart, b. Oct. 24, 1873; son Jonathan Brillhart and Mary Frailey.

Family of ANNA HERR (884) and HENRY BEAR.

2871. Anna Eliza, Manor, Pa., b. Nov. 5, 1807; d. May 14, 1848; m. July 26, 1827, Benjamin Brackbill (1422).

Family of ELIZABETH HERR (885) and JOHN BAKER.

2872. Anna, Manor, Pa., b. Apr. 21, 1811.
2873. Magdalene, Manor, Pa., b. Nov. 17, 1813.
2874. Christian, Manor, Pa., b. Apr. 13, 1817; m. Mary Hostetter.
2875. Barbara, Manor, Pa., b. Aug. 24, 1821.
2876. John, Manor, Pa., b. Sept. 17, 1828; d. Oct. 9, 1831.

Family of HENRY HERR (886) and SARAH FORNEY.

2877. Anna, Hanover, Pa., m. Martin Wenger.
2878. Sarah, Annville, Pa., m. John Rinehart, son Joseph Rinehart and ———.
2879. John, Annville, Pa.
2880. Henry, California.

Family of ABRAHAM HERR (887) and ELIZABETH ENSMINGER

2881. Jonathan, Annville, Pa., m. Eliza Brightbill, dau. Abraham Brightbill and ———.
2882. Rudolph, Annville, Pa., b. Mar. 11, 1827; m. Jan. 7, 1847, Sarah A. Groh, b. Nov. 2, 1827; d. Mar. 17, 1899; dau. Abraham Groh and ———.
2883. Abraham, Annville, Pa., m. Elizabeth Moyer, dau. Martin Moyer and ———.
2884. Frances, Dayton, O., m. Peter Reist, son Jacob Reist and ———.

Family of SAMUEL HERR (888) and FRANCES LONG.

2885. Mary, Englewood, O., b. Oct. 6, 1819; d. Dec. 17, 1886; m. Nov. 28, 1838, David Rasor, b. Apr. 30, 1817; d. May 1, 1863; son Daniel Rasor and Elizabeth ———.

2886. Abraham, Brighton, Mo., b. July 1, 1821; d. Nov. 14, 1861; m. Mar. 26, 1846, Mary Stutzman, b. Mar. 3, 1822; d. June 19, 1881; dau. David Stutzman and Frances Long.

2887. Ann, Englewood, O., b. Apr. 7, 1823; d. Nov. 27, 1879; m. Nov. 16, 1843, Wid. Levi Falkner, b. Sept. 20, 1822; son ——— and Margaret Nicodemus.

2888. Fanny, N. Manchester, Ind., b. Sept. 8, 1826; m. Wid. Jacob Butterbaugh.

2889. Samuel L., Englewood, O., b. Apr. 6, 1828; m. Jan. 20, 1853, Catharine Hocker, b. Oct. 21, 1832; dau. John Hocker and Catharine Kern.

2890. Christian, Englewood, O., b. Feb. 2, 1830; m. Oct. 23, 1860, Julia Huffer, b. Nov. 1, 1841; dau. John Huffer and Sarah Olinger.

2891. Esther, Englewood, O., b. Dec. 1, 1831; d. Mar. 14, 1855; m. Mar., 1853, Wid. Henry Longenecker, b. Sept. 20, 1822.

2892. Elizabeth, Ludlow Falls, O., b. June 30, 1835; m. Sept. 14, 1852, John Heisey, b. Nov. 28, 1827; son Martin Heisey and Elizabeth Engle.

2893. Sarah, Union, O., b. June 25, 1836; m. 1855, David Shaw, b. Nov. 15, 1833.

2894. John, Willow Spring, Kans., b. Feb. 11, 1838; m. 1863, Harriet Spitler, dau. Jacob Spitler and ———.

Family of CHRISTIAN HERR (889) and ELIZABETH SHENK.

2895. Anna, Campbellstown, Pa., b. 1820; m. Reuben Reist, son Jacob Reist and ———.

2896. Joseph, Campbellstown, Pa., m. Elizabeth Horst, dau. Henry Horst and ———; m. Anna Herr (3915).

2897. Fanny, Campbellstown, Pa., m. Wid. Elias Brubaker, son Benjamin Brubaker and ———.   •

2898. Christian, Campbellstown, Pa., m. Sabina Snyder.

2899. Elizabeth, Campbellstown, Pa., m. Moses Brubaker, son Benjamin Brubaker and ———.

2900. Samuel, Campbellstown, Pa., m. ——— Brittenstine, dau. John Brittenstine and ———.

2901. Mary, Campbellstown, Pa., m. John Flickinger, son Samuel Flickinger and ———.

2902. Mollie, Campbellstown, Pa., m. Elias Brubaker, son Benjamin Brubaker and ———.

2903. Barbara, Campbellstown, Pa.

2904. Abraham, Campbellstown, Pa., m. Sarah Marks, dau. John Marks and ———.

2905. Lydia, Campbellstown, Pa., m. Jonas Snyder.

Family of ANNA HERR (891) and SAMUEL SHENK.

2906. Henry, Annville, Pa., m. Mary Kreider, dau. Christian Kreider and ———.

2907. Abraham, Annville, Pa., m. ———Moyer, dau. Martin Moyer and ———.

2908. Anna, Annville, Pa., m. Jacob Cornong, son Philip Cornong and ———.

2909. Maria, Annville, Pa., m. Henry Ellenberger, son Henry Ellenberger and ———; m. ———.

2910. Elizabeth, Annville, Pa.

Family of HENRY HERR (895) and FANNY SHOPP.

2911. Henry, Harrisburg, Pa.

2912. David Shopp, Harrisburg, Pa., b. June 21, 1833; d. Oct. 24, 1892; m. Dec. 28, 1854, Sarah Ann Neidig, b. Dec. 14, 1837; dau. Samuel Neidig and Elizabeth Miller.

2913. Eliza, Harrisburg, Pa.

Family of JOHN HERR, Sr. (897) and SUSAN RUDY.

2914. Catharine, Louisville, Ky., b. Mar. 5, 1796; d. Nov. 6, 1841; m. Sept. 17, 1815, John Hikes, b. Dec. 14, 1789; d. Aug. 20, 1874; son George Hikes and Barbara ———.

2915. John, Jr., St. Matthews, Ky., b. Apr. 11, 1798; d. Dec. 9, 1863;
m. Apr. 10, 1822, Susan Oldham, b. Apr. 10, 1804; d. Nov. 26,
1872; dau. Conway Oldham and Frances Ross.

2916. Frederick, St. Matthews, Ky., b. July 9, 1800; d. Dec. 23, 1848;
m. Feb. 4, 1821, Nancy Oldham, b. Oct. 18, 1801; d. Dec. 17,
1875; dau. Conway Oldham and Frances Ross.

2917. George, St. Matthews, Ky., b. July 6, 1802: d. Oct. 10, 1875; m.
Feb. 6. 1825, Sarah Simcoe, b. Jan. 28, 1808; d. May 3. 1873;
dau. Simeon Simcoe and Elizabeth Whayne.

2918. Eliza, St. Matthews, Ky., b. Aug. 26, 1804; d. Oct. 20, 1842; m.
Mar. 21, 1822, George Rudy, b. Sept. 2, 1794; d. Oct. 19, 1864.

2919. Alfred, Lyndon, Ky., b. Nov. 20, 1806; d. Jan. 31, 1884; m. Dec.
7, 1830, Mary A. Shirley, b. July 13, 1813; d. Apr. 16, 1884; dau,
Lewis Shirley and Elizabeth H. Broaddus.

Family of Wid. JOHN HERR, Sr. (897) and ELIZABETH WHAYNE SIMCOE.

2920. Emily, Lexington, Ky., m. John W. Oldham.

2921. Annie, St. Matthews, Ky., b. June 27, 1820; d. Oct. 27, 1894; m.
Oct. 8, 1840, Norbourne Arterburn, b. May 26, 1813; d. Apr.
9, 1878; son William Arterburn and Rachael Smoot.

Family of ELIZABETH HERR (898) and HENRY SWOPE.

2922. Jacob, Taneytown, Md., b. Aug. 14, 1793; d. Sept. 7, 1794.

2923. Eliza, Gettysburg, Pa., b. May 13, 1795; d. Sept. 4, 1863; m.
Mar. 12, 1812, Samuel S. Forney, b. Mar. 6, 1790; d. Aug. 2,
1879; son Adam Forney and Rachael Shriver.

2924. Dr. John, Taneytown, Md., b. Aug. 16, 1797; d. Sept. 3. 1871;
m. Apr. 12, 1825, Mary J. Boyle, b. 1800; d. July 30, 1846.

2925. Jesse, Taneytown, Md., b. Aug. 31, 1800; d. Sept. 21, 1805.

2926. Mary, Taneytown, Md., b. May 10, 1803; d. Apr. 17, 1840; m.
William Crapster.

2927. Caroline, Taneytown, Md., b. Oct. 11, 1804; d. 1805.

2928. Dr. Samuel, Taneytown, Md., b. Nov. 21, 1806; m. 1847. Henrietta Boyle, b. 1807; d. 1884.

2929. Daniel Herr, Taneytown, Md., b. Nov. 16, 1808; d. Apr. 9, 1873;
m. Margaret Bruce Scott.

2930. Clara A., Gettysburg, Pa., b. Feb. 17, 1812; d. July 1, 1860; m. June 10, 1847, Henry Wantz, b. Aug. 26, 1811; d. 1863; son Henry Wantz and ————.

2931. Henry, Liberty, Md., b. Mar. 4, 1817; d. May 3, 1897; m. May 20, 1847, Matilda Jones, b. Dec. 30, 1834; d. June 13, 1893; dau. Abraham Jones and ————.

Family of CHRISTIAN B. HERR (900) and ELIZABETH SHENK.

2932. Anna S., Millersville, Pa., m. Christian Brubaker (2816).

2933. Elizabeth, Millersville, Pa., m. Amos Funk.

2934. Adaline, Millersville, Pa.

2935. Susanna, Millersville, Pa.

Family of JOHN HERR (910) and ANN HESS.

2936. Martha, Quarryville, Pa., b. Oct. 16, 1831; d. May 21, 1900; m. David Keen, b. Mar. 4, 1825; d. Apr. 14, 1904; son Henry Keen and Julia Ann Mowrer.

2937. Catharine, Quarryville, Pa., b. Nov. 1, 1834.

2938. Benjamin, Quarryville, Pa., b. Sept. 20, 1837.

2939. Mary Ann, Quarryville, Pa., b. Mar. 9, 1840; m. Dec. 8, 1859, Adam Keen, b. Nov. 10, 1830; son Henry Keen and Julia Ann Mowrer.

2940. Amos Henry, Quarryville, Pa., b. Mar. 14, 1842.

Family of Wid. JOHN HERR (910) and MARGARET ANN RALSTON.

2941. Jemima C. Elizabeth, Camargo, Pa., b. Jan. 11, 1853; m. Dec. 22, 1874, Abraham Myers, b. June 28, 1837; son Jacob Myers and Susan McMichael.

2942. John Martin, Camargo, Pa., b. July 28, 1855; d. Nov. 12, 1894.

2943. William D., Camargo, Pa., b. Oct. 28, 1858; m. 1880, Frances E. Good, dau. Henry Good and Mary Charles.

2944. Anna M. L., W. Willow, Pa., b. Aug. 19, 1861; m. May 18, 1882, Henry Boettner, b. Dec. 23, 1860; son Constantine Boettner and ————.

2945. Emma E. L. S., Buck, Pa., b. Dec. 15, 1864; d. July 4, 1889; m. Mar. 24, 1882, Miller J. Ressler, son Rudolph Ressler and Elizabeth Gochenour.

Family of ELIZABETH HERR (911) and MARTIN BARR (1210).

2946. Cyrus S., Burnham, Pa., b. Aug. 5, 1832; m. Nov. 5, 1858, Mary
A. Riley, b. Aug. 17, 1833; dau. John Riley and Mary ———.

2947. Caroline Herr, Seymour, Ind., b. Sept. 10, 1834; d. Dec. 24,
1891; m. Jan. 10, 1860, Henry L. Uhler, b. Dec. 14, 1832; d.
May 30, 1885; son Levi Uhler and Mary Light.

2948. Salome E., Philadelphia, Pa., b. Oct. 26, 1837; m. Samuel B.
Sides, son Samuel Sides and ———.

Family of Wid. ELIZABETH HERR BARR (911) and JAMES CRESWELL.

2949. Catherine Kezia, New Providence, Pa., b. Oct. 13, 1840; d. Aug.
1, 1898; m. Jan. 7, 1858, John Eckman, b. Aug. 12, 1830; d.
Dec. 8, 1889; son Henry Eckman and Elizabeth Hickman.

2950. David Maris, Fairview, Pa., b. Oct. 25, 1842; m. ———; m.
———; m. ———.

2951. Emma Ann, Carmago, Pa., b. Feb. 23, 1845; d. Apr. 5, 1852.

2952. Mattie Adaline, Bellevue, O., b. Mar. 25, 1847; m. Dec. 9, 1869,
Hiram E. Snavely, b. Dec. 22, 1845; son Christian Snavely and
Elizabeth Howry.

2953. George Martin, Camargo, Pa., b. Mar. 21, 1849; m. Dec. 28,
1871, Christiana Keen, b. Feb. 17, 1852; dau. Christian Keen
and Sophia Althouse.

2954. Mary Jane, Camargo, Pa., b. July 23, 1851; d. Apr. 8, 1852.

Family of JULIA ANN HERR (913) and JACOB BARR.

2955. Rev. Gideon, Camargo, Pa., m. Catharine Binkley.

2956. Francis, Camargo, Pa.

2957. Catharine, Camargo, Pa., m. Daniel Sides, son Samuel Sides
and Maria Benner.

2958. Asbury, Camargo, Pa.

2959. David, Camargo, Pa.

Family of MARIA HERR (914) and JOSEPH SMITH.

2960. David, Bartville, Pa.

2961. John, Bartville, Pa.

2962. Catharine, Bartville, Pa.

2963. Sarah, Bartville, Pa.

Family of SAMUEL B. HERR (915) and MAGDALENA BRUBAKER.

2964. David Martin, Ashbury, Mo., b. Apr. 7, 1842; m. Sallie Heaps.

2965. Benj. Franklin, Paradise, Pa., b. Sept. 14, 1844; m. Sept. 12, 1867, Amanda L. Longenecker (3626).

2966. Catharine E., Bridgeport, Pa., b. Mar. 11, 1846; d. Apr. 7, 1852.

2967. Amos H., Bridgeport, Pa., b. Oct. 2, 1847; d. Apr. 11, 1852.

2968. Susan E., Bridgeport, Pa., b. Dec. 16, 1848; d. Mar. 31, 1852.

2969. Elias B., Bridgeport, Pa., b. Mar. 13, 1850; d. Apr. 2, 1852.

2970. Mary A., Bridgeport, Pa., b. Feb. 10, 1853; m. Jacob Steinman.

2971. Martha Ellen, Strasburg, Pa., b. Feb. 7, 1855; m. Henry S. Hersh.

2972. Emma L., Lancaster, Pa., b. Aug. 30, 1856; m. Apr. 9, 1876, John F. Johnson, b. Apr. 11, 1852; son William S. Johnson and Mary A. Erb.

2973. Alice E., Iva, Pa., b. July 15, 1858; m. John Zanders.

2974. Samuel J., Leaman Place, Pa., b. Nov. 23, 1859; m. Nov. 23, 1881, Ellen N. Gochenour, b. Aug. 30, 1863; dau. Simon S. Gochenour and Anna J. Breneman.

2975. Susanna C., Edmond, Kans., b. Dec. 1, 1862; m. Thomas Boling.

2976. Albert L., Strasburg, Pa., b. May 21, 1865; m. Emma Mowery.

2977. Addison F., Lancaster, Pa., b. Apr. 25, 1868; d. June 30, 1900; m. Namona Miller.

Family of CATHARINE HERR (916) and JOHN HERR (922).

2978. Mary Ann, Perry Co., Pa., m. Michael Miller.

2979. Amanda, Millersville, Pa.

2980. Benjamin, Millersville, Pa.

Family of BENJAMIN HERR (917) and MARY RANCK.

2981. Abraham, Bird-in-Hand, Pa., b. Feb. 25, 1827; d. Dec. 20, 1893; m. Amanda Groff, dau. Levi Groff and Martha Wenger.

2982. Jacob, Bird-in-Hand, Pa., b. Mar. 18, 1828; m. Dec. 6, 1855, Susan Myers, b. Nov. 16, 1828; d. July 24, 1884; dau. Solomon

Myers and Elizabeth Hoover; m. Dec. 7, 1886, Sarah Diller, b. Nov. 23, 1838; dau. Lewis Diller and Sophronia Grabill.

2983. Anna, Bird-in-Hand, Pa., b. Mar. 6, 1830; d. May 14, 1830.

2984. John R., Bird-in-Hand, Pa., b. May 23, 1831; m. Dec. 13, 1860, Anna Groff, dau. Samuel Groff and Mary Hoover.

2985. Benjamin B., Bird-in-Hand, Pa., b. Dec. 5, 1833; d. Oct. 10, 1864; m. Nov., 1859, Anna Hershey, b. Mar. 13, 1836; d. Sept. 22, 1860; dau. John Hershey and Martha Musser.

2986. Martin R., Bird-in-Hand, Pa.. b. Sept. 24. 1836; d. Apr. 16, 1894; m. Nov. 7, 1861, Hettie Landis, b. Apr. 19, 1838; dau. Christian Landis and Mary Landis.

2987. Margaret Ann, Bird-in-Hand, Pa., b. Nov. 12, 1838; m. Nov. 28, 1882, James Casey, d. Mar. 10, 1897.

2988. Elias R., Lancaster, Pa., b. July 12, 1845; m. Lydia Groff, dau. Samuel Groff and Mary Hoover.

Family of ELIZABETH HERR (918) and SAMUEL L. KAUFFMAN.

2989. John Herr, Lancaster, Pa., b. Nov. 1, 1840; m. July 4, 1865, Emma E. Longenecker (3623).

2990. Lewis, Lancaster, Pa.

2991. Margaret, Lancaster, Pa., b. 1845; m. Samuel Heidelbach, b. 1843.

Family of ABRAHAM HERR (919) and ANNA BYERLY.

2992. Abraham, May, Pa., b. Oct. 8, 1851; d. Dec. 17, 1853.

Family of MARY HERR (920) and ELISHA HAMEL.

2993. Robert, Quarryville, Pa., m. Mary Fritz.

2994. Mary Elizabeth, Quarryville, Pa.

2995. William H., Quarryville, Pa., b. May 11, 1852; d. Aug. 11, 1852.

Family of Wid. JOHN HERR (922) and CATHARINE TEMPLETON.

2996. Susan, Perry Co., Pa.

2997. John, Bird-in-Hand, Pa.

2998. Elias, Bird-in-Hand, Pa.

2999. Levi, Perry Co., Pa.
3000. Catharine, Perry Co., Pa.
3001. Adam Mann, Perry Co., Pa.

Family of ADAM HERR (923) and MARIA BRENEMAN.

3002. Fanny, Millersville, Pa., m. Daniel Shenk. .
3003. Mary, Millersville, Pa., m. Andrew Killheffer.
3004. Henry, Quarryville, Pa., b. Aug. 23, 1845; m. Mary A. Levenite, dau. Samuel Levenite and ——— Bitner.
3005. Lizzie, Millersville, Pa., m. Christian Neff, son John Neff and ———.
3006. John, Millersville, Pa., m. Fanny Neff, dau. Jacob Neff and ———.
3007. Benjamin, Letort, Pa., m. Ida Groff, dau. Isaac Groff and ———.

Family of MARY BARR (924) and DAVID NEWSWENGER.

3008. Daughter, Quarryville, Pa.
3009. Daughter, Quarryville, Pa.
3010. David, Lancaster, Pa., m. Eliza Clements, dau. Jacob Clements and Eliza Winters.
3011. Susan, Quarryville, Pa.
3012. Abraham, Quarryville, Pa.
3013. Benj. Franklin, Quarryville, Pa.

Family of CHRISTIANA BARR (925) and ELIJAH ESHLEMAN.

3014. Abraham, Camargo, Pa.
3015. Jacob, Smithville, Pa., m. Barbara Eshleman, dau. Benjamin Eshleman and Barbara Speck.
3016. Henry, Fairmount, Pa.
3017. Anna, Fairmount, Pa.
3018. Susan, Fairmount, Pa.

Family of FRANCES BARR (928) and HENRY S. HOOVER (1281).

3019. Emma, Quarryville. Pa.
3020. Anna, Quarryville, Pa., m. Amos Groff, son Benjamin Groff and Eliza Lefevre.

3021. Elam, Strasburg, Pa.
3022. Susan, Strasburg, Pa.
3023. Christian, New Providence, Pa.
3024. Frances, New Providence, Pa.

Family of ANNA BARR (929) and Wid. HENRY S. HOOVER (1281).

3025. Emma, New Providence, Pa.

Family of CATHARINE BARR (930) and GEORGE MOWRER.

3026. Mary, New Providence, Pa.
3027. Benjamin, New Providence, Pa.
3028. Susan, New Providence, Pa.
3029. Elizabeth, New Providence, Pa.
3030. Christian, Chestnut Level, Pa.
3031. Franklin, Refton, Pa.
3032. Catharine, New Providence, Pa.
3033. Emma, New Providence, Pa.
3034. Christiana, New Providence, Pa.

Family of ABRAHAM BARR (931) and ELIZABETH GROFF.

3035. Cyrus, Buck, Pa.
3036. Mary, Quarryville, Pa.
3037. Emma, Quarryville, Pa.
3038. Letitia, Quarryville, Pa.
3039. Elizabeth, Quarryville, Pa.
3040. Esther, Quarryville, Pa.
3041. Franklin, Mountville, Pa.
3042. Martin, Quarryville, Pa.

Family of CHRISTIAN R. HERR (932) and ELIZA BALMER.

3043. Henry B., Phalanx, O., b. Dec. 22, 1829; m. June 5, 1859, Elizabeth Stroeble, b. Apr. 6, 1839; dau. David Stroeble and ———.
3044. Daniel, Rock Hill, Pa., b. July 8, 1831; m. Feb. 22, 1854, Mary A. Eisenberger, b. Oct. 24, 1834; dau. Jacob Eisenberger and Elizabeth Myers.

3045. Maria, New Danville, Pa., b. Jan. 18, 1833; d. Feb. 2, 1833.
3046. Christian, Millersville, Pa., b. Jan. 8, 1834; d. Apr. 7, 1895; m. Aug. 17, 1854, Elizabeth Benedict, b. Feb. 16, 1833; dau. Amos Benedict and ———.
3047. Elizabeth, New Danville, Pa., b. Mar. 11, 1836; d. July 20, 1896.
3048. Emanuel, New Danville, Pa., b. July 31, 1838; d. Aug. 4, 1838.
3049. Jacob, New Danville, Pa., b. Feb. 28, 1842; m. Mar. 9, 1862, Barbara A. Kendig, b. Dec. 29, 1841; dau. Christian Kendig and Mary Frantz.

Family of Wid. CHRISTIAN R. HERR (932) and ELIZABETH BARR.

3050. Martin R., Lancaster, Pa., b. Oct. 11, 1846; d. May 17, 1901; m. June 10, 1869, Martha Kreider, b. Apr. 19, 1848; d. Oct. 13, 1893; dau. Henry Kreider and ———.

Family of EMANUEL HERR (933) and MARY MUSSELMAN.

3051. Peter, Millersville, Pa., b. June 1, 1841; d. Apr. 30, 1843.
3052. John, Millersville, Pa., b. Sept. 5, 1843; d. Jan. 24, 1895.
3053. Elizabeth, Millersville, Pa., b. Aug. 22, 1846.
3054. Mary Ann, Lancaster, Pa., b. Mar. 29, 1849; m. Henry Harnish.
3055. Emanuel, Jr., Millersville, Pa., b. May 13, 1852; d. Oct. 12, 1894; m. Elizabeth Charles.
3056. Jacob, Millersville, Pa., b. Nov. 15, 1854; d. Dec. 5, 1856.
3057. Amanda, Millersville, Pa., b. Jan. 14, 1859; d. June 28, 1896.

Family of MARY HERR (934) and JACOB K. SHENK.

3058. Christian H., Millersville, Pa., b. Oct. 25, 1833; m. Eliza Thompson.
3059. Anna Maria, Millersville, Pa., b. Feb. 6, 1836; d. Dec. 29, 1892; m. John S. Benner, son Christopher Brenner and ———.
3060. Daniel, Millersville, Pa., b. June 30, 1838; d. May 7, 1839.
3061. Jacob Franklin, Millersville, Pa., b. Apr. 13, 1840; d. Jan. 19, 1847.
3062. Elizabeth, Millersville, Pa., b. Feb. 26, 1843; m. 1860, Henry Bowman, b. 1835; son Jacob Bowman and Susan Grabill.

12

3063. Henry, Millersville, Pa., b. Aug. 25, 1845; d. Mar. 9, 1882; m. Ida Hoke.

3064. Abraham, Millersville, Pa., b. Mar. 21, 1848; d. Nov. 16, 1854.

3065. John Jacob, Lancaster, Pa., b. Mar. 21, 1851.

Family of HENRY HERR (935) and ELIZABETH BRENEMAN.

3066. Emanuel, Glen Roy, Pa., d. Mar. 17, 1898.

3067. Jacob B., Willow Street, Pa., m. Elizabeth Herr.

3068. Henry B., Quarryville, Pa., m. Levina Graybill.

3069. Benjamin, Quarryville, Pa.

3070. Margaret, Landisville, Pa., m. Mar. 6, 1879, John R. Stauffer, b. Oct. 25, 1848.

3071. Amos, Landisville, Pa., b. June 9, 1860.

Family of CATHARINE HERR (937) and JACOB HERTZLER.

3072. Christian, Millersville, Pa., m. Elizabeth Haverstick.

3073. Jacob, Landisville, Pa., m. Sarah Buckwalter.

3074. Rev. Benjamin, Lancaster, Pa., d. Oct. 28, 1906; m. Anna Hostetter, dau. Jacob ——— and ———.

Family of CHRISTIAN HERR (938) and MARY MYERS.

3075. Magdalene, Hatton, Pa., b. Mar. 23, 1830; d. Aug. 8, 1900; m. May 28, 1851, George Tanger, b. Oct. 30, 1824; son John Tanger and Ann Gochenauer.

3076. Samuel M., Hatton, Pa., b. May 4, 1831; d. Mar. 30, 1879; m. Jan. 8, 1852, Maria Kauffman, b. Jan. 15, 1826; d. Oct. 5, 1906; dau. Tobias Kauffman and Anna Johns.

3077. Mary, Hatton, Pa., b. July 20, 1832; d. Sept. 19, 1833.

3078. Christian K., Carlisle, Pa., b. Feb. 19, 1834; d. Mar. 29, 1905; m. Oct. 30, 1856, Catharine Spangler, b. Sept. 29, 1836; d. Nov. 27, 1878; dau. Jacob Spangler and Catharine Kunkle; m. Mar. 3, 1881, Sara Kauffman, b. Sept. 30, 1844; dau. John Kauffman and Martha Seachrist.

3079. Barbara, Salem Church, Pa., b. Nov. 12, 1837; d. May 17, 1899; m. Feb. 29, 1857, Manassa Lerew, b. Jan. 27, 1834; d. Nov. 26, 1860; son Henry Lerew and Rachel Belty Coovers; m. Dec. 20,

1866, Abraham Strickler, b. July 15, 1834; d. Sept. 2, 1887; son Ulrich Strickler and Catharine Hertzler.

3080. Jacob M., Allen, Pa., b. Jan. 22, 1844; d. Apr. 15, 1907; m. Nov. 5, 1867, Annie Hertzler, b. Dec. 3, 1849; dau. John Hertzler and Fanny Erb.

Family of DANIEL HERR (939) and SUSAN MARGARETTA HORNBERGER.

3081. Henry, Millersville, Pa., b. Sept. 11, 1831; d. Mar. 15, 1834.

3082. Daniel H., Lancaster, Pa., b. Jan. 14, 1835; m. Apr. 14, 1879, Emma L. Adams, b. Nov. 28, 1858; dau. Jacob Adams and Mary Strauss.

3085. Stephen B., Philadelphia, Pa., b. Oct. 8, 1836; d. Jan. 3, 1900; m. 1874, Amanda Murr, dau. George Murr and ———.

3084. Christian G., Lancaster, Pa., b. Jan. 7, 1839; d. Dec. 22, 1902; m. Emma Miller, dau. William Miller and ———.

3085. Susan Margaret, Lancaster, Pa., b. Mar. 9, 1840; m. John Kreider; m. John H. McCulley.

3086. Jacob, Lancaster, Pa., b. Mar. 4, 1843; d. Sept. 24, 1843.

3087. Catharine H., Lancaster, Pa., b. Nov. 10, 1844; m. Nov. 12, 1868, Samuel M. Frantz, b. Mar. 15, 1846; son Christian N. Frantz and Elizabeth Miller.

3088. Mary Magdalene, Lancaster, Pa., b. Feb. 18, 1847; m. Dec. 24, 1868, John L. Binkley, b. Oct. 28, 1845.

3089. Anna Elizabeth, Lancaster, Pa., b. Mar. 3, 1850; m. Dec. 25, 1874, Edgar M. Levan, b. Dec. 25, 1850; d. Aug. 22, 1890; son Isaac N. Levan and ———.

3090. John Peter, Millersville, Pa., b. May 10, 1852; d. Aug. 13, 1861.

Family of JACOB HERR (943) and MARY KREIDER.

3091. George, Baumgardners, Pa., b. May 27, 1847.

3092. Christian, Lampeter, Pa., b. Nov. 24, 1848.

3093. Jacob K., Lampeter, Pa., b. Aug. 9, 1850; d. July 17, 1902.

3094. Maria, Conestoga, Pa., b. Apr. 20, 1852.

3095. Henry, Conestoga, Pa., b. Oct. 4, 1854; d. Jan. 3, 1856.

3096. Catharine, Lancaster, Pa., b. Sept. 25, 1856; m. Samuel Gochenour.

3097. Elizabeth, Lancaster, Pa., b. Jan. 4, 1859.

3098. Barbara, Lancaster, Pa., b. Sept. 8, 1861 ; m. John L. Herr.

3099. Benjamin, E. Lampeter, Pa., b. Dec. 19, 1864.

3100. Lydia, E. Lampeter, Pa.

Family of CHRISTIAN S. HERR (958) and CAROLINE STONER.

3101. Martha Ann, Rosemont, Pa., b. Nov. 4, 1843 ; m. Feb. 18, 1867, John Peart, b. Mar. 31, 1840; son Daniel Peart and Elizabeth Hoenilie.

3102. Susan, Washington, Pa., b. 1845 ; d. 1860.

3103. Abraham, Morrison, Colo., b. Feb. 29, 1848 ; m. Agnes Bailey, dau. Marshall Bailey and Maria Bailey.

3104. Jacob G., Washington, Pa.

3105. Mary, Washington, Pa.

3106. Caroline, Washington, Pa.

Family of CHRISTIAN O. HERR (977) and AMELIA STONER.

3107. David S., Pleasant Grove, Pa., b. Oct. 11, 1844 ; m. Sept. 25, 1889, Mary L. Rhoads, b. Sept. 22, 1850; d. June 1, 1901 ; dau. Charles J. Rhoads and Jane Bell.

3108. Silas S., Pleasant Grove, Pa., b. Apr. 21, 1846 ; m. May 19, 1870, Adaline Frey, b. Dec. 1, 1852; dau. Frederick Frey and Elizabeth ———.

3109. Annie, Lebanon, Pa., b. Sept. 3, 1848 ; m. Mar. 31, 1870, Rev. Amos M. Stirk, b. June 15, 1838; d. Feb. 6, 1900; son Robert Stirk and Mary Snyder.

3110. Barbara, Lima, Pa., b. July 20, 1849 ; m. Nov. 5, 1872, Peter W. Pratt, b. May 12, 1847; son Thomas Pratt and Hannah Haycock.

3111. Mary Amanda, Brooklyn, N. Y., b. Mar. 29, 1851 ; m. Jacob Frey, b. July 18, 1849; son Frederick Frey and ———.

3112. Amelia, Altoona, Pa., b. Aug. 19, 1852 ; m. Oct. 3, 1877, David Ohlweiler, b. July 3, 1849; son Frederick Ohlweiler, and Anna M. Kuhl.

3113. Alice, Lancaster, Pa., b. Mar. 8, 1857 ; m. Oct. 25, 1882, John B. Fisher, b. May 9, 1855; son George Fisher and Catharine Brown.

3114. Christian S., Altoona, Pa., b. Oct. 3, 1860; m. Sept. 14, 1896, Nettie B. Peck, b. Feb. 20, 1864; dau. Isaac Peck and Esther ———.

3115. Jacob H., Altoona, Pa., b. Oct. 3, 1860; d. Dec. 3, 1903; m. Sept. 18, 1884, Mary E. Davis, b. June 19, 1864; dau. Amos C. Davis and Elizabeth Coho.

3116. Martha E., Lebanon, Pa., b. Dec. 29, 1862; m. July 23, 1885, Edwin U. Sowers, b. Sept. 1, 1864; son John Sowers and Catharine Uhler.

3117. Elmer E., Trenton, N. J., b. Sept. 16, 1867; m. Nov. 9, 1893; Catharine C. Dean, b. Mar. 6, 1874; dau. James S. Dean and Clara P. Patterson.

Family of DAVID O. HERR (977) and MARY ANN HUBER (3188).

3118. John, Creswell, Pa., m. Anna Gardner, dau. John Gardner and ———.

3119. Emma H., Millersville, Pa., b. Mar. 1, 1854; m. John Shenk, son Jacob K. Shenk and ———; m. May 26, 1901, Frank M. Miller, son John H. Miller and Mary Ann Book.

3120. Lizzie H., Goshen, Pa., m. Jacob Herr.

3121. Anna Mary, Creswell, Pa.

3122. Ida, Creswell, Pa., m. ——— Herr.

3123. Adaline, Willow Street, Pa., m. Aldus Mylin.

3124. Susan, Willow Street, Pa.

3125. Fanny, Willow Street, Pa.

Family of Dr. ELIAS B. HERR (980) and LIZZIE S. MILLER.

3126. Harry Miller, Lancaster, Pa., b. Apr. 14, 1856.

3127. Jacob Edwin, Lancaster, Pa., b. Apr. 23, 1863; d. May 20, 1882.

3128. Mary A., Lancaster, Pa.

Family of BARBARA HERR (981) and HENRY H. STEHMAN (3143).

3129. Olivia, Lancaster, Pa., b. Feb. 8, 1856; m. Christian Brubaker, son Jacob Brubaker and ——— Erb.

3130. Alice, Millersville, Pa., b. Jan. 17, 1858; m. Aldus Barr, son Benjamin Barr and ——— Buckwalter.

3131. Anna Mary, Landisville, Pa., b. Dec. 29, 1859; m. Jonas L. Minnich, son Simon Minnich and ——— Brubaker.

3132. Henry J., Millersville, Pa., b. Dec. 8, 1861; m. Ida Knatwell, dau. ——— and Harriet Shuman.

3133. Isaiah D., Mt. Joy, Pa., b. May 12, 1863; m. Lillie Mylin, dau. Eli Mylin and ——— Charles.

Family of ISAIAH HERR (982) and ANNA E. BRADY.

3134. Alfred B., Creswell, Pa., b. June 2, 1858; m. Jan. 3, 1878, Minnie M. Benedict, dau. Michael Benedict and Fanny Hiller.

3135. Emma, Washington, Pa., m. Jacob Mann, son Henry Mann and ———.

3136. Annie, Washington, Pa.

3137. Ada, Washington, Pa.

3138. Mary, Washington, Pa.

3139. Isaiah, Washington, Pa.

3140. Infant, Washington, Pa.

Family of ANNA HERR (983) and JOHN STEHMAN.

3141. Benjamin, Mountville, Pa., b. Nov. 22, 1826; d. Dec. 20, 1842.

3142. John B., Mountville, Pa., b. Aug. 15, 1827; m. Jan. 25, 1849, Anna Garber, b. Oct. 22, 1829; dau. Jonas Garber and Catharine Gamber.

3143. Henry H., Millersville, Pa., b. Sept. 4, 1829; m. Apr. 17, 1855, Barbara Herr (981).

3144. Abraham, Mountville, Pa., b. June 22, 1834; d. Nov. 26, 1866.

3145. Christian Bachman, Mountville, Pa., b. Apr. 18, 1843; d. Jan. 30, 1865.

3146. Hiram, Mountville, Pa., b. Oct. 23, 1842; d. Dec. 7, 1848.

Family of JOHN HERR (985) and ELIZABETH REINECKER.

3147. Anna M., York, Pa., b. Aug. 10, 1843; d. Sept. 25, 1881; m. Oct. 12, 1871, Prof. W. H. Shelly, b. Aug. 16, 1840; son Jacob M. Shelly and Elizabeth Snyder.

3148. Henry R., York, Pa., b. Sept. 15, 1844; d. Oct. 31, 1882; m. Dec. 20, 1867, Margaret Upp, b. Oct. 1, 1834; dau. George Upp and Eliza McIlvaine.

3149. Edward, York, Pa., b. July, 1846; m. Dec. 20, 1881, Emma B. Landis, b. Mar. 1, 1848; dau. David Landis and Elizabeth Ellint.

3150. Mary E., York, Pa., b. Mar. 7, 1848; d. Dec. 16, 1897.

3151. Lizzie, York, Pa., b. Apr. 7, 1849.

3152. John, York, Pa., b. Apr. 7, 1849; d. July 13, 1849.

3153. John, York, Pa., b. Aug. 18, 1850; d. June 23, 1851.

3154. George R., York, Pa., b. July 18, 1852.

3155. Michael, Philadelphia, Pa., b. Aug. 6, 1855; m. Oct. 25, 1882, Augusta Walz, b. Apr. 8, 1860; dau. Joseph Walz and ———.

Family of BENJAMIN HERR (986) and ELIZABETH STEHMAN.

3156. Hiram, Marietta, Pa., m. Charlotte Watson, dau. Nathaniel Watson and ———

3157. Betsey, Marietta, Pa., m. ——— Rohrer.

3158. Benjamin, Maytown, Pa., m. ——— Miller.

3159. Mary, Marietta, Pa., m. John Miller.

3160. Amanda, Elizabethtown, Pa., m. Henry Gish.

3161. Cyrus, Marietta, Pa., b. Mar. 29, 1846; d. Mar. 24, 1900; m. Nov. 3, 1869, Emma H. Sultzbach, dau. Henry Sultzbach and Helena Olberdorff.

Family of CHRISTIAN B. HERR (987) and ELIZA HALDEMAN,

3162. J. Haldeman, Columbia, Pa., b. Oct., 1837.

3163. Mary, Thornburg, Pa., b. July 15, 1839; m. Jan. 1, 1863, Joseph H. Brinton, b. Aug. 15, 1858; son Lewis Brinton and Anna C. Garrison.

3164. Anna E., Lancaster, Pa., b. Aug. 14, 1841; m. Mar. 26, 1863, Dr. Granville B. Wood, b. Nov. 19, 1834; d. Mar. 6, 1879; son Samuel Wood and Hannah Brown.

3165. C. Bachman, Millersville, Pa., b. Aug., 1843; m. Anna Hostetter, dau. Jacob Hostetter and Anna Witmer.

3166. Benjamin, Millersville, Pa.

3167. Albertus, Millersville, Pa.

Family of ABRAHAM H. HERR (989) and NARCISSA HOFFMAN.

3168. Austin, Washington, D. C., b. Mar. 13, 1852; d. Sept. 6, 1900; m. Nov. 13, 1873, Fannie W. Welch, b. Apr. 22, 1852; dau. James S. Welch and Jane ———.

3169. Warren, Baltimore, Md., b. Oct. 1, 1853; d. July 3, 1864.

3170. Mary, Harper's Ferry, Md., b. Feb. 22, 1855; d. Apr. 25, 1856.

3171. Rev. Charles, Jersey City, N. J., b. Oct. 20, 1856; m. June 14, 1881, Helen Dougal, b. Aug. 24, 1854; dau. William H. Dougal and Mary V. Adler.

3172. Frances, Chicago, Ill., b. Feb. 4, 1858; m. Feb. 10, 1880, William E. Niblach, b. Sept. 5, 1854; son William E. Niblach and Eliza A. Sherman.

3173. Henry, Washington, D. C., b. Sept. 19, 1859; d. Mar. 23, 1876.

3174. William, Washington, D. C., b. July 20, 1861; d. July 22, 1876,

Family of HENRY C. HERR (991) and MARY A. BRENEMAN.

3175. Henry, Mt. Joy, Pa.

Family of ABRAHAM DONER HERR (1001) and MARY ANNA MULVANEY.

3176. Franklin H., New York, N. Y., b. Apr. 19, 1846; m. Henrietta B. Higgins.

3177. Emma L., Lancaster, Pa., b. Sept. 15, 1847.

3178. Ernest Edwin, Lancaster, Pa., b. Feb. 20, 1850.

3179. Laura Kate, New York, N. Y., b. Nov. 5, 1852.

3180. Albert Doner, New York, N. Y., b. Jan. 17, 1855.

3181. Louis Theodore, Canton, Ill., b. Mar. 25, 1857.

3182. Albert William, Philadelphia, Pa., b. Sept. 23, 1859; m. Minnie Hughes.

3183. Clarence M., Philadelphia, Pa., b. June 22, 1861; m. Della Mc-Ewen.

3184. Harry, Chicago, Ill., b. Mar. 7, 1864.

3185. Julia, Canton, Ill., b. Jan. 18, 1866; m. Mar. 1, 1882, Dr. Louis Goettinger, b. Nov. 11, 1859; son John Goettinger and Elizabeth Spurlock.

3186. Mary Florence, W. Philadelphia, Pa., b. Oct 28, 1867; m. Maurice Goettinger.

3187. Fanny E., b. July 17, 1870.

Family of ELIZABETH KENDIG (1008) and JOHN HUBER.

3188. Mary Ann, Willow Street, Pa., b. July 18,, 1832; d. Nov. 19, 1876; m. Oct. 2, 1850, David O. Herr (977).

Family of BARBARA KENDIG (1010) and MARTIN MYLIN.

3189. Hon. Amos H., Lancaster, Pa., b. Sept. 29, 1837; m. Feb. 26, 1884, Wid. Caroline Emily Hepburn Powell, b. May 15, 1847; dau. John Hepburn and Caroline Wheeler.

Family of JOHN KENDIG (1011) and MARY HERR (1784).

3190. Martha Frances, Lancaster, Pa., b. Mar. 6, 1843; d. May 4, 1898.
3192. Addah Louisa, Lancaster, Pa., b. Nov. 18, 1844; d. Mar. 14, 1901; m. Nov. 15, 1864, Franklin H. Bare, b. June 7, 1840; son Martin Bare and Elizabeth Harnish.
3192. Martin Herr, San Jacinto, Cal., b. Nov. 18, 1844; d. Dec. 9, 1904.
3193. John E., Willow Street, Pa., b. Dec. 1, 1846; d. Dec., 1846.
3194. John B., Willow Street, Pa., b. May 21, 1849; m. Oct. 21, 1873, Susan Brackbill, b. Nov. 24, 1854; dau. Henry E. Brackbill and Maria Eaby.
3195. Mary, Millersville, Pa., b. Oct. 8, 1851; m. Christian H. Herr (4144).
3196. Elizabeth, Lancaster, Pa., b. Oct. 4, 1854.
3197. Barbara Alice, Lancaster, Pa., b. Mar. 17, 1859.

Family of ABRAHAM H. KENDIG (1013) and MARIA ROHRER.

3198. Lizzie, Millersville, Pa., b. Apr. 4, 1849; m. Tobias Brenk; m. W. H. Huber.
3199. Mary Ann, Millersville, Pa., b. Feb. 10, 1850; d. Oct. 3, 1865.

Family of Wid. ABRAHAM H. KENDIG (1013) and ELIZABETH SHEPHERD.

3200. Henry, New Carlisle, O., b. May 12, 1853; m. 1871, Harriet E. Davis, b. Jan. 27, 1853; dau. James Davis and Diana ———; m. Feb. 27, 1873, Mary Miller, dau. Abraham Miller and Barbara ———.

3201. John W., New Carlisle, O., b. Oct. 26, 1855; d. Dec. 18, 1855.

3202. Alice, New Carlisle, O., b. Apr. 7, 1859; d. July 18, 1863.

3203. Albert, New Carlisle, O., b. Aug. 3, 1861; d. Aug. 3, 1863.

3204. Susan E., New Carlisle, O., b. Nov. 12, 1864; m. Oct. 2, 1883, John Greider; m. 1894, Henry C. Williams.

Family of CHRISTIAN H. WITMER (1015) and MARIA S. MANN.

3205. Elizabeth M., Suspension Bridge, N. Y., b. Dec. 13, 1832.

3206. Jacob, Niagara Falls, N. Y., b. July 23, 1835; m. May 26, 1859, Elizabeth Young, b. Dec. 20, 1839; d. June 3, 1878; dau. Jonas Young and Lydia Hittle; m. July 15, 1880, Wid. Maria Hancock, b. Nov. 15, 1838; dau. William ——— and Rebecca Wenham.

3207. Abraham, Suspension Bridge, N. Y., b. May 26, 1837; d. May 10, 1899; m. E. Augusta Dart.

3208. John Mann, Niagara Falls, N. Y., b. Oct. 15, 1842; m. June 6, 1872, Julia A. Baer, b. Nov. 14, 1848; dau. Jonas Baer and Sarah Ann House.   (

3209. Fanny Maria, York, Pa., b. Jan. 12, 1844; m. Feb. 27, 1873, William H. Emig, b. Dec. 22, 1840; d. Mar. 9, 1899; son John Emig and Sarah Kniesly.

3210. Abraham, Suspension Bridge, N. Y., b. Dec. 13, 1832; d. Dec. 14, 1832.

3211. Son, Suspension Bridge, N. Y., b. Feb. 11, 1832; d. Feb. 20, 1832.

3212. Daughter, Suspension Bridge, N. Y., b. Feb. 11, 1832; d. Feb. 22, 1832.

3213. Son, Suspension Bridge, N. Y., b. Apr. 11, 1839; d. Apr. 11, 1839.

Family of ABRAHAM WITMER (1017) and CATHARINE STRICKLER.

3214. Son, Lock Haven, Pa., b. 1836.

Family of DAVID WITMER (1018) and FANNY MARTIN (2414).

3215. Anna, Niagara Falls, N. Y., b. Dec. 11, 1839; m. William A. McAuley.

3216. Christian, Niagara Falls, N. Y., b. Apr. 29, 1841; m. Matilda K. Schenck.

3217. Esther, Niagara Falls, N. Y., b. Nov. 2, 1842; m. ———— Crabtree.

3218. Fanny, Niagara Falls, N. Y., b. Oct. 21, 1844.

3219. Daughter, Niagara Falls, N. Y., b. Nov. 13, 1846; d. Nov., 1846.

3220. Sarah, Youngstown, N. Y., b. Jan. 21, 1848; m. ———— Canfield.

3221. Barbara, Youngstown, N. Y., b. May 11, 1850; m. ———— Lambkins, d. Aug. 18, 1882.

3222. Harriet, Youngstown, N. Y., b. June 17, 1852; m. Sept., 1871, ———— Schenck.

3223. David, Youngstown, N. Y., b. Jan. 10, 1859; d. Apr. 7, 1862.

Family of JOSEPH WITMER (1019) and CATHARINE KAUFFMAN.

3224. Maria, Suspension Bridge, N. Y.

3225. Katharine, Suspension Bridge, N. Y.

Family of TOBIAS WITMER (1021) and ANNA LONG FRICK (2421).

3226. Esther Elizabeth, Williamsville, N. Y., b. Sept. 9, 1838.

3227. Christian F., Williamsville, N. Y., b. Apr. 11, 1840; m. Sept. 4, 1878, Mary S. Cotton, b. Nov. 27, 1848; dau. Elisha L. Cotton and Mary A. Bunnel.

3228. Anna B., Tacoma, Wash., b. Oct. 14, 1842; m. Dec. 29, 1870, John V. Richardson, son John Richardson and Fanny Vinecke.

3229. Tobias, Jr., Buffalo, N. Y., b. Feb. 7, 1844; d. Dec. 26, 1898; m. June 19, 1878, Caroline Urban, dau. George Urban and Margaret Kern.

3230. Elvira M., Lancaster, N. Y., b. Nov. 27, 1848; m. June 16, 1875, Henry B. Zavitz, son Joseph Zavitz and Rebecca Miller.

3231. Catharine A., Williamsville, N. Y., b. Nov. 25, 1850; d. June 17, 1899.

3232. Mary E., Snyder, N. Y., b. Mar. 27, 1852; m. Sept. 5, 1882, Rev. Edgar A. Pardee, b. Nov. 21, 1847; son Augustus Pardee and Susan Newcomb.

3233. Ellen, Lancaster, N. Y., b. Sept. 27, 1853; m. Apr. 18, 1882, Levant F. Hillman, son Thompson Hillman and —— Ayer.

3234. Abraham L., Williamsville, N. Y., b. June 18, 1855; m. Oct. 31, 1893, Vinetta M. Strange, b. Sept. 20, 1870; dau. John H. Strange and Nancy A Gibler.

3235. Emily Ann, Niagara Falls, N. Y., b. Oct. 25, 1857; m. Dec. 31, 1885, Daniel Schmitt, son Daniel Schmitt and ——.

3236. Joseph F., Corning, N. Y., b. Nov. 25, 1859; m. Dec. 22, 1887, Virginia C. Jones.

3237. Victor M., Milwaukee, Wis., b. Sept. 3, 1861.

3238. Clara F., Buffalo, N. Y., b. Dec. 11, 1862; m. Sept. 9, 1885, Elmer E. Browning, son William Browning and ——.

3239. Alice V., Williamsville, N. Y., b. Oct. 8, 1865; d. July 13, 1887.

Family of FRANCES MARIA WITMER (1023) and JACOB S. LEIB.

3240. Abraham W., Fortuna, Mo., b. Nov. 3, 1849.

3241. Jacob H., Fortuna, Mo., b. Jan. 13, 1851; d. Jan. 9, 1854.

3242. Christian H., Well City, Mo., b. May 14, 1854.

3243. Joseph M., Excelsior, Mo., b. Aug. 29, 1856.

Family of ELIZABETH HABECKER (1033) and CHRISTIAN HABECKER

3244. Christian H., Rohrerstown, Pa., b. Oct. 22, 1853; m. Oct. 17, 1876, Susan F. Schenck, b. Oct. 13, 1852.

Family of MARIA HABECKER (1035) and Dr. PETER WISSLER HIESTAND.

3245. B. Frank, Millersville, Pa., b. Apr. 27, 1857.

3246. Ira C., Millersville, Pa., b. Sept. 6, 1860; m. Feb. 24, 1892, Elizabeth Yecker, b. May 31, 1868; dau. Blasius Yecker and Mary Schreck.

3247. Elizabeth, Millersville, Pa., b. July, 1862; d. Aug. 14, 1863.

Family of ESTHER SCHOFF (1036) and BENJAMIN LANDIS (4183).

3248. Frances M., Landis Valley, Pa., b. Jan. 31, 1837.

3249. John S., Landis Valley, Pa., b. Mar. 24, 1841; m. Dec. 24, 1862, Helen Hershey, b. Aug. 13, 1843; dau. John H. Hershey and Anna Staman.

3250. Benjamin H., Landis Valley, Pa., b. Nov. 23, 1852; d. Feb. 5, 1857.

Family of JOSEPH HABECKER (1037) and ANNA HERR (1835).

3251. Frank David, Sanborn, N. Y., b. Nov. 27, 1846; m. Dec. 12, 1888, Catharine A. Schenck, b. July 16, 1857; dau. Jacob Schenck and Myra J. Batchelder.
3253. Joseph H., Sanborn, N. Y., b. Apr. 6, 1851; d. Apr. 29, 1853.
3253. Benjamin J., Sanborn, N. Y., b. May 6, 1854; m. Feb. 6, 1884, Ella E. Metz (5412).

Family of BENJAMIN HERR (1043) and MARY ANN HERR (3748).

3254. Benjamin, Lancaster, Pa.
3255. Mary Lucinda, Darby, Pa., b. Mar. 19, 1855; m. July 27, 1871, Eli Huber, b. July 7, 1849; d. May 11, 1901; son Jacob Huber and Frances Aler.
3256. John Franklin, Lancaster, Pa., b. Dec. 26, 1857; m. Sept. 20, 1879, Annie Isabella Steube, b. Nov. 22, 1860; dau. John L. Steube and Fannie E. Brown.
3257. Martha Matilda, Darby, Pa., m. Benjamin F. Gaul.
3258. Naomi, Lancaster, Pa., b. Apr. 14, 1863; m. Nov. 9, 1881, Amet J. Kline, b. Dec. 13, 1861; son William Kline and Mary Renels.
3259. Susan, Lancaster, Pa., b. June 5, 1856; m. John B. Yunginger, b. June 10, 1856.
3260. Charles Dennis, Lancaster, Pa., m. Emma I. Engles, dau. Joseph Engles and Mary Mehaffey.

Family of DAVID CROFT (1052) and MARY FLEMING.

3261. Amelia, Allegheny, Pa., b. Jan. 22, 1851.
3262. Edwin, Longmont, Col., b. July 18, 1852; m. 1880, Sarah ———.
3263. Ida, Allegheny City, Pa., b. Mar. 19, 1854; m. May 17, 1881, Hugh A. Heckard, b. Apr. 1, 1855; d. July 25, 1895; son John Heckard and Caroline Montgomery.
3264. John, Allegheny City, Pa., b. Dec. 30, 1855.
3265. Arthur, Bakerstown, Pa., b. Nov. 5, 1857; m. Elizabeth Thompson.

3266. Alma, Allegheny City, Pa., b. Nov. 5, 1857.

3267. Bertha, Allegheny City, Pa.

Family of Wid. DAVID CROFT (1052) and SARAH SMITH.

3268. Sarah E., Allegheny City, Pa., b. Jan. 31, 1861; d. July 4, 1874.

3269. Clara, Pittsburg, Pa., b. Sept. 1, 1862; m. C. D. W. Caton.

3270. Flora, Pittsburg, Pa., b. May 13, 1865.

Family of MAGDALENE CROFT (1053) and J. B. CAMPBELL.

3271. James, Cincinnati, O., b. Oct., 1851.

3272. Anne Melissa, Pittsburg, Pa., b. Sept. 9, 1853; m. July 19, 1877, John G. Hall.

Family of SARAH CROFT (1054) and EPHRAIM McKELVEY.

3273. Henry C., Pittsburg, Pa., b. Sept. 17, 1858; m. July, 1886, Ida Dill.

3274. Frank M., Pittsburg, Pa., b. Aug. 20, 1864; m. Oct. 7, 1890, Mary I. McCormick, b. Oct. 4, 1860; dau. Joseph McCormick and Mary Espy.

3275. Edward W., Wilmerding, Pa., b. Jan. 9, 1866; m. Apr. 8, 1887, Harriet E. Lindsay, b. May 11, 1867; dau. Morris Lindsay and Sarah Leaman.

Family of JOHN CROFT (1055) and Wid. MARIETTA W. PIERCE.

3276. Sarah Annie, Pittsburg, Pa., b. Oct. 9, 1858; d. Apr. 21, 1886.

3277. Catharine Marietta, Pittsburg, Pa., b. May 20, 1862; m. June 21, 1882, Eugene B. McAbee, b. May 29, 1855; son Thomas H. McAbee and Mary J. ———.

3278. Bertha E., Pittsburg, Pa., b. Mar. 22, 1867; d. May 30, 1901; m. Oct. 1, 1887, Edward B. Reilly, b. Nov. 15, 1859; d. Mar. 30, 1901; son George W. Reilly and Lydia Ann Dennis.

3279. Minnie, C., Iola, Kans., b. Oct. 24, 1870; m. Oct. 3, 1894, Robert Langley, son Thomas Langley and Mary Ann White.

Family of SARAH HERR (1058) and JOSEPH SPANG.

3280. Charles A., Allegheny City, Pa., b. Sept. 16, 1870; m. Jan. 28, 1896, Jennie F. Waite, b. Oct. 30, 1870; dau. Thomas C. Waite and Mary Crawford.

3281. Joseph M., Allegheny City, Pa., b. Sept. 13, 1880.

Family of ELIZABETH HERR (1059) and SAMUEL H. SUTTER.

3282. Anna M., Sharpsburg, Pa., b. May 19, 1871.

3283. Bertha M., Sharpsburg, Pa., b. July 23, 1879.

Family of JOHN HERR (1061) and LOUISA J. RICE.

3284. Benjamin T., Bennett, Pa., b. Sept. 8, 1874.

3285. Ida Evelyn, Bennett, Pa., b. Dec. 1, 1876; m. Jan. 22, 1901, Philip Frendenberger.

3286. William Thorton, Bennett, Pa., b. July 12, 1879.

3287. John Albert, Bennett, Pa., b. Sept. 18, 1881.

3288. Lulu Edna, Bennett, Pa., b. July 21, 1884.

3289. Harry Wesley, Bennett, Pa., b. Nov. 13, 1887.

3290. Clarence Henry, Bennett, Pa., b. Feb. 1, 1890.

Family of BENJAMIN HERR (1062) and V. ELLEN WRIGHT.

3291. Mabel, Lancelot, Pa., b. Mar., 1881; m. John Kretzer.

3292. Nellie, Lancelot, Pa., b. Mar., 1883.

3293. Charles, Lancelot, Pa.

3294. Benjamin, Lancelot, Pa.

3295. Earl, Lancelot, Pa., b. Sept., 1889.

3296. Olive, Lancelot, Pa.

3297. Ada, Lancelot, Pa.

3298. Frank, Lancelot, Pa.

3299. Eula, Lancelot, Pa.

3300. Verne, Lancelot, Pa.

Family of MARY HERR (1063) and WILLIAM STEVENSON.

3301. Alda E., Warren, O., b. Aug. 4, 1886.

3302. Harry, Warren, O., b. 1888.

3303. William, Warren, O.

Family of HIRAM HERR (1067) and MARY A. JOHNSON.

3304. Samuel F., Aspinwall, Pa., b. Aug. 12, 1868; m. Sept. 2, 1896, Margaret E. Kerr, b. Feb. 4, 1870; dau. Milton B. Kerr and Mary E. Covert.

3305. Roland, Lanctster, Pa., b. Jan. 5, 1871.
3306. Andrew G., Minneapolis, Minn., b. Oct. 26, 1874; m. Oct. 16, 1901, Josie M. Watt, b. Feb. 2, 1877; dau. William T. Watt and Isabella B. Jones.

Family of MAGDALENA HERR (1069) and Rev. DAVID WILLIAMS.

3307. Anne Flora, Boston, Mass., b. Feb. 4, 1864.
3308. Stewart Herr, Philadelphia, Pa., b. June 18, 1868.
3309. Jesse Herr, Philadelphia, Pa., b. Aug. 11, 1870; d. May 7, 1898.
3310. Ira Jewell, Philadelphia, Pa., b. Nov. 20, 1872; m. Feb. 17, 1898, Mary H. Jones (3316).

Family of SARAH A. HERR (1070) and Rev. DAVID JONES.

3311. Robert Marshall, Pittsburg, Pa., b. Nov. 29, 1861; d. Oct. 13, 1891.
3312. Frederick, Pittsburg, Pa, b. July 27, 1864; m. Nov. 8, 1899, Catharine S. Taft, dau. Orrville W. Taft and Eliza Mallory.
3313. Charles H., Tifton, Ga., b. Oct. 25, 1866; d. Nov. 21, 1897.
3314. Ernest Elbert, Pittsburg, Pa., b. Apr. 9, 1869.
3315. Blanche Adaline, Pittsburg, Pa., b. May 3, 1871.
3316. Mary Horton, Philadelphia, Pa., b. Nov. 13, 1872; m. Feb. 17, 1898, Ira J. Williams (3310).
3317. Ethel Herr, Pittsburg, Pa., b. Apr. 2, 1876; m. June 9, 1898, Dr. Lawrence Litchfield, b. Nov. 8, 1862; son Gen. Allynore Litchfield and Susan Carver.
3318. Theodore Simpson, Pittsburg, Pa., b. June 26, 1878; d. July 17, 1888.

Family of Rev. JOSEPH DANIEL HERR (1071) and MARY E. WOOD.

3319. Rev. Benj. Laisdell, Delhi, N. Y., b. Nov. 18, 1861; m. May 16, 1885, Frances L. Frank, b. Dec. 15, 1861; dau. Alpheus N. Frank and Placontia Pitman.

Family of Wid. JOSEPH DANIEL HERR (1071) and ANNA M. GIVEN.

3320. Ella Elliot, Pittsburg, Pa., b. Sept. 11, 1868; d. Oct. 21, 1868.
3321. Mary Lillian, Boston, Mass., b. Oct. 10, 1873.

3322. Joseph Daniel, Jr., New York, N. Y., b. Mar. 6, 1877; m. Nov. 12, 1901, Bessie M. Miller, b. May 29, 1879; dau. Dr. Charles J. Miller and Jennie E. Moyer.

Family of BENJAMIN HERR (1074) and MARY HENRITZE.

3323. Charles John, S. Brooklyn, O., b. Feb. 23, 1861; m. Sept. 25, 1884, Ella F. Streigel, d. Feb. 28, 1889; dau. Conrad Streigel and Elizabeth Koch; m. Mar. 24, 1891, Pauline A. Bliem, dau. John Bliem and Anna Buchholtz.
3324. Mary, Cleveland, O., b. Nov. 15, 1862; m. ——— Gelkie.

Family of Dr. HENRY S. HERR (1078) and REBECCA A. BASH.

3325. Flora Belle, Cleveland, O., b. Sept. 28, 1873.
3326. Howard Henry, Cleveland, O., b. Oct. 20, 1878.

Family of ESTHER FEILBACH (1084) and GEORGE C. GUMBART.

3327. Charles, Macomb, Ill., b. July 13, 1864; d. Sept. 17, 1864.
3328. Louis F., Macomb, Ill., b. Nov. 25, 1865; m. Apr. 22, 1891, Eleanor M. Elting, b. July 23, 1859; dau. Philip H. Elting and Margaret McSperritt.
3329. Otto D., Macomb, Ill., b. Mar. 31, 1869.
3330. Georgianna, Macomb, Ill., b. Mar. 1, 1871; m. Mar. 9, 1898, Rev. Willis J. Sanborn, b. Feb. 18, 1865; son Joseph N. Sanborn and Ruth K. Smith.
3331. Conrad G., Macomb, Ill., b. Nov. 5, 1872.
3332. Elizabeth, Macomb, Ill., b. Jan. 2, 1875; d. Apr. 22, 1875.

Family of ELIZABETH H. FEILBACH (1085) and CHARLES A. BURROWS.

3333. Louisa F., Wapello, Iowa, b. Nov. 16, 1861; m. Oct. 20, 1902, Fosdick Fitzgerald.
3334. George G., Pittsburg, Pa., b. Mar. 19, 1863.
3335. Bessie, Parkersburg, Pa., b. Aug. 7, 1867; d. July 13, 1868.
3336. Carl A., Allegheny, Pa., b. Aug. 16, 1882; m. Jan. 16, 1906, Esther Jeanette Simon.

13

Family of **MARY M. FEILBACH** (1086) and **THEODORE LOUGEAY.**

3337. Alice C., Philadelphia, Pa., b. Nov. 12, 1870; m. Feb. 6, 1893, Joshua McClintock, son ———— and Penelope Hearst.

3338. Harry, St. Louis, Mo., b. May 12, 1880.

Family of **HENRIETTA FEILBACH** (1087) and **JAMES L. McKEE.**

3339. Edward, Brooklyn, N. Y., b. Sept. 20, 1870; m. Mar. 21, 1900, Emma Whitford, b. June 20, 1874.

Family of **BENJAMIN H. FEILBACH** (1088) and **MARY L. LANTZ.**

3340. Emma L., Pittsburg, Pa., b. Mar. 21, 1868.

3341. Bertha, Pittsburg, Pa., b. Nov. 25, 1870.

3342. Esther G., Pittsburg, Pa., b. Feb. 7, 1875; m. Dec. 24, 1900, Milton I. Kamerer, b. Feb. 27, 1880; son Jacob Kamerer and ———— Beyerly.

3343. Louis W., Pittsburg, Pa., b. Sept. 14, 1877; m. Oct. 23, 1900, Carrie M. Moore, b. June 10, 1876; dau. Irwin W. Moore and Elsie ————.

Family of **MARY E. HERSHEY** (1090) and **GEORGE LEHMAN.**

3344. Jessie Belle, Erie, Pa., b. Sept. 12, 1868; m. Apr. 16, 1896, Frank R. Callaghan, b. Aug. 10, 1867; son Jeremiah S. Callaghan and Eliza L. Reed.

3345. Elinor, Erie, Pa., b. Nov. 8, 1874.

3346. Sarah, Erie, Pa., b. Aug. 20, 1876; d. Dec. 23, 1896.

Family of **JOHN HERR** (1097) and **ELIZA MORRISON.**

3347. David H., Strasburg, Pa., b. Dec. 1, 1840; d. Aug. 14, 1845.

3348. Mary Jane, Springville, Pa., b. June 8, 1842; d. Mar. 17, 1872.

3349. Joseph B., Strasburg, Pa., b. July 1, 1846; d. Sept. 1, 1863.

3350. John Wesley, Gap, Pa., b. Mar. 4, 1853; m. Sept. 14, 1881, Elizabeth L. Wasson, b. June 27, 1838; dau. Usher Wasson and Annie Smith.

Family of ABRAHAM HERR (1099) and LEAH MAYER SOUDERS.

3351. Mary Ann, Lampeter, Pa., b. Dec. 19, 1831; m. Sept. 26, 1853, Dr. Aaron Witmer, d. Nov. 15, 1900; son Jacob Witmer and Sarah Lefever.

3352. Fanny, Strasburg, Pa., b. July 31, 1833; d. Oct. 22, 1878.

3353. Leah, Strasburg, Pa., b. Aug. 18, 1835; d. Nov. 4, 1847.

3354. Esther, Strasburg, Pa., b. June 18, 1837; d. Dec. 16, 1844.

3355. Susan, Philadelphia, Pa., b. Aug. 1, 1839; m. Dec. 25, 1863, Joseph E. Wenger, son John Wenger and —— Erb.

3356. Abraham H., Strasburg, Pa., b. Oct. 1, 1841; m. Mar. 6, 1866, Catharine Harnish, dau. Elias Harnish and ——.

3357. Christian M., Strasburg, Pa., b. Feb. 11, 1844; m. Feb. 5, 1867, Catharine R. Griest, b. Feb. 22, 1847; dau. Amos Griest and Catharine Eckman.

3358. Elam S., Kansas City, Mo., b. June 6, 1846; m. Jan. 28, 1868, Mary Barr, b. June 3, 1847; d. Aug. 30, 1902; dau. Benjamin Barr and Barbara Groff.

3359. Lavinia, Strasburg, Pa., b. Nov. 22, 1848; m. Oct. 31, 1876, Rev. Reuben S. Nolt, b. Feb. 23, 1848; son Jonas Nolt and Elizabeth Schreder,

3360. Emma L., Strasburg, Pa., b. Apr. 11, 1851.

Family of ESTHER ANN HERR (1102) and MATHEW BARTHOLOMY.

3361. Amanda, Lancaster, Pa.

3362. Mary Ann, Lancaster, Pa.

3363. Benjamin F., Lancaster, Pa.

3364. David H., Lancaster, Pa., b. June 4, 1848; m. June 26, 1872, Elizabeth Eckman (7679).

Family of JOHN HOOVER (1103) and MARTHA KREIDER.

3365. Samuel, Strasburg, Pa., b. Dec. 6, 1833; d. May 30, 1836.

3366. Frances K., Sterling, Ill., b. July 27, 1835; d. Nov. 7, 1903; m. Jan. 27, 1861, Mary Snavely, b. Nov. 22, 1839; dau. Jacob Snavely and Barbara Hess.

3367. Elizabeth, Marion, Pa., b. May 27, 1837; d. Sept. 1, 1842.

3368. Mary, Sterling, Ill., b. Dec. 21, 1839; d. July 15, 1862; m. Jan. 20, 1861, Abraham S. Weaver, b. Oct. 23, 1835; son Rev. John Weaver and Anna Snavely.

3369. Ann, Sterling, Ill., b. Sept. 24, 1842; d. May 26, 1889; m. Dec. 1, 1864, Wid. Abraham S. Weaver, b. Oct. 23, 1835; son Rev. John Weaver and Anna Snavely.

3370. Isaac S., Sterling, Ill., b. Jan. 1, 1845; m. Nov. 2, 1870, Mary Martin, b. Nov. 8, 1841; d. Sept. 30, 1894; dau. Samuel Martin and Mary Cox.

3371. Martha E., Sterling, Ill., b. Sept. 11, 1847.

3372. Benjamin F., Sterling, Ill., b. Oct. 22, 1849; d. Mar. 29, 1873.

Family of JACOB HOOVER (1104) and ESTHER HOFFMAN.

3373. Elias, Lampeter, Pa., m. Maria Kreider, dau. Henry Kreider and ————.

3374. Martha, Lampeter, Pa., m. Abraham Mellinger.

3375. Lizzie, Lampeter, Pa., m. Jacob Harnish.

3376. Mary, Lampeter, Pa., m. John Landis.

3377. Emma, Lampeter, Pa.

3378. Hettie, Lampeter, Pa.

3379. Jacob, Lampeter, Pa.

3380. Lavinia, Lampeter, Pa.

Family of MARY HOOVER (1106) and BENJAMIN LANDIS.

3381. Mary, Enterprise, Pa., m. David Long, son David Long and ————.

3382. Leah, Enterprise, Pa., m. Abraham Landis, son Benjamin Landis and ———— Frick.

Family of SUSAN HOOVER (1109) and JOHN N. LANDIS.

3383. David H., Sterling, Ill., b. Mar. 1, 1839; d. July 11, 1854.

3384. Mary Ann, Sterling, Ill., b. Sept. 9, 1840; d. July 24, 1851.

3385. Phares H., Sterling, Ill., b. Mar. 6, 1842; m. Dec. 23, 1875, Ann E. Shuler, b. Apr., 1857; dau. Frederick Shuler and Eliza Rosenburg.

3386. Abraham J., Sterling, Ill., b. Nov. 4, 1843; d. Jan. 16, 1869; m. Jan. 16, 1867, Anna F. Summy, b. 1841; dau. Daniel Summy and Anna Frick.

3387. Emma, Mt. Hope, Pa., b. Dec. 15, 1845; d. Dec. 26, 1849.

3388. Anna M., Sterling, Ill., b. Feb. 8, 1848; m. Dec. 10, 1878, Emanuel G. Landis, b. Dec. 9, 1844; son John Landis and Eva Good.

3389. Elizabeth, Sterling, Ill., b. Jan. 3, 1850; d. Feb. 2, 1861.

3390. John H., Sterling, Ill., b. Mar. 1, 1852; d. Mar. 6, 1852.

3391. Martha E., Glen Elder, Kans., b. Apr. 23, 1853; m. Dec. 25, 1873, Benjamin F. Landis, b. Dec. 25, 1850; son John L. Landis and Maria Hershey.

Family of MARTHA HOOVER (1111) and ISAAC WEAVER.

3392. Susan, Lancaster, Pa.

3393. Mary, Lancaster, Pa.

3394. Isaac H., Lancaster, Pa.

Family of LEVI HERR (1114) and LEAH WARFEL.

3395. John, Marticville, Pa., m. Frances Huber.

Family of HENRY G. HERR (1118) and NAOMI A. DILLER.

3396. Susanna B., Lancaster, Pa., b. Oct. 10, 1844.

3397. Mary Jane, Lancaster, Pa., b. Oct. 3, 1846.

3398. Diller P., New Holland, Pa., b. Jan. 31, 1848.

3399. Abby Ann, Bausman's, Pa., b. Feb. 19, 1850; m. Harry Bausman.

3400. John E., Rawlinsille, Pa., b. Nov. 24, 1854; m. Annie Trout.

Family of SUSANNA HERR (1120) and Wid. HENRY WITMER.

3401. Henry H., Paradise, Pa., b. Feb. 1, 1843; d. Sept. 22, 1864.

Family of ANN HERR (1121) and GEORGE LEFEVER.

3402. Susan Salome, Lancaster, Pa., b. Nov. 14, 1837.

3403. Franklin P., Bart, Pa., b. Dec. 17, 1839; m. Oct. 9, 1867, Catharine F. Ash, b. Sept. 18, 1846; dau. Franklin P. Ash and Mary M. Folmer.

3504. Benjamin H., Strasburg, Pa., b. Jan. 30, 1842; d. Feb. 8, 1848.
3405. Annie Maria, Strasburg, Pa., b. Mar. 13, 1845; d. Jan. 24, 1848.
3406. George Newton, Strasburg, Pa., b. July 31, 1850; m. July 31, 1874, Laura Long, dau. Addison Long and Mary Wilson.

Family of AMANDA HERR (1122) and AMOS L. WITMER.

3407. Ezra Herr, Nottaway, Va., b. Dec. 11, 1841; m. June 14, 1866, Anna B. Sweigart, b. May 4, 1840; dau. Charles Sweigart and Catharine Ranck.
3408. Ira David, Paradise, Pa., b. Oct. 5, 1843; d. Mar. 15, 1863.
3409. Susan Jane, Strasburg, Pa., b. Mar. 31, 1845; d. Nov. 12, 1874; m. Sept. 19, 1867, Aldus J. Groff (4245).
3410. Alonzo Potter, Paradise, Pa., b. Sept. 14, 1847; m. Oct. 26, 1870, Harriet A. Caruthers, b. Oct. 7, 1846; dau. Jason Caruthers and Sarah Pennington.
3411. Leah Dale, Philadelphia, Pa., b. Feb. 20, 1850; m. Jan. 28, 1880, T. Fillmore Caruthers, b. July 27, 1848; son Jason Caruthers and Sarah Pennington.
3412. Maria Louisa, Lancaster, Pa., b. July 7, 1852; m. Oct. 1, 1873, Emanuel R. Hershey, b. May 2, 1847; son Abraham Hershey and Barbara Eby.
2413. Evaline Juliet, Harrisburg, Pa., b. May 15, 1855; m. Jan. 28, 1885, Alexander W. Carlile, b. Dec. 3, 1854; son Samuel Carlile and Caroline Henderson.
3414. Jessie A., Lancaster, Pa., b. Feb. 20, 1857; m. Sept. 5, 1888, Hon. Charles I. Landis, b. Nov. 18, 1856; son Jesse Landis and Elizabeth Daniels.

Family of DAVID GROFF (1123) and NANCY GROVE (1322).

3415. Abraham, New Providence, Pa., m. Anna M. Starr.
3416. Benjamin, New Prividence, Pa., m. Hannah Brower.
3417. David, El Paso, Ill., b. Aug. 26, 1817; m. Barbara Grove (3882).
3418. Eliza, El Paso, Ill., m. Isaac Vanousdall.
3419. Nancy, El Paso, Ill., m. Samuel Dillman.
3420. Daniel, El Paso, Ill., m. Diana Grove (3883).
3421. Mary A., El Paso, Ill., m. David Jones.
3422. Henry, El Paso, Ill., m. Elizabeth Grove (3885).

Family of ANN GROFF (1124) and HENRY WEAVER.

3423. Anna, Lampeter, Pa.
3424. Fanny, Lampeter, Pa., m. Amos Lantz.
3425. Samuel, Lampeter, Pa., m. Martha Zittle; m. Rachael Zittle.
3426. John, Lampeter, Pa., m. Maria MacElroy.
3427. Eliza, Lampeter, Pa.
3428. Susan, Chester. Pa., m. George Lantz.
3429. Leah, Lampeter, Pa., m. Jacob Frailiph; m. Martin Cassel.

Family of BETSEY GROFF (1125) and EMANUEL KENDIG (2206).

3430. Elias, Roanoke, Ill., b. May 24, 1813; m. Elizabeth Wine.
3431. Benjamin, Washington, Ill., b. Sept. 29, 1814; m. Delilah Shot. well.
3432. Eliza, Washington, Ill., b. July 8, 1816; d. May 2, 1844; m. Dec. 12, 1833, Benjamin W. Kendig (1794).
3433. Abraham H., Fisherville, Va., b. June 8, 1818; m. Elizabeth Wenger, b. Jan., 1831; dau. Marion Wenger and Mary Grove.
3434. Mary, Fisherville, Va., b. Apr. 24, 1822; m. Wid. John S. Robison.
3435. Anna, Roanoke, Va., b. Feb. 8, 1824; m. Dec. 24, 1846, David Trout Fauber, b. Nov. 15, 1822; d. May 20, 1893; son Samuel C. Fauber and Jane Trout.
3436. Henry, Roanoke, Va., b. Oct. 30, 1825; m. Margaret Anderson.
3437. Elizabeth, Roanoke, Va., b. Jan. 18, 1828; m. H. B. Jones.
3438. Barbara, Roanoke, Va., b. Aug. 28, 1829; m. Jan. 25, 1849, James Rufus Gish, b. Jan. 24, 1826; son —— and Elizabeth Houtz.
3439. Ellen, Stuarts Draft, Va., b. Sept. 25, 1831; m. Joseph N. Brown.

Family of MARTIN HERR (1136) and MARIA BRUBAKER.

3440. Elizabeth, New Danville, Pa., b. Aug. 22, 1825; d. July 14, 1831.
3441. Susan, New Providence, Pa., b. Sept. 6, 1827; d. Feb. 29, 1848; m. Adam Baer, b. July 4, 1826; son Henry Baer and Susan Kendig.

3442. Hannah, Hagerstown, Md., b. Oct. 27, 1829; m. Oct. 15, 1850, Wid. Adam Baer, b. July 4, 1826; son Henry Baer and Susan Landis.

3443. Mary Ann, New Danville, Pa., b. Apr. 28, 1832; d. May 31, 1879; m. Jan. 3, 1853, Jacob L. Hess, b. Mar. 5, 1827; d. Apr. 6, 1897; son Jacob Hess and Elizabeth Light.

3444. Elizabeth, New Danville, Pa., b. Nov. 4, 1834; m. Dec. 9, 1856, Samuel H. Shenk, b. Feb. 3, 1829; d. Apr. 16, 1904; son Henry Shenk and Susan Hoover.

3445. Frances, New Danville, Pa., b. June 11, 1837; d. July 14, 1838.

3446. Magdalene, New Danville, Pa., b. May 31, 1839; m. Dec. 2, 1862, John B. Myers, b. Sept. 16, 1836; son David Myers and Barbara Burkholder.

3447. Martin B., New Danville, Pa., b. Nov. 8, 1841; m. Nov. 24, 1864, Anna H. Shenk, b. Feb. 20, 1839; dau. Rev. Henry Shenk and Susan Hoover.

3348. Barbara, New Danville, Pa., b. Aug. 21, 1844; d. Sept. 1, 1844.

3449. Rev. Abraham B., New Danville, Pa., b. Aug. 21, 1845; m. Nov. 12, 1867, Anna Ranck, b. May 8, 1840; d. Feb. 6, 1886; dau. Jacob Ranck and Susan Leaman; m. Sept. 27, 1887, Susan M. Shenk, b. Aug. 19, 1850; dau. John H. Shenk and Magdalena Musser.

Family of SUSAN HERR (854) and JOHN CHARLES (1025).

3450. Esther, Millersville, Pa., m. Joseph Habecker (1034).

Family of GEORGE L. HERR (1137) and MARY ELIZABETH HERR (1153).

3451. Levi, Tipton, Ia., b. Aug. 25, 1834; d. Feb. 22, 1899.

3452. Benjamin, Wilton, Ia., b. Apr. 23, 1837; d. Aug. 4, 1865; m. 1860, Mary A. Cooper, b. Nov. 11, 1840; dau. James Cooper and Amanda Cochran.

3453. Christian, Wilton, Ia., b. Nov. 21, 1839; d. Mar. 11, 1881; m. Dec. 12, 1863, Margaret Hyde, b. Dec. 12, 1849; d. Jan. 20, 1891.

3454. Mary Elizabeth, Tipton, Ia., b. Dec. 28, 1841; d. June 27, 1881; m. Mar. 15, 1865, Edwin D. Reeve, b. Dec. 28, 1839; d. Nov. 6, 1903; son Edward Reeve and ———.

3455. George W., Wilton, Ia., b. Mar. 24, 1844; m. Mar. 14, 1867, Susan Wallace, b. Apr. 21, 1850; dau. Thomas Wallace and Tacy Harris.

3456. Frances, Benton Co., Ia., b. Sept. 8, 1846; d. Aug. 26, 1871; m. Mar. 14, 1867, Charles Aldrich.

3457. Eliza Ann, Brush, Colo., b. Feb. 25, 1849; m. Dec. 19, 1867, Joseph A. Wallace, b. Sept. 15, 1847.

3458. John, Wilton, Ia., b. July 17, 1851; d. May 12, 1894, Floy Carl, d. Nov. 24, 1890; dau. —— and Sarah ——.

3459. Adaline, Afton, Ia., b. June 17, 1855; m. Reuben Nauman, b. Mar. 20, 1851; son Jacob Nauman and ——.

Family of ANNA HERR (1138) and JOHN BACHMAN.

3460. Eliza, Lancaster, Pa., b. Sept. 16, 1823; d. July 7, 1874; m. Abraham Warfel, son Abraham Warfel and ——; m Dec. 23, 1852, Martin F. Kendig, b. June 6, 1826; d. Dec. 1, 1885; son Martin Kendig and Mary Forry.

3461. Benjamin Herr, Sedalia, Mo., b. Aug. 6, 1825; d. Oct. 21, 1870; m. Martha Barr, dau. Samuel Barr and ——.

3462. Esther, Lancaster, Pa., b. Dec. 14, 1827; d. Jan. 11, 1904; m. Dec. 24, 1846, Simon R. Weaver (4321).

3463. Maria, Willow Street, Pa., b. Dec. 3, 1829; m. Henry Dabler.

3464. Lydia Ann, New Providence, Pa., b. Dec. 30, 1831; d. June 3, 1874; m. Sept. 25, 1855, Abraham Stoner, b. Jan. 23, 1820; d. Feb. 7, 1859; son Abraham Stoner and ——; m. Levi Leonard, d. Apr. 27, 1877.

3465. Hannah, St. Louis, Mo., b. Mar. 20, 1834; m. May 30, 1860, Christian Zercher, b. Apr. 20, 1834; son John Zercher and . Esther Shaub.

3466. Frances, Lancaster, Pa., b. Apr. 28, 1836; m. Israel Landis.

3467. Amos W., Philadelphia, Pa., b. May 30, 1839; m. Jane Ranck.

3468. John M., Lancaster, Pa., b. Aug. 6, 1841; m. July 21, 1865, Mary B. Harnish, b. Dec. 23, 1845; d. Jan. 13, 1872; dau. Jacob Harnish and Elizabeth Bare; m. Jan. 28, 1873, Susan Harnish, b. Nov. 20, 1842; dau. Jacob Harnish and Elizabeth Bare.

3469. Abraham, Lampeter, Pa., b. Aug. 13, 1843; m. Catharine Houser, dau. Jacob Houser and ——.

3470. Amanda, Lancaster, Pa., b. Feb. 4, 1846; m. June 18, 1865, Benjamin Weaver, b. Mar. 17, 1844; son Abraham Weaver and Eliza Kreider.

Family of CHRISTIAN HERR (1140) and SUSANNA STIVER.

3471. Ira, West Liberty, Ia., b. 1834; d. 1846.
3472. John, Lorimor, Ia., b. Oct. 6, 1836; d. Apr. 25, 1904; m. Sept. 27, 1860, Mary E. McVey, b. Dec. 15, 1839; dau. Cephas McVey and Tacy L. Gregg.
3473. Benjamin, West Liberty, Ia., b. July 3, 1839; m. Sept. 16, 1865, Rebecca R. Wilson, b. May 4, 1847; dau. David Wilson and Abigail Swem.
3474. Maria, Johnsville, O., b. Feb. 16, 1842; d. July, 1904; m. May, 1860, Joseph L. Reed, b. 1830; d. Nov., 1875; m. 1879, Rev. E. L. Briggs.
3475. Ellen, Salem, O., b. Oct. 31, 1844; m. Feb. 18, 1869, Milton A. Budlong, b. Aug. 24, 1848; son Milton S. Budlong and Guila Ann Alvord.
3476. Daniel, Puyallup, Wash., b. Dec. 31, 1847; m. Dec. 31, 1874, Cynthia A. Craven, b. Nov. 2, 1855; dau. John D. Craven and Eliza M. Duncan.
3477. Amos H., Pendleton, O., b. Jan. 17, 1851; d. Apr. 1, 1905; m. July 3, 1873, Maggie Dise, b. May 8, 1851; dau. Jacob Dise and Mary A. Light.
3478. Jane Swisshelm, West Liberty, Ia.

Family of Wid. CHRISTIAN HERR (1140) and SARAH JANE CHADWICK.

3479. Jennie, Akron, O., m. 1878, R. Decater Springer, d. Sept., 1885.
3480. Charles Sumner, Johnsville, O.
3481. Willard C., Akron, O.
3482. Oliver P. M., Akron, O.

Family of BENJAMIN HERR (1143) and ELIZA HERR (1370).

3483. Mary Ann, Smithville, Pa., b. Aug. 27, 1842; d. Jan. 10, 1880; m. Sept. 12, 1867, John Hart, b. June 7, 1839; son Samuel Hart and Susan Newport.

3484. Benjamin M., Lancaster, Pa., b. Oct. 8, 1844; m. Feb. 28, 1872, Elizabeth Rhinier, b. Mar. 18, 1854; dau. Daniel Rhinier and Elizabeth Beats.

3485. Eliza, Rawlinsville, Pa., b. Nov. 19, 1846; d. Jan. 23, 1882; m. Dec. 20, 1866, John P. Morton, b. Aug. 14, 1842; son John S. Morton and Ann Spence.

3486. Catharine, Rawlinsville, Pa., b. Jan. 12, 1849; d. Sept. 23, 1854.

3487. Hannah, Landisville, Pa., b. July 23, 1852; m. Dec. 25, 1873, George W. Hess, b. Apr. 21, 1850; son Samuel Hess and Leah Warfel.

3488. Susan, Salunga, Pa., b. Feb. 25, 1854; d. May 8, 1877.

3489. Samuel M., Salunga, Pa., b. Oct. 24, 1856; d. Dec. 7, 1885.

3490. Martha, Salunga, Pa., b. Jan. 15, 1860; d. Apr. 11, 1889.

3491. Emma, Lancaster, Pa., b. Feb. 24, 1864; m. Nov. 18, 1886, Jacob W. Harnish, b. May 21, 1865; son Martin Harnish and Susan Harnish.

Family of DAVID HERR (1145) and MARY HOWRY.

3492. Sophia E., Lancaster, Pa., b. Apr. 28, 1839; m. Benjamin F. Daily, son John Daily and Nancy ———.

3493. Frances, Lancaster, Pa., b. Aug. 27, 1841; m. Amos M. Sourbeer, son Reuben Sourbeer and Mary Musser.

3494. David, Columbia, Pa., b. 1843; m. Sept. 17, 1865, Mary Focht, b. Aug. 25, 1844; dau. Adam Focht and Margaret Rhinehart.

Family of FRANCES HERR (1147) and BENJAMIN W. LANTZ (4346).

3495. Ann Maria, Baumgardners, Pa., b. Sept. 15, 1847; m. John Kreider.

3496. Hercules, Altoona, Pa., b. Jan. 22, 1849; m. Georgia Barr.

3497. Hettie Ann, Dover, Del., b. July 28, 1850; d. Nov. 9, 1898; m. Pernial A. Bash.

3498. Frances E., Millersville, Pa., b. Sept. 4, 1852; m. Dec. 12, 1878, Michael S. Lefever, b. June 27, 1847; son Adam Lefever and Elizabeth ———.

3499. John, Lancaster, Pa., b. Sept. 16, 1854; m. Ella Stoner.

3500. Ida, Bird-in-Hand, Pa., b. July 4, 1856; m. ——— Stevens.

3501. Emma, Safe Harbor, Pa., b. Jan. 15, 1858; d. Dec. 25, 1864.

3502. Samuel, Safe Harbor, Pa., b. Sept. 12, 1860; d. July 2, 1865.

3503. Harry, Altoona, Pa.

Family of BENJAMIN SNAVELY (1148) and FRANCES HERR (1405).

3504. Ann, West Willow, Pa., b. Jan. 7, 1835; m. Jan. 8, 1863, Aaron B. Shenk (8652).

3505. Elam Herr, Herrville, Pa., b. Jan. 1, 1841; d. Sept. 29, 1853.

3506. Benjamin H., Lancaster, Pa., b. May 29, 1846; m. Oct. 27, 1868, Annie Herr (4106).

Family of ELIZA SNAVELY (1149) and MARTIN HERR (1162).

3507. Fanny Malinda, Wheatland Mills, Pa., b. May 23, 1845; d. Aug. 16, 1900.

3508. Martin Snavely, Wheatland Mills, Pa., b. Oct. 10, 1847.

3509. Eliza Maria, Wheatland Mills, Pa., b. Oct. 19, 1850; d. Sept. 8, 1851.

Family of FANNY SNAVELY (1150) and JOSEPH HERR (1414).

3510. Anna Maria, West Willow, Pa., b. Mar. 14, 1845; d. Oct. 7, 1864.

3511. Henry S., West Willow, Pa., b. Sept. 16, 1846; m. Feb. 23, 1881, Abbie P. Hess, b. June 30, 1857; dau. John B. Hess and Elizabeth McCrabb.

3512. Susan H., Buffalo, Minn., b. Dec. 6, 1848; m. Mar. 5, 1878, Christian M. Rutt, b. Aug. 23, 1849; son David Rutt and Martha Miller.

3513. Christian S., Lancaster, Pa., b. Oct. 26, 1852; d. Apr. 15, 1902; m. Ellen K. Baker, dau. David Baker and Catharine Kauffman; m. Sue Yecker.

Family of ANN SNAVELY (1152) and FRANCIS MYLIN.

3514. Maria, New Providence, Pa.

Family of DAVID H. BRACKBILL (1159) and Wid. MARTHA B. REILEY.

3515. Ann Maria, Lancaster, Pa., b. Apr. 20, 1865; m. Nov. 16, 1886, Charles F. Seachrist, b. July 9, 1862; son John C. Seachrist and Catherine ———.

Family of ELIZA ANN BRACKBILL (1160) and JOHN MUSSELMAN.

3516. Franklin B., Strasburg, Pa., b. Mar. 30, 1835; m. Dec. 15, 1858, M. Adrian Musser (4875).

3517. Milton M., Wheatland Mills, Pa., b. Apr. 17, 1837; d. June 5, 1842.

3518. Christian, Lancaster, Pa., b. Jan. 18, 1839; d. Feb. 4, 1908; m. Oct. 11, 1864, M. Luetta Musser (4885).

3519. Ann Eliza, Wheatland Mills, Pa., b. Jan. 13, 1841; d. Feb. 7, 1841.

3520. Emma S., Lancaster, Pa., b. Apr. 24, 1842; m. Oct. 4, 1866, Dr. Ambrose J. Herr (4867).

3521. Martha M., Lancaster, Pa., b. Nov. 12, 1843.

3522. Barbara A., Lancaster, Pa., b. Dec. 13, 1845.

3523. Eliza Ann, Lampeter, Pa., b. May 27, 1848; d. June 14, 1885; m. Oct. 27, 1868, Dr. John Henry Musser (4876).

3524. Mary Myra, Lancaster, Pa., b. July 20, 1850; m. Nov. 24, 1875, Dr. Henry E. Musser (4644).

3525. Harriet F., Refton, Pa., b. Oct. 24, 1852; d. May 30, 1878; m. Oct. 14, 1874, Reuben D. Herr (4113).

3526. Ada Louisa, Wheatland Mills, Pa., b. Oct. 24, 1852; d. June 13, 1855.

Family of FRANCIS HERR (1161) and LYDIA BARR.

3527. Christiana, Slackwater, Pa., b. Feb. 24, 1826; m. Nov. 15, 1849, Nathaniel Mayer, b. June 3, 1827; son Christian Mayer and Mary Miller.

3528. Catharine, Slackwater, Pa., b. Apr. 15, 1829; m. Henry Stehman, son Tobias Stehman and Mary Mylin.

Family of BETSEY HERR (1164) and FREDERICK ZARRACHER.

3529. Benj. Franklin, Crookston, Minn., b. Oct. 29, 1844; m. Feb. 25, 1871, Annie Hennings, b. May 6, 1837; dau. Saxe Hennings and Betsey Guthern.

3530. Christiana, Philadelphia, Pa., b. Jan. 24, 1849; m. Oct. 5, 1868, Edwin C. Kelley, b. Feb. 13, 1844; son Peter Kelley and Elizabeth Cooper.

3531. Martin H., Harrisburg, Pa., d. 1861.

Family of **HENRY ECKMAN** (1165) and **ELIZABETH McMULLEN.**

3532. Jacob, Jackson, Mich.
3533. Henry, Lancaster, Pa., b. Apr. 23, 1827; d. Mar. 3, 1882; m. May 4, 1848, Anna Hoke, b. Jan. 28, 1825; d. Nov. 23, 1893; dau. Joseph L. Hoke and Sarah Mehaffy.
3534. Hester, Mapleton, O., m. Grabill Binkley, b. Jan. 7, ——.
3535. John B., Lampeter, Pa., d. infant.

Family of **ANN MARTIN** (1167) and **JONATHAN BUSHONG.**

3536. Hiram, Lancaster, Pa.
3537. Levi, Lancaster, Pa.
3538. Leah, Lancaster, Pa., m. Jacob Shaub.
3539. Martha, Lancaster, Pa., b. Mar. 11, 1819.
3540. Jonathan, Lancaster, Pa.

Family of **MATTIE MARTIN** (1168) and **HENRY MEHAFFY.**

3541. John, West Willow, Pa., b. Apr. 1, 1828; m. Catharine Pfoutz, b. June 9, 1834; dau. Jacob Pfoutz and Catharine Harnish.
3542. Lydia Ann, Lancaster, Pa., b. Oct. 3, 1832; d. Mar. 14, 1892; m. Sept. 26, 1850, George Byerly, b. July 7, 1823; d. Jan. 28, 1897; son George Byerly and Mary Klink.
3543. Ann, Conestoga Center, Pa., b. 1840; d. 1884.

Family of **GEORGE MARTIN** (1170) and **ALICE ANN SHAUB** (1719).

3544. Mattie, E. Germantown, Ind., b. Sept. 2, 1821; d. 1882; m. George Wiker, son George Wiker and ———.
3545. John, Gap, Pa., b. Mar. 10, 1823; d. Oct. 7, 1894, Mary Breneman, dau. Melchoir Breneman and ———.
3546. Catharine, Rawlinsville, Pa., b. June 16, 1825; d. Jan. 3, 1900; m. Nov. 26, 1846, George W. Drumm, b. Sept. 6, 1824; d. Aug. 1, 1900; son George Drumm and Mary Creamer.
3547. Elizabeth, Rawlinsville, Pa., b. Nov. 8, 1827; d. June 3, 1889; m. Nov. 15, 1849, Christian Hackman, b. Feb. 26, 1826; d. Apr. 12, 1889; son Henry Hackman and Susan Aument.

Family of Wid. GEORGE MARTIN (1170) and Wid. ANN TANGER.

3548. Samuel, Lancaster, Pa., b. Apr. 12, 1835; d. July 27, 1868; m. July 29, 1858, Emma Miller, b. July 14, 1837; dau. John Miller and Esther Kreider.

3549. Ann, Lancaster, Pa., b. Dec. 12, 1836; m. 1866, Samuel Drumm, son Peter Drumm and ———.

3550. Hannah, Lancaster, Pa., b. July 11, 1838; d. June 19, 1886.

3551. Jacob, Lancaster, Pa., b. Mar. 7, 1841; d. Mar. 17, 1876; m. 1862, Anna Gast, b. Sept. 24, 1843; dau. Christian Gast and Maria Eckert.

3552. Henry C., Lancaster, Pa., b. July 6, 1844; m. Mar. 16, 1869, Mary L. Eichler, b. Feb. 6, 1848; dau. Simon Eichler and Mary Ann Peterman.

3553. Mary, Lancaster, Pa., b. Feb. 6, 1847.

Family of HENRY MARTIN (1171) and CATHARINE SMITH.

3554. John E., Lancaster, Pa., m. ———Shirk, dau. H. ——— and Mary A. ———.

3555. Pamella, Lancaster, Pa., m. William Baldwin., son Anthony W. Baldwin and Maria Bowman; m. George Beck.

3556. Sidon, Lancaster, Pa.

3557. Samuel, Safe Harbor, Pa., b. Nov. 11, 1836; m. May 21, 1861, Lizzie J. Kenersley, b. Mar. 29, 1838; dau. John Kenersly and Elizabeth Fluck.

3558. Catharine, Lancaster, Pa.

3559. Letitia, Lancaster, Pa.

3560. Lillie, Lancaster, Pa.

3561. Henry, Lancaster, Pa.

Family of ELIZABETH MARTIN (1172) and JOHN E. LEFEVRE.

3562. George Martin, Hubers, Pa., b. July 9, 1833; m. Dec. 10, 1855, Susanna Winters, b. Sept. 29, 1837; dau. Michael Winters and Mary Stoneroad; m. Mary Ann Winters, dau. Silas Winters and Catharine ———.

3563. Susan, Hubers, Pa., m. Benjamin Shaub.

3564. John H., Camargo, Pa.

3565. Harrison, Aurora, Ill., m. Catharine Harmon, dau. Henry Harmon and ———.
3566. Abraham, Quarryville, Pa.
3567. Eliza Ann, Lancaster, Pa.
3568. Abner, Lancaster, Pa.
3569. Daniel, Lancaster, Pa.

Family of SAMUEL MARTIN (1173) and MARIA MARRON.

3570. George, Lancaster, Pa.
3571. John, Lancaster, Pa.
3572. Martha, Lancaster, Pa., m. ——— Hurslock.
3573. Samuel, Safe Harbor, Pa.

Family of EDWARD KENDIG (1174) and Wid. SARAH KISSECKER.

3574. Christian, Middletown, Pa.

Family of HENRY S. KENDIG (1183) and LAMYRA V. PITTENGER.

3575. Harry D., Denver, Colo., b. Mar. 17, 1857; m. May 24, 1882, Sarah E. Petry, b. July 17, 1858; dau. John N. Petry and Miriam Newton.

Family of MARGARET KENDIG (1186) and DAVID WEAVER.

3576. Mary, Willow Street, Pa., m. George Hastings.
3577. Harry, Reading, Pa.
3578. Elizabeth, Witers Mill, Pa., m. Jacob Worth.

Family of SAMUEL KENDIG (1188) and CATHARINE AUMENT.

3579. George, Philadelphia, Pa., m. Maggie B. Lefever, dau. Daniel Lefever and ———.
3580. Samuel C., Chicago, Ill.
3581. Eliza, Lancaster, Pa.
3582. Scott, Lancaster, Pa.

Family of MICHAEL KENDIG (1189) and CATHARINE SHELLY.

3583. Maria, Middletown, Pa., b. May 19, 1844; m. John Phillips.
3584. Lizzie, Manheim, Pa., b. Aug. 6, 1847; m. Price Shull.

3585. William, Manheim, Pa., b. Oct. 31, 1848; d. Dec. 25, 1893.
3586. Annie S., Manheim, Pa., b. June 29, 1850; m. Nov. 15, 1874, Jacob S. Shaeffer.
3587. Justine, Manheim, Pa., b. July 3, 1851.
3588. Abraham, Middletown, Pa., b. Dec. 25, 1852.
3589. Henry S., Royalton, Pa., b. June 9, 1854; m. Aug. 8, 1878, Sarah A. Weidman, b. Oct. 28, 1854; dau. Michael D. Weidman and Sarah F. Elker.
3590. John, Harrisburg, Pa., b. Sept. 27, 1856.
3591. Harriet, Middletown, Pa., b. Mar. 7, 1857; m. Aaron Brandt.
3592. Hiram, Middletown, Pa., b. Aug. 27, 1858.
3593. Frances, Middletown, Pa., b. Aug. 12, 1861; m. Thomas Dougherty.

Family of MARIA KENDIG (1191) and JOHN HOOVER.

3594. William, Middletown, Pa.
3595. Susan, Willow Street, Pa., m. Eli Cramer.
3596. Mary, Lancaster, Pa., m. Amos Leachey.

Family of HIRAM KENDIG (1192) and ANNIE E. FETTER.

3597. Mary E., Lancaster, Pa., b. Apr. 14, 1849; d. Oct. 29, 1879.
3598. Emma A., Lancaster, Pa., b. Mar. 6, 1851; m. William Lawrence.
3599. William Glim, Lancaster, Pa., b. Dec. 24, 1854.
3600. Ella Margaret, Lancaster, Pa., b. July 14, 1857; d. Mar. 10, 1900.
3601. Harry Hiram, Lancaster, Pa., b. June 17, 1860; d. Dec. 12, 1879.
3602. Lyda Salina, Lancaster, Pa., b. Oct. 5, 1862; m. John U. Troy.
3603. Clara Louisa, Lancaster, Pa., b. Dec. 18, 1852; d. Aug. 6, 1853.
3604. Frank Hermon, Lancaster, Pa., b. Dec. 20, 1864; d, May 24, 1865.

Family of ELIZABETH KENDIG (1193) and JOHN PENNEL.

3605. Mary Ann, Lancaster, Pa., b. Sept. 5, 1845; m. James Irwin, b. Apr. 6, 1838; d. July 8, 1893; son David Irwin and Margaret Rogers.
3606. Harry C., Chicago, Ill., b. Apr. 23, 1848; d. May 15, 1905; m.

Sept. 21, 1875, Ella M. Holtslander, b. Sept. 21, 1856; dau. Henry Holtslander and Jennie Gondieloch.

Family of CATHARINE WITHERS (1198) and JOHN R. HOPKINS.

3607. Dr. Howard H., Baltimore, Md., b. Jan. 26, 1814; d. Aug. 2, 1850; m. Nov. 25, 1844, Mary McConkey, b. Dec. 16. 1820, d. June 29, 1880; dau. William McConkey and Tabitha Monsell.

Family of MICHAEL WITHERS (1199) and ANNA MARY SMITH.

3608. Clara A., Lancaster, Pa., b. Nov. 30, 1828; d. Dec. 13. 1903; m. Nov. 25. 1856, Col. Emlen Franklin, b. Apr. 7, 1827; son Hon. Walter Franklin and Annie Emlen.
3609. Dr. M. Augustus, Pottstown, Pa., b. Nov. 6, 1829; m. Jan. 23, 1856, Louisa Musselman (4851).
3610. Mary Jane, Lancaster, Pa., m. John Wagner; d. Apr. 27, 1902.
3611. Louisa W., Lancaster, Pa., m. Dr. Andrew J. Carpenter.
3612. Annie E., Pittsburg, Pa., m. Feb. 27, 1866, Bernard Wolff, b. Mar., 1828; d. Apr., 1901; son Bernard Wolff and Judith Ann Heyser.

Family of ANN WITHERS (1200) and Dr. RICHARD T. HOUGHY.

3613. George F., Cincinnati, O.
3614. Laura F., Cincinnati, O., m. John B. Thompson.

Family of GEORGE WITHERS (1201) and ELIZABETH METZGER.

3615. Dr. Michael M., Maytown, Pa., b. Jan. 17, 1830; d. Jan. 20, 1888; m. June 21, 1866, Elizabeth C. Fahnestock, b. Oct. 6, 1836; dau. Dr. Wm. B. Fahnestock and Maria Reigart.
3616. Dr. George W., Willow Street, Pa., b. July 25, 1831; d. Jan. 12, 1870; m. Mary A. Shultz, dau. Christian Shultz and Maria Diffenbach.
3617. Howard H., Lancaster, Pa., b. Jan. 9, 1833; d. Sept. 15, 1895.
3618. Ann Elizabeth, Lancaster, Pa.
3619. Catharine J., Lancaster, Pa., m. John J. Shertz, son Henry Shertz and ———.

Family of JACOB BARR (1204) and SUSAN BARR (1229).

3620. Aaron, Quarryville, Pa., b. Sept. 14, 1831; d. Jan. 1, 1835.

Family of JOHN BARR (1211) and ANNA GROFF.

3621. Henry, Marticville, Pa., m. Anna Wademan.

3622. Anna, Mt. Joy, Pa., m. Peter Wademan.

Family of MARTIN B. LONGENECKER (1216) and HARRIET HAWKE.

3623. Emma E., Lancaster, Pa., b. Feb. 10, 1844; m. July 4, 1865, John H. Kauffman (2989).

3624. Daniel Franklin, Ronks, Pa., b. Sept. 12, 1845; m. Sept. 12, 1867, Lydia Sharp, b. Sept. 21, 1847; dau. William Sharp and Anna Bowman.

3625. Susanna, Paradise, Pa., b. Nov. 13, 1846; m. Samuel Keplinger, son Samuel Keplinger and Elizabeth ———.

3626. Amanda L., Paradise, Pa., b. Mar. 13, 1849; m. Sept. 12, 1867, Benjamin F. Herr (2965).

3627. Mary Ann, Leesburg, Pa., b. Feb. 9, 1854; d. Mar. 6, 1854.

3628. Jacob, Paradise, Pa., b. Apr. 18, 1855; m. Martha Rounds.

Family of MARY LONGENECKER (1217) and JACOB MARTIN.

3629. Mary Emma, Paradise, Pa.

3630. Susanna, Paradise, Pa.

3631. Samuel, Paradise, Pa.

Family of ELIZA LONGENECKER (1218) and JOHN HICKMAN.

3632. Aldus, New Providence, Pa.

3633. Milton, New Providence, Pa.

3634. Clayton, New Providence, Pa.

3635. Emma, New Providence, Pa.

3636. Gideon, New Providence, Pa.

3637. Edward, Paradise, Pa.

3638. Jefferson, New Providence, Pa.

3639. Mary, New Providence, Pa.

3640. Willie, New Providence, Pa.

Family of FANNY BARR (1223) and THOMAS LYLE.

3641. Lydia Ann, Millersville, Pa.

3642. Margaret, Quarryville, Pa., m. July 30, 1861, Samuel Witmer, b. Apr. 22, 1837; son David Witmer and Elizabeth McComsey.

Family of MARY BARR (1226) and JOHN HARSH.

3643. Sophia, Camargo, Pa., b. Dec. 18, 1820; d. Dec. 19, 1820.

2644. Ann Elizabeth, Camargo, Pa., b. Mar. 20, 1822; d. May 21, 1822.

Family of Wid. MARY B. HARSH (1226) and OILVER WATSON.

3645. Anna T., Strasburg, Pa., b. Dec. 12, 1826; m. Dec. 1, 1846, Henry Fraelich, b. Jan. 8, 1824; d. Aug. 9, 1864.

3646. George Washington, Strasburg, Pa., b. Feb. 15, 1828; d. May 11, 1828.

3647. Mary E, Strasburg, Pa., b. May 2, 1829; d. Nov. 19, 1832.

3648. Jacob B., Hepler, Kans., b. Apr. 13, 1831; m, Oct. 24, 1850, Hannah A. Howett, b. Feb. 13, 1823.

3649. John A., Unicorn, Pa., b. July 21, 1832; d. Jan. 12, 1838.

3650. Susan M., Bart, Pa., b. Feb. 8, 1834; d. Nov. 22, 1866; m. Feb. 23, 1854, Jacob Helm.

3651. Fanny N., Quarryville, Pa., b. Nov. 7, 1835; d. Oct. 11, 1883; m. Oct. 23, 1852, Skipwith Howett, b. Nov. 7, 1815; d. Oct. 1, 1892; son George Howett and Hannah Brown.

3652. Mary L., Quarryville, Pa., b. June 23, 1837.

3653. Elam, Strasburg, Pa., b. Oct. 12, 1838; d. Sept. 9, 1839.

3654. Martha, Strasburg, Pa., b. Dec. 5, 1839; d. June 1, 1850.

3655. Margaret, Lancaster, Pa., b. Aug. 21, 1841; m. Dec. 20, 1860, Thomas Eager, b. June 22, 1827; d. Sept. 28, 1895.

3656. Emanuel, Strasburg, Pa., b. May 19, 1844; d. June 22, 1844.

Family of ANNA BARR (1228) and FREDERICK STIVELY.

3657. Jacob, Martic, Pa., m. Sallie Stafford.

3658. Fanny, New Providence, Pa., b. Oct. 7, 1833; m. Feb. 18, 1858, John M. Shenk (5784).

3659. Frederick, Camargo, Pa.

3660. Mary, Camargo, Pa., m. David Miller.

3661. Abraham L., Collins, Pa., b. Mar. 5, 1844; m. Apr. 20, 1898, Emma F. Herr (4025).

3662. Elizabeth, Collins, Pa.

3663. John, Buck, Pa.

Family of ELIZABETH SHAUB (1238) and ABRAHAM METZ.

3664. Susanna, Lampeter, Pa., m. Martin Metz.

Family of HENRY SHAUB (1239) and ELIZA MILLER.

3665. Mary, Strasburg, Pa., b. Mar. 3, 1833; d. July 9, 1895; m. Nov. 18, 1856, Tobias Herr (1920).

3666. Jacob, Strasburg, Pa., b. Jan. 25, 1834; d. Jan. 25, 1837.

3667. Hettie, Refton, Pa., b. Jan. 9, 1836; m. Levi Rohrer.

3668. Elizabeth, Leaman Place, Pa., b. Jan. 16, 1837; d. Aug. 7, 1876; m. John Denlinger.

3669. Susan, Leaman Place, Pa., b. Mar. 5, 1838; d. Aug. 27, 1858.

3670. Fanny, Leaman Place, Pa., b. July 29, 1839; d. Nov. 9, 1862.

3671. Henry, Lampeter, Pa., b. Dec. 30, 1840; m. Dec. 3, 1867, Fanny Landis, b. Nov. 12, 1846; dau. Benjamin Landis and Elizabeth Kreider.

3672. Abraham, Millersville, Pa., b. Mar. 23, 1842; m. Mary Huber, dau. Christian Huber and ———.

3673. Anna, Strasburg, Pa., b. Sept. 25, 1843; d. June 25, 1848.

3674. Elias, Strasburg, Pa., b. Dec. 22, 1845; d. Jan. 7, 1893; m. Anna Ranck, dau. John Ranck and ———.

Family of MARTIN SHAUB (1240) and ANN GOCHENOUR.

3675. George, Quarryville, Pa.

3676. Samuel, New Providence, Pa.

3677. Mary, New Providence, Pa.

Family of JOHN W. MARTIN (1813) and SUSAN SHAUB (1242).

3678. Henry Michael, Lancaster, Pa., b. Aug. 4, 1841.

3679. Abraham, Lancaster, Pa., b. Dec. 11, 1842; d. Mar. 23, 1862.

3680. Elias, Lancaster, Pa., b. Mar. 25, 1844.

3681. Jacob, Lancaster, Pa., b. Feb. 3, 1846.

3682. John, Lancaster, Pa., b. Aug. 21, 1847.

3683. Amos, Lancaster, Pa., b. Nov. 10, 1848.

3684. Anna, Lancaster, Pa., b. Feb. 1, 1850; d. Feb. 12, 1850.

3685. Levi, Lancaster, Pa., b. Jan. 29, 1851.

3686. Mary, Lancaster Pa., b. Aug. 31, 1852.

3687. Hettie Ann, Lancaster. Pa., b. May 26, 1854.

3688. Samuel S., Lancaster, Pa., b. Feb. 9, 1856.

3689. David Witmer, Lancaster, Pa., b. Nov. 9, 1857.

3690. Benjamin S., Lancaster, Pa., b. Sept. 26, 1859.

Family of JACOB SHAUB (1244) and ELIZABETH ECKMAN.

3691. John M., Binkleys, Pa.

3692. Lizzie, Binkleys, Pa.

3693. Sarah, Binkleys, Pa.

3694. Jacob, Buck, Pa.

3695. Albert, West Willow, Pa.

3696. Susanna, West Willow, Pa.

Family of HENRY SHAUB (1249) and HARRIET HOOVER.

3697. Martin L., Newark, O., b. Feb. 22, 1831; d. Sept. 29, 1866; m. Nov. 16, 1852, Caroline Hoover, b. Jan. 16, 1835; d. Nov. 16, 1884; dau. ———— and Margaret Hoover.

3698. Frank, Newark, O., m. Wid. Rosa Gipple.

Family of MARTIN SHAUB (1250) and ESTHER STROHM (1876).

3699. Amanda, Morrison, Ill., b. Dec. 25, 1838; m. Nov. 11, 1863, Oscar Woods, b. Oct. 18, 1836; son Leonard Woods and Mary L. Sinnett.

3700. Eliza A., Exeter, Neb., b. Jan. 21, 1841.

3701. Jerome, Anaconda, Cal., b. Dec. 5, 1842; m. Dec. 31, 1868, Rhoda Goddard, d. Aug. 14, 1900; dau. Snell Goddard and Cornelia Barnes.

3702. Henry, Alexandria, O., b. Nov. 11, 1844; d. Dec. 19, 1855.

3703. John, Glendive, Mont., b. Oct. 8, 1846; d. Apr. 6, 1894; m.

Apr. 18, 1871, Emma Fisher, b. June 23, 1842; dau. William Fisher and Nancy DeWolf.

3704. Franklin, Exeter, Neb., b. Mar. 26, 1849; m. Nov. 27, 1889, Wid. Emma Austin, dau. David Tollansbee and Mary J. Eads.

3705. Orren P., Tacoma, Wash., b. July 31, 1851; m. Sept. 20, 1882, Carrie Sanford, b. Sept. 16, 1864; dau. George M. Sanford and Susan M. Hays. .

3706. Elim, Alexandria, O., b. June 16, 1853; m. Sept. 9, 1880, Josephine Foster, b. Apr. 25, 1860; dau. George E. Foster and Mary Stenson.

3707. Alice, Exeter, Neb., b. Apr. 23, 1855; m. May 8, 1890, Wid. Albert Vennum, b. Dec. 4, 1845; son Edward Vennum and Susan Jackson.

3708. Lura, Exeter, Neb., b. June 15, 1857; d. Oct. 10, 1887; m. Nov. 28, 1882, Albert Vennum, b. Dec. 4, 1845; son Edward Vennum and Susan Jackson.

3709. Florence, Exeter, Neb., b. Aug. 8, 1859; d. May 2, 1895.

3710. Francis, Alexandria, O., b. Aug. 8, 1859; d. Feb. 28, 1864.

Family of JACOB SHAUB (1251) and LEAH ELIZABETH BUSHONG.

3711. Martha A., Johnstown, O., b. May 24, 1837; d. Aug. 5, 1837.

3712. Emma, Johnstown, O., b. Apr. 30, 1838; m. Apr. 15, 1858, George W. Mouser, b. June 5, 1836; son Abraham Mouser and Martha Hancock.

3713. Elizabeth, Johnstown, O., b. Apr. 27, 1839; d. June 5, 1898; m. Dec. 9, 1867, George W. Barstow, b. May 30, 1824.

3714. Benjamin, Johnstown, O., b. Dec. 24, 1840; d. Sept. 13, 1841.

3715. Mary C., Johnstown, O., b. Jan. 24, 1842; d. July 18, 1842.

3716. Wesley, Johnstown, O., b. Mar. 28, 1843; d. Sept. 20, 1843.

3717. Edwin, Johnstown, O., b. Sept. 11, 1844; d. Oct. 2, 1844.

3718. Cora, Johnstown, O., b. Oct. 15, 1846; d. Oct. 15, 1846.

3719. Anna, Johnstown, O., b. Jan. 11, 1849; d. July 14, 1849.

Family of ISAAC SHAUB (1252) and ANN THORN.

3720. Almira, Granville, O., b. June 27, 1845; m. July 26, 1864. John Krug, b. June 9, 1839; son Samuel Krug and Dorothy Myers.

3721. Lemath, Johnstown, O., b. Nov. 4, 1846; m. Sept. 20, 1882, Judson Peck, b. May 13, 1846; son Horace Peck and Rozilla Boume.

3722. Roland J., Johnstown, O., b. Mar. 7, 1848; m. Dec. 23, 1875, Jennie Stephens, b. Apr. 25, 1852; dau. Jackson Stephens and Joanna Dull.

3723. Theresa A., Johnstown, O., b. July 13, 1849; d. Mar. 26, 1852.

3724. James M., Creswell, Pa., b. Apr. 8, 1851; m. Nov. 17, 1880, Agnes Cadwell, b. Dec. 17, 1862; dau. George Cadwell and Mary E. Kingsbury; m. Sept. 7, 1887, Carrie Scott, b. Sept. 30, 1861; dau. Benjamin B. Scott and Mary Lewis.

3725. Edwin, Spokane Falls, Wash., b. Dec. 29, 1853; d. Aug. 25, 1885; m. May 24, 1877, Inez Franklin.

3726. Elmer, Creston, Ia., b. Aug. 26, 1855; m. Oct. 4, 1877, Ella Alspack, b. May 22, 1849; dau. Henry B. Alspack and Charata Coffman.

3727. Ida E., Granville, O., b. Feb. 6, 1857; m. Dec. 13, 1876, Allen A. Avery, b. Nov. 24, 1850; son Christopher Avery and Axia Hayes.

3728. Luna, Granville, O., b. Oct. 28, 1858; m. Feb. 9, 1882, David H. Ramey, b. Mar. 14, 1850; son Elisha Ramey and Rosanna Herigall.

3729. Altha, Granville, O., b. July 12, 1860.

3730. Olive, Granville, O., b. Dec. 10, 1861.

3731. Burt E., Johnstown, O., b. May 22, 1863; m. Feb. 14, 1889, Lydia C. Glynn, b. Nov. 2, 1868; dau. John Glynn and Elizabeth Brown.

3732. Milton B., Johnstown, O., b. Apr. 12, 1867; m. Ora Conway, dau. Howard Conway and Rebecca Mann.

Family of CHRISTIANA SHAUB (1253) and LEWIS JAMISON.

3733. Milton B., Johnstown, O., b. Nov. 20, 1842; d. Aug. 15, 1892; m. Mar. 31, 1868, Lydia E. Emerson, b. Nov. 12, 1842; dau. Roe Emerson and Charity Faultenburg.

3734. Mary E., Johnstown, O., b. Mar. 7, 1846; d. Sept. 12, 1847.

3735. Nora A., Johnstown, O., b. Aug. 28, 1847.

3736. Alexander S., Johnstown, O., b. Aug. 21, 1849; m. Dec. 1, 1874, Abigail M. Woodbury, b. May 8, 1856; d. Oct. 12, 1877; dau. William B. Woodbury and Josephine Piper.

3737. Emma E., Akron, O., b. Aug. 24, 1851; m. Jan. 3, 1878, Anson J. Stambach, b. Apr. 27, 1849; son Henry W. Stambach and Susan Wallick.

3738. Martha A., Johnston, O., b. Dec. 5, 1854; d. Aug. 23, 1855.

Family of BARBARA HERR (1275) and DAVID GROFF.

3739. Christian, Strasburg, Pa., m. Elizabeth Overly.

3740. Frances, Strasburg, Pa.

3741. Barbara, Strasburg, Pa.

Family of ABRAHAM HERR (1275) and HANNAH WHITE.

3742. Anna, Mountville, Pa., b. Aug. 22, 1824; m. George Tangert, b. Nov. 11, 1822; d. Nov. 9, 1864; son George Tangert and Anna Miller.

3743. Lavinia, Reading, Pa., b. Aug. 19, 1827; m. John McCann, b. Apr. 15, 1825; d. Aug. 12, 1870; son Edwin McCann and Sarah Rany.

3744. Mary Ann, York, Pa., b. Oct. 4, 1831; d. Dec. 3, 1885; m. Dec. 2, 1852, Henry B. Stone, b. Mar. 28, 1830; son Abraham Stone and Rebecca Brower.

3745. Eliza, Mountville, Pa., b. Feb. 10, 1837; m. Levi Sener, b. Mar. 22, 1839; son Jacob Sener and Leah Balmer.

3746. Abraham, Reading, Pa., b. July 26, 1839; m. Aug. 18, 1861, Louisa Furgeson, b. July 19, 1839; dau. Robert Furgeson and Hannah Slaughter.

3747. Martha, Mountville, Pa., b. May 27, 1842; d. Aug. 24, 1870; m. 1868, Jacob S. Clair, b. May 27, 1840; d. Oct 3, 1876; son Jacob Clair and Sarah Snead.

Family of JOHN HERR (1277) and SUSANNA MOWRER.

3748. Mary Ann, Lancaster, Pa., b. May 18, 1836; m. Aug. 13, 1853, Benjamin Herr (1043); m. Apr. 20, 1875, Thomas Bellamy,

b. July 26, 1827; d. Aug. 11, 1893; son George Bellamy and
——— Ploughrit.
3749. Abraham, Strasburg, Pa., b. Sept. 16, 1837; d. Oct. 13, 1837.

Family of Wid. JOHN HERR (1277) and MARY BARTHOLOMEW.

3750. Susanna, Lancaster, Pa., b. Sept. 17, 1842.
3751. Elizabeth B., Strasburg, Pa., b. Jan. 17, 1845; m. Oct. 5, 1865,
Henry B. Miller, b. Feb. 2, 1837; d. Dec. 12, 1890; son Jacob
Miller and Christiana Miller.
3752. Martin, Strasburg, Pa., b. Sept. 22, 1847; d. Aug. 1, 1848.

Family of NANCY HERR (1278) and WILLIAM SHANES.

3753. Mary Ann, New Providence, Pa., m. Joshua Wilson.
3754. Joseph, New Providence, Pa.
3755. Elizabeth, New Providence, Pa., m. Cruikshank.

Family of MARTIN HERR (1279) and ELIZABETH MILLER.

3756. John M., Chrome, Pa., b. Dec. 23, 1833; m. Catharine Lefever,
dau. Daniel Lefever and Martha Shenk; m. May 1, 1877, Amy
Ann, b. Aug. 13, 1844; d. Mar. 10, 1898.
3757. Sarah Ann, Buck, Pa., b. Dec. 17, 1835; d. Mar. 20, 1864; m.
Sept. 27, 1855, Daniel F. Lefever, b. June 5, 1832; son Daniel
Lefever and Martha Shenk.
3758. Abraham Miller, Buck, Pa., b. Dec. 23, 1836; d. Apr. 4, 1837.
3759. Mary Barbara, Lancaster, Pa., b. Nov. 2, 1843; m. Dec. 26,
1865, Wid. Daniel F. Lefever, b. June 5, 1832; son Daniel Lefever and Martha Shenk.
3760. Elizabeth, New Providence, Pa., b. July 17, 1850; m. Oct. 27,
1870, John Broome, b. Jan. 20, 1847; son Samuel Broome and
Jane Witmer.
3761. Martin V., Columbia, Pa., b. Aug. 8, 1852; m. Aug. 8, 1878,
Laura E. Hess, b. Nov. 27, 1856; dau. Elias Hess and Mary
A. Gosage.

Family of ANN HOOVER (1282) and JACOB H. HOOVER (1288).

3762. Christian, Strasburg, Pa., b. Nov. 9, 1842; m. Martha Herr
(2776).

3763. Amos, Sterling, Ill., m. Barbara Groff, dau. Martin Groff and ———; m. Sarah Hoak.

3764. Mary Ann, Strasburg, Pa.

3765. Frances, Strasburg, Pa., m. Elias Espenshade, son Samuel Espenshade and ———.

3766. Jacob, Strasburg, Pa.

3767. Aaron, Strasburg, Pa.

3768. Susanna, Strasburg, Pa.

3769. Elias, Soudersburg, Pa., b. May 2, 1858; m. Dec. 22, 1881, Lydia A. Wiker, b. Sept. 26, 1862; dau. Christian Wiker and Elizabeth Price.

Family of MARIA HOOVER (1285) and MARTIN HOOVER (1289).

3770. Aaron, Willow Street, Pa., b. July 28, 1853; d. Feb. 16, 1854.

3771. Anna Mary, Willow Street, Pa., b. June 16, 1856; d. Feb. 14, 1858.

3772. Emma Susan, Willow Street, Pa., b. Oct. 28, 1861; m. David Hoover, son Christian Hoover and ———.

3773. Frances, Willow Street, Pa., m. Henry Shenk.

Family of CHRISTIANA HOOVER (1287) and HENRY HOOVER (1290).

3774. Franklin Benjamin, Strasburg, Pa.

3775. Anna Mary, Strasburg, Pa.

Family of ELIZA HOOVER (1292) and CYRUS ZITTLE.

3776. Susanna, Lancaster, Pa., b. Dec. 23, 1858; m. John Brackbill, son Benjamin Brackbill and ———.

3777. Daniel, Downingtown, Pa., b. Mar. 3, 1862; m. Ida Deets.

3778. Cyrus, Philadelphia, Pa., b. Feb. 22, 1865; m. Martha Round.

3779. Jacob Franklin, Edisonville, Pa., b. Jan. 12, 1867; m. Esther Fritz.

3780. Hettie, Lancaster, Pa.

Family of HENRY GROFF (1295) and ROSANNA MYERS.

3781. John, Ashland, O., b. Oct. 19, 1802; d. July 31, 1882; m. Oct. 16, 1828, Ann Herr (1361).

3782. Jacob, New Providence, Pa., m. Susan Stonedale.
3783. Thomas, New Providence, Pa., m. Mary Nowland.
3784. Benjamin, New Providence, Pa.
3785. Annie, Ephrata, Pa., m. John Barr, son Martin Barr and Nancy Herr.
3786. Susan, Martic, Pa., m. John Myers.
3787. Elizabeth, Martic, Pa.

Family of ISAAC GROFF (1296) and BETSEY ESHLEMAN.

3788. Abraham, Manheim, Pa., m. Lydia Esbenshade.
3789. Michael, Refton, Pa.
3790. Isaac, Strasburg, Pa., m. Marinda Showalter.
3791. John, New Providence, Pa., m. Maria Brubaker.
3792. Susan, Wheatland Mills, Pa., m. Benjamin Groff, son John Groff and Maria Hackman.
3793. Fannie, Strasburg, Pa., m. Abraham Groff; m. John Murdock.
3794. Eliza, Quarryville, Pa., m. David Mourer.
3795. Mary, Bartville, Pa., m. Benjamin Fritz.
3796. Mattie, Intercourse, Pa., m. John Leaman.
3797. Annie, Intercourse, Pa., m. William Hagy.
3798. Lydia, Millersville, Pa., m. Henry Lintner.

Family of MICHAEL GROFF (1297) and REBECCA CARPMAN.

3799. Rudolph, Lancaster, Pa., d. 1882; m. Christiana Herr (1360).
3800. Christian, Quarryville, Pa., m. Phœbe Knopt.
3801. John, Smithville, Pa., m. Laura Longenecker.
3802. Benjamin, Lancaster, Pa., m. Elizabeth Hoover (1108).
3803. Isaac, West Earl, Pa., m. Margaret Campbell.
3804. Elizabeth, West Earl, Pa.

Family of Wid. MICHAEL GROFF (1297) and MATTIE WADE.

3805. Maria, Quarryville, Pa.
3806. Susan, Quarryville, Pa., m. Samuel Davis.
3807. Martha, Quarryville, Pa.
3808. Michael, Quarryville, Pa.
3809. Abraham, Quarryville, Pa.

AND HIS DIRECT LINEAL DESCENDANTS.

Family of JOHN GROFF (1298) and ELIZABETH GROFF.

3810. George, Paradise, Pa., b. Oct. 7, 1810; d. Mar. 20, 1880; m. Mar. 10, 1835, Ann Eshleman (1437).

3811. Isaac, Paradise, Pa., m. Mary Groff, dau. Rev. John Groff and Judith Nisley; m. Elizabeth Kanour.

3812. Susan, Chester Co., Pa., m. John Drips.

3813. Alice, Strasburg, Pa., m. Alfred Clark.

3814. John, Maryland, b. Mar. 12, 1822; m. Feb. 27, 1847, Lizzie Barr (1758).

3815. Dr. Jacob, Strasburg, Pa., m. Hattie Lefevre, dau. Levi Lefevre and ———.

3816. Lizzie, Strasburg, Pa., m. Martin M. Rohrer.

3817. Louisa, Strasburg, Pa., m. Henry Girvin.

Family of SIMON GROFF (1299) and SUSAN GOCHENOUR.

3818. Nancy, Clearfield, Pa., b. Aug. 21, 1810; d. Dec. 2, 1843; m. 1827, Henry Hart, b. 1800; d. 1863; son Benjamin Hart and Susan Hess.

3819. Elizabeth, Witmer, Pa., b. Oct. 21, 1811; d. Aug. 1, 1867; m. Oct. 18, 1832, John Hess, b. Aug. 23, 1806; d. June 22, 1894: son Christian Hess and Catharine Brua.

3820. Abraham, Chestnut Level, Pa., b. Aug. 5, 1813; d. Nov. 6, 1875; m. July 4, 1839, Hannah Peoples, d. Jan. 3, 1897.

3821. Leah, Lampeter, Pa., b. May 27, 1819; d. Dec. 10, 1854; m. Samuel Weaver, son Samuel Weaver and Mary Raub.

3822. Susan, Lampeter, Pa.

Family of Wid. SIMON GROFF (1299) and BARBARA HERR (1359).

3823. Simon, New Providence, Pa., b. Nov. 16, 1841; d. Sept. 2, 1872; m. Aug. 14, 1862, Frances Eckman, b. Sept. 25, 1841; dau. Daniel Eckman and Elizabeth Longenecker.

Family of JACOB GROFF (1300) and MARY RUSH.

3824. Annie, Conestoga Center, Pa., m. Jacob Breneman.

3825. Susan, Lime Valley, Pa., m. Benjamin Ressler.

3826. John, Quarryville, Pa., m. ——— Kreider.

3827. Adam, New Providence, Pa., m. Lizzie Stinaman.

3828. Amos, Herrville, Pa., d. 1899; m. ——— Groff, dau. Joseph
      Groff and ———.

3829. Lizzie, Refton, Pa., m. Christian Good.

3830. Hettie, Smithville, Pa., m. Simon Good.

Family of DANIEL GROFF (1301) and SUSAN SIDES.

3831. Isaac, Paradise, Pa., m. ——— Mowrer.

3832. Susan, Paradise, Pa.

3833. Lizzie, Paradise, Pa., m. ——— Winters.

3834. Barbara, Paradise, Pa., m. ——— Mowrer.

3835. Samuel, Gordonville, Pa., m. ——— Winters.

3836. Martin, Ledger, Pa., m. ——— Templeton.

3837. Henry, Safe Harbor, Pa., m. ——— Seigman.

Family of JOSEPH GROFF (1302) and BARBARA SIDES.

3838. Ann, Smithville, Pa., m. Samuel Anthony.

3839. John, Smithville, Pa., m. Ann Swisher.

3840. Joseph H., Kirkwood, Pa., b. Jan. 4, 1834; d. Jan. 31, 1908; m.
      Aug. 28, 1855, Mary Elizabeth Kinnard, b. Apr. 7, 1839.

3841. Simon, Kirkwood, Pa., m. Sallie Thompson.

3842. Benjamin, Witmer, Pa.

3843. Christiana, Collins, Pa., m. William Hagens.

3844. Maria, Reamstown, Pa., m. Levi DeBolt.

3845. Fanny, Reamstown, Pa., m. C. ——— Grimes.

Family of MARTIN GROFF (1303) and SUSAN MOONEY.

3846. Newton, Kirkwood, Pa., m. ——— Aument.

3847. Albert, East Petersburg, Pa.

3848. Harry, Strasburg, Pa.

3849. Susan, Strasburg, Pa.

3850. Leah, Washington, Pa., m. John Helm.

Family of SUSAN GROFF (1304) and JOHN ECKMAN.

3851. Eliza, New Providence, Pa., m. Jacob Eckman.
3852. Daniel, Quarryville, Pa., m. Leah Hoak.
3853. John, New Providence, Pa., m. ———— Longenecker; m. ————
Snavely.
3854. Susan, New Providence, Pa., m. Henry Eckman.
3855. Kate, Strasburg, Pa., m. Joseph Foulk.

Family of ELIZABETH GROFF (1305) and JOHN GOCHENOUR.

3856. Susan, Willow Street, Pa., m. Henry Gull.

Family of ANNIE GROFF (1306) and MARTIN GULL.

3857. Kate, Willow Street, Pa., m. David Mourer.
3858. Henry, Willow Street, Pa., m. Susan Gochenour; m. Wid. Nancy
Gull.
3859. Betsey, Willow Street, Pa., m. John Meck.
3860. Susan, Willow Street, Pa., m. David Rush.
3861. Annie, Willow Street, Pa., m. Jacob Light.

Family of SIMON GROVE (1319) and REBECCA REINHART.

3862. Barbara, Hermitage, Va.
3863. Jacob, Hermitage, Va.
3864. Benjamin, Hermitage, Va.
3865. Hannah, Hermitage, Va.
3866. Leah, Hermitage, Va.
3867. Mary A., Hermitage, Va.
3868. Abraham, Hermitage, Va.
3869. Henry, Hermitage, Va.
3870. Isaac, Hermitage, Va.
3871. Susan, Hermitage, Va.
3872. Sallie, Hermitage, Va.
3873. Lizzie, Hermitage, Va.

Family of BENJAMIN GROVE (1320) and SUSAN BROWNING.

3874. Mary J., Hermitage, Va.

3875. John, Hermitage, Va.
3876. Elizabeth, Hermitage, Va.
3877. Thomas, Hermitage, Va.

Family of MARY GROVE (1321) and ABRAHAM REINHART.

3878. Mary, Hermitage, Va.
3879. Henry, Hermitage, Va.
3880. Martha, Hermitage, Va.

Family of ABRAHAM GROVE (1323) and SARAH GRINER.

3881. Mary Ann, Hermitage, Va., m. Richard Brackin.
3882. Barbara, El Paso, Ill., b. May 16, 1828; m. David Grafft (3417).
3883. Diana, Hermitage, Va., m. Daniel Grafft (3420).
3894. John, Hermitage, Va., m. Margaret Roost.
3885. Elizabeth, Hermitage, Va., m. Henry Grafft (342).
3886. Eliza, Hermitage, Va., m. Lewis Hoit.
3887. Virginia, Hermitage, Va., m. Henry Konkler.
3888. William, Hermitage, Va.

Family of ELIZABETH GROVE (1324) and JOHN GROFF (2223).

3889. Barbara, Hermitage, Va., b. Dec. 4, 1820; m. Albert F. ————.
3890. Anna, Hermitage, Va., b. Aug. 27, 1822; d. Apr. 29, 1836.
3891. Samuel, Hermitage, Va., b. Feb. 16, 1825.
3892. Susanna, Hermitage, Va., b. Feb. 2, 1826; d. Nov. 22, 1859.
3893. John H., Hermitage, Va., b. July 19, 1832; d. Feb. 27, 1894;
    m. Mary Jane Schreckhise.
3894. Elizabeth, Hermitage, Va., b. Apr. 24, 1831; d. Sept. 5, 1831.
3895. Mary, Hermitage, Va., b. Mar. 25, 1828; m. William Ross.
3896. Martin B., South English, Iowa, b. May 9, 1835.
3897. Abraham J., Hermitage, Va., b. May 22, 1838; d. May 30, 1864.
3898. Elizabeth T., Hermitage, Va., b. Jan. 18, 1841; d. May 7, 1851.

Family of JACOB GROVE (1325) and MARGARET HOOVER.

3899. Eve, Hermitage, Va., m. Jacob Stambach.
3900. Barbara, Hermitage, Va., m. Joseph Withrow.

3901. Sarah, Hermitage, Va., m. William Withrow.

3902. Benjamin, Hermitage, Va.

3903. Michael, Hermitage, Va., m. Sarah Richardson.

3904. Abraham, Hermitage, Va.

Family of HENRY GROVE (1326) and ELIZABETH HOOVER.

3905. Eve, Hermitage, Va., m. James Wright.

3906. Mary, Hermitage, Va., m. Christian Miller.

3907. Eliza, Hermitage, Va., m. Philip Mail.

3908. Abraham, Hermitage, Va., m. Mary Neargate.

3909. Ann, Hermitage, Va., m. George Areholtz.

3910. Sarah, Hermitage, Va., m. C. ——— Gizleman.

3911. David, Hermitage, Va., m. Malinda Sands.

3912. Martha, Hermitage, Va.

3913. Ellen, Hermitage, Va.

Family of HENRY HERR (1335) and KATIE GARBER.

3914. Jacob, Myerstown, Pa., b. Nov. 8, 1819; d. Mar. 5, 1897; m. Dec. 3, 1844, Sarah Pfoutz, b. Dec. 21, 1824; dau. Jacob Pfoutz and Elizabeth Eby.

Family of ISAAC HERR (1336) and ELIZABETH ROYER.

3915. Annie, Campbellstown, Pa., b. Apr. 12, 1822; m. Wid. Joseph Herr (2896).

3916. Jacob, Lancaster, Pa., b. Aug. 21, 1823; m. 1867, Elizabeth Reese, b. 1850; dau. Joshua Reese and ———.

3917. Susanna, New Providence, Pa., b. Nov. 5. 1824; d. Aug. 5, 1841.

3918. Tobias R. Strasburg, Pa., b. Jan. 15, 1826; d. 1902; m. Katie Book, dau. John Book and Ann Geist.

3919. Mary, New Providence, Pa., b. Feb. 8, 1827; d. Sept. 27, 1827.

3920. Samuel, New Providence, Pa., b. July 4. 1828; d. Apr. 18, 1830.

3921. Daniel B., New Providence, Pa., b. Mar. 7. 1830; d. Aug. 5, 1839.

3922. Elizabeth, New Providence, Pa., b. June 24, 1832; d. Aug. 7, 1839.

14

3923. Benjamin M., New Providence, Pa., b. Feb. 7, 1834; d. June 18, 1834.

3924. Sarah, New Providence, Pa., b. Apr. 14, 1835.

3925. Henry, Lebanon, Pa., b. May 23, 1836; m. Mary Yortz.

3926. Amos, Lancaster, Pa., b. Jan. 12, 1838; m. Jan. 18, 1866, Anna M. Landis, b. May 22, 1840; d. Sept. 25, 1895; dau. John Landis and Barbara Stauffer.

3927. Lydia Ann, Strasburg, Pa., b. June 5, 1839; m. Abraham Hostetter, son David Hostetter and ——— Miller.

3928. Elizabeth. Buck, Pa., b. Nov. 1, 1840; m. David Kreider, son George Kreider and ——— Swarr.

3929. Rebecca, Landisville, Pa., b. Nov. 25, 1842; m. Henry Stehman, son Henry Stehman and ——— Swarr.

Family of FANNY HERR (1337) and JOHN URBAN.

3930. Delilah, Willow Street, Pa., m. John Eckman.

3931. Harriet, Willow Street, Pa.

3932. Hiram, Baltimore, Md., m. ——— Shingle; m. ———.

3933. Mattie, Willow Street, Pa., m. Henry Konkle.

Family of HENRY KRUG (1338) and SUSAN GRIMES.

3934. Elizabeth. Martic, Pa., m. David Hoover.

3935. Catharine, Union, O., m. Josiah McMullen.

3936. Susan, Cockeysville, Md., m. Archibald Warren.

Family of Wid. HENRY KRUG (1327) and ELIZABETH HOOVER.

3937. Mary, Union, O.

3938. Benjamin, Union, O., b. Dec. 4, 1829: d. Sept. 5, 1903; m. Mar. 31, 1859, Susanna Herr (3953).

3939. Frances, Union, O.

3940. Esther, Union, O.

Family of DANIEL KRUG (1340) and SUSAN JOHNSON.

3941. Esther, Strasburg, Pa., b. Jan. 3, 1825; d. Feb. 15, 1886; m. Sept. 10, 1856, Joseph Landis, b. Nov. 22, 1818; d. Dec. 6, 1893; son Henry Landis and Susan Detwiler.

3942. Samuel, Lancaster, Pa., b. Apr. 18, 1829; d. Aug. 24, 1851.
3943. John, Lancaster, Pa.

Family of MARY KRUG (1343) and JOHN WILLIAMS.

3944. Christiana, Union, O., m. W. ——— M. Sanders.
3945. Samuel, Union, O.
3946. Esther, Union, O., m. ——— Philips.
3947. Mary, Union, O.
3948. Rachael, Union, O.
3949. Elias, Union, O.

Family of BARBARA KRUG (1346) and JONATHAN STEELE.

3950. Mary, Lycoming, Pa.
3951. Elizabeth, Lycoming, Pa.
3952. Susan, Lycoming, Pa.

Family of SAMUEL M. HERR (1347) and MARY BOWMAN (1386).

3953. Susanna, Union, O., b. Mar. 29, 1836; d. June 2, 1884; m. Mar. 31, 1859, Benjamin Krug (3938).
3954. Henry B., Dayton, O., b. July 30, 1837.
3955. Levi, Union, O., b. Dec. 23, 1840; d. May 19, 1867.

Family of MARY HERR (1350) and JESSE BRENBERGER.

3956. Elizabeth, Ithaca, O., b. Jan. 6, 1831; m. Mar. 18, 1869, Noah Brenner, b. Oct. 26, 1832; d. Nov. 27, 1887; son Lewis Brenner and Mary Swank.
3957. Benjamin, Seven Mills, O., b. May 25, 1832; d. 1840.
3958. Henry, Ithaca, O., b. Sept. 9, 1833; d. Sept. 7, 1885; m. Wid. Eliza M. Sharp, dau. Abraham Huffer and ———.
3959. Ann, Seven Mills, O., b. Jan. 22, 1835.
3960. Susan, Seven Mills, O., b. Nov. 2, 1836; d. Nov. 2, 1837.
3961. Rachael, Johnsville, O,, b. Dec. 28, 1838.
3962. Mary Ann, Trenton, Mo., b. Sept. 9, 1840; d. Aug. 18, 1906; m. Oct. 27, 1865, Jefferson Rynearson, b. Sept. 13, 1834; son Burnett Rynearson and Mary Ann Drake.

3963. Hannah Jane, Monument, Kas., b. Dec. 24, 1841; m. Dec. 15, 1863, Philemon Caywood, b. June 26, 1839; son Albert Caywood and Rhoda Rynearson.

3964. Sarah Catharine, Union, O., b. Mar. 8, 1843.

3965. Christiana M., Ithaca, O., b. Sept. 8, 1845; d. Mar. 14, 1868.

3966. Jesse Franklin, Dayton, O., b. Mar. 8, 1847; m. May 8, 1877.

3967. Daniel Frederick, Seven Mills, O., b. Aug., 1848; d. Feb., 1850.

Family of BENJAMIN HERR (1353) and MARY MILLER.

3968. Son, Helena, O., b. May 17, 1839; d. May 18, 1839.

3969. Sarah Ann, Helena, O., b. May 14, 1840; d. Mar. 15, 1871.

3970. Samuel, Akron, O., b. Oct. 13, 1841.

3971. John, Helena, O., b. Jan. 31, 1843; m. Dec. 25, 1876, Emma· J. Oppermann, b, Mar. 1, 1855; dau. William Oppermann and Ruth ———.

3972. Elizabeth, Bellevue, O., b. Mar. 12, 1844; m. Josiah Wenger.

3973. Mary Jane, Gibsonburg, O., b. July 30, 1845; m. Nov. 14, 1867, Eli Hufford, b. Mar. 27, 1841; son Jacob Hufford and Rebecca

3974. George, Helena, O., b. June 5, 1847; d. July 28, 1850.

3975. Christiana, Toledo, O., b. Mar. 17, 1849; m. Feb. 24, 1895, William E. Richards.

3976. David, Fremont, O., b. Aug. 5, 1851; d. July 22, 1904; m. Dec. 9, 1881, Marcella J. Russell.

3977. Susanna, Helena, O., b. June 21, 1854; m. Oct. 14, 1875, Quintus Seiple, b. May 10, 1855; son Edward Seiple and Elizabeth Lambert.

3978. Hannah Maria, Akron, O., b. June 21, 1854.

3979. Joseph, Gibsonburg, O., b. June 5, 1857; m. Jan. 10, 1883, Lily J. Hufford, b. Nov. 2, 1862; dau. Simon Hufford and Sarah

Family of CHRISTIANA HERR (1356) and JACOB M. HUBER.

3980. Martha, Landisville, Pa., b. July 30, 1846.

3981. Susan, Lancaster, Pa., b. Mar. 15, 1848; m. Dec. 2, 1869, John M. Musselman, b. Feb. 19, 1842; d. Apr. 15, 1900; son Christian Musselman and Martha Minnick.

3982. Franklin, Lampeter, Pa., b. Nov. 23, 1849; d. July 31, 1853.

3983. Jacob, Landisville, Pa., b. Mar. 24, 1852; m. May 10, 1880, Naomi M. Swisher, b. Aug. 10, 1862; d. Dec. 17, 1898; dau. Albert Swisher and Elizabeth McElree.

3984. John, Braddock, Pa., b. Feb. 26, 1854; m, Feb. 15, 1877, Sara A. Kurtz, b. Aug. 14, 1851; dau. Daniel Kurtz and Elizabeth Stoner.

3985. Mary Elizabeth, Landisville, Pa., b. Apr. 22, 1856; d. July 12, 1892.

3986. Emma Salome, Landisville, Pa., b. Apr. 4, 1858; m. Sept. 16, 1877, Daniel K. Wolf, b. Sept. 11, 1850; son Nicholas Wolf and Annie Kern.

3987. Ellen, Landisville, Pa., b. July 26, 1860; m. Oct. 9, 1881, Frank M. Musselman, b. Oct. 9, 1859; son Christian Musselman and Martha Minnick.

3988. Ann Rachel, Landisville, Pa., b. Dec. 23, 1863; d. May 8, 1864.

3989. Enos, Lancaster, Pa., b. July 1, 1865; m. Mar. 15, 1888, Elizabeth Wertz, b. Nov. 17, 1859; dau. Henry Wertz and Mettie Herr.

3990. Levi, Landisville, Pa., b. Oct. 20, 1867; m. Nov. 4, 1897, Annie M. Kern, b. Dec. 14, 1872; dau. John B. Kern and Adaline H. Sweigart.

3991. Ida, Rohrerstown, Pa., b. Sept. 18, 1869; d. June 12, 1873.

Family of RACHEL HERR (1357) and SAMUEL KLINE.

3992. Joseph, Medway, O., b. Aug. 18, 1852; d. Jan. 2, 1854.

3993. Sarah Ann, Medway, O., b. Nov. 26, 1854; d. Sept. 23, 1855.

3994. Mary Jane, Enon, O., b. June 28, 1857; d. Feb. 2, 1859.

3995. John Edwin, Osborn, O., b. Feb. 29, 1860; m. Sept. 1, 1887, Mary Grable, b. July 16, 1865; dau. Harvey K. Grable and Mary Harrison.

3996. Anna, Enon, O., b. May 12, 1862; m, Oct. 24, 1880, David B. Beard, b. Jan. 24, 1859; son John Beard and Margaret Shellenberger.

3997. Jacob, Enon, O., b. Mar. 19, 1864.

3998. Elizabeth, Medway, O., b. Aug. 29, 1865; m. Sept., 1885. George K. Schauer.

3999. Emma, Enon, O., b. Apr. 21, 1867; d. Jan. 2, 1887.
4000. Benjamin, Enon, O., b. June 1, 1869; d. Feb. 12, 1870.

Family of SUSAN HERR (1358) and BENJAMIN HUBER.

4001. Benjamin, Hubers, Pa., m. Catharine Benedict.
4002. Mary, Hubers, Pa., m. Jacob Eshleman, son David Eshleman
and ——— Harnish.

Family of JOSEPH HERR (1362) and ELIZABETH MILLER.

4003. Jonas, Dayton, O.
4004. Aaron, Dayton, O.
4005. Martin, Dayton, O.
4006. John, Ashland, O.
4007. Albert, Ashland, O.
4008. B. Frank, Ashland, O.
6643. Louisa, Osborn, O., b. Mar. 10, 1858; m. Feb. 9, 1882,Albert
Neff, b. Mar. 17, 1856;d. Feb. 5, 1884; son Jacob Neff and
Mary Harnish.

Family of ELIZABETH HERR (1363) and JOHN C. BALDWIN.

4009. Mary Emma, Millersville, Pa., b. Dec. 6, 1842; m. Henry Shaub.
4010. Adeline, Millersville, Pa., b. Aug. 22, 1844; m. Amaziah Baldwin.
4011. Henrietta, Lancaster, Pa., b. Sept. 19, 1846; m. M. ———
Franklin Hoak.
4012. Alpheus, Harrisburg, Pa., b. Mar. 6, 1849.
4013. Elizabeth, Millersville, Pa., b. Feb. 26, 1851.
4014. Elmira M., Millersille, Pa., b. Apr. 20, 1853.
4015. Benjamin Franklin, Martinsville, Pa., b. Dec. 14, 1854; m. Leah
Witmer.
4016. John Charles, Philadelphia, Pa., b. Dec. 14, 1854.
4017. Martin Anthony, Martinsville, Pa., b. Jan. 5, 1855; d. 1899; m.
——— Barr.
4018 William Lincoln, Martinsville, Pa., b. May 25, 1859.

Family of MARTIN HERR (1364) and MARIA MARTIN (1753).

4019. Letitia Esther, Quarryville, Pa., b. Jan. 19, 1840.

4020. Anna Maria, Quarryville, Pa., b. Feb. 19, 1842; m. Nov. 29, 1866, Elam L Herr (1888).

4021. Jacob Martin, Lancaster, Pa., b. Oct. 2, 1844; m. Apr. 23, 1874, Elizabeth Shuler, b. Nov. 23, 1836; dau. William Shuler and Catharine Cost.

4022. Susan Melvina, Lancaster, Pa.. b. Apr. 23, 1847; m. Dec. 13, 1869, David Skeen, b. Sept. 18, 1835; d. June 3, 1884; son Stephen Skeen and Jane Pierce.

4023. B. Franklin, Monta Vista, Colo., b. Aug. 11, 1849; m. 1876, Ella Hill, d. Aug., 1883; dau. William Hill and Emily Jones; m. Jan. 16, 1889, Sarah J. Hill, dau. William Hill and Emily Jones.

4024. Elam Kendig, Bloomfield, Ia., b. Sept. 17, 1853; m. Dec. 21, 1881, Lillie Raub, b. Mar. 1, 1856; dau. Dr. John K. Raub and Leah Peoples.

4025. Emma Florence, Collins, Pa., b. Feb. 3, 1856; m. Apr. 20, 1898. Abraham L. Stively (3661).

4026. Ella Marian, Quarryville, Pa., b. Aug. 29, 1858; m. Dec. 24, 1884, John W. McElheney, b. Oct. 15, 1858; son David S. McElheney and Sarah A. Guiles.

4027. William R., Buchanan, Salt Lake, U., b. Oct. 1, 1861.

Family of BENJAMIN HERR (1365) and ELIZABETH BARR.

4028. Antoinette, New Providence, Pa.

4029. Adelia, New Providence, Pa.

4030. Eliza Ann, New Providence, Pa.

Family of FANNIE HERR (1366) and PETER REESE.

4031. Elias, New Providence, Pa.

4032. Martin, New Providence, Pa.

4033. Josiah, Lancaster, Pa.

4034. Susan, New Providence, Pa.

4035. Simon, New Providence, Pa.

Family of SUSAN HERR (1367) and GEORGE TSHUDY.

4036. Hiram, Buck, Pa., b. 1844; m. Delilah Cochran, b. 1845; dau. Daniel Cochran and ——— Sigman.

Family of ISAAC HERR (1371) and MARY B. SHAUB.

4037. Alice Ann, Smithville, Pa., b. Dec. 25, 1852; m. Dec. 25, 1878, Elias H. Wiggins (11768).

4038. Mary Elizabeth, Smithville, Pa., b. Jan. 17, 1854; m. Dec. 23, 1879, Edwin C. Aston, b. Sept. 2, 1852; son Edwin W. Aston and Margaret V. Taylor.

Family of Wid. ISAAC HERR (1371) and FRANCES BRENEMAN.

4039. John Henry, Baltimore, Md., b. July 8, 1856; m. Jan. 27, 1878, Emma L. Kuhns, b. Apr. 12, 1858; dau. George Kuhns and Mary ———.

4040. Margaret Ann, Baltimore, Md., b. Aug. 31, 1858; d. Sept. 13, 1858.

4041. Catharine, Baltimore, Md., b. June 25, 1860; d. Aug. 2, 1860.

4042. Susan, Camargo, Pa., b. Mar. 1, 1862; m. Elmer Ressler.

4043. Benjamin Franklin, Camargo, Pa., b. Sept. 28, 1863.

4044. Amanda, Camargo, Pa., b. Sept. 5, 1866.

4045. Annie Jane. Herrville, Pa., b. Feb. 17, 1869; m. Aug. 12, 1883, Benjamin Good, b. July 29, 1834; son Jacob Good and Maria

4046. Elizabeth, Strasburg, Pa., b. Mar. 30, 1870; m. Benjamin Rhineer.

4047. Daniel Martin, New Danville, Pa., b. Sept. 24, 1872.

Family of GEORGE DIFFENBACH (1375) and BARBARA ROHRER.

4048. Maria, Strasburg, Pa., b. Dec. 20, 1805; d. Feb. 9, 1831; m. June 27, 1824, Henry Witmer, b. July 18, 1798; d. Apr. 3, 1847; son David Witmer and Esther Kendig.

4049. Eliza, Strasburg, Pa., b. Feb. 5, 1808; d. July 17, 1868.

4050. Barbara, Lancaster, Pa., b. Dec. 24, 1809; d. July 19, 1901; m. Feb. 21, 1839, Francis D. Connelly, b. Jan. 9, 1812; d. Apr. 20, 1888; son John Connelly and Mary Clark.

4051. Nancy, Strasburg, Pa., b. Sept. 8, 1812; d. Sept. 18, 1812.

4052. John R., Lancaster, Pa., b. Sept. 13, 1813; d. Feb. 10, 1903; m. Sept. 29, 1840, Martha Breneman, b. May 8, 1818; dau. Abraham Breneman and Sarah McCann.

4053. George W., Strasburg, Pa., b. Mar. 28, 1816; d. Apr. 3, 1830.

4054. Henry H., Strasburg, Pa., b. Apr. 3, 1818; d. Sept. 26, 1871.

4055. Adam F., Kasota, Minn., b. Nov. 17, 1820; m. Sophia Markoff.

Family of JOHN BOWMAN (1384) and Wid. ELIZABETH WINTERS.

4056. Benjamin, Smithville, Pa.

4057. Joseph, Smithville, Pa., m. Barbara Everly.

4058. Elizabeth, Smithville, Pa., b. June 20, 1813; d. 1868; m. May 1, 1833, Stephen Wiggins, b. July 19, 1812; son Robert Wigginsa nd Hannah Hambleton.

Family of Rev. HENRY BOWMAN (1385) and ELIZABETH WEAVER (1470).

4059. Rev. Jacob, Refton, Pa., b. July 3, 1820; d. Sept. 23, 1868; m. Dec. 6, 1845, Maria M. Frantz, b. Nov. 5, 1821; d. Nov. 21, 1906; dau. Christian N. Frantz and Elizabeth Miller.

Family of Rev. Wid. HENRY BOWMAN (1385) and SUSAN WEAVER.

4060. Elizabeth, Martinsville, Pa., b. Aug. 31, 1823; d. Nov. 5, 1875; m. Dec. 22, 1850, Henry F. Trout, b. Apr. 5, 1825; son John Trout and Mary Free.

4061. John, Forgy, O., b. Jan. 2, 1825; d. Feb. 24, 1897; m. Nov. 9, 1852, Maria P. Frick (2456).

4062. Ann, Providence, Pa., b. Jan. 16, 1827; d. July 29, 1856.

4063. Esther, Lancaster, Pa., b. Dec. 26, 1828; d. Oct. 8, 1863; m. Nov. 22, 1852, Christian Kreider, b. May 4, 1830; son John Kreider and Nancy Houser.

4064. Henry, Refton, Pa., b. Oct. 21, 1830; d. Mar. 9, 1894; m. Nov. 22, 1853, Susanna Frantz, b. Jan. 29, 1834; d. Nov. 1, 1855; dau. Christian N. Frantz and Elizabeth Miller; m. Oct. 28, 1858, Susanna Barr, b. Apr. 24, 1834; d. Apr. 26, 1900; dau. Martin Barr and Lizzie Harnish.

Family of Rev. Wid. HENRY BOWMAN (1385) and Wid. MARY BRENEMAN.

4065. Francis, Bird-in-Hand, Pa., b. Oct. 29, 1835; m. Nov. 7, 1859, Anna Herr (1868).

4066. Amos, Lampeter, Pa., b. Sept. 25, 1839; m. Jan. 31, 1869, Barbara Weaver (4343).

Family of ESTHER BOWMAN (1387) and JOHN HARNISH.

4067. Mary, Osborn, O., b. Oct. 21, 1830; m. Mar. 9, 1852, Jacob Neff, b. Nov. 15, 1815; son John Neff and Elizabeth ———.

4068. Henry, Medway, O., b. Mar. 9, 1832; m. Dec. 7, 1858, Elizabeth Miller, b. July 13, 1836; d. June 22, 1885; dau. Benjamin Miller and Barbara Hershey.

4069. Hettie, Medway, O., b. Apr. 13, 1834; m. May 14, 1857, John M. Zeller, b. Aug. 31, 1828; son Henry Zeller and Mary Miller.

4070. Jacob, Osborn, O., b. Oct., 1837; d. Oct., 1853.

4071. Anna, Osborn, O., b. Oct. 28, 1839; m. Mar. 7, 1861, Levi Kauffman, b. Sept. 5, 1833; son Christian Kauffman and Anna Erb.

4072. John S., Medway, O., b. May 1, 1843; d. May 27, 1888; m. Dec. 6, 1864, Catharine S. Davis, b. July 29, 1841; dau. Phenias Davis and Eliza Hardman.

4073. Amos B., Dayton, O., b. Apr. 12, 1845; m. Apr. 16, 1867, Agnes A. Philby, dau. William Philby and Susan Schriver.

4074. Emma, Medway, O., b. Oct. 23, 1849; m. Jan. 23, 1873, Cyrus Helman, b. Dec. 30, 1847; son John Helman and Mary Sheirick.

4075. Elizabeth, Osborn, O.

Family of DAVID ROHRER (1389) and SUSAN McALLISTER.

4076. John Wesley, Lampeter, Pa.

4077. Edwin, Lampeter, Pa.

Family of Rev. BENJAMIN HERR (1391) and NANCY BRENEMAN.

4078. Christian B., Lancaster, Pa., b. Dec. 6, 1824; d. Mar. 3, 1894; m. Sept. 17, 1850, Lizzie Myers, b. Nov. 19, 1827; dau. Martin Myers and Elizabeth Musser.

4079. Ann, Lime Valley, Pa., b. Sept. 5, 1833; m Sept. 29, 1855, John B. Brackbill (4165).

Family of ELIAS HERR (1392) and BETSEY HERSHEY.

4080. Jeremiah, Lancaster, Pa., b. June 26, 1836; d. July 16, 1903; m. Nov. 29, 1859, Elizabeth Landis, b. Nov. 5, 1837; d. Oct. 29, 1891; dau. Benjamin Landis and Elizabeth Seachrist.

4081. Mary Ann, Strasburg, Pa., b. Oct., 1838; m. Nov. 6, 1860, Rev.

Elias Groff, b. Jan. 1, 1838; son Emanuel Groff and Mary Landis.

4082. Andrew, Lime Valley, Pa., b. Mar. 10, 1841; m. Oct. 27, 1863, Susan Hess (4135).

4083. Elias, Limeton, Va., b. Sept. 26, 1843; m. Oct. 31, 1865, Elizabeth B. Leaman, b. Oct. 13, 1845; d. Sept., 1901; dau. Henry Leaman and Sarah ————.

4084. Benjamin F., Lancaster, Pa., b. Oct. 14, 1845; m. Nov. 2, 1871, Amanda R. Haverstick, b. Nov. 2, 1843; dau. Jacob Haverstick and Elizabeth Rush.

Family of MARIA HERR (1393) and JOHN BRACKBILL (1423).

4085. Christian, Strasburg, Pa., b. Aug. 1, 1828; m. Dec. 23, 1852, Susanna Lefever, b. Oct. 24, 1829; dau. Abraham Lefever and Ann Fritz.

4086. Benjamin, Willow Street, Pa., b. May 6, 1831; m. Sept. 26, 1854, Annie Lefever, b. Nov. 5, 1831; dau. Abraham Lefever and Ann Fritz.

4087. Ann, Willow Street, Pa., b. Apr. 19, 1833; d. Apr. 4, 1847.

4088. John H., Strasburg, Pa., b. Apr. 13, 1835; d. Feb. 12, 1905; m. Feb. 15, 1860, Fannie Herr (1590).

4089. Elias, Strasburg, Pa., b. Mar. 25, 1837.

4090. Son, Strasburg, Pa., b. Feb. 19, 1839; d. Feb. 19, 1839.

4091. Amos, Strasburg, Pa., b. Feb. 19, 1840.

4092. Son, Strasburg, Pa., b. Apr. 12, 1842; d. Apr. 30, 1842.

4093. Maria, New Providence, Pa., b. May 9, 1844; m. Oct. 30, 1862, Hon. Hiram Peoples, b. Feb. 14, 1835; son John Peoples and Susanna Miller.

4094. Joseph, Reading, Pa., b. July 9, 1846; m. Salinda Hershey.

4095. Elizabeth, Strasburg, Pa., b. July 28, 1848; d. Oct. 14, 1849.

Family of CHRISTIAN HERR (1394) and SUSANNA BRACKBILL (1426).

4096. John B., Lampeter, Pa., b. Nov. 10, 1834; d. Mar. 10, 1903; m. Oct. 21, 1856, Fanny Hess (4133).

4097. Son, Lancaster, Pa., b. Mar. 14, 1837; d. Mar. 14, 1837.

4098. Levi, Lancaster, Pa., b. June 14, 1838; m. Nov. 6, 1860, Susanna

L. Groff, b. July 7, 1839; d. July 9, 1902; dau. Emanuel Groff and Mary Landis.

4099. Christian, Lancaster, Pa., b. Dec. 22, 1840; m. Nov. 1, 1864, Emma S. Miller (1875).

4100. Eliza Ann, Lime Valley, Pa., b. Nov. 19, 1843; m. Nov. 3, 1864, Ebey Hershey, b. Nov. 22, 1843; d. Jan., 26, 1900; son Samuel Hershey and Elizabeth Ebey.

Family of JOSEPH HERR (1395) and ESTHER STAUFFER.

4101. Mary Ann, Lampeter, Pa., b. May 29, 1857; m. Nov. 30, 1881, Frank E. Witmer (7213).

4102. Emma, Lampeter, Pa., b. Jan. 29, 1859; d. Feb. 21, 1865.

4103. Hettie Ann, Lampeter, Pa., b. Oct. 13, 1860; d. Jan. 14, 1865.

4104. Lizzie, Baumgartners, Pa., b. Apr. 24, 1862; m. Nov., 1896, Rufus Gerlach, b. May 18, 1860; son David Gerlach and Catharine Kauffman.

Family of Rev. AMOS HERR (1396) and BETSEY ROHRER.

4105. Hettie, Strasburg, Pa., b. June 11, 1844; m. Oct. 31, 1865, Jacob L. Ranck, b. May 27, 1842; son Jacob Ranck and Susanna Leaman.

4106. Annie, Lancaster, Pa., b. Apr. 1, 1846; m. Oct. 27, 1868, Benjamin H. Snavely (3506).

4107. Christian R., Lancaster, Pa., b. Dec. 28, 1847; m. Jan. 16, 1872, Mary Hertzler, b. Aug. 16, 1849; dau. Rudolph Hertzler and Mary Shoff.

4108. Elizabeth, New Danville, Pa., b. June 10, 1854; m. Oct. 13, 1875, Amos M. Landis, b. Dec. 20, 1852; son David Landis and Frances Mayer.

Family of DANIEL HERR (1397) and ANN C. BRENEMAN (1570).

4109. Daughter, Refton, Pa., b. Aug. 13, 1841; d. Aug. 13, 1841.

4110. Enos B., Refton, Pa., b. Dec. 2, 1843; d. Sept. 19, 1869; m. Oct. 1, 1868, Mary E. Herr (4868).

4111. Elizabeth Ann, Lancaster, Pa., b. Nov. 30, 1846; m. Sept. 29, 1868, Christian B. Herr (1596).

4112. Henry B., Refton, Pa., b. Sept. 28, 1848; d. Mar. 31, 1850.
4113. Reuben D., Refton, Pa., b. July 7, 1850; d. Feb., 1907; m. Oct. 14, 1874, Harriet F. Musselman (3525); m. Nov. 9, 1886, H. Louisa Coho, b. Jan. 2, 1855; d. Nov. 9, 1900; dau. John L. Coho and Elizabeth Kurtz.

Family of JOHN HERR (1401) and ANNA STAUFFER (1449).

4114. Levi, Lexington, Ky., b. Jan. 13, 1816; d. May 22, 1891; m. Dec. 4, 1849, Frances M. Dunning, b. Mar. 4, 1830; d. Apr. 13, 1888; dau. Lucius B. Dunning and Mary T. White.
4115. Mary, Columbus, O., b. Sept. 30, 1817; d. Jan. 21, 1848; m. Apr. 28, 1836, Francis Johnson, b. Mar. 9, 1808; son Thomas Johnson and Elizabeth Stewart.
4116. Elizabeth, Columbus, O., b. Oct. 25, 1819.
4117. Samuel, Galena, O., b. Jan. 17, 1822; d. Aug. 6, 1865; m. Aug. 26, 1856, Margaret S. McIlhenny, b. July 28, 1829; dau. Hugh McIlhenny and Sarah Williams.
4118. John, Columbus, O., b. June 1, 1824; m. July 18, 1850, Ann Shultz, b. Dec. 25, 1827; dau. Jacob Shultz and Catharine Carpenter.
4119. Benjamin, Columbus, O., b. July 26, 1826; d. Oct. 26, 1843.
4120. Ann, Columbus, O., b. Jan. 14, 1829; c. Jan. 1, 1832.
4121. Henry, Columbus, O., b. May 21, 1831; d. Sept. 24, 1839.
4122. Christian S., Reese Station, O., b. Oct. 7, 1833; m. Dec. 21, 1865, Susan Stutzenberger, b. June 28, 1844; dau. Jacob Stutzenberger and Elizabeth Frank.
4123. Francis, Reese Station, O., b. Apr. 8, 1836; m. Anna Clark.
4124. Amanda, Columbus, O., b. June 25, 1838.

Family of BARBARA HERR (1403) and DAVID STROHM.

4125. Henry, Lampeter, Pa., m. ——— ——— Whip.
4126. Isaac, Lampeter, Pa.
4127. Fanny, Lampeter, Pa.
4128. Mary, Lampeter, Pa.
4129. John, Lancaster, Pa.,

Family of ELIZABETH HERR (1404) and HENRY HESS.

4130. Samuel, Lancaster, Pa., b. June 21, 1829; m. Sept. 24, 1852, Barbara A. Lintner, b. Jan. 22, 1832; dau. Christian Lintner and Elizabeth Sener.

4131. Benjamin B., Willow Street, Pa., b. Dec. 21, 1830.

4132. Anna, Rockville, Pa., b. June 4, 1834; m. Oct. 12, 1854, Rudolph Shenk, b. Nov. 15, 1826; son Henry Shenk and Susan Hoover.

4133. Fanny, Lampeter, Pa., b. Nov. 9, 1836; m. Oct. 21, 1856, John B. Herr (4096).

4134. Mary, Willow Street, Pa., b. Sept. 4, 1839; m. June 1, 1858, Benjamin Harnish, b. Dec. 21, 1830; son Michael Harnish and Elizabeth Warfel.

4135. Susanna, Lime Valley, Pa., b. Feb. 28, 1842; m. Oct. 27, 1863, Andrew Herr (4082).

4136. Henry W., Orrville, O., b. Apr. 26, 1845; d. Feb. 2, 1905; m. Oct. 24, 1865, Catharine Hoover (8660).

Family of ABRAHAM HERR (1406) and ANN STONER.

4137. Fanny, Rohrerstown, Pa., b. Mar. 20, 1833; m. Oct. 18, 1856, John K. Bender, b. Oct. 18, 1827; d. May 27, 1894; son Michael Bender and ——— Gluik.

4138. Ann, Lancaster, Pa., b. June 8, 1834; m. Oct. 18, 1860, George H. Leaman, b. Sept. 24, 1839; son Samuel Leaman and Barbara Heller.

4139. Abraham S., Bird-in-Hand, Pa., b. Oct. 30, 1835; d. Mar. 15, 1905; m. Oct. 9, 1862, Elizabeth Burkholder, b. Mar. 10, 1834; d. Dec. 4, 1896; dau. John Burkholder and Mary Kreider.

4140. Isaac, Lancaster, Pa., b. May 29, 1837; d. Mar. 24, 1904; m. Nov. 29, 1860, Mary H. Leaman, b. Apr. 28, 1837; dau. Samuel Leaman and Barbara Heller.

Family of CHRISTIAN HERR (1408) and SUSAN HESS.

4141. Jacob H., Willow Street, Pa., b. Aug. 26, 1840; m. Jan. 13, 1880, Wid. Catharine Kreider, b. July 8, 1835; dau. Christian Mylin and Elizabeth Ferree.

4142. Joseph, Lancaster, Pa., b. Jan. 6, 1842; d. Dec. 27, 1902; m. Jan. 26, 1879, Etta Eberly, b. Mar. 23, 1853; dau. John Eberly and Mary Hoak.

4143. Maria, Lancaster, Pa., b. June 23, 1844; d. May 9, 1847.

4144. Christian H., Millersille, Pa., b. Mar. 5, 1846; d. Feb. 21, 1898; m. Oct. 15, 1872, Mary Kendig (3195).

4145. Barbara, Lancaster, Pa., b. Oct. 28, 1850; m. Nov. 28, ——, Jacob B. Lindeman, son John Lindeman and Frances ——.

4146. Elizabeth, Lancaster, Pa., b. Sept. 15, 1853.

4147. Abraham, Lancaster, Pa., b. Oct. 5, 1855.

Family of MARIA HERR (1413) and JOHN HARNISH.

4148. Amos, Willow Street, Pa., b. Sept. 9, 1840; d. Aug. 17, 1841.

4149. Maria, Willow Street, Pa., b. Apr. 28, 1844; d. Oct. 18, 1851.

4150. John, Willow Street, Pa., b. Mar. 26, 1846; d. Feb. 8, 1850.

4151. Elizabeth, New Danville, Pa., b. Mar. 4, 1848; m. Nov. 18, 1869, Abraham B. Harnish, b. Oct. 16, 1845; d. Sept. 17, 1906.

4152. David F., Herrville, Pa., b. May 20, 1850; m. 1879, Kate Herman, b. 1855; dau. John Herman and Elizabeth ——.

4153. Martin S., Herrville, Pa., b. Feb. 19, 1853; d. Aug. 1, 1872.

4154. Emma H., Herrville, Pa., b. Aug. 31, 1855; m. Dec. 27, 1894, Jacob B. Wissler, d. Aug. 25, 1898; m. 1902, Harry F. Eshbach.

4155. Annie Selma, Herrville, Pa., b. Dec. 24, 1857; d. Feb. 7, 1870.

Family of MARTIN HERR (1415) and CATHARINE E. MILLER.

4156. Emma Adaline, Bausman, Pa., b. Aug. 7, 1849; m. H. —— Smith.

4157. Christian, Quarryville, Pa., b. Feb. 3, 1851; d. Mar. 11, 1851.

4158. Mary Catharine, New Providence, Pa., b. Aug. 30, 1852; m. —— Edwards.

4159. Elim Miller, Quarryville, Pa., b. Nov. 21, 1853.

4160. Anna Elizabeth, Quarryville, Pa., b. Apr. 18, 1857; d. May 9, 1858.

4161. Martin, Quarryville, Pa., b. Sept. 17, 1858; m. Feb. 13, 1879, Lydia A. Rineer, b. Nov. 17, 1861; dau. Benjamin Rineer and Eliza Keen.

4162. Benjamin Franklin, Quarryville, Pa., b. Jan. 24, 1860.
4163. John Henry, Quarryville, Pa., b. Mar. 31, 1862.

Family of DAVID HERR (1416) and MARY GROFF.

4164. John, Quarryville, Pa.

Family of BENJAMIN BRACKBILL (1422) and ANN ELIZA BAIR (2871).

4165. John B., Soudersburg, Pa., b. Aug. 3, 1828; d. Mar. 13, 1861;
m. Sept. 29, 1855, Ann Herr (4079).
4166. Ann, Soudersburg, Pa., b. Apr. 3, 1831; m. Nov. 8, 1853, Daniel
Leaman, b. Oct. 1, 1821; son Joseph Leaman and Lydia Hartman.
4167. Susanna, Soudersburg, Pa., b. June 10, 1835; m. Oct. 2, 1855,
Samuel L. Leaman, b. June 10, 1830; son George Leaman and
Hettie Lefevre.
4168. Amanda, Soudersburg, Pa., b. July 17, 1838.
4169. Eliza, Soudersburg, Pa., b. May 3, 1848; d. May 21, 1849.

Family of ELIZABETH BRACKBILL (1424) and JACOB HOUSER.

4170. Eliza, Rocky Springs, Pa., b. Dec. 29, 1828; m. Nov. 12, 1850,
John B. Kreider, b. May 6, 1825; son Henry Kreider and Catharine Barr.
4171. Son, Lancaster, Pa., b. Nov. 22, 1831; d. Nov. 22, 1831.
4172. Anna, Lancaster, Pa., b. May 11, 1833; m. Oct. 25, 1853, Christian Lefevre, b. Nov. 24, 1823; son Henry Lefevre and Elizabeth Hess.
4173. Son, Lancaster, Pa., b. Dec. 4, 1836; d. Dec. 4, 1836.
4174. Maria, Lampeter, Pa., b. Aug. 6, 1838; m. Nov. 22, 1860, John
N. Meck, b. Aug. 9, 1832; son George Meck and Martha
Nuding.
4175. Susanna, Lampeter, Pa., b. Mar. 30, 1842; m. Nov. 28, 1864,
Aaron Weaver, b. June 5, 1839; son Peter B. Weaver and
Fanny Groff.
4176. Son, Lampeter, Pa., b. Mar. 31, 1845; d. Mar. 31, 1845.
4177. Jacob B., Lampeter, Pa., b. July 10, 1848.

Family of CHRISTIAN BRACKBILL (1425) and BARBARA LANDIS.

4178. Henry L., Fairview, Pa., b. Sept. 17, 1830; m. Sept. 30, 1851, Susan W. Rudy, b. May 14, 1832; dau. Daniel Rudy and Anna M. Weidler.

4179. Eliza Ann, Fairview, Pa., b. May 16, 1832; m. Aug. 29, 1850, John H. Risser, b. July 9, 1829; son John Risser and Lizzie Herr.

4180. Maria, Fairview, Pa., b. May 2, 1836; d. Feb. 3, 1851.

4181. Christian L., Fairview, Pa., b. Aug. 30, 1841; m. Apr. 21, 1863, Amanda E. Baker, b. May 29, 1846; dau. Henry Baker and Sarah Erb.

Family of JOHN LANDIS (1428) and ELIZABETH RUDY.

4182. Maria, Manor, Pa., b. June 20, 1807; m. May 11, 1830, Rudolph Gamber, b. Dec. 11, 1798; son William Gamber and Anna Harzler.

4183. Benjamin, Manor, Pa., b. Apr. 24, 1810; m. Mar. 12, 1835, Esther Schoff (1036).

4184. Anna, Manor, Pa., b. Jan. 2, 1812; m. Aug. 31, 1830, John Forry, b. June 12, 1798; d. Oct. 30, 1865; son John Forry and Fanny Sides.

4185. Fanny, Manor, Pa., b. Jan. 16, 1814; m. Jan. 7, 1834, George Weidler, b. Dec. 12, 1810; d. Jan. 27, 1859; son George Weidler and Lizzie Bollinger.

4186. John, Manor, Pa., b. Feb. 27, 1816; d. Mar. 31, 1831.

Family of Wid. JOHN LANDIS (1428) and ANNA HOOVER.

4187. Susanna, Manor, Pa., b. Apr. 5, 1818.

4188. Elizabeth, Manor, Pa., b. Dec. 11, 1819; d. May 19, 1865.

4189. Jacob H., Millersville, Pa., b. Apr. 18, 1822; d. Mar. 2, 1904; m. Feb. 26, 1852, Anna S. Herr (859).

4190. David, Millersville, Pa., b. Oct. 13, 1823; m. Dec. 9, 1845, Fanny Myers, b. Apr. 25, 1825; dau. Martin Myers and Elizabeth Musser.

4191. Tobias, Millersville, Pa., b. Dec. 21, 1824.

4192. Magdalene, Lancaster, Pa., b. July 24, 1826; d. June, 1866; m. Nov. 25, 1852, Rudolph S. Herr (860).

Family of BENJAMIN LANDIS (1430) and MAGDALENE BRUBAKER.

4193. Elizabeth, Landis Valley, Pa., b. Mar. 17, 1811 ; m. Jan. 2, 1840, Jacob Kohr, b. Aug. 20, 1810; son Jacob Kohr and Anna Frantz.

4194. Magdalene, Landis Valley, Pa., b. Nov. 12, 1812; d. Dec. 13, 1828.

4195. Christian B., Landis Valley, Pa., b. Nov. 24, 1814; m. Dec., 12, 1837, Fanny Denlinger, b. Sept. 16, 1820; d. May 6, 1852; dau. John Denlinger and Fanny Hurst; m. May 7, 1857, Anna Hostetter, b. May 8, 1821 ; d. Nov. 25, 1861 ; dau. Daniel Hostetter and Susanna Rudy.

4196. Anna, Landis Valley, Pa., b. Dec. 4, 1817; m. Jan. 17, 1837, Andrew Brubaker, b. Sept. 25, 1814; son Jacob Brubaker and Barbara Shenk.

4197. Benjamin, Landis Valley, Pa., b. Dec. 16, 1818; d. June 24, 1824.

4198. Fanny, Landis Valley, Pa., b. Nov. 19, 1822; d. Jan. 10, 1823.

4199. Sarah, Landis Valley, Pa., b. Nov. 5, 1824; d. May 11, 1828.

Family of SUSANNA ESHLEMAN (1431) and MICHAEL B. BARR.

4200. Hiram Eshleman, Quincy, Ill., b. Oct. 2, 1814; m. Dec. 27, 1838, Elizabeth Briant, b. Jan. 17, 1817; dau. William Briant and Lydia Barnet.

4201. Mary Elizabeth, Quincy, Ill., b. July 20, 1816; m. Mar. 18, 1841, William Homan, b. May 18, 1805; son Joseph Homan and —— Getzinger.

4202. Melchor Newton, Monmouth, Ill., b. Jan. 11, 1818; m. June 26, 1864, M. —— J. H. Uncles, b. Feb. 25, 1843; dau. John Uncles and Rebecca Sowther.

4203. Elijah. Quincy, Ill., b. Feb. 20, 1820; d. Oct. 10, 1864; m. May 26, 1859, Lizzie Kindle, b. Nov. 20, 1827; dau. Francis Kindle and Rebecca Stowe.

4204. Susan, Baltimore, Md., b. Feb. 2, 1822; m. Mar. 25, 1846, Cyrus J. Miller, son George Miller and —— Rice.

4205. Amanda, Lancaster, Pa., b. Jan. 29, 1824; m. Mar. 26, 1856, Dr. John McCalla, b. Nov. 21, 1814; son Alexander McCalla and Elizabeth Mitchel.

4206. Dr. Edwin Wesley, St. Louis, Mo., b. Aug. 7, 1825; m. Aug. 25, 1859, Mary Blosdel, b. Sept. 4, 1838; d. Aug. 30, 1863; dau. John C. Blosdel and ——.

4207. Frances Louisa, St. Louis, Mo., b. July 14, 1827; d. Dec. 10, 1864; m. Dec. 28, 1853, Hiram Mars, b. Jan. 7, 1829; son Andrew Mars and Elizabeth Whips.

4208. Harvey F., Quincy, Ill., b. Dec. 24, 1829; d. Oct. 8, 1900; m. Oct. 16, 1873, C. Isabil Tuthill, b. Nov. 15, 1846; dau. Russell Tuthill and Dannetta Bigelow.

4209. Daughter, Quincy, Ill., b. Jan. 23, 1832; d. Jan. 24, 1832.

4210. Emma Cela, Erie, Pa., b. Aug. 25, 1835; m. Aug. 24, 1864, Rev. J. —— D. Barstow, b. Jan. 1, 1834; son John C. Barstow and Melinda A. Plumber.

Family of BENJAMIN B. ESHLEMAN (1432) and MARY E. STAUFFER.

4211. William D., Bart, Pa., b. Jan. 24, 1819; d. Aug. 8, 1852.

4212. Dr. Isaac S., Fresno, Cal., b. May 22, 1820; d. June 13, 1902; m. Nov. 27, 1851, Mary D. Jayne, b. Mar. 14, 1830; d. Jan. 19, 1903; dau. Dr. David Jayne and Hannah Sheppard.

4213. James Harvey, Topeka, Kans., b. Sept. 1, 1821; d. Dec. 10, 1897; m. May 24, 1849, Mary E. Cooper, b. June 1, 1830; d. Oct. 24, 1889; dau. Truman Cooper and Julia A. Pusey.

4214. John J., Lancaster, Pa., b. Apr. 14, 1823; d. ——.

4115. Martin B., Faggs, Manor, Pa., b. Jan. 1, 1825; d. Mar. 17, 1895; m. Jan. 14, 1857, Mary E. Good, b. Oct. 4, 1833; dau. Jacob Good and Sarah A. Davis.

4216. Sarah M., Philadelphia, Pa., b. Jan. 9, 1827; m. Aug. 24, 1848, Rev. George W. Young, b. Aug. 8, 1820; d. Nov. 12, 1864; son Thomas S. Young and Eloise Orvis.

4217. H. Louisa, Spruce Grove, Pa., b. Jan. 31, 1828; m. Sept. 25, 1855, Joseph Hastings, b. Nov. 25, 1826; son Peter Hastings and Sarah Andrews.

4218. Benjamin Franklin, New Orleans, La., b. Mar. 9, 1830; m. Dec. 22, 1868, Fannie H. Leverick, b. July 19, 1846; dau. William E. Leverick and Fannie Inskeep.

4219. Ann, Strasburg, Pa., b. Oct. 30, 1832; m. Jan. 26, 1858, Jacob

Bachman, b. Jan. 21, 1825; d. Mar. 9, 1888; son Jacob Bachman and Barbara Eshleman.

4220. Kate A., Fresno, Cal., b. Dec. 8, 1834; d. Oct. 10, 1891; m. May 25, 1869, Benjamin Garret, b. Oct. 17, 1836; son Enos Garret and Sarah J. Hipple.

4221. J. Albert, Erie, Pa., b. May 20, 1837; m. June 15, 1865, Clara V. Eckendorff, b. June 20, 1842; dau. Gustavus Eckendorff and Margaret Rise; m. Laura Neill, d. June 29, 1901; dau. Rev. James Neill and ———.

4222. Emma F., Philadelphia, Pa., b. Nov. 18, 1839; d. Mar. 4, 1878; m. Oct. 15, 1868, Joseph R. Craig, b. Oct. 6, 1838; son Robert Craig and Margaret Burns.

4223. Edwin D. H., Philadelphia, Pa., b. Oct. 5, 1841; m. Oct. 19, 1876, Annie V. Musselman (4857).

Family of MARIA ESHLEMAN (1434) and JOHN WARFEL.

4224. Martha E., Strasburg, Pa., b. Apr. 9, 1825; d. Nov. 7, 1886.

4225. Jacob E., Strasburg, Pa., b. July 26, 1826; d. June 2, 1855.

4226. John B., Lancaster, Pa., b. Sept. 19, 1830; d. Apr. 18, 1908; m. Jan. 16, 1853, Mary A. Girvin (5945).

4227. Albert K., Lancaster, Pa., b. June 11, 1836; m. Jan. 10, 1859, Mary N. Groff (5870).

4228. Silas N., Strasburg, Pa., b. July 29, 1838.

4229. Amos, Strasburg, Pa,. b. May 8, 1840; d. Aug. 17, 1840.

4230. Anna M., Strasburg, Pa., b. Feb. 12, 1842; d. Aug. 24, 1842.

Family of JACOB ESHLEMAN (1436) and JANE JULIET WITMER.

4231. Jacob Witmer, Leaman Place, Pa., b. Feb. 21, 1832; d. Mar. 3, 1838.

4232. David Witmer, Leaman Place, Pa., b. Feb. 21, 1832; d. Mar. 10, 1832.

4233. Mary Jane, Leaman Place, Pa., b. Aug. 6, 1833; d. Sept. 10, 1834.

4234. Milton Brackbill, Newport, Pa., b. Feb. 4, 1835; d. Feb. 25, 1899; m. Sept. 19, 1867, Jennie M. Williams, b. Oct. 6, 1841; d. Apr. 18, 1872; dau. John Williams and Jane Moore; m. Dec. 2, 1873, Annie M. Lightner, b. Dec. 8, 1843; dau. Peter E. Lightner and Christiana Musser.

4235. Daughter, Leaman Place, Pa., b. Nov. 28, 1836; d. Nov. 28, 1836.

4236. Ferree Witmer, Leaman Place, Pa., b. Oct. 31, 1837; d. Dec. 31, 1870; m. Jan. 28, 1869, Clarissa R. Musselman (4856).

4237. Amos Lightener, Leaman Place, Pa., b. Nov. 19, 1839; m. Feb. 4, 1875, Esther E. Hoover, b. Dec. 12, 1845; dau. Jacob Hoover and Esther E. Witmer.

4238. Elam Witmer, Leaman Place, Pa., b. Nov. 19, 1841; m. June 11, 1873, Isabella A. Lightner, b. May 14, 1853; dau. John L. Lightner and Eliza Bender.

4239. Eliza Emaline, Leaman Place, Pa., b. Nov. 6, 1843; d. July 9, 1893.

4240. Silas Kendrick, Leaman Place, Pa., b. June 13, 1845; m. Dec. 15, 1874, Emma H. Slaymaker, b. Jan. 12, 1852; dau. John M. Slaymaker and Emma H. Jack.

4241. Edwin Sample, Leaman Place, Pa., b. Apr. 17, 1847; d. July 18, 1851.

4242. Juliet Frances, Leaman Place, Pa., b. Jan. 17, 1849; d. Aug. 6, 1851.

4243. Son, Leaman Place, Pa., b. Apr. 5, 1851; d. Apr. 5, 1851.

Family of ANN ESHLEMAN (1437) and GEORGE GROFF (3810).

4244. Son, Paradise, Pa., b. June 17, 1836; d. June 17, 1836.

4245. Aldus John, Lancaster, Pa., b. June 13, 1837; m. Sept. 19, 1867, Susan J. Witmer (3409); m. Nov. 7, 1877, Augusta Parker, b. Sept. 3, 1852; dau. Edward Parker and Amelia Sylvia.

4246. Mary Virginia, Strasburg, Pa., b. Oct. 23, 1839.

4247. Silas Eshleman, Strasburg, Pa., b. Mar. 6, 1842; m. Feb. 27, 1878, Sarah E. Keneagy, b. Dec. 25, 1851; dau. Henry Keneagy and Sarah A. Rowe.

4248. Emma E., Paradise, Pa., b. June 10, 1844.

Family of Dr. JOHN K. ESHLEMAN (1440) and FANNY EDGE.

4249. Mary, Downingtown, Pa., b. Apr. 18, 1841; d. Aug. 23, 1864.

4250. Ruth Anna, Valley Brook Farm, Pa., b. Jan. 22, 1843; m. Sept. 5, 1872, William McClure Lloyd, b. Mar. 2, 1842; d. June 26, 1887; son Samuel H. Lloyd and Mary M. McClure.

4151. Lizzie, Downingtown, Pa., b. June 30, 1847; m. June 24, 1875, Abraham R. McIlvaine, b. Nov. 18, 1847; son John McIlvaine and Elizabeth R. Mattack.

4252. John Jay, Downingtown, Pa., b. July 6, 1853; d. Nov. 1, 1861.

Family of MARTHA ESHLEMAN (1442) and CHRISTIAN H. LEFEVRE.

4253. Laura, Lancaster, Pa., b. Nov. 29, 1841; d. Mar., 1876.

Family of JOHN BRACKBILL (1443) and ANN GROFF.

4254. Harvey, Strasburg, Pa., b. July 10, 1826; d. Oct. 7, 1898; m. Jan. 26, 1857, Caroline C. Rauch, b. May 29, 1830; d. Feb. 3, 1903; dau. Christian H. Rauch and Mary M. Romig.

4255. Mary Ann, Lancaster, Pa., b. Sept. 19, 1833; d. Oct. 29, 1907; m. May 15, 1855, Cyrus N. Herr (1557).

4256. Phenias, Strasburg, Pa., b. Oct. 23, 1835; d. Mar. 5, 1851.

Family of BENJAMIN BRACKBILL (1445) and SUSANNA HOWRY.

4257. Mary Elizabeth, Vintage, Pa., b. Nov. 21, 1837.

4258. Elam H., Kinzers, Pa., b. July 2, 1839; m. Dec. 16, 1869, Barbara Hershey, b. Aug. 1, 1848; dau. Christian Hershey and Magdalena Metzler.

4259. Elias E., Vintage, Pa., b. Aug. 23, 1841.

4260. Susanna, Vintage, Pa., b. Feg. 4, 1844.

4261. Lydia Ann, Vintage, Pa., b. Mar. 23, 1846; d. Dec. 7, 1888; m. Nov. 19, 1874, Peter Hess, b. Jan. 13, 1844; son Christian Hess and Judith Zimmerman.

4262. Benjamin O., Vintage, Pa., b. Sept. 19, 1848; d. Sept. 26, ——; m. Anna Martin, dau. Joseph Martin and —— Oberholtzer.

4263. Jacob F., Vintage, Pa., b. May 19, 1850.

4264. Henry P., Vintage, Pa., b. May 11, 1853; m. Emma Diller.

Family of HENRY BRACKBILL (1447) and MARIA EABY.

4265. Amaziah E., Paradise, Pa., b. Sept. 2, 1847; m. —— Denlinger.

4266. ——.

4267. Naomi Ada, Paradise, Pa., b. Nov. 30, 1849; m. Grabill Diller.

4268. Elmira Clara, Strasburg, Pa., b. July 19, 1851; m. Abraham H. Denlinger.

4269. Susanna R., Strasburg, Pa., b. Nov. 24, 1853.

4270. Preston Eaby, Strasburg, Pa., b. June 18, 1856.

4271. Seymour H., Strasburg, Pa., b. Oct. 19, 1858.

Family of MARIA STAUFFER (1448) and SAMUEL BARR.

4272. Catharine, Lampeter, Pa., b. Oct. 21, 1816; d. Apr. 18, 1840; m. Dec. 22, 1836, Benjamin Herr (442).

4273. Son, Willow Street, Pa., b. July 9, 1818; d. July 9, 1818.

4274. Ann, Willow Street, Pa., b. June 17, 1819; m. Oct. 1, 1839, Henry Shenk, b. June 5, 1818; d. Jan. 6, 1854; son Henry Shenk and Susan Huber; m. Mar. 6, 1866, Wid. Abraham K. Miller, b. June 27, 1817; son Christian Miller and Martha.

4275. Maria, Lancaster, Pa., b. June 27, 1821; m. Nov. 22, 1842, Michael L. Huber, b. Sept. 19, 1819; son Jacob Huber and Anna Landis.

4276. Benjamin, Lancaster, Pa., b. Aug. 17, 1823; m. Dec. 18, 1845, Barbara Groff, b. Aug. 23, 1826; dau. John Groff and Susan Rife.

4277. Elizabeth, Conestoga Center, Pa., b. Sept. 25, 1825; m. Feb. 20, 1851, Abraham Kendig, b. Oct. 22, 1824; son Martin Kendig and Fanny Mylin.

4278. Magdalene, Willow Street, Pa., b. Dec. 15, 1827; m. June 10, 1851, Benjamin Bachman, b. Aug. 6, 1825; son John Bachman and Ann Herr.

4279. Frances, Salunga, Pa., b. Jan. 13, 1830; d. Feb. 24, 1851; m. Nov. 27, 1849, Christian Greider, b. July 31, 1825; d. Mar. 7, 1854; son Christian Greider and Susan Miller.

4280. Barbara, Willow Street, Pa., b. Mar. 4, 1832; d. Mar. 15, 1836.

4281. Son, Willow Street, Pa., b. Mar. 4, 1832; d. Mar. 4, 1832.

Family of JACOB BRACKBILL (1452) and BARBARA GREENLEAF.

4282. Benjamin Landis, Salisburyville, Pa., b. Dec. 28, 1833; d. June 17, 1892; m. Dec. 25, 1855, Susan Carpenter, b. Dec. 4, 1831; dau. John Carpenter and Sarah Kendig.

4283. Isaac Veazy, Salisburyville, Pa., b. Nov. 23. 1835; d. Mar. 3, 1837.

4284. Frances Elizabeth, Salisburyville, Pa., b. Jan. 17, 1838; d. May 27, 1841.

4285. Martha Ann, Salisburyville, Pa., b. May 8, 1840; m. David Levison, son John Levison and Jane Graham.

4286. Salome Maria, Salisburyville, Pa., b. Sept. 16, 1842; m. Nov. 24, 1863, Solomon Linville, b. Dec. 26, 1832; son William Linville and Ann Supplee.

4287. Christian Houser, Salisburyville, Pa., b. Sept. 30, 1844.

Family of BARBARA BRACKBILL (1455) and BENJAMIN HOOVER.

4288. Elizabeth, Paradise, Pa., b. Jan. 15, 1838; m. Benjamin Eby, b. May 7, 1838; son Samuel Eby and Anna Frantz.

4289. Maria, Strasburg, Pa., b. Sept. 23, 1839; d. Jan. 15, 1842.

4290. Anna, Strasburg, Pa., b. Sept. 23, 1839; d. Jan. 8, 1842.

4291. Son, Strasburg, Pa., b. Aug. 23, 1841; d. Aug. 26, 1841.

4292. Salome, Strasburg, Pa., b. Sept. 24, 1842.

4293. Benjamin Franklin, Gordonville, Pa., b. Jan. 20, 1845; d. Mar. 23, 1901; m. Hettie Rutter, b. July 14, 1843; dau. Jonathan Rutter and Barbara Hurst.

4294. Christian Brackbill, Kinzers, Pa., b. Sept. 3, 1846; m. Mary Reeser, b. June 30, 1849; d. Apr. —, 1907.

4295. Amanda, Strasburg, Pa., b. Oct. 20, 1848.

4296. John Milton, New Holland, Pa., b. Nov. 7, 1850; m. Oct. 14, 1875, Mary E. Rutter, b. July 23, 1853; d. Feb. 15, 1883; dau. Emanuel Rutter and Anna Hershey; m. Nov. 19, 1885, Lucetta M. Ranck, b. June 19, 1846; dau. John Ranck and Elizabeth ———.

4297. Amos Hershey, Kinzers, Pa., b. Nov. 21, 1852; m. Fianna Wenger, b. Feb. 20, 1855; dau. Jonas Wenger and Susan Ernst.

4298. Barbara Ann, Strasburg, Pa., b. Nov. 29, 1856.

4299. Henry Myers, Magdalene, Fla., b. July 23, 1863; m. Mar. 22, 1892, Anna E. Stauffer, b. Sept. 2, 1861.

Family of BENJAMIN BRACKBILL (1456) and MAGDALENE CARPENTER.

4300. John C., Kinzers, Pa., b. June 16, 1838; m. Dec. 15, 1863, Hettie Frantz, b. Oct. 1, 1842; dau. Joseph Frantz and Barbara Kreider.

4301. Elizabeth, Intercourse, Pa., b. Dec. 10, 1839; m. Dec. 12, 1861, John M. Hershey, b. Apr. 29, 1839; son John Hershey and Magdalene Musser.
4302. Anna, Bethania, Pa., b. Mar. 12, 1842.
4303. Barbara, Bethania, Pa., b. July 11, 1844; m. Dec. 20, 1866, Adam Longenecker, son Adam Longenecker and ———— Miller.
4304. Benjamin A., Bethania, Pa., b. Feb. 25, 1847; d. June 16, 1847.
4305. Magdalene, Bethania, Pa., b. Dec. 19, 1850.
4306. Amos H., Kinzers, Pa., b. Mar. 28, 1854.
4307. Josiah A., Kinzers, Pa., b. Feb. 19, 1857.
4308. Eli M., Kinzers, Pa., b. Aug. 20, 1860.

Family of SUSANNA BRACKBILL (1457) and LEVI HOOVER.

4309. Emma Elizabeth, Strasburg, Pa., b. Aug. 29, 1854.
4310. Owen B., Strasburg, Pa., b. Nov. 3, 1861.
4311. Vincent Keys, Strasburg, Pa., b. Apr. 3, 1864.

Family of JOSEPH BRACKBILL (1459) and ELIZABETH METZLER.

4312. Rev. Christian Metzler, Gap, Pa., b. Dec. 5, 1853; m. Elizabeth Denlinger.
4313. Anna, Gap, Pa., b. Feb. 18, 1856.
4314. Levi H., Gap, Pa., b. Aug. 18, 1858; m. Nov. 22, 1883, Susan Ranck, b. Nov. 16, 1863; dau. Benjamin Ranck and Lydia Hershey.
4315. Elizabeth, Gap, Pa., b. Dec. 25, 1862; m. John K. Eaby.
4316. Joseph Warner, Paradise, Pa., b. June 13, 1866; m. Alice Frantz, dau. Joseph Frantz and ————.

Family of SAMUEL WEAVER (1453) and MAGDALENE RUSH.

4317. Jacob, Lampeter, Pa., b. Dec. 18, 1810.
4318. Samuel, Lampeter, Pa., b. July 5, 1813.
4319. Catharine, Lampeter, Pa., b. Feb. 21, 1816; d. Feb. 5, 1845.
4320. Hiram, Lampeter, Pa., b. Feb. 4, 1821; d. 1867; m. Louisa L. Lawson, b. Dec. 14, 1827.
4321. Simon R., Lampeter, Pa., b. Apr. 6, 1824; d. Aug. 19, 1871; m. Dec. 24, 1846, Esther Bachman (3462).

4322. David, Lampeter, Pa., b. Mar. 18, 1827; m. June 14, 1852, Sarah Esbenshade, b. Oct. 20, 1834; dau. Adam Esbenshade and Mary Kreider.

4323. Martha, Lancaster, Pa., b. Apr. 1, 1830; m. Nov. 10, 1856, Alpheus Carpenter, b. July 17, 1827; son Henry Carpenter and Betsey Groff.

Family of MATTIE WEAVER (1466) and MARTIN HARNISH.

4324. David, Conestoga, Center, Pa., b. Mar. 22, 1823; m. Mar. 28, 1847, Mary A. Lauber, b. Mar. 10, 1821; d. Feb. 5, 1849; dau. Martin Lauber and Catharine Kyle; m. Oct. 27, 1850, Annie Myers, b. Mar. 16, 1825; d. Dec. 21, 1859; dau. Daniel Myers and Barbara Metzler; m. Nov. 17, 1860, Catharine Lauber, b. Mar. 9, 1819; dau. Martin Lauber and Catharine Kyle.

4325. Elizabeth, Conestoga Center, Pa., b. Jan. 31, 1828; m. Nov. 3, 1846, John L. Denlinger, b. Nov. 16, 1822; son Jacob Denlinger and Mary Landis.

4326. Susanna, Millport, Pa., b. Oct. 11, 1831; m. Nov. 7, 1850, Benjamin Harnish, b. Dec. 14, 1828; son Michael Harnish and Susan Hess.

Family of JOHN WEAVER (1467) and BETSEY KREIDER.

4327. Martin, Lampeter, Pa., b. Aug. 6, 1820; m. Nov. 28, 1843, A. Catharine Herr (1553).

4328. Christian, Lampeter, Pa., b. May 14, 1823; m. Nov. 6, 1849, Rebecca Brubaker, b. Feb. 14, 1831; dau. Samuel Brubaker and Esther Stehman.

4329. Amos, Lampeter, Pa., b. May 22, 1825; m. Dec. 10, 1850, Mary Harnish, b. Feb. 16, 1831; dau. Michael Harnish and Susan Hess.

4330. Elizabeth, Lampeter, Pa., b. May 2, 1827.

4331. Anna, Lampeter, Pa., b. Mar. 25, 1829; d. Feb. 24, 1899.

4332. John K., Lampeter, Pa., b. Mar. 15, 1832; m. 1871, Rebecca M. Frantz, b. Oct. 30, 1835; d. Dec. 20, 1900; dau. Christian N. Frantz and Elizabeth K. Miller.

4333. Cyrus J., Lenover, Pa., b. Mar. 2, 1835; m. Oct. 7, 1856, Mary

Witmer, b. July 3, 1835; dau. Abraham Witmer and Susan New-comer.

4334. Frank J., Lancaster, Pa., b. Apr. 7, 1838; m. Feb. 27, 1870, Mary Buckwalter, b. Nov. 4, 1837; dau. Benjamin Buckwalter and Elizabeth Mylin.

4335. Dr. Jacob G., Strasburg, Pa., b. Apr. 9, 1840.

Family of Rev. JOSEPH WEAVER (1468) and BARBARA BARR.

4336. Isaac, Wheatland Mills, Pa., b. Sept. 8, 1820; d. Oct. 27, 1887; m. Oct. 20, 1850, Catharine Barr, b. Aug. 23, 1824; dau. Benjamin Barr and Mary Mylin.

4337. Ephraim, Lampeter, Pa., b. Apr. 4, 1823; d. June 17, 1868.

4338. Ann, Waynesboro, Pa., b. July 25, 1825; d. Sept. 11, 1845; m. Nov. 19, 1844, John Frantz, b. Aug. 10, 1811; son Rev. Christian Frantz and Ann Frick.

4339. Jacob, Wheatland Mills, Pa., b. Aug. 4, 1827; d. Dec. 22, 1843.

4340. Mary, Lancaster, Pa., b. May 17, 1830.

4341. Elizabeth, Wheatland Mills, Pa., b. July 25, 1832; d. Nov. 10, 1857; m. Oct. 1, 1854, Rev. Christian N. Witmer, b. Apr. 16, 1831; d. Sept. 2, 1879; son Abraham Witmer and Susan New-comer.

4342. Susanna, Lancaster, Pa., b. Apr. 27, 1835.

Family of Rev. Wid. JOSEPH WEAVER (1468) and Wid. ESTHER BRUBAKER.

4343. Barbara, Lampeter, Pa., b. Mar. 27, 1844; m. Jan. 31, 1869, Amos Bowman (4066).

4344. Annie E., Lancaster, Pa., b. July 17, 1848; m. 1892, John Kurtz, son Jacob Kurtz and Sarah Shirk.

Family of HETTIE WEAVER (1471) and JACOB LANTZ.

4345. Ephraim, Lampeter, Pa., b. Aug. 16, 1820; d. Oct. 24, 1821.

4346. Benjamin W., Wrightsville, Pa., b. Sept. 27, 1821; m. Oct. 20, 1846, Fanny Herr (1147).

4347. Elizabeth, Lampeter, Pa., b. Apr. 16, 1824; d. May 26, 1824.

4348. Jacob, Lampeter, Pa., b. Oct. 1, 1825; d. Apr. 30, 1830.

4349. Isaac, Chester, Pa., b. May 3, 1827; d. 1902; m. Jan. 8, 1853, Barbara Esbenshade, b. Mar. 3, 1828; dau. Adam Esbenshade and Mary Kreider.

4350. Esther, Lancaster, Pa., b. Aug. 2, 1829; m. July 28, 1848, Martin Myers, b. Aug. 11, 1828; son Daniel Myers and Barbara Metzler.

4351. John, Lampeter, Pa., b. Jan. 8, 1831; m. May 20, 1858, Margaret Wilson, b. Oct. 9, 1835; dau. William Wilson and Margaret Shultz.

4352. Abraham, Lampeter, Pa., b. Feb. 25, 1833.

4353. Anna, Lampeter, Pa., b. July 27, 1834.

4354. Susanna, Lampeter, Pa., b. July 6, 1836.

4355. Samuel, Lampeter, Pa., b. Oct. 27, 1837.

4356. Leah, Lampeter, Pa., b. Apr. 26, 1839.

Family of SAMUEL KENDIG (1476) and SUSAN BARR.

4357. Ann Catharine, Lancaster, Pa., b. Jan. 25, 1823; b. Nov. 16, 1871; m. Mar. 21, 1843, John Metzgar, b. July 24, 1818; d. Jan. 21, 1877; son John Metzgar and Elizabeth Miller.

4358. Elizabeth, Lampeter, Pa., b. Aug. 12, 1824; d. July 24, 1836.

4359. Amanda, Lampeter, Pa., b. Oct. 30, 1825; d. Sept. 3, 1829.

4360. Susanna, Cincinnati, O., b. Dec. 22, 1826; d. July 31, 1863; m. Henry H. Breneman (1579).

4361. Jacob, Lampeter, Pa., b. Dec. 11, 1828; d. Nov. 25, 1829.

4362. Rev. Amos B., Brockton, Mass., b. Sept. 19, 1830; m. Sept. 7, 1853, Miriam Post, b. May 1, 1834; d. Nov. 5, 1856; dau. John Post and Elizabeth ———; m. Apr. 6, 1857, Mary Bancroft, b. Jan. 5, 1834; d. June 2, 1900; dau. Dr. Benjamin Bancroft and Eunica Doolittle.

4363. Son, Lampeter, Pa., b. Dec. 25, 1831; d. Feb. 26, 1833.

Family of HENRY GOOD WEAVER (1478) and ANNA M. SHIRK (1485).

4364. Mathias Shirk, Philadelphia, Pa., b. Nov. 25, 1816; d Oct. 29, 1847; m. Sept. 15, 1842, Eliza H. Burgert, b. Nov. 1, 1820; d. Dec. 26, 1895; dau. Daniel Burgert and Sarah Baum.

4365. Mary Ann, Decorah, Ia., b. Apr. 8, 1818; d. Apr. 9, 1879; m. June 1, 1841, Cyrus Adams.

4366. Frances Eliza, Springfield, O., b. Mar. 15, 1821; d. June 15, 1849; m. Apr. 6, 1843, William Sawyer.

4367. Caroline Amelia, Toledo, O., b. Nov. 20, 1822; d. Feb. 21, 1899; m. Oct. 14, 1845, Franklin Sawyer.

4368. Harriet Sarah, Bourbon, Ind., b. Aug. 26, 1824.

4369. Martha Catharine, Decorah, Ia., b. May 27, 1827; d. Oct. 6, 1900; m. Aug., 1853, Wid. William Sawyer.

4370. Henry Davies, Bourbon, Ind., b. Mar. 15, 1830; m. Sept. 18, 1865, Jane E. Parks.

Family of ELIZABETH SHIRK (1482) and DAVID DIFFENDERFER.

4371. Ann, Lake, O., b. Oct. 14, 1812; m. ——— Stoner.

4372. Charles, Lake, O., b. Nov. 25, 1818.

Family of FRANCES SHIRK (1487) and Rev. DIEDRICH WILLERS.

4373. Anna Gevina, Varick, N. Y., b. Apr. 27, 1824; d. June 27, 1824.

4374. Margaret Amelia, Fayette, N. Y., b. July 25, 1825; m. Mar. 21, 1850, Charles Bachman, b. Jan. 28, 1829.

4375. Emma, Fayette, N. Y., b. Dec. 7, 1826; d. Feb. 15, 1872; m. Dec. 16, 1847, John L. Reed, b. June 29, 1824; son Jacob Reed and Catharine Smith.

4376. Frances, Seneca Falls, N. Y., b. June 3, 1828; d. May 22, 1859; m. Feb. 18, 1847, George Pontius, b. Dec. 19, 1822; d. Dec. 17, 1890; son George Pontius and Margaret ———.

4377. Theodore, Varick, N. Y., b. Aug. 30, 1831; d. Oct. 9, 1831.

4378. Diedrich, Fayette, N. Y., b. Nov. 3, 1833; m. Mar. 16, 1892, Wid. Mary A. Randall, b. Oct. 29, 1843; dau. Thomas Mac-Donald and Sarah McDonald.

4379. Caroline Lydia, Fayette, Pa., b. May 21, 1836; d. July 13, 1907; m. Jan. 20, 1875, Wid. John L. Reed, b. June 29, 1824; d. Aug. 22, 1906; son Jacob Reed and Catharine Smith.

4380. Calvin, Albany, N. Y., b. Dec. 9, 1840; d. Apr. 9, 1875; m. Apr. 3, 1872, Elizabeth R. Kennedy, b. Mar. 17, 1849.

Family of LYDIA SHIRK (1490) and DANIEL GAMBEE.

4381. Theodore W., Lake, O., b. Apr. 27, 1840.

4382. Albert Shirk, Lake, O., b. Oct. 2, 1841.

4383. Henry Marcellus, Lake, O., b. July 1, 1843.

Family of CAROLINE SHIRK (1491) and THOMAS CUNNINGHAM.

4384. Oliver W., Goshen, Ind.

4385. Henry, Ligonia, Ind.

4386. Frances, Canton, O., d. Feb. 11, 1903; m. ——— Shively.

4387. Carrie, Canton, O., m. Charles Campbell.

Family of MATTHIAS W. SHIRK (1492) and MARGARET SCHULTZ.

4388. Carrie, Wooster, O., m. ——— Snyder.

4389. Mary J., Wooster, O., m. ——— Cutter.

4390. Harry C., Danville, Ill.

Family of ANN CATHARINE WITMER (1493) and ALSTON BOYD.

4391. Mary Julianna, Greenfield, Mass., b. Dec. 20, 1827; d. Nov. 19, 1847.

Family of JULIANNA WITMER (1495) and JOHN RUSSELL.

4392. Ann Catharine, Greenfield, Mass., b. Oct. 14, 1831; m. 1851, George Denison; m. June 19, 1879, James S. Grinnell, b. July 24, 1821; d. Oct. 7, 1900; son George Grinnell and Eliza S. Perkins.

4393. John E., Leicester, Mass., b. Jan. 20, 1834; d. Oct. 28, 1903; m. Mar. 18, 1856, Caroline Nelson, b. Dec. 14, 1834; dau. John Nelson and Sylvia Bigelow.

4394. Charles W., Cedarhurst, L. I., b. Nov. 20, 1836; d. Mar. 27, 1903; m. Oct. 8, 1861, Lucy A. Merriam, b. Mar. 30, 1841; d. Aug. 16, 1879; dau. Lewis Merriam and Lucy Alvord; m. Aug. 1, 1888, Estelle Sotolonga, b. Dec. 24, 1871; dau. Reuben Sotolonga and Janet Crowley.

4395. Francis Burg, Greenfield, Mass., b. Dec. 12, 1839; d. July 4, 1870; m. Jan. 15, 1862, Isabella Clapp, b. Jan. 15, 1840; dau. Henry W. Clapp and Anna Hilliard.

Family of MARY C. GRAFF (1497) and ABRAHAM T. HAMILTON.

4396. Andrew G., Rudyville, Ky., b. Jan. 9, 1835; d. Apr. 3, 1895; m. Sept. 24, 1865, Fannie D. Hamilton, b. June 22, 1845; d. June 28, 1891; dau. James Hamilton and Sarah F. ———; m. Jan. 4, 1893, Josephine Hutchinson, b. Sept. 7, 1873; dau. William H. Hutchinson and Nancy Edgar.

4397. William M., Erie, Pa., b. Apr. 22, 1837; m. Feb. 11, 1866, Sallie A. James, b. Nov. 24, 1843.

4398. Witmer G., Erie, Pa., b. Apr. 22, 1837; m. Feb. 3, 1876, Annie Reid, b. Sept. 10, 1851; dau. John D. Reid and Elizabeth Briggs.

Family of ABRAHAM WITMER GRAFF (1498) and CAROLINE McMURTRIE.

4399. Mary G., Milroy, Pa., b. Aug. 6, 1849; m. Nov. 16, 1882, George H. Fulton.

4400. Caroline, Milroy, Pa., b. May 5, 1851; m. June 22, 1897, Charles E. Aurand.

4401. John, Osborne, Kans., b. June 15, 1853; m. Dec. 15, 1880, Mary Taylor, dau. John Taylor and Mary A. Alexander.

4402. Harriet Stoner, Milroy, Pa., b. Oct. 28, 1855; m. Dec. 8, 1875, John D. Sterrett, b. Dec. 4, 1853; son Robert Sterrett and Susan Shaw.

4403. Jacob W., Milroy, Pa., b. Aug. 20, 1858; d. Mar. 9, 1859.

Family of CHARLOTTE FERREE (1500) and DAVID LOGAN.

4404. ———, Mill Hall, Pa.
4405. ———, Mill Hall, Pa.
4406. ———, Mill Hall, Pa.
4407. ———, Mill Hall, Pa.
4408. ———, Mill Hall, Pa.
4409. ———, Mill Hall, Pa.
4410. ———, Mill Hall, Pa.
4411. ———, Mill Hall, Pa.
4412. David, Mill Hall, Pa., b. Jan. 23, 1827; d. Apr. 14, 1894.
4413. ———, Mill Hall, Pa.

Family of REBECCA FERREE (1506) and JACOB KAUFFMAN.

4414. Abraham Carpenter, Mill Hall, Pa., b. May 11, 1832; d. July 26, 1899; m. Jan. 22, 1863, Henrietta Linn, dau. James Linn and Mary Morrison; m. Martha ———.

4415. William B., Philadelphia, Pa., d. Feb., 1905.

4416. Edward, Mill Hall, Pa.

11816. Albert, Webster Grove, Mo.

11817. David, Flano, Tex.

11818. Charles, St. Louis, Mo.

11819. Jacob, St. Louis, Mo.

Family of HARRIET HARTMAN (1519) and MARK WILSON (1512).

4417. Eliza, Jamesport, Mo., b. Sept. 5, 1818; m. Oct., 1836, John Robinson.

4418. Matilda, Jeromeville, O., b. Sept. 5, 1820; m. Feb., 1841, Martin Lutz, d. 1872.

4419. Caroline, Lisbon, Ind., b. Apr. 6, 1823; d. 1902; m. 1845, Lorenzo Tyler.

4420. George Hartman, Ft. Wayne, Ind., b. Nov. 14, 1825; m. 1855, Ellen A. Allen.

4421. Samuel Ellis, Rochester, N. Y., b. Feb. 16, 1828.

4422. Daniel E., Marion, Ind., b. Feb. 27, 1830; m. Sept. 30, 1856, Abigail Bevans, b. Sept. 16, 1830; dau. Henry Bevans and Elizabeth ———.

4423. Harriet Ann, Jeromeville, O., b. Nov. 10, 1834; d. Apr. 17, 1862.

4424. Mark L., Lake Fort, O., b. Jan. 18, 1837; d. Aug., 1864; m. 1862, ———.

4425. Christian David, Kendallville, Ind., b. Apr. 5, 1844.

Family of GEORGE HARTMAN (1518) and SARAH WILSON (1514).

4426. Rev. Albert, Great Bend, Kans., b. Jan. 5, 1821; d. Jan. 13, 1897; m. Dec. 16, 1851, Jane Evans, b. Dec. 27, 1827; dau. Jacob Evans and Hannah N. Morris.

4427. Catharine Herr, Lock Haven, Pa., b. Dec. 20, 1822; d. Feb. 27, 1901; m. July 22, 1863, Martin Herr (586).

4428. Rev. Jacob, Chicago, Ill., b. Feb. 13, 1825; m. Sept. 21, 1854, Ellen Miller, b. Nov. 5, 1832.

4429. Elizabeth, Chicago, Ill., b. Feb. 5, 1827; d. Apr. 29, 1853; m. July 5, 1851, David R. Carrier.

4430. Leonard L., Shintown, Pa., b. Nov. 19, 1828; m. Sept. 2, 1862, Clara A. M. Armstrong, b. Aug. 9, 1841; d. Mar. 9, 1900; dau. McIntire Armstrong and Lucy Bigelow.

4431. Harriet F., Chattannoga, Tenn., b. Dec. 13, 1830; d. Aug. 3, 1880; m. Dec. 19, 1860, Daniel W. Bressler (4531).

4432. David Shaver, Chattanooga, Tenn., b. July 14, 1833; d. Jan. 30, 1838.

4433. Samuel Wilson, Chattanooga, Tenn., b. Aug. 31, 1835; d. Jan. 24, 1838.

4434. Rebecca, Salona, Pa., b. Sept. 25, 1837; d. Feb. 1, 1844.

4435. Sarah H., Salona, Pa., b. Sept. 20, 1840; m. July 28, 1860, Cyrus W. Rote, b. Mar. 16, 1838; son Griffin Rote and Jane Moyer.

4436. Anson, Salona, Pa., b. Oct. 20, 1842; d. Feb. 12, 1844.

4437. David, Salona, Pa., b. Nov. 29, 1844; d. Dec. 23, 1844.

Family of DAVID HARTMAN (1520) and MARY MILLER.

4438. Harriet, Landisville, Pa., b. Jan. 2, 1831; d. Jan. 19, 1831.

4439. Samuel Leidy, Lancaster, Pa., b. Nov. 23, 1832.

4440. Tobias Miller, Landisville, Pa., b. Oct. 21, 1834; d. Mar. 10, 1837.

4441. Jacob, Landisville, Pa., b. Apr. 8, 1836; d. Mar. 18, 1837.

4442. David, Lancaster, Pa., b. Feb. 17, 1838.

4443. Anna Elizabeth, Landisville, Pa., b. Jan. 10, 1840.

4444. John Lehman. Landisville, Pa., b. Sept. 10, 1841; d. Feb. 20, 1845.

4445. Mary H., Phiadelphia, Pa., b. May 6, 1843; m. May 3, 1870, Luther S. Kauffman, b. Nov. 5, 1846; son Samuel Kauffman and Maria Heisler.

4446. Henry Hess, Phillipsburg, Pa., b. Dec. 17, 1844.

4447. Sarah E., Lancaster, Pa., b. Feb. 10, 1847; d. Mar. 28, 1848.

4448. Barbara, Lancaster, Pa., b. Feb. 15, 1850; d. Feb. 16, 1851.

Family of Rev. CHRISTIAN HARTMAN (1521) and CAROLINE V. BOYD.

4449. John Newton, Springfield, Ill., b. Nov. 23, 1837; d. Aug. 18, 1865; m. May 13, 1862, Margaret C. Conrad.

4450. Wilson McKendry, Rochefort, Mo., b. Mar. 31, 1839; m. May 10, 1887, Mary D. Shaull.

4451. Josephine P., Rochefort, Mo., b. Aug. 2, 1840.

4452. Edwin Mayberry, Rochefort, Mo., b. Dec. 21, 1841; d. July 8, 1860.

4453. William Woodward, Salona, Pa., b. Apr. 4, 1843; m. Mar. 25, 1880, Julia Shaull.

4454. Sarah E. Frances, Salona, Pa., b. Nov. 11, 1845; m. Apr. 29, 1879, G. —— A. Shaull.

15

Family of SAMUEL HARTMAN (152) and LUCY HOLCOMB.

4455. Charles Carroll, Salona, Pa., b. Jan. 23, 1833; d. Apr., 1889.
4456. Nathan Holcomb, Salona, Pa., b. July 31, 1834.
4457. George Bressler, Salona, Pa., b. Apr. 1, 1837.
4458. Sarah Amanda, Salona, Pa., b. Mar. 28, 1839.
4459. Thomas Huling, Salona, Pa., b. Jan. 4, 1841; d. Dec., 1860.
4460. Richard Watson, Salona, Pa., b. Feb. 23, 1845.
4461. Daniel Watson, Salona, Pa., b. Feb. 8, 1847.
4462. Elizabeth, Salona, Pa., b. Apr. 6, 1849; d. Aug. 8, 1850.
4463. Harriet Frances, Salona, Pa., b. Dec. 25; d. Oct., 1880.
4464. Samuel Willis, Salona, Pa., b. Feb. 8, 1857.

Family of Rev. DANIEL HARTMAN (1523) and MARY E. DAVIS.

4465. Elizabeth Caroline, Philadelphia, Pa., b. Feb. 2, 1840; m. June 15, 1865, John F. Glosser, b. Oct. 20, 1838; son Frederick Glosser and Anna M. Oaks.
4466. John Davis, Cumberland, Md., b. Oct. 16, 1843.
4467. Sarah Frances, West Chester, Pa., b. Jan. 21, 1846; d. 1846.
4468. Charles Tidings, Florence, Mass., b. May 16, 1855; m. 1873, Lizzie R. Pennock, b. 1856; dau. John L. Pennock and ———; m. Aug. 5, 1896, Diana E. Stiedler, b. July 15, 1866; dau. Jacob Stiedler and Susan Johnson.

Family of FRANCES ANN HARTMAN (1525) and BENJAMIN H. BAIRD.

4469. Christian William, Island, Pa., b. Jan. 9, 1845.
4470. Elizabeth F., Clearfield, Pa., b. Sept. 2, 1846; m. Apr. 15, 1879, Francis G. Harris, b. Nov. 6, 1845; son John Harris and Elinor Graham.
4471. Dr. Edmund Jaynes, Lock Haven, Pa., b. Nov. 3, 1849; m. Apr. 4, 1878, Harriet A. Buck, b. Aug. 6, 1852; dau. Christian Buck and Catharine Beck.
4472. Mary Harriet, Lock Haven, Pa., b. Apr. 19, 1852.
4473. Rebecca Emily, Lock Haven, Pa., b. Oct. 31, 1854.
4474. Alfred Tennyson, Island, Pa., b. Feb. 11, 1862; m. July 23, 1886, Rena Ritchie.

Family of SARAH ANN BRESSLER (1526) and JOHN DUNLOP McCORMICK.

4475. Eliza Ellen, Lock Haven, Pa, b. Jan. 6, 1843; d. Aug. 10, 1844.

4476. Catharine F., Lock Haven, Pa., b. Mar. 28, 1844; m. Nov. 25, 1869, Clark R. Gearhart, b. Dec. 19, 1842; son Charles Gearhart and Sarah Metter.

4477. Charles B., Mill Hall, Pa., b. Oct. 9, 1845; d. Dec. 22, 1897.

4478. William D., Philadelphia, Pa., b. Jan. 28, 1848.

Family of GEORGE BRESSLER (1527) and PHOEBE ANN BADGER.

4479. John Edward, Renovo, Pa., b. Dec. 19, 1846; m. 1869, Sarah Elizabeth Bamer, b. June 12, 1850; dau. Christian Bamer and Catharine Fraser.

4480. Eliza Frances, Salona, Pa., b. Sept. 4, 1848; m. Aug. 12, 1869, Joseph McKibben, b. July 25, 1845; son ―――― and Eliza Askey.

Family of Wid. GEORGE BRESSLER (1527) and JOSEPHINE VANNATTA.

4481. Harry E., Avoca, Ark.

4482. Augustus E., Athens, Pa.

4483. Huston, Athens, Pa.

4484. Emory, Athens, Pa.

4485. ――――, Mill Hall, Pa., m. B. ―――― J. Bowers.

4486. William C., Mill Hall, Pa.

4487. Clara, Mill Hall, Pa., m. W. ―――― H. Hunter.

Family of Dr. CHARLES BRESSLER (1528) and SARAH TOWNER.

4488. Ella M., York, Pa.

4489. Dr. W. ―――― C., York, Pa.

4490. A. ―――― C., York, Pa.

4491. Emma B., York, Pa.

4492. Clara B., York, Pa.

4493. George B., Lancaster, Pa.

Family of HENRY BRESSLER (1529) and ISABELLA HENDERSON.

4494. Lida, Lock Haven, Pa., m. ―――― Shoemaker.

4495. ――――, Lock Haven, Pa.

4496. ――――, Lock Haven, Pa.

4497. ――――, Lock Haven, Pa. ,

4498. ———, Lock Haven, Pa.
4499. ———, Lock Haven, Pa.

Family of JOHN J. BRESSLER (1530) and REBECCA SLENKER.

4500. Josephine, Flemington, Pa., b. Feb. 13, 1848.
4501. John P., Flemington, Pa., b. Jan. 19, 1850; m, Mattie Kitchen.
4502. George, Flemington, Pa., b. Mar. 11, 1852; d. Jan. 12, 1857.
4503. Edward S., Flemington, Pa., b. July 18, 1854.
4504. Ida, Flemington, Pa., b. Jan. 12, 1856; d. Aug. 12, 1862.
4505. Jacob, Flemington, Pa., b. Mar. 17, 1858; d. July, 1860.
4506. Thomas, Flemington, Pa., b. Dec. 23, 1861; m. Maggie Bloom.
4507. Charles H., Lock Haven, Pa., b. July 20, 1865; m. Mary M. Troxel, dau. Benj. F. Troxel and Alameda Stoner.
4508. Minnie C., Flemington, Pa., b. June 20, 1868; m. S. ——— Grant Leitzel, b. Aug. 1, 1867.

Family of HARRIET F. HARTMAN (4431) and DANIEL W. BRESSLER (1531).

4509. George L., Williamsport, Pa., b. May 6, 1863; m. Sept. 7, 1899, Mary E. Rosser, b. June 27, 1879; dau. Titus M. Rosser and Clara Crispen.
4510. Robert Luther, Williamsport, Pa., b. Sept. 9, 1864; d. Dec. 4, 1864.
4511. Charles Wallace, Williamsport, Pa., b. Jan. 1, 1867; d. Jan. 16, 1867.
4512. Albert Shuman, Williamsport, Pa., b. Jan. 1, 1867; d. Mar. 20, 1868.

Family of FRANKLIN NEFF (1543) and ELIZABETH MUSSER.

4513. Martha Elizabeth, East Mill Creek, Utah, b. Apr. 25, 1848.
4514. Letitia, Salt Lake, Utah, b. Feb. 21, 1853; d. May —, 1853.

Family of Wid. FRANKLIN NEFF (1543) and FRANCES MARIA STILLMAN.

4515. Frances M., East Mill Creek, Utah, b. Sept. 19, 1855; d. Nov. 14, 1865.
4516. Mary M., East Mill Creek, Utah, b. Sept. 6, 1857.
4517. John F., East Mill Creek, Utah, b. Aug. 7, 1859; d. Dec. 7, 1865.

4518. Barbara M., East Mill Creek, Utah, b. Mar. 15, 1861; d. Mar. 19, 1864.

4519. Rozella S., East Mill Creek, Utah, b. May 27, 1863.

4520. May S., East Mill Creek, Utah, b. Oct. 30, 1866.

4521. Alice A., East Mill Creek, Utah, b. Nov. 22, 1868.

4522. Seymour H., East Mill Creek, Utah, b. Dec. 23, 1870.

4523. Alforetta, East Mill Creek, Utah, b. Jan. 16, 1872.

Family of AMOS HERR NEFF (1544) and MARTHA A. DILWORTH.

4524. Ida, East Mill Creek, Utah, b. Feb. 5, 1849; d. Jan. 8, 1901; m. Valaren Russell.

4525. Eva, Medway, Utah, b. Dec. 4, 1850; m. David Huffaker.

4526. Amos Barr, East Mill Creek, Utah, b. Aug. 13, 1853; m. Lucy Seeley.

4527. Cyrus, East Mill Creek, Utah, b. Apr. 22, 1855; m. Grace Boyce.

4528. Martha Ann, Sugar House, Utah, b. Aug. 8, 1857; m. Franklin Smith.

4529. Mary Barr, Salt Lake, Utah, b. May 16, 1859; m. Isaac Young.

4530. John Dillworth, East Mill Creek, Utah, b. Aug. 11, 1861; m. Lilian Evans.

Family of Wid. AMOS HERR NEFF (1544) and CATHARINE E. THOMAS.

4531. Harriet S., East Mill Creek, Utah, b. Sept. 16, 1865.

4532. Amanda Barr, Big Cottonwood, Utah, b. Oct. 16, 1867; m. Edward C. Bagley.

4533. David, East Mill Creek, Utah, b. June 13, 1871.

4534. Samuel, East Mill Creek, Utah, b. June 13, 1871; m. Ina Brinton.

4535. Catharine A., East Mill Creek, Utah, b. Oct. 1, 1873; d. Nov. 2, 1876.

4536. Aldus D., East Mill Creek, Utah, b. July 16, 1875; d. Nov. 4, 1876.

4537.. Alice M., East Mill Creek, Utah, b. May 18, 1877.

Family of Wid. AMOS HERR NEFF (1544) and ELIZA A. HUGHES.

4538. William L., East Mill Creek, Utah, b. Nov. 12, 1876; d. May 15, 1880.

4539. Frank Herr, East Mill Creek, b. Nov. 11, 1878.

4540. Anna L., East Mill Creek, Utah, b. Feb. 10, 1881.

4541. Eugene J., East Mill Creek, Utah, b. Mar. 29, 1883.

4542. Katie B., East Mill Creek, Utah, b. May 21, 1885.

4543. Albert Hughes, East Mill Creek, Utah, b. May 21, 1890.

4544. Julian, East Mill Creek, Utah, b. Mar. 22, 1893.

Family of MARY ANN NEFF (1546) and ORIN PORTER ROCKWELL.

4545. Mary Ann, Salt Lake, Utah, b. Mar. 11, 1855.

4546. Sarah N., Salt Lake, Utah, b. Aug. 5, 1856.

4547. John Orin, Salt Lake, Utah, b. Oct. 23, 1858.

4548. David Porter, Salt Lake, Utah, b. Feb. 19, 1861.

4549. Forrest Neff, Draper, Utah, b. Dec. 19, 1862; d. Jan. 23, 1864.

4550. Letitia Barr, Salt Lake, Utah, b. Aug. 28, 1864.

4551. Joseph Neff, Salt Lake, Utah, b. Aug., 1866; d. Oct., 1866.

Family of SUSANNA NEFF (1547) and ELI H. PIERCE.

4552. Eli Harvey, Salt Lake, Utah, b. Sept. 27, 1851; m. Etta Madren.

4553. Mary Barr, Salt Lake, Utah, b. Sept. 21, 1853; m. O. ——— G. Snow.

4554. Leonidas Thomas, Brigham City, Utah, b. June 21, 1855; m. Gena Snow.

4555. Susanna Octavia, Mendon, Utah, b. Mar. 27, 1857; m. Joseph Hardman.

Family of Wid. SUSANNA NEFF PIERCE (1547) and WILLIS HENRY BOOTHE.

4556. Amanda Viola, Collinston, Utah, b. Oct. 17, 1860; m. Evan Morgan.

4557. Olive Matilda, Salt Lake, Utah, b. Apr. 27, 1862; m. Wid. W. ——— D. Johnson.

4558. Willis Henry, Salt Lake, Utah, b. Sept. 16, 1864; m. Sept. 28, 1897, Sarah Rich, b. Dec. 13, 1873; dau. John T. Rich and Agnes Young.

4559. John Neff, Collinston, Utah, b. Mar. 6, 1866; m. Mar. 3, 1898, Fannie P. Wilde, b. May 3, 1874; dau. Thomas Wilde and Fannie Gunn.

4560. Benjamin Franklin, Brigham City, Utah, b. Sept. 16, 1868; m. June 2, 1897, Louisa M. Stark.

4561. Morris Artemus, Collinston, Utah, b. Feb. 26, 1872; m. Oct. 14, 1900, Jennie Alvord.

Family of BENJAMIN BARR NEFF (1548) and MARTHA A. BITNER.

4562. Martha Louisa, Draper, Utah, b. May 22, 1859; d. Feb. 8, 1883; m. Dec., 1881, Isaac Dunyon.

4563. Anna Bitner, Salt Lake, Utah, b. Oct. 2, 1860; d. Feb. 19, 1865.

4564. Benjamin Barr, Sandy, Utah, b. Nov. 2, 1862; m. Ida Jenkins.

4565. John Breneman, Sandy, Utah, b. Sept. 24, 1864; m. Phœbe Hardcastle.

4566. Mary Elizabeth, Estado Morelos, Mexico, b. June 11, 1866; d. Nov. 22, 1891; m. Oct. 19, 1887. Hubert L. Hall, b. Feb. 22, 1858; son Isaac Clark Hall and Susanna Ryder.

Family of Wid. BENJAMIN BARR NEFF (1548) and MARY E. LOVE.

4567. Lillian Estelle, Salt Lake, Utah, b. Aug. 7, 1871.

4568. Nancy Maria, Salt Lake, Utah, b. Feb. 17, 1873.

4569. Henrietta Love, Salt Lake, Utah, b. Dec. 20, 1875.

4570. Andrew Love, Salt Lake, Utah, b. Feb. 17, 1878.

Family of Wid. BENJAMIN BARR NEFF (1548) and MARIA A. BOWTHORPE.

4571. Virtue Leanora, Holliday, Utah, b. Feb. 28, 1872; m. Feb. 11, 1893, Hyrum Neilson, b. Feb. 12, 1869; son Carl C. Neilson and Maria ———.

4572. William Cyrus, Salt Lake, Utah, b. Dec. 22, 1874; m. Oct. 1, 1902, Carolyn Henricksen.

4573. Franklin T., Salt Lake, Utah, b. Sept. 4, 1877.

4574. Deseret C., Salt Lake, Utah, b. Sept. 22, 1879.

4575. Maria Pearl, Salt Lake, Utah, b. April 27, 1880.

Family of JOHN NEFF (1550) and ANN ELIZA BENEDICT.

4576. Delia Benedict, East Mill Creek, Utah, b. Apr. 16, 1864; m. July 10, 1889, Albert Spencer, d. Oct. 4, 1898.

4577. Marian Barr, East Mill Creek, Utah, b. July 10, 1866; m. Dec. 24, 1890, Charles F. Stillman.

4578. Mary Bitner, East Mill Creek, Utah, b. July 10, 1866; m. June 21, 1893, Samuel A. Cornwall.

4579. Ruth Irene, East Mill Creek, Utah, b. Jan. 14, 1869; d. Oct. 26, 1869.

4580. Frances Emeline, East Mill Creek, Utah, b. Mar. 31, 1872; m. Dec. 23, 1898, James O. Smith.

4581. Esther Eliza, East Mill Creek, Utah, b. Sept. 29, 1874; m. Jan. 4, 1901, Peter M. Hixon.

4582. Lillian Edna, East Mill Creek, Utah, b. Mar. 22, 1877; d. Sept. 2, 1878.

4583. Susan Eugenia, East Mill Creek, Utah, b. Aug. 31, 1882.

4584. Lawrence Elaine, East Mill Creek, Utah, b. May 21, 1886.

Family of ELIZABETH NEFF (1551) and CHARLES STILLMAN.

4585. Mary Elizabeth, East Mill Creek, Utah, b. Oct. 23, 1858.

4586. John Neff, East Mill Creek, Utah, b. Mar. 21, 1860; d. Nov. 22, 1865.

4587. Harriet Seymour, East Mill Creek, Utah, b. Nov. 21, 1861.

4588. Delia Barr, East Mill Creek, Utah, b. Sept. 20, 1863.

4589. Charles Franklin, East Mill Creek, Utah, b. Sept. 26, 1865.

4590. Samuel Seymour, East Mill Creek, Utah, b. June 13, 1867.

4591. Forrest Neff, East Mill Creek, Utah, b. Sept. 27, 1869.

4592. Frances Minerva, East Mill Creek, Utah, b. June 30, 1871.

4593. Cyrus Neff, East Mill Creek, Utah. b. May 30, 1873.

4594. Letitia Barr, East Mill Creek, Utah, b. Apr. 3, 1875.

4595. Brigham Jason, East Mill Creek, Utah, b. May 11, 1877.

4596. Barbara Matilda, East Mill Creek, Utah. b. Apr. 3, 1879.

4597. Joseph Julian, East Mill Creek, Utah. b. Jan. 12, 1881.

4598. Susanna Ethel, East Mill Creek, Utah, b. Apr. 21, 1883.

Family of ANN C. HERR (1553) and MARTIN WEAVER (4327).

4599. Frances E., Ronks, Pa., b. June 8, 1846; m. Dec. 1, 1872, John H. Weaver, b. Oct. 1, 1842; son Rev. Henry Weaver and Annie Howry.

4600. Annie Mary, Fertility, Pa., b. Sept. 19, 1849; m. Dec. 10, 1876, Daniel Girvin, b. Nov. 25, 1839; son Samuel Girvin and Elizabeth Diffenbach.

4601. Enos Herr, Lancaster, Pa., b. Aug. 3, 1851; m. Oct. 8, 1879, Mary N. Musser (4900); m. Feb. 6, 1898, Annie Esbenshade (11069).

4602. Ida Naomi, Lancaster, Pa., b. Aug. 27, 1854; m. Dec. 26, 1875, Rev. John Kohr, b. Mar. 30, 1847; son Rev. John Kohr and Esther Denlinger.

Family of AMOS F. HERR (1554) and ANN M. FRANTZ.

4603. Virgil Frantz, Wheatland Mills, Pa., b. Oct. 19, 1850; d. Sept. 21, 1855.

4604. Ida Elizabeth, Waynesboro, Pa., b. Nov. 9, 1851; m. Dec. 2, 1875, Amos R. Frantz, b. Sept. 10, 1850; son John Frantz and Catharine Ryder.

4605. Francis Christian, Ottawa, Kans., b. Dec. 1, 1852; m. July 6, 1882, Lillian R. Seiler, b. Jan. 4, 1851; dau. Jacob Seiler and Susan Fridley.

4606. Horace Jacob, Wheatland Mills, Pa., b. July 5, 1854; d. Oct. 4, 1866.

4607. Homer Andrew, Philadelphia, Pa., b. Dec. 18, 1855; m. Aug. 15, 1889, Lillian A. Howard, b. Mar. 10, 1864; d. Mar. 27, 1897; dau. Asbury Howard and Catharine Garrison; m. June 20, 1906, Margaret T. Detwiler.

4608. Willis Cyrus, Strasburg, Pa., b. June 2, 1857; m. Jan. 4, 1889, Emma E. Phenegar, b. Feb. 21, 1867; dau. Isaac Phenegar and Elmira Weaver.

4609. Mary Frances, Wheatland Mills, Pa., b. Jan. 9, 1859.

4610. Anna Amanda, Lancaster, Pa., b. Nov. 22, 1861; m. May 7, 1885, Abraham Lincoln Mayer, b. Jan. 17, 1860; son Benjamin Mayer and Elizabeth Wenger.

4611. Elizabeth Rebecca, Wheatland Mills, Pa., b. Apr. 8, 1863; d. Feb. 26, 1865.

4612. Edith Charlotte, Waynesboro, Pa., b. Aug. 17, 1865; m. Apr. 24, 1895, John Elmer Frantz (6205).

4613. Harry Neff, Lancaster, Pa., b. Mar. 30, 1868; m. Ida L. Stoner, dau. Henry K. Stoner and Sarah M. Porter.

4614. Lottie Lavinia, Wheatland Mills, Pa., b. Feb. 28, 1871.

5463. Son, Wheatland Mills, Pa., b. 1874; d. Infant.

Family of CYRUS N. HERR (1557) and MARY ANN BRACKBILL (4255).

4615. Ira Harvey, Lancaster, Pa., b. Mar. 31, 1856; m. May 2, 1888, H. Mary Brown, dau. Davis A. Brown and Rachael Patton.

4616. Annie Frances, Lancaster, Pa., b. Oct. 6, 1857.

4617. Milo Brackbill, Lancaster, Pa., b. Mar. 13, 1860; m. June 23, 1892, Elizabeth M. Breneman (4651).

4618. Almon Howard, Wheatland Mills, Pa., b. July 22, 1862; d. Dec. 19, 1863.

4619. Harry Francis, Wheatland Mills, Pa., b. Jan. 22, 1864; d. Mar. 23, 1864.

4620. Allan Cyrus, Chicago, Ill., b. Aug. 7, 1867.

4621. Herman Horace, Wheatland Mills, Pa., b. Sept. 2, 1870; d. Dec. 2, 1893.

4622. Cyrus Anson, Wheatland Mills, Pa., b. Mar. 18, 1872; d. Apr. 2, 1872.

4623. Bertha Mary, Lancaster, Pa., b. Apr. 30, 1874.

Family of FRANKLIN J. HERR (1560) and SALLIE FRANTZ.

4624. Ella Frances, Lancaster, Pa., b. July 28, 1859.

4625. Elmer Francis, Lancaster, Pa., b. Mar. 8, 1861; d. June 3, 1862.

4626. Walter Christian, Goshen, Ind., b. Sept. 18, 1862; m. Apr. 27, 1888, Anna S. Hartman, b. Sept. 18, 1865: dau. George H. Hartman and Anna M. Bender.

4627. Ada Elizabeth, Philadelphia, Pa., b. Mar. 26, 1864; d. Jan. 31, 1897.

4628. Laura Amanda, Lancaster, Pa., b. Oct. 1, 1865.

4629. Lizzie Charlotte, Lancaster, Pa., b. Apr. 7, 1867; m. Apr. 12, 1897, Dr. Frank G. Hartman, b. Dec. 29, 1869; son Daniel Hartman and Catharine Gast.

4630. Harold Frantz, Dawson City, Alaska, b. Aug. 23, 1868.

4631. Sallie Miller, Lancaster, Pa., b. Oct. 23, 1869; m. June 6, 1900,

Wid. Dr. John M. Shartle, b. Nov. 19, 1856; son John Shartle and Maria Miller.

4632. Francis Neff, Lancaster, Pa., b. Aug. 3, 1871; m. June 19, 1895, Annie L. Comp, b. June 9, 1870; dau. Alfred Comp and Catharine Metzger.

4633. Horace Benjamin, Lancaster, Pa., b. May 12, 1873.

4634. Arthur Alfred, Lancaster, Pa., b. Mar. 18, 1875; m. June 12, 1901, Anna J. Laubenstein, b. Feb. 13, 1878; dau. Ezekiel Laubenstein and Anna Alexander.

4635. Fannie Susan, Wheatland Mills, Pa., b. June 17, 1876; d. Sept. 13, 1877.

4636. Anna Maria, Lancaster, Pa., b. Oct. 13, 1879.

4637. Mary Eva, Lancaster, Pa., b. July 11, 1881.

Family of LETITIA NEFF (1561) and Dr. BENJAMIN MUSSER.

4638. Anna Letitia, Lancaster, Pa., b. Oct. 4, 1848; d. June 11, 1891; m. June 10, 1879, Allan A. Herr (4872).

Family of JEFFERSON N. NEFF (1564)) and EMMA MUSSER.

4639. Harry Musser, Denver, Col., b. July 17, 1861.

Family of MARY VIRGINIA NEFF (1569) and JOHN E. HERSHEY (5644).

4640. Annie Frances, Waynesboro, Pa., b. May 24, 1870.

4641. Aldus Neff, Waynesboro, Pa., b. Oct. 14, 1871.

Family of ELIZABETH BRENEMAN (1572) and HENRY MUSSER.

4642. Dr. Milton B., Philadelphia, Pa., b. Oct. 20, 1846; d. Mar. 4, 1888; m. Sept. 24, 1873, Carrie M. Swayne, b. June 4, 1846; dau. Mahlon F. Swayne and Jane L. Greiner.

4643. Ada, Strasburg, Pa., b. Aug. 28, 1847; d. Aug. 29, 1847.

4644. Henry Elmer, Witmer, Pa., b. Feb. 17, 1852; d. Sept. 22, 1906; m. Nov. 24, 1875, Mary M. Musselman (5324).

4645. Charles Martin, Strasburg, Pa., b. May 1, 1857; d. Nov. 30, 1865.

Family of HENRY N. BRENEMAN (1574) and ANN M. POTTS (5975).

4646. Winona Sue, Willow Street, Pa., b. Sept. 15, 1858; m. Abraham F. Strickler, b. May 16, 1857; son Jesse Strickler and Frances Stoner.

4647. Park Potts, Lancaster, Pa., b. Oct. 14, 1859.

4648. Harry Miller, Strasburg, Pa., b. May 6, 1862; d. Oct. 27, 1866.

4649. Annie M., Lancaster, Pa., b. Dec. 31, 1863; m. Feb. 14, 1884, John L. Groff, b. Mar. 4, 1864; son Dr. Jacob E. Groff and Hettie Lefever.

4650. Joseph Potts, Lancaster, Pa., b. Apr. 2, 1865; m. Oct. 19, 1898, Barbara Hollinger, b. Mar. 18. 1866; dau. Amos Hollinger and Elizabeth ————.

4651. Elizabeth Musser, Lancaster, Pa., b. Sept. 26, 1866; m. Jan. 23, 1892, Milo B. Herr (4617).

4652. Maud Marian, Duluth, Minn., b. Dec. 23, 1867; m. June, 1906, John W. Bayly.

4653. Herbert Neff, Newark, O., b. May 10, 1869.

4654. Jennie May, Lancaster, Pa., b. May 17, 1871.

4655. Eliza Lucille, Lancaster, Pa., b. May 16, 1874; m. May 9, 1905, Ira H. Bare, son Frank H. Bare and Ada Kendig.

4656. Frank Witmer, Lancaster, Pa., b. Aug. 2, 1877; d. Sept. 10, 1877.

Family of AMAZIAH M. HERR (1582) and SUSAN BRENEMAN (1577).

4657. Charles Breneman, Strasburg, Pa., b. July 23, 1861.

4658. Mary Elizabeth, Lancaster, Pa., b. Dec. 7, 1862; m. Feb. 9, 1896, Dr. Martin H. Musser (5238).

4659. Edgar Henry, Strasburg, Pa., b. June 6, 1866.

4660. Susan Breneman, Strasburg, Pa., b. Mar. 20, 1875; d. June 23, 1878.

Family of CHRISTIAN H. BRENEMAN (1578) and LOUISA A. BRENNER.

4661. Ella Louisa, Lancaster, Pa., b. Dec. 24, 1855; m. Feb. 14, 1884, Leon Von Ossko, b. Dec. 6, 1855; son Baron Alexander G. Von Ossko and Paula Schaneffelin.

4662. Mary Frances, Lancaster, Pa., b. Jan. 18, 1857; d. 1861.

Family of HENRY H. BRENEMAN (1579) and SUSAN KENDIG (4360).

4663. Cassius K., San Antonio. Tex., b. Sept. 4, 1847; m. July 3, 1873, Wid. Susan A. Henry, dau. Benjamin F. Burks and Susan H. Winn.

4664. Herbert L., Cincinnati, O., b. Feb. 26, 1849; m. Feb. 9, 1876, Eunice C. Swift, b. Sept. 10, 1849; dau. Briggs Swift and Martha P. Hubbell.

4665. Charles W., Cincinnati, O., b. Apr. 18, 1853; m. Oct. 24, 1878, Bessie Campbell, b. Sept. 30, 1856; dau. George W. Campbell and Elizabeth W. Little.

4666. Susan K., Cincinnati, O., b. Sept. 3, 1854; d. July 18, 1860.

Family of Wid. HENRY H. BRENEMAN (1579) and EMMA B. SHENK (9728).

4667. Mary Dawson, Cincinnati, O., b. Nov. 27, 1866; d. Dec. 15, 1866.

4668. Mary, Cincinnati, O., b. June 28, 1869; d. July 10, 1880.

4669. Susan Wilson, Cincinnati, O., b. Jan. 17, 1875; d. July 5, 1880.

4670. Bessie, Cincinnati, O., b. Mar. 13, 1880; d. Jan. 6, 1883.

Family of BENJAMIN EZRA HERR (1585) and HETTIE PFOUTZ.

4671. Mary Maud, Willow Street, Pa., b. Feb. 8, 1878.

4672. Clyde Mylin, Willow Street, Pa., b. Mar. 6, 1879.

Family of MARY LOUISA HERR (1587) and WESLEY WELLINGTON NESSLY.

4673. Ray Herr, Lancaster, Pa.

4674. Mary Catharine, Landisburg, Pa.

Family of ADA NAOMI HERR (1588) and Dr. SAMUEL FOREMAN.

4675. Carrie Louisa, Lancaster, Pa., b. Nov. 28, 1878.

4676. Edgar Herr, Lancaster, Pa., b. Sept. 19, 1880; d. Mar. 26, 1882.

4677. Frederick Herbert, Lancaster, Pa., b. Feb. 16, 1882.

4678. Edith Elizabeth, Lancaster, Pa., b. Jan. 12, 1886.

Family of FANNY HERR (1590) and JOHN H. BRACKBILL (4088).

4679. Susan Bertha, Strasburg, Pa., b. Jan. 2, 1861.

4680. Eustace H., Strasburg, Pa., b. Mar. 10, 1863.

4681. Harry C., Strasburg, Pa., b. Mar. 12, 1865.

11803. R. John, Reading, Pa.

11804. Lillie, Strasburg, Pa.

11805. Austin, Strasburg, Pa.

11806. Ira H., Strasburg, Pa.

11807. Carl, Strasburg, Pa.

Family of MARY ANN HERR (1595) and Rev. Wid. CHRISTIAN N. WITMER.

4682. Harry Herr, Lancaster, Pa., b. Aug. 23, 1869.

4683. Dr. B. Franklin, Lancaster, Pa., b. May 1, 1872.

4684. Anna M., Lancaster, Pa., b. Dec. 12, 1874; d. July 24, 1892.

Family of CHRISTIAN B. HERR (1596) and ELIZABETH ANN HERR (4111).

4685. Enos B., Refton, Pa., b. Sept. 14, 1869; d. July 21, 1870.

4686. Harry B., Lancaster, Pa., b. June 21, 1871; m. Nov. 4, 1896, Minnie L. Groff, b. Aug. 8, 1873; dau. Henry L. Groff and Anna Landis.

4687. Daniel Jefferson, Refton, Pa., b. July 5, 1873; m. Sept. 4, 1900, Cora Groff, b. July 7, 1875; dau. Henry L. Groff and Anna Landis.

4688. Anna Catharine, Lancaster, Pa., b. Mar. 31, 1876; m. Sept. 5, 1900, Frank R. Houser, b. Oct. 20, 1872; son Jacob B. Houser and Susan Rohrer.

Family of SENER MILLO HERR (1579) and MARY MAUD HERR (4895).

4689. Infant, Lampeter, Pa., b. Apr. 18, 1878; d. Apr. 18, 1878.

4690. Benjamin Ralph, Lampeter, Pa., b. July 29, 1879; d. Dec. 19, 1879.

4691. John Roy, Lampeter, Pa., b. Sept. 13, 1880; d. Jan. 13, 1881.

4692. Marguerite Musser, Lampeter, Pa., b. Nov. 16, 1881.

4693. May Maud, Lampeter, Pa., b. May 3, 1883.

4694. Millo Sener, Lampeter, Pa., b. Mar. 29, 1885.

4695. Anna Laura, Lampeter, Pa., b. Mar. 23, 1887.

4696. Martha Sener, Lampeter, Pa., b. Dec. 19, 1888.

4697. Pauline Emma, Lampeter, Pa., b. Mar. 30, 1893.

Family of JOHN ALDUS HERR (1604) and MARY BOWMAN (8240).

4698. Paul Bowman, Lampeter, Pa., b. Dec. 15, 1897; d. Mar. 7, 1898.

4699. Mary Hilda, Lampeter, Pa., b. Aug. 28, 1899.

4700. Anna Irene, Lampeter, Pa., b. June 29, 1901; d. Oct. 25, 1901.

Family of AMANDA HERR (1605) and DAVID HESS.

4701. Anna E., Leola, Pa., b. June 29, 1868; m. July 28, 1890, Milton R. Rupp, b. Nov. 16, 1864; son David R. Rupp and Sarah S. Kurtz.
4702. Ida B., New York, N. Y., b. Mar. 10, 1870.

Family of BENJAMIN M. HERR (1606) and ALICE W. MOYER.

4703. Benjamin Ira, Strasburg, Pa., b. Nov. 9, 1878.
4704. Alice Florence, Shippensburg, Pa., b. Feb. 22, 1881; m. Oct. 14, 1902, Howard A. Ryder, b. Oct. 2, 1875; son Adam Ryder and Mame Longenecker.

Family of HEBRON M. HERR (1607) and REBECCA ANN HERSHEY.

4705. Emma Gertrude, Lancaster, Pa., b. Jan. 6, 1877.
4706. Reba Ann, Lancaster, Pa., b. Aug. 18, 1888.

Family of JACOB R. HERR (1608) and SUSAN F. BRENEMAN.

4707. Willis B., Willow Street, Pa., b. Dec. 24, 1882; d. May 27, 1904.
4708. Jay W. B., Willow Street, Pa., b. Aug. 21, 1896.

Family of Rev. FRANK M. HERR (1610) and MARY ELIZABETH HERSHEY.

4709. Mabel Anna, Lancaster, Pa., b. Aug. 22, 1882.
4710. Jacob Hershey, Lancaster, Pa., b. July 10, 1887.
4711. Miriam Elizabeth, Lancaster, Pa., b. Apr. 5, 1894.

Family of AMOS C. HERR (1611) and MARY H. SHENK (7433).

4712. Edith L., Strasburg, Pa., b. Mar. 4, 1883.
4713. Musser S., Strasburg, Pa., b. Jan. 21, 1885.
4714. Mary, Strasburg, Pa., b. Nov. 21, 1893; d. Apr. 28, 1894.
4715. Herbert, Strasburg, Pa., b. Oct. 6, 1895.

Family of MARY ANN HERR (1613) and AMOS H. McALLISTER.

4716. Anna Maud, Conestoga Center, Pa., b. Oct. 28, 1885.
4717. John Wesley H., Millersville, Pa., b. Oct. 19, 1892.

Family of HENRY ROHRER (1623) and ELIZABETH STONER.

4718. Fanny, Intercourse, Pa., b. Jan. 3, 1817; d. 1875; m. June, 1875, Benjamin Leman.

4719. Christian, Strasburg, Pa., b. Aug. 3, 1818; d. 1897; m. Maria Buckwalter.

4720. Jacob, Strasburg, Pa., b. Oct. 3, 1820; d. 1892; m. Mary Ann Barge.

4721. Martin, Strasburg, Pa., b. Mar. 2, 1822; d. Aug. 6, 1884; m. Nov. 24, 1846, Catharine Meck, b. Aug. 11, 1823; d. Feb. 9, 1885; dau. John Meck and Susanna Forrer.

4722. Henry, Hagerstown, Md., b. Dec. 31, 1823.

4723. Maria, Clark Co., O., b. Oct. 10, 1825; m. Abraham Kendig.

4724. Catharine, New Danville, Pa., b. Aug. 29, 1828; m. Abraham Snavely, d. Nov., 1891.

4725. John S., Lancaster, Pa., b. Nov. 26, 1833; m. June 30, 1864, Anna E. Waidley, b. Apr. 26, 1845; dau. Levi Waidley and Julia A. Shroy.

4726. Elizabeth, Strasburg, Pa., b. May 24, 1837; d. 1874; m. Feb. 14, 1859, Lewis Hilt, b. Sept. 19, 1834; d. 1876.

Family of MARTIN ROHRER (1625) and ELIZABETH KREIDER.

4727. Christian, Dayton, O.

4728. Maria, Dayton, O., d. 1900; m. ——— Grimes.

4729. Martha, Dayton, O., m. ——— Williamson.

Family of ELIZABETH ROHRER (1626) and MARTIN KREIDER.

4730. Henry, Lampeter, Pa., m. ——— Urban.

4731. Martin, Lampeter, Pa., m. ——— Groff.

4732. Tobias R., Fertility, Pa., b. Oct. 17, 1827; d. Dec. 12, 1903; m. 1850, Anna Kreider, b. Sept. 22, 1832; d. Dec. 5, 1889; dau. John Kreider and Mary Denlinger.

4733. John, Lampeter, Pa., m. ——— Esbenshade.

4734. Daniel, Lampeter, Pa., m. ——— Meck.

4735. Mary, Lampeter, Pa., m. Henry Rowe.

4736. Lizzie, Lampeter, Pa., m. Henry Doner.

Family of CATHARINE ROHRER (1627) and EMANUEL BARR.

4737. Mary, Muscatine, Ia., b. Nov. 2, 1824; d. July 5, 1849; m. Mar. 14, 1844, Daniel W. Kauffman.

4738. Elizabeth, Lancaster, Pa., b. Oct. 10, 1826; d. Aug. 13, 1888; m. Aug. 20, 1846, Christian R. Herr.

4739. Adam Rohrer, Lancaster, Pa., b. Oct. 17, 1831; m. Jan. 27, 1859, Emma M. Reed, dau. Peter Reed and Margaret ————.

Family of CHRISTIAN ROHRER (1628) and MARGARET EMERICK.

4740. David, Germantown, O.

4741. John H., Germantown, O.

4742. Maria, Germantown, O., m. ———— Gruber.

4743. Josephine, Shelbyville, Ind., m. ———— Byers.

4744. Elizabeth, Yankton, Dak., m. Samuel Kaucher.

Family of SAMUEL ROHRER (1629) and REBECCA WISE.

4745. John, Dayton, O.

4746. Christian, Dayton, O.

4747. Samuel, Dayton, O.

4748. Susan, Dayton, O.

4749. Warren, Dayton, O.

4750. Mary Ann, Dayton, O., m. ———— Kiser.

4751. Adaline, Cleveland, O., m. ———— Snyder.

4752. Caroline, Dayton, O., m. ———— Gebheart.

Family of DANIEL ROHRER (1630) and SARAH LAUDERBACH.

4753. Martin, DeGraff, O.

4754. Abraham, Mansfield, O.

4755. Christian F., Fremont, O.

4756. Mary Ann, Urbana, O.

Family of JACOB ROHRER (1631) and ELIZABETH KENDIG.

4757. Son, Tippecanoe City, O., b. Oct. 22, 1849; d. Oct. 22, 1849.

4758. Mary Ann, Tippecanoe City, O., b. Oct. 15, 1853; m. Jan. 17, 1875, Thomas C. Leonard, son Joseph Leonard and Margaret

4759. John Henry, Tippecanoe City, O., b. Dec. 25; m. Apr. 7, 1885, Rose Benham, b. Feb. 13, 1863; dau. Joseph Benham and Margaret E. Shafford.

4760. Daniel Webster, Tippecanoe City, O., b. Aug. 28, 1860.

4761. Son, Tippecanoe City, O., b. Apr. 2, 1863; d. Apr. 2, 1863.

4762. Ida R., Tippecanoe City, O., b. Feb. 6, 1866; m. Dec. 20, 1887, Abraham R. Garver, b. Dec. 20, 1860; son Benjamin C. Garver and Ruth A. Rohrer.

Family of BARBARA HERR (1644) and Rev. TOBIAS KREIDER.

4763. Tobias H., Bird-in-Hand, Pa., b. June 28, 1853; m. Jan. 30, 1873, Susan Shiffer, b. Mar. 27, 1852; dau. John Shiffer and Martha Bowermaster.

Family of JACOB F. HERR (1646) and SUSAN WITMER.

4764. Isaiah, Strasburg, Pa., b. Dec. 1, 1846; d. Feb. 7, 1849.

4765. Jacob Witmer, Refton, Pa., b. Feb. 14, 1848; m. Oct. 15, 1873, Ella Travis.

4766. Maggie, Smithville, Pa., b. Apr. 11, 1849; m. Oct. 15, 1871, Elam Hess, son David Hess and Louisa Hetler.

4767. Luriston B., Lancaster, Pa., b. July 15, 1850; m. Dec. 26, 1879, Anna F. Clark, b. Dec. 18, 1854; dau. Edwin Clark and Mary A. Davis.

4768. Sarah Ann, Strasburg, Pa., b. Oct. 12, 1851; d. Apr. 9, 1853.

4769. Susan, Strasburg, Pa., b. Mar. 25, 1853; d. Aug. 20, 1853.

4770. Mary Vegeta, Strasburg, Pa., b. July 2, 1854.

4771. Barbara, Strasburg, Pa., b. Mar. 13, 1856; d. Mar, 1, 1857.

4772. George M., Strasburg, Pa., b. Mar. 13, 1857; d. Jan. 1, 1858.

4773. Tobias L., Strasburg, Pa., b. Apr. 20, 1859; d. Aug. 16, 1862.

4774. Aaron C., Strasburg, Pa., b. Apr. 20, 1859; d. Feb. 1, 1886.

4775. Mary N., Strasburg, Pa., b. Aug. 18, 1862; d. Aug. 27, 1863.

4776. Omer Elmer, Lancaster, Pa., b. Feb. 29, 1864; m. Nov. 19, 1886, Annie Ester, b. Oct. 17, 1864; dau. Benjamin K. Ester and Ellenora Harlan.

4777. Newton F., Monterey, Pa., b. July 25, 1866.

Family of MARTHA HEINEY (1655) and MICHAEL HAVERSTICK.

4778. Frances, Marticville, Pa,. b. Oct. 7, 1814; d. June 29, 1881; m. John Miller.

4779. Michael, Washington, Ia., b. Aug. 22, 1817; m. Leah Beck, b. June 13, 1820; d. Jan. 17, 1892; dau. Joseph Beck and Rebecca Foringer.

4780. Isaac, ———, Ind., b. Oct. 13, 1819.

4781. Eve, Marticville, Pa., b. Oct. 26, 1821; d. Dec. 11, 1901; m. Simon Lehman, d. Mar. 12, 1877.

4782. Socrates, ———, Ill., b. Mar. 27, 1824.

4783. George, ———, Cal., b. May 3, 1827.

Family of ELIZABETH HEINEY (1656) and WILLIAM REAM.

4784. Frances, Rohrerstown, Pa., m. Adam Deitrich.

4785. Susan, Rohrerstown, Pa., m. John Eshleman.

4786. Jacob, Rohrerstown, Pa.

Family of FRANCES HEINEY (1660) and DAVID S. HEINEY.

4787. Eli, Rohrerstown, Pa.

4788. David, Rohrerstown, Pa., d, May 1, 1899.

4789. Samuel, Lancaster, Pa., b. Apr. 11, 1831; d. May 17, 1876; m. Jan. 5, 1858, Christiana Hess, b. Nov. 4, 1839; d. Dec. 21, 1874; dau. Rudolph Hess and Polly Johnson.

4790. Isaac, Marticville, Pa., m. ——— McCarter.

4791. George, Lancaster, Pa., m. Elizabeth Good, dau. John Good and Susan Eshleman.

4792. Maria, Mt. Nebo, Pa., m. William Warfel. ·

Family of ISAAC HEINEY (1665) and Wid. ELIZABETH ZERCHER.

4793. Martha H., New Danville, Pa., b. Mar. 2, 1840; m. Nov. 17, 1859, Michael B. Haverstick, b. Dec. 21, 1836; son Michael Haverstick and Leah Beck.

4794. Frances H., Lancaster, Pa., b. Nov. 18, 1841; m. Aug. 15, 1861, Abraham Fisher, b. July 6, 1840; son Henry Fisher and Anna McAllister.

4795. Isaac, Lancaster, Pa., b. Nov. 12, 1843; m. 1868, Emma Simmons, dau. Isaac Simmons and ——— Goodman.

Family of SUSAN HEINEY (1667) and JACOB KAUFFMAN.

4796. Abraham, Masson, O., b. July 29, 1834; d. 1868.

4797. Daughter, Millersville, Pa., b. Jan. 20, 1834; d. Feb. 3, 1834.

Family of JACOB GROFF (1669) and MARY HOWRY.

4798. Elizabeth, Bird-in-Hand, Pa., b. Sept. 1, 1842; m. Nov. 10, 1864, S. —— W. Ranck.

4799. Rev. John H., Middletown, Pa., b. Dec. 8, 1843; m. Nov. 27, 1866, Elizabeth Kurtz, b. Dec. 29, 1841; d. Nov. 29, 1873; dau. Henry Kurtz and Leah Rupp; m. Nov. 15, 1877, Sarah C. Eckert, b. July 14, 1848; dau. Henry Eckert and ——.

4800. Phœbe, Middletown, Pa., b. Sept. 19, 1845; d. Apr. 30, 1876.

4801. Jacob, Middletown, Pa., b. Mar. 31, 1851; d. Mar. 31, 1852.

4802. Mary, Des Moines, Ia., b. July 24, 1855; d. May 11, 1891; m. Frank Jaquith.

4803. Abraham L., Harrisburg, Pa., b. June 7, 1857; m. May 27, 1880, Elizabeth Weidman, b. Oct. 1, 1856; dau. George Weidman and Pamilla Heilman.

Family of RICHARD B. GROFF (1670) and Wid. JUDITH ESHLEMAN.

4804. Sylvanus Antha, Morengo, Ia., b. Aug. 16, 1843; d. Nov. 29, 1861.

4805. Susan Antha, Morengo, Ia., b. Dec. 31, 1844; m. Nov. 29, 1866, Dr. William L. Huston, b. Mar. 19, 1830; son John Huston and Elizabeth Langfelt.

4806. Charles Harold, Live Oak, Fla., b. Dec. 12, 1846; d. Oct. 10, 1886; m. Oct. 11, 1869, Elizabeth A. Dunham, b. May 5, 1848; dau. Joseph Dunham and Mary Woodyard.

4807. Eddie B., Marengo, Ia., b. Oct. 10, 1848; d. Mar. 15, 1858.

Family of BENJAMIN GROFF (1671) and EVELINE DECKER.

4808. Infant, Belmond, Ia.

4809. Mary E., Belmond, Ia., b. Feb. 22, 1843; m. July 4, 1869, Elias P. Ripley, b. July 11, 1837; son Henry Ripley and Margaret Surgart.

4810. Amine Bedora, Viroqua, Wis., b. Sept. 5, 1844; m. Oct. 4, 1867, Charles C. Brown, b. Feb. 24, 1844; son James Brown and Mary A. Bird.

Family of SUSAN GROFF (1673) and THOMAS WIGGINS.

4811. Joseph B., Broughton, Ill., b. Nov. 3, 1853; m. Mar. 29, 1883, Mary Jackman.

4812. Christian G., Norwood, O., b. Sept. 15, 1855; m. Feb. 22, 1888, Elizabeth J. Power, b. Oct. 27, 1860; dau. Charles C. Power and Laura E. Skinner.

4813. Leonard H., Daylers, La., b. Mar. 12, 1857.

4814. Sarah, Miamiville, O., b. Dec. 12, 1862.

4815. Susan, Miamiville, O., b. May 14, 1864.

4816. Margaret, Miamiville, O., b. Mar. 4, 1867.

4817. William, Miamiville, O., b. Oct. 1, 1869.

4818. Augusta, Miamiville, O., b. June 24, 1872.

Family of DAVID GROFF (1674) and SARA MAJOR.

4819. Ida, Lawrenceville, Ill., b. Mar. 6, 1858; m. Apr. 1, 1886, James A. Seed, b. Aug. 15, 1860; son William Seed and Lydia Smith.

4820. Ova, Wooddale, Kans., b. Jan. 8, 1860.

4821. Ada, Lawrenceville, Ill., b. June 24, 1861; m. May 24, 1887, Frank Sircomb, b. May 15, 1851.

4822. Carrie, Lawrenceville, Ill., b. Jan. 24, 1864; d. May 13, 1874.

4823. Homer, Claremont, Ill., b. Dec. 22, 1868; m. Dec. 24, 1891, Letitia Allen, b. Jan. 1, 1871; dau. Epperson Allen and ————.

4824. James, Campbell, Mo., b. Sept. 1, 1875.

4825. Robert, Louisville, Ky., b. Mar. 19, 1879; d. June 20, 1903.

Family of MARTIN LUTHER GROFF (1675) and ELIZABETH CAMPBELL.

4826. Elictta, Weston, O., b. Dec. 11, 1862.

4827. George, Haney, O., b. Oct. 8, 1864; m. Oct. 10, 1888, Zella Lamb, b. Dec. 19, 1867; dau. Ottorburn Lamb and Jennie Cartright.

4828. Homer, North Creek, O., b. Mar. 30, 1866; m. Feb. 12, 1891, Ora Andrews, b. Jan. 21, 1873; dau. John Andrews and Laura Price.

4829. Charles, Haney, O., b. Oct. 20, 1868; m. Feb. 22, 1898, Etta Flier, b. Nov. 14, 1871; dau. Joseph Flier and Ellen E. Kamerly.

4830. Ona, Bettsville, O., b. Aug. 2, 1871.

4831. Vinnie, Bettsville, O., b. Dec. 19, 1873.

4832. Maude, Weston, O., b. June 7, 1877.

Family of CATHARINE GROFF (1676) and HIRAM HALL.

4833. Linnie P., Yankton, S. Dak., b. Aug. 26, 1862; m. Oct. 24, 1878, Albert H. Orvis, b. May 19, 1857; son Chester Orvis and Esther A Ware.

4834. Edward, Shell Rock, Ia., b. Nov. 16, 1865; m. Sept. 24, 1890, Ella Mallony.

Family of ELIZABETH S. GROFF (1677) and JACOB BAKER.

4835. Jefferson S., Philadelphia, Pa., b. Dec. 16, 1859; m. Oct. 31, 1889, Martha Spear, dau. James Spear and Matilda Mullen.

4836. Oliver J., Curwensville, Pa., b. Mar. 10, 1862; m. Mar. 7, 1886, Lelia Legg.

4837. Elmira C., Soudersburg, Pa., b. Apr. 1, 1864; m. July 5, 1883, Amos Rathfon, b. Nov. 23, 1859; son Michael Rathfon and

4838. Christian G., Philadelphia, Pa., b. Mar. 22, 1866; m. Oct. 6, 1889, Rosa Makinley, dau. William Makinley and ———.

Family of MARY GROFF (1678) and ELI CAPELLA.

4839. Alexander, Haney, O., b. May 11, 1859; m. Apr. 9, 1877, Catharine Hatch, b. June 18, 1874; dau. John Hatch and Elizabeth Weaver.

4840. Martin, Custer, O., b. Feb. 26, 1861; m. Oct. 7, 1880, Annie Andrews, b. Sept. 28, 1871.

4841. William, Custer, O., b. Apr. 24, 1863; m. May 1, 1897.

4842. Josephine, Cansburg, O., b. July 11, 1865; m. Feb. 2, 1879, David Slater.

4843. Sylvia, Weston, O., b. May 18, 1867; m. May 23, 1880, Matt Paff.

4844. Elizabeth, Ottaway, O., b. May 7, 1869; m. Oct. 17, 1883, Martin Smith.

4845. Reva, Millers City, O., b. May 18, 1871; m. Nov. 26, 1883, Joseph Rheumaker.

4846. Frank, Custer, O., b. May 17, 1874.

4847. Lue, Custer, O., b. Mar. 31, 1876; m. Aug. 16, 1897, Mary Feeland, b. June 23, 1877.

4848. Jennie, Custer, O., b. Mar. 28, 1880.

4849. Frederick, Custer, O., b. Sept. 22, 1883.

Family of ANNA ESHLEMAN (1679) and HENRY MUSSELMAN.

4850. Amos Forrer, Baltimore, Md., b. July 28, 1830; d. Sept. 16, 1906.

4851. Mary Louisa, Pottstown, Pa., b. Sept. 27, 1832; m. Jan. 23, 1856, Dr. Michael A. Withers (3609).

4852. Elmira S., Strasburg, Pa., b. Feb. 16, 1835; m. June 9, 1858, James W. Linville, b. Jan. 27, 1825; d. Nov. 19, 1881; son James Linville and Sarah Quigley.

4853. Benjamin H. Franklin, Lancaster, Pa., b. June 25, 1837; d. Aug. 27, 1895; m. Nov. 19, 1873, Anna J. Herr (4871).

4854. Martha Ann, Strasburg, Pa., b. Dec. 26, 1839; d. Dec. 16, 1840.

4855. Josephine E., Leaman Place, Pa., b. Sept. 17, 1841; m. Feb. 15, 1866, Dr. Brainard Leaman, b. Mar. 28, 1842; d. Jan. 28, 1904; son Rev. John Leaman and Martha McClurg.

4856. Clarissa R., Philadelphia, Pa., b. Dec. 23, 1843; d. Dec. 26, 1900; m. Jan. 28, 1869, Ferree W. Eshleman (4236).

4857. Annie V., Overbrook, Pa., b. Aug. 6, 1846; m. Oct. 19, 1876, Edwin D. H. Eshleman (4225).

4858. David G. Eshleman, Germantown, Pa., b. Jan. 11, 1849; m. Nov. 8, 1883, Katie R. Robinson, b. May 16, 1850; dau. John P. Robinson and Priscilla Barnhurst.

4859. Edwin Charles, Philadelphia, Pa., b. Nov. 23, 1851; m. Mar. 4, 1874, Emily D. Bishop, b. July 24, 1852; dau. Rev. William Bishop and Mary A. Steacy.

Family of DAVID G. ESHLEMAN (1682) and CAROLINE O. CARPENTER.

4860. Anna Julia, Milan, Italy, b. Oct. 20, 1849; d. Oct. 21, 1879; m. May 28, 1872, John H. McMurdy, b. June, 1847; d. June 5, 1875; son Rev. Robert McMurdy and ——— Russell.

4861. Mary Ross, Lancaster, Pa., b. Oct. 23, 1851; d. Jan. 3, 1852.

4862. Eliza Ross, Denver, Col., b. Aug, 13, 1853; m. Nov. 28, 1875, Frank M. Taylor, b. Apr. 5, 1850; son Henry A. Taylor and Catharine C. Osborne.

4863. Harriet Burrows, Cripple Creek, Col., b. Oct. 1, 1856; m. Apr. 12, 1876, Paul F. Mohr, son Paul Mohr and Fredricka Deiterline; m. Edward C. Stimson, son Charles W. Stimson and Harriet Junkins.

4864. George Ross, Lancaster, Pa., b. Sept. 30, 1864; m. June 1, 1893, Emma E. Spencer, dau. Sheldon S. Spencer and Emma Foltz.

Family of BENJAMIN G. HERR (1683) and MARY EMMA WITMER.

4865. Theodore Witmer, Denver, Col., b. Dec. 7, 1833; m. June 15, 1859, Annie Musser, b. May 19, 1833; d. Sept. 29, 1871; dau. Dr. Martin Musser and Anna Hostetter; m. Jan. 1, 1873, Wid. Emma M. Neff, b. Nov. 25, 1838; d. Dec. 25, 1904; dau. Dr. Martin Musser and Anna Hostetter.

4866. Lorenzo David, Denver, Col., b. Nov. 5, 1835; m. Oct. 10, 1871, Hannah E. Weaver, b. Sept. 18, 1849; dau. Jacob Weaver and Catharine Eynson.

4867. Dr. Ambrose John, Lancaster, Pa., b. Mar. 1, 1838; m. Oct. 4, 1866, Emma S. Musselman (3520).

4868. Mary Elizabeth, Lancaster, Pa., b. Apr. 26, 1840; m. Oct. 1, 1868, Enos B. Herr (4110).

4869. Hiero Benjamin, Chicago, Ill., b. Nov. 12, 1842; m. June 25, 1868, Mattie A. Shenk (9729).

4870. Francis Lightner, Lancaster, Pa., b. Aug. 3, 1844; m. Oct. 6, 1874, Sallie A. Myers, b. Aug. 25, 1850; d. Feb. 2, 1882; dau. Henry Myers and Elvina A. Fetter.

4871. Anna Jane, Lancaster, Pa., b. Oct. 4, 1846; m. Nov. 19, 1873, Benjamin F. Musselman (4853).

4872. Allan Adam, Lancaster, Pa., b. Feb. 17, 1849; m. June 11, 1879, Annie L. Musser (4638); m. Oct. 10, 1894, Anna McC. Jones, b. Sept. 25, 1845; dau. Richard W. Jones and Mary J. McClelland.

4873. Juliet Sylvia S., Lancaster, Pa., b. July 30, 1851.

4874. Alice Emma, Strasburg, Pa., b. Dec. 25, 1853; d. Dec. 29, 1856.

PORTRAIT OF THEODORE W. HERR, GENEALOGIST;
COMPILER AND PUBLISHER OF THIS BOOK.

280b

Family of ELIZABETH HERR (1686) and Rev. Dr. DANIEL MUSSER.

4875. Mary Adrienne, Strasburg, Pa., b. Feb. 1, 1837; m. Dec. 15, 1858, Frank B. Musselman (3516).

4876. John Henry, Lampeter, Pa., b. Jan. 5, 1845; m. Oct. 27, 1868, Eliza A. Musselman (3523).

Family of ANNA HERR (1687) and HENRY FRANTZ.

4877. Dr. John Herr, Old Point Comfort, Va., b. Oct. 14, 1837; d. Mar. 2, 1882; m. May 27, 1868, Louisa Sewall, b. Mar. 10, 1851; d. July 18, 1894; dau. James Sewall and Anne M. Pinkney.

4878. Ada Elizabeth, Paradise, Pa., b. Nov. 6, 1838; d. May 30, 1844.

4879. Jacob Milton, San Francisco, Cal., b. June 8, 1841; d. Feb. 26, 1907; m. Jan. 19, 1876, Lida Gillette, b. June 18, 1846; dau. Gersham Gillette and Elizabeth Moe.

4880. Henry Benjamin, West Allis, Wis., b. Jan. 4, 1843; m. Oct. 20, 1877, Nellie L. Stone, b. Apr. 20, 1853; d. July 14, 1886; dau. Chauncey H. Stone and Julia A. Harrington; m. Dec. 21, 1887, Della A. Stone, b. Mar. 10, 1857; dau. Chauncey H. Stone and Julia A. Harrington.

4881. Joseph Ira, Los Angeles, Cal., b. Oct. 21, 1845; m. Oct. 1, 1902, Alice L. Reed, b. Dec. 6, 1869; dau. Asa W. Reed and Phidelia Gay.

4882. Mary Emma, Rock Island, Ill., b. Feb. 11, 1848; m. Jan. 4, 1870, Levi M. Haverstick, b. Jan. 4, 1842; d. Nov. 25, 1881; son Benjamin Haverstick and Lydia Mylin.

4883. Albert Daniel, San Bernardino, Cal., b. Oct. 20, 1853; m. Wid. Sarah Waldman Williams, b. Nov. 4, 1863; dau. Martin Waldman and Marion Lee.

4884. Anna Naomi, Lancaster, Pa., b. May 22, 1859.

Family of MARTHA M. HERR (1688) and Dr. JACOB H. MUSSER.

4885. Mary Luetta, Witmer, Pa., b. Aug. 20, 1841; d. June 27, 1902; m. Oct. 11, 1864, Christian Musselman (3518).

4886. John Herr, Witmer, Pa., b. Apr. 3, 1843; d. Dec. 3, 1847.

4887. Annie Elizabeth, Lancaster, Pa., b. July 15, 1847; m. Feb. 21, 1875 (8233).

4888. Francis Martin, Lancaster, Pa., b. Dec. 31, 1849; d. Sept. 12, 1885; m. May 26, 1875, Ruth A. Cooper, b. Jan. 8, 1853; dau. Mark P. Cooper and Sydney Conard.

4889. John Jacob, Witmer, Pa., b. July 3, 1852; d. Feb. 22, 1856.

4890. Willis Benjamin, Lancaster, Pa., b. Oct. 28, 1854; m. Jan. 21, 1885, Katherine W. Kauffman, b. Sept. 12, 1860; dau. Junius B. Kauffman and Katherine Bonebaugh.

4891. Omar Henry. Manheim, Pa., b. May 23, 1857; m. Sept. 1, 1901, Anna B. Krauss, b. July 15, 1871; dau. John Krauss and Barbara Hachtel.

Family of JOHN F. HERR (1689) and MARTHA MUSSER.

4892. Walter M., Strasburg, Pa., b. Jan. 26, 1849; d. Nov. 29, 1849.

4893. Ada Elizabeth, Strasburg, Pa., b. Apr. 21, 1851; d. Nov. 26, 1853.

4894. Laura Ann, Strasburg, Pa., b. Apr. 6, 1853.

4895. Mary Maud, Lampeter, Pa., b. Oct. 12, 1854; m. Oct. 12, 1876, Sener Millo Herr (1597).

4896. Benjamin Maurice, Gap, Pa., b. Aug. 2, 1856.

4897. Henry Rufus, Strasburg, Pa., b. Mar. 10, 1858; m. Mary V. Diller, b. Feb. 21, 1866; dau. George Diller and Hannah Rutter.

4898. John Ellsworth, Strasburg, Pa., b. June 6, 1861; m. Feb. 9, 1887, Edith M. Eberman (9887).

Family of NAOMI HERR (1691) and Wid. Dr. BENJAMIN MUSSER.

4899. Dr. John Herr, Philadelphia, Pa., b. June 22, 1856; m. Sept. 16, 1880, Agnes G. Harper, dau. John M. Harper and Susan B. Robb.

4900. Mary Naomi, Lancaster, Pa., b. Aug. 23, 1858; d. Oct. 4, 1895; m. Oct. 8, 1879, Enos H. Weaver (4601).

Family of HARRIET MARTIN (1715) and JACOB REDSECKER.

4901. Sarah A., Mt. Washington, Md., b. July 4, 1831; m. Henry S. Greenawalt, d. Aug. 9, 1867.

4902. George Henry, Mt. Washington, Md., b. Jan. 3, 1832; d. Nov. 7, 1835.

4903. Mary A., Mt. Washington, Md., b. July 13, 1834; d. May 12, 1889; m. Abraham Beetem, b. 1826; d. May 8, 1900.
4904. Harriet S., Mt. Washington, Md., b. Aug. 13, 1836; d. June 11, 1895; m. Charles Kunkel.
4905. Jacob H., Lebanon, Pa., b. Feb. 15, 1839.
4906. Anna E., Baltimore, Md., b. Feb. 28, 1842; d. Feb. 19, 1892; m. William H. Bougher.
4907. Abraham Ream, Pittsburg, Pa., b. Mar. 17, 1844; m. Martha T. Peffer.
4908. John B. C., b. Oct. 26, 1846; d. May 23, 1849.

Family of JACOB ESHLEMAN (1716) and BARBARA A. MILLER.

4909. Emanuel, Martinsville, Pa., b. Oct. 3, 1830; d. Jan. 2, 1902; m. Sept. 6, 1870, Anna B. Eshleman, dau. Elijah Eshleman and Christian Bear.
4910. Martha, Strasburg, Pa., b. Nov. 2, 1832; d. June 25, 1872; m. Peter Wenger, son Emanuel Wenger and Annie Griffy.
4911. Christian, Lampeter, Pa., b. Aug. 10, 1834; m. Mary Cassel, dau. Samuel Cassel and Barbara Hunchberger.
4912. Abraham, Martinsville, Pa., b. Feb. 23, 1837; d. Apr. 5, 1882; m. Mary Mowrer.
4913. Mary, Lancaster, Pa., b. Apr. 10, 1839; m. John H. Kreider, son John Kreider and ——— Houser.
4914. Jacob, Lancaster, Pa., b. Mar. 17, 1841; m. 1861, Anna Harnish, dau. Elias Harnish and ——— Urban.
4915. Infant, Lancaster, Pa.
4916. Barbara Anne, Lancaster, Pa., b. Mar. 17, 1846; m. May 14, 1867, John W. Eshleman, b. Oct. 7, 1844; son John W. Eshleman and Susan Rheem.
4917. Infant, Lancaster, Pa.
4918. Emma, Lancaster, Pa., b. May 27, 1851.

Family of CHRISTIAN MARTIN (1744) and MARY KEMMORY.

4919. Amos, Philadelphia, Pa.
4920. Christian, Lancaster, Pa
4921. Samuel, Philadelphia, Pa.

Family of SUSAN MARTIN (1748) and CHRISTIAN W. BINKLEY.

4922. Louisa, Strasburg, Pa., b. Sept. 18, 1844; d. Apr. 25, 1860.

4923. Elias L., Dayton, O., b. May 1, 1846; m. Hattie A. Patterson.

4924. Ann Eliza, Strasburg, Pa., b. Feb. 6, 1848; m. Dec. 25, 1866, John F. Ingram, b. Mar. 7, 1845; son James Ingram and Sarah Myers.

4925. Samuel M., Strasburg, Pa., b. Jan. 5, 1850; d. Apr. 3, 1863.

4926. Susan, Strasburg, Pa., b. Dec. 15, 1852; d. Dec. 22, 1852.

4927. Mary Frances, Lancaster, Pa., b. July 6, 1854; m. Samuel Bally.

4928. Martha Emma, Lancaster, Pa., b. Apr. 10, 1856; m. Jacob Benner.

4929. Elmira Catharine, Strasburg, Pa., b. Nov. 3, 1857; m. Elim Holl, son John Holl and Martha Cramer.

4930. Christian, Manheim, Pa., b. June 22, 1860; m. Esther Kendig, dau. Michael Kendig and ———— Reilly.

4931. Harry E., Philadelphia, Pa., b. Apr. 7, 1862; d. Jan. 11, 1892.

4932. Sue, Rothville, Pa., b. June 14, 1864; m. Joseph Hess, son Joseph Hess and ———— Weidler.

4933. John Franklin, Elizabethtown, Pa., b. Feb. 16, 1869; m. Wid. Amanda Engle, dau. Jacob Stauffer and ————.

Family of ESTHER ANN MARTIN (1754) and GEORGE H. MILLER.

4934. Benjamin F., Lancaster, Pa., b. Jan. 7, 1846; b. Dec. 19, 1863.

4935. Maria L., Lancaster, Pa., b. Apr. 7, 1847; d. May 10, 1847.

4936. Jacob M., Lancaster, Pa., b. June 10, 1848; m. Jennie Funk.

4937. Esther A., Lancaster, Pa., b. Mar. 6, 1850.

4938. Catharine E., Oxford, Pa., b. Dec. 19, 1852; m. Harvey M. Groff, d. 1901.

4939. Addie A., Lancaster, Pa., b. Mar. 4, 1853; d. Mar. 4, 1853.

4940. Henry C., Lancaster, Pa., b. Apr. 11, 1854; d. Mar. 22, 1857.

4941. John W., Lancaster, Pa., b. Sept. 5, 1855; d. Jan. 17, 1857.

4942. George W., Lancaster, Pa., b. Nov. 10, 1855; m. Sallie McLaughlin, dau. John McLaughlin and Hettie ————.

4943. Charles E., Philadelphia, Pa., b. Jan. 12, 1858.

4944. William W., Fairmount, Pa., b. Aug. 13, 1859; m. Linnie Eshleman, dau. Henry Eshleman and Elizabeth ————.

4945. Isaac N., Lancaster, Pa., b. May 30, 1861.

4946. Laura L., Lancaster, Pa., b. Sept. 23, 1862; d. Nov. 26, 1881.

4947. Mary E., Lancaster, Pa., b. July 5, 1864.

4948. Elmer E., Lancaster, Pa., b. May 24, 1866; d. Apr. 3, 1867.

4949. Emma S., Lancaster, Pa., b. Sept. 2, 1867; d. Dec. 31, 1903.

Family of FANNIE BARR (1755) and JACOB M. MAYER.

4950. John B., Landisville, Pa., b. Jan. 13, 1836; m. Nov. 20, 1864, Elizabeth Swartley, b. Sept. 13, 1844; d. May 6, 1877; dau. Christian Swartley and Catharine Huber; m. Catharine Gross, b. Feb. 16, 1846.

4951. Christian N., Creston, Ia., b. Sept. 19, 1837; m. Sept. 27, 1866, Elizabeth Hartman, b. June 6, 1844; dau. George Hartman and Judith Creitz.

4952. Mary Emma, New Providence, Pa., b. Aug. 5, 1839; d. Sept. 16, 1842.

Family of ANNA BARR (1756) and JOHN H. LONGENECKER.

4953. John Barr, Towson, Md., b. July 23, 1842.

4954. Henry Clay, Towson, Md., b. Aug. 25, 1844; m. Nov. 15, 1874, Eliza P. Martin, dau. Dr. Joseph L. Martin and ——— Metcalf.

4955. Mary Louisa, Towson, Md., b. Mar. 23, 1848.

4956. Catharine Stoner, Towson, Md., b. Oct. 1, 1854.

4957. Emma Lizzie, Towson, Md., b. Sept. 20, 1856.

Family of MARTIN BARR (1757) and MARGARET GORE.

4958. Ronaldo Sabedus, Glyndon, Md., b. Apr. 23, 1856.

4959. Eugene, Glyndon, Md., b. Nov. 5, 1857.

4960. Luetta, Glyndon, Md., b. June 27, 1859.

4961. Catharine Gore, Glyndon, Md., b. Aug. 1, 1861.

Family of ELIZABETH BARR (1758) and JOHN GROFF (3814).

4962. Ida Marion, Towson, Md., b. May 28, 1848; m. Joshua Tracey.

4963. Anna Elizabeth, Charleston, W. Va., b. Feb. 5, 1850; m. James K. Gies.

4964. Charles Clayton, Charleston, W. Va., b. Oct. 9, 1851; m. Mary R. Fisher, b. Mar. 1, 1854.

4965. William Barr, Philadelphia, Pa., b. Aug. 8, 1853; m. Margaret French.

4966. Mary Louisa, Philadelphia, Pa., b. Dec. 25, 1857; d. Feb. 22, 1858.

Family of CATHARINE BARR (1761) and JOHN B. KEAGY.

4967. Clara Agnes, Towsontown, Md., b. Jan. 31, 1857.

4968. Miller Storm, Towsontown, Md., b. May 16, 1858.

4969. Harry Clay, Towsontown, Md., b. Sept. 17, 1859.

4970. Winfield Scott, Towsontown, Md., b. Sept. 28, 1861.

4971. Anna Elizabeth, Towsontown, Md., b. Jan. 22, 1863.

Family of FANNY BARR (1763) and JOHN H. HARMAN.

4972. Charles Herbert, Owings Mills, Md., b. Sept. 18, 1845; d. Aug. 1, 1864.

4973. Daniel Martin, Owings Mills, Md., b. Mar. 12, 1847.

4974. Susan Catharine, Owings Mills, Pa., b. July 21, 1848; d. Mar. 12, 1850.

4975. Mary E., Owings Mills, Pa., b. Dec. 22, 1850.

4976. John Henry, Owings Mills, Md., b. Apr. 26, 1852; d. May 24, 1854.

4977. Susanna, Owings Mills, Md., b. Dec. 17, 1853.

4978. Catharine L., Owings Mills, Md., b. May 15, 1855.

4979. John Barr, Owings Mills, Md., b. Dec. 16, 1857.

4980. Fanny, Owings Mills, Md., b. June 14, 1863; d. Aug. 1, 1863.

Family of FRANCIS B. GROFF (2235) and HETTIE ANN BARR (1764).

4981. Mary Alice, Philadelphia, Pa., b. Sept. 7, 1850.

4982. Dr. Charles Abraham, Philadelphia, Pa., b. Feb. 20, 1852.

4983. Annie Miller, Philadelphia, Pa., b. Feb. 19, 1854.

4984. Martin Barr, Philadelphia, Pa., b. Sept. 8, 1855; d. Apr. 21, 1856.

4985. Martha Elizabeth, Philadelphia, Pa., b. Aug. 7, 1858; m. Dec. 3, 1884, Hamilton I. Rothrock, b. Feb. 26, 1849; son Larkin J. Rothrock and Sarah Miller.

4986. Francis B., Philadelphia, Pa., b. Aug. 22, 1860.

Family of JOHN N. BARR (1765) and SALLIE M. DARR.

4987. Grace Ella, Brunswick, Mo., b. Sept. 25, 1855.
4988. Lillie Stone, Brunswick, Mo., b. June 28, 1857.
4989. Kate Kreider, Brunswick, Mo., b. Sept. 25, 1859.
4990. Jessie, Brunswick, Mo., b. Nov. 17, 1861.

Family of MARTIN W. BARR (1766) and HARRIET CORNELIUS.

4991. Harry C., Washington, D. C., b. Nov. 25, 1855; d. Jan. 20, 1860.
4992. Martin Potts, Washington, D. C., b. Mar. 29, 1859.
4993. William Yancey, Washington, D. C., b. Jan. 10, 1861.

Family of MARTIN H. KREIDER (1860) and ANN CATHARINE BARR (1767).

4994. Frank B., Sterling, Ill., b. July 8, 1851.
4995. Annie Elizabeth, Sterling, Ill., b. July 29, 1853.
4996. Martin, Sterling, Ill., b .Mar. 1, 1862.
4997. Katie, Sterling, Ill., b. Jan. 20, 1864.

Family of Dr. DAVID MILLER BARR (1769) and SUSAN L. DICKSON.

4998. Samuel Dickson, Philadelphia, Pa., b. July 27, 1865; m. Apr. 23, 1889, Julia Hughes.
4999. John, Philadelphia, Pa., b. Dec. 18, 1868; d. Dec. 18, 1868.
5000. Annie Elizabeth, Long Branch, N. J., b. Sept. 2, 1870.
5001. Ambrose Witmer, Green Bay, Wis., b. June 26, 1874; d. June 26, 1900.
5002. Minnie Sears, Philadelphia, Pa., b. Oct. 5, 1875; m. June 24, 1897, Francis P. Witmer, b. Apr. 2, 1873; son Ambrose Witmer and Imogene Potts.
5003. Susan Dickson, Long Branch, N. J., b. Oct. 26, 1880.
5004. Maud Miller, Long Branch, N. J., b. Oct. 20, 1882.
5005. Lavinia Laurence, Long Branch, N. J., b. Jan. 13, 1886.

Family of ANNA HARTMAN (1774) and JOHN STAUFFER.

5006. Jacob H., Leola, Pa., b. Jan. 11, 1838; m. Anna Baldwin.
5007. Anna, Millersville, Pa., b. July 6, 1839; d. Sept. 14, 1849.
5008. John H., Millersville, Pa., b. Jan. 16, 1841; m. May 28, 1867, Catharine Barr, b. Nov. 5, 1843; dau. Jacob K. Barr and Christiana Dickle.

Family of CHRISTIAN B. HARTMAN (1777) and CATHARINE IMMEL.

5009. John Augustus, Hill Grove, O., b. Jan. 18, 1847; m. Mar. 9, 1871, Mary A. Noggle, b. May 21, 1852; dau. John Noggle and Elizabeth ———; m. June 1, 1899, Alice Wheeler, b. Aug. 30, 1852.

5011. Infant, Hill Grove, O.

Family of ELIZABETH HARTMAN (1779) and HENRY KAUFFMAN.

5012. Henry Clay, Mill Grove, O.
5013. Solomon, Mill Grove, O.
5014. Sarah, Mill Grove, O.

Family of JOSEPH RUTTER (2479) and HENRIETTA HARTMAN (1780).

5015. Christian H., New Holland, Pa., b. June 26, 1849; d. Mar. 15, 1874.
5016. Esther, New Holland, Pa., b. Nov. 8, 1852; d. Feb. 1, 1855.
5017. Anna Elizabeth, New Holland, Pa., b. May 20, 1858; m. Apr. 26, 1892, John Barton, b. Jan. 7, 1846; son Henry Barton and Margaretta ———.

Family of Dr. SAMUEL B. HARTMAN (1781) and SARAH ANN MARTZELL.

5018. Henry, Lancaster, Pa., b. Jan. 7, 1863; d. Oct. 21, 1881.
5019. Maribel, Lancaster, Pa., b. June 1, 1872; m. June, 1895, Frederick W. Shumacker.

Family of BENJAMIN ESHLEMAN (1728) and ELIZABETH GYGER.

5020. John Gyger, Greenland, Pa., b. Feb. 24, 1833; d. Aug. 4, 1855.
5021. Mary Frances, Greenland, Pa., b. June 23, 1836; d. July 4, 1836.
5022. Mary Tabitha, Philadelphia, Pa., b. Feb. 18, 1843; d. July 19, 1882; m. Feb. 18, 1863, Hon. Isaac E. Hiester, b. May 29, 1824; d. Feb. 6, 1871; son William Hiester and Lucy Ellmaker; m. Dr. Richard J. Levis.
5023. Benjamin Franklin, Lancaster, Pa., b. Mar. 10, 1847; d. Dec. 17, 1903; m. Dec. 21, 1876, Mary Mercur, b. May 4, 1855; dau. Hon. Ulysses Mercur and Sarah Davis.
5024. Lizzie Frances, Lancaster, Pa., b. Dec. 9, 1855; d. Feb., 1905; m. Feb., 1882, Martin Bates, son Martin Bates and ———.

Family of MARTHA HERR (1785) and GABRIEL WENGER.

5025. Martin Herr, Lancaster, Pa., b. Aug. 9, 1842; m. Oct. 28, 1866, Louisa Brown, b. Feb. 9, 1846; dau. Peter Brown and Anna Reamsnyder.

5026. Francina, Lampeter, Pa., b. Jan. 22, 1845; d. Jan. 4, 1852.

5027. Mary Elizabeth, Lampeter, Pa., b. May 27, 1848; d. Aug. 12, 1858.

Family of JOHN K. WITMER (1791) and LAURA FRITTER.

5028. Ann Elizabeth, Strasburg, Pa.

5029. Susanna Florida, Strasburg, Pa., b. Nov. 8, 1852; d. Sept. 2, 1859.

5030. John Martin, Strasburg, Pa., b. Feb. 4, 1855; d. Mar. 16, 1857.

Family of BENJAMIN W. KENDIG (1794) and ELIZA KENDIG (3432).

5031. Hedessa E., Washington, Ill., m. George W. Leonard.

5032. David, Washington, Ill.

5033. William F., Washington, Ill., m. Mary Ann McKenna.

Family of Wid. BENJAMIN W. KENDIG (1794) and ELIZABETH T. PAGE.

5034. Eliza A., Washington, Ill.

5035. Mary M., Washington, Ill.

5036. Clara E., Washington, Ill.

5037. Adino B., Washington, Ill.

5038. Delilah E., Washington, Ill.

Family of MARY KENDIG (1796) and ANDREW CRESS.

5039. Susanna, Washington, Ill., m. Absalom Wallace.

5040. Benjamin K., Washington, Ill., m. Mary L. Bierd.

5041. Payton M., Washington, Ill., m. Lizzie Krantz.

5042. Mary E., Washington, Ill., m. John Wenger.

5043. George W., Washington, Ill.

5044. Andrew J., Washington, Ill.

5045. Calvin B., Washington, Ill.

Family of MAGDALENE KENDIG (1797) and JACOB J. BANTA.

5046. Ellen, Washington, Ill.

5047. Mary, Washington, Ill., m. Miles Morgan.

16

5048. Leah, Washington, Ill.
5049. Martha, Washington, Ill.

Family of DAVID KENDIG (1798) and ELIZABETH McCORD.

5050. Virginia A., Washington, Ill., b. Apr. 23, 1846; m. Mar. 4, 1866, John W. Wilson, b. Aug. 31, 1848; son William Wilson and Sarah G. McClure.
5051. Eliza Jane, Salem, Mo., b. Sept. 10, 1847; m. Oct. 21, 1869, Jasper N. McMurtrey, b. Apr. 2, 1842; d. Feb. 25, 1897; son Alexander McMurtrey and Rebecca Powell.
5052. Missouri E., Washington, Ill., b. Apr. 19, 1850.
5053. Laura Esther, Kansas City, Mo., b. June 30, 1852; m. Jan. 6, 1881, Gilbert G. Mapes. ,,
5054. Marion Alexander, Winfield, Kans., b. Apr. 26, 1855; m. Jan. 5, 1881, Jennie E. Nesmith, b. May 24, 1860; dau. Arthur E. Nesmith and Mary A. McGinnis.

Family of HENRY W. KENDIG (1799) and ELIZABETH ARNOLD.

5055. Melissa B., Washington, Ill.
5056. Clarissa Ellen, Washington, Ill.
5057. Anna M., Washington, Ill.
5058. George Henry, Washington, Ill.

Family of LEAH KENDIG (1800) and JACOB GROVE.

5059. Simon, Washington, Ill.
5060. Columbus, Washington, Ill.
5061. Melissa, Washington, Ill.
5062. Sebastian. Washington, Ill.
5063. Eliza J., Washington, Ill.

Family of HETTIE KENDIG (1801) and DAVID HILDEBRAND.

5064. Susan F., Waynesboro, Va.
5065. William H.. Waynesboro, Va.
5066. David D., Waynesboro, Va.
5067. Jacob M., Waynesboro, Va.
5068. Mary A., Waynesboro, Va.
5069. Martin, Waynesboro, Va.

Family of MARY KENDIG (1802) and JOHN ROEBUSH.

5070. Virginia S., Waynesboro, Va.
5071. David H., Waynesboro, Va.
5072. Mary J., Waynesboro, Va.
5073. John C., Waynesboro, Va.
5074. William M., Waynesboro, Va.
5075. Archie M., Waynesboro, Va.
5076. Elizabeth M., Wyanesboro, Va.

Family of MARIA WITMER (1803) and JOHN ERB.

5077. Susan, Bonview, Pa., b. May 19, 1841.
5078. Amaziah W., Mt. Nebo, Pa., b. May 6, 1842; d. June 19, 1872; m. 1869, Laura A. Ward.
5079. Anna Elizabeth, Battle Creek, Mich., b. Apr. 26, 1844; d. May 11, 1886; m. Mar. 16, 1865, John Rathfon, b. Sept. 19, 1844; son John Rathfon and Wid. Catharine Pfoutz.
5080. John, Mt. Nebo, Pa., b. Apr. 7, 1847; d. Dec. 26. 1882; m. Dec. 25, 1871, Letitia A. Witmer, d. Feb. 14, 1884; dau. Elias Witmer and Susan ———.
5081. Mahlon, Mt. Nebo, Pa., b. Dec. 13, 1849; m. Mar. 26, 1868, Emma L. Acheson, b. May 27, 1848; dau. Cunningham Acheson and Annie ———.
5082. Amanda, Conestoga Center, Pa., b. Dec. 11, 1851; d. Dec. 4, 1852.
5083. Henry, Mt. Nebo, Pa., b. Apr. 10, 1853; m. Mar. 15, 1877, Ida Moss, b. Oct. 29, 1851; dau. James Moss and Rebecca ———.
5084. Mary Jane, Bonview, Pa., b. Oct. 8, 1854.
5085. Emanuel, Lancaster, Pa., b. July 25, 1856; d. Apr. 21. 1891; m. Jan. 3, 1884, Lillian Bell McGuigan, b. Feb. 21, 1861; dau. James A. McGuigan and Marinda ———.
5086. Clayton, Bonview, Pa., b. Mar. 17, 1858; m. Jan. 3. 1884, Esther H. Wissler, b. Apr. 11, 1863; dau. Elias N. Wissler and Anna C.———.
5088. William, Bonview, Pa., b. Nov. 26, 1863; m. Nov. 27, 1890, Emma D. Stevenson, b. Mar. 15, 1866; dau. Samuel C. Stevenson and Mary ———.

Family of ELIAS WITMER (1804) and SUSAN MARKLEY.

5089. Letitia, Strasburg, Pa.

Family of MARTIN B. WITMER (1806) and BARBARA HILLER.

5090. Susan, Mt. Nebo, Pa.
5091. John, Mt. Nebo, Pa.
5092. Charles, Mt. Nebo, Pa.
5093. Frank, Mt. Nebo, Pa.

Family of ESTHER MARTIN (1814) and JACOB S. HERSHEY.

5094. Mary, Intercourse, Pa., b. Nov. 23, 1853.
5095. Hettie, Intercourse, Pa., b. Jan. 28, 1855.
5096. Susanna, Intercourse, Pa., b. Oct. 16, 1856.
5097. Jacob, Intercourse, Pa., b. Oct. 8, 1860.
5098. John W., Intercourse, Pa., b. June 10, 1863.

Family of ESTHER MARTIN (1815) and BENJAMIN GOCHENOUR.

5099. Benjamin M., Willow Street, Pa., b. Mar. 19, 1856.
5100. Samuel M., Willow Street, Pa., b. Aug. 24, 1857.
5101. Jacob M., Willow Street, Pa., b. Sept. 6, 1859; d. Sept. 23, 1863.
5102. Martha A., Willow Street, Pa., b. Nov. 12, 1862.
5103. Esther A., Willow Street, Pa., b. Nov. 23, 1865.

Family of SUSAN MARTIN (1816) and JAMES SPENCE.

5104. John M., Rawlinsville, Pa.; b. Apr. 22, 1844; d. Feb. 23, 1879; m. Sept. 24, 1867, Susan Dunkelberger, b. Sept. 9, 1843; dau. Solomon Dunkelberger and ———— Corl.
5105. Samuel, Rawlinsville, Pa., b. July 28, 1845; d. Apr. 13, 1888.
5106. Emma, Duncannon, Pa., b. May 8, 1847; m. Dec. 5. 1868, John B. Sheaffer, b. Jan. 18, 1844; d. Oct. 9, 1872; son William Sheaffer and Margaret Bear; m. Nov. 7, 1878, James T. Owen, b. Oct. 26, 1842; son Abel D. Owen and Margaret Findley.
5107. David W., Rawlinsville, Pa., b. Feb. 7, 1849.
5108. Abraham L., Rawlinsville, Pa., b. Aug. 21, 1850; d. Jan. 24, 1897.
5109. Martha, Rawlinsville, Pa., b. Feb. 22, 1853; d. June 25, 1883.

Family of MARY MARTIN (1817) and DAVID MILLER.

5110. Martha A., Rawlinsville, Pa., b. Sept. 10, 1848.
5111. Elizabeth C., Rawlinsville, Pa., b. Feb. 26, 1850.
5112. John W., Rawlinsville, Pa., b. Sept. 20, 1851.
5113. Mary E., Rawlinsville, Pa., b. Nov. 26, 1853.
5114. Samuel W., Rawlinsville, Pa., b. Feb. 23, 1856.
5115. Sarah E., Rawlinsville, Pa., b. Mar. 1, 1858.
5116. Esther L., Rawlinsville, Pa., b. Apr. 1, 1860.
5117. David C., Rawlinsville, Pa., b. Mar. 12, 1862.
5118. Benjamin D., Rawlinsville, Pa., b. Sept. 26, 1864.
5119. Susan C., Rawlinsville, Pa., b. Mar. 16, 1866.

Family of DAVID MARTIN (1818) and ELIZABETH RESSEL.

5120. Benjamin F., Rawlinsville, Pa., b. Sept. 1, 1860.
5121. Martha A., Rawlinsville, Pa., b. Feb. 22, 1862.
5122. Samuel R., Rawlinsville, Pa., b. Mar. 14, 1864.
5123. Anna Maria, Rawlinsville, Pa., b. Aug. 20, 1865.
5124. David C., Rawlinsville, Pa., b. Nov. 27, 1866.

Family of BENJAMIN W. MARTIN (1823) and SUSAN GOOD.

5125. Andrew G., Rawlinsville, Pa., b. Aug. 28, 1864.
5126. Frances M., Rawlinsville, Pa., b. Aug. 28, 1866.

Family of ELIZABETH MARTIN (1824) and SAMUEL B. KENDIG.

5127. Martha, Lancaster, Pa., b. Oct. 29, 1862.
5128. Aaron M., Lancaster, Pa., b. Feb. 21, 1864.
5129. Mary, Lancaster, Pa., b. Dec. 31, 1865; d. Sept. 5, 1866.
5130. Anna Elizabeth, Lancaster, Pa., b. June 28, 1867.

Family of HENRY HERR (1836) and HARRIET METZ.

5131. Andrew M., Clarence Center, N. Y., b. July 28, 1850; d. Mar.
12, 1895; m. Feb. 15, 1872. Eliza Eshleman, b. Apr. 3, 1851;
dau. Jacob Eshleman and Catharine Rhodes.
5132. Esther, Williamsville, N. Y., b. Feb. 20, 1852; m. Mar. 6, 1881,
Frederick Brelos, b. Jan. 19, 1851; son Michael Brelos and
Margaret ———.

5133. Edwin, New York, N. Y., b. Aug. 20, 1854; d. Sept. 9, 1901; ,
m. May 8, 1893, Hattie E. Seager, b. Mar. 30, 1865; dau. Russell Seager and Jerusha Snow.

5134. Francis, Shawnee, N. Y., b. May 9, 1857; d. Apr. 1. 1858.

Family of Rev. ELI HERR (1838) and MELVINA L. EGGERT.

5135. Dr. Benjamin F., Millersville, Pa., b. May 26, 1852; m. Susanna Herr (1871).

5136. Dr. John, Port Huron, Mich., b. Dec. 16, 1853; m. Apr. 3, 1879, Lucy A. Grove, b. Sept. 10, 1853; dau. Peter Grove and Jane Miller.

5137. Dr. Christian A., Osborne, O., b. Nov. 12, 1855; m. Sept. 12, 1880, Emma J. Kissinger, d. May 5, 1891; dau. Jacob C. Kissinger and Sarah Kline.

5138. Dr. Abraham Gantz, Port Huron, Mich., b. Sept. 2, 1858; m. June 22, 1879, Sarah A. Eley, b. Oct. 8, 1862; d. Jan. 4, 1881; dau. John Eley and Susan Staley; m. June 17, 1896, Gertrude M. Granger, b. June 28, 1874.

5139. Henry C., Port Huron, Mich., b. Sept. 9, 1860; m. Dec. 8, 1891, Jennie M. Green, b. Oct. 9, 1859; dau. Gardner Green and Lavina M. Grove.

5140. Anna, Buffalo, N. Y., b. July 10, 1862.

5141. Esther, Osborne, O., b. Feb. 7, 1865; d. Dec. 19, 1866.

5142. Harvey E., Osborne, O.

5143. Alta A., Buffalo, N. Y., b. May 28, 1870; m. Sept. 25, 1895, Frank D. Reigle (5153).

Family of MARY HERR (1839) and HENRY TREICHLER.

5144. Eli Julian, Sanborn, N. Y., b. Mar. 17, 1849; m. Dec. 17, 1873, Elizabeth F. Landis (6231).

5145. Melissa J., Williamsville, N. Y., b. Oct. 17, 1850; m. Oct. 26, 1884, John Snearly, b. July 21, 1856; son George Snearly and Esther Metz.

5146. Henry B., Sanborn, N. Y., b. Mar. 17, 1853; m. Jan. 26, 1882, Sarah Rose, b. Sept. 14, 1852; dau. George Rose and Sarah Farley.

5147. Elma A., Sanborn, N. Y., b. Mar. 16, 1858; d. Aug. 9, 1879.

Family of SUSAN HERR (1840) and ANDREW REIGLE.

5148. Mary A., Sanborn, N. Y., b. July 18, 1853; m. Dec. 15, 1881, Lyman G. Hoover, b. Mar. 10, 1840; d. Jan. 29, 1898; son George Hoover and Sarah Zachariah.

5149. Harriet E., Sanborn, N. Y., b. Feb. 8, 1856; m. Sept. 1, 1878, Henry Haubeil, b. May 28, 1851; son George Haubeil and Susan Reed.

5150. Arthur H., Sanborn, N. Y., b. Dec. 11, 1857; d. June 24, 1884.

5151. Alice C., Sanborn, N. Y., b. Feb. 20, 1860; m. Sept. 24, 1890, John D. Edsall, b. Oct. 8, 1853; son John Edsall and Anna Hathway.

5152. Anna M., Sanborn, N. Y., b. Jan. 10, 1862; d. Feb. 6, 1890; m. Dec. 20, 1883, William Subbera, b. Aug. 20, 1852; son David Subbera and Jane Lambert.

5153. Frank D., Buffalo, N. Y., b. July 6, 1866; m. Sept. 25, 1895, Alta A. Herr (5143).

5154. Etta G., La Salle, N. Y., b. Mar. 22, 1868; d. Jan. 24, 1903; m. Sept. 29, 1886, Frank E. Wilson, b. Aug. 15, 1863; son ——— and Ann Craddock.

5155. Henry A., La Salle, N. Y., b. July 18, 1871; d. Oct., 14, 1874.

Family of ELIZABETH HERR (1841) and JOHN SCHMECK.

5156. Franklin H., Pekin, N. Y., b. Aug. 29, 1863; d. Aug., 1879.

5157. John M., Pekin, N. Y., b. Sept. 21, 1865; d. Aug., 1879.

5158. Herbert, Pekin, N Y., b. Aug. 1, 1871; d. Aug. 1, 1871.

5159. Mary, Pekin, N. Y., b. Aug. 1, 1871; d. Aug. 1, 1871.

Family of ESTHER HERR (1842) and ABRAHAM B. GANTZ.

5160. Rev. Edwin John, Minneapolis, Minn., b. May 30, 1853; m. Mar. 28, 1876, Frances L. St. Clair, b. Nov. 17, 1855; dau. H. Smith St. Clair and Ora M. Sherman.

5161. Dr. Henry H., Albia, Ia., b. Apr. 30, 1857; m. July 6, 1881, Nora L. St. Clair, b. Mar. 27, 1858; d. Feb. 13, 1897; dau. H. Smith St. Clair and Ora M. Sherman; m. May 27, 1900, Susan B. Humeston, b. July 15, 1868; dau. Daniel D. Humeston and Florence L. Hazen.

Family of DAVID LONG (1843) and MARY K. MILLER.

5162. Henry M., Williamsville, N. Y., b. May 30, 1842; m. Dec. 25, 1864, Isabella E. Summy, b. Sept. 11, 1846; dau. George W. Summy and Susan Snearly.

5163. Esther S., Williamsville, N. Y., b. Oct. 28, 1843; m. Nov. 22, 1863, Wid. Jacob Shisler, b. Jan. 9, 1837; son Isaac Shisler and Ann Beam.

5164. Mary E., Athol Springs, N. Y., b. Sept. 11, 1845; d. Aug. 6, 1901; m. Nov. 26, 1863, George B. Summy, b. Sept. 11, 1842; son George W. Summy and Susan Snearly.

5165. John D., Williamsville, N. Y., b. July 25, 1847; m. Mar. 18, 1874, Sarah E. Miller, b. Nov. 24, 1846; dau. Benjamin Miller and Susanna Fulner.

5166. Elias A., Chicago, Ill., b. May 1, 1849; m. Dec. 3, 1872, Josephine Baker, b. July 5, 1849; d. Dec. 19, 1894; dau. George Baker and Elizabeth Frick.

5167. Daniel B., Buffalo, N. Y., b. Feb. 5, 1851; m. Sept. 10, 1884, Hattie A. Savage, b. June 30, 1856; d. Oct. 31, 1886; dau. Simeon Savage and ———— Rice.

5168. Susan L., Buffalo, N. Y., b. Jan. 6, 1853; m. Oct. 15, 1892, Thomas F. Morley, b. Aug. 13, 1860; son Thomas Morley and Elizabeth Forsythe.

5169. Anna M., Lewiston, N. Y., b. Nov. 19, 1854; m. Oct. 31, 1883, Charles E. Sweitzer, b. Apr. 23, 1850; son George Sweitzer and Elizabeth Fisher.

5170. David N., Buffalo, N. Y., b. Oct. 26, 1856; m. Apr. 4, 1880, Mary A. Landis, b. Sept. 9, 1853; dau. Benjamin Landis and Mary Hoover.

5171. Dr. Benjamin G., Buffalo, N. Y., b. Sept. 2, 1858; m. May 1, 1884, Mary Grove, b. June 9, 1858; dau. Charles C. Grove and Harriet Driesbach.

5172. Dr. Eli H., Buffalo, N. Y., b. July 24, 1860; m. Jan. 3, 1884, Alice E. Eggert, b. Feb. 20, 1861; dau. Oliver J. Eggert and Susan Frick.

Family of DANIEL LONG (1844) and SARAH MILLER.

5173. Emanuel C., Williamsville, N. Y., b. June 5, 1845; m. Jan. 28, 1869, Anna B. Seachrist, b. Aug. 18, 1846; dau. Frederick Seachrist and Catharine Bishop.

5174. Elizabeth L., Williamsville, N. Y., b. Mar. 14, 1847.

5174. Franklin B., Williamsville, N. Y., b. Mar. 24, 1849; d. Feb. 25, 1853.

5176. Emily C., Williamsville, N. Y., b. Feb. 3, 1851; d. Oct. 16, 1872.

Family of SUSAN HERR (1845) and ELIAS FOGELSONGER.

5177. Emma E., Lockport, N. Y., b. Dec. 22, 1853; m. ——— Wing.

5178. Willard E., Buffalo, N. Y.

Family of GEORGE W. HERR (1851) and CAROLINE J. HOLTON.

5179. Maude Carrie, Rochester, N. Y., b. Aug. 5, 1878; m. Apr. 6, 1897, Thomas E. Lannin, b. Jan. 31, 1875; son Thomas Lannin and Martha ———.

5180. George Holton, Rochester, N. Y., b. Dec. 21, 1887.

Family of HENRY H. METZLER (1852) and NANCY HERSHEY.

5181. Mary Ann, Mastersonville, Pa., b. Nov. 20, 1844; m. Oct. 16, 1866, Henry Ober, b. Sept. 13, 1844; son Christian Ober and Barbara Ruhl.

5182. Christian, Mt. Joy, Pa., b. July 16, 1846; m. Dec. 22, 1870, Elizabeth Helt, b. Apr. 26, 1845; dau. Peter Helt and Katie Shiffer.

5183. Fanny, Old Line, Pa., b. Oct. 20, 1847; d. Mar. 30, 1884; m. Oct. 29, 1868, Paul G. Gibble, b. Mar. 30, 1844; son Joseph W. Gibble and Catharine Greiner.

5184. John, Sporting Hill, Pa., b. Sept. 24, 1849; m. Oct. 31, 1872, Mary Diffenderfer, b. Feb. 13, 1854; dau. B. Franklin Diffenderfer and Mary Flory.

5185. Elizabeth, Milton Grove, Pa., b. Oct. 10, 1851; m. Feb. 22, 1872, Isaac G. Kopp, b. Feb. 24, 1850; son Levi Kopp and Rebecca Greiner.

5185. Henry, Old Line, Pa., b. July 2, 1853; m. Nov. 9, 1875, Elizabeth
E. Heisey, b. Sept. 12, 1857; d. Jan. 27, 1877; dau. Christian
Heisey and Elizabeth Elser; m. Oct. 1, 1878, Mary E. Sterner,
b. Apr. 11, 1855; dau. Daniel Sterner and Joanna Wolf.

5187. Jacob, Farmersville, Ill., b. Sept. 1, 1855; m. Elizabeth Huber.

5188. Isaac, Galva, Kans., b. Aug. 7, 1858; m. Katie Witmer.

5189. Samuel, Sedalia, Wash., b. June 27, 1861.

5190. Phares, Salunga, Pa., b. Feb. 1, 1864.

5191. Annie, Sporting Hill, Pa., b. Nov. 22, 1867.

Family of MARTIN H. METZLER (1853) and SUSAN METZLER.

5192. Annie, Lancaster, Pa., b. Nov. 8, 1848; m. June 20, 1872, John S.
Wolfe, b. Oct. 23, 1846; son Jacob Wolfe and Mary Shober.

5193. Amos, Lititz, Pa., b. Aug. 20, 1850; m. Dec. 1, 1874, Catharine
Andes, b. June 23, 1849; dau. George Andes and Annie Mathiot.

5194. Benjamin, Chestnut Hill, Pa., b. Dec. 27, 1853; m. Dec. 20, 1877,
Elizabeth B. Hiestand, b. Dec. 2, 1857; dau. Abraham Hiestand
and Fannie Brubaker.

5195. Levi, Sporting Hill, Pa., b. Dec. 24, 1855; d. Apr. 15, 1857.

5196. Emma Susan, East Petersburg, Pa., b. Sept. 3, 1860; m. Apr.
23, 1891, Amos M. Kissinger, son Samuel Kissinger and Eliza
———.

5197. David, Sporting Hill, Pa., b. Feb. 11, 1864; d. July 27, 1883.

5198. Reuben, East Petersburg, Pa., b. Feb. 4, 1866.

Family of JOHN H. METZLER (1854) and ESTHER SHELLY.

5199. Abraham, Lime Rock, Pa., b. Nov. 18, 1853; m. Oct. 22, 1874,
Mary Hernley, b. Sept. 8, 1855; dau. Peter Hernley and Barbara Hershey.

5200. Elias, Mt. Joy, Pa., b. Aug. 27, 1855; m. Nov. 17, 1881, Rebecca
Gingrich, b. Sept. 24, 1861; dau. Samuel Gingrich and Rebecca
Schlott.

5201. Daniel, Mt. Joy, Pa., b. Mar. 5, 1858; m. Oct. 9, 1879, Elizabeth
M. Erb, b. Feb. 4, 1860; dau. Samuel Erb and Elizabeth
Mumma.

5202. Elizabeth, Manheim, Pa., b. Aug. 5, 1862; m. Oct. 26, 1882,
Abraham Hernley, b. June 22, 1860; son Peter Hernley and
Barbara Hershey.

Family of Wid. JOHN H. METZLER (1854) and MARY BRADLEY.

5203. Emma B., Manheim, Pa., b. Aug. 3, 1875; m. Oct. 16, 1895, Jacob B. Snavely, b. Jan. 11, 1871; son Jacob H. Snavely and Susan Brubaker.

Family of SUSAN H. METZLER (1855) and MARTIN GEPHER.

5204. Aaron, Mastersonville, Pa., b. Nov. 24, 1850; m. Oct. 12, 1875, Susan Ruhl, b. Jan. 29, 1859; dau. Benjamin Ruhl and Annie W. Brandt.

5205. Henry, Mastersonville, Pa., b. Oct. 24, 1856; d. Nov. 10, 1879.

5206. Emma, Mt. Joy, Pa., b. Feb. 27, 1866.

Family of BENJAMIN METZLER (1856) and BARBARA W. NISSLEY.

5207. Daniel, Rohrerstown, Pa., b. Nov. 2, 1856.

5208. Susan, Petersburg, Pa., b. July 29, 1858; m. Jan. 22, 1882, Jacob S. Huttenstein, b. Apr. 24, 1855; son Henry Huttenstein and Maria Stamen.

5209. Harriet N., Elizabethtown, Pa., b. Oct. 24, 1860; d. Jan. 30, 1892; m. Oct. 19, 1886, Amos Witmer, b. Sept. 29, 1863; son Martin Witmer and Mary Ann Leib.

5210. Jacob, Centerville, Pa., b. Dec. 1, 1863; d. Nov. 20, 1864.

5211. Barbara N., Clay, Pa., b. Nov. 17, 1865; d. Mar. 30, 1900; m. Nov. 24, 1887, Peter B. Stauffer, b. Aug. 14, 1864; son Elam Stauffer and Maria Burkholder.

5212. Annie, East Petersburg, Pa., b. Apr. 9, 1870; d. Jan. 20, 1897, Phares S. Bemesderfer, b. Dec. 16, 1869; son George M. Bemesderfer and Mary B. Sahn.

Family of ABRAHAM METZLER (1858) and LEVICIA ALEXANDER.

5213. Ida Alexander, Sterling, Ill., b. June 30, 1876; m. Nov. 20, 1895, John H. Morton (7595).

5214. Horace A., Manheim, Pa., b. Jan. 20, 1881.

5215. Edna May, Sterling, Ill., b. May 10, 1885.

Family of FANNY METZLER (1859) and SAMUEL BARNES.

5216. Malinda, Manheim, Pa., b. Mar. 29, 1866; d. Jan. 6, 1879.

5217. Fanny, Manheim, Pa., b. Apr. 13, 1867; d. Jan. 6, 1879.

5218. Elizabeth, Manheim, Pa., b. Sept. 29, 1868; d. Jan. 5, 1879.

5219. Alice, Manheim, Pa., b. Mar. 17, 1870; d. Jan. 11, 1878.

5220. Emma, Manheim, Pa., b. June 30, 1871.

5221. Samuel, Manheim, Pa., b. May 15, 1874; d. Nov. 30, 1878.

5222. David, Elstonville, Pa., b. Dec. 19, 1879.

Family of SUSAN KREIDER (1863) and Wid. PETER EBERLY.

5223. Catharine, Spring Valley, O., b. Oct. 30, 1861; m. Frank S. Evans.

5224. Effie, Spring Valley, O.

Family of ISAAC KREIDER (1864) and MAGGIE O'DONNELL.

5225. Mary Elizabeth, Philadelphia, Pa., b. Aug. 8, 1875; d. May 4, 1876.

Family of Wid. ISAAC KREIDER (1864) and SALLIE BILLINGS.

5226. Tillie K., West Philadelphia, Pa.

Family of MARTHA KREIDER (1865) and JOHN S. SMITH.

5227. Daniel Sherman, Lancaster, Pa., b. Sept. 21, 1864; m. May 11, 1897, Zama J. Frasher, b. Feb. 14, 1864; dau. Jacob M. Frasher and Grace E. Johnson.

5228. Edgar Kreider, Lampeter, Pa., b. Aug. 26, 1866; d. July 5, 1878.

5229. Ida Elizabeth, Lancaster, Pa., b. Feb. 2, 1868; m. Apr. 7, 1896, Henry C. Demuth, Jr., b. Sept. 25, 1859; son Henry C. Demuth and Elizabeth McDonald.

5230. John Somerfield, Lancaster, Pa., b. Oct. 20, 1870; m. Apr. 2, 1893, Florence C. Norbeck, b. July 3, 1873; dau. Jacob Norbeck and Ann L. Feagley.

5231. Alfred Cookman, Lancaster, Pa., b. June 28, 1873; m. June 19, 1901, Lillian L. Hostetter, b. Feb. 9, 1877; dau. David R. Hostetter and Mary A. Kuhns.

Family of ANNA HERR (1868) and FRANCIS BOWMAN (4065).

5232. Annetta, Bird-in-Hand, Pa., b. Oct. 4, 1860.

Family of AMOS K. HERR (1869) and ELIZABETH KOHR.

5233. Son, Lancaster, Pa., b. Feb. 17, 1880; d. Feb. 19, 1880.

5234. John K., Lancaster, Pa., b. Jan. 13, 1882.

Family of Dr. BENJAMIN F. HERR (5135) and SUSANNA HERR (1871).

5235. Frances M., Millersville, Pa., b. Aug. 28, 1881.

Family of SUSANNA HERR (1872) and DANIEL MUSSER.

5236. Mary Ann, Strasburg, Pa., b. Dec. 28, 1859; d. Nov. 11, 1860.

5237. Emma Elizabeth, Strasburg, Pa., b. June 7, 1861; d. Feb. 18, 1884; m. Sept. 10, 1882, Hiram M. Dellinger, b. Jan. 5, 1859; son Michael B. Dellinger and Anna B. Miller.

5238. Martin Henry, Lancaster, Pa., b. Oct. 2, 1862; m. Feb. 9, 1896, Mary E. Herr (4658).

5239. Walter, Strasburg, Pa., b. Feb. 29, 1876; d. Feb. 29, 1876.

Family of DANIEL K. HERR (1873) and SUSANNA MUSSER.

5240. Albert Martin, Lancaster, Pa., b. July 19, 1862; m. Feb. 24, 1897, Elizabeth A. Irwin, b. Dec. 8, 1870; dau. Andrew Irwin and Mary A. Clendenon.

Family of CHRISTIAN HERR (4099) and EMMA S. MILLER (1875).

5241. Enos M., Lime Valley, Pa., b. Oct. 7, 1865; d. Feb. 23, 1876.

5242. Martha Ella, Junction, Pa., b. Apr. 3, 1869; m. Oct. 4, 1893, Henry R. Snavely, b. July 26, 1865; son Henry Snavely and Barbara Reist.

5243. Susan Bertha, Lancaster, Pa., b. Mar. 29, 1872; m. Dec. 6, 1905, William Burkholder Rush, b. July 28, 1874: son Henry Gaul Rush and Catharine Burkholder.

5244. Edgar Christian, Lancaster, Pa., b. Sept. 29, 1873.

5245. Son, Lime Valley, Pa., b. Feb. 3, 1875; d. Feb. 3, 1875.

5246. Emma Minerva, Lancaster, Pa., b. Nov. 1, 1876.

5247. Herbert F., Lime Valley, Pa., b. Jan. 9, 1890; d. Oct. 13, 1891.

Family of HENRY STROHM (1877) and MARY KAUFFMAN.

5248. John W., Iowa City, Ia.

5249. Henry Clay, Iowa City, Ia.

Family of JOHN STROHM (1879) and FANNY MYLIN.

5250. Henry, Lancaster, Pa., b. Feb. 18, 1855; d. Dec. 7, 1895; m. Feb. 19, 1890, Barbara M. Kinsey, b. Mar. 1, 1857; d. Dec. 23, 1892; dau. Henry Kinsey and Catharine Mylin.

5251. Benjamin Franklin, Mohave, Cal., b. July 28, 1856; m. Mar. 21,
1898, Elizabeth Messinger, b. July 6, 1862; dau. George Messinger and Fannie Niswender.

5252. Elmer, Needles, Cal., b. Mar. 21, 1861; m. Sept. 3, 1893, Elizabeth Wagner, b. Aug. 6, 1876; dau. J. ——— J. Wagner and
Lydia ———.

Family of JOHN F. STROHM (1883) and ELIZABETH JANE LORD.

5253. Estella Maud, St. Louis, Mo., b. Nov., 1866.

Family of ELIZA ANN HERR (1887) and DANIEL ESBENSHADE.

5254. Serenus B., Paradise, Pa., b. Apr. 13, 1857; m. Nov. 15, 1882,
Emma N. Caskey, b. Apr. 26, 1861; dau. James Caskey and
Susan Neff.

5255. Reuben L., Strasburg, Pa., b. June 21, 1861; m. Dec. 10, 1886,
Elizabeth Herr (6136).

5256. John S., Lancaster, Pa., b. Dec. 18, 1864; m. Apr. 19, 1899,
Martha Leaman, dau. John Leaman and Martha Rockafield.

Family of ELAM L. HERR (1888) and ANNA MARIA HERR (4020).

5257. Thaddeus, Strasburg, Pa., b. Mar. 22, 1868; m. Mar. 25, 1897,
Ella N. Rohrer, b. Aug. 25, 1872; dau. Christian Rohrer and
Eliza Leaman.

Family of HANFORD B. HERR (1895) and HANNAH G. STEPHENS.

5258. Edgar M., Lancaster, Pa., b. July 7, 1869; m. Nov., 1899, Ella
Frey, dau. George Frey and Elizabeth ———.

5259. Gertrude L., Lancaster, Pa., b. Mar. 2, 1871.

5260. Charles F., Lancaster, Pa., b. July 12, 1874; d. Mar. 2, 1876.

5261. Hattie O., Lancaster, Pa., b. Feb. 12, 1877.

5262. Nellie S., Lancaster, Pa., b. Apr. 23, 1879; d. Sept. 11, 1879.

Family of ANN ELIZABETH HERR (1896) and DAVID A STEPHENS.

5263. Walter H., Middletown, Pa., b. Mar. 18, 1868; d. July 6, 1870.

5264. Bertha Louisa, Reading, Pa., b. Feb. 21, 1871; m. July 3, 1897,
George W. Fehr.

5263. Blanchard B., Philadelphia, Pa., b. May 23, 1873; m. June 4,
1900, Kathryn Marshall, b. Dec. 22, 1875; dau. Joseph H. Marshall and Kathryn Cassidy.

5266. Ada Evilla, Reading, Pa., b. Feb. 11, 1876.

5267. Ida Hoyt, Reading, Pa., b. Dec. 28, 1878.

5268. Mary Amanda, Reading, Pa., b. Oct. 25, 1882.

Family of Dr. MARTIN LIGHT HERR (1898) and ROSINA E. HUBLEY.

5269. Sarah Maria, Lancaster, Pa., b. June 22, 1871; d. Nov. 29, 1899.

5270. Dr. William H., Lancaster, Pa., b. July 24, 1873; m. Apr. 16, 1901, Caroline H. Wright, b. June 1, 1875; dau. Thomas F. Wright and Susan Haywood.

5271. John L., Cresson, Pa., b. June 21, 1875; m. Nov., 1902, Clara Gohn.

5272. Anna Elizabeth, Lancaster, Pa., b. July 17, 1880.

5273. Robert Martin, Lancaster, Pa.

Family of ADAM FRANKLIN HERR (1900) and MARIA BENEDICT.

5274. Rose Marie, Lancaster, Pa., b. July 1, 1874.

5275. John Philip, Lancaster, Pa., b. Sept. 6, 1878.

Family of ANNIE ELIZABETH HERR (1900) and JOSEPH WARREN YOCUM.

5276. Howard Herr, Lancaster, Pa., b. Oct. 30, 1876.

Family of FANNIE HERR (1902) and JEROME KIEFFER.

5277. Anna Mary, Lancaster, Pa., b. Aug. 23, 1875; d. July 12, 1898.

Family of ALPHEUS N. HERR (1906) and ESTHER M. MILLER.

5278. Henry Miller, Lancaster, Pa., b. Aug. 30, 1870.

5279. Marion, Strasburg, Pa., b. July 28, 1871.

Family of FRANCIS W. HERR (1907) and ARRILLA J. SERGEANT.

5280. Elmer David, Orrville, O., b. Oct. 25, 1872.

5281. Lettie Naomi, Orrville, O., b. Jan. 13, 1873; m. June 25, 1899, Samuel Jackson, b. Aug. 27, 1875; son James A. Jackson and Susan Martin.

5282. Willis Ephraim, Orrville, O., b. Nov. 14, 1875.

5283. Samuel Melvin, Orrville, O., b. Jan. 22, 1878.

5284. Serenus Abner, Orrville, O., b. Oct. 5, 1879.

5385. Grace Greenwood, Orrville, O., b. Sept. 28, 1884.

5386. Winnie May, Orrville, O., b. Nov. 2, 1886.

Family of LETTIE ANNA HERR (1908) and SAMUEL T. GAILEY.

5287. Infant, Orrville, O.

5288. Infant, Orrville, O.

Family of CATHARINE NAOMI HERR (1910) and LEVI BRENEMAN.

5289. David Clyde, Akron, O., b. Mar. 17, 1875.

5290. Esther Elizabeth, Burton City, O., b. Nov. 9, 1877; m. Feb. 28, 1901, D. ——— Frank Spindler, son Daniel John Spindler and Margaret Ghouse.

5291. Anna May, Orrville, O., b. May 6, 1881; m. Sept. 21, 1902, Samuel S. Musselman, b. July 23, 1875; son Zachariah Musselman and Kate ———.

5292. Ralph Emerson, Orrville, O., b. July 7, 1884.

5293. Samuel Robert, Orrville, O., b. Mar. 7, 1887.

5294. Frank Woodman, Orrville, O., b. May 7, 1892.

Family of MARY MALINDA HERR (1911) and SAMUEL TROUT.

5295. Infant, Mt. Vernon, O.

5296. Infant, Mt. Vernon, O.

Family of DAVID GRANT HERR (1913) and IDA M. KURTZ.

5297. Dee Dee Fay, Orrville, O., b. Aug. 29, 1891.

5298. Ruth Minnette, Orrville, O., b. Oct. 5, 1893.

5299. Frances Naomi, Orrville, O., b. Nov. 7, 1896.

Family of BENJAMIN F. HERR (1916) and MARY ANN WILKENSON.

5300. Henry, Livingston, Ala., b. Aug. 7, 1857.

5301. Susan, Livingston, Ala., b. Sept. 3, 1859; d. 1862.

5302. Franklin W., McManus, La., b. Mar. 29, 1861; m. Sept. 26, 1895, Jessie S. McKay, b. Aug. 6, 1872; dau John St. C. McKay and Lucy Cady.

5303. Ernest, Livingston, Ala., b. Nov. 10, 1865; d. May 10, 1878.

5304. Mary, Livingston, Ala., b. Mar. 23, 1873.

Family of HENRY CLAY HERR (1917) and FRANCES A. KINSEY.

5305. Emily K., Cinnamon, N. J., b. Jan. 21, 1861; m. Nov. 2, 1899, Benjamin Lippincott, b. July 1, 1862; son William R. Lippincott and Anna M. Bollinger.

5306. Frank Strohm, Moorestown, N. J., b. Aug. 20, 1862; m. Mar. 26, 1895, Frances B. Smith, b. May 2, 1870; dau. Benjamin Smith and Sarah E, ———.

5307. Harry Lincoln, Moorestown, N. J., b. Apr. 19, 1865; d. July 19, 1865.

5308. Henry C., Moorestown, N. J., b. Jan. 18, 1868; m. June 27, 1894, Rachael L. DeCow, b. Sept. 5, 1869; dau. Samuel DeCow and Martha Lippincott.

5309. Margaret Maud, Moorestown, N. J., b. July 19, 1876.

Family of SARAH ANN HERR (1918) and JOSEPH COOPER.

5310. Fannie Estelle, Philadelphia, Pa., b. Sept. 1, 1859; d. Sept. 18, 1864.

5311. Carrie Salome, Philadelphia, Pa., b. Sept. 22, 1861.

5312. Ernest Herr, Philadelphia, Pa., b. Dec. 12, 1863; m. Margaretta Hergeshimer.

Family of TOBIAS HERR (1920) and MARY SHAUB (3665).

5313. Henry S., Strasburg, Pa., b. May 9, 1860; m. Dec. 5, 1880, Sarah A. Mowrer.

5314. Frank J., Willow Street, Pa., b. Oct. 31, 1857; m. Ida L. Witmer, b. May 27, 1863; dau. Martin L. Witmer and ———.

5315. Elizabeth A., Strasburg, Pa.

5316. Emma M., Strasburg, Pa.

5317. Enos, Strasburg, Pa.

Family of EVE ANN HERR (1921) and CHRISTIAN BRENEMAN.

5318. Emma, Hubers, Pa., b. Oct. 1, 1857; m. Elmer Lefever.

5319. Miriam, New Danville, Pa., b. Oct. 9, 1862; m. Adam Dombach.

Family of BENJAMIN M. HERR (1922) and ANNA MARY MORGAN.

5320. Edwin M., Los Angeles, Cal., b. Apr. 22, 1866.

5321. Josephine, Bloomington, Ill., b. Sept. 8, 1871; m. Sept. 23, 1897, Edward Pankhurst.

Family of ELIZABETH HERR (1923) and BENJAMIN GOCHENOUR.

5322. Emma, New Danville, Pa.

5323. Harry, New Danville, Pa.

5324. Ezra, New Danville, Pa.

5325. Adam, New Danville, Pa.

5326. Mary, New Danville, Pa.

5327. Benjamin, New Danville, Pa.

5328. Edwin, New Danville, Pa.

Family of SALENA HERR (1927) and BENJAMIN L. GAMBER (8501).

5329. John Herr, New Providence, Pa., b. May 4, 1860; m. Agnes Strickler.

5330. Henry H., Manheim, Pa., b. July 25, 1861; m. Nov. 5, 1889, Anna S. Neff, b. July 27, 1867; dau. Benjamin Neff and Anna

5331. Mary Ann, Millersville, Pa., b. Oct. 1, 1862; m. Jacob Charles.

5332. Susan H., Lancaster, Pa., b. Dec. 4, 1863; m. Sept. 29, 1885, Isaac Landis Brubaker, b. Mar. 14, 1862; son John D. Brubaker and Maria Shirk.

5333. Annie H., Washington Borough, Pa., b. Nov. 2, 1866; m. Christian Habecker.

5334. Rudolph H., Washington Borough, Pa., b. Sept. 8, 1868.

5335. Fannie H., Washington Borough, Pa., b. Aug. 18, 1870.

5336. Salena H., Lancaster, Pa., b. June 2, 1874; m. Phares Denlinger.

5337. Ada May, Washington Borough, Pa., b. May 1, 1883.

Family of JOHN L. HERR (1928) and FANNY L. BRUBAKER (8537).

5338. Landis B., Lancaster, Pa., b. Jan. 25, 1865, m. Jan. 6, 1897, Mary A. Book, b. July 15, 1865; dau. Daniel L. Book and Maria Lemon.

5339. John, Lancaster, Pa., b. Sept. 8, 1866; d. Oct. 7, 1881.

5340. Annie, Lancaster, Pa., b. May 16, 1869; m. Nov. 3, 1894, Emlin B. Mylin, b. Feb. 15, 1865; son Benjamin B. Mylin and Mary Good.

5341. Fannie B., Strasburg, Pa., b. Aug. 13, 1872; m. Dec. 12, 1900, Elias B. Groff (8316).

Family of ESTHER HERR (1932) and MARTIN HENRY.

5342. Benjamin, Millersville, Pa.

5343. Franklin, Millersville, Pa.

5344. Elvina, Millersville, Pa.

5345. Adeline, Millersville, Pa., m. Benjamin Charles.

5346. Ann Maria, Millersville, Pa.

Family of ANN HERR (1934) and SOLOMON MARTIN.

5347. Elizabeth, Millersville, Pa.

5348. Mary Ann, Millersville, Pa.

5349. John, Millersville, Pa.

5350. Michael, Millersville, Pa.

5351. Phares, Millway, Pa.

Family of JOHN B. HERR (1935) and SUSAN ESHLEMAN.

5352. Henry, Millersville, Pa.

5353. Mary Ann, Millersville, Pa.

5354. John J., Millersville, Pa.

5355. Fanny, Millersville, Pa.

5356. Susan, Millersville, Pa.

Family of CATHARINE HERR (1936) and JOHN A. GARBER.

5357. Frances E., Elizabethtown, Pa., b. Apr. 7, 1862; m. May 17, 1887, David Z. Witmer, b. Nov. 27, 1864; son John Witmer and Elizabeth Zug.

5358. Anna Mary, Maytown, Pa., b. June 25, 1863.

5359. Amelia H., Maytown, Pa., b. Sept. 30, 1864.

5360. Franklin H., Lancaster, Pa., b. Jan. 21, 1867.

5361. Paris H., Columbia, Pa., b. Jan. 22, 1869; m. Nov. 4, 1896, Elizabeth Herr, b. Mar. 5, 1876; dau. Aaron Herr and Catharine Dombach.

5362. Elmer Jay, Bainbridge, Pa., b. Dec. 4, 1875; m. Nov. 27, 1900, Caroline Seachrist, b. Sept. 6, 1880; dau. Joseph Seachrist and Caroline Girdler.

5363. Florence K., Florin, Pa., b. Oct. 17, 1877; m. July 7, 1901, Paris G. Shelly, b. Oct. 8, 1876; son Henry G. Shelly and Frances Grider.

5364. Josephine Clare, Maytown, Pa., b. Feb. 20, 1880.

Family of JACOB K. HERR (1941) and MALILA WIDDOW.

5365. David, Columbia, Pa
5366. Rosa, Columbia, Pa.
5367. George W., Columbia, Pa.
5368. Laura V., Columbia, Pa.
5369. Malila Magdalena, Columbia, Pa.

Family of MAGDALENA HERR (1844) and CHRISTIAN E. HOSTETTER.

5370. Emma M., Millersville, Pa., b. Jan. 16, 1866; m. Sept. 13, 1883, Elmer D. Erisman.

Family of JOHN C. HERR (1945) and MARY KAUFFMAN.

5371. Emma, Millersville, Pa., b. Aug. 15, 1856; m. ———; m. ———.
5372. Isaac, Millersville, Pa., b. Feb., 1859; d. Dec. 21, 1862.

Family of JOSEPH C. HERR (1947) and ELMIRA HICKMAN.

5373. Clarence, Columbia, Pa.
5374. William W., Carlisle, Pa.
5375. Nellie, Carlisle, Pa.

Family of ESTHER HERR (1948) and HIRAM T. ALBERT.

5376. Howard Frank, Columbia, Pa.
5377. David, Columbia, Pa.
5378. Elmer Herr, Columbia, Pa.
5379. Emily, Columbia, Pa.
5380. Lizzie Minerva, Columbia, Pa.
5381. Magdalena, Columbia, Pa.
5382. Paris L., Columbia, Pa.
5383. Grace S., Columbia, Pa.

Family of ELIZABETH HERR (1949) and HENRY A. SNYDER.

5384. Henry H., Lancaster, Pa., b. Nov. 1, 1865.
5385. John, Lancaster, Pa., b. Aug. 2, 1867.
5386. Abraham, Lancaster, Pa.
5387. Elizabeth, Lancaster, Pa.
5388. Anna, Lancaster, Pa.
5389. Alice, Lancaster, Pa.

Family of ADELINE E. HERR (1950) and RULEF S. GILE.

5390. Rulef H., Milwaukee, Wis., b. Nov. 20, 1854; m. Jan. 3, 1875, Charlotte I. Herrick, b. July 15, 1855; d. Oct. 23, 1894; dau. Orville Herrick and Martha A. ———; m. June 1, 1899, Mary E. Dougherty.

Family of ELDRIDGE GERRY HERR (1953) and MARY EMELINE CHILD.

5391. Charles C., Goshen, Ind., b. June 27, 1867; m. Feb. 23, 1893, Kate M. Baker, b. Aug. 10, 1867.

Family of EUGENE MARKHAM HERR (1956) and NETTIE E. ROE.

5392. Harold E., South Bend, Ind., b. June 9, 1883.
5393. Helen, South Bend, Ind., b. July 18, 1887.

Family of SUSAN KENDIG (1967) and SAMUEL FONDERSMITH.

5394. Naomi, Millersville, Pa., b. June 28, 1844.
5395. Aldus Henry, Millersville, Pa., b. Jan. 8, 1851.

Family of MARTHA KENDIG (1968) and Wid. WILLIAM FRAZER.

5396. Charles K., Millersville, Pa., b. Jan. 1, 1847.
5397. Leah S., Millersville, Pa., b. July 25, 1851.
5398. Annie E., Millersville, Pa., b. July 24, 1855.

Family of MARY CARPENTER (1971) and ABRAHAM HOOVER.

5399. Sarah Ann, Strasburg, Pa., b. Jan. 31, 1854; d. Nov. 28, 1855.
5400. Susan Lucinda, Strasburg, Pa., b. Oct. 6, 1855; d. Mar. 25, 1865.
5401. Mary Ellen, Strasburg, Pa., b. Nov. 17, 1856.
5402. Margaret Elizabeth, Strasburg, Pa., b. Jan. 15, 1859.
5403. Martha Louisa, Strasburg, Pa., b. Oct. 26, 1860.
5404. Juliet Rebecca, Strasburg, Pa., b. July 30, 1863.
5405. Catharine Salome, Strasburg, Pa., b. Mar. 29, 1865.
5406. David Eby, Strasburg, Pa., b. May 18, 1867.

Family of SUSAN CARPENTER (1972 and B. LANDIS BRACKBILL.

5407. Jacob, Eden, Pa., b. Dec. 15, 1856.
5408. Anna Barbara, Strasburg, Pa., b. July 11, 1858; m. Nov. 29, 1883, Martin H. Baer (7421).

5409. Mary Elizabeth, Strasburg, Pa., b. May 3, 1860.

5410. Emma Salome, Strasburg, Pa., b. Nov. 18, 1861; d. Mar. 11, 1864.

5411. Andrew Carpenter, Strasburg, Pa., b. Aug. 3, 1863.

Family of ESTHER ANN SNEARLY (1973) and CHRISTIAN C. METZ.

5412. Ellie Endora, Williamsville, N. Y., b. Mar. 25, 1857; m. Feb. 6, 1884, Benjamin J. Habecker (3253).

5413. Catharine Lillian, Williamsville, N. Y., b. Dec. 20, 1863; d. Feb. 14, 1876.

5414. Cora Ada, Williamsville, N. Y., b. Mar. 26, 1865; m. Jan. 18, 1896, Charles J. Pfohl, b. June 13, 1860; son Joseph Pfohl and Susan Spath.

Family of MARY M. SNEARLY (1974) and JACOB S. LAPP.

5415. Ella Endora, Williamsville, N. Y., b. Sept. 17, 1854; d. May 28, 1857.

5416. Emma Ezala, Williamsville, N. Y., b. Dec. 28, 1856; d. June 4, 1863.

5417. Adelbert Erasmus, Spokane, Wash., b. Feb. 17, 1858.

Family of SARAH SNEARLY (1975) and FRANKLIN METZ.

5418. Gertrude E., Williamsville, N. Y., b. Sept. 30, 1877.

Family of ANNA MARIA HERR (1982) and EDWARD J. SHAFFER.

5419. Samuel David, Baltimore, Md., b. Feb. 10, 1865; d. Oct. 12, 1870.

5420. Charles Clifton, Baltimore, Md., b. Oct. 31, 1866; d. Oct. 1, 1870.

5421. Edward Leon, Baltimore, Md., b. June 6, 1868; d. July 10, 1891.

5422. Frank Oden, Baltimore, Md., b. Aug. 16, 1869; d. Oct. 31, 1870.

5423. Claudius, Baltimore, Md., b. Feb. 24, 1872; d. June 20, 1875.

5424. Theodore Harry, Baltimore, Md., b. Jan. 23, 1874.

5425. Martin Luther, Baltimore, Md., b. Feb. 23, 1877.

5426. Claton, Baltimore, Md., b. Oct. 23, 1880.

5427. Claudius, Baltimore, Md., b. Oct. 12, 1882.

5428. Paul, Baltimore, Md., b. Feb. 23, 1884.

Family of ESTHER HERR (491) and MARTIN ESHLEMAN.

5429. Franklin, Strasburg, Pa., b. Apr. 4, 1807; d. 1810.
5430. Abraham, Strasburg, Pa., b. Aug. 31, 1808; d. Mar., 1875; m. Anna Harnish, dau. Michael Harnish and Mary ———; m. Mary Guss.
5431. Frances, Strasburg, Pa., b. Feb. 10, 1810; d. 1810.
5432. Eliza, Lancaster, Pa., b. Aug. 28, 1811; d. Mar. 29, 1865; m. Joseph Harnish, son Michael Harnish and Mary ———.
5433. Martin, Lancaster, Pa., b. Oct. 5, 1813; d. Oct. 10, 1829.
5434. John, Lancaster, Pa., b. Mar. 8, 1815; m. Jan. 15, 1839, Susan Barr, b. Aug. 1, 1814; dau. Benjamin Barr and Susanna Bear.
5435. Frances, Waynesboro, Pa., b. July 26, 1818; d. Nov. 11, 1900; m. Jan. 2, 1840, Rev. Christian Hershey, b. Dec. 24, 1812; d. Mar. 6, 1875; son Isaac Hershey and Anna Frantz.
5436. Esther, Strasburg, Pa., b. Sept. 30, 1822; d. Feb. 28, 1824.

Family of ANNA HERR (492) and HENRY MYLIN.

5437. Martha, Lampeter, Pa., b. Oct. 25, 1803; d. Feb. 26, 1891; m. Mar. 18, 1823, John Landis, b. Nov. 17, 1795; d. Mar. 24, 1856; son John Landis and Elizabeth Burkholder.
5438. Francis, Lampeter, Pa., b. 1804; d. 1805.

Family of Wid. ANNA HERR MYLIN (492) and JACOB WEAVER (1462).

5439. ———, Wheatland Mills, Pa.
5440. ———, Wheatland, Mills, Pa.
5441. ———, Wheatland Mills, Pa.
5442. ———, Wheatland Mills, Pa.
5443. ———, Wheatland Mills, Pa.
5444. ———, Wheatland Mills, Pa.

Family of FRANCIS K. HERR (1983) and ELLEN R. TRUMP.

5445. Bessie Ober, Westminster, Md., b. June 13, 1876.
5446. Charles Trump, Westminster, Md., b. Aug. 14, 1878; d. Oct. 31, 1882.
5447. Sarah LaRue, Westminster, Md., b. Feb. 12, 1882.
5448. Eva Pauline, Westminster, Md., b. July 10, 1884.
5449. Frank Trump, Westminster, Md., b. Apr. 6, 1887.
5450. Ober Samuel, Westminster, Md., b. Oct. 17, 1888.

Family of HETTIE HERR (1984) and Dr. LUTHER TRUMP.

5451. George Herbert, Westminster, Md., b. Nov. 8, 1875; d. Apr. 21, 1898.

5452. Adda LaRue, Westminster, Md., b. Sept. 4, 1877.

5453. Emma Estelle, Westminster, Md., b. Nov. 30, 1879.

5454. Francis Herr, Westminster, Md., b. Mar. 6, 1881; d. Mar. 20, 1881.

5455. Lizzie Ober, Westminster, Md., b. July 11, 1882; d. Sept. 1, 1882.

5456. Ober Herr, Westminster, Md., b. May 2, 1884; d. Aug., 1884.

Family of ANN KEAGY (1987) and GEORGE HECKROTH.

5457. Benjamin, Mt. Joy, Pa.

5458. Amanda, Mt. Joy, Pa.

5459. Katie, Mt. Joy, Pa.

5460. Clifford, Mt. Joy, Pa.

Family of SARAH KEAGY (1991) and EDWIN STORM.

5466. Willie Heckoth, Washington, D. C., b. 1859.

5467. Estella Blandel, Washington, D. C., b. 1861.

5468. Samuel M., Washington, D. C., b. 1863.

5010. Rosalia Adelia, Washington, D. C., b. 1865.

Family of ELIZABETH MOORE (1998) and JOSEPH DUDDING.

5469. George, Hannibal, Mo., b. Oct. 3, 1843; d. Apr., 1863.

5470. Mary Catharine, Hannibal, Mo., b. 1845; d. 1899; m. 1868, Wallace Armour.

5471. Henry Sylvester, Hannibal, Mo., b. Apr. 16, 1846; d. 1848.

5472. Henry Sarver, Hannibal, Mo., b. 1849; m. 1887, Lillian Kelsey.

5473. Elizabeth, St. Louis, Mo., b. Dec. 16, 1850; m. 1888, Nathaniel Carlin, d. 1887; son Thomas Carlin and ———.

5474. Emma Caplinger, Springfield, Ill., b. 1852; m. Feb. 4, 1875, William C. McConnell, b. Oct. 15, 1852; son William McConnell and Mary McKelvey.

5475. Frank, Springfield, Ill., b. July, 1855; m. Percallie ———.

Family of FRANCES HERR MOORE (1999) and JOHN P. CADOGAN.

5476. William Henry, Quincy, Ill., b. Jan. 27, 1855; d. Sept. 9, 1892; m. Feb. 5, 1879, Sarah J. Herr (2038).

5477. Fannie, Quincy, Ill., b. Aug. 20, 1857.

5478. Ida, Quincy, Ill., b. June 26, 1859; m. Nov. 1, 1877, Charles B. Hatcher, b. July 3, 1852; son Solomon J. Hatcher and Mary E. Menart.

5479. George McClellan, Macon, Mo., b. Mar. 14, 1862; m. 1891, Georgia Nolan, b. 1865; dau. J. ——— P. Nolan and Elizabeth Cattick.

5480. Lillian, Quincy, Ill., b. Feb. 3, 1864; d. 1865.

5481. Carlotta, Quincy, Ill., b. Apr. 8, 1866; d. 1900; m. 1891, William E. Hatcher, b. 1862; son Solomon J. Hatcher and Mary E. Menart.

5482. Katherine, Quincy, Ill., b. Aug. 3, 1868.

Family of WILLIAM HENRY MOORE (2000) and SUSAN MARY BOYNTON.

5483. Nora Ethel, St. Louis, Mo., b. Nov. 6, 1855; m. Sept. 27, 1877, Horace B. Steel, b. July 13, 1855; son James Steel and Katie MacGovern.

5484. Lemuel Boynton, St. Louis, Mo., b. Dec. 29, 1857; d. Aug., 1858.

5485. Annie Virginia, St. Louis, Mo., b. July 28, 1859; m. Feb. 24, 1881, William P. Morgan, b. June 23, 1856; son Stephen D. Morgan and Emma B. Wright.

5486. Lottie Boynton, St. Louis, Mo., b. Jan. 1, 1862; m. 1880, William Sutton; m. Mar. 25, 1895, Joseph E. Papin, b. Sept. 27, 1868; son Pierre M. Papin and Mary E. DeMaulins.

5487. Mary Bradford, St. Louis, Mo., b. Sept. 25, 1864; m. Apr. 29, 1897, Joseph T. Logan, b. July 21, 1869; son John C. Logan and Martha E. Carter.

5488. Milton Henry, St. Louis, Mo., b. Jan. 11, 1869; m. Dec. 19, 1894, Jeanette M. Wilson, b. 1869; dau. George Wilson and Josephine Farris.

5489. Susan Burrill, Wellston, Mo., b. Dec. 2, 1872; m. June 11, 1902,

James M. Wood, b. Sept. 18, 1871; son Patrick H. Wood and Emma Kee MacNatt.

5490. Dr. Roy Dudley, Central, Mo., b. Feb. 14, 1877; m. Oct. 3, 1899, Ella M. Rowe, b. Nov. 23, 1874; dau. Abner Rowe and Caroline Stuart.

5491. George Kenneth, Wellston, Mo., b. July 29, 1880.

Family of SARAH CATHARINE MOORE (2001) and GEORGE LEWIS.

5492. James William, Denver, Col., b. Nov. 18, 1854; m. May 6, 1875, Mary E. Winston, b. Jan. 13, 1855; dau. John Winston and Mary J. Roby.

5493. John Edgar, Pittsburg, Pa., b. Feb. 12, 1857; d. June 7, 1901; m. Edna Graham.

5494. Lottie, Hannibal, Mo., b. May 6, 1859; d. Dec. 10, 1859.

5495. Jessie K., Huntington, W. Va., b. Aug. 2, 1861; d. Aug. 22, 1888; m. Sept. 8, 1880, J. Walter Winget, b. Oct. 31, 1854; son Elias V. Winget and Ellen M. A. Spence.

Family of GEORGE CRANE MOORE (2003) and MARY ELIZABETH HATCHER.

5496. John Edward, Hannibal, Mo., b. Jan. 24, 1865; m. 1890, Susan M. Taylor, b. Dec. 6, 1869; dau. William W. Taylor and Susan Myers.

5497. George Victor, Hannibal, Mo., b. Nov. 6, 1867; m. 1895, Etha Stevens, b. Aug. 16, 1870; dau. Benjamin Q. Stevens and Harriet E. McLeod.

5498. Maude, Hannibal, Mo., b. Sept. 14, 1873.

Family of JOHN SUMMERFIELD MOORE (2004) and ETHLINDA ROCKWOOD.

5499. George Paul, Pittsburg, Pa., b. Apr. 14, 1865; m. Oct. 14, 1901, Wid. Ruth Will Craig, b. May 2, 1874; dau. George L. Will and Adelia Van Huff.

5500. Laura Summerfield, Denver, Col., b. Oct. 28, 1871; m. Aug. 26, 1891, Edward L. Staats, b. Nov. 21, 1864; son Dow L. Staats and Catharine Clute.

5501. Harry G., Cincinnati, O., b. Aug. 2, 1873; m. May 24, 1902, Wid. Nellie M. Guyman, b. Jan. 13, 1872; dau. John A. Conway and Elizabeth Wait.

Family of GEORGE L. WILSON (2007) and SARAH B. GRAY.

5502. Samuel Gray, Newbury, Pa., b. Feb. 5, 1864; d. Mar. 14, 1889.
5503. Helen Elizabeth, Williamsport, Pa., b. Dec. 14, 1865; m. Aug. 19, 1897, Clarence L. Peaslee, b. Jan. 19, 1871; son Rev. Isaac D. Peaslee and Martha Browne.
5504. Florence Theresa, Newbury, Pa., b. June 25, 1869.
5505. Cornelia Gray, Newbury, Pa., b. May 7, 1879.

Family of SARAH CATHARINE WILSON (2008) and JOHN ELDER WILSON.

5506. Frances F., Glidden, Iowa, b. July 20, 1860; m. Apr., 1894, Addison Kyle, son Charles Kyle and Anna Campbell.
5507. Edmund, Glidden, Iowa, b. June, 1862.

Family of CHARLOTTE E. WILSON (2010) and IRA CANFIELD STONER.

5508. Bessie Marie, New York, N. Y., b. July 19, 1871; m. May 24, 1894, Dr. Joseph H. Krape, b. Aug. 21, 1868; son John M. Krape and Abigail Reber.
5509. Katharine Isabelle, Philadelphia, Pa., b. Sept. 15, 1876; m. June 20, 1899, William A. Swyers, b. 1873; son Joseph Swyers and Ellen Baker.
5510. George Wilson, New York, N. Y., b. Oct. 4, 1884.

Family of SARAH FRANCES HERR (2017) and GEORGE W. H. SCHRIFFLER.

5511. Charles C., Salona, Pa., b. Sept. 8, 1869; d. Mar. 1, 1871.
5512. Annie Catherine, Lock Haven, Pa., b. Mar. 13, 1872.
5513. Louise H., Lock Haven, Pa., b. Mar. 13, 1878.
5514. Florence M., Lock Haven, Pa., b. Aug. 2, 1884.

Family of MARY AMANDA HERR (2018) and J. REESE CRISPEN.

5515. Edmund Herr, Lock Haven, Pa., b. May 9, 1871; m. Sept. 26, 1896, Annie L. Shultz, b. Mar. 1, 1875; dau. William Shultz and Sarah Parsell.
5516. Charles L., Salona, Pa., b. Oct. 4, 1873; d. June 20, 1874.
5517. Clarence C., Philadelphia, Pa., b. June 10, 1875.
5518. Anson LeRoy, Philadelphia, Pa., b. Mar. 24, 1878.
5519. Francis R., Philadelphia, Pa., b. Apr. 25, 1883.

Family of ANSON MARTIN HERR (2021) and ALVERNA M. KELLER.

5520. Florence Mildred, Burlington, N. J., b. Apr. 27, 1900.

Family of WESLEY URIAH HERR (2023) and MARGARET WALTERS.

5521. Walter Matson, Salona, Pa., b. Dec. 21, 1892.

5522. Harold Mark, Salona, Pa., b. June 8, 1894.

Family of GEORGE LEIDY HERR (2026) and CHRISTINA R. MYERS.

5523. John Myers, Mill Hall, Pa., b. Jan. 19, 1881; m. Dec., 1899, Anna Field.

5524. Jennie Pearl, Mill Hall, Pa., b. Jan. 29, 1883; d. Feb. 14, 1888.

5525. Emory R., Mill Hall, Pa., b. Dec. 5, 1885.

5526. Edward Guy, Mill Hall, Pa., b. Sept. 10, 1887.

Family of JOHN MAYBERRY HERR (2027) and ROSE A. BRUMGARD.

5527. Mary E., Indianapolis, Ind., b. Dec. 27, 1887.

5528. Donald, Indianapolis, Ind., b. Aug. 31, 1889.

Family of EMORY ELSE HERR (2028) and CORA B. GUYER.

5529. Robert Guyer, Scranton, Pa., b. Nov. 4, 1890.

5530. Mary Catherine, Sunbury, Pa., b. Apr. 1, 1893.

5531. Irvin Emory, Scranton, Pa., b. Mar. 4, 1894.

Family of EMMA FRANCES HERR (2031) and ELY E. HYATT.

5532. Harriet Rebecca, East Smithfield, Pa., b. Aug. 27, 1857; d. Apr. 12, 1878; m. Dec. 21, 1876, Elmer Jakeway, b. 1856; son George Jakeway and Harriet ———.

5533. Charlotte Salina, Salona, Pa., b. Sept. 18, 1859; m. Jan. 28, 1886, John R. Thompson, b. June 9, 1859; son James Thompson and Hannah Limon.

5534. George Thomas, Salona, Pa., b. Nov. 11, 1861; m. Feb. 16, 1888, Effie E. McKibben (8882).

5535. Harry Clinton, Lewisburg, Pa., b. Jan. 31, 1869; m. Marion A. Browne, b. June 2, 1868; dau. Reuben F. Browne and Susan Frick.

5536. Annie Catharine, Tremont, Ill., b. May 24, 1872; m. Feb., 1894,

Thomas H. Harris, b. 1874; son William Harris and Frances Fetter.

5537. Jane Frances, Salona, Pa., b. Apr. 18, 1875.

Family of DANIEL BARNET HERR (2033) and GERTRUDE C. HILLS.

5538. George Minor, Quincy, Ill., b. Aug. 23, 1869; m. Oct. 27, 1897, Alice G. Barber, dau. William Barber and Sarah Cromwell.

5539. Harry Perry, Pune, Ida., b. Dec. 16, 1870.

5540. Arthur Barnet, Quincy, Ill., b. July 16, 1873; m. Nov. 2, 1896, Mary E. Callendine, b. Sept. 25, 1875; dau. George Callendine and Mary Voorhies.

5541. Walter Socrates, Quincy, Ill., b. Mar. 13, 1875.

5542. Eugene Evarts, Peoria, Ill., b. Mar. 7, 1877.

5543. Emma Elliot, Quincy, Ill., b. June 22, 1880.

5544. Pearl May, Quincy, Ill., b. May 8, 1885.

5545. John, Quincy, Ill., b. Mar. 8, 1887; d. July 13, 1887.

5546. Philip Sheridan, Quincy, Ill., b. Mar. 20, 1889.

5547. Charles Osmer, Quincy, Ill., b. Dec. 24, 1892.

5548. Chester Daniel, Quincy, Ill., b. Dec. 24, 1892.

5549. Herbert, Quincy, Ill., b. Feb. 9, 1895.

Family of GEORGE WILSON HERR (2036) and ANNIE ELIZA FREDERICK.

5550. Wilson Frederick, Salona, Pa., b. May 29, 1873; m. Mar. 28, 1895, Annie F. Heard, b. July 8, 1873; dau. Horace M. Heard and Henrietta Stoner.

5551. Jessica Frances, Salona, Pa., b. Jan. 26, 1875.

Family of SARAH JANE HERR (2038) and WILLIAM HENRY CADOGAN.

5552. Mabel Catharine, Lewisburg, Pa., b. Jan. 21, 1880.

5553. John Niles, Lewisburg, Pa., b. July 18, 1882.

5554. George Henry, Lewisburg, Pa., b. Sept. 3, 1889.

Family of JOHN E. PARRY (2041) and ANNIE J. SMITH.

5555. Anna R., Philadelphia, Pa., b. Nov., 1867.

5556. Lucy, Manchester, Eng., b. Jan., 1869.

Family of ABRAHAM SHOFF (2045) and JANE SIMMONS.

5557. William Augustus, Warren, Pa., b. Jan. 28, 1848; d. Mar. 7, 1885; m. Emma Dunn.

5558. George Herr, Dubois, Pa., b. Jan. 17, 1850; m. Nov. 1, 1890, Harriet Snodgrass, b. May 22, 1869; dau. John Snodgrass and Mary Minihan.

5559. Rebecca Elizabeth, Lock Haven, Pa., b. June 22, 1852; d. Oct. 31, 1877.

5560. Wilson, Buffalo, N. Y., b. Sept. 17, 1854; d. Oct. 25, 1888; m. 1877, Frances C. Iler, b. Feb. 4, 1858; dau. Frank Iler and Catherine ———.

5561. Henry Eugene, Lock Haven, Pa., b. Oct. 7, 1856; d. Nov. 7, 1885.

5562. Jane Ellen, Lock Haven, Pa., b. Dec. 29, 1852; d. Jan. 27, 1883.

5563. Albert M., Buffalo, N. Y., b. May 11, 1869; m. July 1, 1899, Carrie Howard, b. June 12, 1879; dau. J. ——— P. Howard and Hattie Langdon.

5564. Emma, Williamsport, Pa., b. June 20, 1866; d. July 18, 1893; m. John Buzzy.

5565. James Grant, Buffalo, N. Y., b. May 23, 1868; m. Nellie Berngan, b. Apr. 26, 1871.

Family of CYNTHIA JANE HERR (2050) and ROBINSON M. THOMPSON.

5566. Hannah Frances, Ridgeway, Pa., b. Feb. 6, 1856; m. Aug. 24, 1881, Norman T. Arnold, son William Arnold and Margaret Kinson.

5567. Wilford Downs, Ridgeway, Pa., b. Feb. 4, 1858; m. Sept. 4, 1883, Mary Shilling, b. Mar. 7, 1861; dau. Jacob Shilling and Elizabeth Rute.

5568. Elizabeth B., Ridgeway, Pa., b. Nov. 4, 1859.

5569. Sarah Ann, Ridgeway, Pa., b. Aug. 1, 1861.

5570. Ulysses S. Grant, Ridgeway, Pa., b. Nov. 24, 1863; d. Feb. 2, 1885; m. May 1, 1884, Ida M. Arnold, dau. William Arnold and Margaret Kinson.

5571. Rev. William Sherman, Somerville, Mass., b. Apr. 21, 1866; m. Sept. 11, 1890, Grace Newell, b. Nov. 4, 1866; dau. Rev. Frederick Newell and Jane T. Slater.

5572. Benjamin Franklin, Pittsburg, Pa., b. Feb. 20, 1868; m. June 2, 1900, Helen Quigley, b. Feb. 1, 1875; dau. John B. Quigley and Louise Brungard.

5573. Robert Burke, Ridgeway, Pa., b. Mar. 12, 1872.

Family of ELIZA HERR (2051) and JOSEPH FARLEY.

5574. John Henry, Williamsport, Pa., b. July 4, 1863 ; d. Sept. 26, 1899.

5575. Clara Hannah, Horsehead, N. Y., b. Oct. 8, 1864 ; m. Sept., 1890, John Nichols, son James Nichols and Ellen ———.

5576. Martin Herr, Sayres, Pa., b. Aug. 5, 1866; m. May 16, 1892, Alice Kimball, b. June 20, 1872; dau. John J. Kimball and Elmira Paugh.

5577. George Wilson, Williamsport, Pa., b. Mar. 9, 1868; d. Feb. 26, 1871.

5578. Bessie Catharine, Williamsport, Pa., b. Feb. 20, 1870; d. Mar. 1, 1871.

5579. Anna Maie, Williamsport, Pa., b. Jan. 5, 1872.

5580. Sarah Jane, Williamsport, Pa., b. Feb. 14, 1874.

5581. Daniel Hartman, Williamsport, Pa., b. Sept. 29, 1876.

5582. Mabel Gay, Williamsport, Pa., b. June 15, 1881 ; d. Aug. 13, 1883.

Family of JOHN MILLER HERR (2052) and ELIZA A. WINKLEBLECK.

5583. Allison Hartman, Beech Creek, Pa., b. Oct. 3, 1872.

5584. Harry Miller, Beech Creek, Pa., b. Aug. 18, 1874; m. Emma Lewis.

5585. Edmund, Beech Creek, Pa., b. Sept. 1, 1875 ; d. Sept. 22, 1875.

5586. Ida May, Beech Creek, Pa., b. Sept. 11, 1876.

5587. Joseph Farley, Beech Creek, Pa., b. Nov. 17, 1878.

5588. Charles Ellsworth, Beech Creek, Pa., b. Feb. 23, 1880.

5589. Samuel Blaine, Beech Creek, Pa., b. Oct. 26, 1883.

5590. John Edwin, Beech Creek, Pa., b. Feb. 10, 1886.

Family of MARTIN WILSON HERR (2055) and LYDIA AGNES BURRELL.

5591. Charles Burrell, Salona, Pa., b. Apr. 26, 1875 ; m. Sept. 12, 1900, Clara E. Stoner, b. Mar. 17, 1877; dau. William H. Stoner and Catharine E. Meals.

5592. Samuel Claude, Salona, Pa., b. Apr. 26, 1877.

Family of JAMES EDWIN HERR (2061) and ANNETTA M. YOUNG.

5593. Eleanor Snodgrass, Mifflinburg, Pa., b. Aug. 13, 1867; d. Jan. 3, 1871.

5594. Jane Irvin, Mifflinburg, Pa., b. Nov. 1, 1868.

5595. Jessie Chambers, Mifflinburg, Pa., b. July 6, 1870.

5596. Rev. Arthur Bell, Potts Grove, Pa., b. May 7, 1872.

5597. Stella Holmes, Mifflinburg, Pa., b. Dec. 15, 1873.

5598. Mabel Young, Mifflinburg, Pa., b. May 15, 1875.

5599. Donald David, Mifflinburg, Pa., b. Mar. 6, 1880.

Family of EMILY SHRINER HERR (2067) and JOSEPH HANNA.

5600. Frank, Lock Haven, Pa., b. 1872; d. 1873.

5601. Mary Louise, Lock Haven, Pa., b. Nov. 22, 1874.

5602. Augusta Joseph, Lock Haven, Pa., b. Dec. 18, 1876.

Family of Wid. EMILY S. HANNA (2067) and THOMAS A. BLACKBURN.

5603. Harry Malcolm, Lock Haven, Pa., b. Dec. 31, 1882.

Family of HARRY GRAHAM HERR (2068) and AUGUSTA HOTALING.

5604. Walter D., Athens, N. Y., b. Feb., 24, 1876; m. Apr. 3, 1899, Laura D. Whitney, dau. Willard M. Whitney and Louisa M. Barthil.

5605. Mabel Louise, Athens, N. Y., b. May 7, 1881.

Family of GEORGE EDWARD HERR (2069) and CATHARINE C. GRITNER.

5606. Effie Jane, Lock Haven, Pa., b. Sept. 7, 1871; m. June 28, 1894, Benjamin R. Snyder, b. Mar. 4, 1874; son William Snyder and Anna Raugh.

5607. Charles Edward, Lock Haven, Pa., b. Mar. 11, 1874; m. June 11, 1895, Mary J. Cree, b. May 28, 1877; dau. David Cree and Orpha Poorman.

5608. Mary Emma, Lock Haven, Pa., b. Feb. 3, 1876; d. May 8, 1878.

5509. Pearl Gertrude, Lock Haven, Pa., b. June 29, 1879.

5610. Nellie May, Lock Haven, Pa., b. Mar. 7, 1881.

5611. Georgiana, Lock Haven, Pa., b. Aug. 1, 1884.

5612. Clarence R., Lock Haven, Pa., b. June 20, 1887; d. Sept. 11, 1887.

5613. Claire Louise, Lock Haven, Pa., b. Apr. 20, 1892.

Family of MARY LOUISE HERR (2070) and ALGERNON S. FLEMING.

5614. Henrietta Louise, Saxton, Pa., b. Jan. 28, 1881.

5615. Julia Herr, Saxton, Pa., b. Oct., 9, 1886; d. Jan. 27, 1888.

Family of ANNIE M. HERR (2073) and Dr. GEORGE WILEY RAE.

5616. MacDelaney, Lock Haven, Pa., b. Sept. 25, 1886.
5617. Catharine Louise, Lock Haven, Pa., b. Dec. 23, 1889.

Family of WALTER DIFFENBACH HERR (2075) and CATHARINE HUFFORD.

5618. Emma Elizabeth, Lock Haven, Pa., b. May 11, 1885; d. June 13, 1887.
5619. Harry Malcolm, Lock Haven, Pa., b. Jan. 8, 1888.
5620. Margaret Dorotha, Lock Haven, Pa., b. Mar. 23, 1890.
5621. Walter Drew, Lock Haven, Pa., b. June 25, 1892.
5622. Constance Curtin, Lock Haven, Pa., b. Mar. 30, 1895.
5623. Edna Rebecca, Lock Haven, Pa., b. Dec. 30, 1898.

Family of ABRAHAM ESHLEMAN (5430) and ANNA HARNISH.

5624. Michael, Strasburg, Pa.
5625. Anna, Strasburg, Pa.

Family of Wid. ABRAHAM ESHLEMAN (5430) and MARY GUSS.

5626. Harriet, Strasburg, Pa.
5627. Lizzie, Strasburg, Pa.
5628. Mary, Strasburg, Pa.
5629. Edwin, Strasburg, Pa.

Family of ELIZA ESHLEMAN (5432) and JOSEPH HARNISH.

5630. Martin, Lancaster, Pa., m. Anna Hershey.
5631. Lizzie, Lancaster, Pa.
5632. Fanny, Kansas City, Mo., m. John K. Landis.
5633. Joseph, Lancaster, Pa.
5634. Emma, Lancaster, Pa.

Family of JOHN ESHLEMAN (5434) and SUSAN BARR.

5635. Daughter, Lancaster, Pa., b. Jan. 15, 1840; d. Jan. 15, 1840.
5636. Benjamin B., Lancaster, Pa., b. Aug. 18, 1841; d. July 19, 1859.
5637. Daughter, Lancaster, Pa., b. May 1, 1845; d. May 1, 1845.
5638. Susanna B., Lancaster, Pa., b. Aug. 17, 1846.
5639. Elizabeth, Lancaster, Pa., b. Apr. 30, 1849.
5640. Ann, Lancaster, Pa., b. June 14, 1851; d. Dec. 31, 1851.
5641. Martin, Lancaster, Pa., b. Nov. 1, 1854.

17

Family of **FRANCES ESHLEMAN** (5435) and Rev. **CHRISTIAN HERSHEY.**

5642. Fianna, Waynesboro, Pa., b. Mar. 17, 1841; m. Dec. 9, 1866, Rev. Henry B. Strickler, b. Nov. 13, 1840; son Jacob Strickler and Ann Stauffer.

5643. Naomi, Waynesboro, Pa., b. Aug. 12, 1842.

5644. John E., Waynesboro, Pa., b. Mar. 1, 1844; m. Oct. 11, 1868, Mary V. Neff (1569); m. Oct. 22, 1876, Sarah Mumma, b. Feb. 1, 1842; dau. Samuel Mumma and Nancy Newcomer.

5645. Amos, Derry, Pa., b. Aug. 15, 1845; m. Nov. 12, 1867, Frances Beam, b. July 26, 1846; dau. Jacob Beam and Frances Forney.

5646. Martin, Philadelphia, Pa., b. Jan. 24, 1847; m. Nov. 20, 1884, Grace Muench, b. May 11, 1860; dau. Robert L. Muench and Ellen E. Zollinger.

5647. Daniel, Steelton, Pa., b. Dec. 14, 1850; m. Dec. 25, 1871, Henrietta Cramer, b. Aug.. 1849; dau. Joseph Cramer and Elizabeth Kettering.

Family of **MARTHA MYLIN** (5437) and **JOHN LANDIS.**

5648. Anna, East Lampeter, Pa., b. Apr. 24, 1824; d. Aug. 18, 1824.

5649. Mary Ann, Sinking Valley, Pa., b. May 28, 1825; d. Dec. 26, 1901; m. Nov. 16, 1842, John B. Diffenbach, b. Jan. 15, 1813; d. Aug. 2, 1874; son Henry Diffenbach and Mary Bressler.

5650. Susan, Sinking Valley, Pa., b. Oct. 18, 1826.

5651. Eliza M., Fertility, Pa., b. Jan. 27, 1829.

5652. Amos, Lancaster, Pa., b. Feb. 23, 1832; d. Sept. 12, 1898; m. Nov. 24, 1859, Hettie A. Rohrer, b. Aug. 8, 1840; dau. Christian Rohrer and Hettie Buckwalter.

5653. Daniel M., Lancaster, Pa., b. Nov. 6, 1833; d. Feb., 1904; m. Mar. 22, 1860, Christiana McAllister, b. Sept. 14, 1830; dau. John McAllister and Rachael Miller.

5654. John M., Lancaster, Pa., b. Jan. 3, 1835; d. Mar. 22, 1903.

5655. Esther Ann, East Lampeter, Pa., b. Feb. 20, 1837; d. Aug. 5, 1838.

5656. Jacob M., Fertility, Pa., b. Nov. 15, 1841.

5657. Frances, Fertility, Pa., b. May 25, 1845; d. Sept. 6, 1845.

Family of ANN ELIZA BINKLEY (4924) and JOHN F. INGRAM.

5658. Cora S., Strasburg, Pa., b. June 30, 1867.
5659. Bertha A., Lancaster, Pa., b. Oct. 22, 1868; m. Nov. 20, 1893, Milton B. Eaby, b. Sept. 15, 1867; son Elias Eaby and Mary Buckwalter.
5660. Pearl A., Strasburg, Pa., b. Dec. 22, 1880.
5661. Park B., Strasburg, Pa., b. Oct. 23, 1883.
5662. Earl J., Strasburg, Pa., b. Aug. 1, 1887.

Family of SUE BINKLEY (4932) and JOSEPH HESS.

5663. Ralph, Rothville, Pa.

Family of DANIEL L. HERR (2076) and MARGARET McLAUGHLIN.

5664. Elizabeth Margaret, Lock Haven, Pa., b. Sept. 10, 1887.
5665. Mary Catharine, Lock Haven, Pa., b. Dec. 11, 1888.
5666. Louisa Claire, Lock Haven, Pa., b. Mar. 4, 1891.

Family of ANNA MARY HERR (2079) and Dr. AMOS W. SHELLEY.

5667. Sara Herr, Baltimore, Md., b. August 31, 1875; m. Dec. 31, 1896, Rev. David T. Neely, b. June 13, 1871; son John Neely and Margaret J. Ewing.
5668. Gertrude May, Port Royal, Pa., b. May 7, 1877; d. Aug. 19, 1877.
5669. Edith, Port Royal, Pa., b. Nov. 26, 1878; d. Jan. 7, 1879.
5670. Mary Dull, Port Royal, Pa., b. July 29, 1880.
5671. Jay Warren, Port Royal, Pa., b. Apr. 17, 1882.
5672. Anna Margaretta, Port Royal, Pa., b. Feb. 10, 1884.
5673. Penrose Herr, Port Royal, Pa., b. Sept. 24, 1886.

Family of CLARA ANN ADAMS (2085) and A. WASHINGTON McCOY.

5674. Willis C., Elkhart, Ind., b. June 14, 1857; m. Nov. 27, 1889, Saloma Garber.
5675. Minnie A., Goshen, Ind., b. Dec. 19, 1858; m. Apr. 9, 1885, Jonathan W. Lehman, b. Mar. 17, 1855; son Moses Lehman and Mary ———.
5676. Edward J., Bellefontaine, O., b. Mar. 7, 1861; m. Sept., 1884, Susie Damson.

5677. Lewis D., Elkhart, Ind., b. Jan. 18, 1864; m. Mar. 6, 1892, Effie Shick.

5678. Anna May, Chicago, Ill., b. Apr. 25, 1871; m. Mar. 9, 1893, Charles Krepps.

Family of ESLIE C. ADAMS (2087) and CARRIE E. STEVENS.

5679. Mary P., Garden City, Kans., b. Jan. 18, 1869; d. Oct. 9, 1870.

5680. Robert P., Garden City, Kans., b. Dec. 10, 1871; d. Nov. 15, 1886.

5681. Eslie C., Garden City, Kans., b. June 30, 1874.

5682. Thomas S., Garden City, Kans., b. Dec. 11, 1877.

Family of MARY J. ADAMS (2089) and JAMES NEWELL.

5683. Phœbe Lorena, Gering, Neb., b. Mar. 12, 1869; m. Aug. 21, 1887, William Fritz, b. Aug. 27, 1860.

5684. Frederick A., Juniata, Neb., b. July 3, 1870; m. Feb. 15, 1895, Katie C. Shields, b. Oct., 1867; d. Feb. 28, 1898; dau. Louis Shields and ———; m. June 14, 1899, Fannie H. Aylsworth, b. Oct. 27, 1872; dau. Wallace G. Aylsworth and Hattie Burlingham.

5685. Mary J., Pine Bluffs, Wyo., b. Sept. 27, 1879.

5686. Sarah E., Pine Bluffs, Wyo., b. Oct. 14, 1880.

Family of MARY L. FUHRMAN (2093) and LEWIS HIMMELRIGHT.

5687. Laura Alice, Red Haw, O., b. Sept. 7, 1866; m. Aug. 12, 1903, M. ——— D. Wright.

5688. Maudilla, Santiago, Chili, South America, b. Apr. 26, 1868; m. Aug. 17, 1899, Charles H. Westenberger, son George Westenberger and Jane Berry.

5689. Nellie Catherine, West Salem, O., b. Mar. 31, 1870; m. Dec. 25, 1901, Henry C. Sechrist, son Henry Sechrist and Julia A. Shoemaker.

5690. Ada Belle, Untali, Africa, b. Oct. 2, 1873; m. June 18, 1901, Edward L. Sechrist, b. Aug. 15, 1873; son Henry Sechrist and Julia A. Shoemaker.

Family of AARON ELIJAH ADAMS (2104) and ELLA JANE PAXSON.

5691. Arthur Everett, St. Louis, Mo., b. June 28. 1867; m. June 14, 1893, Ida L. Dinkins, b. Mar., 1874.

5692. Frank Paxson, Elkhart, Ind., b. Dec. 8. 1869; m. July 3, 1894, Hattie B. Godfrey, b. Feb., 1874.

5693. Clara Edna, Farmington, Mo., b. July 15. 1873; m. June 17, 1894, Rev. J. S. Meracle, b. Apr. 1, 1867.

5694. Son, Redford, Mo., b. July 27, 1889; d. July 28, 1889.

Family of AMBROSE IRA ADAMS (2105) and AMANDA JANE WHITE.

5695. Arthur J., Bristol, Ind.

5696. Albert Elijah, Bristol, Ind.

5697. Ira Ambrose, Bristol, Ind.

Family of MARTHA ANN ADAMS (2106) and HENRY T. MENGES.

5698. Prof. William Henry, Delaware, O., b. Mar. 23, 1874.

5699. Susan Evelyn, Bristol, Ind., b. July 9, 1875; d. Sept. 3, 1881.

5700. Oliver Adelbert, Baltimore, Md., b. Oct. 10, 1877.

5701. Laura Alda, Bristol, Ind., b. Feb. 9, 1880; d. Sept., 1892.

5702. Bertha Leona, Belgrade, Me., b. Feb. 8, 1882; m. Percy Everett Hanson, b. June 27, 1882; son John T. Hanson and Julius Scates.

5703. Hubert Theophilus, Baltimore, Md., b. Jan. 10, 1884.

5704. Mabel Luella, Baltimore, Md., b. Sept. 11, 1885.

5705. Benjamin Harrison, Baltimore, Md., b. June 9, 1888.

Family of LENA HERR (2107) and Dr. CHARLES KINNAMAN.

5606. Belle, Cleveland, O., b. July 29, 1872; m. Dec. 28, 1892, Charles Swearington, b. Nov. 23, 1871; son George Swearington and Maggie A. Longfitt.

5607. Carson H., Cleveland, O., b. July 31, 1877.

Family of HARRY LEANDER HERR (2108) and FLOY CHESNEY.

5708. Cora, Bucyrus, O., b. 1893.

5709. Isabella, Bucyrus, O., b. 1896.

5710. Harriet, Bucyrus, O., b. 1899.

Family of **EPHRAIM CARPENTER** (2122) and **HARRIET RHODES**.

5711. Montgomery, Vogansville, Pa., b. Aug. 27, 1840; d. June 10, 1845.

5712. Eliza, Vogansville, Pa., b. July 14, 1846; d. Aug. 28, 1856.

5713. Virdilla F., Naperville, Ill., b. Nov. 7, 1848; m. Feb. 2, 1871, Elias S. Zook, b. Apr. 2, 1846; son Elias Zook and Maria Sheaffer.

5714. Mary Ann, Naperville, Ill., b. Dec. 28, 1850; m. June 6, 1871, Edwin S. Fry, b. July 20, 1851; son George Fry and Catharine Snyder.

5715. Arkansas, Vogansville, Pa., b. Feb. 22, 1855; d. May 11, 1883.

Family of **FIANNA CARPENTER** (2130) and **JACOB SHEETS**.

5716. Volney C., Brunersville, Pa., b. May 25, 1855.

Family of **URIAH CARPENTER** (2131) and **HARRIET MILLER**.

5717. Sumpter, Brunersville, Pa., b. July 9, 1854.

5718. Wayne, Brunersville, Pa., b. Oct. 8, 1855.

5719. Francis, Brunersville, Pa., b. May 3, 1858.

Family of **JOHN W. FORNEY** (2164) and **MATILDA REITZEL**.

5720. Philip Reitzel, Philadelphia, Pa., b. Dec. 28, 1840.

5721. James, Philadelphia, Pa., b. Jan. 17, 1844; m. Jane S. Richardson.

5722. John W., Philadelphia, Pa., b. Aug. 8, 1846.

5723. Mary Stokes, Philadelphia, Pa., b. Nov. 24, 1854; m. Harry G. Thunder.

5724. Anna Hoover, Philadelphia, Pa., b. Feb. 3, 1858; m. George W. Fitter.

5725. Tillie May, Philadelphia, Pa., b. May 17, 1862.

Family of **CHARLES B. FORNEY** (2167) and **AMELIA STEHMAN**.

5726. Stehman, Steelton, Pa.

5727. Charles, Steelton, Pa.

5728. Sumpter, Steelton, Pa.

5729. Sarah, Steelton, Pa.

Family of **SARAH FORNEY** (2168) and **JOHN LINGLE**.

5730. Infant, Harrisburg, Pa.

5731. Infant, Harrisburg, Pa.

Family of WEIN FORNEY (2169) and LYDIA GUMPH.

5732. Peter William, Washington, D. C., b. Oct. 7, 1851; d. Oct. 27, 1885; m. 1880, Julia Grier.

5733. Anna F., Chestnut Hill, Pa., b. May 1, 1853; m. June 30, 1885, Chauncey H. Brush, b. Apr. 5, 1883; son Abner Brush and Laura Hubbard.

5734. Clara, Harrisburg, Pa., b. 1854; d. 1855.

5735. Wein, Chicago, Ill., b. Nov. 18, 1862.

Family of DANIEL C. FORNEY (2170) and CATHERINE RHINEHART.

5736. Emma, Harrisburg, Pa., b. 1854; d. 1886; m. 1877, William W. Ely, d. 1886.

5737. Clara, Providence, R. I., m. Feb. 4, 1880, Walter J. Comstock, b. Dec. 12, 1853; son Jonathan H. Comstock and Mary D. Hall.

Family of JACOB FORNEY (2171) and EMMA DEBOLT.

5738. Michael, Harrisburg, Pa.

Family of HENRY GROFF (2179) and —— GOCHENOUR.

5739. Amos, New Providence, Pa., b. 1837; d. July 3, 1902; m. Barbara Groff, dau. John Groff and Catherine Eshleman.

Family of JOHN GROFF (2180) and CATHERINE ESHLEMAN.

5740. Joseph, New Providence, Pa., m. Susan Myers.

5741. Barbara, New Providence, Pa., m. Amos Groff, b. 1837; d. July 3, 1902; son Henry Groff and —— Gochenour.

5742. Martin, New Providence, Pa., m. Barbara Hoover.

5743. Eliza, New Providence, Pa., m. Martin Eshleman, son Jacob Eshleman and Anna Groff.

5744. Levi, New Providence, Pa., m. Betsey Thomas, dau. Adam Thomas and Ann Eshleman.

5745. John, New Providence, Pa., m. Hettie Eshleman, dau. Jacob Eshleman and Anna Groff.

5746. Kate, New Providence, Pa.

Family of JACOB GROFF (2181) and —— BLEECHER.

5747. Elias, Strasburg, Pa., m. Susan Herr (5243).

5748. Ephraim, New Providence, Pa., m. Eliza Eckman.

Family of Wid. JACOB GROFF (2181) and BARBARA MILES.

5749. Benjamin, New Providence, Pa.

5750. Barbara, New Providence, Pa.

5751. Fanny, New Providence, Pa.

5752. Henry, New Providence, Pa.

Family of JOSEPH GROFF (2182) and NANCY SMITH.

5753. Joseph, Quarryville, Pa., m. Elizabeth Crawford.

5754. Sarah, Quarryville, Pa., m. Robert Trimble.

5755. Isaac, Paradise, Pa., m. Wid. Louisa Troxler.

5756. Benjamin, Quarryville, Pa.

5757. Catherine E., Quarryville, Pa., m. Frank McCrabb.

5758. Elias, Quarryville, Pa.

Family of ABRAHAM GROFF (2183) and FANNY GROFF.

5759. Lizzie, Strasburg, Pa., m. Abraham Witmer.

5760. Aaron, Strasburg, Pa.

5761. Kate, Lampeter, Pa., m. Dr. George Miller.

5762. Fanny, Lampeter, Pa., m. Harry Miller.

5763. Abraham, Lampeter, Pa.

5764. Joseph, Lampeter, Pa.

Family of SAMUEL GROFF (2185) and BARBARA RANK.

5765. Rachael, Willow Street, Pa.

5766. Jessie, Willow Street, Pa., m. ———— Miller.

5767. David, Strasburg, Pa., m. Barbara Shaub.

5768. Samuel, Strasburg, Pa.

5769. Rebecca, Strasburg, Pa., m. Martin Reese.

5770. Isaac, Strasburg, Pa.

5771. Jacob, Strasburg, Pa.

Family of ANNA GROFF (2186) and JACOB ESHLEMAN.

5772. Elijah, New Proidence, Pa., m. Christiana Barr, dau. Abraham Barr and ————.

5773. Kate, New Providence, Pa., m. Solomon Cockel.

5774. Hettie, New Providence, Pa., m. John Groff, son John Groff and Catherine Eshleman .

5775. Martin, New Providence, Pa., m. Eliza Groff, dau. John Groff and Catherine Eshleman.

5776. Anna, New Providence, Pa., m. Harvey Whiteside.

5777. Eliza, New Providence, Pa.

5778. Benjamin, New Providence, Pa.

5779. Hiram, New Providence, Pa.

Family of CATHARINE GOCHENOUR (2194) and JOHN SHENK.

5780. Martha S., New Providence, Pa., b. June 27. 1810; m. Daniel Lefever, son Philip Lefever and ———.

5781. Joseph C., New Providence, Pa., b. Oct. 14, 1812; m. Ann M. Eckman, dau. Martin Eckman and ———.

5782. Benjamin F., Lancaster, Pa., b. Mar. 13, 1815; m. Barbara Barr, b. May 23, 1817; d. Apr, 27, 1846; dau. Christian Barr and Susan Breneman; m. Catherine Christ, b. Sept. 16, 1817; d. Sept. 5, 1900; dau. John Christ and ———.

5783. Esther, New Providence, Pa., b. Nov. 9, 1817; m. Jan. 29, 1860, Daniel Bair, b. Aug. 7, 1818; son John Bair and Elizabeth Miller.

5784. John M., New Providence, Pa., b. Dec. 29, 1818; m. Feb. 18, 1858, Frances C. Stively (8658).

5785. Catherine, New Providence, Pa., b. Nov. 5, 1820; m. Jan. 1, 1846, John Hess, b. Nov. 2, 1821; son John Hess and Martha Musser.

Family of BENJAMIN GROFF (2198) and LIZZIE LEFEVRE.

5786. Daniel, New Providence, Pa.

5787. Amos, New Providence, Pa.

Family of AMOS GROFF (2200) and SUSAN HARMAN.

5788. Mary E., Lanacster, Pa., m. Martin Kreider, son Martin Kreider and ———.

5789. Martha M., Lancaster, Pa., m. Martin Kreider, son Jacob Kreider and ———.

5790. Hannah M., Lancaster, Pa.

5791. Emma L., Lancaster, Pa.

5792. Clara E., Lancaster, Pa.

Family of MARTHA GROFF (2201) and JOHN MILLER.

5793. Mary Emma, Martic, Pa.
5794. Benjamin, Martic, Pa.
5795. Elizabeth, Martic, Pa.
5796. Joseph, Martic, Pa.

Family of FRANK GROFF (2202) and ABIGAIL J. McCRABB.

5797. Olivia Jane, Martic, Pa.
5798. Oliver Larenzo, Lancaster, Pa.
5799. Oscar Bigham, Martic, Pa.
5800. Ovintheus Francis, Martic, Pa.

Family of Wid. FRANK GROFF (2202) and MARIA BRECKWELL.

5801. Oliptheus L., Martic, Pa.
5802. Martha M., Martic, Pa.
5803. Amos Ellsworth, Martic, Pa.

Family of Wid. BENJAMIN KENDIG (2203) and ABIGAIL PATTERSON.

5804. Elizabeth, Washington, Ill., b. July 4, 1826; d. 1847; m. Jonathan R. Wilson.
5805. Anna, Washington, Ill., b. Jan. 1, 1828; d. Apr. 26, 1835.
5806. Susanna, Washington, Ill., b. Feb. 18, 1830; m. Benjamin G. Kendig (5811).
5807. Samuel, Washington, Ill., b. Mar. 4, 1832; m. Catherine Brubaker.
5808. Emanuel, Washington, Ill., b. Feb. 7, 1835; m. Margaret Wallace.

Family of ISAAC KENDIG (2205) and MARY GROFF.

5809. Mary, Waynesboro, Va., m. Henry Stehman.

Family of JOSEPH KENDIG (2207) and BARBARA KREIDER.

5810. Amos, Washington, Ill., m. Elizabeth Brubaker.
5811. Benjamin G., Washington, Ill., m. Susanna Kendig (5806).
5812. Ann, Washington, Ill., m. Enoch Biggs.
5813. Barbara, Washington, Ill., m. Henry Jewit.
5814. Joseph, Washington, Ill., m. ——— Wilson,

5815. Martin, Washington, Ill., m. Mary Shaub.
5816. Henry, Washington, Ill., m. Sarah Devour.
5817. Tobias, Washington, Ill., m. Anna Kendig (5826).
5818. Mary, Washington, Ill., b. 1820; m. John Herr (1039).
5819. Katie, Washington, Ill., m. David Groff, son Wid. Joseph Groff and Wid. Maria Stauffer.

Family of MARY KENDIG (2208) and PETER ANDREWS.

5820. Maria, Lampeter, Pa., m. Levi Landis.
5821. Jacob, Lampeter, Pa.
5822. Lydia, Lampeter, Pa.
5823. Benjamin, Lampeter, Pa., m. Lizzie Kreider.

Family of Wid. MARTIN KENDIG (2209) and MARIA STAUFFER.

5824. Henry, Waynesboro, Va., m. Bettie Spitler.
5825. Jacob, Juniata, Neb., m. Phoebe, Zircle.

Family of SAMUEL KENDIG (2211) and MARTHA BOSLER.

5826. Anna, Martinsville, Pa., m. Tobias Kendig (5817).
5827. Mary, Martinsville, Pa.
5828. Joseph, Martinsville, Pa., m. Barbara Bowermaster; m. Anna Brubaker.
5829. Henry, Martinsville, Pa., m. Barbara Slote.
5830. John, Binkley's Bridge, Pa., m. Wid. Barbara Kendig, dau. Tobias Kreider and ———.
5831. Hettie, Baumgartners, Pa., m. Christian Breneman.
5832. Mattie, Baumgartners, Pa.
5833. Samuel, Hartman's Bridge, Pa., m. Lizzie Martin.
5834. Jacob, Enterprise, Pa., m. Lizzie Reinhart.

Family of JOHN G. KENDIG (2212) and SUSAN HARTMAN.

5835. Christian, Strasburg, Pa., b. Dec. 22, 1829; d. Jan. 4, 1886; m. Oct. 25, 1855, Anna Witmer, b. Oct. 13, 1830; dau. Rev. David Witmer and Anna Root.
5836. Mary Ann, Mountville, Pa., b. Feb. 1, 1832; d. Jan. 22, 1892; m. Dec. 6, 1853, Abraham R. Witmer, son Rev. David Witmer and Anna Root.

5837. Henry, Mountville, Pa., b. Dec. 10, 1834; d. Oct. 30, 1861.
5838. Susanna, Mountville, Pa., b. Mar. 24, 1840.
5839. John Jacob, Mountville, Pa., b. Oct. 30, 1843; d. Jan. 28, 1847.

Family of ABRAHAM KENDIG (2213) and Wid. CATHERINE HARTMAN.

5840. Elvira, Hinkletown, Pa., m. Wid. Benjamin Bolmer.
5841. Levi, Neffsville, Pa., m. Susan Bolmer, dau. Benjamin Bolmer
       and ———.
5482. Hezekiah, Neffsville, Pa.
5843. Abraham, Hahnstown, Pa., m. Susan Bair.
5844. Katy, Hahnstown, Pa.
5845. Betsey, Hahnstown, Pa.
5846. B. Rohrer, Hahnstown, Pa.

· Family of HENRY KENDIG (2214) and ANNA EABY.

5847. Isaac, Enterprise, Pa.
5848. Fanny, Enterprise, Pa.

Family of CATHERINE GROFF (2215) and JOHN WELSH.

5849. James D., Drumore, Pa., m. Mary Boyd.
5850. Jacob H., Drumore, Pa., m. Annie Bitting.

Family of ELIZABETH GROFF (2216) and JOHN BROWN.

5851 Mary E., Little Britain, Pa., m. Pusey Tollinger, son Casper
      Tollinger and Elizabeth Reyburn.

Family of DAVID GROFF (2217) and ANN LONGENECKER.

5852. Eliza, Washington, Ill., m. Christian Schoaf.
5853. Susan, Washington, Ill., m. John Bair.
5854. Martha, Washington, Ill., m. Elias Fry.
5855. Mary, Washington, Ill., m. David Posey.
5856. Fanny, Washington, Ill., m. Daniel Diffenbach.
5857. Daniel, Washington, Ill.
5858. Anna, Washington, Ill.
5859. Naomi, Washington, Ill.

Family of BENJAMIN GROFF (2218) and MARIA BALSLEY.

5860. George, Harrisburg, Pa., m. Lizzie Lane.
5861. Sarah, Harrisburg, Pa.
5862. Mary, Milton, Pa., m. Archibald Rahn.
5863. Anna, Milton, Pa., m. Mowry Nichols.
5864. Charlotte, Milton, Pa.
5865. Jacob, Milton, Pa., m. Mary Gross.
5866. Eliza, Milton, Pa., m. Harry Funk.
5867. Wesley K., Milton, Pa.

Family of MARTIN GROFF (2219) and MARY ESHLEMAN (2245).

5868. Alice Ann, Strasburg, Pa., b. July 13, 1832.
5869. Susan K., Strasburg, Pa., b. Dec. 15, 1834.
5870. Mary N., Strasburg, Pa., b. Sept. 8, 1835; m. Jan. 10, 1859, Albert K. Warfel (4227).
5871. Joanna, Strasburg, Pa., b. Aug. 1, 1837.
5872. John M., Strasburg, Pa., b. Dec. 11, 1839.
5873. Ann Salome, Strasburg, Pa., b. Mar. 6, 1843; d. Aug. 3, 1846.

Family of SUSAN GROFF (2220) and CHRISTIAN LEFEVRE.

5874. Wesley, Martic, Pa., m. Sallie Bachman.
5875. Lizzie, Martic, Pa., m. William Philips.
5876. John F., Lancaster, Pa., m. Elizabeth ———.
5877. Jacob, Martic, Pa.
5878. Kate, Martic, Pa.
5879. Benjamin, Martic, Pa.
5880. Emma, Martic, Pa.
5881. George, Martic, Pa.
5882. Frank, Martic, Pa.

Family of JACOB GROFF (2221) and JANE STEELE.

5883. Jennie Barr, Martic, Pa., b. Apr. 5, 1851.

Family of HENRY GROVE (2224) and ANNA STOVER.

5884. Martin, Waynesboro, Va., b. Dec. 25, 1823.
5885. Barbara, Waynesboro, Va., b. Dec. 19, 1825.
5886. Michael, Waynesboro, Va., b. July 5, 1827; d. May 5, 1867.

5887. Anna, Waynesboro, Va., b. Dec. 12, 1830.

5888. Catherine, Waynesboro, Va., b. Mar. 22, 1836.

5889. Susan, Waynesboro, Va., b. May 18, 1838.

5890. Henry, Waynesboro, Va., b. Jan. 2, 1841.

5891. Mary, Waynesboro, Va., b. Dec. 8, 1843.

5892. Matthias, Waynesboro, Va., b. Nov. 10, 1846.

Family of JOSEPH GROVE (2225) and NANCY BROWER.

5893. Fanny, Hermitage, Va., b. Jan. 7, 1834.

5894. John, Hermitage, Va., b. Nov. 25, 1836; d. 1836.

5895. Christian, Hermitage, Va., b. July 3, 1838.

5896. Jacob, Hermitage, Va., b. Dec. 19, 1841.

5897. Mary, Hermitage, Va., b. July 9, 1845.

5898. Elizabeth, Hermitage, Va.. b. Oct. 16, 1848.

Family of MARY GROVE (2226) and JOSEPH WENGER.

5899. Nancy, Spring Hill, Va., b. Mar., 1832.

5900. Martin, Spring Hill, Va., b. Oct., 1834.

5901. Mary, Spring Hill, Va., b. Apr., 1840.

5902. Levi, Spring Hill, Va., b. 1844.

5903. Eliza, Spring Hill, Va., b. 1846.

Family of ISAAC GROVE (2229) and CATHERINE WENGER.

5904. Elizabeth E., Lemore, Cal., b. Aug. 10, 1839; m. Dec. 20, 1860, Jacob F. Flory, b. Aug. 2, 1839. son Daniel Flory and Christiana Sniteman.

5905. Barbara A., New Hope, Va., b. Oct. 18, 1840; d. Oct. 17, 1881; m. Dec. 7, 1865, John A. Stover. b. Sept. 26, 1843; son Jacob Stover and ———.

5906. Joseph, New Hope, Va., b. Mar. 24, 1842; d. Dec. 30, 1862.

5907. Nancy, New Hope, Va., b. Mar. 23, 1844; m. Feb. 18, 1865, William B. Garber, b. Sept. 19, 1842; son Samuel Garber and Anna Peters.

5908. Mary, Barren Ridge, Pa., b. Aug. 29, 1845; d. Mar. 6, 1886; m. Dec. 19, 1867, Samuel Wampler, b. Oct. 9, 1837; son Jonas Wampler and ———.

5909. Catherine, New Hope, Va., b. Jan. 20, 1848; d. Oct. 25, 1877; m. Sept. 12, 1872, Joseph Garber, son Samuel Garber and Anna Peters.

5910. Susanna, Laurel Hill, Va., b. Jan. 17, 1850; m. Oct. 12, 1871, Henry F. Borden, b. Dec. 2, 1849; son James Borden and Martha Coffman.

5911. Isaac N., Freyers Cave, Va., b. Nov. 23, 1851; m. Dec. 25, 1873, Elizabeth Landis, b. Sept. 13, 1854; dau. John W. Landis and Anna Harshberger.

5912. Noah, Somerville, Va., b. May 17, 1854; m. Mar. 27, 1878, Ella L. Wood, b. Aug. 3, 1855; dau. Thomas Wood and Sarah Phelps.

5913. Jacob A., Koiners Store, Va., b. Dec. 7, 1856; m. Mar. 28, 1878, Emma E. Craig, b. July 31, 1856; dau. William A. Craig and Catherine C. Via.

Family of MARTHA GROFF (2234) and ABRAHAM FRANTZ (2433).

5914. Ann Elizabeth, Waynesboro, Pa., b. Jan. 8, 1839; m. May 25, 1873, John Bonebrake, b. June 6, 1833; son Jacob Bonebrake and Susan Hollinger.

5915. Elam G., Gwyn Brook, Md., b. Nov. 2, 1840; m. Oct. 31, 1865, Martha B. Funk, b. Oct. 25, 1845; dau. Henry Funk and Susan Miller.

5916. Ezra G., Waynesboro, Pa., b. Dec. 8, 1842; d. Sept. 14, 1848.

5917. Mary Alice, Waynesboro, Pa., b. Nov. 6, 1844; d. Apr. 4, 1894.

5918. Benjamin Franklin, Ringgold, Md., b. Feb. 23, 1847; m. Dec. 19, 1872, Martha L. Funk, b. Feb. 7, 1851; dau. Henry W. Funk and Margaret Good.

5919. Abraham G., Waynesboro, Pa., b. Oct. 10, 1849; d. July 24, 1852.

5920. Christian G., Lancaster, Pa., b. Nov. 30, 1851; m. Dec. 9, 1880, Georgie Myers, b. July 30, 1853; dau. David M. Myers and Mary A. Slagle.

5921. Martin, Waynesboro, Pa., b. Mar. 27, 1854; d. Aug. 8, 1855.

5922. Ida Martha, Waynesboro, Pa., b. June 7, 1856; m. Dec. 17,

1878, Willis Overholtzer Frantz, b. Jan. 17, 1858; son Henry L. Frantz and Elizabeth Overholtzer.

5923. Ella Louisa, Waynesboro, Pa., b. Aug. 24, 1858; d. Dec. 29, 1904; m. Feb. 13, 1883, John E. Denlinger, b. Feb. 13, 1862; son David Denlinger and Susan Myers.

Family of ABRAHAM GROFF (2237) and SUSAN HOFFMAN.

5924. Ernest Abraham, Catonsville, Md., b. July 14, 1859.
5925. Mary Louisa, Catonsville, Md., b. Nov. 11, 1860.
5926. Luetta Musser, Catonsville, Md., b. Oct. 21, 1864.
5927. Willis, Catonsville, Md., b. June 26, 1866; d. July 13, 1866.

Family of JACOB B. GROFF (2238) and MARY ANN MILLER.

5928. Henry C., Washington, D. C., m. Kate Jeffries.
5929. Jacob C., Washington, D. C.
5930. Mary Kate, Washington, D. C.
5931. David W., Washington, D. C.
5932. Emma May, Washington, D. C.
5933. Frank, Washington, D. C.
5934. Samuel, Washington, D. C.

Family of MARY GROFF (2239) and MARTIN PFOUTZ.

5935. Abraham G., Strasburg, Pa., b. Feb. 25, 1850.
5936. Martin Miller, Strasburg, Pa., b. Oct. 8, 1851; d. Oct. 6, 1874.
5937. Francis H., Strasburg, Pa., b. Aug. 25, 1853.
5938. Samuel B., Strasburg, Pa., b. Aug. 19, 1855; m. Apr. 14, 1887, Sallie M. Foulk, dau. Miller Foulk and ——— Speihlman.
5939. Jacob W., Strasburg, Pa., b. July 2, 1857; d. Sept. 2, 1857.

Family of BEN. FRANKLIN GROFF (2240) and ELIZABETH ANN DENMEAD.

5940. Mary Rachel, Baltimore, Md., b. Jan. 11, 1871; m. June 28, 1899, Clarence S. Farquharcon, b. Apr. 16, 1870; son Clarence S. Farquharcon and Elizabeth Sonner.
5941. Clara Denmead, Baltimore, Md., b. Nov. 9, 1873; m. Dec. 14, 1898, William D. Wight, b. Mar. 4, 1872; son John H. Wight and Elizabeth Davidson.
5942. Guy Baldwin, Spokane, Wash., b. Oct. 10, 1875.
5943. William Denmead, Spokane, Wash., b. Aug. 27, 1879.

Family of SUSANNA ESHLEMAN (2241) and ISAAC GIRVIN.

5944. John E., Philadelphia, Pa., b. Feb. 18, 1829; m. Oct. 13, 1852, Emma Bowman, b. Jan. 11, 1830; dau. Joseph Bowman and Anna Brua.

5945. Mary Ann, Lancaster, Pa., b. July 22, 1830; m. Apr. 16, 1853, John B. Warfel (4226).

5946. Ann Elizabeth, Lancaster, Pa., b. Jan. 5, 1832; d. Dec. 17, 1882.

5947. Susan, Lancaster, Pa., b. Oct. 14, 1833; d. Dec. 15, 1882.

5948. Robert Milton, Philadelphia, Pa., b. Feb. 3, 1836; d. Mar. 17, 1900; m. July 10, 1867, Wid. Sue B. Saunders, b. Dec. 18, 1843, dau. John M. Harper and Susan B. Robb.

Family of NANCY ESHLEMAN (2242) and DANIEL POTTS.

5949. Mary Ann, Strasburg, Pa., b. May 15, 1828; d. Sept. 5, 1828.

5950. Benjamin, Strasburg, Pa., b. Dec. 15, 1830; d. Sept. 21, 1851.

5951. John, Strasburg, Pa., b. Aug. 10, 1832; d. Feb. 12, 1833.

5952. Daniel E., Strasburg, Pa., b. Mar. 18, 1835; d. Sept. 12, 1887; m. Sept. 24, 1861, Catherine McElroy, b. Jan. 10, 1839; d. Nov. 19, 1895; dau. George McElroy and Catherine Herr.

5953. Jacob, Strasburg, Pa., b. Sept. 1, 1836; d. Mar. 10, 1837.

5954. Angelica, Strasburg, Pa., b, Mar. 1, 1838; d. Apr. 17, 1890; m. Oct. 4, 1859, Edward M. Eberman, b. July 16, 1826; d. Dec. 8, 1873; son John Eberman and Sarah Fahnestock.

5955. Son, Strasburg, Pa., b. Aug. 1, 1841; d. Aug. 22, 1841.

Family of BENJAMIN ESHLEMAN (2247) and JUDITH BARR.

5956. Benjamin, Marengo, Ia., b. Jan. 17, 1834; d. June 12, 1847.

Family of Dr. ABRAHAM ESHLEMAN (2250) and LIZZIE MASON.

5957. Alice Narcissa, Strasburg, Pa., b. Jan. 4, 1855.

Family of MARIA POTTS (2254) and STEPHEN HASTINGS.

5958. Frances, Millport, Pa., b. May 18, 1830; m. Dec. 2, 1850, James C. Dunlap, b. Jan. 14, 1829; son Andrew Dunlap and Mary Miller.

5959. Maria, Millport, Pa., b. Dec. 31, 1831; m. Nov. 6, 1852, Samuel Curtis, b. Dec. 5, 1822; son John Curtis and Barbara Shenk.

Family of Wid. MARIA HASTINGS (2254) and JOHN ECHTERNACH.

5960. Eliza, Strasburg, Pa., b. Dec. 2, 1838; m. Dec. 22, 1864, Frederick Stamm, b. Feb. 19, 1833; d. Mar., 1908; son David Stamm and Eve Cook.

5961. Margaret, Strasburg, Pa., b. Dec. 15, 1840.

5962. Joseph, Strasburg, Pa., b. July 10, 1842.

5963. John, Strasburg, Pa., b. Sept. 8, 1845.

5964. Daniel, Strasburg, Pa., b. Mar. 23, 1848.

5965. Louisa, Strasburg, Pa., b. Feb. 10, 1851.

Family of FANNY POTTS (2255) and MATTHIAS SHIRK.

5966. Joseph Henry, Willow Street, Pa., b. Nov. 22, 1831; m. Jan. 19, 1865, Lizzie Eckman, b. 1842; dau. John Eckman and Mary

5967. Samuel, Soudersburg, Pa., b. Nov. 13, 1834.

5968. Amos, Soudersburg, Pa., b. Mar. 25, 1838; m. Sept. 29, 1860, Martha A. Appleton, b. July 29, 1838; dau. John Appleton and Matilda Leaman.

5969. Ann Elizabeth, Willow Street, Pa., b. Dec. 12, 1840.

5970. Frances Maria, Strasburg, Pa., b. June 28, 1843.

5971. David, Willow Street, Pa., b. Apr. 28, 1846; d. Apr. 28, 1846.

5972. Jefferson, Willow Street, Pa., b. May 18, 1848.

5973. Mary Ann, Willow Street, Pa., b. Apr. 26, 1852.

Family of Wid. JACOB E. POTTS (2256) and Wid. CATHERINE McELROY.

5974. Junius Brutus, Strasburg, Pa., b. Apr. 10, 1843.

Family of JOSEPH POTTS (2258) and ELIZA MILLER.

5975. Annie Maria, Lancaster, Pa., b. Sept. 7, 1835; m. Mar. 17, 1858, Henry N. Breneman (1574).

5976. Joseph Miller, Strasburg, Pa., b. July 21, 1837.

Family of DAVID E. POTTS (2260) and CATHARINE WARREN.

5977. Samuel, Lancaster, Pa., b. Oct. 5, 1841.

5978. Joseph Warren, Lancaster, Pa., b. Oct. 31, 1843.

5979. James Warren, Lancaster, Pa., b. Aug. 18, 1845; d. Nov. 7, 1863.

5980. Ann Elizabeth, Lancaster, Pa., b. June 23, 1847.

5981. Emma Catherine, Lancaster, Pa., b. July 3, 1849; d. Jan. 8, 1862.

5982. Mary Louisa, Lancaster, Pa., b. Feb. 23, 1852; d. Dec. 20, 1863.

5983. David, Lancaster, Pa., b. Nov. 3, 1853.

5984. John Frank, Lancaster, Pa., b. Nov. 17, 1856.

5985. Mary Ella, Lancaster, Pa., b. June 14, 1859.

5986. Jacob F., Lancaster, Pa., b. Jan. 18, 1861.

Family of MARIA BACHMAN (2263) and WILLIAM P. PARKER.

5987. Elizabeth, Greencastle, Pa., b. July 25, 1845; m. Mar. 1, 1864, George Costly.

5988. William P., Greencastle, Pa., b. Dec. 14, 1851.

Family of ANNA BACHMAN (2266) and DAVID S. LONGENECKER.

5989. Edwin R., Owings Mills, Md., b. Sept. 19, 1850.

5990. John, Owings Mills, Md., b. Feb. 1, 1854.

5991. Annie Sheridan, Owings Mills, Md., b. Aug. 12, 1864.

Family of JACOB BACHMAN (2268) and ANN ELIZABETH ESHLEMAN.

5992. Frank, Pittsburg, Pa., b. Dec. 9, 1858.

Family of FANNY BACHMAN (2269) and JOHN R. JAMESON.

5993. Annie L., Quincy, Ill., b. Dec. 25, 1857.

Family of FRANCES MILLER (2272) and WILLIAM HASTINGS.

5994. Mary, Colerain, Pa., b. Sept. 3, 1837; d. Oct. 5, 1838.

5995. William M., Carlisle, Pa., b. Mar. 15, 1839; m. Dec. 24, 1861, Caroline Snyder, b. July 21, 1838; dau. Henry Snyder and Elizabeth Neff.

Family of JOHN MILLER (2273) and LUCETTA CULVER.

5996. Fanny Hastings, Carlisle, Pa., b. Nov. 15, 1846.

5997. Joseph Culver, Carlisle, Pa., b. Dec. 12, 1848.

5998. M. Catherine, Carlisle, Pa., b. Jan. 7, 1851; d. Aug. 1, 1852.

5999. M. Elizabeth, Carlisle, Pa., b. Feb. 5, 1853.

6000. David Paul, Carlisle, Pa., b. Mar. 4, 1855.

340   GENEALOGICAL RECORD OF HANS HERR

6001. John Eshleman, Carlisle, Pa., b. Aug. 2, 1857.
6002. Edwin Cary, Carlisle, Pa., b. Oct. 14, 1859.
6003. Harold Bachman, Carlisle, Pa., b. Oct. 11, 1861.
6004. Louisa, Carlisle, Pa., b. Sept. 10, 1863.

Family of SAMUEL MILLER (2274) and MARTHA I. EVANS.

6005. Mary Louisa, Lebanon, Pa., b. Feb. 7, 1848.
6006. S. Catherine, Lebanon, Pa., b. Aug. 26, 1849; d. Aug. 5, 1852.
6007. Emma Isabella, Lebanon, Pa., b. Aug. 14, 1851.
6008. Elizabeth, Lebanon, Pa., b. June 4, 1854.
6009. David, Lebanon, Pa., b. Oct. 21, 1856.
6010. Robert, Lebanon, Pa., b. Sept. 25, 1858.
6011. John Taylor, Lebanon, Pa., b. Oct. 2, 1860.
6012. Samuel Eshleman, Lebanon, Pa., b. July 1, 1863.

Family of DAVID MILLER (2275) and ELIZABETH STAUFFER.

6013. Mary Elsie, Middlesex, Pa., b. Sept. 21, 1857.
6014. Annie Eliza, Middlesex, Pa., b. Nov. 7, 1859.
6015. Harry S., Middlesex, Pa., b. July 22, 1864.

Family of ABNER MILLER (2278) and ELIZABETH STONER.

6016. Isaac, Boiling Springs, Pa., b. July 3, 1862.
6017. Ira, Boiling Springs, Pa., b. Sept. 2, 1863.
6018. Son, Boiling Springs, Pa., b. Jan. 10, 1865; d. Apr. 17, 1865.

Family of AMOS MILLER (2279) and CATHERINE STAUFFER.

6019. Elmer Jacob, Chambersburg, Pa., b. Dec. 30, 1862.

Family of RUDOLPH HERR (2296) and Wid. MARY BENDER.

6020. John K., New Danville, Pa., b. June 20, 1850.
6021. Abraham, New Danville, Pa.
6022. Rudolph, New Danville, Pa.

Family of Wid. RUDOLPH HERR (2296) and ANNA STONER.

6023. Barbara Ann, New Danville, Pa., b. Mar. 16, 1867.

Family of MARY HERR (2306) and MARTIN BEAR.

6024. Henry H., Sterling, Ill., b. Oct. 2, 1851; m. Jan. 4, 1894, Wid. Susan Wiles, b. Sept. 4, 1853; dau. Daniel Paffinberger and Sophia ———.

6025. Jonas H., Galts, Ill., b. Jan. 16, 1853; m. Sept. 12, 1876, Annie Rutt, dau. Jacob Rutt and ——— Harnley.

6026. Elizabeth Herr, Sterling, Ill., b. Jan. 2, 1854; m. Feb. 26, 1878, John P. Herz, b. Feb. 11, 1866; son Jacob Herz and Clementina Dahl.

6027. Ezra, Dixon, Ill., b. Aug. 17, 1859; d. Sept. 29, 1895; m. Feb. 24, 1886, Mamie Hobbs, b. Feb. 8, 1867; dau. George W. Hobbs and Carrie Page.

6028. Abraham, Emerson, Ill., b. May 19, 1861; d. June 13, 1890.

6029. Catherine, Sterling, Ill., b. Aug. 13, 1863; m. Dec. 23, 1887, Samuel Myers, b. Mar. 4, 1865; son Francis Myers and Elizabeth Burger.

6030. Franklin, Sterling, Ill., b. Aug. 15, 1866; d. Sept. 17, 1896; m. Dec. 19, 1888, Margaret M. John, b. Nov. 24, 1867; d. Dec. 10, 1889; dau. George D. John and Mary A. Miller.

Family of TOBIAS H. HERR (2307) and ANNIE H. MELLINGER.

6031. Henry H., Millersville, Pa., b. Aug. 30, 1861.

Family of MARTHA HERR (2309) and NICHOLAS C. BAKER.

6032. Harry H., Millersville, Pa., b. Mar. 4, 1860; d. Sept. 1, 1861.

6033. Mary H., Freeport, Ill., b. Aug. 15, 1862; m. Dec. 31, 1884, William J. Laible, son Christian R. Laible and Mary Clump.

6034. Franklin H., Brooklyn, N. Y., b. Dec. 22, 1864; m. 1888, Marian Gartin.

6035. Nathan Clinton, Elgin, Ill., b. Feb. 1, 1867; m. June, 1889, Laura Randall.

6036. Catherine H., Freeport, Ill., b. Aug. 10, 1868; d. Sept. 19, 1869.

Family of AMOS H. HERR (2310) and MARY F. HARNISH.

6037. David, Neffsville, Pa., b. Nov. 22, 1859; m. Nov. 12, 1885, Lizzie H. Shreiner, dau. George D. Shreiner and Anna B. Hollinger.

6038. Josiah, Neffsville, Pa., b. Aug. 26, 1861; d. Mar. 19, 1862.

6039. Jonas, Ephrata, Pa., b. Apr. 14, 1863; m. Sept. 19, 1889, Fanny B. Mumma, b. Sept. 11, 1865; dau. Jonas Mumma and Mary A. Brubaker.

6040. Henry, Neffsville, Pa., b. Mar. 12, 1865; d. Sept. 21, 1901; m. Oct. 30, 1888, Emma L. Baker, b. Feb. 21, 1869; dau. Joseph M. Baker and Sarah H. Longenecker.

6041. Amos, Neffsville, Pa., b. July 3, 1867; m. Nov. 9, 1893, Mary K. Kauffman, b. Nov. 23, 1869; dau. Christian K. Kauffman and Barbara K. Kindig.

6042. Elam, Binkley's Bridge, Pa., b. June 30, 1869; m. July 21, 1897, Minnie W. Esbenshade, dau. Henry B. Esbenshade and Adaline S. Weidler.

6043. Enos, Binkley's Bridge, Pa., b. Apr. 9, 1872; d. Dec. 21, 1872.

6044. Susan, Windom, Pa., b. Dec. 27, 1873; m. Feb. 16, 1899, Martin H. Funk, son Amos G. Funk and Elizabeth S. Herr.

6045. Zenas, Neffsville, Pa., b. June 4, 1875.

6046. Emma, Neffsville, Pa., b. June 2, 1877; d. Aug. 3, 1877.

Family of FRANCES HERR (2311) and ISAAC KAUFFMAN.

6047. Uriah, Mountville, Pa., b. May 8, 1859.

6048. Catherine, Mountville, Pa., b. Jan. 31, 1861; d. Jan. 16, 1862.

6049. Annie M., Mountville, Pa., b. Dec. 28, 1862.

6050. Addie, Mountville, Pa., b. Aug. 17, 1865.

6051. Henry, Mountville, Pa., b. Dec. 2, 1866.

6052. Frances, Mountville, Pa., b. Dec. 6, 1868.

Family of ABRAHAM HERR (2312) and MARTHA SHENK.

6053. Ephraim, East Petersburg, Pa., b. Oct. 1, 1864.

6054. Franklin, East Petersburg, Pa., b. Aug. 4, 1867.

6055. Susan, East Petersburg, Pa., b. June 11, 1869.

6056. Henry, East Petersburg, Pa., b. Aug. 19, 1875; d. Mar. 19, 1876.

6057. Ellen, East Petersburg, Pa., b. Oct. 18, 1877.

6058. Annie, East Petersburg, Pa., b. Aug. 25, 1880.

Family of CHRISTIAN HERR (2315) and MARY FUNK.

6059. Martin L., Lancaster, Pa., b. Aug. 15, 1870.
6060. Mattie, Lancaster, Pa., b. May 2, 1873; d. June 21, 1902; m. George W. Millhouse.
6061. Son, Lancaster, Pa., b. July 5, 1876; d. July 5, 1876.
6664. Son, Lancaster, Pa., b. July 5, 1876; d. July 5, 1876.
6062. Harvey G., Lancaster, Pa., b. June 1, 1879.

Family of ELIZABETH HORNBERGER (2316) and DAVID SNAVELY.

6063. Eliza, Springfield, O., m. ———— Snyder.
6064. Barbara, Springfield, O., m. ———— Miller.
6065. David H., Springfield, O., b. Jan. 27, 1845; m. Dec. 25, 1878, Dora Goodfellow, b. Sept. 17, 1756; dau. Thomas Goodfellow and Mary Sexton.
6066. Fanny, Springfield, O., m. ———— Marsh.
6067. Stephen, Springfield, O., m. ———— McLain.
6068. Henry, Springfield, O.
6069. Magdalene, Springfield, O., m. David Exter.
6070. Mary Susan, Springfield, O.
6071. George, Springfield, O.
6072. Jacob, Springfield, O.
6073. Caroline, Springfield, O.

Family of STEPHEN HORNBERGER (2318) and ANNA KIBLINGER.

6074. Stephen, Omaha, Neb.
6075. Alice Amelia, Pontiac, Ill., b. Feb. 22, 1848; d. May 28, 1874; m. Oct. 6, 1870, D. ———— C. Eyler.
6076. Rebecca Jane, Road House, Ill., b. Oct., 1850.
6077. Ann, Springfield, O.

Family of SUSAN HORNBERGER (2319) and BENJAMIN H. KAUFFMAN.

6078. Henry, Philadelphia, Pa.
6079. Aaron, Philadelphia, Pa.
6080. Mary, Philadelphia, Pa., m. John Strine, son Rev. ———— Strine and ————.

Family of MARY ANN HORNBERGER (2320) and HENRY R. MINICH.

6081. Barbara, Philadelphia, Pa., m. John H. Martin.
6082. Christiana, Philadelphia, Pa., m. Alexander Braisling.
6083. Stephen, Philadelphia, Pa.
6084. Franklin, Philadelphia, Pa.

Family of JOHN METZGAR (2324) and MARY METZGAR.

6085. Michael Henry, Lancaster, Pa.
6086. Jacob Augustus, Philadelphia, Pa.
6087. Son, Philadelphia, Pa.

Family of HENRY METZGAR (2325) and MARGARET DORWART.

6088. Jacob Albert, Millersville, Pa., m. Mary Ferree.

Family of EMANUEL METZGAR (2326) and ELIZABETH ESHLEMAN.

6089. Mary Elizabeth, Millersville, Pa.

Family of MARY METZGAR (2327) and REUBEN MONDERBACH.

6090. Morris, Millersville, Pa.
6091. Martin, Millersville, Pa.

Family of MARTIN METZGAR (2328) and ELIZABETH DORWART.

6092. George Albert, Millersville, Pa.

Family of MARY SEACHRIST (2353) and JACOB KREIDER.

6093. Jacob, Millersville, Pa., m. Anna Charles.
6094. John, Millersville, Pa., m. Anna Neff, dau. Jacob Neff and ——— Miller.
6095. Esther, Millersville, Pa., m. Jacob Miller, son John Miller and Anna Heller.
6096. Mary, Millersville, Pa., m. Jacob Rohrer, son Daniel Rohrer and Mary Kreider.

Family of JOHN HERR (2360) and ANNIE FREY.

6097. Jonas, Safe Harbor, Pa., b. Dec. 15, 1857; m. Oct. 20, 1878, Kate Keperling, dau. Abraham Keperling and Leah Ressel.
6098. ———, Safe Harbor, Pa.

6099. ———, Safe Harbor, Pa.
6100. ———, Safe Harbor, Pa.
6101. ———, Safe Harbor, Pa.

Family of BARBARA HERR (2368) and HENRY EBY.

6102. Henry, Buyerstown, Pa., b. Jan. 26, 1860; d. Aug. 11, 1879.
6103. Susanna, Buyerstown, Pa., d. Dec. 11, 1870.
6104. Abraham, Kinzers, Pa., b. Nov. 22; m. Salome Denlinger.
6105. Anna, San Francisco, Cal., m. ——— Kennedy.
6106. Christian, Buyerstown, Pa., b. 1869; d. Mar. 13, 1871.

Family of ELIZABETH HERR (2369) and SIMON RESSLER.

6107. Henry H., Lancaster, Pa., b. Feb. 29, 1864; d. May 7, 1864.
6108. Joseph A., Lancaster, Pa., b. Apr. 10, 1865; m. Naomi Hershey, b. Nov. 9, 1864: dau. Henry H. Hershey and Elizabeth Leaman.
6109. Mattie, Lancaster, Pa., b. Oct. 29, 1867; m. Josiah Book.
6110. Martin W., Lancaster, Pa., b. June 16, 1870.
6111. Jacob Miller, Lancaster, Pa., b. Nov. 8, 1872.
6112. Aaron O., Lancaster, Pa., b. Sept. 7, 1875.
6113. Simon E., Lancaster, Pa., b. Aug. 20, 1878.
6114. Phares H., New Providence, Pa., b. Dec. 26, 1880.

Family of MARY HERR (2370) and CHARLES FOREMAN.

6115. Henry, Smithville, Pa., b. Dec. 30, 1862.
6116. Annie, Smithville, Pa., b. Apr. 24, 1864.
6117. Hannah, Smithville, Pa., b. Mar. 9, 1866; m. Daniel Harkins.
6118. Susanna, Smithville, Pa., b. Mar. 16, 1872.

Family of HENRY HERR (2373) and MAGDALENA BUCKWALTER.

6119. Enos, New Providence, Pa., b. May 4, 1867; m. Anna Harnish.
6120. John, New Providence, Pa., b. Sept. 21, 1868; m. Nov. 28, 1891, Mary E. Huber, b. Apr. 1, 1869; dau. Jonas Huber and Susan Graver.
6121. Harry, New Providence, Pa., b. Mar. 22, 1870.
6122. Annie, New Providence, Pa., b. Aug. 28, 1871.

6123. Ida, New Providence, Pa., b. Jan. 26, 1873.

6124. Walter, New Providence, Pa., b. May 27, 1875; d. Oct. 23, 1879.

6125. Mattie, New Providence, Pa., b. July 2, 1878.

6126. Aaron, New Providence, Pa., b. Sept. 9, 1881.

Family of ABRAHAM B. HERR (2375) and SUSANNA S. ROHRER.

6127. Henry R., Lancaster, Pa., b. May 15, 1873; m. Oct. 1, 1903, Eva May Hutton, b. Apr. 11, 1878; dau. William K. Hutton and Carrie Sawyer.

6128. Jacob, Lancaster, Pa., b. Mar. 27, 1875; d. Apr. 21, 1875.

6129. Nora, Lancaster, Pa., b. Oct. 24, 1882; d. Oct. 25, 1882.

Family of LYDIA HERR (2376) and HENRY GOOD.

6130. Anna Luetta, Bareville, Pa., b. Oct. 23, 1873; m. Dec. 22, 1894, Nathan Rupp.

6131. Ira, Bareville, Pa., b. Feb. 10, 1879.

6132. Mary, Bareville, Pa., b. Feb. 10, 1881.

6133. Lydia May, Bareville, Pa., b. Aug. 18, 1885.

Family of EMANUEL HERR (2396) and MARY WITMER.

6134. David, Witmer, Pa.

6135. Hettie, Witmer, Pa.

6136. Lizzie, Witmer, Pa., m. Reuben L. Esbenshade (5255).

Family of ELIAS HERR (2397) and MARY L. ROHRER.

6137. Aaron, Greenland, Pa., b. Dec. 8, 1866; d. Oct. 23, 1872.

6138. Elam R., Lancaster, Pa., b. Jan. 13, 1874.

Family of ADAM H. HERR (2399) and CATHERINE KILHEFFER (2862).

6139. Chester G., Lancaster, Pa., b. Feb. 7, 1881.

6140. Edmund B., Lancaster, Pa., b. Apr. 13, 1882; m. Apr. 14, 1901, Catherine Rote, b. Nov. 11, 1882; dau. Columbus Rote and Eva B. Acker.

6141. Minnie, Lancaster, Pa., b. July 15, 1884; d. Jan. 10, 1885.

6142. Solomon K., Lancaster, Pa., b. Apr. 11, 1886.

6143. Mildred, Lancaster, Pa., b. Oct. 16, 1890.

6144. Florence, Lancaster, Pa., b. July 24, 1894.

Family of CHRISTIAN SCHEETZ (2400) and CATHERINE GRABILL.

6145. Abraham, Lancaster, Pa., b. Nov. 27, 1838; m. Oct. 15, 1860, Louisa Marshall, b. Aug. 1, 1837; dau. Junius P. Marshall and Sidney Wilson.

6146. Henry, Millersville, Pa., m. Annie Odstodt.

6147. Sarah, Millersville, Pa., m. Philip A. Urich.

6148. Kate, Millersville, Pa.

6149. Christopher, Milersville, Pa., d. Infant.

Family of FREDERICK SCHEETZ (2401) and FANNIE ROHRER.

6150. Barbara, Petersburg, Pa., b. Dec. 17, 1840.

6151. Aaron, Lancaster, Pa., b. May 22, 1843.

Family of JOHN P. FRICK (2408) and HANNAH HERSHEY.

6152. William Henry, York, Pa., b. July 28, 1840; d. July 17, 1873.

6153. Benjamin Franklin, York, Pa., b. June 9, 1841; m. Dec. 21, 1871, Emma J. Sechrist, b. Jan. 29, 1852; dau. Jacob A. Sechrist and Mary Snyder.

6154. John P., York, Pa., b. Feb. 24, 1843; m. Sept. 7, 1869, Mary L. Myers, b. June 2, 1845; dau. Rev. Thomas Myers and Sarah A. Norris.

6155. Abraham, York, Pa., b. June 22, 1844; d. Feb. 12, 1877; m. Mar. 8, 1867, Anna E. Bond, b. Dec. 17, 1849; d. May 27, 1875; dau. Daniel Bond and Annie Frick.

6156. Mary Ellen, York, Pa., b. July 7, 1846; m. Mar. 6, 1874, Martin J. Skinner, b. Dec. 5, 1842; d. Jan. 9, 1879.

6157. Daniel Brandt, York, Pa., b. Oct. 17, 1851; d. May 17, 1852.

6158. Joseph Hershey, York, Pa., b. Jan. 16, 1856; d. Nov. 3, 1882.

Family of MARIA FRICK (2409) and LEVI SLAGLE WINTERODE.

6159. John Luther, Finksburg, Md., b. June 2, 1837; d. Jan. 12, 1881; m. Barbara Cross.

6160. Jacob Frick, Pikesville, Md., b. Aug. 18, 1839; d. Feb. 12, 1869.

6161. Anna Mary, Baltimore, Md., b. June 1, 1841; m. Aug. 9, 1860, William A. Burk, b. Apr. 23, 1830; d. Aug. 19, 1897; son Andrew Burk and Casander ———.

6162. Henry Michael, Baltimore, Md., b. Oct. 13, 1843; d. Mar. 20, 1861.

6163. Amanda Elizabeth, Baltimore, Md., b. Mar. 7, 1846; m. Oct. 19, 1869, Asbury Watts, b. July 31, 1835; son Benjamin Watts and Rachel ———.

6164. George Carroll, Baltimore, Md., b. Oct. 3, 1848; m. 1873, Mary Louisa Watts, dau. Benjamin Watts and Rachel ———.

6165. William Rufus, Baltimore, Md., b. Feb. 5, 1851; d. Jan. 24, 1883; m. Fannie Lewin.

6166. Flora Belle V., Manchester, Md., b. Dec. 20, 1852; d. Aug. 5, 1853.

6167. Charlotte Ann, b. May 28, 1854; d. May 24, 1857.

6168. Amelia Florence, Manchester, Md., b. Apr. 6, 1857; d. Sept. 16, 1857.

6169. Levi Preston, Arcadia, Md., b. July 17, 1859; d. Oct. 5, 1889.

Family of CHRISTIAN FRICK (2410) and MATILDA SPECK.

6170. John, Abbottstown, Pa., b. Oct. 30, 1852; d. Dec. 29, 1890; m. Lydian Krout, b. May, 1857; dau. Michael Krout and ———.

6171. Laura E., Dillsburg, Pa., b. Oct., 1852; m. Dec. 16, 1875, Frederick Bentz, b. Aug. 15, 1851; son Jacob L. Bentz and Elizabeth Slothone.

6172. Elizabeth Ann, Malvern, Ia., b. May 19, 1854; m. Oct. 30, 1879, Joseph Deardorf.

6173. Jacob Martin, Hall, Pa., b. Nov. 22, 1855; m. Oct. 30, 1879, Hattie B. Speck, b. Oct. 30, 1855.

6174. Charlotte, Manchester, Md., b. Sept. 4, 1858.

Family of ENGLEHART A. FRICK (2413) and CECELIA JANE SHOWER.

6175. George Arnold, Norfolk, Va., b. Apr. 6, 1861.

6176. Mary Elizabeth, Manchester, Md., b. Nov. 22, 1863; d. Aug. 20, 1879.

6177. Clarence Englehart, Charlotte, N. C., b. June 15, 1866.

6178. Rachael Shower, Shelly, N. C., b. Jan. 4, 1869; d. Aug. 25, 1887.

6179. Emma Virginia, Shelly, N. C., b. July 4, 1871.

Family of **ANNA ELIZA SUMMY** (2424) and **NELSON JAMES HILLMAN**.

6180. Aldo J., Wilhelm, N. J., b. Aug. 7, 1854; d. Mar., 1858.
6181. Clara, South Bend, Ind., b. Mar. 8, 1859; m. June 18. 1884, Francis A. Marsh, b. Jan. 18, 1856; son William W. Marsh and Sylvia C. ———.
6182. Florence B., Washington, D. C., b. Aug. 15, 1867.

Family of **ORLANDO DAVID SUMMY** (2427) and **IDA MARIA IRWIN**.

6183. Herbert Irwin, Washington, D. C., b. Aug. 30, 1872; d. Jan. 26, 1878.
6184. Carolyn May, Washington, D. C., b. May. 4, 1876; m. Sept. 7, 1897, James C. Kirby, b. Sept. 12, 1874; son Thomas L. Kirby and M. Virginia Jackson.

Family of **BENJAMIN WEST SUMMY** (2429) and **KATE STRONG**.

6185. Katherine, Vienna, Va., b. Apr. 17, 1887.
6186. Helen, Vienna, Va., b. Nov. 6, 1888.
6187. Margaret J., Vienna, Va., b. Oct. 30, 1893; d. May 5, 1895.

Family of **FRANK L. SUMMY** (2430) and **ISABELLE M. STEPHENSON**.

6188. William Frank, Washington, D. C., b. May 12, 1881.
6189. Ethel Isabelle, Washington, D. C., b. Mar. 20, 1888.

Family of **ISAAC FRANTZ** (2431) and **ANNA NEWCOMER**.

6190. David, Galveston, Tex., b. Apr. 16, 1837.
6191. Mary, Lawrence, Kans., b. July 16, 1835; m. James Elliott.
6192. Salinda, Chambersburg, Pa., b. Apr. 17, 1839; d. Feb. 28, 1873; m. William Spear.
6193. Anna Barbara, Berwick, Pa., b. Apr. 28, 1841; d. Apr. 16, 1890; m. July 8, 1868, Rev. Henry S. Mendenhall, b. Aug. 1, 1829; d. Feb. 5, 1899.
6194. Martha, Chambersburg, Pa., b. June 12, 1844; m. Nov. 25, 1873, Joseph Bomberger, b. Aug. 22, 1847; son Joseph Bomberger and Sarah Erb.

Family of **CHRISTIAN FRANTZ** (2435) and **LEAH STAUFFER**.

6195. Elizabeth, Mercersburg, Pa., b. Aug. 23, 1843; m. Oct. 23, 1866, Simon P. Hawbicker, b. Nov. 14, 1843.

6196. Sarah, Mercersburg, Pa., b. Sept. 5, 1845; m. Oct. 25, 1864, Thomas O. Dailey, b. Dec. 24, 1839; d. Sept. 5, 1898.

6197. Albert, Mercersburg, Pa., b. Oct. 30, 1847.

6198. Benjamin, Mercersburg, Pa., b. Dec. 29, 1849; m. Jan. 16, 1896, Annie L. Frick.

6199. Annie, Mercersburg, Pa., b. June 5, 1852; d. June 5, 1900.

6200. Christian, Mercersburg, Pa., b. May 13, 1854; m. Dec. 22, 1880, Sarah Noble.

6201. Jacob, Mercersburg, Pa., b. Sept. 5, 1856; m. Sept. 13, 1896, Annie Stauffer.

6202. Martha, Mercersburg, Pa., b. Oct. 15, 1858; d. May 2, 1875.

6203. Emma, Mercersburg, Pa., b. June 30, 1861; d. Aug. 25, 1865.

6204. Etta, Mercersburg, Pa., b. May 10, 1864.

6205. John E., Mercersburg, Pa., b. Feb. 27, 1867; m. Apr. 24, 1895, Edith C. Herr (4612).

Family of Dr. BENJAMIN FRANTZ (2437) and MARY A. RYDER.

6206. Samuel Ryder, Waynesboro, Pa., b. Sept. 25, 1850; m. Mar. 18, 1879, Mary E. Benson, b. Mar. 24, 1850; dau. Samuel Benson and Elizabeth Fegan.

6207. Charlotte Elizabeth, Lucerne, Ind., b. Sept. 23, 1851; m. Mar. 3, 1874, George M. D. Bell, b. Jan. 30, 1846; son George Bell and Mary A. Mickley.

6208. Caroline, Harrisburg, Pa., b. Feb. 19, 1853; m. Feb. 10, 1876, John A. Marshbank, b. June 8, 1851; son John D. Marshbank and Sophia McIntyre.

6209. Joseph, Waynesboro, Pa., b. Oct. 24, 1854; m. Mar. 5, 1879, Gertrude Smith, b. June 29, 1857; dau. Samuel K. Smith and Jemima Breneman.

6210. Mary, Waynesboro, Pa., b. Dec. 8, 1856; d. Apr. 10, 1857.

6211. Isaac, Waynesboro, Pa., b. Feb. 20, 1858; d. Mar. 31, 1901.

6212. Abraham, Philadelphia, Pa., b. Nov. 13, 1861.

6213. Anna, Waynesboro, Pa., b. July 23, 1864.

6214. John, Waynesboro, Pa., b. Feb. 10, 1867; m. Aug. 20, 1891, Mary V. Mundey, b. June 13, 1869; dau. Thaddeus J. Mundey and Rose Bloominhour.

6215. Mary Ryder, Waynesboro, Pa., b. Nov. 5, 1873.

6216. Herman Benjamin, Waynesboro, Pa., b. May 18, 1875.

Family of ANNA FRANTZ (2438) and Rev. MARTIN HOOVER.

6217. Christian, Providence, R. I., b. Oct. 28, 1856; d. Apr. 1, 1874.

6218. Emma, Waynesboro, Pa., b. Apr. 19, 1858.

Family of GEORGE FRICK (2442) and FREDERICKA OPPENLANDER.

6219. Franklin, Waynesboro, Pa., b. Sept. 23, 1850; d. Aug. 7, 1872.

6220. Abraham O., Waynesboro, Pa., b. June 16, 1852; m. Sept. 17, 1878, Louisa Hatter, dau. Martin Hatter and Fredericka Lyons; m. Mar. 7, 1888, Margie Mehaffy, dau. Samuel Mehaffy and Margaret Cassel.

6221. Martin, Waynesboro, Pa., b. Feb. 20, 1854; d. Sept. 17, 1855.

6222. Ezra O., Waynesboro, Pa., b. Jan. 12, 1856; m. Feb. 26, 1885, Catherine Mehaffy, b. Aug. 28, 1861; dau. Samuel Mehaffy and Margaret Cassel.

6223. Amos M., Waynesboro, Pa., b. Dec. 2, 1857; m. Dec. 20, 1883, Mollie Stover, dau. Christian Stover and ——— Shenk.

6224. Anna Elizabeth, Waynesboro, Pa., b. Mar. 24, 1860; d. Oct. 17, 1867.

6225. Frederick, Waynesboro, Pa., b. Mar. 1, 1863; m. May 8, 1887, Amanda Sprenkley, b. Aug. 9, 1859; dau. Isaiah Sprenkley and Susan Frantz.

6226. Anna Mary, Waynesboro, Pa., b. Nov. 19, 1865; m. July 19, 1892, Victor Good, b. Aug. 7, 1857; son David Good and Elizabeth Deitrich.

Family of ELIZABETH P. FRICK (2453) and JACOB NEFF HAVERSTICK.

6227. Harvey Frick, Lancaster, Pa., b. July 11, 1858; m. Nov. 3, 1880, Annie E. Stoner (7530).

Family of LYDIA P. FRICK (2454) and BENJAMIN N. LANDIS.

6228. Franklin F., Waynesboro, Pa., b. Feb. 25, 1845; m. Nov. 21, 1869, Elizabeth H. Hershey, b. Dec. 11, 1845; dau. Samuel Hershey and Elizabeth Harnish.

6229. Ezra F., La Belle, N. Y., b. Dec. 28, 1846; m. Feb. 18, 1872, Catherine Anthes.

6230. Mary Ann, Lancaster, Pa., b. Sept. 1, 1848; m. Dec. 24, 1868, Jacob D. Kohr, b. Apr. 14, 1845; son John Kohr and ———.

6231. Elizabeth F., Sanborn, N. Y., b. May 24, 1850; m. Dec. 17, 1873, Eli J. H. Treichler (5144).

6232. Salome, Waynesboro, Pa., b. Feb. 27, 1852; m. Mar. 6, 1881, Jacob K. Miller.

6233. Abraham B., Waynesboro, Pa., b. Apr. 14, 1854; m. Jan. 7, 1877, Leah H. Landis, b. Feb. 9, 1855; dau. Benjamin Landis and Mary Hoover.

6234. Emma, Waynesboro, Pa., b. Feb. 15, 1856; m. May 17, 1891, Jacob G. Frick, b. Apr. 10, 1865.

Family of ANNA P. FRICK (2455) and JACOB M. FRANTZ.

6235. Franklin F., Lancaster, Pa., b. July 19, 1846; m. May 1, 1871, Mary C. Best, b. Dec. 14, 1850; d. Oct. 20, 1900; dau. John Best and Anna M. Albright.

6236. Benjamin, Lancaster, Pa., b. June 28, 1848; d. Aug. 21, 1851.

6237. Christian, Lancaster, Pa., b. Aug. 16, 1850; d. Sept. 12, 1851.

6238. Jacob F., New Rochelle, N. Y., b. July 29, 1852; m. Oct. 3, 1878, Gertrude L. Osborn, b. Mar. 15, 1857; dau. Joseph H. Osborne and Joanna Kemble.

6239. Andrew, Lancaster, Pa., b. Jan. 14, 1855; m. July 26, 1881, Susanna Herr Bausman (2855).

6240. Son, Lancaster, Pa., b. Apr. 6, 1857; d. Apr. 6, 1857.

6241. Abraham, Wilmington, Del., b. Sept. 2, 1858; m. Jan. 14, 1885, Carrie Remson, b. Sept. 22, 1863; dau. John Remson and Jane Osborne.

6242. Charles, Lancaster, Pa., b. June 23, 1862; d. Feb. 3, 1864.

6243. Mary Elizabeth, Millersville, Pa., b. Oct. 30, 1864; d. Sept. 16, 1897; m. Apr. 6, 1892, Wid. Dr. Jacob M. Shartle, b. Nov. 19, 1856; son John Shartle and Maria Miller.

6244. Anna, Greensburg, Pa., b. Jan. 18, 1867; m. Sept. 17, 1890, Rev. Stanley L. Krebs, b. Feb. 14, 1864; son Walter E. Krebs and Isabella Lefevre.

6245. Edward, Lancaster, Pa., b. Feb. 14, 1872.

Family of MARIA P. FRICK (2456) and JOHN BOWMAN (4061).

6246. Jacob F., Galesburg, Ill., b. Oct. 4, 1853; m. Oct. 18, 1876, Elizabeth A. Brackbill (8305).

6247. Abraham F., Dayton, O., b. Oct. 8, 1855; m. Nov. 28, 1875, Anna M. Allen, b. June 22, 1855; dau. Andrew J. Allen and Mary J. Bond.

6248. John, Springfield, O., b. Feb. 26, 1858; m. Dec. 9, 1885, Susan Dunkle, b. Sept. 15, 1859; dau. John Dunkle and Mahala Hackman.

6249. Anna, Forgy, O., b. May 6, 1860; m. Oct. 16, 1890, Luther M. Frick, b. Aug. 25, 1850; son John D. Frick and Louisa A. Stoner.

6250. Henry, Forgy, O., b. Feb. 17, 1862; d. Nov. 1, 1862.

6251. Franklin, Normal, Ill., b. Oct. 11, 1863; m. Myrtle Boyd.

6252. Harvey, Forgy, O., b. Mar. 3, 1866.

6253. Amos, Forgy, O., b. Mar. 14, 1869; d. Sept. 19, 1869.

6254. Ezra, Forgy, O., b. Mar. 14, 1869; d. Sept. 2, 1869.

6255. Mary, Osborne, O., b. Oct. 13, 1870; m. Mar. 5, 1899, Phares D. Swartley, b. Mar. 19, 1861; son Joseph Swartley and Martha Denlinger.

6256. Salinda, Forgy, O., b. Feb. 12, 1873; d. June 15, 1881.

6257. Ernest, Forgy, O., b. Nov. 19, 1875.

Family of Dr. ABRAHAM P. FRICK (2457) and MARY K. SMITH.

6258. Euclid Bernardo, Cuba, West Indies, b. July 29, 1867; m. Oct. 30, 1889, Sarah E. Bunting, b. Sept. 15, 1866; dau. John H. Bunting and Anna C. Ogburn.

Family of ANNA ROYER (2466) and MOYER HOOVER.

6259. Mary Elizabeth, Leacock, Pa., b. Mar. 18, 1849; m. June 5, 1878, Elam S. Hershey.

6260. Emma Rebecca, Leacock, Pa., b. June 11, 1851.

6261. Hiram M., Leacock, Pa., b. July 14, 1853; m. Eva Loundagin.

6262. Alice Ann, Lancaster, Pa., b. Jan. 25, 1855; m. Harvey S. Bowers.

6263. Amelia Salome, Leacock, Pa., b. July 16, 1857; m. Jacob M. Bowers.

18

6264. Ada Rachel, Leacock, Pa., b. July 16, 1857; m. Robert R. Lindsey.
6265. Laura Louisa, Leacock, Pa., b. May 20, 1859; m. Rev. James M. Shelly.

Family of RACHAEL ROYER (2467) and JACOB A. BAIR.

6266. Henry M., Leacock, Pa., b. Dec. 30, 1853; d. Mar. 28, 1877.
6267. Josephine R., Leacock, Pa., b. Sept. 26, 1855; m. Jan. 25, 1877.
6268. Anna M., Leacock, Pa, b. May 28, 1858.
6269. Katherine A., Leacock, Pa., b. June 20, 1860.
6270. Elizabeth, Leacock, Pa., b. Nov. 24, 1862.
6271. Clara E., Leacock, Pa., b. Mar. 13, 1865.
6272. Rachael S., Leacock, Pa., b. May 11, 1868; m. May 8, 1896.
6273. Jacob R., Leacock, Pa., b. June 27, 1870; m. Dec. 21, 1872.
6274. J. ——Clement, Leacock, Pa., b. Feb. 1, 1873.

Family of JOHN R. RUTTER (2476) and CAROLINE SNADER.

6275. Hettie A., New Holland, Pa., b. May 17, 1841.
6276. Amos S., New Holland, Pa., b. Oct. 11, 1842; m. May 4, 1869, Sarah L. Entriken, b. Feb. 17, 1848.
6277. Joseph, New Holland, Pa., b. Oct. 30, 1845; d. July 2, 1863.
6278. John S., New Holland, Pa., b. Nov. 5, 1846; d. Feb. 3, 1847.
6279. Jacob, New Holland, Pa., b. Dec. 9, 1847.
6280. Elias, New Holland, Pa., b. Mar. 29, 1850; d. Jan. 16, 1869.
6281. Susanna, New Holland, Pa., b. Sept. 1, 1852.
6282. Jerry S., Lancaster, Pa., b. Sept. 5, 1854; m. Feb. 2, 1884, Kate L. Peters, b. Apr. 15, 1859.

Family of Wid. JOHN R. RUTTER (2476) and ANNA FREYMEYER.

6283. Elizabeth, New Holland, Pa., b. July 16, 1856.
6284. Mary A., New Holland, Pa., b. July 16, 1860.
6285. Amanda, New Holland, Pa., b. Feb. 12, 1862.
6286. Salome, New Holland, Pa., b. July 27, 1868.

Family of JONATHAN R. RUTTER (2481) and RACHAEL HOOVER.

6287. Amanda, Intercourse, Pa., b. Oct. 22, 1854; d. June 6, 1857.
6288. Lucinda, Intercourse, Pa., b. Jan. 17, 1856; d. Apr. 10, 1896; m. Dec. 22, 1887, Amos Lefevre.

6289. Amelia, Intercourse, Pa., b. July 18, 1857; d. Sept. 1, 1880.

6290. Emma Louisa, Intercourse, Pa., b. Mar. 14, 1859; d. Oct. 25, 1864.

6291. Franklin H., Intercourse, Pa., b. May 16, 1860; d. May 23, 1861.

6292. Amos G., Intercourse, Pa., b. Apr. 6, 1862; m. Nov. 30. 1886, Laura Good, b. July 2, 1864; dau. William Good and Savilla Sweigart.

6293. Jason E., Intercourse, Pa., b. —— 10, 1864; m. June 13, 1896, Laura Ranck, b. Sept. 16, 1867; dau. Daniel W. Ranck and Sue Emrey.

6294. Harry H., Intercourse, Pa., b. Sept. 18, 1866; d. Apr. 29, 1867.

6295. Aaron H, Intercourse, Pa., b. Mar. 21, 1868; m. Nov. 15, 1896, Jane Johnson.

6296. Catherine W., Intercourse, Pa., b. Dec. 3, 1871.

Family of AMOS RUTTER (2482) and CATHERINE E. MENTZER.

6297. Eugene M., New Holland, Pa., b. Mar. 7, 1859; m. Mar. 6, 1884, Annie E. Gehr, b. Feb. 14, 1860; dau. John Gehr and Catherine E. McIntyre.

6298. Lillian May, New Holland, Pa.

Family of LEAH RUTTER (2485) and PHILIP SHEAFFER.

6299. Martin, Bareville, Pa., m. Caroline Graybill; m. Charlotte Myers.

Family of HENRY FRICK (2493) and MARIA METZ.

6300. Orlando, Williamsville, N. Y., b. Oct. 29, 1853.

6301. Barbara, Williamsville, N. Y., b. Aug. 1, 1855.

6302. Sarah Maria, Williamsville, N. Y., b. Jan. 6, 1858.

6303. William Henry, Williamsville, N. Y., b. May 4, 1860.

Family of ANNIE HERSHEY (2497) and ISAAC KULP.

6304. John H., Bachmanville, Pa., b. Sept. 25, 1855.

6305. Emma, Parkesburg, Pa., b. June 9, 1857; m. Daniel Dorsheimer.

6306. Menno, Parkesburg, Pa., b. Aug. 13, 1861; d. Feb. 28, 1897.

6307. Henry, Parkesburg, Pa., b. Nov. 1867; d. Dec., 1886.

Family of MARTIN HERSHEY (2498) and MARY ANN SHARTLE.

6308. Amos S., Bloomington, Ind., b. July 4, 1867; m. Sept. 6, 1892, Lillian Wilcox, dau. A. ——— J. Wilcox and Angelina Wantman.

6309. Ida S., Harrisburg, Pa., b. Dec. 28, 1869; m. Sept. 17, 1891, Clinton M. Hershey, b. Dec. 22, 1868; son Christian L. Hershey and Fannie Mumma.

Family of ELIZABETH HERSHEY (2499) and Rev. Wid. MARTIN HOOVER.

6310. Annie, Waynesboro, Pa., b. Feb. 6, 1867.

6311. Leah, Waynesboro, Pa., b. Sept. 8, 1871.

Family of MENNO FRICK HERSHEY (2503) and MALINDA MOTTER.

6312. John M., Baltimore, Md., b. Dec. 30, 1865.

6313. Omer, Baltimore, Md., b. Sept. 23, 1867; m. June 5, 1892, Sylvia Sheaffer.

Family of MARIA HERSHEY (2505) and JACOB WENGER.

6314. Morris, Paradise, Pa., b. Oct. 22, 1871.

6315. Harry, Paradise, Pa., b. June 20, 1874; d. Oct. 25, 1893.

6316. John, Paradise, Pa., b. Oct. 1, 1875; d. Dec. 10, 1875.

6317. Letitia, Paradise, Pa., b. Dec. 1, 1876.

6318. Mary, Paradise, Pa., b. Sept. 27, 1880.

6319. Fannie, Paradise, Pa., b. Apr. 17, 1883.

Family of MARY BALMER (2506) and REUBEN STRICKLER.

6320. Albert, Sporting Hill, Pa., b. Feb. 24, ——; d. July 8, 1867.

Family of ANNA BALMER (2507) and HENRY BEAMSDERFER.

6321. Anna Mary, Manheim, Pa., b. —— 24, 1876; d. Nov. 5, 1896.

Family of HENRY L. FRICK (2512) and SARAH E. GRINER.

6322. Henrietta, Coldwater, O., m. John Cole.

6323. Margaret Ann, Coldwater, O., m. George Arbaugh.

6324. Sarah Jane, Coldwater, O., m. James Andrews; m. Jesse Meyers.

6325. Jacob, Celma, O.

6326. Eva Elizabeth, Celma, O., m. Samuel Claigg.

6327. Agnes, Coldwater, O., m. Calvin Yancy.

6328. William Henry, Celma, O., m. Elizabeth Kittle.

6329. Edward, Chicago, Ill.

6330. Jacob, Coldwater, O.

Family of DAVID W. FRICK (2516) and MARGARET ANN SNIDER.

6331. Laura Gertrude, Minster, O., b. Nov. 10, 1867; m. Mar. 12, 1885, Henry H. Jaspers.

6332. Mary Maud, Chatham, Ont., Can., b. Mar. 2, 1869; m. Feb. 12, 1890, Lewis Paul.

6333. Joanna Kate, Chatham, Ont., Can., b. Jan. 8, 1873; m. Sept. 9, 1894, Henry Fritz.

6334. Jacob Daniel, Chatham, Ont., Can., b. Nov. 1, 1875; d. Apr. 12, 1877.

6335. Addie Belle, Jackson, Mich., b. Apr. 19, 1878; m. Jan. 21, 1901, Melvin H. Rowley.

Family of DAVID BLOCHER (2519) and CATHERINE WINNOWER.

6336. Elizabeth, Buffalo, N. Y.

6337. Sarah, Buffalo, N. Y.

6338. Fanny, Buffalo, N. Y.

6339. Eliza, Buffalo, N. Y.

6340. Susan, Buffalo, N. Y.

6341. Clara, Buffalo, N. Y.

6342. May, Buffalo, N. Y., m. Frank Hoover.

6343. Nancy, Buffalo, N. Y.

Family of DANIEL BLOCHER (2525) and ELIZABETH METZ.

6344. Harriet, Buffalo, N. Y., b. 1845; m. Tobias Berry.

6345. Amelia, Buffalo, N. Y., b. Nov. 10, 1847; m. John Longenecker.

6346. Maria, Buffalo, N. Y., b. Oct. 1, 1850.

6347. Ida May, Buffalo, N. Y., b. Aug. 27, 1863.

Family of HENRY BLOCHER (2526) and CATHERINE LEOPARD.

6348. Harriet, Buffalo, N. Y., m. John Nelson.

6349. Andrew, Buffalo, N. Y., m. Nettie Nelson.

6350. Henry, Buffalo, N. Y., m. Amelia ———.

Family of JOHN BLOCHER (2527) and ELIZA NEFF.

6351. Nelson, Buffalo, N. Y., b. Feb. —, 1848; d. ———, 1883.

Family of BENJAMIN F. ESHLEMAN (2537) and FANNY GRUMBINE.

6352. Elizabeth, Rothsville, Pa., m. ——— Leeking.

Family of SAMUEL ESHLEMAN (2538) and ——— CEARFOSS.

6353. Samuel, Maugansville, Md.
6354. Lillian, Maugansville, Md.
6355. William F., Warahachie, Tex.

Family of JOHN ESHLEMAN (2544) and ELIZABETH STRITE.

6356. Daniel, Smithburg, Md., b. June 18, 1849; m. Dec. 4, 1873, Susanna Horst, b. Mar. 31, 1855; d. Apr. 10, 1889; dau. Christian Horst and Leah Smith; m. Dec. 10, 1891, Annie E. Shank, b. Dec. 31, 1853; d. Mar. 25, 1901; dau. Joseph Shank and Mary Snavely; m. Sept. 6, 1903, Susanna Myers, b. Feb. 23, 1847; dau. Henry Myers and Sophia Shank.
6357. Mary Anna, Smithburg, Md., b. Dec. 23, 1850.
6358. John S., Leitersburg, Md., b. Sept. 16, 1852; d. Sept. 7, 1892; m. Nov. 4, 1875, Ann Malinda Strite (6444).
6359. Elizabeth, Marion, Pa., b. Sept. 2, 1854; m. Nov. 20, 1884, John L. Shank, b. Sept. 21, 1857; son Frederick Shank and Mary Lesher.
6360. Henry, Marion, Pa., b. Oct. 27, 1856; d. July 12, 1859.
6361. Samuel P., Orrville, O., b. July 6, 1859; m. Jan. 28, 1886, Elizabeth Bechtel.

Family of Wid. JOHN ESHLEMAN (2544) and FANNY SIEGRIST.

6362. Emma, Hagerstown, Md., b. Sept. 20, 1867.
6363. Leah, Hagerstown, Md., b. Nov. 4, 1868; m. Jan. 7, 1896, Peter Horst, b. Aug. 16, 1852; son Abraham Horst and Barbara Eshleman.
6364. Catherine, Hagerstown, Md., b. Nov. 1, 1870; d. Aug., 1871.
6644. Jacob C., Hagerstown, Md., b. Jan. 29, 1875.

Family of SAMUEL ESHLEMAN (2545) and SUSAN LESHER.

6365. Anna, Reid, Md., m. Daniel Landis.
6366. ——, Reid, Md.
6367. ——, Reid, Md.

Family of JONAS ESHLEMAN (2546) and MARY WHISLER.

6368. Jacob W., Hagerstown, Md., m. Maria Baer.
6369. Leah, Hagerstown, Md.
6370. Catherine, Hagerstown, Md., m. Samuel Parrett.
6371. Mary, Maugansville, Md., m. David Horst.
6372. Abraham, Landisville, Pa.
6373. Annie, Maugansville, Md., m. Samuel H. Martin.
6374. Martha, Maugansville, Md., m. Martin Risser.
6375. Henry, Landisville, Pa.
6376. Jonas W., Mason and Dixon, Pa., b. Sept. 6, 1871; m. Sept. 6, 1893, Nora F. Gearhart, b. Sept. 2, 1875; m. —— Bally; m. Elizabeth Miller.

Family of NANCY ESHLEMAN (2551) and HENRY KURTZ.

6377. ——, North Lawrence, O.
6378. ——, North Lawrence, O.
6379. ——, North Lawrence, O.

Family of Wid. NANCY ESHLEMAN (2551) and SAMUEL SHOWALTER.

6380. ——, North Lawrence, O.
6380. ——, North Lawrence, O.
6382. ——, North Lawrence, O.

Family of CHRISTIAN ESHLEMAN (2552) and MARY GARDNER.

6383. ——, North Lawrence, O.
6384. ——, North Lawrence, O.
6385. ——, North Lawrence, O.

Family of DAVID ESHLEMAN (2556) and HARRIET ROWLAND.

6386. ——, Mt. Caln, Tex.
6387. ——, Mt. Caln, Tex.
6388. ——, Mt. Caln, Tex.

6389. ———, Mt. Caln, Tex.
6390. ———, Mt. Caln, Tex.
6391. ———, Mt. Caln, Tex.

Family of SAMUEL ESHLEMAN (2558) and ANNA MARTIN.

6392. ———, North Lawrence, O.
6393. ———, North Lawrence, O.
6394. ———, North Lawrence, O.
6395. ———, North Lawrence, O.
6396. ———, North Lawrence, O.
6397. ———, North Lawrence, O.
6398. ———, North Lawrence, O.
6399. ———, North Lawrence, O.
6400. ———, North Lawrence, O.
6401. ———, North Lawrence, O.
6402. ———, North Lawrence, O.

Family of JONAS ESHLEMAN (2559) and FANNY MARTIN.

6403. Jacob, North Lawrence, O.
6404. Jonas, North Lawrence, O.
6405. John, North Lawrence, O.
6406. Abraham, North Lawrence, O.

Family of Wid. JONAS ESHLEMAN (2559) and MARTHA MARTIN.

6407. Amos, North Lawrence, O.
6408. Ezra, North Lawrence, O.
6409. Daniel, North Lawrence, O.
6410. Henry, North Lawrence, O.
6411. Lizzie, Luverne, Minn., m. W. ——— K. Wise.
6412. Nancy, Luverne, Minn.
6413. Mary, Luverne, Minn.
6414. Martha, Luverne, Minn.

Family of DAVID STRITE (2597) and ELIZABETH HORST.

6415. Mary Ann, Reid, Md., m. ——— Hykes.
6416. Martha L., Leitersburg, Md.
6417. John A., Leitersburg, Md.

6418. Elizabeth C., Leitersburg, Md.

6419. David G., Leitersburg, Md.

6420. Franklin M., Maugansville, Md.

6421. Ida C., Mason and Dixon, Pa., m. Joseph H. Eshleman (11874).

6422. Emma S., Leitersburg, Md., m. Henry L. Strite (6446).

Family of JOHN STRITE (2599) and EVA SHANK.

6423. Henry Clinton, Leitersburg, Md.

6424. Clinton, Leitersburg, Md.

6425. Samuel, San Francisco, Cal.

6426. Harvey, San Francisco, Cal.

Family of Wid. JOHN STRITE (2599) and MARY SHANK.

6427. John F., Leitersburg, Md.

6428. Benjamin, Leitersburg, Md.

Family of SAMUEL STRITE (2604) and ESTHER ANN HOOVER SHANK.

6429. Abraham C., Hagerstown, Md., b. Sept. 7, 1860; m. June 15, 1899, Louella Claggett, b. Sept. 10, 1874; dau. George W. Claggett and Sarah E. Carson.

6430. Jacob A., Chambersburg, Pa., b. June 19, 1864; m. May 21, 1891, Emma N. Durboraw, b. July 7, 1870; dau Daniel W. Durboraw and Martha L. Slick.

6431. Samuel M. (Lieut. U. S. N.), Hagerstown, Md., b. June 2, 1866.

6432. Mary E., Hagerstown, Md., b. Oct. 6, 1867.

6433. Emma K., Leitersburg, Md., b. July 15, 1869; m. Apr. 4, 1901, Franklin D. Bell, b. Dec. 4, 1865; son Upton Bell and Mary Bell.

6434. John C., Leitersburg, Md., b. Feb. 28, 1871; m. Nov. 22, 1906, Louisa Temperance Miller, b. Mar. 5, 1878; dau. Benjamin F. Miller and Matilda Ecker.

6435. Louis E. McC., Hagerstown, Md., b. Aug. 19, 1872.

6436. William A., Hagerstown, Md., b. Sept. 3, 1875; m. Nov. 25, 1897, Ella Elizabeth Bear, b. Apr. 7, 1877; dau. Levi Bear and Adalaide Koontz.

6437. Dr. Clarence E. (U. S. N.), Hagerstown, Md., b. Sept. 12, 1877.

6438. Cora M., Hagerstown, Md., b. Jan. 24, 1884.

Family of DANIEL STRITE (2605) and JENNY YOUNG.

6439. Daniel D., Hagerstown, Md.

Family of ELIZABETH STRITE (2616) and ADAM BAKER.

6440. Daughter, Shady Grove, Pa., d. infant.
6441. ———, Shady Grove, Pa.
6442. ———, Shady Grove, Pa.
6443. ———, Shady Grove, Pa.

Family of JOSEPH STRITE (2618) and CATHERINE LESHER.

6444. Ann Malinda, Leitersburg, Md., b. Oct. 21, 1857; d. Dec. 24,
1884; m. John S. Eshleman (6358).
6445. Maria Elizabeth, Cearfoss, Md., b. May 31, 1860; m. Dec., 1884,
Jacob H. Reiff, son Israel Reiff and ——— Hege.
6446. Henry L., Leitersburg, Md., b. Feb. 19, 1862; m. Emma S.
Strite (6422).
6447. Martha A., Leitersburg, Md., b. Sept. 8, 1863; m. Jan. 6, 1886,
Samuel H. Ebersole, son Abraham Ebersole and ———.
6448. Andrew C., Leitersburg, Md., b. Dec. 22, 1866; m. Annie Landis
dau. Abraham Landis and Sarah Landis; m. Elizabeth Landis.

Family of ABRAHAM HERR (2637) and ANNA REIDER.

6449. Catherine, Bellaire, Pa., b. May, 1844; m. Dec. 13, 1866, Henry
N. Risser, b. Nov. 16, 1842; d. Mar, 21, 1897; son Abraham
Risser and Mary Nissley.
6450. Rev. John R., Enterprise, Kans., b. May 1, 1845; m. Nov. 22,
1866, Mary B. Heiser, b. Aug. 28, 1846; dau. Henry Heiser
and Mary Bronser.
6451. Annie, Deodate, Pa., b. Nov. 4, 1846; m. Oct. 25, 1868, Cyrus
G. Shenk, b. May 21, 1839; son John M. Shenk and Mary A.
Gingrick.
6452. Abraham R., Kiowa, Kans., b. Feb. 23, 1848; d. June 14, 1886;
m. May 16, 1869, Elizabeth A. Shenk, b. Jan. 14, 1848; dau.
John M. Shenk and Mary A. Gingrick.
6453. George R., Donegal, Kans., b. June 13, 1849; m. Jan. 1, 1884,
Martha L. Engle, b. Nov. 12, 1857; dau. John Engle and
Magdalene Lindemuth.

6454. Lydia, Elizabethtown, Pa., b. Jan. 28, 1856; d. Jan. 25, 1900.
6455. Annie R., Abilene, Kans., b. Mar. 2, 1857; m. Nov. 14, 1882, John Engle Gish, b. Aug. 17, 1856; son Benjamin Gish and ———— Engle.
6456. Sarah, Bellair, Pa., b. Aug. 5, 1859; m. Dec. 18, 1884, Peter Risser, b. Apr. 4, 1858; son Samuel Risser and Frances Stauffer.
6457. Jacob R., Elizabethtown, Pa., b. Aug. 27, 1863; m. Amanda Risser, d. July 16, 1895; dau. John Risser and Frances Risser.
6458. Isaac R., Elizabethtown, Pa., b. Mar. 7, 1862; m. May 1, 1901, Nora E. Cassel, b. Nov. 27, 1869; dau. Henry H. Cassel and Annie Minich.
6459. Amos R., Elizabethtown, Pa., b. June 5, 1863; m. Nov. 24, 1887, Catherine R. Gish, b. Jan. 11, 1866; dau. Jacob Gish and Elizabeth Rutt.
6460. Rev. David, Elizabethtown, Pa., b. Aug. 28, 1868; d. Dec. 11, 1899.

Family of MARY HERR (2639) and JOHN SHIFFER.

6461. Annie, Mt. Joy, Pa., m. John Martin.
6462. Mary, Steeleville, Pa., m. Benton, McElwee.
6463. Catherine, Bridgewater, Mass., m. John Freeman.
6464. Susan, Furniss, Pa., m. Townsend McCommings.
6465. Rebecca, Mt. Joy, Pa., b. Jan. 11, 1868; m. July 30, 1890, Christian Nixdorf, b. Dec. 25, 1862; son Christian Nixdorf and ————.
6466. Daughter, Mt. Joy, Pa.

Family of JOHN G. HERR (2652) and LEAH STAUFFER.

6467. Jonas S., Lancaster, Pa., b. Dec. 10, 1857; d. July 21, 1858.
6468. Elizabeth, Lancaster, Pa., b. Dec. 28, 1858; d. Dec. 29, 1858.
6469. Maria, Lancaster, Pa., b. Dec. 3, 1861; d. Nov. 20, 1862.
6470. John Adam, Lancaster, Pa., b. Feb. 20, 1864; d. June 29, 1870.
6471. Son, Lancaster, Pa., b. Mar. 3, 1866; d. Mar. 3, 1866.
6472. Ada Stauffer, Grand Rapids, Mich., b. Jan. 21, 1870.

Family of JOHN L. HERR (2666) and SUSANNA MYERS.

6473. Calvin A., Columbia, Pa., b. Oct. 26, 1869; m. June 2, 1897, Carrie Shultz, b. Mar. 12, 1873; dau. Simon Shultz and Ellen ———.

6474. Alla, Millersville, Pa.

6475. Samuel, Windom, Pa.

6476. Emma, Windom, Pa.

Family of CHRISTIAN BINKLEY HERR (2695) and SUSAN J. YOUNG.

6477. Ella, Millersville, Pa., b. Apr. 28, 1876; m. Oct. 7, 1897, Abraham S. Brubaker, b. Dec. 31, 1874; son Abraham Brubaker and Mary ———.

6478. Katie, Steelton, Pa., b. Dec. 5, 1877; m. Jan. 26, 1899, Abraham N. Barley, b. Jan., 1876; son Martin Barley and Lizzie ———.

6479. Harry Y., Millersville, Pa., b. Mar. 11, 1880.

6480. Mary, Millersville, Pa., b. Oct. 1, 1882.

Family of FANNIE ELLENBERGER (2704) and JOHN M. HOOVER.

6481. John E., Yeoman, Ind., b. Sept. 2, 1872, Catherine Stonecipher, b. July 6, 1852; dau. Nathan Stonecipher and Mahala Humbert; m. Etta Gosler, b. July 18, 1858; dau. Jefferson Gosler and Susan Burt.

6482. Rudolph, Cambridge, Ind., b. Nov. 22, 1850; m. Mar. 18, 1877, Mary E. Shafer, b. Nov. 22, 1850; dau. Adam Shafer and Rachel Gebhart.

6483. Benjamin F., Cambridge, Ind., b. Feb., 1852; d. Dec. 21, 1863.

6484. Amos, Cambridge. Ind., b. Aug. 25, 1853; d. Dec. 17, 1863.

6485. Mary, Dublin, Ind., b. Apr. 10, 1855; m. Jan. 13, 1880, David N. Shellenberger, b. Feb. 25, 1855; son George Shellenberger and Mary Neff.

6486. Christian, Cambridge, Ind., b. Nov. 4, 1856; d. May 11, 1860.

6487. Elizabeth. Cambridge, Ind., b. May 26, 1859; d. Dec. 11, 1863.

6488. Susanna, Cambridge, Ind., b. Feb. 2, 1862; d. Aug. 8, 1864.

6489. Daniel, Cambridge. Ind., b. Oct. 5, 1865; m. Jan. 9, 1887, Lydia Shafer, b. Nov. 20, 1867; dau. Adam Shafer and Rachel Gebhart.

Family of MARY ELLENBERGER (2705) and MOSES MYERS.

6490. Rudolph, Cambridge, Ind., b. May 19, 1856; d. Dec. 17, 1857.
6491. Frances, Cambridge, Ind., b. June 15, 1859; d. Dec. 25, 1863.
6492. Lydia, Cambridge, Ind., b. Sept. 8, 1860; d. Jan. 5, 1864.
6493. Moses E., Cambridge, Ind., b. Oct. 3, 1862; m. Mar. 29, 1883, Mary E. Graver (6512).
6494. Isaiah, Cambridge, Ind., b. Sept. 24, 1864; m. Jan. 3, 1892, Lavina Cripe, b. Feb. 23, 1861; dau. Louis Cripe and Lavina Byerly.
6495. Jeremiah E., Hagerstown, Md., b. Oct. 12, 1866; m. Aug. 2, 1891, Laura Huhn, b. July 4, 1872; dau. John Huhn and Anna Hufnagle.

Family of CHRISTIAN ELLENBERGER (2706) and CATHERINE LEONARD.

6496. Frances, Cambridge, Ind., b. Feb. 23, 1859; d. Jan. 8, 1864.
6497. Jacob N., Cambridge, Ind., b. Jan. 31, 1860; d. Jan. 9, 1864.

Family of ELIZABETH HERR (2710) and JOHN M. WISSLER.

6498. Benjamin F., Richmond, Ind., b. July 30, 1848; m. Aug. 5, 1869, Sylvania Needler, b. Jan. 25, 1850.
6499. Christian P., New Lisbon, Ind., b. Sept. 19, 1850; m. Martha Lowell, b. Mar. 17, 1850.
6500. John R., Cambridge, Ind., b. Oct. 8, 1857; d. Nov. 28, 1864.
6501. Jacob L., Cambridge, Ind., b. Aug. 13, 1860; d. Apr. 1, 1862.
6502. William H., Cambridge, Ind., b. Feb. 10, 1867; d. Oct. 8, 1868.

Family of JACOB NEFF HERR (2712) and MARGARET ELIZABETH MALIN.

6503. Rev. Horace Dumont, Muscatine, Ia., b. Mar. 12, 1852; m. Aug. 16, 1874, Mary A. Howard, b. Oct. 11, 1855; dau. Isaiah Howard and Mary A. Berg.

Family of MARY HERR (2714) and JOHN W. ELABARGER.

6504. John B., Dublin, Ind., b. Jan. 29, 1859; d. Nov. 17, 1887; m. Anna Huddleston.
6505. Emma E., Anderson, Ind., b. Jan. 9, 1861; m. Sylvester Trimmer.

6506. Daniel K., Richmond, Ind., b. Dec. 12, 1863; m. Lowie Scudder.
6507. Christian H., Dublin, Ind., b. July 11, 1866; m. Susan Leonard.
6508. Alford L., Muncie, Ind., b. Dec. 24, 1867; m. Rachael Cox.
6509. Horace D., Dublin, Ind., b. Apr. 22, 1872; m. Myrtle Huddleston.
6510. Isaiah E., Dublin, Ind., b. July 22, 1875.

Family of ANNA HERR (2715) and JOHN GRAVER.

6511. Elizabeth H., Cambridge, Ind., b. Dec. 13, 1860; m. Jan. 22, 1880, Andrew K. Zeigler.
6512. Mary E., Cambridge, Ind., b. Aug. 14, 1862; m. Mar. 29, 1883, Moses E. Myers (6493).
6513. Amanda G., Cambridge, Ind., b. Nov. 14, 1864; d. Apr. 24, 1888.
6514. Anna E., Cambridge, Ind., b. Nov. 23, 1867; d. Feb. 13, 1900; m. Sept. 12, 1888, Clarence M. Pierce.
6515. Christian H., Cambridge, Ind., b. Nov. 23, 1872; m. Feb. 22, 1894, Edna Shaffer.

Family of SUSAN HERR (2716) and ISAIAH ELABARGER.

6516. Alice, Dublin, Ind., b. Jan. 19, 1862; d. Mar. 2, 1886.
6517. Edward, Dublin, Ind.
6518. Elizabeth, Dublin, Ind., b. July 7, 1866; d. Oct. 15, 1883.
6519. Rudolph, St. Louis, Mo.
6520. John, Terre Haute, Ind.

Family of CHRISTIAN HERR (2717) and CATHERINE BYERS.

6521. Elizabeth, New Carlisle, O., b. Dec. 20, 1878; m. Feb. 7, 1899, Welborn Snider, b. June 6, 1876.
6522. Orville B., New Carlisle, O., b. Nov. 18, 1884.

Family of BENJAMIN S. HERR (2718) and ELIZABETH ELABARGER.

6523. John R., Cambridge, Ind., b. Apr. 11, 1870.

Family of BARBARA E. FUNK (2719) and GEORGE STEINBERGER.

6524. David Orrin, Springfield, O., b. Mar. 25, 1857.
6525. Mary Elizabeth, Springfield, O., b. May 4, 1859; m. May 11,

1880, Arthur D. Holman, b. 1856; d. Sept. 21, 1903; son Robert L. Holman and Martha Hildreth.

6526. Son, Springfield, O., b. Apr. 11, 1861; d. May 3, 1861.
6527. John Burtis, Springfield, O., b. Apr. 6, 1862; m. Oct. 18, 1886, Clara Benedict, d. Aug. 25, 1891; dau. John Benedict and Rosa Miller; m. Feb., 1896, Lulu Peters, b. Aug. 7, 1870; d. Nov. 28, 1903; dau. Myers Peters and Martha Light.
6528. George Christian, Springfield, O., b. Apr. 18, 1873; d. Dec. 10, 1895.
6529. Jacob Edward, Springfield, O., b. Feb. 17, 1878; d. Nov. 27, 1880.

Family of HENRY JEFFERSON FUNK (2720) and COURTNEY LEMON.

6530. Sterling, Springfield, O., b. Jan. 10, 1861; d. Nov. 3, 1878.
6531. Pearl, Springfield, O., b. Jan. 31, 1876.

Family of Wid. HENRY J. FUNK (2720) and MARY E. BAKER.

6532. Helen, Springfield, O.
6533. Harry, Springfield, O.

Family of CATHERINE C. FUNK (2722) and GEORGE W. DEAVER.

6534. Frank, Springfield, O.
6535. Charles C., Springfield, O.

Family of CHRISTIAN C. FUNK (2724) and IDA OLIVE CORBLY.

6536. Martha A., Seattle, Wash., b. Aug. 7, 1877; m. Louis A. Parshall.
6537. Blanche E., Seattle, Wash., b. Dec. 15, 1874.

Family of ANNA MARTHA FUNK (2726) and Dr. BROWN F. BROWNFIELD.

6538. Charles Percival, Danville, Ill., b. June 4, 1866; d. May 27, 1885.
6539. Ardoth Avada, Springfield, O., b. Sept. 28, 1875.

Family of BENJAMIN F. FUNK (2727) and CYNTHIA E. LAYTON.

6540. Dr. J. —— Arthur, Hamadan, Persia, b. June 17, 1873; m. Apr. 11, 1905, Sue S. Leinbach, dau. Nathan Barto Leinbach and Catherine Campbell.

6541. Alvorda Olive, West New Brighton, N. Y., b. Dec. 3, 1874; d. Mar. 16, 1887.

6542. Walter Audley, Central City, Col., b. Aug. 14, 1876; m. Apr., 1904, Chandos McNeil.

6543. Merton Layton, Brooklyn, N. Y., b. Apr. 29, 1879.

6544. Charles Earl, Boulder, Col., b. Apr. 4, 1881.

6545. Chester Carlisle, Boulder, Col., b. Apr. 21, 1884; d. Aug., 1885.

Family of WILLIAM H. HERR (2732) and CLARA STONE BOBLITS.

6546. Edgar A., Lancaster, Pa., b. Apr. 28, 1881.

6547. Thomas A., Altoona, Pa., b. Aug. 6, 1883.

6548. Henry H., Altoona, Pa., b. Sept. 14, 1889; d. July 21, 1890.

6549. Elizabeth, Altoona, Pa., b. Jan. 3, 1892.

Family of FREDERICK HERR (2734) and JENNIE DONNELLY.

6550. Sarah E., Altoona, Pa., b. Mar. 14, 1886; d. May 6, 1890.

6551. John D., Altoona, Pa., b. Jan. 6, 1888.

6552. Martha, Altoona, Pa., b. Oct. 19, 1889; d. Nov. 20, 1889.

6553. Margaret, Altoona, Pa., b. May 21, 1891.

6554. Franklin P., Altoona, Pa., b. May 31, 1894.

6555. Infant, Altoona, Pa., b. Oct. 12, 1899; d. Oct. 13, 1899.

Family of MINERVA HERR (2737) and CHARLES METZGAR.

6556. Cora Rebecca, Altoona, Pa., b. Aug. 14, 1891.

6557. Charles David, Altoona, Pa., b. May 8, 1895.

Family of ANNA AMERICA HERR (2740) and ALBERT FERRY WYON.

6558. Violet E., Pittsburg, Pa., b. Sept. 19, 1875; m. June 5, 1901, Harry E. Kunzman.

6559. Albert, Indianapolis, Ind., b. Nov. 29, 1876; d. July 21, 1877.

6560. John Elmer, Indianapolis, Ind., b. Oct. 1, 1879.

6561. Effie Gertrude, Indianapolis, Ind., b. Oct. 1, 1881.

6562. Mary Estella, Indianapolis, Ind., b. Sept. 7, 1887.

6563. Evelyn Lucile, Indianapolis, Ind., b. Sept. 22, 1890.

6564. Richard Herr, Indianapolis, Ind., b. June 10, 1899; d. Feb. 16, 1900.

Family of **ABRAHAM SEYMOUR HERR** (2746) and **ELLEN E. FOSTER.**

6565. Ida Mae, Shelby, O., b. July 29, 1893.
6566. Ralph Foster, Shelby, O., b. Mar. 17, 1895.
6567. Esther Irene, Shelby, O., b. Dec. 16, 1896.
6568. Howard Lee, Shelby, O., b. Oct. 18, 1901.

Family of **MARTIN LUTHER LECHLIDER** (2772) and **JULIA R. HOUCK.**

6569. Julia Kathleen, Harmony Grove, Md., b. Aug. 5, 1894.
6570. Marian Louisa, Harmony Grove, Md., b. Feb. 3, 1896.

Family of **FANNY HERR** (2775) and **JOHN KRANTZ.**

6571. Lizzie, Strasburg, Pa.
6572. Annie, Strasburg, Pa.
6573. Mary, Strasburg, Pa.
6574. Emma, Strasburg, Pa.

Family of **ELIZABETH MUMMA** (2787) and **SAMUEL ERB.**

6575. John, Hempfield, Pa.
6576. Samuel, Hempfield, Pa.
6577. Fanny, Hempfield, Pa.
6578. Elizabeth, Hempfield, Pa.
6579. Henry, Hempfield, Pa.
6580. Mary, Hempfield, Pa.

Family of **CHRISTIAN MUMMA** (2788) and **ANNA BOWERS.**

6581. Fianna, Hempfield, Pa.

Family of Wid. **CHRISTIAN MUMMA** (2788) and Wid. **ANNA BARR.**

6582. Simon, Hempfield, Pa.

Family of **JONAS MUMMA** (2789) and **MARY ANN BRUBAKER.**

6583. Eli, Hempfield, Pa.
6584. John, Hempfield, Pa.
6585. Fanny, Hempfield, Pa.
6586. Mary Ann, Hempfield, Pa.

Family of FANNY MUMMA (2790) and JOSEPH HERSH.

6587. John, Hempfield, Pa.

6588. Henry, Hempfield, Pa.

6589. Joseph, Hempfield, Pa.

6590. Jacob, Hempfield, Pa.

6591. Christian, Hempfield, Pa.

6592. Fanny, Hempfield, Pa.

Family of AMOS H. HERR (2793) and MARY H. DOERSTLER.

6593. Sarah A., Oregon, Pa., b. Mar. 9, 1862; m. Harvey F. Hollinger, son Levi Hollinger and ——— Frey.

6594. Lizzie D., Manheim, Pa., b. Oct. 10, 1864; m. Milton K. Shenberger, son Henry Shenberger and Katherine Ressler.

6595. Amos D., Lancaster, Pa., b., Jan. 7, 1866; m. Nov. 10, 1887, Mary J. Mumma, b. Mar. 16, 1868; dau. Uriah Mumma and Mary Muckle.

6596. Mary D., Oregon, Pa., b. Oct. 4, 1867; m. Joseph G. Spangler.

6597. John D., Lancaster, Pa, b. Feb. 14, 1870.

6598. Clayton D., Lancaster, Pa., b. Mar. 19, 1874.

6599. Elvin D., Millersville, Pa., b. July 29, 1879; d. May 29, 1893.

6600. Clarence D., Safe Harbor, Pa., b. Mar. 8, 1886; m. Mabel Doerstler, dau. Jacob Doerstler and Elmire ———.

Family of AMOS SHELLY (2806) and FRANCES NISSLEY.

6601. Ada, Mt. Joy, Pa., b. July 6, 1890.

6602. Amos, Mt. Joy, Pa., b. June 10, 1884.

6603. Ellen, Mt. Joy, Pa., b. Feb. 9, 1893; d. Oct. 8, 1897.

6604. Emma, Mt. Joy, Pa., b. June 27, 1882; d. July 1, 1882.

Family of JOHN L. GAMBER (8504) and FANNY HERR (2830).

6605. Barbara Alice, Landis Valley, Pa., b. Apr. 3, 1862.

6606. Fanny Matilda, Landis Valley, Pa., b. Jan. 7, 1864.

6607. John, Landis Valley, Pa.

Family of DANIEL D. HERR (2831) and ADALINE S. HARNISH.

6608. ———, Mountville, Pa.

6609. ———, Mountville, Pa.

6610. ———, Mountville, Pa.
6611. ———, Mountville, Pa.
6612. ———, Mountville, Pa.
6613. ———, Mountville, Pa.
6614. ———, Mountville, Pa.

Family of Hon. JOHN H. LANDIS (2832) and ELIZABETH A. THOMAS.

6615. Mary Anna, Millersville, Pa., b. Feb. 19, 1883.
6616. Francis Thomas, Millersville, Pa., b. Dec. 23, 1885.

Family of MARY ANN LANDIS (2834) and CLAYTON S. WENGER.

6617. Clarence L., West Earl, Pa., b. June 30, 1877.
6618. Eugene F., West Earl, Pa., b. Apr. 27, 1880.
6619. J. ——— Joel, West Earl, Pa., b. Jan. 5, 1884.

Family of SUSAN LANDIS (2835) and LINNAEUS R. RIEST.

6620. Linnaeus L., Lancaster, Pa., b. Feb. 27, 1885.
6621. John Jacob, Lancaster, Pa., b. Aug. 5, 1892.
6622. Anna, Lancaster, Pa., b. Jan. 15, 1895.

Family of DAVID H. LANDIS (2838) and ELLA H. SHELLY.

6623. Ralph, Windom, Pa., b. July 28, 1891.
6624. Nelson, Windom, Pa., b. Feb. 2, 1894.
6625. Edith, Windom, Pa., b. June 1, 1899.

Family of SUSANNA H. BAUSMAN (2855) and ANDREW F. FRANTZ.

6626. Philip B., Lancaster, Pa., b. Dec. 13, 1881.
6627. Anna Mary, Lancaster, Pa., b. Aug. 15, 1883.
6628. Jacob Paul, Lancaster, Pa., b. July 18, 1885.
6629. Maud B., Lancaster, Pa., b. May 6, 1887.
6630. Ruth Herr, Lancaster, Pa., b. Dec. 3, 1888.
6631. Elizabeth Frick, Lancaster, Pa., b. Oct. 2, 1890.
6632. John Andrew, Lancaster, Pa., b. June 3, 1892.
6633. David Herr, Lancaster, Pa., b. Dec. 18, 1895.
6634. Abraham Peters, Lancaster, Pa., b. Jan. 24, 1897.
5464. Susan, Lancaster, Pa., b. Oct. 4, 1903.

Family of BARBARA E. KILLHEFFER (2859) and JOHN F. KONHE.

6635. Mabel, West Toledo, O., b. Apr. 21, 1883.

6636. Rebecca, West Toledo, O., b. Sept. 27, 1884; m. Nov. 1, 1901, Marshall Suydam.

Family of SARAH E. KILLHEFFER (2860) and M. W. TSHUDY.

6637. John, West Toledo, O., b. Mar. 1, 1880; d. Jan. 3, 1887.

Family of ALEXANDER C. KILLHEFFER (2861) and MARY LOUISE AYRES.

6638. D. ——— Herbert, Cleveland, Tenn, b. Dec. 22, 1895.

6639. Elizabeth H., Cleveland, Tenn., b. May 20, 1898.

Family of MARY H. KILLHEFFER (2864) and W. F. WAGNER.

6645. Joseph, Shoff, Pa., b. Oct. 22, 1892.

6646. Frederick, Shoff, Pa., b. Apr. 2, 1895.

6647. Leah, Shoff, Pa., b. Nov. 5, 1896.

6648. Caroline, Shoff, Pa., b. Jan. 10, 1899.

Family of ANNIE KILLHEFFER (2865) and HARRY J. LIND.

6649. Charles J., Shoff, Pa., b. Mar. 11, 1886.

Family of CHRISTIAN BAKER (2874) and MARY HOSTETTER.

6650. Magdalene, Manor, Pa.

6651. John, Manor, Pa.

6652. Elizabeth, Manor, Pa.

6653. Catherine, Manor, Pa.

Family of JONATHAN HERR (2881) and ELIZA BRIGHTBILL.

6654. John, Annville, Pa., m. Mary Heilman.

6655. Abraham E., Annville, Pa., m. Annie Imboden.

6656. Elizabeth, Annville, Pa., m. William Bordner.

6657. Clara, Annville, Pa., m. Charles H. Lichty.

6658. Minnie, Annville, Pa.

6659. Ida, Annville, Pa., m. George Wanvenkle.

Family of RUDOLPH HERR (2882) and SARAH ANN GROH.

6660. Henry, Annville, Pa., m. Sarah Weltmer.

6661. John E., Annville, Pa., m. Lavina Forney.

6662. Aaron Groh, Annville, Pa., b. Aug. 24, 1856; m. Jan. 11, 1887, Louise M. Walker, b. Mar. 17; 1866; dau. George Walker and Mary Tildon.
6663. William O., Annville, Pa., m. Emma E. Eby.
6664. Albert, Annville, Pa., m. Kate Ulrich.
6665. Sarah A., Annville, Pa., m. C. Eby Geiger.

Family of ABRAHAM HERR (2883) and ELIZABETH MOYER.

6666. Cyrus, Annville, Pa., m. ——— Booker.
6667. David, Annville, Pa., m Mary Brandt.
6668. Mary, Annville, Pa., m. Dr. ——— Mengle.
6669. Lavina, Annville, Pa., m. Rudolph Graybill.
6670. Anna, Annville, Pa., m. M—— Groh.
6671. Permilla, Annville, Pa., m. Amos Lentz.
6672. Abraham, Annville, Pa.
6673. Jacob, Annville, Pa.
6674. Martin, Annville, Pa.
6675. Fannie, Annville, Pa., m. J. ——— Lentz.

Family of FRANCES HERR (2884) and PETER REIST.

6676. Abraham, Dayton, O.
6677. Elizabeth, Dayton, O.
6678. Rudolph, Dayton, O.
6679. Jacob, Dayton, O.
6680. Lawrence, Dayton, O.
6681. Frank, Dayton, O.

Family of MARY HERR (2885) and DAVID RASOR.

6682. Lavina, Englewood, O., b. Aug. 31, 1839.
6683. Samuel, Englewood, O., b. June 6, 1841; d. May 25, 1900.
6684. Josiah, Osgood, O., b. Dec. 8, 1844.
6685. Daniel B., Englewood, O., b. Mar. 16, 1848; m. Jan. 29, 1872, Lydia Fetter, b. Apr. 9, 1851; dau. Peter Fetter and Mary Ann ———.
6686. David F., Englewood, O., b. Sept. 1, 1851; m. Hannah Fetter.
6687. Harvey E., Englewood, O., b. Mar. 14, 1856.

Family of ABRAHAM HERR (2886) and MARY STUTZMAN.

6688. Henry E., Porter, Col., b. June 23, 1847; m. Oct. 4, 1881, Mary C. Long, b. Jan. 16, 1854; d. July 18, 1886; dau. Peter Long and Matilda Dovenbarger; m. Aug. 17, 1895, Alice O'Neil, b. Dec. 2, 1862; dau. James O'Neil and Alice Connelly.

6689. Hiram, Rico, Col., b. Sept. 28, 1849; m. May 8, 1894, Alice Kendall, b. June 6, 1872; dau. Willis J. Kendall and Frances Barnum.

6690. Samuel E., Durango, Col., b. Nov. 15, 1851; m. Jan. 16, 1889, Annetta Hewitt, b. Mar. 9, 1861; dau. Benjamin L. Hewitt and Nancy E. Neff.

6691. Frances, Overbrook, Kans., b. Jan. 25, 1854; d. Sept. 28, 1889; m. Nov. 15, 1881, Adam Hilkey, b. Nov. 10, 1856; son James E. Hilkey and Hannah Clarke.

6692. David M., Silverton, Col., b. June 14, 1857; d. Sept. 22, 1902.

6693. Jesse, Silverton, Col., b. Oct. 4, 1859.

6694. Abraham, West Wilton, O., b. Jan. 20, 1862; d. Feb. 1, 1864.

Family of ANN HERR (2887) and Wid. LEVI FAULKNER.

6695. Angeline, Englewood, O., b. Dec. 9, 1844; d. Aug. 13, 1850.

6696. C. ——— W., Center, O., b. Dec. 14, 1847; m. Jan. 28, 1872, Mary A. Kinsey.

6697 D. ——— C., West Milton, O., b. Oct. 12, 1850; m. Dec. 9, 1875, Clara Morse.

6698. Frances M., Englewood, O., b. Aug. 9, 1852; m. Apr. 12, 1877, George W. Good.

6699. Leren E., West Milton, O., b. Feb. 11, 1854; m. Mar. 27, 1881, Laura A. Morse.

6700. Mary A., Englewood, O., b. Aug. 26, 1857; m. Mar. 2, 1880, W. ——— Martindale.

6701. Theodore, Englewood, O., b. Apr. 10, 1860; m. Jan. 4, 1887, Anna Bitzer.

6702. Jerome, Dayton, O., b. Apr. 5, 1862; m. Oct. 28, 1886, Effie Flack.

Family of SAMUEL L. HERR (2889) and CATHERINE HOCKER.

6703. Martha Ann, Jamton, O., b. Jan. 26, 1854; d. Apr. 1, 1857.

6704. Edna, Brookville, O., b. Dec. 20, 1855; m. May 11, 1876, Theodore F. Sinks, b. Sept. 8, 1854; son George Sinks and Susan Coats.

6705. Mary C., Jamton, O., b. Dec. 4, 1858; d. Oct. 3, 1860.

6706. David, Springfield, O., b Nov. 1, 1861; m. Nov. 24, 1892, Emma Mellinger, b. June 18, 1864; dau. John Mellinger and Rachel Snyder.

6707. Lavina, Englewood, O., b. Oct. 8, 1863; m. Oct. 10, 1882, Calvin E. Kruger.

6708. Levi, Clayton, O., b. Apr. 22, 1867; m. Feb. 22, 1893, Iva C. Ullery, b. Oct. 20, 1871; dau. Jacob Ullery and Leah Beyers.

6709. Ohmer J., Englewood, O., b. June 21, 1874; d. Sept. 12, 1894.

Family of CHRISTIAN HERR (2890) and JULIA HUFFER.

6710. Susan, Trotwood, O., b. May 11, 1861; m. Mar. 4, 1881, Samuel Landis, b. June 9, 1856; d. Apr. 18, 1898; son Samuel Landis and ———.

6711. Ellen, Trotwood, O., b. Aug. 23, 1863; d. Nov. 7, 1893; m. Dec. 8, 1881, William Mumma, b. July 16, 1857; son Henry Mumma and Lena Berns.

6712. Charles Edgar, Durango, Col., b. Jan. 31, 1866; m. Jan. 26, 1888, Alice B. Lloyd, b. Jan. 13, 1866; dau. James Lloyd and Clementine Eakins.

6713. John, Durango, Col., b. Mar. 10,1876.

Family of ELIZABETH HERR (2892) and JOHN HEISEY.

6714. Albert, Clayton, O., b. Oct. 7, 1853.

6715. Mary, Garland, O., b. Oct. 14, 1854.

6716. Samuel, Ludlow Falls, O., b. Apr. 4, 1856.

6717. David, Pleasant Hill, O., b. Sept. 18, 1858.

6718. Jacob, Dayton, O., b. Feb. 9, 1862.

6719. Anna, Center, O., b. Dec. 1, 1863.

6720. Alice, Englewood, O., b. July 28, 1867.

6721. Ida, Ludlow Falls, O., b. Feb. 15, 1869.

6722. Ora, Ludlow Falls, O., b. Oct. 25, 1875.

6723. Bertha, Dayton, O., b. Oct. 1, 1879.

Family of SARAH HERR (2893) and DAVID SHAW.

6724. Mary J., Union, O., b. June 19, 1857.

6725. Frances, Union, O., b. Oct. 3, 1859.

6726. Edwin, Union, O., b. July 28, 1861.

6727. William, Union, O., b. Oct. 26, 1869.

6728. Harry, Union, O., b. May 25, 1876; d. May 25, 1876.

Family of LYDIA HERR (2905) and JONAS SNYDER.

6729. Christian, Cleona, Pa.

6730. Harvey, Cleona, Pa.

6731. Lizzie Hostetter, Cleona, Pa.

Family of HENRY HERR (2911) and ———.

6732. Henry, Lancaster, Pa.

6733. Theodore M., Lancaster, Pa.

6734. Morris, Lancaster, Pa.

6735. Edward, Harrisburg, Pa., m. Mary Garman.

6736. Elizabeth, Oberlin, Pa., m. Henry Handshue.

6737. Lincoln, Oberlin, Pa.

6738. Sarah, Harrisburg, Pa., m. John Brightbill.

6739. Frances, Camp Hill, Pa., m. Daniel Holler.

6740. Annie, Harrisburg, Pa.

Family of DAVID SHOPP HERR (2912) and SARAH ANN NEIDIG.

6741. Franklin Neidig, Harrisburg, Pa., b. Mar. 24, 1856; d. June 1, 1871.

6742. Elizabeth Irene, Harrisburg, Pa., b. May 23, 1858; m. Feb. 12, 1880, Henry C. Ross.

6743. Russell, Harrisburg, Pa., b. May 23, 1861; d. Oct. 2, 1867.

6744. Milton, Harrisburg, Pa., b. Apr. 25, 1864; d. Aug. 13, 1864.

6745. Fannie May, Harrisburg, Pa., b. Apr. 19, 1868; m. Aug. 14,

AND HIS DIRECT LINEAL DESCENDANTS.

1889,Wm. R. Denehey, b. June 6, 1867; son William R. Denehey and Mary Shearer.

Family of CATHERINE HERR (2914) and JOHN HIKES.

6746. Susan, St. Matthews, Ky., b. July 5, 1816; d. Nov. 2, 1881; m. Nov. 4, 1835, Andrew Low, d. June 2, 1879.

6447. Mary, St. Matthews, Ky., b. Sept. 21, 1817; d. Jan. 6, 1889; m. Dec. 24, 1840, Dr. John S. Seaton.

6748. Barbara, Louisville, Ky., b. June 23, 1820; m. Sept. 10, 1840, Emory Low, b. Apr. 16, 1808; d. 1851; son Jabez Low and ———.

6749. Eliza G., St. Matthews, Ky., b. Mar. 16, 1822; d. Nov. 5, 1855; m. July 31, 1849, Roland Whitney.

6750. John L., St. Matthews, Ky., b. July 22, 1824; d. Nov. 3, 1873; m. Nov. 1, 1854, Martha Glover.

6751. Catherine, St. Matthews, Ky., b. Nov. 18, 1826; d. Jan. 27, 1893; m. Sept. 18, 1849, Benjamin F. Cawthorn.

6752. Sarah, St. Matthews, Ky., b. Mar. 12, 1832; d. Oct. 29, 1837.

Family of JOHN HERR (2915) and SUSAN OLDHAM.

6753. Conway O., St. Matthews, Ky., b. Jan. 16, 1823; d. June 15, 1876.

6754. John F., St. Matthews, Ky., b. Feb. 12, 1825; d. Nov. 10, 1849.

6755. William T., Anchorage, Ky., b. Jan. 29, 1827; d. Jan. 30, 1875; m. Mar. 16, 1849, Mary Shanklin.

6756. Susan, Louisville, Ky., b. Feb. 5, 1829; d. Aug. 10, 1888; m. Nov. 30, 1853, Dr. Samuel B. Mills.

6757. Frances Ruth, Louisville, Ky., b. Apr. 18, 1831; m. Mar. 9, 1852, Dr. John E. Sutcliff, son John E. Sutcliff and Tillie Clarkson.

6758. Martha W., Louisville, Ky., b. Aug. 27, 1833; d. July 7, 1896; m. Oct. 18, 1855, George A. Owen, b. Dec. 27, 1830; d. Oct. 14, 1898; son William Owen and Martha Cautchfield.

6759. Henry Clay, Owensboro, Ky., b. Apr. 9, 1836; d. Dec. 3, 1894; m. May 9, 1866, Mildred C. Taylor, b. July 23, 1843; dau. Jonathan G. Taylor and Susan Elizabeth Hawes.

6760. Mary Emma, Chicago, Ill., b. Sept. 16, 1838; m. Sept. 15, 1857, Joshua B. Parks, son Floyd Parks and ——— Macky.

6761. Albert G., Lyndon, Ky., b. Dec. 30, 1840; d. Oct. 1, 1899; m. Nov. 2, 1864, Martha E. Guthrie, b. Apr. 28, 1846; dau. James Guthrie and Fannie Smith.

Family of FREDERICK HERR (2916) and NANCY OLDHAM.

6762. Amanda, St. Matthews, Ky., m. James Shanklin.

6764. Susan Frances, St. Matthews, Ky., m. George Rudy, son Daniel Rudy and Mary Shively.

6765. Ellen M., St. Matthews, Ky., m. Alfred I. Field.

6766. James M., Owensboro, Ky., b. Feb. 17, 1834; m. Nov. 9, 1858, Nancy A. Tate, b. Mar. 11, 1835.

6767. George Warner, Louisville, Ky., b. Oct. 22, 1836; m. Dec. —, 1858, Georgie Landrum, b. ———, 1841; d. Aug. —, 1865; dau. Carter Landrum and Sidonia Keller; m. Mary Brobston, b. Apr. 20, 1846; d. Mar. —, 1899; dau. George Brobston and Elizabeth Randall.

6768. John C., Louisville, Ky., m. Mary Clarkson.

6769. Samuel L., Louisville, Ky., m. Bettie Clarkson.

Family of GEORGE HERR (2917) and SARAH SIMCOE.

6770. Susan Elizabeth, Smith Mills, Ky., b. May 28, 1825; d. July 28, 1852; m. Feb. 25, 1841, Henry A. Fenley, b. Aug. 18, 1821; d. June 11, 1852; son Isaac Fenley and Mary H. Allison.

6771. Richard S., St. Matthews, Ky., b. Mar. 19, 1827; d. Jan. 3, 1878; m. Nov. 9, 1852, Margaret Rudy, d. Jan. 11, 1854; m. June 25, 1857, Jane Ormsby, d. June 30, 1860; dau. Stephen Ormbsy and ——— Shirley.

6772. Priscilla, St. Matthews, Ky., b. May 24, 1830; m. Oct. 14, 1852, John C. Rudy.

6773. George Walker, Louisville, Ky., b. June 26, 1832; d. Sept. 5, 1867; m. Feb. 20, 1855, Lucy Snead, d. Mar. 11, 1868.

6774. William Frederick, Louisville, Ky., b. Sept. 15, 1839; d. Sept. 15, 1866; m. May 14, 1860, Susan E. Ross, b. Mar. 26, 1842; dau. David Ross and Elizabeth Caldwell.

6775. Rosetta Annie, Louisville, Ky., b. Oct. 26, 1841; d. Aug. 26, 1885; m. Nov. 14, 1860, Henry C. Anderson, b. Oct. 15, 1834; son Robert T. Anderson and Adaline B. Spottswood.

6776. Lewis Taylor, St. Matthews, Ky., b. Apr. 27, 1844; d. Dec. 26, 1889; m. Sept. 16, 1873, Annie Brobston, b. Oct. 1, 1847; dau. George Brobston and Elizabeth Randall.

Family of ELIZA HERR (2918) and GEORGE RUDY.

6777. Susan Jane, Sedalia, Mo., m. George Shively; m. William H. Powell.

6778. John, Sedalia, Mo., m. Fanny Tucker.

6779. Kate, St. Matthews, Ky., m. ———— Tucker.

6780. Annie, Louisville, Ky., m. Lewis Washburn.

6781. Sarah, St. Matthews, Ky., m. Crawford Arterburn.

6782. Madora, Nevada City, Mo., m. John Rafferty.

6783. Samuel, Sedalia, Mo.

Family of ALFRED HERR (2919) and MARY A. SHIRLEY.

6784. John Lewis, Lyndon, Ky., b. Mar. 24, 1832; m. Feb. 10, 1857, Susan Uttinger, b. July 4, 1835; dau. Jacob Uttinger and Cynthia Hall.

6785. William Wallace, Owensboro, Ky., b. June 9, 1834; m. Jan. 11, 1866, Kittie B. Todd, b. Oct. 7, 1841; d. Apr. 15, 1875; dau. Robert S. Todd and Elizabeth Humphreys.

6786. Jane Helen, St. Matthews, Ky., b. Jan. 8, 1836; d. Apr. 22, 1891; m. Mar. 6, 1861, Samuel S. Hite, b. Oct. 29, 1828; son Jacob Hite and Elizabeth Snead.

6787. Robert W., St. Matthews, Ky., b. Mar. 18, 1838; m. May 28, 1879, Minnie Ormsby, b. Jan. 24, 1856; dau. Hamilton Ormsby and Edmonia Taylor.

Family of ANNIE HERR (2921) and NORBOURNE ARTERBURN.

6788. Sarah Ophelia, Worthington, Ky., b. Jan. 23, 1842; m. Albert W. Hardin.

6789. Elizabeth R., Louisville, Ky., b. July 16, 1844; m. Oct. 18, 1864,

Thomas C. Richards, b. Apr. 15, 1839; d. Mar. 29, 1872; son William Richards and Priscilla A. Grundy; m. July 13, 1876, John Shanks, b. Jan. 20, 1844; d. Aug. 30, 1891; son Talifero Shanks and Elizabeth Bradfield; m. Feb. 12, 1896, Wid. Henry C. Anderson, b. Oct. 15, 1834; son Robert T. Anderson and Adaline B. Spottswood.

6790. Son, Louisville, Ky., b. Dec. 1, 1847; d. Dec. —, 1847.

6791. William C., Louisville, Ky., b. Dec. 15, 1852.

6792. Edward, Louisville, Ky., b. July 10, 1854.

6793. Mary Emma, Worthington, Ky., b. Jan. 8, 1849; m. Robert H. Hoskins.

6794. Anna Tarlton, Worthington, Ky., b. Dec. 10, 1856; m. R. —— Y. Hardin.

6795. Clifton C., Yonkers, N. Y., b. Aug. 5, 1859; m. Jan. 23, 1883, Georgia J. Bell, b. Oct. 4, 1864; dau. Thomas Bell and Susan Ann Sheilds.

Family of ELIZA SWOPE (2923) and SAMUEL S. FORNEY.

6796. Elizabeth, Gettysburg, Pa., b. Dec. 12, 1812; d. Feb. 19, 1858; m. Oct. 14, 1834, Dr. Jesse Gilbert, b. Mar. 7, 1807; d. Aug. 28, 1838; son Bernard Gilbert and Susanna Gilbert; m. Edward B. Buehler.

6797. Henry Swope, Gettysburg, Pa., b. Feb. 1, 1815; d. Jan. 5, 1884; m. Dec. 2, 1844, Maria C. Benson, b. Sept. 28, 1823; d. Nov. 28, 1877; dau. Peter Benson and Elizabeth Ludwig.

6798. Mary Jane, Baltimore, Md., b. Feb. 12, 1817; d. Feb. 27, 1884; m. Sept. 24, 1840, John C. Bridges, b. Mar. 7, 1817; d. June 22, 1892; son John S. Bridges and ———.

6799. Louisa A., Denver, Col., b. Oct. 24, 1819; m. May 11, 1842, Horace Rathvon, b. Nov. 17, 1816; d. Nov. 7, 1875; son Michael Rathvon and Barbara Alleman.

6800. Josephine, Gettysburg, Pa., b. Nov. 7, 1825; m. Mar. 30, 1852, Rev. William D. Roedel, b. Jan. 15, 1828; d. Dec. 12, 1866; son Jacob Roedel and Justina Diller.

6801. David S., Allisonia, Va., b. Jan. 9, 1828; m. Oct. 20, 1878,

Nancy J. Warden, b. Aug. 4, 1857; dau. William H. Warden and Malinda Heymore.

6802. John Swope, Gettysburg, Pa., b. Feb. 17, 1830; m. Feb. 21, 1861, Mary Shriver.

6803. Samuel S., Gettysburg, Pa., b. July 7, 1832: d. Apr. 13, 1837.

6804. Sarah Amelia, Gettysburg, Pa., b. July 25, 1836; d. May 8, 1837.

Family of Dr. JOHN SWOPE (2924) and MARY JOSEPHINE BOYLE.

6805. Helen Josephine, Emmetsburg, Md., b. Apr. 11, 1826.

6806. Adelaide E., Westminster, Md., b. May 10, 1832; d. Nov. 1, 1868; m. Dr. William A. Mathias, b. Mar. 8, 1821; d. Apr. 17, 1864.

Family of MARY SWOPE (2926) and WILLIAM CRAPSTER.

6807. Mary, Taneytown, Md.

6808. Capt. Milton, St. Louis, Mo., m. ———; m. ———.

Family of DANIEL HERR SWOPE (2929) and MARGARET BRUCE SCOTT.

6809. Elizabeth, Taneytown, Md., d. Infant.

Family of CLARA A. SWOPE (2930) and HENRY WANTZ.

6810. Elizabeth S., Lutherville, Md., b. Mar. 6, 1848; d. Oct. 23, 1875; m. Oct. 8, 1867, William H. Cockey, b. ———, 1837; d. Mar. 21, 1879; son John G. Cockey and Mary Ann Bell.

6811. Mary J., Taneytown, Md., b. June 7, 1853; m. Jan. 19, 1875, Edward E. Reindollar, b. Feb. 18, 1853; son David Reindollar and Amelia J. Hiteshue.

Family of MARTHA HERR (2936) and DAVID KEEN.

6812. Antha Letitia, Liberty Square, Pa., b. Jan. 14, 1851; m. Nov. 11, 1875, Joseph D. Ecklen, b. Feb. 11, 1849; d. Feb. 6, 1890; son James Ecklen and Isabella Dickey.

6813. John Henry, Ephrata, Pa., b. July 6, 1852; m. Isabella Rockey, dau. Samuel Rockey and Isabella Spicer; m. Annie E. Eckman, dau. Martin Eckman and Rebecca Howett.

6414. Ann Eliza, May, Pa., b. Sept. 14, 1853; m. Michael Fritz, son Benjamin Fritz and Mary Groff.
6815. Mary Emma, Quarryville, Pa., b. Feb. 6, 1855; d. Oct. 19, 1857.
6816. Franklin Elmer, Quarryville, Pa., b. Jan. 12, 1857; m. Annie Eckman, dau. Balser Eckman and ———Bryson.
6817. Martha Catharine, Camargo, Pa., b. Oct. 10, 1858; m. Daniel H. Eckman, b. Apr. 30, 1860; son Daniel B. Eckman and Mary J. Hess.
6818. William E., Christiana, Pa., b. Apr. 14, 1860.
6819. Ada Sue, New Danville, Pa., b. Nov. 18, 1862; m. Jan. 19, 1882, Conrad Hess, b. Nov. 5, 1856; son Abraham Hess and Ann Zeigler.
6820. Easley H., Christiana, Pa., b. Mar. 8, 1864; m. M—— Ella Irwin, dau. Dr. William Irwin and Eliza J. Mullin.
6821. Effie Maria, Mechanics' Grove, Pa., b. June 11, 1867; m. Dec. 18, 1889, Galen Groff, b. Dec. 8, 1863; son Samuel G. Groff and Fannie Winters.
6822. David Martin, Christiana, Pa., b. Nov. 25, 1871.
6823. Amos, Christiana, Pa., b. Dec. 18, 1873; d. Dec. 21, 1873.

Family of MARY ANN HERR (2939) and ADAM KEEN.

6824. Sue Catharine, Quarryville, Pa., b. Sept. 1, 1860; m. Dec. 6, 1878, William D. Hess, son Daniel D. Hess and Catharine Lefever.
6825. Edith Lemia, Quarryville, Pa., b. Sept. 3, 1861; d. June 4, 1874.
6826. William Burnside, Quarryville, Pa., b. June 27, 1863; m. June 14, 1899, S. Elizabeth Breneman, b. Nov. 9, 1863; dau. Franklin Breneman and Sarah Heidelbaugh.
6827. Harry Grant, Lancaster, Pa., b. May 1, 1864; m. Frances Mylin, dau. Eli Mylin and Martha Charles.
6828. Mary Emma, Quarryville, Pa., b. June 3, 1871; m. Dec. 4, 1889, George M. Gregg, b. Feb. 16, 1865; son Daniel M. Gregg and Hannah A. Gregg.

Family of JEMIMA C. ELIZABETH HERR (2941) and ABRAHAM MYERS.

6829. John A——, Camargo, Pa., b. Oct. 1, 1875.
6830. C—— William, Camargo, Pa., b. Dec. 31, 1878.

Family of WILLIAM D. HERR (2943) and FRANCES ELIZABETH GOOD.

6831. Emma Goldina, Camargo, Pa., b. June 19, 1880.
6832. Olga Mary, Camargo, Pa., b. Mar. 25, 1882.
6833. Margaret E. F., Camargo, Pa., b. Dec. 31, 1883.
6834. Florence C., Camargo, Pa., b. Dec. 19, 1885.
6835. John H., Camargo, Pa., b. Feb. 2, 1888.
6836. William D., Camargo, Pa., b. Feb. 4, 1890.
6837. Charles A., Camargo, Pa., b. May 23, 1892.
6838. Milton Smith, Camargo, Pa., b. Dec. 18, 1894.
6839. Viola E., Camargo, Pa., b. June 30, 1897.
6840. Pauline M., Camargo, Pa., b. Sept. 7, 1899.

Family of ANNA M. L. HERR (2944) and HENRY BOETTNER.

6841. Margaret M., Camargo, Pa., b. July 22, 1883.
6842. Myerl C., Camargo, Pa., b. May 14, 1885.
6843. Miriam, Camargo, Pa., b. June 2, 1888.
6844. W. —— Ray, Camargo, Pa., b. Oct. 23, 1890.
6845. Alice B., Camargo, Pa., b. Feb. 4, 1893.
6846. Harry Ernest, Camargo, Pa., b. Dec. 14, 1895.
6847. Hugh Dewey, Camargo, Pa., b. Mar. 17, 1899.

Family of EMMA E. L. SUSAN HERR (2945) and MILLER J. RESSLER.

6848. Lee, Buck, Pa., b. Oct. 16, 1882.
6849. Clarence, Buck, Pa., b. Aug. 16, 1884.
6850. Goldina V., Buck, Pa., b. July 2, 1886.

Family of CYRUS S. BARR (2946) and MARY ANN RILEY.

6851. Henry, Smyrna, Pa., b. Oct. 4, 1859; m. Mar. 3, 1892, Alice Johnson, dau. Andrew Johnson and Mary Davis.
6852. E. —— Galen, Smyrna, Pa., b. Apr. 3, 1864; d. July 6, 1894.
6853. John M., Willow Street, Pa.

6854. Mary A., Buck, Pa., d. Jan. 9, 1900.
6855. Edward, Smyrna, Pa.
6856. George A., Parkesburg, Pa.
6857. Carrie, Burnham, Pa.

Family of CAROLINE H. BARR (2947) and HENRY L. UHLER.

6858. Edward C., Nespelen, Wash., b. Nov. 21, 1860.
6859. William Levi, Seymour, Ind., b. Feb. 27, 1862; m. May 20, 1899, Mary J. Lucas, b. July 29, 1868.
6860. Mary Ellen, Surprise, Ind., b. Nov. 7, 1863; d. May —, 1892; m. Ephraim R. White.
6861. Alfred H., Nespelen, Wash., b. Dec. 24, 1865.
6862. Caroline B., Denver, Col., b. Sept. 28, 1867; m. May 15, 1901, William E. Condon, b. Apr. 7, 1868; son Harrison Condon and Elizabeth A. Shaw.
6863. Elizabeth M., El Paso, Tex., b. July 17, 1869.
6864. Effie P., Denver, Col., b. Dec. 6, 1874; m. May 22, 1901, Charles A. Whitmore, b. May 8, 1872; son Cyrus P. Whitmore and Catharine Kelley.

Family of SALOME E. BARR (2948) and SAMUEL B. SIDES.

6865. Edward, Philadelphia, Pa.

Family of CATHARINE K. CRESSWELL (2949) and JOHN ECKMAN.

6866. Clara Elizabeth, New Providence, Pa., b. June 26, 1858.
6867. Charles, Lancaster, Pa., b. Feb. 1, 1860; d. Aug. 26, 1888; m. Aug. 24, 1881, Rosa T. Kerchner, b. Sept. 4, 1859; dau. John Kerchner and Barbara Kuhn.
6868. Dora, Hawkesville, Pa., b. Oct. 16, 1861; d. June 28, 1882.
6869. Estella, New Providence, Pa., b. Feb. 8, 1863; m. Oct. 25, 1894, Lewis Eckman, b. Aug. 30, 1863; son Benjamin Eckman and Elizabeth ———.
6870. Martha, New Providence, Pa., b. Sept. 25, 1865.
6871. John G., New Providence, Pa., b. Apr. 17, 1868; d Aug. 27, 1886.

6872. Darius J., Lancaster, Pa., b. Sept. 14, 1870; m. Nov. 2, 1897, Ella Doner, b. July 26, 1873; dau. Abraham Doner and Esther Brubaker.

6873. Winona S., New Providence, Pa., b. Feb. 27, 1873.

6874. K. ———— Bernice, New Providence, Pa., b. Nov. 22, 1875.

6875. Oscar D., New Providence, Pa., b. Apr. 21, 1878.

6876. Edith A., New Providence, Pa., b. June 6, 1882.

Family of MARTHA ADALINE CRESSWELL (2952) and HIRAM E. SNAVELY.

6877. Ollie, Strasburg, Pa., b. Nov. 19, 1870; d. Mar. 19, 1871.

6878. Olan C., Strasburg, Pa., b. Feb. 5, 1872; m. Nov. 17, 1897, Ida S. Feilbach, dau. Christian M. Feilbach and Regina Schaffer.

6879. Arthur K., Strasburg, Pa., b. Dec. 4, 1873.

6880. Alonzo S., Strasburg, Pa., b. Aug. 26, 1876.

6881. Carrie, Stryker, O., b. June 10, 1881; d. Aug. 10, 1881.

Family of GEORGE M. CRESSWELL (2953) and CHRISTIANA KEEN.

6882. John Henry, Quarryville, Pa., b. Sept. 15, 1872.

6883. Christian James, Camargo, Pa., b. May 4, 1875; m. Mar. 12, 1900, Sarah A. Lefever, dau. John Lefever and Susan Eshleman.

6884. Mary Elizabeth, Quarryville, Pa., b. Mar. 4, 1877.

6885. Annie Sophia, Quarryville, Pa., b. Aug. 24, 1878; m. Dec. 22, 1898, Woodward Althouse, son Isaac Althouse and Kezia McCallister.

6886. Daniel Walter, Quarryville, Pa., b. July 29, 1880; d. Dec. 9, 1891.

6887. Samuel Newton, Quarryville, Pa., b. Aug. 29, 1884.

6888. Estella Agnes, Quarryville, Pa., b. June 9, 1891.

Family of EMMA L. HERR (2972) and JOHN F. JOHNSON.

6889. William H., Lancaster, Pa., b. Mar. 24, 1877; d. Aug. 11, 1886.

6890. Edith Z., Lancaster, Pa., b. Feb. 14, 1879; m. Oct. 22, 1899, George Share.

6891. C. ———— May, Lancaster, Pa., b. Jan. 22, 1881; m. Jan. 6, 1900, Edgar A. Ulmer.

19

6892. Gurtie E., Lancaster, Pa., b. Apr. 27, 1883.
6893. Joseph F., Lancaster, Pa., b. Jan. 27, 1888.
6894. Jay H., Lancaster, Pa., b. June 1, 1891; d. Apr. 1, 1893.
6895. Clara L., Lancaster, Pa., b. May 28, 1894.
6896. Emma N., Lancaster, Pa., b. Nov. 17, 1896.

Family of SAMUEL J. HERR (2974) and ELLA NORA GOCHENOUR.

6897. Parke A., Orange, N. J., b. Oct. 1, 1882.
6898. Mabel V., Leaman Place, Pa., b. May 25, 1884.
6899. Fanny B., Leaman Place, Pa., b. Dec. 13, 1885.
6900. Emma E., Leaman Place, Pa., b. Sept. 5, 1887.
6901. Simon S. G., Leaman Place, Pa., b. July 19, 1889.
6902. Alma M., Leaman Place, Pa., b. Nov. 29, 1891.
6903. Clyde L., Leaman Place, Pa., b. Aug. 26, 1894.
6904. Blanche B., Leaman Place, Pa., b. Feb. 13, 1897.
6905. M. Pearl, Leaman Place, Pa., b. Mar. 15, 1899.
6906. Lillian M., Leaman Place, Pa., b. Mar. 25, 1901.

Family of ABRAHAM HERR (2981) and AMANDA GROFF.

6907. Infant, Bird-in-Hand, Pa.
6908. Levi G., Bird-in-Hand, Pa., b. Aug. 31, 1880.

Family of JACOB R. HERR (2982) and SUSAN MYERS.

6909. Benjamin M., New Holland, Pa., b. Dec. 12, 1856; d. Nov. 16, 1894; m. Nov. 14, 1882, Emma Sheaffer, b. Apr. 20, 1855; dau. Adam Sheaffer and Mary Fry.
6910. Solomon R., Leacock, Pa., b. Oct. 4, 1858; m. Jan. 10, 1889, Lydia A. Landis, b. May 10, 1856; dau. Christian R. Landis and Esther Risser.
6911. Martin, Bird-in-Hand, Pa., b. Apr. 30, 1860; d. Dec. 28, 1860.
6912. Jacob M., Bird-in-Hand, Pa., b. Oct. 26, 1861; d. Apr. 30, 1888; m. Nov., 1882, Annie Sheaffer, b. Jan. 7, 1863; d. Sept. 30, 1898; dau. Adam Sheaffer and Mary Fry.
6913. Daniel, Bird-in-Hand, Pa., b. July 27, 1863; d. July 11, 1864.
6914. Samuel, Soudersburg, Pa., b. June 27, 1865; m. Jan. 1, 1889,

Emma Denlinger, b. Jan. 18, 1862; dau. Martin Denlinger and Ann Groff.

6915. Elizabeth, Bird-in-Hand, Pa., b. Feb. 20, 1867; d. Mar. 5, 1867.

6916. Abraham, Lampeter, Pa., b. Feb. 7, 1868; m. Oct. 15, 1895, Annie Shaffer, b. Dec. 9, 1868; dau. John Shaffer and Martha Sensenig.

Family of JOHN R. HERR (2984) and ANNA GROFF.

6917. Amos G., Bird-in-Hand, Pa., b. Aug. 31, 1863; m. Dec. 25, 1884, Mary A. Kreider, b. Oct. 27, 1865; dau. David L. Kreider and Mary K. Landis.

6918. Mary Emma, Bird-in-Hand, Pa., b. Nov. 19, 1865; d. June 28, 1900.

6919. Anna Elizabeth, Bird-in-Hand, Pa., b. Aug. 31, 1868.

6920. Cora L., Bird-in-Hand, Pa., b. Mar. 23, 1871; d. Apr. 8, 1872.

6921. Samuel H., Bird-in-Hand, Pa., b. Oct. 24, 1873; m. Jan. 16, 1900, Mary Ressler, dau. William Ressler and Elizabeth ———.

6922. Benjamin W., Bird-in-Hand, Pa., b. Aug. 15, 1875.

6923. Lydia G., Bird-in-Hand, Pa., b. Sept. 24, 1877; m. ——— Buckwalter.

Family of MARTIN R. HERR (2986) and ESTHER LANDIS.

6924. Mary L., Leacock, Pa., b. Jan. 26, 1863; m. Nov. 16, 1886, Christian B. Nolt, b. Oct. 29, 1861; son Jonas H. Nolt and Maria D. Burkholder.

6925. Benjamin, Bird-in-Hand, Pa., b. Mar. 8, 1864; d. Feb. 28, 1865.

6926. Annie, Strasburg, Pa., b. Dec. 6, 1865; m. Josiah Mellinger.

6927. Daughter, Bird-in-Hand, Pa., b. May 29 1867; d. May 29, 1867.

6928. Amanda, Lancaster, Pa., b. Oct. 7, 1868; m. Abraham L. Herr (8427).

6929. Lydia, Bird-in-Hand, Pa., b. Sept. 26, 1870; d. Aug. 6, 1874.

6930. Elam, Bird-in-Hand, Pa., b. Sept. 9, 1874; d. Aug. 16, 1878.

6931. Landis R., Bird-in-Hand, Pa., b. Mar. 4, 1876; d. Aug. 18, 1876.

6932. Elizabeth, Dillerville, Pa., b. July 14, 1877.

6933. Esther A., Dillerville, Pa., b. Aug. 7, 1879.

6934. Emma, Bird-in-Hand, Pa., b. Oct. 24, 1881; d. Apr. 8, 1884.
6935. Ella, Dillerville, Pa., b. Apr. 3, 1885.

Family of ELIAS R. HERR (2988) and LYDIA GROFF.

6936. Mary Ann, Lancaster, Pa.
6937. Margaret S., Lancaster, Pa.

Family of JOHN H. KAUFFMAN (2989) and EMMA E. LONGENECKER (3623).

6938. Mary Elizabeth, Lancaster, Pa., b. Apr. 12, 1856; m. Aug. —, 1888, John J. A. Hoover, b. ———, 1864.
6939. Harriet Wildy, Lancaster, Pa., b. Nov. 19, 1868; d. Apr. 19, 1896.

Family of HENRY B. HERR (3043) and ELIZABETH STROEBLE.

6940. Milton M., Akron, O., b. Apr. 10, 1861; m. Nov. 10, 1897, Harriet Miller, b. Oct. 10, 1878; dau. Riley D. Miller and Eliza J. Philpotts.
6941. Christian S., Phalanx, O., b. Nov. 9, 1863; m. Feb. 21, 1900, Lena Miller, b. Mar. 23, 1871; dau. Riley D. Miller and Eliza J. Philpotts.
6942. Washington M., Akron, O., b. July 4, 1866; m. Sept. 2, 1893, Margaret R. Powell, b. July 5, 1876; dau. James Powell and Emily Bishop.
6943. Barton, Warren, O., b. Jan. 26, 1868; m. Jan. 23, 1895, Fleda Gleick, b. May 25, 1875; dau. George Gleick and Elmyra Heintzleman.
6944. Henry D., Champion, O., b. Nov. 16, 1870; m. Aug. 15, 1895, Gertrude B. Murphy, b. Oct. 21, 1870; dau. John Murphy and Laura J. Shaffer.
6945. Charles, Warren, O., b. Sept. 17, 1873.
6946. John, Warren, O., b. Apr. 26, 1876.
6947. Lauren, Phalanx, O., b. June 27, 1879.

Family of DANIEL B. HERR (3044) and MARY ANN EISENBERGER.

6948. Mary A., Salunga, Pa., b. Feb. 22, 1855; m. ——— Garber.
6949. Barton M., Lancaster, Pa., b. Mar. 1, 1859.

6950. Christian E., Lancaster, Pa., b. Aug. 7, 1861.

6951. Daniel G., Shoffs, Pa., b. July 23, 1866.

6952. Lillie A., Shoffs, Pa., b. July 26, 1869; d. Mar. 18, 1889; m. —————— Morrison.

Family of CHRISTIAN B. HERR (3046) and ELIZABETH BENEDICT.

6953. Aldus B., Millersville, Pa., b. Nov. 12, 1854; m. Dec. 23, 1880, Annie E. Kauffman, b. Nov. 2, 1859; d. June 13, 1898; dau. Abraham Kauffman and Elizabeth ————.

6954. Franklin, New Danville, Pa., b. Jan. 9, 1856.

6955. Elam, Millersville, Pa., b. Feb. 15, 1859.

6956. Elizabeth, Millersville, Pa., b. Feb. 22, 1861; m. Isaac Hess.

6957. Ada, Latrobe, Pa., b. Mar. 23, 1866; m. Nov. 25, 1898, William G. Drumm, b. Feb. 22, 1865; son Daniel L. Drumm and Lavina A. ————.

6958. Emma, Millersville, Pa., b. Dec. 31, 1872; m. June 12, 1890, Jacob J. Lehr, b. Sept. 23, 1867; son Emanuel H. Lehr and Adaline B. ————.

Family of JACOB B. HERR (3049) and BARBARA ANN KINDIG.

6959. Emma Frances, Millersville, Pa., b. Dec. 9, 1863; m. Sept. 24, 1885, John B. Eshback, b. Jan. 14, 1865; son John B. Eshback and Barbara K. ————.

6960. Mary Elizabeth, New Providence, Pa., b. June 2, 1866; m. Nov. 17, 1887, Samuel E. Brubaker, b. Oct. 14, 1866; son Jacob B. Brubaker and Maria W. ————.

6961. Christian Kendig, Millersville, Pa., b. Jan. 14, 1868; m. Oct. 9, 1890, Frances F. Charles, b. Sept. 15, 1869; dau. Joseph W. Charles and Frances L. Forry.

6962. Edwin, New Danville, Pa., b. Sept. 28, 1782; d. Nov. 24, 1872.

6963. Eli, New Danville, Pa., b. Mar. 30, 1875; m. Feb. 26, 1902, Celia M. Mylin, dau. Eli Mylin and ————.

6964. Annie May, New Danville, Pa., b. May 18, 1880; m. Jan. 18, 1903, Charles Weller.

Family of MARTIN R. HERR (3050) and MARTHA KREIDER.

6965. Clara K., Lancaster, Pa., b. Jan. 8, 1870; m. July 17, 1889, Samuel F. Wendler, son John Wendler and Louisa G. Miller.

6966. Christian H., Intercourse, Pa., b. Mar. 15, 1871; m. Feb. 9, 1895, Margaret E. Deitrich, b. Oct. 29, 1876; dau. James M. Deitrich and Lydia A. Smith.

6967. Martin K., Intercourse, Pa., b. Feb. 19, 1888.

Family of ELIZABETH SHENK (3062) and HENRY BOWMAN.

6968. Charles E., Millersville, Pa., b. ———, 1861.

6969. Henry Luther, Millersville, Pa., b. ———, 1862.

6970. Jacob S., Millersville, Pa., b. ———, 1866.

6971. Mary, Millersville, Pa., b. ———, 1870.

Family of SAMUEL M. HERR (3076) and MARIA KAUFFMAN.

6972. Viola A., Boiling Springs, Pa., b. Oct. 12, 1852.

6973. John J., Boiling Springs, Pa., b. Sept. 24, 1854; m. Aug. 26, 1877, Jennie Messinger, b. Apr. 15, 1858; dau. John Messinger and Catharine Leidigh.

6974. S. Milton, Berwick, Pa., b. Aug. 8, 1857; m. Annie Barbour.

6975. Jacob Edwin, Boiling Springs, Pa., b. Sept. 21, 1859; m. Dec. 16, 1879, Emma Shupp, b. Apr. 30, 1858; d. June 5, 1888; m. Aug. 20, 1890, Mary Guttshall, b. July 3, 1860; dau. John Guttshall and Mina Barbour.

6976. Newton K., Boiling Springs, Pa., b. Apr. 24, 1862.

Family of CHRISTIAN K. HERR (3078) and CATHARINE SPANGLER.

6977. Viola, Hatton, Pa., b. Aug. 1, 1857; d. Aug. 7, 1863.

6978. Emerson, Carlisle, Pa., b. July 13, 1859.

6979. Barbara Mae, Philadelphia, Pa.

6980. Jacob, Boiling Springs, Pa., b. Nov. 1, 1862; m. Mayme Galigar.

6981. Henry, Boiling Springs, Pa., b. Nov. 1, 1862; m. Susan Burns.

6982. Abraham, Boiling Springs, Pa.

6983. Christian, Lincoln, Neb., b. June 11, 1867; m. Eva Sterns.

12402. William W., Carlisle, Pa., b. Mar. 7, 1874; m. Apr. 13, 1897,

Dora M. Myers, b. Jan. 31, 1875; dau. James A. Myers and Susan S. Yost.

12403. George, Davy, Neb., b. July 9, 1871; m. Ida Purbaugh.

12404. Mary Catharine, Philadelphia, Pa.

Family of JACOB M. HERR (3080) and ANNIE HERTZLER.

6984. Maurice L., Allegheny, Pa., b. Oct, 11, 1868; m. Nov. 18, 1893, Jessie McFail, b. June 10, 1859; dau. Henry G. Griffin and Sarah R. Dayton.

6985. Amos A., Boiling Springs, Pa., b. May 3, 1871; m. Nov. 16, 1900, Ella Shalto, b. Jan. 1, 1876; dau. David Shalto and Mary A. Beecher.

6986. Mary E., Millersville, Pa., b. Apr. 2, 1873; m. May 23, 1898, Abraham S. Longenecker, son Adam Longenecker and Lizzie ———.

6987. Fannie I., Mechanicsburg, Pa., b. Apr. 21, 1875; m. Nov. 25, 1897, George B. Hoover, son John S. Hoover and Mary Beltzhoover.

6988. Frank E., Millersville, Pa., b. Nov. 30, 1878; m. June 14, 1905, Anna H. Landis (8390).

6989. Annie F., Dillsburg, Pa., b. Apr. 1, 1880; m. Apr. 5, 1906, Jacob W. Kniesly, b. Oct. 29, 1872; son George W. Kniesly and Hattie Ann Elicker.

6990. John M., Boiling Springs, Pa., b. Aug. 27, 1882.

6991. Grace E., Boiling Springs, Pa., b. Sept. 6, 1884.

6992. Jacob O., Boiling Springs, Pa., b. Apr. 7, 1888.

6993. Mattie Mabel, Boiling Springs, Pa., b. Aug. 6, 1890.

Family of DANIEL H. HERR (3082) and EMMA L. ADAMS.

6994. Paul A., Lancaster, Pa., b. Jan. 23, 1880.

Family of STEPHEN B. HERR (3083) and AMANDA MURR.

6995. Stephen Edgar, Philadelphia, Pa.

6996. James, Philadelphia, Pa.

Family of CHRISTIAN G. HERR (3084) and EMMA MILLER.

6997. William M., Lancaster, Pa.
6998. Charles C., Lancaster, Pa.

Family of SUSAN MARGARET HERR (3085) and JOHN KREIDER.

6999. Stephen H., Lancaster, Pa.

Family of CATHARINE H. HERR (3087) and SAMUEL M. FRANTZ.

7000. Daniel Herr, Lancaster, Pa., b. Feb. 6, 1870; m. Apr. 1, 1892, Amelia D. Weller, b. Oct. 1, 1871.
7001. Charles Stephen, Lancaster, Pa., b. July 27, 1871; m. Jan. 2, 1893, Elizabeth Smith, b. Sept. 29, 1864; dau. Albert Smith and Harriet Rosenburg.
7002. Elizabeth Herr, Lancaster, Pa., b. May 4, 1873; m. Oct. —, 1897, Marshall W. Warren, b. Feb. 28, 1856; son Archibald Warren and Susan ———.
7003. Harry Herr, Lancaster, Pa., b. Nov. 1, 1874; d. May 27, 1880.
7004. Emma, Lancaster, Pa., b. June 26, 1877; d. June 6, 1880.
7005. Jennie, Lancaster, Pa., b. Sept. 13, 1879; d. Sept. 13, 1879.
7006. Edgar H., Lancaster, Pa., b. Apr. 30, 1882; d. Aug. 9, 1903; m. Apr. 16, 1903, May L. Leibold, b. 1883; d. Aug. 9, 1909; dau. Isaac Leibold and ———.

Family of MARY M. HERR (3088) and JOHN L. BINKLEY.

7007. Elizabeth Virginia, Lancaster, Pa., b. Mar. 6, 1870; m. Dec. 24, 1899, John W. Bush, b. Mar. 23, 1868.
7008 Maude, Lancaster, Pa., b. Apr. 27, 1872; m. Oct. 17, 1894, William S. Barnholt, b. May 28, 1872.
7009. Mary Belle, Lancaster, Pa., b. Jan. 15, 1878; m. Dec. 25, 1897, George S. Morrison.
7010. John Martin, Lancaster, Pa., b. Feb. 10, 1879.
7011. Florence, Lancaster, Pa., b. Oct. 21, 1881.

Family of ANN ELIZABETH HERR (3089) and EDGAR MARSHALL LEVAN.

7012. Edgar Herr, Lancaster, Pa., b. Sept. 19, 1877.

Family of MARTHA ANN HERR (3101) and JOHN PEART.

7013. Caroline, Rosemont, Pa., b. Sept. 4, 1870.

Family of SILAS S. HERR (3108) and ADALINE FREY.

7014. David V., Pleasant Grove, Pa., b. Jan. 9, 1871; d. June 6, 1877.

7015. Minnie, Pleasant Grove, Pa., b. Oct. 4, 1872; d. June 3, 1877.

7016. Ambrose, Pleasant Grove, Pa., b. Jan. 4, 1875; d. June 6, 1877.

7017. Calvin F., Pleasant Grove, Pa., b. Jan. 4, 1875; m. Dec. 19, 1900, Kathryn Beaver, b. Sept. ———, 1876; dau. ——— ——— and Elizabeth ———.

7018. Florence A., Little Britain, Pa., b. May 4, 1877; m. Sept. 4, 1901, Leiper W. Scott, b. July 23, 1878.

7019. Clara F., Pleasant Grove, Pa., b. Mar. 15, 1880.

7020. James G., Pleasant Grove, Pa., b. Dec. 6, 1882.

7021. Emmitt L., Pleasant Grove, Pa., b. June 16, 1887.

Family of ANNIE HERR (3109) and Rev. AMOS M. STIRK.

7022. Levi Acker, Allentown, Pa., b. May 12, 1872; m. Oct. 10, 1893, Minnie Hoffman, b. Sept. 8, 1872; dau. Winfield G. Hoffman and Sarah E. Butz.

7023. Archie Robert, Lebanon, Pa., b. Oct. 22, 1875; m. July 3, 1894, Gertie R. Ressler, b. Nov. 25, 1875; d. Jan. 13, 1895; dau. Nathan G. Ressler and Alice Neidig.

7024. Alice Elma, Lebanon, Pa., b. Feb. 23, 1882.

7025. Floyd Herr, Lebanon, Pa., b. June 12, 1884.

Family of BARBARA HERR (3110) and PETER WORRALL PRATT.

7026. Clarence Herr, Altoona, Pa., b. Jan. 17, 1874; m. Nov. 17, 1897, Viola K. Hoar.

7027. Ida Mary, Philadelphia, Pa., b. June 4, 1875; m. June 7, 1899, Frank J. Woodward.

7028. Phineas, Altoona, Pa., b. May 1, 1877; m. June 12, 1902, Emma Powell.

7029. Iradell, Altoona, Pa., b. Nov. 17, 1880; m. Dec. 18, 1902, Bertha A. Neff.

7030. Edna Earl, Lima, Pa., b. Dec. 8, ———.

7031. Thomas Clifford, Lima, Pa., b. July 31, 1886.

Family of MARY AMANDA HERR (3111) and JACOB FREY.

7032. Amelia H., Lebanon, Pa., b. June 3, 1872; m. Everett D. Burkett, b. Mar. 28, 1856.

7033. Elma A., Lebanon, Pa., b. Sept. 29, 1878.

Family of AMELIA HERR (3112) and DAVID OHLWILER.

7034. Clarence H., Altoona, Pa., b. Aug. 25, 1879.

7035. David Ralph, Altoona, Pa., b. Nov. 16, 1881.

Family of ALICE HERR (3113) and JOHN B. FISHER.

7036. Mary Herr, Lancaster, Pa., b. June 27, 1885; d. July 1, 1885.

7037. Edna Herr, Lancaster, Pa., b. July 4, 1887.

7038. John Clyde, Lancaster, Pa., b. Dec. 8, 1892.

Family of CHRISTIAN S. HERR (3114) and NETTIE B. PECK.

7039. D. Frederick, Altoona, Pa., b. Apr. 4, 1893.

Family of JACOB H. HERR (3115) and MARY E. DAVIS.

7040. Edna D., Altoona, Pa., b. Oct. 15, 1885.

7041. Raymond D., Altoona, Pa., b. Dec. 18, 1890.

Family of MARTHA HERR (3116) and EDWIN UHLER SOWERS.

7042. Claude Herr, Lebanon, Pa., b. May 14, 1886.

Family of ELMER E. HERR (3117) and KATHARINE DEAN.

7043. Edwin Dean, Trenton, N. J., b. Sept. 17, 1895.

Family of ALFRED B. HERR (3134) and MINNIE M. BENEDICT.

7044. Frank Hiller, Creswell, Pa., b. Aug. 4, 1879.

7045. Fanny Mae, Creswell, Pa., b. June 18, 1881.

7046. Ella Benedict, Creswell, Pa., b. Sept. 12, 1884.

7047. James Mowery, Creswell, Pa., b. Feb. 3, 1893.

7048. Elizabeth, Creswell, Pa.

7049. Oscar, Creswell, Pa.

Family of JOHN B. STEHMAN (3142) and ANNA GARBER.

7050. Jonas G., Mountville, Pa., b. May 6, 1850; m. Jan. 8, 1874, Annie Doner, b. Nov. 29, 1848; dau. John Doner and Elizabeth Landis.

7051. Dr. Henry B., Pasadena, Cal., b. Feb. 9, 1852; m. Apr. 26, 1881, Elizabeth Miller, b. Feb. 1, 1856; dau. Henry Miller and Eliza Regar.

Family of ANNA M. HERR (3147) and Prof. W—— H. SHELLEY.

7052. Annie E., York, Pa., b. Sept. 19, 1881.

Family of HENRY R. HERR (3148) and MARGARET UPP.

7053. John, St. Louis, Mo., b. Dec. 4, 1868; m. Dec. 27, 1898, Lottie H. Dessin, b. July 2, 1876; dau. August W. Dessin and Hannah Greiner.

7054. Fannie, York, Pa., b. Feb. 30, 1875.

7055. George U., York, Pa., b. May 24, 1879.

7056. Elizabeth, York, Pa., b. Aug. 17, 1881.

Family of EDWARD R. HERR (3149) and EMMA B. LANDIS.

7057. Llewellyn, York, Pa.

7058. Edward, York, Pa.

Family of MICHAEL HERR (3155) and AUGUSTA WALZ.

7059. Joseph Michael, Philadelphia, Pa., b. Aug. 24, 1883; d. Aug. 28, 1901.

7060. Anna Barbara, Philadelphia, Pa., b. May 2, 1885; d. Aug. 28, 1901.

Family of MARY HERR (3163) and JOSEPH H. BRINTON.

7061. Arthur H., Thornburg, Pa., b. Mar. 22, 1864; m. Dec. 18, 1899, Marian Jones, dau. Dr. ——— Jones and ———.

7062. Annie G., Thornburg, Pa., b. Apr. 5, 1865.

7063. Mary H., Thornburg, Pa., b. Mar. 6, 1867.

7064. Lillian H., Thornburg, Pa., b. May 6, 1868.

7065. Christian F., New York, N. Y., b. Sept. 14, 1870.

7066. Edith R., London, Eng., b. Apr. 14, 1876; m. Nov. 20, 1903, Edward McKenna.

Family of ANNA E. HERR (3164) and Dr. GRANVILLE B. WOOD.

7067. H. Mary, Lancaster, Pa., b. May 13, 1866; d. Jan. 19, 1887; m. July 22, 1886, George H. Brinton, b. Oct. —, 1859; son George Brinton and Crissy Brinton.

Family of C. BACHMAN HERR (3165) and ANNA HOSTETTER.

7068. Benjamin, Phoenix, Ariz., b. Jan. 2, 1868.

7069. Charles S., Safe Harbor, Pa., b. Sept. 7, 1870; m. Sept. 7, 1888, Lettie Waller, b. Oct. 2, 1871; dau. Joseph Waller and Esther Weil.

Family of Rev. CHARLES HERR (3171) and HELEN DOUGAL.

7070. William Dougal, Jersey City, N. J., b. Apr. 2, 1882; d. Oct. 17, 1895.

7071. Helen Hoffman, Jersey City, N. J., b. May 19, 1884.

7072. Margaret, Jersey City, N. J., b. Jan. 2, 1886.

7073. Philip Hoffman, Jersey City, N. J., b. Oct. 15, 1887; d. Jan. 3, 1892.

7074. Malvina Adler, Jersey City, N. J., b. Dec. 3, 1889.

7075. Narcissa, Jersey City, N. J., b. July 14, 1892; d. Jan. 14, 1895.

Family of FRANCES HERR (3172) and WILLIAM C. NIBLACK.

7076. Narcissa, Chicago, Ill., b. May 2, 1882; m. May 29, 1901, James W. Thorn.

7077. Austin H., Chicago, Ill., b. Sept. 12, 1885.

7078. Lydia, Chicago, Ill., b. Mar. 4, 1889.

Family of JOHN B. KENDIG (3194) and SUSAN BRACKBILL.

7079. Roy Brackbill, Willow Street, Pa., b. Nov. 1, 1874; m. June 21, 1899, Emma A. Brubaker.

7080. Charles Herr, Willow Street, Pa., b. Jan. 25, 1877; m. Apr. 20, 1899, Bertha Mylin.

7081. Jay Brackbill, Willow Street, Pa., b. June 29, 1878; d. Sept. 14, 1878.

Family of LIZZIE KENDIG (3198) and TOBIAS BRENK.

7082. Anna, Millersville, Pa.

7083. May, Millersville, Pa.

7084. Abraham, Millersville, Pa.

7085. Elizabeth, Millersville, Pa.

Family of Wid. LIZZIE K. BRENK (3198) and W—— H. HUBER.

7086. William, Millersville, Pa.

7087. Nellie, Millersville, Pa.

7088. Florence, Millersville, Pa.

Family of SUSAN E. KENDIG (3204) and JOHN GREIDER.

7089. Arthur, Willow Street, Pa.

7090. Bessie, Willow Street, Pa.

7091. Claude, Willow Street, Pa.

Family of JOHN M. WITMER (3208) and JULIA A. BAER.

7092. Fanny M., Suspension Bridge, N. Y., b. May 26, 1873.

7093. Emma A., Suspension Bridge, N. Y., b. Dec. 26, 1874.

7094. Edith M., Suspension Bridge, N. Y., b. May 10, 1877.

7095. Julia A., Suspension Bridge, N. Y., b. Mar. 5, 1880.

7096. Christian H., Suspension Bridge, N. Y., b. Jan. 9, 1882.

7097. Grace A., Suspension Bridge, N. Y., b. Feb. 4, 1884.

7098. Howard B., Suspension Bridge, N. Y., b. Aug. 10, 1892.

Family of FANNY MARIA WITMER (3209) and WILLIAM HENRY EMIG.

7099. Maria Elizabeth, Pittsburg, Pa., b. Feb. 22, 1874; m. June 21, 1900, J. Horace Rudy, b. Sept. 30, 1870; son John Rudy and Emma Fillmore.

7100. John W., Toledo, O., b. May 3, 1875; m. Feb. 7, 1899, Maude Boughton, b. Feb. 19, 1874; dau. William H. Boughton and Wilhelmina Noor.

7101. Charles H., York, Pa., b. Dec. 11, 1876.

7102. Jacob W., York, Pa., b. Apr. 20, 1879.

7103. William Ed., York, Pa., b. July 15, 1880.

7104. Howard A., York, Pa., b. Mar. 2, 1888.

Family of CHRISTIAN FRICK WITMER (3227) and MARY SOPHIA COTTON.

7105. Grace, Williamsville, N. Y., b. June 24, 1879.

7106. Ralph, Williamsville, N. Y., b. Oct. 29, 1880.

7107. Mary, Williamsville, N. Y., b. Dec. 2, 1882.

7108. Christian Cotton, Williamsville, N. Y., b. Oct. 26, 1884.

7109. Anna Elizabeth, Williamsville, N. Y., b. Apr. 30, 1887.

Family of MARY EMMALINE WITMER (3232) and Rev. EDGAR ALLEN PARDEE.

7110. Elmer Witmer, Snyder, N. Y., b. Dec. 16, 1886.

7111. Alice Vinnie, Snyder, N. Y., b. Aug. 17, 1889.

7112. Eulalie Augusta, Snyder, N. Y., b. June 5, 1891.

Family of ABRAHAM L. WITMER (3234) and VINETTA MAY STRANGE.

7113. Walter Abraham, Williamsville, N. Y., b. Mar. 15, 1896.

7114. John Tobias, Williamsville, N. Y., b. July 6, 1898.

7115. Edgar Louis, Williamsville, N. Y., b. Oct. 9, 1901.

Family of CHRISTIAN HABECKER (3244) and SUSAN F. SCHENCK.

7116. Albert S., Rohrerstown, Pa., b. Mar. 7, 1877.

7117. Christian S., Rohrerstown, Pa., b. Sept. 5, 1878.

7118. Ira M., Rohrerstown, Pa., b. Apr. 24, 1880.

7119. Isaac N., Rohrerstown, Pa., b. Nov. 2, 1881.

7120. Ida M., Rohrerstown, Pa., b. Aug. 11, 1883.

7121. Anna L., Rohrerstown, Pa., b. May 21, 1885; d. ——, 1885.

7122. Emily Susan, Rohrerstown, Pa., b. Apr. 18, 1887; d. Mar. 23, 1892.

7123. Ella Nora, Rohrerstown, Pa., b. Nov. 28, 1888.

7124. Bessie S., Rohrerstown, Pa., b. Nov. 8, 1890; d. ——, 1890.

7125. John S., Rohrerstown, Pa., b. Aug. 2, 1892.

7126. Son, Rohrerstown, Pa.

Family of JOHN S. LANDIS (3249) and HELEN HERSHEY.

7127. Mary Alice, Landis Valley, Pa., b. Nov. 27, 1863.
7128. Annie, Landis Valley, Pa., b. July 29, 1865.
7129. Benjamin H., Landis Valley, Pa., b. Jan. 24, 1868; d. Jan. 31, 1868.

Family of FRANKLIN D. HABECKER (3251) and CATHARINE A. SCHENCK.

7130. Myra Anna, Sanborn, N. Y., b. Sept. 22, 1889.
7131. Kate Louise, Sanborn, N. Y., b. Sept. 7, 1892.
7132. Gertrude Ada, Sanborn, N. Y., b. Mar. 21, 1895.
7133. Frances Leons, Sanborn, N. Y., b. Oct. 22, 1897.
7134. Leon Benjamin, Sanborn, N. Y., b. July 25, 1900.

Family of BENJAMIN J. HABECKER (3253) and ELLA E. METZ (5412).

7135. Emma A., Sanborn, N. Y., b. Dec. 17, 1896; d. Dec. 20, 1896.

Family of MARY LUCINDA HERR (3255) and ELI HUBER.

7136. Oliver Jacob, Philadelphia, Pa, b. Nov. 12, 1871; m. Nov. 27, 1893, Mary E. Thompson, dau. Charles Thompson and Elizabeth Beaumont.
7137. Elmer Emmet, Darby, Pa., b. Nov. 30, 1872.
7138. Ida Blanche, Philadelphia, Pa., b. Feb. 15, 1874; m. May 27, 1891, Jacob N. Miller, son Samuel Miller and ———.
7139. Lillie May, Lancaster, Pa., b. Jan. 8, 1876; d. Mar. 23, 1877.
7140. Charles Dennis, Darbey, Pa., b. July 13, 1877.
7141. Fanny Maria, Darby, Pa., b. Nov. 13, 1878; m. June 27, 1900, David Williams, son David Williams and Elizabeth Ponting.
7142. Thomas Bellany, Darby, Pa., b. Jan. 18, 1881.
7143. Guy Arville, Darby, Pa., b. Feb. 6, 1885.
7144. John Franklin, Darby, Pa., b. Aug. 6, 1892.

Family of JOHN FRANKLIN HERR (3256) and ANNIE ISABELLA STEUBE.

7145. Ila May, Lancaster, Pa., b. Feb. 7, 1881; d. July 7, 1881.
7146. Chester Musser, Lancaster, Pa., b. Jan. 28, 1890.
7147. Mabel Ruth, Lancaster, Pa., b. Sept. 20, 1894.
7148. Everett J., Lancaster, Pa., b. June 10, 1896.

Family of MARTHA MATILDA HERR (3257) and BENJAMIN F. GAUL.

7149. Mary Ann, Darby, Pa., b. Sept. 23, 1877.

7150. Edgar Elam, Darby, Pa., b. Aug. 3, 1879.

7151. Eli Marshal, Darby, Pa., b. Nov, 2, 1880.

7152. Bertha May, Darby, Pa., b. Apr. 24, 1882.

7153. Rufus Andrew, Darby, Pa., b. Oct. 15, 1883.

7154. Benjamin Frederick, Darby, Pa., b. Feb. 23, 1888.

7155. Oliver Franklin, Darby, Pa., b. Feb. 21, 1890.

7156. Martha Matilda, Darby, Pa., b. Oct. 23, 1896.

Family of NAOMI HERR (3258) and AMER J. KLINE.

7157. Charles D., Lancaster, Pa., b. May 6, 1883; d. Aug. 13, 1883.

7158. Myrtle M., Lancaster, Pa., b. Apr. 21, 1886; d. Mar. 6, 1908.

7159. Edna May, Lancaster, Pa., b. Dec. 28, 1892.

7160. John J., Lancaster, Pa., b. May 3, 1899.

Family of SUSAN HERR (3259) and JOHN B. YUNGINGER.

7161. Emily Dora, Lancaster, Pa., b. Nov. 15, 1886.

7162. Annabel, Lancaster, Pa., b. Jan. 16, 1888.

7163. Reuben, Lancaster, Pa., b. Feb. 14, 1890; d. Nov. 14, 1890.

Family of CHARLES DENNIS HERR (3260) and EMMA I. ENGLES.

7164. Hattie May, Lancaster, Pa., b. May 10, 1885.

7165. Lawrence F., Lancaster, Pa., b. May 9, 1888; d. Oct. 4, 1896.

7166. John C., Lancaster, Pa., b. Feb. 2, 1891.

7167. Pauline M., Lancaster, Pa., b. Dec. 15, 1893; d. Feb. 23, 1908.

7168. Mabel R., Lancaster, Pa., b. June 9, 1895.

7169. Luther P., Lancaster, Pa., b. Feb. 27, 1898.

Family of EDWIN CROFT (3262) and SARAH ———.

7170. David, Longmont, Col.

7171. Josephine, Longmont, Col.

Family of IDA CROFT (3263) and HUGH A. HECKARD.

7172. Lila, Allegheny City, Pa., b. Sept. 9, 1885.

7173. Ida, Allegheny City, Pa., b. Feb. 18, 1891.

Family of ARTHUR CROFT (3265) and ELIZABETH THOMPSON.

7174. Annie, Bakerstown, Pa.

Family of CLARA CROFT (3269) and C—— D. W. CATON.

7175. Elinor, Pittsburg, Pa.

Family of ANNE MELISSA CAMPBELL (3272) and JOHN G. HALL.

7176. Edna Allen, Pittsburg, Pa., b. Aug. 10, 1878.
7177. John G., Pittsburg, Pa., b. Mar. 18, 1882.

Family of HENRY C. McKELVEY (3273) and IDA DILL.

7178. Frank M., Canton, Ill., b. Sept. 6, 1887.
7179. Raymond, Canton, Ill., b. Aug. 5, 1889.
7180. Olive Irene, Canton, Ill., b. Jan. —, 1892.
7181. Pauline Ethel, Canton, Ill., b. Dec. —, 1894.
7182. Henry C., Canton, Ill., b. Oct. —, 1898.

Family of FRANK M. McKELVEY (3274) and MARY IDA McCORNICK.

7183. Joseph Clifton W., Pittsburg, Pa., b. Jan. 20, 1895.

Family of EDWARD W. McKELVEY (3275) and HARRIET ELIZ. LINDSAY.

7184. Marcus L., Wilmerding, Pa., b. June 30, 1888.
7185. Malvern B., Wilmerding, Pa., b. Jan. 13, 1890.
7186. Margaretta, Wilmerding, Pa., b. May, 10, 1892.
7187. Preston Willis, Wilmerding, Pa., b. Sept. 24, 1897.

Family of CATHARINE MARY CROFT (3277) and EUGENE B. McABEE.

7188. Clifford Eugene, Pittsburg, Pa., b. Sept. 30, 1886; d. July 8, 1887.
7189. Ruth Belle, Pittsburg, Pa., b. Oct. 6, 1888.
7190. Grace, Pittsburg, Pa., b. Sept. 6, 1891.
7191. Bertha, Pittsburg, Pa., b. Mar. 5, 1894; d. Mar. 8, 1894.

Family of BERTHA E. CROFT (3278) and EDWARD B. REILLEY.

7192. Maud, Pittsburg, Pa., b. Nov. 9, 1887; d. Nov. 17, 1907.

7193. Harrison, Iola, Kans., b. Mar. 30, 1892.
7194. Lloyd, Iola, Kans., b. Feb. 1, 1896.
7195. Mary, Iola, Kans., b. Oct. 6, 1899.

Family of MINNIE C. CROFT (3279) and ROBERT LANGLEY.

7196. Milford, Iola, Kan.
7197. Hazel, Iola, Kan.

Family of SAMUEL FRANKLIN HERR (3304) and MARGARET E. KERR.

7198. Henry Bruce, Aspinwall, Pa., b. June 11, 1892.
11963. Edward F., Aspinwall, Pa., b. Sept. 9, 1903.

Family of IRA JEWELL WILLIAMS (3310) and MARY H. JONES (3316).

7199. Ira Jewell, Philadelphia, Pa., b. Sept. 24, 1899.
7200. David Alexander, Philadelphia, Pa., b. July 22, 1901.

Family of FREDERICK JONES (3312) and CATHARINE S. TAFT.

7201. Frederick H., Pittsburg, Pa., b. Nov. 6, 1900.

Family of ETHLWYN H. JONES (3317) and Dr. LAWRENCE LITCHFIELD.

7202. Ethel Carver, Pittsburg, Pa., b. May 10, 1899.
7203. Lawrence, Pittsburg, Pa., b. June 17, 1900.

Family of CHARLES JOHN HERR (3323) and ELLA F. STREIGEL.

7204. Edward C., Brooklyn, O., b. Aug. 9, 1887.

Family of LOUIS F. GUMBART (3328) and ELEANOR M. ETTING.

7205. Harold Etting, Macomb, Ill., b. Dec. 25, 1893.
7206. George Conrad, Macomb, Ill., b. July 30, 1898.

Family of ALICE LOUGEAY (3337) and JOSHUA McCLINTOCK.

7207. David, Philadelphia, Pa., b. Mar. 11, 1899.
7208. Daughter, Philadelphia, Pa., b. Apr. —, 1902.
7209. Son, Philadelphia, Pa., b. Aug. —, 1903.

Family of JESSIE BELLE LEHMAN (3344) and FRANK REED CALLAGHAN.

7210. Jessie Fae, Erie, Pa., b. Nov. 30, 1898.
7211. Frank Reed, Erie, Pa., b. Oct. 19, 1900.

Family of MARY JANE HERR (3348) and ———.

7212. Isaac W. Herr, Springfield, Pa.

Family of MARY ANN HERR (3351) and Dr. AARON WITMER.

7213. Franklin Elmer, Lampeter, Pa., b. July 27, 1855; m. Nov. 30, 1881, Mary Ann Herr (4101).
7214. Abraham, Lampeter, Pa., m. Mary Bachman, dau. Eli Bachman and Elizabeth Miller.
7215. Elam, Lancaster, Pa., m. Elizabeth Bachman, dau. Eli Bachman and Elizabeth Miller.
7216. Hettie, Lancaster, Pa.
7217. Christian, Lancaster, Pa.

Family of SUSAN HERR (3355) and JOSEPH E. WENGER.

7218. Laura, Philadelphia, Pa.
7219. Clarence, Philadelphia, Pa., m. Alice Lockwood.

Family of ABRAHAM H. HERR (3356) and CATHARINE HARNISH.

7220. Frances, Lancaster, Pa., m. John Cross.
7221. Elam, Lancaster, Pa., m. Mary Brenner.
7222. Alfred G., Lancaster, Pa., m. Agnes Brenner.
7223. Franklin M., Lancaster, Pa., b. ———, 1874; d. ———, 1902.
7224. Catharine, Philadelphia, Pa.
7225. Bertha, Lancaster, Pa.
7226. Jonas, Strasburg, Pa.

Family of CHRISTIAN M. HERR (3357) and CATHARINE R. GREIST.

7227. Lillie K., Strasburg, Pa., b. Nov. 20, 1867; m. Frank Mowery, son Daniel Mowery and Emma Weaver.
7228. Laura J., Strasburg, Pa., b. Feb. 5, 1869; d. June 20, 1878.
7229. Ida R., Lancaster, Pa., b. Dec. 15, 1871.

7230. Francis V., Lancaster, Pa., b. Aug. 19, 1872; m. Orie Stewart.
7231. Edgar C. M., Strasburg, Pa, b. Jan. 11, 1874; d. Feb. 22, 1878.
7232. Lena May, Lancaster, Pa., b. June 4, 1879; m. June 16, 1900, Albert E. Miller.
7233. Clarence E., Lancaster, Pa., b. Aug. 3, 1886.
7234. Nettie, Strasburg, Pa.

Family of ELAM S. HERR (3358) and MARY BARR.

7235. Alice C., Belton, Mo., b. Oct. 15, 1868; m. Jan. 28, 1890, Sidney Belcher, b. Apr. 9, 1868; son James O. Belcher and Amanda Phillips.
7236. Abraham M., Belton, Mo., b. Mar. 26, 1870.
7237. Barbara A., Belton, Mo., b. Apr. 15, 1871; d. July 4, 1889.
7238. Emma F., Kansas City, Mo., b. Oct. 16, 1872.
7239. Benjamin B., Kansas City, Mo., b. Dec. 2, 1876; m. Aug. 28, 1900, Fanny B. Landis, dau. Noah Landis and ———.
7240. John H., Lancaster, Pa., b. June 28, 1876; d. Aug. 3, 1876.
7241. David E., Belton, Mo., b. Jan. 25, 1879; d. July 24, 1879.
7242. Ellis F., Belton, Mo., b. May 18, 1881; d. July 8, 1881.
7243. Charles S., Belton, Mo., b. Nov. 17, 1882; d. Feb. 19, 1883.
7244. Lettie Leah, Belton, Mo., b. Nov. 6, 1884; d. Feb. 14, 1889.

Family of LAVINIA HERR (3359) and REUBEN S. NOLT.

7245. Elizabeth L., Strasburg, Pa., b. Nov. 5, 1877.
7246. Emma F., Strasburg, Pa., b. Oct. 11, 1878.
7247. Letitia, Strasburg, Pa., b. Dec. 22, 1880.
7248. Annie M., Strasburg, Pa., b. May 6, 1882.
7249. Willis H., Strasburg, Pa., b. July 31, 1883.
7250. Harry S., Strasburg, Pa., b. Apr. 13, 1885.
7251. Frances, Strasburg, Pa., b. Jan. 1, 1887.

Family ELIZABETH ECKMAN (7679) and DAVID H. BARTHOLOMEW (3364).

7252. Annie Elizabeth, Lancaster, Pa., b. Apr. 20, 1873; d. July 9, 1881.
7253. David Baughman, Philadelphia, Pa., b. Sept. 9, 1874.

7254. Henry Matthew, Lancaster, Pa., b. June 13, 1876; m. Oct. 6, 1897, Hannah M. Hunter, b. Dec. 15, 1874; dau. Daniel M. Hunter and Susan A. Haines.

7255. Mary Ann, Lancaster, Pa., b. Nov. 3, 1877.

7256. Amy Geneva, Lancaster, Pa., b. Apr. 5, 1883.

7257. Guy Clifford, Lancaster, Pa., b. Dec. 21, 1884.

7258. Annie Hester, Lancaster, Pa., b. Jan. 18, 1887.

7259. Elizabeth May, Lancaster, Pa., b. May 18, 1889; d. Feb. 28, 1897.

7260. Sarah Eckman, Lancaster, Pa., b. Dec. 11, 1891.

7261. John Williams, Lancaster, Pa., b. July 8, 1893; d. Dec. 11, 1899.

7262. Edith May, Lancaster, Pa., b. Jan. 22, 1895; d. Dec. 15, 1899.

Family of FRANCIS K. HOOVER (3366) and MARY SNAVELY.

7263. John H., Sterling, Ill., b. Apr. 17, 1862; m. Elizabeth Lefever, dau. Adam Lefever and Emma Sickman.

7264. Edward, Sterling, Ill., b. Aug. 14, 1864.

7265. William, Sterling, Ill., b. Sept. 17, 1866; m. Florence Eshleman, dau. Jacob K. Eshleman and Elizabeth Hendricks.

7266. Harriet, Sterling, Ill., b. Feb. 22, 1869; m. John Reitzel.

7267. Isaac, Sterling, Ill., b. Nov. 30, 1871.

7268. Henry, Sterling, Ill., b. Nov. 15, 1874.

7269. Benjamin, Sterling, Ill., b. June 17, 1877.

7270. Frank K., Sterling, Ill., b. Apr. 28, 1881.

7271. Infant, Sterling, Ill.

Family of MARY HOOVER (3368) and ABRAHAM S. WEAVER.

7272. Mary, Sterling, Ill., b. July 15, 1862; d. ———, 1864.

Family of ANN HOOVER (3369) and Wid. ABRAHAM S. WEAVER.

7273. Benjamin, Sterling, Ill., b. June 22, 1866.

7274. Martha Luetta, Waverly, Ia., b. Jan. 28, 1868; m. July 7, 1892, Amos B. Ahrens, b. Sept. 12, 1866; son Alend Henry Ahrens and Gertina F. Sokeer.

7275. A. ——— Cora, Sterling, Ill., b. Oct. 7, 1870.

7276. Emma G., Sterling, Ill., b. June 12, 1875.

Family of ISAAC S. HOOVER (3370) and MARY MARTIN.

7277. Mary Martha, Sterling, Ill., b. Feb. 27, 1876.

Family of PHARES H. LANDIS (3385) and ANN ELIZA SHULER.

7278. Frank F., Sterling, Ill., b. Jan. 6, 1877.
7279. Harvey S., Sterling, Ill., b. Oct. 28, 1878; d. Feb. 14, 1896.
7280. Cora E., Sterling, Ill., b. Dec. 5, 1880.
7281. Bertha M., Sterling, Ill., b. Oct. 2, 1882.
7282. Arthur R., Sterling, Ill., b. Feb. 2, 1884.
7283. Ida Susan, Sterling, Ill., b. Aug. 8, 1887.
7284. Walter, E., Sterling, Ill., b. July 9, 1890; d. Jan. 15, 1892.
7285. John I., Sterling, Ill., b. Sept. 15, 1891; d. Jan. 14, 1892.
7286. Verna Ruth, Sterling, Ill.
7287. Martha Ann, Sterling, Ill.

Family of MARTHA E. LANDIS (3391) and BENJAMIN F. LANDIS.

7288. Ida B., Cawker, Kans., b. Jan. 3, 1876; m. Feb, 16, 1898, Alvah
    E. Sapp, b. Aug. 9, 1875; son Ananias Sapp and Sarah Boring.
7289. Raymond J., Cawker, Kans., b. June 6, 1877; d. Oct. 12, 1887.
7290. Orra E., Cawker, Kans., b June 17, 1879.
7291. Gertrude M., Cawker, Kans., b. Jan. 16, 1885; d. June 29, 1886.
7292. Myrtle A., Cawker, Kans., b. Jan. 3, 1892.

Family of JOHN HERR (3395) and FRANCES HUBER.

7293. Franklin M., Mt. Nebo, Pa., b. May 5, 1861; m. May 15, 1881,
    Rebecca Armstrong, b. Dec. 14, 1862; dau. William Armstrong
    and Rachael Getz.

Family of FRANKLIN P. LEFEVER (3403) and CATHARINE F. ASH.

7294. Elmer Irving, Coatesville, Pa., b. Sept. 24, 1868; m. Oct. —,
    1901, Lillian Allison Welsh.
7295. Acton Ash, Lancaster, Pa., b. Feb. 5, 1870; m. Emma Wettig,
    dau. Frederick Wettig and Ellen ———.
7296. Elizabeth S., Smyrna, Pa., b. Aug. 14, 1872; m. Oct. —, 1901,
    Maris S. Townsend, son Jacob R. Townsend and Susan ———.

7297. Anna, Lancaster, Pa., b. May 15, 1875; d. Aug. 22, 1877.
7298. Benjamin Herr, Philadelphia, Pa., b. Mar. 15, 1877.
7299. Mary Edith, Bart, Pa., b. Aug. 13, 1879.

Family of EZRA H. WITMER (3407) and ANNIE B. SWEIGART.

7300. Susan Amanda, Philadelphia, Pa., b. June 27, 1867.
7301. Elbertha Catharine, Paradise, Pa., b. Aug. 30, 1869; d. Apr. 29, 1890.
7302. Charles B Herr, Chrome, Va., b. Mar. 22, 1872.
7303. Evelyn Jessie, London Grove, Pa., b. July 30, 1874; m. Aug. 22, 1900, Edwin S. Martin, b. Apr. 7, 1872; son Aaron Martin and Mary A. Baker.
7304. John Amos, Philadelphia, Pa., b. Feb. 26, 1878; m. Dec. 1, 1903, Frances V. Bogardus, b. Mar. 4, 1881; dau. Marcus Brooke Bogardus and Anna A. Carnac.

Family of SUSAN JANE WITMER (3409) and ALDUS J. GROFF (4245).

7305. Anna Mae, Strasburg, Pa., b. Jan. 8, 1870; d. Dec. 11, 1873.
7306. Charles Howard, Berwyn, Pa., b. July 1, 1871; m. Aug. 5, 1898, Carrie Longenecker, dau. Harry Longenecker and Mary Roland.
7307. Fannie Eshleman, Lancaster, Pa., b. May 8, 1873; d. Apr. 21, 1903.

Family of ALONZO P. WITMER (3410) and HARRIET A. CARUTHERS.

7308. Lorin Jason, Philadelphia, Pa., b. Jan. 29, 1872; m. Sept. 4, 1895, Harriet E. Chittenden, dau. Richard L. Chittenden and Ella Howard.
7309. Gertrude Emma, Lancaster, Pa., b. Oct. 1, 1875; m. May 15, 1900, Samuel E. Meister, son Emil Meister and Amelia Kleinschmidt.
7310. William LaRue, Philadelphia, Pa., b. Aug. 3, 1883.
7311. Amos Lightner, Paradise, Pa., b. June 9, 1885; d. July 21, 1886.
5464. Mary Irma Amelia, Philadelphia, Pa., b. July 7, 1891.

Family of LEAH D. WITMER (3411) and T. FILLMORE CARUTHERS.

7312. Eugene Witmer, Philadelphia, Pa., b. Dec. 8, 1880.
7313. Frank D. Earsley, Philadelphia, Pa., b. Jan. 19, 1891.

Family of **MARIA LOUISA WITMER** (3412) and Dr. **EMANUEL R. HERSHEY.**

7314. Leon Witmer, Lancaster, Pa., b. Dec. 19, 1875; m. Feb. 18, 1906, Pearl Hale, dau. James George Hale and Eugenia McCrary.

7315. Ivan D. W., Lancaster, Pa., b. Feb. 22, 1882.

7316. Alva L., Lancaster, Pa., b. Feb. 16, 1888.

Family of **EVALINE J. WITMER** (3413) and **ALEXANDER W. CARLILE.**

7317. Guy Witmer, Harrisburg, Pa., b. Dec. 3, 1888; d. June 9, 1891.

7318. Genevieve, Harrisburg, Pa., b. Dec. 27,, 1892; d. Oct. 3, 1902.

8690. Julian Alexander, Harrisburg, Pa., b. July 27, 1901.

Family of **ABRAHAM GROFF** (3415) and **ANNA MORNINGSTARR.**

7319. George, New Providence, Pa.

7320. David, New Providence, Pa., m. Levanda Sweigart.

7321. John, New Providence, Pa.

7322. Ann Elizabeth, New Providence, Pa.

7323. Lydia, New Providence, Pa.

7324. Mary Catharine, New Providence, Pa.

Family of **BENJAMIN GROFF** (3416) and **HANNAH BROWERS.**

7325. Isaac Henry, New Providence, Pa., m. Mary C. Ludwig.

7326. Nancy, New Providence, Pa., m. Jerry S. Oppenshain.

7327. Sarah Ann, New Providence, Pa.

7328. John, New Providence, Pa., m. Nancy McCooly.

7329. Harriet, New Providence, Pa., m. Willard Griswell.

7330. David, New Providence, Pa.

7331. Isabel, New Providence, Pa.

7332. Margaret, New Providence, Pa.

7333. Maria L., New Providence, Pa.

7334. Daniel, New Providence, Pa.

Family of **DAVID GRAFFT** (3417) and **BARBARA GROVE** (3882).

7335. Emanuel, El Paso, Ill., b. Mar. 22, 1848; d. June 16, 1851.

7336. John J., El Paso, Ill., b. Mar. 16, 1850.

7337. Sarah Ann, El Paso, Ill., b. Dec. 21, 1851.
7338. Mary Elizabeth, El Paso, Ill., b. June 7, 1855; d. Mar. 13, 1857.
7339. Eliza Ellen, El Paso, Ill., b. May 4, 1857.
7340. Nancy Jane, El Paso, Ill., b. Mar. 19, 1862.
7341. Diana May, El Paso, Ill., b. Sept. 25, 1864.

Family of ELIZA GRAFFT (3418) and ISAAC VANOUSDALL.

7342. Peter, El Paso, Ill.
7343. David, El Paso, Ill.
7344. Martin, El Paso, Ill.
7345. Rachael, El Paso, Ill.
7346. Ann Maria, El Paso, Ill.
7347. Henry H., El Paso, Ill.
7348. Susetta C., El Paso, Ill.
7349. Mary France, El Paso, Ill.
7350. Maria, El Paso, Ill.,
7351. John, El Paso, Ill.
7352. Isaac, El Paso, Ill.
7353. Henry, El Paso, Ill.
7354. Elizabeth, El Paso, Ill.
7355. Lillie May, El Paso, Ill.

Family of NANCY GRAFFT (3419) and SAMUEL DILLMAN.

7356. Josephine, El Paso, Ill.
7357. Mary J., El Paso, Ill.
7358. William Henry, El Paso, Ill.
7359. Arthur, El Paso, Ill.
7360. Levanda, El Paso, Ill.
7361. Isabel, El Paso, Ill.
7362. Frank, El Paso, Ill.

Family of DANIEL GRAFFT (3420) and DIANA GROVE (3883).

7363. William, Wyers Cave, Va.
7364. Mary E., Wyers Cave, Va.
7365. John J., Waynesborough, Va.

Family of MARY ANN GRAFFT (3421) and DAVID JONES.

7366. William Edgar, El Paso, Ill.
7367. Flora Bell, El Paso, Ill.
7368. Luella, El Paso, Ill.

. Family of HENRY GRAFFT (3422) and ELIZABETH GROVE (3885).

7369. Charles, Koiners Store, Va.
7370. Emma, Koiners Store, Va.
7371. Virginia, Koiners Store, Va.
7372. Sarah E., Koiners Store, Va.

Family of ELIAS KENDIG (3430) and ELIZABETH WINE.

7373. John E., Roanoke, Ill., b. Sept. 2, 1840.
7374. Daniel H., Washington, Ill., b. June 6, 1843.
7375. David M., Washington, Ill., b. May 18, 1845.
7376. Andrew J., Washington, Ill., b. Sept. 19, 1847.
7377. Mary F., Washington, Ill., b. Feb. 23, 1850.
7378. Absolom P., Roanoke, Ill., b. Mar. 13, 1852.
7379. James R., Roanoke, Ill., b. Oct. 24, 1854.

Family of ABRAHAM H. KENDIG (3433) and ELIZABETH WENGER.

7380. Emanuel David, Fishersville, Va., b. May 19, 1850.
7381. Leona Jane, Fishersville, Va., b. Mar. 17, 1853.

Family of MARY KENDIG (3434) and Wid. JOHN S. ROBINSON.

7382. Emanuel Thomas, Blue Ridge, Va., b. Aug. 22, 1843; m. Aug. 22, 1872, Frances Susan Noffsinger, b. Sept. 11, 1853; dau. William Noffsinger and America E. Graybill.
7383. Elizabeth Ann, Roanoke, Ill., b. Sept. 28, 1844; m. Dec. 25, 1862, William McKendree Jeter, b. Feb. 22, 1842; d. Aug. 11, 1883; son James Jeter and Sarah Paterson.
7384. Melissa Ellen, Roanoke, Ill., m. Abraham Barnhart.
7385. Martha Lee, Colfax, Ill., m. Philip Brown.
7386. Eliza D. Mott, Colfax, Ill.
7387. Clara Salina, Bloomington, Ill., m. Palo Fisher.

7388. John Henry, Venus, Ark., m. Elva Shook.

7389. Emma Dora, Roanoke, Ill., m. Thomas Brown.

7390. James Rufus, Henry, Ill., m. Marietta Anderson.

Family of ANNA KENDIG (3435) and DAVID TROUT FAUBER.

7391. Lavina I., Roanoke, Ill., b. Oct. 24, 1847; d. Mar. 31, 1879; m. ———— Heppard.

7392. Samuel H., Onargo, Ill., b. May 30, 1850.

7393. Emanuel D., Roanoke, Ill., b. Mar. 7, 1852.

7394. Eliza Ann, Roanoke, Ill., b. Apr. 9, 1854; d. Dec. 24, 1859.

7395. Barbara E., Roanoke, Ill., b. May 12, 1856; m. Jan. 27, 1880, Edward M. Cox, b. Apr. 15, 1854; son William Cox and Katharine Fagelly.

7396. Mary K., Sibley, Ia., b. Apr. 7, 1858; m. Feb. 18, 1877, Samuel M. Bullington, b. May 26, 1851.

7397. Virginia M., Roanoke, Ill., b. Feb. 16, 1860; m. Mar. 4, 1883, John W. Heppard, b. Aug. 15, 1856; son Jacob Heppard and Susan Spears.

7398. James W., Roanoke, Ill., b. July 26, 1863; m. Aug. 2, 1883, Minnie C. Peterson, b. Mar. 4, 1868; dau. Herman Peterson and Elizabeth Bowers.

7399. Eliza Alice, Roanoke, Ill., b. Nov. 19, 1865; d. Apr. 12, 1894; m. Feb. —, 1889, Joseph S. Risser, b. Dec. 8, 1863; son John Risser and Anna Forney.

7400. Minnie Lee, Stewarts Draft, Va., b. May 26, 1868; m. Dec. 24, 1889, Frank J. Engle; m. June 1, 1898, Dr. W———. B. Dodge.

Family of HENRY KENDIG (3436) and MARGARET ANDERSON.

7401. Terrisia, Roanoke, Ill., b. Nov. 9, 1847.

7402. Susan J., Roanoke, Ill., b. Mar. 1, 1849.

7403. James E., Roanoke, Ill., b. Jan. 3, 1855.

7404. Emma D., Roanoke, Ill., b. Aug. 28, 1857.

Family of ELIZABETH KENDIG (3437) and HENRY B. JONES.

7405. Emanuel H., Sweetman, Va., b. Mar. 15, 1852; m. Feb. 14, 1877, Sarah Ellen Brooks, dau. Jacob Brooks and Freyborn Rider.

7406. James R., Sweetman, Va., b. June 12, 1854; m. Susan ————.
7407. Abraham A., Fishersville, Va., b. Mar. 19, 1858; m. Ida ————.
7408. Frances M., Roanoke, Ill., b. Apr. 24, 1860.
7409. Lucy M., Roanoke, Ill., b. June 24, 1863; m. Robert S. Sutter.
7410. Charles W., Charlotte, N. C., b. July 11, 1865; m. Cora ————.
7411. Jacob W., Roanoke, Ill., b. May 18, 1868.

Family of ELLEN KENDIG (3439) and JOSEPH N. BROWN.

7412. John C., Roanoke, Ill., b. Sept. 20, 1856.
7413. Thomas E., Roanoke, Ill., b. Mar. 15, 1858.
7414. Benjamin F.. Roanoke, Ill.. b. Feb. 14, 1860.
7415. Sarah E., Roanoke, Ill., b. Feb. 3, 1862.
7416. Charles H., Stuarts Draft, Va., b. July 31, 1864.
7417. Mary E., Stuarts Draft, Va., b. Jan. 24. 1867.

Family of HANNAH HERR (3442) and Wid. ADAM BAER.

7418. Infant, Hagerstown, Md., b. Jan. 3, 1852; d. Jan. 3, 1852.
7419. Henry H., Hagerstown, Md., b. May 15, 1853; m. Nov. 17,
    1874, Susan L. Horst, b. Jan. 5, 1851; d. Sept. 23, 1884; dau.
    Abraham Horst and Mary Lesher; m. ————, 1885, Wid.
    Barbara M. Risser, b. Aug. 10, 1858, dau. Abraham Martin
    and Barbara Wenger.
7420. Maria, Hagerstown, Md., b. Aug. 6, 1856; m. May 10, 1877,
    Jacob W. Eshleman, b. July 26, 1856; son Jonas Eshleman and
    Mary Whisler.
7421. Martin, Menges Mills, Pa., b. Feb. 26, 1860; m. Nov. 29, 1883,
    Annie B. Brackbill (8688).
7422. Adam, Paramount, Md., b. Sept. 18, 1865; m. Dec. 26, 1895,
    Bertha Metz, b. Feb. 19, 1871; dau. Jacob Metz and Elizabeth
    Ebersole.

Family of MARY ANN HERR (3443) and JACOB L. HESS.

7423. Elizabeth, Lancaster, Pa., b. Mar. 15, 1853; d. Nov. 20, 1855.
7424. Martin, Lancaster, Pa., b. Oct. 5, 1855; m. Mary Huber, dau.
    David Huber and Maria McCartney.

7425. Barbara, Lancaster, Pa., b. May 25, 1858; m. Jacob Sigler.

7426. Henry H., New Danville, Pa., b. July 3, 1860.

7427. Martha, New Danville, Pa., b. July 7, 1863; d. Feb. 19, 1864.

7428. Anna, New Danville, Pa., b. Nov. 6, 1864; d. Aug. 10, 1865.

7429. Jacob L., New Danville, Pa., b. Feb. 6, 1866.

7430. Mary, New Danville, Pa., b. Nov. 2, 1868; m. Mar. 17, 1892, John W. Eshleman (9232).

7431. Frances, New Danville, Pa., b. Jan. 27, 1872.

7432. Susanna, New Danville, Pa., b. July 8, 1875.

Family of ELIZABETH HERR (3444) and SAMUEL H. SHENK.

7433. Mary, Strasburg, Pa., b. Feb. 14, 1858; m. Feb. 28, 1882, Amos C. Herr (1611).

7434. Henry H., Lancaster, Pa., b. Oct. 22, 1860; m. Sept. 16, 1890, Elizabeth Herr (8310).

7435. Anna, New Danville, Pa., b. Jan. 22, 1863; m. Nov. 22, 1883, Jacob B. Harnish, b. June 1, 1861; son Jacob Harnish and Barbara Buckwalter.

7436. Elizabeth, New Danville, Pa., b. Aug. 23, 1866; d. Nov. —, 1898.

7437. Martin, New Danville, Pa., b. Oct. 28, 1872; m. Mary Bomberger, dau. Christian Bomberger and ————.

7438. Magdalena, New Danville, Pa., b. Nov. 17, 1875.

Family of MAGDALENA HERR (3446) and JOHN B. MYERS.

7439. David, New Danville, Pa., b. Nov. 15, 1863.

7440. Ada, New Danville, Pa., b. Sept. 19, 1865.

7441. Anna, New Danville, Pa., b. Oct. 27, 1867.

7442. Martin, New Danville, Pa., b. Aug. 7, 1870; m. Dec. 20, 1893, Elizabeth H. Snavely (7623).

7443. Elam, New Danville, Pa., b. Aug. 3, 1873.

7444. Henry, New Danville, Pa., b. Feb. 17, 1877.

7445. John, New Danville, Pa., b. Apr. 7, 1880; d. Mar. 18, 1884.

Family of MARTIN B. HERR (3447) and ANNA H. SHENK.

7446. Mary, New Danville, Pa., b. Mar. 13, 1868; d. Aug. 25, 1868.

7447. Susan S., New Danville, Pa., b. Sept. 3, 1869; m. Dec. 4, 1895, Harry L. Herr (8329).

7448. Martha, Mechanicsburg, Pa., b. Mar. 4, 1874; m. Aug. 3, 1898, Martin R. Nissley, b. June 3, 1876; son Christian L. Nissley and Catharine Reist.

7449. Annie, New Danville, Pa., b. July 24, 1881.

Family of Rev. ABRAHAM B. HERR (3449) and ANNIE RANCK.

7450. Susan, New Danville, Pa., b. Dec. 19, 1868; m. Nov. 11, 1890, Emanuel Groff (8314).

7451. Amos, New Danville, Pa., b. Jan. 28, 1872; d. Mar. 1, 1872.

7452. Mary, New Danville, Pa., b. Oct. 20, 1873; d. Mar. 16, 1874.

7453. Henry R., New Danville, Pa., b. Feb. 3, 1875; m. Dec. 29, 1897, Ada H. Groff (8318).

7454. Elizabeth, New Danville, Pa., b. Dec. 10, 1877; m. Nov. 15, 1900, Amos H. Snavely (7626).

7455. Annie, New Danville, Pa., b. Jan. 6, 1880; d. Nov. 11, 1887.

7456. Martin, New Danville, Pa., b. May 9, 1881: d. July 29, 1881.

7457. Abraham, New Danville, Pa., b. May 22, 1882.

7458. Amanda, New Danville, Pa., b. Nov. 15, 1884.

Family of Wid. Rev. ABRAHAM B. HERR (3449) and SUSAN M. SHENK.

7459. Mattie S., New Danville, Pa., b. July 10, 1888; d. July 10, 1888.

Family of BENJAMIN HERR (3452) and MARY AMELIA COOPER.

7460. Eva, Cleveland, O., b. Mar. 9, 1861; m. Feb. 8, 1883, Michael S. Craley, b. Sept. 6, 1848; son Michael Craley and Elizabeth Flesh.

7461. Alice, Everette, Ill., b. Feb. 28, 1863; m. Dec. 31, 1890, Herman R. Weaver, b. Nov. 27, 1848; son Joseph Weaver and Melissa Benedict.

Family of CHRISTIAN HERR (3453) and MARGARET HYDE.

7462. Emma, Brookfield, Mo., m. Apr. 27, 1886, Joseph Lyford, b. Aug. 15, 1865.

7463. Franklin, Ainsworth, Ia., m. Mar. 24, 1892, Viola Stevens, b. May 15, 1867.

7464. William, Wilton, Ia., b. Jan. 24, 1873; m. Feb. 14, 1900, Edith Haggerty.
7465. Nellie, Larwill, Ind., b. June 12, 18—; m. Aug. 21, 1900, Sherman Byall.
7466. ———, Larwill, Ind.
7467. ———, Larwill, Ind.
7468. ———, Larwill, Ind.

Family of MARY E. HERR (3454) and EDWIN D. REEVE.

7469. George Albert, Tipton, Ia., b. Feb. 9, 1866; m. Dec. 10, 1889, Annetta L. Bolton, b. Nov. 22, 1868; dau. John H. Bolton and Cornelia Culver.
7470. Francis Wayland, West Branch, Ia., b. July 28, 1868; m. Jan. 28, 1892, Fannie Folsom, d. June —, 1895; m. Nov. 15, 1898, Arminta May Owen.
7471. Frances Lawrence, Tipton, Ia., b. Feb. 7, 1871; m. Feb. 4, 1892, Charles K. Pierce, b. Dec. 21, 1870; son Andrew Pierce and Julia Mary Lyle.
7472. Mary Susan, West Branch, Ia., b. May 26, 1874; m. Apr. 10, 1894, Homer Morton.
7473. James Marion, Tipton, Ia., b. July 16, 1876; m. Apr. 1, 1892, Lola Kemp.
7474. Edwin, Tipton, Ia., b. Nov. 27, 1878.

Family of GEORGE W. HERR (3455) and SUSAN WALLACE.

7475. Dr. Arthur Wallace, Cleveland, O., b. Mar. 18, 1868; m. June 21, 1897, Dr. Ida M. Shively, b. Feb. 29, 1868; dau. Jacob Shively and Harriet Gibson.
7476. Minnie, Wilton, Ia., b. Aug. 23, 1870; m. Nov. 21, 1891, Oily Stuttler, b. Sept. 4, 1863; son Jessie Stuttler and Malinda Robinson.
7477. Jesie Belle, Muscantine, Ia., b. May 13, 1873; m. June 7, 1900, Clifford Covell, b. May 28, 1873; son Julius Covell and Augusta Stuart.
7478. Myrtle Irene, Wilton, Ia., b. Aug. 20, 1875; m. Mar. 21, 1901,

Royal Kelly, son Abner Kelly and Martha Barr.

7479. Eva Laura, Wilton, Ia., b. Feb. 21, 1878.

7480. Mary Bertha, Wilton, Ia., b. Oct. 19, 1880.

7481. Herbert Nele, Wilton, Ia., b. Mar. 4, 1885.

7482. Walter Leonard, Wilton, Ia., b. Oct. 2, 1890.

Family of FRANCES HERR (3456) and CHARLES ALDRICH.

7483. Edward, Benton Co., Ia.

7484. Mary, Benton Co., Ia.

Family of ELIZA ANN HERR (3457) and JOSEPH A. WALLACE.

7485. George H., Nassau, Minn., b. Dec. 27, 1868.

7486. Josephine G., Brush, Col., b. Dec. 7, 1870; m. Mar. 11, 1895, James E. Armstrong.

7487. Raymond W., Brush, Col., b. Mar. 28, 1873; d. Oct. 30, 1894.

7488. Thomas A., Brush, Col., b. Dec. 7, 1875.

7489. William A., Brush, Col., b. May 24, 1879.

7490. Mabel E., Brush, Col., b. Feb. 8, 1882.

7491. Ernest L., Brush, Col., b. July 22, 1885; d. ———, 1885.

7492. Everett L., Brush, Col., b. May 3, 1888.

Family of JOHN HERR (3458) and FLOY CARL.

7493. George L., Wilton, Ia.

7494. Edwin, Wilton, Ia.

7495. Pearl, Muscatine, Ia., m. Samuel Braumbaugh.

7496. Roland, Wilton, Ia.

7497. ———, Wilton, Ia.

7498. ———, Wilton, Ia.

Family of ADALINE HERR (3459) and REUBEN NAUMAN.

7499. Mary Katharine, Afton, Ia., b. Sept. 27, 1875; m. Apr. 3, 1897, Charles Siddens, b. Sept. 30, 1876.

7500. John Edwin, Afton, Ia., b. Sept. 30, 1877.

7501. Susan Albina, Afton, Ia., b. Nov. 7, 1897.

7502. Reatus Earl, Afton, Ia., b. Nov. 7, 1881.

7503. Ada Pearl, Afton, Ia., b. Dec. 19, 1882.

7504. Bessie May, Afton, Ia., b. Apr. 9, 1886.

7505. Merel Leroy, Afton, Ia., b. Dec. 9, 1887.

7506. Roland Levi, Afton, Ia., b. Aug. 24, 1889.

7507. Minnie Lela, Afton, Ia., b. Feb. 13, 1891.

7508. Clarence Lloyd, Afton, Ia., b. June 23, 1892.

7509. Vernon Raymond, Afton, Ia., b. May 13, 1895.

7510. Muda Glee, Afton, Ia., b. Sept. 18, 1896.

7511. Ruby Gladys, Afton, Ia., b. Nov. 15, 1900.

Family of Wid ELIZA B. WARFEL (3460) and MARTIN F. KENDIG.

7512. Mary A. B., Lancaster, Pa., b. June 9, 1854; m. Abraham Stiffle.

7513. John B., Lancaster, Pa., b. July 9, 1856; m. Jan. 3, 1882, Elizabeth Brill, b. Jan. 22, 1855; dau. Martin Brill and Charlotte Hedrick.

7514. Francis E., Lancaster, Pa., b. Dec. 14, 1859; d. June 1, 1891.

7515. Martin H., Lancaster, Pa., b. Aug. 16, 1863; d. July 6, 1880.

7516. Franklin B., Lancaster, Pa., b. Nov. 9, 1865; m. Jan. 22, 1889, Mary Reinfried, b. May 27, 1861; dau. Peter Reinfried and Elizabeth Powel.

7517. Harry W., Lancaster, Pa., b. Sept. 22, 1869.

Family of ESTHER BACHMAN (3462) and SIMON R. WEAVER (4321)

7518. Maris B., Lampeter, Pa., b. Jan. 8, 1848; m. Esther Zittle, dau. Elijah Zittle and ——— Miller.

7519. Ann Elizabeth, Bart, Pa., b. Nov. 2, 1849; m. Taylor Stafford.

7520. Franklin Rush, Rawlinsville, Pa., b. June 10, 1851; d. Sept. 23, 1856.

7521. John Bachman, Gordonville, Pa., b. Oct. 12, 1853; m. Feb. —, 1884, Mary Morrow, b. Apr. 17, 1860; dau. Ishmael Morrow and Rosa Shreiner.

7522. Martha Jane, Lancaster, Pa., b. May 14, 1855; m. Nov. 15, 1877, Philip Hottenstein, b. ———, 1848; son Philip Hottenstein and ——— Sheaffer.

20

7523. Esther Alice, Rawlinsville, Pa., b. Feb. 14, 1858; d. Feb. 14, 1858.

7524. Mary Emma, Gap, Pa., b. Dec. 28, 1859; m. William Sterling, son William Sterling and ———— Eagens.

7525. Charles Herr, West Town, Pa., b. Feb. 1, 1861; m. Annie Kreider, dau. Isaac Kreider and Mary Denlinger.

7526. Simon Wesley, Kinzers, Pa., b. Sept. 23, 1862; m. Laura Rutter.

7527. Benjamin Franklin, Kinzers, Pa., b. June 20, 1864; m. Annie Kemerer, dau. Joseph Kemerer and ———— Futer.

7528. Effie Kate, Germantown, Pa., b. Apr. 20, 1866; m. Samuel Harking, son Samuel Harking and ———— Rhoads.

Family of LYDIA ANN BACHMAN (3464) and ABRAHAM STONER.

7529. Frances Ann, Quarryville, Pa., b. May 25, 1856; m. June 27, 1867, Charles H. Geiger, b. Oct. 6, 1853; son Christopher Geiger and Anna Beates.

7530. Annie E., Philadelphia, Pa., b. Oct. 13, 1857; m. Nov. 3, 1880, Harvey F. Haverstick (6227).

Family of Wid. LYDIA ANN B. STONER (3464) and LEVI LEONARD.

7531. Willis B., New Providence, Pa., b. Jan. 11, 1863; d. Jan. 17. 1863.

7532. John A., New Providence, Pa., b. Feb. 4, 1864; d. Aug. 21, 1864.

7533. Abraham H., Philadelphia, Pa., b. Feb. 4, 1864; m. Apr. 2, 1890, Susan Patrick, b. Sept. 5, 1868; dau. John Patrick and Elizabeth ————.

7534. DeWilton, New Providence, Pa., b. Jan. 27, 1866; d. Mar. 8, 1871.

7535. Charles B., New Providence, Pa., b. Nov. 19, 1867.

7536. David Maurice, Brooklyn, N. Y., b. Feb. 28, 1871.

7537. Infant, New Providence, Pa., b. Nov. 2, 1872; d. Nov. 2, 1872.

7538. Harry M., New Providence, Pa., b. May 29, 1874; d. June 16, 1874.

Family of FRANCES BACHMAN (3466) and ISRAEL C. LANDIS.

7539. John, Lancaster, Pa.

7540. Elmer, Lancaster, Pa.

Family of JOHN M. BACHMAN (3468) and MARY B. HARNISH.

7541. Eliza A., Rock Hill, Pa., b. July 15, 1865; d. Apr. 1, 1868.

7542. John H., Rock Hill, Pa., b. Feb. 12, 1867; d. June 26, 1867.

7543. Jacob B., Lancaster, Pa., b. Feb. 12, 1867; m. —— Susan ———.

7544. Ada Ann, Rock Hill, Pa., b. June 13, 1869; d. Sept. 28, 1878.

Family of Wid. JOHN M. BACHMAN (3468) and SUSAN HARNISH.

7545. Benjamin F., Lancaster, Pa., b. Mar. 16, 1875; m. Oct. 4, 1899, Maude E. Leinbach, b. July 18, 1878; dau. Ezra S. Leinbach and Emma M. Greider.

7546. John Ira, Pittsburg, Pa., b. Nov. 27, 1876.

7547. Lee Roy, Lancaster, Pa., b. June 7, 1878; m. Apr. 17, 1900, Ella M. Rohrer, b. May 6, 1880; dau. Mifflin E. Rohrer and Louise Spicer.

7548. Arthur G., Lancaster, Pa., b. June 8, 1880.

Family of AMANDA BACHMAN (3470) and BENJAMIN WEAVER.

7549. Elizabeth, Lancaster, Pa., b. Aug. 1, 1865; d. Aug. 16, 1865.

7550. Laura, Lancaster, Pa., b. Mar. 11, 1867; d. Mar. 25, 1900; m. George W. Fisher, son William Fisher and Caroline Gump.

7551. Edith, Lancaster, Pa., b. May 22, 1869; m. ———, 1889, William Weigand, b. Apr. 2, 1867; son Edward Weigand and Jemima ———.

7552. Ella M., Lancaster, Pa., b. Nov. 2, 1872; m. June 25, 1892, Ralph Marroquin, b. Oct. 24, 1868.

Family of JOHN HERR (3472) and MARY E. McVEY.

7553. Benjamin Francis, Harrisonville, Mo., b. Mar. 21, 1862; m. May 7, 1886, Celia M. Jessup, b. Nov. 15, 1865; d. Aug. 24, 1887; dau. Lewis Jessup and Lucy Pierce; m. Jan. 25, 1897, Annie B. St. John, b. Aug. 15, 1865; dau. Ronald B. St. John and Emily Prather.

7554. Maria Adele, Macksburg, Ia., b. May 10, 1866; m. Feb. 25, 1886, William H. Rowe, b. Apr. 28, 1860; son Martin Rowe and Rebecca Gray.

7555. Annie Eva, Colorado Springs, Col., b. Feb. 11, 1870; m. Mar. 27, 1892, Burton L. Townsend, b. Jan. 25, 1871; son Levi T. Townsend and Lois L. Thompson.

7556. Hattie Belle, Woodhull, Ill., b. May 15, 1877; m. Aug. 27, 1899, Maurice Garrison, b. Dec. 22, 1873; son William B. Garrison and Caroline Rickey.

Family of BENJAMIN HERR (3473) and REBECCA ROSE WILSON.

7557. Frances, Downey, Ia., b. July 29, 1867; m. Jan. 25, 1887, Edward Wells, b. Sept. 1, 1863.

7558. George, West Liberty, Ia., b. Mar. 12, 1870; m. Feb. 20, 1895, Hattie Verry, b. Aug. 29, 1879; d. Dec. 15, 1898.

7559. Bertha E., West Liberty, Ia., b. Apr. 15, 1876.

7560. Carrie M., West Liberty, Ia., b. Jan. 11, 1878; m. Feb. 22, 1899, Edwin James, b. May 22, 1873.

Family of MARIA HERR (3474) and JOSEPH L. REED.

7561. Charles, Superior, Neb.

7562. Harry, Chicago, Ill.

Family of ELLEN HERR (3475) and MILTON A. BUDLONG.

7563. Edwin S., Salem, Ore., b. July 6, 1870; m. Apr. 10, 1890, Alice Thomas, b. Jan. 12, 1871; dau. Obijah P. Thomas and Maria Millan.

7564. Harry A., Mill City, Ore., b. July 7, 1872; m. Oct. 10, 1894, Ida May Work, b. May 9, 1876; dau. Charles W. Work and Carrie Rains.

7565. Alena Ellen, Salem, Ore., b. June 18, 1876; m. Oct. 27, 1897, Clifford D. Vaughn, b. Jan. 25, 1867; son James Vaughn and Ada McCreary.

7566. Rollin Howard, Salem, Ore., b. Feb. 15, 1882; d. Oct. 9, 1896.

6763. Amelia Alice, Franklin Co., Neb., b. July 24, 1874; d. Oct. 8, 1880.

Family of DANIEL HERR (3476) and CYNTHIA A. CRAVEN.

7567. Frances M., Puyallup, Wash., b. Nov. 30, 1875.

7568. Bessie B., Puyallup, Wash., b. Dec. 22, 1877; m. Sept. 27, 1905, Carl Lars Struve, b. Apr. 28, 1878; son Jacob G, Struve and Mary Gruber.

7569. Harley Weaver, Puyallup, Wash., b. Apr. 7, 1880; d. July 2, 1893.

7570. Ethel B., Puyallup, Wash., b. Aug. 14, 1882.

7571. Theron Craven, Puyallup, Wash., b. Mar. 22, 1885; d. July 2, 1893.

7572. Leila Leota, Puyallup, Wash., b. June 2, 1887.

7573. Archie John, Puyallup, Wash., b. Sept. 4, 1889.

7574. Norman, Puyallup, Wash., b. June 20, 1892.

7575. Wallace, Puyallup, Wash., b. July 16, 1895.

Family of AMOS HERR (3477) and MAGGIE DISE.

7576. Fannie May, Pendleton, Ore., b. Feb. 21, 1874; m. July 14, 1894, Joseph P. Francis, b. Nov. 27, 1865; son James P. Francis and Mary Ann Gidley.

7577. Charles Laird, Lincoln, Neb., b. Apr. 11, 1876; m. Rose Schermain.

7578. Amos Daily, Letcher, Cal., b. June 16, 1878; m. July 11, 1900, Libbie Weaver, b. Mar. 26,1885; dau. Ely Weaver and Mattie A. ———.

7579. Hubert Parnell, Letcher, Cal., b. Feb. 13, 1880.

7580. Maggie May, Bozeman, Mont., b. May 21, 1882; m. William A. Merryman.

7581. Grover Cleveland, Lincoln, Neb., b. Dec. 2, 1884.

7582. Roy DeWitt, Lincoln, Neb., b. Feb. 21, 1887.

Family of JENNIE HERR (3479) and R. DECATUR SPRINGER.

7583. Victor Leland, Akron, O., b. Jan. 1, 1879; d. Sept. —, 1885.

Family of MARY ANN HERR (3483) and JOHN HART.

7584. Naomi, Willow Street, Pa., b. Feb. 18, 1862; m. Aug. 18, 1885, William E. McFalls, b. Dec. 12, 1862; son William F. McFalls and Harriet Daily.

Family of BENJAMIN M. HERR (3484) and ELIZABETH RHINIER.

7585. Clara J., New Danville, Pa., b. Aug. 19, 1872; d. Jan. 8, 1878.

7586. Benjamin F., Lancaster, Pa, b. Apr. 15, 1874.

7587. Elizabeth R., New Danville, Pa., b. Jan. 30, 1876; d. Dec. 29, 1877.

7588. Ella N., Lancaster, Pa., b. Dec. 22, 1877.

7589. Bertha B., Lancaster, Pa., b. Oct. 4, 1880.

7590. Martin B., New Danville, Pa., b. Mar. 15, 1883; d. Mar. 8, 1884.

7591. Annie M., Lancaster, Pa., b. Aug. 29, 1886.

7592. Barbara A., New Danville, Pa., b. Mar. 8, 1888; d. Mar. 10, 1888.

7593. Samuel H., New Danville, Pa., b. Aug. 23, 1891.

7594. Mabel R., New Danville, Pa., b. Feb. 14, 1894; d. Feb. 7, 1897.

Family of ELIZA HERR (3485) and JOHN BEAM MORTON.

7595. John Herr, Sterling, Ill., b. Nov. 11, 1867; d. Aug. 14, 1899; m. Nov. 23, 1895, Ida A. Metzler (5213).

7596. Benjamin Franklin, Rawlinsville, Pa., b. Jan. 23, 1870; d. Sept. 16, 1871.

7597. Rev. Galen Wesley, Barron, Wis., b. Aug. 3, 1872; m. May 10, 1900, Lucy A. Sweitzer, b. Feb. 19, 1880; dau. Cornelius Sweitzer and Lena Asrweigo.

7598. Mary Elizabeth, Lime Valley, Pa., b. July 12, 1875; m. Apr. 25, 1897, Samuel S. Brenberger, b. Jan. 8, 1872; son Martin Brenberger and Mary ———.

7599. William Elmer, Lancaster, Pa., b. Apr. 15, 1878; m. Nov. 30, 1899, Emma Bessie Eager (7814).

Family of HANNAH HERR (3487) and GEORGE W. HESS.

7600. Benjamin H., Landisville, Pa., b. Nov. 21, 1874; d. Nov. 17, 1878.

7601. Susan M., Landisville, Pa., b. Apr. 27, 1878.

7602. Henry H., Landisville, Pa., b. Apr. 9, 1880.

7603. Samuel, Landisville, Pa., b. June 19, 1883.

7604. Elizabeth, Landisville, Pa., b. Sept. 30, 1885.

7605. Ira N., Landisville, Pa., b. June 22, 1888.
7606. Walter R., Salunga, Pa., b. May 30, 1891.
7607. Nora, Salunga, Pa., b. Mar. 13, 1893.
7608. Harold W., Salunga, Pa., b. Nov. 15, 1894; d. Jan. 16, 1897.
7609. Winona, Salunga, Pa., b. Sept. 11, 1896.

Family of MARTHA HERR (3490) and ———.

7610. Jacob H. Breneman, Salunga, Pa.

Family of EMMA HERR (3491) and JACOB M. HARNISH.

7611. Clarence, Lancaster, Pa., b. June 28, 1887.
7612. Lillie Lily, Lancaster, Pa., b. Oct. 4, 1889.
7613. H——— Earl, Lancaster, Pa., b. June 13, 1892.
7614. Ruby M., Lancaster, Pa., b. Apr. 24, 1896.
7615. Jay Davey, Lancaster, Pa., b. May 21, 1898.

Family of DAVID HERR (3494) and MARY FOCHT.

7616. Melvin, Camden, N. J., b. July 19, 1866; m. June 1, 1891, Carrie
    Nichols, b. Oct. 6, 1865; dau. Joseph Nichols and Hannah
7617. Carrie, Safe Harbor, Pa., b. Dec. 29, 1868; d. Dec. 28, 1870.
7618. Carrie A., Safe Harbor, Pa., b. May 5, 1872; m. Mar. 30, 1890,
    Samuel Lyte, b. Oct. 31, 1871; son William Lyte and Maggie
    Spence.
7619. Adam Barton, Safe Harbor, Pa., b. Apr. 25, 1874; d. July 28,
    1876.
7620. David A., Safe Harbor, Pa., b. Apr. 5, 1877; m. Feb. 20, 1896,
    Amelia F. Rineer, b. Oct. 26, 1878; dau. Harman C. Rineer and
    Susan Aston.

Family of FRANCES E. LANTZ (3498) and MICHAEL S. LEFEVER.

7621. Leah A., Millersville, Pa.

Family of AARON B. SHENK (8652) and ANN SNAVELY (3504).

7622. Benjamin, Willow Street, Pa., b. June 9, 1867.

Family of ANNIE HERR (4106) and BENJAMIN H. SNAVELY (3506).

7623. Elizabeth H., Willow Street, Pa., b. July 27, 1869; m. Dec. 20,
    1893, Martin Myers (7442).

7624. Harry H., Lancaster, Pa., b. June 11, 1871; m. Apr. 14, 1897, Amanda Book, b. Oct. 13, 1873; dau. Samuel Book and Mary A. Buckwalter.

7625. Ida Frances, Refton, Pa., b. Jan. 6, 1873; m. Oct. 18, 1899, Ira B. Graybill, b. Nov. 14, 1870; son Simon E. Graybill and Emma Breneman.

7626. Amos H., Lime Valley, Pa., b. July 29, 1875; m. Nov. 15, 1900, Elizabeth R. Herr (7454).

7627. B. Frank, Lancaster, Pa., b. Sept. 15, 1878; m. Oct. 18, 1905, Anna Blanche Lichty, dau. Clarence V. Lichty and ——— Stauffer.

7628. Ella Naomi, Maytown, Pa., b. Jan. 3, 1882; m. Jan. 19, 1905, Benjamin F. Garber, son David L. Garber and Emma Hershey.

Family of FANNY MALINDA HERR (3507) and ———.

7629. Albert F. Herr, Wheatland Mills, Pa., b. July 10, 1863; m. Dec. 24, 1885, Elizabeth K. Harting, b. Sept. 18, 1866; dau. Hiram Harting and Catharine K. Howry.

Family of HENRY SNAVELY HERR (3511) and ABBIE P. HESS.

7630. Anna M., West Willow, Pa., b. Oct. 7, 1883.

7631. Granville B., West Willow, Pa., b. July 14, 1888.

7632. Carrie Elizabeth, West Willow, Pa., b. Sept. 14, 1894.

7633. Emma Fannie, West Willow, Pa., b. Sept. 30, 1896.

7634. Harry S., West Willow, Pa., b. Dec. 27, 1885; d. Sept. 20, 1886.

7635. Walter C., West Willow, Pa., b. Sept. 2, 1890; d. Mar. 12, 1892.

Family of SUSAN HERR (3512) and CHRISTIAN M. RUTT.

7636. Ida H., Buffalo, Minn., b. Feb. 11, 1879; d. July 29, 1880.

7637. Edith, Buffalo, Minn., b. Aug. 5, 1881.

7638. Edna, Buffalo, Minn., b. Apr. 2, 1883; d. July 15, 1890.

Family of CHRISTIAN S. HERR (3513) and ELLEN K. BAKER.

7639. Harry B., Pittsburg, Pa.

7640. Ella B., Witmer, Pa., b. Oct. 23, 1876; m. Nov. 24, 1897, I——— N. Sheaffer.

7641. Fannie B., Lancaster, Pa., b. Jan. 9, 1879; m. July 14, 1899, Charles Mahler, son Jacob Mahler and ———; m. Sept. 15, 1904, Conrad Kempf, son John Kempf and Elizabeth ———.

7642. Nora B., Lancaster, Pa., b. Feb. 24, 1882.

7643. Frank B., Witmer, Pa.

6642. Christian B., Witmer, Pa., b. May 18, 1889; d. Oct. —, 1889.

Family of ANN MARIA BRACKBILL (3515) and CHARLES F. SEACHRIST.

7644. Marriot Brosius, Lancaster, Pa., b. Apr. 16, 1888.

7645. David Herr, Lancaster, Pa., b. July 14, 1891.

Family of M. ADRIENNE MUSSER (4875) and FRANKLIN B. MUSSELMAN.

7646. E—— Elizabeth, Strasburg, Pa., b. Jan. 25, 1861.

7647. Frank L., Strasburg, Pa., b. May 5, 1865.

7648. John, Philadelphia, Pa., b. Nov. 20, 1874.

Family of Dr. AMBROSE J. HERR (4867) and EMMA S. MUSSELMAN (3520).

7649. Daughter, Lancaster, Pa., b. July 6, 1867; d. July 6, 1867.

7650. Daughter, Lancaster, Pa., b. July 6, 1867; d. July 6, 1867.

7651. Florence Emma, York, Pa., b. Oct. 13, 1871; m. Nov. 8, 1894, Rev. Henry H. Apple, b. Nov. 8, 1869; son Thomas G. Apple and Emma Miller.

Family of Dr. J. HENRY MUSSER (4876) and ELIZA A. MUSSELMAN (3523).

7652. Edith E., Lampeter, Pa., b. July 15, 1871; m. Oct. 5, 1898, Jay Bachman, b. Oct. 21, 1871; son John Bachman and Elizabeth Rohrer.

7653. Will M., Lampeter, Pa., b. Oct. 9, 1872; m. Aug. 31, 1898, Bertha C. Eshleman (9234).

7654. Mary Ada, Lampeter, Pa., b. Aug. 24, 1878; d. Oct. 13, 1887.

Family of Dr. HENRY E. MUSSER (4644) and MYRA MUSSELMAN (3524).

7655. Charles Milton, Witmer, Pa., b. Jan. 26, 1877; m. Oct. 24, 1907, Wid. Elizabeth Bair Locher. dau. Daniel W. Bair and Edith Drumm.

7656. Guy Musselman, Philadelphia, Pa., b. May 31, 1879.

7657. Park Neff, Denver, Col., b. Mar. 4, 1881; m. Apr. 2, 1904, Helen Viancourt, b. Apr. 23, 1887; dau. Moses F. Viancourt and Frances Anna Graham.

Family of REUBEN D. HERR (4113) and HARRIET F. MUSSELMAN (3525).

7658. Miriam Musselman, Lancaster, Pa., b. Feb. 24, 1876; m. Apr. 10, 1902, Duncan W. Patterson.

7659. Carolyn Musselman, Lancaster, Pa., b. Sept. 12, 1877; m. Frederick Franklin.

Family of CHRISTIANA HERR (3527) and NATHANIEL MAYER.

7660. Mary Alice, Slackwater, Pa., b. Dec. 24, 1850.

7661. Franklin Herr, Slackwater, Pa., b. Feb. 21, 1852; d. Aug. 3, 1853.

7662. Emma Catharine, Slackwater, Pa., b. Sept. 1, 1853.

7663. Lydia Louisa, Slackwater, Pa., b. Feb. 21, 1855; d. Sept. 9, 1856.

7664. Christian Nathaniel, Slackwater, Pa., b. Feb. 23, 1857.

7665. John David, New Providence, Pa., b. Dec. 27, 1858.

7666. Christiana Elizabeth, New Providence, Pa., b. June 17, 1861.

Family of BENJAMIN F. ZARRACHER (3529) and ANNIE HENNINGS.

7667. Elizabeth Herr, Hillsboro, North Dakota, b. June 1, 1873; m. June 28, 1899, James F. Hetler.

Family of CHRISTIANA HERR ZARRACHER (3530) and EDWIN C. KELLEY.

7668. John E., Philadelphia, Pa., b. Feb. 12, 1870.

7669. Frederick, Philadelphia, Pa., b. Apr. 1, 1872.

7670. Edwin C., Philadelphia, Pa., b. Nov. 1, 1873.

7671. Elizabeth, Philadelphia, Pa., b. Aug. 15, 1884.

7672. Sarah, Philadelphia, Pa., b. Feb. 1, 1889.

7673. Joseph Hooker, Philadelphia, Pa., b. Apr. 5, 1892.

Family of JACOB ECKMAN (3532) and ———.

7674. William, Jackson, Mich.

7675. Lillian, Lancaster, Pa., m. Abraham Parmer.
7677. Esther, Lancaster, Pa., m. Samuel Parmer.

Family of HENRY ECKMAN (3533) and ANNA HOKE.

7677. Aldus, Water Valley, Miss., b. July 29, 1849; d. Oct. 20, 1896; m. Julia Litzel, b. Aug. 7, 1855.
7678. Henry, Lancaster, Pa., b. Sept. 3, 1850; m. Jan. 31, 1878, Mary Pries, b. July 29, 1853; dau. George Pries and Barbara Harman.
7679. Elizabeth, Lancaster, Pa., b. Dec. 29, 1851; m. June 26, 1872, David H. Bartholomew (3364).
7680. John, Lancaster, Pa., b. Oct. 3, 1853; d. May 25, 1884; m. Apr. 24, 1881, Letitia M. Helm, b. Oct. 1, 1855; dau. Michael Helen and Lavinia Lynch.
7681. Jacob, Lancaster, Pa., b. Sept. 17, 1857; d. Mar. 27, 1901; m. Anna M. Wickle, b. Oct. 17, 1864; d. Mar. 30, 1889; dau. John Wickle and Sarah E. Hummel; m. July 14, 1898, Adaline L. Hoak, b. Mar. 29, 1865; dau. John Hoak and Christiana
7682. Mary, Lancaster, Pa., b. Nov. 26, 1859; m. Feb. 13, 1879, George W. Banzhoff, b. Dec. 22, 1856; son Henry W. Banzhoff and Ann Kleiss.
7683. Anna, Philadelphia, Pa., b. Nov. 20, 1861.
7684. Sarah, Lancaster, Pa., b. Nov. 27, 1863; d. Mar. 6, 1864.
7685. Sarah, Lancaster, Pa., b. Jan. 13, 1866; d. Dec. 27, 1866.

Family of HESTER ECKMAN (3534) and GRABILL BINKLEY.

7686. H—— C——, Ashgrove, Mo.
7687. Benjamin F., Dallas, Tex., b. Mar. 12, 1853; m. Nov. 30, 1879, Catherine Bee Lockhart, b. Dec. 9, 1861; d. June 12, 1882; dau. Rev. John C. R. Lockhart and Martha Sarah Bates; m. Apr. 19, 1883, Catharine Etta Wiggins, b. May 11, 1854; dau. William —— and Rosaline Cutbirth.
7688. Rachael, Esher, Cleveland, O.
7689. Felix, Esher, Cleveland, O.

Family of LYDIA ANN MEHAFFY (3542) and GEORGE BYERLY.

7690. Sarah Lavinia, Lancaster, Pa., b. Oct. 26, 1852; m. July 2, 1874, John W. Hubley, b. July 2, 1848; son Isaac Hubley and Margaret A. ———.

7691. Martha Alice, Lancaster, Pa., b. Feb. 17, 1854; m. Feb. 7, 1883, Alonzo R. Poisel, b. Jan. 12, 1859; son Joseph Poisel and Isabella Reber.

7692. Anna Mary, Lancaster, Pa., b. Aug. 26, 1856; d. Aug. 23, 1858.

7693. William Henry, Lancaster, Pa., b. Apr. 7, 1863; d. Jan. 23, 1866.

7694. George William, Lancaster, Pa., b. Nov. 25, 1869; m. Dec. 27, 1887, Mary E. Pontz, b. Mar. 1, 1872; dau. Jacob Pontz and Mary Palmer.

Family of MARTHA MARTIN (3544) and GEORGE WIKER.

7695. Charles, Germantown, Ind.

7696. Jacob, Germantown, Ind.

Family of JOHN MARTIN (3545) and MARY BRENEMAN.

7697. George, Gap, Pa.

7698. Frank, Gap, Pa.

7699. William, Gap, Pa.

7700. Alice, Gap, Pa.

7701. Elizabeth, Gap, Pa.

Family of CATHARINE MARTIN (3546) and GEORGE W. DRUMM.

7702. Mary Ann, Rawlinsville, Pa., b. Dec. 4, 1847; d. Jan. 9, 1867.

7703. George Martin, Mountville, Pa., b. Dec. 9, 1849; m. Sept. 20, 1873, Frances H. Sheirick, b. Nov. 17, 1856; dau. John H. Sheirick and Elizabeth Herr.

7704. Martha Jane, Rawlinsville, Pa., b. Sept. 27, 1852; m. June 24, 1875, Daniel Kreider, b. Sept. 23, 1849; son Jacob Kreider and Charlotte Groff.

7705. Catharine Elizabeth, Rawlinsville, Pa., b. Apr. 6, 1855; d. Oct. 27, 1858.

7706. John Milton, Mt. Nebo, Pa., b. Oct. 20, 1857; m. Feb. 7, 1880, Sarah A. Armstrong, dau. William Armstrong and ———.

7707. Peter Cartright, Rawlinsville, Pa., b. Apr. 8, 1860; m. June 8, 1896, Jane Jenkins, b. Nov. 25, 1871; dau. Lewis Jenkins and Mary Ann Alexander.

7708. Frances Elenora, Lancaster, Pa., b. Apr. 25, 1862; m. Nov. 20, 1880, Jacob O. Hart, b. Oct. 10, 1858; son Jacob Hart and Susan Pyfer.

7709. Samuel Grant, Rawlinsville, Pa., b. May 13, 1865; m. May 3, 1889, Annie Dunkel, dau. Orasheo Dunkel and ———.

Family of ELIZABETH MARTIN (3547) and CHRISTIAN HACKMAN.

7710. John Martin, Wooddale, Del., b. Aug. 26, 1850.

7711. Benjamin, Wooddale, Del., b. Aug. 13, 1852.

7712. George W., Wilmington, Del., b. Jan. 30, 1855; m. Sarah L. McFalls.

7713. Annie, Mt. Nebo, Pa., b. Feb. 14, 1857; m. Feb. 5, 1880, Henry Douts, son ——— and Mary A. Onail.

7714. Hannah, Colemanville, Pa., b. Apr. 1, 1859; m. Albertis Hart.

7715. Elizabeth, Mt. Nebo, Pa., b. Aug. 26, 1861; m. Jan. 12, 1881, George Hickey, son George Hickey and Mary A. Harvey.

7716. Susan, Wooddale, Del., b. Jan. 6, 1864.

7717. Henry C., Sparrow Point, Md., b. Sept. 19, 1867; m. Mary Stiles.

Family of JACOB MARTIN (3551) and ANNA GAST.

7718. William G., Trenton, N. J., b. Sept. 12, 1862.

7719. Harry Stevens, Lancaster, Pa., b. Nov. 16, 1864; d. July 8, 1867.

7720. Lulu, Lancaster, Pa., b. Feb. 24, 1866; m. Jan. 1, 1901, Edward R. Kant, b. Feb. 22, ———; son William R. Kant and Elizabeth Hassmer.

7721. George, Lancaster, Pa., b. June 4, 1868; d. Nov. 21, 1872.

7722. Howard, Jersey City, N. J., b. May 29, 1870.

Family of HENRY C. MARTIN (3552) and MARY L. EICHLER.

7723. John S., Lancaster, Pa., b. Feb. 9, 1870.

7724. George E., Lancaster, Pa., b. June 2, 1874.

7725. Henry C., Lancaster, Pa., b. Sept. 5, 1877; d. Oct. 15, 1877.

Family of GEORGE MARTIN LEFEVER (3562) and SUSANNA WINTERS.

7726. Fanny, Smithville, Pa., b. Mar. 19, 1856; m. July 22, 1875, Jacob
Fellenbaum, son Reuben Fellenbaum and ——— Witmer; m.
Mar. 24, 1884, James M. Clark.

7727. Martha, Smithville, Pa., b. Mar. 30, 1857.

7728. Eliza Ann, Smithville, Pa., b. Apr. 13, 1860.

7729. Thaddeus, Smithville, Pa., b. Dec. 2, 1861.

Family of Wid. GEORGE M. LEFEVER (3562) and MARY ANN WINTERS.

7730. Ida Blanche, Oak Bottom, Pa., b. Aug. 11, 1867; m. Oct. 16,
1890, Harry A. Lefever (7951).

7731. Minnie Belle, Oak Bottom, Pa., b. Jan. 19, 1869; m. Mar. 2,
1892, Charles J. Resh, son Jacob Resh and Mary Barnett.

7732. Charles Augustus, New Providence, Pa., b. Aug. 30, 1870; m.
Estella Trimble, dau. Thomas Trimble and Harriet Moore.

7733. William Bernard, New Providence, Pa., b. Nov. 23, 1873; m.
Nov. 24, 1898, Ella S. Eckman, dau. Franklin Eckman and
Elizabeth Rowe.

7734. Walter Clement, New Providence, Pa., b. June 23, 1875; m.
Jan. 6, 1898, Annie Moore, dau. Robert Moore and Eliza
Ritchey.

7735. Ella Bessie, New Providence, Pa., b. July 25, 1877; m. Aug. 11,
1898, William S. Barnett, son Joseph Barnett and Harriet
Shenk.

7736. Laura Catharine, New Providence, Pa., b. June 13, 1881; d.
Nov. 27, 1897.

Family of HARRY DAY KENDIG (3575) and SARAH ELIZABETH PETRY.

7737. Myra Virginia, Denver, Col., b. Feb. 14, 1883; m. May 12, 1903,
Charles A. Frey, b. Aug. 9, 1882; son Charles A. Frey and
Mary Ellen Haines; m. June 19, 1907, Nelson Douglas Bennett,
b. June 21, 1878; son James Seymour Bennett and Mary Kings-
ford.

7738. Miriam, Denver, Col., b. Aug. 22, 1889; d. Feb. 5, 1892.
7739. Hal, Denver, Col., b. Dec. 30, 1891.
7740. May Belle, Denver, Col., b. Apr. 28, 1896.

Family of HENRY S. KENDIG (3589) and SARAH ANN WEIDMAN.

7741. Michael, Royalton, Pa., b. May 30, 1879.
7742. Elizabeth, Royalton, Pa., b. Aug. 8, 1881.
7743. Franklin, Royalton, Pa., b. Nov. 14, 1883.
7744. Edwin, Royalton, Pa., b. Mar. 24, 1885.
7745. Harry, Royalton, Pa., b. Aug. 12. 1887.
7746. Walter, Royalton, Pa., b. Aug. 11, 1891; d. Aug. 18, 1891.
7747. John, Royalton, Pa., b. May 30, 1895.

Family of Dr. HOWARD H. HOPKINS (3607) and MARY McCONKEY.

7748. Mary Howard, Baltimore, Md., b. Sept. 18, 1845; d. July 20, 1846.
7749. Son, Baltimore, Md., b. Oct. 28. 1846; d. Oct. 28, 1846.
7750. Dr. Howard Hanford, New Market, Md., b. Feb. 2, 1848; m. Sept. 1, 1869, Margaret M. Downey, b. Aug. 27, 1850; dau. William Downey and Margaret J. Wright.
7751. Kate Howard, Baltimore, Md., b. Sept. 24, 1849; d. July 18, 1850.

Family of CLARA A. WITHERS (3608) and Col. EMLIN FRANKLIN.

7752. Walter Withers, Lancaster, Pa., m. Ella Engles, b. June 15, 1869.
7753. Emlen Augustus, Denver, Col., b. Feb. 23, 1864; m. Mar. 3, 1885, Christine Pflum, b. June 15, 1869; dau. Peter Pflum and Elizabeth ———: m. Dec. 5, 1895, Noma Cain, b. Dec. 4, 1876; dau. Samuel Cain and Sarah Simmons.
7754. Anna Josephine, Lancaster, Pa.

Family of Dr. M. AUG. WITHERS (3609) and M. LOUISE MUSSELMAN (4851).

7755. Mary, Pottstown, Pa., b. Jan. 16, 1857; m. Horace Evans, b. Dec. 19, 1854; son Abner Evans and Anna May.

Family of LOUISA W. WITHERS (3611) and Dr. ANDREW J. CARPENTER.

7756. Joseph A. E., Lancaster, Pa.

Family of ANNIE E. WITHERS (3612) and BERNARD WOLFF.

7757. Paul C., Pittsburg, Pa.

7758. Mary B., Pittsburg, Pa.

7759. Bernard W., Pittsburg, Pa., b. Feb. 21, 1872; d. Jan. 18, 1890.

Family of Dr. MICHAEL M. WITHERS (3615) and ELIZ. C. FAHNESTOCK.

7760. Mae Reinstine, Maytown, Pa., b. Dec. 17, 1868; m. Feb. 17, 1892, Jacob K. Miller, b. Oct. 24, 1856; son Jacob H. Miller and Esther S. Kreider.

Family of CATHARINE J. WITHERS (3619) and JOHN J. SHERTZ.

7761. Elizabeth Withers, Lancaster, Pa.

7762. George Howard, Lancaster, Pa.

7763. Henry Hartman, Lancaster, Pa.

7764. John Clarence, Lancaster, Pa.

7765. Anna Catharine, Lancaster, Pa., b. Feb. 26, 1880.

Family of DANIEL F. LONGENECKER (3624) and LYDIA SHARP.

7766. Jessie Amanda, Lancaster, Pa., b. Mar. 4, 1868; m. Oct. 15, 1891, John F. Bowman, b. Aug. 3, 1869; son Isaac M. Bowman and Charlotte ———.

7767. Bertha, Mountain Lake, Minn., b. Oct. 17, 1871; m. Nov. 3, 1892, Dr. S—— D. Sour, b. Oct. 14, 1860; son William L. Sour and Mary A. Weitzel.

7768. Elmira Belle, Parkton, Pa., b. Feb. 25, 1875; m. John Hooley.

7769. Aldus Earle, Ronks, Pa., b. Sept. 29, 1879.

7770. Anna Pearl, Ronks, Pa., b. Oct. 9, 1887.

Family of SUSANNA LONGENECKER (3625) and SAMUEL KEPLINGER.

7771. Elizabeth C., Paradise, Pa., b. May 16, 1870.

7772. Ella Nora, Paradise, Pa., b. Sept. 9, 1875.

Family of AMANDA L. LONGENECKER (3626) and BENJ. F. HERR (2965).

7773. Clement Lorenzo, Paradise, Pa., b. Feb. 16, 1868.

Family of ANNIE T. WATSON (3645) and HENRY FRAELICH.

7774. Susanna, Wheatland Mills, Pa., b. Feb. 17, 1850; m. May 5, 1872, George Arment.

7775. Elizabeth, Wheatland Mills, Pa., b. Mar. 8, 1859; m. Apr. 21, 1868, Josiah Zittle, son Elijah Zittle and ———.

7776. John, Middletown, Pa., b. Jan. 3, 1851.

7777. Amos, Lancaster, Pa., b. Apr. 28, 1853.

7778. Henry, Fertility, Pa., b. May 6, 1854; d. Dec. 23, 1856.

7779. Mary, Lititz, Pa., b. Feb. 24, 1856.

7780. Annie, Lititz, Pa., b. Nov. 12, 1857; d. Dec. 29, 1858.

7781. Levi, Lititz, Pa., b. Apr. 23, 1860; d. Aug. 4, 1860.

7782. Elmira, Lititz, Pa., b. Sept. 23, 1861; d. Sept. 23, 1861.

7783. Alwilda, Lititz, Pa., b. Mar. 26, 1863; d. Aug. 12, 1864.

Family of JACOB B. WATSON (3648) and HANNAH A. HOWETT.

7784. Hannah Mary, Hepler, Kas., b. Aug. 31, 1851.

7785. Emma Ann, Hepler, Kas., b. Nov. 8, 1854.

7786. Elias G., Hepler, Kas., b. July 28, 1855.

7787. Thaddeus Herr, Hepler, Kas., b. Feb. 17, 1856.

7788. Jacob King, Hepler, Kas., b. Sept. 13, 1858.

7789. John B., Hepler, Kas., b. July 18, 1860.

7790. George Oliver, Hepler, Kas., b. Sept. 27, 1862.

7791. Elmer Rice, Hepler, Kas., b. June 25, 1864; d. Aug. 30, 1864.

7792. Miriam Howett, Hepler, Kas., b. Oct. 17, 1866; d. Dec. 30, 1867.

Family of SUSAN M. WATSON (3650) and JACOB HELM.

7793. Martin, Bart, Pa.

7794. William, Bart, Pa.

7795. Irene, Bart, Pa.

7796. Lillie, Bart, Pa.

7797. Mary, Bart, Pa.

7798. Oliver, Bart, Pa.

7799. Walter, Bart, Pa.

Family of FANNY N. WATSON (3651) and SKIPWITH HOWETT.

7800. Mary H., Furniss, Pa., b. July 7, 1855; m. Jan. 5, 1888, William Rineer, b. June 12, 1860; son Jacob Rineer and Lydia Hawk.

7801. Amos W., Lancaster, Pa., b. ————, 1857; m. Clara Johnson.

7802. Annie Laura, Strasburg, Pa., b. Nov. 12, 1869.

Family of MARGARET WATSON (3655) and THOMAS EAGER.

7803. Edwin L., Philadelphia, Pa., b. June 31, 1861.

7804. George F., Strasburg, Pa., b. Dec. 2, 1862; d. Feb. 3, 1863.

7805. Richard J., Lancaster, Pa., b. Jan. 11, 1864.

7806. Annie M., Lancaster, Pa., b. May 5, 1865.

7807. Milton B., Philadelphia, Pa., b. Aug. 9, 1866.

7808. Frank W., Philadelphia, Pa., b. Nov. 21, 1867; d. Nov. 14, 1888.

7809. Susan J., Smithville, Pa., b. Sept. 7, 1869; m. Grant Williams.

7810. Barbara H., Lancaster, Pa., b. Feb. 28, 1871.

7811. Charles H., Lancaster, Pa., b. Jan. 8, 1874; d. Nov. 11, 1897.

7812. John H., Lancaster, Pa., b. May 31, 1876; d. Apr. 2, 1899.

7813. Howard L., Lancaster, Pa., b. Mar. 6, 1878.

7814. Emma Bessie, Lancaster, Pa., b. Sept. 22, 1879; m. Nov. 30, 1899, William E. Morton (7599).

7815. William D., New York, N. Y., b. Feb. 6, 1881.

7816. Eva, Lancaster, Pa., b. Apr. 16, 1883; m. Walter Oblander.

7817. Nora M., Lancaster, Pa., b. Feb. 15, 1887; d. Oct. 18, 1899.

7818. Maggie M., Lancaster, Pa., b. Feb. 15, 1887; d. June 15, 1899.

Family of JOHN M. SHENK (5784) and FRANCES C. STIVELY (3658).

7819. Anna Catharine, New Providence, Pa., b. Dec. 22, 1858.

7820. Esther Elizabeth, New Providence, Pa., b. Mar. 13, 1860.

7821. John Frederick, New Providence, Pa., b. Mar. 12, 1861.

Family of EMMA F. HERR (4025) and ABRAHAM L. STIVELY (3661).

7822. Mary Herr, Collins, Pa., b. Oct. 25, 1900.

Family of HENRY SHAUB (3671) and FANNY LANDIS.

7823. Lizzie L., Lime Valley, Pa., b. Sept. 17, 1868; m. Jan. 8, 1891, John Stoner, son John Stoner and ————.

7824. Annie, Bird-in-Hand, Pa., b. Feb. 24, 1870.

7825. Enos, Lampeter, Pa., b. July 19, 1871; m. Jan. 13, 1897, Ella S. Myers, dau. John Myers and ————.

7826. Eleanora, Strasburg, Pa., b. Mar. 13, 1873; m. Nov. 7, 1899, Harry Groff, son Rev. Elias Groff and ———.

7827. Benjamin L., Refton, Pa., b. July 27, 1874; m. Apr. 12, 1899, Sue E. Herr (8324).

7828. Frances, Refton, Pa., b. Oct. 17, 1876.

7829. Ada, Refton, Pa., b. Sept. 11, 1883.

7830. Lettie, Refton, Pa., b. Mar. 5, 1886.

Family of MARTIN L. SHAUB (3697) and CAROLINE HOOVER.

7831. Della, Newark, O., b. Jan. 19, 1854; m. May 28, 1874, William D. Nash.

7832. Mary Cornelia, Newark, O., b. Apr. 29, 1856; m. Oct. 8, 1878, John P. Goodwin, b. Feb. 1, 1852; son John P. Goodwin and Ellen Wheeler.

7833. Hattie L., Newark, O., b. Dec. 26, 1858; d. Dec. 5, 1880.

7834. Jesse Franklin, Cincinnati, O., b. Apr. 29, 1864; m. June 2, 1892, Clara D. Williams, b. Mar. 12, 1869; dau. Aldridge J. Williams and Mary A. Dodd.

Family of AMANDA SHAUB (3699) and OSCAR WOODS.

7835. Frances, Chicago, Ill., b. Sept. 2, 1866; m. Nov. 8, 1888, George B. Horr, b. Sept. 30, 1863; son Ralph Horr and Martha Barker.

7836. Edna, Morrison, Pa., b. Jan. 21, 1869; m. June 3, 1890, Frank B. Carpenter, b. July 17, 1866; son John D. Carpenter and Charity Lester.

7837. Louis, Morrison, Pa., b. Apr. 28, 1876; m. July 26, 1900, Ivy Tuttle, b. Oct. 2, 1878; dau. Lauren E. Tuttle and Emily A. Ustick.

Family of JEROME SHAUB (3701) and RHODA GODDARD.

7838. Lew C., Morrison, Ill., b. Oct. 14, 1869; d. Aug. 17, 1870.

7839. Frederick, St Louis, Mo., b. Jan. 8, 1873; m. July 21, 1892, Stella M. Blake, dau. Henry C. Blake and Laura E. Haight.

7840. Elmer J., Anaconda, Col., b. Dec. 4, 1874; m. Sept. 10, 1900, Eliza M. Bridgeman, b. Nov. 18, 1877; dau. James Bridgeman and Margaret Bowen.

7841. Esther C., Granville, O., b. July 20, 1883.

7842. Walter J., Alexander, O., b. July 9, 1888.

Family of JOHN SHAUB (3703) and EMMA FISHER.

7843. Ella Etta, Glendive, Mont., b. Apr. 10, 1872.

7844. Charles, Glendive, Mont., b. Apr. 28, 1874.

7845. William, Glendive, Mont., b. July 29, 1876.

Family of FRANKLIN SHAUB (3704) and Wid. EMMA AUSTIN.

7846. Fina, Exeter, Neb., b. May 20, 1891.

7847. Clifford M., Exeter, Neb., b. Sept. 17, 1893.

Family of ORREN P. SHAUB (3705) and CARRIE SANFORD.

7848. Gertrude Helen, Tacoma, Wash., b. Nov. 21, 1886.

7849. Lola Florence, Denver, Col., b. Jan. 11, 1889; d. Aug. 28, 1889.

7850. Monroe Emerson, Tacoma, Wash., b. June 23, 1890.

Family of ELIM SHAUB (3706) and JOSEPHINE FOSTER.

7851. Ethel A., Alexandria, O., b. Mar. 25, 1888.

Family of LURA SHAUB (3708) and ALBERT VENNUM.

7852. Vallie, Exeter, Neb., b. Sept. 16, 1883.

7853. Jay, Exeter, Neb., b. Nov. 20, 1884.

7854. Arthur, Exeter, Neb., b. Aug. 11, 1886.

Family of EMMA SHAUB (3712) and GEORGE W. MOUSER.

7855. Amanda D., Kirkersville, O., b. Feb. 4, 1859; m. Mar. 8, 1882, Theodore B. Clark, b. Dec. 8, 1861; son William Clark and Ann Glancock.

7856. Howard L., Johnstown, O., b. Apr. 7, 1861; d. Mar. 24, 1864.

7857. Blanch M., Afton, Ia., b. Dec. 13, 1862; m. Mar. 28, 1888, James A. Foster, b. Aug. 15, 1859; d. Nov. 3, 1900; son Isaac Foster and Pemelia Miller.

7858. Leah B., Johnstown, O., b. June 17, 1865; m. Apr. 15, 1885, Philip T. Jones, b. Apr. 14, 1864; son David Jones and Eliza Foster.

7859. Jacob E., Johnstown, O., b. Dec. 15, 1867; d. Sept. 10, 1875.

7860. Winnie M., Johnstown, O., b. Jan. 11, 1876; m. June 30, 1896, Noah H. Overturf, b. June 25, 1874; son James W. Overturf and Emma Bush.

7861. Emma E., Johnstown, O., b. Nov. 15, 1878.

7862. George Ernest, Johnstown, O., b. July 17, 1881.

Family of ALMIRA SHAUB (3720) and JOHN KRUG.

7863. Cora D., Granville, O., b. Aug. 24, 1865; m. Aug. 18, 1898, George C. Case, b. Aug. 24, 1851; son William Case and Alcinda Whiteford.

7864. Minnie May, Granville, O., b. Jan. 26, 1867; d. Mar. 23, 1868.

7865. Maude Ann, Granville, O., b. Sept. 30, 1876.

Family of LEMATH SHAUB (3721) and JUDSON PECK.

7866. Olive, Johnstown, O., b. July 25, 1883.

7867. Eva, Johnstown, O., b. Nov. 21, 1886.

7868. Infant, Johnstown, O., b. Oct. 17, 1889; d. Oct. 17 1889.

Family of ROLAND J. SHAUB (3722) and JENNIE STEPHENS.

7869. James I., Johnstown, O., b. Apr. 17, 1879; m. Oct. 15, 1900, Mary Jaggers, b. Jan. 19, 1880; dau James Jaggers and Rebecca Simpson.

7870. Hattie S., Johnstown, O., b. Dec. 24, 1885.

Family of JAMES M. SHAUB (3724) and AGNES CADWELL.

7871. Virgie Almira, Creswell, Pa., b. Nov. 27, 1881.

7872. George Wendell, Creswell, Pa., b. Jan. 31, 1885.

Family of Wid. JAMES M. SHAUB (3724) and CARRIE SCOTT.

7873. Grace Marian, Creswell, Pa., b. July 19, 1888.

7874. Lewis Edwin, Creswell, Pa., b. Nov. 15, 1892; d. Nov. 20, 1892.

7875. Altha, Creswell, Pa., b. June 25, 1898.

Family of EDWIN SHAUB (3725) and INEZ FRANKLIN.

7876. Jennie, Spokane Falls, Wash., b. Mar. 9, 1878.

7877. Lucy, Spokane Falls, Wash., d. Infant.
7878. Etta, Spokane Falls, Wash., b. ———, 1882.
7879. George, Spokane Falls, Wash.

Family of ELMER SHAUB (3726) and ELLA ALSPACK.

7880. L. Josephine, Creston, Ia., b. July 8, 1878; m. Oct. 4, 1897, Alonzo J. Brown.
7881. Bessie E., Creston, Ia., b. Feb. 2, 1887.
7882. Ruth M., Creston, Ia., b. July 4, 1892.
7883. A. Pauline, Creston, Ia., b. Nov. 10, 1896.

Family of IDA E. SHAUB (3727) and ALLEN A. AVERY.

7884. Harry R., Granville, O., b. Oct. 9, 1881.
7885. Adah Shaub, Granville, O., b. June 27, 1889.

Family of LUNA SHAUB (3728) and DAVID H. RAMEY.

7885. Carl Shaub, Granville, O., b. Nov. 10, 1882.
7886. Anna Margaret, Granville, O., b. June 19, 1894.

Family of BURT E. SHAUB (3731) and LIDA GLYNN.

7887. Edith Adelaide, Johnstown, O., b. Aug. 22, 1894.
7888. Harold Glynn, Johnstown, O., b. June 23, 1898.

Family of MILTON SHAUB (3732) and ORA CONWAY.

7889. Howard, Johnstown, O., b. Apr. 2, 1892.
7890. Bonnie, Johnstown, O., b. Apr. 17, 1893.
7891. Aubrey, Johnstown, O.

Family of ALEXANDER S. JAMISON (3736) and ABIGAIL M. WOODBURY.

7892. Clarence E., Granville, O., b. Mar. 10, 1876; m. Dec. 23, 1896, Orpha B. Cooperider, b. June 24, 1878; dau. D—— B. Cooperider and Mary Feaman.

Family of EMMA E. JAMISON (3737) and ANSON J. STAMBACH.

7893. Clarence J., East Akron, O., b. Nov. 29, 1878.
7894. Walter P., East Akron, O., b. June 18, 1881; m. Katharine May

Davis, b. Aug. 23, 1886; dau. Morey Cada Davis and Emma Elizabeth ———.

7895. Nellie M., East Akron, O., b. Dec. 8, 1883; d. Mar. 21, 1900.

Family of ANNA HERR (3742) and GEORGE TANGERT.

7896. Amanda, Philadelphia, Pa., b. Dec. 17, 1842; m. Apr. 24, 1861, Levi Poulton, b. May 20, 1835; d. Apr. 6, 1891; son Smith Poulton and Azubah Springer.

7897. Mary Jane, Philadelphia, Pa., d. ———, 1899; m. ———, 1863, Thomas Stewart.

7898. Harry, Philadelphia, Pa.

7899. Emma, Lancaster, Pa., m. Isaac Lively.

Family of LAVINIA HERR (3743) and JOHN McCANN.

7900. Robert, Haysville, O., b. Nov. 26, 1848; d. Dec. 20, 1867.

7901. Franklin, Reading, Pa., b. July 5, 1850; d. June 23, 1882.

7902. Abraham, Reading, Pa., b. Apr. 15, 1854.

7903. Lile, Reading, Pa., b. July 3, 1856; m. Sept. 25, 1882, Albert Henning.

7904. David. Reading, Pa., b. Mar. 26, 1858; m. Jan. 5, 1885, Ella Saylor, d. July 5, 1893.

7905. Elias, Reading, Pa., b. Mar. 16, 1861; m. Dec. 22, 1889, Carrie Ray.

7906. Martha, Reading, Pa., b. May 2, 1863; d. Sept. 21, 1887; m. Harry Whitman.

7907. Charles, Reading, Pa., b. Dec. 6, 1868; d. Mar. 15, 1890.

7908. John, Reading, Pa., b. Dec. 5, 1870; d. Feb. 5, 1889.

Family of MARY ANN HERR (3744) and HENRY B. STONE.

7909. Hannah Rebecca, Heidleburg. Pa.. b. Mar. 13, 1853; d. Dec. 8, 1868.

7910. Oliver Abraham, York, Pa., b. Jan. 2, 1856; m. Feb. 25, 1883, Ella Lease, b. Sept. ʒ, 1860; dau. Aaron Lease and Harriet Trimmer.

7911. Mary Ellesta, York, Pa., b. June 2, 1858; d. Mar. 23, 1893; m.

July 15, 1887, Henry R. Serff, b. Dec. 5, 1860; son Henry Serff
and Louisa Rudisill.

7912. Amanda Elmira, New Cumberland, Pa., b. Sept. 22, 1860; d.
Nov. 27, 1860.

7313. Dora Franciscus, York, Pa., b. Aug. 19, 1862; m. Sept. 19,
1886, Peter Law, b. Feb. 10, 1864; son Samuel Law and Susan
Banblitz.

7914. Henry Brower, York, Pa., b. Oct. 15, 1865; m. Feb. 11, 1892,
Mary A. Griever, b. May 22, 1869; dau. Henry Griever and
Louisa Banblitz.

7915. Laura Lucinda, York, Pa., b. Sept. 6, 1869; d. Aug. 15, 1891;
m. Mar. 14, 1888, Edward Schrum, b. July 15, 1862; son
Andrew Schrum and Louisa Banblitz.

7916. John Clinger, York, Pa., b. May 9, 1872; m. Oct. 7, 1891,
Myrtle M. Snyder, b. Sept. 11, 1871; dau. Henry Snyder and
Sarah McClary.

Family of ABRAHAM HERR (3746) and LOUISA FURGESON.

7917. Elmer E., Philadelphia, Pa., b. May 31, 1862; m. May —, 1880,
Catharine A. Shrack, b. Oct. —, 1862; dau. Bennival Shrack
and Rebecca Bidler; m. ———.

7918. Hannah Eliza, Mountville, Pa., b. Aug. 18, 1864; d. Aug. 21,
1864.

7919. Martha Ann, Mountville, Pa., b. Oct. 11, 1865; d. Nov. 9, 1865.

7920. Margaret, Reading, Pa., b. June 14, 1867; d. June 23, 1867.

7921. Abraham, Reading, Pa., b. July 28, 1868; d. Aug. 9, 1868.

7922. Luther, Philadelphia, Pa., b. Oct. 29, 1870; m. Apr. 6, 1889,
Katie V. Hartman, b. May 3, 1871; dau. Henry Hartman and
Hannah Lease.

7923. Walter S., Reading, Pa., b. July 1, 1875; m. Dec. 25, 1897, Ella
J. Pottieger, b. Sept. 5, 1875; dau. William Pottieger and
Esther Kauffman.

7924. Oliver Jay, Reading, Pa., b. Jan. 31, 1880; d. Feb. 7, 1880.

Family of MARTHA HERR (3747) and JACOB S. CLAIR.

7925. Thaddeus S., Mountville, Pa.

Family of Wid. MARY ANN HERR (3748) and THOMAS BELLAMY.

7926. Emma Anna, Lancaster, Pa., b. Apr. 24, 1871.

7927. Leona Winona, Lancaster, Pa., b. Aug. 5, 1874.

7928. Adaline Amanda, Atlantic City, N. J., b. July 30, 1876; m. George Schoen.

7929. Nora Corella, Lancaster, Pa., b. June 8, 1878.

Family of ELIZABETH HERR (3751) and HENRY B. MILLER.

7930. Charles Henry, Pittsburg, Pa., b. Nov. 30, 1866, m. Oct. 9, 1900, Edna Ward, b. June 22, 1881, dau. Francis M. Ward and Virginia Jane Bryan.

7931. Enos Herr, Strasburg, Pa., b. Sept. 8, 1868, m. Nov. 25, 1897. A. Elizabeth Miller, dau. Oliver B. Miller and Elizabeth Hoover.

7932. John Milton, Strasburg, Pa., b. Apr. 11, 1870; m. Nov. 14, 1896, Bertha Murphy, dau. Milton Murphy and Julia McComsey.

Family of JOHN M. HERR (3756) and CATHARINE LEFEVER.

7933. Frank, White Rock, Pa.

7934. Elizabeth, White Rock, Pa.

7935. Elam, White Rock, Pa.

7936. Mary, White Rock, Pa.

7937. Harry, White Rock, Pa.

7938. Aldus, White Rock, Pa.

Family of Wid. JOHN M. HERR (3756) and AMY ANN ———.

7939. Witmer H., Chrome, Pa., b. Dec. 7, 1877; d. Aug. 19, 1878.

7940. Effie C., Chrome, Pa., b. Apr. 8, 1879.

7941. Joseph A., Chrome, Pa., b. May 31, 1880.

7942. Hannah M., Chrome, Pa., b. Apr. 2, 1881; d. Sept. 17, 1881.

7943. Walter L., Chrome, Pa., b. June 22, 1882.

7944. Charles M., Chrome, Pa., b. Aug. 26, 1885.

7945. Samuel D., Chrome, Pa., b. June 25, 1886; d. Oct. 29, 1886.

7946. Hattie Wood, Chrome, Pa., b. Dec. 8, 1888.

7947. Clara Bell, Chrome, Pa., b. Jan. 13, 1890; d. June 24, 1890.

Family of SARAH ANN HERR (3757) and DANIEL F. LEFEVER.

7948. John M., Buck, Pa., b. June 21, 1856.

7949. Daniel Franklin, Buck, Pa., b. Aug. 5, 1859; m. Minnie Barr, dau. Cyrus Barr and Mary A. Riley.

7950. Martha Elizabeth, Lancaster, Pa., b. Mar. 14, 1861; m. Elmer E. Keen, son Jacob Keen and Elizabeth Mowrer.

7951. Harry Ankrim, Oak Bottom, Pa., b. Oct. 18, 1863; m. Oct 16, 1890, Ida B. Lefever (7730).

Family of MARY BARBARA HERR (3759) and Wid. DANIEL F. LEFEVER.

7952. Ida Palmo, Lancaster, Pa., b. May 4, 1868.

7953. James Irwin, Refton, Pa., b. Nov. 22, 1869; m. Nov. 22, 1894, Emma Book, b. June 10, 1872; dau. Elam Book and Eliza Laird.

7954. Mary Laberta, Parkesburg, Pa.., b. Aug. 16, 1872; m. Aug. 3, 1893, George Barr, b. Sept. 16, 1870; son Cyrus Barr and Mary A. Riley.

7955. Esther Luella, Refton, Pa., b. Apr. 6, 1874; m. Sept. 27, 1900, Frank Mowrer, b. Sept. 13, 1869; son Daniel Mowrer and Sarah Tweed.

7956. Charles Herr, Lancaster, Pa., b. June 1, 1883.

Family of ELIZABETH HERR (3760) and JOHN BROOME.

7957. J—— Frank, Burnham, Pa., b. Feb. 18, 1871; m. Carrie Barr.

7958. Harry Witmer, New Providence, Pa., b. Apr. 23, 1872; m. Dec. 14, 1899, Emma Lynes, dau. John Lynes and Joanna Money.

7959. Martin Miller, New Providence, Pa., b. Feb. 5, 1876.

7960. Annie Elizabeth, New Providence, Pa., b. Dec. 17, 1883.

Family of MARTIN V. HERR (3761) and LAURA E. HESS.

7961. Willie Francis, Columbia, Pa., b. Sept. 12, 1879.

7962. Harry Martin, Columbia, Pa., b. Feb. 14, 1881; d. Mar. 30, 1901.

7963. Elsie Laura, Columbia, Pa., b. Feb. 14, 1883.

7964. Frederick Cleveland, Columbia, Pa., b. Jan. 6, 1885.

7965. Mary Elizabeth, Columbia, Pa., b. Mar. 11, 1887; d. Jan. 27, 1888.
7966. Miller Hess, Columbia, Pa., b. Oct. 29, 1888.
7967. Charles Raub, Columbia, Pa., b. Nov. 13, 1891.
7968. Ada Virginia, Columbia, Pa., b. Oct. 23, 1894; d. Jan. 21, 1895.
7969. David Roy, Columbia, Pa., b. Nov. 19, 1900.

Family of ELIAS HOOVER (3769) and LYDIA ANN WIKER.

7970. Anna May, Strasburg, Pa., b. May 31, 1883; d. Sept. 24, 1900.
7971. Christian W., Strasburg, Pa., b. Dec. 27, 1884.
7972. Elizabeth Ida, Strasburg, Pa., b. July 16, 1886; d. Oct. 15, 1892.
7973. Jacob W., Strasburg, Pa., b. Apr. 25, 1888.
7974. Susan Esther, Strasburg, Pa., b. Apr. 21, 1889; d. July 13, 1889.
7975. Clarence W., Strasburg, Pa., b. Sept. 13, 1890.
7976. Cora Belle, Strasburg, Pa., b. Feb. 14, 1893.
7977. Martha Edna, Strasburg, Pa., b. Apr. 23, 1895.
7978. Elias W., Strasburg, Pa., b. Aug. 12, 1896.
7979. Harry W., Strasburg, Pa., b. Apr. 12, 1898.
7980. Sarah Elsie, Strasburg, Pa., b. Feb. 5, 1901.

Family of ANN GROFF (3818) and HENRY HART.

7981. Simon, Colemanville, Pa., b. ———, 1828; m. ———, 1851, Leah McGrady, b. ———, 1821; d. ———, 1888; dau. John McGrady and Elizabeth Wilson.
7982. Martha, Martinsville, Pa., m. Peter Cramer, d. ———, 1870.
7983. Susan, Martinsville, Pa.
7984. Amos, Martinsville, Pa.
7985. Goram, Martinsville, Pa.
7986. Mary Ann, Martinsville, Pa.
7987. Benjamin, Martinsville, Pa.

Family of ELIZABETH GROFF (3819) and JOHN HESS.

7988. Leah, Wheatland Mills, Pa., b. May 29, 1833; d. Feb. 27, 1897; m. Feb. 7, 1871, Levi Bushong, b. Feb. 27, 1815; d. Jan. 8, 1892.

7989. Simon G., Witmer, Pa., b. Aug. 14, 1835; d. July 3, 1893.

7990. Susan, Witmer, Pa., b. Feb. 4, 1838.

7991. Mary, Witmer, Pa., b. May 3, 1840; m. Dec. 25, 1860, Joel Miller, b. Feb. 25, 1825; d. Aug. 2, 1895; son William Miller and Jane Knox.

7992. Catharine, Witmer, Pa., b. Apr. 13, 1842; m. Nov. 7, 1865, John K. Esbenshade, b, Apr. 3, 1832; son Adam Esbenshade and Mary Kreider.

7993. Sarah, Witmer, Pa., b. June 20, 1844; d. Aug. 3, 1844.

7994. Frances, Witmer, Pa., b. Aug. 22, 1845; d. June 19, 1893.

7995. Martha, Witmer, Pa., b. Sept. 18, 1846; d. July 10, 1875.

7996. Elizabeth, Witmer, Pa., b. July 28, 1850; d. May 6, 1851.

7997. John B., Witmer, Pa., b. Nov. 19, 1852; m. Oct. 11, 1877, Belle Plank, b. July 21, 1852; dau. William Plank and Susan Snader.

7998. Christian, Lampeter, Pa., b. June 8, 1856; d. Aug. 9, 1856.

Family of ABRAHAM GROFF (3820) and HANNAH PEOPLES.

7999. Mary Louisa, New Providence, Pa., b. Nov. 1, 1840; d. Nov. 20, 1840.

8000. Milton, Lancaster, Pa., b. Dec. 25, 1842; m. Martha Hart.

8001. Aldus, Mechanics' Grove, Pa., b. Dec. 1, 1844; m. Jan. 1, 1880, Sarah Hoover, dau. Jacob Hoover and ———.

8002. Anna, Lancaster, Pa., b. Jan. 8, 1848.

8003. Theron S., Lancaster, Pa., b. Oct. 31, 1849; m. Apr. 11, 1875, Louisa B. Hess, b. Apr. 1, 1853; dau. Elias Hess and Mary A. Gorsuch.

Family of LEAH GROFF (3821) and SAMUEL WEAVER.

8004. Susan, Strasburg, Pa., m. Samuel Stauffer.

8005. Abraham, Lampeter, Pa.

8006. Henry Newton, Lancaster, Pa., m. Sarah Erb; m. Mary Kreider.

8007. Martha Ann, Lancaster, Pa., m. Benjamin Bowman.

8008. Mary Catharine, Strasburg, Pa., m. John Fraelich.

Family of SIMON GROFF (3823) and FRANCES ECKMAN.

8009. Galen, Allegheny, Pa., b. May 17, 1863; m. Oct. 26, 1884,

Frances M. Nale, b. Feb. 14, 1867; dau. J. Edwin Nale and Florence Hinman.

Family of MARY ANN GROVE (3881) and RICHARD BRACKIN.

8010. Lydia A., Hermitage, Va.

8011. Harvey D., Hermitage, Va.

8012. Sarah B., Hermitage, Va.

8013. Eliza A., Hermitage, Va.

8014. Lula Leota, Hermitage, Va.

8015. Archie John, Hermitage, Va.

8016. Norman Herr, Waynesboro, Va.

Family of JOHN GROVE (3884) and MARGARET ROOST.

8017. Sarah E., Hermitage, Va.

8018. Abraham, Hermitage, Va.

8019. Jane, Koiners Store, Va.

8020. Jeanette, Koiners Store, Va.

Family of ELIZA E. GROVE (3886) and LEWIS HOIT.

8021. Joseph, Hermitage, Va.

8022. Calvin, Hermitage, Va.

8023. Perry, Hermitage, Va.

8024. Taylor, Hermitage, Va.

8025. Franklin, Hermitage, Va.

Family of VIRGINIA GROVE (3887) and HENRY KONKLER.

8026. Joseph E., Hermitage, Va.

Family of JOHN H. GROVE (3893) and MARY JANE SCHRECKHISE.

8027. George M., Hildebrand, Va.

8028. James M., Waynesboro, Va., b. Dec. 1, 1870; m. Apr. 10, 1895, Mary L. Hamer, b. Jan. 29, 1874; d. July 26, 1901; dau. John J. Hamer and Martha M. Smith; m. Oct. 19, 1903, Mary Christina Coiner, b. Oct. 19, 1871; dau. J—— D. Coiner and Carrie ———.

8029. William J., Hermitage, Va., b. June 27, 1862; m. Oct. 30, 1888, Ida Miller Coiner, b. June 2, 1886; d. Mar. 12, 1900; dau. Elijah Coiner and Bettie Read.
8030. Dr. Herbert D., Boise City, Tex.
8031. Ada G., Columbia, S. C., m. C—— H. Freed.
8032. Rebecca J., Hermitage, Va., m. Dr. R—— F. Davis.
8033. Infant, Hermitage, Va.

Family of EVE GROVE (3905) and JAMES WRIGHT.

8034. Sarah, Hermitage, Va.
8035. Mary, Hermitage, Va.
8036. Hannah, Hermitage, Va.
8037. Eliza, Hermitage, Va.
8038. Henry, Hermitage, Va.
8039. David, Hermitage, Va.
8040. John, Hermitage, Va.
8041. Angeline, Hermitage, Va.
8042. Milton, Hermitage, Va.

Family of MARY GROVE (3906) and CHRISTIAN MILLER.

8043. Barbara A., Hermitage, Va.
8044. Henry, Hermitage, Va.
8045. Sarah E., Hermitage, Va.

Family of ELIZA GROVE (3907) and PHILIP MAIL.

8046. Lenora, Hermitage, Va.
8047. Frederic, Hermitage, Va.
8048. Elizabeth, Hermitage, Va.
8049. Henry, Hermitage, Va.
8050. John, Hermitage, Va.
8051. Daniel, Hermitage, Va.

Family of ABRAHAM GROVE (3908) and MARY NEARGATE.

8052. Emma, Hermitage, Va.
8053. Edward, Hermitage, Va.
8054. Minnie, Hermitage, Va.

Family of ANN GROVE (3909) and GEORGE AREHOLTZ.

8055. Ellen, Hermitage, Va.
8056. George, Hermitage, Va.

Family of SARAH GROVE (3910) and C. GIZLEMAN.

8057. Franklin, Hermitage, Va.
8058. Henry, Hermitage, Va.
8059. Ellen, Hermitage, Va.
8060. Margaret, Hermitage, Va.
8061. Mary A., Hermitage, Va.

Family of DAVID GROVE (3911) and MALINDA SANDS.

8062. Elizabeth, Hermitage, Va.

Family of JACOB HERR (3914) and SARAH PFOUTZ.

8063. Rev. John, Myerstown, Pa., b. Feb. 10, 1848; m. May 13, 1869, Anna Zug, b. May 10, 1848; dau. Abraham Zug and Lydia Wolf.
8064. Catharine, Cardova, Md., b. July 28, 1851; m. May 21, 1878, Daniel Geib, b. Jan. 26, 1846; son Abraham Geib and Catharine Royer.
8065. Elizabeth, Fontana, Pa., b. Nov. 28, 1861; m. Oct. 13, 1883, Alfred B. Gingrich, b. Oct. 25, 1861; son William Gingrich and Susan Bucher.

Family of TOBIAS R. HERR (3918) and KATIE BOOK.

8066. Amanda, Strasburg, Pa., m. Henry Stauffer, son Jonathan Stauffer and ——— Hoover.
8067. John B., Harrisburg, Pa., m. Anna Weaver, dau. John Weaver and ———.
8068. Abraham L., Kansas City, Mo., b. July 26, 1852; d. Nov. 30, 1879; m. Dec. 14, 1873, Christiana Eicherly, b. Jan. 1, 1846; dau. George Eicherly and Caroline Detts.
8069. Christian B., New Providence, Pa., b. Jan. 22, 1855; m. Oct. 18, 1877, Anna E. Keen, dau. Josiah Keen and Catharine Brubaker.

8070. Edward B., Strasburg, Pa., m. Elizabeth Smeltz, dau. Isaac Smeltz and Mary Keen.
8071. Franklin B., Strasburg, Pa., b. Mar. 28, 1863; d. Aug. 1, 1863.
8072. Fremont, Strasburg, Pa., b. Feb. 25, 1864; d. Feb. 25, 1864..

Family of AMOS HERR (3926) and MARIA LANDIS.

8073. Franklin L., Lancaster, Pa., b. Jan. 4, 1867.
8074. Henry L., Lancaster, Pa., b. Feb. 27, 1869.
8075. Landis, Lancaster, Pa., b. Dec. 28, 1871.
8076. John L., Lancaster, Pa., b. Feb. 15, 1873.
8077. Clarence L., Lancaster, Pa., b. Feb. 14, 1875; m. Oct. 20, 1901, Bertha Skeen, dau. Hiram Skeen and ———.
8078. Amos L., Lancaster, Pa., b. Jan. 10, 1877; d. Jan. 20, 1877.
8079. Sherman L., Lancaster, Pa., b. Apr. 16, 1878; d. Sept. 2, 1895.
8080. Edward Ross, Ephrata, Pa., b. July 31, 1880.

Family of LYDIA A. HERR (3927) and ABRAHAM HOSTETTER.

8081. Letitia, Strasburg, Pa., m. Andrew Harnish, son Jonas Harnish and ———.
8082. Amaziah, Paradise, Pa.
8083. Isaac, Gap, Pa.

Family of ELIZABETH HERR (3928) and DAVID KREIDER.

8084. Henry H., Lancaster, Pa.
8085. Isaac H., Lancaster, Pa., m. Mary ———.

Family of DELILAH URBAN (3930) and JOHN ECKMAN.

8086. Lizzie, Lancaster, Pa., m. J. Henry Shirk, son Matthias Shirk and ———.
8087. Frank, Buck, Pa.
8088. Mary, Buck, Pa.

Family of CATHARINE KRUG (3935) and JOSIAH McMULLEN.

8089. William, Airhill, O.
8090. Henry, Airhill, O.

8091. Susan, Airhill, O.
8092. Lizzie, Airhill, O.
8093. Mary Ann, Airhill, O.

Family of SUSAN KRUG (3936) and ARCHIBALD WARREN.

8094. William, Cockeysville, Md.
8095. Catharine, Cockeysville, Md.
8096. Lizzie, Cockeysville, Md.
8097. James, Cockeysville, Md.
8098. Amada, Cockeysville, Md.
8099. Susan, Cockeysville, Md.

Family of BENJAMIN KRUG (3938) and SUSANNA HERR (3953).

8100. Leander J., Union, O., b. Feb. 11, 1860.
8101. Ann Josephine, Union, O., b. July 24, 1861.
8102. Mary Elizabeth, Union, O., b. Aug. 26, 1864; d. Sept. 12, 1864.
8103. Jennie Alice, Union, O., b. Aug. 7, 1866; m. Aug. 15, 1886, John F. Cissner, b. Dec. 22, 1857.
8104. Minnie Ida, Union, O., b. Aug. 26, 1868.
8105. Samuel Henry, Union, O., b. June 11, 1871; d. Dec. 23, 1872.
8106. Charles F., Union, O., b. Oct. 30, 1872; m. Mar. 3, 1896, Maud M. Hissong, b. Mar. 1, 1878; dau. Jacob Hissong and Sarah Miller.
8107. Elmer H., Union, O., b. Nov. 12, 1876; d. Mar. 4, 1877.
8108. Emma F., Union, O., b. Apr. 3, 1878; d. June —, 1886.
8109. Leroy, Uuion, O., b. Oct. 8, 1880.

Family of ESTHER KRUG (3941) and JOSEPH LANDIS.

8110. Daniel K., Strasburg, Pa., b. Apr. 28, 1858; d. Aug. 29, 1894; m. Feb. 13, 1890, M. Alice Trout, b. Jan. 1, 1862; dau. Abraham Trout and Elizabeth Mancha.
8111. Benjamin K., Strasburg, Pa., b. Aug. 3, 1859; d. Oct. 4, 1881.

Family of HANNAH JANE BRENBERGER (3963) and PHILEMON CAYWOOD.

8112. Leslie Grant, Monument, Kans., b. Sept. 6, 1864.

21

8113. Ellison M., Monument, Kans., b. Nov. 13, 1867.

8114. Rhoda Ellen, Monument, Kans., b. Aug. 15, 1869; d. Nov. 14, 1896; m. Feb. —, 1891, H—— L. Dedrick, b. Sept. 31, 1857.

8115. Mary Elizabeth, Page, Kans., b. Dec. 15, 1870; m. Aug. 4, 1889, F—— E. Wegener, son Charles E. Wegener and Mary A. ——.

8116. Gracie I., Honolulu, Hawaii, b. Oct. 30, 1872.

8117. Effie Amanda, Page, Kans., b. Sept. 8, 1875; m. Jan. 3, 1897, L—— D. Wegener, b. Jan. 19, 1874; son Charles E. Wegener and Mary A. ——.

8118. Mattie Edna Pearl, Monument, Kans., b. Sept. 4, 1879.

8119. Jesse Brenberger, Monument, Kans., b. Jan. 3, 1881.

Family of JOHN HERR (3971) and EMMA JANE OPPERMAN.

8120. Jesse, Helena, O., b. Aug. 10, 1879; m. Aug. 10, 1899, Lurah Garn.

8121. Harry, Helena, O., b. Nov. 8, 1880; d. Oct. 6, 1881.

8122. Myrtle, Helena, O., b. Feb. 14, 1883; d. Mar. 18, 1883.

8123. Fannie, Helena, O., b. Dec. 22, 1889.

Family of ELIZABETH HERR (3972) and JOSIAH WENGARD.

8124. Infant, Lancaster, Pa.

8125. Minnie, Lancaster, Pa.

8126. Sarah Eveline, Lancaster, Pa., b. Apr. 10, 1870.

8127. John Osker, Lancaster, Pa., b. ——, 1872.

Family of MARY JANE HERR (3973) and ELI HUFFORD.

8128. Emma, Gibsonburg, O., b. Aug. 9, 1868; m. Sept. 24, 1891, Richard Smith.

8129. Clarence D., Gibsonburg, O., b. May 24, 1871; d. June 29, 1879.

8130. Marcella, Gibsonburg, O., b. May 19, 1873; d. June 28, 1894; m. Oct. 11, 1893, Hugh Havens.

8131. James A., Gibsonburg, O., b. Jan. 28, 1875.

8132. Arvilla, Gibsonburg, O., b. Oct. 9, 1877; d. July 31, 1898; m. June 10, 1896, Elmer Claypool.

8133. Mylin W., Gibsonburg, O., b. Dec. 30, 1879.

8134. Eli B., Gibsonburg, O., b. July 7, 1882.

8135. Francis E., Gibsonburg, O., b. Dec. 25, 1885.

Family of SUSANNA HERR (3977) and QUINTUS SEIPLE.

8136. Rozella E., Helena, O., b. Jan. 11, 1877; m. Sept. 6, 1905, Henry A. Rhodes.

8137. Edwin B., Marshall, Ill., b. Nov. 28, 1879; m. Sept. 7, 1904, Cordelia Whittington.

8138. Alton, Helena, O., b. Aug. 3, 1884.

8139. Morris, Helena, O., b. Nov. 8, 1887.

8140. Lettie R., Helena, O., b. June 15, 1892.

Family of JOSEPH HERR (3979) and LILY J. HUFFORD.

8141. Harry J., Gibsonburg, O., b. Oct. 24, 1883; d. July 20, 1886.

8142. Hattie May, Gibsonburg, O., b. July 20, 1886.

Family of SUSAN H. HUBER (3981) and JOHN M. MUSSELMAN.

8143. Christian, Millersville, Pa., b. July 8, 1871; d. Mar. 28, 1887.

8144. Ella, Lancaster, Pa., b. July 22, 1873; m. Aug. 8, 1894, Harry Gerhart, b. May 21, 1871.

8145. Jacob, Lancaster, Pa., b. June 1, 1875.

8146. Amos, Lancaster, Pa., b. June 23, 1877.

8147. John, Lancaster, Pa., b. Mar. 7, 1879.

8148. Benjamin G., Lancaster, Pa., b. June 5, 1881.

8149. Susan, Lancaster, Pa., b. June 5, 1883.

8150. Martha, Lancaster, Pa., b. Feb. 13, 1885.

8151. Ida, Lancaster, Pa., b. June 12, 1887.

8152. Franklin, Lancaster, Pa., b. Feb. 5, 1890.

8153. Fannie, Lancaster, Pa., b. Jan. 6, 1893.

Family of JOHN H. HUBER (3984) and SARA ANNA KURTZ.

8154. Ada Martha, Braddock, Pa., b. July 11, 1879.

8155. John Jacob, Braddock, Pa., b. Mar. 21, 1881.

8156. Myra Elizabeth, Johnstown, Pa., b. Aug. 9, 1882; d. Jan. 7, 1893.

8157. Harry Daniel, Braddock, Pa., b. Nov. 25, 1883.

8158. Elsie Viola, Waynesboro, Pa., b. Feb. 7, 1888; d. July 15, 1888.

Family of EMMA SALOME HUBER (3986) and DANIEL K. WOLF.

8159. Annie C., Landisville, Pa., b. Aug. 27, 1878; d. May 8, 1886.

8160. Jacob H., Landisville, Pa, b. July 19, 1880.

8161. Ella H., Landisville, Pa., b. Mar. 3, 1882.

8162. Daniel H., Landisville, Pa., b. Oct. 20, 1884; d. Dec. 11, 1884.

8163. Emma Salome, Landisville, Pa., b. July 31, 1886.

8164. Edna Lovessa, Landisville, Pa., b. Apr. 4, 1891.

8165. Alice Irene, Landisville, Pa., b. June 2, 1893.

8166. Elmer H., Landisville, Pa., b. May 6, 1895; d. Aug. 7, 1896.

Family of ENOS H. HUBER (3989) and ELIZABETH WERTZ.

8167. Martha May, Lancaster, Pa., b. July 3, 1889.

8168. Cora, Lancaster, Pa., b. Jan. 8, 1892.

Family of LEVI H. HUBER (3990) and ANNIE MARGIE KERN.

8169. Della K., Landisville, Pa., b. Nov. 2, 1898.

Family of ANNA KLINE (3996) and DAVID B. BEARD.

8170. John Samuel, Enon, O., b. Oct. 8, 1881.

8171. Elmer Herr, Enon, O., b. Jan. 16, 1883.

8172. Harry Kline, Enon, O., b. June 14, 1885.

8173. Esther Thelma, Enon, O., b. Jan. 2, 1900.

Family of BENJAMIN HUBER (4001) and CATHARINE BENEDICT.

8174. Elmer Franklin, Lancaster, Pa., b. Sept. 24, 1868; m. Nov. 17, 1899, Amanda Grau.

8175. Harry, Creswell, Pa., b. June 7, 1876.

8176. Minnie Herr, Creswell, Pa., b. Feb. 18, 1879.

Family of SUSAN M. HERR (4022) and DAVID SKEEN.

8177. Ida May, Lancaster, Pa., b. Feb. 6, 1870; d. Sept. 7, 1870.

8178. Son, Lancaster, Pa., b. June 11, 1871; d. June 28, 1871.

8179. Lucy Blanche, Coatesville, Pa., b. Sept. 4, 1872; m. Nov. 10, 1892, William J. Landis, son Ezra Landis and Martha Weaver.
8180. Charles Earl, Pottsville, Pa., b. May 31, 1874.
8181. Nora Lillian, Lancaster, Pa., b. July 25, 1876.
8182. William Ross, Lancaster, Pa., b. Aug. 24, 1878; d. Mar. 23, 1899.
8183. Maud Estelle, Lancaster, Pa., b. Mar. 1, 1881.
8184. Ella Florence, Lancaster, Pa., b. Sept. 26, 1883; m. Ray Metzger.
8185. Frank, Lancaster, Pa.
8186. Harry, Lancaster, Pa., b. Oct. 11, 1868; d. July 28, 1869.
8187. Adam A., Lancaster, Pa.

Family of ELAM K. HERR (4024) and LILLIE RAUB.

8188. Ella Blanche, Bloomfield, Ia., b. Sept. 27, 1883.
8189. Charles Raub, Bloomfield, Ia., b. Sept. 17, 1886; d. Sept. 21, 1886.
8190. Miriam, Bloomfield, Ia., b. May 28, 1892.
8191. Dorothy Leah, Bloomfield, Ia., b. Sept. 5, 1894; d. Oct. 6, 1896.

Family of ELLA MARIAN HERR (4026) and JOHN W. McELHENEY.

8192. Clair H., Quarryville, Pa., b. July 22, 1887.
8193. Franklin H., Quarryville, Pa., b. Aug. 9, 1892.
8194. Emma C., Quarryville, Pa., b. June 23, 1897.
8195. Esther Rose, Quarryville, Pa., b. May 29, 1900.

Family of HIRAM TSHUDY (4036) and DELILAH COCHRAN.

8196. George W., Buck, Pa., b. Nov. 5, 1868.
8197. Benjamin F., Buck, Pa.
8198. Ada Ann, Buck, Pa., b. Nov. 28, 1872.
8199. Harry Milton, Buck, Pa., b. Feb. 16, 1874.
8200. Celia Sarah, Buck, Pa., b. Feb. 28, 1877.
8201. Catharine Ellen, Buck, Pa., b. May 16, 1879.
8202. Blanche, Buck, Pa., b. Mar. 4, 1892.

Family of **ALICE ANN HERR** (4037) and **ELIAS H. WIGGINS** (11768).

8203. Cora Belle, New Providence, Pa., b. June 21, 1879; m. Oct. 11, 1900, John L. F. Andrews, b. July 29, 1875; son Benjamin K. Andrews and Elizabeth L. Kreider.

8204. Miriam Irene, Smithville, Pa., b. Feb. 2, 1884.

8205. James Beaver, Smithville, Pa., b. July 1, 1886.

8206. Mary Alice, Smithville, Pa., b. Nov. 21, 1891.

Family of **MARY ELIZABETH HERR** (4038) and **EDWIN C. ASTON**.

8207. Jennie May, Harristown, Pa., b. Sept. 11, 1881; m. Mar. 31, 1908, Richard Joseph Lewin, son Wiskin Lewin and Rebecca Lord.

8208. Benjamin Franklin, Willow Street, Pa., b. Oct. 1, 1883.

8209. Margaret Viola, Lancaster, Pa., b. Oct. 28, 1885.

8210. Alice Elizabeth, West Willow, Pa., b. Feb. 5, 1888; m. Mar. 28, 1907, Joseph E. Rankin, son Joseph Rankin and ———— Eshleman.

8211. Anna Belle, West Willow, Pa., b. June 9, 1890.

8212. Leah Herr, West Willow, Pa., b. Dec. 22, 1893.

8213. Charles Westley, West Willow, Pa., b. Jan. 25, 1896.

Family of **JOHN HENRY HERR** (4039) and **EMMA L. KUHNS**.

8214. Samuel Clarence, Baltimore, Md., b. Feb. 7, 1897.

8215. Lizzie Jane, Baltimore, Md., b. June 27, 1882; d. Feb. 4, 1884.

8216. Stella Louella, Baltimore, Md., b. June 17, 1884.

Family of **MARIA DIFFENBACH** (4048) and **HENRY WITMER**.

8217. Laura Lavina, Strasburg, Pa., b. Oct. 31, 1825; d. Oct. 24, 1890; m. Apr. 28, 1846, Edwin T. Fetter, b. Nov. 27, 1822; d. Sept. 3, 1852; son Frederick Fetter and Anna Jarrell.

8218. Maria Louisa, Crofton, Pa., b. Sept. 12, 1827; m. May 19, 1846, Dr. Samuel Keneagy, d. Apr. 10, 1892.

8219. Barbara Esther, Paradise, Pa., b. Aug. 12, 1830; d. Nov. 19, 1830.

Family of BARBARA DIFFENBAUGH (4050) and FRANCIS D. CONNELLY.

8220. John Diffenbach, Lancaster, Pa., b. Mar. 15, 1840; m. Dec. 29, 1862, Sarah E. Miller, b. Aug. 11, 1844; dau. John Miller and Wid. Martha Musser.

8221. Mary Elizabeth, Lancaster, Pa., b. Sept. 13, 1842; d. July 12, 1863.

8222. George Francis, Lancaster, Pa., b. Sept. 7, 1844: d. Aug. 22, 1848.

8223. Son, Lancaster, Pa., b. July 4, 1850; d. July 4, 1850.

Family of JOHN R. DIFFENBAUGH (4052) and MARTHA BRENEMAN.

8224. George B., Marietta, Pa., b. Aug. 9, 1841; d. May 18, 1842.

8225. Anna Mary, Marietta, Pa., b. Apr. 29, 1847; d. Feb. 19, 1864.

8226. Sarah Barbara, Lancaster, Pa., b. Apr. 3, 1853.

8227. Elizabeth, Lancaster, Pa., b. Nov. 17, 1856.

Family of ADAM F. DIFFENBAUGH (4055) and SOPHIA MARKROFF.

8228. Barbara, Kasota, Minn., b. Sept. 20, 1857.

8229. Anna Jane, Kasota, Minn., b. Aug. 24, 1860.

8230. Frances Adalene, Kasota, Minn., b. July 19, 1862.

8231. John Christian, Kasota, Minn., b. Mar. 11, 1867.

8232. Charles Francis, Kasota, Minn., b. June 27, 1871; d. Mar. 29, 1873.

Family of Rev. JACOB BOWMAN (4059) and MARIA M. FRANTZ.

8233. Ezra F., Lancaster, Pa., b. Feb. 24, 1847; d. May 7, 1901; m. Feb. 21, 1875, Annie E. Musser (4887).

8234. Christian, Waynesboro, Pa., b. May 27, 1848; d. Nov. 25, 1872.

8235. Anna, Binkley's Bridge, Pa., b. Aug. 9, 1850; d. Jan. 8, 1873.

8236. Henry F., Lancaster, Pa, b. Sept. 9, 1852; d. Apr. 22, 1881.

8237. Elizabeth, Shoffs, Pa., b. Apr. 22, 1855; m. Jan. 5, 1889, Benjamin E. Flory, b. July 14, 1856; son Daniel Flory and Catharine Eby.

8238. Jacob, Strasburg, Pa., b. June 2, 1857; d. Apr. 7, 1868.

8239. Enos, Strasburg, Pa., b. Nov. 16, 1858; d. July 19, 1859.

8240. Mary, Willow Street, Pa., b. Apr. 22, 1860; m. Jan. 27, 1897, J. Aldus Herr (1604).

8241. Daughter, Strasburg, Pa., b. May 23, 1862; d. May 28, 1862.

8242. Son, Strasburg, Pa., b. Oct. 20, 1864; d. Oct. 20, 1864.

Family of ELIZABETH BOWMAN (4060) and HENRY F. TROUT.

8243. Emma Susanna, Strasburg, Pa., b. July 14, 1852; d. Dec. 4, 1897.

8244. Elam Bowman, Iva, Pa., b. Jan. 22, 1854; m. Apr. 15, 1876, Catharine Hess, b. Oct. 16, 1854; dau. David Hess and Elizabeth Heitler.

8245. Annie Elizabeth, Strasburg, Pa., b. Aug. 10, 1856; m. Oct. 4, 1875, Amos B. Leaman, b. Apr. 2, 1849; son Abraham Leaman and Elizabeth Buckwalter.

8246. Henry Free, Bart, Pa., b. Oct. 26, 1858; m. Feb. 12, 1899, Catharine Nagle, b. June 4, 1866; dau. John Nagle and Elizabeth Miller.

8247. Franklin John, Bart, Pa., b. June 2, 1861; m. Dec. 29, 1886, Elizabeth A. Huber, b. Feb. 3, 1868; dau. Amos Huber and Anna Kohr.

8248. Amos Theodore, Strasburg, Pa., b. Nov. 17, 1863; d. July 16, 1865.

8249. Elmer Jacob, Lancaster, Pa., b. Sept. 10, 1867; m. Feb. 13, 1890, Phoebe A. Howry, b. Aug. 25, 1869; dau. Rev. Christian Howry and Susan Shroad.

Family of Wid. HENRY BOWMAN (4064) and SUSANNA BARR.

8250. Lydia Ann, Refton, Pa., b. July 27, 1859; d. Apr. 19, 1860.

8251. Naomi, Mountville, Pa., b. Oct. 31, 1860; m. Oct. 18, 1882, Benjamin Weaver, b. Feb. 7, 1858; son Isaac Weaver and Katie Bear.

8252. Amaziah, Refton, Pa., b. May 4, 1862; d. Apr. 1, 1881.

8253. Martin B., Lancaster, Pa., b. Aug. 17, 1863.

8254. Elizabeth A., Refton, Pa., b. July 23, 1865.

8255. Henry, Lancaster, Pa., b. June 4, 1867.

8256. Jacob, Millersville, Pa., b. Dec. 19, 1868.

8257. Susanna, Refton, Pa., b. July 23, 1870; d. Apr. 29, 1871.

8258. Benjamin Franklin, Lancaster, Pa., b. July 30, 1875.

Family of MARY HARNISH (4067) and JACOB NEFF.

8259. John, Osborn, O., b. Dec. 5, 1852; d. Aug. 28, 1853.

8260. Amos, Osborn, O., b. July 10, 1854; d. June 20, 1870.

8261. Albert, Osborn, O., b. Mar. 17, 1856; d. Feb. 5, 1884; m. Feb. 9, 1882, Louisa Herr (4643).

8262. Esther, Osborn, O., b. Sept. 14, 1857; m. Feb. 15, 1876, Christian K. Brenner, b. Sept. 5, 1847; son Jacob Brenner and Anna Kauffman.

8263. Elizabeth, Osborn, O., b. Dec. 8, 1859.

8264. Frank, Osborn, O., b. Oct. 3, 1861; m. Anna Kline, dau. Jacob Kline and Catharine Showalter.

8265. Mary, Osborn, O., b. Apr. 1, 1863; m. Rev. Christian A. Herr.

8266. Jacob, Medway, O., b. Dec. 20, 1864; m. Blanche Huffman, dau. Charles Huffman and Barbara Frick.

8267. Emma, Medway, O., b. Oct. 14, 1866; m. Jacob Tippy, son Jacob Tippy and Lucinda Tripper.

8268. Henry, Osborn, O., b. Apr. 25, 1869; m. Ella Wolfe, dau. W——— S. Wolfe and Elizabeth Koogler.

8269. Christian, Osborn, O., b. Mar. 18, 1871.

Family of ESTHER HARNISH (4069) and JOHN M. ZELLER.

8270. Alonzo, Medway, O., b. Apr. 3, 1858; m. Jan. 29, 1882, Mary E. Brosey, b. Nov. 15, 1861.

8271. Henry, Medway, O., b. Sept. 15, 1859.

8272. John, Medway, O., b. Oct. 7, 1861.

8273. Lorenzo, Medway, O., b. Oct. 3, 1863; d. Nov. 23, 1869.

8274. Frank, Medway, O., b. Jan. 7, 1866.

8275. William, Medway, O., b. Aug. 9, 1868.

8276. Christian, Medway, O., b. Dec. 15, 1870.

8277. Cyrus, Medway, O., b. Oct. 8, 1873.

Family of ANNA HARNISH (4071) and LEVI KAUFFMAN.

8278. Laura H., Osborn, O., b. Jan. 19, 1862.

8279. Benjamin F., Osborn, O., b. Mar. 11, 1863.

8280. Esther H., Osborn, O., b. Aug. 4, 1865; m. Dec. 30, 1885, Henry K. Smith, b. Nov. 8, 1862.

8281. Hattie, Osborn, O., b. Aug. 4, 1865; d. Aug. 7, 1865.

8282. Susan S., Osborn, O., b. Sept. 7, 1867; d. Nov. 22, 1880.

8283. Anna E., Osborn, O., b. July 4, 1871.

8284. Emma B., Osborn, O., b. Oct. 27, 1873; m. N—— R. Bear, son S—— D. Bear and Anna Rung.

8285. Elizabeth, Osborn, O., b. Feb. 19, 1876.

8286. Cora, Osborn, O., b. June 8, 1884; d. Aug. 30, 1884.

8287. Dora, Osborn, O., b. June 8, 1884.

Family of JOHN S. HARNISH (4072) and CATHARINE S. DAVIS.

8288. Albert G., Medway, O. b. Mar. 13, 1867.

8289. Elizabeth C., Medway, O., b. Mar. 13, 1869; d. Dec. 7, 1872.

8290. Joseph D., Medway, O., b. Feb. 19, 1871; d. Oct. 22, 1895.

8291. Martha J., Medway, O., b. Apr. 27, 1873.

8292. Henry B., Medway, O., b. June 5, 1874; d. July 25, 1875.

8293. Esther B., Medway, O., b. July 27, 1876.

Family of AMOS B. HARNISH (4073) and AGNES A. PHILBY.

8294. Clara S., Dayton, O., b. Jan. 17, 1868.

8295. Elizabeth J., Cincinnati, O., b. Sept. 26, 1872; m. Sept. 21, 1898, George G. Ruhlman, b. Mar. 23, 1867; son Henry Ruhlman and Louisa Veith.

8296. Annie J., Dayton, O., b. Dec. 11, 1874.

Family of EMMA HARNISH (4074) and CYRUS HELMAN.

8297. Henry, Medway, O., b. Nov. 30, 1876.

8298. Mary, Medway, O., b. Oct. 19, 1878.

8299. John, Medway, O., b. Nov. 12, 1879.

Family of CHRISTIAN B. HERR (4078) and LIZZIE MYERS.

8300. Henry M., Lancaster, Pa., b. Sept. 25, 1851; m. Nov. 21, 1877, Emma Haverstick, b. May 16, 1854; dau. John Haverstick and Maria S. Hershey.

8301. Martin B., Lancaster, Pa., b. Apr. 20, 1853; m. Barbara Stoner, b. Oct. 3, 1846; dau. Jacob Stoner and Susan Funk.

8302. Benjamin F., Rohrerstown, Pa., b. Aug. 25, 1855; m. Nov. —, 1881, Mary E. Barr, b. Sept. 3, 1857; d. Aug. 16, 1903; dau. Benjamin Barr and Anna W. Erb.

8303. Lizzie, Millersville, Pa., b. Jan. 14, 1858; m. Nov. 19, 1879, Henry M. Stehman, b. Oct. 21, 1855; d. Sept. 2, 1888; son Tobias Stehman and Mary Mylin.

8304. Theodore William, Lime Valley, Pa., b. Jan. 4, 1861; m. Sept. 4, 1894, Emma L. Stonecker, b. Mar. 19, 1860; dau. Jacob Stonecker and Salome Karchner.

Family of ANN HERR (4079) and JOHN B. BRACKBILL (4165).

8305. Lizzie Ann, Galesburg, Ill., b. Mar. 8, 1857; m. Oct. 8, 1876, Jacob F. Bowman (6246).

8306. Benjamin H., Lime Valley, Pa., b. July 9, 1858; m. Oct. 8, 1883, Anna M. Hostetter, b. Sept. 7, 1862; dau. David Hostetter and Salome Brubaker.

8307. John Elmer, Columbus, O., b. Jan. 20, 1860; m. May 27, 1885, Alice J. Strock, b. Aug. 27, 1859; dau. —— and Elizabeth Keller.

Family of JEREMIAH HERR (4080) and ELIZABETH LANDIS.

8308. Annie E., Lancaster, Pa., b. Sept. 6, 1860; d. Nov. 10, 1864.

8309. Elias L., Lancaster, Pa., b. July 31, 1862; d. Mar. 31, 1809; m. Sept. 20, 1887, Katie W. Brubaker, b. Feb. 9, 1869; d. June 4, 1897; dau. Benjamin L. Brubaker and Annie B. ——.

8310. Lizzie, Lancaster, Pa., b. Jan. 15, 1865; m. Sept. 16, 1890, Henry H. Shenk (7434).

8311. Emma L., Lancaster, Pa., b. May 25, 1867.

Family of MARY ANN HERR (4081) and Rev. ELIAS GROFF.

8312. Lizzie H., Martinsville, Pa., b. June 25, 1862; m. Dec. 23, 1886, John F. Hess, b. Jan. 1, 1861; son Daniel Hess and Eliza J. Wade.

8313. Enos H., Strasburg, Pa., b. Aug. 16, 1864; m. Dec. 5, 1895, Martha Brubaker, b. Mar. 5, 1873; dau. Abraham Brubaker and Annie Bowman.

8314. Emanuel L., New Danville, Pa., b. Oct. 22, 1866; m. Nov. 13, 1890, Susan R. Herr (7450).

8315. Emma Sue, New Danville, Pa., b. Jan. 11, 1869.

8316. Elias B., Strasburg, Pa., b. Nov. 26, 1870; m. Dec. 12, 1900, Fannie B. Herr (5341).

3317. Harry, Strasburg, Pa., b. Apr. 14, 1873; m. Nov. 7, 1900, Ella Shaub, b. Apr. 3, 1873; dau. Henry Shaub and Fannie Landis.

8318. Ada H., West Willow, Pa., b. Feb. 16, 1875; m. Dec. 29, 1897, Henry R. Herr (7653).

8319. John Elmer, West Willow, Pa., b. Dec. 31, 1879.

Family of ANDREW HERR (4082) and SUSAN HESS (4135).

8320. Lizzie F., Refton, Pa., b. Dec. 30, 1864; m. Oct. 25, 1888, Jacob E. Witmer, b. ———, 1864; d. Mar. 25, 1901; son George Witmer and ——— Peoples.

8321. Milton H., Lime Valley, Pa., b. Dec. 2, 1866; d. Jan. 23, 1867.

8322. Lucena V., Lime Valley, Pa., b. Dec. 22, 1867; d. Sept. 28, 1870.

8323. Annie M., Lime Valley, Pa., b. Apr. 10, 1870; d. Mar. 19, 1871.

8324. Susan E., Lancaster, Pa., b. Jan. 2, 1872; m. Apr. 12, 1899, Benjamin L. Shaub (7827).

8325. Harry H., Lime Valley, Pa., b. July 22, 1874; d. Sept. 26, 1882.

8326. Mary E., Lancaster, Pa., b. Sept. 2, 1876· m. Nov. 14, 1900, Jacob W. Breneman, b. ———, 1874; son Amos Breneman and ———.

8327. Amos A., Lime Valley, Pa., b. Nov. 20, 1880; d. Dec. 4, 1880.

Family of ELIAS HERR (4083) and ELIZABETH B. LEAMAN.

8328. Annie L., Lime Valley, Pa., b. Feb. 7, 1867; d. Nov. 17, 1870.

8329. Harry L., New Danville, Pa., b. June 6, 1869; m. Dec. 4, 1895. Susan S. Herr (7447).

8330. Sarah Frances, Limeton, Va., b. Jan. 19, 1873; m. Dec. 22, 1897, Joseph L. Borden, b. Jan. 9, 1874; son Benjamin F. Borden and Sarah C. Pitman.

8331. Addie S., Philadelphia, Pa., b. Aug. 28, 1875; m. Sept. 16, 1896, Charles W. Haldeman, b. June 1, 1871; son Isaac F. Haldeman and Anna Grabill.

8332. Reuben E., Limeton, Va., b. Jan. 2, 1881.

8333. Ira L., Limeton, Va., b. Aug. 29, 1882.

Family of BENJAMIN F. HERR (4084) and AMANDA R. HAVERSTICK.

8334. Alice, Lancaster, Pa., b. Aug. 27, 1873.

8335. Mary, Millersville, Pa., b. Aug. 19, 1875; m. Harry Breneman.

8336. Estella, Lancaster, Pa., b. Aug. 3, 1879; m. Oct. 15, 1903, John M. Rutter.

Family of CHRISTIAN BRACKBILL (4085) and SUSANNA LEFEVRE.

8337. Annie Maria, Lancaster, Pa., b. Oct. 14, 1853.

8338. Ellis, Lancaster, Pa., b. July 5, 1855; d. Sept. 11, 1855.

8339. Maria V., Lancaster, Pa., b. June 25, 1858.

8340. Susan E., Lancaster, Pa., b. Mar. 23, 1860.

8341. Abraham, Lancaster, Pa., b. July 21, 1861; d. Nov. 19, 1862.

8342. Martha M., Lancaster, Pa., b. Mar. 2, 1863.

8343. Mark, Lancaster, Pa., b. May 11, 1865; d. Oct. 12, 1865.

Family of BENJAMIN BRACKBILL (4086) and ANNA LEFEVRE.

8344. John A., Lampeter, Pa., b. Oct. 18, 1855.

8345. Christian E., Lampeter, Pa., b. May 2, 1858.

8346. Maria Ella, Lanpeter, Pa., b. Sept. 13, 1860.

8347. Benjamin A., Lampeter, Pa., b. Jan. 28, 1863.

8348. Thaddeus H. Lincoln, Lampeter, Pa., b. Sept. 23, 1864.

Family of MARIA BRACKBILL (4093) and HIRAM PEOPLES.

8349. John B., Lancaster, Pa., b. Sept. 15, 1863; m. Luella L. Lefever, dau. Daniel Lefever and ———.

8350. Ida Sue, Bart, Pa., b. Apr. 3, 1865; m. Nov. 22, 1888, Dr. Charles E. Helm, b. Feb. 11, 1859; son Daniel Helm and Susan Eckman.

8351. Angie Winona, Lancaster, Pa., b. Mar. 9, 1868.

8352. Annie Carlotta, Lancaster, Pa., b. Nov. 9, 1869; m. Oct. 8, 1907, Henry L. Stager, b. May 30, 1853; son Henry F. Stager and Elizabeth Litch.

8353. Maria, Lancaster, Pa., b. Oct. 27, 1871; m. Martin Rush, son John Rush and ——— Breneman.

Family of JOHN B. HERR (4096) and FRANCES HESS (4133).

8354. Christian H., Lampeter, Pa., b. Sept. 18, 1857; m. Oct. 25, 1882, Amanda Book, b. Dec. 21, 1860; dau. Daniel Book and Mary Leaman.
8355. Henry B., Lampeter, Pa., b. July 21, 1859; m. Nov. 21, 1884, Barbara Harnish, b. Jan. 21, 1855; dau. Emanuel Harnish and Leah Good.
8356. Milton J., Lampeter, Pa., b. July 24, 1861; d. Mar. 31, 1864.
8367. Elizabeth N., Intercourse, Pa., b. Jan. 6, 1864; m. Oct. 25, 1888, Samuel E. Ranck, b. Dec, 21, 1861; son David Ranck and Elizabeth Esbenshade.
8358. Susan I., Lampeter, Pa., b. May 19, 1866; d. Jan. 11, 1869.
8359. John L., Lampeter, Pa., b. July 23, 1869; d. Feb. 12, 1879.
8360. Anna M., Lancaster, Pa., b. Aug. 26, 1872; m. Benjamin B. Groff, b. Dec. 10, 1867; son Jacob Groff and Mary Buckwalter.

Family of LEVI HERR (4098) and SUSANNA L. GROFF.

8361. Newton, Ronks, Pa., b. Jan. 20, 1867.
8362. Mary, Ronks, Pa., b. Sept. 18, 1870.
8363. Emma, Ronks, Pa., b. Mar. 24, 1875.

Family of ELIZA ANN HERR (4100) and EBY HERSHEY.

8364. Susan Naomi, Lime Valley, Pa., b. July 19, 1866.
8365. Mary Elizabeth, Lime Valley, Pa., b. Dec. 21, 1867; m. Sept. 27, 1897, Dr. Sylvester J. Finley, b. May 5, 1870; son Dr. Sylvester J. Finley and Josephine A. Cameron.
8366. Christian Milton, Lime Valley, Pa., b. Aug. 16, 1869.
8367. Anna Estella, Lime Valley, Pa., b. Mar. 25, 1872.
8368. Cora Belle, Lime Valley, Pa., b. Mar. 14, 1875.
8369. John Atlee, Lime Valley, Pa., b. July 15, 1878.

Family of MARY ANN HERR (4101) and FRANK E. WITMER (7213).

8370. Ida May, Lampeter, Pa., b. Sept. 12, 1882.
8371. Jacob Herr, Lampeter, Pa., b. July 11, 1891.

8372. Elmer J., Lampeter, Pa., b. Oct. 23, 1893.

8373. Frank A., Lampeter, Pa., b. Sept. 27, 1896.

8374. Esther M., Lampeter, Pa., b. Apr. 22, 1899.

Family of ELIZABETH HERR (4104) and RUFUS GERLACH.

8375. Henry H., Willow Street, Pa., b. Mar. 4, 1898.

Family of ESTHER HERR (4105) and JACOB L. RANCK.

8376. Elizabeth, Strasburg, Pa., b. May 29, 1868; d. Feb. 18, 1880.

8377. Amanda, Strasburg, Pa., b. Aug. 13, 1870; d. Aug. 4, 1880.

8378. Amos H., Strasburg, Pa., b. June 4, 1872; d. Feb. 23, 1874.

8379. Reuben H., Strasburg, Pa., b. Apr. 7, 1875; d. May 8, 1876.

8380. Milton H., Strasburg, Pa., b. June 2, 1877.

8381. Anna Naomi, Strasburg, Pa., b. June 28, 1880.

8382. Sarah Etta, Strasburg, Pa., b. Apr. 5, 1883.

Family of CHRISTIAN R. HERR (4107) and MARY HERTZLER.

8383. Naomi Etta, Lime Valley, Pa., b. Mar. 8, 1873.

8384. Elizabeth Esther, Witmer, Pa., b. Nov. 4, 1874; m. Nov. 15, 1899, John Stauffer, b. Aug. 21, 1876; son Amos P. Stauffer and Elizabeth Wenger.

8385. Amos H., Lancaster, Pa., b. June 28, 1876; m. Feb. 26, 1902, Anna Hollinger.

8386. Frank Elvin, Lime Valley, Pa., b. Dec. 7, 1878.

8387. Jay M., Lime Valley, Pa., b. Nov. 26, 1881.

8388. Christian D., Lime Valley, Pa., b. Dec. 31, 1888.

8389. Mary, Lancaster, Pa., b. Nov. 6, 1890; d. May 13, 1892.

Family of ELIZABETH HERR (4108) and AMOS M. LANDIS.

8390. Anna H., New Danville, Pa., b. Oct. 5, 1877; m. June 14, 1905, Frank E. Herr (6988).

8391. Mary Frances, New Danville, Pa., b. Nov. 29, 1879; m. Mar. 31, 1907, Charles H. Mumma, b. Oct. 21, 1872; son John Mumma and Elizabeth Hertzler.

8392. Elizabeth A., New Danville, Pa., b. July 24, 1882.

8393. David M., New Danville, Pa., b. Dec. 9, 1885.

8394. Esther Mae, New Danville, Pa., b. May 20, 1896.

Family of MARY ELIZABETH HERR (4868) and ENOS B. HERR (4110).

8395. Enos Etta, Lancaster, Pa., b. Nov. 1, 1869.

Family of Wid. REUBEN D. HERR (4113) and H. LOUISA COHO.

8396. Claire Coho, Refton, Pa., b. Dec. 30, 1887.

Family of LEVI HERR (4114) and FRANCES MARY DUNNING.

8397. Mary Emma, Lexington, Pa., b. Apr. 7, 1852; d. Aug. 26, 1852.
8398. Lee Pierce, Lexington, Pa., b. Aug. 3, 1853; d. Oct. 2, 1887; m. Nov. 4, 1880, Emily V. Walker, b. Oct. 31, 1861; dau. Rev. Hiram P. Walker and Catharine Kenner.
8399. Ethelbert Dudley, Lexington, Pa., b. July 2, 1856; m. 1887, Tillie K. Pollock, b. Nov. 10, 1857; dau. Thurman Pollock and Jane ————.
8400. Charles Edmond, Lexington, Pa., b. Sept. 13, 1858; m. Jan. 15, 1886, Gertrude Pollock, b. Oct. 30, 1886; d. Dec. 10, 1889; dau. Thurman Pollock and Jane ————.

Family of MARY HERR (4115) and FRANCIS JOHNSON.

8401. William H., Centre, O., b. Jan. 29, 1838; d. Oct. 4, 1862; m. Aug. 31, 1859, Abigail M. Stimpson, b. Apr. 27, 1840; dau. Stephen Stimpson and Abigail Shaw.
8402. Elizabeth A., Columbus, O., b. Mar. 11, 1840.
8403. Sarah Jane, New Albany, O., b. June 15, 1842; d. ————, 1882; m. Feb. 2, 1864, Byron C. Babbett, b. Dec. 14, 1841; son Lovell W. Babbett and Lydia Hockman.
8404. Son, Columbus, O., b. Sept. 12, 1845; d. Sept. 22, 1845.
8405. Samuel B., Columbus, O., b. Sept. 28, 1846; d. Apr. 10, 1849.

Family of SAMUEL HERR (1417) and MARGARET S. McILHENNY.

8406. John, Dayton, O., b. Sept. 14, 1859; d. Feb. 14, 1895.
8407. Charles F., Toledo, O., b. July 17, 1861; m. Oct. 3, 1888, Elizabeth M. Hacker, b. July 21, 1866; d. June 6, 1900.

Family of JOHN HERR (4118) and ANN SHULTZ.

8408. Frances A., Columbus, O., b. Apr. 9, 1852.
8409. Catharine, Columbus, O., b. Mar. 16, 1854.

8410. Christian, Columbus, O., b. Oct. 5, 1861.

8411. John Grant, Columbus, O., b. Oct. 20, 1864.

Family of CHRISTIAN S. HERR (4122) and SUSAN STUTTZENBERGER.

8412. Walter, Reese Station, O.

Family of SAMUEL HESS (4130) and BARBARA A. LINTER.

8413. Lizzie, Lancaster, Pa., b. June 14, 1852.

8414. B—— Lintner, Lancaster, Pa., b. Mar. 7, 1854.

8515. Charles Carpenter, Lancaster, Pa., b. Dec. 28, 1858.

8416. Christian L——, Lancaster, Pa., b. June 18, 1861.

8417. Laura Anna, Lancaster, Pa., b. Sept. 7, 1863.

Family of ANNA HESS (4132) and RUDOLPH SHENK.

8418. Henry H., Rockville, Pa., b. Nov. 2, 1855.

8419. Benjamin, Rockville, Pa., b. Sept. 23, 1857; d. Sept. 28, 1858.

8420. Aldus H., Rockville, Pa., b, Feb. 4, 1859.

8421. Lizzie, Rockville, Pa., b. Oct. 10, 1861.

8422. Enos, Rockville, Pa., b. July 17, 1864.

Family of ISAAC HERR (4140) and MARY HERR LEAMAN.

8423. Barbara L., Lampeter, Pa., b. Jan. 30, 1862.

8424. Anna, Lampeter, Pa., b. Aug. 26, 1863; d. Sept. 10, 1864.

8425. Elizabeth, Lampeter, Pa., b. Apr. 6, 1865; m. Nov. 23, 1893, Martin Zimmerman, b. Jan. 14, 1865; son Isaac Zimmerman and Katharyn Messner.

8426. Hettie, Lampeter, Pa., b. June 7, 1866; m. Nov. 20, 1889, Frank S. Lefever, b. Dec. 22, 1864; son Daniel Lefever and Martha Sensenig.

8427. Abraham, Lampeter, Pa., d. Aug. 29, 1867; m. Nov. 17, 1896, Amanda L. Herr (6928).

8428. Mary Ann, Lampeter, Pa., b. June 18, 1870.

8429. Isaac L——, Lampeter, Pa., b. Aug. 22, 1871.

8430. Samuel L——, Lampeter, Pa., b. Feb. 17, 1873.

8431. Emma L., Lampeter, Pa., b. July 6, 1875; m. Oct. —, 1901, Abraham D. Metzler, son Abraham Metzler and ——.

8432. George L., Lampeter, Pa., b. Nov. 13, 1877; m. Oct. 28, 1903, Mary L. Landis, dau. Aaron D. Landis and ——.

8433. Daughter, Lampeter, Pa., b. Nov. 7, 1878; d. Nov. 7, 1878.

8434. Benjamin, Lampeter, Pa., b. Jan. 29, 1882.

Family of JOSEPH HERR (4142) and ETTA EBERLY.

8435. Annie E., Lancaster, Pa., b. Mar. 21, 1883.

Family of CHRISTIAN HERR (4144) and MARY KENDIG.

8436. Mary Frances, Windom, Pa., b. May 25, 1874; m. Dec. 16, 1900, Henry M. Kauffman, b. Sept. 21, 1862; son Samuel M. Kauffman and Martha ———.

8437. Christian Willis, Millersville, Pa., b. Aug. 31, 1875.

8438. Enos K., Millersville, Pa., b. Mar. 12, 1878.

8439. John K., Philadelphia, Pa., b. July 1, 1880.

8440. Franklin, Millersville, Pa., b. June 26, 1883; d. July 4, 1883.

8441. Ira, Millersville, Pa., b. Apr. 17, 1885.

8442. Guy, Millersville, Pa., b. Aug. 19, 1887.

8443. M—— Kendig, Millersville, Pa., b. Mar. 24, 1890.

8444. Raymond, Millersville, Pa., b. Feb. 17, 1895.

Family of ELIZABETH HARNISH (4157) and ABRAHAM B. HARNISH.

8445. Ella Viola, Lancaster, Pa., b. Apr. 13, 1872; m. Apr. 19, 1894, Benjamin E. Lefever, b. May 1, 1870; son Benjamin R. Lefever and Mary ———.

8446. Cora Kate, New Danville, Pa., b. Apr. 21, 1876.

8447. Annie Elizabeth, New Danville, Pa., b. Feb. 23, 1889.

Family of DAVID F. HARNISH (4152) and KATE HERMAN.

8448. Celia, Hollingers, Pa., b. Dec. 17, 1879; m. June —, 1907, Tobias Dunkin, b. ———, 1885.

8449. John, Willow Street, Pa., b. Oct. 12, 1882.

Family of MARTIN HERR (4161) and LYDIA A. RINEER.

8450. Clyde Benjamin, Lancaster, Pa., b. Sept. 8, 1879; m. Apr. 23, 1901, Sadie S. Book, dau. Josiah Book and Cora Shirk.

8451. Mary Frances, Lancaster, Pa., b. Aug. 13, 1881.

8452. Blanche Elizabeth, Lancaster, Pa., b. Feb. 11, 1884.

8453. Maud Catherine, Lancaster, Pa., b. Oct. 15, 1885.

8454. Agnes Armeda, Lancaster, Pa., b. Feb. 27, 1889.

8455. Clara Emily, Lancaster, Pa., b. Aug. 25, 1893; d. Aug. 19, 1896.

8456. Jay Martin, Lancaster, Pa., b. June 30, 1897.

8457. Jasper Johnson, Lancaster, Pa., b. July 4, 1900; d. Aug. 3, 1902.

Family of ANN BRACKBILL (4166) and DANIEL LEAMAN.

8458. Elizabeth, Soudersburg, Pa., b. Nov. 14, 1854.

8459. Christian B., Soudersburg, Pa., b. May 22, 1857.

8460. Susan, Soudersburg, Pa., b. Mar. 23, 1859.

8461. Benjamin Franklin, Soudersburg, Pa., b. Mar. 24, 1864; d. Mar. 20, 1866.

8462. Enos B., Soudersburg, Pa., b. Mar. 1, 1867.

Family of SUSANNA BRACKBILL (4167) and SAMUEL L. LEAMAN.

8463. Millard B——, Lancaster, Pa., b. Feb. 12, 1857.

8464. George Wesley, Lancaster, Pa., b. Jan. 10, 1859.

8465. Benjamin Elmer, Lancaster, Pa., b. Dec. 13, 1862.

8466. Enos Brackbill, Lancaster, Pa., b. Dec. 6, 1864.

Family of ELIZA HOUSER (4170) and JOHN B. KREIDER.

8467. Elam Henry, Rocky Springs, Pa., b. Oct. 9, 1851; d. Mar. 24, 1857.

8468. Franklin J., Rocky Springs, Pa., b. May 17, 1853.

8469. Aaron, Rocky Springs, Pa., b. Feb. 11, 1855.

8470. Ezra, Rocky Springs, Pa., b. Jan. 5, 1857.

8471. Lizzie, Rocky Springs, Pa., b. Nov. 14, 1858; d. Oct. 20, 1859.

8472. Emma C., Rocky Springs, Pa., b. Sept. 11, 1860; d. Nov. 27, 1862.

8473. Enos, Rocky Springs, Pa., b. July 29, 1862; d. Sept. 16, 1863.

8474. Lydia, Rocky Springs, Pa., b. Sept. 26, 1863.

8475. Henry, Rocky Springs, Pa., b. Feb. 5, 1866.

Family of ANNA HOUSER (4172) and CHRISTIAN LEFEVRE.

8476. Elizabeth, Lancaster, Pa., b. Sept. 24, 1854.

8477. Jacob H., Lancaster, Pa., b. Feb. 16, 1858.

8478. Anna Maria, Lancaster, Pa., b. June 5, 1860.

8479. Henry L., Lancaster, Pa., b. June 25, 1861.

8480. Christian E., Lancaster, Pa., b. Feb. 4, 1864.

Family of MARIA HOUSER (4174) and JOHN N. MECK.

8481. George Henry, Lampeter, Pa., b. Sept. 7, 1861.

8482. Jacob Aldus, Lampeter, Pa., b. Dec. 16, 1863.

Family of HENRY L. BRACKBILL (4178) and SUSAN W. RUDY.

8483. Hiram, Lancaster, Pa., b. Aug. 24, 1852.

8484. Daniel Ryan, Lancaster, Pa., b. Oct. 18, 1854.

8485. Henry, Lancaster, Pa., b. Sept. 11, 1856; d. Mar. 24, 1857.

8486. Elizabeth, Lancaster, Pa., b. Jan. 17, 1858.

8487. Christian, Lancaster, Pa., b. Feb. 17, 1860.

8488. Clinton, Lancaster, Pa., b. Jan. 17, 1862.

8489. Annie Emma, Lancaster, Pa., b. Jan. 21, 1864.

Family of ELIZA ANN BRACKBILL (4179) and JOHN H. RISSER.

8490. Abner B., Brunnersville, Pa., b. June 29, 1851.

8491. Barbara Ann, Brunnersville, Pa., b. Sept. 13, 1852.

8492. Phares, Brunnersville, Pa., b. Sept. 30, 1854; d. July 5, 1859.

8493. Amos, Brunnersville, Pa., b. Mar. 12, 1856; d. June 19, 1859.

8494. Levi, Brunnersville, Pa., b. Aug. 27, 1857.

8495. Elias, Brunnersville, Pa., b. Aug. 2, 1859.

8496. Eliza, Brunnersville, Pa., b. May 18, 1861.

8497. Mary, Brunnersville, Pa., b. July 8, 1863.

8498. Infant, Brunnersville, Pa., b. May 30, 1866; d. May 30, 1866.

Family of CHRISTIAN L. BRACKBILL (4181) and AMANDA E. BAKER.

8499. David Amandus, Fairview, Pa., b. Apr. 11, 1864.

Family of MARIA LANDIS (4182) and RUDOLPH GAMBER.

8500. Son, Landis Valley, Pa., b. Apr. 13, 1831; d. Apr. 13, 1831.

8501. Benjamin L., Windom, Pa., b. Apr. 1, 1832; m. Jan. 13, 1859, Salena Herr (1927).

8502. Catherine, Landis Valley, Pa., b. July 1, 1835; d. Sept. —, 1866; m. Feb. 12, 1856, Daniel S. Herr (861).

8503. Son, Landis Valley, Pa., b. Aug. 1, 1836; d. Aug. 1, 1836.

8504. John L., Landis Valley, Pa., b. May 25, 1838; m. Aug. 27, 1861, Fanny Herr (2830).

8505. Anna, Landis Valley, Pa., b. Aug. 29, 1843.

8506. Francis, Landis Valley, Pa., b. July 6, 1846; d. July 16, 1846.

Family of ANNA LANDIS (4184) and JOHN FORRY.

8507. Fanny, Columbia, Pa., b. Mar. 12, 1833; m. Nov. 12, 1850, Joseph Charles, b. Feb. 25, 1825; son John Charles and Fannie Witmer.

8508. Anna, Millersville, Pa., b. May 1, 1835; m. Oct. 11, 1853, Christian Eschbach, b. Jan. 29, 1833; son Christian Eschbach and Mary Brant.

8509. Daniel, Millersville, Pa., b. May 6, 1838; m. June 30, 1857, Martha Swarr, b. July 31, 1840; dau. John Swarr and Susan Frick.

8510. Elizabeth, Millersville, Pa., b. Aug. 2, 1841; m. Sept. —, 1865, Isaac S. Groff, son Isaac Groff and Barbara Sensenig.

8511. Susan, Millersville, Pa., b. Apr. 30, 1846; m. Mar. 11, 1866, Samuel B. Sensenig, b. Jan. 27, 1845; son Isaac W. Sensenig and Eliza B. Bowman.

Family of FANNY LANDIS (4185) and GEORGE WEIDLER.

8512. Elizabeth L., Landis Valley, Pa., b. July 19, 1834; m. Nov. 2, 1856, John B. Brubaker, b. Dec. 18, 1827; son Joseph Brubaker and Maria Bucher.

8513. Salinda, Landis Valley, Pa., b. Feb. 10, 1836; m. Nov. 20, 1860, Daniel Harnish, b. July 21, 1831; son David Harnish and Susan Forry.

8514. Anna, Landis Valley, Pa., b. Aug. 19, 1837; m. Nov. 18, 1863, Daniel Burkholder, son Joseph Burkholder and Betsey Rife.

8515. Fanny Matilda, Landis Valley, Pa., b. Apr. 25, 1839; m. Oct. 18, 1860, Benjamin D. Landis (8527).

8516. Abraham, Landis Valley, Pa., b. May 4, 1841.

8517. George, Landis Valley, Pa., b. June 27, 1843.

8518. Caroline, Landis Valley, Pa., b. Oct. 16, 1845.

8519. Elmira, Landis Valley, Pa., b. Jan. 12, 1849.

8520. Susan, Landis Valley, Pa., b. Sept. 6, 1851.

8521. John, Landis Valley, Pa., b. Sept. 29, 1853.

Family of DAVID LANDIS (4190) and FANNY MYERS.

8522. Urias, Millersville, Pa., b. Jan. 11, 1847; d. Apr. 8, 1847.

8523. Mary Ann, Millersville, Pa., b. Feb. 4, 1848; d. June 22, 1849.

8524. Fanny, Millersville, Pa., b. Dec. 1, 1850.

8525. Amos, Millersville, Pa., b. Dec. 20, 1852.

8526. Elizabeth, Millersville, Pa., b. Mar. 17, 1855; d. Nov. 23, 1856.

Family of CHRISTIAN B. LANDIS (4195) and FANNY DENLINGER.

8527. Benjamin D., Lancaster, Pa., b. July 11, 1839; m. Oct. 18, 1860, Fanny M. Weidler (8515).

8528. Elizabeth, Lancaster, Pa., b. Mar. 13, 1841; m. David Rudy, son Charles Rudy and Betsy Barr.

8529. John, Lancaster, Pa., b. Mar. 6, 1843; m. Emma Ault, dau. Jonas Ault and ——— Miller.

8530. Christian D., Lancaster, Pa., b. Jan. 10, 1845.

8531. Tobias, Lancaster, Pa., b. Aug. 16, 1846; d. May 21, 1862.

8532. Amos, Lancaster, Pa., b. Sept. 5, 1848.

8533. Jacob, Lancaster, Pa., b. Aug. 17, 1850.

8534. Son, Lancaster, Pa., b. May 3, 1852; d. May 4, 1852.

Family of Wid. CHRISTIAN B. LANDIS (4195) and ANNA HOSTETTER.

8535. Susanna H., Lancaster, Pa., b. Apr. 19, 1858.

8536. Fanny H., Landis Valley, Pa., b. June 13, 1859.

Family of ANNA LANDIS (4196) and ANDREW BRUBAKER.

8537. Fanny L., Wheatland Mills, Pa., b. Oct. 13, 1837; m. Dec. 23, 1863, John L. Herr (1928).

8538. Elizabeth, Landis Valley, Pa., b. Jan. 19, 1839; d. Feb. 22, 1839.

8539. Jacob, Rohrerstown, Pa., b. Feb. 23, 1840; m. Fanny C. Herr (2828).

8540. Barbara, Landisville, Pa., b. Feb. 27, 1842; m. John Hertzler, son John Hertzler and Elizabeth Breneman.

8541. Benjamin, Mountville, Pa., b. Feb. 17, 1844; m. Anna Wissler, dau. John Wissler and Catherine Bair.

8542. Anna, Landis Valley, Pa., b. June 5, 1846.

8543. Lizzie Matilda, Landis Valley, Pa., b. Aug. 4, 1859.

8544. Emma, Landis Valley, Pa., b. May 2, 1863.

8545. Mary, Landis Valley, Pa., b. May 25, 1865.

Family of HIRAM E. BARR (4200) and ELIZABETH BRIANT.

8546. Susan F., Quincy, Ill., b. Dec. 25, 1839; m. Jan. 19, 1865, Samuel C. Orten, b. Mar. 17, 1837; son Nesbit Orten and Lucinda Spradling.
8547. Breneman, Quincy, Ill., b. Nov. 11, 1841.
8548. William H., Quincy, Ill., b. Oct. 16, 1844.
8549. Lydia S., Quincy, Ill., b. Nov. 3, 1846.
8550. George F., Quincy, Ill., b. Oct. 9, 1849.
8551. Newton H., Quincy, Ill., b. May 21, 1853.
8552. Mary E., Quincy, Ill., b. Dec. 6, 1856.

Family of MARY ELIZABETH BARR (4201) and WILLIAM HOMAN.

8553. John Sullivan, Quincy, Ill., b. Feb. 7, 1842.
8554. William, Quincy, Ill., b. Jan. 27, 1843.
8555. Susan Emaline, Quincy, Ill., b. May 27, 1844; d. Nov. 8, 1849.
8556. Mary Josephine, Quincy, Ill., b. Mar. 4, 1846.
8557. George, Quincy, Ill., b. Aug. 14, 1847.
8558. Benjamin F., Quincy, Ill., b. Oct. 26, 1855.
8559. Edwin Barr, Quincy, Ill., b. July 24, 1858.

Family of MELCHOR NEWTON BARR (4202) and M—— J. H. UNCLES.

8560. Morris Lincoln, Monmouth, Ill., b. Apr. 20, 1865.

Family of ELIJAH BARR (4203) and LIZZIE KINDLE.

8561. Frank W., Quincy, Ill., b. Sept. 25, 1860; d. Sept. 15, 1861.
8562. Mary L., Quincy, Ill., b. Dec. 20, 1862; d. May 30, 1864.
8563. Mary Augusta, Quincy, Ill., b. Apr. 29, 1865.

Family of AMANDA BARR (4205) and Dr. JOHN McCALLA.

8564. Frances Louisa, Lancaster, Pa., b. Mar. 11, 1857; d. Nov. 14, 1864.

Family of FRANCES L. BARR (4207) and HIRAM MARS.

8565. Antoinette L., St. Louis, Mo., b. Sept. 17, 1858.

Family of Dr. ISAAC S. ESHLEMAN (4212) and MARY D. JAYNE.

8566. Hannah S., Oakland, Cal., b. Aug. 23. 1852; m. Mar. 15, 1879, Alfred Magoon, son John Magoon and ———.

8567. Mima E., Fresno, Cal., b. Jan. 23, 1857; m. Sept. 20, 1899, Dr Walter N. Sherman, b. Sept. 21, 1855; son Dr. Walter R. Sherman and Almira Callahan.

Family of JAMES HERVEY ESHLEMAN (4213) and MARY E. COOPER.

8568. Louis Eugene, East Oakland, Cal., b. July 27, 1850; m. Nov. 25, 1873, Ella E. Barnes, b. Jan. 6, 1855; dau. Simpson Barnes and Angeline Burgoyne.

8569. William DeWitt, East Oakland, Cal., b. Oct. 20, 1854; d. July 12, 1892.

8570. Gertrude, Topeka, Kans., b. June 13, 1856; m. Aug. 28, 1876, John Waite, b. Sept. 28, 1844; son Joseph Waite and ———.

8571. Wid. Gertrude, Topeka, Kans., b. June 13, 1856; m. Oct. 6, 1886, Hugh Curry, b. Aug. 29, 1850.

8572. Mary Elizabeth, Gap, Pa., b. May 17, 1858; d. Nov. 13, 1861.

8573. Fannie, Oakland, Cal., b. Oct. 15, 1865.

8574. Laura, Oakland, Cal., b. Dec. 29, 1868.

Family of MARTIN B. ESHLEMAN (4215) and MARY E. GOOD.

8575. Sarah E., Cochranville, Pa., b. Dec. 23, 1857; m. Oct. 1, 1884, Johnson P. Hill, b. June 20, 1853; d. Oct. 6, 1889; son William Hill and Phoebe Guthrie.

8576. Mary E., Philadelphia, Pa., b. Sept. 9, 1860.

8577. William, Cochranville, Pa., b. Jan. 3, 1864; d. Jan. 5, 1864.

8578. Dr. John Martin, Parkesburg, Pa., b. Nov. 28, 1865; m. Sept. 21, 1892, Anna B. Smith, b. May 15, 1866; dau. John B. Smith and Susanna G. Criswell.

8579. Laura C., Philadelphia, Pa., b. Apr. 29, 1867.

8580. Isaac Stauffer, Parkesburg, Pa., b. Apr. 14, 1871; d. Aug. 3, 1871.

8581. Mabel, Cochranville, Pa., b. June 10, 1873; d. Oct. 14, 1873.

8582. Ellis Good, Philadelphia, Pa., b. May 16, 1876.

Family of SARAH M. ESHLEMAN (4216) and Rev. GEORGE W. YOUNG.

8583. Mary Elizabeth, Zanesville, O., b. Oct. 25, 1849; m. Oct. 25, 1871, Capt. George Hull.

8584. George W., Zanesville, O., b. May 18, 1851.

8585. B—— Franklin, Columbus, O., b. Feb. 28, 1853.

8586. Sarah A., Columbus, O., b. Jan. 16, 1855; m. ——, 1879, Harold Lewis, son Samuel Lewis and Emily Roberts.

8587. Martin B., Philadelphia, Pa., b. Aug. 27, 1857; m. Ella Roberts.

8588. Marianna R., Philadelphia, Pa., b. Sept. 3, 1860.

Family of H. LOUISA ESHLEMAN (4217) and JOSEPH HASTINGS.

8589. Celeste B., Spruce Grove, Pa., b. Sept. 17, 1856.

8590. Edgar E., Omaha, Neb., b. June 4, 1859; m. Nov. 18, 1896, Harriet I. Hart, b. Jan. 1, 1870; dau. Franklin E. Hart and Ione C. Lampher.

8591. Joseph Albert, Spruce Grove, Pa., b. Oct. 22, 1861.

8592. Mary Emma, Spruce Grove, Pa., b. Dec. 13, 1865; m. May 3, 1888, Walter L. Kauffman, b. Nov. 17, 1863; son Samuel L. Kauffman and Catherine Bucherfield.

Family of BENJAMIN FRANK ESHLEMAN (4218) and FANNIE H. LEVERICK.

8593. Maria Elizabeth, New York, N. Y., b. Feb. 8, 1870; m. May 14, 1891, John W. Castles, b. Mar. 25, 1858; son George W. Castles and Sarah A. Sears.

8594. William Edward, New Orleans, La., b. Sept. 25, 1871; d. Jan. 29, 1872.

8595. Benjamin Franklin, New Orleans, La., b. Sept. 4, 1873; d. Oct. 10, 1880.

8596. Fannie Leverick, New Orleans, La., b. June 9, 1875; m. Feb. 5, 1896, Fountain B. Craig, b. Nov. 5, 1870; son Robert E. Craig and Emilie Barksdale.

8597. Sidney St. John, New Orleans, La., b. Dec. 6, 1877.

8598. Dr. Charles Leverick, New Orleans, La., b. May 18, 1880.

8599. Marie Celeste, New Orleans, La., b. Sept. 23, 1883.

8600. Isaac Stauffer, New Orleans, La., b. Jan. 29, 1885.

Family of ANN ELIZABETH ESHLEMAN (4219) and JACOB BACHMAN.

8601. Frank E., Port Henry, N. Y., b. Dec. 9, 1858; m. Oct. 20, 1887, Bessie Timberlake, b. June 24, 1867; dau. R—— H. Timberlake and Henrietta Evans.

Family of Wid. J. ALBERT ESHLEMAN (4221) and LAURA NEILL.

8602. Benjamin, Erie, Pa., b. Aug. 3, 1900.

Family of EMMA F. ESHLEMAN (4222) and JOSEPH R. CRAIG.

8603. Frederick D., Philadelphia, Pa., b. July 28, 1874; m. Annie J. Clarke, dau. James Clarke and Rebecca Cox.

8604. Joseph Robert, Philadelphia, Pa., b. Nov. 9, 1875; d. July 11, 1876.

8605. L. Fletcher, Philadelphia, Pa., b. Feb. 24, 1878.

Family of EDWIN ESHLEMAN (4223) and ANNIE V. MUSSELMAN (4857).

8606. Mary Clara, Philadelphia, b. Oct. 18, 1878.

8607. Anna Louisa, Philadelphia, Pa., b. June 27, 1881.

8608. Helen Elizabeth, Philadelphia, Pa., b. Jan. 26, 1884; d. Apr. 17, 1884.

8609. Edwina Celeste, Philadelphia, Pa., b. July 7, 1887.

Family of JOHN B. WARFEL (4226) and MARY A. GIRVIN (5945).

8610. Ila, Lancaster, Pa., b. Sept. 22, 1853; m. Feb. 10, 1881, William F. Beyer, b. Oct. 11, 1853; son Thomas Beyer and Mary A. McCleneghan.

8611. Jessie F., Lancaster, Pa., b. Mar. 26, 1857.

8612. John G., Lancaster, Pa., b. Mar. 15, 1860; m. Oct. 12, 1887, Elizabeth A. Baehler, b. Mar. 8, 1865; dau. Leonard J. Baehler and Sophia L. Lunaker.

8613. Robert Girvin, Lancaster, Pa., b. Oct. 28, 1862; d. Jan. 4, 1871.

Family of ALBERT K. WARFEL (4227) and MARY NAOMI GROFF (5870).

8614. Ottis Groff, Lancaster, Pa., b. Jan. 21, 1860.

8615. Harry E., Lancaster, Pa., b. June 12, 1864; d. July 6, 1864.

8616. Ovid Barr, Lancaster, Pa., b. July 15, 1865.

Family of MILTON B. ESHLEMAN (4234) and JENNIE M. WILLIAMS.

8617. Victor Eugene, Philadelphia, Pa., b. July 2, 1871; m. Emma Taylor, dau. Edward Taylor and ———.

Family of Wid. MILTON B. ESHLEMAN (4234) and ANNIE M. LIGHTNER.

8618. Fannie Eliza, Newport, Pa., b. Sept. 8, 1877.

8619. Jacob Edwin, Newport, Pa., b. Mar. 3, 1879.

Family of AMOS L. ESHLEMAN (4237) and ESTHER E. HOOVER.

8620. Juliet Evaline, Leaman Place, Pa., b. Nov. 27, 1875.

8621. George Lightner, Leaman Place, Pa., b. Feb. 28, 1877.

8622. Ferree Witmer, Leaman Place, Pa., b. Sept. 16, 1878.

8623. Ellen Emaline, Leaman Place, Pa., b. Apr. 11, 1880.

8624. Amos Carl, Leaman Place, Pa., b. June 1, 1882.

8625. Jacob David, Leaman Place, Pa., b. Feb. 4, 1887.

Family of ELAM W. ESHLEMAN (4238) and ISABELLA A. LIGHTNER.

8626. Howard Lightner, Leaman Place, Pa., b. Nov. 22, 1874.

8627. Emma Jessie, Leaman Place, Pa., b. Feb. 1, 1877.

8628. Ernest Witmer, Leaman Place, Pa., b. Nov. 26, 1881.

8629. Elam Eugene, Leaman Place, Pa., b. Mar. 3, 1883.

Family of SILAS K. ESHLEMAN (4240) and EMMA H. SLAYMAKER.

8630. Eliza Evaline, Paradise, Pa., b. July 5, 1880.

8631. Silas Kendrick, Paradise, Pa., b. July 3, 1886.

Family of Wid. ALDUS JOHN GROFF (4345) and AUGUSTA PARKER.

8632. Elsie Parker, Boston, Mass., b. Aug. 10, 1878; m. Nov. 28, 1900, Henry C. L. Miller.

8633. Mary Amelia, Lancaster, Pa., b. Dec. 4, 1879.

8634. George Edward, Pittsburg, Pa., b. May 9, 1881.

8635. James Parker, Pittsburg, Pa., b. Dec. 5, 1882.

8636. Josephine Musselman, Lancaster, Pa., b. Mar. 6, 1885.

8637. Alice Natalia, Lancaster, Pa., b. Jan. 13, 1887.

8638. Florence Chandler, Lancaster, Pa., b. Aug. 27, 1888.

8639. Arthur Mar, Lancaster, Pa., b. Mar. 6, 1891.

8640. Donald, Lancaster, Pa., b. Nov. 2, 1893.

8641. Dorothy, Lancaster, Pa., b. Nov. 2, 1893.

Family of SILAS E. GROFF (4247) and SARAH E. KENEAGY.

8642. Mary Rowe, Strasburg, Pa., b. Sept. 26, 1888.

8643. John Eshleman, Strasburg, Pa., b. May 22, 1890.

Family of HARVEY BRACKBILL (4254) and CAROLINE C. RAUCH.

8644. Edgar Clayton, Lancaster, Pa., b. Apr. 6, 1858.

8645. Emlen Howard, Strabsurg, Pa., b. May 9, 1859; d. Apr. 1, 1860.

8646. Cora Elizabeth, Strasburg, Pa., b. Sept. 22, 1860.

8647. Marian Virgilia, Strasburg, Pa., b. July 27, 1862; d. Oct 26, 1862.

8648. Sarah M, Strasburg, Pa., b. Apr. 6, 1867; d. Aug. 13, 1867.

8649. Bertha, Strasburg, Pa., b. Apr., 12, 1869; d. May 5, 1869.

8650. William R., Lancaster, Pa., b. Dec. 21, 1871; m. June 5. 1900, Amanda B. Groff, b. June 19, 1879; dau. Isaac Groff and Amanda Bowman.

8651. Laura A., Strasburg, Pa., b. Nov. 30, 1873; d. Sept. 14, 1874.

Family of ANN BARR (4274) and HENRY SHENK.

8652. Aaron B., Willow Street, Pa., b. July 8, 1840; m. Jan. 8, 1863, Ann Snavely (3504).

8653. Son, Willow Street, Pa., b. May 26, 1842; d. May 27, 1842.

8654. Samuel, Willow Street, Pa., b. Aug. 22, 1843; m. Jan. 15, 1867, Fanny Burkholder, dau. Jacob Burkholder and ———.

8655. Henry, Willow Street, Pa., b. Jan. 21, 1846; d. Aug. 7, 1849.

8656. Josiah, Willow Street, Pa., b. Mar. 30, 1848.

8657. David, Willow Street, Pa., b. July 20, 1850.

8658. Alpheus, Willow Street, Pa., b. Jan. 26, 1853; d. Feb. 7, 1856.

Family of MARIA BARR (4275) and MICHAEL L. HUBER.

8659. Jacob B., Lancaster, Pa., b. Dec. 22, 1843; d. Sept. 12, 1846.

8660. Catherine, Lancaster, Pa., b. July 15, 1845; m. Oct. 24, 1865, Henry Hess (4136).

8661. Mary Ann, Lancaster, Pa., b. Nov. 2, 1847.

8662. Emma E., Lancaster, Pa., b. Oct. 20, 1849.

8663. Hiram B., Lancaster, Pa., b. July 2, 1852; d. Mar. 18, 1858.

8664. Lizzie, Lancaster, Pa., b. July 6, 1855.

8665. Martha, Lancaster, Pa., b. May 20, 1858.

Family of BENJAMIN BARR (4276) and BARBARA GROFF.

8666. Mary Ann, Lancaster, Pa., b. June 3, 1847.

8667. Susan, Lancaster, Pa., b. Oct. 27, 1848; d. Dec. 9, 1848.

8668. Samuel, Lancaster, Pa., b. Oct. 30, 1849.
8669. Emma E., Lancaster, Pa., b. Apr. 30, 1851.
8670. Catherine, Lancaster, Pa., b. Dec. 21, 1852.
8671. Frances, Lancaster, Pa., b. Nov. 21, 1854.
8672. Benjamin, Lancaster, Pa., b. Jan. 8, 1856.
8673. John, Lancaster, Pa., b. Feb. 19, 1857.
8674. Barbara, Lancaster, Pa., b. June 30, 1859.
8675. Anna, Lancaster, Pa., b. Jan. 6, 1862.
8676. Sarah, Lancaster, Pa., b. Apr. 6, 1864.

Family of ELIZABETH BARR (4277) and ABRAHAM KENDIG.

8677. Annie, Conestoga Centre, Pa., b. Nov. 20, 1852.
8678. Elizabeth, Conestoga Centre, Pa., b. Nov. 7, 1856; d. Mar. 31, 1857.

Family of MAGDALENE BARR (4278) and BENJAMIN BACHMAN.

8679. Anna, Willow Street, Pa., b. Apr. 19, 1852.
8680. Elizabeth, Willow Street, Pa., b. Aug. 12, 1853.
8681. Martha, Willow Street, Pa., b. May 22, 1855.
8682. Mary Ada, Willow Street, Pa., b. Sept. 2, 1857.
8683. Emma, Willow Street, Pa., b. Sept. 13, 1859; d. Dec. 29, 1861.
8684. Amos B., Willow Street, Pa., b. Feb 8, 1862.
8685. Benjamin, Willow Street, Pa., b. Dec. 16, 1864.

Family of FRANCES BARR (4279) and CHRISTIAN GREIDER.

8686. Frances B., Salunga, Pa., b. Feb. 18, 1851.

Family of SALOME MARIA BRACKBILL (4286) and SOLOMON LINVILLE.

8692. Elace Ann, Salisburyville, Pa., b. Dec. 26, 1864; d. July 29, 1865.
8693. Martha Salome, Salisburyville, Pa., b. Nov. 2, 1866.

Family of JOHN C. BRACKBILL (4300) and HETTIE FRANTZ.

8694. Milton Joseph, Bethany, Pa., b. Mar. 14, 1865.
8695. Benjamin Franklin, Bethany, Pa., b. Nov. 25, 1866.

Family of ELIZABETH BRACKBILL (4301) and JOHN M. HERSHEY.

8696. John B., Gordonville, Pa., b. Nov. 2, 1862; m. Anna M. Eby.
8697. Magdalene, Paradise, Pa., b. Dec. 26, 1864; m. Joseph M. Hershey, b. Apr. 29, 1839.

12112. Elizabeth, Gordonville, Pa., b. Nov. 8, 1867.

12113. Hettie, Gordonville, Pa., b. Feb. 13, 1870.

12114. Mary, Gordonville, Pa., b. July 22, 1881.

Family of DAVID WEAVER (4322) and SARAH ESBENSHADE.

8698. Adam, Lampeter, Pa., b. July 3, 1853.

8699. Martha Luetta, Lampeter, Pa., b. Oct. 27, 1854.

8700. Mary Emma, Lampeter, Pa., b. Oct. 3, 1856; d. Sept. 8, 1860.

8701. Samuel, Lampeter, Pa., b. June 18, 1858.

8702. Franklin, Lampeter, Pa., b. Apr. 9, 1860.

8703. Ezra, Lampeter, Pa., b. Mar. 17, 1862

8704. Lizzie, Lampeter, Pa., b. Oct. 17, 1865; d. June 10, 1866.

Family of MARTHA WEAVER (4323) and ALPHEUS CARPENTER.

8705. Katie Amelia, Lancaster, Pa., b. July 15, 1858.

8706. William S., Lancaster, Pa., b. May 29, 1863.

Family of DAVID HARNISH (4324) and MARY ANN LAUBER.

8707. Josiah, Conestoga Centre, Pa., b. Feb. 2, 1849; d. Dec. 25, 1864.

Family of ELIZABETH HARNISH (4325) and JOHN L. DENLINGER.

8708. Mary Ann, Bird-in-Hand, Pa., b. Nov. 11, 1848.

8709. Naomi, Bird-in-Hand, Pa., b. Dec. 31, 1850; d. Apr. 27, 1852.

8710. Elam, Bird-in-Hand, Pa., b. May 16, 1853.

8711. Franklin, Bird-in-Hand, Pa., b. June 6, 1860.

8712. Jacob, Bird-in-Hand, Pa., b. July 10, 1862.

8713. Freeman Lincoln, Bird-in-Hand, Pa., b. Mar. 23, 1865.

Family of SUSANNA HARNISH (4326) and BENJAMIN HARNISH.

8714. Jacob M., Millport, Pa., b. Sept. 10, 1852.

8715. Benjamin F., Millport, Pa., b. Jan. 15, 1855.

8716. Elam, Millport, Pa., b. Aug. 12, 1857.   .

8717. Emma Jane, Millport, Pa., b. June 27, 1860.

8718. Martha N., Millport, Pa., b. Sept. 29, 1862; d. Jan. 16, 1863.

8719. John Aaron, Millport, Pa., b. Apr. 7, 1864.

Family of CHRISTIAN WEAVER (4328) and REBECCA BRUBAKER.

8720. Ezra J., Lampeter, Pa., b. Dec. 20, 1850.

8721. Ann Elizabeth, Lampeter, Pa., b. Feb. 10, 1852.

8722. Alpheus, Lampeter, Pa., b. May 18, 1853; d. July 24, 1854.

8723. John S., Lampeter, Pa., b. June 10, 1855.

8724. Christian R., Lampeter, Pa., b. Mar. 11, 1857.

8725. Ira, Lampeter, Pa., b. Jan. 14, 1859.

8726. Alpheus, Lampeter, Pa., b. Sept. 11, 1861.

8727. Francis, Lampeter, Pa., b. July 25, 1863.

8728. Henry S., Lampeter, Pa., b. Oct. 8, 1865.

Family of AMOS WEAVER (4329) and MARY HARNISH.

8729. Emma Elizabeth, Lampeter, Pa., b. Dec. 23, 1851.

8730. Franklin M., Lampeter, Pa., b. Nov. 4, 1853.

8731. Susanna H., Lampeter, Pa., b. Nov. 24, 1855.

8732. Aldus H., Lampeter, Pa., b. Nov. 28, 1857.

8733. Amos H., Lampeter, Pa., b. May 31, 1860

8734. Phares J., Lampeter, Pa., b. Jan. 16, 1863.

8735. Martin H., Lampeter, Pa., b. Mar. 31, 1865.

Family of JOHN K. WEAVER (4332) and REBECCA M. FRANTZ.

8736. Son, Enterprise, Pa., b. June 22, 1872; d. June 22, 1872.

8737. John Frantz, Enterprise, Pa., b. Mar. 1, 1876.

Family of CYRUS J. WEAVER (4333) and MARY WITMER.

8738. Florence Witmer, Lenover, Pa., b. Aug. 14, 1859.

8739. Mary Elizabeth, Lenover, Pa., b. Aug. 6, 1862; d. Jan. 3, 1888.

8740. Susan Harriet, Paradise, Pa., b. Jan. 25, 1866; m. Dec. 25, 1888, Wid. Hiram M. Denliger, b. Jan. 5, 1859; son Michael B. Denlinger and Anna B. Miller.

8741. A—— Maud, Lenover, Pa., b. Dec. 16, ——.

Family of FRANK J. WEAVER (4334) and MARY BUCKWALTER.

8742. Harry B., Bird-in-Hand, Pa., b. Aug. 16, 1872; m. June 18, 1902, Minnie E. Hess, dau. David Hess and Barbara ——.

8743. Charles M., Lancaster, Pa., b. Aug. 23, 1874; d. ——, 1875.

8744. Benjamin Ellis, Lancaster, Pa., b. Oct. 8, 1876; m. Mar. 12, 1902, Ella M. Houser, dau. Christian Houser and Emma ——.

8745. Elizabeth Elma, Lancaster, Pa., b. Dec. 24, 1880.

Family of ISAAC WEAVER (4336) and CATHARINE BARR.

8746. Mary, Wheatland Mills, Pa., b. Apr. 12, 1852.
8747. Joseph, Wheatland Mills, Pa., b. Oct. 23, 1853.
8748. Aaron, Wheatland Mills, Pa., b. Mar. 11, 1856.
8749. Benjamin, Wheatland Mills, Pa., b. Feb. 7, 1858.
8750. Milton, Wheatland Mills, Pa., b. Feb. 28, 1860.
8751. Elizabeth, Wheatland Mills, b. Mar. 28, 1863; d. Mar. 27, 1897.

Family of ELIZABETH WEAVER (4341) and Rev. CHRISTIAN N. WITMER.

8752. John Alfred, Philadelphia, Pa., b. July 21, 1855; d. Dec. 30, 1884.
8753. Anna Eliza, Lancaster, Pa., b. Sept. 25, 1856; d. May 29, 1858.

Family of ISAAC LANTZ (4349) and BARBARA ESBENSHADE.

8754. Jacob, Atglen, Pa., b. Dec. 25, 1853; d. Feb. 14, 1855.
8755. Isaac Newton, Atglen, Pa., b. July 18, 1855.
8756. Mary Emma, Atglen, Pa., b. Feb. 16, 1857.
8757. Elizabeth Ann, Atglen, Pa., b. Sept. 16, 1858; d. Sept. 23, 1858.
8758. John Elmer, Strasburg, Pa., b. June 1, 1860.
8759. Benjamin Franklin, Strasburg, Pa., b. Feb. 13, 1862.
8760. Ellen, Strasburg, Pa., b. Sept. 16, 1865; d. Sept. 30, 1865.
8761. Hettie, Strasburg, Pa., b. Sept. 16, 1865; d. Oct. 7, 1865.

Family of ESTHER LANTZ (4350) and MARTIN MYERS.

8762. Jacob, Lancaster, Pa., b. Oct. 29, 1849; d. Aug. 26, 1850.
8763. Hettie Ann, Lancaster, Pa., b. May 21, 1851; d. June 30, 1851.
8764. Adam, Lancaster, Pa., b. Jan. 31, 1853; d. Feb. 18, 1853.
8765. Emma, Lancaster, Pa., b. May 20, 1854.
8766. Daniel, Lancaster, Pa., b. June 16, 1856; d. June 28, 1856.
8767. Martin Aldus, Lancaster, Pa., b. Nov. 8, 1857.

Family of JOHN LANTZ (4351) and MARGARET WILSON.

8768. Eddie E., Lampeter, Pa., b. Jan. 1, 1859.
8769. Letitia, Lampeter, Pa., b. Jan. 29, 1862.
8770. Jacob, Lampeter, Pa., b. Mar. 20, 1863.
8771. Margaret, Lancaster, Pa., b. June 29, 1864.

Family of ANN CATHERINE KENDIG (4357) and JOHN METZGAR.

8772. Adelaide Louisa, Reading, Pa., b. Apr. 21, 1844; m. Feb. 1, 1870, Hon. Daniel Ermentrout, b. Jan. 24, 1837; d. Sept. 19, 1899; son William Ermentrout and Julia Silvis.

8773. Samuel Kendig, Lancaster, Pa., b. Feb. 1846; d. May 26, 1847.

8774. Mary Kate, St. Paul, Minn., b. Jan. 4, 1848; m. Aug. 15, 1865, Edward R. Walker, son Edward L. Walker and Fanny Oats; m. Franklin H. Clark.

8775. Susan Elizabeth, Minneapolis, Minn., b. Nov. 23, 1849; m. Thaddeus Stevens Dickey.

8776. John Kendig, Lancaster, Pa., b. June 3, 1856; m. Edith Mullin.

Family of Rev. Wid. AMOS B. KENDIG (4362) and MARY BANCROFT.

8777. Carrie, Egypt, Mass., b. Apr. 7, 1858; m. May 4, 1886, George Frank Kellogg, b. July 25, 1857; d. Oct. 7, 1904; son Charles Kellogg and Arthusa Webster.

8778. Annie, Brookline, Mass., b. June 17, 1860; m. Apr. 7, 1885, Silas Pierce, b. Aug. 16, 1860; son Silas Pierce and Almira Hall.

Family of MATHIAS SHIRK WEAVER (4346) and ELIZA H. BURGERT.

8779. Henry Mathias, Mansfield, O., b. July 13, 1843; m. June 10, 1874, Helen S. Purdy, b. Sept. 28, 1850; dau. James Purdy and Mary Hodge.

8780. George E., Springfield, O., b. Oct. 6, 1845; d. Mar. 6, 1847.

Family of MARGARET AMELIA WILLERS (4374) and CHARLES BACHMAN.

8781. Carlton, W., Fayette, N. Y., b. Jan. 31, 1852; m. May 23, 1875, Frances J. Gardiner, b. Apr. 18, 1854; d. Mar. 31, 1879; m. Apr. 15, 1884, Maud Emery, b. Dec. 28, 1863; d. Aug. 27, 1891; m. Dec. 25, 1894, Wid. Mary E. Burdette, b. Mar. 21, 1845.

Family of EMMA WILLERS (4375) and JOHN L. REED.

8782. Cynthia Amelia, Coldwater, Mich., b. July 8, 1849; m. Nov. 21, 1900, William B. Downer.

22

8783. Frances Catherine, Fayette, N. Y., b. May 18, 1851; m. Oct. 15, 1879, Jans N. Lorentsen.

8784. Franklin, Fayette, N. Y., b. May 9, 1853; d. Oct. 29, 1853.

Family of FRANCES WILLERS (4376) and GEORGE PONTIUS.

8785. Edla Virginia, Seneca Falls, N. Y., b. Feb. 25, 1874, John B. Dennis, b. Feb. 22, 1842.

8786. George Willers, Seneca Falls, N. Y., b. Apr. 12, 1851; m. June 12, 1878, Lillian J. Schermerhorn, b. Apr. 8, 1857.

8787. Cora Frances, Albany, N. Y., b. Aug. 8, 1853.

8788. Carrie Amelia, Albany, N. Y., b. Apr. 20, 1859; m. Jan. 16, 1895, Charles M. Perkins.

Family of CALVIN WILLERS (4380) and ELIZABETH R. KENNEDY.

8789. Diedrich K., Seneca Falls, N. Y., b. Nov. 9, 1873; m. Jan. 19, 1898, Martha M. Lunn, b. Oct. ——, 1877.

8790. Calvina, Farmers Village, N. Y., b. Dec. 21, 1875; m. Jan. 23, 1904, Benjamin R. Howlett.

Family of JOHN E. RUSSELL (4393) and CAROLINE NELSON.

8791 John N., Leicester, Mass., b. Oct. 6, 1859, d. May 11, 1860.

Family of CHARLES W. RUSSELL (4394) and LUCY A. MERRIAM.

8792. Laura Merriam, Greenfield, Mass., b. Sept. 14, 1863; m. Sept. 21, 1886, Arthur Duncan Moir, b. Apr. 4, 1864; son James Moir and Mary McElroy.

8793. Anna Witmer, Richmond Hill, L. I., b. Nov. 30, 1864.

8794. John Burg, New York, N. Y., b. Feb. 19, 1867; m. Oct. 14, 1897, Evalyn T. Kane, dau. Cornelius V. S. Kane and Eveline T. Dayton.

8795. Lucy Edwards, Richmond Hill, L. I., b. Sept. 24, 1869; m. Oct. 28, 1891, Alrich H. Man, b. May 4, 1858; son Albon P. Man and Elizabeth Hubbolt.

8796. George Denison, Richmond Hill, L. I., b. Nov. 25, 1873.

Family of Wid. CHARLES W. RUSSEL (4394) and ESTELLA SOTOLONGO.

8797. Charles Witmer, Cedarhurst, L. I., b. July 26, 1889.

Family of FRANCIS BURG RUSSELL (4395) and ISABELLA CLAPP.

8798. Kate Denison, Greenfield, Mass., b. June 20, 1868.

Family of ANDREW GROFF HAMILTON (4396) and FANNIE D. HAMILTON.

8799. Witmer H., Rudyville, Ky., b. Sept. 28, 1867; d. Oct. 3, 1867.

Family Wid. ANDREW G. HAMILTON (4396) and JOSEPHINE HUTCHINSON.

8800. Andrew Groff, Rudyville, Ky., b. Sept. 30, 1895.

Family of WILLIAM M. HAMILTON (4397) and SALLIE A. JAMES.

8801. Witmer, Erie, Pa., b. Oct. 3, 1867; d. Oct. 8, 1867.
8802. Mabel M., Mechanicsburg, Pa., b. Jan. 24, 1870.
8803. Carrie, Erie, Pa., b. June 22, 1871; m. Bert Chennick.
8804. Harry B., Erie, Pa., b. May 23, 1879.

Family of WITMER G. HAMILTON (4398) and ANNIE REID.

8805. Elizabeth Mary, Saxton, Pa., b. Sept. 1, 1877; m. June 1, 1899, Willis Bole.
8806. Joseph Abraham, Saxton, Pa., b. Nov. 8, 1878.
8807. Frank Burg, Saxton, Pa., b. June 6, 1881.
8808. Maud Elizabeth, Saxton, Pa., b. June 5, 1884.
8809. Fannie May, Saxton, Pa., b. June 2, 1886.
8810. Caroline Graff, Saxton, Pa., b. June 6, 1891.

Family of MARY G. GROFF (4399) and GEORGE H. FULTON.

8811. H. —— Caroline, Milroy, Pa., d. June 2, 1886.

Family of JOHN GRAFF (4401) and MARY TAYLOR.

8812. Percy Witmer, Osborne, Kans.
8813. Caroline McMurtrie, Osborn, Kans., d. Oct. —, 1897.

Family of HARRIET S. GRAFF (4402) and JOHN D. STERRETT.

8814. Carrie Graff, Milroy, Pa., b. Dec. 13, 1876; d. July 30, 1877.
8815. Robert Witmer, Milroy, Pa., b. Aug. 30, 1878.
8816. Mary M., Milroy, Pa., b. Oct. 21, 1879; d. June 24, 1880.
8817. John D., Milroy, Pa., b. Feb. 12, 1882; d. Feb. 3, 1889.
8818. Helen Jane, Milroy, Pa., b. June 2, 1883.

8819. William S., Milroy, Pa., b. Jan. 3, 1885; d. Feb. 5, 1889.

8820. Andrew Graff, Milroy, Pa., b. May 14, 1886.

8821. C. ——— Hurlbut, Milroy, Pa., b. Oct. 1, 1889.

Family of ABRAHAM C. KAUFFMAN (4414) and HENRIETTA LINN.

8822. Caroline B., Niagara Falls, N. Y., b. Jan. 25, 1864; m. Nov. 29, 1883, John C. Kryder, b. Sept. 5, 1862; son Saul Kryder and Henrietta Cook.

Family of Wid. ABRAHAM C. KAUFFMAN (4414) and MARTHA ———.

8823. Dorothy, Saginaw, Mich., b. Jan. —, 1899.

Family of DANIEL E. WILSON (4422) and ABIGAIL BEVANS.

8824. Harry, Marion, Ind.

8825. Ada, Marion, Ind.

Family of Rev. ALBERT HARTMAN (4426) and JANE EVANS.

8826. Hannah C., Hutchinson, Kans., b. Dec. 26, 1852; m. ———, 1876, J. ——— William Lorrey, b. Nov. 4, 1874.

8827. George J., Newton, Kans., b. Oct. 21, 1854; m. Jan. 27, 1878, Hettie A. Stanford, b. Jan. 22, 1848; dau. George Stanford and Elizabeth Rippey.

8828. Issacher A. J., Great Bend, Kans., b. Apr. 4, 1860; d. Mar. 24, 1895.

Family of Rev. JACOB HARTMAN (4428) and ELLEN MILLER.

8829. Son, Chicago, Ill., b. Sept. 14, 1855; d. Sept. 14, 1855.

8830. Eva Frances, Chicago, Ill., b. Nov. 5, 1856; d. Jan. 7, 1883; m. Charles E. Slocum.

8831. George Miller, Chicago, Ill., b. Feb. 15, 1861; d. Feb. 2, 1888.

8832. Daughter, Chicago, Ill., b. Feb. 22, 1864; d. July 22, 1864.

8833. Alice May, Chicago, Ill., b. July 4, 1865; m. Robert C. Becker.

8834. Ida Belle, Chicago, Ill., b. Dec. 29, 1867; d. June 8, 1886.

8835. Raymond, Chicago, Ill., b. May 26, 1870.

Family of ELIZABETH HARTMAN (4429) and DAVID R. CARRIER.

8836. Albert, Chicago, Ill., b. Apr. 15, 1853; d. May, 1874.

Family of LEONARD L. HARTMAN (4430) and CLARA A. M. ARMSTRONG.

8837. Clara Armstrong, Salona, Pa., b. July 27, 1869; m. James E. Caldwell, b. June 12, 1866; son Watson Caldwell and Harriet McGuire.

8838. Sarah Evangeline, Shintown, Pa., b. Jan. 18, 1873; m. Jan. 18, 1894, John W. Kepler.

8839. Daisy Darling, Kansas City, Kans., b. Apr. 2, 1875.

Family of SARAH H. HARTMAN (4435) and CYRUS W. ROTE.

8840. Ellen, Salona, Pa., b. ———, 1861.

8841. George, Harrisburg, Pa., b. ———, 1864.

8842. William, Salona, Pa., b. ———, 1870.

8843. Max, Salona, Pa., b. ———, 1884.

Family of MARY H. HARTMAN (4445) and LUTHER S. KAUFFMAN.

8844. Edith, Philadelphia, Pa., b. Dec. 28, 1871.

8845. Mary Lenole, Philadelphia, Pa., b. Nov. 5, 1874.

8846. Anna Cecelia, Philadelphia, Pa., b. Feb. 28, 1878.

8847. Helen Ione, Philadelphia, Pa., b. Sept. 3, 1881.

8848. Jennie Lutueria, Philadelphia, Pa., b. Sept. 9, 1885.

Family of ELIZABETH C. HARTMAN (4465) and JOHN FREDERICK. GLOSSER.

8849. Carrie Hartman, Paoli, Pa., b. Oct. 12, 1866; m. Feb. 21, 1889, Otto F. Peeler, b. June 15, 1865; d. Mar. 15, 1896; son Charles Peeler and Pauline Bergner.

8850. Anna Mary, Paoli, Pa., b. July 22, 1870.

8851. John Francis, Mansfield, O., b. Jan. 31, 1873; m. Dec. 27, 1899, Anna Dubosc, b. July 7, 1876; dau. Francis P. Dubosc and Sarah J. Hunter.

8852. Herbert Hartman, Buffalo, N. Y., b. Aug. 29, 1876; m. Aug. 1900, Ruth M. Streeter, b. Aug. 27, 1869; dau. William F. Streeter and Mary E. Frear.

8853. Florence Elizabeth, Paoli, Pa., b. Sept. 8, 1879.

8854. Ruth, Paoli, Pa., b. Apr. 28, 1883; d. Apr. 28, 1883.

Family of CHARLES T. HARTMAN (4468) and LIZZIE RACHEL PENNOCK.

8855. Infant, Florence, Mass., b. ———, 1874; d.———, 1874.

8856. Guy Daniel, Florence, Mass., b. ———, 1875; d. ———, 1878.

Family of Wid. CHARLES T. HARTMAN (4468) and DIANNA E. STIEDLER.

8857. Daniel Hastings, Florence, Mass., b. July 5, 1898.

8858. Foster, Florence, Mass., b. Mar. 4, 1902; d. Mar. 4, 1903.

Family of ELIZABETH F. BAIRD (4470) and FRANCIS G. HARRIS.

8859. Benjamin Bruce, Clearfield, Pa., b. Nov. 27, 1880; d. Mar. 20, 1882.

8860. Helen Frances, Clearfield, Pa., b. July 3, 1883; d. Aug. 25, 1884.

8861. Frank Baird, Clearfield, Pa., b. Nov. 11, 1886; d. Jan. 4, 1887.

Family of Dr. EDMUND J. BAIRD (4471) and HARRIET ANNE BUCK.

8862. Donald Creighton, Lock Haven, Pa., b. Nov. 19, 1879.

8863. Florence Elizabeth, Lock Haven, Pa., b. Nov. 22, 1883.

8864. Helen Mary, Lock Haven, Pa., b. Sept. 6, 1891; d. Mar. 13, 1896.

Family of ALFRED TENNYSON BAIRD (4474) and RENA RITCHIE.

8865. Arthur Dunn, Island, Pa., b. July 6, 1888.

8866. Francis Hartman, Island, Pa., b. Apr. 10, 1890.

8867. Edmund Clarence, Island, Pa., b. Apr. 3, 1892.

8868. May Elizabeth, Island, Pa., b. Mar. 6, 1894.

8869. George Eben, Island, Pa., b. Apr. 23, 1896.

8870. Rena Ellen, Island, Pa., b. Apr. 1, 1899.

8871. Catherine, Island, Pa., b. Dec. 12, 1900.

8872. Teddy, Island, Pa., b. May 21, 1903.

Family of CATHERINE F. McCORMICK (4476) and CLARK R. GEARHART.

8873. Sarah E., Lock Haven, Pa., b. Dec. 1, 1871.

8874. Elenor F., Lock Haven, Pa., b. Jan. 20, 1873; m. May 20, 1900, Arthur B. Salmon, b. Jan. 23, 1872; son David Salmon and Ella ———.

8875. George M., Lock Haven, Pa., b. July 17, 1875.

8876. Frederick D., Lock Haven, Pa., b. Nov. 19, 1881.
8877. C. —— McC., Lock Haven, Pa.
8878. Annie E., Lock Haven, Pa.
8879. Harry A., Lock Haven, Pa.
8880. Frank C., Lock Haven, Pa.
8881. Infant, Lock Haven, Pa.

Family of ELIZA FRANCES BRESSLER (4480) and JOSEPH McKIBBEN.

8882. Effie, Salona, Pa., b. June 27, 1870; m. George T. Hyatt (5534).
8883. Harry Armstrong, Manilla, Philippines, b. Feb. 18, 1873.
8884. Clarence Edward, Juda, Wis., b. ——, 1880.

Family of GEORGE L. BRESSLER (4509) and MARY EVA ROSSER.

8885. Dorothea Frances, Williamsport, Pa., b. July 19, 1900.

Family of WILLIS HENRY BOOTHE (4558) and SARAH RICH.

8886. Afton, Salt Lake, Utah, b. Oct. 8, 1898.
8887. Lucille, Salt Lake, Utah, b. Nov. 1, 1900.
8888. June, Salt Lake, Utah, b. Mar. 19, 1903.

Family of MORRIS A. BOOTHE (4561) and JENNIE ALVORD.

8889. ——, Collinston, Utah, b. Oct. ——, 1901.

Family of MARTHA LOIUSA NEFF (4562) and ISAAC DUNYON.

8890. Isaac Dunyon, Draper, Utah, b. Jan. 27, 1883.

Family of MARY ELIZABETH NEFF (4566) and HUBERT L. HALL.

8891. Martha Ernestine, Morelos, Mex., b. Sept. 25, 1889.
8892. Huberta, Morelos, Mex., b. July 16, 1888.
8893. Mary Elizabeth Neff, Morelos, Mex., b. Nov. 5, 1891.

Family of VIRTUE LEANORA NEFF (4571) and HYRUM NEILSON.

8894. Leanora Myrtle, Holliday, Utah, b. July 27, 1895; d. Nov. 1, 1897.
8895. Estella L., Holliday, Utah, b. Nov. 18, 1897.
8896. Hyrum Leroy, Holliday, Utah, b. Jan. 18, 1900.

Family of **FRANCES E. WEAVER(4599) and JOHN HENRY WEAVER.**

8897. Elmer F., Ronks, Pa., b. May 26, 1875.

8898. Charles M., Ronks, Pa., b. Jan. 6, 1879.

8899. Cora W., Ronks, Pa., b. Feb. 6, 1880.

Family of **ANNIE M. WEAVER (4600) and DANIEL GIRVIN.**

8900. Meta, Fertility, Pa., b. Feb. 11, 1879.

8901. Anna, Fertility, Pa., b. Jan. 18, 1881.

8902. Emily, Fertility, Pa., b. Oct. 8, 1884.

Family of **MARY NAOMI MUSSER (4900) and ENOS H. WEAVER (4601).**

8903. Myrtle May, Lancaster, Pa., b. July 10, 1880.

8904. Anna Naomi, Lancaster, Pa., b. Feb. 22, 1883; m. Sept. 3, 1905,
Roy Rathvon Alexander, b. Sept. 17, 1878; son Merrit Lorenzo
Alexander and Louise Rathvon.

8905. Maud Herr, Lancaster, Pa., b. Jan. 19, 1886.

8906. Martin Musser, Lancaster, Pa., b. Feb. 28, 1889,

8907. Mary Catherine, Lancaster, Pa., b. June 17, 1891.

8908. Ruth Emma, Lancaster, Pa., b. Jan. 29, 1893.

Family of **Wid. ENOS H. WEAVER (4601) and ANNIE ESBENSHADE.**

8909. Catherine, Lancaster, Pa., b. Oct. 18, 1900.

Family of **IDA NAOMI WEAVER (4602) and Rev. JOHN KOHR.**

8910. Enos W., Lancaster, Pa., b. Sept. 13, 1879; m. Feb. 5, 1903,
Viola Gottshall, b. Mar. 4, 1860.

8911. Anna M., Lancaster, Pa., b. Nov. 27, 1890; d. June 4, 1891.

Family of **IDA ELIZABETH HERR (4604) and AMOS R. FRANTZ.**

8912. Grace Herr, Washington Grove, Md., b. Aug. 29, 1878; m. Oct.
3, 1902, Archibald Roberton Bullock, b. Feb. 25, 1855; son
James Bullock and Catharine Wineblock.

8913. Anna Herr, York, Pa., b. Apr. 8, 1882.

8914. Son, York, Pa., b. Aug 11, 1885; d. Aug. 11, 1885.

Family of **FRANCIS C. HERR (4605) and LILLIAN H. SEILER.**

8915. Parvin S., Ottoway, Kans., b. Feb. 5, 1884; d. Apr. 3, 1895.

Family of HOMER ANDREW HERR (4607) and LILLIAN A. HOWARD.

8916. Herbert Homer, Philadelphia, Pa., b. July 18, 1890.
8917. Catherine Anna, Philadelphia, Pa., b. Mar. 22, 1897; d. Mar. 22, 1897.

Family of WILLIS C. HERR (4608) and EMMA EUGENIA PHENEGAR.

8918. Robert Phenegar, Strasburg, Pa., b. Oct. 6, 1890.
8691. Richard Phenegar, Strasburg, Pa., b. Apr. —, 1901.

Family of ANNA AMANDA HERR (4610) and ABRAHAM LINCOLN MOYER.

8919. Miriam H., Lancaster, Pa., b. Apr. 15, 1886; d. Oct. 15, 1886.
8920. Lena Herr, Lancaster, Pa., b. July 24, 1887.
8921. Anna Elizabeth, Lancaster, Pa., b. July 12, 1890.
8922. Marguerite, Lancaster, Pa., b. Mar. 8, 1893.
8923. Amos, Lancaster, Pa., b. May 30, 1894.

Family of EDITH C. HERR (4612) and JOHN ELMER FRANTZ (6205).

8924. Raymond Herr, Waynesboro, Pa., b. July 7, 1896.

Family of IRA HARVEY HERR (4615) and H—— MARY BROWN.

8925. Anna B., Lancaster, Pa., b. Oct. 14, 1889.

Family of ELIZABETH C. HERR (4629) and Dr. FRANK G. HARTMAN.

8926. Richard David, Lancaster, Pa., b. June 29, 1900; d. Mar. 2, 1901.
8927. Sarah Catherine, Lancaster, Pa., b. Jan. 29, 1902.

Family of FRANCIS N. HERR (4632) and ANNIE L. COMP.

8928. Sarah E., Lancaster, Pa., b. Apr. 16, 1896.
8929. Catherine Elizabeth, Lancaster, Pa., b. Sept. 9, 1897.
8930. Robert Frantz, Lancaster, Pa., b. Nov. 14, 1899.

Family of ALLAN A. HERR (4872) and ANNIE LETITIA MUSSER (4638).

8931. Letitia Neff, Lancaster, Pa., b. Mar. 30, 1881.
8932. Benjamin Musser, Lancaster, Pa., b. July 15, 188·
8933. Mary Emma, Lancaster, Pa., b. June 30, 1885.
8934. Florence, Lancaster, Pa., b. Apr. 10, 1887; d. Apr. 3, 1888.

Family of Dr. **MILTON B. MUSSER** (4642) and **CATHARINE M. SWAYNE.**

8935. Harry Milton, Lancaster, Pa., b. Sept. 28, 1876.

8936. Lawrence Guenie, Lancaster, Pa., b. Mar. 4, 1880.

8937. Anna W., Lancaster, Pa., b. June 20, 1884.

Family of **WINONA S. BRENEMAN** (4646) and **ABRAHAM F. STICKLER.**

8938. Harry J., Willow Street, Pa., b. Nov. 24, 1891.

Family of **JOSEPH POTTS BRENEMAN** (4650 and **BARBARA HOLLINGER.**

8939. Harry H., Strasburg, Pa., b. Dec. 2, 1899.

Family of **ELLA LOUISA BRENEMAN** (4661) and **LEON VON OSSKO.**

8940. Franklin R., Lancaster, Pa., b. Sept. 6, 1885; d. Jan. 19, 1886.

Family of **CASSIUS K. BRENEMAN** (4663) and **SUSAN A. BURKS HENRY.**

8941. Henry Kendig, San Antonia, Tex., b. Apr. 23, 1874.

Family of **HERBERT L. BRENEMAN** (4664) and **EUNICE C. SWIFT.**

8942. Martha S., Cincinnati, O., b. Aug. 4, 1879.

8943. Helen, Cincinnati, O., b. Nov. 30, 1881.

Family of **CHARLES W. BRENEMAN** (4665) and **BESSIE CAMPBELL.**

8944. Henry C., Cincinnati, O., b. Oct. 11, 1880.

Family of **HARRY B. HERR** (4686) and **MINNIE L. GROFF.**

8945. Anna Elizabeth, Lancaster, Pa., b. Dec. 27, 1899.

12385. Willis Groff, Lancaster, Pa., b. Aug. 10, 1905.

12386. Harry Groff, Lancaster, Pa., b. June 21, 1907.

Family of **FANNY ROHRER** (4718) and **BENJAMIN LEMAN.**

8946. Elizabeth, Gordonville, Pa., m. Henry H. Hershey.

8947. Benjamin, Linestown, Pa., m. Barbara Groff.

8948. Henry, Intercourse, Pa., m. Fanny Hershey.

8949. Amos, Intercourse, Pa., b. Feb. 18, 1853; m. Dec. 5, 1885; Anna Hershey, b. Aug. 31, 1852; d. Sept. 16, 1877; dau. Peter L. Hershey and Anna Landis; m. Elizabeth Heller, b. Aug., 1858; d. June 28, 1893; dau. Isaac Heller and Wid. —— Stauffer.

8950. Catherine, Intercourse, Pa.

8951. Emma, Intercourse, Pa., d. Aug. —, 1896.

Family of CHRISTIAN ROHRER (4719) and MARIA BUCKWALTER.

8952. Martin B., Strasburg, Pa., m. Emma Groff.

8953. Henry S., Strasburg, Pa., m. Anna Haverstick.

8954. Ezra, Strasburg, Pa.

8955. Elizabeth, Strasburg, Pa., d. Mar. 6, 1907; m. John Bachman, d. ———, 1894.

8956. Emma, Strasburg, Pa.

8957. Mary, St. Louis, Mo.

8958. Ida, Soudersburg, Pa., m. Elias Mellinger.

8959. Elmira, Strasburg, Pa.

8960. Ellen, Strasburg, Pa.

Family of JACOB ROHRER (4720) and MARY ANN BARGE.

8961. Anna Maria, Strasburg, Pa.

8962. Witmer J., Strasburg,

8963. Frank, Strasburg, Pa.

8964. J. ——— Newton, Strasburg, Pa.

8965. Barbara, Strasburg, Pa., m. Martin Lefever.

Family of MARTIN ROHRER (4721) and CATHERINE MECK.

8966. Henry M., Lancaster, Pa.

8967. John F., Lancaster, Pa.

8968. ———, Lancaster, Pa.

8969. ———, Lancaster, Pa.

8970. ———, Lancaster, Pa.

8971. ———, Lancaster, Pa.

8972. ———, Lancaster, Pa.

Family of HENRY ROHRER (4722) and ———.

8973. Christian, Hagerstown, Md.

8974. John, Hagerstown, Md.

8975. Chase, Hagerstown, Md.

8976. Else, Hagerstown, Md.

8977. Laura, Hagerstown, Md.

8978. Francis, Hagerstown, Md.

Family of MARIA ROHRER (4723) and ABRAHAM KENDIG.

8979. ———, Clark Co., O.

8980. ———, Clark Co., O.

Family of CATHERINE ROHRER (4724) and ABRAHAM SNAVELY.

8981. Rohrer, New Danville, Pa.

8982. Stoner, New Danville, Pa.

Family of JOHN S. ROHRER (4725) and ANNA E. WAIDLEY.

8983. Hector L., New York, b. May 4, 1866; m. Oct. 5, 1902, ———.

8984. Estella J., Allegheny, Pa., b. Dec. 27, 1868; m. July 3, 1890, Lewis V. Steeb, b. Feb. 14, 1869; son John Steeb and Eliza J. Truxell.

8985. Jennie Elizabeth, Lancaster, Pa., b. Sept. 25, 1871; d. Mar. 18, 1878.

8986. Nellie Barr, Lancaster, Pa., b. June 25, 1875.

8987. Jennie Blanche, Lancaster, Pa., b. Feb. 25, 1879.

8988. Amy V., Lancaster, Pa., b. Nov. 19, 1882.

8989. Florida Gladys, Lancaster, Pa., b. June 14, 1886.

Family of ELIZABETH ROHRER (4726) and LEWIS HILT.

8990. Harry, New Danville, Pa.

8991. Elmer, New Danville, Pa.

8992. Sylvia, New Danville, Pa., m. Albert Hersh.

8993. Estella, New Danville, Pa.

Family of TOBIAS R. KREIDER (4732) and ANNA KREIDER.

8994. Mary, Lancaster, Pa., b. Sept. 19, 1851; m. Oct. 21, 1869, Henry D. Rohrer.

8995. Lizzie, Kinzers, Pa., b. Mar. 10, 1853; m. Benjamin Leaman; m. Rev. Isaac Eby.

8996. Martin, Lancaster, Pa., b. Jan. 17, 1855; m. Amanda Diffenbaugh.

8997. Annie, Lancaster, Pa., b. May 12, 1856; d. Aug. 15, 1879; m. Christian Stauffer.

8998. John, Fertility, Pa., b. Oct. 5, 1858; m. Lizzie Kreider.

8999. Hettie, Lancaster, Pa., b. Feb. 6, 1861; d. June 24, 1880,

Family of MARY ANN ROHRER (4758) and THOMAS CORWIN LEONARD.

9000. Estella Leonard, Tippecanoe City, O., b. Mar. 22, 1877; d. Feb. 9, 1881.

9001. Harry Rohrer, Tippecanoe City, O., b. Dec. 27, 1897; d. Apr. 27, 1887.

9002. Walter, Tippecanoe City, O., b. Dec. 27, 1881; d. Dec. 15, 1888.

9003. Elden, Tippecanoe City, O., b. Mar. 22, 1885.

9004. Lewis, Tippecanoe City, O., b. Nov. 6, 1888.

9005. Marjorie, Tippecanoe City, O., b. July 29, 1892.

Family of JOHN HENRY ROHRER (4759) and ROSE BENHAM.

9006. Charlie, Tippecanoe City, O., b. Apr. 18, 1887; d. Mar. 20, 1890.

9007. Harry Benham, Tippecanoe City, O., b. Sept. 9, 1890.

9008. Elizabeth, Tippecanoe City, O., b. May 12, 1892.

9009. Robert, Tippecanoe City, O., b. Nov. 16, 1896.

Family of IDA ROHRER (4762) and ABRAHAM R. GARVER.

9010. Ruth Elizabeth, Tippecanoe City, O., b. Oct. 18, 1888.

9011. Karl Rohrer, Tippecanoe City, O., b. Nov. 1, 1890.

9012. Jacob Christian, Tippecanoe City, O., b. Jan. 16, 1896.

Family of TOBIAS H. KREIDER (4763) and SUSAN SHIFFER.

9013. Anna M., Bird-in-Hand, Pa., b. Aug. 20, 1874.

9014. Amos S., Strasburg, Pa., b. Feb. 26, 1876.

9015. Tobias S., Bird-in-Hand, Pa., b. Aug. 30, 1877.

9016. John S., Bird-in-Hand, Pa., b. Mar. 6, 1878.

9017. Ida B., Bird-in-Hand, Pa., b. June 26, 1879.

9018. Barbara, Bird-in-Hand, Pa., b. Aug. 5, 1881.

9019. Mary, Bird-in-Hand, Pa., b. Sept. 25, 1889.

9020. Zuriel S., Bird-in-Hand, Pa., b. Apr. 10, 1891.

Family of JACOB W. HERR (4765) and ELLA TRAVIS.

9021. Infant, Refton, Pa.

9022. Susan, Refton, Pa.

9023. George, Refton, Pa.

9024. Emma, Refton, Pa.

Family of MAGGIE HERR (4766) and ELAM HESS.

9025. Enos, Smithville, Pa.

9026. Elenora, Smithville, Pa.

9027. Abbie Vezeta, Smithville, Pa.

9028. Alvin, Smithville, Pa.

9029. Ida Sue, Smithville, Pa.

Family of LURISTON B. HERR (4767) and ANNA F. CLARK.

9030. Eugene Le Fevre, Lancaster, Pa., b. Sept. 20, 1879; m. Jan. 17, 1906, Anna Griel Miller, b. Feb. 27, 1883; dau. Jacob G. Miller and Mary Ann Griel.

9031. Edwin Clark, Lancaster, Pa., b. Oct. 7, 1883.

9032. Anna Miriam, Lancaster, Pa., b. Sept. 20, 1885.

9033. Lauriston Benjamin, Lancaster, Pa., b. Dec. 27, 1891.

Family of OMER E. HERR (4776) and ANNIE ESTER.

9034. Harry Kunkle, Lancaster, Pa., b. Nov. 20, 1887.

9035. Oscar Ellsworth, Lancaster, Pa., b. June 8, 1890; d. July 9, 1890.

9036. Ella Nora, Lancaster, Pa., b. June 8, 1890.

9037. Mazie Anna, Lancaster, Pa., b. Jan. 23, 1892.

9038. Benjamin Franklin, Lancaster, Pa., b. Aug. 6, 1894.

9039. Ida May, Lancaster, Pa., b. Mar. 2, 1897.

Family of SAMUEL HEINEY (4789) and CHRISTIANA HESS.

9040. Sarah M., Lancaster, Pa., b. Aug. 8, 1860.

9041. Frances M., Strasburg, Pa., b. Oct. 5, 1862; m. Joseph Miller.

9042. Eve Ann, Manheim, Pa., b. Oct. 10, 1864; m. Michael Weidman.

9043. Maris E., Ganetson, S. D., b. Apr. 3, 1866; m. Edith Suekey.

9044. Emlen, Harrisburg, Pa., b. Oct. 13, 1867; m. Elizabeth Hackman.

9045. Lizzie, Lancaster, Pa., b. May 12, 1869; d. Mar. 27, 1897.

Family of MARTHA H. HEINEY (4793) and MICHAEL B. HAVERSTICK.

9046. Isaac, Columbia, Pa., b. Nov. 17, 1860; d. May 28, 1896; m. Emma Reese, dau. John Reese and ———.

9047. Ambrose, St. Maria, Can., b. Oct. 14, 1863; m. Mabel Leisure.

9048. Eve Ann, Binkley's Bridge, Pa., b. Mar. 26; 1866; m. Daniel Mowrer, son Hiram Mowrer and ——— Tweed.

9049. Frances, Columbia, Pa., b. Oct. 25, 1868; m. Michael Kneisley, son Michael Kneisley and Susan Good.

9050. Aaron, San Antonia, Tex., b. Aug. 25, 1871.

9051. Amos, Polo, Ill., b. Jan. 12, 1874.

9052. Michael, New Danville, Pa., b. July 19, 1876; m. Mar. 20, 1901, Lillie Peters, dau. Benjamin Peters and ———.

Family of FRANCES H. HEINEY (4794) and ABRAHAM FISHER.

9053. Elizabeth, Lancaster, Pa., b. Dec. 1, 1861; d. Mar. 6, 1893; m. John Martin, son Isaac Martin and Caroline Lutz.

9054. Harry, Lancaster, Pa., b. Oct. 20, 1863; m. Dec. 30, 1886, Emma Lehman, dau. John K. Lehman and Lucy E. Houghton.

9055. Abraham, Lancaster, Pa., b. Nov. 13, 1865; d. Sept. 2, 1893.

9056. Elmer, Nine Points, Pa., b. Sept. 5, 1867; m. Dec. 23, 1890, Emma Quay.

9057. Frances H., Lancaster, Pa., b. Apr. 17, 1870.

9058. Mary A., Lancaster, Pa., b. Oct. 26, 1872; m. Oct. 26, 1897, William P. Hoover, b. Nov. 24, 1870; son Cornelius L. Hoover and Gertrude Perrine.

9059. Isaac, Lancaster, Pa., b. Sept. 14, 1874; d. Aug. 21, 1887.

9060. Aldus H., Lancaster, Pa., b. Oct. 28, 1876; m. Oct. 22, 1897, Mary Protheroe, dau. William Protheroe and Jennie S. Powell.

9061. Emma May, Lancaster, Pa., b. May 26, 1879; m. Sept. 6, 1897, George Gunzenhauser, son ——— Gunzenhauser and Minnie Kerchner.

9062. Barbara H., Lancaster, Pa., b. Nov. 18, 1882.

9063. Clayton, Lancaster, Pa., b. Apr. 10, 1889.

Family of ELIZABETH GROFF (4798) and S—— W. RANCK.

9064. Howard, Bird-in-Hand, Pa.

9065. Emma, Bird-in-Hand, Pa.

9066. Bertha, Bird-in-Hand, Pa.

Family of Rev. JOHN H. GROFF (4799) and ELIZABETH KURTZ.

9067. Susan E., Johnstown, Pa., b. Aug. 20, 1867; d. July 30, 1891; m. Mar. 3, 1888, Henry Thomas.

9068. Mary A., Philadelphia, Pa., b. Dec. 12, 1870.

Family of MARY GROFF (4802) and FRANK JAQUITH.

9069. Mary, Des Moines, Ia.

9070. Esther, Des Moines, Ia.

Family of ABRAHAM L. GROFF (4803) and ELIZABETH WEIDMAN.

9071. Edna Esther, Harrisburg, Pa., b. Apr. 16, 1881.

9072. George Weidman, Harrisburg, Pa., b. Mar. 29, 1884.

9073. Elizabeth Howry, Harrisburg, Pa., b. Dec. 24, 1891.

Family of SUSAN A. GROFF (4805) and Dr. WILLIAM L. HUSTON.

9074. Herbert Marc, Ruthven, Ia., b. Nov. 8, 1869.

9075. Agnes Maud, Fort Madison, Ia., b. Nov. 4, 1872; m. Sept. 20, 1893, George Kraft, b. Sept. 15, 1863; son John Kraft and Elizabeth Bender.

9076. Frank B., Marengo, Ia., b. Dec. 18, 1875.

9077. Elizabeth Langfelt, Marengo, Ia., b. July 8, 1881.

Family of CHARLES H. GROFF (4806) and ELIZABETH A. DUNHAM.

9078. Frances May, Live Oak, Fla., b. Sept. 26, 1870; m. Dec. 2, 1891, Charles J. Fox, b. June 22, 1868; d. Oct. 19, 1900; son Col. Isaiah I. Fox and Eugenia Williams.

9079. Maud Louise, Newbury, Fla., b. Oct. 10, 1872; m. Jan. 2, 1896, Peyton S. Fortson, b. Aug. —, 1872; son Rev. John H. Fortson and Belle Anderson.

9080. Richard Barr, Live Oak, Fla., b. Nov. 8, 1875.

9081. Joseph Charles, Live Oak, Fla., b. Mar. 8, 1878.

9082. Harry C., Live Oak, Fla., b. Jan. 12, 1880.

9083. Otto Delancy, Live Oak, Fla., b. Sept. 3, 1882.

9084. Judith Anthea, Live Oak, Fla., b. July 1, 1886.

Family of MARY E. GROFF (4809) and ELIAS P. RIPLEY.

9085. May, Belmond, Ia., b. Aug. 20, 1870; d. Jan. 8, 1871.
9086. Lena Belle, Clarion, Ia., b Jan. 18, 1872; m. Dec. 21, 1899.
9087. Floyd Glenn, Clarion, Ia., b. Nov. 27, 1873; d. Dec. 9, 1893.
9088. Galen Groff, Minot, North Dakota, b. Mar. 27, 1876.
9089. D. ——— Florine, Belmond, Ia., b. Apr. 23, 1879.

Family of AMINE B. GROFF (4810) and CHARLES C. BROWN.

9090. Otto Groff, Viroqua, Wis., b. Nov. 15, 1869.
9091. Benjamin Clinton, Viroqua, Wis., b. Nov. 15, 1872.

Family of CHRISTIAN G. WIGGINS (4812) and ELIZABETH JOSETT POWER.

9092. Howard R., Norwood, O., b. Apr. 28, 1889.
9093. Edna Myra, Norwood, O., b. Jan. 3, 1892.
9094. Charles M., Norwood, O., b. June 24, 1896
9095. Delbert S., Norwood, O., b. Nov. 11, 1900.

Family of IDA GROFF (4819) and JAMES A. SEED.

9096. Caroline Alice, Lawrenceville, Ill., b. Mar. 31, 1888.
9097. James Raymond, Lawrenceville, Ill., b. Nov. 2, 1889.
9098. Oscar Vernon, Lawrenceville, Ill., b. Apr. 23, 1891.
9099. Sarah Olena, Lawrenceville, Ill., b. Sept. 12, 1893.
9100. May Inez, Lawrenceville, Ill., b. Jan. 9, 1895.
9101. Jennie Mabel, Lawrenceville, Ill., b. July 7, 1897; d. Mar. 10, 1903.
9102. Edna Barr, Lawrenceville, Ill., b. Mar. 27, 1900.
9103. Homer Willard, Lawrenceville, Ill., b. Jan. 4, 1902.

Family of LINNIE P. HALL (4833) and ALBERT H. ORVIS.

9104. Carrie, Yankton, South Dakota, b. June 14, 1886.
9105. Hattie, Yankton, South Dakota, b. Apr. 9, 1888.
9106. Maud, Yankton, South Dakota, b. Dec. 26, 1890; d. July 12, 1899.
9107. Herbert C., Yankton, South Dakota, b. Mar. 27, 1900.

Family of JEFFERSON S. BAKER (4835) and MARTHA SPEAR.

9108. Albert S., Philadelphia, Pa., b. Aug. 26, 1890; d. Aug. 29, 1890.

9109. James S., Philadelphia, Pa., b. July 2, 1893.

Family of OLIVER J. BAKER (4836) and LELIA LEGG.

9110. Letitia, Currensville, Pa.

9111. Orris, Currensville, Pa.

Family of ELMIRA C. BAKER (4837) and AMOS RATHFON.

9112. Gertrude M., Soudersburg, Pa., b. June 17, 1885.

9113. Charles J., Soudersburg, Pa., b. Mar. 16, 1887.

9114. Baker J., Soudersburg, Pa., b. Dec. 12, 1891.

Family of CHRISTIAN G. BAKER (4838) and ROSA MAKINLEY.

9115. Lizzie, Philadelphia, Pa.

9116. Grant, Philadelphia, Pa.

9117. Viola, Philadelphia, Pa.

9118. Makinley, Philadelphia, Pa.

Family of ELMIRA S. MUSSELMAN (4852) and JAMES W. LINVILLE.

9119. Henry M., Strasburg, Pa., b. Feb. 29, 1860; d. Aug. 25, 1865.

9120. Ellie, Strasburg, Pa., b. Nov. 13, 1861; d. Aug. 30, 1865.

9121. Sara L., Strasburg, Pa., b. July 11, 1864.

9122. Charles, Strasburg, Pa., b. Mar. 13, 1867; d. Jan. 8, 1891.

9123. Josephine L., Strasburg, Pa., b. Nov. 16, 1869; d. Mar. 22, 1874.

9124. Raymond C., Strasburg, Pa., b. Oct. 4, 1873.

Family of ANNA J. HERR (4871) and BENJAMIN F. MUSSELMAN (4853).

9125. Infant, Strasburg, Pa., b. Feb. 21, 1875; d. Feb. 21, 1875.

9126. Benjamin Ovid, Lancaster, Pa., b. Mar. 19, 1876; m. Jan. 12,
    1904, Louisa Flora Miller, b. Aug. 28, 1876; dau. Ernest A.
    Frederick Miller and Catharine F. Becker.

9127. Allen Herr, Lancaster, Pa., b. May 7, 1877; d. Aug. 27, 1877.

9128. Mary Emma, Lancaster, Pa., b. Jan. 26, 1880.

Family of JOSEPHINE E. MUSSELMAN (4855) and Dr. BRAINARD LEAMAN.

9129. Charles McClung, Leaman Place, Pa., b. Nov. 6, 1867; d. Feb.
    26, 1868.

9130. Harry Musselman, Leaman Place, Pa., b. July 8, 1871 ; d. Aug. 21, 1871.

9131. Dr. Walter John, Leaman Place, Pa., b. Dec. 26, 1874.

Family of DAVID G. E. MUSSELMAN (4858) and KATIE R. ROBINSON.

9132. D. ———— Paul, Philadelphia, Pa., b. Sept. 8, 1886.

Family of EDWIN C. MUSSELMAN (4859) and EMILY D. BISHOP.

9133. Henry Bishop, Danville, Va., b. Feb. 20, 1876 ; m. June 26, 1902, Carrie Watkins.

9134. Mary Louise, Strasburg, Pa., b. Aug. 23, 1880.

9135. Dorinda Bishop, Strasburg, Pa., b. May 15, 1885.

Family of ANNA JULIA ESHLEMAN (4860) and JOHN H. McMURDY.

9136. John Hobart, Denver, Col., b. Mar. 8, 1873 ; m. Apr. 28, 1900, Wid. Mary F. Diller, b. Jan. 30, 1873 ; dau. Junius B. Kauffman and Katherine Bonebaugh.

Family of ELIZA R. ESHLEMAN (4862) and FRANK M. TAYLOR.

9137. David Paul, Denver, Col., b. Apr. 14, 1881.

9138. Henry A., Denver, Col.

Family of HARRIET B. ESHLEMAN (4863) and PAUL F. MOHR.

9139. Rose Maxwell, Cripple Creek, Col., b. Feb. 1, 1885 ; d. Aug. 8, 1897.

Family of THEODORE W. HERR (4865) and ANNIE MUSSER.

9140. Edwin Musser, Edgewood Park, Pa., b. May 3, 1860; m. Aug. 27, 1890, Katherine Forsyth, b. Mar. 18, 1863; d. Aug. 12, 1893; dau. William T. Forsyth and Rachel A. Wheatley; m. June 14, 1900, Mary Forsyth, b. Mar. 10, 1861; dau. William T. Forsyth and Rachel A. Wheatley.

9141. Mary Emma, Denver, Col., b. June 20, 1861 ; d. Jan. 5, 1885.

9142. Willis Benjamin, Seattle, Wash., b. Aug. 24, 1863; m. July 6, 1904, Jean Holmes, b. Mar. 28, 1874; dau. Adam Holmes and Ann Keyes.

9143. Anna Elizabeth, Seattle, Wash., b. Mar. 9, 1866; m. Aug. 10, 1886, James W. Clise, b. Dec. 16, 1856; son Samuel F. Clise and Nancy R. McKenzie.

9144. Arthur Theodore, Denver, Col., b. Sept. 20, 1871; m. Jan. 1, 1900, Florella E. James, b. Oct. 3, 1880; dau. Dr. Henry James and Florella Schmidt.

Family of Wid. THEODORE W. HERR (4865) and Wid. EMMA M. NEFF.

9145. Ernest Claude, Denver, Col., b. Nov. 13, 1873; d. June 11, 1893.

9146. Herbert Thacker, Denver, Col., b. Mar. 19, 1876; m. Feb. 10, 1896, Irene F. Viancourt, b. Aug. 3, 1876; dau. Moses F. Viancourt and Frances A. Grahame.

9147. Martha Juliet, Denver, Col., b. June 19, 1880; d. June 19, 1880.

Family of LORENZO D. HERR (4866) and HANNAH E. WEAVER.

9148. Irene Emma, Denver, Col., b. July 31, 1872; m. Sept. 18, 1895, George A. Blue, b. Sept. 7, 1869; son Calvin Blue and Phoebe A. Vicc.

9149. Cora Juliet, Denver, Col., b. Jan. 30, 1877; m. Oct. 20, 1897, Harvey A. McHenry, b. Jan. 6, 1873; son David T. McHenry and Valeria L. Bowman.

Family of HIERO BENJAMIN HERR (4869) and MATTIE A. SHENK (9729).

9150. Percy Benjamin, Chicago, Ill., b. Jan. 20, 1870; d. Jan. 10, 1901; m. Nov. 17, 1900, Caroline O. Hoskins, dau. Oliver Hoskins and ———.

9151. Ruby Emma, Lancaster, Pa., b. June 4, 1872; m. Oct. 23, 1895, William S. Russell, b. May 2, 1862; son Richard Russell and Matilda Stoffell.

9152. Martha Adele, Denver, Col., b. May 7, 1875; d. June 9, 1875.

Family of FRANCIS L. HERR (4870) and SARAH A. MYERS.

9153. Mabel Elmira, Oakmont, Pa., b. July 17, 1876; m. Oct. 1, 1903, Dr. Guy Levis Alexander, b. Oct. 13, 1871; son Vincent K. Alexander and Harriet Levis.

9154. Alice Amelia, Lancaster, Pa., b. Oct. 24, 1878.

Family of Dr. JOHN HERR FRANTZ (4877) and LOUISA SEWALL.

9155. John Pinkney, Lutherville, Md., b. Aug. 5, 1869; m. June 1, 1893, Louisa Denmead, b. Dec. 14, 1862; dau. Benjamin F. Denmead and Margaret E. Hutchins.

9156. Harry, Fort D. A. Russell, Wyo., b. ———, 1870; d. ———, 1870.

9157. Annie Sewall, Hampton, Va., b. Nov. 6, 1872; d. Mar. 10, 1900; m. Dec. 24, 1890, John C. Boyenton, b. Dec. 26, 1868; son John W. Boyenton and Elizabeth M. Champlin.

Family of JACOB MILTON FRANTZ (4879) and LIDA GILLETTE.

9158. Jay Wilde, San Francisco, Cal., b. Jan. 3, 1892.

1469. Ada Gillette, San Francisco, Cal.

Family of HENRY BENJAMIN FRANTZ (4880) and NELLIE L. STONE.

9159. Amy Adell, Milwaukee, Wis., b. Sept. —, 1878; d. Dec. —, 1881.

9160. Harry Stone, West Allis, Wis., b. June 18, 1881.

9161. Bessie Adell, Milwaukee, Wis., b. Oct. 22, 1883; m. Oct. 21, 1903, Harold Mead Stratton, b. Nov. 12, 1878; son Prescot B. Stratton and Martha Elizabeth Lull.

Family of MARY EMMA FRANTZ (4882) and LEVI MICHAEL HAVERSTICK.

9162. Ruth, Rock Island, Ill., b. Mar. 14, 1871.

9163. Ralph, Rock Island, Ill., b. Aug. 24, 1872.

9164. Frantz Maurice, New York, N. Y., b. Mar. 21, 1875; m. Oct. 15, 1902, Eleanor S. Harris, b. May 25, 1876; dau. Moses Harris and Abba Boutelle.

9165. Miriam Anna, Rock Island, Ill., b. Mar. 2, 1879.

Family of ANNIE ELIZ. MUSSER (4887) and EZRA F. BOWMAN (8233).

9166. Martha Maria Musser, Lancaster, Pa., b. July 19, 1876.

9167. John Jacob, Lancaster, Pa., b. Aug. 10, 1878.

9168. Charles Ezra, Lancaster, Pa., b. Dec. 11, 1879.

9169. Luetta Musser, Lancaster, Pa., b. July 27, 1881.

9170. Christian, Lancaster, Pa., b. Mar. 17, 1885.

9171. Henry, Lancaster, Pa., b. Mar. 17, 1885; d. Feb. 5, 1902.

Family of Dr. FRANCIS M. MUSSER (4888) and RUTH A. COOPER.

9172. Clara May, Lancaster, Pa., b. Mar. 9, 1876; m. Aug. 13, 1902, Elmer J. Eshleman (9235).

9173. Mabel Cooper, Lancaster, Pa., b. July 7, 1877.

9174. Frank Arthur, Lancaster, Pa., b. July 15, 1882.

9175. Mary Luetta, Lancaster, Pa., b. Mar. 14, 1886.

Family of WILLIS BENJ. MUSSER (4890) and KATHERINE W. KAUFFMAN.

9176. Mira Lloyd, Ardmore, Pa., b. Nov. 14, 1885.

9177. Frederic Omar, Ardmore, Pa., b. Oct. 31, 1887.

9178. Willis Benjamin, Ardmore, Pa., b. Feb. 3, 1889.

9179. Julia Dorsey, Ardmore, Pa., b. Aug. 11, 1891.

Family of HENRY RUFUS HERR (4897) and MARY V. DILLER.

9180. John Forrer, Strasburg, Pa., b. June 4, 1889.

9181. George Diller, Strasburg, Pa., b. Jan. 22, 1891.

Family of JOHN ELLSWORTH HERR (4898) and EDITH M. EBERMAN (9887).

9182. Helen Alberta, Strasburg, Pa., b. June 2, 1887.

9183. Brenda Angelica, Strasburg, Pa., b. Dec. 24, 1888.

9184. Elsie Martha, Strasburg, Pa., b. Feb. 4, 1890.

9185. Eberman, Strasburg, Pa., b. July 7, 1897; d. July 9, 1897.

9186. Edward Ellsworth, Strasburg, Pa., b. Sept. 8, 1899; d. Nov. 3, 1901.

Family of Dr. JOHN H. MUSSER (4899) and AGNES G. HARPER.

9187. Mary H., Philadelphia, Pa., b. Aug. 5, 1881; m. Nov. 6, 1902, Dr. Richard M. Pearce, b. Mar. 3, 1874; son Richard M. Pearce and Sarah Smith.

9188. John Herr, Philadelphia, Pa., b. June 9, 1883.

9189. Naomi, Philadelphia, Pa., b. Oct. 14, 1885.

9190. Agnes G., Philadelphia, Pa., b. Aug. 5, 1887.

9191. Dorothy, Philadelphia, Pa., b. June 20, 1889; d. Apr. 16, 1891.

Family of SAMUEL ESHLEMAN (4909) and ANNIE B. ESHLEMAN.

9192. Enos, Martinsville, Pa.

9193. Ira, Martinsville, Pa., m. Matilda Stively.

9194. Edith Annie, Strasburg, Pa., b. Apr. 17, 1876; d. Feb. 15, 1883.

9195. Emma, Martinsville, Pa.

9196. Ellis, Martinsville, Pa., b. Mar. 8, 1879; d. Jan. 2, 1883.

9197. John, New Providence, Pa.

9198. Susan, Martinsville, Pa.

9199. Anna, Martinsville, Pa.

9200. Emma, Martinsville, Pa., m. John Kreider, son Christian K. Kreider and ———.

9201. Emlin, Martinsville, Pa.

9565. Infant, Martinsville, Pa.

Family of MARTHA ANN ESHLEMAN (4910) and PETER WENGER.

9202. Elmira M., Gordonville, Pa., b. Apr. 17, 1867; m. July 20, 1882, Jacob Younginger, b. Aug. 21, 1856; son John Younginger and Dorothy Gebhart.

9203. Emma Salome, Lancaster, Pa., m. Levi Mellinger.

9204. Franklin E., Paradise, Pa., b. July 21, 1870; m. Nov. 11, 1891, Luella May Glouner, b. July 15, 1872; dau. Elam Glouner and Delilah Sides.

Family of CHRISTIAN ESHLEMAN (4911) and MARY CASSEL.

9205. Annie G., Martinsville, Pa., b. Aug. 12, 1857; d. Mar. 9, 1881.

9206. Franklin, Martinsville, Pa,, m. Grace Hall.

9207. Lillie, Lampeter, Pa., m. Benjamin Byer.

9208. Samuel, Martinsville, Pa., m. Emma Harnish.

9209. Christian, Shippensburg, Pa., m. Annie Albright.

9210. Mary, Shippensburg, Pa., b. Sept. 9, 1864; d. Apr. 1, 1889; m. Dr. Jacob Miller Shartle, b. Nov. 19, 1856; son John Shartle and Maria Miller.

9211. Eletta, Shippensburg, Pa.

9212. Barbara E., Shippensburg, Pa., b. Feb. 21, 1872; d. Jan. 24, 1890.

9213. Elam, Lampeter, Pa., m. Mary Shaw.

9214. John, Lampeter, Pa.

9215. Willis, Lampeter, Pa., m. Sadie Bear.

9216. Infant, Lampeter, Pa.

Family of ABRAHAM ESHLEMAN (4912) and MARY MOWRER.

9217. Mowrer, Martinsville, Pa.

9218. Barbara, Martinsville, Pa., m. John Lefever.

9219. Serenas, Camargo, Pa., m. Ella Orr.

9220. Emma, Martinsville, Pa., m. Milo Weaver.

9221. Jacob, Martinsville, Pa., m. Cora Diffenbaugh.

9222. Ezra, Sterling, Ill., m. Carrie Clinton.

Family of MARY ESHLEMAN (4913) and JOHN H. KREIDER.

9223. Elam, Paradise, Pa., m. Hettie Miller.

9224. Infant, Lancaster, Pa.

9225. Ida, Lancaster, Pa., m. Martin Bowman.

Family of JACOB ESHLEMAN (4914) and ANNA HARNISH.

9226. Elias H., Iva, Pa., b. May 5, 1862; m. Oct. 14, 1884, Susan E. Brubaker.

9227. Mary F., Shippensburg, Pa., b. July 17, 1863; m. Jan. 9, 1889, Grabill B. Stoner.

9228. Miller J., Strasburg, Pa., b. July 31, 1865; d. Aug. 31, 1866.

9229. John W., Lancaster, Pa., b. Nov. 13, 1868; d. Jan. 23, 1869.

9230. Harry M., York, Pa., b. Aug. 13, 1870; m. Dec. 30, 1890.

9231. Elizabeth Ann, Leola, Pa., b. July 24, 1873; m. Apr. 16, 1891, Franklin B. Metzgar.

Family of BARBARA ANN ESHLEMAN (4916) and JOHN W. ESHLEMAN.

9232. John William, Passaic, N. J., b. Dec. 18, 1869; m. Mar. 17, 1892, Mary Hess (7430).

9233. Franklin Edgar, Lancaster, Pa., b. Sept. 17, 1871; m. Nov. 22, 1895, Elizabeth Bare, dau. Franklin Bare and Adda Kendig.

9234. Bertha Catherine, Lampeter, Pa., b. Dec. 12, 1873; m. Aug. 31, 1898, Will M. Musser (7653).

9235. Elmer Jacob, Lancaster, Pa., b. Dec. 6, 1876; m. Aug. 13, 1902, Clara M. Musser (9172).

9236. Susan Blanche, Lancaster, Pa., b. Mar. 4, 1879.

9237. Herbert Roy, Lancaster, Pa., b. Jan. 19, 1881.

9238. Howard Jay, Lancaster, Pa., b. Dec. 1, 1883.

9239. Miller Rheem, Lancaster, Pa., b. Jan. 4, 1888; d. Feb. 28, 1890.

9240. Violet Ruth, Lancaster, Pa., b. Jan. 27, 1893.

Family of GEORGE W. MILLER (4942) and SALLIE McLAUGHLIN.

9241. Earl, Lancaster, Pa., b. Dec. 31, 1894.

Family of JOHN B. MAYER (4950) and ELIZABETH SWARTLEY.

9242. Frances C., Lampeter, Pa., b. Dec. 22, 1867; m. John K. Fritz.

9243. Ophelia M., Landisville, Pa., b. Aug. 21, 1870; d. June 5, 1874.

9244. Ira S., Philadelphia, Pa., b. Mar. 4, 1873.

9245. Elizabeth S., Landisville, Pa., b. Apr. 30, 1877; d. May 6, 1877.

Family of Wid. JOHN B. MAYER (4950) and CATHERINE GROSS.

9246. Anna G., Landisville, Pa., b. June 17, 1881; d. Feb. 1, 1903.

9247. Hattie E., Landisville, Pa., b. Sept. 30, 1883.

9248. Ida G., Landisville, Pa., b. June 7, 1886.

Family of CHRISTIAN N. MAYER (4951) and ELIZABETH HARTMAN.

9249. Hattie Emma, Wilton, Ia., b. Aug. 31, 1867; m. Sept. 9, 1886, Frank Hood, b. Apr. 28, 1858; son Robert Hood and Sarah Fulton

9250. Fannie Viola, Creston, Ia., b. Oct. 11, 1870; d. Oct. 22, 1870.

9251. Mary Etta, Creston, Ia., b. Oct. 24, 1871; d. Oct. 8, 1892; m. Dec. 2, 1891, Carlton Shields, son James Shields and Cornelia Williamson.

9252. John Henry, Creston, Ia., b. June 5, 1875.

9253. Anna Elizabeth, Des Moines, Ia., b. Dec. 14, 1876; m. Aug. 10, 1898, Adriel H. Maxwell, son Marion L. Maxwell and Ann

9254. Melvin, Creston, Ia., b. Jan. 31, 1880; d. Feb. 11, 1880.

9255. Stella, Creston, Ia., b. Jan. 31, 1880; d. Feb. 14, 1880.

9256. Elmer Clifton, Creston, Ia., b. July 4, 1882.

9257. Roy Barr, Creston, Ia., b. July 10, 1885.

9258. Ray Hartman, Creston, Ia., b. July 10, 1885.

Family of HENRY C. LONGENECKER (4954) and ELIZA PALMER MARTIN.

9259. Edith Martin, Towson, Md., b. Dec. 25, 1875; m. July 14, 1900, William S. Heck.

9260. Eliza Delano, Towson, Md., b. Nov. 9, 1878.

Family of JACOB H. STAUFFER (5006) and ANNA BALDWIN.

9261. ——, Leola, Pa.
9262. ——, Leola, Pa.
9263. ———, Leola, Pa.

Family of JOHN H. STAUFFER (5008) and CATHERINE BARR.

9264. Ann E., Port Hunter, Pa., b. Nov. 14, 1868; m. May —, 1895, Rev. T. Norton Hyde.
9265. Jacob, Millersville, Pa., b. Sept. 7, 1870; d. Nov. 2, 1870.
9266. John Barr, New Castle, Pa., b. Nov. 6, 1871.
9267. Owen H., Philadelphia, Pa., b. Nov. 4, 1874; m. Edith Phipps.
9268. William Hayden, Fort Yates, North Dakota, b. July 9, 1879.
9269. Charles Auburn, Millersville, Pa., b. Feb. 24, 1881.
9270. Infant, Millersville, Pa.

Family of JOHN AUGUSTUS HARTMAN (5009) and MARY A. NOGGLE.

9271. Ann Elizabeth, New Madison, O.
9272. Kate, New Madison, O., b. Feb. 12, 1874; m. U—— S. Loofbourrow.
9273. Edith, New Paris, O., b. May 27, 1875; m. Homer B. Rose.
9274. Alice, Eaton, O., b. Apr. 29, 1877; m. R—— E. Mikesell.
9275. Ida, New Madison, O., b. Mar. 28, 1880.
9276. Cora, New Madison, O., b. Aug. 24, 1882.
9277. Harry A., New Madison, O., b. Mar. 1, 1886.

Family of MARIBEL HARTMAN (5019) and FREDERICK W. SHUMACHER.

9278. Maribel, Lancaster, Pa., b. July 8, 1896.

Family of MARY TABITHA ESHLEMAN (5022) and Hon. ISAAC E. HIESTER.

9279. Son, Philadelphia, Pa.

Family of BENJAMIN FRANKLIN ESHLEMAN (5023) and MARY MERCUR.

9280. Mary Mercur, Lancaster, Pa., b. Sept. 14, 1877; m. Oct. 23, 1901, David Reno Locher, b. Jan. 7, 1874; son Charles H. Locher and Lila Reno.
9281. Frank Mercur, Lancaster, Pa., b. Feb. 12, 1880.

9282. Ulysses Mercur, Lancaster, Pa., b. Mar. 9, 1883.

9283. Benjamin Gyger, Lancaster, Pa., b. Oct. 10, 1885.

9284. Rodney, Lancaster, Pa., b. May 30, 1887.

9285. Amy, Lancaster, Pa., b. Aug. 24, 1889.

Family of VIRGINIA A. KENDIG (5050) and JOHN W. WILSON.

9286. Iva Ellen, Washington, Ill., b. Dec. 2, 1866; d. Oct. 15, 1875.

9287. Naomi Jane, Washington, Ill., b. Jan. 19, 1871; d. Dec. 29, 1897.

9288. Marion Porter, Washington, Ill., b. Sept. 4, 1875; d. Aug. 9, 1896.

9289. Gertrude Givens, Washington, Ill., b. Feb. 2, 1880.

Family of ELIZA JANE KENDIG (5051) and JASPER NEWTON McMURTREY.

9290. Jessie Florence, Salem, Mo., b. Oct. 17, 1870; d. July 24, 1872.

9291. David Walter, Salem, Mo., b. Apr. 8, 1872; d. Oct. 23, 1872.

9292. Tessie Rebecca, Salem, Mo., b. Nov. 16, 1873.

9293. Clifford Jasper, Salem, Mo., b. Dec. 3, 1875.

9294. Averdeene, Salem, Mo., b. Jan. 28, 1880.

9295. Allen Percy, Salem, Mo., b. Nov. 26, 1881; d. Apr. 4, 1883.

Family of MARION ALEXANDER KINDIG (5054) and JENNIE E. NESMITH.

9296. Vera Irene, Winfield, Kans., b. Feb. 14, 1886.

9297. Arthur David, Winfield, Kans., b. July 16, 1889.

9298. Daughter, Winfield, Kans., b. Aug. 12, 1898; d. Aug. 13, 1898.

Family of ANNA ELIZABETH ERB (5079) and JOHN RATHVON.

9299. Anna M., Battle Creek, Mich., b. Jan. 9, 1866; d. Mar. 19, 1880.

9300. John F., Battle Creek, Mich., b. Mar. 16, 1867; d. Apr. 15, 1890.

9301. Catherine J., Mt. Rosa, Ont., b. Nov. 16, 1868; m. Feb. 10, 1896, Emanuel Reeb, b. Apr. 22, 1862; son Andrew Reeb and Margaret Perlett.

9302. Levi, Conestoga Center, Pa., b. Feb. 7, 1872; d. July 22, 1872.

9303. Clara, Battle Creek, Mich., b. May 4, 1873; d. June 23, 1897.

9304. Ezra, Humberston, Ont., b. July 10, 1875.

9305. Horace, Humbertson, Ont., b. Aug. 24, 1877; m. Dec. 3, 1903, Anna Kramer, b. May 29, 1879; dau. David Kramer and Margaret ———.

9306. Elmer, Battle Creek, Mich., b. Aug. 24, 1877; d. Sept. 13, 1877.

9307. Ida, Battle Creek, Mich., b. July 4, 1879; d. May 3, 1880.

9308. Benjamin, Port Colborne, Ont., b. July 11, 1880.

9309. Clayton, Clifton, Ont., b. Aug. 18, 1881.

9310. Alice, Port Colborne, Ont., b. Dec. 31, 1883.

9311. Lillie, Port Colborne, Ont., b. Mar. 22, 1885.

Family of JOHN M. SPENCE (5104) and SUSAN DUNKLEBERGER.

9312. James T., Carlisle, Pa.

9313. ———, Carlisle, Pa.

9314. ———, Carlisle, Pa.

9315. ———, Carlisle, Pa.

Family of EMMA SPENCE (5106) and JOHN B. SHEAFFER.

9316. Rev. William James, Reedville, Pa.

9317. Monroe W., Reading, Pa.

9318. Rebecca J., Petersburg, Pa., m. Austin Minnich.

9319. ———.

Family of Wid. EMMA SPENCE SHEAFFER (5106) and JAMES T. OWEN.

9320. Abraham Spence, Duncannon, Pa.

Family of DAVID W. SPENCE (5107) and ———.

9321. Blanche, Rawlinsville, Pa., m. ——— Clugston.

9322. Harry, Rawlinsville, Pa.

9323. Mabel, Rawlinsville, Pa.

9324. Elsie, Rawlinsville, Pa.

9325. Albert, Rawlinsville, Pa.

Family of MARTHA SPENCE (5109) and ———.

9326. Laura, Duncannon, Pa., b. Aug. 9, 1871; m. Feb. 12, 1890, Thomas J. Hunter, b. July 12, 1871; son Amos Hunter and Barbara Ann Pines.

Family of ANDREW M. HERR (5131) and ELIZA ESHLEMAN.

9327. Clara, Clarence Center, N. Y., b. May 20, 1873; m. Dec. 22, 1892, Henry S. Longenecker, b. Nov. 26 1869; son John E. Longenecker and Amelia Blucher.

9328. Alice, Clarence Center, N. Y., b. July 28, 1875.

9329. Harriet, Clarence Center, N. Y., b. Mar. 15, 1877.

9330. Cora, Clarence Center, N. Y., b. Dec. 15, 1879.

9331. Catherine, Clarence Center, N. Y., b. June 13, 1881.

9332. Mary, Clarence Center, N. Y., b. June 13, 1881.

9333. Ida, Clarence Center, N Y., b. Oct. 14, 1883.

Family of ESTHER HERR (5132) and FREDERICK BRELOS.

9334. Harriet A., Williamsville, N. Y., b. Jan. 25, 1882; d. Apr. 7, 1888.

9335. Henry, Williamsville, N. Y., b. Oct. 25, 1884.

9336. Mary S., Williamsville, N. Y., b. Dec. 10, 1887; d. Apr. 20, 1888.

9337. Alice, Williamsville, N. Y., b. Aug. 6, 1891.

9338. Ida E., Williamsville, N. Y., b. Mar. 3, 1895.

Family of Dr. CHRISTIAN A. HERR (5137) and EMMA J. KISSINGER.

9339. Sarah Melvina, Osborne, O., b. Dec. 4, 1882.

9340. Benjamin F., Osborne, O., b. Mar. 30, 1884.

9341. Anna E., Osborne, O., b. Nov. 22, 1887.

Family of Dr. ABRAHAM GANTZ HERR (5138) and SARAH A. ELEY.

9342. Percival E., Detroit, Mich., b. Apr. 1, 1880.

Family of HENRY C. HERR (5139) and JENNIE M. GREEN.

9343. Ruth L., Port Huron, Mich., b. Dec. 24, 1894.

Family of ALTA A. HERR (5143) and FRANK D. REIGLE (5153).

9344. Merrill H., Buffalo, N. Y., b. July 28, 1896; d. Apr. 9, 1897.

9345. Ronald F., Buffalo, N. Y., b. May 7, 1898; d. Feb. 3, 1899.

Family of ELI J. TREICHLER (5144) and ELIZABETH F. LANDIS (6231).

9346. Charles F., Sanborn, N. Y., b. Sept. 24, 1874; m. Jan. 6, 1897, Mary E. Rose, b. Feb. 9, 1873; dau. Gaylen Rose and Myra Robinson.

9347. Mary L., Sanborn, N. Y., b. June 23, 1876.
9348. Lorin W., Waynesboro, Pa., b. May 2, 1878.
9349. Wilber E., Cleveland, O., b. Feb. 10, 1880; d. May 26, 1901.
9350. Claude L., Sanborn, N. Y., b. Feb. 9, 1882.
9351. Elma Maude, Sanborn, N. Y., b. Mar. 20, 1884.
9352. Edna A., Sanborn, N. Y., b. Jan. 30, 1887.
9353. Abraham B., Sanborn, N. Y., b. Mar. 24, 1889.
9354. Henry J., Sanborn, N. Y., b. Mar. 21, 1891.
9355. Hazel M., Sanborn, N. Y., b. Apr. 15, 1894.

Family of MELISSA J. TREICHLER (5145) and JOHN SNEARLY.

9356. Mary Elma, Williamsville, N. Y., b. Jan. 21, 1890.
9357. Esther Anna, Williamsville, N. Y., b. Dec. 1, 1892; d. Dec. 1, 1892.

Family of HENRY B. TREICHLER (5146) and SARAH ROSE.

9358. Merwyn Willis, Sanborn, N. Y., b. Nov. 25, 1884.
9359. Victor Leo, Sanborn, N. Y., b. Feb. 15, 1886; d. Sept. 7, 1886.
9360. Harriet Melissa, Sanborn, N. Y., b. Nov. 1, 1889.
9361. Laura Irene, Sanborn, N. Y., b. June 8, 1897.

Family of MARY A. REIGLE (5184) and LYMAN G. HOOVER.

9362. Ada Sarah, Sanborn, N. Y., b. Nov. 15, 1882.
9363. Melvin G., Sanborn, N. Y., b. Mar. 17, 1887.
9364. Harold A., Sanborn, N. Y., b. Oct. 11, 1892.

Family of HARRIET E. REIGLE (5149) and HENRY HAUBEIL.

9365. Frank A., Sanborn, N. Y., b. Aug. 23, 1879.
9366. Alice S., Sanborn, N. Y., b. Apr. 3, 1882.
9367. Edith M., Getzville, N. Y., b. Jan. 16, 1884.
9368. Nora E., Sanborn, N. Y., b. Jan. 22, 1887.
9369. Anna H., Sanborn, N. Y., b. June 13, 1891.

Family of ANNA M. REIGLE (5152) and WILLIAM SUBBERA.

9370. Arthur M., Sanborn, N. Y., b. Apr. 16, 1885.
9371. E. ——— Leroy, Sanborn, N. Y., b. Nov. 9, 1886.
9372. Maud M., Sanborn, N. Y., b. Sept. 26, 1888.

Family of ETTA G. REIGLE (5154) and FRANK E. WILSON.

9373. Neil A., La Salle, N. Y., b. Dec. 13, 1887; d. Apr. 9, 1897.
9374. Ellsworth C., La Salle, N. Y., b. Oct. 8, 1889.
9375. Mildred, La Salle, N. Y., b. Oct. 31, 1891.
9376. Francis, La Salle, N. Y., b. Sept. 15, 1894.
9377. Harry, La Salle, N. Y., b. Jan. 21, 1897.
9378. Evelyn Ada, La Salle, N. Y., b. Jan. 28, 1901.

Family of Rev. EDWIN JOHN GANTZ (5160) and FRANCES L. ST. CLAIR.

9379. Esther, St. Louis, Mo.
9380. Emma Ora, Iola, Kans., b. Aug. 8, 1878.
9381. Ethel St. Clair, St. Louis, Mo., b. Sept. 16, 1881.

Family of Dr. HENRY H. GANTZ (5161) and NORA L. ST. CLAIR.

9382. Edna St. Clair, Albia, Ia., b. July 7, 1882.
9383. Edwin St. Clair, Albia, Ia., b. Mar. 18, 1884.
9384. Winnefred S., Albia, Ia., b. Dec. 4, 1885.
9385. Abraham B., Albia, Ia., b. Mar. 14, 1892.
9386. Esther Ora, Humeston, Ia., b. Apr. 5, 1894; d. Oct. 3, 1894.

Family of HENRY M. LONG (5162) and ISABELLA E. SUMMY.

9387. Cora Belle, Williamsville, N. Y., b. Jan. 26, 1868; m. Dec. 25, 1889, Milton J. Hoffman, b. Dec. 1, 1861; son John Hoffman and Susanna Gelen.

Family of ESTHER SOPHIA LONG (5163) and Wid. JACOB SHISLER.

9388. Anna Maria, Williamsville, N. Y., b. Oct. 20, 1864; d. Dec. 26, 1871.
9389. Susan Amelia, Williamsville, N. Y., b. Oct. 7, 1866; d. July 30, 1881.
9390. Sarah Ellen, Williamsville, N. Y., b. Mar. 10, 1869; d. Dec. 29, 1891; m. July 3, 1889, Henry L. Oswald, b. Nov. 19, 1863; son George Oswald and Magdalena Crout.
9391. Margaret Emma, Williamsville, N. Y., b. Aug. 23, 1871.
9392. Christian Beam, Williamsville, N. Y., b. May 28, 1874; m. June

27, 1897, Sarah A. Dresenberg, b. Oct. 26, 1864; dau. John Dresenberg and Margaret Weaver.

9393. Laura Augusta, La Salle, N. Y., b. Nov. 6, 1876; m. Nov. 6, 1895, Franklin E. Rogers, b. Aug. 12, 1875; son John Rogers and Margaret Williams.

9394. Fannie Elma, Lindsay, O., b. Apr. 8, 1879; m. Nov. 24, 1897, Burr S. Rogers, b. Nov. 18, 1877; son John Rogers and Margaret Williams.

9395. Estella A., Williamsville, N. Y., b. June 20, 1882; d. Aug. 13, 1882.

Family of MARY ELIZABETH LONG (5164) and GEORGE B. SUMMY.

9396. Elmer E., Athol Springs, N. Y., b. Sept. 1, 1864; m. Sept. 3, 1888, Susan Gibson, dau. James Gibson and Lydia ———.

9397. Esther E., Wichita, Kans., b. June 22, 1866; m. Oct. 1, 1888, Charles P. Mueller, b. June 13, 1862; son Paul J. Mueller and Mary Chappiene.

9398. Charles E., Athol Springs, N. Y., b. June 30, 1868; m. Sept. 11, 1888, Alice G. Aykroyd, b. Oct. 7, 1868; dau. William H. Aykroyd and Ellen E. Stering.

9399. Allen Eugene, Athol Springs, N. Y., b. Nov. 22, 1869; d. Nov. 28, 1869.

9400. Gertrude Emma, Painted Post, N. Y., b. May 11, 1871; d. Mar. 10, 1875.

9401. Albert E., Painted Post, N. Y., b. May 27, 1873; m. Apr. 27, 1899, Mary L. Fisher, dau. Rev. David Fisher and Mary Jenkins.

9402. David Long, Cynwyd, Pa., b. Mar. 10, 1875; m. Nov. 11, 1899, Virginia Weeks, dau. John H. Weeks and Laura Piers.

Family of ELIAS A. LONG (5166) and JOSEPHINE BAKER.

9403. George Baker, Chicago, Ill., b. Sept. 21, 1873; m. Sept. 19, 1894, Lillian W. McGee, b. June 25, 1874; dau. John McGee and Anna Woolley.

9404. Frances Elizabeth, Chicago, Ill., b. Nov. 28, 1875; m. July 18, 1899, Harold B. Wright.

9405. Helena May, Chicago, Ill., b. May 28, 1886.

Family of DANIEL B. LONG (5167)) and HATTIE ALICE SAVAGE.

9406. Cyrus Savage, Buffalo, N. Y., b. Oct. 30, 1886; d. Jan. 14, 1887.

Family of SUSAN L. LONG (5168) and THOMAS F. MORLEY.

9407. Thomas Henry, Buffalo, N. Y., b. July 17, 1893.

9408. Arthur Long, Buffalo, N. Y., b. Mar. 6, 1895.

9409. Clarence Benjamin, Buffalo, N. Y., b. Jan. 3, 1897; d. Apr. 4, 1901.

Family of ANNA M. LONG (5169) and CHARLES EDWARD SWITZER.

9410. Harriet Elizabeth, Rochester, Mich., b. Mar. 23, 1887.

9411. Isabel L., Rochester, Mich., b. Oct. 3, 1888.

9412. Milton Eli, Winsville, N. Y., b. Sept. 30, 1890.

9413. Mary Pearl, Lewston, N. Y., b. May 3, 1893.

9414. Charles Allen, Lewston, N. Y., b. Feb. 13, 1895.

9415. Fanny Gertrude, Lewston, N. Y., b. June 13, 1897.

Family of Dr. BENJAMIN G. LONG (5171) and MARY GROVE.

9416. Olive Harriet, Buffalo, N. Y., b. May 13, 1885.

9417. Ethel Clara, Buffalo, N. Y., b. Feb. 10, 1887.

9418. Russel Graham, Buffalo, N. Y., b. May 21, 1889; d. May 29, 1892.

9419. Florence Grace, Buffalo, N. Y., b. June 30, 1891.

9420. Clementine G., Buffalo, N. Y., b. Nov. 30, 1898; d. Dec. 21, 1904.

Family of Dr. ELI HERR LONG (5172) and ALICE E. EGGERT.

9421. Edith May, Buffalo, N. Y., b. Feb. 26, 1885.

9422. Austin O., Buffalo, N. Y., b. Jan. 27, 1888.

9423. Raymond D., Buffalo, N. Y., b. Feb. 23, 1891.

9424. Edwin E., Buffalo, N. Y., b. Sept. 12, 1897.

Family of EMANUEL C. LONG (5173) and ANNA BISHOP SEACHRIST.

9425. Ella E., Williamsville, N. Y., b. Jan. 24, 1870; m. Feb. 16, 1890, Christian Weckesser, son Henry Weckesser and Catherine Zimmerman.

23

9426. Frank H., Williamsville, N. Y., b. Apr. 14, 1874.
9427. Mary C., Williamsville, N. Y., b. Jan. 25, 1876.
9428. Abraham F., Williamsville, N. Y., b. Mar. 7, 1878.
9429. Esther A., Williamsville, N. Y., b. Apr. 30, 1880.
9430. Benjamin M., Williamsville, N. Y., b. Mar. 30, 1882.
9431. Cora L., Williamsville, N. Y., b. June 28, 1884.
9432. Ruth E., Williamsville, N. Y., b. Sept. 11, 1886.
9433. Edward S., Williamsville, N. Y., b. Nov. 8, 1888.

Family of MAUD C. HERR (5179) and THOMAS E. LANNIN.

9434. Orton Herr, Rochester, N. Y., b. Mar. 26, 1898.

Family of MARY ANN METZLER (5181) and HENRY OBER.

9435. Fanny, Mastersonville, Pa., b. Dec. 15, 1867.
9436. Agnes, Mastersonville, Pa., b. Apr. 25, 1869.
9437. Philip, Mastersonville, Pa., b. Aug. 8, 1871.
9438. Susan, Mastersonville, Pa., b. Nov. 15, 1873.
9439. Nathan, Mastersonville, Pa., b. Oct. 18, 1878.
9440. Anna, Mastersonville, Pa., b. Dec. 13, 1885.

Family of CHRISTIAN H. METZLER (5182) and ELIZABETH HELT.

9441. Aaron, Mt. Joy, Pa., b. Nov. 27, 1871.
9442. Clayton, Mt. Joy, Pa., b. Mar. 22, 1876.

Family of FANNIE H. METZLER (5183) and PAUL G. GIBBLE.

9443. Phares M., Mastersonville, Pa., b. Oct. 7, 1869.
9444. Ellen, Mastersonville, Pa., b. Nov. 26, 1876.
9445. Fannie, Mastersonville, Pa., b. July 5, 1879.
9446. Katie, Mastersonville, Pa., b. July 14, 1881.
9447. Minnie, Mastersonville, Pa., b. Oct. 30, 1883.

Family of JOHN H. METZLER (5184) and MARY DIFFENDERFER.

9448. Franklin, Sporting Hill, Pa., b. Jan. 5, 1884.
9449. Louisa, Sporting Hill, Pa., b. Jan. 5, 1884.

Family of ELIZABETH H. METZLER (5185) and ISAAC G. KOPP.

9450. Alice M., Milton Grove, Pa., b. Jan. 14, 1873; d. Jan. 18, 1875.
9451. Elizabeth, Milton Grove, Pa., b. Aug. 4, 1874.
9452. Isaac, Milton Grove, Pa., b. Nov. 9, 1875.
9453. Levi, Milton Grove, Pa., b. Apr. 9, 1884.

Family of HENRY H. METZLER (5186) and ELIZABETH HEISEY.

9454. Amos, Lititz, Pa., b. Jan. 21, 1877.

Family of JACOB H. METZLER (5187) and ELIZABETH HUBER.

9455. Ida May, Girard, Ill.
9456. Ada, Girard, Ill.

Family of ANNIE METZLER (5192) and JOHN S. WOLF.

9457. Maggie Ellen, Lancaster, Pa., b. Sept. 13, 1873.
9458. Nora Ada, Lancaster, Pa., b. Apr. 1, 1876; d. July 12, 1878.
9459. Martin Van, Lancaster, Pa., b. Feb. 12, 1880.
9460. John, Lancaster, Pa., b. Aug. 6, 1888.

Family of AMOS M. METZLER (5193) and CATHERINE ANDES.

9461. Annie Olivia, Sporting Hill, Pa., b. July 1, 1875; m. ——— Ginder, son ——— Ginder and Annie Mathiot.
9462. Martin Willis, Lititz, Pa., b. July 7, 1877; d. Aug. 31, 1877.
9463. Amos Walton, Lititz, Pa., b. June 25, 1879.
9464. George Franklin, Lititz, Pa., b. July 20, 1881.
9465. Clayton Ellsworth, Lititz, Pa.
9466. Katie Viola, Lititz, Pa., b. Nov. 13, 1883.
9467. David Francis, Lititz, Pa., b. Mar. 22, 1885; d. Sept. 16, 1885.
9468. Lizzie Naomi, Lititz, Pa., b. Jan. 8, 1887.

Family of BENJAMIN M. METZLER (5194) and ELIZABETH B. HIESTAND.

9469. Susan Bertha, Mt. Joy, Pa., b. Oct. 26, 1878; d. Nov. 22, 1886.
9470. Frances Elizabeth, Mt. Joy, Pa., b. Feb. 11, 1880.
9471. Benjamin Emory, Mt. Joy, Pa., b. Dec. 29, 1881.
9472. Martin Allen, Mt. Joy, Pa., b. June 12, 1884.
9473. James, Mt. Joy, Pa.

Family of **EMMA SUSAN METZLER** (5196) and **AMOS M. KISSINGER.**

9474. Edgar Harrison, East Petersburg, Pa., b. Oct. 2, 1891.
9475. Wayne Oscar, East Petersburg, Pa., b. Jan. 23, 1895.

Family of **ABRAHAM S. METZLER** (5199) and **MARY HERNLEY.**

9476. Herman, Sporting Hill, Pa., b. Feb. 21, 1876.
9477. Monroe, Sporting Hill, Pa., b. Jan. 29, 1878.
9478. Abraham, Sporting Hill, Pa., b. Oct. 23, 1885.

Family of **ELIAS S. METZLER** (5200) and **REBECCA GINGRICH.**

9479. Dora G., Mt. Joy, Pa., b. Oct. 8, 1887.
9480. Bessie, Mt. Joy, Pa., b. Jan. 26, 1889.
9481. Martin, Mt. Joy, Pa., b. Aug. 15, 1892.

Family of **DANIEL S. METZLER** (5201) and **ELIZABETH ERB.**

9482. Minnie E., Mt. Joy, Pa., b. June 8, 1880.
9483. Alice, Mt. Joy, Pa., b. May 7, 1882; d. Apr. 18, 1883.
9484. Henry, Mt. Joy, Pa., b. Feb. 18, 1885.
9485. John E., Mt. Joy, Pa., b. Aug. 15, 1886.

Family of **ELIZABETH S. METZLER** (5202) and **ABRAHAM HERNLEY.**

9486. Dora, Manheim, Pa., b. Mar. 4, 1884.
9487. Minnie, Manheim, Pa., b. July 11, 1887.
9488. Barbara, Manheim, Pa., b. May 26, 1889.
9489. Peter, Manheim, Pa., b. July 18, 1891.
9490. Lizzie, Manheim, Pa., b. Sept. 19, 1893.
9491. Martha, Manheim, Pa., b. Mar. 18, 1897.
9492. Esther, Manheim, Pa., b. Aug. 31, 1899.

Family of **AARON GEPHER** (5204) and **SUSAN RUHL.**

9493. Louisa R., Mastersonville, Pa., b. May 30, 1880.
9494. Cora, Mastersonville, Pa., b. Mar. 13, 1883.
9495. Amelia, Mastersonville, Pa., b. Mar. 9, 1885.

Family of SUSAN METZLER (5208) and JACOB HUTTENSTEIN.

9496. Cora, Petersburg, Pa., b. July 4, 1883.

9497. Wallace, Petersburg, Pa., b. Apr. 14, 1888.

Family of HARRIET N. METZLER (5209) and AMOS WITMER.

9498. Elam, Elizabethtown, Pa., b. Oct. 31, 1887.

Family of BARBARA N. METZLER (5211) and PETER B. STAUFFER.

9499. Benjamin, Clay, Pa., b. Sept. 11, 1888.

9500. Ellen, Clay, Pa., b. Nov. 29, 1890.

Family of ANNIE METZLER (5212) and PHARES S. BEAMESDERFER.

9501. Elise M., East Petersburg, Pa., b. June 17, 1899.

9502. Norman M., East Petersburg, Pa., b. Oct. 5, 1900.

Family of IDA ALEXANDER METZLER (5213) and JOHN HERR MORTON.

9503. Ralph Emerson, Sterling, Ill., b. Aug. 28, 1886.

9504. Myra Ethel, Sterling, Ill., b. Dec. 5, 1898.

Family of CATHERINE EBERLY (5223) and FRANK S. EVANS.

9505. Herman, Spring Valley, O., b. Oct. 5, 1885.

9506. Lawrence, Spring Valley, O., b. Feb. 14, 1895.

Family of DANIEL SHERMAN SMITH (5227) and ZANNA JANE FRASHER.

9507. Grace Elizabeth, Lancaster, Pa., b. May 29, 1900.

Family of IDA ELIZABETH SMITH (5229) and HENRY C. DEMUTH.

9508. Henry C., Lancaster, Pa., b. Aug. 7, 1897.

9509. Christopher, Lancaster, Pa., b. Sept. 12, 1899.

Family of JOHN SOMERFIELD SMITH (5230) and FLORENCE C. NORBECK.

9510. Martha Louisa, Lancaster, Pa., b. Jan. 7, 1898.

Family of EMMA ELIZABETH MUSSER (5237) and HIRAM M. DELLINGER.

9511. Infant, Paradise, Pa., b. Feb. 16, 1884; d. Feb. 18, 1884.

Family of MARTHA ELLA HERR (5242) and HENRY R. SNAVELY.

9512. Rosalia H., Junction, Pa., b. Feb. 1, 1895.
9513. Ella H., Junction, Pa., b. June 3, 1897.
9514. Helen H., Junction, Pa., b. Oct. 3, 1899.

Family of ELMER STROHM (5252) and ELIZABETH WAGNER.

9515. Alice, Needles, Cal., b. Nov. 21, 1894.
9516. Orpha, Needles, Cal., b. Oct. 27, 1896.

Family of SERENUS B. ESBENSHADE (5254) and EMMA N. CASKEY.

9517. Gertrude B., Paradise, Pa., b. May 9, 1885.
9518. Stella E., Paradise, Pa., b. July 9, 1894.
9519. Edith S., Paradise, Pa., b. Aug. 26, 1896.
9520. Ruth C., Paradise, Pa., b. July 27, 1898.

Family of JOHN S. ESBENSHADE (5256) and MARTHA LEAMAN.

9521. John Thomas, Lancaster, Pa., b. May 8, 1900.

Family of THADDEUS HERR (5257) and ELLA NORA ROHRER.

9522. Harold R., Strasburg, Pa., b. Oct. 22, 1898.

Family of BERTHA L. STEPHENS (5264) and GEORGE W. FEHR.

9523. Miriam Stephens, Reading, Pa., b. Aug. 16, 1898.
9524. Charles Augustus, Reading, Pa., b. May 8, 1901.

Family of LETTIE NAOMI HERR (5281) and SAMUEL JACKSON.

9525. Verna Deene, Orrville, O., b. Dec. 4, 1900.

Family of ESTHER ELIZ. BRENEMAN (5290) and D. FRANK SPINDLER.

9526. Mildred Naomi, Burton City, O., b. Feb. 18, 1902.

Family of FRANKLIN W. HERR (5302) and JESSIE S. McKAY.

9527. Ernest McKay, McManus, La., b. Sept. 15, 1897.
11815. Jessie McKay, McManus, La., b. Aug. 10, 1904; d. June 5, 1905.

Family of EMILY HERR (5305) and BENJAMIN LIPPINCOTT.

9528. Francis B., Cinnamon, N. J., b. Feb. 19, 1901; d. Feb. 22, 1901.

Family of FRANKLIN STROHM HERR (5306) and FRANCES BRIGGS SMITH.

9529. Ruth Eastburn, Moorestown, N. J., b. Apr. 24, 1896.
9530. Lawrence Janney, Moorestown, N. J., b. Jan. 29, 1899.

Family of HENRY CLAY HERR (5308) and RACHAEL L. DeCOW.

9531. Samuel K., Moorestown, N. J., b. June 11, 1895; d. June 13, 1895.
9532. Robert E., Moorestown, N. J., b. ———, 1897; d. ———, 1897.
9533. Edith Strohm, Moorestown, N. J., b. Apr. 26, 1899.
9534. Henry P., Moorestown, N. J., b. Nov. —, 1902.

Family of ERNEST H. COOPER (5312) and MARGARETTA HERGESHIMER.

9535. Edith Eva, Philadelphia, Pa.

Family of EMMA BRENEMAN (5318) and ELMER LEFEVER.

9536. Charles B., Hubers, Pa., b. Jan. 28, 1881.
9537. Harry, Hubers, Pa., b. Jan. 16, 1882.
9538. Ray, Hubers, Pa., b. Jan. 5, 1895.
9539. Miriam, Hubers, Pa., b. July 21, 1900.

Family of MIRIAM BRENEMAN (5318) and ADAM DOMBACH.

9540. Christian B., New Danville, Pa., b. Dec. 28, 1887.
9541. Martin, New Danville, Pa., b. Mar. 9, 1889.
9542. Ralph, New Danville, Pa., b. July 20, 1890.
9543. Emma Salome, New Danville, Pa., b. Apr. 17, 1892.
9544. Lloyd, New Danville, Pa., b. June 22, 1893.
9545. Miriam, New Danville, Pa., b. Aug. 12, 1894; d. Feb. 8, 1895.
9546. Jennie, New Danville, Pa., b. Sept. 7, 1895.
9547. Chester, New Danville, Pa., b. Apr. 7, 1899.

Family of LANDIS B. HERR (5338) and MARY A. BOOK.

9548. Raymond B., Lancaster, Pa., b. Dec. 1, 1897.

9549. Florence B., Lancaster, Pa., b. Oct. 24, 1899.
6640. Landis, Lancaster, Pa.
6641. Laura, Lancaster, Pa.

Family of ANNIE B. HERR (5340) and EMLIN B. MYLIN.

9550. Edna H., Strasburg, Pa., b. Sept. 11, 1896.
9551. Fannie E., Strasburg, Pa., b. Nov. 3, 1899.

Family of FRANCES E. GARBER (5357) and DAVID Z. WITMER.

9552. John G., Elizabethtown, Pa., b. Aug. 30, 1888; d. Oct. 12, 1894.
9553. Chester Z., Elizabethtown, Pa., b. Jan. 18, 1890.
9554. Ava Ray, Elizabethtown, Pa., b. Feb. 19, 1891.
9555. Florence E., Elizabethtown, Pa., b. Oct. 17, 1892.
9556. David Paul, Elizabethtown, Pa., b. Mar. 6, 1894.
9557. Bernice Ruth, Elizabethtown, Pa., b. Jan. 27, 1897.

Family of PARIS H. GARBER (5361) and ELIZABETH HERR.

9558. Raymond H., Columbia, Pa., b. Sept. 14, 1897.
9559. Elmer H., Columbia, Pa., b. Dec. 8, 1899.
9560. John A., Coumbia, Pa., b. Sept. 30, 1902.

Family of ELMER JAY GARBER (5362) and CAROLINE SEACHRIST.

9561. Pauline Mildred, Bainbridge, Pa., b. June 21, 1901.

Family of RULEF H. GILE (5390) and CHARLOTTE I. HERRICK.

9562. Julia Agnes, Milwaukee, Wis., b. Mar. 4, 1876; d. Nov. 9, 1880.
9563. Ray Elmer, Milwaukee, Wis., b. July 4, 1883.
9564. Earl Gordon, Milwaukee, Wis., b. Jan. 22, 1889.

Family of CORA ADA METZ (5414) and CHARLES J. PFOHL.

9566. Harold C., Williamsville, N. Y., b. May 2, 1897.

Famly of MARY CATHERINE DUDDING (5470) and WALLACE ARMOUR.

9567. Georgie, Hannibal, Mo.
9568. Hazel, Hannibal, Mo.
9569. Bert, Hannibal, Mo.

Family of **HENRY SARVER DUDDING** (5472) and **LILLIAN KELSEY**.

9570. Olin W., Hannibal, Mo.

Family of **ELIZABETH DUDDING** (5473) and **NATHANIEL CARLIN**.

9571. Clarence E., St. Louis, Mo.
9572. Mary E., St. Louis, Mo.
9573. Josephine S., St. Louis, Mo.
9574. Nathaniel H., St. Louis, Mo.

Family of **EMMA C. DUDDING** (5474) and **WILLIAM C. McCONNELL**.

9575. May Lewis, Springfield, Ill., b. Dec. 31, 1876.

Family of **IDA CADOGAN** (5478) and **CHARLES B. HATCHER**.

9576. Ida Matilda, Quincy, Ill., b. Dec. 25, 1878.
9577. John Cadogan, Quincy, Ill., b. Mar. 1, 1880.
9578. Charles Kenneth, Quincy, Ill., b. Nov. 8, 1885.

Family of **NORA ETHEL MOORE** (5483) and **HORACE B. STEEL**.

9579. William Henry, St. Louis, Mo., b. Sept. 14, 1878; d. Nov. —, 1883.
9580. Russell Leigh, St. Louis, Mo., b. Nov. 7, 1879; d. June 12, 1902; m. June 4, 1900, Irma Haskell, dau. William H. Haskell and Mary Austin.
9581. Bert Cecil, St. Louis, Mo., b. Aug. 28, 1881; d. Nov. 24, 1899.
9582. Robert Eugene, St. Louis, Mo., b. Sept. 10, 1883.

Family of **ANNIE VIRGINIA MOORE** (5485) and **WILLIAM P. MORGAN**.

9583. Lottie Bell, St. Louis, Mo., b. Oct. —, 1883; d. June 21, 1888.
9584. William Patrick, St. Louis, Mo., b. June 3, 1891.

Family of **MARY BRADFORD MOORE** (5487) and **JOSEPH T. LOGAN**.

9585. Lottie Mae, St. Louis, Mo., b. July 27, 1898.
9586. Carleton Moore, St. Louis, Mo., b. Oct. —, 1902.

Family of **MILTON HENRY MOORE** (5488) and **JEANETTE MARIA WILSON**.

9587. Dorothy Mildred, St. Louis, Mo., b. Feb. 6, 1896.

9588. Lucille Athenaise, St. Loius, Mo., b. July 3, 1898.

9689. Donald Winston, St. Louis, Mo., b. Mar. 24, 1901.

Family of Dr. ROY DUDLEY MOORE (5490) and ELLA MARIE ROWE.

9590. Carolyn Virginia, Central, Mo., b. Nov. 26, 1901.

Family of JAMES WILLIAM LEWIS (5492) and MARY ELLEN WINSTON.

9591. Carrie Emma, Denver, Col., b. Feb. 17, 1876; m. Jan. 30, 1895, William B. Turner, son Capt. E. P. Turner and Lucy Baker.

9592. Bessie Cecil, Galveston, Tex., b. Nov. 9, 1877; m. Dec. 4, 1900, Pierce F. Groome, b. Nov. 6, 1877.

9593. George Winston, Quincy, Ill., b. Aug. 14, 1879; d. Apr. 2, 1883.

9594. Edna Florence, Topeka, Kans., b. May 3, 1881; d. Oct. 21, 1884.

9595. Jessie Kate, Denver, Col., b. Sept. 9, 1885.

9596. William Arthur, Quincy, Ill., b. Aug. 7, 1888; d. Mar. 7, 1889.

9597. Mary Gladys, Quincy, Ill., b. July 30, 1890; d. Apr. 2, 1891.

9598. James Walter, Quincy, Ill., b. July 14, 1892; d. Feb. 13, 1893.

Family of JESSIE KENDALL LEWIS (5495) and J. WALTER WINGET.

9599. Lewis Earl, Atlanta, Ga., b. Oct. 21, 1881.

9600. Alma, Huntington, West Va., b. Jan. 25, 1884; m. June 14, 1905, Norman Elmer Cummings, b. June 28, 1876; son William R. Cummings and Estella Hayes.

Family of LAURA S. MOORE (5500) and EDWARD L. STAATS.

9601. Elenor Rockwood, Denver, Col., b. Feb. 12, 1902.

Family of HELEN ELIZABETH WILSON (5503) and CLARENCE L. PEASLEE.

9602. Helen Wilson, Williamsport, Pa., b. Sept. 14, 1898.

9603. Clarence Loomis, Williamsport, Pa., b. June 4, 1901; d. Aug. 30, 1901.

Family of BESSIE MARIE STONER (5508) and Dr. JOSEPH H. KRAPE.

9604. Reber Wilson, Kent, O., b. Feb. 23, 1895; d. Aug. 11, 1895.

9605. Zell Marie, Kent, O., b. July 29, 1896.

9606. Bessie Isabel, Kent, O., b. Dec. 1, 1899.

Family of EDMUND HERR CRISPEN (5515) and ANNIE LOUISA SHULTZ.

9607. Frederick Shultz, Lock Haven, Pa., b. Feb. 29, 1897.

Family of HARRIET REBECCA HYATT (5532) and ELMER JAKEWAY.

9608. Harriet Frances, Athens, Pa., b. Apr. 12, 1878.

Family of CHARLOTTE S. HYATT (5533) and JOHN R. THOMPSON.

9609. Randolph Hyatt, Salona, Pa., b. Sept. 11, 1886.
9610. Clinton Thomas, Salona, Pa., b. Feb. 27, 1888.
9611. Helen Catherine, Salona, Pa., b. Apr. 4, 1890.
9612. Emma Louise, Salona, Pa., b. Mar. 4, 1897.

Family of GEORGE T. HYATT (5534) and EFFIE E. McKIBBEN (8882).

9613. Ethel Frances, Salona, Pa., b. Nov. 22, 1888; d. May 1, 1897.
9614. Ely McKibben, Salona, Pa., b. Sept. 5, 1889.
9615. Sarah Jeanette, Salona, Pa., b. Feb. 8, 1892.
9616. Charlotte Marie, Salona, Pa., b. Feb. 8, 1892.
9617. Georgiana, Salona, Pa., b. Aug. 19, 1893.
9618. Fernando Pulaski, Salona, Pa., b. Feb. 4, 1895.

Family of HARRY CLINTON HYATT (5535) and MARIAN A. BROWNE.

9619. Grace Elizabeth, Lewisburg, Pa., b. Sept. 10, 1891; d. Oct. 14, 1891.
9620. Susan Ernestine, Lewisburg, Pa., b. Oct. 20, 1892.
9621. Marian Eleanor, Lewisburg, Pa., b. Apr. 27, 1897.
9622. Clinton B., Lewisburg, Pa., b. June 3, 1901.

Family of ANNIE CATHERINE HYATT (5536) and THOMAS H. HARRIS.

9623. Marian Frances, Fremont, Ill., b. Dec. 9, 1894.
9624. Benjamin, Fremont, Ill., b. May 17, 1896.

Family of ARTHUR BARNET HERR (5540) and MARY ELLEN CALLENDINE.

9625. Irwin Barnet, Quincy, Ill., b. Feb. 25, 1899.

Family of WILSON FREDERICK HERR (5550) and ANNA FLORENCE HEARD.

9626. Horace Leigh, Salona, Pa., b. Aug. 6, 1895.

9627. Paul Frederick, Salona, Pa., b. Apr. 4, 1897.

9628. Ellenor M., Salona, Pa., b. Oct. 13, 1898.

Family of GEORGE H. SHOFF (5558) and HARRIET SNODGRASS.

9629. Earl, Dubois, Pa., b. Aug. 16, 1889.

9630. Guy, Dubois, Pa., b. Oct. 14, 1891.

Family of WILSON SHOFF (5560) and FRANCES C. ILER.

9631. Henry Eugene, Buffalo, N. Y., b. Feb. 1, 1878.

9632. George Albert, Lock Haven, Pa., b. Dec. 11, 1880; d. Jan. 18, 1881.

Family of ALBERT M. SHOFF (5563) and ———.

9633. Stanley M., Buffalo, N. Y., b. May 6, 1891.

Family of HANNAH T. THOMPSON (5566) and NORMAN T. ARNOLD.

9634. Laura, Ridgeway, Pa., b. Feb. 24, 1883.

9635. Robert, Ridgeway, Pa., b. July 27, 1884; d. Feb. 15, 1885.

9636. Paul Thompson, Ridgeway, Pa., b. Mar. 22, 1889.

9637. William Benjamin, Ridgeway, Pa., b. Feb. 17, 1894.

Family of WILFORD DOWNS THOMPSON (5567) and MARY SHILLING.

9638. Caroline Elizabeth, Ridgeway, Pa., b. July 22, 1884.

9639. Mabel Cynthia, Ridgeway, Pa., b. Feb. 13, 1886; d. June 5, 1894.

9640. Robert LeRoy, Ridgeway, Pa., b. July 4, 1887.

9641. Clyde Jacob, Ridgeway, Pa., b. Aug. 31, 1889.

9642. Benjamin Franklin, Ridgeway, Pa., b. Feb. 19, 1894.

9643. Russell Wilford, Ridgeway, Pa., b. May 11, 1896.

Family of ULYSSES S. GRANT THOMPSON (5570) and IDA M. ARNOLD.

9644. Herbert LeRoy, Ridgeway, Pa.

Family of Rev. WILLIAM S. THOMPSON (5571) and GRACE NEWELL.

9645. Dwight Newell, Somerville, Mass., b. Jan. 18, 1892.

Family of MARTIN H. FARLEY (5576) and ALICE KIMBALL.

9646. Marie Bell, Sayres, Pa., b. Feb. 19, 1893.
9647. Mildred Louisa, Sayres, Pa., b. Jan. 14, 1895.

Family of WALTER D. HERR (5604) and LAURA D. WHITNEY.

9648. Marion Graham, Athens, N. Y., b. May 9, 1900.

Family of CHARLES EDWARD HERR (5607) and MARY JANE CREE.

9649. Alvan Lester, Lock Haven, Pa., b. July 20, 1896.
9650. Katharyn Agnes, Lock Haven, Pa., b. Jan. 22, 1899.

Family of FIANNA HERSHEY (5642) and Rev. HENRY B. STRICKLER.

9651. Emerson H., Waynesboro, Pa., b. Apr. 12, 1869.
9652. Ambrose B., Waynesboro, Pa., b. Sept. 29, 1871.
9653. Fannie N., Waynesboro, Pa., b. Apr. 6, 1876; m. Dec. 31, 1901,
Charles H. Quereau, b. May 1, 1856; son George W. Quereau
and Susan H. Smith.

Family of AMOS HERSHEY (5645) and FRANCES BEAM.

9654. Naomi B., Derry, Pa., m. William Ginrich.
9655. May, Derry, Pa.

Family of MARTIN HERSHEY (5646) and GRACE MUENCH.

9656. Mary Elizabeth, Philadelphia, Pa.
9657. Esther Grace, Philadelphia, Pa.

Family of MARY ANN LANDIS (5649) and JOHN B. DIFFENBACH.

9658. John Franklin, Lancaster, Pa., b. Oct. 9, 1843; d. Feb. 2, 1863.
9659. Martha Ann, Hutchinson, Kans,. b. Oct. 25, 1846; m. R. C. Van
Eman.
9660. Mary Emetta, Hutchinson, Kans., b. July 22, 1849; d. May 30,
1850.
9661. Emma Eliza, Chilton, Mo., b. July 16, 1851.
9662. Jacob Landis, Chilton, Mo., b. Oct. 23, 1853; m. June 15, 1895,
Emma Huffman, b. Nov. 19, 1875; dau. William F. Huffman
and Caroline Wagner.

9663. Ellen Frances, Chilton, Mo., b. July 16, 1856; d. July 10, 1884.
9664. Willis, South McAlester, I. T., b. Jan. 16, 1859.
9665. Henry, Lancaster, Pa., b. Feb. 14, 1861; d. Apr. 16, 1861.
9666. Franklin, Lancaster, Pa., b. Aug. 30, 1863; d. Feb. 5, 1864.
9667. Henry Landis, Chilton, Mo., b. Jan. 17, 1868.

Family of AMOS LANDIS (5652) and HETTIE ROHRER.

9668. Emma, Lampeter, Pa., b. May 18, 1863; m. Nov. 24, 1887, Phares
K. Doner, b. Apr. 25, 1868; son Henry Doner and Elizabeth
Kreider.
10817. John R., Lampeter, Pa., b. Dec. 10, 1860.

Family of DANIEL M. LANDIS (5653) and CHRISTIANA McALLISTER.

9669. Martha Lucretia, Fertility, Pa., b. June 7, 1861; d. ———, 1878.
9670. Harriet Elizabeth, Lancaster, Pa., b. Feb. 7, 1863; m. Mar. 21,
1893, Jacob D. Shuman, b. Mar. 5, 1860; son Henry Shuman
and Elizabeth ———.
9671. William Grant, Fertility, Pa., b. July 29, 1865; d. ———, 1872.

Family of BERTHA A. INGRAM (5659) and MILTON B. EBY.

9672. Arline B., Lancaster, Pa., b. Dec. 11, 1894.

Family of WILLIS C. McCOY (5674) and SALOMA GARBER.

9673. Howard R., Elkhart, Ind., b. Jan. 21, 1890.
9674. Anna M., Elkhart, Ind., b. Mar. 29, 1892.
9675. Inez R., Elkhart, Ind., b. Dec. 6, 1894.
9676. Myron G., Elkhart, Ind., b. Oct. 4, 1897.
9677. Sadie B., Elkhart, Ind., b. Feb. 5, 1899.
9678. Eva L., Elkhart, Ind., b. May 4, 1901.

Family of MINNIE A. McCOY (5675) and JONATHAN W. LEHMAN.

9679. Edgar E., Goshen, Ind., b. Jan. 22, 1886.
9680. Claude A., Goshen, Ind., b. Jan. 5, 1888.

Family of EDWARD J. McCOY (5676) and SUSIE DAMSON.

9681. Charles, Bellefontaine, O., b. July ———, 1885.

9682. Herman W., Bellefontaine, O.
9683. Edward, Bellefontaine, O.
9684. Harry, Bellefontaine, O.
9685. Gaynell, Bellefontaine, O.
9686. Claire, Bellefontaine, O.
9687. Minnie, Bellefontaine, O.

Family of LEWIS D. McCOY (5677) and EFFIE SHICK.

9688. Don L., Elkhart, Ind., b. Mar. 10, 1893.
9689. Thomas J. Mahlon, Elkhart, Ind.

Family of ANNA MAY McCOY (5678) and CHARLES KREPPS.

9690. Ruth M., Chicago, Ill., b. Jan. 16, 1894.
9691. Emma M., Chicago, Ill., b. Aug. 20, 1896.
9692. Leona M., Chicago, Ill., b. Aug. 11, 1897.
9693. Gerald C., Chicago, Ill., b. Sept. 4, 1898.
9694. Ida A., Chicago, Ill., b. Oct. —, 1900.

Family of PHOEBE LORENA NEWALL (5683) and WILLIAM FRITZ.

9695. Ethel Lorena, Gering, Neb., b. Sept. 3, 1889.
9696. Charles Newell, Gering, Neb., b. Nov. 13, 1890.

Family of Wid. FREDERICK A. NEWELL (5684) and FANNIE AYLESWORTH.

9697. Frederick A., Juniata, Neb., b. Aug. 3, 1900.

Family MAUDILLA HIMMELRIGHT (5688) and CHARLES WESTENBERGER.

9698. Mary Grace, Chili, S. America., b. Sept. 22, 1901.

Family of NELLIE C. HIMMELWRIGHT (5689) and HENRY SECHRIST.

9699. Gladys Evangeline, W. Salem, O., b. Dec. 6, 1902.

Family of ADA BELLE HIMMELRIGHT (5690) and EDWARD L. SECHRIST.

9700. Hazel Bell, Untali, Africa, b. May 17, 1903.

Family of ARTHUR EVERETT ADAMS (5691) and IDA LEE DINKINS.

9701. Clara Grace, Annapolis, Mo., b. Apr. 14, 1894.
9702. Everett Dinkins, Annapolis, Mo., b. Feb. 17, 1900.

Family of **FRANK PAXSON ADAMS** (5692) and **HATTIE B. GODFREY.**

9703. Lorrence Roderick, Elkhart, Ind., b. Sept. 25, 1901.

Family of **CLARA EDNA ADAMS** (5693) and Rev. **J. SHERMAN MERACLE.**

9704. William Adams, Farmington, Mo., b. Apr. 17, 1895; d. Aug. 17, 1895.
9705. Edna Luella, Terre Haute, Ind., b. Apr. 27, 1897.
9706. Theda Maud, Terre Haute, Ind., b. Dec. 25, 1899; d. Apr. 13, 1900.
9707. Warren Elliott, Terre Haute, Ind., b. Sept. 2, 1902.

Family of **BELLE KINNAMAN** (5706) and **CHARLES SWEARINGTON.**

9708. Howard, Cleveland, O., b. Sept. 10, 1893.
9709. Albert, Cleveland, O., b. Aug. 12, 1895.

Family of **VIRDILLA F. CARPENTER** (5713) and **ELIAS S. ZOOK.**

9710. Clayton Ephraim, Naperville, Ill., b. Oct. 11, 1872.
9711. Edwin, Vogansville, Pa., b. Oct. 11, 1873; d. Dec. 16, 1873.
9712. Daniel, Naperville, Ill., b. Dec. 8, 1874.
9713. Edith Estella, Vogansville, Pa., b. Mar. 13, 1876; d. Aug. 21, 1876.
9714. LeRoy, Naperville, Ill., b. May 25, 1877; d. July 11, 1896.
9715. Samuel, Naperville, Ill., b. Dec. 20, 1880.
9716. Mary, Naperville, Ill., b. Nov. 24, 1881.
9717. Emma May, Naperville, Ill., b. May 8, 1884.

Family of **MARY ANN CARPENTER** (5714) and **EDWIN S. FRY.**

9718. Cora C., Naperville, Ill., b. Feb. 29, 1872; m. May 15, 1890.
9719. Hattie, Plainfield, Ill., b. Dec. 19, 1873; m. Apr. 21, 1892.
9720. George, Hinkley, Ill., b. Feb. 13, 1876.

Family of **CLARA FORNEY** (5737) and **WALTER J. COMSTOCK.**

9721. Walter J., Providence, R. I., b. Dec. 5, 1880.
9722. Katherine Farnum, Providence, R. I., b. May 30, 1882; d. Sept. 22, 1882.

Family of LIZZIE GROFF (5759) and ABRAHAM WITMER.

9723. Laura, Strasburg, Pa.
9724. Kate, Strasburg, Pa.

Family of KATE GROFF (5761) and Dr. GEORGE MILLER.

9725. Ellie, Lancaster, Pa., m. William W. Westhaeffer.
9726. Kate, Lancaster, Pa.

Family of FANNY GROFF (5762) and HARRY MILLER.

9727. Eddie, Lancaster, Pa.

Family of BENJAMIN F. SHENK (5782) and BARBARA BARR.

9728. Emma B., Philadelphia, Pa., b. June 24, 1837; m. Dec. 22, 1864, Wid. Henry H. Breneman (1579); m. Jan. 22, 1892, Wid. Dr. D. Miller Barr (1769).
9729. Martha A., Chicago, Ill., b. Oct. 18, 1843; m. June 25, 1868, Hiero B. Herr (4869).
9730. Francis, Chicago, Ill.

Family of Wid. BENJAMIN F. SHENK (5782) and CATHERINE CHRIST.

9731. Elizabeth, Lancaster, Pa.
9732. Henry L., Lancaster, Pa.
9733. Myra L., Lancaster, Pa.

Family of CATHERINE SHENK (5785) and JOHN HESS.

9734. Laura M., New Providence, Pa., b. Nov. 16, 1852.
9735. Martha Catherine, New Providence, Pa., b. Nov. 10, 1858.

Family of SUSANNA KENDIG (5806) and BENJAMIN G. KENDIG.

9736. William T., Washington, Ill.
9737. Sarah J., Washington, Ill.
9738. George W., Wasington, Ill.
9739. Isaac H., Washington, Ill.
9740. Andrew J., Washington, Ill.
9741. John W., Washington, Ill.
9742. Charles, Washington, Ill.

Family of SAMUEL KENDIG (5807) and CATHERINE BRUBAKER.

9743. Louisa, Washington, Ill.
9744. Andrew W., Washington, Ill.
9745. Mary N., Washington, Ill.
9746. Leah Ellen, Washington, Ill.

Family of EMANUEL KENDIG (5808) and MARGARET WALLACE.

9747. Charles H., Washington, Ill.

Family of AMOS KENDIG (5810) and ELIZABETH BRUBAKER.

9748. Tobias B., Washington, Ill.
9749. Daniel F., Washington, Ill.
9750. Andrew W., Washington, Ill.
9751. Mary M., Washington, Ill.
9752. Elizabeth A., Washington, Ill.
9753. Ellen A., Washington, Ill.

Family of ANN KENDIG (5812) and ENOCH BIGGS.

9754. Joseph H., Washington, Ill.
9755. Ellen, Washington, Ill.
9756. Francis, Washington, Ill.
9757. Wesley, Washington, Ill.
9758. Enoch, Washington, Ill.

Family of BARBARA KENDIG (5813) and HENRY JEWIT.

9759. Sylvester, Washington, Ill.
9760. Benjamin, Washington, Ill.
9761. Gilbert, Washington, Ill.

Family of MARTIN KENDIG (5815) and MARY SHAUB.

9762. Alfred, Wahsington, Ill.
9763. Charles, Washington, Ill.

Family of TOBIAS KENDIG (5817) and ANNA KENDIG (5826).

9764. Susan, Washington, Ill., m. ——— Sears.

9765. Mattie, Washington, Ill., m. ——— Ashman.
9766. Barbara, Washington, Ill.
9767. Hettie, Washington, Ill.
9768. Samuel, Washington, Ill.
9769. Joseph, Washington, Ill.
9770. Emma, Washington, Ill.

Family of MARY KENDIG (5818) and JOHN HERR.

9771. Amos, Washington, Ill.
9772. Christian, Washington, Ill.
9773. Henry, Washington, Ill.
9774. David, Washington, Ill.
9775. Delilah, Washington, Ill.
9776. Susan A., Washington, Ill.
9777. Mary E., Washington, Ill.

Family of HENRY KENDIG (5824) and BETTIE SPITLER.

9778. Charles, Waynesboro, Va.

Family of JACOB KENDIG (5825) and PHOEBE ZIRCLE.

9779. John, Juniata, Va.
9780. Charles, Juniata, Va.
9781. Mary, Juniata, Va.
9782. Henry, Juniata, Va.

Family of JOSEPH KENDIG (5828) and BARBARA BOWERMASTER.

9783. Simon, Martinsville, Pa.

Family of Wid. JOSEPH KENDIG (5828) and ANNA BRUBAKER.

9784. Martha, Martinsville, Pa.
9785. Benjamin, Martinsville, Pa.
9786. Elias, Martinsville, Pa.
9787. Tobias, Martinsville, Pa.
9788. Hettie Ann, Martinsville, Pa.

Family of JOHN KENDIG (5830) and Wid. BARBARA KREIDER KENDIG.

9889. Emma, Binkley's Bridge, Pa.
9790. Rebecca, Binkley's Bridge, Pa.

Family of HETTIE KENDIG (5831) and CHRISTIAN BRENEMAN.

9791. Mattie C., Baumgardners, Pa.
9792. Henry K., Baumgardners, Pa.
9793. Mary K., Baumgardners, Pa.

Family of SAMUEL KENDIG (5833) and LIZZIE MARTIN.

9794. Mattie, Strasburg, Pa.
9795. Aaron, Strasburg, Pa.

Family of JACOB KENDIG (5834) and LIZZIE REINHART.

9796. Emlen Franklin, Enterprise, Pa.

Family of CHRISTIAN H. KENDIG (5835) and ANNA WITMER.

9797. Witmer J., Lancaster, Pa., b. Mar. 11, 1857; m. Apr. 12, 1883, Rebecca Kinports, b. Jan. 31, 1852; dau. John H. Kinports and Mary Stern.
9788. David H., Reading, Pa., b. Nov. 10, 1859; m. Oct. 6, 1881, Annie S. Heller, b. July 23, 1859; son Isaac D. Heller and Barbara Stauffer.
9799. Susan Elizabeth, Lancaster, Pa., b. Dec. 29, 1861.
9800. Ann Mary, Lancaster, Pa., b. Mar. 19, 1864.

Family of MARY ANN KENDIG (5836) and ABRAHAM R. WITMER.

9801. Amelia, Refton, Pa., b. Oct. 9, 1854; m. Oct. 17, 1877, John Hess, b. Aug. 16, 1851; son Benjamin Hess and Susan Leaman.
9802. Stephen, Harrisburg, Pa., b. July 22, 1856; d. Apr. 24, 1861.
9803. David, Harrisburg, Pa., b. Feb. 7, 1858; m. Ella Kinard, dau. Leonard Kinard and Elizabeth Hummel.
9804. Susan, Mountville, Pa., b. Aug. 26, 1859; d. Feb. 9, 1888; m. May 6, 1884, Henry Weidler, b. Sept. 20, 1858; son David Weidler and Mary Witmer.

9805. Annie B., Mountville, Pa., b. Nov. 17, 1861; m. Sept. 9, 1887, Paul H. Bletz, b. Oct. 9, 1861; son Frederick Bletz and Charlotte Hamilton.

Family of ELIZABETH E. GROVE (5904) and JACOB F. FLORY.

9806. Christiana Catharine, Hanford, Cal., b. Oct. 15, 1862; m. May 8, 1890, Frederick E. Brown, b. July 31, 1866; son William Brown and Ellen M. Walcot.

9807. Joseph Henry, Dos Palos, Cal., b. Mar. 2, 1864; m. May 6, 1890, Alice Webber, b. Mar. 14, 1872; dau. Sidney Webber and Laura E. Sterns.

9808. Isaac Daniel, Newman, Cal., b. Oct. 4, 1865; m. Nov. 6, 1889, Ida Broadhurst, b. Dec. 15, 1865; dau. Stephen Broadhurst and Rebecca O. H. McCombs.

9809. Sarah Elizabeth, Lemore, Cal., b. June 10, 1867; m. Dec. 27, 1888, George W. Barker, b. Dec. 27, 1863; d. Aug. 30, 1907; son Skidmore Barker and Margaret Mills.

9810. Charles Franklin, Lemore, Cal., b. Aug. 12, 1870; m. Jan. 13, 1892, Minta Brouhard, b. Nov. 22, 1878; dau. William N. Brouhard and Euphemia Shield.

9811. Jacob Andrew, Lemore, Cal., b. Dec. 2, 1873; m. Dec. 27, 1899, Constance Doty, b. May 29, 1872; dau. Cloise E. Doty and Anna V. Hunt.

Family of BARBARA A. GROVE (5905) and JOHN A. STOVER.

9812. Dr. William Miller, San Luis Obispo, Cal., b. Feb. 10, 1867; m. Oct. 12, 1898, Annie E. Mitchell.

9813. Charles Franklin, San Luis Obispo, Cal., b. Aug. 10, 1868.

9814. Edward Pilson, Stanton, Va., b. Aug. 9, 1876.

Family of NANCY GROVE (5907) and WILLIAM B. GARBER.

9815. Charles W., Lemore, Cal., b. Mar. 16, 1870; m. Jan. 29, 1890, Belle Monck, dau. Robert Monck and Susan Bunser.

9816. Homer B., Lemore, Cal., b. Aug. 30, 1874; m. Aug. 11, 1897, Mazie Monger, dau. Hiram Monger and ———.

Family of MARY GROVE (5908) and SAMUEL WAMPLER.

9817. Ida C., Stanton, Va., b. Aug. 20, 1869; d. Oct. 29, 1896; m. Nov. 13, 1895, Frank Diehl.

9818. Bertie C., Stanton, Va., b. Jan. 13, 1871; m. Dec. 17, 1890, Jacob M. Jones.

9819. Bettie, Stanton, Va., b. Aug. 7, 1872; m. Dec. 25, 1891, Taylor Weller.

9820. Luther R., Newport News, Va., b. Aug. 24, 1874.

9821. Mamie B., Newport News, Va., b. Apr. 14, 1876; m. Mar. 20, 1895, William Harris.

9822. Elmer S., Newport News, Va., b. Feb. 28, 1878.

9823. Jennie V., Newport News, Va., b. Nov. 28, 1879; m. Aug. 23, 1901, Hiram Driver.

9824. Isaac Grove, Newport News, Va., b. Apr. 5, 1882; d. Sept. 30, 1884.

9825. Charles, Rolla, Va., b. Feb. 23, 1884.

Family of SUSANNA GROVE (5910) and HENRY F. BORDEN.

9826. Effie L., Laurel Hill, Va., b. Mar. 7, 1873; m. Dec. 19, 1895, I. —— F. Dellinger.

9827. Arthur G., Laurel Hill, Va., b. Sept. 13, 1877; m. Dec. 23, 1896, M. —— C. Woodson.

Family of ISAAC N. GROVE (5911) and ELIZABETH LANDIS.

9828. John H., Bowden, N. D., b. Jan. 28, 1875.

9829. William M., Mead, Washington, b. Aug. 25, 1876.

9830. Walter C., Freyers Cave, Va., b. Apr. 25, 1880.

9831. Isaac E., Freyers Cave, Va., b. Jan. 31, 1882.

9832. Grace J., Freyers Cave, Va., b. Nov. 14, 1884.

9833. Charles M., Freyers Cave, Va., b. Mar. 22, 1886.

9834. Catherine, Freyers Cave, Va., b. Nov. 2, 1888.

9835. Elizabeth, Freyers Cave, Va., b. Nov. 6, 1890.

9836. Orrie, Freyers Cave, Va., b. Dec. 21, 1892.

9837. Earl, Freyers Cave, Va., b. Jan. 26, 1897.

9838. Goldie E., Freyers Cave, Va., b. Dec. 13, 1899.

Family of NOAH GROVE (5912) and ELLA LEE WOOD.

9839. Sallie Estell, Somerville, Va., b. Feb. 20, 1879; m. Feb. 10, 1897. Henry W. Teats, b. Nov. 24, 1865.
9840. Winnie Kate, Somerville, Va., b. July 25, 1881; d. Feb. 12, 1886.
9841. Howard Lee, Somerville, Va., b. Nov. 20, 1883.
9842. Ella Florence, Somerville, Va., b. May 16, 1886.
9843. Mamie Pearl, Somerville, Va., b. Mar. 26, 1888.
9844. Henry Laid, Somerville, Va., b. Sept. 25, 1890.
9845. Lona Blanche, Somerville, Va., b. Sept. 3, 1892.
9846. Noah Isaac, Somerville, Va., b. July 6, 1895.

Family of JACOB A. GROVE (5913) and EMMA E. CRAIG.

9847. Araminta Florence, Koiner's Store, Va., b. Jan. 4, 1879.
9848. Flora May, Koiner's Store, Va., b. May 2, 1886.
9849. William Isaac, Koiner's Store, Va., b. May 3, 1890.

Family of ANN ELIZABETH FRANTZ (5914) and JOHN BONEBRAKE.

9850. Jay, Manila, Philippine Islands, b. Dec. 5, 1875.

Family of ELAM G. FRANTZ (5915) and MARTHA B. FUNK.

9851. Ernest M., Gwynn Brook, Md., b. Nov. 27, 1866; m. Dec. 31, 1891, Florence Kendig, b. July 2, 1869; dau. Martin Kendig and Barbara Trout.
9852. Arthur J., Gwynn Brook, Md., b. Sept. 7, 1868; d. Apr. 5, 1870.
9853. Ella S., Glyndon, Md., b. Dec. 15, 1872; m. Oct. 11, 1893, Newton J. Geist, b. Apr. 19, 1866; son Jacob D. Geist and Susan Trout.
9854. Ada E., Gwynn Brook, Md., b. Apr. 28, 1879.
9855. Iva M., Gwynn Brook, Md., b. Nov. 1, 1881.
9856. Etha M., Gwynn Brook, Md., b. Oct. 11, 1883.

Family of BENJAMIN FRANK FRANTZ (5918) and MARTHA L. FUNK.

9857. Harry Abraham, Ringgold, Md., b. Sept. 26, 1875.
9858. Mabel Good, Ringgold, Md., b. Nov. 14, 1879.
9859. Clare Groff, Ringgold, Md., b. Dec. 29, 1880.

9860. Margaret Funk, Ringgold, Md., b. Dec. 5, 1881.
9861. Anna Luella, Ringgold, Md., b. Jan. 5, 1883. .
9862. Frank Bernard, Ringgold, Md., b. Aug. 14, 1884.
9863. Alice B., Ringgold, Md., b. June 26, 1885; d. Sept. 24, 1885.
9864. Arthur Marle, Ringgold, Md., b. Feb. 1, 1891.

Family of CHRISTIAN G. FRANTZ (5920) and GEORGIE MYERS.

9865. Maud Alice, Lancaster, Pa., b. Oct. 15, 1881.
9866. Leila May, Lancaster, Pa., b. Nov. 3, 1883.
9867. Wilber M., Lancaster, Pa., b. Feb. 24, 1887.
9868. Ruth Ellen, Lancaster, Pa., b. Apr. 19, 1889.
9869. Mary Martha, Lancaster, Pa., b. Nov. 23, 1891.
9870. Harry Christian, Lancaster, Pa., b. Dec. 25, 1893.
9871. Lillian Gertrude, Lancaster, Pa., b. Mar. 1, 1895.

Family of ELLA LOUISA FRANTZ (5923) and JOHN DENLINGER.

9872. David Earl, Waynesboro, Pa., b. Nov. 6, 1883.

Family of CLARA DENMEAD GROFF (5941) and WILLIAM DAVISON WIGHT.

9873. Elizabeth Groff, Baltimore, Md., b. Nov. 14, 1899.
8689. Margaret Hyatt, Baltimore, Md., b. Sept. 28, 1902.

Family of JOHN E. GIRVIN (5944) and EMMA BOWMAN.

9874. Dr. Edwin Robert, Philadelphia, Pa., b. July 2, 1853; m. May 20, 1895, Marie E. Loveland, b. Oct. 16, 1875; dau. Samuel W. Loveland and Clara E. Crouse.
9875. Clara E., Philadelphia, Pa., b. Sept. 12, 1854; d. Aug. 3, 1877; m. Oct. 14, 1875, Joseph M. Horton, b. Apr. 22, 1840; d. Nov. 16, 1880; son Nathan W. Horton and Rosanna Miller.
9876. Frank, Philadelphia, Pa., b. Mar. 18, 1856; d. Sept. 20, 1863.
9877. Annie F., Philadelphia, Pa., b. Mar. 4, 1859; d. Oct. 1, 1880.

Family of Dr. ROBERT M. GIRVIN (5948) and Wid. SUSAN B. SAUNDERS.

9878. Susan, West Philadelphia, Pa., b. July —, 1868; d. July —, 1868.

9879. John Harper, West Philadelphia, Pa., b. Sept. 17, 1869.

9880. Charles Jeffries, West Philadelphia, Pa., b. Jan. 3, 1873.

9881. Robert M., West Philadelphia, Pa., b. May 29, 1874; m. Oct. 7, 1903, Alice Kennedy Hill.

9882. Mary, Philadelphia, Pa., b. Sept. 21, 1877.

9883. Helene M., Philadelphia, Pa., b. Aug. 30, 1884.

Family of DANIEL E. POTTS (5952) and CATHERINE McELROY.

9884. Annie Virgilia, Philadelphia, Pa., b. July 13, 1862.

9885. Mary E., Strasburg, Pa., b. Feb. 16, 1864; d. Apr. 4, 1865.

Family of ANGELICA POTTS (5954) and EDWARD M. EBERMAN.

9886. Frank Potts, Gap, Pa., b. Dec. 16, 1860; m. 1883, Frances E. Fitch, dau. ——— and Lucy Langan.

9887. Edith Mary, Strasburg, Pa., b. Oct. 21, 1862; m. Feb. 9, 1887, John Ellsworth Herr (4898).

9888. Ella L., West Chester, Pa., b. Aug. 20, 1866; m. Jan. 18, 1899, Gibbons G. Cornwell, b. Aug. 18, 1861; son Robert T. Cornwell and Lydia A. Jackson.

Family of FRANCES HASTINGS (5958) and JAMES C. DUNLAP.

9889. Andrew John, Millport, Pa., b. Mar. 31, 1852.

9890. Maria Louisa, Millport, Pa., b. June 5, 1853.

9891. Stephen Hastings, Millport, Pa., b. Sept. 25, 1854.

9892. Clara Eliza, Millport, Pa., b. Nov. 27, 1856; d. Dec. 12, 1856.

9893. Emma Josephine, Millport, Pa., b. Feb. 22, 1858.

9894. Alice Isabella, Millport, Pa., b. Oct. 26, 1859.

9895. Frank McClellan, Millport, Pa., b. Dec. 5, 1861.

9896. Mary Elizabeth, Millport, Pa., b. Apr. 7, 1863; d. Apr. 29, 1863.

Family of MARIA HASTINGS (5959) and SAMUEL CURTIS.

9897. George Brown, Fertility, Pa., b. Sept., 1853; d. Mar. 9, 1854.

9898. Maria Adella, Fertility, Pa., b. Dec. 19, 1854.

9899. Stephen John, Fertility, Pa., b. Mar. 24, 1857.

9900. Hattie Barbara, Fertility, Pa., b. Apr. 18, 1860.

9901. William Hastings, Fertility, Pa., b. June 28, 1862.

Family of AMOS SHIRK (5968) and MARTHA ANN APPLETON.

9902. William Henry, Soudersburg, Pa., b. Oct. 16, 1861.

9903. Frances Ella, Soudersburg, Pa., b. Sept. 16, 1863; d. Dec. 11, 1863.

Family of JONAS H. BEAR (6025) and ANNIE RUTT.

9904. Roy R., Sterling, Ill., b. July 7, 1877; m. June 13, 1901, Lulu M. Woodyard.

9905. Bert R., Sterling, Ill., b. Mar. 1, 1883.

9906. Hazel M., Sterling, Ill., b. Mar. 27, 1895.

Family of ELIZABETH BAER (6026) and JOHN P. HERZ.

9907. Infant, Sterling, Ill., b. Jan. 17, 1879; d. Jan. 17, 1879.

9908. Mary Alice, Sterling, Ill., b. Mar. 14, 1880.

9909. Clement, Sterling, Ill., b. Mar. 8, 1882.

9910. Henry Martin, Sterling, Ill., b. Mar. 8, 1884; m. Margaret Susanna Stultz, b. Apr. 4, 1887; dau. Bernard Stoltz and Margaret S. Hummel.

9911. John A. Logan, Sterling, Ill., b. Feb. 20, 1887; d. Mar. 14. 1887.

9912. Harrison, Sterling, Ill., b. Aug, 23, 1888; d. ———, 1888.

9913. Abraham, Sterling, Ill., b. Sept. 25, 1889.

9914. Ira Virgil, Sterling, Ill., b. Jan. 31, 1893.

9915. La Verna Ann, Sterling, Ill., b. Apr. 29, 1896.

Family of EZRA BAER (6027) and MAMIE HOBBS.

9916. Maude, Chicago, Ill., b. Sept. 7, 1887.

Family of CATHERINE BAER (6029) and SAMUEL MYERS.

9917. Guy, Sterling, Ill., b. July 1, 1890.

9918. Eva, Sterling, Ill., b. Nov. 26, 1895.

Family of FRANKLIN BAER (6030) and MARGARET M. JOHN.

9919. Lloyd, Sterling, Ill., b. Dec. 8, 1889.

Family of JONAS HERR (6039) and FANNY B. MUMMA.

9920. Mary M., Ephrata, Pa., b. Dec. 22, 1894.

Family of HENRY HERR (6040) and EMMA L. BAKER.
9921. Joseph B., Neffsville, Pa., b. July 21, 1889.
9922. S. Mabel, Neffsville, Pa., b. May 26, 1891.
9923. Mary, Neffsville, Pa., b. May 22, 1893.
9924. Harry, Neffsville, Pa., b. May 16, 1895.

Family of AMOS HERR (6041) and MARY K. KAUFFMAN.
9925. C. ——— Kauffman, Neffsville, Pa., b. June 6, 1896.
9926. Paul, Neffsville, Pa., b. July 19, 1898.
9927. Grace, Neffsville, Pa., b. Apr. 10, 1901.

Family of ELAM HERR (6042) and MINNIE W. ESBENSHADE.
9928. Henry Elam, Binkley's Bridge, Pa., b. Aug. 15, 1897.

Family of SUSAN HERR (6044) and MARTIN H. FUNK.
9929. Mary Elizabeth, Neffsville, Pa., b. Sept. 9, 1899; d. May 1, 1904.

Family of DAVID H. SNAVELY (6065) and DORA GOODFELLOW.
9930. Mary, Springfield, O., m. ——— Redman.
9931. Glenna, Springfield, O.
9932. Thomas, Springfield, O.
9933. David Herr, Springfield, O.

Family of ALICE AMELIA HORNBERGER (6075) and D——— C. EYLER.
9934. Mary, Pontiac, Ill., b. Mar. 15, 1872; d. Apr. 12, 1873.

Family of BARBARA MINNICH (6081) and JOHN H. MARTIN.
9935. Mary, Philadelphia, Pa.
9936. Catherine, Philadelphia, Pa.

Family of JACOB KREIDER (6093) and ANNA CHARLES.
9937. Mary, Millersville, Pa.
9938. Jacob, Millersville, Pa.

Family of ESTHER KREIDER (6095) and JACOB MILLER.
9939. Jacob, Millersville, Pa.
9940. John, Millersville, Pa.

Family of MARY KREIDER (6096) and JACOB ROHRER.

9941. Jacob, Millersville, Pa.,
9942. Mary, Millersville, Pa.
9943. Daniel, Millersville, Pa.

Family of JONAS HERR (6097) and KATE KEPERLING.

9944. Ralph, Safe Harbor, Pa., b. May 9, 1878.
9945. Howard, Safe Harbor, Pa., b. Sept. 18, 1881.
9946. Chester, Safe Harbor, Pa., b. Aug. 18, 1891.

Family of JOSEPH A. RESSLER (6108) and NAOMI HERSHEY.

9947. Aaron H., Lancaster, Pa., b. July 29, 1890.
9948. Roy M., Lancaster, Pa., b. Dec. 16, 1891.
9949. Charlotte V., Lancaster, Pa., b. June 25, 1894.
9950. Harry A., Lancaster, Pa., b. Sept. 13, 1895.

Family of ENOS HERR (6119) and ANNA HARNISH.

9951. Annie May, New Providence, Pa., b. Sept. 17, 1892.
9952. Enos Earl, New Providence, Pa., b. Sept. 15, 1895.

Family of JOHN HERR (6120) and MARY E. HUBER.

9953. Elmer, New Providence, Pa., b. Sept. 16, 1893.
9954. Clarence, New Providence, Pa., b. Feb. 14, 1895; d. Dec. 10, 1895.
9955. John, New Providence, Pa., b. July 17, 1897.
9956. Ira, New Providence, Pa., b. Feb. 10, 1899.

Family of ABRAHAM SCHEETZ (6145) and LOUISA MARSHALL.

9957. Henry Marshall, Allegheny, Pa., m. Emma Koener.
9958. May Alma, Lancaster, Pa., d. Infant.

Family of BENJAMIN FRANKLIN FRICK (6153) and EMMA J. SECHRIST.

9959. Mary Ellen, York, Pa., b. Sept. 2, 1872; d. ———, 1872.
9960. Clara Emma, York, Pa., b. June 19, 1874.
9961. John Jacob, York, Pa., b. Dec. 20, 1875; d. Nov. 17, 1896.

9962. Hattie S., York, Pa., b. Dec. 23, 1877; d. Oct. 6, 1892.
9963. Hannah H., York, Pa., b. June 9, 1880.
9964. Frances Snyder, York, Pa., b. Dec. 29, 1884.
9965. Susanna Wesley, York, Pa., b. Sept. 11, 1886.

Family of JOHN P. FRICK (6154) and MARY LOUISA MYERS.

9966. Morris Hershey, York, Pa., b. Apr. 15, 1871.
9967. Alice, York, Pa., b. Jan. 11, 1873.
9968. Arthur, York, Pa., b. Sept. 6, 1880.

Family of ABRAHAM FRICK (6155) and ANNIE ELIZABETH BOND.

9969. Charles Carrol, York, Pa., b. Dec. 4, 1867; m. Nov. 22, 1900, Louisa M. Spangler.
9970. Benjamin Franklin, York, Pa., b. Jan. 23, 1870; d. Apr. 24, 1889.
9971. Joseph Hershey, York, Pa., b. July 9, 1872; d. July 16, 1875.
9972. Nellie, York, Pa., b. Oct. 27, 1874; d. Feb. 7, 1875.

Family of MARY ELLEN FRICK (6156) and MARTIN J. SKINNER.

9973. Clara Belle, York, Pa., b. Apr. 28, 1875.
9974. Ivan, York, Pa., b. Dec. 1, 1877.

Family of JOHN LUTHER WINTERODE (6159) and BARBARA CROSS.

9975. Daisy Maria, Finksburg, Md.
9976. Lucy, Finksburg, Md.

Family of ANNA M. WINTERODE (6161) and WILLIAM A. BURK.

9977. Florence Ander, Baltimore, Md., b. June 22, 1861; d. Dec. 9, 1901.
9978. Andrew, Baltimore, Md., b. Aug. 13, 1862; d. July 20, 1863.
9979. George Augustus, Baltimore, Md., b. Oct. 15, 1863; d. Feb. 14, 1899; m. Oct. —, 1891, Sarah A. Skillman.

Family of AMANDA E. WINTERODE (6163) and ASBURY WATTS.

9980. Carrie Louise, Baltimore, Md., b. Aug. 12, 1870; d. Sept. 30, 1871.
9981. Mary Augusta, Baltimore, Md., b. Jan. 25, 1872; d. July 22, 1872.

9982. Cornelia Estelle, Baltimore, Md., b. July 7, 1873; m. Jan. 12, 1890, S. Herbert Anderson.
9983. Cardiff Taggart, Baltimore, Md., b. July 15, 1875.
9984. Frances Asbury, Baltimore, Md., b. July 27, 1877.
9985. Harry Preston, Baltimore, Md., b. Oct. 29, 1880.
9986. Maud Adalaide, Baltimore, Md., b. June 15, 1882.
9987. Vivian Frick, Baltimore, Md., b. Jan. 3, 1890.

Family of GEORGE CARROLL WINTERODE (6164) and MARY L. WATTS.

9988. Dr. Robert Preston, Baltimore, Md., b. Jan. —, 1875.

Family of WILLIAM RUFUS WINTERODE (6165) and FANNIE LEWIN.

9989. Louis Levi, Baltimore, Md.
9990. Williametta, Baltimore, Md.

Family of JOHN FRICK (6170) and LYDIAN KROUT.

9992. Daisy May, Abbottstown, Pa., b. Feb. 18, 18—; m. May —, 1901, John J. McMaster, b. May 9, 1880.
9993. Preston Eugene, Abbottstown, Pa., b. Feb. 12, 1882.
9994. Hattie Bell, Abbottstown, Pa., b. Jan. 4, 1885.

Family of LAURA E. FRICK (6171) and FREDERICK BENTZ.

9995. George E., Malvern, Ia., b. Jan. 17, 1880.
9996. Harry F., Dillsburg, Pa., b. Aug. 22, 1884.
9997. Orrie B., Dillsburg, Pa., b. Dec. 3, 1891.

Family of ELIZABETH ANN FRICK (6172) and JOSEPH DEARDORF.

9998. ———, Malvern, Ia.
9999. ———, Malvern, Ia.
10000. ———, Malvern, Ia.
10001. ———, Malvern, Ia.
10002. ———, Malvern, Ia.
10003. ———, Malvern, Ia.

Family of JACOB M. FRICK (6173) and HATTIE B. SPECK.

10004. ———, Hall, Pa.

10005. ———, Hall, Pa.

10006. ———, Hall, Pa.

Family of ANNA B. FRANTZ (6193) and Rev. HENRY S. MENDENHALL.

10007. Luther Wesley, Pittsburg, Pa., b. May 2, 1869.

10008. Prudence Elizabeth, Berwick, Pa., b. Mar. 4, 1874; m. Franklin Faust.

10009. Gertrude Winnifred, Berwick, Pa., b. Aug. 1, 1877.

10010. Abethenia P., Berwick, Pa., b. Dec. 1, 1882.

Family of ELIZABETH FRANTZ (6195) and SIMON P. HAWBICKER.

10011. Elmer Frantz, Mercersburg, Pa., b. Dec. 26, 1867; m. Oct. 25, 1891, Alice C. Piper.

10012. Leah Nancy, Mercersburg, Pa., b. June 23, 1870; d. Aug. 29, 1890; m. May 16, 1889, Richard Tolman, d. Feb. 26, 1891.

10013. Anna Maria, Mercersburg, Pa., b. Aug. 6, 1872; m. Jan. 14, 1898, Charles Rigdon.

10014. Lucy May, Mercersburg, Pa., b. Feb. 21, 1875; d. Apr. 19, 1891.

10015. Etta Virginia, Mercersburg, Pa., b. Nov. 16, 1876; m. Mar. 25, 1896, Frank Stiles.

10016. William Noble, Mercersburg, Pa., b. Aug. 29, 1881.

10017. Sarah Elizabeth, Mercersburg, Pa.

10018. Jason Eby, Mercersburg, Pa., b. Aug. 19, 1884.

10019. Rudolph Moore, Mercersburg, Pa., b. Oct. 20, 1887.

Family of SARAH FRANTZ (6196) and THOMAS O. DAILEY.

10020. Harry F., Mercersburg, Pa., b. Dec. 11, 1865.

10021. Leah F., Mercersburg, Pa., b. Nov. 3, 1869; m. Sept. 17, 1889, Edwin H. Constantine, b. May 23, 1867.

10022. William P., Mercersburg, Pa., b. Apr. 13, 1873.

10023. Katie S., Mercersburg, Pa., b. Feb. 14, 1874; d. Aug. —, 1878.

10024. Annie M., Mercersburg, Pa., b. Apr. 26, 1876; d. Nov. —, 1877.

10025. Nellie M., Mercersburg, Pa., b. Jan. 3, 1879.

10026. Daisy B., Mercersburg, Pa., b. Feb. 7, 1887.

10027. Mary C., Mercersburg, Pa., b. May 27, 1889.

10028. Etta Rebecca, Mercersburg, Pa., b. July 21, 1891.

Family of BENJAMIN FRANTZ (6198) and ANNIE L. FRICK.

10029. Mark, Mercersburg, Pa., b. Sept. 24, 1897.

Family of CHRISTIAN FRANTZ (6200) and SARAH NOBLE.

10030. Jerome, Mercersburg, Pa., b. Oct. 17, 1881.

10031. Fannie S., Mercersburg, Pa., b. Oct. 11, 1883.

10032. Frank, Mercersburg, Pa., b. Mar. 23, 1885.

10033. Ruth, Mercersburg, Pa., b. July 3, 1887.

10034. Leah, Mercersburg, Pa., b. Sept. 9, 1889; d. Mar. 3, 1893.

10035. Emerson, Mercersburg, Pa., b. Dec. 6, 1891.

10036. Walter, Mercersburg, Pa., b. Apr. 30, 1894.

10037. Christian, Mercersburg, Pa., b. Aug. 16, 1896.

Family of SAMUEL RYDER FRANTZ (6206) and MARY E. BENSON.

10038. Arthur Benson, Waynesboro, Pa., b. Mar. 26, 1880.

10039. Mary, Waynesboro, Pa., b. Apr. 30, 1881.

10040. Katie Stickell, Waynesboro, Pa., b. Apr. 1, 1883.

10041. Herbert, Waynesboro, Pa., b. Feb. 12, 1887.

10042. Robert Benjamin, Waynesboro, Pa., b. Mar. 30, 1894.

Family of CHARLOTTE E. FRANTZ (6207) and GEORGE M. D. BELL.

10043. Mary F., Lucerne, Ind., b. May 3, 1875.

10044. Lottie K., Lucerne, Ind., b. Sept. 25, 1876.

10045. Bessie R., Lucerne, Ind., b. Nov. 3, 1881.

10046. Leila J., Lucerne, Ind., b. July 13, 1883.

10047. George, Lucerne, Ind., b. Apr. 19, 1891.

Family of CAROLINE FRANTZ (6208) and JOHN ANDREW MARSHBANK.

10048. Benjamin Frantz, Harrisburg, Pa., b. Dec. 9, 1876.

10049. Andrew Ross, Harrisburg, Pa., b. Mar. 17, 1879.

10050. John David, Harrisburg, Pa., b. Apr. 11, 1881.
10051. Carl Wolf, Harrisburg, Pa., b. Mar. 20, 1883.

Family of JOSEPH FRANTZ (6209) and GERTRUDE SMITH.

10052. Joseph S., Waynesboro, Pa., b. Apr. 14, 1880.
10053. Paul, Waynesboro, Pa., b. Apr. 20, 1881.
10054. Jemima Helen, Waynesboro, Pa., b. Mar. 15, 1882.
10055. Thomas Breneman, Waynesboro, Pa., b. Sept. 12, 1884.
10056. Hattie Imogene, Waynesboro, Pa., b. Dec. 19, 1886.
10057. Eber, Waynesboro, Pa., b. Dec. 7, 1888; d. July 17, 1889.

Family of JOHN FRANTZ (6214) and MARY V. MUNDY.

10058. Margaret Estelle, Waynesboro, Pa., b. Sept. 13, 1892.
10059. Charlotte Ryder, Waynesboro, Pa., b. Aug. 24, 1894.
10060. John Benjamin, Waynesboro, Pa., b. June 6, 1900.

Family of EZRA O. FRICK (6222) and CATHERINE MEHAFFY.

10061. Fredericka, Waynesboro, Pa., b. Dec. 23, 1885.
10062. Margaret K., Waynesboro, Pa., b. Sept. 15, 1889; d. June 30, 1890.

Family of FREDERICK FRICK (6225) and AMANDA SPRENKLEY.

10063. Ruth, Waynesboro, Pa., b. Apr. 9, 1889.
10064. Naomi, Waynesboro, Pa., b. June 2, 1895.

Family of ANNIE MARY FRICK (6226) and VICTOR GOOD.

10065. George Frick, Waynesboro, Pa., b. May 17, 1896.
10066. Fredericka Deitrich, Waynesboro, Pa., b. Nov. 1, 1897.

Family of ANNIE E. STONER (7530) and HARVEY F. HAVERSTICK (6227).

10067. Daughter, Lancaster, Pa., b. Dec. 2, 1881; d. Dec. 2, 1881.
10068. Rena F., Lancaster, Pa., b. Dec. 5, 1882.
10069. Edna V., Lancaster, Pa., b. Mar. 15, 1884.
10070. Anna E., Lancaster, Pa., b. Sept. 2, 1885.
10071. Winona S., Lancaster, Pa., b. Mar. 4, 1887.

24

10072. Mary, Lancaster, Pa., b. Jan. 9, 1889.

10073. Francis, Lancaster, Pa., b. Dec. 18, 1891.

10074. Son, Lancaster, Pa., b. Jan. 18, 1893; d. Jan. 18, 1893.

10075. William, Lancaster, Pa., b. Oct. 31, 1898.

Family of FRANKLIN F. LANDIS (6228) and ELIZABETH H. HERSHEY.

10076. Ida May, Waynesboro, Pa., b. Dec. 1, 1870; m. Thomas B. Smith, b. Mar. 10, 1860; son Samuel K. Smith and Jemima C. Breneman.

10077. Benjamin H., Waynesboro, Pa., b. Dec. 25, 1871; d. Apr. 11, 1878.

10078. Mary H., Waynesboro, Pa., b. Apr. 28, 1873; d. Apr. 19, 1881.

10079. Elizabeth, Anderson, Ind., b. Sept. 11, 1874; m. Jan. 31, 1901, Chauncey B. Hershey, b. Aug. 28, 1870; son Samuel Hershey and Mary Bachman.

10080. Anna, Waynesboro, Pa., b. Oct. 30, 1878.

10081. Adriana, Waynesboro, Pa., b. Nov. 19, 1881; d. Nov. 24, 1881.

10082. Frank H., Waynesboro, Pa., b. May 5, 1883; d. July 13, 1884.

10083. Mark Homer, Waynesboro, Pa., b. Dec. 16, 1885.

Family of EZRA F. LANDIS (6229) and CATHERINE ANTHES.

10084. Charles A., Chicago, Ill., b. July 10, 1873.

10085. Amelia A., Niagara Falls, N. Y., b. June 3, 1875; m. A—— B. Wentworth.

10086. Grace Elizabeth, Niagara Falls, N. Y., b. Jan. 27, 1877.

10087. Edith A., Niagara Falls, N. Y., b. Sept. 11, 1879.

10088. Mary, Niagara Falls, N. Y., b. July 9, 1881.

10089. Adriana, Niagara Falls, N. Y., b. July 27, 1883.

10090. Catherine, Niagara Falls, N. Y., b. May 17, 1885.

10091. Leah. Niagara Falls, N. Y., b. Nov. 23, 1888; d. June 20, 1889.

Family of MARY ANN LANDIS (6230) and JACOB D. KOHR.

10092. Franklin L., Lancaster, Pa., b. Jan. 3, 1870; m. June 10, 1896, Barbara K. Harnish.

10093. Anna L., Lancaster, Pa., b. Oct. 21, 1871; m. Feb. 20, 1895, Jacob L. Kreider, b. Sept. 20, 1868.

10094. Alice, Ronks, Pa., b. May 1, 1875; m. May 3, 1899, Elmer Weaver.

10095. Howard, Lancaster, Pa., b. Aug. 5, 1877.

10096. Esther L., Lancaster, Pa., b. Sept. 7, 1883.

10097. Lydia, Lancaster, Pa., b. July 8, 1885.

10098. John, Lancaster, Pa., b. Feb. 10, 1890.

Family of SALOME FRICK LANDIS (6232) and JACOB K. MILLER.

10099. Mary L., Waynesboro, Pa., b. Feb. 12, 1882.

10100. Anna, Waynesboro, Pa., b. Aug. 7, 1883.

10101. Lydia, Waynesboro, Pa., b. June 3, 1885.

10102. Elizabeth, Waynesboro, Pa., b. May 23, 1887.

10103. Jacob Frick, Waynesboro, Pa., b. July 10, 1889.

10104. Salome Edna, Waynesboro, Pa., b. Aug. 6, 1891.

10105. Emma Salinda, Waynesboro, Pa., b. Nov. 7, 1893.

10106. Ruth Lillian, Waynesboro, Pa., b. Aug. 3, 1895.

10107. Harold, Waynesboro, Pa., b. Dec. 22, 1897.

Family of ABRAHAM B. LANDIS (6233) and LEAH HOOVER LANDIS.

10108. Mary H., Waynesboro, Pa., b. Oct. 8, 1877; d. Dec. 30, 1880.

10109. Mark, Waynesboro, Pa., b. Apr. 18, 1879; d. Jan. 6, 1881.

10110. Benjamin, Waynesboro, Pa., b. Dec. 22, 1880.

10111. Henry, Waynesboro, Pa., b. Jan. 20, 1883.

10112. Ruth Evaline, Waynesboro, Pa., b. July 13, 1885.

10113. Esther, Waynesboro, Pa., b. Feb. 2, 1889.

10114. Franklin, Waynesboro, Pa., b. July 15, 1894.

Family of EMMA FRICK LANDIS (6234) and JACOB GANTZ FRICK.

10115. Mary Catherine, Waynesboro, Pa., b. Feb. 11, 1892.

10116. Abraham F., Waynesboro, Pa., b. Oct. 17, 1893; d. July 5, 1895.

10117. Anna Lydia, Waynesboro, Pa., b. Apr. 10, 1895.

10118. Elizabeth Mary, Waynesboro, Pa., b. Mar. 22, 1897.

10119. Paul Franklin, Waynesboro, Pa., b. Jan. 19, 1899.

Family of Dr. FRANKLIN F. FRANTZ (6235) and MARY CATHERINE BEST.

10120. George Best, Lancaster, Pa., b. Feb. 25, 1875; d. July 23, 1872.

10121. Louis, Lancaster, Pa., b. Sept. 28, 1873; d. July 21, 1874.

10122. Harvey, Lancaster, Pa., b. Jan. 12, 1875; d. Mar. 21, 1907.

10123. Irene Elizabeth, Columbia, Pa., b. May 20, 1876.

10124. John, Columbia, Pa., b. Oct. 31, 1877.

10125. Edna, Ephrata, Pa., b. July 5, 1879; m. Aaron R. Shearer.

10126. Homer, Schenectady, N. Y., b. Feb. 5, 1881.

10127. Beulah, Ephrata, Pa., b. Sept. 14, 1882; m. Thaves Baker.

10128. James Oscar, Lancaster, Pa., b. Aug. 14, 1884; d. Apr. 26, 1896.

10129. Esther Bertha, Lancaster, Pa., b. Nov. 23, 1886.

10130. Miriam, Lancaster, Pa., b. Aug. 14, 1888; d. Aug. 20, 1889.

10131. Thomas Elliott, Lancaster, Pa., b. Jan. 6, 1890; d. June 28, 1890.

10132. Helen Adalide, Lancaster, Pa., b. Jan. 3, 1892; d. Apr. 14, 1896.

10133. Franklin Frick, Lancaster, Pa., b. Dec. 27, 1894; d. May 8, 1896.

Family of Dr. JACOB F. FRANTZ (6238) and GERTRUDE L. OSBORN.

10134. Anna Viola, Greensburg, Pa., b. July 13, 1879; m. Oct. 16, 1902, Franklin Good, b. Feb. 6, 1872; son George W. Good and Maria Lenhart.

10135. Charles Norman, New Rochelle, N. Y., b. May 4, 1881; d. Aug. 17, 1900.

10136. Ethel, New Rochelle, N. Y., b. Jan. 2, 1885.

10137. LeRoy, New Rochelle, N. Y., b. Apr. 28, 1888.

10138. Jacob Harold, New Rochelle, N. Y., b. Dec. 29, 1889.

10139. Horace G., New Rochelle, N. Y., b. Apr. 15, 1891.

10140. Donald O., New Rochelle, N. Y., b. May 16, 1892; d. Dec. 29, 1895.

Family of ABRAHAM E. FRANTZ (6241) and CARRIE REMSON.

10141. Howard, Wilmington, Del., b. Nov. 24, 1885.

10142. Arthur, Wilmington, Del., b. Apr. 13, 1889.

10143. Mildred, Wilmington, Del., b. June 19, 1892.

10144. Genevieve, Wilmington, Del., b. Dec. 18, 1895.

Family of MARY ELIZ. FRANTZ (6243) and Wid. Dr. JACOB M. SHARTLE.

10145. Harold F., Millersville, Pa., b. May 2, 1894.

10146. Daughter, Millersville, Pa., b. Sept. 16, 1897; d. Sept. 16, 1897.

Family of ANNA F. FRANTZ (6244) and Rev. STANLEY L. KREBS.

10147. Catherine, Reading, Pa., b. Sept. 26, 1891; d. Oct. 19, 1892.

10148. Stanley Walter, Greensburg, Pa., b. Jan. 9, 1896.

8687. Anna Belle, Greenburg,s Pa., b. July 13, 1892.

8688. Josephine, Greensburg, Pa., b. July 16, 1905.

Family of JACOB F. BOWMAN (6246) and ELIZABETH A. BRACKBILL (8305).

10149. Lillian M., Galesburg, Ill., b. Aug. 31, 1878.

10150. Jacob Warren, Galesburg, Ill., b. Feb. 4, 1895.

Family of ABRAHAM FRICK BOWMAN (6247) and ANNA M. ALLEN.

10151. Leota Irene, Dayton, O., b. Nov. 28, 1879; m. Oct. 18, 1900, Joseph D. Chamberlain, b. Mar. 10, 1878; son Joseph D. Chamberlain and Margaret C. ———.

Family of MARY BOWMAN (6255) and PHARES D. SWARTLEY.

10152. ———, Osborne, O., b. Jan. 30, 1902.

Family of EUCLID B. FRICK (6258) and SARAH E. BUNTING.

10153. Edward Walter, Aransas, Tex., b. Jan. 27, 1892; d. Jan. 29, 1892.

10154. Robert Bunting, Porto Rico, Cuba, b. Apr. 24, 1893.

Family of MARY ELIZABETH HOOVER (6259) and ELAM S. HERSHEY.

10155. Floyd B., Leacock, Pa.

10156. Warren H., Leacock, Pa.

10157. Anna Esther, Leacock, Pa.

Family of HIRAM M. HOOVER (6261) and EVA LOUNDAGIN.

10158. Anna, Leacock, Pa.
10159. Elam, Leacock, Pa.
10160. Emory, Leacock, Pa.

Family of ALICE ANN HOOVER (6262) and HARVEY S. BOWERS.

10161. Frederick, Leacock, Pa.
10162. Martha, Leacock, Pa.
10163. Elam, Leacock, Pa.
10164. Maria, Leacock, Pa.

Family of AMELIA SALOME HOOVER (6263) and JACOB M. BOWERS.

10165. Rose, Leacock, Pa.
10166. Clare, Leacock, Pa.
10167. Naomi, Leacock, Pa.

Family of ADA RACHEL HOOVER (6264) and ROBERT R. LINDSEY.

10168. Grace, Leacock, Pa.
10169. Bertha, Leacock, Pa.
10170. Hiram, Leacock, Pa.
10171. Grover, Leacock, Pa.

Family of LAURA LOUISA HOOVER (6265) and Rev. JAMES M. SHELLEY.

10172. Ivan, Leacock, Pa.
10173. Russell, Leacock, Pa.
10174. Ethel, Leacock, Pa.

Family of JERRY S. RUTTER (6282) and KATE L. PETERS.

10175. Ella E., Lancaster, Pa., b. Apr. 5, 1885.
10176. Mabel Elizabeth, Lancaster, Pa., b. July 18, 1887

Family of LUCINDA RUTTER (6288) and AMOS LEFEVER.

10177. Aaron, Intercourse, Pa., b. Nov. 16, 1888.
10178. Laura, Intercourse, Pa., b. July 27, 1891.
10179. John, Intercourse, Pa., b. Feb. 23, 1893.
10180. Walter, Intercourse, Pa., b. Feb. 3, 1894.

Family of AMOS G. RUTTER (6292) and LAURA GOOD.

10181. Bertha, Intercourse, Pa., b. May 28, 1890.

Family of JASON E. RUTTER (6293) and LAURA RANCK.

10182. Earl, Intercourse, Pa., b. Dec. 29, 1896; d. June 7, 1907.

Family of AARON H. RUTTER (6295) and JANE JOHNSON.

10183. Bessie M., Intercourse, Pa.
10184. Viola B., Intercourse, Pa.

Family of EUGENE M. RUTTER (6297) and ANNIE ELIZABETH GEHR.

10185. Lillian May, New Holland, Pa., b. Feb. 7, 1885.
10186. Mary Eugenie, New Holland, Pa., b. Oct. 21, 1888.
10187. Pauline Kathryn, New Holland, Pa., b. Aug. 2, 1894.
10188. Emily Gehr, New Holland, Pa., b. Nov. 24, 1901.

Family of MARTIN SHEAFFER (6299) and CAROLINE GRAYBILL.

10189. Cora, Bareville, Pa.
10190. Martin, Bareville, Pa.
10191. Caroline, Bareville, Pa.

Family of AMOS S. HERSHEY (6308) and LILLIAN WILCOX.

10192. Mary Frieda, Bloomington, Ind., b. Oct. 7, 1898.

Family of IDA S. HERSHEY (6309) and CLINTON M. HERSHEY.

10193. Mary, Harrisburg, Pa., b. Sept. 6, 1893.
10194. Elma, Harrisburg, Pa., b. Sept. 28, 1895.

Family of OMER HERSHEY (6313) and SYLVIA SHEAFFER.

10195. Helen, Baltimore, Md., b. May 10, 1893.
10196. Louisa, Baltimore, Md., b. Dec. 31, 1895.

Family of HENRY BLOCHER (6350) and AMELIA ———.

10197. Lillie, Buffalo, N. Y.
10198. Altie, Buffalo, N. Y.

Family of JOHN ESHLEMAN (6358) and ANN MALINDA STRITE (6444).

10199. Cyrus H., Harrisburg, Pa., b. Oct. 18, 1878; m. Apr. 16, 1903, Mollie K. Koontz, b. Jan. 6, 1878; dau. James W. Koontz and Sarah C. Creager.

10200. Minnie K., Leitersburg, Md., b. Mar. 9, 1880; m. Aug. —, 1897, Melchor E. Strite (12089).

10201. John Ira, Leitersburg, Md., b. Feb. 9, 1883; m. Nora Cordell, dau. Daniel Cordell and ——— Wingert.

Family of ABRAHAM C. STRITE (6429) and LOUELLA CLAGGETT.

10202. Josephine, Hagerstown, Md., b. May 24, 1905.

10203. Samuel, Hagerstown, Md., b. Aug. 10, 1906.

10204. ———, Hagerstown, Md.

10205. ———, Hagerstown, Md.

Family of JACOB A. STRITE (6430) and EMMA N. DURBORAW.

10206. Edwin D., Chambersburg, Pa., b. May 2, 1892.

10207. Albert, Chambersburg, Pa., b. May 2, 1897.

10208. Robert, Chambersburg, Pa., b. June 27, 1901.

10209. ———, Chambersburg, Pa.

Family of MARIA ELIZABETH STRITE (6445) and JACOB H. REIFF.

10210. Clarence E., Cearfoss, Md.

Family of ANDREW C. STRITE (6448) and ANNIE LANDIS.

10211. Ida M., Leitersburg, Md.

10212. Irvin L., Leitersburg, Md.

Family of Wid. ANDREW C. STRITE (6448) and ELIZABETH LANDIS.

10213. Earl, Leitersburg, Md.

10214. Lewis, Leitersburg, Md.

Family of CATHERINE HERR (6449) and HENRY N. RISSER.

10215. Abraham L., Campbellstown, Pa., b. Feb. 20, 1869; m. Oct. 16, 1890, Emma K. Bachman.

10216. Aaron S., Bellaire, Pa., b. May 20, 1870.

10217. Mary A., Hummelstown, Pa., b. Dec. 21, 1874; m. Dec. 21, 1897, Jeremiah H. Gingrich.

10218. H. Allen, Bellaire, Pa., b. Feb. 8, 1879.

Family of Rev. JOHN R. HERR (6450) and MARY B. HEISER.

10219. Anna M., Bengal, India, b. Mar. 8, 1870; m. James H. Sparrow.

10220. Emma H., Fabor, Ia., b. May 28, 1873.

10221. Alice H., Interprise, Kans., b. Nov. 28, 1876; m. Dec. 23, 1896, Levi K. Markley, b. Mar. 16, 1870; son Solomon Markley and Sarah ———.

Family of ANNA HERR (6451) and CYRUS G. SHENK.

10222. Albert B., Derry Church, Pa., b. Oct. 23, 1869; m. Oct. 15, 1891, Mary Longenecker, b. Aug. 30, 1869; dau. Benjamin Longenecker and Anna Gingrich.

10223. John A., Elizabethtown, Pa., b. Apr. 13, 1871.

10224. Hiram H., Annville, Pa., b. Dec. 9, 1872; m. June 26, 1900, Bertha Strickler, b. Apr. 7, 1874; dau. Adam Strickler and Sarah Brightbill.

10225. Cyrus E., Annville, Pa., b. July 23, 1882; m. Mabel Goss, b. Mar. 23, 1880; dau. John G. Goss and Elizabeth Epler.

10226. Anna H., Elizabethtown, Pa., b. Sept. 12, 1888.

Family of ABRAHAM REIDER HERR (6452) and ELIZABETH ANN SHENK.

10227. Allen Ethan, Medicine Lodge, Kans., b. May 17, 1870; m. Jan. 16, 1894, Laura Melvina Taylor, b. Jan. 16, 1894; d. Nov. 2, 1904; dau. George R. Taylor and S. Frances King.

10228. Abraham Lincoln, Chickasha, Okla., b. Oct. 18, 1871; m. Bertha Damntain.

10229. Uriah Clayton, Medicine Lodge, Kans., b. Nov. 11, 1873; m. Jan. 14, 1897, Lillian V. Painter, b. Oct. 19, 1875; dau. David F. Painter and Cynthia A. Morton.

10230. John Nevin, Kiowa, Kans., b. Mar. 3, 1875; m. May 9, 1901, Edith Potter, b. July 8, 1879; dau. Orman J. Potter and Elvira Button.

10231. Ida May, Kiowa, Kans., b. Jan. 6, 1877.

10232. Mercy Hope, Kiowa, Kans., b. July 17, 1878; d. Aug. 22, 1878.

Family of GEORGE R. HERR (6453) and MARTHA L. ENGLE.

10233. Elva, Donegal, Kans., b. Aug. 15, 1886.

10234. Ivan, Donegal, Kans., b. Aug. 15, 1886.

Family of JACOB HERR (6457) and AMANDA RISSER.

10235. Edgar R., Elizabethtown, Pa., b. Oct. 4, 1884.

10236. Annie R., Elizabethtown, Pa., b. Aug. 3, 1886; m. Aug. 6, 1907, J. Warren Chapman.

10237. Frances R., Elizabethtown, Pa., b. Aug. 16, 1889.

10238. Edith R., Elizabethtown, Pa., b. Feb. 14, ——.

10239. Mary R., Elizabethtown, Pa., b. Apr. 21, ——.

10240. Ira R., Elizabethtown, Pa., b. Feb. 13, 1894.

Family of AMOS R. HERR (6459) and CATHERINE GISH.

10241. Ada G., Elizabethtown, Pa., b. Sept. 27, 1888.

10242. Walter Abram, Elizabethtown, Pa., b. Feb. 13, 1890.

10243. Oscar G., Elizabethtown, Pa., b. Jan. 19, 1892.

12467. Ralph G., Elizabethtown, Pa., b. July 4, 1902.

Family of REBECCA SHIFFER (6465) and CHRISTIAN NIXDORF.

10244. Irene, Mt. Joy, Pa., b. Mar. 8, 1891.

10245. Arthur Earl, Mt. Joy, Pa., b. June 8, 1896.

Family of CALVIN A. HERR (6473) and CARRIE SHULTZ.

10246. Infant, Columbia, Pa., b. Dec. 5, 1898.

Family of JOHN E. HOOVER (6481) and CATHERINE STONECIPHER.

10247. Dora Ellen, Yeoman, Ind., b. Dec. 31, 1877.

Family of RUDOLPH HOOVER (6482) and MARY ELLEN SHAFER.

10248. William H., Cambridge, Ind., b. Apr. 8, 1880.

Family of MARY HOOVER (6485) and DAVID N. SHELLENBERGER.

10249. Rudolph, Dublin, Ind., b. Jan. 31, 1889.

Family of DANIEL HOOVER (6489) and LYDIA SHAFER.

10250. Fanny Myrtle, Cambridge, Ind., b. Feb. 11, 1888.
10251. Mamie, Cambridge, Ind., b. May 3, 1890.
10252. Ethel, Cambridge, Ind., b. Nov. 30, 1892.
10253. Charles, Cambridge, Ind., b. Nov. 2, 1895.

Family of MOSES E. MYERS (6493) and MARY E. GRAVER (6512).

10254. Nora Mabel, Cambridge, Ind., b. Sept. 15, 1884.
10255. John Edison, Cambridge, Ind., b. Apr. 12, 1889.

Family of JEREMIAH E. MYERS (6495) and LAURA HUHN.

10256. Herbert O., Hagerstown, Ind., b. Nov. 3, 1894.

Family of BENJAMIN F. WISSLER (6498) and SYLVANIA NEEDLER.

10257. Clark D., Richmond, Ind., b. Sept. 18, 1870; m. Jan. —, 1899,
Etta Viola Gebhart.
10258. Carrie, Richmond, Ind., b. Jan 18, 1875; d. ———, 1877.
10259. Cora, Richmond, Ind., b. Feb. 12, 1876.
10260. Emory, Richmond, Ind., b. Mar. 25, 1879; m. May 5, 1901.
10261. Elizabeth, Richmond, Ind., b. Aug. 7, 1882.
10262. Frank, Richmond, Ind., b. Nov. 29, 1889.
10263. Arthur, Richmond, Ind., b. Apr. 27, 1892.

Family of CHRISTIAN P. WISSLER (6499) and MARTHA LOWELL.

10264. Lawrence O., New Lisbon, Ind., b. July 7, 1875; m. Oct. 26,
1899, Sinnie Hatfield.
10265. Carl A., New Lisbon, Ind., b. May 28, 1889.

Family of Rev. HORACE D. HERR (6503) and MARY ANN HOWARD.

10266. Margaret Elva, Kansas City, Mo., b. June 7, 1875; m. May
27, 1897, Daniel W. Vaughan, b. June 29, 1872.
10267. Isaiah Woodworth, Abilene, Kans., b. Oct. 8, 1877; d. Aug.
26, 1883.
10268. Horace Howard, Winslow, Ariz., b. Mar. 30, 1880.
10269. Gertrude Ann, Muscatine, Ia., b. Feb. 23, 1884.

10270. Bertha Delle, Muscatine, Ia., b. June 6, 1886.

10271. Mildred Ida, Muscatine, Ia., b. Oct. 23, 1888.

Family of ELIZABETH H. GRAVER (6511) and ANDREW K. ZEIGLER.

10272. Cora, Cambridge, Ind.

10273. Clara, Cambridge, Ind.

Family of ANNA E. GRAVER (6514) and CLARENCE M. PIERCE.

10274. Ansel R., Cambridge, Ind.

10275. George C., Cambridge, Ind.

Family of CHRISTIAN H. GRAVER (6515) and EDNA SHAFFER.

10276. Elva G., Cambridge, Ind.

10277. Orrie O., Cambridge, Ind.

10278. Howard S., Cambridge, Ind.

10279. Ivan H., Cambridge, Ind.

Family of MARY ELIZ. STEINBERGER (6525) and ARTHUR DeW. HOLMAN.

10280. John Roy, Springfield, O., b. Nov. 5, 1887.

Family of JOHN BURTIS STEINBERGER (6527) and CLARA BENEDICT.

10281. Lillie May, Springfield, O., b. Jan. 1, 1888.

Family of Wid. JOHN B. STEINBERGER (6527) and LULU PETERS.

10282. James Elwood, Springfield, O., b. June 1, 1897.

Family of JOHN HERR (6654) and MARY HEILMAN.

10283. Eugene, Annville, Pa.

10284. Paul, Annville, Pa.

10285. Naomi, Annville, Pa.

Family of ABRAHAM E. HERR (6655) and ANNIE IMBODEN.

10286. Cora, Annville, Pa.

10287. Will, Annville, Pa.

10288. ———, Annville, Pa.

Family of CLARA HERR (6657) and CHARLES H. LICHTY.

10289. Arthur, Annville, Pa.
10290. ———, Annville, Pa.
10291. ———, Annville, Pa.
10292. ———, Annville, Pa.

Family of HENRY HERR (6660) and SARAH WELTMER.

10293. Minnie, Annville, Pa.
10294. Nettie, Annville, Pa.
10295. Sadie, Annville, Pa., m. Harry Kelchner.

Family of JOHN E. HERR (6661) and LAVINA FORNEY.

10296. Rudolph F., Annville, Pa.
10297. Lottie, Annville, Pa.
10298. Susan, Annville, Pa.
10299. John F., Annville, Pa.
10300. Harry, Annville, Pa., d. ———, 1884.

Family of AARON G. HERR (6662) and LOUISA MAUD WALKER.

10301. L. ——— Dewitt, Annville, Pa., b. Mar. 4, 1888.

Family of WILLIAM O. HERR (6663) and EMMA E. EBY.

10302. Will Eby, Annville, Pa.

Family of ALBERT, HERR (6664) and KATE ULRICH.

10303. Clarence, Annville, Pa.
10304. Denver, Annville, Pa.
10305. Mabel, Annville, Pa.
10306. Nathan, Annville, Pa.
10307. Albert, Annville, Pa.

Family of LAVINA HERR (6669) and RUDOLPH GRAYBILL.

10308. John, Annville, Pa.

Family of DANIEL B. RASOR (6685) and LYDIA FETTER.

10309. Althea May, Englewood, O., b. June 9, 1874; d. Aug. 27, 1888.

Family of HENRY E. HERR (6688) and MARY C. LONG.

10310. Ernest S., Porter, Col. b. Mar. 8, 1883.
10311. Orlo P., Porter, Col., b. Sept. 21, 1884; d. ———, 1887.
10312. Marvin P., Porter, Col., b. Mar. 6, 1886; d. July 29, 1886.

Family of Wid. HENRY E. HERR (6688) and ALICE O'NEIL.

10313. John Maxwell, Porter, Col., b. Nov. 18, 1896.

Family of HIRAM HERR (6689) and ALICE KENDALL.

10314. Frances Nellie, Rico, Col., b. Apr. 19, 1895.

Family of SAMUEL E. HERR (6690) and ANNETTA HEWITT.

10315. Henry Hewitt, Durango, Col., b. Oct. 25, 1889; d. June 3, 1900.

Family of FRANCES HERR (6691) and ADAM HILKEY.

10316. Myrtle, Overbrook, Kans., b. Dec. 2, 1882.
10317. Walter F., Overbrook, Kans., b. Sept. 13, 1889.

Family of EDNA HERR (6704) and THEODORE F. SINKS.

10318. Edwin C., Salem, O., b. Oct. 21, 1877.
10319. Walter H., Salem, O., b. Sept. 5, 1883.

Family of DAVID HERR (6706) and EMMA MELLINGER.

10320. Harry S., Springfield, O., b. Apr. 15, 1894.
10321. Paul M., Springfield, O., b. Feb. 18, 1900; d. June 2, 1901.

Family of LAVINIA HERR (6707) and CALVIN E. KRUGER.

10322. Chester H., Dayton, O., b. Aug. 6, 1886.
10323. Lelia C., Dayton, O., b. Sept. 25, 1891.

Family of LEVI HERR (6708) and IVA C. ULLERY.

10324. Ohmer U., Englewood, O., b. Feb. 4, 1896.

Family of SUSAN HERR (6710) and SAMUEL LANDIS.

10325. Effie E., Trotwood, O., b. Jan. 27, 1882.

10326. Ira C., Trotwood, O., b. Dec., 1, 1884.
10327. David, Trotwood, O., b. Mar. 22, 1889.
10328. Jesse C., Trotwood, O., b. June 21, 1891.
10329. John N., Trotwood, O., b. June 19, 1895.
10330. Charles E., Trotwood, O., b. Apr. 12, 1898.

Family of ELLEN HERR (6711) and WILLIAM MUMMA.

10331. Charles C., Trotwood, O., b. Nov. 7, 1882.
10332. Mary M., Trotwood, O., b. Mar. 8, 1886.
10333. John W., Trotwood, O., b. Aug. 15, 1892.

Family of CHARLES E. HERR (6712) and ALICE B. LLOYD.

10334. Charles E., Durango, Col., b. Dec. 6, 1888.
10335. Howard Lloyd, Durango, Col., b. Sept. 19, 1899.

Family of ELIZABETH IRENE HERR (6742) and HENRY C. ROSS.

10336. David Herr, Harrisburg, Pa., b. Mar. 14, 1882; d. Feb. 11, 1898.
10337. James Spencer, Harrisburg, Pa., b. Oct. 15, 1893.
10338. Elizabeth, Harrisburg, Pa., b. Feb. 25, 1896.

Family of FANNIE MAY HERR (6745) and WILLIAM R. DENEHEY.

10339. Robert Herr, Harrisburg, Pa., b. Sept. 5, 1891.
10340. William Clark, Harrisburg, Pa., b. Feb. 4, 1894.
10341. Sarah, Harrisburg, Pa., b. Oct. 14, 1895.

Family of SUSAN HIKES (6746) and ANDREW LOW.

10342. Theodore, St. Matthews, Ky., d. Feb. 10, 1902.
10343. Florence, St. Matthews, Ky., m. Robert Dupuy.

Family of MARY HIKES (6747) and Dr. JOHN S. SEATON.

10344. Blanche, Louisville, Ky.
10345. Eliza, Louisville, Ky., m. ——— King.
10346. Crittenden, Louisville, Ky., m. Emma Carpenter.
10347. Curran L., Louisville, Ky., m. Carrie Kennedy.

Family of BARBARA HIKES (6748) and EMORY LOW.

10348. Emory, Louisville, Ky., b. Mar. 15, 1843; m. Nov. 18, 1896.
10349. Katie, Louisville, Ky., b. Feb. 1, 1847; d. Sept. 29, 1861.

Family of JOHN L. HIKES (6750) and MARTHA GLOVER.

10350. Annie, St. Matthews, Ky.
10351. Laura, St. Matthews, Ky.

Family of WILLIAM HERR (6755) and MARY SHANKLIN.

10352. James S., St. Matthews, Ky.

Family of FRANCES HERR (6757) and Dr. JOHN E. SUTCLIFFE.

10353. John Herr, Louisville, Ky., b. Apr. 13, 1859; m. Flora Bolling,
b. Apr. 8, 1871; dau. Dr. William H. Bolling and Ida Force.
10354. Sarah May, Louisville, Ky., b. Oct. 30, 1855; m. Oct. 30, 1876,
Robert Nelson Locke, b. Mar. 6, 1847; son Thomas E. Locke
and Lucy A. Nelson.
10355. Cora, Louisville, Ky., b. Jan. 5, 1853; m. Nov. 20, 1873,
Clarence A. Warren, b. Dec. 22, 1846; son Levi Legg Warren
and Mary Ann Wood.
10356. Edward Caldwell, Louisville, Ky.

Family of MARTHA W. HERR (6758) and GEORGE A. OWEN.

10357. Fannie, Louisville, Ky., b. July 18, 1856; m. Oct. 30, 1877,
Leander C. Woolfolk, b. May 27, 1843; son Thomas J. Woolfolk and Adaline Caldwell.

Family of HENRY CLAY HERR (6759) and MILDRED C. TAYLOR.

10358. Susan Mildred, Owensboro, Ky., m. Nov. 7, 1895, Dr. Daniel
M. Griffith, b. Sept. 19, 1867; son Daniel M. Griffith and
Virginia S. Todd.
10359. John G. Taylor, Owensboro, Ky.

Family of MARY EMMA HERR (6760) and JOSHUA B. PARKS.

10360. John, Chicago, Ill.

10361. Bettie, Chicago, Ill.

10362. Walter, Chicago, Ill.

10363. Cora, Chicago, Ill.

Family of ALBERT G. HERR (6761) and MARTHA E. GUTHRIE.

10364. Ada Guthrie, St. Louis, Mo., b. Oct. 15, 1865; d. Aug. 3, 1897.

10365. Fannie Belle, Louisville, Ky., b. Oct. 20, 1867; m. Apr. 15, 1891, Winfred Snook, d. ———, 1891.

10366. James Guthrie, St. Louis, Mo., b. Jan. 28, 1870; m. June 21, 1892, Fanny McClellan, b. Feb. —, 1871; dau. Robert M. McClellan and Fanny Taylor.

10367. Albert Gordon, Chicago, Ill., b. Aug. 3, 1873.

10368. George A. Owen, Louisville, Ky., b. Mar. 16, 1881; d. July 4, 1883.

10369. Aileene Marshall, Louisville, Ky., b. July 1, 1885.

Family of AMANDA HERR (6762) and JAMES SHANKLIN.

10370. John, Louisville, Ky., m. Sallie Wright.

10371. Jane Ellen, Louisville, Ky., m. James Wallace.

Family of SUSAN FRANCES HERR (6764) and GEORGE RUDY.

10372. M. Ellen, Louisville, Ky., m. Alvin Wood.

10373. Kate B., Louisville, Ky., m. Alfred Borie.

10374. James Herr, Owensboro, Ky., m. Sallie Magness.

10375. Fannie Herr, Rathbone, Oklahoma, b. May 11, 1850; m. George H. Simcoe, b. June 30, 1846; son Richard B. Simcoe and Maria B. Oldham.

10376. Frederick Oldham, St. Matthews, Ky., m. Ella Hubbard, dau. Thomas Hubbard and Lydia Rudy.

Family of ELLEN M. HERR (6765) and ALFRED J. FIELD.

10377. Frederick, St. Matthews, Ky., m. Caddie Gordon.

10378. Ella M., St. Matthews, Ky.

10379. Elizabeth, Lebanon, Ky., m. Thomas McElroy.

Family of JAMES M. HERR (6766) and NANCY A. TATE.

10380. Samuel, Owensboro, Ky., b. Nov. 28, 1865.

10381. Hugh, Owensboro, Ky., b. Mar. 22, 1875; m. Ellinor Holmes, dau. Col. James Holmes and ———.

10382. Frederick, Owensboro, Ky., b. Mar. 23, 1860; d. May 10, 1890; m. Anne McCreary, dau. Hon. T. C. McCreary and ———.

Family of GEORGE WARREN HERR (6767) and GEORGIE LANDRUM.

10383. Jennie, Louisville, Ky., b. Nov. 7, 1859; m. Nov. 22, 1876, Claudius Duvall, b. Oct. 22, 1849; son Claudius Duvall and Julia A. Mercer.

10384. Emma L., Chattanooga, Tenn., b. Aug. 6, 1861; m. John T. Howard.

10385. William E., Louisville, Ky., b. Mar. 4, 1863.

Family of Wid. GEORGE W. HERR (6767) and MOLLIE BROBSTON.

10386. George Frederick, Los Angeles, Cal., b. Sept. 8, 1870; m. Feb. 11, 1892, Mary E. Stewart.

10387. Lou Ella Mills, Lyndon, Ky., b. June 25, 1875; m. June 17, 1896, Covington A. Herr (10445).

10388. Ellen F., Covington, Ky., m. Charles D. Jefferson.

10389. Elizabeth, Lyndon, Ky.

Family of JOHN C. HERR (6768) and MOLLIE CLARKSON.

10390. Eula, St. Matthews, Ky., m. ——— Graham.

10391. Ione, St. Matthews, Ky., m. John Kitchen.

Family of SUSAN ELIZABETH HERR (6770) and HENRY A. FENLEY.

10392. George W., Henderson, Ky., b. Sept. 2, 1842; d. Dec. 12, 1866.

10393. Jeffries R., Henderson, Ky., b. Sept. 2, 1844; d. Dec. 27, 1864.

10394. Rebecca H., Waldon, Fla., b. Nov. 7, 1846; m. Apr. 19, 1867, Joseph McClellan, b. May 16, 1840; d. Nov. 14, 1877; son James McClellan and Jane Walker; m. Mar. 29, 1880, George E. Dane, b. Oct. 16, 1850; son John W. Dane and Caroline Lloyd.

10395. Infant, Louisville, Ky., b. ———, 1848; d. ———, 1848.

10396. Sarah A., Geneva, Ky., b. June 1, 1850; d. June —, 1889; m. April —, 1871, Robert H. Abbott, d. Feb. 8, 1899; son Dood Abbott and Ann Law.

10397. Susan P., Corydon, Ky., b. July 28, 1852; m. Apr. 30, 1872, Robert Thomas, b. Jan. 21, 1836; son Owen Thomas and Elizabeth Ashley.

Family of Wid. RICHARD S. HERR (6771) and JANE ORMSBY.

10398. Ormsby, Louisville, Ky., b. July 19, 1858; d. Oct. 2, 1865.

10399. George L., Louisville, Ky., b. Mar. 14, 1860; m. Addie B. Williams; m. Lillie Joyce.

Family of PRISCILLA HERR (6772) and JOHN C. RUDY.

10400. James S., St. Matthews, Ky.

10401. George, St. Matthews, Ky.

10402. Taylor, St. Matthews, Ky.

10403. Adelle, Lyndon, Ky., m. Benjamin F. Ewing.

Family of GEORGE WALKER HERR (6773) and LUCY SNEAD.

10404. Richard S., Louisville, Ky.

10405. Lizzie, Louisville, Ky., m. Robert Skillman.

10406. Cornelia, Louisville, Ky., m. Henry Gale.

Family of WILLIAM FREDERICK HERR (6774) and SUSAN E. ROSS

10407. Edward O., Louisville, Ky., b. Jan. 24, 1861; m. Aug. 17, 1886, Viola Coleman, b. Dec. 15, 1864; dau. John Coleman and Winnifred Mullany.

10408. Bettie, Louisville, Ky., b. July 15, 1862; d. Sept. 14, 1864.

Family of ROSETTA ANNIE HERR (6775) and HENRY C. ANDERSON.

10409. Harlan Herr, Louisville, Ky., b. Sept. 17, 1861; m. Nov. 14, 1889, Minnie B. Kent, b. Mar. 1, 1866; d. Apr. 12, 1899; dau. William S. Kent and Anna B. ——; m. June 12, 1901, Mildred Figg, b. Apr. 14, 1883; dau. George W. Figg and Priscilla

10410. Minnie S., Brooklyn, N. Y., b. May 22, 1866; m. Oct. 4, 1889, Edgar C. Bird, b. Dec. 4, 1864.

10411. Sally Herr, Louisville, Ky., b. Feb. 19, 1869.

10412. Henry Clay, Louisville, Ky., b. Oct. 22, 1872.

10413. Flora Schackelford, Louisville, Ky., b. Dec. 17, 1881.

Family of LEWIS TAYLOR HERR (6776) and ANNIE BROBSTON.

10414. Mary Sarah, St. Matthews, Ky., b. Sept. 14, 1874.

10415. Hattie C., St. Matthews, Ky., b. Feb. 21, 1876.

10416. Bessie Hite, St. Matthews, Ky., b. Dec. 1, 1877; m. Hamilton Frazer.

10417. Oliver, St. Matthews, Ky., b. July 16, 1879.

10418. Annie Adela, St. Matthews, Ky., b. July 12, 1881.

10419. George Brobston, St. Matthews, Ky., b. Sept. 26, 1885.

Family of JANE RUDY (6777) and GEORGE SHIVELY.

10420. George, Sedalia, Mo.

Family of CATHERINE RUDY (6779) and ———TUCKER.

10421. Ida, St. Matthews, Ky., m. John Williams.

10422. Sarah, St. Matthews, Ky., m. Wid. Norborne Arterburn (10430).

Family of ANNIE RUDY (6780) and LEWIS WASHBURN.

10423. Sarah, Louisville, Ky.

10424. Dulany, Louisville, Ky.

10425. Emma B., Louisville, Ky.

10426. George R., Louisville, Ky., b. June 15, 1860; m. Apr. 27, 1892, Mary Moore, dau. William Moore and Annie Thompson.

10427. Jennie, Louisville, Ky.

10428. Ellen, Louisville, Ky.

10429. Irene, Louisville, Ky.

Family of SARAH RUDY (6781) and CRAWFORD ARTERBURN.

10430. Norborne, St. Matthews, Ky., m. Susan Hall; m. Sally Tucker. dau. ——— Tucker and Kate Rudy.

10431. Kate, Louisville, Ky., m. James McBurnie.

Family of MADORA RUDY (6782) and JOHN RAFFERTY.

10432. George R., Nevada City, Mo.

10433. James, Nevada City, Mo.

10434. ———.

10435. ———.

10436. ———.

10437. ———.

10438. ———.

10439. ———.

Family of JOHN LEWIS HERR (6784) and SUSAN UTTINGER.

10440. Mary Bell, St. Matthews, Ky., b. Apr. 1, 1858; d. July 22, 1893; m. Mar. 30, 1876, Elam R. Simcoe, b. Oct. 31, 1845; d. Mar. 20, 1891; son Jeremiah Simcoe and Sarah Rudy.

10441. Alfred U., Louisville, Ky., b. Jan. 5, 1861; m. Oct. 18, 1882, Alice M. Osborn, b. Dec. 18, 1863; dau. William Osborn and Mildred I. Simcoe.

10442. William W., Louisville, Ky., b. Sept. 28, 1863; m. Oct. 8, 1884, Jennie R. Smith, b. Oct. 18, 1864; dau. Samuel Smith and ———.

10443. Lewis H., Lyndon, Ky., b. Nov. 1, 1866.

10444. Benson O., Lyndon, Ky., b. July 20, 1869; m. Sept. 11, 1901.

10445. Covington A., Lyndon, Ky., b. May 27, 1874; m. June 17, 1896, Lou Ella Herr (10387).

10446. Ninette, Lyndon, Ky., b. Jan. 21, 1877; m. Apr. 9, 1895, Alfred H. Hite (10452).

Family of WILLIAM WALLACE HERR (6785) and CATHERINE B. TODD.

10447. Hardin H., Louisville, Ky., b. Nov. 11, 1866.

10448. Robert Todd, Louisville, Ky., b. Apr. 24, 1868; d. July 24, 1869.

10449. John Shirley, Owensboro, Ky., b. Mar. 18, 1870.

10450. Mattie Todd, Louisville, Ky., b. Apr. 16, 1872; d. July 1, 1885.

10451. Willie Chenowith, Louisville, Ky., b. Apr. 7, 1875; d. July 19, 1875.

Family of JANE HELEN HERR (6786) and SAMUEL S. HITE.

10452. Alfred H., St. Matthews, Ky., b. Nov. 6, 1865; m. Apr. 9, 1895, Ninette Herr (10446).

10453. Robert W., St. Matthews, Ky., b. Sept. 30, 1868; m. Jan. 27, 1896, Bird Booker.

Family of ROBERT W. HERR (6787) and NINNINE ORMSBY.

10454. Hamilton O., St. Matthews, Ky., b. Apr. 3, 1880.

10455. Robert W., St. Matthews, Ky., b. Jan. 17, 1886.

Family of ELIZABETH R. ARTERBURN (6789) and THOMAS C. RICHARDS.

10456. Norbourne A., Crescent Hill, Ky., b. June 30, 1866; m. Jan. 27, 1893, Pattie L. Gill, b. Dec. 25, 1870; dau. James A. Gill and Margaret Johnson.

10457. William Thomas, Bisbee, Ariz., b. Mar. 19, 1869.

10458. Robert H., Louisville, Ky., b. Jan. 18, 1871; d. Aug. 11, 1878.

10459. Annie B., Louisville, Ky., b. Apr. 27, 1872; d. May 29, 1872.

Family of Wid. ELIZABETH R. RICHARDS (6789) and JOHN SHANKS.

10460. Harvey C., Louisville, Ky., b. Jan. 25, 1878.

10461. Eddie S. K., Louisville, Ky., b. Apr. 20, 1883.

Family of CLIFTON C. ARTERBURN (6795) and GEORGIA J. BELL.

10462. Albert, Yonkers, N. Y., b. Dec. 12, 1883.

10463. Anna Herr, Yonkers, N. Y., b. Sept. 17, 1885.

10464. Susan L., Yonkers, N. Y., b. Mar. 2, 1889.

10465. Bettie S., Yonkers, N. Y., b. Oct. 4, 1890.

10466. Thomas C., Yonkers, N. Y., b. May 24, 1892.

10467. Martha G., Yonkers, N. Y., b. Apr. 7, 1895.

10468. Mabel C., Yonkers, N. Y., b. June 17, 1898.

10469. Sarah, Yonkers, N. Y., b. Jan. 14, 1901.

Family of ELIZABETH FORNEY (6796) and Dr. JESSE GILBERT.

10470. Clara J., Gettysburg, Pa., b. Nov. 29, 1835; m. Nov. 5, 1856, Rev. David Swope, b. Dec. 25, 1824; d. Nov. 21, 1881; son Adam Swope and Lydia Spangler.

10471. Jessie Elizabeth, Washington, Ia., b. Feb. 17, 1838; d. ———,
1881; m. Nov. 23, 1865, Dr. Max Marburg, b. Aug. 1, 1838.

Family of Wid. ELIZABETH F. GILBERT (6796) and EDW. B. BUEHLER.

10472. Ella R., Hagerstown, Md., b. ———, 1853; m. Sept. 5, 1883,
Rev. Edwin H. Delk.

10473. Mary Caroline, Salisbury, N. C., b. Oct. 1, 1855; m. Nov. 27,
1878, Lewis H. Clement.

10474. Elizabeth, Washington, D. C., b. Nov. 1, 1857; m. Jan. 25,
1893, Louis D. Wine, b. ———, 1855; son Daniel Wine and
Sarah Darrell.

Family of HENRY S. FORNEY (6797) and MARIA C. BENSON.

10475. Samuel S., Baltimore, Md., b. Sept. 28, 1845; d. Aug. 18,
1861.

10476. Alice M., Towson, Md., b. Oct. 19, 1847.

10477. Julia T., Towson, Md., b. Aug. —, 1849; d. Sept. 27, 1883;
m. Oct. 10, 1882, Rev. Willard Troxell.

10478. Josephine R., Baltimore, Md., b. July 11, 1859; d. Mar. 18,
1862.

Family of MARY JANE FORNEY (6798) and JOHN C. BRIDGES.

10479. Helen J., Baltimore, Md., b. Sept. 16, 1841; m. Nov. 16, 1869,
Samuel D. Schumaker, son Rev. S. S. Schumaker and ———.

10480. Susan C., Baltimore, Md., b. Oct. 2, 1843; d. Dec. 22, 1844.

10481. John Patterson, Baltimore, Md., b. Feb. 24, 1846; d. ———,
1859.

10482. M. Julia, Philadelphia, Pa., b. June 17, 1848; m. Dec. 17,
1872, Prof. Samuel P. Satdler, b. July 18, 1847; son Rev.
Benjamin Satdler and ———.

10483. Frances V., Gettysburg, Pa., b. Nov. 15, 1850; m. July 10,
1876, Dr. A. Sargent Tinges, b. Apr. 25, 1850; d. Aug. 24,
1888; son ——— Tinges and Sarah White.

10484. Allen C., Gettysburg, Pa., b. Aug. 25, 1853.

10485. John S., Baltimore, Md., b. Dec. 4, 1856; m. June 4, 1879,
Mary E. Wills, dau. Hon. David Wills and ———.

Family of LOUISA A. FORNEY (6799) and HORACE RATHVON.

10486. Horace, Lancaster, Pa., b. June 6, 1843; d. June 3, 1853.

10487. Samuel F., Denver, Col., b. Mar. 7, 1845; m. June 11, 1868, Mary L. Rhine, b. ———, 1845; dau. Christian Rhine and Elizabeth Brenner; m. May 11, 1878, Emily H. Magraw, b. Sept. 15, 1853; dau. Henry S. Magraw and Emily W. Hopkins.

10488. Elizabeth, Lancaster, Pa., b. Jan. 31, 1847; d. Apr. 20, 1871.

10489. William R., Florence, Col., b. Dec. 31, 1854; m. Dec. 27, 1877, Elizabeth K. Stauffer, b. Nov. 8,1855; d. Oct. 19, 1880; dau. Martin B. Stauffer and Elizabeth C. Pfoutz; m. Apr. 20, 1883, Ella Stauffer, b. Jan. 15, 1863; dau. Martin B. Stauffer and Elizabeth C. Pfoutz.

Family of DAVID S. FORNEY (6801) and NANCY J. WARDEN.

10490. Daisy, Allisonia, Va., b. Nov. 5, 1880; d. Sept. 10, 1881.

10491. Elsie, Allisonia, Va., b. Aug. 5, 1882.

10492. Clara Mabel, Allisonia, Va., b. Nov. 23, 1884.

10493. Josephine R., Allisonia, Va., b. Mar. 21, 1886.

10494. Samuel Walker, Allisonia, Va., b. July 17, 1889.

Family of JOHN S. FORNEY (6802) and MARY SHRIVER.

10495. Louisa, Carlisle, Pa., m. George Lower.

10496. Susan Elizabeth, Gettysburg, Pa.

10497. David Julian, Gettysburg, Pa.

Family of ADELAIDE E. SWOPE (6806) and Dr. WILLIAM A. MATHIAS.

10498. Mary Josephine, Westminster, Md., b. Nov. 20, 1853; d. Mar. 18, 1887; m. Dr. Edward D. Wells.

10499. John Swope, Westminster, Md., b. Oct. 11, 1855; m. Sept. 26, 1878, Mary L. Lynch, b. Mar. 3, 1858.

10500. Agnes R., Westminster, Md., b. Sept. 27, 1857; d. Nov. —, 1872.

10501. Helen Louisa, Westminster, Md., b. Apr. 8, 1859; d. Feb. —, 1861.

10502. William A., Westminster, Md., b. Aug. 15, 1861; d. ———, 1861.

Family of ELIZABETH S. WANTZ (6810) and WILLIAM H. COCKEY.

10503. Infant, Lutherville, Md.

10504. Infant, Lutherville, Md.

Family of MARY J. WANTZ (6811) and EDWARD E. REINDOLLAR.

10505. Elizabeth Swope, Taneytown, Md., b. Aug. 26, 1876.

10506. Mary Henrietta, Taneytown, Md., b. Oct. 24, 1878; m. Jan. 30, 1898, Charles E. Yount, b. Apr. 15, 1878; son Francis M. Yount and Mary Sadler.

10507. Clarissa Amelia, Taneytown, Md., b. May 27, 1882.

10508. Josephine Eugene, Taneytown, Md., b. Oct. 8, 1886.

10509. Edward Eugene, Taneytown, Md., b. May 29, 1890.

10510. David Henry, Taneytown, Md., b. Nov. 24, 1897.

Family of ANTHA LETITIA KEEN (6812) and JOSEPH D. ECKLIN.

10511. Harry W., Liberty Square, Pa., b. Aug. 25, 1876; m. Dec. 20, 1899, Cora E. Houser, b. Mar. 8, 1878; dau. J. Franklin Houser and Sarah M. ———.

10512. Easley J., Liberty Square, Pa., b. Apr. 22, 1879.

10513. Ivy Belle, Liberty Square, Pa., b. Aug. 21, 1881.

10514. Martha Myrtle, Liberty Square, Pa., b. June 22, 1884; d. Oct. 3, 1884.

10515. David K., Liberty Square, Pa., b. Aug. 23, 1886; d. July 16, 1889.

10516. Joseph C., Liberty Square, Pa., b. Apr. 27, 1888.

Family of JOHN HENRY KEEN (6813) and ISABELLA ROCKEY.

10517. Clara, Ephrata, Pa.

10518. Essie, Ephrata, Pa.

10519. Charles, Ephrata, Pa.

10520. Letitia, Ephrata, Pa.

10521. Nettie, Ephrata, Pa.

10522. John, Ephrata, Pa.

Family of Wid. JOHN HENRY KEEN (6813) and ANNIE E. ECKMAN.

10523. Luella, Ephrata, Pa.

10524. Martin, Ephrata, Pa.
10525. Harry, Ephrata, Pa.
10526. Lillie, Ephrata, Pa.
10527. Anna M., Ephrata, Pa.

Family of ANNIE E. KEEN (6814) and MICHAEL FRITZ.

10528. Charles B., May, Pa.
10529. Martin D., May, Pa.
10530. Elsie K., May, Pa.
10531. Mary E., May Pa.

Family of MARTHA CATHERINE KEEN (6817) and DANIEL H. ECKMAN.

10532. Jacob Keen, Camargo, Pa., b. Jan. 1, 1879.
10533. Daniel Martin, Camargo, Pa., b. Apr. 7, 1882.
10534. Effie May, Camargo, Pa., b. Nov. 23, 1885.
10535. Bertha Maud, Camargo, Pa., b. July 8, 1888.
10536. Lottie Viola, Camargo, Pa., b. May 8, 1891.

Family of ADA SUE KEEN (6819) and CONRAD HESS.

10537. Anna M., New Danville, Pa., b. Oct. 28, 1883.
10338. Abraham M., New Danville, Pa., b. July 24, 1885.
10539. Alice May, New Danville, Pa., b. Oct. 10, 1886.
10540. Ada Mary, New Danville, Pa., b. May 14, 1888.
10541. David A., New Danville, Pa., b. June 17, 1889.
10542. Susie Naomi, New Danville, Pa., b. Oct. 27, 1890; d. May 2, 1892.
10543. Barbara V., New Danville, Pa., b. Feb. 4, 1892; d. Mar. 1, 1892.
10544. Martha Ann, New Danville, Pa., b. Mar. 30, 1893.
10545. Emma R., New Danville, Pa., b. Oct. 7, 1894.
10546. Ruth Elizabeth, New Danville, Pa., b. Dec. 13, 1895.
10547. John Ziegler, New Danville, Pa., b. Mar. 13, 1898.
10548. Beula Viola, New Danville, Pa., b. Aug. 12, 1899.
10549. Verna Pauline, New Danville, Pa., b. Aug. 3, 1901.

Family of EASLEY H. KEEN (6820) and M. ELLA IRWIN.

10550. Marvin, Christiana, Pa.

10551. Easley Arthur, Christiana, Pa.

10552. William Rollin, Christiana, Pa.

Family of EFFIE M. KEEN (6821) and GAREN GROFF.

10553. Ernest K., Mechanics Grove, Pa., b. Oct. 28, 1893.

10554. Martha M., Mechanics Grove, Pa., b. July 25, 1896.

10555. Fannie M., Mechanics Grove, Pa., b. June 4, 1900.

Family of SUSAN CATHERINE KEEN (6824) and WILLIAM D. HESS.

10556. Virgey Keen, Quarryville, Pa., b. May 6, 1880; m. Dec. 21, 1899, Alvin Hess.

10557. Adam Roy, Quarryville, Pa., b. June 22, 1883.

10558. Anna Catherine, Quarryville, Pa., b. Nov. 11, 1884.

10559. Odessa Maria, Quarryville, Pa., b. Aug. 7, 1886.

10560. Edith Adell, Quarryville, Pa., b. Jan. 28, 1888.

10561. William Jackson, Quarryville, Pa., b. Oct. 16, 1889.

10562. Ernest Lefever, Quarryville, Pa., b. Nov. 26, 1891.

10563. Mary Ruth, Quarryville, Pa., b. Nov. 17, 1893.

10564. Bertha May, Quarryville, Pa., b. Dec. 17, 1895.

10565. Frances Levina, Quarryville, Pa., b. Dec. 2, 1897.

Family of HARRY GRANT KEEN (6827) and FRANCES MYLIN.

10566. Lula, Lancaster, Pa.

10567. Mylin, Lancaster, Pa.

10568. Martha, Lancaster, Pa.

Family of MARY EMMA KEEN (6828) and GEORGE M. GREGG.

10569. Willard Keen, Quarryville, Pa., b. Dec. 18, 1890.

10570. Hannah Mary, Quarryville, Pa., b. Apr. 8, 1892.

10571. Blanche, Quarryville, Pa., b. Dec. 12, 1895.

10572. Grace Agnes, Quarryville, Pa., b. Sept. 26, 1897.

10573. George Harold, Quarryville, Pa., b. Oct. 12, 1899.

Family of HENRY BARR (6851) and ALICE JOHNSON.

10574. Mary Eva, Smyrna, Pa., b. Jan. 3, 1893.

10575. Ethel, Smyrna, Pa., b. Oct. 26, 1900.

Family of CAROLINE B. UHLER (6862) and WILLIAM E. CONDON.

10576. Edward, Denver, Col., b. Mar. 2, 1902.

Family of CHARLES ECKMAN (6867) and ROSA T. KERCHNER.

10577. John C., Lancaster, Pa., b. Apr. 25, 1883.

10578. Mary I., Lancaster, Pa., b. Jan. 17, 1885.

10579. Victor A., Lancaster, Pa., b. Aug. 25, 1887; d. ———, 1889.

Family of ESTELLA ECKMAN (6869) and LEWIS ECKMAN.

10580. Gertrude Elizabeth, New Providence, Pa., b. Jan. 19, 1896.

10581. Arthur Lloyd, New Providence, Pa., b. Apr. 14, 1897.

Family of DARIUS J. ECKMAN (6872) and ELLA DONER.

10582. Esther Creswell, Lancaster, Pa., b. July 31, 1898.

Family of ANNIE SOPHIA CRESWELL (6885) and WOODARD ALTHOUSE.

10583. Helen Elizabeth, Quarryville, Pa., b. Apr. 28, 1899.

Family of EDITH Z. JOHNSON (6890) and GEORGE SHARE.

10584. Pauline, Lancaster, Pa., b. Mar. 26, 1900.

10585. Dorothy, Lancaster, Pa., b. May 15, 1902.

Family of C. MAY JOHNSON (6891) and EDGAR A. ULMER.

10586. Allen Edgar, Lancaster, Pa., b. May 5, 1901.

10587. Lester, Lancaster, Pa., b. Feb. 25, 1903.

Family of BENJAMIN M. HERR (6909) and EMMA SHEAFFER.

10588. Jason A., Bareville, Pa., b. Oct. 10, 1885.

Family of JACOB M. HERR (6912) and ANNIE SHEAFFER.

10589. Willis, Bird-in-Hand, Pa., b. Sept. 9, 1887; d. Oct. 13, 1887.

Family of SAMUEL M. HERR (6914) and EMMA DENLINGER.

10590. Anna, Soudersburg, Pa., b. Dec. 7, 1889.
10591. Emma D., Soudersburg, Pa., b. Nov. 10, 1890.

Family of ABRAHAM M. HERR (6916) and ANNIE SHEAFFER.

10592. Noah S., Lampeter, Pa., b. Mar. 20, 1897.
10593. Enos S., Lampeter, Pa., b. Nov. 11, 1898.
10594. John Jacob, Lampeter, Pa., b. June 10, 1900.

Family of AMOS G. HERR (6917) and MARY A. KREIDER.

10595. Infant, Bird-in-Hand, Pa., b. Mar. 12, 1887; d. Mar. 12, 1887.
10596. Edith K., Bird-in-Hand, Pa., b. Feb. 2, 1888.
10597. Anna May, Bird-in-Hand, Pa., b. May 24, 1890.
10598. Edna Mary, Bird-in-Hand, Pa., b. Oct. 16, 1898.

Family of MARY L. HERR (6924) and CHRISTIAN B. NOLT.

10599. Ella Nora, New Holland, Pa., b. Oct. 7, 1889.
10600. Daughter, New Holland, Pa., b. Aug. 12, 1890; d. Aug. 14, 1890.
10601. Martin Landis, New Holland, Pa., b. Apr. 18, 1892.
10602. Jonas H., New Holland, Pa., b. Apr. 23, 1893; d. Apr. 16, 1895.
10603. Enos W., New Holland, Pa., b. May 30, 1897.
10604. Emma H., New Holland, Pa., b. Aug. 4, 1898; d. Aug. 14, 1898.
10605. Minnie H., New Holland, Pa., b. Sept. 17, 1901.

Family of MARY ELIZABETH KAUFFMAN (6938) and JOHN J. A. HOOVER.

10606. John Kauffman, Lancaster, Pa., b. ———, 1891.
10607. Harriet Josephine, Lancaster, Pa., b. ———, 1895.
10608. Henry Albert, Lancaster, Pa., b. ———, 1900.

Family of MILTON M. HERR (6940) and HARRIET MILLER.

10609. Helen, Akron, O., b. Jan. 23, 1898.

Family of WASHINGTON M. HERR (6942) and MARGARET R. POWELL.

10610. Anna May, Akron, O., b. Sept. 23, 1897.

Family of BARTON HERR (6943) and FLEDA GLEICK.

10611. George Henry, Warren, O., b. May 12, 1897; d. Aug. 15, 1897.
10612. Hazel Irene, Warren, O., b. Oct. 28, 1901.

Family of HENRY D. HERR (6944) and GERTRUDE B. MURPHY.

10613. Ruth Irene, Champion, O., b. Apr. 12, 1896.

Family of ALDUS B. HERR (6953) and ANNIE E. KAUFFMAN.

10614. Lottie, Millersville, Pa., b. Jan. 28, 1892; d. Jan. 29, 1892.

Family of ADA HERR (6957) and WILLIAM G. DRUMM.

10615. Edgar Hargrave, Latrobe, Pa., b. Dec. 25, 1899.
10616. Marian Orlando, Latrobe, Pa., b. Feb. 10, 1901.

Family of EMMA HERR (6958) and JACOB J. LEHR.

10617. Marian Elizabeth, Millersville, Pa., b. Sept. 8, 1894.
10618. Hilda Adaine, Millersville, Pa., b. Sept. 24, 1898.

Family of EMMA FRANCES HERR (6959) and JOHN B. ESHBACH.

10619. Christian H., Millersville, Pa., b. May 9, 1888.
10620. Edgar, Millersville, Pa., b. Apr. 17, 1890.
10621. Walter, Millersville, Pa., b. June 22, 1900; d. Mar. 22, 1901.

Family of MARY E. HERR (6960) and SAMUEL E. BRUBAKER.

10622. Lillie Herr, Lancaster, Pa., b. Apr. 24, 1889.
10623. Jacob, Bausman, Pa., b. Nov. 25, 1891.
10624. Clayton, Bausman, Pa., b. Nov. 25, 1896.

Family of CHRISTIAN K. HERR (6961) and FRANCES FORRY CHARLES.

10625. Mabel May, Millersville, Pa., b. May 25, 1891.
10626. Barbara Frances, Millersville, Pa., b. Dec. 29, 1892.
10627. Myrtle Charles, Millersville, Pa., b. Apr. 30, 1894.

Family of CHRISTIAN H. HERR (6966) and MARGARET E. DEITRICH.

10628. Lydia M., Intercourse, Pa., b. Aug. 22, 1895.

10629. Florence M., Intercourse, Pa., b. Mar. 9, 1896.

10630. Clara M., Intercourse, Pa., b. Feb. 13, 1900.

10631. Claude R., Intercourse, Pa., b. Oct. 31, 1901.

Family of DANIEL HERR FRANTZ (7000) and AMELIA DEITZ WELLER.

10633. Lauretta Weller, Lancaster, Pa., b. Apr. 1, 1893.

10634. Mary Elizabeth, Lancaster, Pa., b. May 12, 1895.

10635. Freddie McKinley, Lancaster, Pa., b. Feb. 13, 1897.

10636. Charles Franklin, Lancaster, Pa., b. Nov. 3, 1899.

Family of ELIZABETH H. FRANTZ (7002) and MARSHALL WM. WARREN.

10637. Raymond Marshall, Lancaster, Pa., b. Aug. 4, 1898.

10638. Robert Frantz, Lancaster, Pa., b. Oct. 16, 1899.

Family of ELIZABETH VIRGINIA BINKLEY (7007) and JOHN W. BUSH.

10639. Mary Rebecca, Lancaster, Pa., b. Oct. 4, 1900.

Family of MAUDE BINKLEY (7008) and WILLIAM S. BARNHOLT.

10640. Lawrence Lewis, Lancaster, Pa., b. Sept. 2, 1895.

10641. Mary Elizabeth, Lancaster, Pa., b. Dec. 28, 1896; d. May 6, 1897.

Family of LEVI ACKER STIRK (7022) and MINNIE HOFFMAN.

10642. Charles Edward, Allentown, Pa., b. Aug. 9, 1894.

10643. Miriam Amelia, Allentown, Pa., b. Apr. 28, 1896.

10644. Martha Elizabeth, Allentown, Pa., b. Aug. 30, 1901.

Family of IDA MARY PRATT (7027) and FRANK J. WOODWARD.

10645. Tacy Davis, Malvern, Pa., b. June 6, 1901.

Family of JONAS G. STEHMAN (7050) and ANNIE DONER.

10646. Clara Elva, York, Pa., b. Dec. 30, 1874; m. Dec. 28, 1898, Charles B. Pennypacker, b. Nov. 16, 1869; son John Y. Pennypacker and Martha G. Brady.

10647. Anna Estella, Mountville, Pa., b. July 26, 1876.

10648. John Doner, Mountville, Pa., b. Mar. 11, 1878.

10649. Elizabeth Lucretia, Mountville, Pa., b. June 24, 1881.
10650. Jonas Warren, Mountville, Pa., b. Oct. 13, 1887.

Family of Dr. HENRY B. STEHMAN (7051) and ELIZABETH MILLER.

10651. Elizabeth M., Pasedena, Cal., b. Sept. 5, 1882.
10652. John M., Pasedena, Cal., b. Feb. 6, 1886.
10653. Genevieve, Pasedena, Cal., b. Dec. 22, 1887.
10654. Henry, Pasedena, Cal., b. Dec. 21, 1893. .

Family of CHARLES S. HERR (7069) and LETTIE WALLER.

10655. Christian B., Safe Harbor, Pa., b. July 4, 1889.
10656. Benjamin F., Safe Harbor, Pa., b. Jan. 13, 1891.
10657. Maria Belle, Safe Harbor, Pa., b. Nov. 24, 1892.
10658. Joseph H., Safe Harbor, Pa., b. Aug. 23, 1894.
10659. Charles McK., Safe Harbor, Pa., b. Sept. 23, 1897.

Family of JOHN W. EMIG (7100) and MAUDE BOUGHTON.

10660. Eleanor B., Evanston, Ill., b. July 31, 1902.

Family of ALICE C. HERR (7235) and SIDNEY BELCHER.

10661. Emma Golda, Belton, Mo., b. Apr. 18, 1891.
10662. Sallie Gladys, Belton, Mo., b. Dec. 22, 1893.
10663. Lela Marie, Belton, Mo., b. Sept. 2, 1895.
10664. Sidney Forrest, Belton, Mo., b. June 4, 1897.
10665. Amy Lavena, Belton, Mo., b. Dec. 14, 1898.
10666. Ethel Pauline, Belton, Mo., b. Dec. 12, 1900.

Family of BENJAMIN B. HERR (7239) and FANNY B. LANDIS.

10667. Benjamin Russell, Kansas City, Mo., b. Sept. 25, 1901.

Family of HENRY M. BARTHOLOMEW (7254) and HANNAH MARY HUNTER.

10668. Elizabeth, Lancaster, Pa.
10669. Merritt, Lancaster, Pa.

Family of MARTHA LUETTA WEAVER (7274) and AMOS B. AHRENS.

10670. Anna Gurtena, Waverly, Ia., b. Feb. 28, 1894.

Family of FRANKLIN M. HERR (7293) and REBECCA ARMSTRONG.

10671. Dora E., Mt. Nebo, Pa., b. Apr. 9, 1882.
10672. Lloyd, Mt. Nebo, Pa., b. Oct. 18, 1884.
10673. John, Mt. Nebo, Pa., b. Aug. 29, 1887.
10674. Blanche, Mt. Nebo, Pa., b. Apr. 17, 1891.
10675. Amos, Mt. Nebo, Pa., b. Mar. 23, 1893.
10676. Mary, Mt. Nebo, Pa., b. Mar. 17, 1896.
10677. Esther, Mt. Nebo, Pa., b. Apr. 2, 1899.

Family of ELMER IRVING LEFEVER (7294) and LILLIAN ALLISON WELSH.

10678. Robert Franklin, Coatesville, Pa., b. Nov. 1, 1903.

Family of ACTON LEFEVER (7295) and EMMA WETTIG.

10679. Helen Katherine, Lancaster, Pa.
10680. Adeline, Lancaster, Pa.
10681. Acton Ash, Jr., Lancaster, Pa., b. July 19, 1903.

Family of ELIZABETH ANN ROBINSON (7383) and WILLIAM McK. JETER.

10682. James Henry, Bloomington, Ill., b. Feb. 1, 1866; m. Emma Katie Hoffman.
10683. Cora Lee, Mt. Vernon, Ill., b. May 18, 1870; m. Nov. 21, 1888, William Albert Porch.
10684. Charles Franklin, Welsh, La., b. Mar. 10, 1872; m. Feb. 1, 1894, Flora J. Swartsly.
10685. John Raymond, Roanoke, Ill., b. Oct. 10, 1873.
10686. Walter McKendree, Lacon, Ill., b. Apr. 6, 1876; m. Nov. —, 1902, Maud S. Shreve.
10687. Mamie Belle, Roanoke, Ill., b. Mar. 23, 1880.
10688. Robert Hammond, Roanoke, Ill., b. Apr. 2, 1882; m. Oct. 5, 1903, Mabel Shermer.

Family of BARBARA ELLEN FAUBER (7395) and EDWARD M. COX.

10689. Minnie Winfield, Roanoke, Ill., b. Oct. 8, 1881.
10690. Arleigh David, Roanoke, Ill., b. Sept. 17, 1886.
10691. Letta Dell, Roanoke, Ill., b. Oct. 14, 1889.

25

Family of **MARY K. FAUBER** (7396) and **SAMUEL M. BULLINGTON.**

10692. Pearl Edith, Sibley, Ia., b. July 29, 1879; d. Feb. 4, 1881.

10693. Olive Elsie, Sibley, Ia., b. Dec. 28, 1881; m. Jan. 11, 1901, Alfred Hall.

10694. Minnie Ann, Sibley, Ia., b. Dec. 5, 1883; m. Dec. 13, 1901, Lewis Argubright.

10695. Elvena Gem, Sibley, Ia., b. May 22, 1885.

10696. Verna Rozella, Sibley, Ia., b. Mar. 7, 1889.

10697. Estella Mae, Sibley, Ia., b. Apr. 11, 1892.

10698. Edna Bernice, Sibley, Ia., b. Apr. 18, 1894.

10699. Oma Gladys, Sibley, Ia., b. Nov. 28, 1898.

Family of **VIRGINIA MARGARET FAUBER** (7397) and **JOHN W. HEPPARD.**

10700. David Clarence, Roanoke, Ill., b. Mar. 17, 1879.

10701. Prosper D., Roanoke, Ill., b. Apr. 24, 1885.

10702. Progress, Roanoke, Ill., b. Feb. 26, 1887.

10703. Zelda M., Roanoke, Ill., b. Nov. 17, 1889; d. June 3, 1893.

Family of **JAMES WILLIAM FAUBER** (7398) and **MINNIE C. PETERSON.**

10704. William Ray, Roanoke, Ill., b. July 24, 1889.

10705. Hazel Blanche, Roanoke, Ill., b. Oct. 22, 1890.

10706. Frank Cleveland, Roanoke, Ill., b. Sept. 2, 1892.

10707. Edna Pearl, Roanoke, Ill., b. Dec. 25, 1894.

10708. Burtrall Glen, Roanoke, Ill., b. Aug. 6, 1896.

10709. Virginia Alice, Roanoke, Ill., b. July 21, 1898.

10710. Burl Herman, Roanoke, Ill., b. Sept. 23, 1900.

10711. Minnie Lee, Roanoke, Ill., b. Feb. 13, 1903.

Family of **ELIZA ALICE FAUBER** (7399) and **JOSEPH S. RISSER.**

10712. Lester Lyman, Roanoke, Ill., b. Oct. 21, 1889.

10713. Sybil Evangeline, Roanoke, Ill., b. Sept. 27, 1891.

Family of **HENRY H. BAER** (7419) and **SUSAN L. HORST.**

10714. Mary, Hagerstown, Md., b. Oct. 16, 1875.

10715. Anna, Hagerstown, Md., b. Apr. 8, 1877.

10716. Abraham, Hagerstown, Md., b. Aug. 7, 1879.

10717. Susan, Hagerstown, Md., b. Mar. 23, 1881.

10718. Amanda, Hagerstown, Md., b. Aug. 27, 1882.

Fomily of Wid. HENRY H. BAER (7419) and Wid. BARBARA M. RISSER.

10719. Henry M., Hagerstown, Md., b. June 22, 1886.

10720. Adam, Reid, Md., b. Feb. 2, 1890.

10721. Isaac, Hagerstown, Md., b. May 30, 1892.

10722. Leah, Hagerstown, Md., b. Oct. 24, 1893.

10723. Elizabeth, Hagerstown, Md., b. Jan. 28, 1896.

10724. Benjamin, Hagerstown, Md., b. Nov. 24, 1898.

10725. Martha, Hagerstown, Md., b. Jan. 6, 1902.

Family of MARIA BAER (7420) and JACOB W. ESHLEMAN.

10726. Emma B., Reid, Md., b. Nov. 30, 1879; m. Levi H. Martin, b. Nov. 25, 1877; son John W. Martin and Amanda L. Horst.

10727. Adam B., Reid, Md., b. Aug. 1, 1881; m. Aug. 16, 1900, Nettie Grove.

10728. Fanny, Reid, Md., b. Dec. 4, 1884.

10729. Jonas, Hagerstown, Md., b. May 1, 1891; d. Oct. 7, 1893.

Family of MARTIN H. BAER (7421) and ANNA BARBARA BRACKBILL (8688).

10730. Infant, Menges Mills, Pa,, b. Mar. 27, 1886; d. Mar. 31, 1886.

10731. Mary, Menges Mills., Pa., b. July 25, 1889.

10732. Harry, Menges Mills, Pa., b. June 17, 1891.

10733. Hannah, Menges Mills, Pa., b. Dec. 28, 1895.

Family of ELIZABETH HERR (8310) and HENRY H. SHENK (7434).

10734. Emma H., Lancaster, Pa., b. July 20, 1891.

Family of ANNA H. SHENK (7435) and JACOB B. HARNISH.

10735. Lizzie S., New Danville, Pa., b. Feb. 7, 1885.

10736. Franklin S., New Danville, Pa., b. May 27, 1888.

10737. Olive Anna, New Danville, Pa., b. Sept. 4, 1892.

Family of MARTIN H. SHENK (7437) and MARY BOMBERGER.

10738. Samuel B., New Danville, Pa., b. Feb. 7, 1897.

Family of SUSAN S. HERR (7447) and HARRY L. HERR (8329).

10739. Emma Vera, New Danville, Pa., b. Apr. 13, 1898.
10740. Harry Elvin, New Danville, Pa., b. Sept. 26, 1899.

Family of EVA HERR (7460) and MICHAEL S. CRALEY.

10741. Frank, Cleveland, O., b. Nov. 24, 1883.
10742. Rea, Cleveland, O., b. Aug. 19, 1885.
10743. Carrie, Cleveland, O., b. Aug. 18, 1887.
10744. Rodger, Cleveland, O., b. Apr. 7, 1890.
10745. Yvonne, Cleveland, O., b. Feb. 15, 1896.
10746. Arline, Cleveland, O., b. Nov. 6, 1899.

Family of ALICE HERR (7461) and HERMAN R. WEAVER.

10747. Louise Melissa, Everette, Ill., b. Sept. 16, 1898.

Family of GEORGE ALBERT REEVE (7469) and ANNETTA L. BOLTON.

10748. Harold A., Tipton, Ia.
10749. Ralph L., Tipton, Ia.
10750. Raymond D., Tipton, Ia.
10751. Cecil V., Tipton, Ia.
10752. Mary G., Tipton, Ia.
10753. Donald, Tipton, Ia.

Family of Wid. FRANCIS W. REEVE (7470) and ARMINTA A. OWEN.

10754. Edna, Tipton, Ia., b. July 20, 1900.
10755. Clarence Okley, Tipton, Ia., b. Sept. 5, 1903.
10756. Lawrence Owen, Tipton, Ia., b. Sept. 5, 1903.

Family of FRANCES L. REEVE (7471) and CHARLES K. PIERCE.

10757. Hazel Reeve, Tipton, Ia., b. Dec. 3, 1892; d. Apr. 12, 1893.
10758. Floyd Verne, Tipton, Ia., b. Nov. 6, 1893.
10759. Mary Gladys, Tipton, Ia., b. July 22, 1897.

10760. Bertha May, Tipton, Ia., b. July 5, 1899.

10761. Bernice Rae, Tipton, Ia., b. July 5, 1899.

10762. Harry Marion, Tipton, Ia., b. Aug. 12, 1900.

Family of MARY SUSAN REEVE (7472) and HOMER MORTON.

10763. Homer Edwin, West Branch, Ia., b. Oct. —, 1898.

Family of JAMES MARION REEVE (7473) and LOLA KEMP.

10764. Hazel Catherine, Tipton, Ia., b. Oct. —, 1892.

Family of MINNIE MAY HERR (7476) and OILY STUTLER.

10765. Howard, Wilton Junction, Ia., b. Oct. 14, 1890.

10766. Fay, Wilton Junction, Ia., b. Jan. 21, 1893.

10767. Wallace, Wilton Junction, Ia., b. Mar. 4, 1901.

Family of JESSIE BELLE HERR (7477) and CLIFFORD COVELL.

10768. Norma G., Muscatine, Ia., b. May 28, 1901.

10769. Dorris G., Muscatine, Ia., b. June 17, 1902.

Family of MARY KATHERINE NAUMAN (7499) and CHARLES SIDDENS.

10770. Jesse, Afton, Ia., b. Apr. 3, 1899.

Family of JOHN B. KENDIG (7513) and ELIZABETH BRILL.

10771. Letitia E., Lancaster, Pa., b. Aug. 10, 1882.

10772. Daisy M., Lancaster, Pa., b. Nov. 4, 1884.

10773. Katherine Mabel, Lancaster, Pa., b. July 16, 1886; d. Feb. 24, 1890.

10774. Lily Belle, Lancaster, Pa., b. Apr. 2, 1888; d. Feb. 9, 1892.

10775. John Martin, Lancaster, Pa., b. Dec. 27, 1889; d. Feb. 12, 1892.

10776. Walter B., Lancaster, Pa., b. Sept. 22, 1891.

10777. Esther E., Lancaster, Pa., b. Nov. 5, 1897.

Family of JOHN BACHMAN WEAVER (7521) and MARY MORROW.

10778. Eva M., Gordonville, Pa., b. July 16, 1889.

Family of MARTHA JANE WEAVER (7522) and PHILIP HOTTENSTEIN.

10779. Emma May, Greensburg, Pa., b. Aug. 27, 1878; m. Charles Fisher.
10780. Anna, Lampeter, Pa., b. Jan. 18, 1880; m. Christian Snyder.

Family of FRANCES ANN STONER (7529) and CHARLES H. GEIGER.

10781. Anna Beates, Refton, Pa., b. Jan. 17, 1877; m. Apr. 10, 1902, Hervey E. Shertz, b. Oct. 30, 1872; son Hervey Shertz and Barbara Bachman.
10782. John Bachman, Philadelphia, Pa., b. Oct. 31, 1878.
10783. Laura Stoner, Quarryville, Pa., b. Sept. 6, 1880.
10784. Helen, Quarryville, Pa., b. Nov. 5, 1882.
10785. Mary, Quarryville, Pa., b. Jan. 31, 1887.
10786. Charles Henry, Quarryville, Pa., b. July 26, 1889; d. Sept. 21, 1895.
10787. Frances Stoner, Quarryville, Pa., b. July 9, 1897.

Family of EDITH WEAVER (7551) and WILLIAM WEIGAND.

10788. Zetta M., Lancaster, Pa., b. Jan. 16, 1892.
10789. Helen E., Lancaster, Pa., b. Mar. 14, 1894.
10790. Harold H., Lancaster, Pa., b. Dec. 1, 1896.
10791. Benjamin M., Lancaster, Pa., b. Aug. 24, 1899.

Family of BENJAMIN FRANCIS HERR (7553) and CELIA MAY JESSUP.

10792. Sylvia Galelta, Macksburg, Ia., b. Dec. 25, 1886.

Family of Wid. BENJAMIN FRANCIS HERR (7553) and ANNIE B. ST. JOHN.

10793. Thelma B., Harrisonville, Mo., b. Feb. 8, 1898.
10794. Throla V., Harrisonville, Mo., b. June 11, 1900.
10795. John Dar, Harrisonville, Mo., b. Oct. 22, 1901.

Family of MARIA ADELE HERR (7554) and WILLIAM HENRY ROWE.

10796. Dessie Vey, Macksburg, Ia., b. May 10, 1887.
10797. Francis Neal, Macksburg, Ia., b. Oct. 4, 1889.
10798. Maurice Dayton, Macksburg, Ia., b. Nov. 8, 1898.

10799. Theron Dale, Macksburg, Ia., b. Feb. 26, 1901 ; d. Mar. 12, 1901.

Family of ANNIE EVA HERR (7555) and BURTON L. TOWNSEND.

10800. Dee Evaline, Macksburg, Ia., b. Jan. 11, 1895.
10801. Bessie M., Macksburg, Ia., b. Mar. 18, 1897.

Family of FRANCES HERR (7557) and EDWARD WELLS.

10802. Ralph, Downey, Ia., b. Oct. 24, 1887.

Family of GEORGE HERR (7558) and HATTIE VENY.

10803. Verma, West Liberty, Ia., b. Mar. 8, 1896.
10804. Clifford, West Liberty, Ia., b. Jan. 27, 1898.

Family of FRANCES MAY HERR (7576) and JOSEPH P. FRANCIS.

10805. Joseph Philip, Bozeman, Mont., b. May 12, 1895.
10806. Everett, Bozeman, Mont., b. Mar. 3, 1902.

Family of AMOS DAILEY HERR (7578) and LIBBIE BRADFORD.

10807. Harry D., Letcher, Cal., b. July 22, 1901.

Family of MAGGIE MAY HERR (7580) and WILLIAM A. MERRYMAN.

10808. Louis, Bozeman, Mont.

Family of NAOMI HART (7584) and WILLIAM E. McFALLS.

10809. Charles, Willow Street, Pa., b. June 13, 1887.
10810. Florence, Willow Street, Pa., b. Sept. 12, 1888.
10811. Ira, Willow Street, Pa., b. Sept. 5, 1890.
10812. Elsie, Willow Street, Pa., b. May 15, 1892.
10813. Stella, Willow Street, Pa., b. Jan. 17, 1894.
10814. Nora, Willow Street, Pa., b. Apr. 14, 1895.
10815. Hattie, Willow Street, Pa., b. Feb. 10, 1900.
10816. John, Willow Street, Pa., b. June 7, 1901.

Family of MARY ELIZ. MORTON (7598) and SAMUEL S. BRENBERGER.

10819. John, Lime Valley, Pa.

Family of **WILLIAM ELMER MORTON** (7599) and **EMMA B. EAGER** (7814).

10820. John Allen, Lancaster, Pa., b. Jan. 7, 1902.

Family of **MELVIN HERR** (7616) and **CAROLINE NICHOLS.**

10821. Carrie, Camden, N. J., b. Apr. 27, 1892.
10822. Marion, Camden, N. J., b. Nov. 1, 1894.
10823. Isabella, Camden, N. J., b. June 3, 1896; d. Aug. 8, 1896.

Family of **CARRIE A. HERR** (7618) and **SAMUEL LYTE.**

10824. Ethel, Safe Harbor, Pa., b. July 20, 1890; d. July 23, 1890.
10825. Minnie Gertrude, Safe Harbor, Pa., b. Aug. 15, 1891.
10826. Glerma O., Safe Harbor, Pa., b. Jan. 11, 1894.

Family of **DAVID A. HERR** (7620) and **AMELIA F. RINEER.**

10827. Gladys Olivette, Safe Harbor, Pa., b. Aug. 11, 1896.
10828. Dorothy Geraldine, Safe Harbor, Pa., b. Nov. 16, 1899.

Family of **ELIZABETH H. SNAVELY** (7623) and **MARTIN MYERS** (7442).

10829. Mervin S., West Willow, Pa., b. Apr. 29, 1895.
10830. Arthur S., West Willow, Pa., b. Apr. 30, 1896.
10831. Anna Elizabeth, West Willow, Pa., b. Jan. 28, 1898.
10832. Maud H., West Willow, Pa., b. Sept. 8, 1899.

Family of **IDA FRANCES SNAVELY** (7625) and **IRA B. GRAYBILL.**

10833. Edwin B., Lancaster, Pa., b. Sept. 27, 1901.
10834. Robert, Lancaster, Pa.

Family of **AMOS H. SNAVELY** (7626) and **ELIZABETH R. HERR** (7454).

10835. Anna H., Lancaster, Pa., b. Mar. 2, 1902.

Family of **ALBERT F. HERR** (7629) and **ELIZABETH K. HARTING.**

10836. Infant, Wheatland Mills, Pa., b. July 22, 1886; d. July 27, 1886.
10837. Eliza Maria, Wheatland Mills, Pa., b. Oct. 10, 1887.
10838. Fanny Matilda, Wheatland Mills, Pa., b. Sept. 23, 1889.

10839. May Myrtle, Wheatland Mills, Pa., b. Apr. 24, 1893.
10840. Edwin Franklin, Wheatland Mills, Pa., b. Nov. 22, 1896.
10841. Infant, Wheatland Mills, Pa., b. July 8, 1901.

Family of EDITH E. MUSSER (7652) and JAY BACHMAN.

10842. Harry M., Lampeter, Pa., b. Nov. 3, 1899.
10843. John, Lampeter, Pa., b. Dec. 9, 1901.

Family of WILL M. MUSSER (7653) and BERTHA C. ESHLEMAN (9234).

10844. John Henry, Lampeter, Pa., b. Aug. 10, 1899.
10845. Robert B., Lampeter, Pa., b. July 29, 1902.

Family of ELIZABETH HERR ZARRACHER (7667) and JAMES F. HETLER.

10846. Annie Gertrude, Hillsboro, North Dakota, b. Mar. 23, 1901.

Family of ALDUS ECKMAN (7677) and JULIA LITZEL.

10847. Aldus A., Water Valley, Miss., b. July 17, 1878.
10848. Eugene, Water Valley, Miss.
10849. Julia, Water Valley, Miss.
10850. Arthur, Water Valley, Miss.
10851. Mabel, Water Valley, Miss.
10852. Ferol, Water Valley, Miss.
10853. August, Water Valley, Miss.
10854. William, Water Valley, Miss.
10855. Lena Bell, Water Valley, Miss.
10856. Henry, Water Valley, Miss.
10857. Mata, Water Valley, Miss.

Family of HENRY ECKMAN (7678) and MARY PRIES.

10858. May Edna, Lancaster, Pa., b. Aug. 23, 1880.
10859. Guy Henry, Lancaster, Pa., b. Mar. 31, 1885.

Family of JOHN ECKMAN (7680) and LETITIA MARY HELM.

10860. Harry John, Lancaster, Pa., b. Jan. 3, 1882.

Family of JACOB ECKMAN (7681) and ANNA M. WICKLE.

10861. Laura S., Lancaster, Pa., b. Apr. 12, 1887; d. Sept. 13, 1897.

10862. Eva, Lancaster, Pa., b. Nov. 2, 1888.

Family of MARY ECKMAN (7682) and GEORGE W. BANZHOFF.

10863. Infant, Lancaster, Pa., b. Dec. 9, 1879; d. Dec. 9, 1879.

10864. Bertha May, Lancaster, Pa., b. Apr. 6, 1881.

10865. Charles Augustus, Lancaster, Pa., b. Mar. 26, 1885.

10866. George Washington, Lancaster, Pa., b. Nov. 20, 1887.

10867. Henry, Lancaster, Pa., b. Feb. 14, 1889; d. Nov. 16, 1895.

Family of FELIX BINKLEY (7689) and ———.

10868. Aramantha, East Canton, O.

10869. Minnie, Osnaburg, O., m. ——— Ake.

Family of SARAH L. BYERLY (7690) and JOHN W. HUBLEY.

10870. Grace E., Lancaster, Pa., b. Apr. 10, ———; d. Apr. 19, ———.

Family of MARTHA A. BYERLY (7691) and ALONZO R. POISEL.

10871. Ray Byerly, Lancaster, Pa., b. Nov. 3, 1884.

10972. Marie Alice, Lancaster, Pa., b. May 30, 1887.

10873. Grace Hubley, Lancaster, Pa., b. Apr. 12, 1892; d. July 12, 1892.

Family of GEORGE W. BYERLY (7694) and MARY E. PONTZ.

10874. Jacob Pontz, Lancaster, Pa., b. Sept. 16, 1888.

10875. George Robert, Lancaster, Pa., b. Sept. 8, 1890.

10876. Norman Ethelbert, Lancaster, Pa., b. Mar. 7, 1897.

Family of GEORGE MARTIN DRUMM (7703) and FRANCES HERR SHEIRICK.

10877. John Milton, Mercersburg, Pa., b. Mar. 29, 1873.

10878. Ellenora S., Mountville, Pa., b. Jan. 26, 1875.

10879. Ida S., Mountville, Pa., b. Sept. 27, 1877.

10880. Elizabeth S., Mountville, Pa., b. Oct. 16, 1880; m. Apr. 30, 1908, Rudolph S. Herr.

10881. Katherine, Mountville, Pa., b. Dec. 1, 1885.

Family of MARTHA JANE DRUMM (7704) and DANIEL KREIDER.

10882. Samuel H., Rawlinsville, Pa., b. Dec. 1, 1876.
10883. George M., Rawlinsville, Pa., b. Oct. 16, 1878.
10884. Wilmer A., Rawlinsville, Pa., b. Feb. 16, 1880.
10885. Lillie F., Rawlinsville, Pa., b. Sept. 26, 1881.
10886. Daniel P., Rawlinsville, Pa., b. Aug. 31, 1883.
10887. Charles G., Rawlinsville, Pa., b. Feb. 8, 1885.
10888. John M., Rawlinsville, Pa., b. May 16, 1887.

Family of JOHN M. DRUMM (7706) and SARAH ANN ARMSTRONG.

10889. Irene, Mt. Nebo. Pa., b. May 6, 1880.
10890. George W., Mt. Nebo, Pa., b. Mar. 28, 1882.
10891. Mary Olivia, Mt. Nebo. Pa., b. Sept. 14, 1884.
10892. Catherine E., Mt. Nebo, Pa., b. Oct. 14, 1886.
10893. Jay Raymond, Mt. Nebo, Pa., b. May 20, 1889.
10894. Lester A., Mt. Nebo, Pa., b. Feb. 12, 1892.
10895. Myrtle E., Mt. Nebo, Pa., b. May 20, 1894.

Family of PETER CARTRIGHT DRUMM (7707) and JANE JENKINS.

10896. Leigh V., Rawlinsville, Pa., b. Dec. 31, 1897.
10897. Elnora A., Rawlinsville, Pa., b. Dec. 12, 1899.
10898. Ruth, Rawlinsville, Pa., b. Oct. 13, 1902.

Family of FRANCES ELLENORA DRUMM (7708) and JACOB O. HART.

10899. Katie May, Corwin, Pa., b. Apr. 27, 1882.
10900. Susie Ethel, Corwin, Pa., b. Dec. 14, 1883.
10901. Bessie Reba, Corwin, Pa., b. Apr. 8, 1886.
10902. Bertha Auba, Corwin, Pa., b. Oct. 13, 1889.

Family of SAMUEL G. DRUMM (7709) and ANNIE DUNKEL.

10903. George W., Rawlinsville, Pa., b. Jan. 1, 1890.
10904. Ethel, Rawlinsville, Pa., b. June 16, 1895.
10905. Ira, Rawlinsville, Pa., b. Apr. 28, 1898.

Family of ANNIE HACKMAN (7713) and HENRY DOUTS.

10906. Mary E., Mt. Nebo, Pa., b. Jan. 9, 1881.

10907. George E., Mt. Nebo, Pa., b. Nov. 3, 1882.
10908. John R., Mt. Nebo, Pa., b. Oct. 16, 1884.
10909. William C., Mt. Nebo, Pa., b. Sept. 8, 1886.
10910. Benjamin H., Mt. Nebo, Pa., b. July 27, 1888.
10911. Emerson, Mt. Nebo, Pa., b. June 20, 1890.
10912. Walter F., Mt. Nebo, Pa., b. Sept. 16, 1892.
10913. Katie M., Mt. Nebo, Pa., b. Oct. 16, 1894.
10914. Ella M., Mt. Nebo, Pa., b. Apr. 20, 1896.
10915. Charles D., Mt. Nebo, Pa., b. Nov. 24, 1898.

Family of HANNAH HACKMAN (7714) and ALBERTIS HART.

10916. Walter, Colemanville, Pa.
10917. Jessie, Colemanville, Pa.
10918. Clyde, Colemanville, Pa.
10919. Lena, Colemanville, Pa.
10920. Edgar, Colemanville, Pa.
10921. Ruth, Colemanville, Pa.

Family of ELIZABETH HACKMAN (7715) and GEORGE HICKEY.

10922. Dora M., Mt. Nebo, Pa., b. Jan. 10, 1883; d. Dec. 3, 1889.
10923. Oretta M., Mt. Nebo, Pa., b. Dec. 11, 1884.
10924. Walter F., Mt. Nebo, Pa., b. Jan. 25, 1886; d. Oct. 6, 1900.
10925. Charles H., Mt. Nebo, Pa., b. Aug. 14, 1888.
10926. Ella R., Mt. Nebo, Pa., b. Oct. 27, 1891.
10927. George C., Mt. Nebo, Pa., b. Aug. 29, 1895.
10928. Katie E., Mt. Nebo, Pa., b. July 1, 1898.
10929. Infant, Mt. Nebo, Pa.

Family of FANNY LEFEVER (7726) and JACOB FELLENBAUM.

10930. Miller, Smithville, Pa., b. Feb. 8, 1876.
10931. Martin L., Smithville, Pa., b. Nov. 17, 1877.
10932. William B., Smithville, Pa., b. Dec. 1, 1879.

Family of Wid. FANNY FELLENBAUM (7726) and JAMES M. CLARK.

10933. Anna V., Smithville, Pa., b. Mar. 4, 1885.

10934. Edward S., Smithville, Pa., b. Aug. 10, 1888.

10935. Robert, Smithville, Pa., b. Feb. 14, 1892.

10936. Mary E., Smithville, Pa., b. Oct. 19, 1893.

10937. Thaddeus J., Smithville, Pa., b. Jan. 15, 1896.

10938. Lilly R., Smithville, Pa., b. Mar. 25, 1899.

Family of Dr. HOWARD H. HOPKINS (7750) and MARGARET M. DOWNEY.

10939. Mary McConkey, New Market, Md., b. Sept. 8, 1870.

10940. Dr. William Downey, Mt. Airy, Md., b. Apr. 27, 1873.

10941. Dr. Howard Hanford, New Market, Md., b. Dec. 21, 1875; m. Apr. 10, 1901, Alice E. Wood, b. Apr. 6, 1877; dau. Newton Wood and Anna M. Griffith.

10942. Margaret Downey, New Market, Md., b. Apr. 24, 1879.

10943. Catherine Withers, New Market, Md., b. Mar. 27, 1881, d. Mar. 27, 1881.

10944. James Stephenson, Bel Air, Md., b. Mar. 20, 1884.

Family of EMLEN A. FRANKLIN (7753) and CHRISTIAN PFLUM.

10945. Clara Anne, Denver, Col., b. Dec. 20, 1885.

10946. Emlen, Denver, Col., b. Sept. 28, 1887.

Family of Wid. EMLEN A. FRANKLIN (7753) and NOMA CAINS.

10947. Walter, Denver, Col., b. Feb. 1, 1896.

Family of MARY WITHERS (7755) and HORACE EVANS.

10948. Louis Withers, Pottstown, Pa., b. Sept. 27, 1880.

10949. George Withers, Pottstown, Pa., b. May 14, 1884.

Family of JESSIE AMANDA LONGENECKER (7766) and JOHN F. BOWMAN.

10950. Anna L., Lancaster, Pa., b. Apr. 6, 1892.

10951. Ethel M., Lancaster, Pa., b. Aug. 30, 1893.

10952. Ruby M., Lancaster, Pa., b. Dec. 11, 1894.

10953. Verna B., Lancaster, Pa., b. Dec. 29, 1896.

10954. Mary L., Lancaster, Pa., b. Oct. 19, 1898.

Family of BERTHA LONGENECKER (7767) and Dr. S—— D. SOUR.

10955. Daughter, Mountain Lake, Minn., b. Aug. 30, 1893.

Family of SUSANNA FRAELICH (7774) and GEORGE ARMENT.

10956. Harry, Greenland, Pa., m. Lizzie Heibeck, dau. Tobias Heibeck and Christiana Snyder.

10957. Annie, Wheatland Mills, Pa.

Family of ELIZABETH FRAELICH (7775) and JOSIAH ZITTLE.

10958. Elmer, Wheatland Mills, Pa., b. Mar. 27, 1872.

10959. Laura, Wheatland Mills, Pa., b. ———, 1875; m. Jacob Bachman, son Abraham Bachman and Kate Howbet.

10960. Ella, Wheatland Mills, Pa., b. Sept. 30, 1876; m. Harry Good.

10961. Ida May, Wheatland Mills, Pa., b. Mar. 17, 1888.

Family of AMOS FRAELICH (7777) and ———.

10962. Lizzie, Lancaster, Pa.

10963. Alice, Lancaster, Pa.

Family of MARY HOWETT (7800) and WILLIAM RINEER.

10964. Howard, Furniss, Pa., b. June 22, 1888.

10965. Charles, Furniss, Pa., b. Sept. 8, 1889.

10966. Bessie Belle, Furniss, Pa., b. Aug. 19, 1891.

10967. Florence Elnora, Furniss, Pa., b. Nov. 19, 1894.

10968. Milton J., Furniss, Pa., b. Mar. 2, 1896; d. Aug. 10, 1896.

10969. Emma S., Furniss, Pa., b. Aug. 5, 1898; d. Aug. 7, 1898.

Family of AMOS WATSON HOWETT (7801) and CLARA JOHNSON.

10970. Florence May, Lancaster, Pa.

10971. Cora Estelle, Lancaster, Pa.

10972. Ella Theressa, Lancaster, Pa.

10973. Charles Earl, Lancaster, Pa.

10974. Mabel, Lancaster, Pa.

10975. Clarence, Lancaster, Pa.

10976. Mary, Lancaster, Pa.

10977. Johnson, Lancaster, Pa.

Family of LIZZIE L. SHAUB (7823) and JOHN STONER.

10978. Harry S., Lime Valley, Pa.

10979. Frances E., Lime Valley, Pa.

Family of ENOS L. SHAUB (7825) and ELLA S. MYERS.

10980. Mabel E., Lampeter, Pa.

Family of BENJAMIN L. SHAUB (7827) and SUE E. HERR (8324).

10981. Myrtle E., Refton, Pa., b. Sept. 10, 1901.

Family of MARY C. SHAUB (7832) and JOHN P. GOODWIN.

10982. Franklin, Newark, O., b. Oct. 13, 1881.
10983. Carrie, Newark, O., b. May 9, 1884.
10984. Frederick, Newark, O., b. Sept. 25, 1886.

Family of JESSE FRANKLIN SHAUB (7834) and CLARA D. WILLIAMS.

10985. Frank Gordon, Cincinnati, O., b. May 4, 1898.

Family of FRANCES WOODS (7835) and GEORGE B. HORR.

10986. Leonard W., Chicago, Ill., b. Feb. 21, 1890.
10987. Marion, Chicago, Ill., b. Sept. 6, 1894.

Family of EDNA WOODS (7836) and FRANK B. CARPENTER.

10988. Florence, Cleveland, O., b. Aug. 24, 1893.
10989. John Woods, Cleveland, O., b. Dec. 30, 1895.

Family of FREDERICK SHAUB (7839) and STELLA M. BLAKE.

10990. Glenn Albert, St. Louis, Mo., b. Feb. 7, 1894.
10991. Elmer Carl, St. Louis, Mo., b. Oct. 24, 1896; d. Feb. 18, 1900.

Family of AMANDA D. MOUSER (7855) and THEODORE B. CLARK.

10992. Hattie Mae, Macbride, O., b. May 11, 1883; m. Raymon O. Clark, b. July 27, 1881; son James Clark and Martha ———.
10993. Harry Porter, Karkersville, O., b. Nov. 21, 1884.
10994. Emma Blanche, Karkersville, O., b. Nov. 10, 1886.

Family of LEAH B. MOUSER (7858) and PHILIP T. JONES.

10995. Frederick T., Johnstown, O., b. May 29, 1888.
10996. Daughter, Johnstown, O., b. Nov. 4, 1898; d. Dec. 27, 1898.

Family of CORA D. KRUG (7863) and GEORGE C. CASE.

10997. Son, Granville, O., b. June 4, 1901.

Family of AMANDA TANGERT (7896) and LEVI POULTON.

10998. Joseph Smith, Harrisburg, Pa., b. Nov. 4, 1863; m. Bertha Deese.

10999. George Henry, New Market, Pa., b. Dec. 12, 1865; d. Aug. 31, 1871.

11000. Florence Missouri, New Market, Pa., b. Jan. 28, 1868; d. Aug. 21, 1871.

11001. Silas William, New Market, Pa., b. Mar. 11, 1870; d. Sept. 5, 1871.

11002. Clarence Elliott, Malvern, Pa., b. Feb. 27, 1872; m. Feb. 20, 1895, Annie Baker, b. Mar. 5, 1871; dau. Peter A. Baker and Catherine Bixler.

11003. Minerva Irene, Philadelphia, Pa., b. Feb. 21, 1875.

11004. Blanche Tangert, Philadelphia, Pa., b. Feb. 4, 1877; m. Sept. 20, 1902, Philip S. Harkins.

Family of OLIVER ABRAHAM STONE (7910) and ELLA LEASE.

11005. William Arthur, York, Pa., b. Oct. 18, 1884.

Family of MARY ELLECTA STONE (7911) and HENRY R. SERFF.

11006. Clinton Bright, York, Pa., b. Aug. 28, 1891.

Family of DORA F. STONE (7913) and PETER LAW.

11007. Curtis Elmer, York, Pa., b. Apr. 14, 1887; d. Apr. 7, 1892.

11008. Oliver Arthur, York, Pa., b. July 5, 1889.

11009. Daisy Gertrude, York, Pa., b. Jan. 26, 1892; d. Apr. 14, 1893.

11010. Blanche Virgie, York, Pa., b. Nov. 28, 1895.

Family of HENRY B. STONE (7914) and MARY ANN GRIEVER.

11011. Lloyd Henry, York, Pa., b. July 5, 1893.

11012. May Alberta, York, Pa., b. July 22, 1895.

11013. Dorothy, York, Pa., b. Mar. 9, 1898.

Family of LAURA LUCINDA STONE (7915) and EDWARD SCHRUM.

11014. Mary Ellecta, York, Pa., b. May 15, 1889.

Family of JOHN CLINGER STONE (7916) and MYRTLE M. SNYDER.

11015. Walter Gray, York, Pa., b. Dec. 13, 1892.
11016. Myrtle May, York, Pa., b. May 21, 1895.

Family of ELMER E. HERR (7917) and CATHERINE A. SHRACK.

11017. Lulu, Reading, Pa., b. Mar. 12, 1882.
11018. Villa N., Philadelphia, Pa., b. Apr. 7, 1884.
11019. Chester A., Philadelphia, Pa., b. May 29, 1886.

Family of LUTHER HERR (7922) and KATIE V. HARTMAN.

11020. Walter Abraham, West Philadelphia, Pa., b. Oct. 6, 1890.
11021. Frank Raymond, West Philadelphia, Pa., b. Feb. 14, 1892.
11022. Helen Louisa, West Philadelphia, Pa., b. July 24, 1893.
11023. Florence Hannah, West Phiadelphia, Pa., b. Oct. 28, 1894; d. Aug. 16, 1895.
11024. Miriam Naomi, West Philadelphia, Pa., b. June 9, 1896.
11025. Luther, West Philadelphia, Pa., b. Jan. 28, 1898.
11026. Maria, West Philadelphia, Pa., b. July 24, 1900.
11027. Carrie, West Philadelphia, Pa., b. July 24, 1900.

Family of CHARLES HENRY MILLER (7930) and EDNA WARD.

11028. Annie Charlene, Pittsburg, Pa., b. Apr. 10, 1902.

Family of DANIEL F. LEFEVER (7949) and MINNIE BARR.

11029. Daniel Claire, Buck, Pa., b. Aug. 31, 1886.
11030. George Raymond, Buck, Pa., b. Sept. —, 1888.

Family of MARTHA ELIZ. LEFEVER (7950) and ELMER ELLSWORTH KEEN.

11031. Agnes Viola, Lancaster, Pa.
11032. Charles Elmer, Lancaster, Pa., b. May 6, 1894.

Family of HARRY ANKRIM LEFEVER (7951) and BLANCH LEFEVER (7730).

11033. Earl Franklin, Oak Bottom, Pa., b. May 29, 1891.

11034. Ella Catherine, Oak Bottom, Pa., b. Sept. 12, 1892.

11035. Harry Norwood, Oak Bottom, Pa., b. Nov. 9, 1893.

11036. Mary Corrinne, Oak Bottom, Pa., b. Feb. 5, 1896.

11037. Paul Ankrim, Oak Bottom, Pa., b. May 25, 1898.

11038. Florence Ruth, Oak Bottom, Pa., b. Feb. 12, 1900.

Family of JAMES IRWIN LEFEVER (7953) and EMMA BOOK.

11039. Ralph Irwin, Atglen, Pa., b. July 22, 1895; d. Sept. 11, 1895.

11040. Agnes Elizabeth, New Providence, Pa., b. Feb. 18, 1897.

11041. Myrtle Luella, New Providence, Pa., b. Dec. 16, 1899.

11042. Florençe May, New Providence, Pa., b. Mar. 18, 1901.

Family of MARY LABERTA LEFEVER (7954) and GEORGE BARR.

11043. Franklin Park, Parkesburg, Pa., b. Jan. 14, 1894.

11044. Cyrus Roy, Parkesburg, Pa., b. Apr. 2, 1895.

11045. Mary Viola, Parkesburg, Pa., b. May 4, 1896.

11046. Anna Martha, Parkesburg, Pa., b. Apr. 8, 1898.

Family of ESTHER LUELLA LEFEVER (7955) and FRANK MOWRER.

11047. Mary Elizabeth, Refton, Pa., b. July 1, 1901; d. July 6, 1901.

Family of SIMON HART (7981) and LEAH McGRADY.

11048. Emory, Lancaster, Pa., b. Oct. 19, 1851; m. Aug. 11, 1872,
Adaline Sterneman, b. May 18, 1853; dau. David Sterneman
and Anna Eckman.

11049. Milton, Lancaster, Pa., b. May 18, 1853.

11050. Albertus, Colemanville, Pa., b. ———, 1855.

11051. Allen J., Colemanville, Pa., b. ———, 1857.

11052. Harry C., Kenilworth, Pa., b. ———, 1859.

11053. Elmer E., Lancaster, Pa., b. ———. 1861.

11054. Lillie F., Mt. Nebo, Pa., b. ———, 1863.

11055. Goram, Kenilworth, Pa., b. ———, 1867.

Family of LEAH HESS (7988) and LEVI BUSHONG.

11056. Elizabeth, Witmer, Pa., b. Oct. 8, 1872; m. July 28, 1896,
William M. Cosner, b. Apr. 10, 1875; son Joseph Cosner and
Margaret McCarty.

Family of MARY HESS (7991) and JOEL MILLER.

11057. Frances Alice, Leacock, Pa., b. June 18, 1862; m. Feb. 1, 1883, Justus F. Bard, b. July 15, 1856; son Samuel Bard and Leah Steck.

11058. Elizabeth J., Lancaster, Pa., b. July 13, 1865; m. Dec. 23, 1891, Harry M. Eshleman, son Jacob Eshleman and Anna Harnish.

11059. William H., Witmer, Pa., b. Aug. 16, 1867.

11060. Charles W., Witmer, Pa., b. Dec., 1869; d. Feb. 15, 1871.

11061. Annie M., Witmer, Pa., b. Nov 23, 1871.

11062. Edward G., Witmer, Pa., b. Mar. 25, 1875.

11063. Joel R., Witmer, Pa., b. June 14, 1877; d. Nov. 8, 1877.

11064. John C., Witmer, Pa., b. Apr. 24, 1879; d. Oct. 1, 1880.

11065. Howard N., Witmer, Pa., b. Feb. 3, 1883.

Family of CATHERINE HESS (7992) and JOHN K. ESBENSHADE.

11066. Henry H., Waynesboro, Pa., b. Aug. 28, 1866; m. Mar. 3, 1892, Ida Frick, b. July 15, 1865; dau. Jacob Frick and Elizabeth Funk.

11067. Elizabeth, Lancaster, Pa., b. Feb. 27, 1868.

11068. Lettie, Witmer, Pa., b. July 18, 1872.

11069. Annie, Lancaster, Pa., b. July 18, 1872; m. Feb. 6, 1898, Wid. Enos H. Weaver (4601).

11070. John K., Strasburg, Pa., b. Dec. 23, 1874; d. Dec. 27, 1892.

Family of JOHN B. HESS (7997) and BELLE PLANK.

11071. Elmer R., Witmer, Pa., b. Jan. 31, 1878; d. Sept. 4, 1881.

Family of MILTON GROFF (8000) and MARTHA HART.

11072. Aldus H., Lancaster, Pa.

11073. Clarence, Lancaster, Pa., m. Ida ———.

11074. Elizabeth, Lancaster, Pa.

11075. Hannah, Lancaster, Pa.

11076. Anna, Lancaster, Pa.

Family of THERON S. GROFF (8003) and LOUISA B. HESS.

11077. Anna Laura, Lancaster, Pa., b. Oct. 3, 1875.

11078. Sarah Louisa, Lancaster, Pa., b. Jan. 23, 1884.

11079. Theron B., Lancaster, Pa., b. May 14, 1889; d. Apr. 27, 1893.

Family of GALEN GROFF (8009) and FRANCES M. NALE.

11080. Florence May, Allegheny, Pa., b. May 4, 1887.

Family of JAMES M. GROVE (8028) and MARY L. HAMER.

11081. Ollie May, Waynesboro, Va., b. May 1, 1896.

11082. Ada Lucille, Waynesboro, Va., b. Dec. 17, 1897; d. Apr. 14, 1900.

11083. Katherine Grace, Waynesboro, Va., b. Oct. 4, 1899.

11084. John Davis, Waynesboro, Va., b. July 18, 1901.

Family of Dr. WILLIAM J. GROVE (8020) and IDA MILLER COINER.

11085. Frederick Coiner, Hermitage, Va., b. Aug. 15, 1890; d. Apr. 13, 1892.

11086. Luther Davis, Hermitage, Va., b. May 21, 1892.

11087. Simon Miller, Hermitage, Va., b. Nov. 23, 1893.

11088. John Edgar, Hermitage, Va., b. Oct. 25, 1895.

11089. May Elizabeth, Hermitage, Va., b. Jan. 21, 1899.

Family of Rev. JOHN HERR (8063) and ANNA ZUG.

11090. Jonas, Myerstown, Pa., b. Apr. 24, 1870; d. July 12, 1870.

11091. Henry, Myerstown, Pa., b. Aug. 5, 1871.

11092. Ada, Richland, Pa., b. Feb. 18, 1874; d. Nov. 26, 1907; m. May 4, 1895, Prof. F—— Leonard Reber, b. Sept. 29, 1873; son Daniel Reber and Elizabeth Smith.

11093. Annie, Myerstown, Pa., b. July 18, 1876; d. Mar. 2, 1877.

11094. Elizabeth, Myerstown, Pa., b. Mar. 5, 1879.

11095. Jacob, Myerstown, Pa., b. Aug. 18, 1883.

11096. John, Myerstown, Pa., b. Mar. 2, 1887.

11097. Abraham, Myerstown, Pa., b. Oct. 4, 1891; d. Nov. 7, 1892.

Family of CATHERINE HERR (8064) and DANIEL GEIB.

11098. Laura, Cardova, Md., b. Apr. 24, 1879; m. Nov. 29, 1899,

Martin J. Hutchinson, b. Jan. 3, 1875; son James A. Hutchinson and Susanna Sanger.

11099. Sallie, Cardova, Md., b. Mar. 29, 1881.

11100. Emma, Cardova, Md., b. Dec. 6, 1882.

11101. David, Cardova, Md., b. Aug. 26, 1884.

11102. Rufus, Cardova, Md., b. Aug. 3, 1886; d. Sept. 8, 1898.

11103. Jacob, Cardova, Md., b. July 14, 1888.

11104. John, Cardova, Md., b. July 24, 1891.

Family of ELIZABETH HERR (8065) and ALFRED B. GINGRICH.

11105. Harry, Fontana, Pa., b. Jan. 20, 1885.

11106. Sarah, Fontana, Pa., b. Dec. 21, 1886.

11107. Jacob, Fontana, Pa., b. Aug. 14, 1888.

11108. William, Fontana, Pa., b. Nov. 9, 1890.

11109. Alfred, Fontana, Pa., b. Nov. 3, 1892.

11110. Simon, Fontana, Pa., b. Nov. 13, 1894.

11111. Daughter, Fontana, Pa., b. Dec. 10, 1896; d. Dec. 10, 1896.

11112. Susan, Fontana, Pa., b. June 3, 1898.

11113. John, Fontana, Pa., b. Aug. 3, 1900.

Family of CHRISTIAN BOOK HERR (8069) and ANNA E. KEEN.

11114. Harry Willis, Camargo, Pa., b. Mar. 8, 1878; d. Oct. 27, 1897.

11115. Clarence Sylvester, Camargo, Pa., b. Jan. 24, 1893.

Family of CHARLES F. KRUG (8061) and MAUD M. HISSONG.

11116. Alma, Union, O., b. May 31, 1897; d. Oct. 1, 1897.

11117. Allie, Union, O., b. May 31, 1897; d. Sept. 30, 1897.

11118. Benjamin F., Union, O., b. June 24, 1899; d. Sept. 22, 1900.

Family of DANIEL K. LANDIS (8110) and M—— ALICE TROUT.

11119. Mary Elizabeth, Strasburg, Pa., b. Apr. 23, 1893.

Family of RHODA ELLEN CAYWOOD (8114) and H—— L. DEDRICK.

11120. Ira Estella, Monmouth, Kans., b. Nov. 26, 1892.

11121. Earl Henry, Monmouth, Kans., b. July 21, 1894.

11122. Leslie Earl, Monmouth, Kans., b. Mar. 26, 1896.

Family of MARY ELIZABETH CAYWOOD (8115) and F—— E. WEGENER.

11123. Myrtle, Page, Kans., b. Feb. 7, 1893.
11124. Gladys Christine, Page, Kans., b. Sept. 10, 1900.

Family of JESSE HERR (8120) and LURAH GARN.

11125. Orren, Helena, O., b. Feb. 5, 1901.

Family of ELLA H. MUSSELMAN (8144) and HARRY GERHART.

11126. Fannie Elizabeth, Lancaster, Pa., b. Jan. 5, 1895.
11127. John M., Lancaster, Pa., b. June 20, 1896.
11128. Willis, Lancaster, Pa., b. Nov. 25, 1898; d. Aug. 14, 1899.
11129. Margaret, Lancaster, Pa., b. Nov. 27, 1900.

Family of LUCY BLANCHE SKEEN (8179) and WILLIAM J. LANDIS.

11130. Martha Skeen, Coatesville, Pa., b. Jan. 11, 1894.

Family of LAURA LAVINA WITMER (8217) and EDWIN T. FETTER.

11131. Frederick Henry, Milburn, Tex., b. Feb. 4, 1847; d. Apr. 27, 1884; m. Apr. 20, 1874, Mary E. Montan.
11132. Annie Maria, Lancaster, Pa., b. Feb. 4, 1849; m. Feb. 27, 1872, Henry Hershey, b. Apr. 28, 1839; son Jacob Hershey and Eliza Miller.

Family of MARIA LOUISA WITMER (8218) and Dr. SAMUEL KENEAGY.

11133. Agnes, Crafton, Pa.
11134. Christie, Crafton, Pa.

Family of JOHN D. CONNELLY (8220) and SARAH E. MILLER.

11135. William Miller, Pratt, Kans., b. May 29, 1864.
11136. Francis D., York, Pa., b. Jan. 20, 1867; m. Grace Heidler.
11137. George W., Lancaster, Pa., b. Sept. 29, 1869.
11138. Martha B., Lancaster, Pa., b. Feb. 23, 1880.

Family of ELIZABETH F. BOWMAN (8237) and BENJAMIN E. FLORY.

11139. Jacob B., Shoffs, Pa., b. Oct. 28, 1890.

11140. Daniel, Shoffs, Pa., b. Jan. 5, 1892.

11141. Mary, Shoffs, Pa., b. Oct. 1, 1893.

11142. Anna Letitia, Shoffs, Pa., b. Jan. 25, 1895.

11143. Benjamin, Shoffs, Pa., b. Aug. 21, 1896.

11144. Paul, Shoffs, Pa., b. Oct. 4, 1898.

Family of ELAM B. TROUT (8244) and CATHERINE HESS.

11145. Harry David, Iva, Pa., b. Nov. 27, 1876; m. Dec. 8, 1898, Mary Ressler, b. Apr. 10, 1877; dau. Freeland Ressler and Eva Cramer.

11146. Park Hess, Iva, Pa., b. Oct. 23, 1878.

11147. Cora Elizabeth, Iva, Pa., b. May 10, 1880.

11148. Ada Louisa, Iva, Pa., b. Oct. 20, 1881; d. Mar. 9, 1882.

Family of ANNIE ELIZABETH TROUT (8245) and AMOS B. LEAMAN.

11149. Bertha M., Lancaster, Pa., b. Oct. 5, 1876; m. Jan. 19, 1897, Abraham Denlinger, son Benjamin Denlinger and Maria Wenger.

11150. Harry M., New Providence, Pa., b. Sept. 18, 1878; m. Nov. 30, 1899, Rachel Hess, b. Mar. 5, 1875; dau. Samuel Hess and Emma Martin.

11151. Emily V., Strasburg, Pa., b. Nov. 30, 1884.

Family of HENRY F. TROUT (8246) and CATHARINE NAGLE.

11152. Elva E., Bart, Pa., b. Mar. 1, 1900.

Family of FRANKLIN J. TROUT (8247) and ELIZABETH A. HUBER.

11153. Florence H., Bart, Pa., b. Jan. 29, 1888.

11154. Walter H., Bart, Pa., b. June 29, 1889.

11155. Enos F., Bart, Pa., b. Mar. 13, 1891.

11156. Anna E., Bart, Pa., b. May 17, 1892.

11157. John Henry, Bart, Pa., b. Aug. 10, 1893.

11158. Esther H., Bart, Pa., b. Aug. 19, 1897.

11159. Mark H., Bart, Pa., b. Jan. 7, 1899.

11160. Naomi H., Bart, Pa., b. June 3, 1900.

Family of ELMER J. TROUT (8249) and PHOEBE A. HOWRY.

11161. Beulah May, Lancaster, Pa., b. Mar. 4, 1891; d. Apr. 8, 1893.
11162. Maud Ethel, Lancaster, Pa., b. July 5, 1894.
11163. Paul Henry, Lancaster, Pa., b. Dec. 20, 1899.

Family of NAOMI BOWMAN (8251) and BENJAMIN WEAVER.

11164. Mabel, Mountville, Pa., b. Aug. 25, 1883.
11165. Benjamin Omar, Mountville, Pa., b. May 28, 1886.

Family of ESTHER NEFF (8262) and CHRISTIAN K. BRENNER.

11166. Mary Anna, Osborn, O., b. Apr. 24, 1876.
11167. Jacob Neff, Osborn, O., b. July 27, 1878.

Family of ALONZO ZELLER (8270) and MARY E. BROSEY.

11168. Henry, Medway, O., b. Jan. 5, 1883; d. Feb. 7, 1883.
11169. Charles, Medway, O., b. Oct. 7, 1884.

Family of ESTHER H. KAUFFMAN (8280) and HENRY K. SMITH.

11170. Ward Leroy, Osborn, O., b. Apr. 11, 1886.

Family of HENRY M. HERR (8300) and EMMA HAVERSTICK.

11171. Christian H., Lancaster, Pa., b. Dec. 30, 1878; d. Dec. 31, 1878.
11172. Guy H., Philadelphia, Pa., b. July 16, 1880.
11173. Ivan M., Lancaster, Pa., b. June 26, 1882.
11174. Roy M., Philadelphia, Pa., b. Feb. 27, 1884.
11175. Ralph, Philadelphia, Pa., b. Aug. 6, 1885.
11176. Clarence, Philadelphia, Pa., b. Dec. 19, 1887.

Family of MARTIN B. HERR (8301) and BARBARA STONER.

11177. Norman, Lancaster, Pa., b. Aug. 19, 1892.

Family of BENJAMIN F. HERR (8302) and MARY E. BEAR.

11178. Benjamin Bear, Rohrerstown, Pa., b. June 1, 1883.

Family of ELIZABETH M. HERR (8303) and HENRY M. STEHMAN.

11179. Hebron H., Millersville, Pa., b. Nov. 3, 1880.
11180. B. ——— Frank, Millersville, Pa., b. June 24, 1884.
11181. L. ——— Mary, Millersville, Pa., b. Oct. 18, 1888.

Family of BENJAMIN H. BRACKBILL (8305) and ANNA M. HOSTETTER.

11182. Bertha S., Lime Valley, Pa., b. Feb. 24, 1885.
11183. Son, Lime Valley, Pa., b. July 23, 1886; d. July 23, 1886.
11184. Elizabeth F., Lime Valley, Pa., b. Feb. 26, 1888.
11185. David H., Lime Valley, Pa., b. Feb. 2, 1891.
11186. Anna H., Lime Valley, Pa., b. Feb. 2, 1895.
11187. E. ——— Miriam, Lime Valley, Pa., b. Mar. 2, 1897.

Family of JOHN ELMER BRACKBILL (8307) and ALICE J. STROCK.

11188. Ralph Strock, Jeromeville, O., b. Apr. 18, 1886.
11189. Anna Elizabeth, Jeromeville, O., b. Nov. 1, 1888.

Family of ELIAS L. HERR (8309) and KATIE W. BRUBAKER.

11190. Benjamin B., Lancaster, Pa., b. Aug. 22, 1888.
11191. Anna B., Lancaster, Pa., b. June 20, 1890.

Family of LIZZIE H. GROFF (8312) and JOHN F. HESS.

11192. Ara G., Martinsville, Pa., b. Aug. 11, 1889.
11193. Elias E., Martinsville, Pa., b. Apr. 21, 1894.
11194. Elvin W., Martinsville, Pa., b. Mar. 24, 1898.

Family of ENOS H. GROFF (8313) and MARTHA BRUBAKER.

11195. Lester E., Strasburg, Pa., b. Nov. 26, 1896.
11196. Abraham B., Strasburg, Pa., b. May 4, 1898.
11197. Ada, Strasburg, Pa., b. Sept. 14, 1899.
11198. Earl Leroy, Strasburg, Pa., b. Sept. 27, 1901.

Family of EMANUEL L. GROFF (8314) and SUSAN R. HERR (7450).

11199. Mary H., New Danville, Pa., b. Sept. 29, 1891.
11200. Abraham, New Danville, Pa., b. Apr. 29, 1894; d. Aug. 20, 1894.

11201. Anna, New Danville, Pa., b. May 4, 1895.
11202. Esther, New Danville, Pa., b. Nov. 15, 1897.
11203. Susan, New Danville, Pa., b. Sept. 23, 1899.

Family of ADA H. GROFF (8318) and HENRY R. HERR (7453).

11204. Elias G., West Willow, Pa., b. Apr. 5, 1899.
11205. Emma Elizabeth, West Willow, Pa., b. Nov. 12, 1901.

Family of ELIZABETH F. HERR (8320) and JACOB E. WITMER.

11206. Clair H., Refton, Pa., b. Apr. 14, 1890.
11207. Susan E., Refton, Pa., b. Apr. 10, 1892.
11208. Arthur G., Refton, Pa., b. Sept. 29, 1895.
11209. Anna E., Refton, Pa., b. Sept. 25, 1898.

Family of SUSAN E. HERR (8324) and BENJAMIN L. SHAUB (7827).

11210. Myrtle H., Lancaster, Pa., b. Sept. 10, 1901.

Family of SARAH FRANCES HERR (8330) and JOSEPH LEVI BORDEN.

11211. Benjamin Elias, Limeton, Va., b. Nov. 22, 1898.
11212. Joseph Homer, Limeton, Va., b. Oct. 22, 1900.

Family of ADDIE S. HERR (8331) and CHARLES WALDO HALDEMAN.

11213. Charles Waldo, Philadelphia, Pa., b. Nov. 15, 1897.
11214. Anna Elizabeth, Philadelphia, Pa., b. Apr. 13, 1900.

Family of IDA SUE PEOPLES (8350) and Dr. CHARLES E. HELM.

11215. Leigh P., Bart, Pa., b. Oct. 24, 1889.
11216. Hiram, Bart, Pa., b. Aug. 29, 1891.
12513. Miriam, Bart, Pa., b. May 12, 1905.

Family of CHRISTIAN H. HERR (8354) and AMANDA BOOK.

11217. Ada F., Lampeter, Pa., b. Oct. 24, 1883.
11218. Harry D., Lampeter, Pa., b. Feb. 1, 1885.
11219. Roy B., Lampeter, Pa., b. May 24, 1886.
11220. Christian L., Lampeter, Pa., b. Jan. 3, 1888.

11221. Amanda B., Lampeter, Pa., b. Oct. 29, 1889.
11222. Walter J., Lampeter, Pa., b. July 29, 1891.
11223. Ira L,, Lampeter, Pa., b. July 28, 1893.
11224. Mary A., Lampeter, Pa., b. May 7, 1895.
11225. Clarence B., Lampeter, Pa., b. Feb. 26, 1898.
11226. Maud C., Lampeter, Pa., b. Feb. 26, 1900.

Family of HENRY B. HERR (8355) and BARBARA HARNISH.

11227. John H., Lampeter, Pa., b. Sept. 16, 1885.
11228. Anna B., Lampeter, Pa., b. June 17, 1887.
11229. Bessie F., Lampeter, Pa., b. Jan. 19, 1890.
11230. Mary C., Lampeter, Pa., b. Dec. 20, 1891.
11231. Cora E., Lampeter, Pa., b. Nov. 17, 1894.
11232. Victor E., Lampeter, Pa., b. Feb. 25, 1897.

Family of ELIZABETH N. HERR (8357) and SAMUEL E. RANCK.

11233. Fannie H., Intercourse, Pa., b. May 8, 1890; d. Dec. 25, 1891.
11234. Harry E., Intercourse, Pa., b. Sept. 22, 1892.
11235. David H., Intercourse, Pa., b. Mar. 16, 1895.
11236. John E., Intercourse, Pa., b. Aug. 29, 1898; d. Feb. 27, 1899.
11237. Bertha E., Intercourse, Pa., b. May 20, 1900.

Family of ANNA M. HERR (8360) and BENJAMIN B. GROFF.

11238. Elizabeth H., Lancaster, Pa., b. Jan. 25, 1895.
11239. John H., Lancaster, Pa., b. Nov. 12, 1898.
11240. Fannie M., Lancaster, Pa., b. Apr. 22, 1901.

Family of MARY ELIZ. HERSHEY (8365) and. Dr. SYLVESTER J. FINLEY.

11241. Meriam Vesta, Lime Valley, Pa., b. Dec. 5, 1897.

Family of ELIZABETH ESTHER HERR (8384) and JOHN STAUFFER.

11242. Mary Elizabeth, Witmer, Pa., b. Oct. 7, 1900.

Family of LEE P. HERR (8398) and EMILY V. WALKER.

11243. Alonzo Leo, Lexington, Ky., b. Aug. 30, 1881.
11244. Hiram Walker, Lexington, Ky., b. Mar. 29, 1886.

Family of ETHELBERT D. HERR (8399) and TILLIE K. POLLOCK.

11245. Willie D., Bloomington, Ill., b. Oct. 19, 1879; m. Mar. 23, 1907, Lulu Powell.

Family of CHARLES E. HERR (8400) and GERTRUDE POLLOCK.

11246. Robert E., Bloomington, Ill., b. Nov. 25, 1886.

Family of WILLIAM H. JOHNSON (8401) and ABIGAIL M. STIMPSON.

11247. William Carrol, Columbus, O., b. Aug. 15, 1860.
11248. John Francis, Columbus, O., b. Aug. 19, 1862; d. Nov. 13, 1862.

Family of SARAH J. JOHNSON (8403) and BYRON C. BABBETT.

11249. Francis Lovell, Kirkersville, O., b. Nov. 15, 1864.

Family of ELIZABETH L. HERR (8425) and MARTIN ZIMMERMAN.

11250. Mary Katharyn, Lampeter, Pa., b. Aug. 22, 1898.

Family of ESTHER L. HERR (8426) and FRANK S. LEFEVER.

11251. Anna H., Lampeter, Pa., b. Sept. 22, 1890.
11252. Ada, Lampeter, Pa., b. Sept. 25, 1891.
11253. Isaac, Lampeter, Pa., b. Oct. 30, 1893.
11254. Mary, Lampeter, Pa., b. June 21, 1895.
11255. Daniel, Lampeter, Pa., b. Nov. 4, 1896; d. Feb. 23, 1897.
11256. Leaman, Lampeter, Pa., b. Feb. 22, 1898.
11257. Cora, Lampeter, Pa., b. Aug. 9, 1901.

Family of ABRAHAM L. HERR (8427) and AMANDA L. HERR (6928).

11258. Esther H., Lampeter, Pa., b. July 17, 1899.

Family of EMMA L. HERR (8431) and ABRAHAM METZLER.

11259. Abraham, Lampeter, Pa.

Family of ELLA V. HARNISH (8445) and BENJAMIN E. LEFEVER.

11260. Clayton, Willow Street, Pa., b. Aug. 16, 1893.

11261. Emma, Willow Street, Pa., b. Mar. 8, 1895.
11262. Cora, Willow Street, Pa., b. Nov. 24, 1897.

Family of FANNY FORRY (8507) and JOSEPH CHARLES.

11263. Benjamin, Columbia, Pa., b. Aug. 8, 1851.
11264. Anna, Columbia, Pa., b. Oct. 13, 1852; d. Sept. 29, 1857.
11265. Ephraim, Columbia, Pa., b. Oct. 7, 1854; d. Sept. 24, 1857.
11266. Christiana, Columbia, Pa., b. July 25, 1856.
11267. John, Columbia, Pa., b. Dec. 16, 1857.
11268. David, Columbia, Pa., b. Mar. 12, 1859.
11269. Elizabeth, Columbia, Pa., b. Mar. 4, 1861.
11270. Joseph, Columbia, Pa.
11271. Susan, Columbia, Pa.
11272. Jacob, Columbia, Pa.

Family of ANNA FORRY (8508) and CHRISTIAN ESCHBACH.

11273. Henry F., Lancaster, Pa., b. Sept. 29, 1854; m. Sept. 26, 1876, Barbara M. Denlinger, b. Aug. 24, 1856; d. Dec. 21, 1899; dau. Abraham Denlinger and Elizabeth ———; m. Feb. 13, 1902, Wid. Emma K. Wissler Harnish, b. Aug. 31, 1855; dau. ——— Wissler and ———.

Family of DANIEL FORRY (8509) and MARTHA SWARR.

11274. Anna, Millersville, Pa., b. July 4, 1858.
11275. Martha, Millersville, Pa., b. Oct. 9, 1860; d. Dec. 16, 1861.
11276. John, Millersville, Pa., b. Oct. 23, 1862.
11277. Henry, Millersville, Pa., b. Aug. 16, 1865.
11278. Daniel, Millersville, Pa., b. Jan. 18, 1868.

Family of SUSAN FORRY (8511) and SAMUEL B. SENSENIG.

11279. Isaac F., Earl, Pa., b. Aug. 24, 1867; d. Sept. 12, 1867.

Family of ELIZABETH L. WEIDLER (8512) and JOHN B. BRUBAKER.

11280. Weidler, Landis Valley, Pa., b. May 4, 1858.
11281. Thaddeus, Landis Valley, Pa., b. Oct. 1, 1862.
11282. Susan, Landis Valley, Pa., b. Aug. 22, 1864.

Family of **SALINDA L. WEIDLER** (8513) and **DANIEL HARNISH.**

11283. Clara, Landis Valley, Pa., b. Sept. 3, 1862.
11284. Ellen, Landis Valley, Pa., b. Mar. 12, 1864.

Family of **ANNA WEIDLER** (8514) and **DANIEL BURKHOLDER.**

11285. Ephraim W., Landis Valley, Pa., b. Apr. 6, 1864.

Family of **FANNY M. WEIDLER** (8515) and **BENJAMIN D. LANDIS** (8527).

11286. Anna, Landis Valley, Pa., b. July 31, 1861.

Family of **LOUIS E. ESHLEMAN** (8568) and **ELLA E. BARNES.**

11287. Maud, East Oakland, Cal., b. Sept. 16, 1875; m. Jan. 20, 1896, Herman D. Kribbs, b. Dec. 27, 1874; son Herman Kribbs and Lucy Finch.
11288. Stella, East Oakland, Cal., b. Feb. 2, 1879.
11289. Henry E., East Oakland, Cal., b. Mar. 28, 1881.
11290. Edwin B., East Oakland, Cal., b. Mar. 13, 1885.

Family of **GERTRUDE ESHLEMAN** (8570) and **JOHN WAITE.**

11291. Frank L., Topeka, Kans., b. Mar. 3, 1877.
11292. Julia, Topeka, Kans., b. June 13, 1880.
11293. Gertrude, Topeka, Kans., b. Aug. 9, 1883; d. Nov. 10, 1885.

Family of Wid. **GERTRUDE E. WAITE** (8570) and **HUGH CURRY.**

11294. Metta Lorine, Topeka, Kans., b. Sept. 3, 1887.
11295. Eliza Eshleman, Topeka, Kans., b. Sept. 4, 1893.

Family of **SARAH E. ESHLEMAN** (8575) and **JOHNSON P. HILL.**

11296. Clarence Martin, Cochranville, Pa., b. Dec. 28, 1886.
11297. Mary Jones, Cochranville, Pa., b. Mar. 12, 1887.
11298. Laura, Cochranville, Pa., b. Apr. 27, 1889; d. May 11, 1889.

Family of Dr. **JOHN MARTIN ESHLEMAN** (8578) and **ANNA B. SMITH.**

11299. Thomas Edwin, Parkesburg, Pa., b. Oct. 4, 1898.
11300. Walter Barclay, Parkesburg, Pa., b. May 16, 1901.
11301. John Martin, Parkesburg, Pa., b. May 16, 1901.

Family of MARY ELIZABETH YOUNG (8583) and Capt. GEORGE BULL.

11302. Blake, St. Joseph, Mo., b. Oct. 18, 1872; d. Oct. 20, 1892.
11303. George, St. Joseph, Mo., b. ———, 1879.
11304. Robert, St. Joseph, Mo.

Family of SARAH A. YOUNG (8586) and HAROLD LEWIS.

11305. Edwin, Philadelphia, Pa.

Family of EDGAR E. HASTINGS (8590) and HARRIET IONE HART.

11306. Winifred Ione, Omaha, Neb. b. June 8, 1900.

Family of MARY EMMA HASTINGS (8592) and WALTER L. KAUFFMAN.

11307. Louise, Spruce Grove, Pa., b. Dec. 4, 1893.

Family of MARIA ELIZ. ESHLEMAN (8593) and JOHN WESLEY CASTLES.

11308. John Wesley, New Orleans, La., b. Mar. 10, 1893.
11309. Frances, New Orleans, La., b. Apr. 29, 1894.

Family of FANNY LEVERICK ESHLEMAN (8596) and FOUNTAIN B. CRAIG.

11310. Fanny Hampton, New Orleans, La., b. Feb. 5, 1897.
11311. Robert Emmet, New Orleans, La., b. June 4, 1898.
11312. Elizabeth, New Orleans, La., b. July 1, 1902.

Family of FRANK E. BACHMAN (8601) and BESSIE TIMBERLAKE.

11313. Marion Evans, Port Henry, N. Y., b. Sept. 15, 1888.
11314. Luella Lucille, Port Henry, N. Y., b. Oct. 21, 1891.
11315. Henrietta Elizabeth, Port Henry, N. Y., b. Jan. 24, 1893.

Family of ILA WARFEL (8610) and WILLIAM F. BEYER.

11316. Robert Arthur, Lancaster, Pa., b. Feb. 28, 1883; m. 1907, Caroline Myers.
11317. John Warfel, Lancaster, Pa., b. June 10, 1884.
11318. Thomas, Lancaster, Pa., b. Jan. 26, 1890.

Family of JOHN G. WARFEL (8612) and ELIZABETH AGNES BAEHLER.

11319. Mary Sophia, Lancaster, Pa., b. Oct. 20, 1888.
11320. John Leonard, Lancaster, Pa., b. July 14, 1890.

Family of WILLIAM R. BRACKBILL (8650) and AMANDA B. GROFF.

11321. Harvey Groff, Lancaster, Pa., b. Mar. 2, 1901.

12021. William Victor, Lancaster, Pa., b. May 7, 1902; d. Oct. 20, 1902.

12022. Ralph Rauch, Lancaster, Pa., b. Oct. 29, 1904.

Family of HENRY M. WEAVER (8789) and HELEN S. PURDY.

11322. Henry Purdy, Mansfield, O., b. Apr. 23, 1876.

Family of CARLTON W. BACHMAN (8781) and FRANCIS J. GARDNER.

11323. Howard G., Fayette, N. Y., b. Oct. 23, 1876; m. July 21, 1900, Elizabeth M. Moreland, b. Sept. 9, 1880.

Family of FRANCES CATHERINE REED (8783) and JANS N. LORENTSEN.

11324. Frederick W., Waterloo, N. Y., b. July 20, 1880.

11325. Emma L., Waterloo, N. Y., b. May 2, 1884; m. Apr. 25, 1906, George W. Johnson.

Family of EDLA VIRGINIA PONTIUS (8785) and JOHN BEECHER DENNIS.

11326. Pauline Virginia, Hamilton, Can., b. May 9, 1875; m. Aug. 17, 1897, Oliver H. Young, b. Sept. 28, 1869.

11327. George P., Hamilton, Can., b. Sept. 28, 1876.

11328. Vivian, Hamilton, Can., b. Apr. 19, 1878; d. Jan. 25, 1899; m. Nov. 16, 1898, Robert McClelland.

11329. Grace, Hamilton, Can., b. Mar. 31, 1880.

11330. Mabel, Hamilton, Can., b. Mar. 4, 1882.

11331. Cora, Hamilton, Can., b. Oct. 6, 1883; d. Aug. 25, 1896.

11332. Francis W., Hamilton, Can., b. Sept. 20, 1885.

11333. Edla, Hamilton, Can., b. Apr. 20, 1887.

11334. Beecher, Hamilton, Can., b. July 4, 1889.

11335. Carrie, Hamilton, Can., b. Apr. 15, 1891.

Family of GEORGE W. PONTIUS (8786) and LILLIAN J. SCHERMERHORN.

11336. Frances Isabel, Seneca Falls, N. Y., b. Mar. 26, 1879.

11337. George W., Seneca Falls, N. Y., b. Apr. 30, 1882.
11338. Carlisle, Seneca Falls, N. Y., b. June 14, 1890.
11339. Murray, Seneca Falls, N. Y., b. Oct. 30, 1899.

Family of LAURA M. RUSSELL (8792) and ARTHUR DUNCAN MOIR.

11340. Jean, Greenfield, Mass., b. Oct. 16, 1889.
11341. Arthur Duncan, Greenfield, Mass., b. Feb. 6, 1893.
11342. William Wilmerding, Greenfield, Mass., b. Sept. 22, 1901.

Family of JOHN BURG RUSSELL (8794) and EVELINE TROWBRIDGE KANE.

11343. John Edwards, 2333 Broadway, N. Y., b. Aug. 10, 1901.
11344. Theodore Burg, 2333 Broadway, N. Y., b. Sept. 23, 1903.

Family of LUCY EDWARDS RUSSELL (8795) and UHLRICH H. WRAN.

11345. Uhlrich Hubbell, Greenfield, Mass., b. Aug. 25, 1892.
11346. Mary Elizabeth, Greenfield, Mass., b. Oct. 11, 1893.
11347. James Nelson, Greenfield, Mass., b. Aug. 22, 1899.

Family of CAROLINE B. KAUFFMAN (8822) and JOHN C. KRYDER.

11348. Charles C., Niagara Falls, N. Y., b. June 11, 1885.
11349. Mary H., Niagara Falls, N. Y., b. June 13, 1886.

Family of CLARA A. HARTMAN (8837) and JAMES E. CALDWELL.

11350. Marguerite Amelia, Salona, Pa., b. Mar. 6, 1891.
11351. Robert Warren, Salona, Pa., b. Dec. 22, 1891.
11352. Harriet, Salona, Pa., b. Dec. 13, 1893.
11353. Daisy Jessamine, Salona, Pa., b. Feb. 22, 1896.
11354. Catherine Louisa, Salona, Pa., b. July 8, 1898.

Family of SARAH E. HARTMAN (8838) and JOHN W. KEPLER.

11355. John Wilbur, Shintown, Pa., b. Apr. 26, 1895.
11356. William McKinley, Shintown, Pa., b. Apr. 6, 1897.
11357. Albert Monroe, Shintown, Pa., b. Feb. 27, 1899.

Family of CARRIE HARTMAN GLOSSER (8849) and OTTO F. PEELER.

11358. Elizabeth Carrie, Paoli, Pa., b. Aug. 21, 1890; d. Jan. 31, 1891.
11359. Carl, Paoli, Pa., b. Mar. 18, 1892; d. Oct. 14, 1892.

26

Family of **JOHN FRANCIS GLOSSER** (8851) and **ANNA DUBOSC.**

11360. Frederick H., Mansfield, O., b. Oct. 16, 1900.
11361. Edwin Francis, Mansfield, O., b. June 3, 1903.

Family of **ELENOR F. GEARHART** (8874) and **ARTHUR B. SALMON.**

11362. Richard T., Lock Haven, Pa., b. May 1, 1901.

Family of **BERTHA LEONA MENGES** (5702) and **PERCY EVERETT HANSON.**

11363. Oliver Walter, Belgrade, Me., b. Nov. 13, 1905.

Family of **ELIAS HERSHEY SNEATH** (11960) and **ANNA SHELDON CAMP.**

11364. Herbert Camp, New Haven, Conn., b. Mar. 31, 1895.
11365. Katherine Williams, New Haven, Conn., b. June 17, 1899.
11366. Richard Sheldon, New Haven, Conn., b. Feb. 11, 1901.

Family of **EMMA EUGENIA SNEATH** (11961) and **HARRY CLARKE BRUNER.**

11367. Caroline Sneath, Columbia, Pa., b. Apr. 21, 1895.
11368. Harry Clarke, Columbia, Pa., b. Sept. 29, 1897.

Family of **ELIZABETH ROHRER** (8955) and **JOHN BACHMAN.**

11369. Jay, Strasburg, Pa.
11370. Daughter, Shannon, Pa.
11371. Son, Shannon, Pa.

Family of **ESTELLA J. ROHRER** (8984) and **LEWIS V. STEEB.**

11372. Anna Lyda, Allegheny, Pa., b. May 23, 1892.
11373. Gladys Estella, Allegheny, Pa., b. June 14, 1894.
11374. Carrie May, Allegheny, Pa., b. May 11, 1898.
11375. Blanche Rebecca, Allegheny, Pa., b. Nov. 2, 1902.

Family of **MARY KREIDER** (8994) and **HENRY D. ROHRER.**

11376. Abraham K., Lancaster, Pa., b. Nov. 16, 1872; m. Apr. 2, 1902, Anna Edgerly.
11377. Harry, Lancaster, Pa., b. Jan. 21, 1882.
11378. Ella, Lancaster, Pa., b. Mar. 4, 1888.

Family of LIZZIE KREIDER (8995) and BENJAMIN LEAMAN.

11379. Lizzie, Kinzers, Pa., m. Landis Hershey.
11380. Ada, Leaman Place,, Pa., m. Isaac Hershey.

Family of Wid. LIZZIE K. LEAMAN (8995) and ISAAC EBY.

11381. Eva May, Kinzers, Pa.
11382. Ruth, Kinzers, Pa.

Family of MARTIN KREIDER (8996) and AMANDA DIFFENBAUGH.

11383. Frank, Lancaster, Pa.
11384. Ida, Lancaster, Pa.
11385. Annie, Lancaster, Pa.
11386. Tobias, Lancaster, Pa.
11387. Elam, Lancaster, Pa.
11388. Benjamin, Lancaster, Pa.
11389. Martin, Lancaster, Pa.

Family of ANNIE KREIDER (8997) and CHRISTIAN STAUFFER.

11390. Annie, Lancaster, Pa., m. David Groff.
11391. Susan, Farmersville, Pa., m. Elam Hurst.

Family of JOHN KREIDER (8998) and LIZZIE KREIDER.

11392. Luetta, Fertility, Pa.
11393. Emma, Fertility, Pa.
11394. Anna, Fertility, Pa.

Family of SUSAN E. GROFF (9067) and HENRY THOMAS.

11395. Florence, Johnstown, Pa., b. Dec. 25, 1888.
11396. Elizabeth, Johnstown, Pa., b. Apr. 1, 1890; d. July 30, 1891.

Family of AGNES MAUD HUSTON (9075) and GEORGE KRAFT.

11397. Kenneth Huston, Fort Madison, Ia., b. Nov. 12, 1896.

Family of FRANCES MAY GROFF (9078) and CHARLES JAMES FOX.

11398. Robert Harold, Live Oak, Fla., b. Aug. 8, 1892.

Family of **MAUD LOUISE GROFF** (9079.) and **PEYTON S. FORTSON**.

11399. Charles Harold, Live Oak, Fla., b. Jan. 5, 1897.
11400. Elizabeth Belle, Live Oak, Fla., b. May 7, 1898; d. June 22, 1899.

Family of **ANNA ELIZABETH HERR** (9143) and **JAMES WILLIE CLISE**.

11401. Ruth, Seattle, Wash., b. July 16, 1888.
11402. Charles Francis, Seattle, Wash., b. Sept. 16, 1890.
11403. Willis Herr, Seattle, Wash., b. Oct. 9, 1892; d. Mar. 19, 1898.
11404. James William, Seattle, Wash., b. Sept. 1, 1900.

Family of **HERBERT T. HERR** (9146) and **IRENE F. VIANCOURT**.

11405. Herbert Thacker, Denver, Col., b. Feb. 18, 1898.
11406. Muriel Viancourt, Denver, Col., b. Aug. 21, 1901.

Family of **IRENE EMMA HERR** (9148) and **GEORGE A. BLUE**.

11407. Irene Madora, Denver, Col., b. Aug. 4, 1896.
11408. Georgie Herr, Denver, Col., b. July 8, 1898; d. Oct. 28, 1898.

Family of **CORA JULIET HERR** (9149) and **HARVEY ALVA McHENRY**.

11409. Lorenzo Alva, Denver, Col., b. Jan. 15, 1899.
11410. Hiero Herr, Denver, Col., b. Nov. 19, 1903.

Family of **RUBY EMMA HERR** (9151) and **WILLIAM SEWARD RUSSELL**.

11411. Richard Herr, Easton, Pa., b. Aug. 23, 1899.

Family of **JOHN PINKNEY FRANTZ** (9155) and **LOUISA DENMEAD**.

11412. Margaret Pinkney, Lutherville, Md., b. Mar. 29, 1894.
11413. Louisa Sewall, Lutherville, Md., b. May 2, 1895.
11414. John Pinkney, Lutherville, Md., b. Feb. 17, 1897.
11415. Donald Herr, Lutherville, Md., b. Feb. 15, 1900.

Family of **ANNIE SEWELL FRANTZ** (9157) and **JOHN C. BOYENTON**.

11416. John Frantz, Hampton, Va., b. July 24, 1895.

Family of JOHN WILLIAM ESHLEMAN (9232) and MARY HESS (7430).

11417. John Hess, New Danville, Pa., b. ———, 1893.
11418. Virginia, New Danville, Pa., b. ———, 1894.
11419. Pauline, New Danville, Pa., b. ———, 1897.

Family of FRANKLIN EDGAR ESHLEMAN (9233) and ELIZABETH BARE.

11420. Paul, Lancaster, Pa., b. ———, 1896.
11421. Mary, Lancaster, Pa., b. ———, 1898.

Family of HATTIE EMMA MAYER (9249) and FRANK HOOD.

11422. Fred. Elmer, Shannon City, Ia., b. Aug. 26, 1887.
11423. Mattie Belle, Shannon City, Ia., b. July 9, 1889.
11424. Arthur Ray, Shannon City, Ia., b. Mar. 14, 1895.
11425. Harry Strohm, Shannon City, Ia., b. June 14, 1898.
11426. Carl Roy, Shannon City, Ia., b. Jan. 4, 1901.
11427. Mary Jane, Shannon City, Ia., b. Jan. 26, 1903.
11964. Eugene Frank, Shannon City, Ia., b. Aug. 6, 1905.

Family of MARY ETTA MAYER (9251) and CARLTON SHIELDS.

11428. Earl Leo, Creston, Ia., b. Aug. 28, 1892.

Family of Rev. WILLIAM JAMES SHEAFFER (9316) and ———.

11429. Emma H., Reedville, Pa.
11430. Harold, Reedville, Pa.
11431. Isabel, Reedville, Pa.
11432. Donald, Reedville, Pa.
11433. Lewis, Reedville, Pa.

Family of REBECCA J. SHEAFFER (9318) and AUSTIN MINNICH.

11434. George R., Petersburg, Pa.
11435. Claribel, Petersburg, Pa.
11436. William, Petersburg, Pa.
11437. Sarah, Petersburg, Pa.
11438. Emma, Petersburg, Pa.

Family of CLARA HERR (9327) and HENRY S. LONGENECKER.

11439. Myra May, Clarence Centre, N. Y., b. Aug. 9, 1893.
11440. Gertrude, Clarence Centre, N. Y., b. Feb. 27, 1896.
11441. Mabel, Clarence Centre, N. Y., b. May 15, 1898.

Family of CHARLES F. TREICHLER (9346) and MARY E. ROSE.

11442. Leora Rose, Sanborn, N. Y., b. June 8, 1898.
11443. Galen Mark, Sanborn, N. Y., b. July 4, 1900.

Family of CORA BELLE LONG (9387) and MILTON J. HOFFMAN.

11444. Jewett M., Williamsville, N. Y., b. Dec. 30, 1890.
11445. Russell L., Williamsville, N. Y., b. July 17, 1892.
11446. Henry M., Williamsville, N. Y., b. July 16, 1893.
11447. Isabelle C., Williamsville, N. Y., b. Apr. 4, 1898.
11448. Augustus S., Williamsville, N. Y., b. Mar. 8, 1901.

Family of SARAH ELLEN SHISLER (9390) and HENRY LEON OSWALD.

11449. Elcie Fern, Williamsville, N. Y., b. Dec. 8, 1890.

Family of CHRISTIAN B. SHISLER (9392) and SARAH ANN DRESENBERG.

11450. Evelyn May, Williamsville, N. Y., b. Jan. 29, 1900.
11451. Mildred Esther, Williamsville, N. Y., b. May 19, 1901.

Family of LAURA AUGUSTA SHISLER (9393) and FRANKLIN E. ROGERS.

11452. Allan Franklin, Wheatfield, N. Y., b. Dec. 4, 1896.
11453. Howard Edwin, Wheatfield, N. Y., b. Dec. 17, 1898.
11454. Olive Elma, Wheatfield, N. Y., b. Aug. 17, 1901.

Family of FANNIE E. SHISLER (9394) and BURR STEVEN ROGERS.

11455. Florence May, Williamsville, N. Y., b. Dec. 5, 1898.
11456. Floyd Raymond, Lindsey, O., b. Mar. 28, 1902.

Family of ELMER E. SUMMY (9396) and SUSAN GIBSON.

11457. Marion, Athol Springs, N. Y., b. July 13, 1891.
11458. Edna, Athol Springs, N. Y.
11459. Bernetta, Athol Springs, N. Y.
11460. Dorothy, Athol Springs, N. Y.

Family of ESTHER E. SUMMY (9397) and CHARLES P. MUELLER.

11461. Harriet Stevens, Wichita, Kans., b. June 15, 1891.
11462. Laura, Wichita, Kans., b. Jan. 26, 1894.
11463. Mildred, Wichita, Kans., b. Oct. 9, 1897.

Family of CHARLES EDWARD SUMMY (9398) and ALICE G. AYKROYD.

11464. Alice E., Buffalo, N. Y., b. Oct. 24, 1890.
11465. George E., Buffalo, N. Y., b. Mar. 7, 1892.
11466. Charlotte, Buffalo, N. Y., b. July 2, 1894.
11467. Harold, Buffalo, N. Y., b. Apr. 27, 1898.

Family of DAVID LONG SUMMY (9402) and VIRGINIA WEEKS.

11468. Elizabeth L., Cynwyd, Pa., b. Jan. 17, 1902.

Family of GEORGE BAKER LONG (9403) and LILLIAN W. McGEE.

11469. Hillan McGee, Chicago, Ill., b. Aug. 28, 1895.

Family of FRANCES ELIZABETH LONG (9404) and HAROLD B. WRIGHT.

11470. Gilbert Munger, Chicago, Ill., b. Mar. 17, 1901.

Family of ELLA E. LONG (9425) and CHRISTIAN WECKESSER.

11471. Louise Ella, Williamsville, N. Y., b. Nov. 9, 1891.
11472. Esther Florence, Williamsville, N. Y., b. Apr. 3, 1893.
11473. Ruth Adelle, Williamsville, N. Y., b. Feb. 22, 1895.
11474. Ernest Prosper, Williamsville, N. Y., b. Feb. 20, 1897.
11475. Constant E., Williamsville, N. Y., b. July —, 1899.

Family of RUSSELL LEIGH STEEL (9580) and IRMA HASKELL.

11476. Irma Monette, St. Louis, Mo., b. Mar. 29, 1901.

Family of CARRIE EMMA LEWIS (9591) and WILLIAM BAKER TURNER.

11477. William Baker, Denver, Col., b. Aug. 1, 1897.

Family of NAOMI B. HERSHEY (9654) and WILLIAM GINGRICH.

11478. Katie May, Derry, Pa., b. Dec. —, 1895.

Family of **MARTHA A. DIFFENBAUGH** (9659) and **R—— C. VAN EMAN.**

11479. Frances May, Hutchinson, Kans., b. May 14, 1888.

Family of **JACOB L. DIFFENBAUGH** (9662) and **EMMA HUFFMAN.**

11480. Lucille Huffman, Clinton, Mo., b. Apr. 21, 1896.

Family of **HARRIET ELIZABETH LANDIS** (9670) and **JACOB D. SHUMAN.**

11481. Dorothy L., Lancaster, Pa., b. Oct. 18, 1896.

Family of **WITMER J. KENDIG** (9797) and **REBECCA KINPORTS.**

11482. Walter R., Lancaster, Pa., b. Dec. 27, 1883.
11483. John L., Lancaster, Pa., b. May 25, 1890.

Family of **DAVID H. KENDIG** (9798) and **ANNIE S. HELLER.**

11484. Cleon R., Reading, Pa., b. Sept. 16, 1882.
11485. Mabel A., Reading, Pa., b. June 8, 1884.
11486. Christian H., Reading, Pa., b. Jan. 31, 1886.
11487. David H., Reading, Pa., b. Nov. 30, 1887.
11488. Mary E., Reading, Pa., b. Oct. 23, 1889.
11489. Mildred S., Reading, Pa., b. Jan. 30, 1892.
11490. Herbert A., Reading, Pa., b. Sept. 21, 1895.

Family of **CHRISTIANA CATHERINE FLORY** (9806) and **FRED. E. BROWN.**

11491. Jessie May, Hanford, Cal., b. Nov. 30, 1891.
11492. Jacie May, Hanford, Cal., b. Nov. 30, 1891.
11493. Roy Jacob, Hanford, Cal., b. Oct. 15, 1893.
11494. Earl William, Hanford, Cal., b. Dec. 6, 1896.
11495. Ray Alvin, Hanford, Cal., b. Dec. 4, 1900.
11496. Clyde Grove, Hanford, Ca., b. Feb. 13, 1902.

Family of **JOSEPH HENRY FLORY** (9807) and **ALICE WEBBER.**

11497. Everett Edward, Dos Palos, Cal., b. Jan. 27, 1891.
11498. Laurane Henry, Dos Palos, Cal., b. Aug. 29, 1893.
11499. Lyle Kenneth, Dos Palos, Cal., b. Aug. 27, 1898.

2523x5

Family of ISAAC DANIEL FLORY (9808) and IDA BROADHURST.

11500. Lambert Grove, Newman, Cal., b. Sept. 16, 1891.
11501. Leta Goldie, Newman, Cal., b. Jan. 24, 1894.

Family of SARAH ELIZABETH FLORY (9809) and GEORGE W. BARKER.

11502. Isaac Clayton, Lemoore, Cal., b. Nov. 27, 1889.
11503. Hazel Margarite, Lemoore, Cal., b. Oct. 28, 1891.
11504. Berdina Elizabeth, Lemoore, Cal., b. July 27, 1893.
11722. Mabry, Lemoore, Cal., b. ———, 1903.

Family of CHARLES FRANKLIN FLORY (9810) and MINTA BROUHARD.

11505. Vesta Pearl, Lemoore, Cal., b. June 28, 1893.
11506. Charles Clio, Lemoore, Cal., b. Dec. 5, 1899.

Family of JACOB ANDREW FLORY (9811) and CONSTANCE DOTY.

11507. Dolores, Lemoore, Cal., b. Nov. 16, 1900.
11508. Lena Atwood, Lemoore, Cal., b. May 15, 1902.

Family of Dr. WM. MILLER STOVER (9812) and ANNIE ELIZ. MITCHELL.

11509. Ethel Virginia, San Luis Obispo, Cal., b. Dec. 9, 1899.
11510. Raymen Beverly, San Luis Obispo, Cal., b. Feb. 13, 1902.

Family of CHARLES W. GARBER (9815) and BELLE MAUCK.

11511. Ernest Mauck, Lemore, Cal., b. Nov. 6, 1890.
11512. Addie Susan, Lemoore, Cal., b. Jan. 6, 1893.

Family of HOMER B. GARBER (9816) and MAZIE MONGER.

11513. Hallie I., Lemoore, Cal., b. May 31, 1898.
11514. Mazie Madaline, Lemoore, Cal., b. Jan. 28, 1900.

Family of BERTIE C. WAMPLER (9818) and JACOB M. JONES.

11515. Boyd Grove, Staunton, Va., b. Oct. 29, 1890.
11516. Meda E., Staunton, Va., b. Jan. 9, 1893.
11517. Irma C., Staunton, Va., b. July 5, 1895.
11518. Jacob Earl, Staunton, Va., b. Oct. 14, 1897.
11519. Mary Vera, Staunton, Va., b. Jan. 8, 1902.

Family of BETTIE WAMPLER (9819) and TAYLOR WELLER.

11520. Erskine, Staunton, Va., b. Nov. 17, 1891.
11521. John E., Staunton, Va., b. Jan. 26, 1894.

Family of MAMIE B. WAMPLER (9821) and WILLIAM HARRIS.

11522. Mabel B., Newport News, Va., b. Mar. 31, 1899.
11523. Anna Belle, Newport News, Va., b. Sept. 10, 1901.

Family of ARTHUR G. BORDEN (9827) and M—— C. WOODSON.

11524. Ethel L. Nora, Laural Hill, Va., b. Nov. 12, 1897.

Family of SALLIE ESTELLE GROVE (9839) and HENRY W. TEATS.

11525. Ruby Ernistine, Somerville, Va., b. Mar. 6, 1898.
11526. Noble Oscar, Somerville, Va., b. Aug. 20, 1899.
11527. Ella Violet, Somerville, Va., b. May 8, 1901.

Family of ERNEST M. FRANTZ (9851) and FLORENCE KENDIG.

11528. Marie, Gwynn Brook, Md., b. Jan. 30, 1897.

Family of ELLA S. FRANTZ (9853) and NEWTON J. GEIST.

11529. Elam J., Glyndon, Md., b. July 12, 1895.
11530. Arthur F., Glyndon, Md., b. Mar. 6, 1897.

Family of Dr. EDWIN R. GIRVIN (9814) and MARIE ELIZ. LOVELAND.

11531. Robert Loveland, Philadelphia, Pa., b. July 16, 1897.

Family of CLARA E. GIRVIN (9875) and JOSEPH MILLER HORTON.

11532. John Girvin, Philadelphia, Pa., b. July 22, 1876.

Family of ELLA L. EBERMAN (9883) and GIBBONS GRAY CORNWELL.

11533. Mary Gray, West Chester, Pa., b. July 21, 1900; d. July 30, 1900.
11534. Gibbons Gray, West Chester, Pa., b. Aug. 8, 1902.

Family of CHARLES CARROLL FRICK (9969) and LOUISA M. SPANGLER.

11535. C—— C., York, Pa., b. Oct. 29, 1901.

Family of **GEORGE AUGUSTUS BURK** (9979) and **SARAH ANN SKILLMAN**.

11536. Mary Elizabeth, Baltimore, Md., b. Oct. 23, 1893.
11537. Anna Winterode, Baltimore, Md., b. Sept. 8, 1895.
11538. George Augustus, Baltimore, Md., b. Apr. 1, 1898.

Family of **CORNELIA E. WATTS** (9982) and **S—— HERBERT ANDERSON**.

11539. Dorothy Frick, Baltimore, Md., b. Sept. —, 1902.

Family of **ELMER F. HAWBICKER** (10011) and **ALICE C. PIPER**.

11540. Harriet Lena, Mercersburg, Pa., b. Oct. 26, 1892.
11541. James Russell, Mercersburg, Pa., b. Sept. 10, 1894.

Family of **LEAH NANCY HAWBICKER** (10012) and **RICHARD TOLMAN**.

11542. LeRoy Scott, Mercersburg, Pa., b. Aug. 10, 1890.

Family of **LEAH F. DAILEY** (10021) and **EDWIN H. CONSTANTINE**.

11543. Henry Frederick, Mercersburg, Pa., b. Jan. 21, 1891; d. Mar. 4, 1892.
11544. Thomas Paul, Mercersburg, Pa., b. Feb. 16, 1893; d. Oct. 2, 1895.
11545. Dorothy Jane, Mercersburg, Pa., b. Sept. 7, 1900.

Family of **IDA MAY LANDIS** (10076) and **THOMAS B. SMITH**.

11546. Elizabeth L., Waynesboro, Pa., b. Dec. 2, 1893.
11547. Frank L., Waynesboro, Pa., b. Aug. 27, 1898.
11965. Thomas Breneman, Waynesboro, Pa., b. June 18, 1900.

Family of **AMELIA A. LANDIS** (10085) and **A—— B. WENTWORTH**.

11548. Nellie L., Niagara Falls, N. Y., b. Feb. 17, 1896.
11549. Albert L., Niagara Falls, N. Y., b. Aug. —, 1898.

Family of **FRANKLIN L. KOHR** (10092) and **BARBARA K. HARNISH**.

11550. Mary Elizabeth, Lancaster, Pa., b. Oct. 28, 1899.

Family of **ANNA L. KOHR** (10093) and **JACOB L. KREIDER**.

11551. Esther K., Lancaster, Pa., b. Dec. 10, 1895.

11552. Jessie Anna, Lancaster, Pa., b. Oct. 13, 1897.

11553. Mary K., Lancaster, Pa., b. Apr. 17, 1901.

Family of ALICE KOHR (10094) and ELMER WEAVER.

11554. J. —— Lloyd, Ronks, Pa., b. Sept. 26, 1900.

Family of CYRUS H. ESHLEMAN (10199) and MOLLIE K. KOONTZ.

11555. Frederick K., Harrisburg, Pa., b. Apr. 13, 1906.

Family of MINNIE K. ESHLEMAN (10200) and MELCHOR E. STRITE.

11556. Ellsworth, Leitersburg, Md.

11557. Charlotte, Leitersburg, Md.

11558. Russell, Leitersburg, Md.

11559. Walter W., Leitersburg, Md.

Family of JOHN IRA ESHLEMAN (10201) and NORA CORDELL.

11560. Hazel, Harrisburg, Pa.

11561. Marie, Harrisburg, Pa.

11562. Catherine Louise, Harrisburg, Pa.

Family of ALICE HERR (10221) and LEVI K. MARKLEY.

11563. Preston H., Donegal, Kans., b. Mar. 30, 1899.

Family of MARGARET ELVA HERR (10266) and DANIEL WAITE VAUGHAN.

11564. Daniel Waite, Kansas City, Mo., b. July 10, 1898.

11565. Margaret Ann, Kansas City, Mo., b. Sept. 4, 1900.

Family of FLORENCE LOW (10343) and ROBERT DUPUY.

11566. Andrew, Los Angeles, Cal.

11567. Robert, Los Angeles, Cal.

11568. Florence, Los Angeles, Cal., m. William Johnson.

Family of CURRAN L. SEATON (10347) and CARRIE KENNEDY.

11569. Mary, Buffalo, N. Y., m. Edward L. Blimhaus.

Family of GEORGE R. WOOD (11582) and MINNIE EMMIT.

11570. Ethel, Louisville, Ky.
11571. Virginia, Louisville, Ky.
11572. Minah, Louisville, Ky.

Family of SARAH MAY SUTCLIFF (10354) and ROBERT NELSON LOCKE.

11573. Fanny Sutcliff, Louisville, Ky., b. Aug. 18, 1877; d. Dec. 8, 1878.
11574. Lucy Nelson, Louisville, Ky., b. May 3, 1879; d. July 30, 1894.
11575. Cora Sutcliff, Louisville, Ky., b. Jan. 18, 1883; m. Nov. 11, 1902, Edwin Kirtley Milton, son Eben Milton and Margaret Kirtley.

Family of CORA SUTCLIFF LOCKE (11575) and EDWIN KIRTLEY MILTON.

11576. Edwin Kirtley, Jr., Louisville, Ky., b. Oct. 29, 1903.

Family of FANNIE OWEN (10357) and LEANDER C. WOOLFOLK.

11577. Matalea, Louisville, Ky., b. May 4, 1880; m. Feb. 19, 1901, William H. Mourning, b. Dec. 2, 1873; son Garland H. Mourning and Jennie Morse.

Family of SUSAN MILDRED HERR (11358) and Dr. DANIEL M. GRIFFITH.

11578. Mildred Taylor, Owensboro, Ky., b. Dec. 22, 1899.
11579. Mary Ridgely, Owensboro, Ky., b. Mar. 6, 1903.

Family of JAMES GUTHRIE HERR (10366) and FANNY McCLELLAN.

11580. James Guthrie, St. Louis, Mo., b. Aug. 5, 1893.
11581. Gladys, St. Louis, Mo., b. Apr. 10, 1898.

Family of M—— ELLEN RUDY (10372) and ALVIN WOOD.

11582. George R., Louisville, Ky., m. Minnie Emmit.
11583. Frances Otae, Louisville, Ky.

Family of CATHERINE B. RUDY (10373) and ALFRED BORIE.

11584. Alfred Wood, Louisville, Ky.

11585. William Dean, Louisville, Ky.

11586. George Rudy, Louisville, Ky.

11587. Minnie Ola, Louisville, Ky.

11588. Francis Edward, Louisville, Ky.

11589. Ellen Adele, Louisville, Ky.

Family of JAMES H. RUDY (10374) and SALLIE MAGNESS.

11590. Fannie, Owensboro, Ky., m. Christopher Edelen.

11591. Margaret, Owensboro, Ky., m. John Daly.

11592. George, Owensboro, Ky., m. Kittie Fuqua.

11593. John, Owensboro, Ky., m. Ella Doris.

11594. Nannie, Owensboro, Ky., m. William Morrison.

11595. Lee, Owensboro, Ky.

11596. Wallace, Owensboro, Ky.

Family of FRANCES HERR RUDY (10375) and GEORGE HERR SIMCOE.

11597. Hope Brooke, Chillicothe, Mo., b. July 28, 1872; m. Sept. 7, 1892, Albert F. Stockton, b. Oct. 9, 1869; son James Stockton and Mary Hussey.

11598. Lou Ella, Clipper, Tex., b. Sept. 7, 1874; m. Oct. 18, 1899, Thomas Bingham.

11599. Albert Rudy, Rathbone, Oklahoma, b. Dec. 19, 1880.

Family of FREDERICK OLDHAM RUDY (10376) and ELLA HUBBARD.

11600. James H., St. Matthews, Ky., m. Carrie Edinger.

11601. Norbourne Oldham, St. Matthews, Ky., b. July 1, 1880; m. June 30, 1903, Ella Thomas, b. Nov. 12, 1880; dau. P. ———— I. Thomas and Frances ————.

Family of HUGH HERR (10381) and ELEANOR HOLMES.

11602. Marian, Owensboro, Ky., b. Sept. 10, 1900.

Family of FREDERICK HERR (10382) and ANNA McCREARY.

11603. Clara, Owensboro, Ky., b. July 4, 1884.

Family of JENNIE HERR (10383) and CLAUDIUS DUVALL.

11604. Georgia Mary, Louisville, Ky., b. Mar. 22, 1878.

11605. Mary Scott, Louisville, Ky., b. May 13, 1881; m. June 9, 1903, Albert S. Pope.

11606. Virginia Allen, Louisville, Ky., b. July 31, 1884.

11607. Neniene Ovington, Louisville, Ky., b. June 26, 1895.

Family of EMMA L. HERR (10384) and JOHN T. HOWARD.

11608. Edwin Allen, Chattanooga, Tenn.

11609. Nevelle B., Chattanooga, Tenn.

Family of LOU ELLA HERR (10387) and COVINGTON A. HERR (10445).

11610. Lindenbarger, Lyndon, Ky., b. Aug. 18, 1900.

Family of REBECCA H. FENLEY (10394) and JOSEPH McCLELLAN.

11611. Lillie M., Henderson, Ky., b. May 29, 1869; d. Jan. 15, 1883.

11612. Sarah E., Vanceburg, Ky., b. July 13, 1871; m. Mar. 27, 1897, Marcelus Plummer, b. Oct. 10, 1862; son Lewis Plummer and ———.

11613. M. ——— Adelia, Vanceburg, Ky., b. Nov. 14, 1873; m. Apr. 15, 1895, A. Harman Holderness, b. May 2, 1873; son William H. Holderness and ———.

11614. George A., Maxville, Fla., b. Feb. 29, 1876; d. Apr. 6, 1882.

Family of Wid. REBECCA H. McCLELLAN (10394) and GEORGE E. DANE.

11615. Carrie S., Jacksonville, Fla., b. Feb. 15, 1882.

11616. Hattie R., Jacksonville, Fla., b. Feb. 28, 1884; d. Nov. 21, 1901.

11617. Bessie R., Jacksonville, Fla., b. Apr. 10, 1886.

Family of SUSAN P. FENLEY (10397) and ROBERT THOMAS.

11618. Mary Arminda, Corydon, Ky., b. Feb. 12, 1873.

11619. Sarah Elizabeth, Corydon, Ky., b. Nov. 9, 1874; d. Sept. 30, 1875.

11620. Rebecca Alison, Evansville, Ind., b. Sept. 15, 1877; m. Oct. 24, 1899, Frank C. Gore.

11621. Lillie Fenley, Corydon, Ky., b. Aug. 5, 1881.

11622. Annis Robert, Corydon, Ky., b. Apr. 6, 1885.

11623. Hendry Owen, Corydon, Ky., b. Dec. 3, 1888.

11624. Ruth Eliza, Corydon, Ky., b. May 12, 1890.

11625. Stanley Abbott, Corydon, Ky., b. Aug. 3, 1894.

12317. Elizabeth, Corydon, Ky., b. —, 1875; d. —, 1876.

Family of HARLAN HERR ANDERSON (10409) and MINNIE BELLE KENT.

11626. Henry Ernest, Louisville, Ky., b. Dec. 13, 1890; d. Aug. 29, 1898.

11627. Annabel, Louisville, Ky., b. June 18, 1894.

11628. Florence, Louisville, Ky., b. Mar. 25 1896; d. Sept. 17, 1896.

11629. Minnie Louisa, Louisville, Ky., b. May 4, 1897; d. Jan. 25, 1898.

Family of Wid. HARLAN HERR ANDERSON (10409) and MILDRED FIGG.

11630. Mayme Herr, Louisville, Ky., b. Sept. 4, 1902.

Family of MINNIE SPOTTSWOOD ANDERSON (10410) and EDGAR C. BIRD.

11631. Edgar Courtney, Brooklyn, N. Y., b. Aug. 25, 1890.

Family of GEORGE R. WASHBURN (10426) and MARY MOORE.

11632. Annie Louise, Pewee Valley, Ky., b. Jan. 27, 1893.

11633. Mary Elizabeth, Pewee Valley, Ky., b. Feb. 7, 1900.

Family of MARY B. HERR (10440) and ELAM RUPERT SIMCOE.

11634. Jessie Herr, New Madrid, Mo., b. July 8, 1878; m. Sept. 6, 1899, Henry Clay Hunter, b. Apr. 12, 1880; son Albert B. Hunter and Ella M. Pack.

11635. Maude Ewing, Lyndon, Ky., b. Apr. 27, 1883; m. Dec. 4, 1905, Mack Bush Wise, b. June 22, 1883.

11636. Samuel Hite, Lyndon, Ky., b. Oct. 26, 1887.

Family of ALFRED U. HERR (10441) and ALICE M. OSBORN.

11637. Ruth Lee, Louisville, Ky., b. Aug. 17, 1883.

11638. John L., Louisville, Ky., b. Jan. 2, 1886.

11639. Woodward, Louisville, Ky., b. Aug. 31, 1888.

Family of **WILLIAM W. HERR** (10442) and **JENNIE RUTH SMITH.**

11640. Susie M., Louisville, Ky., b. Nov. 24, 1887.
11641. Laura, Louisville, Ky., b. Jan. 11, 1890.
11642. Elan Rupert, Louisville, Ky., b. Oct. 27, 1891.

Family of **NORBOURNE A. RICHARDS** (10456) and **PATTIE LEE GILL.**

11643. Elizabeth A., Crescent Hill, Ky., b. Oct. 30, 1893.
11644. Thomas Gill, Crescent Hill, Ky., b. July 4, 1896.
11645. Margaret J., Crescent Hill, Ky., b. Oct. 14, 1900.
11646. Francis T., Crescent Hill, Ky., b. Oct. 14, 1900.

Family of **CLARA J. GILBERT** (10470) and Rev. **DAVID SWOPE.**

11647. Luther G., Johnstown, Pa., b. Nov. 20, 1857; d. Mar. 25, 1858.
11648. Gilbert E., Newville, Pa., b. Jan. 24, 1860; d. June 17, 1899; m. Sept. 24, 1890, Belle McK. Hays, b. Oct. 12, 1867; dau. John S. Hays and Jennie E. McFarlane.
11649. Jessie Elizabeth, Middleburg, N. Y., b. Apr. 19, 1863; d. Nov. 14, 1878.
11650. Josephine R., Middleburg, N. Y., b. Aug. 7, 1866; d. May 13, 1867.

Family of **JESSIE ELIZABETH GILBERT** (10471) and Dr. **MAX MARBURG.**

11651. Gertrude, Washington, Ia., b. Mar. 15, 1869; d. Jan. 29, 1886.

Family of **ELLA R. BUEHLER** (10472) and Rev. **EDWIN H. DELK.**

11652. Edward B., Hagerstown, Md., b. Sept. 21, 1884.
11653. Margaret Esther, Hagerstown, Md., b. Nov. 13, 1892.

Family of **MARY CAROLINE BUEHLER** (10473) and **LOUIS H. CLEMENT.**

11654. Hayden C., Salisburg, N. C., b. Sept. 25, 1879.
11655. Edward B., Salisburg, N. C., b. Sept. 18, 1881.
11656. John M., Salisburg, N. C., b. Mar. 26, 1884; d. June 29, 1884.
11657. Donald, Salisburg, N. C., b. Nov. 7, 1886.
11658. Louis Heyl, Salisburg, N. C., b. Mar. 2, 1891.

Family of ELIZABETH BUEHLER (10474) and LOUIS D. WINE.

11659. Louis D. J., Washington, D. C., b. Dec. 24, 1893.
11660. Elizabeth Buehler, Washington, D. C., b. Jan. 17, 1899.

Family of M. JULIA BRIDGES (10482) and Prof. SAMUEL P. SADTLER.

11661. Samuel S., Philadelphia, Pa., b. Nov. 15, 1873.
11662. Frederick B., Philadelphia, Pa., b. Feb. 21, 1876; d. Apr. 15, 1880.
11663. Ella, Philadelphia, Pa., b. Apr. 1, 1878.
11664. Philip B., Philadelphia, Pa., b. Feb. 21, 1884.
11665. Alice H., Phiadelphia, Pa., b. Apr. 9, 1881.

Family of FRANCES V. BRIDGES (10483) and Dr. ALFRED S. TINGES.

11666. Mary Howard, Gettysburg, Pa., b. June 22, 1877; d. ———, 1877.
11667. Kate White, Philadelphia, Pa., b. Nov. 12, 1878.
11668. Ida V., Philadelphia, Pa., b. Dec. 28, 1880.
11669. George Herbert, Philadelphia, Pa., b. Sept. 16, 1885.

Family of JOHN S. BRIDGES (10485) and MARY E. WILLS.

11670. John S., Baltimore, Md., b. Dec. 19, 1880.
11671. David Wills, Baltimore, Md., b. Jan. 12, 1883.
11672. Mary E., Baltimore, Md., b. Jan. 15, 1889.
11673. James W., Baltimore, Md., b. Apr. 10, 1892; d. July 19, 1893.

Family of SAMUEL F. RATHVON (10487) and MARY L. RHINE.

11674. Elizabeth B., Chicago, Ill., b. June 19, 1870; m. Sept. 28, 1897, Henry Slaymaker, son Henry Slaymaker and Letitia Montgomery.

Family of Wid. SAMUEL F. RATHVON (10487) and EMILY H. MAGRAW.

11675. Emily H., Sterling, Kans., b. July 6, 1879; d. June 10, 1880.
11676. Horace H., Denver, Col., b. Aug. 8, 1880.
11677. Henry M., Denver, Col., b. Oct. 16, 1882.
11678. Mary Louisa, Denver, Col., b. Jan. 12, 1884.

11679. Annie Cochran, Denver, Col., b. Feb. 1, 1887.

11680. Blanche S., Denver, Col., b. Oct. 22, 1888.

11681. Nathaniel P., Denver, Col., b. Apr. 26, 1891.

Family of WILLIAM R. RATHVON (10489) and ELIZABETH K. STAUFFER.

11682. Martin T., Florence, Col., b. Sept. 12, 1880; m. May 5, 1904, Josephine Palin.

Family of LOUISA FORNEY (10495) and GEORGE LOWER.

11683. Josephine, Carlisle, Pa., d. ———, 1896.

Family of MARY JOSEPHINE MATHIAS (10498) and Dr. EDW. D. WELLS.

11684. Edward J., Westminster, Md., b. Sept. 7, 1877.

11685. Mary A., Westminster, Md., b. Jan. 1, 1879; d. ———, 1881.

11686. William T., Westminster, Md., b. Jan. 22, 1880.

11687. Frank H., Westminster, Md., b. July 21, 1881.

11688. John G., Westminster, Md., b. Oct. 12, 1882.

11689. Mary J., Westminster, Md., b. July 12, 1884.

11690. Dyer, Westminster, Md., b. Nov. 24, 1885; d. ———, 1886.

Family of Dr. JOHN SWOPE MATHIAS (10499) and MARY L. LYNCH.

11691. Edward L., Westminster, Md., b. Jan. 9, 1880.

11692. Samuel S., Westminster, Md., b. June 27, 1882.

11693. William A., Westminster, Md., b. Nov. 29, 1884.

11694. Mary J., Westminster, Md., b. Dec. 11, 1887.

11695. John B., Westminster, Md., b. Jan. 23, 1890; d. July 16, 1890.

11696. Charles R., Westminster, Md., b. Mar. 11, 1892.

11697. John Swope, Westminster, Md., b. Feb. 9, 1895.

11698. Joseph J., Westminster, Md., b. Feb. 9, 1895.

Family of MARY H. REINDOLLAR (10506) and CHARLES E. YOUNT.

11699. Ralph, Taneytown, Md., b. May 28, 1899.

Family of VIRGEY KEEN HESS (10556) and ALVIN HESS.

11700. Mary Catherine, Quarryville, Pa., b. Apr. 17, 1901.

Family of CLARA ELVIRA STEHMAN (10646) and CHAS. B. PENNYPACKER.

11701. Mary Anita, York, Pa., b. Oct. 25, 1899.

Family of MINNIE ANN BULLINGTON (10694) and LEWIS ARGUBRIGHT.

11702. Howard Lester, Sibley, Ia.

Family of EMMA B. ESHLEMAN (10726) and LEVI H. MARTIN.

11703. Hannah E., Reid, Md., b. Aug. 17, 1900.
11704. Cora E., Reid, Md., b. Mar. 18, 1892; d. Apr. 29, 1902.

Family of ANNA BEATES GEIGER (10781) and HERVEY EDGAR SHERTS.

11705. Charles Geiger, Refton, Pa., b. Apr. 11, 1903.

Family of Dr. HOWARD HANFORD HOPKINS (10941) and ALICE E. WOOD.

11706. Howard Hanford, New Market, Md., b. Feb. 6, 1902.

Family of JOSEPH SMITH POULTON (10998) and BERTHA DEESE.

11707. Ross Edward, Harrisburg, Pa.
11708. Claude Elliott, Harrisburg, Pa.
11709. Frank Hoffman, Harrisburg, Pa.
11710. Ruth Violet, Harrisburg, Pa.

Family of CLARENCE ELLIOTT POULTON (11002) and ANNA BAKER.

11711. Clyde Wilbur, Malvern, Pa., b. Dec. 11, 1898.
11712. Mildred Edwinna, Malvern, Pa., b. Sept. 3, 1900.
11713. Catherine Emaline, Malvern, Pa., b. Jan. 5, 1903.

Family of EMORY HART (11048) and ADALINE STERNEMAN.

11714. C. —— Minnie, Lancaster, Pa., b. Apr. 11, 1872; m. Will
       Murphey.
11715. William, Lancaster, Pa., b. Oct. 27, 1874; d. Nov. 19, 1899.
11716. Ella F., Lancaster, Pa., b. Jan. 21, 1877.
11717. Anna F., Lancaster, Pa., b. June 4, 1879.
11718. Bertha, Lancaster, Pa., b. Apr. 8, 1882; d. Dec. 27, 1884.
11719. Ray, Lancaster, Pa., b. July 11, 1889; d. Apr. 14, 1899.

11720. Harry, Lancaster, Pa., b. Sept. 24, 1892.

11721. Pearl, Lancaster, Pa., b. Oct. 15, 1896.

Family of ADA HERR (11092) and F—— LEONARD REBER.

11723. Harry H., Richland, Pa., b. Mar. 4, 1901.

Family of HARRY W. HERR (11114) and ——.

11724. Daniel Mowrer, Camargo, Pa., b. Mar. 3, 1898.

Family of HARRY DAVID TROUT (11145) and MARY RESSLER.

11725. Harry D., Iva, Pa., b. June 29, 1899.

Family of MAUD ESHLEMAN (11287) and HERMAN D. KRIBBS.

11726. Harriet, East Oakland, Cal.

11727. Harold, East Oakland, Ca.

Family of PAULINE VIRGINIA DENNIS (11326) and OLIVER H. YOUNG.

11728. Mary, Hamilton, Can., b. Mar. 19, 1898; d. Aug. 2, 1899.

11729. Violet, Hamilton, Can., b. Nov. 29, 1899.

11730. Oliver David, Hamilton, Can., b. Feb. 19, 1902.

Family of FLORENCE DUPUY (11568) and WILLIAM JOHNSON.

11731. William, Los Angeles, Cal.

11732. Florence, Los Angeles, Cal.

11733. Margaret May, Los Angeles, Cal.

Family of JOHN HERR SUTCLIFF (10353) and FLORA BOLLING.

11734. John Edward, Louisville, Ky., b. Oct. 25, 1901.

11735. Ida Bolling, Louisville, Ky., b. Oct. 21, 1903.

Family of CORA SUTCLIFF (10355) and CLARENCE AUGUSTUS WARREN.

11736. John Sutcliff, Louisville, Ky., b. Oct. 3, 1874; m. Feb. 10, 1903, Cora M. McGregor.

11737. Francis Wood, Louisville, Ky., b. Jan. 14, 1878.

11738. Levi Legg, Louisville, Ky., b. Oct. 12, 1879.

11739. Fanny Sutcliff, Louisville, Ky., b. Aug. 19, 1895.

Family of MATALEA WOOLFOLK (11577) and WILLIAM H. MOURNING.

11740. Matalea Caldwell, Louisville, Ky., b. Mar. 27, 1903.

Family of HENRY MYERS (2096) and CATHERINE BRENEMAN.

11741. Carrie A., Argyle, Mich., b. Dec. 29, 1879; m. James Mc-
Naughten.
11742. Verne, Argyle, Mich., b. June 29, 1881.
11743. Clarence C., Argyle, Mich., b. July 20, 1884.
11744. Ernest B., Argyle, Mich., b. Oct. 15, 1882.

Family of SARAH MYERS (2097) and HARMON SMITH.

11745. George, Shabbond, Mich.
11746. Charles, Shabbond, Mich.
11747. Lulu, Shabbond, Mich.
11748. Amy, Shabbond, Mich.
11749. Owen, Shabbond, Mich.
11750. Edward, Shabbond, Mich.
11751. Earl, Shabbond, Mich.

Family of LOU ELLA SIMCOE (11598) and THOMAS BINGHAM.

11752. Mary Frances, Clipper, Tex., b. Sept. 13, 1900.

Family of SARAH E. McCLELLAN (11612) and MARCELUS PLUMMER.

11753. Helen F., Vanceburg, Ky., b. July 6, 1900.
11754. Sarah A., Vanceburg, Ky., b. Oct. 10, 1901.

Family of M. ADELIA McCLELLAN (11613) and A. HARMAN HOLDERNESS.

11755. Norman H., Vanceburg, Ky., b. Feb. 23, 1898.
11756. Edith B., Vanceburg, Ky., b. Feb. 8, 1900.
11757. Roy M., Vanceburg, Ky., b. Oct. 31, 1901.

Family of ELIZA LUCILLE BRENEMAN (4655) and IRA H. BARE.

11758. Winona Breneman, Lancaster, Pa., b. July 20, 1906.

Family of ELIZABETH BOWMAN (4058) and STEPHEN WIGGINS.

11759. Samuel, Rawlinsville, Pa., b. Apr. 11, 1835.

11760. David, Rawlinsville, Pa., b. June 1, 1836.

11761. Benjamin, Smithville, Pa., b. Apr. 3, 1838.

11762. John F., New Providence, Pa., b. July 8, 1839; m. Mary Book, dau. George Book and Mary ———.

11763. Clayton, New Providence, Pa., b. May 31, 1845; d. June 9, 1904.

11764. Hannah C., Smithville, Pa., b. Apr. 4, 1843; d. Nov. 11, 1904; m. Feb. 1, 1866, John G. Keemer, b. Feb. 1, 1866; m. Martin Warfel.

11765. Mary Ann, Shenk's Ferry, Pa., b. Aug. 25, 1846; m. William H. Fowden.

11766. Ellen, New Providence, Pa., b. Mar. 6, 1848; m. ——— Shaub.

11767. Harriet, Lancaster, Pa., b. Dec. 9, 1849; m. William Shaub.

11768. Elias H., New Providence, Pa., b. Mar. 18, 1852; m. Dec. 25, 1878, Alice Ann Herr (4037).

11769. Martha, New Providence, Pa., b. Nov. 2, 1853.

11770. Harvey, New Providence, Pa., b. Sept. 16, 1855.

11771. Angeline, New Providence, Pa.

Family of HANNAH C. WIGGINS (11764) and JOHN G. KEEMER.

11772. Elizabeth A., New Providence, Pa., b. Mar. 1, 1867; d. Feb. 22, 1868.

11773. Jennie W., New Providence, Pa., b. June 10, 1868; d. Mar. 18, 1870.

11774. Mary Emma, Germantown, Pa., b. Jan. 4, 1874; m. Theo. ——— Smith.

11775. Martha W., Haddington, N. J., b. Nov. 11, 1876; m. ——— Ferns.

11776. James Q. A. G., Lancaster, Pa., b. July 9, 1881; m. Nov. 30, 1904, Mae Trissler, b. Sept. 21, 1878.

11777. John Henry Clay, Philadelphia, Pa., b. Mar. 24, 1884.

Family of EDWIN S. BUDLONG (7563) and ALICE THOMAS.

11778. Stella Alena, Mill City, O., b. Jan. 17, 1891.

Family of HARRY A. BUDLONG (7564) and IDA MAY WORK.

11779. Percy Ernest, Mill City, O., b. Aug. 15, 1895.
11780. Sadie Ellen, Mill City, O., b. Mar. 8, 1897; d. Jan. 8, 1899.
11781. Nettie Hazel, Mill City, O., b. July 26, 1899.

Family of ALENA ELLEN BUDLONG (7565) and CLIFFORD VAUGHN.

11782. Veda Beryl, Salem, Or., b. Dec. 3, 1898.

Family of ANNE HERSHEY (968) and DANIEL W. WITMER.

11783. Maria Anna, Mountville, Pa., b. Aug. 11, 1830.
11784. Benjamin, Mountville, Pa., b. July 19, 1831.
11785. Elizabeth, Mountville, Pa., b. Apr. 19, 1833; d. Apr. 27, 1908;
      m. Oct. 23, 1853, Jacob Sneath, b. Nov. 11, 1828; d. Oct. 3,
      1906; son Robert Sneath and Mary Todd.
11786. Elias, Mountville, Pa., b. May 8, 1835.
11787. Catherine, Lancaster, Pa., b. Mar. 1, 1838; m. Levi Myers.
11788. Abraham, Mountville, Pa., b. July 25, 1840.
11789. Jacob, Mountville, Pa., b. Dec. 11, 1841.
11790. Henry Clay, Mountvile, Pa., b. Feb. 25, 1844.
11791. Sarah, Mountville, Pa., b. Mar. 7, 1847.

Family of HENRY H. FUNK (810) and CATHERINE H. KILHEFFER (865).

11792. Mary K., Raymore, Mo., m. 1872, ——— Hostetter.
11793. Barbara E., Lancaster, Pa., m. Martin B. Burkhart.
11794. Benjamin F., Lancaster, Pa.
11795. Christian C., Lancaster, Pa.
11796. Henry J. K., Neffsville, Pa., m. June —, 1902,
11797. Catherine C., Lancaster, Pa.

Family of BARBARA E. FUNK (11793) and MARTIN B. BURKHART.

11798. Mary E., Lancaster, Pa., m. Walter Harding.
11799. John, Lancaster, Pa.
11800. Henry, Lancaster, Pa., m. ———, dau. Myson Peters and
      Martha Light.

Family of MARY E. BURKHART (11798) and WALTER HARDING.

11801. Daughter, Lancaster, Pa., b. ———, 1893.

Family of HENRY BURKHART (11800) and ———.

11802. Gerald, Lancaster, Pa.

Family of CALVINA WILLERS (8790) and BENJAMIN R. HOWLETT.

11808. Calvin Willers, Farmer's Village, N. Y., b. May 8, 1905.

Family of MARY ANN BRENBERGER (3962) and JEFFERSON BYNEARSON.

11809. Wesley Sherman, Trenton, Mo., b. Oct. 13, 1866; m. Mar. 15, 1906, Mary Florence Williams.
11810. Catherine Drucilla, Ithaca, N. Y., b. ———, 1867; d. ———, 1867.
11811. Clarence Jesse, St. Joseph, Mo., b. Oct. 7, 1872; m. June, 1898, Estella Pennock.
11812. Daisy May, St. Joseph, Mo., b. Dec. 30, 1876.

Family of MABEL ELVINA HERR (9153) and Dr. GUY LEVIS ALEXADNER.

11813. Frances Levis, Pittsburg, Pa., b. Mar. 2, 1907.

Family of BESSIE ADELL FRANTZ (9161) and HARRY M. STRATTON.

11814. John Frantz, Milwaukee, Wis., b. Apr. 2, 1907.

Family of REBECCA FERREE (1506) and JACOB KAUFFMAN.

11816. Albert, Webster, Grove, Mo.
11817. David, Flano, Tex.
11818. Charles, St. Louis, Mo.
11819. Jacob, St. Louis, Mo.

Family of WILLIAM B. KAUFFMAN (4415) and ———.

11820. Albert F., Keener, Mo.
11821. Elizabeth R., Kylerstown, Pa., m. ——— Watts.
11822. Edward, Bainbridge, N. Y., b. Sept. 12, 1849; m. Sept. 15, 1878, Harriet Bloom.

Family of EDWARD KAUFFMAN (11822) and HARRIET BLOOM.

11823. Mae Edna, Bainbridge, N. Y., b. July 22, 1880; m. Apr. 15, 1900, Harry M. Smith.

Family of MAE EDNA KAUFFMAN (11823) and HARRY M. SMITH.

11824. Mildred E., Bainbridge, Pa., b. June 26, 1901.

Family of JACOB GROFF (100) and ———.

11825. Susanna, New Providence, Pa., b. ———, 1765; m. July 17, 1784, Frederick Brown.
11826. Elizabeth, New Providence, Pa.
11827. Barbara, New Providence, Pa.
11828. Michael, New Providence, Pa.

Family of SUSANNA GROFF (11825) and FREDERICK BROWN.

11829. John, Columbia, Pa., b. June 14, 1788; d. June 27, 1847; m. Mar. 7, 1813, Catherine Minnich, b. June 25, 1789; d. Dec. 10, 1849; dau. Jacob Minnich and Elizabeth Wolf.
11830. Barbara, New Providence, Pa., b. Mar. 9, 1790; m. ——— Myers.
11831. Catherine, New Providence, Pa., b. Aug. 14, 1792.
11832. Henry W., New Providence, Pa., m. ——— Hoak.

Family of JOHN BROWN (11829) and CATHERINE MINNICH.

11833. Rebecca, Brooklyn, N. Y., b. Nov. 19, 1824; d. Apr. 3, 1888; m. Jan. 1, 1847, William J. Kuhns, b. Jan. 26, 1825; d. June 27, 1885; son Jacob Kuhns and Ann Maria Boss.
11834. Levi, Brooklyn, N. Y., m. Mary Ann Rigby Snedecker.
11835. John Groff, Brooklyn, N. Y., m. Mary Ann ———.
11836. George Washington, Brooklyn, N. Y., b. July 1, 1848; m. ——— Dickinson; m. Louisa Webb.
11837. Jacob Minnich, Brooklyn, N. Y., m. Josephine Grugon.
11838. Frederick, Brooklyn, N. Y., m. ——— Lucas; m. Wid. Mary Eliza Brown.

Family of BARBARA BROWN (11830) and ——— MYERS.

11839. Benjamin Brown, New Providence, Pa.
11840. Aaron, New Provilence, Pa.
11841. John M., New Providence, Pa., m. ——— Groff.
11842. David, New Providence, Pa., m. ——— Jones.
11843. Isaac, New Providence, Pa., m. ——— Kean.
11844. Frederick M., New Providence, Pa., m. ——— Keller; m. ———.
11845. Abraham, New Providence, Pa., m. ——— Meyer.

Family of HENRY BROWN (11832) and ——— HOAK.

11846. Alfred, Strasburg, Pa.
11847. Christian, Strasburg, Pa.
11848. Benjamin, Strasburg, Pa., m. ——— Sides.
11849. Jacob, Strasburg, Pa.
11850. Daughter, Strasburg, Pa., m. ——— Shenk.
11851. Daughter, Strasburg, Pa., m. ——— Warfel.
11852. Daughter, Strasburg, Pa., m. ——— Johnson.
11853. Daughter, Strasburg, Pa., m. Samuel Lines.

Family of BENJAMIN BROWN (11848) and ——— SIDES.

11854. Benjamin, Strasburg, Pa., m. ——— Keen.

Family of REBECCA BROWN (11833) and WILLIAM J. KUHNS.

11855. George Washington, Brooklyn, N. Y., b. July 7, 1848; d. Apr. 10, 1849.
11856. Walter Brown, Brooklyn, N. Y., b. Nov. 11, 1850; d. July 9, 1852.
11857. Catherine Angeline, Brooklyn, N. Y., b. Nov. 8, 1858; d. Sept. ———.
11858. Henry Clarence, Brooklyn, N. Y., b. Sept. 30, 1853; d. Mar. 7, 1903.
11859. Oscar, Middletown, Conn., b. Feb. 21, 1856; m. Apr. 6, 1893, Lillie Bell Conn, b. Apr. 6, 1868; dau. Reuben Price Conn and Harriet Elizabeth Harding.

Family of HARVEY F. BARR (4208) and C—— ISABEL TUTHILL.

11860. Russell Tuthill, Quincy, Ill., b. Mar. 25, 1875; m. Oct. 6, 1904, Mary Winn, b. Aug. 9, 1878; dau. Thomas Winn and Eliza Willard.

11861. Harvey Willard, Quincy, Ill., b. June 28, 1877.

11862. Earl Eshleman, Quincy, Ill., b. June 2, 1880.

11863. Wilson Rogers, Quincy, Ill., b. May 3, 1884.

Family of RUSSELL TUTHILL BARR (11860) and MARY WINN.

11864. ————, Quincy, Ill.

11865. ————, Quincy, Ill.

Family of OSCAR KUHNS (11859) and LILLIE BELL CONN.

11866. Austin Hubbard, Middletown, Conn., b. Mar. 27, 1894.

Family of BENJAMIN F. BINKLEY (7687) and CATHERINE BEE LOCKHART.

11867. Allie Frances, Renner, Tex., b. June 5, 1881; m. Nov. 25, 1903, James Clay Wells, b. Aug. 26, 1881; son James M. Wells and Adeline P. McLeary.

Family of JOSEPH ESHLEMAN (2543) and SUSANNA HORST.

11868. John H., Gap, Pa., b. Mar. 24, 1848; m. ————, 1869, Esther Denlinger, dau. Daniel Denlinger and Margaret Hershey.

11869. Anna, Gap, Pa., b. Jan. 3, 1851; d. Dec. 22, 1897.

11870. Peter H., State Line, Pa., b. May 5, 1852; m. ————, 1875, Elizabeth Stoner, dau. Isaac Stoner and Mary Stauffer.

11871. Christian H., Hagerstown, Md., b. Jan. 16, 1854; m. 1879, Elizabeth L. Lesher, dau. Abraham Lesher and Susan Reiff.

11872. Mary, Hagerstown, Md., b. Jan. 22, 1856; d. Feb. 25, 1906; m. ————, 1876, John Hostetter, son Jacob Hostetter and Mary Weikert.

11873. Elizabeth, Denbigh, Va., b. Mar. 23, 1858; d. Apr. 9, 1897; m. ————, 1889, Franklin Brunk, son George Brunk and Mary Weaver.

11874. Joseph H., Mason and Dixon, Pa., b. Dec. 15, 1859; m. ————, 1882, Ida C. Strite (6421).

11875. Abraham, Mason and Dixon, Pa., b. Jan. 27, 1862; d. Oct. 30, 1862.

11876. David H., Mason and Dixon, Pa., b. Aug. 17, 1863; m. ———, 1886, Mary L. Reiff, d. Dec. 14, 1887; dau. Israel Reiff and Elizabeth Lesher; m. 1890, Elizabeth C. Reiff, d. Aug. 13, 1898; m. 1902, Mary M. Horst, dau. Samuel Horst and Elizabeth Martin.

11877. Michael H., Reid, Md., b. Sept. 30, 1865; m. 1890, Amanda L. Strite, dau. John Strite and Catherine Lesher.

11878. Daniel R., Reid, Md., b. Sept. 4, 1867; m. ———, 1889, Anna M. Baker, dau. Daniel Baker and Ann Weyant.

11879. Susan, Reid, Md., b. Dec. 31, 1871; m. ———, 1894, Israel Reiff, son Israel Reiff and Elizabeth Lesher.

Family of JOHN H. ESHLEMAN (11868) and ESTHER DENLINGER.

11880. Joseph, Vintage, Pa., b. Jan. 7, 1871; m. ———, 1896, Minnie Cochran, dau. Stephen Cochran and Elizabeth Barnard.

11881. Daniel H., Paradise, Pa., b. Sept. 27, 1872; m. May 30, 1893, Susan E. Brackbill (12034).

11882. Abraham, Leaman Place, Pa., b. Nov. 14, 1874; d. May 20, 1902; m. ———, 1895, Mary Eby, dau. Jacob Eby and Susanna Ranck.

11883. John, Gap, Pa., b. Apr. 16, 1877; m. ———, 1901, Ida E. Brackbill (12036).

11884. Anna, Gap, Pa., b. Aug. 7, 1879.

11885. Susan, Hagerstown, Md., b. Sept. 7, 1881; m. ———, 1905, John D. Risser, son John Risser and Barbara Martin.

11886. Elizabeth, Gap, Pa., b. Mar. 19, 1884; m. ———, 1904, Samuel Martin, son Isaac Martin and Barbara Newswanger.

11887. Esther, Gap, Pa., b. June 1, 1886.

11888. Henry, Gap, Pa., b. Aug. 15, 1888.

11889. Isaac, Gap, Pa., b. July 2, 1891.

Family of PETER H. ESHLEMAN (11870) and ELIZABETH STONER.

11890. Joseph S., State Line, Pa., b. Aug. 30, 1876; d. Dec. 27, 1899.

11891. Samuel H., State Line, Pa., b. Nov. 24, 1877; m. ———,
1899, Anna Myers, d. May 12, 1900; dau. Isaac Myers and
Anna Newman; m. ———, 1903, Mary M. Shuman, dau.
Josiah Shuman and Annis Uhler.

11892. Isaac C., State Line, Pa., b. July 4, 1881.

11893. Son, State Line, Pa., b. Oct. 31, 1882; d. Oct. 31, 1882.

11894. Anna M., State Line, Pa., b. Oct. 8, 1887.

Family of CHRISTIAN ESHLEMAN (11871) and ELIZABETH LESHER.

11895. Susan S., Hagerstown, Md., b. Feb. 25, 1881.

11896. Amos D., Hagerstown, Md., b. May 5, 1886.

11897. Laban L, Hagerstown, Md., b. Dec. 20, 1887.

11898. Abner J., Hagerstown, Md., b. July 6, 1890.

11899. Mary M., Hagerstown, Md., b. Dec. 1, 1892.

Family of MARY ESHLEMAN (11872) and JOHN HOSTETTER.

11900. Jacob E., Hagerstown, Md., b. Jan. 22, 1877.

11901. Susan A., Hagerstown, Md., b. Sept. 17, 1878.

11902. David E., Hagerstown, Md., b. July 25, 1880.

11903. J. ——— Emory, Hagerstown, Md., b. July 26, 1881.

11904. Alpheus M., Hagerstown, Md., b. Nov. 17, 1883.

11905. A——— Irvin, Hagerstown, Md., b. Jan. 26, 1886.

11906. Daniel E., Hagerstown, Md., b. Nov. 13, 1887.

11907. Joseph E., Hagerstown, Md., b. Feb. 28, 1890.

11908. Henry H., Hagerstown, Md., b. Oct. 14, 1893.

11909. Samuel L., Hagerstown, Md., b. June 13, 1896.

Family of ELIZABETH ESHLEMAN (11873) and FRANKLIN BRUNK.

11910. Joseph E., Denbigh, Va., b. May 7, 1888.

11911. George Y., Denbigh, Va., b. Nov. 18, 1890.

11912. Samuel H., Denbigh, Va., b. May 3, 1892.

11913. Henry M., Denbigh, Va., b. Jan. 30, 1895.

Family of JOSEPH H. ESHLEMAN (11874) and IDA C. STRITE.

11914. George S., Maugansville, Md., b. Sept. 14, 1883; m. ———,
1906, Amanda Weaver, dau. John Weaver and Clara Railing.

11915. Martha E., Maugansville, Md., b. Apr. 9, 1887.

11916. S. ——— Clinton, Maugansville, Md., b. June 3, 1889; d. Jan. —, 1890.

11917. Cora S., Maugansville, Md., b. Feb. 11, 1891.

11918. Rhoda M., Maugansville, Md., b. June 30, 1893.

Family of DAVID ESHLEMAN (11876) and MARY REIFF.

11919. Mary E., Cearfoss, Md., b. Dec. 12, 1887.

Family of DAVID ESHLEMAN (11876) and ELIZABETH REIFF.

11920. Katy M., Cearfoss, Md., b. Dec. 4, 1890; d. Dec. 17, 1890.

11921. Israel, Cearfoss, Md., b. Feb. 1, 1892.

11922. Esther, Cearfoss, Md., b. Nov. 14, 1895.

11923. Ida C., Cearfoss, Md., b. July 9, 1898; d. Aug. 13, 1898.

Family of DAVID ESHLEMAN (11876) and MARY HORST.

11924. Samuel H., Cearfoss, Md., b. Jan. 3, 1903; d. May 18, 1903.

11925. Martin E., Cearfoss, Md., b. Oct. 29, 1904.

11926. Anna C., Cearfoss, Md., b. Mar. 1, 1907.

Family of MICHAEL ESHLEMAN (11877) and AMANDA STRITE.

11927. Hattie S., Reid, Md., b. Dec. 3, 1891.

11928. Nancy, Reid, Md., b. Apr. 10, 1893; d. Mar. 23, 1903.

11929. John, Reid, Md., b. Jan. 12, 1895.

11930. Lydia S., Reid, Md., b. Nov. 2, 1896; d. Oct. 24, 1900.

11931. Emory S., Reid, Md., b. Aug. 20, 1897; d. Jan. 1, 1898.

11932. Daughter, Reid, Md., b. June 15, 1901; d. June 15, 1901.

11933. Amanda S., Reid, Md., b. Apr. 1, 1903.

Family of DANIEL ESHLEMAN (11878) and ANNA BAKER.

11934. Bessie V., Kauffman's, Pa., b. Nov. 15, 1894.

11935. Charles S., Kauffman's, Pa., b. Sept. 1, 1892.

11936. Grace M., Kauffman's Pa., b. Aug. 15, 1894.

11937. Ralph McK., Kauffman's, Pa., b. July 23, 1896.

11938. Earl D., Kauffman's, Pa., b. Mar. 8, 1898.

11939. Walter L., Kauffman's, Pa., b. Jan. 28, 1900.

11940. Iva P., Kauffman's, Pa., b. Apr. 1, 1902.
11941. Edna M., Kauffman's, Pa., b. Dec. 30, 1906.

Family of SUSAN ESHLEMAN (11879) and ISRAEL REIFF.

11942. Katie, Waynesboro, Pa., b. Sept. 23, 1896.

Family of DANIEL H. ESHLEMAN (11881) and SUSAN E. BRACKBILL.

11943. Clarence B., Paradise, Pa., b. Dec. 8, 1892.
11944. Christian H., Paradise, Pa., b. Mar. 7, 1895.
11945. Susan E., Paradise, Pa., b. Jan. 19, 1906.

Family of ABRAHAM ESHLEMAN (11882) and MARY EBY.

11946. Elmer E., Leaman Place, Pa., b. Oct. 1, 1896.
11947. John L., Leaman Place, Pa., b. Feb. 13, 1899.
11948. Phoebe, Leaman Place, Pa., b. Mar. 8, 1901.

Family of JOHN ESHLEMAN (11883) and IDA E. BRACKBILL (12036).

11949. Esther B., Gap, Pa., b. Feb. 18, 1904.
11950. Elam H., Gap, Pa., b. Mar. 3, 1906.

Family of SUSAN ESHLEMAN (11885) and JOHN D. RISSER.

11951. John E., Hagerstown, Md., b. Sept. 30, 1905.
11952. Landis E., Hagerstown, Md., b. Mar. 12, 1907.

Family of ELIZABETH ESHLEMAN (11886) and SAMUEL MARTIN.

11953. Marian V., Gap, Pa., b. Sept. 10, 1906.

Family of SAMUEL H. ESHLEMAN (11891) and ANNA MYERS.

11954. Elmer I., State Line, Pa., b. Mar. 29, 1900.

Family of SAMUEL H. ESHLEMAN (11891) and MARY SHUMAN.

11955. Annis E., State Line, Pa., b. Jan. 31, 1905.

Family of EDWIN B. SEIPLE (8137) and CORDELIA WITTINGTON.

11956. ———, Marshall, Ill., b. June 14, 1905.

Family of ANDREW G. HERR (3306) and JOSIE M. WATT.

11957. Frederick Roland, Minneapolis, Minn., b. Apr. 14, 1903.
11958. Robert Louis, Minneapolis, Minn., b. Jan. 5, 1905.

Family of ELIZABETH WITMER (11785) and JACOB SNEATH.

11959. Isaiah Witmer, New Haven, Conn., b. Aug. 22, 1855; m. Sept. 19, 1882, Ella Jane Mark, b. Mar. 20, 1856; dau. George A. Mark and Maria Myers.
11960. Elias Hershey, New Haven, Conn., b. Aug. 7, 1857; m. June 19, 1890, Anna Sheldon Camp, dau. John N. Camp and Sarah Williams.
11961. Emma Eugenia, Columbia, Pa., b. May 11, 1869; m. Oct. 10, 1893, Harry Clarke Bruner, son Henry Bruner and Caroline Millison.

Family of ISAIAH W. SNEATH (11959) and ELLA JANE MARK.

11962. George Mark, New Haven, Conn., b. Sept. 6, 1884.

Family of EMORY ELSE HERR (2028 and MAE COOK MYER.

11966. John Lathrop, Scranton, Pa., b. Jan. 25, 1902.

Family of Wid. EMORY ELSE HERR (2028) and MARY S. GILLIES.

11967. Dorothy S., Scranton, Pa.

Family of ESTHER G. FEILBACH (3342) and MILTON I. KAMERER.

11968. Margaret Marie, Pittsburg, Pa., b. Nov. 24, 1903.
11969. Louis Irvin, Pittsburg, Pa., b. Nov. 28, 1905; d. Aug. 30, 1906.

Family of HENRY HERR (823) and CLARISSA LITTLE.

11970. Fannie, York, Pa., b. June 4, 1860; d. Jan. 2, 1888; m. Feb. ———, 1875, Charles Brunhouse.
11971. Lillie, York, Pa., b. Mar. 30, 1859; m. Dec. 5, 1877, Horace C. Epply, b. Dec. 25, 1859; son George W. Epply and Anna M. ———.

27

Family of FANNIE HERR (11970) and CHARLES BRUNHOUSE.

11972. Harry, Mechanisburg, Pa.

11973. Luther, York, Pa.

Family of LILLIE HERR (11971) and HORACE C. EPPLY.

11974. Annie M., Lancaster, Pa., b. Apr. 20, 1879; d. June 5, 1898; m. July 15, 1897, Nathan Engle, b. Sept. 21, 1875; son Michael H. Engle and Malvinia A. Blake.

11975. George W., Lancaster, Pa., b. Nov. 18, 1882; m. June 2, 1896, Estella Bailey, b. Aug. 28, 1882; dau. William Bailey and Henrietta ———.

11976. H. Robert, York, Pa., b. May 5, 1886.

11977. Mabel L., Lancaster, Pa., b. May 27, 1890.

11978. Florence B., Lancaster, Pa., b. July 27, 1893.

11979. Raymond Herr, Lancaster, Pa., b. Sept. 3, 1895.

Family of SUSANNA HERR (826) and JACOB GUNDRUM.

11982. Harry Francis, York, Pa., b. Apr. 5, 1869; m. Oct. 6, 1896, Lucy May Rodes, b. May 4, 1876; dau. Alexander A. Rodes and Lucy A. E. Naylor.

11983. Charles Albert, York, Pa., b. Oct. 15, 1870; m. Nov. 10, 1900, Olive C. Wagner, b. Jan. 25, 1880; dau. Samuel Wagner and Catherine Snyder.

11984. Jacob William, Bethlehem, Pa., b. Sept. 18, 1873; m. May 21, 1903, Estella May Ruth, b. Dec. 17, 1882; dau. Milton E. Ruth and Catherine Weiss.

11985. Lewis Jacob, Bethlehem, Pa., b. Oct. 27, 1865; d. July 19, 1866.

11986. Frederick William, Bethlehem, Pa., b. Aug. 19, 1867; d. Mar. 2, 1868.

Family of HARRY GUNDRUM (11982) and LUCY MEY RODES.

11987. Franklin Rodes, York, Pa., b. July 22, 1897.

11988. Raymond Herr, York, Pa., b. Sept. 15, 1899.

11989. Henry Francis, York, Pa., b. Mar. 27, 1902.

11990. Mary Elizabeth, York, Pa., b. Apr. 12, 1906.
11991. Robert Alexander, York, Pa., b. Apr. 12, 1906; d. Feb. 27, 1907.

Family of CHARLES GUNDRUM (11983) and OLIVE C. WAGNER.

11992. Ralph Jacob, York, Pa., b. June 2, 1901.
11993. Paul Charles, York, Pa., b. Feb. 2, 1903.
11994. Albert Luther, York, Pa., b. Oct. 30, 1905.

Family of WILLIAM GUNDRUM (11984) and ESTELLA M. RUTH.

11995. J. —— William, Bethlehem, Pa., b. Oct. 21, 1905.

Family of CLARA LOUISA MILLER (2750) and PETER H. SLAYBAUGH.

11996. Annie Elizabeth, Biglerville, Pa., b. Nov. 18, 1873; m. John Albert; m. Benjamin Hummer.
11997. Harry Elmer, Biglerville, Pa., b. Sept. 20, 1877; m. Annie Eckert; m. —— Essic.
11998. Hattie Alverta, Biglerville, Pa., b. Oct. 21, 1882; m. Emory Glosser.

Family of FLORENCE VIRGINIA MILLER (2751) and DANIEL S. BRICKER.

11999. Mary Alverta, Biglerville, Pa., m. William Fohl.
12000. Elmer George, Biglerville, Pa., b. Apr. 9, 1879; m. Hattie Brame.
12001. Stella Amanda, Biglerville, Pa., b. Mar. 20, 1885; m. Taylor Brame.

Family of JOHN HENRY MILLER (2752) and ALICE EPPLEMAN.

12002. Hugh Henry, Aspers, Pa., b. May 27, 1884.
12003. Erma Harriet, Aspers, Pa., b. Oct. 16, 1885.
12004. Walter Scott, Aspers, Pa., b. Mar. 15, 1888.
12005. Abraham, Aspers, Pa., b. Apr. 5, 1891; d. Apr. 5, 1891.
12006. James Gracen, Aspers, Pa., b. Jan. 4, 1894.
12007. Grace M., Aspers, Pa., b. Aug. 15, 1897; d. Aug. 22, 1897.

Family of ROSANNA MARGARET MILLER (2753) and HOWARD BRAME.

12008. Magnertus, Gettysburg, Pa., b. May 11, 1878; d. May 18, 1878.

12009. Cora Amelia, Gettysburg, Pa., b. Apr. 9, 1879; m. George Cleveland.
12010. Effie Jane, Gettysburg, Pa., b. Jan. 16, 1880.
12011. Harriet Naomi, Gettysburg, Pa., b. Oct. 8, 1881; m. May —, 1902, Mervine Topper.
12012. Emery E., Gettysburg, Pa., b. Feb. 18, 1883.
12013. Harvey, Gettysburg, Pa., b. Dec. 27, 1884.
12014. Oscar Howard, Gettysburg, Pa., b. Oct. 24, 1886.
12015. Franklin Ira, Gettysburg, Pa., b. Jan. 25, 1889.
12016. James Roy, Gettysburg, Pa., b. Sept. 8, 1890; d. Apr. 18, 1891.
12017. Edna May, Gettysburg, Pa., b. Mar. 27, 1892.
12018. Goldie, Gettysburg, Pa., b. Jan. 4, 1894.
12019. Archie William, Gettysburg, Pa., b. Mar. 23, 1902.

Family of ELMER HERR MILLER (2754) and LAURA BRAME.

12020. Mary E., Aspers, Pa., b. Aug. 2, 1904.

Family of ANNIE JANE MILLER (2755) and JEROME R. EMERY.

12023. Vertie M., York, Pa., b. May 17, 1891.
12024. Mary Elizabeth, York, Pa., b. Mar. 19, 1893; d. Mar. 31, 1893.

Family of SUSAN HOOVER (3595) and ELI CRAMER.

12025. Lida, Willow Street, Pa.
12026. John, Willow Street, Pa.
12027. Edward, Willow Street, Pa.
12028. Elizabeth, Willow Street, Pa.

Family of MARY HOOVER (3596) and AMOS LEACHEY.

12029. Harry, Lancaster, Pa.
12030. Edith, Lancaster, Pa.

Family of EDWIN B. SEIPLE (8137) and CORDELIA WHITTINGTON.

12031. J —— Waldo Marshall, Ill.

Family of BARBARA HERR (23) and JACOB MILLER.

12032. Christian H., Lampeter, Pa., b. Feb. 5, 1812; d. Jan. 8, 1879; m. Dec. 21, 1837, Martha Herr (522).

Family of ELAM H. BRACKBILL (4258) and BARBARA HERSHEY.

12033. Christian E., Gap, Pa., b. Jan. 13, 1871; m. Nov. 2, 1893, Anna Buckwalter, b. June 14, 1867; dau. Isaac Buckwalter and Magdalena Hershey.

12034. Susan E., Paradise, Pa., b. July 22, 1872; m. May 30, 1893, Daniel H. Eshleman (11881).

12035. Lena H., Kinzers, Pa., b. Sept. 9, 1874; m. Isaac Buckwalter.

12036. Ida E., Gap, Pa., b. Oct. 15, 1876; m. Nov. 28, 1900, John Eshleman (11883).

12037. Harry G., Kinzers, Pa., b. Aug. 21, 1881.

12038. Hettie S., Kinzers, Pa., b. Oct. 31, 1883; m. Isaac E. Hershey (12115).

12039. Anna Mary, Kinzers, Pa., b. Apr. 10, 1879; m. Dec. 3, 1901, David Groff, b. Apr. 17, 1879; son Martin Groff and Elizabeth Hershey.

12054. Elam M., Kinzers, Pa., b. Aug. —, 1886; d. Aug. 29, 1887.

Family of LYDIA ANN BRACKBILL (4261) and PETER HESS.

12040. Christian B., Mechanicsburg, Pa., b. Feb. 16, 1879; m. Dec. 29, 1904, Fannie Horst, dau. Joseph Horst and Maria Frey.

12041. Anna Barbara, Mechanicsburg, Pa., b. Mar. 21, 1884.

12042. Mary Susan, Mechanicsburg, Pa., b. Mar. 8, 1882.

12055. Lizzie Judith, Mechanicsburg, Pa., b. Dec. 12, 1875; d. Apr. 28, 1887.

Family of BENJAMIN O. BRACKBILL (4262) and ANNA MARTIN.

12043. Martin H., Lancaster, Pa., b. Feb. 2, 1882; m. Feb. 17, 1903, Mary C. Weaver, b. Oct. 3, 1879; dau. Ezra Weaver and Elizabeth Zimmerman.

12044. Edith, Lancaster, Pa., b. Nov. 30, 1884.

12045. Mary, Lancaster, Pa., b. May 16, 1887.

12046. Isaac, Lancaster, Pa., b. Apr. 15, 1886.

12047. Joseph, Lancaster, Pa., b. July 6, 1889.

12048. Moses, Lancaster, Pa., b. Aug. 8, 1890.

12056. Abraham B., Lancaster, Pa., b. Jan. 23, 1885; d. July 26, 1905.

Family of HENRY P. BRACKBILL (4264) and EMMA DILLER.

12049. Cora E., Vintage, Pa., b. Oct. 5, 1880; m. Nov. 4, 1903, J—— Ira Ranck, b. June 12, 1880; son John M. Ranck and Martha H. Groff.

12050. Bessie M., Vintage, Pa.

12051. Harry D., Vintage, Pa.

12052. Ira B., Vintage, Pa., b. July 26, 1904.

12053. ————, Vintage, Pa., b. Apr. 16, 1906.

Family of MARTHA STRITE (2602) and JACOB SHANK.

12057. Catharine, Mason and Dixon, Pa., m. Samuel H. Martin.

12058. Elizabeth, Mason and Dixon, Pa.

12059. Mary, Mason and Dixon, Pa., m. Isaac Myers.

12060. Jacob, New Danville, Pa.

12061. Samuel, New Danville, Pa.

12062. Martha, New Danville, Pa., m. John H. Grove.

12063. David, New Danville, Pa.

12064. Emma, New Danville, Pa.

12065. Ida, New Danville, Pa., m. J—— W. Eby.

12066. Rebecca, New Danville, Pa.

Family of CATHARINE STRITE (2603) and LEWIS HARBAUGH.

12067. Daniel, Hagerstown, Md.

12068. Alice, Mason and Dixon, Pa.

12069. Clara, Mason and Dixon, Pa.

12070. Melchor, Mason and Dixon, Pa.

12071. John, Mason and Dixon, Pa.

Family of MARY STRITE (2606) and J—— LEMUEL GILBERT.

12072. Lewis DeLoyd, Waynesboro, Pa.

12073. D—— Clayton, Hagerstown, Md.

12074. Myrtle E., Hagerstown, Md., m. ———— Wolfersberger.

12075. David Allen, Waynesboro, Pa.

Family of MARY STRITE (2622) and CHRISTIAN SHANK.

12076. Abraham, Hagerstown, Md., b. Dec. 5, 1872; m. Nov. 21, 1895, Susan K. Horst, b. ————, 1875; d. Sept. 3, 1899; dau. Samuel Horst and Lydia Lesher; m. Jan. 8, 1801, Susanna M. Horst, dau. Samuel Horst and Elizabeth Martin.

12077. Annie, Hagerstown, Md., b. Oct. 26, 1875; m. Dec. 9, 1895, Jacob Oberholtzer.

12078. Martha, Hagerstown, Md., b. May 26, 1874.

12231. Frederick, Hagerstown, Md., b. ———, 1877; d. ———, 1878.

12232. Aaron, Hagerstown, Md., b. Dec. 22, 1880; m. Nov. 18, 1900, Ida M. Grove, dau. John Grove and Elizabeth Shank.

12233. Noah, Greencastle, Pa., b. Jan. 29, 1884; m. Nov. 22, 1904, Katie Shank, dau. John Shank and Mary Bumbgardner.

12234. Rebecca, Hagerstown, Md., b. Apr. 8, 1886.

12235. Christian, Hagerstown, Md., b. Aug. 23, 1888.

12236. Daniel, Hagerstown, Md., b. June 24, 1890.

Family of ELIZABETH ESHLEMAN (6359) and JOHN L. SHANK.

12079. Harvey E., Marian, Pa., b. Sept. 26, 1887.

12080. Charles E., Marian, Pa., b. Dec. 19, 1892.

12081. Clarence E., Marian, Pa., b. Apr. 11, 1895.

Family of DANIEL ESHLEMAN (6356) and SUSANNA HURST.

12082. Anna M., Smithburg, Md., b. Oct. 28, 1874; d. Apr. 9, 1879.

12083. Harry, Smithburg, Md., b. Mar. 6, 1876: d. Mar. 17, 1876.

12084. Emma S., Smithburg, Md., b. Feb. 16, 1878; d. July 5, 1879.

12085. Rebecca, Hagerstown, Md., b. June 28, 1880; m. Jan. 22, 1903, Aaron Hoover, b. Mar. 10, 1879; son John Hoover and Mary Stauffer.

12186. David Franklin, Smithburg, Md., b. Sept. 29, 1881; m. Mar. 22, 1905, Anna Fishack, b. Feb. 21, 1884; dau. Jeremiah Fishack and Anna R. Williar.

12187. Martin H., Smithburg, Md., b. Nov. 3, 1883.

12188. Samuel H., Smithburg, Md., b. Oct. 2, 1885; d. Aug. 21, 1890.

12189. Daniel H., Smithburg, Md., b. Mar. 31, 1887.

12190. Benjamin H., Smithburg, Md., b. Oct. 14, 1888; d. Apr. 10, 1889.

Family of JACOB W. ESHLEMAN (6368) and MARIA BAER.

12086. Adam B., Hagerstown, Md.

12087. Daughter, Hagerstown, Md.

12088. Daughter, Hagerstown, Md.

Family of JOHN A. STRITE (6417) and ———.

12089. Melchor E., Leitersburg,*Md., m. Minnie K. Eshleman (10200).

12090. Charles, Leitersburg, Md.

12091. D ——— Frank, Leitersburg, Md.

12092. Mary, Leitersburg, Md.

12093. Ira, Greencastle, Pa.

12094. Emma, Greencastle, Pa., m. ——— Snyder.

12095. John C., Greencastle, Pa.

12096. Lizzie, Cearfoss, Md., m. Martin Horst.

Family of IDA C. STRITE (6421) and JOSEPH H. ESHLEMAN.

12097. George S., Mason and Dixon, Pa.

Family of EMMA S. STRITE (6422) and HENRY L. STRITE.

12098. Carrie M., Leitersburg, Md.

12099. Chester, Leitersburg, Md.

12100. Milton, Leitersburg, Md.

Family of MARY ANN PENNEL (3605) and JAMES IRVIN.

12101. E. ——— Side, Lancaster, Pa., b. Aug. 2, 1867.

12102. Harry S., Lancaster, Pa., b. Aug. 22, 1872; m. Apr. 18, 1907, Ella M. Zercher, b. Dec. 4, 1876; dau. John T. Zercher and Lavina M. Weaver.

12103. C——— Ray, Lancaster, Pa., b. May 18, 1880.

Family of HARRY C. PENNEL (3606) and ELLA M. HOLSTANDER.

12104. Clarence Arthur, Chicago, Ill., b. Sept. 9, 1876.

Family of RUTH ANN ESHLEMAN (4250) and WILLIAM McCLURE LLOYD.

12105. Samuel Henry, Downingtown, Pa., b. Aug. 10, 1873; d. June 7, 1874.

12106. John Eshleman, Downingtown, Pa., b. Mar. 28, 1882.

12107. William McClure, Downingtown, Pa., b. Jan. 23, 1887.

Family of ELIZABETH ESHLEMAN (4251) and ABRAHAM R. McILVAINE.

12108. Fanny Edge, Downingtown, Pa., b. July 24, 1878.

12109. John Gilbert, Downingtown, Pa., b. Dec. 4, 1880.

12110. Herbert Robinson, Downingtown, Pa., b. Mar. 16, 1882.
12111. Donald, Downingtown, Pa., b. July 28, 1892.

Family of JOHN B. HERSHEY (8696) and ANNA M. EBY.

12115. Isaac E., Gordonville, Pa., b. Apr. 20, 1884; m. Nov. 30, 1905, Hettie S. Brackbill (12038).
12116. John Aaron, Gordonville, Pa., b. May 20, 1886; d. June 9, 1902.
12117. Henry Rine, Gordonville, Pa., b. Sept. 14, 1898.

Family of MAGDALENA HERSHEY (8697) and JOSEPH M. HERSHEY.

12118. Roy, Paradise, Pa.
12119. John C., Paradise, Pa.
12120. Magdalena, Paradise, Pa., b. Sept. 5, 1904.

Family of MARTHA ELIZ. GROFF (4985) and HAMILTON I. ROTHROCK.

12121. Anna Hershey, Philadelphia, Pa., b. Apr. 10, 1886; d. Mar. 14, 1887.

Family of SUSAN BERTHA HERR (5243) and WILLIAM B. BUSH.

12122. Catharine Herr, Lancaster, Pa., b. Oct. 23, 1906.

Family of CHARLES C. GROFF (4964) and MARY R. FISHER.

12123. George Fisher, Charleston, W. Va., b. Jan. 18, 1880; m. June 6, 1905, Grayce Harley Malcolm.
12124. Charles Clayton, Charleston, W. Va., b. May 29, 1881; d. Feb. 17, 1882.
12125. Forres Claon, Charleston, W. Va., b. Dec. 11, 1882.
12126. Benjamin Barr, Charleston, W. Va., b. Apr. 20, 1884.

Family of ANNIE M. EPPLY (11974) and NATHAN ENGLE.

12127. Roland Blake, Lancaster, Pa., b. Dec. 11, 1898.

Family of HENRY S. HERR (5313) and SARAH A. MOWRER.

12128. Milton M., Lancaster, Pa., b. Mar. 1, 1882.
12129. Anna M., Lancaster, Pa., b. Dec. 14, 1883.
12130. Ray J., Lancaster, Pa., b. July 29, 1885.
12131. Bertha E., Lancaster, Pa., b. Nov. 23, 1889.

12132. Edith M., Lancaster, Pa., b. Oct. 4, 1892.

12133. Park T., Lancaster, Pa., b. Feb. 14, 1894; d. July 28, 1894.

12134. Lestie L., Lancaster, Pa., b. Aug. 11, 1895; d. Jan. 28, 1896.

12135. Harry L., Lancaster, Pa., b. May 20, 1897.

Family of FRANK J. HERR (5314) and IDA WHITMER.

12136. Iven W., Willow Street, Pa., b. Oct. 16, 1888.

12137. Edna Mary, Willow Street, Pa., b. Aug. 24, 1890.

12138. Marion Anna, Willow Street, Pa., b. Oct. 16, 1899.

12139. Myrtle Emma, Willow Street, Pa., b. Oct. 16, 1899.

12140. Frank W., Willow Street, Pa., b. Mar. 30, 1904.

12141. George W., Willow Street, Pa., b. Sept. 20, 1907.

Family of Rev. BENJAMIN HERTZLER (3074) and ANNA HOSTETTER.

12142. Amanda, Safe Harbor, Pa., m. Benjamin Miller, son Abner Miller and ———.

12143. Catharine, Lancaster, Pa., m. Daniel Brubaker.

12144. Anna, Lancaster, Pa., b. Mar. 3, 1864; m. Aug. 19, 1883, Jacob J. Stehman, b. July 28, 1861; son Jacob B. Stehman and Anna Mary Shenk.

Family of EMMA M. HOSTETTER (5370) and ELMER D. ERISMAN.

12145. Edna H., Millersville, Pa., b. Mar. 3, 1885.

12146. Clyde H., Millersville, Pa., b. July 13, 1887.

12147. Elmer H., Millersville, Pa., b. Sept. 29, 1889.

12148. Hilda M., Millersville, Pa., b. Mar. 20, 1899.

Family of CARRIE SHIRK (4387) and ——— SNYDER.

12149. Edgar, Wooster, O.

Family of CLARK D. WISSLER (10257) and ETTA V. GEBHART.

12150. Stanley, Richmond, Ind., b. Mar. 31, 1901.

12151. Mary Viola, Richmond, Ind., b. July 29, 1907.

Family of MARTIN H. BRACKBILL (12043) and MARY C. WEAVER.

12152. Allan G., Lancaster, Pa., b. Jan. 22, 1903.

12153. Martin H., Lancaster, Pa., b. Mar. 26, 1904.

12154. Almeda G., Lancaster, Pa., b. June 4, 1905.

Family of ANNA ESHLEMAN (202) and ——— GINGRICH.

12155. Jacob, Strasburg, Pa.
12156. John, Strasburg, Pa.
12157. Christian, Strasburg, Pa.
12158. David, Strasburg, Pa.
12159. Daniel, Strasburg, Pa.
12160. Abraham, Strasburg, Pa.
12161. Henry, Strasburg, Pa.
12162. Joseph, Strasburg, Pa.
12163. Infant, Strasburg, Pa.

Family of BARBARA ESHLEMAN (204) and ——— HOOVER.

12164. Peter, Strasburg, Pa.
12165. Samuel, Strasburg, Pa.
12166. Jacob, Strasburg, Pa.
12167. John, Strasburg, Pa., b. Feb., 1806; d. Jan. 22, 1899; m. Fanny Buckwalter.
12168. ———, Strasburg, Pa., m. Christian Hess.
12169. ———, Strasburg, Pa., m. Henry Stoner.
12170. ——— ———, Strasburg, Pa., m. Samuel Martin.
12171. ——— ———, Strasburg, Pa., m. ——— Horst.
12172. ——— ———, Strasburg, Pa., m. Andrew Groff.

Family of HENRY HERR GAMBER (5330) and ANNIE S. NEFF.

12173. Elia N., Manheim, Pa., b. Oct. 30, 1890; d. Nov. 7, 1890.
12174. Anna N., Manheim, Pa., b. Oct. 7, 1891.
12175. Selena N., Manheim, Pa., b. June 10, 1893.
12176. Benjamin N., Manheim, Pa., b. Aug. 16, 1894.
12177. Grace N., Manheim, Pa., b. Apr. 27, 1897.
12178. Harry N., Manheim, Pa., b. Nov. 22, 1900.
12179. Ada N., Manheim, Pa., b. Feb. 8, 1907.

Family of EMMA K. STRITE (6433) and FRANKLIN D. BELL.

12180. Frederick Strite, Leitersburg, Md., b. Jan. 18, 1902.
12181. Franklin Arthur, Leitersburg, Md., b. Oct. 25, 1906.

Family of WILLIAM A. STRITE (6436) and ELLA E. BEAR.

12182. Margaret Adelaide, Hagerstown, Md.

Family of Hon. AMOS H. MYLIN (3189) and Wid. CAROLINE H. POWELL.

12183. Barbara Kendig, Lancaster, Pa., b. Jan. 7, 1885.
12184. Helen, Lancaster, Pa., b. Mar. 10, 1887; d. Jan. 4, 1904.
12185. Mercy Hepburn, Lancaster, Pa., b. July 30, 1889.

Family of Wid. DANIEL ESHLEMAN (6356) and ANNA E. SHANK.

12191. Mary E., Smithburg, Md., b. Jan. 18, 1893.
12192. Florence, Smithburg, Md., b. Mar. 9, 1895.
12193. Catharine, Smithburg, Pa., b. Sept. 1, 1896.

Family of JONAS W. ESHLEMAN (6376) and NORA F. GERHART.

12200. Preston G., Mason and Dixon, Pa., b. June 27, 1894.
12201. Samuel I., Mason and Dixon, Pa., b. Nov. 6, 1901.
12202. Chalice R., Mason and Dixon, Pa., b. June 1, 1904.

Family of ELLA B. HERR (7640) and I—— N. SHEAFFER.

12203. C—— Harold, Witmer, Pa., b. Dec. 11, 1897.
12204. B—— Richard, Witmer, Pa., b. Apr. 27, 1905.

Family of FANNIE B. HERR (7641) and CHARLES MAHLER.

12205. Donald, Witmer, Pa., b. Jan. 30, 1898.
12206. Catharine, Witmer, Pa., b. July 20, 1900.

Family of ALMA WINGET (9600) and NORMAN E. CUMMINGS.

12207. Elmer Lewis, Huntington, W. Va., b. May 18, 1906.
12208. William Winget, Huntington, W. Va., b. Jan. 24, 1907.

Family of JOHN ESHLEMAN (2591) and ELLEN STEINBAUGH.

12209. David J., Penbrook, Pa., b. Aug., 1864; m. Elizabeth Aungst.
12210. Emma C., Penbrook, Pa., b. Mar. 23, 1866.
12211. Samuel F., Penbrook, Pa., b. Aug. 27, 1867.
12212. John G., Penbrook, Pa., b. Feb. 4, 1869; d. Aug. 12, 1892.
12213. Elias, Penbrook, Pa., b. Oct. 17, 1870; m. Ida Hetrick.
12214. Emanuel, Penbrook, Pa., b. July 7, 1872; m. Sallie Krebs.

Family of Wid. JOHN ESHLEMAN (2591) and MARY A. STOPFEL.

12215. Mary E., Penbrook, Pa., b. Feb. 10, 1878.

12216. Susan J., Penbrook, Pa., b. Apr. 5, 1879; m. Apr. 22, 1906, Morris M. Wagner.

12217. Christiana, Penbrook, Pa., b. Sept. 3, 1880.

12218. Emma E., Penbrook, Pa., b. Dec. 22, 1881; d. Nov. 26, 1883.

12219. Daniel E., Penbrook, Pa., b. Mar. 17, 1883.

12220. Joseph J., Penbrook, Pa., b. Dec. 16, 1884.

12221. Elizabeth M., Penbrook, Pa., b. Dec. 19, 1886.

12222. Isaac S., Penbrook, Pa., b. Feb. 22, 1888.

12223. Aaron N., Penbrook, Pa., b. Dec. 23, 1889; d. June 29, 1890.

12224. Ralph W., Penbrook, Pa., b. Aug. 11, 1891.

12225. John H., Penbrook, Pa., b. June 23, 1893; d. Aug. 31, 1894.

12226. Louisa A., Penbrook, Pa., b. Jan. 18, 1895.

12227. Emerson I., Penbrook, Pa., b. Mar. 18, 1896.

12228. Paul V., Penbrook, Pa., b. Jan. 22, 1898.

12229. Jonah A., Penbrook, Pa., b. Mar. 10, 1900.

12230. Annie K., Penbrook, Pa., b. Mar. 31, 1904.

Family of ABRAM SHANK (12076) and SUSAN K. HORST.

12237. Amos H., Hagerstown, Md., b. Oct. 11, 1896.

12238. Samuel L., Hagerstown, Md., b. Dec. 30, 1897.

Family of Wid. ABRAM SHANK (12076) and SUSANNA M. HORST.

12239. Fannie K., Hagerstown, Md., b. June 7, 1902.

Family of ANNIE SHANK (12077) and JACOB OBERHOLTZER.

12240. Aaron, Hagerstown, Md., b. Feb. 19, 1897.

12241. Mary K., Hagerstown, Md., b. Nov. 23, 1901.

Family of AARON SHANK (12232) and IDA M. GROVE.

12242. Evarella, Hagerstown, Md., b. Jan. 31, 1902.

12243. Cora G., Hagerstown, Md., b. Dec. 20, 1904; d. May 20, 1905.

Family of ANNIE E. MAYER (9253) and ADRIEL H. MAXWELL.

12244. Bernice Elanor, Des Moines, Ia., b. Aug. 26, 1904.

Family of ELIZABETH HERR (2694) and ABRAHAM KAUFFMAN.

12245. Annie, Columbia, Pa., b. Oct. 3, 1873.

Family of CATHARINE HERR (2699) and BENJAMIN B. ESHBACH.

12246. Mary H., Lancaster, Pa., b. Feb. 15, 1879; m. Amos Brubaker.

12247. John H., Lancaster, Pa., b. Nov. 29, 1881; m. Jan. 5, 1904, Ethel Charles.

12248. Fanny H., Lancaster, Pa., b. Aug. 20, 1883.

12249. Harry H., Lancaster, Pa., b. Oct. 18, 1885; m. Nov. 8, 1906, Bertha Kendig.

12250. Benjamin, Lancaster, Pa., b. June 15, 1888.

12251. Enos H., Lancaster, Pa., b. Apr. 8, 1890.

12252. Katie H., Lancaster, Pa., b. Mar. 29, 1896.

Family of JOHN H. ESHBACH (12247) and ETHEL CHARLES.

12253. Anna Mary, Lancaster, Pa., b. May 16, 1905.

Family of HARRY H. ESHBACH (12249) and BERTHA KENDIG.

12254. Infant, Lancaster, Pa.

Family of HENRY MYERS (1632) and SARAH COBLE.

12255. Christian, Union City, Pa., b. June 14, 1839; d. Sept. 15, 1904; m. Nov. 27, 1862, Martha Jane Mellinger, b. Feb. 18, 1839; dau. Dr. Davis Mellinger and Jane Galloway.

12256. Barbara A., Marietta, Pa., b. July 31, 1844; m. William Beates.

12257. Eli, Marietta, Pa., b. May 18, 1842; d. Dec. 10, 1892; m. Annie Forrel.

12258. Katharine, Marietta, Pa., b. Apr. 20, 1847; d. infancy.

12259. David H., Elizabethtown, Pa., b. Oct. 10, 1848; m. Elizabeth Geyer.

12260. Sarah, Middletown, Pa., b. Feb. 28, 1852; m. Rev. Henry Shope.

Family of Wid. HENRY MYERS (1632) and MARIA ZIMMERMAN.

12261. Simon B., Elizabethtown, Pa., b. Sept. 30, 1854; m. Rebecca Gingrich.

12262. Ellen, Elizabethtown, Pa., b. July 8, 1857; m. Oct. 30, 1879, Ephraim D. Shank, b. May 19, 1856; son Henry Shank and Mary Donacker.

Family of ELLA M. WENGER (9202) and JACOB YUNGINGER.

12263. Walter Ross, Harrisburg, Pa., b. Oct. 29, 1882; m. Oct. 20, 1904, Wilda Blanche Trout, b. May 4, 1882; dau. Frank M. Trout and S—— Alice Cooper.

12264. Edith May, Gordonville, Pa., b. Apr. 25, 1884; m. June 14, 1906, Harry F. Hassel, b. Jan. 1, 1885; son G. Leonard Hassel and Matilda Kinkle.

12265. Clayton Wenger, Strasburg, Pa., b. Nov. 3, 1885; m. Sept. 21, 1907, Margie Elizabeth Feitchner, b. Aug. 6, 1886; dau. Jacob Feitchner and Harriet S. Helm.

12266. Maud Salome, Gordonville, Pa., b. Apr. 26, 1888.

12267. Jacob Franklin, Gordonville, Pa., b. Apr. 20, 1890.

12268. Edgar Lee, Gordonville, Pa., b. Mar. 3, 1892.

12269. Anna Louise, Gordonville, Pa., b. Oct. 30, 1893.

12270. Ada Blanche, Gordonville, Pa., b. June 6, 1896.

12271. Emily Ruth, Gordonville, Pa., b. Sept. 30, 1898.

12272. Jennie Martha, Gordonville, Pa., b. Aug. 11, 1900.

Family of FRANK E. WENGER (9204) and LOUELLA MAY GLOUNER.

12273. Clarence Roy, Paradise, Pa., b. Apr. 22, 1892.

12274. Louella Blanche, Paradise, Pa., b. Jan. 9, 1894.

12275. Franklin P., Paradise, Pa., b. Apr. 20, 1896.

12276. Bessie D., Paradise, Pa., b. May 7, 1897.

12277. Herbert Elim, Paradise, Pa., b. May 13, 1899.

11278. Estella May, Paradise, Pa., b. Aug. 27, 1901.

12279. Lillian Marie, Paradise, Pa., b. Oct. 19, 1903.

12280. Harry G., Paradise, Pa., b. June 6, 1906.

Family of WALTER R. YUNGINGER (12263) and WILDA BLANCHE TROUT.

12281. Edwin Russel, Gordonville, Pa., b. Jan. 15, 1907.

Family of EDITH M. YUNGINGER (12264) and HARRY F. HASSEL.

12282. Bertha May, Gordonville, Pa., b. Oct. 20, 1907.

Family of EMANUEL T. ROBINSON (7382) and FRANCES NOFSINGER.

12283. Mary Leota, Roanoke, Ill., b. Aug. 13, 1874.

12284. Nora Virginia, Welsh, La., b. Mar. 24, 1876; m. Sept. 24, 1901, John William Armstrong, b. July 30, 1876; son John C. Armstrong and Sarah C. Robinson.

12285. John William, Roanoke, La., b. Dec. 24, 1877; m. Mary Emmaline Neely, b. Mar. 29, 1887; dau. M. A. Neely and ———.

12286. Onno Frances, Roanoke, La., b. Dec. 1, 1879; m. July 16, 1902, Joseph B. Firestone, b. ———, 1878; son Nathan Firestone and Mary Rothrock.

12287. Eva Victoria, Roanoke, La., b. Jan. 2, 1882; m. Dec. 24, 1902, Marshal Samuel Watkins, son Culpepper R. Watkins and Sarah E. Wooley.

12288. Clara Alice, Flanagan, Ill., b. Mar. 3, 1884; d. Oct. 27, 1885.

12289. Elbert Cline, Roanoke, La., b. Mar. 9, 1886.

12290. Dora Clarinda, Roanoke, La., b. Jan. 7, 1889; m. July 13, 1907, James Watkins, b. Dec. 21, 1884; son Culpepper R. Watkins and Sarah E. Wooley.

12291. Jessie America, Roanoke, La., b. June 17, 1891.

12292. James Emanuel, Roanoke, La., b. Oct. 9, 1894.

12293. Roda Mabel, Roanoke, La., b. Dec. 17, 1896.

Family of OMA ROBINSON (12286) and JOSEPH B. FIRESTONE.

12294. Leonard Joseph, Roanoke, La., b. July 16, 1903.

12295. Eva Frances, Roanoke, La., b. Oct. 6, 1904.

12296. Marion L., Roanoke, La., b. Dec. 7, 1906.

Family of EVA V. ROBINSON (12287) and MARSHALL S. WATKINS.

12297. Son, Roanoke, La., b. Nov. 17, 1905.

Family of ALLEN ETHAN HERR (10227) and LAURA M. TAYLOR.

12298. George Clayton, Medicine Lodge, Kans., b. Feb. 5, 1895; d. Aug. 16, 1900.

12299. Ethan Allen, Medicine Lodge, Kans., b. Nov. 20, 1896.

12300. Susan Grace, Medicine Lodge, Kans., b. Oct. 29, 1898.

12301. Mabel May, Medicine Lodge, Kans., b. Jan. 30, 1901.

12302. Francis Floyd, Medicine Lodge, Kans., b. Apr. 7, 1903.

Family of ABRAHAM L. HERR (10228) and BERTHA DOWNTAIN.

12303. ———, Chickaska, Okla.
12304. ———, Chickaska, Okla.
12305. ———, Chickaska, Okla.

Family of URIAH CLAYTON HERR (10229) and LILLIAN V. PAINTER.

12306. Opal Angiline, Medicine Lodge, Kans., b. Nov. 11, 1897.
12307. Roland Benjamin, Medicine Lodge, Kans., b. Jan. 29, 1900; d. July 2, 1901.
12308. Jewell Kathryn, Medicine Lodge, Kans., b. Dec. 21, 1904.

Family of JOHN NEVIN HERR (10230) and EDITH POTTER.

12309. Eleanor Lucille, Kiowa, Kans., b. Mar. 4, 1903.

Family of LEVI H. BRACKBILL (4314) and SUSAN RANCK.

12310. Benjamin R., Gap, Pa., b. Mar. 4, 1885.
12311. Bertha M., Gap, Pa., b. Sept. 15, 1886.
12312. Anna E., Gap, Pa., b. June 21, 1888.
12313. Park R., Gap, Pa., b. Aug. 24, 1890.
12314. Elsie S., Gap, Pa., b. Feb. 4, 1894.

Family of ANNA M. BRACKBILL (12039) and DAVID GROFF.

12320. Barbara B., Kinzers, Pa., b. June 25, 1903.
12321. M—— Elizabeth, Kinzers, Pa., b. Jan. 13, 1905.
12322. Clarence V., Kinzers, Pa., b. Aug. 17, 1906.

Family of CHRISTIAN B. HESS (12040) and FANNIE HORST.

12323. Ellen Maria, Mechanicsburg, Pa., b. Oct. 31, 1905.

Family of WALTER A. FUNK (6542) and CHANDOS McNEIL.

12324. Helen Faye, Central City, Col., m. Sept. 3, 1907.

Family of JOHN FORRER (1316) and ELIZABETH KENDIG.

12325. John, Orrville, O., b. July 15, 1816; d. May 1, 1895; m. Jan. 4, 1849, Wid. Sarah Caldner Kenpf, b. Jan. 3, 1817; d. Dec. 31, 1891; dau. David Gardner and Elizabeth Dook.
12326. Henry, Orrville, O., b. Aug. 18, 1823; d. June 27, 1897; m. Oct. 26, 1875, Henrietta Geiss, b. June 1, 1857; dau. Henry Geiss and Catharine Lutz.

12327. Daniel, Orrville, O., b. Sept. 27, 1819; d. Feb. 13, 1904; m. June 4, 1874, Sarah Ann Bigler, b. Apr. 29, 1854; dau. George Bigler and Catharine Amstutz.

12328. Eli, Marshalville, O., b. Feb. 15, 1825; d. July 7, 1907; m. Apr. 3, 1851, Mary Baughman, b. Sept. 23, 1827; d. July 28, 1898.

12329. Martin, Clarksville, Ind., b. Dec. 12, 1814; d. Oct. 4, 1904; m. June 23, 1839, Eliza Heiney, b. Sept. 13, 1820.

12330. Nancy, Orrville, O., b. May 5, 1818; d. Apr. 29, 1901; m. Nov. 12, 1839, Samuel Martin, b. Nov. 6, 1814; d. Apr. 29, 1905; son Henry Martin and Anna Sauders.

12331. Elizabeth, Orrville, O., b. Apr. 23, 1821; d. June 4, 1872.

12332. Martha, Orrville, O., b. Sept. 12, 1827; d. May 13, 1850; m. Martin Kendig.

12333. Elvina, Orrville, O., b. Feb. 8, 1829; d. Oct. 31, 1836.

Family of HENRY FORRER (1317) and MEGDALENA EYMAN.

12334. Henry H., Wooster, O., b. Apr. 12, 1829; d. Aug. 7, 1891; m. Feb. 19, 1852, Anna Hoffman, b. Nov. 13, 1830; dau. Jacob Hoffman and Magdalena Thomas.

12335. Anna, Apple Creek, O., b. Dec. 20, 1819; d. Sept. 22, 1886; m. ———, 1837, Isaac Stauffer, b. Aug. 8, 1811; son Samuel Stauffer and Susanna Kiser.

12336. Susanna, East Union, O., b. Dec. 16, 1821; d. Dec. 25, 1853; m. Dec. 12, 1839, Emanuel F. Sauders, b. Aug. 14, 1816; d. Dec. 4, 1875.

12337. Elizabeth, Seville, O., b. Oct. 23, 1824; d. Mar. 4, 1891; m. Feb. 8, 1844, Israel Miller, b. Aug. 26, 1819; d. Oct. 24, 1891; son Christopher Miller and Susanna Killinger.

12338. Benjamin, Orrville, O., b. Feb. 18, 1827; d. Dec. 18, 1895; m. Mar. 2, 1860, Wid. Catharine Root, b. Apr. 14, 1831; d. Sept. 17, 1906; dau. Henry Brenneman and Fanny Rodfong.

12339. Catharine, Orrville, O., b. Mar. 18, 1834; d. Apr. 1, 1854.

12340. David, Orrville, O., b. Nov. 27, 1837; d. Jan. 4, 1905; m. Dec. 18, 1862, Sarah Weaver, b. Aug. 15, 1842; dau. Joseph Weaver and Martha Myers.

Family of DANIEL FORRER (1318) and ———.

12341. Theodore, Omaha, Neb.

12342. William Henry, Orrville, O.

12343. ———, Orrville, O.

12344. ———, Orrville, O.

12345. ———, Orrville, O.

Family of CHRISTIAN MYERS (12255) and MARTHA JANE MELLINGER.

12346. Sara Jane, Newville, Pa., b. Jan. 13, 1865; m. ——— Martin.

12347. Linda B., Union City, Pa., b. Oct. 3, 1872; m. ——— Buller.

12348. Christian M., Lebanon, Pa., b. Nov. 9, 1874.

Family of HENRY H. FORRER (12334) and ANNA HOFFMAN.

12349. David D., Orrville, O., b. Jan. 14, 1853; m. Sept. 28, 1877, Sarah Jane Forrer (12957).

12350. Daniel W., Orrville, O., b. Jan. 24, 1854; m. Nov. 14, 1878, Mary Ellen Cook, b. Nov. 8, 1855; d. Feb. 6, 1897; dau. Robert Cook and Jennie D. Cummins; m. Apr. 20, 1895, Lorena Moll, b. June 14, 1860; dau. John Moll and Margaret Horne.

12351. Samuel H., Canton, O., b. June 19, 1864; m. Lydia Hofstedler, b. July —, 1864; d. Dec. 27, 1904.

Family of DAVID D. FORRER (12349) and SARAH JANE FORRER.

12352. Clarence, Orrville, O., b. May —, 1879; m. Nov. 29, 1905, Emma Kohler, b. Feb. 18, 1885; dau. Jacob Kohler and Caroline Kinsey.

12353. Otto O., Orrville, O., b. June 12, 1886.

12354. Olive E., Smithville, O., b. Feb. 4, 1881; d. Feb. —, 1906; m. Jan. 12, 1905, Noah S. Steele, b. Aug. 26, 1878; son Isaac Steele and Elizabeth Hoover.

Family of DANIEL W. FORRER (12350) and MARY E. COOK.

12355. Jennie LeAnna, Akron, O., b. Sept. 6, 1879; d. May 5, 1904; m. June 28, 1903, Floyd B. Hackett, b. Mar. 25, 1878; son George W. Hackett and Louisa Blosser.

Family of Wid. DANIEL W. FORRER (12350) and LORENA MOLL.

12356. Leonard E., Orrville, O., b. Apr. 24, 1894.

Family of ANNA HERTZLER (12144) and JACOB J. STEHMAN.

12357. Alice H., Lancaster, Pa., b. July 14, 1888.
12358. Clayton, Lancaster, Pa., b. Oct. 7, 1892.
12359. Edgar, Lancaster, Pa., b. Aug. 28, 1897.
12360. Anna, Lancaster, Pa., b. Sept. 26, 1900.

Family of NORA V. ROBINSON (12284) and JOHN W. ARMSTRONG.

12361. Donoran R., Welsh, La., b. Aug. 29, 1903.

Family of SUSAN H. GAMBER (5332) and ISAAC L. BRUBAKER.

12362. Mary Gamber, Lancaster, Pa., b. May 27, 1888.
12363. Selena Gamber, Lancaster, Pa., b. Jan. 21, 1891.
12364. Wayne Gamber, Lancaster, Pa., b. Feb. 23, 1894.
12365. Harry Gamber, Lancaster, Pa., b. Jan. 7, 1899.

Family of AMOS A. HERR (6985) and ELLA SHATTO.

12366. Fanny Mae, Boiling Springs, Pa., June 23, 1901.
12367. Beula Elnora, Boiling Springs, Pa., b. Jan. 16, 1903.
12368. A—— Albert, Boiling Springs, Pa., b. Jan. 13, 1908.

Family of MARY E. HERR (6986) and ABRAHAM LONGENECKER.

12369. Frank H., Millersville, Pa.

Family of FANNY I. HERR (6987) and GEORGE B. HOOVER.

12370. Helen Herr, Mechanicsburg, Pa., b. Nov. 19, 1905.

Family of FRANK E. HERR (6988) and ANNA H. LANDIS (8390).

12371. Rhoda Landis, Millersville, Pa., b. Feb. 21, 1907.

Family of ANNA F. HERR (6989) and JACOB W. KNEISLEY.

12372. George H., Boiling Springs, Pa., b. June 15, 1907.

Family of BARBARA A. MYERS (12256) and WILLIAM BEATES.

12373. Harry, Conewago, Pa., m. Ella Bishop.
12374. Sarah, Marietta, Pa., m. John Orth.

Family of SARAH MYERS (12260) and Rev. HENRY SHOPE.

12375. Martha, Highspire, Pa., m. Elmer Handshue.

12376. Harry, Highspire, Pa., m. Alice Sunday.

12377. Bertha, Elizabethtown, Pa., m. Edward Miller.

12378. Annie, Highspire, Pa., m. Eli Lentz.

12379. Eli, Middletown, Pa.

12380. William, Middletown, Pa.

12381. Myrtle, Middletown, Pa.

Family of EMMA LANDIS (9568) and PHARES K. DONER.

12382. Claude L., Lampeter, Pa., b. Nov. 12, 1888.

12383. Arthur L., Lampeter, Pa., b. Nov. 24, 1892.

12384. Landis, Lampeter, Pa., b. July 28, 1896.

Family of DANIEL JEFFERSON HERR (4687) and CORA GROFF.

12387. Morris Groff, Lancaster, Pa., b. Feb. 20, 1903.

Family of ANNA C. HERR (4688) and FRANK R. HOUSER.

12388. Harry F., Lancaster, Pa., b. Nov. 2, 1901.

12389. Jacob P., Lancaster, Pa., b. Feb. 13, 1907.

Family of MAGDALENE HERR (3075) and GEORGE TANGER.

12390. Barbara H., Boiling Springs, Pa., b. Jan. 11, 1852; m. Mar.
13, 1884, Daniel B. Hoerner, b. Oct. 1, 1851; son David
Hoerner and Barbara Hoover.

12391. Mary H., Boiling Springs, Pa., b. Feb. 12, 1853; m. Nov. 21,
1872, William H. Kunkle, b. July 9, 1846; son John Kunkle
and Maria Cockin.

12392. Annie M., Carlisle, Pa., b. Feb. 12, 1853; m. Nov. 21, 1872,
Jacob C. Baker, b. Feb. 14, 1848; son Rev. Joseph Baker and
Elizabeth Spangler.

12393. Jacob, Hatton, Pa., b. July 25, 1855; d. Mar. 16, 1868.

12394. John A., Boiling Springs, Pa., b. Oct. 13, 1856; m. Sept. 24,
1878, Mary C. Comman, b. Aug. 6, 1858; dau. William Comman and Sarah Shupp.

12395. Susan S., Hays Grove, Pa., b. Jan. 4, 1859; m. Dec. 18, 1879,
Jacob M. Keller, b. Sept. 27, 1858; son William Keller and
Annie Musselman.

12396. Martha C., Hatton, Pa., b. Oct. 14, 1860; d. May 17, 1900; m.
Sept. 27, 1883, John W. Miller, b. Sept. 24, 1860; son Jacob
Miller and Anna Wolf.

12397. George H., Mount Holly Springs, Pa., b. Oct. 28, 1862; m.
Mar. 10, 1888, Sadie F. Miller, b. Mar. 6, 1863; dau. Jacob
Miller and Anna Wolf.

12398. Christian, Carlisle, Pa., b. Apr. 14, 1865; m. May 1, 1866,
Clara K. Gleim, b. Jan. 26, 1867; dau. John Gleim and Rebecca
Givler.

12399. Emma M., Carlisle, Pa., b. Sept. 2, 1867.

12400. Abram, Carlisle, Pa., b. Nov. 12, 1869; m. Sept. 27, 1888, Ida
Nailor, b. July 4, 1871; dau. Barney Nailor and Mary Bell.

12401. Harry, Carlisle, Pa., b. Apr. 5, 1872; m. Mar. 8, 1894, Mary
E. Yeingst, b. Oct. 22, 1872; dau. William Yeingst and
Margaret Lutz.

Family of BARBARA HERR (3079) and MANASSA LEREW.

12405. William H., Selem Church, Pa., b. Nov. 17, 1858; d. Aug. 16,
1859.

Family of Wid. BARBARA HERR (3079) and ABRAHAM STRICKLER.

12406. Jacob Edwin, Carlisle, Pa., b. July 7, 1868; m. Sept. 26, 1888,
Elizabeth Albright, d. Mar. 29, 1892; m. Nov. 14, 1895, Jennie
Kitch.

12407. Samuel H., Carlisle, Pa., b. Mar. 29, 1872; d. Aug. 19, 1873.

12408. Franklin H., Carlisle, Pa., b. Nov. 12, 1874; d. Aug. 31, 1875.

12409. Mary G., Allen, Pa., b. Apr. 6, 1876.

12410. Emma G., Carlisle, Pa., b. Apr. 6, 1876; m. Nov. 30, 1905,
Alfred E. Engle.

12411. Barbara A., Carlisle, Pa., b. Apr. 5, 1878; m. Jan. 21, 1902,
J—— Frank Greegor.

Family of BARBARA H. TANGER (12390) and DANIEL B. HOERNER.

12412. Mae, Mechanicsburg, Pa., b. Dec. 1, 1886.

12413. Jessie Emma, Mechanicsburg, Pa., b. Nov. 27, 1887.

Family of MARY H. TANGER (12391) and WILLIAM KUNKLE.

12414. Olive M., Boiling Springs, Pa., b. July 23, 1878; m. Dec. 19, 1899, Walter Spangler, son Joseph Spangler and Susan Hobble.

12415. Lena M., Boiling Springs, Pa., b. May 18, 1880; m. Sept. 22, 1900, W—— Spencer Mullin, son Charles F. Mullin and Emma Albright.

12416. Annie M., Boiling Springs, Pa., b. Aug. 1, 1884; m. Jan. 30, 1908, James A. Whitcomb, son Charles Whitcomb and Catharine Spera.

12417. Frank L., Boiling Springs, Pa., b. Jan. 1, 1875.

12418. George T., Boiling Springs, Pa., b. May 3, 1888.

Family of ANNIE M. TANGER (12392) and JACOB C. BAKER.

12419. Clarence E., Carlisle, Pa., b. Feb. 8, 1875; m. Sept. 8, 1896, Edith J. Donnelly, dau. George Donnelly and Margaret Daugherty.

12420. Harry W., Carlisle, Pa., b. Mar. 4, 1877; m. Jan. 3, 1899, Anna R. Shelly, dau. J—— W. Shelly and Frances Rebman.

12421. Ira C., Carlisle, Pa., b. Jan. 24, 1879.

12422. Albert T., Carlisle, Pa., b. Apr. 11, 1881; m. Feb. 3, 1903, Priscilla Book Weakley, dau. Charles Weakley and Anna Leicy.

12423. Emily J., Carlisle, Pa., b. Feb. 22, 1884; m. Aug. 6, 1906, Edwin Einstein, son Joseph Einstein and Ella Rhineheart.

Family of JOHN A. TANGER (12394) and MARY C. CARMAN.

12424. Annie E., Boiling Springs, Pa., b. Aug. 28, 1879; m. Sept. 24, 1897, Harry L. Murtoff, son John Murtoff and Annie Kyle.

12425. Zula, Boiling Springs, Pa.

12426. Mary, Boiling Springs, Pa.

12427. Freda, Boiling Springs, Pa.

Family of SUSAN S. TANGER (12395) and JACOB M. KELLER.

12428. Ray C., Hay's Grove, Pa., b. Oct. 5, 1884.

12429. Don K., Hay's Grove, Pa., b. July 11, 1896.

Family of MARTHA C. TANGER (12396) and JOHN W. MILLER.

12430. Norman C., Hatton, Pa., b. May 25, 1884.
12431. Lloyd F., Hatton, Pa., b. Feb. 11, 1887.
12432. Lawrence, Hatton, Pa., b. Feb. 25, 1897.
12433. Mary B., Hatton, Pa., b. Apr. 12, 1889; m. Oct. 30, 1908, Mervin Etter, son Samuel Etter and Annie Brindle.

Family of GEORGE H. TANGER (12397) and SADIE MILLER.

12434. Leam O., Mount Holly Springs, Pa., b. Apr. 29, 1889.
12435. Lois A., Mount Holly Springs, Pa., b. Nov. 2, 1890.

Family of CHRISTIAN TANGER (12398) and CLARA GLEIM.

12436. Florence M., Carlisle, Pa., b. Oct. 12, 1886.
12437. John G., Carlisle, Pa., b. Dec. 15, 1889.
12438. Mary R., Carlisle, Pa., b. June 27, 1896.

Family of ABRAM TANGER (12400) and IDA NAILOR.

12439. Mervin H., Carlisle, Pa., b. Aug. 5, 1889.

Family of HARRY TANGER (12401) and MARY E. YEINGST.

12440. Argie W., Carlisle, Pa., b. July 12, 1895.
12441. Ray M., Carlisle, Pa., b. Sept. 25, 1896.
12442. Pearl I., Carlisle, Pa., b. July 9, 1898.
12443. Ruth E., Carlisle, Pa., b. Sept. 21, 1900.
12444. Lena A., Carlisle, Pa., b. Feb. 18, 1903.
12445. Loy E., Carlisle, Pa., b. Mar. 8, 1905.
12446. Helen M., Carlisle, Pa., b. May 29, 1907.

Family of JOHN J. HERR (6973) and JENNIE MESSINGER.

12447. Ralph, Boiling Springs, Pa.
12448. Mae, Boiling Springs, Pa.

Family of S—— MILTON HERR (6974) and ANNIE BARBOUR.

12449. Clarence, Berwick, Pa., m. Anna Smith.
12450. Grace M., Berwick, Pa., m. Clayton Stitzel.
12451. Mildred, Berwick, Pa.
12452. Mabel, Berwick, Pa.

12453. Daisy, Berwick, Pa.
12454. Paul, Berwick, Pa.

Family of JACOB EDWIN HERR (6975) and MARY GUTTSHALL.

12455. Clyde, Boiling Springs, Pa.
12456. Edna, Boiling Springs, Pa.
12457. Helen, Boiling Springs, Pa.
12458. John, Boiling Springs, Pa.
12459. Eva, Boiling Springs, Pa.
12460. Merrill, Boiling Springs, Pa.
12461. Charles, Boiling Springs, Pa.
12462. Mary, Boiling Springs, Pa.
12463. Dorsey, Boiling Springs, Pa.
12464. Samuel, Boiling Springs, Pa.
12465. William, Boiling Springs, Pa.
12466. Martha, Boiling Springs, Pa.

Family of HENRY HERR (6981) and SUSAN BURNS.

12468. Laura, Boiling Springs, Pa.

Family of JACOB HERR (6980) and MAYME GALIGAR.

12469. Ethel, Boiling Springs, Pa., m. George Snyder.
12470. Catharine, Boiling Springs, Pa.

Family of GEORGE HERR (12403) and IDA PURBAUGH.

12571. Ray, Davy, Neb.
12472. Raymond, Davy, Neb.

Family of JACOB EDWIN STRICKLER (12406) and ELIZABETH ALBRIGHT.

12473. Barbara Mae, Carlisle, Pa.
12474. Ruth, Carlisle, Pa.

Family of Wid. JACOB EDWIN STRICKLER (12406) and JENNIE KITCH.

12475. Cora, Carlisle, Pa.
12476. Jacob, Carlisle, Pa.
12477. Clara, Carlisle, Pa.

Family of MARY A. KENDIG (1179) and HOTHER HAGE.

12478. Christian Kendig, Williamsport, Pa., b. Sept. 1, 1850.

12479. Hother Brent, Harrisburg, Pa., b. Feb. 3, 1852.

12480. Boletta Kip, England, b. Aug. 18, 1854.

12481. Gertrude Marie, Harrisburg, Pa., b. Oct. 18, 1858.

Family of SARAH ANN KENDIG (1180) and JOHN H. ZIEGLER.

12482. Grace Greenwood, Washington, D. C., b. Nov. 28, 1851; m. Oct. 21, 1873, Louis Fahnestock, b. Jan. 26, 1847; son Adam K. Fahnestock and Sibyl T. Holbrook.

Family of JOHN HERR (2641) and BARBARA PETERS.

12483. Elizabeth, Manheim, Pa., b. Dec. 13, 1857; m. Jan. 20, 1876, Benjamin Witman, b. Jan. 26, 1847; son John Witman and Magdalena Smith.

12484. Henry P., Manheim, Pa., b. Oct. 6, 1860; m. Sept. 25, 1881, Elizabeth Wenger, b. Nov. 14, 1858; dau. Joseph Wenger and Susan Weaver.

12485. Hiram P., Manheim, Pa., b. Nov. 16, 1864; m. Elizabeth Shelly, dau. Rev. Benjamin Shelly and ———.

12486. Annie P., Manheim, Pa., b. Feb. 1, 1873; m. Nov. 28, 1886, Samuel J. Becker, b. July 29, 1861; son Samuel Becker and Harriet Farmer.

12487. Jacob P., Manheim, Pa., b. July 8, 1869; m. Oct. 13, 1889, Mary Spickler, b. May 12, 1868; dau. John Spickler and Catharine Thuma.

12488. Benjamin P., Manheim, Pa., b. Nov. 20, 1871; d. Feb. 19, 1873.

12489. Abraham P., Manheim, Pa., b. Nov. 20, 1873; d. Jan. 23, 1888.

12490. Catharine P., Manheim, Pa., b. Nov. 26, 1875; m. Nov. 8, 1898, Simon Ginder, b. Nov. 9, 1867; son Joseph Ginder and Elizabeth Brubaker.

12491. Joseph P., Manheim, Pa., b. Dec. 14, 1877; d. Dec. 18, 1877.

12492. Minnie P., Elizabethtown, Pa., b. Nov. 24, 1878; m. June 26, 1898, Peter G. Brubaker, b. Oct. 24, 1874; son Amos Brubaker and Catharine Gibble.

12493. Elias P., Lancaster, Pa., b. Feb. 20, 1880; m. June 8, 1905, Emma L. Miller, b. Aug. 29, 1877; dau. Levi Z. Miller and Sarah A. Fritz.

12494. Barbara P., Manheim, Pa., b. Mar. 20, 1881; d. May. 1, 1881.

12495. John P., Manheim, Pa., b. Feb. 25, 1863; m. Nov. 21, 1886, Annie E. Williams, b. Aug. 31, 1867; dau. John Williams and Sarah Engle.

Family of ELIZABETH HERR (12483) and BENJAMIN WITMAN.

12496. John H., Youngstown, O., b. Feb. 6, 1883; m. Mary Hasting.

Family of HENRY P. HERR (12484) and ELIZABETH WENGER.

12497. Joseph W., Manheim, Pa., b. June 24, 1883; m. Nov. 17, 1901, Amelia G. Brant, b. Aug. 22, 1884; dau. Henry W. Brant and Rebecca Greiner.

12498. Henry W., Manheim, Pa., b. Apr. 6, 1882.

12499. Susan W., Manheim, Pa., b. Jan. 5, 1890; d. Mar. 29, 1890.

Family of JOHN H. WHITMAN (12496) and MARY HASTING.

12500. Herman E., Youngstown, O., b. June 25, 1907.

Family of JOHN P. HERR (12495) and ANNIE E. WILLIAMS.

12501. Francis W., Manheim, Pa., b. Feb. 13, 1891.

Family of ANNIE P. HERR (12486) and SAMUEL J. BECKER.

12502. Harriet H., Manheim, Pa., b. July 8, 1892.

Family of JACOB P. HERR (12487) and MARY SPICKLER.

12503. John S., Manheim, Pa., b. Jan. 8, 1897.

Family of CATHARINE P. HERR (12490) and SAMUEL GINDER.

12504. Irwin, Manheim, Pa., b. Jan. 20, 1900.

12505. Mabel, Manheim, Pa., b. Aug. 18, 1901.

12506. David, Manheim, Pa., b. Nov. 29, 1903.

12507. Paul, Manheim, Pa., b. Nov. 10, 1905.

12316. Elizabeth, Manheim, Pa., b. Mar. 10, 1908.

Family of MINNIE P. HERR (12492) and PETER BRUBAKER.

12508. Catharine, Elizabethtown, Pa., b. Sept. 8, 1899.

12509. ———, Elizabethtown, Pa., b. July 6, 1902; d, Mar. 14, 1903.

12510. ———, Elizabethtown, Pa., b. Mar. 17, 1904.

Family of SARAH HERR (6456) and PETER S. RISSER.

12511. Abner Herr, Elizabethtown, Pa., b. Oct. 21, 1886.

12512. Lillian Herr, Elizabethtown, Pa., b. Oct. 13, 1887.

Family of AMOS D. HERR (6595) and MARY J. MUMMA.

12514. Grace M., Millersville, Pa., b. Aug. 21, 1890.

Family of FANNIE R. HERR (6455) and JOHN E. GISH.

12515. Oliver Holmes, Elizabethtown, Pa., b. Sept. 1, 1883.

12516. Walter Scott, Elizabethtown, Pa., b. June 28, 1885; d. Nov. 27, 1905.

12517. Amos Herr, Elizabethtown, Pa., b. Oct. 17, 1886.

12518. Naomi Priscilla, Elizabethtown, Pa., b. Oct. 3, 1888; m. Dec. 25, 1907, Berton Bradley Sexton.

12519. Nathan Arthur, Elizabethtown, Pa., b. Jan. 6, 1890.

12520. Hiram Stanley, Elizabethtown, Pa., b. May 23, 1891.

12521. Anna Lily, Elizabethtown, Pa., b. Sept. 24, 1892.

12522. Ruth Arminta, Elizabethtown, Pa., b. Feb. 8, 1894; d. July 4, 1896.

12523. Lizzie Emma, Elizabethtown, Pa., b. Jan. 27, 1896.

12524. Dorothea Pearl, Elizabethtown, Pa., b. May 15, 1898.

12525. Grace Iola, Elizabethtown, Pa., b. Dec. 5, 1898.

Family of ISAAC E. HERSHEY (12115) and HATTIE S. BRACKBILL.

12526. E—— Ross, Gordonville, Pa., b. Oct. 29, 1906.

Family of CHRISTIAN HERR (841) and MARY HOSTETTER.

12527. Fanny, Millersville, Pa.

12528. Christian, Millersville, Pa.

12529. Susan, Millersville, Pa.

12530. Anna, Millersville, Pa.

12531. Mary, Millersville, Pa.

Family of SUSAN HERR (2849) and JONAS B. NISSLEY.

12532. Daniel, East Petersburg, Pa.
12533. Christian, East Petersburg, Pa.
12534. Jonas, East Petersburg, Pa.

Family of ABRAHAM HERR (863) and SUSAN SEITZ.

12535. Anna, Lancaster, Pa.
12536. Abraham, Lancaster, Pa.
12537. Ella, Lancaster, Pa.

Family of JACOB HERR (848) and CATHARINE LANHART.

12538. Jacob, Maytown, Pa.
12539. Catharine, Maytown, Pa.

Family of Wid. ANNA HERR (842) and ISAAC BRUBAKER.

12540. Anna H., Millersville, Pa., b. Mar. 8, 1857; d. June 10, 1857.
12541. Isaac H., Millersville, Pa., b. June 7, 1858; m. ——, 1878, Elizabeth Brubaker, dau. Christian Brubaker and Anna Herr.

Family of ELIZA HERR (2644) and HIRAM BEATTIE.

12542. Eli, Maytown, Pa.
12543. Emanuel, Maytown, Pa.
12544. Catharine, Reading, Pa., m. Martin Jones.
12545. Mary, Marietta, Pa., m. Charles Gallagher.
12546. Lewis H., Rossmere, Pa., m. Catharine Miller, dau. George Miller and Annie Basler.
12547. Emma, Columbia, Pa., m. John Gipe.
12548. Ella, Maytown, Pa.

Family of CATHARINE BEATTIE (12544) and MARTIN JONES.

12549. William, Reading, Pa.
12550. Edward, New York, N. Y.
12551. Martin, Warnersville, Pa.
12552. John, Reading, Pa.
12553. Ralph, Cherry Hill, Md.

Family of LEWIS H. BEATTIE (12546) and CATHARINE MILLER.

12554. Mary E., Rossmere, Pa., b. Apr. 16, 1890.

12555. Ruth, Rossmere, Pa., b. Aug. 17, 1891.

12556. Edna D., Rossmere, Pa., b. Sept. 10, 1892.

12557. Lewis L., Rossmere, b. Mar. 15, 1894.

12558. Hiram G., Rossmere, b. Oct. 18, 1895.

12559. George E., Rossmere, Pa., b. May 3, 1901.

12560. Catharine S., Rossmere, Pa., b. Apr. 23, 1903.

12561. Anna M., Rossmere, Pa., b. Mar. 26, 1906.

12662. Ralph H., Rossmere, Pa., b. July 30, 1907.

Family of ANNIE HERR (2645) and SAMUEL SHEARER.

12563. Amos, Mount Joy, Pa.

12564. Cassie, Mount Joy, Pa., m. George Hassler.

12565. Daniel, Mount Joy, Pa.

Family of ELIZABETH BENDER (2292) and MARTIN RUDY.

12566. John B,. Hershey, Pa., b. Aug. 10, 1850; m. Sept. 28, 1876, Barbara Ellen Kauffman, b. May 5, 1857; dau. John Kauffman and Sarah Hocker.

12567. Phares B., Lititz, Pa., b. Aug. 14, 1853; m. Annie Bowman.

12568. Mary Ann B., Lititz, Pa., b. Nov. 29, 1851; d. Dec. 6, 1897; m. Oct. 31, 1872, Jacob Witmer.

12569. Elizabeth B., Lititz, Pa., b. Oct. 31, 1854; m. Feb. 12, 1875, Henry Landis.

12570. Martin B., Lititz, Pa., b. Aug. 1, 1856; m. Oct. 13, 1881, Mary H. Huber, b. Jan. 13, 1855.

12571. Clayton B., Lititz, Pa., b. July 7, 1861; d. Aug. 15, 1863.

12572. Lalvina B., Lititz, Pa., b. July 28, 1859; m. Andrew Dunlap.

12573. Jacob B., Lititz, Pa., b. June 7, 1868; m. Annie Royer.

12574. Martha B., Lititz, Pa., b. Mar. 22, 1867.

Family of MARTIN B. RUDY (12570) and MARY H. HUBER.

12575. Lizzie H., Lititz, Pa., b. Aug. 10, 1882; m. Sept. 29, 1904, Christopher C. Good.

12576. Annie H., Lititz, Pa., b. May 1, 1884.

12577. Katie H., Lititz, Pa., b. Mar. 12, 1888.

12578. Emma H., Lititz, Pa., b. Sept. 5, 1890.

Family of ALFRED C. SMITH (5231) and LILLIAN L. HOSTETTER.

12579. Glenna Mary, Lancaster, Pa., b. May 20, 1905.

12580. Johri Herr, Lancaster, Pa., b. Feb. 24, 1907.

Family of JOHN H. HERR (2797) and ELIZABETH W. BALMER.

12581. Enos B., Georgetown, Wash., b. Jan. 19, 1871.

12582. Elizabeth B., Salunga, Pa., b. Dec. 13, 1873; m. Dec. 5, 1897, Reuben D. Raffensberger, b. Aug. 19, 1863; son George Raffensberger and Henrietta Stouch.

12583. Mary B., Salunga, Pa., b. Jan. 25, 1880; m. June 5, 1898, Ira M. Herr, b. Nov. 20, 1876; son Jacob Herr and Amanda Mann.

Family of ANNIE KENDIG (8778) and SILAS PEIRCE.

12584. Carrie Mildred, Brookline, Mass., b. Mar. 14, 1886.

12585. Susan Elizabeth, Brookine, Mass., b. Sept. 25, 1887.

Family of ISAAC HOOVER (1112) and MARGARET FRY.

12586. Mary Ann, Lancaster, Pa., b. Apr. 5, 1856; d. Aug. 9, 1856.

12587. John Franklin, Lancaster, Pa., b. Aug. 25, 1857.

12588. Alice Salome, Sterling, Ill., b. Sept. 26, 1860; m. ——— Miller.

12589. Abraham Lincoln, New Providence, Pa., b. Dec. 25, 1863; d. Apr. 14, 1864.

12590. Elmer Ellsworth, New Providence, Pa., b. Mar. 8, 1865.

12591. Emma Naomi, Lancaster, Pa., b. Mar. 6, 1867; m. June 4, 1893, Benjamin G. Lintner, b. Dec. 9, 1865; son Christian H. Lintner and Martha Groff.

12592. Annie Elizabeth, Waynesboro, Pa., b. Mar. 17, 1869.

12593. Charles Edwin, Lancaster, Pa., b. Mar. 23, 1871; m. Apr. —, 1898, Alice Mary Hoar, dau. Robert Hoar and Mary Ann Eckert.

Family of Wid. ISAAC HOOVER (1112) and MARTHA RHINEHEART.

12594. Harry, Lancaster, Pa., b. Oct. 26, 1881.

Family of **ALBERT B. SHENK** (10222) and **MARY LONGENECKER.**

12595. Edith L., Derry Church, Pa., b. Apr. 24, 1893.
12596. Ira L., Derry Church, Pa., b. Aug. 11, 1894.
12597. Roy A., Derry Church, Pa., b. Sept. 12, 1901.

Family of **HIRAM H. SHENK** (10224) and **BERTHA STRICKLER.**

12598. Sara Lucile, Annville, Pa., b. Nov. 26, 1902.
12599. Anna Esther, Annville, Pa., b. June 12, 1905.

Family of **CHARLES HOWARD GROFF** (7306) and **CARRIE LONGENECKER.**

12600. Honoris Augustus, Berwyn, Pa., b. July 8, 1899.
12601. Madaline, Berwyn, Pa., b. May 24, 1903.

Family of **LORIN JASON WITMER** (7308) and **HARRIET E. CHITTENDEN.**

12602. Eleanor Chittenden, Philadelphila, Pa., b. Apr. 26, 1898.
12603. Pennington Cope, Philadelphia, Pa., b. Apr. 19, 1900.

Family of **GERTRUDE EMMA WITMER** (7309) and **SAMUEL E. MEISTER.**

12604. Samuel Emil, Lancaster, Pa., b. Oct. 9, 1901.
12605. Theodore Witmer, Lancaster, Pa., b. Mar. 5, 1903.

Family of **GRACE GREENWOOD ZEIGLER** (12482) and **LOUIS FAHNESTOCK.**

12606. Louis, Washington, D. C., b. Mar. 13, 1875; m. Dec. 28, 1905, Gertrude Fiery.
12607. Adam Bruce, Washington, D. C., b. May 5, 1878; m. June 4, 1904, Mary Sheridan.
12608. Brent Hege, Washington, D. C., b. July 12, 1882; d. Aug. 14, 1884.
12609. Holbrook, Washington, D. C., b. Apr. 6, 1885.
12610. Bessie Marie, Washington, D. C., b. Jan. 17, 1889.

Family of **EMMA N. HOOVER** (12591) and **BENJAMIN G. LINTNER.**

12611. Martha Elizabeth, Lancaster, Pa., b. Apr. 16, 1894.
12612. Mary Grace, Lancaster, Pa., b. Dec. 25, 1895.
12613. Emma Ruth, Lancaster, Pa., b. Apr. 27, 1897.
12614. Anna May, Lancaster, Pa., b. Jan. 23, 1899.

Family of ANNA FORRER (12335) and ISAAC STAUFFER.

12615. John, Wilersville, O., b. Sept. 17, 1843; m. Sept. 24, 1868, Sarah Ellen Anderson, b. Aug. 13, 1849; dau. Armour Anderson and Jane Orr.

12616. Martha, Apple Creek, O., b. Aug. 3, 1841; d. May 8, 1898, m. John Laudenslager.

12617. Susanna, Lyons, Neb., b. Nov. 29, 1851; m. Cyrus W. Keiffer, b. Feb. 15, 1851.

12618. Eliza, Orrville, O., b. Feb. 10, 1855; m. Sept. 26, 1900, Christian E. Yeagley, b. Oct. 25, 1842; son Christian Yeagley and Christina ———; m. May 30, 1901, Charles Hodges, b. May 22, 1853; son Samuel Hodges and Elizabeth S. ———.

12619. Nancy, Orrville, O., b. Mar. 24, 1860; m. Aug. 28, 1879, John W. McAffee, b. Feb. 24, 1857; son William McAffee and Rebecca ———.

12620. Henry, Orrville, O., b. Mar. 23, 1839; d. Apr. 16, 1842.

12621. Amos, Orrville, O., b. June 28, 1846; d. Jan. 14, 1853.

12622. Benjamin, Orrville, O., b. Apr. 29, 1849; d. Jan. 4, 1853.

Family of SUSANNA FORRER (12336) and EMANUEL F. SAUDERS.

12623. Martha, Middleburg, Ind., b. Mar. 17, 1841; m. David Zimmerman, b. ———, 1830; d. Oct. 29, 1904.

12624. Henry F., Evansport, O., b. June 5, 1843; m. Oct. 29, 1868, Caroline Stauffer.

12625. Nancy, Rittman, O., b. July 16, 1845; m. Jacob Stuckey.

12626. Catharine, Sterling, O., b. June 14, 1849; d. Oct. 5, 1906; m. Jacob M. Star, b. Jan. 22, 1845; d. May 23, 1907.

12627. Susanna, Smithville, O., b. July 15, 1852; m. Jan. 14, 1872, David Kurtz, b. May 15, 1845.

Family of ELIZABETH FORRER (12337) and ISRAEL MILLER.

12628. Susanna, Bryan, O., b. Feb. 4, 1845; d. Nov. 4, 1887; m. Z—— Wenger.

12629. Martha, Creston, O., b. Sept. 17, 1847; m. Jan. 11, 1872, Ezra Martin, b. Feb. 14, 1849; d. July 2, 1878; son Henry Martin and Nancy Shisler; m. Aug. 7, 1895, William F. Miller, b. May 29, 1847; son William Miller and Rebecca Lambert.

28

12630. David K., Chippewa, O., b. May 27, 1853; m. July 3, 1895, Mary Dernhanner.

12631. Christopher, Wooster, O., b. Apr. 18, 1859; m. Feb. 11, 1900, Millie Steel.

12632. Abraham, Seville, O., Sept. 28, 1860; m. Dec. 24, 1885, Mary Harbaugh; m. Jan. 16, 1906, Ella Larke.

12633. Eliza, Sheron Centre, O., b. July 25, 1865; m. Robert McNutt.

12634. Sarah, Sheron Centre, O., b. May 6, 1868.

12635. Henry, Bryan, O., b. Mar. 2, 1849; d. Dec. 2, 1857.

12636. Benjamin, Bryan, O., b. June 11, 1851; d. Aug. 7, 1852.

12637. Israel, Bryan, O., b. Dec. 14, 1855; d. Nov. 29, 1857.

Family of BENJAMIN FORRER (12338) and Wid. CATHARINE ROOT.

12638. Henry B., Orrville, O., b. Nov. 25, 1865; d. Apr. 13, 1867.

Family of DAVID FORRER (12340) and SARAH WEAVER.

12639. Henry B., Orrville, O., b. Nov. 1, 1863; d. Aug. 14, 1864.

12640. Martha, Orrville, O., b. Apr. 29, 1865; d. May 24, 1865.

Family of ELIZABETH B. HERR (12582) and REUBEN D. RAFFENSBERGER.

12641. Miriam Herr, Salunga, Pa., b. Jan. 14, 1903.

Family of MARY B. HERR (12583) and IRA M. HERR.

12642. John Harold, Salunga, Pa., b. Sept. 9, 1900.

12643. Alta Marie, Salunga, Pa., b. Aug. 1, 1903.

12644. Martha Elizabeth, Salunga, Pa., b. May 19, 1906.

Family of JOHN STAUFFER (12615) and SARAH ELLEN ANDERSON.

12645. Isaac Clinton, Wooster, O., b. May 1, 1871; m. Jan. 1, 1895, Keziah Kathryn Brenneman, b. Mar. 13, 1877; dau. Jacob Brenneman and Mary McIntyre.

Family of MARTHA STAUFFER (12616) and JOHN LAUDENSLAGER.

12646. Anna C., Dalton, O., b. Nov. 6, 1864; Daniel Sauer.

12647. Isaac, Apple Creek, O., b. Aug. 1, 1868; m. Barbara Kessler.

12648. Mary J., Orrville, O., b. Sept. 10, 1866; m. Edward Deeds.

12649. William H., Mt. Eaton, O., b. May 27, 1870; m. Mar. 17, 1895, Isa Smedley.

12650. John E., Barberton, O., b. Feb. 17, 1874; m. Jennie Hunter.

12651. Frederick G., Kidron, O., b. Oct. 16, 1876; m. Ida Sauer.

12652. Eliza, Orrville, O., b. Aug. 28, 1881; m. Edward Villard.

Family of SUSANNA STAUFFER (12617) and CYRUS W. KIEFFER.

12653. Anna Eliza, Lyons, Neb., b. Sept. 25, 1871; m. John August Carlson, b. May 1, 1868.

12654. Caroline K., Oakland, Neb. b. Feb. 15, 1874; m. Amandus Ulrich, b. Feb. 24, 1870.

12655. Charles Wesley, Lyons, Neb., b. July 13, 1876; m. Mary Permilla Arnold, b. Mar. 23, 1880.

12656. Harvey Edmund, Lyons, Neb., b. Nov. 7, 1878; m. Minnie Pearl Morse, b. May 5, 1882.

12657. Leah Amanda, Orrville, O., b. Feb. 24, 1881; m. Emory C. Russel, b. Sept. 25, 1877.

12658. Henry Elmer, Lyons, Neb., b. May 28, 1883.

12659. Ida Sabina, Lyon,s Neb., b. Oct. 26, 1885; d. Sept. 30, 1900.

12660. Isaac Sylvester, Lyons, Neb., b. Oct. 26, 1885.

12661. Nora Mae, Lyons, Neb., Sept. 1, 1888.

12662. Susan S., Lyons, Neb., b. Sept. 19, 1890; m. Clinton Standley Philips, b. July 31, 1888.

12663. Sarah Pearl, Lyons, Neb., b. Dec. 5, 1892.

Family of NANCY STAUFFER (12619) and JOHN W. McAFFEE.

12664. Della, Orrville, O., b. Mar. 25, 1880; m. June 24, 1900, Charles Shank.

12665. Norman Arthur, Orrville, O., b. Jan. 2, 1883; m. Dec. 26, 1907, Lena L. Amstutz.

12666. Isaac Ernest, Orrville, O., b. June 21, 1887.

Family of ANNA C. LAUDENSLAGER (12646) and DANIEL SAUER.

12667. Alda Mildred, Dalton, O., b. Aug. 19, 1896.

12668. Ralph Vernon, Dalton, O., b. Mar. 7, 1898.

12669. John Earle, Dalton, O., b. Mar. 7, 1898.

12670. Roy Abraham, Dalton, O., b. May 11, 1900.

12671. Lloyd Henry, Dalton, O., b. Nov. 23, 1902; d. Oct. 6, 1903.

12672. Pearl Lewis, Dalton, O., b. Apr. 5, 1905.

12673. Elmer Roy, Dalton, O., b. Oct. 12, 1907.

Family of ISAAC LAUDENSLAGER (12647) and BARBARA KESSLER.

12674. Gracie, Apple Creek, O., b. Jan. 6, 1894.

12675. Russell, Apple Creek, O., b. Aug. 9, 1897.

12676. Herbert, Apple Creek, O., b. Sept. 13, 1901.

Family of JOHN E. LAUDENSLAGER (12650) and JENNIE HUNTER.

12677. Thomas, Barberton, O., b. Feb. 4, 1902.

12678. Elmer, Barberton, O., b. Mar. 25, 1904.

Family of FREDERICK G. LAUDENSLAGER 12651) and IDA SAUER.

12679. Resa, Kidron, O., b. Apr. 2, 1905.

Family of ELIZA LAUDENSLAGER (12652) and EDWARD VILLARD.

12680. Ona, Orrville, O., b. Aug. 19, 1900.

12681. Edith, Orrville, O., b. July 17, 1904.

12682. Infant, Orrville, O., b. Feb. 24, 1908.

Family of ANNE ELIZA KEIFFER (12653) and JOHN A. CARLSON.

12683. Frederica Agnes, Lyons, Neb., b. Sept. 22, 1892.

12684. Mabel Irene, Lyons, Neb., b. May 16, 1896; d. May 18, 1896.

12685. Roy Alvin, Lyons, Neb., b. Nov. 18, 1897.

Family of CAROLINE KEIFFER (12654) anl AMANDUS ULRICH.

12686. Vida Echel, Oakland, Neb., b. Dec. 6, 1894.

12687. Edna Rebecca, Oakland, Neb., b. June 6, 1896.

12688. Cattie Mae, Oakland, Neb., b. Nov. 27, 1897.

12689. Mina Permilla, Oakland, Neb., b. Aug. 1, 1899.

12690. Cola Alvin, Oakland, Neb., b. June 29, 1901.

12691. Wilford Joseph, Oakland, Neb., b. Nov. 20, 1902.

12692. Lloyd Hylas, Oakland, Neb., b. Apr. 16, 1905.

12693. Fern Marguerete, Oakland, Neb., b. Feb. 12, 1907.

Family of CHARLES WESLEY KEIFFER (12655) and MARY P. ARNOLD.

12694. Una Gladys, Lyons, Neb., b. Apr. 7, 1901.

12695. Lamenta Susanna, Lyons, Neb., b. Mar. 19, 1903.

12696. Permilla Adella, Lyons, Neb. b. Aug. 1, 1905.

12697. Ethel Winifert, Lyons, Neb., b. Feb. 18, 1907.

Family of HARVEY EDMUND KEIFFER (12656) and MINNIE P. MORSE.

12689. Mildred Olin, Lyons, Neb., b. Dec. 29, 1902.

12699. Pearl Susan, Lyons, Neb., b. Apr. 12, 1906.

Family of LEAH AMANDA KIEFFER (12657) and EMORY C. RUSSELL.

12700. Florence Leah, Lyons, Neb., b. Aug. 3, 1901.

12701. Ralph Cyrus, Lyons, Neb., b. Sept. 14, 1902.

12702. Chester Arthur, Lyons, Neb., b. Mar. 24, 1907.

Family of SUSAN S. KEIFFER (12662) and CLINTON STANDLEY PHILIPS.

12703. Lucilla Elizabeth, Lyons, Neb., b. Aug. 18, 1907.

Family of MARTHA MILLER (12629) and EZRA MARTIN.

12704. Edwin, Kenmore, O., b. July 26, 1873; m. Mar. 28, 1907, Alma Bowman, b. June 22, 1884; dau. Joshua B. Bowman and Martha Hillburn.

12705. Amanda, Rittman, O., b. Dec. 14, 1875; m. Oct. 11, 1893, William Fixler, b. May 3, 1866; son Abraham Fixler and Caroline Stine.

12706. Israel, Creston, O., b. Apr. 13, 1878; d. Nov. 29, 1878.

Family of DAVID K. MILLER (12630) and MARY DERHAMMER.

12707. ———, Chippewa Lake, O., d. Infant.

12708. Christopher, Chippewa Lake, O., b. Apr. 5, 1896.

Family of ABRAHAM MILLER (12632) and MARY HARBAUGH.

12709. Infant, Orrville, O.

12710. Grasy, Orrville, O., b. June 9, 1888; m. William Hunter.

Family of Wid. ABRAHAM MILLER (12632) and ELLA LARKE.

12711. Orlena, Orrville, O., b. Jan. 19, 1907.

Family of ELIZA MILLER (12633) and ROBERT McNUTT.

12712. Charles, Sheron Centre, O., b. May 5, 1894.

12713. Clarence, Sheron Centre, O., b. Feb. 7, 1896.

Family of AMANDA MILLER (12705) and WILLIAM FIXLER.

12714. Ralph, Rittman, O., b. July 9, 1894.

12715. Irene, Rittman, O., b. Apr. 18, 1897.

12716. Martha, Rittman, O., b. Nov. 2, 1900.

12717. William, Rittman, O., b. July 13, 1904.

Family of GRASY MILLER (12710) and WILLIAM HUNTER.

12718. Lester William, Orrville, O., b. Sept. 17, 1907.

Family of DELLA McAFFEE (12664) and CHARLES SHANK.

12719. Nora May, Orrville, O., b. Feb. 2, 1901.

12720. Anna Arena, Orrville, O., b. Jan. 28, 1903.

12721. Raymond Edward, Orrville, O., b. July 15, 1907.

12722. Roy Lee, Orrville, O., b. Feb. 27, 1908.

12723. Infant, Orrville, O., b. Jan. 10, 1905; d. Jan. 10, 1905.

Family of WILLIAM H. LAUDENSLAGER (12649) and ISA SMEDLEY.

12724. Nepa, Mt. Eaton, O., b. May 2, 1896.

12725. Mearl, Mt. Eaton, O., b. Mar. 20, 1897.

12726. Infant, Mt. Eaton, O.

12727. Infant, Mt. Eaton, O.

Family of HENRY F. SAUDERS (12624) and CAROLINE STAUFFER.

12728. Emma, Evansport, O., b. Dec. 7, 1869; m. ———, 1865, John F. Carpenter.

12729. Margaret, Sturgis, Mich., b. Aug. 17, 1871; m. Mar. 30, 1893, Henry M. Heer, b. Sept. 14, 1866.

12730. Mary, Evansport, O., b. Nov. 11, 1873; d. Dec. 25, 1885.

12731. W—— W., Bryan, O., b. July 9, 1876; m. Nov. —, 1898, Dena Gibson.

12732. Lottie, Stryker, O., b. Nov. —, 1879; m. Oct. 16, 1898, Wilfred Buehrer, b. Aug. 15, 1874.

12733. Henry H., Evansport, O., b. May 26, 1881.

12734. Levi H., Evansport, O., b. Dec. 18, 1883.

12735. Elmer E., Evansport, O., b. Aug. 10, 1886.

Family of NANCY SAUDERS (12625) and JACOB STUCKEY.

12736. Henry F., Rittman, O., b. ———, 1866.

Family of CATHARINE SAUDERS (12626) and JACOB M. STARN.

12737. David Elmer, Orrville, O., b. June 17, 1871; m. Libbie Idella Hoffman, b. Apr. 27, 1874.

12738. Jacob Wesley, Wooster, O., b. Apr. 24, 1873; m. Ella May Garver, b. June 29, 1880.

12739. Nancy Orrvilla, Sterling, O., m. Henry D. Curie, b. Aug. 13, 1865.

12740. Noah Orrvilla, Sterling, O., b. Mar. 18, 1876; m. Henry D. Currie, b. Aug. 13, 1865.

12740. Noah, Orrville, O., b. Aug. 25, 1879; m. Lydia Gerber.

Family of SUSANNA SAUDERS (12627) and DAVID KURTZ.

12721. John, Orrville, O., b. Dec. 12, 1872; m. Nov. 10, 1901, Gertrude Felix, b. May 19, 1883.

12742. Jacob, Orrville, O., b. Mar. 29, 1875; m. Dec. 24, 1902, Muriel Ferrer, b. May 19, 1883.

12743. David B., Smithville, O., b. Mar. 7, 1877; m. Mar. 9, 1902, Susan Swartz, b. Feb. 4, 1884.

12744. Sarah, Smithville, O., b. Feb. 2, 1879.

12745. Simon, Smithville, O., b. Dec. 13, 1881; m. Dec. 6, 1900, Fanny Musser, b. Sept. 16, 1883.

12746. Amelia, Smithville, O., b. Jan. 8, 1884.

12747. Della M., Smithville, O., b. Mar. 13, 1886.

12748. Lydia A., Smithville, O., b. Feb. 5, 1891.

12749. Nancy C., Smithville, O., b. July 15, 1893; d. May 10, 1905.

Family of EMMA SAUDERS (12728) and JOHN F. CARPENTER.

12750. Martha Elizabeth, Ney, O., b. Feb. 23, 1886; m. Oct. 16, 1906, Frederic Brown.

12751. Susie Dell, Bryan, O., b. Aug. 16, 1887; m. Dec. 30, 1907, Clyde Easterly.

12752. Mary May, Evansport, O., b. Mar. 23, 1889.

12753. Alice Caroline, Evansport, O., b. July 17, 1891.

12754. George W., Evansport, O., b. Apr. 22, 1893.

12755. Charles H., Evansport, O., b. Oct. 24, 1895.

12756. Clara Bell, Evansport, O., b. Sept. 22, 1900.

12757. John W., Evansport, O., b. Mar. 1, 1903.

Family of MARGARET SAUDERS (12729) and HENRY M. HEER.

12758. Clayton C., West Unity, O., b. Nov. 30, 1894.

12759. Nelson V., West Unity, O., b. July 29, 1896.

12760. Otha B., West Unity, O., b. Aug. 8, 1899.

12761. Edna M., West Unity, O., b. Apr. 10, 1902.

Family of W—— W. SAUDERS (12731) and DENA GIBSON.

12762. Walter Willie, Bryan, O., b. Sept. 11, 1899.

12763. Gracie Maria, Bryan, O., b. Feb. 1, 1907.

Family of LOTTIE SAUDERS (12732) and WILFRED BUEHRER.

12764. Forest T., Stryker, O., b. Mar. 5, 1901; d. July 24, 1901.

12765. Ruth, Stryker, O., b. Oct. 29, 1902.

12766. Ellen, Stryker, O., b. May 19, 1903.

12767. Dorris, Stryker, O., b. Feb. 18, 1906.

12768. Denver W., Stryker, O., b. Feb. 28, 1908.

Family of DAVID ELMER STARN (12737) and LIBBIE IDELLA HOFFMAN.

12769. Warren Vernon, Orrville, O., b. Nov. 24, 1895.

12770. Gale Murine, Orrville, O., b. Oct. 8, 1902.

12771. Vincent Orla, Orrville, O., b. Sept. 24, 1904.

Family of JACOB WESLEY STARN (12738) and ELLA MAY GARVER.

12772. Goldie Luella, Wooster, O., b. Aug. 8, 1902.

12773. Curtis Walter, Wooster, O., b. Oct. 13, 1904.

Family of ORRILLA STARN (12739) and HENRY D. CURIE.

12774. William J., Sterling, O., b. Aug. 30, 1896.

12775. Harry B., Sterling, O., b. Jan. 30, 1898.

Family of HENRY F. STUCKEY (12736) and ——.

12776. May, Sterling, O.

12777. Grace, Sterling, O.

12778. Ruth, Sterling, O.

Family of MARTHA ELIZ. CARPENTER (12750) and FREDERIC BROWN.

12779. John Henry, Ney, O., b. Mar. 6, 1907.

Family of JOHN B. RUDY (12566) and BARBARA ELLEN KAUFFMAN.

12780. Edwin Kauffman, Lemoyne, Pa., b. Nov. 2, 1879; m. Aug. 18, 1898, Mabelle May Moyer, b. Apr. 20, 1876; dau. John F. Moyer and Jennie Rudolph.

12781. Irwin Kauffman, Hershey, Pa., b.May 17, 1888.

12782. John Martin, Hershey, Pa., b. Apr. 21, 1891.

Family of EDWIN K. RUDY (12780) and MABELLE MAY MOYER.

12783. Mildred Moyer, Lemoyne, Pa., b. Feb. 4, 1899.

12784. Mary Ellen, Lemoyne, Pa., b. Mar. 18, 1901.

12785. John Moyer, Lemoyne, Pa., b. Mar. 11, 1905.

12786. Edwin Kauffman, Lemoyne, Pa., b. Jan. 29, 1907.

Family of MARTHA SAUDERS (12623) and DAVID ZIMMERMAN.

12787. Henry, Nottawa, Mich., b. July 8, 1861; m. ———, 1885, Jane Lehr.

12788. Peter, Constantine, Mich., b. Sept. 30, 1863; m. Dec. 18, 1888, Minnie Noel.

12789. William, Middleburg, Ind., b. Jan. 20, 1865; m. Mar. 22, 1894, Louise Schmidt, b. May 13, 1871.

12790. John, Middleburg, Ind., b. Sept. 23, 1867; m. Dec. —, 1888, Clara Schrock.

12791. David, Middleburg, Ind., b. Mar. 4, 1869; m. Jan. —, 1891, Susan Golder, b. Sept. 5, 1869.

12792. Simon, Middleburg, Ind., b. Feb. 18, 1871; m. Mar. 21, 1906, Lulu Schmidt, b. Sept. 10, 1877.

Family of HENRY ZIMMERMAN (12787) and JANE LEHR.

12793. Wesley, Nottawa, Mich., b. Nov. 25, 1886; m. Dec. 31, 1907, Nellie Hardman.

12794. Roy, Nottawa, Mich., b. Jan. 9, 1888.

12795. Earl, Nottawa, Mich., b. ———, 1894; d. Dec. 25, 1894.

Family of WILLIAM ZIMMERMAN (12789) and LOUISE SCHMIDT.

12796. Ralph Lamar, Middleburg, Ind., b. Oct. 15, 1897.

Family of JOHN ZIMMERMAN (12790) and CLARA SCHROCK.

12797. Willis, Middleburg, Ind., b. Dec. —, 1889.
12798. Lamar, Middleburg, Ind., b. Mar. 29, 1901.

Family of DAVID ZIMMERMAN (12791) and SUSAN GOLDER.

12799. Martha, Middleburg, Ind., b. Feb. 7, 1892; d. Nov. 26, 1892.
12800. Hazel, Middleburg, Ind., b. Nov. 15, 1893.
12801. Modie, Middleburg, Ind., b. Mar., 29, 1896.
12802. Clarence, Middleburg, Ind., b. Aug. 4, 1898.
12803. Theodore, Middleburg, Ind., b. Oct. 8, 1902.
12804. Evelin, Middleburg, Ind., b. Jan. 12, 1907.

Family of JOHN KURTZ (12741) and GERTRUDE FELIX.

12805. Clarence Olin, Orrville, O., b. Sept. 8, 1905.
12806. Doris Susanna, Orrville, O., b. Nov. 28, 1907.

Family of JACOB KURTZ (12742) and MURIEL FERRER.

12807. Irien Leslie, Orrville, O., b. Mar. 15, 1904.
12808. Dorothy Gertrude, Orrville, O., b. Oct. 27, 1906.

Family of DAVID B. KURTZ (12743) and SUSAN SWARTZ.

12809. Roy Wesley, Orrville, O., b. Dec. 19, 1904.
12810. Eloda Arline, Orrville, O., b. Aug. 16, 1907.

Family of SIMON KURTZ (12745) and FANNY MUSSER.

12811. Ida Mabel, Smithville, O., b. Nov. 10, 1901.
12812. Clyde Leonard, Smithville, O., b. Sept. 5, 1903.
12813. Lloyd William, Smithville, O., b. May 26, 1905.

Family of JOHN MILTON HOOVER (4296) and MARY E. RUTTER.

12814. Clayton R., New Holland, Pa., b. July 31, 1876; d. May 21, 1879.
12815. Anna B., New Holland, Pa., b. Dec. 23, 1877.
12816. Cora S., New Holland, Pa., b. May 15, 1879; m. Nov. 30, 1905, Levi G. Ranck, b. June 4, 1877.
12817. Mabel E., New Holland, Pa., b. Jan. 24, 1881; m. Apr. 5, 1905, George S. Ranck, b. Mar. 16, 1881.

12818. Landis H., New Holland, Pa., b. Feb. 18, 1883; d. July 23, 1883.

Family of ANNA KILHEFFER (870) and JOHN ESHBACH.

12819. Susan, Lancaster, Pa., b. Nov. 3, 1865; m. Henry Kauffman, son Andrew K. Kauffman and Anna Ottstot.

12820. Katie, Strasburg, Pa., m. Jonas Kreider.

12821. Lizzie, Millersville, Pa., m. John Stehman.

12822. Fanny, Lancaster, Pa., m. Simon Sechrist.

12823. Barbara, Lancaster, Pa., d. Infant.

12824. John, Conestoga, Pa., m. Anna Buckwalter.

12825. Elias, Pequea, Pa., m. Delilah Warfel.

12826. Isaiah, Lancaster, Pa., m. Mary Neff.   1

Family of SUSAN ESHBACH (12819) and HARRY KAUFFMAN.

12827. Raymond E., Lancaster, Pa., b. June 9, 1889.

12828. John, Lancaster, Pa., b. Apr. 14, 1891; d. May 21, 1893.

12829. Esther, Lancaster, Pa., b. Oct. 6, 1902.

Family of JOHN F. WIGGINS (11762) and MARY BOOK.

12830. H—— G. I., New Providence, Pa., m. Susie Ager.

12831. Bertha, Lancaster, Pa., m. —— Myers.

12832. Ella, Lancaster, Pa., m. —— Andrews.

12833. Justus B., Lancaster, Pa., b. Jan. 9, 1876; m. Apr. 6, 1905, Clara Hoover, b. June 23, 1881.

12834. Enos, Allen, Pa.

12835. Elizabeth, Allen. Pa.. m. —— Herr.

12836. Elmer J., New Providence, Pa.

Family of EUGENE LEFEVRE HERR (9030) and ANNA GRIEL MILLER.

12837. Rupert Eugene, Lancaster, Pa., b. Oct. 25, 1907.

Family of ANN HERR (131) and HENRY HARTMAN.

12838. Henry, Strasburg, Pa.

12839. Samuel, Strasburg, Pa., b. Aug. 22, 1834; d. Apr. 21, 1908.

12840. Esther, Strasburg, Pa., m. David Hoover.

12841. Frena, Strasburg. Pa., m. Henry Hess.

12842. Ann, Strasburg, Pa.

Family of **SAMUEL HARTMAN** (12839) and ——— **HABECKER**.

12843. Anna, Landisville, Pa., b. Feb. 8, 1825; d. June 23, 1862; m. Andrew Hershey, b. Dec. 16, 1795; d. Mar. 23, 1837.

12844. Benjamin, Manheim, Pa., m. Susan Seitz.

12845. ———, Manheim, Pa.

Family of **MARTIN FRICK** (721) and **CATHARINE D. MILLER**.

12846. Susan, Buffalo, N. Y., b. Jan. 11, 1829; m. Nov. 15, 1849, Oliver J. Eggert.

12847. Joseph W., Peru, Ind., b. Aug. 27, 1830; m. Sept. 12, 1850, Eliza Guyer, b. Jan. 25, 1833.

12848. Eliza, Eggersville, N. Y., b. Feb. 29, 1832; d. June 17, 1832.

12849. Barbara E., Coopersville, Mich., b. Jan. 28, 1834; m. ———, 1851, John Zimmerman.

12850. Martin J., Buffalo, N. Y., b. Feb. 19, 1836; m. Dec. 25, 1856, Fanny Hoil, b. Mar. 26, 1835.

12851. Tobias, Eggertsville, N. Y., b. July 18, 1838; d. Sept. 6, 1838.

12852. Sarah A., Orchard Park, N. Y., b. Aug. 5, 1839; d. Nov. 7, 1897; m. July 4, 1856, Barton Duer.

12854. Daniel W., Buffalo, N. Y., b. Oct. 1, 1841; m. Jan. 9, 1869, Eliza Myers.

12854. Catharine M., Buffalo, N. Y., b. Oct. 2, 1842.

12855. Edward C., Buffalo, N. Y., b. Jan. 11, 1854; m. May 29, 1878, Elmira Miller.

Family of **SUSAN FRICK** (12846) and **OLIVER J. EGGERT**.

12856. Charles A., Eggertsville, N. Y., b. Aug. 22, 1850; d. May 29, 1854.

12857. Edwin B., Buffalo, N. Y., b. Apr. 10, 1856; m. June 10, 1885, Mary Scott, d. Sept. 5, 1894.

12858. Alice, Buffalo, N. Y., b. Feb. 20, 1861; m. Jan. 3, 1884, Eli H. Long.

Family of **JOSEPH W. FRICK** (12847) and **ELIZA GUYER**.

12859. Ellen Alvenah, Peru, Ind., b. Sept. 26, 1865; d. Apr. 19, 1872.

12860. Orlando A., Defiance, O., b Mar. 1, 1852; m. Mollie Otis.

12861. Herschel E., Peru, Ind., b. Mar. 15, 1854; m. Cora Hackley.
12862. Erwin W., Canon City, Col., b. Aug. 31, 1858; m. Lenah Andres.

Family of BARBARA E. FRICK (12849) and JOHN ZIMMERMAN.

12863. Morris, Coopersville, Mich.
12864. Nellie, Coopersville, Mich., m. Horace Perry.

Family of MARTIN J. FRICK (12850) and FANNY HOIL.

12865. Benjamin, Buffalo, N. Y., b. Feb. 21, 1858; d. Feb. 19, 1860.
12866. Henry L., Buffalo, N. Y., b. Jan. 3, 1861.
12867. Esther A., Buffalo, N. Y., b. Feb. 19, 1863.
12868. Ellsworth S., Buffalo, N. Y., b. Mar. 12, 1867.

Family of SARAH A. FRICK (12852) and BARTON DUER.

12869. Merrill, Orchard Park, N. Y., m. Eva Duell.
12870. Mabel, Buffalo, N. Y., m. Eugene Burr.

Family of DANIEL W. FRICK (12853) and ELIZA MYERS.

12871. Estella, Buffalo, N. Y., b. Jan. 12, 1872; m. May 2, 1901, William Weaver.

Family of EDWARD C. FRICK (12855) and ELMIRA MILLER.

12872. Mildred, Buffalo, N. Y.

Family of ORANDO A. FRICK (12860) and MOLLIE OTIS.

12873. Maud, Defiance, O.
12874. Claud, Delance, O.
12875. Everette, Defiance, O.
12876. Chester, Defiance, O.

Family of HERSCHEL E. FRICK (12861) and CORA HACKLEY.

12877. Fred, Peru, Ind.
12878. June, Peru, Ind.

Family of ERWIN W. FRICK (12862) and LENAH ANDRES.

12879. Ervin, Canon City, Col.
12880. Matie, Canon City, Col.

Family of ALICE EGGERT (12858) and ELI H. LONG.

12882. ———, Buffalo, N. Y.
12883. ———, Buffalo, N. Y
12884. ———, Buffalo, N. Y.
12885. ———, Buffalo, N. Y.

Family of MERILL DUER (12869) and EVA DUELL.

12886. ———, Orchard Park, N. Y.
12887. ———, Orchard Park, N. Y.

Family of MABELL DUER (12870) and EUGENE BURR.

12888. ———, Buffalo, N. Y.
12889. ———, Buffalo, N. Y.

Family of ESTELLA FRICK (12871) and WILLIAM WEAVER.

12890. ———, Buffalo, N. Y.
12891. ———, Buffalo, N. Y.

Family of ANN HARTMAN (12843) and ANDREW HERSHEY.

12892. Jacob Hartman, Rohrerstown, Pa., b. June 4, 1826; d. Dec. 6, 1898; m. Dec. 23, 1847, Anna Manning, b. Feb. 4, 1822; d. May 12, 1894; dau. Jacob Manning and ——— Kready.
12893. Benjamin, Landisville, Pa., b. Aug. 3, 1828; d. June 12, 1832.
12894. Barbara Hartman, Manheim, Pa., b. Oct. 27, 1832; m. Sept. 24, 1850 Jacob N. Metzger, b. Dec. 1, 1824; son Andrew Metzger and Elizabeth Newcomer.
12895. Anna, Osborn, O., b. May 21, 1836; m. Nov. 29, 1859, David R. Doner, d. 1877.

Family of BENJAMIN HARTMAN (12844) and SUSANNA SEITZ.

12896. Hetty, Camden, N. J., m. Ephraim Bear.
12897. Mary, Arganta, Ill., m. Jacob Buffenmoyer.
12898. Annie, Manheim, Pa.

Family of HETTY HARTMAN (12896) and EPHRAIM BEAR.

12899. Elizabeth, Camden, N. J.
12900. John, Camden, N. J.

12901. Emma, Camden, N. J.

12902. Annie, Camden, N. J.

12903. George, Camden, N. J.

12904. Mary, Camden, N. J.

12905. Hetty, Camden, N. J.

12906. Benjamin, Camden, N. J.

Family of MARY HARTMAN (12897) and JACOB BUFFENMOYER.

12907. Lulu, Arganta, Ill.

12908. Anna, Arganta, Ill.

12909. John, Arganta, Ill.

12910. Joseph, Arganta, Ill.

12911. Benjamin, Arganta, Ill.

12912. Harriet, Arganta, Ill.

12913. Uriah, Arganta, Ill.

12914. Malinda, Arganta, Ill.

12915. Jacob, Arganta, Ill.

12916. Jennie, Arganta, Ill.

Family of CHRISTIAN HERR (240) and FANNY ESHLEMAN.

12917. John, Mastersonville, Pa., b. Feb. 7, 1774; d. Feb. 17, 1810.

12918. David, Mastersonville, Pa., b. July 19, 1785.

12919. Susan, Mastersonville, Pa., b. Aug. 16, 1784; d. Mar. 19, 1788.

12920. Magdalena, Mastersonville, Pa., b. Dec. 18, 1778; d. Oct. 8, 1779.

12921. Elizabeth, Mastersonville, Pa., b. Feb. 23, 1796; d. ———, 1853; m. Oct. 16, 1814, Joseph Sproat, d. Aug. 14, 1828.

12922. Catharine, Mastersonville, Pa., b. Sept. 27, 1797; m. Nov. 19, 1839, ——— Wright.

12923. Barbara, Mastersonville, Pa., b. Nov. 10, 1801.

12924. Mary, Mastersonville, Pa., b. Jan. 10, 1808; m. John Boyer.

Family of MARY HERR (12924) and JOHN BOYER.

12925. Harriet, Lancaster, Pa., b. Feb. 28, 1845; m. Apr. 8, 1866, William Lechler, b. Feb. 16, 1826; d. June 1, 1902.

12926. Perninal, Mt. Joy, Pa., b. Mar. 30, 1852; m. Jan. 23, 1873, Benjamin Heistand, b. Dec. 9, 1847.

12927. Catharine, Mt. Joy, Pa., m. —— Thornberg.

12928. Henry H., Lancaster, Pa.

12929. John, Elizabethtown, Pa., b. Dec. 27, 1848.

12930. Maria, Elizabethtown, Pa., m. John Snavely.

12931. Ann, Elizabethtown, Pa., m. —— Laross.

Family of JACOB HARTMAN (12892) and ——.

12932. David Hartman, Rohrerstown, Pa., b. Oct. 4, 1848; d. Jan. 27, 1878.

12933. Anna Elizabeth, Rohrerstown, Pa., b. June 27, 1850; d. May 7, 1875.

12934. Andrew Hiestand, Lancaster, Pa., b. Aug. 15, 1852; m. Mary Ellen Brown, dau. John George Brown and Leah Culberson.

12935. Sonora Catharine, Rohrerstown, Pa., b. Nov. 26, 1854; d. April 17, 1902.

12936. Mary Amanda, Rohrerstown, Pa., b. Apr. 3, 1856; d. May 14, 1862.

12937. Sylvania Victoria, Rohrerstown, Pa., b. July 31, 1858; d. Aug. 14, 1884.

12938. Jacob Manning, Rohrerstown, Pa., b. June 28, 1861; d. Nov. 6, 1862.

12939. Henry Elmer, Rohrerstown, Pa., b. July 18, 1863; m. Feb. 21, 1900, Dora Elizabeth Mayer, dau. Henry Musser Mayer and Frances Matilda Hershey.

12940. Sarah M., Rohrerstown, Pa., b. July 16, 1865; d. Sept. 3, 1865.

Family of HENRY ELMER HERSHEY (12949) and DORA ELIZ. MAYER.

12941. Frances Mayer, Rohrerstown, Pa., b. Apr. 3, 1902.

Family of BARBARA HERSHEY (12894) and JACOB N. METZGER.

12942. Andrew Hershey, Philadelphia, Pa., b. June 21, 1851; m. Sept. 19, 1871, —— Hocker, dau. John Hocker and Elizabeth ——.

12943. Elizabeth Ann, Manheim, Pa., b. Apr. 15, 1853; d. Dec. 3, 1855.

12944. Lillie, Manheim, Pa., b. Aug. 10, 1857; d. Aug. 29, 1857.

12945. Emma, Manheim, Pa., b. June 1, 1860; d. June 1, 1860.

12946. Harry Sherman, Manheim, Pa., b. Sept. 17, 1864; d. Oct. 11, 1864.

12947. Walter Mahlon, Manheim, Pa., b. Apr. 15, 1868; d. Apr. 27, 1872.

12948. Calvin Luther, Manheim, Pa., b. Apr. 15, 1868; d. May 9, 1870.

Family of ANDREW HERSHEY METZGER (12948) and ———.

12949. Charles Goldsmith, Philadelphia, Pa., b. July 17, 1873.

12950. Maude Lavinia, Philadelphia, Pa., b. Nov. 21, 1875.

12951. Elsie Serene, Philadelphia, Pa., b. Nov. 22, 1889.

Family of ENOS W. KOHR (8910) and VIOLA GODSHALK.

12952. Walter L., Lancaster, Pa., b. Mar. 10, 1904.

Family of EMMA SALOME WENGER (9203) and LEVI MELLINGER.

12953. Florence May, Lancaster, Pa., b. Sept. 3, 1893.

Family of MARTHA IDA FUNK (6536) and LOUIS A. PARSHALL.

12954. Kathleen Elizabeth, Seattle, Wash., b. May 3, 1904.

Family of JOHN FORRER (12325) and Wid. SARAH GARDNER KEMPF.

12955. Elizabeth Ann., Apple Creek, O., b. Mar. 7, 1850; m. Aug. 26, 1867, George McConnell, b. Aug. 12, 1840; son John McConnell and Jerusha Ried.

12956. Elvina F., Orrville, O., b. Apr. 22, 1852; d. Jan. 27, 1901; m. May 15, 1877, Samuel Plumer, b. May 2, 1840; son Lazarus Plumer and Jane Craig.

21957. Sarah Jane, Orrville, O., b. Sept. 6, 1855; m. David D. Forrer (12349)

Family of HENRY FORRER (12326) and HENRIETTA GEISS.

12958. William Martin, Orrville, O., b. Dec. 10, 1876.

21959. Elizabeth Catharine, Greshan, O., b. Dec. 13, 1878; m. Dec. 24, 1896, Charles Geiss, b. Apr. 8, 1866; son Frederick Geiss and Elizabeth Meyer.

21960. Emma Viola, Cleveland, O., b. May 7, 1881; m. Dec. 24, 1901, George J. Scheuring, b. Nov. 14, 1877; son Anthony Scheuring and Bertha Euchbeurger.

12961. Henry Archie, Cleveland, O., b. Nov. 18, 1883; m. Mar. 10, 1905, Alta Bailey, b. Jan. 29, 1886; dau. William Henry Bailey and Mary Louisa Garver.

12962. Ervin Oliver, Orrville, O., b. May 6, 1886; d. Feb. 6, 1889.

12963. Ira Oscar, Orrville, O., b. May 6, 1886; d. Feb. 6, 1889.

12964. John Elvin, Orrville, O., b. June 5, 1888.

12965. Samuel Plumer, Orrville, O., b. Feb. 19, 1891; d. Jan. 9, 1895.

12966. Elvina Romaine, Orrville, O., b. June 26, 1892.

12967. Esther Belle, Orrville, O., b. June 8, 1897.

Family of DANIEL FORRER (12327) and SARAH ANN BIGLER.

12968. Clara Jane, Orrville, O., b. Mar. 14, 1875; m. Mar. 4, 1891, Charles Banhof, b. Aug. 17, 1871; d. Apr. 17, 1904; son Christian Banhof and Hester Moyer; m. Feb. 13, 1905, Elmer Leroy Tussing, b. Mar. 7, 1886; son Levi Tussing and Mary Ann Snyder.

12969. Daniel J., Orrville, O., b. Jan. 21, 1877; m. Apr. 17, 1908, Mamie Belle Swartz, b. Sept. 26, 1888, dau. Isaac M. Swartz and Nancy Detwiler.

12970. George S. Wadsworth, O., b. Dec. 25, 1880; m. Mar. 2, 1904, Ida Stoll, b. Dec. 6, 1884; dau. Jacob Stoll and Caroline Yoder.

12971. Sadie Jannette, Avalon, Pa., b. Sept. 3, 1882; m. Dec. 25, 1902, Charles B. Walter, b. July 4, 1879; son Samuel Walter and Minerva Winkler.

Family of ELI FORRER (12328) and MARY BAUGHMAN.

12972. Elizabeth, Marshalville, O., b. Mar. 12, 1852; m. Philip Wirth, b. Apr. 29, 1850.

12973. Nancy, Marshalville, O., b. Aug. 18, 1853; m. John W. Kelby, son George Kelby and Caroline Tinsler.

12974. John, Colesburg, Tenn., b. Sept. 9, 1855; m. Anna Hurst, b. June 28, 1856.

12975. Mary, Marshalville, O., b. Feb. 18, 1858; m. George W. Garman, b. June 29, 1853.

12976. Charlotte, Barberton, O., b. May 18, 1860; m. David Etter; m. David Ettling.

12977. William Henry, Barberton, O., b. May 31, 1865; m. Margaret Butzer, b. Aug. 18, 1871.

Family of MARTIN FORRER (12329) and ELIZA HEINEY.

12978. ———, Clarksville, Ind.

12979. ———, Clarksville, Ind.

12980. ———, Clarksville, Ind.

12981. ———, Clarksville, Ind.

12982. ———, Clarksville, Ind.

12983. ———, Clarksville, Ind.

Family of NANCY FORRER (12330) and SAMUEL MARTIN.

12984. John F., Orrville, O., b. Sept. 6, 1841; m. Jan. 10, 1878, Anna Brenneman, b. Apr. 14, 1854; dau. Henry Brenneman and Catharine Lefever.

12985. Emanuel, Orrville, O., b. Mar. 9, 1844; d. Sept. 29, 1904; m. Dec. 23, 1875, Henrietta Nitterauer, b. Jan. 29, 1848; dau. Daniel Nitterauer and Susanna Seabolt.

12986. Elizabeth, Dalton, O., b. May 2, 1846; m. Nov. 5, 1868, Benjamin Huntsberger, b. Aug. 20, 1847; son Christian Huntsberger and Susan Hursh.

12987. Lydia, Massillon, O., b. Sept. 29, 1847; m. Dec. 5, 1867, Cyrus Singer, b. Apr. 20, 1843; son Cyrus Singer and Lydia Gaimen.

12988. Maria, Dalton, O., b. Nov. 22, 1849; m. Nov. 27, 1873, Joseph Wenger, b. Mar. 10, 1852; son Joseph Wenger and Maria Groff.

12989. Daniel F., Columbiana, O., b. Dec. 19, 1851; m. Dec. 15, 1887, Anna Koontz, b. Mar. 31, 1869; dau. Lorance Koontz and Catharine Gerberich.

12990. Elvina, Orrville, O., b. Dec. 25, 1853; m. Jan. 7, 1875, George F. Forrer (13233).

12991. Levi, Orrville, O., b. Dec. 22, 1855; d. Oct. 3, 1862.

12992. Nancy, Orrville, O., b. July 19, 1860.

Family of MARTHA FORRER (12332) and MARTIN KENDIG.

12993. ———, Orrville, O.

Family of ELIZABETH ANN FORRER (12955) and GEORGE McCONNELL.

12994. Perry Elmer, Alliance, O., b. Feb. 18, 1868; m. Sept. 30, 1900,
Clara Gerber, b. Aug. 30, 1878; dau. Carl Gerber and Caroline
Marty.

12995. Sarah Delfis, Apple Creek, O., b. Feb. 7, 1871; d. Feb. 6, 1878.

12996. John Elington, Apple Creek, O., b. Jan. 21, 1873; m. Jan. 20,
1905, Isa Spitler, b. May 26, 1885; dau. C—— A. Spitler and
Malinda Winkler.

12997. Clara Netta, Cleveland, O., b. Nov. 28, 1874; m. June 21, 1904,
William Proper, b. Aug. 26, 1875.

12998. Luella Belle, Marion, O., b. Nov. 26, 1876; m. Oct. 18, 1898,
George Woods, son John Woods and Selina Reed.

12999. Gladder Glenn, Apple Creek, O., b. June 25, 1879.

13000. Cleo Pearl, Apple Creek, O., b. Feb. 9, 1881; m. May 7, 1907,
Orrin Beach.

13001. Justus George, Apple Creek, O., b Feb., 15, 1883.

13002. Edith Ethel, Apple Creek, O., b. May 29, 1885.

13003. Forest Forrer, Apple Creek, O., b. Dec. 17, 1887.

13004. Oliver Earl, Apple Creek, O., b. Aug. 11, 1892.

Family of ELIZABETH CATHARINE FORRER (12959) and CHARLES GEISS.

13005. Carl Frederick, Greshan, O., b. Sept. 30, 1899.

Family of EMMA VIOLA FORRER (12960) and GEORGE J. SCHEURING.

13006. George A., Cleveland, O., b. Mar. 20, 1902.

13007. Clarence E., Cleveland, O., b. June 26, 1906.

Family of HENRY ARCHIE FORRER (12961) and ALTA BAILEY.

13008. George Henry, Cleveland, O., b. Oct. 9, 1905.

13009. Ralph Adren, Cleveland, O., b. July 10, 1907.

Family if **CLARA JANE FORRER** (12968) and **CHARLES BANHOF.**

13010. Vernon, Orrville, O., b. Jan. 17, 1894.

13011. Irene Hester, Orrville, O., b. Nov. 11, 1896.

13012. ———, Orrville, O.

13013. ———, Orrville, O.

13014. ———, Orrville, O.

Family of **GEORGE C. FORRER** (12970) and **IDA STOLL.**

13015. Irene, Wadsworth, O., b. Aug. 22, 1896.

Family of **SADIE JANETTE FORRER** (12971) and **CHARLES B. WALTER.**

13016. Ariel Minerva E., Avalon, Pa., b. Dec. 29, 1903.

13017. Leah Jannette C., Avalon, Pa., b. Nov. 29, 1906.

Family of **ELIZABETH FORRER** (12972) and **PHILIP WIRTH.**

13018. John, Marshalville, O., b. Aug. 13, 1875.

13019. Eli, Marshalville, O., b. June 16, 1877; d. June 24, 1877.

13020. Infant, Marshalville, O., b. June 19, 1878; d. June 19, 1878.

13021. Catharine, Marshalville, O., b. Aug. 17, 1879; d. Dec. 28, 1887.

13022. Mary Elizabeth, Marshalville, O., b. Dec. 17, 1881.

13023. Adam William, Marshalville, O., b. Jan. 25, 1885; d. Dec. 17, 1887.

13024. Philip Henry, Marshalville, O., b. Aug. 28, 1887.

13025. Charles, Marshalville, O., b. Feb. 5, 1890; d. Feb. 21, 1890.

13026. Infant, Marshalville, O., b. June 8, 1891; d. June 19, 1891.

Family of **NANCY FORRER** (12973) and ——— **GRIFFIN.**

13027. Ida May, South Akron, O., b. Oct. 19, 1874; m. Apr. 10, 1902, Jess Millinger.

Family of **NANCY FORRER** (12973) and **JOHN W. KELBLY.**

13028. George Garfield, Marshalville, O., b. Oct. 13, 1880; d. Oct. 15, 1902.

13029. Minnie Minette, Marshalville, O., b. Mar. 5, 1878; d. Sept. 18, 1880.

13030. Rhoda Ellen, Ashland, O., b. Mar. 11, 1883; m. Nov. 14, 1902, Zenas Freace.

13031. Eli F., Jeromeville, O., b. Dec. 31, 1885; m. Nov. 14, 1905, Alta Eagle.

13032. John Harrison, Marshalville, O., b. June 18, 1889; d. July 18, 1889.

13033. Ira Earl, Marshalville, O., b. Nov. 14, 1892; d. Oct. 9, 1896.

Family of JOHN FORRER (12974) and ANNA HURST.

13034. Mary H., Colesburg, Tenn., b. Mar. 16, 1882; d. Oct. 12, 1882.

13035. Elvina, Colesburg, Tenn., b. Oct. 16, 1883; d. Dec. 20, 1903.

13036. Eli, Colesburg, Tenn., b. June 16, 1885.

13037. Francis, Colesburg, Tenn., b. May 16, 1887.

13038. Henry, Colesburg, Tenn., b. May 31, 1888; d. Sept. 5, 1888.

13039. David, Colesburg, Tenn., b. Sept. 15, 1889.

13040. George, Colesburg, Tenn., b. Apr. 7, 1891.

Family of MARY FORRER (12975) and GEORGE W. GARMAN.

13041. Eli E., Doylestown, O., b. June 16, 1878; m. Feb. 13, 1901, Mary Burg, b. Aug. 15, 1877.

13042. John W., Marshalville, O., b. June 30, 1880.

13043. Jacob A., Marshalville, O., b. Dec. 17, 1883.

13044. Eltie M., Doylestown, O., b. Mar. 4, 1885; m. Jan. 10, 1906, Michael Burg, b. Feb. 26, 1884.

13045. Infant, Marshalville, O., b. Sept. 17, 1891; d. Sept. 17, 1891.

13046. Mellie G., Marshalville, O., b. May 22, 1893.

13047. Mary M., Doylestown, O., b. Jan. 10, 1887.

Family of CHARLOTTE FORRER (12976) and ——— UPLINGER.

13048. Harvey, Barberton, O., b. ———, 1888.

Family of CHARLOTTE FORRER (12976) and DAVID ETTER.

13049. Dora May, Barberton, O., b. ———, 1893.

Family of WILLIAM HENRY FORRER (12976) and MARGARET BUTZER.

13050. Mary Elizabeth, Barberton, O., b. Nov. 9, 1904.

13051. Harold Theodore, Barberton, O., b. June 13, 1907.

Family of JOHN F. MARTIN (12984) and ANNA BRENNEMAN.

13052. Amelia, Wooster, O., b. Oct. 13, 1878; m. Mar. 19, 1903, Christian M. Burkhart, son Henry Burkhart and Nancy Martin.

13053. Samuel B., Apple Creek, O., b. Apr. 29, 1890; m. Dec. 28, 1905, Cora Ressler, b. Apr. 14, 1884; dau. George Ressler and Sarah Shisler.

13054. Elmira, Orrville, O., b. Dec. 13, 1881.

13055. Henry, Orrville, O., b. Dec. 13, 1888.

13056. Amanda, Orrville, O., b. Jan. 21, 1898.

Family of ELIZABETH MARTIN (12986) and BENJAMIN HUNTSBERGER.

13057. Samuel M., Dalton, O., b. Oct. 5, 1871; m. Jan. 3, 1897, Ida Ellen Metzler, b. Oct. 29, 1877; dau. Jesse Metzler and Mary Ann Martin.

13058. Nancy, Orrville, O., b. Aug. 12, 1873; m. Oct. 26, 1893, Charles F. Benglesdorf, b. Dec. 30, 1861; son Frederick Benglesdorf and Marie Haase.

13059. Susan, Orrville, O., b. Feb. 6, 1875; d. Apr. 2, 1890.

13060. Ida, Orrville, O., b. Jan. 2, 1877; m. Dec. 2, 1897, Martin Horst, b. May 20, 1873; son Jonas Horst and Mary ———.

13061. Elizabeth, Orrville, O., b. Sept. 7, 1878.

13062. Mary Ann, Dalton, O., b. Nov. 23, 1880; m. Dec. 3, 1899, Jacob Horst, b. May 6, 1877; son David Horst and Anna Hess.

13063. David E., Dalton, O., b. Aug. 2, 1885.

13064. Emma, Dalton, O., b. Dec. 10, 1889.

Family of LYDIA MARTIN (12987) and CYRUS SINGER.

13065. Ella, Orrville, O., b. Sept. 9, 1868; m. Jan. 6, 1891, Christian Brenneman, son David Brenneman and Elizabeth Eshleman.

13066. Cyrus B., Orrville, O., b. Dec. 22, 1872; m. Jan. 17, 1901, Maria F. Allan, b. Nov. 21, 1880; dau. John Allan and Elizabeth Jack.

13067. Nancy, Dalton, O., b. Dec. 8, 1870; m. Mar. 3, 1898, Oliver Homan, b. Oct. 18, 1877; son Henry Homan and Lucy Crites.

13068. Lydia Ann, Dalton, O., b. Oct. 10, 1875; m. Nov. 30, 1899, Samuel Milton Chapman, b. June 8, 1873; son Collins Chapman and Mary Ann Woods.

13069. Samuel M., Dalton, O., b. Aug. 25, 1877; m. Dec. 25, 1899, Clara L. Woods, b. Aug. 7, 1878; dau. Adolph Woods and Maria Messinger.

13070. Levi E., Dalton, O., b. Sept. 2, 1879; m. Jan. 13, 1904, Perley M. Martin, b. Dec. 18, 1885; dau. Daniel Martin and Mary Kapper.

13071. Eugene, Dalton, O., b. Oct. 9, 1881; m. Oct. 13, 1904, Bessie A. Kauffman, b. Apr. 6, 1883; dau. Louis Kauffman and Elizabeth Petit.

13072. David L., Akron, O., b. Nov. 2, 1883; m. June 25, 1907, Mary S. Martin, b. May 24, 1884; dau. John Martin and Mary Heninger.

13073. George F. F., Massillon, O., b. Nov. 30, 1885.

13074. Effie M., North Lawrence, O., b. Nov. 21, 1887; m. May 31, 1906, C—— Clyde Hollinger, son Martin Hollinger and Sarah Eshleman.

13075. Fanny B., Massillon, O., b. Sept. 23, 1889.

13076. Alvin S., Massillon, O., b. Mar. 25, 1892.

Family of MARIA MARTIN (12988) and JOSEPH WENGER.

13077. Clara, North Lawrence, O., b. Jan. 12, 1875; m. Nov. 8, 1894, Frank Horst, b. Nov. 4, 1867; son David Horst and Anna Hess.

13078. Nancy, North Lawrence, O., b. June 28, 1877; m. Mar. 1, 1898, Rev. Daniel Brubaker, b. Mar. 30, 1873; son Martin Brubaker and Magdalene Horst.

13079. Martin, Dalton, O., b. Oct. 25, 1878; m. Dec. 28, 1905, Mary Rudy, b. Nov. 15, 1877.

13080. John, Burton City, O., b. Feb. 5, 1881; d. Sept. 9, 1881.

13081. Mary, North Lawrence, O., b. Sept. 21, 1882; m. Nov. 5, 1907, John H. Martin, b. June 15, 1882; son Joseph S. Martin and Eliza Hess.

13082. Samuel, Dalton, O., b. Sept. 16, 1884.

13083. Emma, Dalton, O., b. Dec. 6, 1886.

13084. Benjamin, Dalton, O., b. Sept. 22, 1888.

13085. Emanuel, Dalton, O., b. Oct. 19, 1890.

13086. Joseph, Dalton, O., b. Dec. 2, 1892.

Family of DANIEL F. MARTIN (12989) and ANNA KOONTZ.

13087. George, Columbiana, O., b. Apr. 24, 1889.

13088. Samuel, Columbiana, O., b. Feb. 2, 1894.

13089. Reuben, Columbiana, O., b. Feb. 9, 1898; d. Mar. 13, 1901.

13090. Clatus, Columbiana, O., b. Aug. 27, 1902.

13091. Simon, Columbiana, O., b. June 20, 1905.

13092. Rhoda, Columbiana, O., b. Jan. 28, 1907.

Family of ELVINA MARTIN (12990) and GEORGE F. FORRER.

13093. Nancy Viola, Orrville, O., b. June 22, 1884.

13094. Ida May, Orrville, O., b. Nov. 22, 1885; m. Jan. 9, 1879, David E. Geiser, b. Apr. 9, 1879; son David Geiser and Katharine Swartz.

13095. Charlotte Ann, Orrville, O., b. Nov. 12, 1890.

13096. Leroy Leelan, Orrville, O., b. Mar. 17, 1893.

Family of PERRY E. McCONNELL (12994) and CLARA GERBER.

13097. Caroline M., Alliance, O., b. Aug. 20, 1906.

Family of LUELLA BELLE McCONNELL (12998) and GEORGE WOODS.

13098. Reed G., Marion, O., b. Oct. 11, 1897.

13099. Edith, Marion, O., b. Dec. 31, 1898; d. May —, 1899.

13100. Rufus, Marion, O., b. Jan. 6, 1900.

13101. Forrest, Marion, O., b. Oct. 28, 1902.

Family of CLEO PEARL McCONNELL (13000) and ORRIN BEACH.

13102. Pearl Virginia, Apple Creek, O., b. Jan. 22, 1908.

Family of IDA MAY GRIFFIN (13027) and JESS MELINGER.

13103. Gilbert Clemens, South Akron, O., b. May 7, 1908.

Family of ELI F. KELBY (13031) and ALTA EAGLE.

13104. John Wesley, Marshalville, O., b. June 10, 1906.

Family of ELI E. GARMAN (13041) and MARY BURG.

13105. Henry G., Doylestown, O., b. Apr. 18, 1902.

Family of ELTIE M. GARMAN (13044) and MICHAEL BURG.

13106. Marcella G., Doylestown, O., b. Sept. 21, 1906.
13107. Lucille G., Doylestown, O., b. Dec. 3, 1907.

Family of AMELIA MARTIN (13052) and CHRISTIAN M. BURKHART.

13108. Henry A., Wooster, O., b. Nov. 1, 1903.
13109. Russel J., Wooster, O., b. Sept. 13, 1905.
13110. Ethel Amelia, Wooster, O., b. Nov. 17, 1907.

Family of SAMUEL B. MARTIN (13053) and CORA RESSLER.

13111. Blanche M., Apple Creek, O., b. Nov. 28, 1906.

Family of SAMUEL M. HUNTSBERGER (13057) and IDA ELLEN METZLER.

13112. Earl Emerson, Dalton, O., b. Aug. 8, 1898.
13113. Ira Jay, Dalton, O., b. Dec. 25, 1899.
13114. Sadie Alice, Dalton, O., b. Apr. 18, 1902.
13115. Stella May, Dalton, O., b. Nov. 19, 1904.
13116. John Henry, Dalton, O., b. Mar. 24, 1907.

Family of NANCY HUNSTBERGER (13058) and FRED. BENGELSDORF.

13117. Nora E., Orrville, O., b. Sept. 8, 1894.
13118. Elmer R., Orrville, O., b. Feb. 15, 1896.
13119. Lena M., Orrville, O., b. Feb. 16, 1898.
13120. Lloyd L., Orrville, O., b. Mar. 4, 1901.
13121. Henry F., Orrville, O., b. Jan. 23, 1903.
13122. Mabel V., Orrville, O., b. May 21, 1905.
13123. Mary E., Orrville, O., b. Nov. 10, 1907.

Family of IDA HUNTSBERGER (13060) and MARTIN HORST.

13124. Arthur Roy, Orrville, O., b. Dec. 14, 1898.
13125. Dora May, Orrville, O., b. Sept. 21, 1901.
13126. Emma Viola, Orrville, O., b. Apr. 30, 1906.

Family of MARY ANN HUNTSBERGER (13062) and JACOB HORST.

13127. Laura Emma, Dalton, O., b. July 28, 1900.
13128. Erma Viola, Dalton, O., b. Aug. 26, 1902.
13129. Ruth Estella, Dalton, O., b. Sept 5, 1904.
13130. Adam, Dalton, Ò., b. Aug. 10, 1907.

Family of ELLA SINGER (13065) and CHRISTIAN BRENNEMAN.

13131. Ira, Orrville, O., b. Oçt. 18, 1891.
13132. Lydia Myrtle, Orrville, O., b. July 6, 1893; d. Oct. 28, 1906.
13133. David Elmer, Orrville, O., b. Aug. 11, 1895.
13134. Nancy Elvina, Orrville, O., b. July 17, 1897.
13135. Anna Elizabeth, Orrville, O., b. June 14, 1899.
13136. Mary Edna, Orrville, O., b. June 11, 1902.
13137. Manard Roy, Orrville, O., b. Apr. 7, 1903.
13138. Effa Viola, Orrville, O., b. Mar. 23, 1908.

Family of CYRUS B. SINGER (13066) anl MARIA F. ALLAN.

13139. Esther V., Orrville, O., b. Jan. 24, 1902.
13140. Raymond F., Orrville, O., b. Aug. 13, 1903.
13141. Ralph C., Orrville, O., b. Sept. 29, 1904.
13142. David Allan, Orrville, O., b. Apr. 3, 1907.

Family of NANCY SINGER (13067) and OLIVER HOMAN.

13143. Lydia I., Dalton, O., b. Oct. 10, 1899.
13144. Velda Mae, Dalton, O., b. Aug. 20, 1903.

Family of LYDIA ANN SINGER (13068) and SAMUEL MILTON CHAPMAN.

13145. Vera Luella, Dalton, O., b. Dec. 11, 1901.
13146. ———, Dalton, O., b. May 16, 1908.

Family of **SAMUEL M. SINGER** (13069) and **CLARA L. WOODS**.

13147. Ethel Marie, Dalton, O., b. Nov. 22, 1901.

Family of **LEVI E. SINGER** (13070) and **PERLEY M. MARTIN**.

13148. C—— Milton, Dalton, O., b. Feb. 20, 1905.
13149. Cyrus E., Dalton, O., b. Aug. 17, 1906.
13150. Daniel M., Dalton, O., b. Nov. 20, 1907.

Family of **EUGENE SINGER** (13071) and **BESSIE A. KAUFFMAN**.

13151. Russel L., Dalton, O., b. Mar. 4, 1905.
13152. Clyde F., Dalton, O., b. Apr. 1, 1907; d. Aug. 14, 1907.

Family of **EFFIE M. SINGER** (13074) and **C—— CLYDE HOLLINGER**.

13153. Viola Mae, North Lawrence, O., b. Aug. 4, 1906; d. Sept. 9, 1906.

Family of **CLARA WENGER** (13077) and **FRANK HORST**.

13154. Nola, North Lawrence, O., b. Jan. 22, 1890.
13155. Earl, North Lawrence, O., b. Sept. 3, 1898.
13156. Samuel, North Lawrence, O., b. Sept. 6, 1901.
13157. Della, North Lawrence, O., b. June 4, 1904.
13158. Mary Ann, North Lawrence, O., b. Oct. 4, 1906.

Family of **NANCY WENGER** (13078) and **Rev. DANIEL BRUBAKER**.

13159. Merl, North Lawrence, O., b. Nov. 1, 1899.
13160. Oren, North Lawrence, O., b. June 7, 1903.
13161. Iva, North Lawrence, O., b. Dec. 27, 1905.

Family of **IDA MAY FORRER** (13094) and **DAVID E. GEISER**.

13162. Ruth Elenor, Orrville, O., b. May 28, 1908.

Family of **ELIZA SNAVELY** (6063) and **Z—— SNYDER**.

13163. Anna M., Springfield, O., b. ——, 1868; m. Jasper Newman, b. ——, 1868; d. ——, 1898.
13164. Daniel Elbert, Springfield, O., b. ——, 1872; m. Jane Callisan.

13165. Mary Edith, Springfield, O., b. ———, 1877; m. Emery Baker.
13166. Ruth Aurelia, Springfield, O., b. ———, 1878.
13167. Ross Omar, Springfied, O., b. ———, 1885.

Family of BARBARA SNAVELY (6064) and DAVID MILLER.

13168. Harry, Springfield, O., b. ———, 1869; m. Ross Grube.
13169. Ebie, Springfield, O., b. ———, 1872; d. ———, 1885.
13170. Orestes, Springfield, O., b. ———, 1876; d. ———, 1902.

Family of FANNY SNAVELY (6066) and EUGENE MARSH.

13171. George, Springfield, O., b. ———, 1872.
13172. Eva, Springfield, O.
13173. Lyman, Springfield, O.
13174. Clara, Springfield, O.
13175. Arthur, Springfled, O., b. ———, 1885.
13176. Lawrence, Springfield, O., b. ———, 1882.
13177. Grace, Springfield, O.

Family of STEPHEN S. SNAVELY (6067) and ANNA McCLAIN.

13178. Nellie A., Springfield, O., m. Charles Cartnell.
13179. Frank S., Springfield, O.

Family of ANNA M. SNYDER (13163) and JASPER NEWMAN.

13180. Olive, Springfield, O., b. ———, 1892.
13181. D—— Leon, Springfield, O., b. ———, 1893.
13182. Glenn H., Springfield, O., b. ———, 1895.

Family of DANIEL ELBERT SNYDER (13164) and JANE CALLISON.

13183. Cletus, Springfield, O., b. ———, 1894.
13184. Jessie, Springfield, O., b. ———, 1896.·
13185. Lottie, Springfield, O., b. ———, 1899.
13186. Bernice, Springfield, O., b. ———, 1903.

Family of MARY EDITH SNYDER (13165) and EMERY BAKER.

13187. Eugene, Springfield, O., b. ———, 1906.
13188. Wayne, Springfield, O., b. ———, 1907.

Family of MARY ELIZABETH SNAVELY (9930) and HARRY REDMOND.

13189. Harold, Springfield, O., b. Oct. 28, 1904.
13190. Elizabeth, Springfield, O., b. Jan. 29, 1906.

Family of WILLIE D. HERR (11245) and LULU POWELL.

13191. Barker Dudley, Bloomington, Ill., b. Dec. 30, 1907.

Family of JOHN H. GROVE (9828) and HANNAH E. KINGERY.

13192. Beatrice V., Bowden, North Dakota, b. Jan. 20, 1904.
13193. Opal V., Bowden, North Dakota, b. Aug. 28, 1905.
13194. Homer D., Bowden, North Dakota, b. Oct. 11, 1907.

Family of ELIZABETH LANDIS (10079) and CHAUNCEY B. HERSHEY.

13195. Robert L., Anderson, Ind., b. Dec. —, 1901.

Family of ANNA VIOLA FRANTZ (10134) and FRANKLIN GOOD.

13196. Gertrude F., Greensburg, Pa., b. Jan. 1, 1904.

Family of ANNA M. HERR (10219) and JAMES H. SPARROW.

13197. Louis M., Bengal, India, b. Mar. 27, 1903.

Family of ELIZABETH HERR (12921) and JOSEPH SPROAT.

13198. Mary Ann, Reading, Pa., b. July 11, 1815; d. ———, 1877;
m. June 9, 1840, William Thomas, b. Dec. 20, 1811; d. July 6,
1876.
13199. Eliza, Reading, Pa., b. Oct. 16, 1816; d. July 30, 1852; m.
——— Douglas.
13200. Joseph, Reading, Pa., b. Feb. 25, 1819; d. June 12, 1892.
13201. Frances, Reading, Pa., b. Mar. 28, 1821.
13202. Jane, Reading, Pa., b. Jan. 18, 1823.

Family of MARY ANN SPROAT (13198) and WILLIAM THOMAS.

13203. Joseph, Philadelphia, Pa., b. June 27, 1841; d. Aug. 7, 1842.
13204. William Henry, Philadelphia, Pa., b. Sept. 27, 1842; m. Oct.
19, 1871, Ellen Rebecca Given, b. Jan. 19, 1849; dau. John B.
Given and Mary Catharine Ramsey.

13205. Susan, Philadelphia, Pa., b. Oct. 9, 1844.

13206. John Herr, Philadelphia, Pa., b. Oct. 25, 1846.

13207. Robert Augustus, Phila., Pa., b. Sept. 5, 1850; d. Sept. 20, 1851.

13208. Henry Johnson, Phila., Pa., b. Jan. 29, 1849; d. July 13, 1849.

13209. Charles, Philadelphia, Pa., b. Apr. 2, 1852; d. July 6, 1852.

13210. Laura Irene, Phila., Pa., June 26, 1859; d. Aug. 9, 1859.

13211. Mary Elizabeth, Philadelphia, Pa., b. Jan. 20, 1856.

Family of WILLIAM HENRY THOMAS (13204) and ELLEN REBECCA GIVIN.

13212. LaRue Dewees, Philadelphia, Pa., b. Oct. 16, 1872.

13213. Mary Virginia, Philadelphia, Pa., b. Nov. 30, 1873.

13214. William Banks, Brooklyn, N. Y., b. Dec. 3, 1875; m. Oct. 27, 1903, Jessie LeBaron Hammond, dau. George LeBaron Hammond and Jennie ———.

13215. Alice Givin, Philadelphia, Pa., b. Nov. 19, 1877.

13216. Susan Baird, Philadelphia, Pa., b. Apr. 10, 1881.

13217. Helen Ramsey, Philadelphia, Pa., b. Nov. 27, 1882.

13218. Marjorie Alexander, Philadelphia, Pa., b. Jan. 17, 1886.

Family of CATHARINE ESHLEMAN (780) and JOHN MILLER.

Continued from page 152.

Continued from page 152.

13219. Fanny, Landisville, Pa., b. Oct. 14, 1833; m. Jacob Trout.

13220. Emanuel, Landisville, Pa., b. Nov. 16, 1835; d. Feb. 1, 1905.

13221. Mary Ann, East Petersburg, Pa., b. Apr. 11, 1837; m. David Graybill.

13222. Catharine Elizabeth, East Petersburg, Pa., b. Sept. 21, 1839; m. Henry Hottenstein.

13223. Henry, Landisville, Pa., b. Feb. 24, 1847.

BURIAL PLACE OF REV. HANS HERR, A. D. 1725, IN MENNONITE CEMETERY, ONE-HALF MILE EAST OF WILLOW STREET, IN LANCASTER COUNTY, PENNA.

INDEX

OF

NAMES OF REV. HANS HERR AND HIS DESCENDANTS.

29

AUGUSTBURGER, Amos, C-68.
    J. W., C-63.
    Marian, C-64.
    Peter, C-67.
    Samuel, C-65.
    Sarah, C-66.
AVERY, Adah Shaub, 7885.
    Harry R., 7884.
BABBETT, Frank Lovell, 11249.
BACHMAN, Abraham, 3409.
    Ada Ann, 7544.
    Amanda, 3470.
    Amos B., 8684.
    Amos W., 3467.
    Anna, 2266, 8679.
    Arthur G., 7548.
    Benjamin, 8685.
    Benjamin F., 2270, 7545.
    Benjamin H., 3461.
    Carlton W., 8781.
    Daughter, 11370.
    Eliza, 3460.
    Eliza Ann, 7541.
    Elizabeth, 2271, 8680.
    Emma, 8683.
    Esther, 3402.
    Fanny, 2269.
    Frances, 3466.
    Frank, 5992.
    Frank E., 8601.
    Hannah, 3465.
    Harry M., 10842.
    Henrietta Elizabeth, 11315.
    Howard G., 11323.
    Jacob, 2267, 2268.
    Jacob B., 7543.
    Jay, 11369.
    John, 2265, 10843.
    John H., 7542.
    John Ira, 7546.
    John M., 3468.
    Lee Roy, 7547.
    Luella Lucille, 11314.
    Lydia Ann, 3464.
    Maria, 2263, 3463.
    Marion Evans, 11313.
    Martha, 8681.
    Mary Ada, 8682.
    Son, 11371.
    Susan, 2264.
BADER, Ada Ruth, C-92.
    Caroline, C-44.
    Catharine, C-49.
    Christian, C-46.
    Conrad, C-16.
    Doyle Wright, C-97.
    Ernest Henry, C-91.
    Felix Roy, C-90.
    Francis, C-98.
    Frank Amos, C-74.
    Frederica, C-43.
    Frederick William, C-72.
    George Nicholas, C-75.
    Glen, C-99.
    Ivan Eloro, C-93.
    John George, C-45.
    Louisa Alice, C-100.
    Mary Elizabeth, C-71, C-89.
    Nicholas Ernest, C-47.
    Orla William, C-94.

    Paul, C-96.
    Ray Loren, C-95.
    William Ernest, C-73.
    William Frederick, C-48.
BAER, Abraham, 10716.
    Adam, 7422, 10720.
    Amanda, 10718.
    Anna, 10715.
    Benjamin, 10724.
    Bert B., 9905.
    Elizabeth, 10723.
    Hannah, 10733.
    Harry, 10732.
    Hazel M., 9906.
    Henry H., 7419.
    Henry M., 10719.
    Infant, 7418, 10730.
    Isaac, 10721.
    Leah, 10722.
    Lloyd, 9919.
    Maria, 7420.
    Martha, 10725.
    Martin, 7421.
    Mary, 10714, 10731.
    Maude, 9916.
    Roy R., 9904.
    Susan, 10717.
BAIR, Anna M., 6268.
    Clara E., 6271.
    Elizabeth, 6270.
    Henry M., 6266.
    J. Clement, 6274.
    Jacob R., 6273.
    Josephine R., 6267.
    Katharine A., 6269.
    Rachel S., 6272.
BAIRD, Alfred Tennyson, 4474.
    Arthur Dunn, 8865.
    Catharine, 8871.
    Christian William, 4469.
    Donald Creighton, 8862.
    Edmund Clarence, 8867.
    Dr. Edmund Jaynes, 4471.
    Elizabeth F., 4470.
    Florence Elizabeth, 8863.
    Frances Hartman, 8866.
    George Eben, 8869.
    Helen Mary, 8864.
    Mary Harriet, 4472.
    May Elizabeth, 8868.
    Rebecca Emily, 4473.
    Rena Ellen, 8870.
    Teddy, 8872.
BAKER, 6441, 6442, 6443.
    Albert, 12422.
    Albert S., 9108.
    Anna, 2812, 2872.
    Barbara, 2875.
    Catharine, 6653.
    Catharine H., 6036.
    Christian, 2809, 2874.
    Christian G., 4838.
    Clarence, 12419.
    Daughter, 6440.
    Elizabeth, 6652, C-79.
    Elmira C., 4837.
    Emily, 12423.
    Eugene, 13187.
    Franklin H., 6034.
    Grant, 9116.
    Harry, 12420.
    Harry H., 6032.
    Henry, 2811.

Ira, 12421.
Jacob, 2810.
James S., 9109.
Jefferson S., 4835.
John, 2866, 6651.
Joseph, C-80.
Letitia, 9110.
Lizzie, 9115.
Magdalena, 2873.
Magdalene, 6650.
Mary H., 6033.
McKinley, 9118.
Nathan Clinton, 6035.
Oliver J., 4836.
Orris, 9111.
Viola, 9117.
William, C-78.
Wayne, 13188.
BALDWIN, Adaline, 4010.
   Alpheus, 4012.
   Benjamin Franklin, 4015.
   Elizabeth, 4013.
   Elmira M., 4014.
   Henrietta, 4011.
   John Charles, 4016.
   Martin Anthony, 4017.
   Mary Emma, 4009.
   William Lincoln, 4018.
BALMER, Anna F., 2507.
   Harriet, 2508.
   Mary, 2506.
BANTA, Ellen, 5046.
   Leah, 5048.
   Martha, 5049.
   Mary, 5047.
BANHOFF, 13012, 13013, 13014.
   Irene Hester, 13011.
   Vernon, 13010.
BANZHOFF, Bertha May, 10864.
   Charles Augustus, 10865.
   George Washington, 10866.
   Henry, 10867.
   Infant, 10863.
BARE, Winona Breneman, 11758.
BARKER, Berdina Elizabeth, 11504.
   Hazel Margarite, 11503.
   Isaac Clayton, 11502.
   Mabry, 11722.
BARNES, Alice, 5219.
   David, 5222.
   Elizabeth, 5218.
   Emma, 5220.
   Fanny, 5217.
   Malinda, 5216.
   Samuel, 5221.
BARNHOLT, Lawrence Lewis, 10640.
   Mary Elizabeth, 10641.
BARR, 11864, 11865.
   Aaron, 3620.
   Abraham, 338, 931.
   Adam Rohrer, 4739.
   Amanda, 4205.
   Ambrose Witmer, 5001.
   Ann, 342, 1208, 4274.
   Ann Catharine, 1767.
   Anna, 124, 1228, 1756, 3622, 8675.
   Anna Martha, 11046.
   Annie, 487.
   Annie Elizabeth, 5000.
   Asbury, 2958.
   Augustus, 1233.
   Barbara, 4280, 8674.
   Benjamin, 481, 1214, 1225, 4276, 8672.

Betsey, 926.
Breneman, 8547.
Carl Eshleman, 11862.
Caroline, 6857.
Caroline Herr, 2947.
Catharine, 930, 1761, 2957, 4272, 8670.
Catharine Gore, 4961.
Christian, 1212, 1231.
Christiana, 925, 1203.
Cyrus, 3035.
Cyrus Roy, 11044.
Cyrus S., 2946.
Daughter, 4209.
David, 1202, 2959.
Dr. David Miller, 1769.
E. Galen, 6852.
Edward, 6855.
Dr. Edwin W., 4206.
Elijah, 4203.
Elizabeth, 484, 1222, 1758, 3039, 4277, 4738.
Eliza Ann, 1762.
Emma, 3037.
Emma Celia, 4210.
Emma E., 8669.
Esther, 1232, 3040.
Esther Ann, 1764.
Ethel, 10575.
Eugene, 4959.
Fannie, 125, 486.
Fanny, 343, 928, 1209.
Fanny B., 1763.
Frances, 1223, 1755, 4279.
Frances Louisa, 4207.
Francis, 2956, 8671.
Frank W., 8561.
Franklin, 3041.
Franklin Park, 11043.
George A., 6856.
George F., 8550.
Rev. Gideon, 2955.
Grace Ella, 4987.
Harry C., 4991.
Harvey F., 4208.
Harvey W., 11861.
Henry, 3621, 6851.
Hiram Eshleman, 4200.
Isaac, 1106.
Jacob, 339, 346, 485, 1204, 1227, 1759.
Jacob Neff, 1770.
Jessie, 4990.
John, 126, 341, 478, 480, 902, 1211, 1224, 1760, 4999, 8673.
John M., 6853.
John N., 1765.
Kate Kreider, 4989.
Lavinia Lawrence, 5005.
Letitia, 3038.
Letitia M., 1772.
Lillie Stone, 4988.
Lizzie, 127.
Luetta, 4960.
Lydia S., 8549.
Magdalena, 482.
Magdalene, 4278.
Maria, 4275.
Martha, 129, 1230.
Martin, 128, 340, 479, 483, 901, 1205, 1210, 1757, 3042.
Martin Potts, 4992.
Martin W., 1766.
Mary, 123, 345, 347, 924, 1207, 3036, 4734.

Mary A., 6854.
Mary Ann, 4666.
Mary Augusta, 8563.
Mary B., 1226.
Mary E., 8552.
Mary Elizabeth, 4201.
Mary Eva, 10574.
Mary G., 1771.
Mary L., 8562.
Mary Viola, 11045.
Maud Miller, 5004.
Melchor Newton, 4202.
Minnie Sears, 5002.
Morris Lincoln, 8560.
Nancy, 929.
Newton H., 8551.
Ronaldo Sabedus, 4958.
Russell Tuthill, 11860.
Salome E., 2948.
Samuel, 1768, 8668.
Samuel Dickson, 4998.
Sarah, 8676.
Simon, 1213.
Son, 4273, 4281.
Susan, 344, 927, 1215, 1229, 4204, 8667.
Susan Dickson, 5003.
Susan F., 8546.
Tobias, 1234.
William H., 8548.
William Yancey, 4993.
Wilson Rogers, 11863.
BARTHOLOMEW, Amanda, 3361.
    Amy Geneva, 7256.
    Annie Elizabeth, 7252.
    Annie Hester, 7258.
    Benjamin F., 3363.
    David Boughman, 7253.
    David H., 3364.
    Edith May, 7262.
    Elizabeth, 10668.
    Elizabeth May, 7259.
    Guy Clifford, 7257.
    Henry Matthew, 7254.
    John William, 7261.
    Mary Ann, 3362, 7255.
    Merritt, 10669.
    Sarah Eckman, 7260.
BAUSMAN, Daughter, 2858.
    David H., 2857.
    John H., 2856.
    Susanna, 2855.
BEACH, Pearl Virginia, 13102.
BEAM, Abraham T., 962.
    Mary, 961.
BEAMESDERFER, Anna Mary, 6321.
    Elsie M., 9501.
    Norman M., 9502.
BEAR, Abraham, 6028.
    Anna Eliza, 2871.
    Annie, 12902.
    Benjamin, 12906.
    Catharine, 6029.
    Elizabeth, 12899.
    Elizabeth Herr, 6026.
    Emma, 12901.
    Ezra, 6027.
    Franklin, 6030.
    George, 12903.
    Henry H., 6024.
    Hetty, 12905.
    John, 12900.
    Jonas H., 6025.

Mary, 12904.
BEARD, Elmer Herr, 8171.
    Esther Thelma, 8173.
    Harry Kline, 8172.
    John Samuel, 8170.
BEATES, Harry, 12373.
    Sarah, 12374.
BEATTIE, Anna M., 12561.
    Catharine, 12544.
    Catharine S., 12560.
    Edna D., 12556.
    Eli, 12542.
    Ella, 12548.
    Emanuel, 12543.
    Emma, 12547.
    George E., 12559.
    Hiram G., 12558.
    Lewis, H., 12546.
    Lewis L., 12557.
    Mary, 12545.
    Mary E., 12554.
    Ralph H., 12562.
    Ruth, 12555.
BECKER, Harriet H., 12502.
BELCHER, Amy Lavena, 10665.
    Emma Golda, 10661.
    Ethel Pauline, 10666.
    Lela Marie, 10663.
    Sallie Gladys, 10662.
    Sidney Forrest, 10664.
BELL, Bessie R., 10445.
    Franklin Arthur, 12181.
    Frederick Strite, 12180.
    George, 10047.
    Leila I., 10046.
    Lottie K., 10044.
    Mary F., 10043.
BELLAMY, Adaline Amanda, 7928.
    Emma Anna, 7926.
    Leona, Winona, 7927.
    Nora Corella, 7929.
BENDER, Ann, 2285.
    Elizabeth, 2292.
    Ephraim, 2286.
    Jacob, 2289.
    John, 2287.
    Joseph, 2290.
    Levi, 2288.
    Martha, 2291.
    Mary, 2293.
    Michael, 2294.
    Rehecca, 2295.
BENGELSDORF, Elmer R., 13118.
    Henry F., 13121.
    Lena M., 13119.
    Lloyd L., 13120.
    Mabel V., 13122.
    Mary E., 13123.
    Nora E., 13117.
BENTZ, George E., 9995.
    Harry F., 9996.
    Orie B., 9997.
BEYER, John Warfel, 11317.
    Robert Arthur, 11316.
    Thomas, 11318.
BIGGS, Ellen, 9755.
    Enoch, 9758.
    Francis, 9756.
    Joseph H., 9754.
    Wesley, 9757.
BINGHAM, Mary Frances, 11752.
BINKLEY, Allie Frances, 11867.
    Ann Eliza, 4924.

BOYD, Mary Julianna, 4391.
BOYER, Ann, 12931.
    Catharine, 12927.
    Harriet, 12925.
    Henry H., 12928.
    John, 12929.
    Maria, 12930.
    Perninah, 12926.
BOYENTON, John Frantz, 11416.
BRACKBILL, Abraham, 8341.
    Abram B., 12056.
    Allan G., 12152.
    Almeda G., 12154.
    Amanda, 4168.
    Amaziah E., 4265.
    Amos, 4091.
    Amos H., 4306.
    Andrew Carpenter, 5411.
    Ann, 4087, 4166.
    Ann Maria, 3515.
    Anna, 110, 403, 1421, 1451, 4302,
        4313.
    Anna Barbara, 5408.
    Anna E., 12312.
    Anna Elizabeth, 11189.
    Anna H., 11186.
    Anna Mary, 12039.
    Annie Emma, 8489.
    Annie Maria, 8337.
    Austin, 11805.
    Barbara, 42, 1455, 4303.
    Benedict, 109.
    Benjamin, 405, 1422, 1445, 1456, 4086.
    Benjamin A., 4304, 8347.
    Benjamin Franklin, 8695.
    Benjamin H., 8306.
    Benjamin L., 4282.
    Benjamin O., 4262.
    Benjamin R., 12310.
    Bertha, 8649.
    Bertha M., 12311.
    Bertha S., 11182.
    Bessie M., 12050.
    Carl, 11807.
    Christian, 406, 1425, 4085, 8487.
    Christian E., 8345, 12033.
    Christian H., 4287.
    Christian L., 4181.
    Christian M., 4312.
    Clinton, 8488.
    Cora E., 12049.
    Cora Elizabeth, 8646.
    Daniel Ryan, 8484.
    Daughter, 1420.
    David Amandus, 8499.
    David H., 1159, 11185.
    E. Miriam, 11187.
    Edgar Clayton, 8644.
    Edith, 12044.
    Elam H., 4258.
    Elam M., 12054.
    Eli M., 4308.
    Elias, 4089.
    Elias E., 4259.
    Eliza, 4169.
    Eliza A., 1160, 4179.
    Elizabeth, 400, 1424, 1454, 4095, 4301,
        4315, 8486.
    Elizabeth F., 11184.
    Ellis, 8338.
    Elmira Clara, 4268.
    Elsie S., 12314.
    Emlen Howard, 8645.

    Emma Salome, 5410.
    Eustace H., 4680.
    Fanny, 107.
    Frances, 111.
    Frances Elizabeth, 4284.
    Harry C., 4681.
    Harry D., 12051.
    Harry G., 12037.
    Harvey, 4254.
    Harvey Groff, 11321.
    Henry, 112, 402, 1447, 8485.   ?
    Henry L., 4178.
    Henry P., 4264.
    Hettie S., 12038.
    Hiram, 8483.
    Ida E., 12036.
    Ira H., 11806.
    Isaac, 12046.
    Isaac Veazy, 4283.
    Jacob, 1446, 1852, 5407.
    Jacob F., 4263.
    John, 108, 399, 1423, 1443, 1453.
    John A., 8344.
    John B., 4165.
    John C., 4300.
    John Elmer, 8307.
    John H., 4088.
    Joseph, 1459, 12047, 4094.
    Joseph Warner, 4316.
    Josiah A., 4307.
    Laura A., 8651.
    Levi H., 4314.
    Lena H., 12035.
    Lillie, 11804.
    Lizzie Ann, 8305.
    Lydia Ann, 4261.
    Magdalene, 4305.
    Maria, 1419, 1444, 1450, 4093, 4180.
    Maria Ella, 8346.
    Maria V., 8339.
    Marian Virgilia, 8647.
    Mark, 8343.
    Martha, 1458.
    Martha Ann, 4285.
    Martha M., 8342.
    Martin H., 12043, 12153.
    Mary, 401, 12045.
    Mary Ann, 4255.
    Mary Elizabeth, 4257, 5409.
    Maudlin, 40.
    Milton Joseph, 8694.
    Moses, 12048.
    Naomi Ada, 4267.
    Park R., 12313.
    Phenias, 4256.
    Preston Eaby, 4270.
    R. John, 11803.
    Ralph Rauch, 12022.
    Ralph Strock, 11148.
    Salome Maria, 4286.
    Sarah M., 8648.
    Seymour H., 4271.
    Son, 106, 4090, 4092, 11183.
    Susan B., 4673.
    Susan E., 8340, 12034.
    Susanna, 404, 1426, 1457, 4167, 4260.
    Susanna R., 4269.
    Thaddeus H. Lincoln, 8348.
    Uhlrich, 41.
    William R., 8650.
    William Victor, 12021.
BRACKIN, Archie John, 8015.
    Eliza A., 8013.

Sarah Ann, 1526.
Thomas, 4506.
Dr. W. C., 4489.
William C., 4486.
BRICKER, Elmer V. George, 12000.
  Mary Alberta, 11999.
  Stella Amanda, 12001.
BRIDGES, Allen C., 10484.
  David Wills, 11671.
  Frances V., 10483.
  Helen J., 10479.
  James W., 11673.
  John Patterson, 10481.
  John S., 10485, 11670.
  M. Julia, 10482.
  Mary E., 11672.
  Susan C., 10480.
BRINTON, Annie G., 7062.
  Arthur H., 7061.
  Christian F., 7065.
  Edith R., 7066.
  Lillian H., 7064.
  Mary H., 7063.
BROOME, Annie Elizabeth, 7960.
  Harry Witmer, 7958.
  J. Frank, 7957.
  Martin Miller, 7959.
BROWN, Alfred, 11846.
  Barbara, 11830.
  Benjamin, 11848, 11854.
  Benjamin C., 9091.
  Benjamin F., 7414.
  Catharine, 11831.
  Charles H., 7416.
  Christian, 11847.
  Clyde Grove, 11496.
  Daughter, 11850, 11851, 11852, 11853.
  Earl William, 11494.
  Frederick, 11838.
  George W., 11836.
  Henry, 11832.
  Jacie May, 11492.
  Jacob, 769, 11849.
  Jacob Minnich, 11837.
  Jessie May, 11491.
  John, 770, 11829.
  John C., 7412.
  John Groff, 11835.
  John Henry, 12779.
  Levi, 11834.
  Maria, 772.
  Mary E., 5851, 7417.
  Otto Groff, 9090.
  Peter, 771.
  Ray Alvin, 11495.
  Rebecca, 11833.
  Roy Jacob, 11493.
  Sarah E., 7415.
  Thomas E., 7413.
BROWNFIELD, Ardoth Avada, 6539.
  Charles Percival, 6538.
BRUA, Catharine, 577.
BRUBAKER, Anna, 2820, 8542.
  Anna H., 12540.
  Barbara, 8540.
  Benjamin, 8541.
  Catharine, 12508.
  Christian, 851, 2819.
  Christian B., 2816.
  Clayton, 10624.
  David, 2814.
  Eliza, 2821.
  Elizabeth, 2818, 8538.

Emma, 8544.
Fanny, 2825.
Fanny L., 8537.
Guy, 12509.
Harry Gamber, 12365.
Henry, 2823.
Isaac H., 12541.
Iva, 13161.
Jacob, 852, 8539, 10623.
Jacob B., 2815.
John, 2813.
Lillie H., 10622.
Lizzie Matilda, 8543.
Mary, 2817, 2822, 8545.
Mary Gamber, 12362.
Merl, 13159.
Nancy, 850.
Oren, 13160.
Rita, 12510.
Selena Gamber, 12363.
Susan, 11282.
Susanna, 2825.
Thaddeus, 11281.
Wayne Gamber, 12364.
Weidler, 11280.
BRUNER, Caroline Sneath, 11367.
  Harry Clarke, 11368.
BRUNHOUSE, Harry, 11972.
  Luther, 11973.
BRUNK, George J., 11911.
  Henry M., 11913.
  Joseph E., 11910.
  Samuel H., 11912.
BUDLONG, Alena Ellen, 7565.
  Amelia Alice, 6763.
  Edwin S., 7563.
  Harry A., 7564.
  Nettie Hazel, 11781.
  Percy Ernest, 11779.
  Rollin Howard, 7566.
  Sadie Ellen, 11780.
  Stella Alena, 11778.
BUEHLER, Elizabeth, 10474.
  Ella R., 10472.
  Mary Caroline, 10473.
BUEHRER, Denver W., 12768.
  Dorris, 12767.
  Ellen, 12766.
  Forest T., 12764.
  Ruth, 12765.
BUFFENMOYER, Anna, 12908.
  Benjamin, 12911.
  Harriet, 12912.
  Jacob, 12915.
  Jennie, 12916.
  John, 12909.
  Joseph, 12910.
  Lulu, 12907.
  Malinda, 12914.
  Uriah, 12913.
BULLINGTON, Edna Bernice, 10698.
  Elvena Gem, 10695.
  Estelle Mae, 10697.
  Olive Elsie, 10693.
  Oma Gladys, 10699.
  Minnie Ann, 10694.
  Pearl Edith, 10692.
  Verna Rozella, 10696.
BURG, Lucille G., 13107.
  Marcella G., 13106.
BURK, 12315.
  Andrew, 9978.
  Anna Winterode, 11537.

CASTLES, Frences, 11309.
    John Wesley, 11308.
CATON, Elinor, 7175.
CAYWOOD, Effie Amanda, 8117.
    Ellison M., 8113.
    Gracie I., 8116.
    Jesse Brenberger, 8119.
    Leslie Grant, 8112.
    Mary Elizabeth, 8115.
    Mattie Edna Pearl, 8118.
    Rhoda Ellen, 8114.
CHAPMAN, 13146.
    Vera Luella, 13145.
CHARLES, Anna, 948, 1028, 5461, 11264.
    Barbara, 950.
    Benjamin, 11263.
    Betsey, 946.
    Catharine, 952.
    Christian, 949, 1026.
    Christiana, 11266.
    David, 11268.
    Elizabeth, 1024, 11269.
    Ephraim, 11265.
    Esther, 1027, 3450.
    Fanny, 951.
    Jacob, 947, 11272.
    John, 1025, 11267.
    Joseph, 1029, 11270.
    Mary, 945.
    Susan, 11271.
CLARK, Anna V., 10933.
    Edward S., 10934.
    Emma Blanche, 10994.
    Harry Porter, 10993.
    Hattie Mae, 10992.
    Lilly R., 10938.
    Mary E., 10936.
    Robert, 10935.
    Thaddeus J., 10937.
CLAIR, Thaddeus S., 7924.
CLEMENT, Donald, 11657.
    Edward B., 11655.
    Hayden C., 11654.
    John M., 11656.
    Louis Heyl, 11658.
CLISE, Charles Francis, 11402.
    James William, 11404.
    Ruth, 11401.
    Willis Herr, 11403.
COCKEY, Infant, 10503, 10504.
COMSTOCK, Katharine Farnum, 9722.
    Walter J., Jr., 9721.
CONDON, Edward, 10576.
CONNELLY, Frances D., 11136.
    George Francis, 8222.
    George W., 11137.
    John Dieffenbach, 8220.
    Martha B., 11138.
    Mary Elizabeth, 9721.
    Son, 8223.
    William Miller, 11135.
CONSTANTINE, Dorothy Jane, 11545.
    Henry Frederic, 11543.
    Thomas Paul, 11544.
COOPER, Carrie Salome, 5311.
    Edith Eva, 9535.
    Ernest Herr, 5312.
    Fannie Estella, 5310.
CORNWELL, Gibbons Gray, 11534.
    Mary Gray, 11533.
COVELL, Dorris G., 10769.
    Norma G., 10768.
COVER, Charles, 2155, 2160.

    Eliza, 2157.
    Isaac, 633, 2161.
    Joel, 632.
    John, 634, 2162.
    Mary, 635, 2156.
    Michael, 2154.
    Rebecca, 2159.
    Sarah, 2158.
    Susanna, 631.
COX, Arleigh David, 10690.
    Letta Dell, 10691.
    Minnie Winfield, 10689.
CRAIG, Elizabeth, 11312.
    Fanny Hampton, 11310.
    Frederick D., 8603.
    Joseph Rohert, 8604.
    L. Fletcher, 8605.
    Robert Emmet, 11311.
CRALEY, Arline, 10746.
    Carrie, 10743.
    Frank, 10741.
    Rea, 10742.
    Rodger, 10744.
    Yvonne, 10745.
CRAMER, Edward, 12027.
    Elizabeth, 12028.
    Harriet, 1197.
    John, 12026.
    Lida, 12025.
    Matilda, 1195.
    Solomon, 1196.
CRAPSTER, Mary, 6817.
    Milton, 6818.
CRESS, Andrew J., 5044.
    Benjamin 5040.
    Calvin B., 5045.
    George W., 5043.
    Mary E., 5042.
    Payton M., 5041.
    Susanna, 5039.
CRESSWELL, Annie Sophia, 6885.
    Christian James, 6883.
    Daniel Walter, 6886.
    Estella Agnes, 6888.
    John Henry, 6882.
    Mary Elizabeth, 6884.
    Samuel Newton, 6887.
CRESWELL, Catharine Kezia, 2949.
    David Maris, 2950.
    Emma Ann, 2951.
    George Martin, 2953.
    Mary Jane, 2954.
    Mattie Adaline, 2952.
CRISPEN, Anson LeRoy, 5518.
    Charles L., 5516.
    Clarence C., 5517.
    Edmund Herr, 5515.
    Frances R., 5519.
    Frederick Shultz, 9607.
CROFT, Alma, 3266.
    Amelia, 3261.
    Annie, 7174.
    Arthur, 3265.
    Benjamin H., 1056.
    Bertha, 3267.
    Bertha E., 3278.
    Catharine Marietta, 3277.
    Clara, 3269.
    David, 1052, 7170.
    Edward, 1051.
    Edwin, 3262.
    Flora, 3270.
    Ida, 3263.

Emerson, 10911.
George E., 10907.
John R., 10908.
Katie M., 10913.
Mary E., 10906.
Walter F., 10912.
William C., 10909.
DRUMM, Catharine E., 10892.
Catharine Elizabeth, 7705.
Edgar Hargrave, 10615.
Elizabeth S., 10880.
Ellenora S., 10878.
Elnora A., 10897.
Ethel, 10904.
Frances Elenora, 7708.
George Martin, 7703.
George W., 10890, 10903.
Ida S., 10879.
Ira, 10905.
Irene, 10889.
Jay Raymond, 10893.
John Milton, 7706, 10877.
Katharine, 10881.
Leigh V., 10896.
Lester A., 10894.
Marian Orlando, 10616.
Martha Jane, 7704.
Mary Ann, 7702.
Mary Olivia, 10891.
Myrtle E., 10895.
Peter Cartright, 7707.
Ruth, 10898.
Samuel Grant, 7709.
DUDDING, Elizabeth, 5473.
Emma Caplinger, 5474.
Frank, 5475.
George, 5469.
Henry Sarver, 5472.
Henry Sylvester, 5471.
Mary Catharine, 5470.
Olin W., 9570.
DUER, 12886, 12887.
Mabell, 12870.
Merrill, 12869.
DUNGON, Isaac, 8890.
DUNLAP, Alice Isabella, 9894.
Andrew John, 9889.
Clara Eliza, 9892.
Emma Josephine, 9893.
Frank McClellan, 9895.
Maria Louisa, 9890.
Mary Elizabeth, 9896.
Stephen Hastings, 9891.
DUPUY, Andrew, 11566.
Florence, 11568.
Robert, 11567.
DUVAL, Georgia Mary, 11604.
Mary Scott, 11605.
Neniene Ovington, 11607.
Virginia Allen, 11606.
EABY, Abraham, 2633.
Christian, 2635.
Frances, 2634.
Henry, 2636.
Mary, 2632.
EAGER, Annie M., 7806.
Barbara H., 7810.
Charles H., 7811.
Edwin L., 7803.
Emma Bessie, 7814.
Eva, 7816.
Frank W., 7808.
George F., 7804.

Howard L., 7813.
John H., 7812.
Maggie M., 7818.
Milton B., 7807.
Nora M., 7817.
Richard J., 7805.
Susan J., 7809.
William D., 7815.
EBERLY, Catharine, 5223.
Effie, 5224.
EBERMAN, Edith Mary, 9887.
Ella L., 9888.
Frank Potts, 9886.
EBY, Abraham, 6104.
Anna, 6105.
Arline B., 9672.
Christian, 6106.
Eva May, 11381.
Henry, 6102.
Ruth, 11382.
Susanna, 6103.
ECHTERNACH, Daniel, 5964.
Eliza, 5960.
John, 5963.
Joseph, 5962.
Louisa, 5965.
Margaret, 5961.
ECKLIN, David K., 10515.
Easley J., 10512.
Harry W., 10511.
Ivy Belle, 10513.
Joseph C., 10516.
Martha Myrtle, 10514.
ECKMAN, Aldus, 7677.
Aldus A., 10847.
Anna, 7683.
Arthur, 10850.
Arthur Lloyd, 10581.
August, 10853.
Bertha Maud, 10535.
Charles, 6867.
Clara Elizabeth, 6866.
Daniel, 3852.
Daniel Martin, 10533.
Darius J., 6872.
Dora, 6868.
Edith A., 6876.
Effie May, 10534.
Eliza, 3851.
Elizabeth, 7679.
Estella, 6869.
Esther, 7676.
Esther Creswell, 10582.
Eugene, 10848.
Eva, 10862.
Ferol, 10852.
Frank, 8087.
Gertrude Elizabeth, 10580.
Guy Henry, 10859.
Harry John, 10860.
Henry, 1165, 3533, 7678, 10856.
Hester, 3534.
Hettie, 1166.
Jacob, 3532, 7681.
Jacob Keen, 10532.
John, 3853, 7680.
John B., 3535.
John C., 10577.
John G., 6871.
Julia, 10849.
K. Bernice, 6874.
Kate, 3855.
Laura S., 10861.

Samuel H., 7392.
Virginia Alice, 10709.
Virginia M., 7397.
William Ray, 10704.
FAULKNER, Angeline, 6695.
C. W., 6696.
D. C., 6697.
Jerome, 6702.
Frences M., 6698.
Leren E., 6699.
Mary A., 6700.
Theodore. 8701.
FEHR, Charles Augustus, 9524.
Miriam Stephens, 9523.
FEILBACH, Benjamin H., 1088.
Bertha, 3341.
Catharine, 1889.
Elizabeth, 1085.
Emma L., 3340.
Esther, 1084.
Esther G., 3342.
Henrietta, 1087.
Louis W., 3343.
Mary M., 1086.
FELLENBAUM, Martin L., 10931.
Miller, 10930.
William B., 10932.
FENLEY, George W., 10392.
Infant, 10395.
Jeffries R., 10393.
Rebecca H., 10394.
Sarah A., 10396.
Susan P., 10397.
FERREE, Charlotta, 1500.
Eliza, 1502.
Fannie, 1504.
George, 1499.
Harriet, 1507.
Joel, 1505.
Mary, 1501.
Rebecca, 1506.
FETTER, Annie Maria, 11132.
Frederick Henry, 11131.
FIELD, Elizabeth, 10379.
Ella M., 10378.
Frederick, 10377.
FINLEY, Miriam Vesta, 11241.
FIRESTONE, Eva Frances, 12295.
Leonard Joseph, 12294.
Marion L., 12296.
FISHER, Abraham, 9055.
Aldus, 9060.
Barbara H., 9062.
Clayton, 9063.
Edna Herr, 7037.
Elizabeth, 9053.
Elmer, 9056.
Emma May, 9061.
Frances H., 9057.
Harry, 9054.
Isaac, 9059.
John Clyde, 7038.
Mary A., 9058.
Mary Herr, 7036.
FIXLER, Irene, 12715.
Martha, 12716.
Ralph, 12714.
William, 12717.
FLEMING, Henrietta Louise, 5614.
Julia Herr, 5615.
FLORY, Anna Letitia, 11142.
Benjamin, 11143.
Charles Clio, 11506.

Charles Franklin, 9810.
Christiana Catharine, 9806.
Daniel, 11140.
Delores, 11507.
Everett Edward, 11497.
Isaac Daniel, 9808.
Jacob Andrew, 9811.
Jacob B., 11139.
Joseph Henry, 9807.
Lambert Grove, 11500.
Laurane Henry, 11498.
Lena Atwood, 11508.
Leta Goldie, 11501.
Lyle Kenneth, 11499.
Mary, 11141.
Paul, 11144.
Sarah Elizabeth, 9809.
Vesta Pearl, 11505.
FOGELSONGER, Emma E., 5177.
Willard E., 5178.
FONDERSMITH, Aldus H., 5395.
Naomi, 5394.
FOREMAN, Annie, 6116.
Carrie Louisa, 4675.
Edgar Herr, 4676.
Edith Elizabeth, 4678.
Frederick Herbert, 4677.
Hannah, 6117.
Henry, 6115.
Susanna, 6118.
FORNEY, Alice M., 10476.
Amanda, 2176.
Anna F., 5733.
Anna Hoover, 5724.
Barbara, 650.
Catharine, 654.
Charles, 5727.
Charles B., 2167.
Charles C., 656.
Clara, 5734, 5737.
Clara Mabel, 10492.
Daisy, 10490.
Daniel C., 2170.
David Julian, 10497.
David S., 6801.
Elizabeth, 6796.
Elsie, 10491.
Emma, 5736.
Frederick, 2166.
George, 2165, 2172, 2173.
Henry Swope, 6797.
Isaac, 655, 2175.
Jacob, 652, 2171.
James, 5721.
John Swope, 6802.
John W., 2164, 2722.
Josephine, 6800.
Josephine R., 10478, 10493.
Julia T., 10477.
Louisa, 10495.
Louisa A., 6799.
Mary Jane, 6798.
Mary Stokes, 5723.
Michael, 5738.
Peter, 649.
Peter William, 5732.
Philip Reitzel, 5720.
Samuel S., 6803, 10475.
Samuel Walker, 10494.
Sarah, 2168, 2177, 5729.
Sarah A., 6804.
Sarah C., 653.
Stehman, 5726.

Ella Louisa, 5923.
Ella S., 9853.
Emerson, 10035.
Emma, 6203, 7004.
Ernest M., 9851.
Esther Bertha, 10129.
Etha M., 9856.
Ethel, 10136.
Etta, 6204.
Ezra G., 5916.
Fannie S., 10031.
Frank, 10032.
Frank Bernard, 9862.
Franklin, 6235.
Franklin Frick, 10133.
Freddie McKinley, 10635.
Genevieve, 10144.
George Best, 10120.
Grace Herr, 8912.
Harry, 9156.
Harry Abraham, 9857.
Harry Christian, 9870.
Harry Herr, 7003.
Harry Stone, 9160.
Harvey, 10122.
Hattie Imogene, 10056.
Helen Adalaide, 10132.
Henry B., 4880.
Herbert, 10041.
Herman Benjamin, 6216.
Homer B., 10126.
Horace G., 10139.
Howard, 10141.
Ida Martha, 5922.
Irene Elizabeth, 10123.
Isaac, 2431, 6211.
Iva M., 9855.
Rev. Jacob, 2434.
Jacob, 6201.
Jacob F., 6238.
Jacob Harold, 10138.
Jacob Milton, 4879.
Jacob Paul, 6628.
James Oscar, 10128.
Jay Wilde, 9158.
Jemima Helen, 10054.
Jennie, 7005.
Jerome, 10030.
John, 2432, 6214, 10124.
John Andrew, 6632.
John Benjamin, 10060.
John E., 6205.
John H., 4877.
John Pinkney, 9155, 11414.
Joseph, 6209.
Joseph Ira, 4881.
Joseph S., 10052.
Katie Stickell, 10040.
Lauretta Weller, 10633.
Leab, 10034.
Leila May, 9866.
Leroy, 10137.
Lillian Gertrude, 9871.
Louis, 10121.
Louisa Sewall, 11413.
Mabel Good, 9858.
Margaret Estelle, 10058.
Margaret Funk, 0860.
Margaret Pinkney, 11412.
Marie, 11528.
Mark, 10029.
Martha, 6194, 6202.
Martin, 5921.

Mary, 6191, 6210, 10039.
Mary Alice, 5917.
Mary Elizabeth, 6243, 10634.
Mary Emma, 4882.
Mary Martha, 9869.
Mary Ryder, 6215.
Maud Alice, 9865.
Maud B., 6629.
Mildred, 10143.
Miriam, 10130.
Paul, 10053.
Philip B., 6626.
Raymond Herr, 8924.
Robert Benjamin, 10042.
Ruth, 10033.
Ruth Ellen, 9868.
Ruth Herr, 6630.
Salinda, 6192.
Samuel, 2436.
Samuel Ryder, 6206.
Sarah, 6196.
Son, 6240, 8914.
Thomas Breneman, 10055.
Thomas Elliott, 10131.
Walter, 10036.
Wilber M., 9867.
FRAZER, Anna E., 5398.
Charles K., 5396.
Leah S., 5397.
FREY, Amelia H., 7032.
Elma A., 7033.
FRICK, 10004, 10005, 10006.
Abraham, 718, 726, 735, 2422, 2445, 2452, 6155.
Abraham F., 10116.
Abraham H., 193.
Abraham O., 6220.
Abraham P., 2457.
Addie Belle, 6235.
Agnes, 6327.
Alice, 9967.
Amos M., 6223.
Angeline, 2515.
Anna, 195, 710, 716, 723, 733, 2441, 2447, 2455, 2494.
Anna E., 2411.
Anna Elizabeth, 6224.
Anna Long, 2421.
Anna Lydia, 10117.
Anna Maria, 2511.
Anna Mary, 6226.
Arthur, 9968.
Barbara, 717, 720, 731, 6301.
Barbara E., 12849.
Benjamin, 2449, 12865.
Benjamin Franklin, 6153, 9970.
C. C., 11535.
Caroline, 2509.
Catharine M., 12854.
Catharine W., 707.
Charles Carrol, 9969.
Charlotte, 6174.
Chester, 12876.
Christian, 713, 755, 2410, 2444.
Christian H., 191.
Clara Emma, 9960.
Clarence Englehart, 6177.
Claud, 12874.
Daisy May, 9992.
Daniel, 290.
Daniel Brandt, 6157.
Daniel W., 12853.
David, 745.

Mary K., 11792.
Merton Layton, 6543.
Pearl, 6531.
Sterling, 6530.
Walter Audley, 6542.
GAILEY, Infant, 5287, 5288.
GAMBEE, Albert Shirk, 4382.
   Henry Marcellus, 4383.
   Theodore W., 4381.
GAMBER, Ada May, 5337.
   Ada, N., 12179.
   Anna, 8505.
   Anna N., 12174.
   Annie H., 5333.
   Barbara Alice, 6605.
   Benjamin L., 8501.
   Benjamin N., 12176.
   Catharine, 8502.
   Elia N., 12173.
   Fanny H., 5335.
   Fanny Matilda, 6606.
   Francis, 8506.
   Grace N., 12177.
   Harry N., 12178.
   Henry H., 5330.
   John, 6607.
   John Herr, 5329.
   John L., 8504.
   Mary Ann, 5331.
   Rudolph H., 5334.
   Selena H., 5336.
   Selena N., 12175.
   Son, 8500, 8503.
   Susan H., 5332.
GANTZ, Abraham B., 9385.
   Edna St. Clair, 9382.
   Edwin J., 5160.
   Edwin St. Clair, 9383.
   Emma Ora, 9380.
   Esther, 9379.
   Esther Ora, 9386.
   Ethel St. Clair, 9381.
   Henry H., 5161.
   Winnefred S., 9384.
GARBER, Addie Susan, 11512.
   Amelia H., 5359.
   Anna May, 5358.
   Charles W., 9815.
   Elmer H., 9559.
   Elmer Jay, 5362.
   Ernest Mauck, 11511.
   Florence K., 5363.
   Frances E., 5357.
   Franklin H., 5360.
   Hallie I., 11513.
   Homer B., 9816.
   John A., 9560.
   Josephine Clare, 5764.
   Mazie Madaline, 11514.
   Pauline Mildred, 9561.
   Paris H., 5361.
   Raymond H., 9558.
GARMAN, Eli E., 13041.
   Eltie M., 13044.
   Henry G., 13105.
   Infant, 13045.
   Jacob A., 13043.
   John W., 13042.
   Mary M., 13047.
   Mellie G., 13046.
GARVER, Jacob Christian, 9012.
   Karl Rohrer, 9011.
   Ruth Elizabeth, 9010.

GAUL, Benjamin Frederick, 7154.
   Bertha May, 7152.
   Edgar Elam, 7150.
   Eli Marshal, 7151.
   Martha Matilda, 7156.
   Mary Ann, 7149.
   Oliver Franklin, 7155.
   Rufus Andrew, 7153.
GEARHART, 2582, 2583.
   Anna E., 8878.
   C. McC., 8877.
   Elenor F., 8874.
   Frank C., 8880.
   Frederick D., 8876.
   George M., 8875.
   Harry A., 8879.
   Infant, 8881.
   Jacob, 2581.
   Sarah E., 8873.
GEIB, David, 11101.
   Emma, 11100.
   Jacob, 11103.
   John, 11104.
   Laura, 11098.
   Rufus, 11102.
   Sallie, 11099.
GEIGER, Anna Beates, 10781.
   Charles Henry, 10786.
   Frances Stoner, 10787.
   Helen, 10784.
   John Bachman, 10782.
   Laura Stoner, 10783.
   Mary, 10785.
GEISER, Ruth Elenor, 13162.
GEISS, Carl Frederick, 13005.
GEIST, Arthur F., 11530.
   Elam J., 11529.
GEPHER, Aaron, 5204.
   Amelia, 9495.
   Cora, 9494.
   Emma, 5206.
   Henry, 5205.
   Louisa R., 9493.
GERHART, Fannie Elizabeth, 11126.
   John M., 11127.
   Margaret, 11129.
   Willis, 11128.
GERLACH, Henry H., 8375.
GIBBLE, Ellen, 9444.
   Fannie, 9445.
   Katie, 9446.
   Minnie, 9447.
   Phares M., 9443.
GILBERT, Clara J., 10470.
   D. Clayton, 12073.
   David Allen, 12075.
   Jessie Elizabeth, 10471.
   Lewis DeL., 12072.
   Myrtle E., 12074.
GILE, Earl Gordon, 9564.
   Julia Agnes, 9562.
   Ray Elmer, 9563.
   Rulef H., 5390.
GINDER, David, 12506.
   Elizabeth, 12316.
   Irvin, 12504.
   Mabel, 12505.
   Paul, 12507.
GINGRICH, Abraham, 12160.
   Alfred, 11109.
   Christian, 12157.
   Daniel, 12159.
   Daughter, 11111.

Noah, 5912.
Noah Isaac, 9846.
Ollie May, 11081.
Opal V., 13193.
Orrie, 9836.
Rebecca J., 8032.
Sallie, 3872.
Sallie Estell, 9839.
Sarah, 3901, 3910, 8017.
Sebastian, 5062.
Simon, 5059.
Simon Miller, 11087.
Susan, 3871, 5889.
Susanna, 5910.
Thomas, 3877.
Virginia, 3887.
Walter C., 9830.
William, 3888.
William Isaac, 9849.
William J., 8029.
William M., 9829.
Winnie Kate, 9840.
GULL, Annie, 3861.
   Betsey, 3859.
   Henry, 3858.
   Kate, 3857.
   Susan, 3860.
GUMBART, Charles, 3327.
   Conrad G., 2331.
   Elizabeth, 3332.
   George Conrad, 7206.
   Georgiana, 3330.
   Harold Etting, 7205.
   Lewis F., 3328.
   Otto D., 3329.
GUNDRUM, Albert Luther, 11994.
   Charles Albert, 11983.
   Franklin Rodes, 11987.
   Frederick William, 11986.
   Harry Frances, 11982.
   Henry Frances, 11989.
   J. William, 11995.
   Lewis Jacob, 11985.
   Mary Elizabeth, 11990.
   Paul Charles, 11993.
   Ralph Jacob, 11992.
   Raymond Herr, 11988.
   Robert Alexander, 11991.
   William Jacob, 11984.
HABECKER, Albert S., 7116.
   Anna L., 7121.
   Barbara, 289, 1038.
   Benjamin J., 3253.
     Bessie S., 7124.
   Christian, 291.
   Christian H., 3244.
   Christian S., 7117.
   David, 293.
   Elizabeth, 1033.
   Ella Nora, 7123.
   Emily Susan, 7122.
   Emma A., 7135.
   Esther, 290, 1031.
   Frances, 292.
   Frances Leons, 7133.
   Frank David, 3251.
   Gertrude Ada, 7132.
   Ida M., 7120.
   Ira M., 7118.
   Isaac, 1030.
   Isaac N., 7119.
   John, 1032.
   John S., 7125.

Joseph, 288, 1034, 1037.
Joseph H., 3252.
Kate Louise, 7131.
Leon Benjamin, 7134.
Maria, 1035.
Myra Anna, 7130.
Son, 7126.
HACKMAN, Annie, 7713.
   Benjamin, 7711.
   Elizabeth, 7715.
   George W., 7712.
   Hannah, 7714.
   Henry C., 7717.
   John Martin, 7710.
   Susan, 7716.
HAGE, Boletta Kip, 12480.
   Christian Kendig, 12478.
   Gertrude Marie, 12481.
   Hother Brent, 12479.
   Hager, Emil, C-34.
   Ernest, C-33.
   George, C-35.
HAGY, Ann, 570.
HALDEMAN, Anna Elizabeth, 11214.
   Charles Waldo, 11213.
HALL, Edna Alleen, 7176.
   Edward, 4834.
   Huberta, 8892.
   John G., 7177.
   Linnie P., 4833.
   Martha Ernestine, 8891.
   Mary Eliz. Neff, 8893.
HAMEL, Robert, 2993.
   Mary Elizabeth, 2994.
   William H., 2995.
HAMILTON, Andrew G., 4390.
   Andrew Groff, 8800.
   Carrie, 8803.
   Caroline Graff, 8810.
   Elizabeth Mary, 8805.
   Frances May, 8809.
   Frank Burg, 8807.
   Harry B., 8804.
   Joseph Abraham, 8806.
   Mabel M., 8802.
   Maud Elizabeth, 8808.
   William M., 4397.
   Witmer, 8801.
   Witmer G., 4398.
   Witmer H., 8799.
HANNA, Augusta Joseph, 5602.
   Frank, 5600.
   Mary Louise, 5601.
HANSON, Oliver W., 11363.
HARBAUGH, Alice, 12068.
   Clara, 12069.
   Daniel, 12067.
   John, 12071.
   Melchor, 12070.
HARDING, Daughter, 11801.
HARMAN, Catharine L., 4978.
   Charles Herbert, 4972.
   Daniel Martin, 4973.
   Fanny, 4980.
   John Barr, 4979.
   John Henry, 4976.
   Mary E., 4975.
   Susan Catharine, 4974.
   Susanna, 4977.
HARNISH, Albert G., 8288.
   Amos, 4148.
   Amos B., 4073.
   Anna, 4071.

John Augustus, 5009.
John B., 1778.
John Davis, 4466.
John Lehman, 4444.
John N., 4449.
Josephine P., 4451.
Kate, 9272.
Leonard L., 4430.
Maribel, 5019.
Mary, 12897.
Mary H., 4445.
Nathan Holcomb, 4456.
Raymond, 8835.
Rebecca, 4434.
Richard David, 8226.
Ricard Watson, 4460.
Samuel, 1522, 12839.
Samuel B., 1781.
Samuel Leidy, 4439.
Samuel W., 4433.
Samuel Willis, 4464.
Sarah Amanda, 4458.
Sarah Catharine, 8927.
Sarah E., 4447.
Sarah E. Frances, 4454.
Sarah Evangeline, 8838.
Sarah Frances, 4467.
Sarah H., 4435.
Son, 8820.
Thomas Huling, 4459.
Tobias Miller, 4440.
William Woodward, 4453.
Wilson McKendry, 4450.
HASSEL, Bertha May, 12282.
HASTINGS, Celeste B., 8589.
    Edgar E., 8590.
    Frances, 5958.
    Joseph Albert, 8591.
    Maria, 5959.
    Mary, 5994.
    Mary Emma, 8592.
    William M., 5995.
    Winifred Ione, 11306.
HATCHER, Charles Kenneth, 9578.
    Ida Matilda, 9576.
    John Cadogan, 9577.
HAUBEIL, Alice S., 9366.
    Anna H., 9369.
    Edith M., 9367.
    Frank A., 9365.
    Nora E., 9368.
HAVERSTICK, Aaron, 9050.
    Ambrose, 9047.
    Amos, 9051.
    Anna E., 10070.
    Daughter, 10067.
    Edna V., 10069.
    Eve, 4781.
    Eve Ann, 9048.
    Frances, 4778, 9049.
    Francis, 10073.
    Frantz Maurice, 9164.
    George, 4783.
    Harvey Frick, 6227.
    Isaac, 4780, 9046.
    Mary, 10072.
    Michael, 4779, 9052.
    Miriam Anna, 9165.
    Ralph, 9163.
    Rena F., 10068.
    Ruth, 9162.
    Socrates, 4782.
    Son, 10074.

William, 10075.
Winona S., 10071.
HAWBICKER, Anna Maria, 10013.
    Elmer Frantz, 10011.
    Etta Virginia, 10015.
    Harriet Lena, 11540.
    James Russell, 11541.
    Jason Eby, 10018.
    Leah Nancy, 10012.
    Lucy May, 10014.
    Rudolph Moore, 10019.
    Sarah Elizabeth, 10017.
    William Noble, 10016.
HECKARD, Ida, 7173.
    Lila, 7172.
HECKROTH, Amanda, 5458.
    Benjamin, 5457.
    Clifford, 5460.
    Katie, 5459.
HEER, Clayton C., 12758.
    Edna M., 12761.
    Nelson V., 12759.
    Otha B., 12760.
HEINEY, David, 4788.
    Eli, 4787.
    Elizabeth, 1656.
    Emlen, 9044.
    Eve Ann, 9042.
    Frances, 1660.
    Frances H., 4794.
    Frances M., 9041.
    George, 1659, 1664, 1668, 4791.
    Infant, 1666.
    Isaac, 1655, 1661, 4790, 4795.
    Jacob, 1657.
    Lizzie, 9045.
    Maria, 4792.
    Maris E., 9043.
    Martha, 1655.
    Martha H., 4794.
    Mary, 1658.
    Nancy, 1663.
    Polly, 1662.
    Samuel, 4789.
    Sarah M., 9040.
    Susan, 1667.
HEISEY, Albert, 6714.
    Alice, 6720.
    Anna, 6719.
    Bertha, 6723.
    David, 6717.
    Ida, 6721.
    Jacob, 6718.
    Mary, 6715.
    Ora, 6722.
    Samuel, 6716.
HELM, Hiram, 11216.
    Irene, 7795.
    Leigh P., 11215.
    Lillie, 7796.
    Martin, 7793.
    Mary, 7797.
    Miriam, 12513.
    Oliver, 7798.
    Walter, 7799.
    William, 7794.
HELMAN, Henry, 8297.
    John, 8299.
    Mary, 8298.
HENRY, Adeline, 5345.
    Ann Maria, 5346.
    Benjamin, 5342.
    Elvina, 5344.

Enos Earl, 9962.
Enos Etta, 8395.
Enos K., 8438.
Enos M., 5241.
Enos S., 10593.
Ephraim, 6053.
Ernest, 5303.
Ernest Claude, 9145.
Ernest Edwin, 3178.
Ernest McKay, 9527.
Ernest S., 10310.
Estella, 8336.
Esther, 74, 77, 141, 152, 259, 387, 491,
    511, 514, 544, 552, 659, 1690,
    1842, 1932, 1948, 2374, 2891,
    3354, 5132, 5141, 10677.
Esther A., 6933.
Esther Ann, 1044, 1102, 2805.
Esther Eugene, 2742.
Esther H., 1984, 11258.
Esther Irene, 6567.
Ethan Allen, 12299.
Ethel, 12469.
Ethel B., 7570.
Ethelbert D., 8399.
Eugene, 10283.
Eugene Evarts, 5542.
Eugene Lefevre, 9030.
Eugene Markham, 1956.
Eula, 3298, 10390.
Eva, 7460, 12459.
Eva Lura, 7479.
Eva Pauline, 5448.
Eve, 146.
Eve Ann, 538, 1921.
Everett J., 7148.
Ezra B., 8070.
Ezra G., 2378.
Fannie, 25, 55, 90, 104, 6675, 7054,
    8123, 11970.
Fannie B., 5341, 7641.
Fannie Belle, 10365.
Fannie I., 6983.
Fannie May, 6745, 7576.
Fanny, 72, 186, 244, 283, 321, 496,
    840, 862, 1366, 1590, 1902, 2775,
    2804, 2888, 3125, 4137, 5355,
    12527, C-24, C-39.
Fanny Ann, 590.
Fanny B., 6899.
Fanny C., 2828.
Fanny E., 3187.
Fanny Mae, 7045, 12366.
Fanny Malinda, 3507.
Fanny Matilda, 10838.
Fanny R., 6456.
Fanny Susan, 4635.
Flora Belle, 3325.
Florence, 6144, 8934.
Florence A., 7018.
Florence B., 9549.
Florence C., 6834.
Florence Emma, 7651.
Florence Hannah, 11023.
Florence M., 10629.
Florence Mildred, 5520.
Frances, 46, 115, 209, 212, 437, 674,
    792, 803, 960, 1147, 1337, 1405,
    1555, 1783, 1870, 2302, 2311,
    2367, 2657, 2701, 2711, 2830,
    2884, 2897, 3002, 3172, 3352,
    3445, 3456, 3493, 6691, 7220,
    7557.

Frances A., 8408.
Frances C., 2029.
Frances E., 1905.
Frances Floyd, 12302.
Frances M., 5235, 7567.
Frances Naomi, 5299.
Frances Nellie, 10314.
Frances R., 10237.
Frances Ruth, 6757.
Francis, 140, 326, 495, 1161, 1692,
    1933, 4123, 5134.
Francis Christian, 4605.
Francis H., 1583.
Francis K., 1983.
Francis Lightner, 4870.
Francis Neff, 4632.
Francis V., 7230.
Francis W., 1907, 12501.
Frank, 3298, 7933.
Frank B., 7643.
Frank E., 6987.
Frank Elvin, 8386.
Frank Hiller, 7044.
Frank J., 5314.
Frank M., 1610.
Frank Raymond, 11021.
Frank Strohm, 5306.
Frank Trump, 5449.
Frank W., 12140.
Franklin, 6054, 6954, 7463, 8440.
Franklin B., 8071.
Franklin H., 3176.
Franklin J., 1560.
Franklin L., 1079, 8073.
Franklin M., 7223, 7293.
Franklin Neidig, 6741.
Franklin P., 2731, 6554.
Franklin W., 5302.
Frederick, 219, 820, 2734, 2916, 10382.
Frederick Cleveland, 7964.
Frederick R., 11957.
Frederica Ann, 2748.
Fremont, 8072.
George, 593, 2917, 3091, 3974, 7578,
    9023, 12403.
George A. Owen, 10368.
George B., 585.
George Brobston, 10419.
George Clayton, 12298.
George Diller, 9181.
George E., 2069, 2739.
George Frederick, 10386.
George Henry, 10611.
George Holton, 5180.
George L., 1137, 7493, 8432, 10399.
George Leidy, 608, 2026.
George M., 4772.
George Minor, 5538.
George R., 3154, 6453.
George U., 7055.
George W., 2036, 3455, 5367, 12141.
George Walker, 6773.
George Warner, 6767.
George Washington, 1851.
Georgiana, 5611.
Gertrude Ann, 10269.
Gertrude L., 5259.
Gladys, 11581.
Gladys Olivette, 10827.
Grace, 9927.
Grace E., 6991.
Grace Greenwood, 5285.
Grace M., 12450, 12514.

Granville B., 7631.
Grover Cleveland, 7581.
Guy, 8442.
Guy H., 11172.
Hamilton O., 10454.
Hanford B., 1895.
Hannah, 1141, 1146, 3442, 3487.
Hannah E., 2736.
Hannah Eliza, 7918.
Hannah M., 7942.
Hannah Maria, 3978.
Rev. Hans, 1.
Hans, H-1.
Hardin H., 10447.
Harley Weaver, 7569.
Harold E., 5392.
Harold Frantz, 4630.
Harold. Mark, 5522.
Harold R., 9522.
Harriet, 591, 821, 5710, 9329.
Harriet C., 2119.
Harriet E., 2015.
Harry, 3184, 6121, 7937, 8121, 9924, 10300.
Harry B., 4686, 7639.
Harry D., 10807, 11218.
Harry Elvin, 10740.
Harry Francis, 4619.
Harry G., 2068.
Harry Groff, 12386.
Harry H., 2030, 8325.
Harry J., 8141.
Harry Kunkle, 9034.
Harry L., 8329, 12135.
Harry Lincoln, 5307.
Harry Malcolm, 5619.
Harry Martin, 7962.
Harry Miller, 3126, 5584.
Harry Neff, 4613.
Harry Perry, 5539.
Harry S., 7634, 10320.
Harry W., 3289.
Harry Willis, 11114.
Harry Y., 6479.
Harvey E., 5142.
Harvey G., 6062.
Hattie Belle, 7556.
Hattie C., 10415.
Hattie May, 7164, 8142.
Hattie O., 5261.
Hattie Wood, 7946.
Hazel Irene, 10612.
Hebron M., 1607.
Helen, 5393, 10609, 12457.
Helen Alberta, 9182.
Helen Elizabeth, 5462.
Helen Hoffman, 7071.
Helen Louisa, 11022.
Henry, 7, 58, 142, 176, 236, 266, 303, 374, 510, 521, 553, 617, 690, 802, 823, 857, 883, 886, 895, 921, 935, 1096, 1274, 1335, 1348, 1602, 1836, 1886, 1902, 2091, 2373, 2667, 2698, 2880, 2911, 3004, 3081, 3095, 3173, 3175, 3925, 4121, 5300, 5352, 6040, 6056, 6660, 6732, 6981, 9773, 11091, C-22.
Henry B., 3043, 3068, 3954, 4112, 8355.
Henry Bruce, 7198.
Henry C., 991, 5139, 5308.
Henry Clay, 1917, 6759.

Henry D., 6944.
Henry E., 2032, 6688.
Henry Elam, 9928.
Henry F., 800.
Henry G., 1118.
Henry H., 2308, 2730, 6031, 6548.
Henry Hewitt, 10315.
Henry L., 2108, 8074.
Henry M., 1593, 8300.
Henry Miller, 5278.
Henry P., 9534, 12484.
Henry R., 3148, 6127, 7453.
Henry Rufus, 4897.
Henry S., 1078, 1848, 3511, 5313.
Henry W., 12498.
Herbert, 4715, 5549.
Herbert F., 5247.
Herbert Homer, 8916.
Herbert Nele, 7481.
Herbert Thacker, 9146, 11405.
Herman H., 4621.
Hettie, 284, 844, 4105, 6135, 8426.
Hettie Ann, 4103.
Hiero Benjamin, 4869.
Hiram, 1067, 3156, 6699.
Hiram P., 12485.
Hiram Walker, 11244.
Homer Andrew, 4607.
Horace Benjamin, 4633.
Horace Dumont, 6503.
Horace Howard, 10268.
Horace Jacob, 4606.
Horace Leigh, 9626.
Howard, 9944.
Howard Henry, 3326.
Howard Lee, 6568.
Howard Lloyd, 10335.
Hubert Parnell, 7579.
Hugh, 10381.
Huldah May, C-59.
Ida, 3122, 6123, 6659. 9333.
Ida B., 2744.
Ida Elizabeth, 4604.
Ida Evelyn, 3285.
Ida Jane, 2062.
Ida Mae, 6565.
Ida May, 5586, 9039, 10231.
Ida R., 7229.
Ila May, 7145.
Infant, 297, 993, 2120, 2728, 3140, 4689, 6555, 6907, 9021, 10246, 10290, 10595, 10836, 10841.
Ione, 10391.
Ira, 3471, 8441, 9950. 10240.
Ira Harvey, 4615.
Ira L., 8333, 11223.
Irene Emma, 9148.
Irvin Emory, 5531.
Irwin Barnet, 9625.
Isaac, 39, 381, 658, 1336, 1371, 4140, 5372.
Isaac H., 2795.
Isaac L., 8429.
Isaac R., 6458.
Isaac W., 7212.
Isabella, 2048, 10823.
Isabella T., 2066.
Isabelle, 5709.
Isaiah, 982, 3139, 4764.
Isaiah Woodworth, 10267.
Israel, 2777.
Ivan, 10234.
Ivan M., 11173.

30

Robert Frantz, 8930.
Robert Guyer, 5529.
Robert Louis, 11948.
Robert Martin, 5273.
Robert Phenegar, 8918.
Robert Todd, 10448.
Robert W., 6787, 10455.
Rohrer Eberly Sener, 1503.
Roland, 3305, 7496.
Roland Benjamin, 12307.
Rosa, 5366.
Rose Marie, 5274.
Rosetta A., 6775.
Rosina, C-8, C-19.
Roy B., 11219.
Roy DeWitt, 7582.
Roy M., 11174.
Ruby Emma, 9151.
Rudolph, 10, 61, 231, 248, 793, 890,
    1144, 2296, 2844, 2854, 2882,
    6022.
Rudolph F., 10296.
Rudolph H., 2640.
Rudolph S., 860.
Rupert Eugene, 12837.
Russell, 6743.
Ruth Eastburn, 8529.
Ruth Irene, 10613.
Ruth L., 9343.
Ruth Lee, 11637.
Ruth Minnette, 5288.
S. Mabel, 9922.
S. Milton, 6974.
Sadie, 10295.
Salena, 1927.
Sallie Miller, 4631.
Salome, C-13.
Samuel, 5, 30, 153, 159, 237, 444,
    603, 612, 888, 1065, 1095, 2900,
    3920, 3970, 4117, 6475, 6914,
    10380, 12464.
Samuel B., 915.
Samuel Blaine, 5589.
Samuel Clarence, 8214.
Samuel Claude, 5592.
Samuel D., 7945.
Samuel E., 6690.
Samuel F., 1066, 3304.
Samuel G., 2053.
Samuel H., 6921, 7593.
Samuel J., 2974.
Samuel K., 1981, 9531.
Samuel L., 2889, 6769, 8430.
Samuel M., 1347, 2034, 3076, 3489.
Samuel Melvin, 5283.
Samuel Millo, 1597, 4694.
Sarah, 154, 557, 562, 581, 599, 1058,
    1891, 1979, 1985, 2878, 2893,
    3924, 6457, C-40.
Sarah A., 1070, 2735, 6593, 6665.
Sarah Ann, 1589, 1919, 2049, 3757,
    3969, 4768.
Sarah E., 6550, 8928.
Sarah Frances, 2017, 8330.
Sarah J., 2038.
Sarah La Rue, 5447.
Sarah M., 5269.
Sarah Melvina, 9330.
Sarah Z., 1083.
Serenus Abner, 5284.
Serenus B., 1894.
Sherman L., 8079.
Sidney, C-81.

Silas S., 3108.
Simon, C-2, C-4, C-5, C-11, C-18, C-27.
Simon S. G., 6901.
Simon Peter, C-52.
Solomon, 835.
Solomon K., 6142.
Solomon R., 6910.
Son, 79, 132, 976, 992, 1940, 2798,
    2845, 2847, 3968, 4097, 5233,
    5245, 6061, 6471, 6644.
Sophia E., 3492.
Stella Holmes, 5597.
Stella Louella, 8216.
Stephen B., 3083.
Stephen Edgar, 6995.
Susan, 147, 151, 249, 378, 386, 438,
    507, 556, 560, 615, 819, 847, 854,
    957, 979, 1040, 1100, 1358, 1367,
    1840, 1845, 1938, 2372, 2643,
    2659, 2716, 2996, 3102, 3122,
    3259, 3355, 3441, 3488, 4042,
    4769, 5301, 5356, 6044, 6055,
    6710, 6756, 7450, 9022, 10298,
    12529, 12919.
Susan A., 9776.
Susan Bertha, 5243.
Susan Breneman, 4660.
Susan C., 2827.
Susan E., 2968, 6770, 8324.
Susan Frances, 6764.
Susan Grace, 12300.
Susan H., 3512.
Susan I., 8358.
Susan Margaret, 3085.
Susan Melvina, 4022.
Susan Mildred, 10358.
Susan S., 7447.
Susan W., 12499.
Susanna, 22, 36, 267, 517, 826, 1120,
    1349, 1400, 1871, 1872, 1893,
    2799, 2841, 2849, 2935, 3740,
    3917, 3953, 3977.
Susanna B., 3396.
Susanna C., 2975.
Susie M., 11640.
Sylvia Galetta, 10792.
Thaddeus, 5257.
Thaddeus S., 1890.
Thelma B., 10793.
Theodore M., 6733.
Theodore William, 8304.
Theodore Witmer, 4865.
Theron Craven, 7571.
Thomas A., 6547.
Throla V., 10794.
Tobias 310, 545, 1925, 2649.
Tobias H., 2307, 2794.
Tobias L., 4773.
Tobias R., 3918.
Tobias W., 1920.
Uriah, 587.
Uriah Clayton, 10229.
Verma, 10803.
Veronica, 135, 1684.
Verne, 3300.
Victor E., 11232.
Villa N., 11018.
Viola A., 6972, 6977.
Viola E., 6839.
Virgil Frantz, 4603.
Wallace, 7575.
Walter, 6124, 8412.
Walter Abraham, 11020.

Laverna Ann, 9915.
Mary Alice, 9908.
HESS, Abbie Vezeta, 9027.
Abraham M., 10538.
Ada Mary, 10540.
Adam Roy, 10557.
Alice M., 10539.
Alvin, 9028.
Anna, 4132, 7428.
Anna Barbara, 12041.
Anna Catharine, 10558.
Anna E., 4701.
Anna M., 10537.
Ara G., 11192.
B. Lintner, 8414.
Barbara, 7425.
Barbara V., 10543.
Benjamin B., 4131.
Benjamin H., 7600.
Bertha May, 10564.
Beula Viola, 10548.
Catharine, 7992.
Charles Carpenter, 8415.
Christian, 7998.
Christian B., 12040.
Christian L., 8416.
David A., 10541.
Edith Adell, 10560.
Elenora, 9026.
Elias E., 10193.
Elizabeth, 7423, 7604, 7096.
Ellen Maria, 12323.
Elmer R., 11071.
Elvin W., 11194.
Emma R., 10545.
Enos, 9025.
Ernest Lefever, 10562.
Fanny, 4033.
Frances, 7431, 7994.
Frances Levina, 10565.
Harold W., 7608.
Henry, 4136.
Henry H., 7426, 7602.
Ida B., 4702.
Ida Sue, 9029.
Ira N., 7605.
Jacob L., 7429.
John B., 7997.
John Zeigler, 10547.
Laura Anna, 8417.
Laura M., 9734.
Leah, 7988.
Lizzie, 8413.
Lizzie Judith, 12055.
Martha, 7427, 7995.
Martha Ann, 10544.
Martha Catharine, 9735.
Martin, 7424.
Mary, 4134, 7430, 7991.
Mary Catharine, 11700.
Mary Ruth, 10563.
Mary Susan, 12042.
Nora, 7607.
Odessa Maria, 10559.
Ralph, 5663.
Ruth Elizabeth, 10546.
Samuel, 4130, 7603.
Sarah, 7993.
Simon G., 7989.
Susan, 7990.
Susan M., 7601.
Susanna, 4135, 7432.
Susie Naomi, 10542.

Verna Pauline, 10549.
Virgey Keen, 10556.
Walter R., 7606.
William Jackson, 10561.
Winona, 7609.
HETLER, Annie Gertrude, 10846.
HICKEY, Charles H., 10925.
Dora M., 10922.
Ella R., 10926.
George C., 10927.
Infant, 10929.
Katie E., 10928.
Oretta M., 10923.
Walter F., 10924.
HICKMAN, Aldus, 3632.
Clayton, 3634.
Edward, 3637.
Emma, 3635.
Gideon, 3636.
Jefferson, 3638.
Mary, 3639.
Milton, 3633.
Willi, 3640.
HIESTAND, B. Frank, 3245.
Elizabeth, 3247.
Ira C., 3246.
HIESTER, Infant, 9279.
HIKES, Annie, 10350.
Barbara, 6748.
Catharine, 6751.
Eliza G., 6749.
John L., 6750.
Laura, 10351.
Mary, 6747.
Sarah, 6752.
Susan, 6746.
HILDEBRAND, David D., 5066.
Jacob M., 5067.
Martin, 5069.
Mary A., 5068.
Susan F., 5064.
William H., 5065.
HILKEY, Myrtle, 10316.
Walter F., 10317.
HILL, Clarence Martin, 11296.
Laura, 11298.
Mary Jones, 11297.
HILLMAN, Alda J., 6180.
Clara, 6181.
Florence B., 6182.
HILT, Elmer, 8991.
Estella, 8993.
Harry, 8991.
Sylvia, 8992.
HIMMELRIGHT, Ada Belle, 5690.
Laura Alice, 5687.
Maudilla, 5688.
Nellie Catharine, 5689.
HITE, Alfred H., 10452.
Robert W., 10453.
HOFFMAN, Augusta S., 11448.
Benjamin, 1926.
Henry M., 11446.
Isabella C., 11447.
Jewett M., 11444.
John, 1924.
Russell L., 11445.
Tobias, 1925.
HOIT, Calvin, 8022.
Franklin, 8025.
Joseph, 8021.
Perry, 8023.
Taylor, 8024.

Margaret Downey, 10942.
Mary Howard, 7748.
Mary McConkey, 10939.
Son, 7749.
William Downey, 10940.
HORNBERGER, Alice Amelia, 6075.
  Ann, 6077.
  Elizabeth, 2316.
  George, 2317.
  Henry, 2321.
  Mary Ann, 2320.
  Rebecca Jane, 6076.
  Stephen, 2318, 6074.
  Susan, 2319.
HORNER, Jessie, 12413.
  Mae, 12412.
HORST, Adam, 13130.
  Arthur Roy, 13124.
  Christian, 801, 2560.
  Daniel, 2567.
  David, 2563, 2565.
  Della, 13157.
  Dora May, 13125.
  Earl, 13155.
  Emma Viola, 13126.
  Erma Viola, 13128.
  John, 2562.
  John V., 2566.
  Joseph, 2564.
  Laura Emma, 13127.
  Martin, 2561.
  Mary Ann, 13158.
  Nola, 13154.
  Ruth Estella, 13129.
  Samuel, 13156.
HORTON, John Girvin, 11532.
HORR, Leonard W., 10983.
  Marion, 10987.
HOSTETTER, A. Irvin, 11905.
  Alpheus M., 11904.
  Amaziah, 8082.
  Daniel E., 11906.
  David E., 11902.
  Emma M., 5370.
  Henry H., 11908.
  Isaac, 8083.
  J. Emory, 11903.
  Jacob E., 11900.
  Joseph E., 11907.
  Letitia, 8081.
  Samuel L., 11909.
  Susan A., 11901.
HOTTENSTEIN, Anna, 10780.
  Emma May, 10779.
HOUGHEY, George F., 3613.
  Laura T., 3614.
HOUSER, Anna 4172.
  Eliza, 4170.
  Harry F., 12388.
  Jacob B., 4177.
  Jacob P., 12389.
  Maria, 4174.
  Son, 4171, 4173, 4176.
  Susanna, 4175.
HOWARD, Edwin Allen, 11608.
  Nevelle B., 11609.
HOWETT, Amos W., 7801.
  Annie Laura, 7802.
  Charles Earl, 10973.
  Clarence, 10965.
  Cora Estelle, 10971.
  Ella Theresa, 10972.
  Florence May, 10970.

  Johnson, 10977.
  Mabel, 10974.
  Mary, 10976.
  Mary H., 7800.
HOWLETT, Calvin Willers, 11808.
HUBER, Ada Martha, 8154.
  Ann Rachael, 3988.
  Benjamin, 4001.
  Catharine, 8660.
  Charles Dennis, 7140.
  Cora, 8168.
  Della K., 8169.
  Ellen, 3987.
  Elmer Emmet, 7137.
  Elmer Franklin, 8174.
  Elsie Viola, 8158.
  Emma E., 8662.
  Emma Salome, 3986.
  Enos, 3989.
  Fanny Maria, 7141.
  Florence, 7088.
  Franklin, 3982.
  Guy Arville, 7143.
  Harry, 8175.
  Harry Daniel, 8157.
  Hiram B., 8663.
  Ida, 3991.
  Ida Blanche, 7138.
  Jacob, 3983.
  Jacob B., 8659.
  John, 3984.
  John Franklin, 7144.
  John Jacob, 8155.
  Levi, 3990.
  Lillie May, 7139.
  Lizzie, 8664.
  Martha, 3980, 8665.
  Martha May, 8167.
  Mary, 4002.
  Mary Ann, 3188, 8661.
  Mary Elizabeth, 3985.
  Minnie Herr, 8176.
  Myra Elizabeth, 8156.
  Nellie, 7087.
  Oliver Jacob, 7136.
  Susan, 3981.
  Thomas Bellamy, 7142.
  William, 7086.
HUBLEY, Grace E., 10870.
HUFFORD, Arvilla, 8132.
  Clarence D., 8129.
  Eli B., 8134.
  Emma, 8128.
  Frances E., 8135.
  James A., 8131.
  Marcella, 8130.
  Mylin W., 8133.
HULL, Blake, 11302.
  George, 11303.
  Robert, 11304.
HUNTER, Lester William, 12718.
HUNTSBERGER, Earl Emerson, 13112.
  Elizabeth, 13061.
  Emma, 13064.
  David E., 13063.
  Ida, 13060.
  Ira Jay, 13113.
  John Henry, 11116.
  Mary Ann, 13062.
  Nancy, 13058.
  Sadie Alice, 13114.
  Samuel M., 13057.
  Stella May, 13115.

Hattie, 8281.
Helen Ione, 8847.
Henry, 228, 879, 2283, 6051, 6078.
Henry Clay, 5012.
Jacob, 881, 11819.
Jennie Lutneria, 8848.
John, 229, 878, 12828.
John Herr, 2989.
Laura H., 8278.
Lewis, 2990.
Louise, 11307.
Mae Edna, 11823.
Magdalena, 2284.
Margaret, 2091.
Mary, 875, 6080.
Mary Elizabeth, 6938.
Mary Lenole, 8845.
Raymond B., 12827.
Sarah, 5014.
Solomon, 5013.
Susan S., 8282.
Uriah, 6047.
William B., 4415.
KEAGY, Amanda, 1989.
Ann, 1987.
Anna Elizabeth, 4971.
Clara Agnes, 4967.
Elizabeth, 1992.
Harry Clay, 4969.
John B., 1989.
Levi, 1990.
Miller Storm, 4968.
Samuel, 1986.
Sarah K., 1991.
Winfield Scott, 4970.
KEECH, Ann, 349.
Barbara, 350.
Fanny, 348.
KEEMER, Elizabeth A., 11772.
James S. A. G., 11776.
Jennie W., 11773.
John H. C., 11777.
Martha W., 11775.
Mary E., 11774.
KEEN, Ada Sue, 6819.
Agnes Viola, 11031.
Amos, 6823.
Ann Eliza, 6814.
Anna M., 10527.
Antha Letitia, 6812
Charles, 10519.
Charles Elmer, 11032.
Clara, 10517.
David Martin, 6822.
Easley Arthur, 10551.
Easley H., 6820.
Edith Lemia, 6825.
Effie Maria, 6721.
Essie, 10518.
Franklin Elmer, 6816.
Harry, 10525.
Harry Grant, 6827.
John, 10522.
John Henry, 6813.
Letitia, 10520.
Lillie, 10526.
Luella, 10523.
Lula, 10566.
Martha, 10568.
Martha Catharine, 6817.
Martin, 10524.
Marvin, 10550.
Mary Emma, 6815, 6828.

Mylin, 10567.
Nettie, 10521.
Sue Catharine, 6824.
William Burnside, 6826.
William E., 6818.
William Rollin, 10552.
KELBLY, Eli F., 13031.
George Garfield, 13028.
Ira Earl, 13033.
John Harrison, 13032.
Minnie Minette, 13029.
Rhoda Ellen, 13030.
KELBY, John Wesley, 13104.
KELLER, Don, 12429.
Ray, 12428.
KELLEY, Edwin C., 7670.
Elizabeth, 7671.
Frederick, 7669.
John E., 7668.
Joseph Hooker, 7673.
Sarah, 7672.
KENDIG, 8979, 8980, 12993.
Aaron, 9795.
Aaron M., 5128.
Abraham, 565, 1007, 1177, 2213, 3588, 5843.
Abraham H., 1013, 3433.
Absalom P., 7378.
Addah Louisa, 3191.
Adino B., 5037.
Albert, 3203.
Alfred, 9762.
Alice, 331, 3202.
Amanda, 4359.
Amos, 1993, 5810.
Amos B., 4362.
Andrew J., 7376, 9740.
Andrew W., 9744, 9750.
Ann, 337, 5812.
Ann Catharine, 4357.
Ann Mary, 9800.
Anna, 3435, 5805, 5826, 8778.
Anna Elizabeth, 5130.
Anna M., 5057.
Anna S., 3586.
Annie, 1995, 8677.
Arthur David, 9297.
B. Rohrer, 5846.
Barbara, 328, 372, 1010, 3438, 5813, 9766.
Barbara Alice, 3197.
Barbara Ann, 1181.
Benjamin, 2203, 3431, 9785.
Benjamin G., 5811.
Benjamin W., 1794.
Betsey, 5845.
Carrie, 8777.
Catharine, 1474.
Charles, 9742, 9763, 9778, 9780.
Charles H., 9747.
Charles Herr, 7080.
Christian, 335, 703, 1176, 3574, 5835.
Christian H., 11486.
Clara E., 5036.
Clara Louisa, 3503.
Clarissa Ellen, 5056.
Cleon R., 11484.
Daisy M., 10772.
Daniel, 369, 704, 1308.
Daniel F., 9749.
Daniel H., 7374.
Daughter, 9298.
David, 574, 1798, 5032.

KEPLER, Albert Monroe, 11357.
    John Wilbur, 11355.
    William McKinley, 11356.
KEPLINGER, Elizabeth C., 7771.
    Ella Nora, 7772.
KERN, Caroline, C-105.
    Emil, C-104.
    Emma, C-109.
    Henry, C-102.
    Mary Elizabeth, C-106.
    Matilda, C-107.
    Rosina, C-103.
    Samuel Walter, C-110.
    William, C-108.
KIEFFER, Anna Eliza, 12653.
    Anna Mary, 5277.
    Caroline K., 12654.
    Charles Wesley, 12655.
    Ethel Winifert, 12697.
    Harvey Edmund, 12656.
    Henry Elmer, 12658.
    Ida Sabina, 12659.
    Isaac Sylvester, 12660.
    Lamenta Susanna, 12695.
    Leah Amanda, 12657.
    Mildred Olin, 12698.
    Nora Mae, 12661.
    Pearl Susan, 12699.
    Permilla Adella, 12696.
    Sarah Pearl, 12663.
    Susan S., 12662.
    Una Gladys, 12694.
KILHEFFER, Alexander C., 2861.
    Alice May, 2870.
    Anna, 870.
    Annie, 2865.
    Barbara E., 2859.
    Catharine, 865, 2862.
    Christian, 869.
    D. Herbert, 6638.
    Daniel, 871.
    David, 868.
    Edmund H., 2863.
    Elizabeth, 866.
    Elizabeth H., 6639.
    Henry H., 874.
    Infant, 2867, 2868.
    Jacob H., 872.
    John, 873.
    Josephine R., 2866.
    Mary, 867.
    Mary H., 2864.
    Sarah E., 2860.
    Son, 2869.
KINNAMAN, Belle, 5706.
    Carson H., 5707.
KISSINGER, Edgar Harrison, 9474.
    Wayne Oscar, 9475.
KLINE, Anna, 3996.
    Benjamin, 4000.
    Charles D., 7157.
    Edna May, 7159.
    Elizabeth, 3998.
    Emma, 3999.
    Jacob, 3997.
    John Edwin, 3995.
    John J., 7160.
    Joseph, 3992.
    Mary Jane, 3994.
    Myrtle M., 7158.
    Sarah Ann, 3993.
KNAISLEY, Barbara, 1636.
    Christian, 1642.

    Daniel, 1639.
    Eliza, 1635.
    George, 1640.
    John, 1638.
    Mary, 1637.
    Samuel, 1641.
KNAPP, Isaac, 2125.
    Mary, 2128.
    Rebecca, 2129.
    Sophia, 2126.
    Susanna, 2127.
KNEISLEY, George H., 12372.
KOHNE, Mabel, 6635.
    Rebecca, 6636.
KOHR, Alice, 10094.
    Anna L., 10093.
    Anna M., 8911.
    Enos W., 8910.
    Esther L., 10096.
    Franklin L., 10092.
    Howard, 10095.
    John, 10098.
    Lydia, 10097.
    Mary Elizabeth, 11550.
    Walter Leon, 12952.
KOPP, Alice M., 9450.
    Elizabeth, 9451.
    Isaac, 9452.
    Levi, 9453.
KONKLER, Joseph E., 8026.
KRAFT, Kenneth Huston, 11397.
KRANTZ, Annie, 6572.
    Emma, 6574.
    Lizzie, 6571.
    Mary, 6573.
KRAPE, Bessie Isabel, 9606.
    Reber Wilson, 9604.
    Zell Marie, 9605.
KREBS, Anna Belle, 8687.
    Catharine, 10147.
    Harriet, 11726.
    Harold, 11727.
    Josephine, 8688.
    Stanley Walter, 10148.
KREIDER, Aaron, 8469.
    Abraham, 2672.
    Amos S., 9014.
    Anna, 11394.
    Anna Elizabeth, 4995.
    Anna M., 9013.
    Annie, 8997, 11385.
    Barbara, 9018.
    Benjamin, 11388.
    Catharine, 2675.
    Charles G., 10887.
    Daniel, 1861, 4734.
    Daniel P., 10886.
    Elam, 9223, 11387.
    Elam Henry, 8467.
    Elizabeth, 2676.
    Ely H., 1862.
    Emma, 11393.
    Emma C., 8472.
    Enos, 8473.
    Esther, 6095.
    Esther K., 11551.
    Ezra, 8470.
    Frances, 2677.
    Frank, 11383.
    Frank B., 4994.
    Franklin J., 8468.
    George M., 10883.
    Henry, 4730, 8475.

Henry H., 8084.
Hettie, 8999.
Ida, 9225, 11384.
Ida B., 9017.
Infant, 9224.
Isaac, 1864.
Isaac H., 8085.
Jacob, 2680, 6093, 9938.
Jessie Anna, 11552.
John, 2674, 4733, 6094, 8998.
John M., 10888.
John S., 9016.
Katie, 4997.
Lillie F., 10885.
Lizzie, 4736, 8471, 8995.
Luetta, 11392.
Lydia, 8474.
Martha, 1865, 2681.
Martin, 4731, 4996, 8996, 11389.
Martin H., 1860.
Mary, 2673, 4735, 6096, 8994, 9019, 9937.
Mary Elizabeth, 5225.
Mary K., 11553.
Samuel H., 10882.
Stephen H., 6999.
Susan, 1863, 2679.
Tillie K., 5226.
Tobias, 2679, 9015, 11386.
Tobias H., 4763.
Tobias R., 4732.
Wilmer A., 10884.
Zuriel S., 9020.
KREPPS, Emma M., 9691.
Gerald C., 9693.
Ida A., 9694.
Leona M., 9692.
Ruth M., 9690.
KRUG, Allie, 11117.
Alma, 11116.
Ann Josephine. 8101.
Barbara, 1346.
Benjamin, 3938.
Benjamin F., 11118.
Betsey, 1342.
Catharine, 3935.
Charles F., 8106.
Christiana, 1344.
Cora D., 7863.
Daniel, 1340.
Elizabeth, 3934.
Elmer H., 8107.
Emma F., 8108.
Esther, 3940, 3941.
Frences, 3939.
Frederick, 1341.
Henry, 1338.
Jennie Alice, 8103.
John, 3943.
Leander J., 8100.
Leroy, 8109.
Mary, 1343, 3937.
Mary Elizabeth, 8102.
Maude Ann, 7865.
Minnie Ida, 8104.
Minnie May, 7864.
Samuel, 1345, 3942.
Samuel Henry, 8105.
Susan, 1339, 3936.
KRUGER, Chester H., 10322.
Lelia C., 10323.
KRYDER, Mary H., 11349.
Charles E., 11348.

KUHNS, Austin Huffard, 11866.
Catharine Angeline, 11857.
George Washington, 11855.
Henry Clarence, 11858.
Oscar, 11859.
Walter Brown, 11856.
KULP, Emma, 6305.
Henry, 6307.
John, 6304.
Menno, 6306.
KUNKLE, Annie, 12416.
Frank, 12417.
George, 12418.
Lena, 12415.
Olive, 12414.
KURTZ, 6377, 6378, 6379.
Amelia, 12746.
Clarence Olin, 12805.
Clyde Leonard, 12812.
David B., 12743.
Della M., 12747.
Doris Susanna, 12806.
Dorothy Gertrude, 12808.
Eloda Arline, 12810.
Ida Mable, 12811.
Irien Leslie, 12807.
Jacob, 12742.
John, 12741.
Lloyd William, 12813.
Lydia A., 12748.
Nancy C., 12749.
Roy Wesley, 12809.
Sarah, 12744.
Simon, 12745.
LANDIS, Aaron, 2833.
Abraham B., 6233.
Abraham J., 3386.
Adriana, 10081, 10089.
Amelia, 10085.
Amos, 5652, 8525, 8532.
Anna, 1427, 4184, 4196, 5648, 10080, 11286.
Anna H., 8390.
Anna M., 3388.
Arthur R., 7282.
Annie, 7128.
Benjamin, 1430, 4183, 4197, 10110.
Benjamin D., 8527.
Benjamin H., 3250, 7125, 10077.
Benjamin K., 8111.
Bertha M., 7281.
Catharine, 10090.
Charles A., 10084.
Charles E., 10330.
Christian B., 4195.
Christian D., 8530.
Cora E., 7280.
Daniel K., 8110.
Daniel M., 5653.
David, 2838, 4190, 10327.
David H., 3383.
David M., 8393.
Edith, 6625.
Edith A., 10087.
Effie E., 10325.
Eliza M., 5651.
Elizabeth, 2836, 3389, 4188, 4193, 6231, 8526, 8528, 10079.
Elizabeth A., 8392.
Elmer, 7540.
Emma, 3387, 6234, 9668.
Esther, 10113.
Esther Ann, 5655.

Esther Mae, 8394.
Ezra F., 6229.
Fanny, 2837, 4185, 4198, 8524.
Fanny H., 8536.
Frances, 5657.
Frances M., 3248.
Francis Thomas, 6616.
Frank F., 7278.
Frank H., 10082.
Franklin, 10114.
Franklin F., 6228.
Gertrude M., 7291.
Grace Elizabeth, 10086.
Harriet Elizabeth, 9670.
Harvey S., 7279.
Henry, 10111.
Ida B., 7288.
Ida May, 10076.
Ida Susan, 7283.
Ira C., 10326.
Jacob, 8533.
Jacob H., 4189.
Jacob M., 5656.
Jessie C., 10328.
John, 1428, 1429, 4186, 7539, 8529.
John H., 2832, 3390.
John I., 7285.
John M., 5654.
John N., 10329.
John R., 10817.
John S., 3249.
Leah, 3382, 10091.
Magdalene, 4192, 4194.
Maria, 4182.
Mark, 10109.
Mark Homer, 10083.
Martha Ann, 7287.
Martha E., 3391.
Martha Lucretia, 9669.
Martha Skeen, 11130.
Mary, 3381, 10088.
Mary Alice, 7127.
Mary Ann, 2834, 3384, 5649, 6230.
    8523.
Mary Anna, 6615.
Mary Elizabeth, 11119.
Mary Frances, 8391.
Mary H., 10078, 10108.
Myrtle A., 7292.
Nelson, 6624.
Orra E., 7290.
Phares H., 3385.
Ralph, 6623.
Raymond J., 7289.
Ruth Evaline, 10112.
Salome, 6232.
Sarah, 4199.
Son, 8534.
Susan, 2835, 5650.
Susanna, 4187.
Susanna H., 8535.
Tobias, 4190, 8531.
Urias, 8522.
Verna Ruth, 7286.
Walter E., 7284.
William Grant, 9671.
LANGLEY, Hazel, 7197.
    Mifford, 7196.
LANNIN, Orton Herr, 9434.
LANTZ, Abraham, 4352.
    Ann Maria, 3495.
    Anna, 4353.
    Benjamin Franklin, 8759.

Benjamin W., 4346.
Eddie E., 8768.
Elizabeth, 4347.
Elizabeth Ann, 8757.
Ellen, 8760.
Emma, 3501.
Ephraim, 4345.
Esther, 4350.
Frances E., 3498.
Harry, 3503.
Hercules, 3496.
Hettie, 8661.
Hettie Ann, 3497.
Ida, 3500.
Isaac, 4349.
Isaac Newton, 8755.
Jacob, 4348, 8710, 8754.
John, 3499, 4351.
John Elmer, 8758.
Leah, 4356.
Letitia, 8769.
Margaret, 8771.
Mary Emma, 8756.
Samuel, 3502, 4355.
Susanna, 4354.
LAPP, Adelbert Erasmus, 5417.
    Emma Ezalia, 5416.
    Ella Endora, 5415.
LAUDENSLAGER, Anna C., 12646.
    Eliza, 12652.
    Elmer, 12678.
    Frederick G., 12651.
    Gracie, 12674.
    Herbert, 12676.
    Infant, 12726, 12727.
    Isaac, 12647.
    John E., 12650.
    Mary J., 12648.
    Mearl, 12725.
    Nepa, 12724.
    Resa, 12679.
    Russell, 12675.
    Thomas, 12677.
    William H., 12649.
LAW, Blanche Virgie, 11010.
    Curtis Elmer, 11007.
    Daisy Gertrude, 11009.
    Oliver Arthur, 11008.
LEACHEY, Edith, 12030.
    Harry, 12029.
LEAMAN, Ada, 11380.
    Benjamin Elmer, 8465.
    Benjamin Franklin, 8461.
    Bertha M., 11149.
    Charles McClug, 9129.
    Christian B., 8459.
    Elizabeth, 8458.
    Emily V., 11151.
    Enos B., 8462.
    Enos Brackbill, 8466.
    George Wesley, 8464.
    Harry M., 11150.
    Harry Musselman, 9130.
    Lizzie, 11379.
    Millard B., 8463.
    Susan, 8460.
    Walter L., 9131.
LECHLIDER, Fannie Boyer, 2773.
    Francis Alexander, 2771.
    Julia Kathleen, 6569.
    Lenora Grace, 2764.
    Lillie May, 2770.
    Marian Louisa, 6570.

Jacob, 1132.
John, 1135.
Maria, 1133.
Martin, 1131.
Samuel, 1134.
LIND, Charles J., 6649.
LINDSEY, Bertha, 10169.
   Grace, 10168.
   Grover, 10171.
   Hiram, 10170.
LINGLE, Infant, 5730, 5731.
LINTNER, Anna May, 12614.
   Emma Ruth, 12613.
   Martha Elizabeth, 12611.
   Mary Grace, 12612.
LINVILLE, Charles, 9122.
   Elace Ann, 8692.
   Ellie, 9120.
   Henry M., 9119.
   Josephine L., 9123.
   Martha Salome, 8693.
   Raymond C., 9124.
   Sarah L., 9121.
LIPPINCOTT, Francis B., 9528.
LITCHFIELD, Ethel Carver, 7202.
   Lawrence, 7203.
LLOYD, John Eshleman, 12106.
   Samuel Henry, 12105.
   William McClure, 12107.
LOCKE, Cora Sutcliffe, 11575.
   Fanny Sutcliffe, 11573.
   Lucy Nelson, 11574.
LOGAN, 4404, 4405, 4406, 4407, 4408, 4409,
      4410, 4411, 4413.
   Carleton Moore, 9586.
   David, 4412.
   Lottie Mae, 9575.
LONG, 12882, 12883, 12884, 12885.
   Abraham F., 9428.
   Anna M., 5169.
   Austin O., 9422.
   Benjamin G., 5171.
   Benjamin M., 9430.
   Clementine G., 9420.
   Cora Belle, 9387.
   Cora L., 9431.
   Cyrus Savage, 9406.
   Daniel, 1844.
   Daniel E., 5167.
   David, 1843.
   David N., 5170.
   Edith May, 9421.
   Edward S., 9433.
   Edwin E., 9424.
   Eli H., 5172.
   Elias A., 5166.
   Elizabeth L., 5174.
   Ella E., 9425.
   Emanuel C., 5173.
   Emily C., 5176.
   Esther A., 9429.
   Esther S., 5163.
   Ethel Clara, 9417.
   Florence Grace, 9419.
   Frances Elizabeth, 9404.
   Frank H., 9426.
   Franklin B., 5175.
   George Baker, 9403.
   Helena May, 9405.
   Henry M., 5162.
   Hillan McGee, 11469.
   John D., 5165.
   Mary C., 9427.

Mary E., 5164.
Olive Harriet, 9416.
Raymond D., 9423.
Russel Graham, 9418.
Ruth E., 9432.
Susan L., 5168.
LOUGEAY, Alice, 3337.
   Harry, 3338.
LONGENECKER, Abraham, 1708.
   Aldus Earle, 7769.
   Amanda L., 3626.
   Anna Pearl, 7770.
   Annie Sheridan, 5991.
   Benjamin, 1700.
   Bertha, 7767.
   Catharine Stoner, 4956.
   Daniel, 1705.
   Daniel F., 3614.
   Edwin R., 5989.
   Edith Martin, 9259.
   Eliza, 1218.
   Eliza Delano, 9260.
   Elmira Belle, 7768.
   Emma E., 3623.
   Emma Lizzie, 4957.
   Fanny, 1219, 1707.
   Frank H., 12369.
   Gertrude, 11440.
   Henry Clay, 4954.
   Jacob, 3628.
   Jessie Amanda, 7766.
   John, 1701, 5990.
   John Barr, 4953.
   John F., 1220.
   Lizzie, 1703.
   Mabel, 11441.
   Mattie, 1706.
   Martin B., 1216.
   Mary, 1217, 1702.
   Mary Ann, 3617.
   Mary Louisa, 4955.
   Myra May, 11439.
   Nancy, 1704.
   Susan, 1699.
   Susanna, 3625.
LORENTSEN, Emma, 11325.
   Frederick W., 11324.
LOW, Emory, 10348.
   Florence, 10343.
   Katie, 10349.
   Theodore, 10342.
LOWER, Josephine, 11683.
LYLE, Lydia Ann, 3641.
   Margaret, 3642.
LYTE, Ethel, 10824.
   Glerma O., 10826.
   Minnie Gertrude, 10825.
MAHLER, Catharine, 12206.
   Donald, 12205.
MAIL, Daniel, 8051.
   Elizabeth, 8048.
   Frederic, 8047.
   Henry, 8049.
   John, 8050.
   Lenora, 8046.
MARBURG, Gertrude, 11651.
MARKLEY, Preston H., 11563.
MARS, Antoinette L., 8565.
MARSH, Arthur, 13175.
   Clara, 13174.
   Eva, 13172.
   George, 13171.
   Grace, 13177.

McCALLA, Frances Louisa, 8564.
McCANN, Abraham, 7902.
    Charles, 7907.
    David, 7904.
    Elias, 7905.
    Franklin, 7901.
    John, 7908.
    Lile, 7903.
    Martha, 7906.
    Robert, 7900.
McCLELLEN, George A., 11614.
    Lillie M., 11611.
    M. Adelia, 11613.
    Sarah E., 11612.
McCLINTOCK, Daughter, 7208.
    David, 7207.
    Son, 7209.
McCONNELL, Caroline M., 13097.
    Clara Netta, 12997.
    Cleo Pearl, 13000.
    Edith Ethel, 13002.
    Forest Forrer, 13003.
    Gladder Glenn, 12999.
    John Elington, 12996.
    Justus George, 13001.
    Luella Belle, 12998.
    May Lewis, 9575.
    Oliver Earl, 13004.
    Perry Elmer, 12994.
    Sarah Delfis, 12995.
McCORMICK, Catharine F., 4476.
    Charles B., 4477.
    Eliza Ellen, 4475.
    William D., 4478.
McCOY, Anna M., 9674.
    Anna May, 5678.
    Charles, 9681.
    Claire, 9686.
    Don L., 9688.
    Edward, 9683.
    Edward J., 5676.
    Eva L., 9678.
    Gaynell, 9685.
    Harry, 9684.
    Herman W., 9682.
    Howard R., 9673.
    Inez, R., 9675.
    Lewis D., 5677.
    Minnie, 9687.
    Minnie A., 5675.
    Myron G., 9676.
    Sadie B., 9677.
    Thomas J. Mahlon, 9689.
    Willis C., 5674.
McELHENY, Clair H., 8192.
    Emma C., 8194.
    Esther Rose, 8195.
    Franklin H., 8193.
McFALLS, Charles, 10809.
    Elsie, 10812.
    Florence, 10810.
    Hattie, 10815.
    Ira, 10811.
    John, 10816.
    Nora, 10814.
    Stella, 10813.
McHENRY, Hiero Herr, 11410.
    Lorenzo Alva, 11409.
McILVAINE, Donald, 12111.
    Fanny Edge, 12108.
    John Gilbert, 12109.
    Herbert Rohinson, 12110.
McKEE, Edward, 3339.

McKELVEY, Edward W., 3275.
    Frank M., 3274, 7178.
    Henry C., 3273, 7182.
    Joseph Clifton W., 7183.
    Malvern B., 7185.
    Marcus L., 7184.
    Margaretta, 7186.
    Olive Irene, 7180.
    Pauline Ethel, 7181.
    Preston Willis, 7187.
    Raymond, 7179.
McKIBBEN, Clarence Edward, 8884.
    Effie, 8882.
    Harry Armstrong, 8883.
McMULLEN, Henry, 8090.
    Lizzie, 8092.
    Mary Ann, 8093.
    Susan, 8091.
    William, 8089.
McMURDY, John Hobert, 9136.
McMURTREY, Allen Percy, 9295.
    Averdeene, 9294.
    Clifford Jasper, 9293.
    David Walter, 9291.
    Jessie Florence, 9290.
    Tessie Rebecca, 9292.
McNUTT, Charles, 12712.
    Clarence, 12713.
MECK, George Henry, 8481.
    Jacob Aldus, 8482.
MEHAFFY, Ann, 3543.
    John, 3541.
    Lydia, A., 3542.
MEISTER, Samuel Emil, 12604.
    Theodore Witmer, 12605.
MELLINGER, Gilbert Clemens, 13103.
MENDENHALL, Abethenia P., 10010.
    Gertrude Winnifred, 10009.
    Luther Wesley, 10007.
    Prudence Elizabeth, 10008.
MENGES, Benjamin Harrison, 5705
    Bertha Leona, 5702.
    Hubert Theophilus, 5703.
    Laura Alda, 5701.
    Mabel Luella, 5704.
    Oliver Adelbert, 5700.
    Susan Evelyn, 5699.
    William Henry, 5698.
MERACLE, Edna Luella, 9705.
    Theda Maud, 9706.
    Warren Elliott, 9707.
    William Adams, 9704.
MERRYMAN, Louis, 10808.
METZ, Catharine Lillian, 5413.
    Cora Ida, 5414.
    Ellie Eudora, 5412.
    Gertrude E., 5418.
    Susanna, 3664.
METZGAR, Adelaide L., 8772.
    Barbara, 2331.
    Charles David, 6557.
    Cora Rebecca, 6556.
    David. 2332.
    Elizabeth, 2330.
    Emanuel, 2326.
    George, 2322.
    George Albert, 6092.
    Henry, 2325.
    Jacob, 2323.
    Jacob Albert, 6088.
    Jacob Augustus, 6087.
    John, 2324.
    John Kendig, 8776.

i

Infant, 2025, 12707, 12709.
Ira, 6017.
Isaac, 6016.
Isaac N., 4945.
Israel, 12637.
Jacob, 2277, 9939.
Jacob Frick, 10103.
Jacob M., 4936.
James Gracen, 12006.
Joel R., 11063.
John, 1966, 2273, 2579, 9940.
John C., 11064.
John Eshlehan, 6001.
John Henry, 2752.
John Milton, 7932.
John Taylor, 6011.
John W., 4941, 5112.
Joseph, 5796.
Joseph Culver, 5997.
Josiah, 1537.
Kate, 9226.
Laura L., 4946.
Lawrence, 12432.
Louisa, 6004.
Loyd, 12431.
Lydia, 10101.
M. Catharine, 5998.
M. Elizabeth, 5999.
Maria L., 4935.
Martha, 1965, 12629.
Martha A., 5110.
Mary, 12433.
Mary Ann, 13221.
Mary E., 4947, 5113.
Mary Elizabeth, 12020.
Mary Elsie, 6013.
Mary Emma, 5793.
Mary L., 10099.
Mary Louisa, 6005.
Norman, 12430.
Orestes, 13170.
Orlena, 12711.
Robert, 6010.
Rosanna Margaret, 2753.
Ruth Lillian, 10106.
S. Catharine, 6006.
Salome Edna, 10104.
Salome F., 1540.
Samuel, 1538, 2274.
Samuel Eshleman, 6012.
Samuel W., 5114.
Sarah, 12634.
Sarah E., 5115, 8045.
Son, 6018.
Susan, 1962.
Susan C., 5119.
Susan Rebecca, 2749.
Susanna, 12628.
Walter Slott, 12004.
William H., 11059.
William W., 4944.
MILTON, Edwin Kirtley, 11576.
MINNICH, Annie K., 11979.
Barbara, 6081.
Christiana, 6082.
Claribel, 11435.
Emma, 11438.
Franklin, 6084.
George R., 11434.
Sarah, 11437.
Stephen, 6083.
William, 11436.

MINNIGH, Anna K., 2766.
Infant, 2767, 2768.
MOHR, Rose Maxwell, 9139.
MOIR, Arthur Duncan. 11341.
Jean, 11340.
William Wilmerding, 11342.
MONDERBACH, Martin, 6091.
Morris, 6090.
MOORE, Anna Virginia, 5485.
Carolyn Virginia, 9590.
Donald Winston, 9589.
Dorothy Mildred, 9587.
Elizabeth, 1998.
Frances Herr, 1999.
George Crane, 2003.
George Kenneth, 5491.
George Paul, 5499.
George Victor, 5497.
Harry G., 5501.
John Edward, 5496.
John S., 2004.
Laura Summerfield, 5500.
Lemuel Boynton, 5484.
Lottie Boynton, 5486.
Lucille Athenaise, 9588.
Mary Bradford, 5487.
Maude, 5498.
Milton Henry, 5488.
Nora Ethel, 5483.
Roy Dudley, 5490.
Sarah Catharine, 2001.
Susan Burrill, 5489.
Uriah Brison, 2002.
William Henry, 2000.
MORGAN, Lottie Bell, 9583.
William Patrick, 9584.
MORLEY, Arthur Long, 9408.
Clarence Benjamin, 9409.
Thomas Henry, 9407.
MORTON, Benjamin Franklin, 7596.
Galen Wesley, 7597.
Homer Edwin, 10763.
John Allen, 10820.
John Herr, 7595.
Mary Elizabeth, 7598.
Myra Ethel, 9504.
Ralph Emerson, 9503.
William Elmer, 7599.
MOSINGER, Anna Maria, C-32.
George Frederick, C-30.
John George, C-15.
William, C-31.
MOURNING, Matalea Caldwell, 11740.
MOUSER, Amanda D., 7855.
Blanch M., 7857.
Emma E., 7861.
George Ernest, 7862.
Howard L., 7856.
Jacob E., 7859.
Leah B., 7858.
Winnie M., 7860.
MOWRER, Benjamin, 3027.
Catharine, 3032.
Christian, 3030.
Christiana, 3034.
Elizabeth, 3029.
Emma 3033.
Franklin, 3031.
Mary, 3026.
Mary Elizabeth, 11047.
Susan, 3028.
MOYER, Amos, 8923.
Anna Elizabeth, 8921.

Lena Herr, 8920.
Marguerite, 8922.
Miriam H., 8919.
MUELLER, Harriet Stevens, 11461.
Laura, 11462.
Mildred, 11463.
MUMMA, Charles C., 10331.
Christian, 2788. ————
Eli, 6583.
Elizabeth, 2787.
Fanny, 2790, 6585.
Fianna, 6581.
John, 6584.
John W., 10333.
Jonas, 2789.
Mary Ann, 6586.
Mary M., 10332.
Simon, 6582.
MUSSELMAN, Ada Louisa, 2026.
Allan Herr, 9127.
Amos, 8146.
Amos Forrer, 4850.
Ann Eliza, 3519.
Annie V., 4857.
Barbara A., 3522.
Benjamin Franklin, 4853.
Benjamin G., 8148.
Benjamin Ovid, 9126.
Christian, 3518, 8143.
Clarissa R., 4856.
D. Paul, 9132.
David G. Eshleman, 4858.
Dorinda Bishop, 9135.
E. Elizabeth, 7646.
Edwin Charles, 4859.
Eliza Ann, 3523.
Ella, 8144.
Elmira S., 4852.
Emma S., 3520.
Fannie, 8153.
Frank L., 7647.
Franklin, 8152.
Franklin B., 3516.
Harriet F., 3525.
Henry Bishop, 9133.
Ida, 8151.
Infant, 9125.
Jacob, 8145.
John, 7648, 8147.
Josephine E., 4855.
Martha, 8150.
Martha Ann, 4854.
Martha M., 3521.
Mary Emma, 9128.
Mary Louisa, 4851.
Mary Louise, 9134.
Mary Myra, 3524.
Milton M., 3517.
Susan, 8149.
MUSSER, Ada, 4643.
Agnes G., 9190.
Anna Letitia, 4638.
Anna W., 8937.
Annie E., 4887.
Benjamin, 1739.
Charles Martin, 4645.
Charles Milton, 7655.
Christian, 1733.
Clara May, 6172.
Daniel, 1737.
Dorothy, 9191.
Edith E., 7652.
Elizabeth, 1732.

Emma Elizabeth, 5237.
Frances, 1741, 2391.
Francis Martin, 4888.
Frank Arthur, 9174.
Frederic Omar, 9177.
Guy Musselman, 7656.
Harry Milton, 8935.
Henry Elmer, 4644.
Hettie, 1742.
John, 1734.
John H., 4886.
John Henry, 4876, 10844.
John Herr, 4899, 9188.
John Jacob, 4889.
Julia Dorsey, 9179.
Lawrence Guenie, 8936.
Mabel Cooper, 9173.
Martha, 1736.
Martin, 1740.
Martin H., 5238.
Mary, 1738, 2390.
Mary A., 5236.
Mary Ada, 7654.
Mary Adrienne, 4875.
Mary H., 9187.
Mary Luetta, 4885, 9175.
Mary Naomi,, 4900.
Milton B., 4642.
Mira Lloyd, 9176.
Nancy, 1735.
Naomi, 9189.
Omar Henry, 4891.
Park Neff, 7657.
Robert B., 10845.
Samuel, 1743.
Walter, 5239.
Will M., 7653.
Willis B., 4890.
Willis Benjamin, 7178.
MYERS, Aaron, 11840.
Abraham, 11845.
Ada, 7440.
Adam, 8764.
Anna, 7441.
Anna Elizabeth, 10831.
Annie, 12198.
Arthur S., 10830.
Barbara A., 12256.
Benjamin, 12197.
Benjamin Brown, 11839.
C. William, 6830.
Carrie A., 11741.
Catharine, 1633.
Christian, 12255.
Christian M., 12348.
Clarence C., 11743.
Daniel, 8766, 12196.
David, 7439, 11842.
David H., 12259.
Elam, 7443.
Eli, 12257.
Elias, 12194.
Eliza, 1221.
Elizabeth, 12199.
Ellen, 12262.
Emma, 8765.
Ernest B., 11744.
Frederick M., 11844.
Frances, 6491.
Eva, 9918.
Guy, 9917.
Henry, 1632, 2096, 7444.
Herbert O., 10256.

Glenn H., 13182.
Olive, 13180.
NEWSWENGER, Abraham, 3012.
Benjamin Franklin, 3013.
Daughter, 3008, 3009.
David, 3010.
Susan, 3011.
NIBLACK, Austin H., 7077.
Lydia, 7078.
Narcissa, 7076.
NISSLY, Christian. 12533.
Daniel, 12532.
Jonas, 12534.
NIXDORF, Arthur Earl, 10245.
Irene, 10244.
NOLT, Annie May, 7248.
Daughter, 10600.
Elizabeth L., 7245.
Ella Nora, 10599.
Emma S., 7246.
Emma H., 10604.
Enos W., 10603.
Francis, 7251.
Harry S., 7250.
Jonas H., 10602.
Letitia, 7247.
Martin Landis, 10601.
Minnie H., 10605.
Willis H., 7249.
OBER, Agnes, 9436.
Anna, 9440.
Fanny, 9435.
Nathan, 9439.
Philip, 9437.
Susan, 9438.
OBERHOLTZER, Aaron, 12240.
Mary K., 12241.
OHLWILER, Clarence H., 7034.
David Ralph, 7035.
ORVIS, Carrie, 9104.
Hattie, 9105.
Herbert C., 9107.
Maud, 9106.
OSWALD, Elsie Fern, 11449.
OVERTURF, Daughter, 10996.
OWEN, Abraham Spence, 9320.
Fanny, 10357.
PARDEE, Alice Vinnie, 7111.
Elmer Witmer, 7110.
Eulalie Augusta, 7112.
PARKER, Elizabeth, 5987.
William P., 5988.
PARKS, Bettie, 10361.
Cora, 10363.
John, 10360.
Walter, 10362.
PARRY, Anna R., 5555.
Charlotte R., 2042.
George A., 2043.
Henry B., 2040.
John E., 2041.
Lucy, 5556.
PEASLEE, Clarence Loomis, 9603.
Helen Wilson, 9602.
PEART, Caroline, 7013.
PECK, Eva, 7867.
Infant, 7868.
Olive, 7866.
PEELER, Carl, 11359.
Eliz. Carrie, 11358.
PIERCE, Carrie Mildred, 12584.
Susan Elizabeth, 12585.
PENNEL, Clarence A., 12104.

PENNYPACKER, Mary Anita, 11701.
PEOPLES, Angie Winona, 8351.
Annie Carlotta, 8352.
Ida Sue, 8350.
John B., 8349.
Maria, 8353.
PENNELL, Harry C., 3606.
Clarence Arthur, 12104.
Mary Ann, 3605.
PFOHL, Harold C., 9566.
PFOUTZ, Abraham G., 5935.
Anna, 597.
Elizabeth, 596.
Francis H., 5937.
Jacob W., 5939.
Martin Miller, 5936.
Samuel B., 5938.
PHILIPS, Lucille Elizabeth, 1-703.
PIERCE, Ansel R., 10274.
Bernice Rae, 10761.
Bertha May, 10760.
Eli Harvey, 4552.
Floyd Ferne, 10758.
George C., 10275.
Harry Marion, 10762.
Hazel Reeve, 10757.
Leonidas Thomas, 4554.
Mary Barr, 4553.
Mary Gladys, 10759.
Susanna Octavia, 4555.
PLUMMER, Helen F., 11753.
Sarah A., 11754.
POISEL, Grace Hubley, 10873.
Marie Alice, 10872.
Ray Byerly, 10871.
PONTIUS, Carlisle, 11338.
Carrie Amelia, 8788.
Cora Frances, 8787.
Edla Virginia, 8785.
Frances Isabelle, 11336.
George W., 11337.
George Willers, 8786.
Murray, 11339.
POTTS, Angelica. 5954.
Ann Elizabeth, 5980.
Annie Maria, 5975.
Annie Virgilia, 9884.
Benjamin, 2259, 5950.
Daniel, 2251, 2252.
Daniel E., 5952.
David, 2260, 5983.
Emma Catharine, 5981.
Fanny, 2255.
Jacob, 5953.
Jacob E., 2256.
Jacob F., 5986.
James Warren, 5979.
John, 2257, 5951.
John Frank, 5984.
Joseph, 2258.
Joseph Miller, 5976.
Joseph Warren, 5978.
Junius Brutus, 5974.
Maria, 2254.
Mary Ann, 5949.
Mary E., 9885.
Mary Ella, 5985.
Mary Louisa, 5982.
Samuel, 2253, 5977.
Son, 2261, 2262, 5955.
POULTON, Blanche Tangert, 11004.
Catharine Emaline, 11713.
Clarence Elliott, 11002.

Claude Elliott, 11708.
Clyde Wilbur, 11711.
Florence Missouri, 11000.
Frank Hoffman, 11709.
George Henry, 10999.
Joseph Smith, 10998.
Mildred Edwina, 11712.
Minerva Irene, 11003.
Ross Edward, 11707.
Ruth Violet, 11710.
Silas William, 11001.
PRATT, Clarence Herr, 7026.
Edna Earl, 7030.
Ida May, 7027.
Iradell, 7029.
Phineas, 7028.
Thomas Clifford, 7031.
RAE, Catharine Louise, 5617.
Mac Delancy. 5616.
RAFFENSPERGER, Miriam Herr, 12641.
RAFFERTY, George R., 10432.
James, 10433.
RAMEY, Anna Margaret, 7886.
Carl Shaub, 7885.
RANCK, Amanda, 8377.
Amos H., 8378.
Anna Naomi, 8381.
Bertha, 9066.
Bertha E., 11237.
David H., 11235.
Elizabeth, 8376.
Emma, 9065.
Fannie H., 11233.
Harry E., 11234.
Howard, 9064.
John E., 11236.
Milton H., 8380.
Reuben H., 8379.
Sarah Etta, 8382.
RASOR, Althea May, 1039.
Daniel B., 6685.
David F., 6686.
Harvey E., 6687.
Josiah, 6684.
Lavina, 6682.
Samuel, 6683.
RATHVON, Alice, 9310.
Anna M., 9299.
Anna Cochran, 11679.
Baker J., 9114.
Benjamin, 9308.
Blanche S., 11680.
Catharine J., 9301.
Charles J., 9113.
Clara, 9303.
Clayton, 9309.
Elizabeth, 10488.
Elizabeth B., 11674.
Elmer, 9306.
Emily H., 11675.
Ezra, 9304.
Gertrude M., 9112.
Henry M., 11677.
Horace, 9305, 10486.
Horace H., 11676.
Ida, 9307.
John F., 9300.
Levi, 9302.
Lillie, 9311.
Martin T., 11682.
Mary Louisa, 11678.
Nathaniel P., 11681.

Samuel F., 10487.
William R., 10489.
BEAM, Frances, 4784.
Jacob, 4786.
Susan, 4785.
REBER, Harry H., 11723.
REDMOND, Elizabeth, 13190.
Harold, 13189.
REDSECKER, Abraham Ream, 4907.
Anna E., 4906.
George Henry, 4902.
Harriet S., 4904.
Jacob H., 4905.
John B. C., 4908.
Mary A., 4903.
Sara A., 4901.
REED, Charles, 7561.
Cynthia Amelia, 8782.
Frances Katharine, 8783.
Franklin, 8784.
Harry, 7562.
REESE, Elias, 4031.
Joel, 2046.
Josiah, 4033.
Martin, 4032.
Samuel, 2047.
Simon, 4035.
Susan, 4034.
REEVE, Cecil V., 10751.
Clarence Okley, 10755.
Donald, 10753.
Edna, 10754.
Edwin, 7474.
Frances Lawrence, 7471.
Francis Wayland, 7470.
George Albert, 7469.
Harold A., 10748.
Hazel Catharine, 10764.
James Marion, 7473.
Lawrence Owen, 10756.
Mary G., 10752.
Mary Susan, 7472.
Ralph L., 10749.
Raymond D., 10750.
REIFF, Clarence E., 10210.
Katie, 11942.
REIGLE, Alice C., 5151.
Anna M., 5152.
Arthur H., 5150.
Etta G., 5154.
Frank D., 5153.
Harriet E., 5149.
Henry A., 5155.
Mary A., 5148.
Merrill H., 9344.
Ronald F., 9345.
REILLY, Harrison, 7193.
Lloyd, 7194.
Mary, 7195.
Maud, 7192.
REINDOLLAR, Clarissa Amelia, 10507.
David Henry, 10510.
Edward Eugene, 10509.
Elizabeth Swope, 10505.
Josephine Eugene, 10508.
Mary Henrietta, 10506.
REINHART, Henry, 3879.
Mary, 3878.
Martha, 3880.
REIST, Abraham, 6676.
Elizabeth, 6677.
Frank, 6681.
Jacob, 6679.

Josephine, 4743.
Laura, 8977.
Maria, 4723, 4728, 4742.
Martha, 4729.
Martin, 1625, 4721, 4753.
Martin B., 8952.
Mary, 8957, 9942.
Mary Ann, 4750, 4756, 4758.
Nellie Barr, 8986.
Robert, 9009.
Samuel, 1629, 4748.
Son, 4757, 4761.
Susan, 4748.
Warren, 4749.
Witmer J., 8962.
ROSS, David Herr, 10336.
    Elizabeth, 10338.
    James Spencer, 10337.
ROTE, Ellen, 8840.
    George, 8841.
    Max, 8843.
    William, 8842.
ROTHROCK, Anna Halsey, 12121.
ROWE, Dessie Vey, 10796.
    Francis Neal, 10797.
    Maurice Dayton, 10798.
    Theron Dale, 10799.
ROYER, Anna, 738, 2466.
    Elizabeth, 741, 2462.
    Esther, 740.
    Henry, 736.
    John, 737, 2471.
    Magalena, 739.
    Mary, 742, 2470.
    Rachael, 2467.
    Saloma, 2468.
    Rebecca, 2469.
RUDY, Adelle, 10403.
    Annie, 6780.
    Annie H., 12576.
    Clayton B., 12571.
    Edwin Kauffman, 12780, 12786.
    Elizabeth B., 12569.
    Emma H., 12578.
    Fannie, 11590.
    Fannie Herr, 10375.
    Frederick Oldham, 10376.
    George, 10401, 11592.
    Irwin K., 12781.
    Jacob B., 12573.
    James H., 11600.
    James Herr, 10374.
    James S., 10400.
    John, 6778, 11593.
    John B., 12566.
    John Martin, 12782.
    John Moyer, 12785.
    Kate, 6779.
    Kate B., 10373.
    Katie H., 12577.
    Lavina B., 12572.
    Lee, 11595.
    Lizzie H., 12575.
    M. Ellen, 10372.
    Madora, 6782.
    Margaret, 10591.
    Martha B., 12574.
    Martin B., 12570.
    Mary Ann B., 12568.
    Mary Ellen, 12784.
    Mildred Moyer, 12783.
    Nannie, 11594.
    Norbourne Oldham, 11601.

Phares B., 12567.
Samuel, 6783.
Sarah, 6781.
Susan Jane, 6777.
Taylor, 10402.
Wallace, 11596.
RUSH, Catharine H., 12122.
RUSSELL, Ann Catharine, 4392.
    Anna Witmer, 8793.
    Charles W., 4394.
    Charles Witmer, 8797.
    Chester Arthur, 12702.
    Francis Burg, 4395.
    Florence Leah, 12700.
    George Denison, 8796.
    John Burg, 8794.
    John E., 4393.
    John Edwards, 11343.
    John N., 8791.
    Kate Denison, 8798.
    Laura Merriam, 8792.
    Lucy Edwards, 8795.
    Ralph Cyrus, 12701.
    Richard Herr, 11411.
    Theodore Burg, 11344.
RUTT, Edith, 7637.
    Edna, 7638.
    Ida H., 7636.
RUTTER, Aaron H., 6295.
    Amanda, 6285, 6287.
    Amelia, 6289.
    Amos, 2482.
    Amos G., 6292.
    Amos S., 6276.
    Anna, 2474, 2477, 2490, 2491.
    Anna Elizabeth, 5017.
    Bertha, 10181.
    Bessie M., 10183.
    Catharine, 2480.
    Catharine W., 6296.
    Christian H., 5015.
    Cyrus, 2492.
    Earl, 10182.
    Elias, 6280.
    Elizabeth, 2487, 6283.
    Ella E., 10175.
    Emily Gehr, 10188.
    Emily Louisa, 6290.
    Esther, 2483, 5016.
    Eugene M., 6297.
    Franklin H., 6291.
    Harry H., 6294.
    Hettie A., 6275.
    Isaac, 2489.
    Jacob, 6279.
    Jason E., 6293.
    Jeremiah H., 2484.
    Jerry S., 6282.
    John, 2488.
    John R., 2476.
    John S., 6278.
    Jonathan, 2473.
    Jonathan R., 2481.
    Joseph, 2479, 6277.
    Leah, 2485.
    Lillian May, 6298, 10185.
    Lucinda, 6288.
    Mabel Elizabeth, 10176.
    Martha, 2475.
    Mary, 2478.
    Mary A., 6284.
    Mary Eugenie, 10186.
    Pauline Kathryn, 10187.

Rachael, 2486.
Salome, 6286.
Susanna, 6281.
Viola B., 10184.
RYNEARSON, Catharine Drucella, 11810.
Clarence Jessie, 11811.
Daisy May, 11812.
Wesley Sherman, 11809.
SADTLER, Alice H., 11665.
Ella, 11663.
Frederick B., 11662.
Philip B., 11664.
Samuel S., 11661.
SALMON, Richard T., 11362.
SANDERS, 12623, 12624, 12625, 12626, 12627.
Elmer E., 12735.
Emma, 12728.
Gracie Maria, 12763.
Henry H., 12733.
Levi H., 12734.
Lottie, 12732.
Margaret, 12729.
Mary, 12730.
W. W., 12731.
Walter Willie, 12762.
SAUER, Aldan Mildred, 12667.
Elmer Roy, 12673.
John Earle, 12669.
Lloyd Henry, 12671.
Pearl Louis, 12672.
Ralph Vernon, 12668.
Roy Abraham, 12670.
SCHEETZ, Aaron, 6151.
Abraham, 6145.
Barbara, 2405, 6150.
Catharine, 2407.
Christian, 2400.
Christopher, 6149.
Frederick, 2401.
Henry, 6146.
Henry Marshall, 9957.
Jacob, 2404.
John, 2403.
Kate, 6148.
May Alma, 9958.
Nancy, 2406.
Sarah, 6147.
Sophia, 2402.
SCHEURING, Clarence E., 13006.
George A., 13007.
SCHMECK, Franklin H., 5156.
Herbert, 5158.
John M., 5157.
Mary, 5159.
SCHRIFFLER, Annie Catharine, 5512.
Charles C., 5511.
Florence M., 5514.
Louise H., 5513.
SCHRUM, Mary Ellecta, 11014.
SEACHRIST, Abraham, 2341.
Anna, 2347, 2351.
Christian, 685, 2342.
Marriot Brosius, 7644.
David Herr, 7645.
Elizabeth, 2346, 2354.
Esther, 2348.
Frances, 2344, 2352.
Gladys Evangeline, 9699.
Hazel Bell, 9700.
Jacob, 2343.
John, 686, 2340.
Judith, 2356.
Maria, 688.

Mary, 2345, 2353.
Michael, 687, 2355.
Tobias, 2349.
SEATON, Blanche, 10344.
Eliza, 10345.
Crittenden, 10346.
Curran L., 10347.
Mary, 11569.
SEED, Caroline Alice, 9096.
Edna Barr, 9102.
Homer Willard, 9103.
James Raymond, 9097.
Jennie Mabel, 9101.
May Inez, 9100.
Oscar Vernon, 9098.
Sarah Olena, 9099.
SEIPLE, 11956.
Alton, 8138.
Edwin B., 8137.
J. Waldo, 12031.
Lettie R., 8140.
Morris, 8139.
Rozella E., 8136.
SERFF, Clinton Bright, 11006.
SENSENIG, Isaac F., 11279.
SHAFFER, Claudius, 5423, 5427.
Clayton, 5426.
Edward Leon, 5421.
Frank Oden, 5422.
Martin Luther, 5425.
Paul, 5428.
Charles Clifton, 5420.
Samuel David, 5419.
Theodore Harry, 5424.
SHANES, Elizabeth, 3755.
Joseph, 3754.
Mary A., 3753.
SHANK, Aaron, 12232.
Abraham, 12076.
Amos H., 12237.
Amy Arena, 12720.
Annie, 12077.
Catharine, 12057.
Charles E., 12080.
Clarence E., 12081.
Christian, 12235.
Cora G., 12243.
Daniel, 12236.
David, 12063.
Elizabeth, 12058.
Emma, 12064.
Evarella, 12242.
Fannie R., 12239.
Frederick, 12231.
Harvey E., 12079.
Ida, 12065.
Jacob, 12060.
Martha, 12062, 12078.
Mary, 12059.
Nora, 12233.
Nora May, 12719.
Raymond Edward, 12721.
Rebecca, 12066, 12234.
Samuel, 12061.
Samuel L., 12238.
Son, 12722.
SHANKLIN, Jane Ellen, 10371.
John, 10370.
SHANKS, Eddie S. K., 10461.
Harvey C., 10460.
SHARE, Dorothy, 10585.
Pauline, 10584.

SHARTLE, Daughter, 10146.
    Harold F., 10145.
SHAUB, A. Pauline. 7883.
    Abraham, 353, 1243, 1254, 3672.
    Ada, 7829.
    Albert, 3695.
    Alice, 3707.
    Alice A., 1719.
    Almira, 3720.
    Altha, 3729, 7875.
    Amanda, 3699.
    Anna, 358, 1256, 3719, 3673.
    Annie, 7824.
    Aubrey, 7891.
    Barbara, 357, 1237, 1247, 1259, 1722.
    Benjamin, 3714, 7827.
    Bessie E., 7881.
    Bonnie, 7890.
    Burt E., 3731.
    Catharine, 1261.
    Charles, 7844.
    Christian, 354, 1257, 1720.
    Christiana, 1253.
    Clifford M., 7847.
    Cora, 3718.
    David, 1260.
    Della, 7831.
    Edith Adelaide, 7887.
    Edwin, 3717, 3725.
    Eleanora, 7826.
    Elias, 3674.
    Elam, 3706.
    Eliza A., 3700.
    Elizabeth, 1238, 1245, 1262, 1718, 3668, 3713.
    Ella Etta, 7843.
    Elmer, 3726.
    Elmer Carl, 10991.
    Elmer J., 7840.
    Emma, 3712.
    Enos, 7825.
    Esther C., 7841.
    Ethel A., 7851.
    Etta, 7878.
    Fanny, 356, 3670.
    Florence, 3709.
    Frances, 7828.
    Francis, 3710.
    Frank, 3698.
    Frank Gordon, 10985.
    Franklin, 3704.
    Frederick, 7839.
    George, 3675, 7879.
    George Wendell, 7872.
    Gertrude Helen, 7848.
    Glenn Albert, 10990.
    Grace Marion, 7873.
    Harold Glynn, 7888.
    Hattie L., 7833.
    Hattie S., 7870.
    Henry, 351, 1239, 1249, 1264, 3671, 3702.
    Hettie, 3667.
    Howard, 7889.
    Ida E., 3727.
    Isaac, 1252.
    Jacob, 1244, 1246, 1251, 3666, 3694.
    James I., 7869.
    James M., 3724.
    Jennie, 7876.
    Jerome, 3701.
    Jessie Franklin, 7834.
    John, 352, 1248, 1255, 1723, 3703.

    John M., 3691.
    L. Josephine, 7880.
    Lemath, 3721.
    Lettie, 7830.
    Lew C., 7838.
    Lewis Edwin, ~874.
    Lizzie, 3692.
    Lizzie L., 7823.
    Lola Florence, 7849.
    Lucy, 7877.
    Luna, 3728.
    Lura, 3708.
    Mabel E., 10980.
    Martha, 1236, 1263, 1724.
    Martha A., 3711.
    Martin, 355, 1240, 1250, 1265.
    Martin L., 3697.
    Mary, 1258, 1721, 3665, 3677.
    Mary C., 3715.
    Mary Cornelia, 7832.
    Milton B., 3732.
    Monroe Emerson, 7850.
    Myrtle E., 10981.
    Myrtle H., 11210.
    Olive, 3730.
    Orren P., 3705.
    Roland J., 3722.
    Ruth M., 7882.
    Samuel, 1241, 3676.
    Sarah, 3693.
    Susan, 1242, 3669.
    Susanna, 3696.
    Theresa A., 3723.
    Tina, 7846.
    Virgie Almira, 7871.
    Walter J., 7842.
    Wesley, 3716.
    William, 7845.
SHAW, Edwin, 6726.
    Frances, 6725.
    Harry, 6728.
    Mary J., 6724.
    William, 6727.
SHEAFFER, 9319.
    B. Richard, 12204.
    C. Harold, 12203.
    Caroline, 10191.
    Cora, 10189.
    Donald, 11432.
    Emma A., 11429.
    Harold, 11430.
    Isabel, 11431.
    Lewis, 11433.
    Martin, 6299, 10190.
    Monroe W., 9317.
    Rebecca J., 9318.
    William James, 9316.
SHEARER, Amos, 12563.
    Cassie, 12564.
    Daniel, 12565.
SHEETS, Volney C., 5716.
SHELLENBERGER, Rudolph, 10249.
SHELLEY, Annie E., 7052.
    Anna Margaretta, 5672.
    David, 2808.
    Edith, 5669.
    Ethel, 10174.
    Gertrude May, 5668.
    Ivan, 10172.
    Jay Warren, 5671.
    Mary Dull, 5670.
    Penrose Herr, 5673.

Clyde F., 13152.
Cyrus B., 13066.
Cyrus E., 13149.
Daniel M., 13150.
David Allen, 13142.
David L., 13072.
Effie M., 13074.
Ella, 13065.
Esther V., 13139.
Ethel Marie, 13147.
Eugene, 13071.
Fanny B., 13075.
George F. F., 13073.
Levi E., 13070.
Lydia Ann, 13068.
Nancy, 13067.
Ralph C., 13141.
Raymond, F., 13140.
Russell L., 13151.
Samuel M., 13069.
SINKS, Edwin C., 10318.
Walter H., 10319.
SKEEN, Adam A., 8187.
Charles Earl, 8180.
Ella Florence, 8184.
Frank, 8185.
Harry, 8186.
Ida May, 8177.
Lucy Blanche, 8179.
Maud Estella, 8184.
Nora Lillian, 8181.
Son, 8178.
William Ross, 8182.
SKINNER, Clara Bell. 9973.
Ivan, 9974.
SLAYBAUGH, Annie Elizabeth, 11996.
Harry Elmer, 11997.
Hattie Alverta, 11998.
SLENTZ, Charles Jacob, 2763.
Eliza Margaret, 2762.
Franklin C., 2765.
Ida B., 2757.
John Edward, 2760.
Julia Katie, 2758.
Mary G., 2756.
Sarah J., 2759.
Luther M., 2764.
William H., 2761.
SMITH, Abraham Herr, 1005.
Albert C., 5231.
Amy, 11748.
Catharine, 2962.
Charles, 11746.
Daniel Sherman, 5227.
David, 2960.
Earl, 11751.
Eliza E., 1006.
Edgar Kreider, 5228.
Edward, 11750.
Elizabeth L., 11546.
Frank L., 11547.
George, 11745.
Glenna Mary, 12579.
Grace Elizabeth, 9607.
Ida Elizabeth, 5229.
John, 2961.
John Herr, 12580.
John Somerfield, 5230.
Lulu, 11747.
Martha Louisa, 9510.
Mildred E., 11824.
Owen, 11749.

Sarah, 2963.
Ward, Le Roy, 11170.
SNAVELY, Alonzo S., 6880.
Amos H., 7626.
Ann 1152, 3504.
Anna H., 10835.
Arthur R., 6879.
Arthur K., 6879.
B. Frank, 7627.
Barbara, 6064.
Benjamin, 1148.
Benjamin H., 3506.
Caroline, 6073, 6881.
David H., 6065.
David Herr, 9933.
Elam Herr, 8505.
Eliza, 1149, 6063.
Elizabeth H., 7623.
Ella H., 9513.
Ella Naomi, 7228.
Fanny, 6066.
Frances, 1150.
Frank S., 13179.
George, 6071.
Glenna, 9931.
Harry H., 7624.
Helen H., 9514.
Henry, 6068.
Ida Frances, 7625.
Jacob, 6072.
Jessie, 13184.
Lottie, 13185.
Magdalene, 6069.
Maria, 1151.
Mary, 9930.
Mary Susan, 6070.
Nellie A., 13178.
Olan C., 6878.
Ollie, 6877.
Rohrer, 8981.
Rosalia H., 9512.
Stephen, 6067.
Stoner, 8982.
Thomas, 9932.
SNEARLY, Esther Anna, 9357.
Emanuel, 1976.
Mary Elma, 9356.
Esther Ann, 1973.
Mary M., 1974.
Sarah, 1975.
SNEATH, Elias Hershey, 11960.
Emma Eugenia, 11961.
George Mark, 11962.
Herbert Camp, 11364.
Isaiah, 11959.
Katharine Williams, 11365.
Richard Sheldon, 11366.
SNYDER, Abraham, 5386.
Alice, 5389.
Anna, 5388.
Anna M., 13163.
Bernice, 13186.
Christian, 6729.
Cletus, 13183.
Daniel Elbert, 13164.
Edgar, 12149.
E. Lizzie Hostetter, 6731.
Elizabeth, 5387.
Harvey, 6730.
Henry H., 5384.
John, 5385.
Mary Edith, 13165.

Charles Franklin, 4589.
Cyrus Neff, 4593.
Delia Barr, 4588.
Forest Neff, 4591.
Frances Minerva, 4592.
Harriet Seymour, 4587.
Joseph Julian, 4597.
John Neff, 4586.
Letitia Barr, 4594.
Mary Elizabeth, 4585.
Samuel Seymour, 4590.
Susanna Ethel, 4598.
STIRK, Alice Elma, 7024.
Archie Robert, 7023.
Floyd Herr, 7025.
Charles Edward, 10642.
Martha Elizabeth, 10644.
Miriam Amelia, 10643.
Levi Acker, 7022.
STIVELY, Abraham L., 3661.
Elizabeth, 3662.
Fanny, 3658.
Frederick, 3659.
Jacob, 3657.
John, ;663.
Mary, 3660.
Mary Herr, 7822.
STONE, Amanda Elmira, 7912.
Dora Franciscus, 7913.
Dorothy, 11013.
Hannah Rebecca, 7909.
Henry Brower, 7914.
John Clinger, 7916.
Laura Lucinda, 7915.
Lloyd Henry, 11011.
May Alberta, 11012.
Mary Ellestra, 7911.
Myrtle May, 11016.
Oliver Abraham, 7910.
Walter Gray, 11015.
William Arthur, 11005.
STONER, Anderson, 1046.
Annie E., 7530.
Bessie Mame, 5508.
Elizabeth, 1048.
Frances Ann, 7529.
Frances E., 10979.
George Wilson, 5510.
Hannah, 1045.
Harry S., 10978.
Catharine Isabelle, 5509.
Mary Ann, 1047.
Susan Jane, 1050.
Thomas, 1049.
STORM, Estelle Blandel, 5467.
Rosalia Adelia, 5010.
Samuel M., 5468.
Willie Heckroth, 5466.
STOVER, Ethel Virginia, 11509.
Charles Franklin, 9813.
Edward Pilson, 9814.
Raymond Beverly, 11510.
William Miller, 9812.
STRATTON, John Frantz, 11814.
STRICKLER, Albert, 6320.
Ambrose B., 9652.
Barbara A., 12411.
Barbara Mae, 12473.
Clara. 12477.
Cora, 12475.
Emerson H., 9651.
Emma G., 12410.
Fannie N., 9653.

Franklin H., 12408.
Harry J., 8938.
Jacob, 12476.
Jacob Edwin, 12406.
Mary G., 12409.
Ruth, 12474.
Samuel H., 12407.
STRITE, 2594, 2595, 2596, 2607, 2608, 2609, 10209.
Abraham, 785, 2617.
Abraham C., 6429.
Albert, 10207.
- Andrew C., 6448.
Ann Malinda, 6444.
Anna, 2611.
Benjamin, 6428.
Carrie M., 12098.
Catharine, 2603, 2619.
Charles, 12090.
Charlotte, 11557.
Chester, 12099.
Christian, 787, 2623.
Clarence E., 6437.
Clinton, 6424.
Cora M., 6438.
D. Frank, 12091.
Daniel, 2605.
Daniel D., 6439.
David, 2597.
David G., 6419.
Earl, 10213.
Edwin D., 10206.
Elizabeth, 2600, 2616.
Elizabeth C., 6418.
Ellsworth, 11556.
Emma, 12094.
Emma K., 6433.
Emma S., 6422.
Franklin M., 6420.
Harvey, 6426.
Henry, 2612, 6423.
Henry L., 6446.
Ida C., 6421.
Ida M., 10211.
Ira, 12093.
Irwin S., 10212.
Jacob, 2601.
Jacob A., 6430.
John, 786, 2599, 2610, 2621.
John A., 6417.
John C., 6434, 12095.
John F., 6427.
Joseph, 790, 2618.
Josephine, 10202.
Lewis, 10214.
Lizzie, 12096.
Louis E. McC., 6435.
Margaret Adelaide, 12182.
Maria Elizabeth, 6445.
Martha, 2602, 2620.
Martha A., 6447.
Martha L., 6416.
Mary, 2606, 2622, 12092.
Mary Ann, 6415.
Mary E., 6432.
Melchor E., 12089.
Milton, 12100.
Nancy, 789, 2598.
Robert, 10208.
Russell, 11558.
Samuel, 788, 2604, 6425, 10203.
Samuel M., 6431.

31

Laura Irene, 13210.
Lillie Fenley, 11621.
Majorie Alexander, 13218.
Mary Arminda, 11618.
Mary Elizabeth, 13211.
Mary Virginia, 13213.
Rebecca Allison, 11620 .
Robert Augustus, 13207.
Ruth Eliza, 11624.
Sara Elizabeth, 11619.
Stanley Abbott. 11615.
Susan, 13205.
Susan Baird, 13216.
William Banks, 13214.
William Henry, 13204.
THOMPSON, Benjamin Franklin, 5572, 9642.
Caroline Elizabeth, 9638.
Clinton Thomas, 9610.
Clyde Jacob, 9641.
Dwight Newell, 9645.
Elizabeth B., 5568.
Emma Louise, 9612.
Hannah Frances, 5566.
Helen Catharine, 9611.
Herbert Leroy, 9644.
Mabel Cynthia, 9639.
Randolph Hyatt, 9609.
Robert Burke, 5573.
Robert Leroy, 9640.
Russell Wilford, 9643.
Sarah Ann, 5569.
Ulysses S. Grant, 5570.
Wilford Downs, 5567.
William Sherman, 5571.
TINGES, George Herbert, 11669.
Ida V., 11668.
Kate White, 11667.
Mary Howard, 11666.
TOLMAN, Leroy Scott, 11542.
TOWNSEND, Bessie M., 10801.
Dee Evaline, 10800.
TREICHLER, Abraham B., 9353.
Charles F., 9346.
Claude L., 9350.
Edna A., 9352.
Eli Julian, 5144.
Elma A., 5147.
Elma Maude, 9351.
Gaylen Mark, 11443.
Harriet Malissa, 9360.
Hazel M., 9353.
Henry B., 5146.
Henry J., 9354.
Laura Irene, 9361.
Leora Rose, 11442.
Lorin W., 9348.
Mary L., 9347.
Malissa J., 5145.
Merwyn Willis, 9358.
Victor Leo, 9359.
Wilber E., 9349.
TROUT, Ada Louisa. 11148.
Amos Theodore, 8248.
Anna E., 11156.
Annie Elizabeth, 8245.
Beulah May, 11161.
Cora Elizabeth, 11147.
Elam Bowman, 8244.
Elmer Jacob, 8249.
Elva E., 11142.
Emma Susanna, 8243.
Enos F., 11155.
Esther H., 11158.

Florence H., 11153.
Franklin John, 8247.
Harry D., 11725.
Harry David, 11145.
Henry Free, 8246.
Infant, 5295, 5296.
John Henry, 11157.
TROUT, Mark H., 11159.
Maud Ethel, 11162.
Naomi H., 11160.
Paul Henry, 11163.
Park Hess, 11146.
Walter H., 11154.
TRUMP, Adda Larue, 5452.
Emma Estelle, 5453.
Francis Herr, 5454.
George Herbert, 5451.
Lizzie Ober, 5455.
Ober Herr, 5456.
TSHUDY, Ada Ann, 8198.
Benjamin F., 8197.
Blanche, 8202.
Catharine Ellen, 8201.
Celia Sarah, 8200.
George W., 8196.
Harry Milton, 8199.
Hiram, 4036.
John, 6637.
TUCKER, Ida, 10421.
Sarah, 10422.
TURNER, William Baker, 11477.
UHLER, Alfred H., 6861.
Caroline B., 6862.
Edward C., 6858.
Effie P., 6864.
Elizabeth M., 6863.
Mary Ellen, 6860.
William Levi, 6859.
ULMER, Allen Edgar, 10586.
Lester, 10587.
ULRICH, Cattie Mae, 12688.
Cola Alvin, 12690.
Edna Rebecca, 12687.
Fern Marguerite, 12693.
Floyd Hylas. 12692.
Mina Permilla, 12689.
Vida Schel, 12686.
Wilford Joseph, 12691.
UPLINGER, Harvey, 13048.
URBAN, Delilah, 3930.
Harriet, 3931.
Hiram, 3932.
Mattie, 3933.
VAN EMAN, Frances May, 11479.
VANOUSDALL, Ann Maria, 7346.
David, 7343.
Elizabeth, 7354.
Henry, 7353.
Henry H., 7347.
Isaac, 7352.
John, 7351.
Lillie May, 7355.
Maria, 7350.
Martin, 7344.
Mary Frances, 7349.
Peter, 7342.
Rachael, 7345.
Susetta P., 4748.
VAUGHAN, Daniel Waite, 11564.
Margaret Ann, 11565.
VAUGHN, Veda Beryl, 11782.
VENNUM, Arthur, 7854.

Laura, 7218.
Letitia, 6317.
Levi, 5502.
Lillian Maria, 12279.
Louella Blanche, 12274.
Martin, 5900, 13079.
Martin Herr, 5025.
Mary, 5901, 6318, 13081.
Mary E., 5027.
Morris, 6314.
Nancy, 58899, 13078.
Salome, 9203.
Samuel, 13082.
WENTWORTH, Albert L., 11549.
    Nellie L., 11548.
WESTENBERGER, Mary Grace, 9698.
WIGGINS, Angeline, 11771.
    Augusta, 4818.
    Benjamin, 11761.
    Bertha, 12831.
    Charles M., 9094.
    Christian G., 4812.
    Clayton, 11763.
    Cora Bell, 8203.
    David, 11760.
    Delbert S., 9095.
    Edna M., 9093.
    Elias, 11768.
    Elizabeth, 12835.
    Ella, 12832.
    Ellen, 11766.
    Elmer J., 12836.
    Enos, 12834.
    H. G., 12830.
    Hannah C., 11764.
    Harriet, 11767.
    Harry, 11770.
    Howard R., 9092.
    James Beaver, 8205.
    John, 11762.
    Joseph B., 4811.
    Justus B., 12833.
    Leonard H., 4813.
    Margaret, 4816.
    Martha, 11769.
    Mary Alice, 8206.
    Mary Ann, 11765.
    Miriam Irene, 8204.
    Samuel, 11759.
    Sarah, 4814.
    Susan, 4815.
    William, 4817.
WIGHT, Elizabeth Groff, 9873.
WIKER, Charles, 7695.
    Jacob, 7696.
WILLERS, Anna Gevina, 4373.
    Calvin, 4380.
    Calvina, 8790.
    Caroline Lydia, 4379.
    Diedrich, 4378.
    Diedrich K., 8789.
    Emma, 4375.
    Frances, 4376.
    Margaret Amelia, 4374.
    Theodore, 4377.
WILLIAMS, Anna Flora, 3307.
    Christiana, 3944.
    David Alexander, 7200.
    Rachael, 3948.
    Esther, 3946.
    Ira J., 3310.
    Ira Jewell, 7199.
    Jessie H., 3309.

Mary, 3947.
Elias, 3949.
Samuel, 3945.
Stewart Herr, 3308.
WILLIAMSON, Harriet, 2078.
    Samuel, 2077.
WILSON, Amanda, 2006.
    Ada, 8825.
    Ann Eliza, 2058.
    Caroline, 4419.
    Catharine, 1517.
    Charles, 2057.
    Charlotte E., 2010.
    Christian David, 4425.
    Cornelia Gray, 5505.
    Daniel E., 4422.
    Edmund, 5507.
    Edmund F., 2005.
    Edward, 2056.
    Eliza, 4417.
    Elizabeth, 1510.
    Ellsworth C., 9374.
    Evelyn Ada, 9378.
    Florence Theresa, 5504.
    Fanny, 1508.
    Frances F., 5506.
    Francis, 9376.
    George, 1511.
    George Hartman, 4420.
    George Leidy, 2007.
    Gertrude Givens, 9289.
    Harriet Ann, 4423.
    Harry, 8824, 9377.
    Helen Elizabeth, 5503.
    Ira, 2059.
    Iva Ellen, 9286.
    Jesse, 1516.
    John, 1513.
    Marion Porter, 9288.
    Matilda, 4418.
    Mark, 1512.
    Mark L., 4424.
    Martin H., 2009.
    Mary, 1509.
    Mildred, 9375.
    Naomi Jane, 9287.
    Neil A., 9373.
    Rebecca, 2060.
    Samuel, 1515.
    Samuel Ellis, 4421.
    Samuel Gray, 5502.
    Sarah, 1514.
    Sarah C., 2008.
WINE, Elizabeth Buehler, 11660.
    Louis D. J., 11659.
WINGET, Alma, 9600.
    Lewis Earl, 9599.
WINTERODE, 9991.
    Amanda Elizabeth, 6163.
    Amelia Florence, 6168.
    Anna Mary, 6161.
    Charlotte Ann, 6167.
    Daisy Maria, 9975.
    Flora Belle V., 6166.
    George Carroll, 6164.
    Henry Michael, 6162.
    Jacob Frick, 6160.
    John Luther, 6159.
    Levi Preston, 6169.
    Louis Levi, 9989.
    Lucy, 9976.
    Robert Preston, 9988.

William Rufus, 6165.
Williametta, 9990.
WIRTH, Adam William, 13023.
 Catharine, 13021.
 Charles, 13019.
 Eli, 13019.
 Infant, 13020, 13026.
 John, 13018.
 Leah Janette C., 13017.
 Mary Elizabeth, 13024.
 Philip Henry, 13024.
WISSLER, Arthur, 10263.
 Benjamin, F., 6498.
 Carl A.. 10265.
 Carrie, 10258.
 Christian P., 6499.
 Clark D., 10257.
 Cora, 10259.
 Elizabeth, 10261.
 Emory, 10260.
 Frank, 10262.
 Jacob L., 6501.
 John R., 6500.
 Lawrence O., 10264.
 Mary Viola, 12151.
 Stanley, 12150.
 William H., 6502.
WITHERS, Ann, 1200.
 Ann Elizabeth, 3618.
 Anna E., 3612.
 Catharine, 1198.
 Catharine J., 3619.
 Clara A., 3608.
 George, 1201.
 George W., 3616.
 Louisa W., 3611.
 M. Augustus, 3609.
 Mae Reinstine, 7760.
 Mary, 7755.
 Mary Jane, 3610.
 Michael, 1199.
 Michael M., 3615.
 Howard H., 3617.
WITMAN, Herman E., 12500.
 John H., 12496.
WITMER, Abraham, 420, 1017, 3207, 3210,
  7214, 11788.
 Abraham L., 3234.
 Alice V., 3239.
 Alonzo Potter, 3410.
 Amelia, 9801.
 Amos, 1827.
 Amos Lightner, 7311.
 Ann Catharine, 1493.
 Ann Elizabeth, 1807, 5028.
 Anna, 1789, 3215.
 Anna B., 9805.
 Anna E., 11209.
 Anna Eliza. 8753.
 Anna Elizabeth, 7109.
 Anna M., 4684.
 Anna R., 3228.
 Arthur G., 11208.
 Ava Ray, 9554.
 B. Franklin, 4683.
 Barbara, 3221.
 Barbara Esther, 8219.
 Benjamin, 1788, 1826, 11784.
 Benjamin Henry, 1810.
 Bernice Ruth, 9557.
 Betsey, 505.
 Catharine, 506, 11787.
 Catharine A., 3231.

Charles, 5092.
Charles B. Herr, 7302.
Chester Z., 9553.
Christian, 3216, 7217.
Christian Cotton, 7108.
Christian F., 3227.
Christian H., 1015, 7096.
Christiana, 1808.
Clair H., 11206.
Clara F., 3238.
D. Herr, 1835.
Daniel, 546, 1786.
Daughter, 3212, 3219.
David, 504, 1018, 3223, 9803.
David Paul, 9556.
Edgar Louis, 7115.
Edith M., 7094.
Elam, 7215, 9498.
Elbertha Catharine, 7301.
Eleanor Chittenden, 12602.
Elias, 1022, 1804, 11786.
Elizabeth, 421; 1790, 11785.
Elizabeth M., 3205.
Ellen, 3233.
Elmer J., 8372.
Elvira M., 3230.
Emily Ann, 3235.
Emma A., 7093.
Esther, 489, 1020, 1787, 1805, 3217.
Esther Ann, 1825.
Esther Elizabeth, 3226.
Esther M., 8374.
Evalina Juliet, 3413.
Evelyn Jessie, 7303.
Ezra H., 3407.
Fanny, 3218.
Fanny M., 7092.
Fannie Maria, 3209.
Florence E., 9555.
Frances M., 1023.
Frank, 5093.
Frank A., 8373.
Franklin, 1828.
Franklin Elmer, 7213.
George, 1833.
Gertrude Emma, 7309.
Grace, 7105.
Grace A., 7097.
Harriet, 3222.
Harry Herr, 4682.
Henry Clay, 11790.
Henry H., 3401.
Hettie, 7216.
Howard B., 7098.
Ida May, 8370.
Ira David, 3408.
Jacob, 3206, 11789.
Jacob Herr, 8371.
Jessie Amanda, 3414.
John, 419, 501, 557, 1809, 1830, **5091.**
John Alfred, 8752.
John Amos, 7304.
John G., 9552.
John H., 1791.
John Martin, 5030.
John Mann, 3208.
John Tobias, 7114.
Joseph, 1019.
Joseph F., 3236.
Judith W., 1792.
Julia, 1811.
Julia A., 7095.
Juliana, 1495.

Wesley, 12793.
William, 12789.
Willis, 12797.
ZITTLE, Cyrus, 3778.
Daniel, 3777.
Ella, 10960.
Elmer, 10958.
Hettie, 3780.
Ida May, 10961.
Jacob Franklin, 3779.

Laura, 10959.
Susanna, 3776.
ZOOK, Clayton Ephraim, 9710.
Daniel, 9712.
Edith Estella, 9713.
Edwin, 9711.
Emma May, 9717.
Leroy, 9714.
Mary, 9716.
Samuel, 9715.

ADDENDA

Data and corrections entered since Record went to press.

15 follows 51.
41. m. Oct. 21, 1722.
65. Catharine Eyerman.
113. Abraham Witmer (Bridge).
238. b. Nov. 18, 1744; d. Dec. 20, 1819; m. Fannie Eshleman.
240. Omit b. 1744; d. 1819.
278. David,
301. d. Oct. 5, 1801.
302. Elizabeth Smith Sarver,
303. Charlotte Sease.
452. Dayton, O.
660. Va. not Pa.
721. d. Feb. 3, 1885; m. May 1, 1828, Catharine D. Miller, b. Oct. 22, 1810; d. Mar. 14, 1885.
800. d. Mar. 31.
827. Lisburn, Pa.
828. Dillsburg, Pa.
829. Mechanicsburg, Pa.
830. Allen, Pa.
831. Allen, Pa.
845. Elizabeth, m. John H. Shirick.
860. Magdalene H. Landis.
867. East Petersburg, Pa.
870. Anna K., b. Oct. 9, 1831, son John Esbach and Elizabeth Shenk.
871. Millersville, Pa.
873. Osborn, O.
1011. Lancaster, Pa.
1067. Kelly Station, Pa.
1179. Hage, son Jans Friedenreich Hage and Giertrude Heitmann.
1317. dau Christian Eyman.
1333. John P. Smithville, O., b. Sep. 10, 1815; d. July 5, 1889; m. Mary Meck, b. Nov. 10, 1823; d. 1899; dau. George Meck and Martha Neuding.
1597. Samuel instead of Sener.
1820. John Q.
2167. d. May 27, 1905; m. Oct. 18, 18—.
2169. Wien,
2797. b. June 2, 1849; Elizabeth Weaver.
2924. Mary Josephine.
3055. m. Nov. 4, 1873, Elizabeth G. Charles, b. Mar. 4, 1855, dau. Abraham Charles and Elizabeth Good.
4079. d. 1905.
4255. d. Oct. 30.
4258. b. July 7.
4513. d. Feb. 12, 1888; m. Allison Eldridge.
4516. m. James M. Fisher.
4517. John Franklin, d. Dec. 27, 1866.
4519. m. Robert P. Fisher.
4520. m. John Wilson.
4522. m. Eudora I. Fisher.
4523. Alfaretta; m. Arta M. Seeley.
4542. Katie to Catharine.
4545. m. David Reid.
4546. m. Edward Stowell.
4550. m. Andrew Stevens.
4552. Madren to Madsen.
4553. O. to Oliver.
4583. m. J. Stokes.

4585. m. Ross Porter.
4587. m. Eli Curtis.
4588. m. John B. Flagg.
4589. m. Marion B. Neff.
4590. m. Selina Osguthorpe.
4591. m. Elizabeth Ellis.
4592. m. Andrew H. Bagley.
4593. m. Elisa Heppler.
4594. m. Joseph H. Moss.
4598. m. Albert Wagstaff.
4644. Dr. Henry Elmer.
4647. Dr. Park Potts, m. June 30, 1908, wid. Mildred Eckert Sutton, dau. George Sutton.
4694. Samuel, not Sener.
4888. Dr. Francis Martin,
4895. Samuel Millo Herr.
4910. Martha Ann, m. Nov. 22, 1856; Peter Wenger, b. Oct. 1, 1830.
5010 follows 5468.
5018. J. Henry.
5022. m. June, 1877.
5023. Benjamin Frank.
5024. d. Nov. —, 1905
5186. Mary E. Stermer and Daniel Stermer.
5209. Oct. 19, 1884.
5472. Lillian Keltz.
5533. Sept.   1859.
5765. m. Jacob Homsher.
5766. Jesse, m. Emma Miller.
5767. m. Mary Shaub.
5770. m. Amanda Bowman.
6064. b. 1842; d. 1879; m. David Miller, b. 1844; d. 1884.
6065. b. Sept. 17, 1856.
6066. Fanny, b. 1847; m. Eugene Marsh.
6067. Stephen S., b. 1849; m. Anna McLain.
6068. Henry C., b. Sept. 2, 1852; d. July 18, 1873.
6069. Magdalene R., b. Oct. 2, 1866; m. David Erter.
6070. b. 1854; d. 1874.
6071. George W., b. May 15, 1860; d. July 8, 1908; m. Lilla Brannan.
6072. Jacob, b. 1839; d. 1844.
6073. Caroline S., b. Nov. 1, 1862; d. July 11, 1890.
6191. Mary Magdalena, m. June 13, 1861.
6243. Dr. Jacob Miller,
6748. d. Nov. 8, 1907.
6749. d. Nov. 15, 1855; m. Roland Whitney, b. Mar. 20, 1817; d. Aug. 7, 1896, son Jacob Whitney and Maria.
6750. b. June 21, 1823; m. Martha A. Glover.
6943. b. Mar. 23, 1870.
6983. Christian D., m. Jan. 26, 1891; Eva Gertrude Sterns, b. Dec. 21, 1871, dau. Calvin Sterns and Frances ———.
7006. May L., Leibold, d. Aug. 9, 1903.
7183. Mother's name is McCormick.
7687. C. R. to Commodore Rogers.
7766. Charlotte Alexander.
7767. S——— D. to Stephen Douglas.

7768. m. April 18, 1901; b. Feb. 19, 1867; son David Hooley and Fannie Hertzler.
8121. Nov. to Dec.
8136. Jan. 11 to Jan. 9.
8137. Nov. 28 to 29.
8141. Oct. to Nov.
8276. Feb. 18, 1879 to Mar. 14, 1880.
8248. July 16 to July 15.
8300. Nov. 21 to Nov. 20.
8305. Artesia, N. Mex.
8388. Lancaster, Pa., d. July 11, 1908.
8397. Lexington, Ky.
8398. Lexington, Ky.
8399. Lexington, Ky., m. Dec. 25, 1876; dau. Jane Biggers.
8426. S. to L.
8774. 2d; m. Nov. 17, 1874.
8775. m. Oct. 1, 1874; son Hon. John Dickey and Elvira Walker Adams.
8776. d. Nov. 3, 1901; m. June 16, 1892. dau. Samuel Mullan and Mary Adair.
9187. M. to Mills.
9482. m. Nov. 26, 1903, John K. Kreider, b. Dec. 2, 1878; son Andrew Kreider.
9483. Alice E.
9484. Henry to Harvey E.
9485. m. Oct. 17, 1907, Ada H. Risser, b. April 23, 1887; dau. Jacob O. Risser.
12318 follows 9485. Samuel E., Mt. Joy, Pa., d. Feb. 4, 1899.
11815 follows 9527. McManus to New Orleans.
9570. b. July 22, 1890, mother's name Lillian Keltz.
9828. m. Mar. 12, 1902, Hannah E. Kingery; dau. David A. Kingery and Mary Hoff.
9921. Neffsville to Lititz.
9925. C—— to Christian.
9962. S. to Sechrist.
9963. H. to Hershey.
9966. M. to N., father's name John J. Frick.
9967. Alice M.
9968. John Arthur, m. ——, 1908, Ruth Linderman.
9969. Carroll, Louisa to Louise.
9973. m. ——, 1904, Harry DeHoff.
9974. m. ——, 1906, Henrietta Lenz.
12315 follows 9979.
9989. b. Dec. 12, 1875; m. Mar. 15, 1900, Catharine Sehringer.
9990. Waterloo, Ia., b. Jan. 24, 1882; m. William G. Bussler.
9991. Bertha Augusta, Waterloo, Iowa, b. Sep. 13, 1877; d. Mar. 4, 1890.
10125. m. Aug. 9, 1895, Aaron R. Shearer, b. Sept. 11, 1872; son Abram S. Shearer and Emma ——.
10127. m. Feb. 26, 1905, Phares Baker, b. Feb. 18, 1885; son Samuel Baker and Sara
10132. Adalide to Adalaide.
10211. Ida to Ada.
12467 follows 10243.
10354. E. to Estep and A. to Armstead.
10355. Cora Sutcliffe, A. to Augustus.
10360. John Floyd, Hot Springs, S. Dak.
10361. d. ——, 1900; m. Wilfred Brown.
10363. Ellis. Kas., m. Frank Atwood.
10372. M. Ellen, b. Nov. 18, 1837; m. Alvin Wood, b. Nov. 31, 1831; d. Feb. 7, 1891; son Dr. Peter Wood and Anna Long.
10498. Son Dr. Thomas Wells and —— Lamotte.
11178. m. Oct. 29, 1907, Nora H. Breneman, b. Sept. 15, 1883; dau. Dr. Henry F. Breneman and Harriet Heidler.

11179. m. Sept. 29, 1904, Cora M. Warfel, b. Nov. 17, 1884; dau. Simon Warfel and Hannah Bowers.
11964 follows 11427.
11457. Marion Louise, La Salle, N. Y., b. July 14, 1891.
11458. Edna Margaret, Buffalo, N. Y., b. Feb. 24, 1893.
11459. Buffalo, N. Y., b. July 29, 1894.
11460. Buffalo, N. Y., b. Sept. 4, 1885.
11575. b. July 12, 1867, son Eben O. and Margarett E.
11684. Westminster to Baltimore, Md.
11686. Westminster to Pittsburg, Pa., m. ——, Bird.
11687. Westminster to Wayne, Mich.
11688. Westminster to Chicago, Ill., m. ——, O'Brien.
11689. Westminster to Wayne, Mich.
11691. Westminster to Kansas City, Mo.
11692. Westminster to Jacksonville, Fla., m. Margarete O'Brien.
11693. Westminster to Detroit Mich.
11736. M. to Mildred, b. April 10, 1882; dau. Alexander W. McGregor and India Johnson.
11742. LaVerne.
11837. b. Jan. 13, 1837; change Grugon to Guyon, m. April 25, 1866; b. June 6, 1848; d. Mar. 9, 1895; dau. Henry C. Guyon and Mary Edsall.
11838. b. Nov. 19, 1817; d. Nov. 17, 1885.
11848. —— to Susan, dau. Andrew Sides and Fanny Herr, mother Susan Sides.
11854. —— to Catharine, dau. Benjamin Keen and Rachel Aulthouse.
11878. Reid, Md., to Kauffman, Pa., M. to Myrtle.
11879. Reid, Md. to Wingerton, Pa.
11943. 1892 to 1893.
11944. 1895 to 1896; after 11987, father is Harry F. Gundrum.
11950. Mar. to Nov.
12034. 1893 to 1892.
12035. m. Nov. 25, 1904; Isaac H., b. Nov. 6, 1885; son Isaac Buckwalter and ——.
12036. m. Nov. 28, 1901.
12351. Add 14 to July; dau. David Hofstedler and Katharine Lichty.
12354. 4 to 24, change —— to 24.
12929. Dec. to Mar. 17, 1843.
12974. Hurst to Horst, dau. Levi Horst and Sarah Rohlan.
12978. John H., Lapel, Ind., b. Mar. 31, 1840; m. Dec. 30, 1868, Charlotte Miller, b. Sept. 15, 1852; d. May 9, 1879; m. Mary E. Setters, b. April 17, 1864.
12979. Katharine, m. Thomas Rambo.
12980. Elizabeth, Noblesville, Md., m; Evert Craig.
12981. Christian, b. April 18, 1850; m. Mar. 2, 1892, Prudence Martin.
12982. Daniel, m. Clara Heiney.
12983. Martin, V. B.
12993. —— to Daniel, b. May 19, 1850, d. Sept. 30, 1850.
13012. —— to infant, b. Nov. 5, 1895; d. Nov. 5, 1895.
13013. —— to infant, b. Nov. 5, 1895; d. Nov. 5, 1895.
13014. —— to infant, b. Jan. 8, 1898; d. Jan. 8, 1898.
13066. Maria to Marian.

APPENDIX

Genealogical Record of Hans Herr (Father of Rev. Hans Herr), born A. D. 1608, and his Lineal Descendants, except those of Rev Hans Herr.

Family of HANS HERR (H1) born 1608 and ———.

A1. Abraham.

1. Rev. Hans, Lampeter, Pa., b. Sept. 17, 1739; d. ——— 1725; m. ——— 1660, Elizabeth Kendig, b. ——— 1644; d. ———1730, dau. John Kendig and Jane Mylin.

J1. Jacob, Switzerland.

C1. Christian, Mursbach, Baden, Ger.; d. ——— 1728; m. ——— Salome Haas; dau. Isaac Haas and ———.

B1. Benjamin, Zatsche Baden, Ger., m. ——— Salome Haas.

Family of CHRISTIAN HERR (C1) and ———.

C2. Simon, Ostevwarden, m. ——— 1671; Magdalena Haas, dau. Isaac Haas and Christiana Roeder.

Family of SIMON HERR (C2) and MAGDALENA HAAS.

C3. Christian, Musbach, Baden, Ger., m. ——— 1728, Salome Haas, dau. Jacob Haas and Caroline Vetter.

Family of CHRISTIAN HERR (C3) and SALOME HAAS.

C4. Simon, Musbach, Baden, Ger., b. Oct. 4, 1741; m. Oct. 4, 1771, Salome Haas, dau. Fritz Haas and Anna Anderly.

Family of SIMON HERR (C4) and SALOME HERR.

C5. Simon, Baden, Ger., b. Sept. 3, 1773; d. Oct. 24, 1845; m. June 1, 1802, Salome Mösinger, dau. George Mösinger and Magdalene Holzwart.

C6. Christina, Baden, Ger., b. Oct. 4, 1776; m. George F. Mösinger.

C7. Michael, Baden, Ger., b. Nov. 20, 1779.

C8. Rosina, Baden, Ger., b. Jan. 10, 1781; m. Conrad Bader, b. Aug. 7, 1784; d. Aug. 7, 1847, son Conrad Bader and Elizabeth Kreider.

Family of SIMON HERR (C5) and SALOME MOSINGER.

C9. Andrew, Landegg, Baden, Ger., m. Barbara Gross, dau. George Gross and Anna Lehman.
C10. Jacob, Landegg, Baden, Ger., d. ———, Infant.
C11. Simon, Strasburg, Ger.
C12. Christian, Bluffton, O., b. Jan. 10, 1810; d. Oct. 2, 1857; m. June 1, 1838, Cathrina Moser, b. Dec. 28, 1821; d. Nov. 6, 1866, dau. Theodore Moser and Verena Luginbuehl.
C13. Salome, Baden, Ger., b. Jan. 20, 1812; d. 1871; m. Karl Hager.
C14. John Michael, Bluffton, O., b. Jan. 9, 1814; d. Jan. 9, 1891; m. Fanny Deppler, b. Dec. 20, 1830, dau. John Jacob Deppler and Fanny Boldiger.

Family of ROSINA HERR (C8) and CONRAD BADER.

C16. Conrad, Baden, Ger., m. Elizabeth Crider.

Family of ANDREW HERR (C9) and BARBARA GROSS.

C17. Andrew, Baden, Ger.
C18. Simon, Baden, Ger.
C19. Rosina, Baden, Ger., m. G. Schneider.
C20. Christina, Baden, Ger., m. Christian Herr.

Family of SIMON HERR (C11) and ———.

C21. Charles, Strasburg, Ger.
C22. Henry, Strasburg, Ger.

Family of CHRISTIAN HERR (C12) and CATHARINE MOSER.

C23. Rev. John, Lima, O., b. Mar. 17, 1840; m. June 17, 1863, Mary A. Schifferly, b. Oct. 13, 1845, dau. Jacob Schifferly and Anna Stetler.
C24. Fanny, Beaver, O., b. May 28, 1842; m. Nov. 19, 1863, Moses Augustburger, son John Augustburger and Anna Balmer.

C25. Catharine, Bluffton, O., b. Oct. 9, 1844; m. Nov. 21, 1867, Peter Thut, son Peter Thut and Lizzie Burkholder.

C26. Christian, Bluffton, O., b. Jan. 10, 1848; m. Sept. 12, 1867, Fanny Basinger, dau. Christian Basinger and Fanny Geiger.

C27. Simon, Bluffton, O., April 17, 1851; m. Apr. 26, 1876, Margaret Termains, dau. Daniel Termains and Martha Wade.

C28. Peter, Silverton, Oregon, b. April 23, 1854; m. Jan. 20, 1883, Louisa A. Geiser, b. Feb. 26, 1865, dau. Peter Geiser and Mary Lehman.

C29. David, Bluffton, O., b. Mar. 20, 1857; d. Feb. 26, 1861.

Family of SALOME HERR (C13) and KARL HAGER..

C33. Ernest, Baden, Ger.

C34. Emil, Baden, Ger.

C35. George, Chicago, Ill.

Family of JOHN MICHAEL HERR (C14) and FANNY DEPPLER.

C36. Catharine, Bluffton, O., b. Mar. 17, 1859; m. Mar. 8, 1881, Isaac Stauffer, b. Dec. 9, 1858; son David Stauffer and Catharine Neuenswander.

C37. Mary, Bluffton, O., b. Sept. 12, 1860; m. Feb. 24, 1884, John Stull, son John Stull and Barbara Kiene.

C38. William, Bluffton, O., b. Aug. 24, 1862; m. Jan. 12, 1898, Alice E. Daniels, b. Feb. 9, 1878, dau. John Daniels and ———.

C39. Fanny, Bluffton, O., b. Oct. 25, 1863; m. Jan. 3, 1888, Charles Green, b. April 20, 1862.

C40. Sarah, Bluffton, O., b. Aug. 7, 1867; m. Aug. 8, 1899, Peter Baditscher, b. Oct. 12, 1866, son John U. Baditscher and Elizabeth Neiswander.

C41. Emma, Bluffton, O.

C42. Louisa, Bluffton, O., b. Nov. 4, 1871; m. Feb. 28, 1900, J. A. Anderson, b. Dec. 29, 1869; son David Anderson and

Family of CONRAD BADER, Jr. (C16) and ELIZABETH CRIDER.

C43. Frederica. Landegg Baden, Ger.

C44. Caroline, Landegg Baden, Ger.

C45. John George, Boulder, Colo, d. Dec. 1, 1895; m. Mary Elizabeth Messinger, b. Aug. 7, 1850; d. Nov. 12, 1855.

C46. Christian, Emardinger, Ger.

C47. Nicholas Ernest, Longmont, Colo., b. Mar. 13, 1828; d. Dec. 5, 1872; m. Dec. 25, 1867, Elizabeth Greub, b. Mar. 4, 18—; dau. Rudolph Greub and Elizabeth Affalter.

C48. William Frederick, Emardinger, Ger.

C49. Catharine, Lima, O., b. Aug. 7, 1836; m. Sept. 28, 1854 Henry Weber, m. Oct. 5, 1860, Ferdinand Becker.

Family of Rev. JOHN HERR (C23) and MARY A. SCHIFFERLY.

C50. Christian Jacob, Lima, O., b. Mar. 4. 1864; m. Nov. 20, 1893, Carrie Williams, dau. Thomas Williams and Mary Holman.

C51. K. Anna, Beaverdam, O., b. Jan. 13, 1866; d. Feb. 19, 1866.

C52. Simon Peter, Bluffton, O., b. May 1, 1867; m. Sept. 20, 1893, Otila Herrman, dau. Dr. Frank Herrman and Christiana Hernley.

C53. Emma Anna, India, Asia, b. Jan. 20, 1869.

C54. John Samuel, Blufftou, O., b. June 6, 1871; d. Nov. 27, 1905; m. Nov. 24, 1898, Eva M. Wood, b. Mar. 24, 1875; dau. Harvey Wood and Matilda Rayls.

C55. Elizabeth F. Herring, O., b. Jan 3, 1873.

C56. Catharine Anna, Lima, O., b. Dec. 29, 1876; m. William Furgeson ; m. Edward Gardner.

C57. William Henry, Elmwood, Cal., b. Dec. 29, 1876; m. Tillie Witmer, dau. Jacob Witmer and ———.

C58. Albert Hiram, Columbus, O., b. April 8, 1879; m. Laura McGinnis.

C59. Huldah May, Herring, O., b. May 19, 1881; m. Oct. —, 1907, Chas. Contris, son Melanthon Contris and Mary ———.

C60. John Calvin, Bluffton, O., b. May 24, 1883; m. ——, Ella Contner.

C61. Walter Scott, Fort Wayne, Ind., b. July 10, 1885.

C62. Charles Frederick, Herring, O., b. Dec. 10, 1887.

Family of FANNY HERR (C24) and MOSES AUGUSTBURGER.

C63. J—— W——, Bluffton, O., b. Jan. 1, 1865; m. Mar. 18, 1889,

Barbara Gratz; b. Dec. 19, 1898, dau. Christian Gratz and Catharine Steiner.

C64. Marian, Beaverdam, O., b. Sept. 27, 1866; m. Jan. 12, 1901, Adolph Folet.

C65. Samuel, Beaverdam, O., b. April 17, 1868; m. Nov. 14, 1895, Sarah Burkholder, dau. Christian Burkholder and Elizabeth Geiger.

C66. Sarah, Beaverdam, O., b. Dec. 7, 1870.

C67. Peter, Beaverdam, O., b. June 9, 1872; d. June 10, 1881.

C68. Amos, Beaverdam, O., b. Mar. 14, 1876; d. Oct. 9, 1891.

Family of PETER HERR (C28) and LOUISA GEISER.

C69. Leona, Silverton, Ore., b. Feb. 1, 1885; m. Jan. 30, 1905, Bert Yates, b. June 20, 1882.

C70. Elvin, Silverton, Ore., b. May 5, 1887.

Family of JOHN GEORGE BADER (C45) and MARY E. MESSINGER.

C71. Mary Elizabeth, Ni Wat, Col., b. Aug. 7, 1850; m. Mar. 14, 1889, William Aberthnot.

C72. Frederick William, Ni Wat, m. May 11, 1879, Ada Root.

Family of NICHOLAS E. BADER (C47) and ELIZABETH GREUB

C73. William Ernest, Loveland, Colo., b. Dec. 21, 1868; m. Feb. 11, 1892, Sarah Elizabeth Welty, b. Mar. 23, 1864; dau. Henry Welty and Elizabeth Beach.

C74. Frank Amos, Longbeach, Cal., b. Aug. 17, 1870; m. Nov. 29, 1893, Laura Erickson.

C75. George Nicholas, Berthoud, Colo., b. Jan. 21, 1873; m. June 6, 1895, Iva Burch, dau. Henry H. Burch and Louise Frederick.

Family of CATHARINE BADER (C49) and HENRY WEBER.

C76. John, Lima, O., b. ———, 1858.

C77. Catharine, Lima, O., b. Apr. 29, 1856; m. Michael Zimmerman.

Fam. Wid. CATHARINE B. WEBER (C19) and FERDINAND BECKER.

C78. William, Lima, O., b. July 10, 1862.

C79. Elizabeth, Denver, Col., b. Nov. 28, 1864; m. Lewis A. Brown.
C80. Joseph, Buckland, O., b. Mar. 30, 1866; m. Frances Auburn.

Family of CHRISTIAN J. HERR (C50) and CARRIE WILLIAMS.

C81. Sidney, Lima, O.

Family of MARY E. BADER (C71) and WILLIAM ABERTHNOT.

C83. Charles Frederick W., Ni Wat, Colo., b. Nov. 30, 1869; m.
      Margaret Coe, dau. George Coe and ———.
C84. William C., Ni Wat, Colo., b. June 12, 1871.
C85. George J., Ni Wat, Colo., b. Feb. 9, 1875.
C86. Melissa, Ni Wat, Colo., b. July 7, 1876.
C87. Sarah May, Ni Wat, b. Jan. 13, 1878.
C88. Sidney Arthur, Ni Wat, Colo., b. Feb. 17, 1880.

Family of FREDERICK WILLIAM BADER (C72) and ACTA ROOT

C89. Mary Elizabeth, Eden Vale, Cal., b. June 25, 1880; m. June 21,
      1906, Herschel Johnson, b. May 28, 1877; son Daniel Johnson
      and Phoebe Ann Jamison.
C90. Felix Roy, Ni Wat, Colo., b. Mar. 23, 1885.

Family of WILLIAM E. BADER (C73) and SARAH E. WELTY.

C91. Ernest Henry, Loveland, Colo., b. Dec. 9, 1892.
C92. Ada Ruth, Loveland, Colo., b. Mar. 1, 1894.
C93. Ivan Eloro, Loveland, Colo., b. Oct. 5, 1897.
C94. Orla William, Loveland, Colo., b. Oct. 18, 1900.
C95. Roy Loren, Loveland, Colo., b. April 7, 1903.
C96. Paul, Loveland, Colo.

Family of FRANK AMOS BADER (C74) and LAURA ERICKSON.

C97. Doyle Wright, Ni Wat, Colo., b. Sept. 24, 1895.
C98. Francis, Ni Wat, Colo., b. Aug. 29, 1900.
C99. Glen, Ni Wat, Colo.

Family of GEORGE NICHOLAS BADER (C75) and IVA M. BURCH.

C100. Louisa Alice, Berthoud, Colo., b. Dec. 10, 1896.

Family of CHRISTINA HERR (C6) and GEORGE F. MOSINGER.

C15. John George, Baden, Ger., b. Feb. —, 1802; d. Nov. 22, 1880; m. Mary Magdalena Holtzward, b. Aug. 7, 1807; d. Jan. 24, 1864.

Family of JOHN G. MOSINGER (C15) and MARY M. HOLTZWARD.

C30. George Frederick, Findlay, O.

C31. William, Findlay, O.

C32. Anna Maria, Baden, Ger., m. Jan. 30, 1839, Abraham Kern, b. Sept. 17, 1828; d. Jan. 14, 1898.

Family of ANNA MARIA MOSINGER (C32) and ABRAHAM KERN.

C102. Henry, Baden, Ger., b. Jan. 15, 1860.

C103. Rosina, Baden, Ger., b. Dec. 2, 1863; m. Jan. —, 1882, Samuel Gratz, son Christian Gratz and Catharine Steiner.

C104. Emil, Baden. Ger., b. Oct. 10, 1866.

C105. Caroline, Baden, Ger., b. June 12, 1869; m. Noah Matter, son Christian Matter and Regina Stauffer.

C106. Mary Elizabeth, Baden, Ger., b. Feb. 8, 1871; m. Henry Trimblehorn.

C107. Matilda, Baden, Ger., b. Nov. 14, 1874.

C108. William, Baden, Ger., b. May 31, 1887.

C109. Emma, Baden, Ger., b. Dec. 20, 1881.

C110. Samuel Walter, Baden, Ger., b. Sept. 23, 1884.

Family of LEONA HERR (C69) and BERT YATES.

C82. Crystal L., Silverton, Ore., b. Oct. 23, 1907.

Family of MARY E. BADER (C89) and HERSCHEL JOHNSON.

C111. Herschel, Jr., Eden Vale, Cal., b. Nov. 24, 1907.

Family of JOHN SAMUEL HERR (C54) and EVA M. WOOD.

C112. Opal Lucille, Ada, Ohio, b. Aug. 30, 1899.

C113. Floe, Ada, Ohio, b. Aug. 16, 1901; d. Feb. 18, 1902.

C114. Alice Lenore, Ada, Ohio, b. Jan. 19, 1903.

C115. Lillian Corinne, Ada, Ohio, b. Feb. 3, 1905.